HANDBOOK OF CONSUMER BEHAVIOR

Thomas S. Robertson
The Wharton School
University of Pennsylvania

Harold H. Kassarjian
Anderson School of Management
University of California, Los Angeles

PRENTICE-HALL, Upper Saddle River, New Jersey 07458

Library of Congress Cataloging-in-Publication Data

Handbook of consumer behavior / [edited by] Thomas S. Robertson,
  Harold H. Kassarjian.
      p.   cm.
   Includes bibliographical references and index.
   ISBN 0-13-372749-1
   1. Consumer behavior. 2. Motivation research (Marketing)
I. Robertson, Thomas S. II. Kassarjian, Harold H.
HF5415.32.H36 1991
658.8'342--dc20   90-40459
                                                   CIP

Editorial/production supervision and
   interior design: Shelly Kupperman
Cover design: Mike Fender Design
Manufacturing buyer: Bob Anderson
Prepress buyer: Trudy Pisciotti

©1998 by Prentice-Hall, Inc.
A Pearson Education Company
Upper Saddle River, NJ 07458

Printed in the United States of America
10 9 8 7 6 5 4 3 2

ISBN   0-13-372749-1

Prentice-Hall International (UK) Limited, London
Prentice-Hall of Australia Pty. Limited, Sydney
Prentice-Hall Canada Inc., Toronto
Prentice-Hall Hispanoamericana, S.A., Mexico
Prentice-Hall of India Private Limited, New Delhi
Prentice-Hall of Japan, Inc., Tokyo
Pearson Education Asia Pte. Ltd., Singapore
Editoria Prentice-Hall do Brasil, Ltda., Rio De Janeiro

CONTENTS

PART THREE: PHILOSOPHY AND METHOD

EDITORIAL REVIEW BOARD

PREFACE

CONSUMER BEHAVIOR THEORY

This book takes as its focus the field of consumer behavior—the scientific study of consumer actions in the marketplace. As an academic discipline it is at a nascent stage of development compared with the more established social sciences, such as psychology, sociology, anthropology, and economics. The field emerged in the mid-twentieth century and has expanded with increasing rigor for the past three or four decades.

The purpose of this *Handbook* is to provide a current account of what is known about consumer behavior and to propose future research directions. The intended audience is scholars and potential scholars engaged in consumer inquiry and theory generation. In order to achieve our central objective, we turned to the leading researchers in the field. Their chapters represent the conceptual underpinnings of the consumer behavior discipline as it presently exists.

Audits and assessments of the consumer behavior field have been conducted with some frequency, although seldom in the depth that we have in mind for this book (Ward and Robertson 1973; Jacoby 1978; Sheth 1979). Reviews of the field have also been presented, particularly those published intermittently in the *Annual Review of Psychology* (Twedt 1965; Perloff 1968; Jacoby 1976; Kassarjian 1982; Bettman 1986; Cohen and Chakravarthi 1990). These reviews and assessments have been of value in summarizing knowledge and (sometimes) in providing critiques of the extant research base.

As the consumer behavior field has evolved, its focus has changed. Its initial foundations, for example, tended to be in economics (Clark 1958) and motivation research; attitude research and learning theory then emerged as important foci; comprehensive models constituted an important stage, and, more recently, cognitive theories have dominated the field, stimulating reaction by postpositivist researchers.

Interestingly, although multiple theoretical approaches have been pursued, they generally have not been pursued in tandem. The research base of the early 1990s is highly concentrated as to its conceptual preference for cognitive psychology and its methodological preference for experimental design. In this volume, we take an enhanced multitheoretical perspective, not only of where the field is today, but also of the recommended future conceptual directions of the field.

There is a compelling need for *theory* in consumer behavior research. A major thrust of this book is to develop key theoretical domains and to posit research directions. As will be seen, at this stage in the field's development, it may be advisable to borrow the most promising theories from sister disciplines rather than to develop unique theories. Perhaps it is the *adaptation* of behavioral concepts to consumer behavior whereby significant contributions to the field may be made. The adaptation process represents creative insight. In some ways the adaptation process is the Schumpeterian distinction (Schumpeter 1939) between *invention*—development of the concept in the basic discipline—and *innovation*—the application engineering of the concept to the applied domain. If we consider consumer behavior to be an applied discipline, then such adaptive innovation processes are a key mission of scholars in this field.

The generation of consumer behavior theory can occur at multiple levels of abstraction. At a *microlevel* there is a considerable amount of research on specific constructs, whether variety-seeking, risk, uncertainty, or expertise. These empirical findings, over time, become the building blocks for theory development. At a *middle-range* level are relatively circumscribed domains of inquiry, such as the works of Hansen (1972), Bettman (1979), or Rogers (1983). At a *macrolevel* are comprehensive models, such as those set forth in the late 1960s by Nicosia (1966), Howard and Sheth (1969), or Engel, Kollat, and Blackwell (1968).

It seems to us that theory development can benefit from all three levels of abstraction. Nevertheless, our bias is toward the upper end of the abstraction hierarchy. Without discouraging the pursuit of microconcepts, which may be quite insightful, we believe that the greatest potential payoffs will result from the pursuit of research tied to and seeking to build middle-range or comprehensive theory. Indeed, most of the chapters in this book seek to elaborate reasonably comprehensive theories for the understanding of consumer behavior.

Now we turn to the sixteen chapters to follow. They represent consumer behavior in the 1990s and present a set of middle-range theories, reviews, and perspectives of where the field is today and where it is going. Cu-

mulatively, the chapters suggest a research agenda leading us into the twenty-first century.

OVERVIEW OF CHAPTERS

The first section of the volume starts with an individual-level approach toward understanding the consumer—physiology, cognition, and conation. Chapter 1 by Joseph Alba, Wesley Hutchinson, and John Lynch is an overview of the growing literature on consumer memory and on its influence on consumer choice. This paper reflects much of what has been accomplished in the past decade and presents a possible agenda for ongoing research.

James Bettman, Eric Johnson, and John Payne author Chapter 2, reviewing existing theories and research on consumer decision making. This chapter presents a discussion of the choice heuristics used by consumers to cope with decisions, some theories for understanding decision making, and a discussion of methods for studying decision processes.

Chapter 3 continues in the same vein, reviewing recent development of individual choice behavior. Robert Meyer and Barbara Kahn review the extensive literature on models of discrete choice that have been developed in recent years. This paper is a discussion of that literature and recommends the most promising extensions for further research.

Perhaps no topic at the individual level of analysis has a longer and more varied history of research than psychophysiology. Richard Bagozzi reviews this topic in Chapter 4, introducing three basic prototypes of research in the field. He discusses research issues, measurement issues, and reviews the relevant literature, again pointing toward the most promising future research directions.

Again and again, authors throughout this book refer to learning and theories of learning. Surely every reasonably educated person has read about Pavlov's famous dog and its skill of salivating at the sound of a bell. In recent years consumer researchers again have begun to show considerable interest in Pavlovian learning and neo-Pavlovian conditioning. Terrence Shimp presents this material in an interesting discussion in Chapter 5, pointing out that classical conditioning is fully cognitive in nature.

With this background, the volume then turns to affect and attitude change. Joel Cohen and Charles Areni present a review of the affect literature—feelings, emotions, and moods. Starting with its physiological roots, Chapter 6 discusses the various lines of research on affect and affect's relationship to cognition, behavior, and attitude change.

Chapter 7, authored by Richard Petty, Rao Unnava, and Alan Strathman, focuses on attitude formation and change. Using the Petty and Cacioppo "Elaboration Likelihood Model" of persuasion as a conceptual glue, theories and empirical research on attitudes are presented and discussed.

From a thorough analysis of the consumer as a thinking, feeling, deciding individual, we turn to a more macro-level approach to consumer behavior—the influence of others and the socio/cultural environment. Valerie Folkes and Tina Kiesler bridge the micro-level and the macro-level views in Chapter 8. They discuss how cognitive processes influence how consumers think about themselves and others. Topics such as schemata, attribution theory, and social comparison theory are presented.

The influence of others in the decision process is perhaps best seen in the area of innovation and new product diffusion. Whereas the previous chapters deal primarily with the influence of psychology on consumer behavior, Chapter 9 by Hubert Gatignon and Thomas Robertson reflects the influence of sociological research as well. It poses a number of research questions emerging from network analysis, diffusion research, social influence, and competitive strategy.

Persuasion, consumer behavior, and marketing are often thought of as synonymous with advertising, television, and mass communications. Chapter 10 by Thomas O'Guinn and Ronald Faber reviews selected areas of research in mass communications. Topics covered include media choice decisions and the influence

of the mass media on consumers. Research and conceptualizations on the cutting edge of mass communication theory are presented.

Few areas in consumer behavior can claim the persistence and longevity of economic psychology. Based on the work of Katona and the Michigan Survey Research group, this views suggests that consumer spending patterns are heavily influenced by consumer expectations of their economic well-being and by consumer sentiments (pessimism, optimism, or confidence). Economic psychology was not destined to enjoy rapid expansion in the United States. In Europe, however, interest has been steadily growing. In Chapter 11, Fred van Raaij presents some of the recent thinking in this area of research—the formation and use of expectations in consumer decision making.

The topic of organizational buying and industrial purchasing is another perspective within the field of consumer behavior. Here, Scott Ward and Frederick Webster present a review of that literature in Chapter 12. This is a topic that tends to have been underresearched in the consumer behavior literature, and Ward and Webster suggest promising research directions.

Then, in Chapter 13, Alan Andreasen presents the intersection of consumer behavior research and public policy. Issues such as consumer satisfaction and discontent, deceptive and misleading advertising, exploitation of the poor, discrimination against women, and consumer protection are presented and discussed.

That brings us to the last section of our *Handbook*—philosophy and methods of research. In Chapter 14, Jerry Wind, Vithala Rao and Paul Green present a review of the various methods for behavioral research that abound in the field—from the collection and analysis of data to its interpretation. These authors also discuss the biases and shortcomings in current research methods.

For the last half of the twentieth century, the dominant philosophy of science view in consumer research has been that of logical positivism (logical empiricism or falsification). Recently, some scholars have criticized this approach as defective and have advocated a more relativistic account of science. J. Paul Peter, in Chapter 15, discusses both the traditional positivisitc approach and the relativistic approach.

Finally, the book ends with a detailed alternative approach to positivism, which the author terms "postmodernism." In Chapter 16, John Sherry, a consumer researcher trained in anthropology, introduces an anthropological approach to the study of consumer behavior. In this chapter, the reader will see many references to the type of research that the postmodernism movement has introduced since its emergence in the mid-1980s.

A WORD OF THANKS

This book has been several years in the making. As editors we owe a great deal to the renowned scholars who took the time and the effort to produce these chapters. We are grateful that some of the "best and the brightest" in this field cared enough to help us bring this endeavor to fruition. Similarly, our editorial board, listed earlier, helped in the selection of the topics and by reviewing the various drafts of the manuscript. We are indebted to these individuals, who contributed their insights so generously.

It is our fervent hope that this volume will be perceived as a lasting scholarly contribution to the field of consumer behavior. If that is achieved, the credit belongs not only to the authors and reviewers, but also to the Prentice-Hall acquisitions editors, Whitney Blake and Chris Treiber, and the production editor, Shelly Kupperman, who helped it all come about. Thank you all.

Thomas S. Robertson
Harold H. Kassarjian

REFERENCES

BETTMAN, JAMES R. (1979). *An Information Processing Theory of Consumer Choice.* Reading, MA: Addison-Wesley.

BETTMAN, JAMES R. (1986). "Consumer Psychology," *Annual Review of Psychology,* 37, 257–289.

CLARK, LINCOLN L. (Ed.) (1958). *Consumer Behavior: Research on Consumer Reactions.* New York: Harper & Brothers.

COHEN, JOEL B., and DIPANKAR CHAKRAVARTI (1990). "Consumer Psychology," *Annual Review of Psychology.*

ENGEL, JAMES F., DAVID T. KOLLAT and ROGER D. BLACKWELL (1968). *Consumer Behavior.* New York: Holt, Rinehart & Winston.

HANSEN, FLEMMING (1972). *Consumer Choice Behavior: A Cognitive Theory.* New York: The Free Press.

HOWARD, JOHN A., and JAGDISH N. SHETH (1979). *The Theory of Buyer Behavior.* New York: Wiley.

JACOBY, JACOB (1976). "Consumer Psychology: An Octennium," *Annual Review of Psychology,* 27, 331–358.

JACOBY, JACOB (1978). "Consumer Research: A State of the Art Review," *Journal of Marketing,* 42 (April), 87–96.

KASSARJIAN, HAROLD H. (1982). "Consumer Psychology," *Annual Review of Psychology,* 33, 619–649.

NICOSIA, FRANCESCO (1966). *Consumer Decision Processes.* Englewood Cliffs, NJ: Prentice-Hall.

OLSHAVSKY, RICHARD W., and DONALD H. GRANBOIS (1979). "Consumer Decision Making—Fact or Fiction," *Journal of Consumer Research,* 6 (September), 93–100.

PERLOFF, ROBERT (1968). "Consumer Analysis," *Annual Review of Psychology,* 19, 437–466.

ROGERS, EVERETT, M. (1983). *Diffusion of Innovations* (3rd edition). New York: The Free Press.

SCHUMPETER, JOSEPH A. (1939). *Business Cycles,* Vol. 11. New York: McGraw-Hill.

SHETH, JAGDISH N. (1979). "The Surpluses and Shortages in Consumer Behavior Theory and Research," *Journal of the Academy of Marketing Science,* 7 (Fall), 414–427.

TWEDT, DIK WARREN (1965). "Consumer Psychology," in *Annual Review of Psychology,* 16, 265–294.

WARD, SCOTT and THOMAS S. ROBERTSON (1973). *Consumer Behavior: Theoretical Sources.* Englewood Cliffs, NJ: Prentice-Hall.

MEMORY AND DECISION MAKING

Joseph W. Alba
University of Florida

J. Wesley Hutchinson
University of Florida

John G. Lynch, Jr. *
University of Florida

The focus in this chapter is on consumer memory and how it influences consumer choice. A small but growing literature exists on consumer memory, and the literature on consumer decision making is vast (see, e.g., reviews in this volume by Meyer and Kahn and by Bettman, Johnson, and Payne). Surprisingly, however, overlap between these two research streams has been minimal. Thus, our primary purpose in writing this chapter is to advocate an agenda for future investigations rather than to review a well-established body of consumer research, though, by necessity, we also partially accomplish the latter. Though speculative, we hope that what we have to say about the role of memory in consumer choice stimulates research that will eventually replace the present conjectures with more solid empirical evidence.

INTRODUCTION

The majority of consumer memory research has focussed on the memory of consumers for advertising—either as the focal dependent variable or as a mediator of advertising's effects on attitudes and persuasion. This research is clearly important in its own right. However,

with very few exceptions, this work has not come to grips with how advertising effects on memory and attitudes are translated into actual behavior, that is, into choice by consumers from among alternative brands or products.

Similarly, despite the enormous attention our field has devoted to psychological analysis of consumer decision processes, the paradigms that have been developed have minimized the role of memory, and only a handful of papers have explicitly considered its role in choice.

*Authorship is listed alphabetically and reflects an equal contribution by each author.

Perhaps the focal topic in the past fifteen years of consumer decision research, as well as in the allied field of behavioral decision theory, has been how task and context factors affect the decision rules used to *combine* information about alternatives in order to arrive at a final choice (e.g., Einhorn 1971; Klein and Bither 1987; Johnson, Payne, and Bettman 1988; Wright 1975; Wright and Weitz 1977). As documented by Bettman et al. in the present volume, the consumer has been viewed as choosing from among alternative compensatory and noncompensatory combination heuristics, trading off effort required to execute the rules with expected accuracy or optimality of the choice.[1]

A prototypical empirical study might test the hypothesis that one rule would be employed in one task condition, whereas a second rule would be employed in a second task condition. Clearly, an adequate test of this hypothesis requires the researcher to be able to specify both the complete set of alternatives and their values on any relevant attributes. This is true whether the researcher plans to infer process indirectly, using shifts in decision outcomes associated with changes in rule use, or to examine process directly, using process tracing data. Typically, tight control over the brands and attributes that the consumer can consider is achieved by employing unfamiliar or hypothetical brands, perhaps displayed in a brands-by-attributes matrix (e.g., Payne 1976; Payne, Bettman, and Johnson 1988). Note that these controls make scientific sense given the very interesting questions this research has been designed to address. If, for example, real and familiar brands were used, subjects might use idiosyncratic inputs that create error variance in decision outcomes. Moreover, if inputs are retrieved from memory rather than given explicitly by the researcher, it is difficult to record exactly what inputs were used and, therefore, to identify the choice heuristic employed.

However, these controls also exact a cost. We argue that by adopting research paradigms that assign memory a subordinate role, decision researchers have framed out of the picture some of the most interesting and practically important questions in real world consumer choice. Our analysis of the role of memory in consumer choice will center on four key questions:

1. Which of the available brands or alternatives are considered, and why?
2. What information is processed in evaluating each brand considered, and why?
3. How are these inputs combined to arrive at a final choice?
4. How do memories of past decisions alter the answers to questions 1, 2, and 3?

As the discussion above implies, existing consumer choice research has been very strong in its analysis of Question 3 but the paradigms adopted to illuminate this issue have obscured the remaining three issues — issues that may explain far more variance in choice outcomes in the real world. Interestingly, even the combination rules used by consumers are influenced by memory, although we shall refer the reader to the chapter on choice processes by Bettman et al. for a fuller review, limiting our focus to the remaining three questions.[2]

---

[1] In this stream of research, the limited capacity of *working* memory has played a central theoretical role, but very few papers have been concerned with the influence of *long-term* memory.

[2] Two of the most interesting results come from the research of Biehal and Chakravarti. First, processing operations at the time of the initial encoding operation affect memory organization (brand-based versus attribute-based), and this influences the brand-versus-attribute-based nature of subsequent choice processing (Biehal and Chakravarti 1982). Second, a very robust result is that with large choice sets composed of physically present brands, one observes a two-step phased decision process. Consumers first engage in some noncompensatory attribute-based screening, whittling the entire set of alternatives down to some two or three candidate brands. Then, they engage in compensatory evaluation of the reduced set — e.g., by additive difference. Biehal and Chakravarti (1986) showed that when consumers must decide from among choice sets that include some physically present brands and some that must be recalled, the two-phase process was rare. Instead, choice processes were fragmented in nature, with three or four phases being typical. The reason for this seems to be in the nature of the processing operations that subjects

Lynch and Srull (1982) used the label "stimulus-based choice" to describe decision making when all relevant brand and attribute information is physically present at the time of choice. They noted that, in the real world, consumers often make choices in which some or all of the relevant information is not directly present when the choice is made. In pure "memory-based choice," all relevant information must be recalled from memory, as when one must remember what one has heard about videotaped movies prior to renting one. In "mixed choice," some of the relevant information is physically present, and some must be recalled from memory, as when a shopper must decide whether to buy one of the shirts physically present in Store B or return to Store A to buy one seen earlier.

Lynch and Srull's focus was primarily on whether the *inputs* to choice were externally available or whether they had to be recalled from memory (Question 2, in the previous list). Nedungadi (1989) pointed out that a similar distinction can be made with respect to whether the identities of the relevant *alternatives* are externally available, or if they have to be recalled from memory (Question 1). For example, if one is in a grocery store choosing a brand of canned tomatoes, all alternatives are shelved together and their names need not be generated from memory. Thus, at least with respect to the generation of a consideration set of alternatives, this decision is stimulus-based, although the consumer may choose to rely solely on inputs retrieved from memory in choosing from among these brands. At the other extreme, as when choosing a restaurant for dinner, the set of candidate alternatives might be purely memory-based. In the same decision, the generation

could execute when some brands had to be recalled. Very efficient initial screening operations, such as comparing all alternatives on the most important dimension, simply require more processing capacity than people have available if they have to keep information about four brands in memory. Therefore, subjects were forced to use more but less efficient steps—e.g., compartmentalizing alternatives in order to first identify the "winner" from among the four "external" brands, then to identify the "winner" from four "memory" brands, and then to decide which of the two "winners" was best.

of candidate alternatives might be "mixed" if the consumer consults the Yellow Pages for a partial list of possibilities, or if he or she is driving past several restaurants while trying to remember what other restaurants in the general area might be appealing.

Our contention is that very few decisions in the real world are purely "stimulus-based" with respect to the generation of alternatives and the inputs used and, therefore, the laboratory paradigms that our field has developed are representative of only a small fraction of the universe of choices in the real world. The reason for this is that memory plays a very large role in many decisions that, in principle, could be purely stimulus-based.

For example, choosing brands of packaged goods from a grocery store display *could* be purely stimulus-based if the shelf environment supplies the names of all relevant alternatives and the package information provides all relevant inputs for choosing. However, in most such decisions, memory factors play a crucial role. This is true for three key reasons that Lynch and Srull (1982) did not recognize when they suggested distinctions among stimulus-based, memory-based, and mixed choices:

1. The external stimulus environment is usually so complex that consumers must recall what they are seeking, both in terms of product categories and brands, in order to find the relevant choice alternatives in the display. For this reason, we assert that, in addition to recognition processes, grocery shopping also involves recall as an important component.

2. Even when the consumer looks at a grocery store display of a product category without preconceptions, memory factors influence the ease with which specific brands "catch one's eye" and enter into the consideration set.

3. Motivation levels are usually too low and time too scarce for consumers to scan all brands displayed in a given product category (Park, Iyer, and Smith 1989)—a phenomenon that cannot be easily captured in laboratory studies of stimulus-based choice. One reason for this low motivation is that consumers have a (perhaps unwarranted) belief that they already possess enough relevant

knowledge to make a choice that satisfied their objectives, and that information in the store environment would not alter their preferences if it were examined. Observational studies of shopping for frequently purchased packaged goods (e.g., Dickson and Sawyer 1986; Hoyer 1984) show extremely low levels of external search. For example, Dickson and Sawyer reported that shoppers buying margarine, coffee, toothpaste, and cold cereal averaged 12 seconds from the time the display was approached to the time the selected brands was placed in their carts, with only 1.2 brands inspected on average. Similarly, in Hoyer's observations of laundry detergent purchases, the median number of packages examined was 1.2, with even fewer packages physically picked up (1.1), suggesting very low levels of using package information at the point of purchase.

Some have looked at data such as these and drawn the conclusion that attempts to explain purchase in terms of "choice" of "information processing" are fundamentally misguided (e.g., Kassarjian 1978, 1982, 1986; Olshavsky and Granbois 1979). We disagree. First, such a conclusion ignores the possibility that purchases accompanied by almost no in-store search could simply be the result of a purely memory-based decision made earlier, such as when one clips a coupon at home and decides to use it the next time one goes to the store. Second, even when such a decision is made in the store, it seems likely that complex processing goes on below the level of conscious awareness (Janiszewski 1990). Third, such a conclusion ignores the effects of knowledge calibration and mental set. Consumers may avoid inspection of particular alternatives because they feel sufficiently knowledgeable about them (Bettman and Park 1980; Johnson and Russo 1984) or because they fail to think flexibly about product usage (cf. Langer 1989), which potentially leads to overconfidence or missed opportunities. Finally, such conclusions suffer from an overly narrow view of the inputs in a decision, presuming that product "attributes" must be processed for a meaningful choice to occur.

MEMORY FOR BRANDS

There has been very little research directly testing hypotheses about the role of memory in the formation of consideration sets. This is surprising for at least two reasons. First, the consideration set (also called the evoked set) is widely recognized as an important concept for understanding decision making (Howard and Sheth 1969; Narayana and Markin 1975; Silk and Urban 1978; Urban 1975). In fact, Hauser (1978) reported an analysis of brand choice in which 78 percent of the explainable variation across consumers was attributable to whether the brand was included in the consumer's consideration set. Only 22 percent of the variation was attributable to consumers' preferences among brands in their consideration sets.[3] Second, the important role of brand awareness (measured by brand recall or brand recognition) is cited in most texts on advertising management (see Rossiter and Percy 1987 for an extensive treatment) and is a central construct in the well-known hierarchy-of-effects model of advertising effectiveness (Lavidge and Steiner 1961; Ray et al. 1973). Moreover, several researchers have reported that brand recall measures (such as top-of-mind awareness) are (1) sensitive to differing levels of advertising exposure and (2) strongly correlated with brand choice (Axelrod 1968; Haley and Case 1979; Nedungadi and Hutchinson 1985).

We suspect that the scarcity of research on memory and consideration sets is because the consideration set has traditionally been thought of as a relatively static construct. That is, consumers are assumed to "have" specific evoked sets that are composed of alternatives which they find acceptable. These sets of alternatives are assumed to be considered on each choice occasion. Variation in choice across occasions is typically assumed to result from changes in brand preference, from changes in attribute importance, or from simple stochastic variation

---

[3]Hauser's measure of variation was based on information theory rather than statistical variance.

(e.g., McAlister and Pessemier 1982). Only recently have changes in the composition of the consideration set been proposed as a possible source of individual level choice variation (e.g., Baker et al. 1986; Hauser and Wernerfelt 1990; Nedungadi 1989).

In the remainder of this section we discuss two general ways in which memory can affect the formation of consideration sets. First, in some situations, consumers must retrieve decision alternatives from memory. For example, in deciding where to eat lunch we might recall several nearby restaurants. In this case, decision-related information serves as a "cue" for retrieval. Second, many shopping situations present the consumer with a large number of potential alternatives. In this case recall is not necessary; however, consumers must recognize an item as a potential alternative before it can be considered. Items that are familiar to the consumer are likely to be recognized more frequently and more quickly than unfamiliar items.

Product Recall: Cue-Based Criteria for Inclusion in the Consideration Set

In the most extreme case, consumers must rely entirely on memory in the formation of a consideration set. An internal need, such as hunger, gives rise to some potential solution, such as finding a restaurant. Somehow the consumer must retrieve particular restaurants from memory. Subjectively, these alternatives simply "come to mind." Most modern theories of memory hypothesize that the process mediating such recall is associative. That is, the current contents of awareness "bring to mind" other ideas and events that are associated with them. This process is referred to as associative cuing, and recently retrieved memory items are said to serve as cues that guide subsequent retrieval. For example, feeling hungry may be associated with restaurants, and the abstract concept of restaurants may be associated with particular restaurants. In some cases, these associations may be direct; in others they may be mediated

by associations to other information such as attributes or specific personal experiences. As retrieval progresses, information that is relevant to the decision is held in "active memory." Other information is allowed to "fade from memory." In general, cues are believed to exert a dominant influence on the quantity and quality of recalled information.[4]

The Size of the Consideration Set. The size of the consideration set is a simple but extremely important aspect of decision making. This is especially true for relatively small size sets because the average choice probability for each alternative drops dramatically as the consideration set size increases (i.e., average choice probabilities are 1.0, 0.5, 0.33, and 0.25 for set sizes of 1, 2, 3, and 4, respectively). In fact, most investigators have reported small set sizes, generally ranging between 2 and 8 (e.g., Hauser and Wernerfelt 1990; Reilly and Parkinson 1985; Urban 1975). In most cases, "checklist" measures, which do not require subjects to recall alternatives, have been used. In situations where alternatives must be recalled, it is likely that set sizes are even smaller.

Similarly, whenever consumers are motivated to increase the size of their consideration set, they will be limited by their ability to recall potential alternatives and may be forced to engage in various types of external search. For example, Hauser and Wernerfelt (1990) presented a model in which the size of the consideration set on a given choice occasion reflects a trade-off between the cost of searching for and evaluating more alternatives and the increase in utility that can be expected from such an increase in consideration set. Clearly, good memory for alternatives reduces many aspects of the cost of search and, therefore, results in "better" choices (i.e., choices with higher expected utilities).

The most relevant experimental paradigm in

---

[4]Detailed theoretical treatments of associative memory can be found in Anderson (1983), Humphreys, Bain, and Pike (1989), Raaijmakers and Shiffrin (1981), and Tulving (1983, 1984, 1985).

memory research for understanding product recall during choice is the category production task (Bousefield and Sedgewick 1944; Gruenewald and Lockhead 1980). Subjects in these experiments are instructed to recall as many instances as possible from a particular category. In marketing research, this paradigm is used to obtain top-of-mind and share-of-mind measures of brand awareness.

Figure 1.1 illustrates two factors that affect the number of recalled items. The most obvious factor is the total number of items known to the subject (i.e., vocabulary size). This number can be estimated by the asymptote of a curved function fitted to recall data (i.e., the dashed line in Figure 1.1) The second, less obvious factor, is the speed with which items are recalled. This can be estimated by the rate parameter of the same fitted function. Thus, when time is limited some consumers may recall more alternatives than others either because they are aware of more alternatives or because they recall items more quickly. In a study of brand name recall for cold remedies, Hutchinson (1983) found that expert consumers differed from novices in estimated vocabulary size, but not in rate of recall. We suspect that there are many situational factors,

such as motivation, that can affect the rate of recall. Further research that manipulates consumer and situational factors is needed in this area.

In many situations, some but not all alternatives are physically present and the consideration set must be "completed" by retrieving additional alternatives. It might be expected that the physically presented items facilitate memory by providing external cues. In some instances (discussed later), this occurs. Within a given category, however, such "part-list" cues typically inhibit the recall of other items (see Nickerson, 1984, for an excellent review). Alba and Chattopadhyay (1985) found similar inhibitory effects for part-list cuing on the recall of shampoo brand names. For example, in one experiment, males recalled about fifteen brands when no cues were provided, but recalled only nine brands when five brands were provided as cues (thus, the total brands available was actually less, fourteen versus fifteen). The degree of inhibition was not always this dramatic; however. For males, recall always decreased as the number of provided brands increased, but interestingly, no effect was found for females. The authors attributed this to greater product familiarity (discussed in more detail subsequently).

FIGURE 1.1 Brand Name Recall as a Function of Time for a Typical Subject

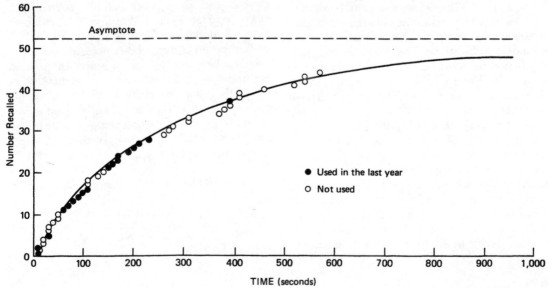

The Likelihood of Recalling Particular Alternatives. In the absence of external information, successful brand recall is a necessary, but not sufficient, condition for inclusion in the consideration set. Unacceptable alternatives will be rejected even though they are recalled. Given small consideration set sizes and the large number of brands in many product categories, recall of brands, per se, is potentially an inefficient first step in the choice process. Several factors mitigate this inefficiency, however. For instance, it is well known that more preferred brands are recalled earlier than less preferred brands (Axelrod 1968; Haley and Case 1979; Nedungadi and Hutchinson 1985; Ward and Loken 1986). Another important factor making recall more efficient during the formation of the consideration set is that decision criteria also serve as retrieval cues. So, if a consumer wants a restaurant that is fast and inexpensive, then restaurants that are highly associated with those properties become more retrievable. All properties are not equally effective in improving recall, however. In the remainder of this section we discuss several factors that have been found to be related to the effectiveness of retrieval cues in facilitating the recall of particular memory items.[5]

In a classic experiment by Freedman and Loftus (1971), category names and specific attributes were used as sequential cues. For example, some subjects were given the cue "fruit" and then "red," whereas others were given "red" and then "fruit" (the target items were the same for both groups, e.g., red fruit). Thus, the first cue served to "prime" semantic memory. Recall was found to be faster when the category came before the attribute. This superiority of category primes was taken as evidence that category terms were highly associated with category members, whereas attribute terms were associ-

ated with a more heterogeneous set of items (e.g., the set of all red objects).

Consistent with this are the well-known effects of item prototypicality on the recall of category members. Members that are typical of the category and resemble most other members are recalled more quickly and frequently than members that are atypical or distinctive (Rosch and Mervis 1975). Nedungadi and Hutchinson (1985) and Ward and Loken (1986) have replicated this result for brands as members of product categories.

Barsalou (1983, 1985) investigated the differences between naturally occurring taxonomic categories, such as, restaurants and fruits, and goal-derived categories, such as "things not to eat on a diet." Barsalou found that both types of categories exhibited a reliable *"graded structure"* as measured by prototypicality ratings. Unlike taxonomic prototypicality (which was correlated within overall similarity), goal-derived prototypicality was correlated with only one or two attributes. It is easy to imagine consumer situations in which the consideration set would be better described as either taxonomic or goal-derived. Of special interest in the present context is the fact that prototypicality ratings were strongly related to recall only for taxonomic categories. A prototypicality effect was present, but greatly reduced, for goal-derived categories.

In subsequent research, Barsalou and Ross (1986) found goal-derived categories (which were defined by single attributes) to be less established in memory than common taxonomic categories (i.e., automatic frequency counting was observed for the latter, but not for the former). They also found, however, that extensive experience with goal-derived categories was sufficient to make them comparable to taxonomic categories.

Recent work by Ratneshwar and Shocker (1988, 1989) has shown that goal-derived product categories that are defined by usage situations can be as well established in memory as taxonomic categories. Moreover, recall based on usage situation cues is strongly related to situation-specific ratings of prototypicality, but not to overall taxonomic prototypicality. This is

---

[5]Here and throughout we focus on recall from semantic memory rather than recall from previously learned lists. Although the literature on list learning is extensive, most naturally occurring choice situations involve recall based on the consumer's general knowledge of the product class rather than recall from some specific previous learning experience. Moreover, most of the factors discussed here have been found for both types of recall.

consistent with the results of Barsalou and Ross (1986) and supports the idea that people use decision criteria as retrieval cues during the formation of consideration sets. Over time such consideration sets come to be well established categories in memory. Of course, many decision-making situations may be more "ad hoc" in nature (cf. Barsalou 1983, 1985). Infrequent purchases, such as "food to buy for a camping trip," seem likely to require consideration sets that are not already defined by appropriate decision criteria and must be assembled from categories in memory.

Taken together, these findings strongly suggest that although people may "know" all of the members of a category or all of the attributes of a brand, and even though they may be able, in principle, to use any attribute to include or eliminate brands from consideration, the accessibility of this information in memory will vary greatly. In particular, the categorical structure of memory and the contextual cues that prime different aspects of that structure are likely to exert a strong influence on which information will be accessible. On the one hand, it should prove difficult for manufacturers to position themselves in a particular "niche" of the market, if that niche does not conform to some well-established category or subcategory. On the other hand, in situations in which the consideration set is essentially an ad hoc category, its composition may be less controlled by memory and, therefore, highly sensitive to advertising and in-store promotional cues (see Alba and Hutchinson 1987). In the first case, decisions will be framed by the consumer (either deliberately or as the result of past decisions based on memory). In the second case, decisions will be framed by contextual cues that result from marketing actions or mere happenstance.

The Composition of the Consideration Set. In addition to influencing the recall of particular alternatives, the categorical structure of memory is likely to influence which brands co-occur in the consideration set. Brand names tend to be recalled in categorical clusters (Hutchinson 1983; see also Bousefield and Sedgewick 1944; Friendly 1979; Gruenewald and Lockhead 1980). This phenomenon is readily apparent in Figure 1.2. Brands that are recalled together are likely to co-occur in the same consideration set. It is well known that the composition of the consideration set can bias choice in a number of ways (e.g., agenda effects—Kahn, Moore, and Glazer 1987; Hauser 1986; Tversky and Sattath 1979; decoy effects—Huber, Payne, and Puto 1982; similarity effects—Tversky 1972; and phantom effects—Farquhar and Pratkanis 1989).

Recently, Nedungadi (1989) has demonstrated that choice outcomes can be affected by manipulating factors that affect brand recall but not brand preference. Nedungadi primed particular brands with a prior task and observed a strong direct effect of priming on choice. That is, brands were chosen more often when they were primed than when not primed. More revealing, however, was the fact that an unprimed brand in the same subcategory as a primed brand was also chosen more frequently (unless the subcategory was always highly accessible). For example, when choosing a place to eat lunch, subjects were more likely to think of hamburger restaurants than sandwich shops. If a previous task had primed a less-preferred sandwich shop, then a more-preferred sandwich shop was chosen with greater frequency even though it had not been directly primed. Presumably, the less-preferred sandwich shop cued the entire subcategory.

Nedungadi's results are consistent with part-list cuing studies in which specific category members have been given as cues for the recall of a list of words from several categories (Nickerson 1984). When single members from each of several of the categories are provided as retrieval cues, total recall is improved. The improvement, however, results because more categories are recalled (i.e., people fail to retrieve entire categories in the uncued condition). The number of items per category is not improved. In fact, if multiple within-category cues are provided, then recall of the remaining category members is inhibited. Also, Alba and Chattopadhyay (1985) reported evidence that subcategory cuing can inhibit recall for other subcategories. Their procedure closely resembled

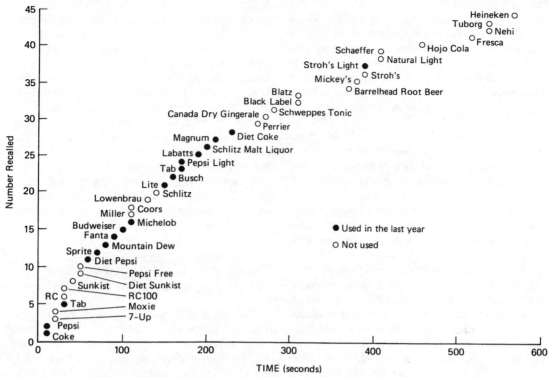

FIGURE 1.2   Clustering in Brand Name Recall for a Typical Subject

the types of cuing that might be expected to result from exposure to comparison advertising.

Taken as a whole, current research suggests that there is a trade-off between the negative and the positive effects of subcategory and brand-level cuing. At one extreme, anything that cues subcategories that would otherwise be forgotten will facilitate recall for members of that subcategory. At the other extreme, whenever several members of the same subcategory are cued, recall of the remaining members will be inhibited. We noted in our earlier discussion of part-list cuing for shampoo brands that only males showed inhibition effects. If females were more knowledgeable about shampoos and differentiated them into several subcategories, then the positive effects of subcategory cuing would have been more likely to occur. In general, we suspect that one critical factor is how strong a subcategory is as a retrieval cue for particular brands. In Nedungadi's experiment, positive effects were only observed for brands that were the most preferred within their subcategory. Presumably, this was because such brands are more strongly associated with the subcategory than are less preferred brands. Again, this is a promising area for future research.

Noncategorical Cues. Most research has supported the idea that semantic memory has a strongly categorical organization. In particular, category names are very effective retrieval cues, and items in the same category or subcategory tend to be recalled at the same time. One important exception to this generalization can be found when people are able to use visual or spatial cues. The usefulness of visual imagery as an aid to memorization is well known and used in many memory improvement techniques (Childers and Houston 1984; Lutz and

Lutz 1977; MacInnis and Price 1987). More relevant in this context is the use of the spatial aspects of the information that is being retrieved. For example, Indow and Togano (1970) reported that recall of Japanese cities was qualitatively different from the normal pattern (e.g., Figure 1.1) when subjects were instructed to recall cities from north to south. Cities were produced at a relatively fast and constant rate (as if people were scanning a mental map). Without such instructions, the pattern of recall was similar to that of most other categories.

In some situations, consumers may develop good mental maps of where alternatives are located—stores in a shopping mall, departments in a grocery store, automobile dealerships in a city, and so forth. These spatial locations may be used to construct considerations sets even though they are relatively unrelated to the categorical structure of the choice alternatives. In fact, Hutchinson, Mantrala, and Raman (1990) found that respondents in brand recall tasks reported using store shelf imagery as a recall cue about as often as they reported using product categories or personal preference. This was true for both taxonomic recall and recall of consideration sets. Interestingly, the store-related response was more frequent for the recall of soft drinks than for the recall of beverages in general. Category-based cues showed an opposite trend, and preference-related cues were equally frequent in the two tasks. Also, for soft-drink recall only, there was a comparably high frequency of respondents reporting the use of vending-machine imagery as a recall cue. These results were preliminary in nature, but clearly illustrate the potential complexity of the recall process during the formation of consideration sets.

Summary. When decision making is completely memory-based, there are at least three ways in which brand recall can affect choice outcomes. First, the number of recalled alternatives has an obvious effect on the size of the consideration set. As the size of the consideration set increases, the probability of choosing any particular alternative decreases. Recall can

be enhanced by factors such as consumer expertise and motivation. Also, brands that are recalled first tend to inhibit the recall of other brands. Second, brands that are preferred or prototypical of the product class tend to be recalled more frequently and more quickly. Thus, such brands enjoy a memory-based advantage relative to their competitors. Finally, brands that are similar tend to be recalled at the same time. This increases the likelihood that they will co-occur in the same consideration sets and thereby compete more directly with each other. In all three cases, recall plays an important role because alternatives that are not recalled obviously cannot be chosen.

Product Recognition: Familiarity-Based Criteria for Inclusion in the Consideration Set

The intended meanings and operational measures of product familiarity have varied widely in the consumer literature (e.g., Alba and Hutchinson 1987; Bettman and Park 1980; Brucks 1985; Johnson and Russo 1981, 1984; Punj and Staelin 1983; Sujan 1985). Often, product familiarity has been treated synonymously with product knowledge. Here we adopt the narrower definition of Alba and Hutchinson (see also Baker et al. 1986; Brucks 1986; Jacoby et al. 1986). Specifically, familiarity is defined as the number of product-related experiences that have been accumulated by the consumer. It is contrasted with expertise, which is the ability to perform product-related tasks successfully. In the context of memory, familiarity is often used as a generic term for the strength of the memory trace of a single stimulus or the strength of the association between two stimuli. This usage is consistent with the present definition insofar as it is commonly assumed that the strength of a memory trace is an increasing function of the number of stimulus exposures.

Although its antecedents may be different, familiarity guides the consumer's attention to specific brands in the same general way that perceptual salience guides attention. Thus, the effects of familiarity on choice are potentially as strong as those found for perceptual salience.[6] For example, Fazio, Powell, and Williams (1989) measured subjects' attitudes towards 100 common consumer brands and measured, through response latencies, the accessibility of those attitudes in memory. At the end of the experiment, ten of the original products were displayed on a table, and subjects were allowed to choose five of these as a reward for participation. The physical prominence of these products was manipulated by displaying five in the front row and five in the back row. When subjects' attitudes were less accessible, there was a stronger tendency for them to choose products in the front row over those in the back row. Indeed, when subjects' attitudes were accessible, there was no significant effect of display prominence on probability of choice. This result implies a trade-off between memory factors and physical salience in controlling the contents of the consideration set.

In this section we discuss results from three fundamental areas of memory research that are related to familiarity: name recognition, brand identification, and the accessibility of product positioning.

Name Recognition. In many ostensibly stimulus-based shopping situations, consumers are presented with a large number of choice alternatives. In the most extreme case, the information immediately available consists of brand names only. For instance, most music stores display cassette recordings alphabetically by artist. If the choice has been made prior to coming into the store, this facilitates finding the desired tape. If, however, the shopper wants to browse, the alphabetical display is of little or no help because it is unrelated to the similarities

and differences that exist among types of music. In such situations, mere familiarity with the artist's name may determine whether particular alternatives are considered. Browsing in the Yellow Pages is similar insofar as the alternatives within a particular category are listed alphabetically. In fact, a moment's reflection reveals that such displays are rather commonplace in many retail and catalog shopping situations. Often there is substantial "competition" among brands merely to be noticed. Brands that are unnoticed cannot be included in the consideration set. In this subsection, we review cognitive research on the recognition of words and suggest how the results of this research may be related to consumer choice.

Word recognition experiments typically present words in some perceptually degraded fashion (e.g., visually masked, briefly exposed, with missing letters, etc.) and require subjects to read each word aloud or simply indicate whether it is an actual English word. Because virtually any memory of the word is sufficient to respond correctly, performance on these tasks is regarded as a measure of the lower threshold of familiarity.

PERCEPTUAL ENHANCEMENT. The results of a large number of experiments indicate that repeated exposures to a word increase the ease with which it is recognized (Morton 1969, 1979). This effect has been labeled perceptual enhancement (Jacoby 1983a). Thus, words that occur frequently in the language (or in stores and advertisements) are perceptually enhanced relative to words that occur infrequently. However, recency of exposure exerts a strong transient effect. A single exposure to a word that occurs infrequently in the language can compensate for the recognition advantage normally enjoyed by high-frequency words. These effects of single exposures have been shown to last for at least a week (Jacoby 1983a; Tulving, Schacter, and Stark 1982), but not for as long as a year (Salasoo, Shiffrin, and Feustel 1985, 1985a).

Perceptual enhancement due to recent exposures appears to be fairly stimulus-specific. Murrell and Morton (1974) found that percep-

---

[6]A good example of the effects of perceptual salience can be found in the results of a supermarket field experiment by Wilkerson, Mason, and Paksoy (1982). They reported that expanded shelf space and special displays had positive effects on sales, as did price reductions. Also, display prominence and price interacted. Price sensitivity increased with display prominence. Indeed, the effects of price discounts given normal display were minimal. This suggests that expanded display simply increased the likelihood that the target brands would be included in consumers' consideration sets.

tual enhancement generalized to semantically related words, but not to words that were visually similar (see also Jacoby and Brooks 1984; Morton 1979; Witherspoon and Allan 1985). For example, prior exposure to "bored" enhanced subsequent recognition of "boring" but not "born." Furthermore, a lack of generalization has been found to printed words from pictures, spoken words, and self-generated words (Jacoby 1983b; Morton 1979). These results suggest that differences in context due to "merely" perceptual factors may reduce the amount of enhancement. Thus, product usage, per se, or exposure to the brand name in word-of-mouth discussions or radio advertising may not facilitate package recognition in the store. This also suggests that the common practice of including photos of the product's package as part of television and magazine advertisements is well advised.

Interestingly, several studies report that perceptually enhanced words actually "feel" easier to read (Witherspoon and Allan 1985; Johnston, Dark, and Jacoby, 1985). This sensation has been called perceptual fluency. Assuming that a feeling of familiarity is generally positive, perceptual fluency may affect attitude as a peripheral cue (Petty, Cacciopo, and Schuman 1981) or as a "mere exposure" effect (Obermiller 1985; Zajonc and Markus 1982). In fact, perceptual enhancement often occurs in the absence of recognition of the word as a previously presented stimulus. Furthermore, Gordon and Holyoak (1983) found that affect due to mere exposure transferred to new stimuli that were similar to the mere exposure stimuli, and that prototypicality was more predictive of affect than repetition per se.

LEXICAL "CODES." In addition to these relatively transient effects for well-known words, quite persistent effects have been demonstrated for repeated exposures to pseudowords (i.e., pronounceable nonwords). These results are especially relevant for brands with essentially nonsense names (e.g., Exxon) or names unrelated to the product concept (e.g., Apple computers), and they are most directly applicable when the brands are either in the introductory

phase of the product life cycle or have significant numbers of first-time purchasers. Nonsense words are initially much more difficult to recognize than well-known words. However, they approach the level of well-known words after as few as five exposures (Feustel, Shiffrin, and Salasoo 1983; Salasoo et al. 1985). Not only does this form of familiarity develop quickly, it is relatively enduring (remaining comparatively strong a year after exposure). Salasoo et al. conclude that a permanent memory "code" is established after a few exposures to a word. Presumably, this code is a principal link between words and their cognitive and affective meanings. Therefore, this level of familiarity is a necessary prerequisite for further development of brand memory.

Brand Identification. Word recognition experiments address forms of familiarity that develop with little or no conscious effort or intention. Stimulus identification experiments, on the other hand, typically involve subjects who are trying to learn specific responses for specific stimuli, or subjects who are trying to remember which one of a set of particular items occurred previously. The amount and the pattern of errors is the dependent measure of principal interest. In the vast majority of these experiments the responses are verbal. Put simply, subjects are attempting to name unfamiliar or poorly remembered items.

Naming is a very basic form of familiarity and may be regarded as the "gateway" to more complicated types of learning and memory. If a brand is not correctly identified, then newly encoded information cannot be integrated with existing knowledge. If a brand is misidentified, then new information is attributed to a competitor (e.g., Keller 1989; Loken, Ross, and Hinkle 1986; Reece 1984). We examine naming because (1) often brands cannot be considered if they cannot be recalled by name and (2) if very few specific brand names are known, consideration sets are likely to be determined by external factors such as salespersons, store inventory, or magazine content (editorial or advertising).

THE MAGIC NUMBER SEVEN, PLUS OR MINUS TWO. In his classic paper on human limitations in information processing capacity, George Miller (1956) reviewed a large number of identification experiments. Unfortunately, this paper and its magical number are mainly cited in reference to the normal limit on immediate memory. The identification results are generally overlooked. These results suggest that about seven levels can be accurately identified on any given perceptual dimension (i.e., about 2.8 bits of information can be "transmitted" in a stimulus-response task). However, dimensions can be combined to increase capacity. Thus, experiments using six or more acoustic dimensions resulted in as many as 150 identifiable sounds. The fundamental insight to be gained from this research is that the ease and accuracy of identification depends critically on how items are represented in memory (i.e., their subjective dimensionality). Thus, it is not surprising to find that consumers can identify only a few size levels of eggs but 31 varieties of ice cream (assuming that ice cream has more perceived attributes than eggs).

THE ROLE OF SIMILARITY. The dimensionality of memory representations not only determines the level of accuracy in identification, it determines which stimuli will be confused with which other stimuli. That is, misidentifications are not random; rather, similar items are confused and dissimilar items are easily distinguished. For example, Loken, Ross, and Hinkle (1986) found that the similarity in physical appearance of two brands was significantly related to consumer perceptions of a common business origin between them. Similarly, Keller (1988) found that brands that were evaluated similarly were more confusable than those that were not evaluated similarly.

A number of early and recent studies have demonstrated that confusion errors are well predicted by mathematical models that are based on multidimensional scaling representations of the stimuli (Luce 1963; Nosofsky 1986; Shepard 1958, 1987; Smith 1980). Moreover, these similarity-based models are naturally extended to account for categorization and recog-

nition tasks (e.g., Medin and Schaffer 1978; Nosofsky 1984, 1986; Nosofsky, Clark, and Shin 1989; Shepard and Chang 1963; Shepard, Hovland, and Jenkins 1961). The central idea, called the "mapping hypothesis," is deceptively simple. It asserts that a wide variety of behavior can be understood within a straightforward stimulus-response framework. Moreover, once the mapping between individual stimuli and identification responses (e.g., names) has been modeled, many other behaviors can be modeled by adding a second mapping from names to the final response. From this perspective, identification and the representations in memory of individual stimuli play a central role in many cognitive processes (Shepard 1987).

Identification provides a natural point of connection between familiarity and positioning. Multidimensional scaling and cluster analyses of similarity and preference data have long been used in marketing research to describe product positioning (i.e., consumer perceptions of competing brands). However, the central role of memory in these types of tasks is seldom discussed. Also, readers interested in mathematical models of consumer behavior will find the identification literature a natural point of connection between memory-based models and traditional models of choice (e.g., the recent work by Nosofsky cited earlier; see also Meyer and Kahn in this volume).

The Accessibility of Product Positioning. Even when consumers observe a particular product in the store they may not consider it for purchase because they do not recognize it as a potential alternative or, more likely, because they do not recognize it fast enough. For example, consumers looking for a headache remedy may only consider the first few brands that catch their attention even though there are twenty such brands on the shelf in front of them (cf. Fazio et al. 1989). In such a "race" for consideration, the accessibility of product positioning may play an important role (cf. Nedungadi 1989).

A number of cognitive researchers have investigated the accessibility of various properties of items, such as attributes or category membership. In a typical experiment, complete or partial sentences, such as "An apple is a fruit." or "apple—fruit," are presented to subjects who must then respond "true" or "false." In some cases, target categories are presented followed by pictures of possible members. Reaction times and error rates have been the principal dependent measures for most types of experiments (often referred to as sentence verification tasks). Several well-known results are relevant to the issue of positioning accessibility. First, category membership is verified more quickly for prototypical members than for atypical members (e.g., McCloskey and Glucksberg 1979; Murphy and Brownell 1985; Rosch and Mervis 1975; Smith, Shoben, and Rips 1974). Also, items are verified more quickly as members of "basic level" categories, than as members of subordinate or superordinate categories (Murphy and Smith 1982; Rosch et al. 1976). Basic level categories are moderately abstract and represent the level of inclusivenss at which within-category similarity is maximized and between-category similarity is minimized (see Murphy 1982; Murphy and Medin 1985; Rosch 1978; Rosch et al. 1976; Smith and Medin 1981; Tversky and Hemenway 1984). For instance, car, rather than vehicle or sedan, and shirt, rather than clothing or tank top, have been identified as basic level categories. Precise theoretical formulations of basic level categories have been elusive; however, it seems likely that perceived similarity alone is an insufficient criterion. For example Murphy and Medin (1985) have argued that basic level categories represent the level of abstraction at which people formulate naive theories about the world. In particular, it is the pattern of perceived causal relations that determine the basic level, and the perceived similarities derive from perceived causation.

An important exception to these results, however, was demonstrated by Murphy and Brownell (1985). They showed that this basic level superiority applied only to items that were typical of the basic level. Items that are atypical of the basic level are verified most quickly at the subordinate level. For example, a picture of a man's dress shirt is verified more quickly as a

shirt than a dress shirt. A tank top, however, is more quickly identified as a tank top than a shirt. Interestingly, most of Murphy and Brownell's stimuli were consumer products, although no brand names were used. Also, Sujan and Bettman (1989) have recently reported several experiments demonstrating that when brand positioning emphasizes very unusual attributes, the brand is perceived as belonging to a "niche" product subcategory rather than as a differentiated competitor in the primary category.

Finally, several studies have shown that these types of accessibility effects are sensitive to context. Roth and Shoben (1983) demonstrated that verification times were related to context-specific prototypicality ratings, but not to context-free ratings. For example, they found that tea was more typical than coffee as a beverage consumed by secretaries during a midmorning break, but coffee was more typical for a truck driver starting his day at a truck stop. This clearly parallels the results of consumer research regarding usage situations (e.g., Belk 1975; Dickson 1982; Ratneshwar and Shocker 1989; Srivastava, Alpert, and Shocker 1984). Similarly, Barsalou was able to identify context-dependent and context-independent attributes for various objects (e.g., "floats" is context-independent for a life preserver, but context-dependent for a basketball).

Summary. There are several ways in which familiarity can affect choice by increasing product recognition. First, familiar brands are likely to be perceptually enhanced. This gives them a competitive advantage in the "race" for consumer attention as consideration sets are being formed in the store. Second, familiarity reduces the misidentification of brands, increasing the likelihood that out-of-store events translate into appropriate in-store results. For example, familiarity should reduce the extent to which advertised benefits are mistakenly attributed to similar competitors. Finally, the accessibility of product positioning affects which brands will be recognized as members of a desired product category. In particular, prototypical alternatives are recognized more quickly. For example, if a consumer is shopping for meat for a cookout, steaks might be easily recognized and fish passed by without a thought because grilled steak is commonplace but grilled fish is somewhat unusual. In all of these cases, ease of recognition has the potential to affect choice because consumers are often making decisions under some form of time pressure and are naturally guided to alternatives that somehow "stand out" from their competitors. In this regard, product recognition is the internal counterpart to perceptual salience.

The foregoing discussion has laid out memory factors that determine what brands are considered for choice. We now turn to an analysis of the determinants of what inputs are used to evaluate those brands that are considered. The next section examines pure memory factors that lead to poor memory for some types of information and good memory for other types. Many of the psychological principles we discuss here are equally relevant to an analysis of factors influencing recall of advertising, as advertising is but one mode of acquiring information about products. However, we will consider work on advertising recall in detail only insofar as it provides theoretically relevant implications for the analysis of consumer choice. Following our review of memory for attributes, we will build the case for why the inputs used for choice cannot be understood solely in terms of selective encoding and recall, because of the task objectives that are peculiar to choice tasks.

MEMORY FOR ATTRIBUTES

As important as it is to remember product alternatives, meaningful brand selection cannot occur without knowledge and understanding of the attributes that characterize those alternatives. This information can be gleaned from a variety of sources, including advertising, direct experience, package information, and word-of-mouth sources. Regardless of the original source of product information in memory, two different questions about attribute information are especially pertinent to consumer decision making. The first deals with the issue of how well consumers can be expected to remember

the form and content of explicit messages. This question has been raised with respect to the absolute amount of information remembered as well as the accuracy with which it is represented in memory. The second question assumes some degree of imprecision in memory and asks whether there are any systematic ways in which information is forgotten or distorted.

Amount and Accuracy

Numerous factors can affect the amount of recall, including such intuitive ones as frequency of exposure, level of involvement, delay interval, and level of expertise. We will touch on several of these factors later in this chapter. At this point, however, a more fundamental question pertains to how well information is remembered under conditions conducive to recall; that is, when involvement is relatively high, time delays are short, and the information is nontechnical and representative of everyday discourse.

Naturally, memory performance will vary as a function of what is measured. For example, recall of the syntactic and lexical details of a message can be quite poor (see Alba and Hasher, 1983, for a discussion). Though such details are generally unimportant, the existence of verbatim memory would lessen the effectiveness of some deceptive methods (discussed subsequently). More worrisome are the findings related to memory for the semantic content of televised and print communications reported by Jacoby and Hoyer (1982, 1989). Though framed in terms of comprehension, this research can be considered in terms of consumer memory in the sense that many of the reported instances of miscomprehension would have been averted had accurate recall of the messages been achieved. Instead, subjects either incorrectly identified or were unable to identify the validity of a significant proportion (nearly one-third) of restated assertions from ads or logical conclusions based on those assertions. This occurred despite immediate testing after message presentation and a level of involvement that likely exceeded that of most real-world contexts.

Researchers and policymakers may debate the merits of emphasizing the relative amounts of accurate versus inaccurate recall reported in this research (cf. Jacoby and Small 1975). In principle, however, memory failure, by itself, need not be a problem of great concern. When consumers feel that their memories contain insufficient information for a decision, external search generally is an option. Whether, in fact, search is conducted is a choice that can be left to the consumer — although policymakers can do much to insure and improve the availability, accessibility, and usability of product-related facts (see Alba and Hutchinson, in press, for a discussion). A significant problem does arise, however, when consumers recall distorted versions of a communication. In such cases, external search is unlikely because consumers misassess the true state of their knowledge. Unfortunately, the interpretive and elaborative processes that distort memory are not uncommon.

Interpretation. A ubiquitous process in discourse processing is the idiosyncratic interpretation of the nominal words and phrases used to convey meaning. The message sender rarely spells out the complete and precise meaning of every assertion, but relies instead on the receiver's ability to make simple inferences. In the best cases this procedure results in smoother communication without loss of accuracy. However, accuracy is clearly a victim of misinterpretation resulting from the receiver's honest misunderstanding of the sender's intent or, more objectionably, from the sender's attempt to deceive. For example, a consumer may interpret "not expensive" as "inexpensive," thereby misconstruing a relatively benign assertion by an advertiser (cf. Harris and Monaco 1978). Alternatively, an automaker may point out that its model has more leg room than Competitor X, more head room than Competitor Y, and more trunk space than Competitor Z, purposely implying that its offering is especially roomy, when, in fact, each comparison is made to a competitor who fares particularly poorly on each specified dimension (Harris 1977).

Unlike the case in which consumers make poor decisions because they resist external search, *caveat emptor* is a less valid response here because misinterpretation may occur despite repeated exposure to deceptive assertions (Alpert, Golden, and Hoyer 1983), forewarnings about the possibility of misinterpretation (Harris, Teske, and Ginns 1975), and even explicit training to avoid it (Bruno 1980). In addition, combined with an inability to recall verbal information verbatim, most memory-based attempts to reinterpret the original message are not likely to succeed.

Even when made accurately, some forms of interpretation may reduce decision quality. This specifically applies to interpretations that simplify an assertion or series of assertions. For example, "rapid acceleration" is a plausible interpretation of the more detailed fact "goes from zero to sixty in six seconds." Similarly, the adjective "comfortable" accurately summarizes the attributes implied in the words "bucket seats," "adjustable steering wheel," "plush carpeting," and "roomy." The practical importance of such interpretations involves their memorability. Across several contexts, simplified or summary information has been shown to be easier to remember than the details from which it is derived (e.g., Kintsch and van Dijk 1978). As a result, its relative impact in judgment should increase over time (cf. Cantor and Mischel 1977; Carlston 1980; Higgins and King 1981; Lingle and Ostrom 1979; Wyer and Srull 1986).

A simple demonstration of this in a consumer context has been provided by Alba, Marmorstein, and Chattopadhyay (1989). They likened abstract inferences to product positionings within a market. They created two fictitious brands of cameras and positioned them in terms of being technically sophisticated (Brand A) or easy to use (Brand B) in separate advertisements. Each ad made pufferylike claims about its dimension of strength but also described specific attributes regarding both technical strength and ease of use. Based strictly on these attributes, however, Brand B dominated Brand A on both dimensions, even though only Brand B's ease-of-use was emphasized. Subjects were shown Brand A and then, immediately afterward or two days later, they were exposed to Brand B. After examining Brand B they were asked to evaluate it relative to Brand A on each dimension. Results showed that regardless of the amount of delay between exposure to the two ads, Brand B was rated superior to Brand A in terms of ease of use by 94 percent of the subjects. Thus, when both the positioning of the brands and their actual attributes favor the brand seen most recently, correct decisions obtain. However, a different pattern was found for technical superiority. When the two ads were seen consecutively, 68 percent of the subjects correctly identified Brand B as superior, presumably on the basis of its superior attributes. When two days separated exposure, this figure was reduced to 36 percent. Apparently, as memory for details of the first brand decreased over time, the more abstract positioning of the alternatives dominated evaluation. Thus, reliance on interpreted information can lead to erroneous decisions even if the interpretation is accurate.

Elaboration and Reconstruction. The second avenue through which memory may be distorted involves elaboration and reconstruction. These processes result in inferences about product attributes that are not implied in the actual product description.

A variety of such inferences have been described elsewhere (Alba and Hutchinson 1987), and we review them only briefly here. Evaluation-based inferences (or "halo effects") result in the transfer of affect from one concept to another (Beckwith and Lehman 1975; Cooper 1981; Nisbett and Wilson 1979). Thus, evaluation of individual attributes of a product may be biased by one's overall perception of the product. Similarity-based inferences derive from the resemblance between two objects. Thus, consumers may assess the quality and features of a new or unfamiliar brand based on its apparent similarity to a known brand (cf. Cohen 1982; Gilovich 1981; Loken et al. 1986). Such analogical reasoning can be quite erroneous if the perceived similarity of the two brands is driven by perceptually salient but nondiagnostic features. Correlational inferences occur when two

attributes are believed to covary frequently and, consequently, information about one is used to infer information about the other (cf. Erikson, Johansson, and Chao 1984; Hoch 1984; John, Scott, and Bettman 1986). The price-quality inference is a common example. Finally, typicality inferences occur when consumers infer that a product possesses a particular attribute because it is typical of brands in that product class (cf. Arkes and Harkness 1980; Crocker 1984; Sujan and Dekleva 1987).

Depending on the inference and the situation, inference making may be virtually irresponsible and unconscious. At other times inferences may be intentionally substituted for search based on the perceived costs of search and the assessed likelihood that the inference is valid. In still other cases, inference making may fail to occur if not prompted externally. Recently, Dick, Biehal, and Chakravarti (in press) have discussed the situational properties that can affect the likelihood and impact of different types of inferences in the decision process. In particular, they note, in addition to the obvious task demands which can prompt or suppress inference making, that (1) information that serves as a basis for an inference must be available *and* accessible and (2) the impact of a particular inference will depend on its perceived diagnosticity vis-à-vis the diagnosticity of other inferences. Thus, for example, evaluation-based inferences require recall of prior judgments, and correlational inferences are contingent on a database from which a rule can be constructed. Because memory for various types of information that form the bases for inferences differ, so too does the potential for each inference to occur. Further, given a situation in which inference making is not constrained by memory, the extent to which an inference is formed and used in making a decision will vary as a function of its perceived reliability. In their particular study, Dick et al. report that correlational inferences are favored over evaluation-based inferences.

This research represents an important initial attempt to examine the independent effects of accessibility and diagnosticity. As an interesting aside, it should be noted that perceived reliability of an inference may be determined not only by the strength of its logical foundation but also by memory itself. That is, inferences may also be firmly incorporated into a consumer's beliefs as a result of memory failure. This can occur in two ways. First, inferences made at the time of information encoding may not be identified as such at the time of informational retrieval. That is, the consumer may forget the source of the inferred belief. More important, research suggests that when a source cannot be identified, there is a tendency to attribute remembered information to an external source (Johnson, Raye, Foley, and Foley 1981). Thus, when the belief consists of an inference, an undeserved level of validity may be ascribed to it. Further, independent of source effects, there exists a bias to believe that facts retrieved from memory are valid (Collins, Warnock, Aiello, and Miller 1975). Overall, then, as time passes, inferences are likely to become more influential in the evaluation process.

The second memory-mediated source of false beliefs involves reconstruction. Not all inferences are generated at the time of exposure. Instead, consumers may accurately encode a message but intrude unstated attributes during later attempts to recall it. Alternatively, an attribute may be encoded accurately but forgotten. At the time of retrieval it may then be inferred, most likely in a way that is consistent with previously held beliefs. Thus, when price information cannot be recalled accurately, errors are in the direction of the consumer's prior expectations (Helgeson and Beatty 1987). In both cases the intrusions are generally plausible and, as with interpretive inferences, the consumer may have little motivation to verify them.

Summary. Verbatim recall of product information is rare. Consumers aware of their memory loss may compensate with additional search but may also infer missing information. More subtly, due to memory failure, inferences that are made may later be misidentified as part of an external message or as part of common knowledge, therby conferring the message with

an unwarranted truth status. This, in turn, should reduce motivation to validate product beliefs with external information. Thus, the effects of memory are pervasive, affecting not only the need for inference making but also the perception of inferences after they are made.

Retrieval Biases

Interpretive and elaborative inferences actively distort memory by creating unintended or untrue meanings. Memory also may be biased in the absence of such distortion through the process of selective retrieval. A subset of the attribute information encoded by a consumer may be accurately retrieved, but what is retrieved may be unrepresentative of all that is known. This should be distinguished from selective search or selective exposure in which there is a failure to learn information. As was true of memory for brands, attribute memory is largely determined by attentional factors, familiarity, the presence of retrieval cues, and the level of competitive interference (see, e.g., Burke and Srull 1988; Keller 1987). These are well known main effects. In the following pages we focus on how these fundamental moderators of memory may favor some attributes over others as inputs to decision making.

Salience. Attention to and recall of product attributes are determined by their salience, which can be affected by a variety of factors. In the best case, salience will be internally driven and correspond to the importance consumers assign to the attributes. Indeed, there exists a long history of research across several domains showing that recall is related directly to the perceived importance of information (e.g., Johnson 1970; Kintsch and van Dijk 1978; Lichtenstein and Brewer 1980; Voss, Vesonder, and Splich 1980). In some cases, as when particular attributes are personally very important, they will be recalled very well even when processing conditions are adverse (Bargh and Thein 1985). In the extreme case, processing of such information may verge on being automatic. Thus, even under highly distracting conditions, consumers may encode and later recall attributes they consider important for evaluation (cf. Ratneshwar, Mick, and Reitinger 1989).

Such outcomes are heartening and suggest that consumers will make decisions that, if not objectively optimal, are at least consistent with their personal values. The problem with this scenario, of course, is that consumers do not always possess well formed beliefs about attribute importance (cf. Fischhoff, Slovic, and Lichtenstein 1980; Jacoby, Troutman, Kuss, and Mazursky 1986; Wind and DeVita 1976). In such cases salience may be determined externally, perhaps via repetition or by the format in which it is conveyed (cf. Finn 1988). In addition, there may be characteristics of the information itself that makes it inherently salient. In a previous section the effects of cuing on brand recall were discussed. In that context, cuing was shown to affect the size and composition of the evoked set. In the context of attributes, such increases in salience may be discussed in terms of "problem framing," whereby the effective weight, of attributes in decision making are altered by manipulations of either the perceptual salience or the memory accessibility of that information (e.g., Gardener 1983; MacKenzie 1986; Wright and Rip 1980).

In the seminal work on this phenomenon, Wright and Rip (1980) demonstrated that repeated reference to certain product dimensions increased their influence in subsequent judgments by consumers. Other studies have shown that decisions can be influenced more subtly simply by increasing the prominence of some facts without explicitly suggesting that they are very important. In addition, some of these studies have shown that memory can mediate the effect. For example, Reyes, Thompson, and Bower (1979) showed that by manipulating the vividness of a piece of information one could vary the influence of that information in a later judgment. Moreover, the vividness manipulation was effective only when the judgment was made well after exposure to the message. When judgment immediately followed message exposure, the critical information was salient regardless of its vividness. After a delay, however, information was more memorable if

presented in a vivid rather than pallid fashion, and, therefore, it was more likely to be incorporated into the decision.

In a similar vein, Gardner (1983) showed that by making a product feature very prominent in an ad, one could increase both its memorability and its effect on attitude (see also MacKenzie 1986). Interestingly, she also found that the enhanced recall of the prominent attribute came at the expense of the nonprominent attributes contained in the ad.

When the presence of salient information results in reduced consideration and usage of nonsalient information during evaluation, the cause is sometimes ambiguous. Attention-related reasons include the differential processing of salient and nonsalient facts at the time of exposure and the tendency to recall only the most easily remembered facts at the time of retrieval (cf. Fischhoff, Slovic, and Lichtenstein 1978). Alternatively, the salience of some facts may inhibit recall of other facts despite effortful attempts to retrieve them. The former has been examined by Kisielius and Sternthal (1984, 1986). They demonstrated that vivid stimuli prompt disproportionate amounts of elaboration, which in turn leads to higher recall and a greater persuasive effect. When the opportunity to elaborate is limited, a corresponding decrease in attitude change results. On the other hand, Alba and Chattopadhyay (1985) demonstrated that recall of product attributes can be inhibited at the time of recall and independently of attention at the time of exposure. Using a part-list cuing procedure, their subjects viewed product attributes under identical conditions but, in line with traditional findings, recall of uncued attributes decreased as a function of the number of attributes cued at the time of retrieval. Subsequent research showed the effect due, at least in part, to the inhibiting effects of the salient cues (Alba and Chattopadhyay 1986). Thus, when some facts are particularly salient, they are continually and unavoidably retrieved during attempts to recall the remaining information. All this suggests that advertisers may be able to inhibit consideration of threatening competitors and unfavorable attributes by making salient in their ads nonthreatening competitors and their own attribute strengths.

As noted, salience need not be determined solely by the messenger. By virtue of their unusualness, inherent vividness, or personal relevance, some types of information will exert a greater influence on memory and judgment than others. For example, visual images may have more impact than verbal descriptions (cf. Childers and Houston 1984). Similarly, people overestimate the relative risk of events that are unusual, newsworthy, and personally salient, perhaps because instances of such events are highly available in memory and are therefore overgeneralized (Lichtenstein, Slovic, Fischhoff, Layman, and Combs 1978; see also Folkes 1988). This suggests that consumers will be suboptimal in the way they purchase insurance, and it explains why relatively low-risk dietary hazards, such as the presence of Alar on apples, elicits such an extreme consumer reaction.

Although the effects of salience have been described primarily in terms of recall, it is important to note that salient concepts can also affect the interpretation of stimulus information, particularly if the stimulus is ambiguous. Thus, awareness of brand name or country of origin may influence how positively or negatively a product attribute is assessed (See Hong and Wyer 1989). Similarly, advertisements that explicitly promote a product dimension may guide how that dimension is evaluated—even when the evaluation is based on direct experience with the product (Hoch and Ha 1986). Other interpretive effects may be much more subtle. For example, a moderately priced product may be perceived as being more (or less) expensive than usual if the consumer has been unobtrusively exposed to a set of relatively inexpensive (or expensive) brands from the same product class (Herr 1989). Thus, the increased salience that results from the temporary priming of one price category biases the perception of products in another. The importance of these interpretive effects, combined with the scarcity of relevant empirical research, makes this an important area for future research.

More consistent with the notion of problem framing are cases in which the unobtrusively primed information affects the recall and usage of particular attributes during product choice. For example, it has been shown that for noncomparable products (e.g., cameras and computers), people may base their evaluations on abstract dimensions that are held in common (Bettman and Sujan 1987; Johnson 1984). By surreptitiously priming a common dimension (e.g., reliability), it is possible to guide consumers into making decisions in terms of that dimension (Bettman and Sujan 1987).

More important, the effects of such priming can interact with memory (Srull and Wyer 1980; see also Higgins, Rholes, and Jones 1977). When subjects are primed with an evaluative dimension prior to exposure to an ambiguous description of an object, evaluation of the object tends to be consistent with the prime. Moreover, the effects of the prime are larger when a long interval occurs between exposure to the description and judgment. This result is consistent with the previously described study by Alba et al. (1989). As delay increases, memory for the original detailed information decreases, whereas higher-order interpretations made salient by the prime remain stable. Thus, over time, evaluations become dominated by and more consistent with the original interpretation of the object.

It should be apparent at this point that the manipulation of salience by others can have very adverse effects on consumer decision making. In general, salient information is given disproportionate amounts of attention and is recalled in disproportionate amounts. Thus, consumers will be biased in their use of information relative to stimulus-based situations or situations in which memory is complete and attributes are given objectively correct importance weights. For example, Edell and Staelin (1983) compared consumers' responses to print ads that varied in the format of information found in one portion of each ad (text alone, pictures alone, or text plus pictures). As predicted, pictures alone seemed to depress support and counterarguments about attributes that a normative sample had rated as important for evaluating the target products. Presumably, the pictures alone allowed attention to dwell on affectively pleasant, easy to process aspects of the pictures that were not truly relevant to judging the brands.

The especially distressing aspect of all this is that salience effects are most likely to influence product novices and other vulnerable segments of the population (Alba and Hutchinson in press). Experts are less likely to conform to an advertiser's framing of a problem and can remember nonsalient information more completely (see Alba and Hutchinson 1987). Novices, on the other hand, find it more difficult to challenge an advertiser's claims and will preferentially recall salient attributes, especially after a delay. Thus, salience manipulations influence those consumers who are least capable of making optimal decisions.

Repetition. As noted, repeated presentation of a stimulus may enhance its salience, which in turn may increase its impact on decision making. Repetition also facilitates recall (Crowder 1976; Sawyer 1973). Thus, heavy advertising should heighten recall of both the brand name and the attributes associated with it. And, as with previously discussed salience effects, differences in recall that result from differential repetition across brands and attributes should exert its greatest influence on memory-based decisions.

We take special note of repetition-related salience not only because repetition is a fundamental advertising variable, but also because research has identified three unintended effects of repetition. First, repetition may affect the amount of attention paid to an ad. Thus, high levels of repetition may lead to "wearout," wherein lower amounts of attention are paid to each additional exposure, and recall ceases to improve (Craig, Sternthal, and Leavitt 1976). However, alterations in presentation, such as when an ad is repeated in different media, may affect the rate of wearout. For example, when a television version of an ad is followed by a radio version, people actively reprocess the former during exposure to the latter (Edell and Keller 1989). Second, repetition may have adverse effects on a consumer's affective reactions to a message, perhaps by producing boredom or an-

noyance or by affording greater opportunity for counterargumentation (Calder and Sternthal 1980). Both effects are undesirable from an advertiser's perspective. A third outcome is undesirable from a consumer's perspective. That is, messages that become familiar through repetition also have a tendency to be perceived as more valid, independent of their actual validity (Bacon 1979; Hasher, Goldstein, and Toppino 1977).

Consistency. Although our emphasis has been on external manipulations, there are numerous internal processes that can lead to many errors in decision making. In general, these processes involve the biased recall of information that is consistent with prior knowledge, beliefs, and decisions.

For example, as discussed in the context of inference, consumers may have a sense of attribute typicality. To the extent that this is true, research suggests that, except for extremely unusual features, recall of product information will increasingly favor typical attributes as time elapses (Schmidt and Sherman 1984; Smith and Graesser 1981; Sujan and Bettman 1989). When little time has elapsed, people have reasonably good memory for both typical and atypical features. Over time, however, episodic recall diminishes and increasing reliance is placed on general knowledge to cue recall. Because general knowledge tends to cue typical features, beliefs about the product should become stereotyped, thereby reducing the consumer's ability to discriminate among brands.

Sawyer (1976) has adopted this notion to assess the potential long-term impact of corrective advertising. He argues that if the corrective claim is not well integrated into general knowledge, recall of information about the offending brands will come to resemble recall prior to exposure to the corrective claim. This argument is based on the atypical nature of the corrective claim compared with what the consumer has long believed to be true about the brand.

In addition to the pure memorability of typical versus atypical claims, retrieval may be influenced by the conceptual foundation of those claims. Specifically, the encoding of a "fact," especially an unfamiliar or nonintuitive one, may initiate attempts to justify or explain it. In the process, beliefs or hypotheses may be constructed that persist after the fact has been discredited (Anderson, Lepper, and Ross 1980). Thus, to the extent that erroneous product beliefs stimulate or are derived from a more encompassing theory, they may be difficult to correct because the theory persists beyond memory for specific claims and counterclaims.

Regardless of the reason for the persistence of an erroneous belief, the problem will be compounded when corrective or qualifying claims are made inconspicuously, inasmuch as the memory constraints on the recall side will be compounded by attentional deficits on the encoding side (cf. Burke, DeSarbo, Oliver, and Robertson 1988).

Biased recall can result not only from objective assessments of typicality but also from errors in reasoning. Foremost among them is the widely reported and pervasive tendency known as confirmation bias, in which information search, interpretation, and recall are conducted in such a way as to confirm rather than disconfirm one's beliefs. This, in part, accounts for the phenomenon of illusory correlation, wherein people overestimate the relationship between variables (e.g., between price and quality). To the extent that correlations are computed from memory, perception of the relationship will be overstated because recall of confirming cases (i.e., high-priced, high-quality products and low-priced, low-quality products) will exceed recall of disconfirming cases (i.e., high-priced, low-quality products and low-priced, high-quality products). (See Crocker 1981.) This offers another reason why strong beliefs may be formed in the absence of strong data.

Analogous confirmatory processes have been reported for recall of information pertaining to actual decisions that are unrelated to personal beliefs and prior hypotheses. In some cases there seems to be a tendency to search for information that affirms an answer or decision (Koriat, Lichtenstein, and Fischhoff 1980). In other cases it appears the information supportive of a previous decision is more accessible

than other information (Dellarosa and Bourne 1984; see also Hoch 1984). Such information is more closely associated with the decision and is cued by the decision at the time of recall. In still other cases, information may be preferentially recalled simply because it is given more attention at the time of exposure. Thus, attributes about chosen brands are recalled at a higher level than attributes of rejected brands (Biehal and Chakravarti 1983; Loken and Hoverstad 1985). Although the opportunity to examine both types of attributes may be equal at the time of choice, most decision rules result in more frequent examination of the ultimately preferred brands.

Related to the situation in which misassessment of knowledge results in inadequate search, preferential recall of decision-consistent attributes should result in overconfidence (Koriat et al. 1980). Thus, consumers may assess their decisions and decision-making abilities more favorably than is justified.

The research discussed thus far portrays a rather dismal picture of the human ability to learn from experience (see also Hoch and Deighton 1989). Through the processes of selective encoding and recall, information that should cause us to broaden our beliefs, moderate our attitudes, and recognize our abilities instead results in stereotyped beliefs, polarized attitudes, and overconfidence in our consumer decisions.

Of course, learning does take place and experience does have salutary effects; the effect of biases is to reduce the rate of learning and thereby increase exposure requirements. However, the empirical evidence on consistency effects is not monolithic. Specifically, the results do not extend uniformly to cases in which information is received less passively than during hpothesis testing. In some instances recall is superior *both* for information that is highly consistent *and* for information that is highly inconsistent with prior beliefs. Thus, assertions that contradict what one believes or has been led to expect may be well recalled because they elicit strong reactions (cf. Judd and Kulik 1980) and/or because they are surprising and initiate attempts to understand them, thereby increasing the extent they become elaborated and connected to other recallable information in memory (Houston, Childers, and Heckler 1987; Srull, Lichtenstein, and Rothbart 1985).

Weber and Crocker (1983) present a more extensive model of adaptation to discrepant information (see also Sujan and Bettman 1989). They outline three types of cognitive reaction that might take place. First are bookkeeping reactions, which make small adjustments to existing knowledge to accommodate the discrepancy. For example, if a consumer buys an overripe apple at an always reliable grocery store, he or she might adjust accordingly and consequently believe that the store is usually reliable. The second reaction is called subtyping. This refers to the construction of an entire subcategory of exceptions to a general rule, as when a consumer who initially believes the only good electronics products are made in Japan does further search and revises the belief to reflect the existence of several European and American firms. The third reaction is more extreme. Conversion reactions result in dramatic alterations in point of view. For example, examination of the *Consumer Reports* article on sparkling waters may result in a switch in the perception of Perrier from seeing it as a chic and unique beverage to seeing it as a pretentious club soda substitute.

Extensive examinations of these reactions have not yet been conducted over time. Evidence described previously suggests that bookkeeping reactions might be least durable. On the other hand, conversion reactions might be quite durable because they represent fundamental changes in outlook.

Summary. As in other areas of human information processing, research on memory has tended to accentuate the negative. Instances of misinterpretation, misallocation of attention and importance weights, and biased memory predominate. It is unclear to what extent such findings result from researcher bias in the selection of experimental contexts or in the presentation of results (cf. Christensen-Szalanski and Beach 1984; 1987; Nisbett, Krantz, Jepson, and Kunda 1983). Nor is it clear to what extent

memory actually affects final purchase (cf. Funder 1987). Two important facts are apparent, however. First, the *potential* effects are large. For example, the causes of the apparent failure of a major public policy initiative, namely corrective advertising (see Armstrong, Gurol, and Russ 1983), can be traced in part to some of the principles of encoding and retrieval discussed here. Second, to whatever extent consumers are affected in the real world, the impact is likely to be felt most strongly by the least knowledgeable segments of the market.

A final methodological point is also worth noting. Recent research on the measurement of advertising impact has addressed the relative merits of recall versus recognition tests and has generally focussed on the sensitivity of each (e.g., Singh, Rothschild, and Churchill 1988). It is important to add that these two measures are unequally affected by the salience effects and the consistency effects described here. Specifically, such effects occur most strongly on recall tests and may virtually disappear on recognition tests (Alba and Hasher 1983; Alba and Hutchinson 1987). Thus, while arguments may be made from a managerial perspective regarding the value of recognition tests to tap awareness and learning of ads, such tests may mask biases that exist in consumer choice contexts that require the free recall of attribute information.

MEMORY AND DECISION MAKING

The preceding section hinted at the role of memory in product evaluation, but the focus was on the remembrance of attributes, per se. In this final section we directly address the issue of memory-based decision making.

Even in mundane consumer decisions, there are dozens of inputs available in memory and in the external environment that could *potentially* be considered in making one's choice, but only a few of these will actually be used as inputs to the choice on a given occasion. For example, one of the authors of this chapter frequently runs out to get a quick take-out lunch, and finds himself standing between Burrito Brothers and

Falafel King restaurants, trying to decide which to partronize. On various occasions within the past month, the decision has been made based on answers to the following questions: "Where did I go yesterday?" "Which line is longer?" "How many minutes do I have until my next appointment?" "Should I be merciful to the people I will be meeting all afternoon, and avoid anything with garlic? — If so, walk one more block to TCBY Yogurt." "How much money do I have in my wallet?" "Maybe I won't get a chance to eat right away — what can I get that won't be inedible if it sits in the bag for awhile?" "Do I want something vegetarian, or something with meat?" "Do I want a big lunch or a small one?" "Are we planning to have tacos for dinner tonight?" Fortunately, all of these issues do not seem to arise on a single occasion — otherwise, our protagonist might consistently find that darkness has fallen before he has been able to make his selection. Instead, in each case the choice is made based on one or two of these considerations. Because of this, the final choice depends crucially on what small subset of the potential inputs the consumer happens to retrieve or to note in the external environment, and to actually incorporate into the decision.

Hoyer's (1984) field observation of laundry detergent purchases (cited earlier) provides more systematic evidence in support of the previous arguments. Immediately after consumers had placed a brand of detergent in their shopping carts, they were approached and asked the reasons for their brand choices. "Choice tactics" cited included price considerations ("cheaper"; "I use less so it costs less"), performance considerations ("works in cold water"; "removes stains"), pure affect ("I like it"; "I love it"), and normative considerations ("my wife told me to buy it"; "my mother always used it"). The most striking aspect of the responses given was that less than 10 percent of all consumers gave more than one reason for their selections.

It could be argued that respondents' true, unobservable decision processes were more complex, and that they simply said only as much as they felt was required to satisfy the interviewer. Similarly, one could argue that the actual decision was made at home, and that,

therefore, the entire set of reasons was no longer accessible in memory. However, one could as easily maintain that these self-reports overstated the degree of thought that entered into the choices and that many consumers simply identified the brand that they bought last time and placed it in their shopping carts without deliberation, or that their choices were based upon pure affect without supporting reasons.

Though these interpretations must remain speculative, we see data like those reported above as evidence that for many repetitive and unimportant choices, decision processes are *extremely* simple. We are struck by the impression that these processes are an order of magnitude less effortful than what is typically observed in laboratory studies of consumers' use of "simplifying heuristics," where, for example, consumers might shift from a compensatory heuristic to the use of a conjunctive rule under adverse task conditions. Indeed, if Hoyer's results are to be taken at face value, one cannot even speak of "multi-attribute" choice rules, as the choice on a given occasion is essentially "uni-attribute" or "uni-input"! Moreover, the qualitative character of the inputs cited suggests that they are retrieved from memory rather than simply read from package or display information, as does the supporting data by Hoyer cited earlier suggesting that external search was minimal.

For all of these reasons, it is important to understand the processes that determine which small sample of inputs from the universe of possibilities might actually be used as a basis for choice. Feldman and Lynch (1988) proposed a simple theoretical framework to address this issue, and Lynch, Marmorstein, and Weigold (1988) modified and elaborated this framework.

Feldman and Lynch's Framework

Feldman and Lynch attempted to explain the likelihood that a potential input in memory (e.g., an attribute, the memory of one's own prior behavior, one's attitude, one's reaction to an advertisement, another person's suggestion, etc.) would actually be used in making a memory-based judgment or decision. Let us call the focal potential Input A. As stated by Lynch et al. (1988), the likelihood that Input A will be used as an input to some judgment or choice is the following:

1. a positive function of the *accessibility* of Input A in memory (e.g., Biehal and Chakravarti 1983, 1986; Keller 1987, 1988; Tybout, Sternthal, and Calder 1983);

2. a positive function of the perceived *diagnosticity* of Input A for the decision—i.e., the degree to which the decision suggested by Input A alone is perceived to allow one to attain one's task objectives (e.g., Costley and Brucks 1989; Lichtenstein and Srull 1985);

3. a negative function of the accessibility of alternative diagnostic inputs (B, C, D) in memory (e.g., Bettman and Sujan 1987; Higgins and Rholes 1978)

4. a negative function of the diagnosticity of alternative inputs (B, C, D) that are accessible in memory (e.g., Hoch and Ha 1986; Levin and Gaeth 1988; Lynch et al. 1988).

These simple propositions are compatible with a number of theoretical mechanisms. Lynch et al. (1988) suggested that decisions arise from an anchoring and adjustment type of process, in which inputs (or related "chunks") are sequentially retrieved with the consumer updating the implications of already considered evidence with each new input retrieved. The order of retrieval is a function of the accessibility of each input, but accessible information can be actively disregarded if it is perceived to be nondiagnostic. The cumulative diagnosticity of evidence considered up to that time is monitored (relatively effortlessly). Memory search stops after a number of searches fail to retrieve new inputs, or when the cumulative diagnosticity counter passes some threshold. This threshold depends on involvement in the decision, among other factors.

In this view, motivational direction can affect the set of cues used in judgment by determining task objectives and, hence, which types of information are diagnostic. For example, in choosing a gift for a friend, one's objective may be to select something of symbolic significance, or to buy something generally "appropriate" before the store closes, or to buy something of lasting value. Motivational intensity can affect inputs either actively, by causing information perceived as nondiagnostic to be ignored, or passively, by causing processing to stop after considering a few salient or accessible inputs—but before retrieving other less accessible inputs that may also be diagnostic.

In the sections that follow, we use this framework to interpret recent research both on determinants of inputs to memory-based judgment, and on determinants of memory-based choice. Though our central concern is with the latter topic, memory-based judgment has received more extensive study both in consumer research and in social psychological work on person impressions and on the link between delayed attitude and the recall of a persuasive message.

Research on the Link Between Recall and Memory-Based Judgment

Reliance on memory for "Facts" or "Attributes". Suppose that consumers are exposed to an advertisement for a product at Time 1 and at Time 2 we measure their attitudes toward the product and their ability to recall specific claims made in the ad. Typically, the set of claims encoded at Time 1 includes elements with varying evaluative implications for how one should evaluate the product, but consumers will remember only some subset of these claims at Time 2. One hypothesis is that the consumer's attitude at Time 2 will be a function of the sum or average of the evaluative implications of the subset recalled at the time (McGuire 1968), or the sum or average of the consumers' recalled cognitive responses (e.g., Edell and Staelin 1983; Greenwald 1968; Kisielius and Sternthal 1984, 1986; Wright 1980). In either case, holding constant the information originally encoded at Time 1, attitude judgments at Time 2 will be more positive if the subset consumers happen to remember at Time 2 is predominantly positive rather than predominantly negative. Therefore, all of the factors reviewed in the previous section on selectivity in memory for attributes might be predicted to have straightforward consequences for judgment outcomes.

For example, in the mock jury decision-making study by Reyes et al. (1980) cited earlier, the relative vividness of evidence favoring the prosecution and defense was manipulated, holding constant the content of the evidence. This manipulation had no effect on immediate judgments of the defendant's guilt or innocence. (Kisielius and Sternthal 1984, 1986; McGill and Anand 1989; and Schedler and Manis, 1986, have reported conditions under which vividness affects such immediate judgments.) When the same subjects returned after a 48-hour delay, subjects were asked to remember as many of the defense and prosecution arguments as possible, and then were asked to judge guilt or innocence again, as if they "were deciding the case now for the first time." Recall data showed that when prosecution rather than defense evidence had been vivid, subjects recalled more of the former evidence; the reverse was true when defense evidence had been relatively more vivid. In line with this, subjects judged the defendant to be more guilty when the prosecution rather than the defense evidence had been relatively more vivid.

This notion that there should be a strong correlation between the evaluative implications of specific information recalled about an attitude object and memory-based attitude judgments is intuitively quite plausible. However, in a conceptual replication of the Reyes et al. study, Schedler and Manis (1986) used causal modeling analysis to conclude that vividness affected both memory for facts and judgments of guilt or innocence, but that memory did not mediate the effects of vividness on judgments. Moreover, in the context of advertising, several field studies report a weak relationship between ad recall and persuasion (Gibson 1983; Grass and Wallace 1969; Ross 1982). Other laboratory studies have failed to find evidence of recall-judgment correlations, or these studies found that such correlations are observed in some circumstances but not in others (e.g., Beattie and Mitchell 1985; Dickson 1982; Hastie and Park 1986; Keller 1987; Lichten-

stein and Srull 1985; Loken and Hoverstadt 1985; Sherman, Zehner, Johnson, and Hirt 1983). In a related way, other experimental variables seem to have different effects on memory for specific attributes than on overall judgments (e.g., Anderson and Hubert 1963; Dreben, Fiske, and Hastie 1979; Riskey 1979), and studies show that the persistence of persuasion over time is unrelated to the persistence of recall (e.g., Watts and McGuire 1964).

Reliance on Memory for Abstractions, Inferences, and Summary Judgments. A partial explanation for the perplexing results cited above is that consumers' memory-based judgments are based on recalled abstractions, inferences, and summary judgments that were generated at the time of initial exposure to specific product information. In Feldman and Lynch's (1988) parlance, the accessibility of such alternative diagnostic inputs should decrease reliance on retrieved details. As noted earlier in this chapter, such abstractions can be retrieved and used indepedently of the raw attribute information on which they were originally based.

A classic illustration of this phenomemon comes from Lingle and Ostrom's (1979) research in social cognition on person impressions. Subjects made stimulus-based judgments of their suitability for some specified occupation based on one to seven traits (e.g., "How good a lawyer would a conscientious, shy, and intelligent person be?"). Next, subjects were asked to judge the suitability of the same person for either a similar or a dissimilar occupation without further exposure to the original trait information. There was no effect of the number of traits initially presented on the time required to make the second judgment, suggesting that subjects were not retrieving and reintegrating the original trait information, but were instead relying on their retrieved initial judgments. Other authors have also found support for such judgment retrieval processes (e.g., Lingle, Geva, Ostrom, Lieppe, and Baumgardner 1979; Lingle, Dukerich, and Ostrom 1983; Loken 1984).

Lingle and Ostrom's concept of judgment retrieval parallel's Wright's (1975) "affect referral" heuristic, whereby consumers do not process any specific attribute information in making brand choices but simply choose the alternative for which their retrieved affect is most positive. It is interesting to consider the potential role of such processes in explaining the rapid decisions reported in the observational studies of supermarket shopping behavior cited earlier. It should be apparent that these affect/judgment referral processes require low levels of effort, but may be highly adaptive if no new brands are introduced, product modifications are infrequent, and one's usage purpose remains unchanged.

The notion that initial summary judgments, once made, can take on lives of their own and affect related judgments and behavior is illustrated by Sherman, Ahlm, Berman, and Lynn's (1978) study of contrast effects on judgment, and their relation to subsequent behavior. Subjects rated the importance of recycling in the context of either a set of important or a set of unimportant issues. As might be expected, recycling was judged to be more important if rated in the context of unimportant rather than important issues. However, contrast effects on rating of the importance of recycling carried over to subsequent recycling behavior (i.e., more recycling behavior in the "unimportant context" condition in which recycling was rated as relatively important) only when the ratings were made salient. (See Higgins and Lurie, 1983, for a related example of how contrast effects influence initial categorizations that are, in turn, used as a basis for memory-based judgments independent of the information that led to those categorizations.)

Effects of Delay on Reliance on Specific Facts Versus Summary Evaluations. Given that memory-based judgments seem to be based on the evaluative implications of recalled specific facts in some studies and on recalled summary evaluations and abstractions in others, what can explain the conditions under which consumers rely on each type of input to make memory-based judgments? Several authors have suggested that reliance on summary evaluations and abstractions might increase over

time because the ability to retrieve specific facts decays more rapidly than the ability to retrieve more global judgments (Alba and Hutchinson 1987; Carlston 1980; Chattopadhyay and Alba 1988; Higgins and Rholes 1978; Kardes 1986; Lingle et al. 1979). However, the empirical evidence for this assertion has been mixed at best. Some findings seem clearly consistent with this conjecture, such as the Alba et al. (1989) results cited earlier on the persistence of memory for abstract positioning information rather than for the specific detail conveyed in advertising. However, other studies have been less supportive. For example, Kardes (1986), failed to find an effect of time on the influence of initial judgments.

At this point, one can only speculate about the reasons for the inconsistencies among studies with respect to whether or not the impact of abstractions and prior summary judgments increases over time relative to the impact of recalled specific details. First, we should note that "all things being equal" claims made by some authors that memory for specific detail should decay more rapidly than summary judgments are usually accompanied by an admission that the distinction between summary judgments and details in memory is almost unavoidably confounded with other factors related to memorability, such as distinctiveness and amount of interfering information. For instance, in the oft-cited study by Lingle et al. (1979, Experiment 2), subjects were asked to judge the suitability of a person for an occupation based on a small photograph and detailed information about eleven traits. Either one day or one week later, subjects returned for a second session and were shown the photo they had seen earlier. They were then asked to recall the exact rating they had assigned on a twenty-one point scale, and to recognize the original eleven traits in a list including these traits and an additional eleven trait foils. Recognition accuracy declined significantly over time, while memory for their evaluations did not. Ninety-seven percent of all subjects were able to reproduce their previous ratings within a scale point.

First, given that subjects had only one judgment to remember and eleven traits, the superior recall and persistence of the former is not surprising. By the same token, we should not be surprised to find poor memory for prior abstract judgments and summary evaluations under conditions in which many such judgments are made about closely related objects within a single experimental session (Baumgardner, Leippe, Ronis, and Greenwald 1983; Keller 1987). Indeed, it seems possible to arrange conditions so that many different abstract judgments about brands or persons are made based on a small amount of detailed information. Here, memory for the detailed information might be better and more persistent over time than memory for the judgments.

Second, it is obvious that if, in a given study, memory for detailed information has dissipated completely after a delay, while memory for abstractions and summary evaluations has not, memory-based judgments will be dominated by the latter and not the former. However, under conditions in which both types of information are remembered but to different degrees, it seems necessary to consider more than just the relative accessibilities of these types of information. Clearly, the perceived diagnosticity of each also plays an important role (cf. Baker and Lutz, 1988; Keller 1989). This theme will arise repeatedly in the sections that follow.

"On Line" Versus "Memory-Based" Judgment and the Effects of Processing Goals at the Time of Initial Exposure to a Brand. An apparent consensus has formed that memory-based evaluations will correlate with the evaluative implications of recalled specific facts primarily when there is no existing attitude toward the target. Whether such an attitude exists is, in turn, a function of a number of factors (see Hastie and Park, 1986, for a review), including processing goals at the time of initial encoding. Beattie and Mitchell (1985), Lichtenstein and Srull (1985, 1987), Hastie and Park (1986), and Loken and Hoverstadt (1985) have all theorized that if consumers initially receiving information about a brand have a goal of forming an evaluation or impression of that brand, the evaluation will be formed "on-line." As a consequence, in making subsequent memory-based judgments about

that brand they will be able to retrieve that evaluation directly rather than compute an evaluation based on specific facts retrieved. If, however, the processing goal at the time the consumer initially receives information about a brand does not lead to the formation of a brand impression "on-line," subsequent memory-based judgments will depend on the evaluative implications of specific facts retrieved.

Hastie and Park's (1986) theoretical review argued that this "memory-based" versus "on-line" distinction is the central variable that explains when memory-based judgments about an object will or will not correlate with the evaluative implications of recalled facts about that object. Their theory implies that whenever some overall summary judgment is available in memory because it was formed "on-line," it will be used in preference to specific facts.

This hypothesis has intuitive appeal and is consistent with other heuristics people use to simplify decision making, particularly affect referral (Wright 1975). We would argue, though, that this hypothesis is incomplete as an account of most nonroutinized cases of memory-based consumer decision making for three reasons that can be cast in terms of Feldman and Lynch's accessibility-diagnostic framework. First, it presumes that overall judgments will be accessible whenever they are available in memory. As noted earlier, associative interference among brands may make it difficult to recall memory for one's overall evaluations of consumer products (Baumgardner et al. 1983; Keller 1987, 1989a). Second, it understates the role of attribute recall under conditions in which prior judgments exist by focussing on episodic recall—for example, by focussing on recall of the content of advertising (Gibson 1983). Consumer purchase may rely more on recall of general knowledge about the brands considered, both because of general knowledge's greater accessibility and perceived diagnosticity.

Third, and most critical, the Hastie and Park (1986) hypothesis presumes that people regard overall evaluations and other summary judgments to be highly diagnostic for later related decisions, even if those later decisions involve somewhat different dimensions, and are more diagnostic for memory-based decisions than for specific recalled factual information. We would argue that this assumption may hold under some (but not all) conditions in the realm of social judgment, but it fits badly with circumstances typical of consumer decision making. It is ironic that research on the distinction between "on-line" versus "memory-based" judgment has given such heavy emphasis to the effects of processing objectives at the time of initial encoding as a determinant of whether or not brand attitudes and other judgments are formed "on-line," but has neglected almost entirely the effect of objectives at the time of memory-based decision making on what types of information are perceived by consumers to be diagnostic (cf. Alba et al. 1989; Baker and Lutz 1987; Biehal and Chakravarti 1982).

In the course of social judgment it is considerably more efficient to recall an evaluation of another individual than to generate one anew from memory each time that individual is encountered. Judgment-referral serves as a sufficiently diagnostic tool because judgments about a person often may be generated in isolation, and a simple affective or evaluative response is all that is required by the decision context. Moreover, people have elaborate "implicit personality theories" about how traits and behaviors of people covary (Kardes 1986; Lingle, Altom, and Medin 1984; Rosenberg and Sedlak 1972), making even prior judgments on somewhat different dimensions diagnostic. In the product domain, though, consumers must deal with so many product classes that their typical level of knowledge about any one is rather low. Thus, they are less likely to have well practiced, accessible inference rules for relating one abstract dimension to another, unless those dimensions cut across many product categories (Simmons 1988). This reduces both the accessibility and the diagnosticity of these earlier, indirectly related judgments at the time of later decisions.

Also, products are rarely considered in isolation, and recalled judgments may provide an inadequate basis for decision making unless they are extreme. Ultimate decisions often require greater deliberation and may hinge on the specific attributes of the product and/or the consumption situation. In essence, we argue that many product judgments possess a choice component. It follows that when alternatives cannot be separated on the basis of the global evaluations tied to them, these evaluations will be nondiagnostic and attribute recall will play a significant role.

Judgment versus Choice: Effects of Task Objectives on Diagnosticities of Inputs

In his classic review of contingent decision making, Payne (1982) considered differences in information processing between stimulus-based judgment and stimulus-based choice. As discussed by Bettman, Johnson, and Payne in Chapter 2 in this volume, judgment processing is "by alternative"—that is, by reviewing and integrating all information about a single brand or object before moving on to judge another brand or object. Choice processing tends to be more dimensional. Consumers seem to prefer to compare alternatives on each dimension in turn and to integrate the results of these comparisons rather than to integrate all information about each brand into a single overall evaluation and then choose the best alternative by comparing overall evaluations.

By extension, it can be argued that in memory-based and mixed-choice tasks in which levels of involvement are at least moderate, the diagnosticity of an input is largely driven by the ability of that input to *discriminate* the best alternative from the rest. This causes the diagnosticity of specific attributes to be, in part, contextually determined (Tversky 1977), increasing the attention paid to discriminating or "determinant" attributes (Myers and Alpert 1968). Conversely, decreasing attention is paid to attributes and overall evaluations that do not discriminate. This focus on discrimination in choice tasks can be contrasted with judgment, in which the goal is often to *categorize* objects, with no requirement to respond to objects differentially if they are largely similar.

For this reason, results from memory-based

and mixed-choice tasks generally violate the earlier mentioned consensus that retrieved specific attributes are used in memory-based decisions only if prior attitudes or judgments do not exist. One such finding comes from Biehal and Chakravarti's (1983, 1986) research on "mixed" choice. In the first phase of their experiment, subjects were exposed to information about four attributes of four hypothetical calculators (A, B, C, and D), and they were instructed either to memorize this information or to choose one of the calculators as a gift. The upshot of this manipulation was that subjects generally had better memory for the brands' attributes when they had memorized this information than when they had acquired it incidentally in making a choice. For subjects making a choice, recall was best for the brand actually chosen.

In a second phase of the experiment, both groups of subjects were asked to make a choice among brands A through D and four new brands (E, F, G, and H). Information about E through H was given externally, but information about the four attributes of A through D, seen earlier, had to be recalled from memory. Moreover, a fifth attribute was described for all eight brands.

Results showed that the brand choices were strongly affected by the ability to retrieve specific attribute information about the initial four brands. Subjects who had initially memorized information about the first four brands had a pattern of choice outcomes virtually identical to those of control subjects who made stimulus-based choices based on full information on the five attributes of all eight brands. However, subjects who had made a prior choice imperfectly recalled the brands they had rejected earlier, and this caused them to tend to select one of the four new external brands—even when these were dominated by one of the four recalled brands.

These results seem contrary to Hastie and Park's (1986) assertion that people will not rely on recalled specific facts in making memory-based decisions when summary evaluations are available. Presumably, subjects who had made prior choices in Biehal and Chakravarti's re-search had some such evaluation in memory, or at least recall of their own past choice or rejection of each brand. Note, though, that overall evaluations are not particularly informative in "mixed" choice, because the knowledge that one had earlier chosen Brand A or evaluated it highly has no necessary implication for whether it is better or worse than some new set of brands, unless one and not the other is extremely good or bad. One might speculate that if the externally described brands had been clearly worse than the remembered brands, recalled overall evaluations might have been sufficiently diagnostic. Thus, choice outcomes might not have depended on the adequacy of memory for the initial brands.

Lynch, Marmorstein, and Weigold (1988) reported two experiments bearing on the effects of the accessibility and diagnosticity of attribute information and recalled overall judgments. Their first experiment employed a mixed-choice task similar to that of Biehal and Chakravarti. Subjects saw *Consumer Reports* information about three television sets and evaluated each one. Some subjects then learned information about several new brands, interfering with their ability to recall specific details. Others saw no such interfering information. Then subjects were asked to make a choice between one of the brands seen initially and a new stimulus brand, with external information presented only for the latter. Interest centered on how ability to retrieve attribute information would influence the utilization of recalled attributes and prior evaluations in choice.

Results indicated that under conditions of low interference with attribute memory, subjects making choices made significant use of retrieved attributes but not of recalled prior evaluations, consistent with the Biehal and Chakravarti results cited previously. Under conditions of poor attribute memory, subjects apparently engaged in minimal attempts to retrieve specific attributes but, surprisingly, gave no evidence of reliance on retrieved overall evaluations. Lynch et al. (1988) speculated that this was because the two alternatives had been calibrated to be equally evaluated, so that overall evaluations were nondiagnostic.

To clarify the role of diagnosticity of recalled evaluations, Lynch et al. (1988) performed a second experiment in which subjects first were shown print ads for four brands and were asked to evaluate each brand on *two* summary dimensions. They were then asked to make a memory-based choice between two of the four brands just seen. Lynch et al. reasoned that if the two summary evaluations favored the same brand, these evaluations would be sufficiently diagnostic as a basis for choice, but if they conflicted they would be nondiagnostic. In line with this, subjects whose evaluations were consistent made significant use of recalled overall evaluations but not of the retrieved specific attribute information conveyed by the ads, whereas the reverse was true for subjects whose evaluations were inconsistent.

Lynch et al. (1988) construed this tendency for diagnosticity of inputs to decisions to depend on their discrimination power in terms of a judgment-versus-choice distinction. However, the research of Chattopadhyay and Alba (1988) indicates that diagnosticity in judgment can be similarly affected if the judgment context is perceived by consumers to call for *comparative* evaluations. They presented subjects with an advertisement for an automobile either in isolation or in the context of another similar automobile. Attitude toward the target brand was measured along with recall of and inferences about the attributes contained in the ad. Results showed that when the product had been presented in isolation, recall was unrelated to attitude. Interestingly, in this case, attitude was predictable from the abstract inferences subjects generated. These inferences were of the type described earlier that summarize several specific attributes. Thus, in the absence of context, attitudes were generated from relatively nonspecific characterizations of the product, such as its amount of comfort or power. However, when the ad was presented after viewing information about a similar automobile, recall was significantly related to attitude, whereas the abstract inferences were not. The presence of an alternative brand moved the decision context more toward choice and, therefore, prompted subjects to rely on memory for specific attributes prior to making a judgment. Because the two products were similar, abstract inferences were not sufficient to discriminate between them and, therefore, did not serve as a basis for evaluation.

The work of Costley and Brucks (1989) also demonstrates the critical role of diagnosticity and discrimination power in comparative judgment, and shows that the same factors governing the use of overall evaluations versus recalled facts determine which recalled facts will and will not be used. They exposed subjects to a target print ad conveying information about two sets of attributes, one positive and one neutral in evaluative implications. Later, subjects were asked to make a comparative evaluation of the recalled brand in comparison with an external brand shown in another ad. The authors manipulated the accessibility of positive versus neutral information about the memory ad in two ways.

First, the external stimulus ad mentioned either the dimensions on which the memory brand was positive, or those on which it was neutral. Theoretically, this should affect the relative accessibility of attributes of the memory brand by serving as a retrieval cue (Keller 1987) or by inhibiting retrieval of uncued attributes (Alba and Chattopadhyay 1986; Hoch 1984; Keller 1989). The authors reasoned that this manipulation would also affect the diagnosticity of the attribute dimension on which the memory brand was positive versus neutral. The diagnosticity of those dimensions would depend upon whether or not the external brand was described in terms of the same dimensions, so that the two brands could be compared and discriminated on those dimensions (Johnson 1988; Payne 1982; Slovic and MacPhillamy 1974). Results showed that this factor explained 16 percent of the variance in recall of positive attributes, and 18 percent of the variance in preferences. The effects on preferences cannot be attributed to diagnosticity alone, because a control group given a stimulus-based choice between the external brand and the brand shown in the "memory" ad showed no effect of which attribute dimensions were mentioned in the ad for the external brand.

A second manipulation varied accessibility of positive versus neutral attributes of the memory brand without manipulating diagnosticity. For half of the subjects, the positive attributes were presented pictorially and the neutral attributes were presented in accompanying text, whereas the reverse was true for the remaining subjects. While this manipulation explained roughly 25 percent of the variance in recall, it explained no significant variance (0.4 percent) in preferences for the memory brand versus the external brand. This suggests that we should be cautious in extrapolating results from other research on recall of visual versus verbal advertising (e.g., Childers and Houston 1984) in order to draw conclusions about the use of this information in decision making. Costley and Brucks interpreted the complete pattern of results to show that accessibility only enhances use of an input if it is also diagnostic—at least under conditions in which alternative inputs are both accessible and diagnostic.

Accessibility and Diagnosticity of Nonattribute Information

Our discussion up to this point has focussed on the memory accessibility and diagnosticity of two generic types of inputs to choice—specific "attribute" information and prior global judgments. Though these types of inputs have received the most research attention to date, it is useful to think more broadly about the types of inputs that might be used in consumer choice, and how their influence might change over time. The first part of this question has been the topic of much persuasion research and has examined the relative persuasiveness of argument or attribute information and other associated cues (variably called peripheral cues or heuristic cues), such as the characteristics of the spokesperson. The results, summarized in Chapter 7 of this volume (Petty et al.), generally show that strong message arguments are most persuasive when the individual is highly involved in the message and that peripheral information is most persuasive under low-involvement conditions.

Unfortunately, there is a surprising dearth of research on the relative persuasiveness of various types of information over time. Theory suggests that the basic result just described should generalize to cases in which memory plays a larger role. Indeed, it has been demonstrated that the persuasive effect of a message decays less over time when the message was originally processed under high- versus low-involvement conditions (Chaiken 1980; Haugtvedt 1989). This result is plausible and intuitive and stems from the higher memorability and salience of the message arguments following more intense processing.

However, there exists virtually no research that examines the relative persuasiveness of different types of information independent of involvement and as a function of time. Psychologists interested in delayed persuasion effects have rarely examined anything other than attribute information or attribute-related thoughts (see Sawyer and Ward, 1979, for a review). In consumer research there has been very little attention paid to persistence and resistance at all (Lesne and Didow 1987). This is rather stunning, given the multitude of cues contained in an ad and the long-term effects advertising is designed to achieve.

Several exceptions to this rule exist. The first involves the long-studied sleeper effect, in which persuasive effects of a message increase over time. The effect is interesting because it includes precisely the feature of interest here, namely, delayed measurement and messages that contain both central arguments and peripheral cues. Recent attempts to demonstrate reliable sleeper effects have succeeded but require that the message arguments and peripheral cues be memorable in the short term and have roughly equivalent but opposite persuasive impact (see Hannah and Sternthal 1984; Mazursky and Schul 1988; Pratkanis, Greenwald, Leippe, and Baumgardner 1988). In a consumer context this might be exemplified by the presentation of legitimate product attributes in an advertisement by a noncredible manufacturer. In such cases, persuasive impact will increase over time when the impact of the source decays more rapidly than the impact of the attributes. Although this research outlines the conditions that must be met in order to produce what previously appeared to be an ephemeral effect, it says little about real-world generalizability because it used procedures that were designed to maximize the long-term impact of the message arguments and the short-term impact of the spokesperson, while at the same time hindering the association between the two. One of the key missing elements in all persuasion research concerns the inherent memorability and impact of different types of information.

The second study to examine central and peripheral information over time did not manipulate memorability of the cues and found a different pattern of results; that is, messages became more persuasive over time as the product attributes became less memorable (Alba et al. 1989). In brief, subjects were presented with an ad for a television. The television performed poorly on three important dimensions but also possessed six good, but relatively unimportant, features. Immediately afterward or two days later a comparison brand was presented and subjects were asked to make a choice. The comparison brand dominated the first brand on the important dimension but lacked the additional features. Results showed that the proportion of subjects choosing the comparison brand decreased over time; that is, choice became less optimal. Debriefing showed that, as time passed, memory for the specific features of the first brand declined, but memory of the fact that it had many attributes remained. Thus, unable to make attribute-by-attribute comparisons, subjects chose the brand with the greatest number of attributes, which by most accounts would be considered a peripheral cue (Petty and Cacioppo 1984).

A third set of studies by Moore and Hutchinson (1983, 1985) also pertains to conditions under which nondiagnostic peripheral cues might actually increase their influence on decisions over time. Subjects were exposed to a series of ads that varied in the evaluative reactions they induced. Some ads were very unpleasant (e.g., irritating ads for personal hygiene products), whereas others induced neutral reactions, and others were very pleasant. Subjects were later asked to judge their liking for the brands based upon brand name alone. Both immediately and two days after exposure, brand liking was a positive function of evaluative reactions to the ads themselves. After seven days, however, ratings of brand liking were a J-shaped function of the evaluations of the ad, so that brands associated with very negative ads were rated higher than those associated with more neutral ads. Presumably, this stemmed from the greater attention and elaboration given to evaluatively extreme ads, so that a single exposure to these ads caused a greater increment in subjective brand familiarity than did exposure to more neutral ads. Over time, specific ad and brand reactions were forgotten, but this subjective familiarity became confusable with weak but positive affect and used as a basis for preference ratings as in "mere exposure" effects (Zajonc 1980).

A final series of studies pertaining to the effect of differential use of attribute and nonattribute information over time comes from the fascinating research of Wilson and his colleagues on the disruptive effects of thinking about reasons for our preferences on attitude behavior relations. (See Wilson, Dunn, Kraft, and Lisle (1989) for a review.) In the paradigm used by Wilson and his colleagues, subjects acquire affective reactions to some attitude object or set of objects through direct experience. All subjects are asked to rate their preferences, and subsequently, their behavior toward the objects is measured. For some subjects, though, the preference measures are preceded by instructions to organize their thoughts by thinking about reasons for their preferences, whereas for the remaining subjects this task is replaced by a filler task. The standard result is that attitude or preference measures from subjects who have thought about reasons for their preferences exhibit low correlations with subsequent behavior, whereas these correlations are strong for subjects who rated their preferences without giving reasons.[7]

---

[7]Millar and Tesser (1986) show that this is true only for behaviors that are consummatory (i.e., performed for the pleasure of the experience, as in Hirschman and Holbrook's 1982 concept of experiential consumption), and that the opposite pattern actually occurs for behaviors that are cognitively driven (i.e., performed for their instrumental value in attaining some objective). Wilson, Kraft, and Dunn (1989) demonstrate that giving reasons reduces attitude behavior correlations only for subjects who are low in prior knowledge about the attitude object.

Wilson et al. explain this result by postulating that much behavior is driven by pure affect, rather than on the basis of cognitions about the attitude object, or more cognitive "attitudes." (See Cohen and Areni in Chapter 6 of this volume for further justification of an affect-versus-attitude or evaluation distinction.) Affective reactions to people, products, and other objects are caused by factors that are only partially accessible to conscious awareness. When asked to give reasons for preferences, consumers come up with responses that seem sensible to them. They may actually think that these reasons are true. But their reasons tend to be either plausible fabrications or selectively retrieved in a way that is biased toward salient cues. When an attitude measure is administered immediately following self-reflection about one's reasons, people persuade themselves that they hold the attitudes implied by these reasons. In essence, they form purely cognitive "attitudes." Because what is most salient will vary considerably among individuals, these purely cognitive attitudes need not differ on average from purely affective responses given to the same measures by subjects who did not give reasons, but these attitudes do have more "error variance."

When subjects who have given reasons then have an opportunity to engage in behavior related to the persons, products, or objects just rated, their initial choices are in line with the reason-driven preferences they just stated. However, if the behavior is more long term, they sometimes receive affective feedback that the alternatives that they thought they liked do not give them that much pleasure. Thus, they revert to making behavioral decisions based on pure affect. For subjects who did not give reasons, their preference judgments, initial behavior, and long-term behavior are all based on the same affective responses. Thus, attitude-behavior correlations are high.

There seem to be two plausible explanations for the differential effects of giving reasons on short-term versus long-term behaviors. The explanation offered by Wilson et al. (1989) is that affective *feedback* invalidates the reconstituted preferences formed in response to giving rea-

sons, causing people to revert to choosing based on noncognitive affect. This is in essence a diagnosticity explanation. Alternatively, memory for the reasons generated or for newly formed preferences based on them may decay rapidly, whereas the affective reactions may be retrieved spontaneously and automatically. The less accessible one's reasons become, the greater the use of the alternative input of affect should be.

In any case, this research has important implications for consumer behavior, both in showing the importance of nonattribute information in influencing preferences and choice and in suggesting how the determinants of behavior can be altered over time due to changes in the accessibility and perceived diagnosticity of potential inputs in memory. It also reaffirms the importance of information processing that goes on below the level of conscious awareness to preferences and behavior, and it provides a challenge to our research that relies so heavily on self-report methods.

Memory, Judgment, and Choice: Implications for Research on the Attitude-Behavior Relationship

Consumer researchers and social psychologists have evinced a long-standing concern with the relationship between attitude toward a brand and behavior toward the same object, and with the factors that affect the strength of this relationship (e.g., Fazio, Powell, and Williams 1989; Fishbein and Ajzen 1975; Wicker 1969). Traditionally, correlation between the two has been taken as presumptive evidence that attitudes *cause* behavior, although the information processing mechanisms by which this might occur have been given little research attention until recently. Research in the 1980s has made it increasingly apparent that the effects of factors influencing attitude-behavior correlations can be understood in terms of the effects of memory on the inputs used for behavioral choice.

In an important review paper, Fazio and Zanna (1978) built the case that attitude-behavior correlations are stronger when attitudes are based on direct experiences with the attitude object rather than on second-hand information about the same object. Smith and Swinyard (1983) made a similar point about the effects of product trial versus advertising, arguing that product trial leads to higher information acceptance than advertising because people rarely derogate themselves as sources of information. This implies that the perceived reliability (and thus diagnosticity) of retrieved information acquired by experience would be relatively high. This higher information acceptance leads to the formation of "higher-order" beliefs and affect that are held with more confidence. This is in contrast to the "lower-order" beliefs and affect formed on the basis of exposure to advertising. In line with this, attitude-behavior correlations were significantly stronger when based on product trial rather than advertising.

One interpretation of these results is that attitude-behavior correlations are higher when consumers use retrieved attitudes directly as inputs to choice, as in Wright's (1975) affect-referral notion, rather than basing behavior on some subset of facts or other nonattitudinal inputs. If attitudes formed from trial are held with more confidence, they may be more diagnostic for choice and thus used more than if they are formed on the basis of advertising (cf. Berger and Mitchell 1989).

Fazio has developed in his 1986 paper (see also Fazio, Chen, McDonel, and Sherman 1982; Fazio, Powell and Herr 1983; Fazio, Powell, Sanbonmatsu, and Kardes 1986; Fazio and Williams 1986; Fazio, Powell, and Williams 1989) a process model that provides a different potential explanation of the effects of direct experience, focusing on attitude accessibility rather than attitude diagnosticity. He argues that, holding constant the polarity of attitudes, attitudes vary on a dimension of accessibility, ranging from nonattitudes (when no attitude has been formed) to attitudes that are available but not readily accessible, to attitudes that are so accessible that they are retrieved spontaneously on mere observation of the attitude object. Arguably, direct experience, as through product trial, heightens the accessibility of an attitude more than does watching

an ad, which may not even prompt the formation of an attitude.

Fazio (1986) maintains that if one's attitude toward the object is accessible, it "colors perceptions" of the object, filtering out attitude-inconsistent information and filtering in attitude-consistent information. In most of his published work, this information being filtered in or out comes from the stimulus environment (e.g., Fazio and Herr 1984; Fazio et al. 1983; Fazio and Williams 1986; Houston and Fazio 1989) rather than from memory.[8] Fazio argues that these filtered perceptions are the proximate cause of behavior. Attitude or affect is not directly used as an input to choice but "guides behavior" only indirectly by screening perceptions. Lynch et al. (1988) suggest two alternative possibilities—that accessible attitudes are used as direct inputs to choice as in Wright's (1975) concept of affect-referral, or that attitudes are used as a basis for retrieving a consideration set of alternative brands or behaviors, with retrieved details used to choose from among the set. Fazio, Powell, and Williams (1989) speculate that in environments in which stimulus information is sparse, the selective perceptions component of their theory may become less important, and people may use retrieved affect directly as an input to choice.

We should note that the designs used by Fazio and his colleagues make it difficult to disentangle two "selective perception" explanations of why accessible attitudes lead to higher attitude-behavior correlations. Their explanation is that accessible attitudes filter in attitude-consistent new information, but filter our new information if it is attitude discrepant. However, it is not possible to rule out the interpreta-

---

[8]This notion has an interesting parallel to the memory literature on schema theory. Some schema theorists have asserted that the activation of a schema prior to exposure to ambiguous new information causes schema-consistent recall by editing out schema-inconsistent details at the time of encoding. Alba and Hasher (1983) review evidence that allows rejection of this assertion. Preferential recall of schema-consistent information seems instead to be due to effects of the activated schema on interpretation, or to the cuing effects of schemata at the time of retrieval. See also Hastie and Park (1986) for a discussion of how this bears on explanations of memory-judgment correlations.

tion that those with accessible attitudes are more likely to filter out *both* attitude-consistent and attitude-inconsistent new information. Because consumers think they already know how the object is to be evaluated, they have less motivation to attend to new information. This parallels the finding in the literature on consumer search that those with higher knowledge see fewer benefits of search and thus search less (Newman 1977; Punj and Staelin 1983).

Note that in this case, if attitudes are measured at Time 1 and consumers are exposed to new information at Time 2, attitudes would change less as a consequence of new information if it is edited out. Thus, if the Time 1 attitude measure is correlated with a measure of behavior at Time 3, attitude-behavior correlations would be higher for consumers who had not changed their attitudes, because they had edited out all new information.

The connection of this hypothesis to Sujan's (1985) work on "piecemeal" processing versus "category-based" processing merits attention (see also Cohen 1982). Sujan studied consumers' stimulus-based judgments of cameras based on ads that either violated or failed to violate the expectations for the camera category (110 cameras versus 35 mm single lens reflex cameras) established by the ad headline. Based on Fiske and Pavelchak's (1986) notion of "schema triggered affect," she predicted that consumers exposed to a novel brand would first attempt to classify it as an instance of a familiar category. If successful, the brand would be evaluated by simply retrieving the affect associated with that category rather than by detailed review of its attributes. If the novel instance could not be matched to a category, its specific attributes would be reviewed and integrated "piecemeal," as in the traditional multiattribute model. Results were consistent with these hypotheses.

Fazio's model, in which filtered perceptions are the direct determinants of behavior, suggests a piecemeal mode of processing. If Sujan is correct, and "category-based" processing is the norm unless the evidence grossly violates category knowledge, one can see that (1) both consistent and moderately inconsistent new in-

formation could be filtered out if categories and their associated affect are highly accessible, leading to higher attitude behavior correlations, and (2) those with accessible categories would, therefore, be more likely to reconstruct when answering researcher's questions about perceptions, leading to the appearance that attitude-consistent new information had been selected into the processing.

CONCLUSION

Historically, memory effects on decision making have typically been discussed in terms of the processing constraints imposed by the limited capacity of short-term memory, often under the heading of information load. In this chapter we have attempted to highlight the potential importance of long-term memory. We have taken the relatively extreme position that the effects of long-term memory are so pervasive and fundamental as to cast doubt on the existence of any purely stimulus-based decisions in the real world. The basis for our position lies not only in the mundane observation that few consumer decisions take place in the presence of complete information but also in the belief that memory exerts itself even in stimulus-intense environments through its effects on attention and perception.

If one accepts our argument concerning the role of memory, then one must also conclude that our understanding of much real-world consumer behavior is dismally low. As noted at the outset, most traditional decision research has treated memory as an annoyance, requiring experimental control, rather than as a target for investigation. Thus, we are left with a meager database from which to generalize. Unfortunately, extrapolation to memory contexts from traditional paradigms may be folly. Memory appears to affect not only the amount of information that enters into the decision process but also the type of information considered and the heuristics used to process it. Also unfortunate is our inability to extrapolate from other domains, such as social judgment, that have explicitly considered the effects of memory.

The character of the decision process may be highly sensitive to the task required. Judgment tasks and choice tasks may invoke significantly different decision strategies.

Our purpose in writing this chapter is not to lament our current state of knowledge but rather to provide incentive for corrective action. The opportunities are clear. However, in order to exploit them a broader conceptualization of memory is necessary, as is a rethinking of the paradigms we choose to employ.

REFERENCES

ALBA, JOSEPH W. AND AMITAVA CHATTOPADHYAY (1985). "The Effects of Context and Part-Category Cues on the Recall of Competing Brands," *Journal of Marketing Research*, 22 (August), 340–349.

ALBA, JOSEPH W., AND AMITAVA CHATTOPADHYAY (1986). "Salience Effects in Brand Recall," *Journal of Marketing Research*, 23 (November), 363–369.

ALBA, JOSEPH W., AND LYNN HASHER (1983). "Is Memory Schematic?", *Psychological Bulletin*, 93 (March), 203–231.

ALBA, JOSEPH W., AND J. WESLEY HUTCHINSON (1987). "Dimensions of Consumer Expertise," *Journal of Consumer Research*, 13 (March), 411–454.

ALBA, JOSEPH W., AND J. WESLEY HUTCHINSON (in press). "Public Policy Implications of Consumer Knowledge," in *Advances in Marketing and Public Policy*, Vol. 2, ed. Paul N. Bloom. Greenwich, CT: JAI Press.

ALBA, JOSEPH W., AND HOWARD MARMORSTEIN (1987). "The Effects of Frequency Knowledge on Consumer Decision Making," *Journal of Consumer Research*, 14, (June), 14–25.

ALBA, JOSEPH W., HOWARD MARMOSTEIN, AND AMITAVA CHATTOPADHYAY (1989). "Memory-Based Preference Reversals," Working Paper, University of Florida, Gainesville, FL.

ALPERT, MARK I., LINDA L. GOLDEN, AND WAYNE D. HOYER (1983). "The Impact of Repetition on Advertisement Miscomprehension and Effectiveness," in *Advances in Consumer Research*, eds. Richard P. Bagozzi and Alice M. Tybout. Ann Arbor, MI: Association for Consumer Research, 130–135.

ANDERSON, CRAIG A., MARK R. LEPPER, AND LEE ROSS (1980). "Perserverance of Social Theories: The Role of Explanation in the Persistence of Discredited Information," *Journal of Personality and Social Psychology*, 39 (December), 1037–1049.

ANDERSON, JOHN (1983). *The Architecture of Cognition.* Cambridge, MA: Harvard University Press.

ANDERSON, NORMAN H., AND STEPHEN HUBERT (1963). "Effects of Concomitant Verbal Recall on Order Effects in Personality Impression Formation," *Journal of Verbal Learning and Verbal Behavior*, 2 (December), 379–391.

ARKES, HAL R., AND ALLAN R. HARKNESS (1983). "Estimates of Contingency Between Two Dichotomous Variables," *Journal of Experimental Psychology: General*, 112 (March), 117–135.

ARMSTRONG, GARY M., METIN N. GUROL, AND FREDERICK A. RUSS (1983). "A Longitudinal Evaluation of the Listerine Corrective Advertising Campaign," *Journal of Public Policy & Marketing*, 2, 16–28.

AXELROD, J. N. (1968). "Advertising Measures that Predict Purchase," *Journal of Advertising Research*, 8 (March), 3–17.

BACON, FREDERICK T. (1979). "Credibility of Repeated Statements: Memory for Trivia," *Journal of Experimental Psychology: Human Learning and Memory*, 5 (May), 241–252.

BAKER, WILLIAM J. WESLEY HUTCHINSON, DANNY MOORE, AND PRAKASH NEDUNGADI (1986). "Brand Familiarity and Advertising: Effects on the Evoked Set and Brand Preference," in *Advances in Consumer Research*, Vol. 13, ed. Richard J. Lutz. Provo, UT: Association for Consumer Research, 637–642.

BAKER, WILLIAM E., AND RICHARD J. LUTZ (1988). "The Relevance-Accessibility Model of Advertising Effectiveness," in *Nonverbal Communications in Advertising*, eds. Sidney Hecker and David M. Stewart. Lexington, MA: Lexington Books, 59–84.

BARGH, JOHN A., AND ROMAN D. THEIN (1985). "Individual Construct Accessibility, Person Memory, and the Recall-Judgment Link: The Case of Information Overload," *Journal of Personality and Social Psychology*, 49 (November), 1129–1146.

BARSALOU, LAWRENCE W. (1983). "Ad Hoc Categories," *Memory and Cognition*, 11 (May), 211–227.

BARSALOU, LAWRENCE W. (1985). "Ideals, Central Tendency, and Frequency of Instantiation as Determinants of Graded Structure," *Journal of Experimental Psychology: Learning, Memory, and Cognition,* 11 (October), 629–654.

BARSALOU, LAWRENCE, W., AND BRIAN H. ROSS (1986). "The Roles of Automatic and Strategic Processing in Sensitivity to Superordinate and Property Frequency," *Journal of Experimental Psychology: Learning, Memory, and Cognition,* 12 (January), 116–134.

BAUMGARDNER, MICHAEL H., MICHAEL R. LEIPPE, DAVID L. RONIS, AND ANTHONY G. GREENWALD (1983). "In Search of Reliable Persuasion Effects: II. Associative Interference and Persistence of Persuasion in a Message-Dense Environment," *Journal of Personality and Social Psychology,* 45 (September), 524–537.

BEATTIE, ANN E., AND ANDREW A. MITCHELL (1985). "The Relationship Between Advertising Recall and Persuasion: An Experimental Investigation," in *Psychological Processes and Advertising Effects: Theory, Research, and Application,* eds. Linda F. Alwitt and Andrew A. Mitchell. Hillsdale NJ: Erlbaum, 129–155.

BECKWITH, NEIL E., AND DONALD R. LEHMANN (1975). "The Importance of Halo Effects in Multi-Attribute Attitude Models," *Journal of Marketing Research,* 12 (August), 265–275.

BELK, RUSSELL W. (1975). "Situational Variables and Consumer Behavior," *Journal of Consumer Research,* 2 (December), 157–164.

BERGER, IDA E., AND ANDREW A. MITCHELL (1989). "The Effect of Advertising on Attitude Accessibility, Attitude Confidence, and the Attitude-Behavior Relationship," *Journal of Consumer Research,* 16 (December), 267–279.

BETTMAN, JAMES R., AND C. WHAN PARK (1980). "Effects of Prior Knowledge and Experience and Phase of the Choice Process on Consumer Decision Processes: A Protocol Analysis," *Journal of Consumer Research,* 7 (December), 234–248.

BETTMAN, JAMES R., AND MITA SUJAN (1987). "Effects of Framing on Evaluation of Comparable and Noncomparable Alternatives by Expert and Novice Consumers," *Journal of Consumer Research,* 14 (September), 141–154.

BIEHAL, GABRIEL, AND DIPANKAR CHAKRAVARTI (1982). "Information Presentation Format and Learning Goals as Determinants of Consumers' Memory Retrieval and Choice Processes," *Journal of Consumer Research,* 8 (March), 431–441.

BIEHAL, GABRIEL, AND DIPANKAR CHAKRAVARTI (1983). "Information Accessibility as a Moderator of Consumer Choice," *Journal of Consumer Research,* 10 (June), 1–14.

BIEHAL, GABRIEL, AND DIPANKAR CHAKRAVARTI (1986). "Consumers' Use of Memory and External Information in Choice: Macro and Micro Perspectives," *Journal of Consumer Research,* 13 (March), 382–405.

BOUSEFIELD, W. A., AND C. H. SEDGEWICK (1944). "An Analysis of Sequences of Restricted Associative Responses," *Journal of General Psychology,* 30 (April), 149–165.

BRUCKS, MERRIE (1985). "The Effects of Product Class Knowledge on Information Search Behavior," *Journal of Consumer Research,* 12 (June), 1–16.

BRUCKS, MERRIE (1986). "A Typology of Consumer Knowledge Content," In *Advances in Consumer Research,* Vol. 13, ed. Richard J. Lutz. Provo, UT: Association for Consumer Research, 58–63.

BRUNO, KRISTIN J. (1980). "Discrimination of Assertions and Implications: A Training Procedure for Adults and Adolescents," *Journal of Educational Psychology,* 72 (December), 850–860.

BURKE, RAYMOND R., AND THOMAS K. SRULL (1988). "Competitive Interference and Consumer Memory for Advertising," *Journal of Consumer Research,* 15 (June), 55–68.

BURKE, RAYMOND R., WAYNE S. DESARBO, RICHARD L. OLIVER, AND THOMAS S. ROBERTSON (1988). "Deception by Implication: An Experimental Investigation," *Journal of Consumer Research,* 14 (March), 483–494.

CALDER, BOBBY J., AND BRIAN STERNTHAL (1980). "Television Commercial Wearout: An Information Processing View," *Journal of Marketing Reseearch,* 17 (May), 173–186.

CANTOR, NANCY, AND WALTER MISCHEL (1979). "Prototypes in Person Perception," in *Advances in Experimental Social Psychology,* Vol. 12 ed. Leonard Berkowitz. New York: Academic Press.

CARLSTON, DONAL E. (1980). "The Recall and Use of Traits and Events in Social Inference Processes," *Journal of Experimental Social Psychology,* 16 (July), 303–328.

CHAIKEN, SHELLY (1980). "Heuristic Versus Systematic Information Processing and the Use of Source Versus Message Cues in Persuasion," *Journal of Personality and Social Psychology,* 39 (November), 752–766.

CHATTOPADHYAY, AMITAVA, AND JOSEPH W. ALBA (1988). "The Situational Importance of Recall and Inference in Consumer Decision Making," *Journal of Consumer Research,* 15 (June), 1–12.

CHILDERS, TERRY L., AND MICHAEL J. HOUSTON (1984). "Conditions for a Picture-Superiority Effect on Consumer Memory," *Journal of Consumer Research,* 15 (September), 643–654.

CHRISTENSEN-SZALANSKI, JAY J. J., AND LEE ROY BEACH (1984). "The Citation Bias: Fad and Fashion in the Judgment and Decision Literature," *American Psychologist,* 39 (January), 75–78.

COHEN, JOEL B. (1982). "The Role of Affect in Categorization: Toward a Reconsideration of the Concept of Attitude," in *Advances in Consumer Research,* Vol. 9, ed. Andrew Mitchell. Provo, UT: Association for Consumer Research, 472–477.

COLLINS, ALLAN, ELEANOR H. WARNOCK, NELLEKE AIELLO, AND MARK L. MILLER (1975). "Reasoning from Incomplete Knowledge," in *Representation and Understanding,* eds. Daniel G. Bobrow and Allan Collins. New York: Academic Press, 383–415.

COOPER, WILLIAM H. (1981). "Ubiquitous Halo," *Psychological Bulletin,* 90 (September), 218–244.

COSTLEY, CAROLYN L., AND MERRIE BRUCKS (1989). "Selective Recall and Information Use in Consumer Preferences," Working Paper Series No. 46 (August), Department of Marketing, University of Arizona, Tucson, AZ.

CRAIG, C. SAMUEL, BRIAN STERNTHAL, AND CLARK LEAVITT (1976). "Advertising Wearout: An Experimental Analysis," *Journal of Marketing Research,* 13 (November), 365–372.

CROCKER, JENNIFER (1981). "Judgment of Covariation by Social Perceivers," *Psychological Bulletin,* 90 (September), 272–292.

CROCKER, JENNIFER (1984). "A Schematic Approach to Changing Consumers Beliefs," in *Advances in Consumer Research,* Vol. 11, ed. Thomas C. Kinnear. Provo, UT: Association for Consumer Research, 472–477.

CROWDER, ROBERT G. (1976). *Principles of Learning and Memory.* Hillsdale, NJ: Erlbaum.

DELLAROSA, DENISE, AND LYLE E. BOURNE, JR. (1984). "Decisions and Memory: Differential Retrievability of Consistent and Contradictory Evidence," *Journal of Verbal Learning and Verbal Behavior,* 23 (December), 669–682.

DICK, ALAN S., GABRIEL BIEHAL, AND DIPANKAR CHAKRAVARTI (1990). "Memory-Based Inferences During Consumer Choice," *Journal of Consumer Research.* (in press.).

DICKSON, PETER R. (1982). "Person-Situation: Segmentation's Missing Link," *Journal of Marketing,* 46 (Fall), 56–64.

DICKSON, PETER R., AND ALAN G. SAWYER (1986). "Point-of-Purchase Behavior and Price Perceptions of Supermarket Shoppers," Marketing Science Institute, Working Paper No. 86–102, Cambridge, MA: MSI.

DREBEN, ELIZABETH K., SUSAN T. FISKE, AND REID HASTIE (1979). "The Independence of Evaluative and Item Information Impression and Recall Order Effects in Behavior-Based Impression Formation," *Journal of Personality and Social Psychology,* 37 (October), 1758–1768.

EDELL, JULIE A., AND RICHARD STAELIN (1983). "The Information Processing of Pictures in Print Advertisements," *Journal of Consumer Research,* 10 (June), 45–61.

EDELL, JULIE A., AND KEVIN LANE KELLER (1989). "The Information Processing of Coordinated Media Campaigns," *Journal of Marketing Research,* 26 (May), 149–163.

EINHORN, HILLEL J. (1971). "Use of Nonlinear, Noncompensatory Models as a Function of Task and Amount of Information," *Organizational Behavior and Human Performance,* 6 (January), 1–27.

ERIKSON, GARY M., JOHNY K. JOHANSSON, AND PAUL CHAO (1984). "Image Variables in Multi-Attribute Product Evaluations: Country-of-Origin Effects," *Journal of Consumer Research,* 11 (September), 694–699.

FARQUHAR, PETER H., AND ANTHONY R. PRATKANIS (1989). "Decisive Advantage Choice Models," Paper Presented at the TIMS Marketing Science Conference, Durham, NC.

FAZIO, RUSSELL H. (1986). "How Do Attitudes Guide Behavior" in *Handbook of Motivation and Cognition,* eds. Richard M. Sorrentino and E. Tory Higgins. New York: Guilford Press, 204–243.

FAZIO, RUSSELL H., JEAW-MEI CHEN, ELIZABETH C. MCDONEL, AND STEVEN J. SHERMAN (1982). "Attitude Accessibility, Attitude-Behavior Consistency, and the Strength of the Object-Evaluation Association," *Journal of Experimental Social Psychology,* 18 (July), 339–357.

FAZIO, RUSSELL H., MARTHA C. POWELL, AND PAUL M. HERR (1983). "Toward a Process Model of the Attitude-Behavior Relation: Accessing One's Attitude upon Mere Observation of the

Attitude Object," *Journal of Personality and Social Psychology*, 44 (April), 723–735.

FAZIO, RUSSELL H., MARTHA C. POWELL, AND CAROL J. WILLIAMS (1989). "The Role of Attitude Accessibility in the Attitude-to-Behavior Process," *Journal of Consumer Research*, 16 (December), 280–288.

FAZIO, RUSSELL H., PAUL M. HERR, AND TIMOTHY J. OLNEY (1984). "Attitude Accessibility Following a Self-Perception Process," *Journal of Personality and Social Psychology*, 47 (August), 277–286.

FAZIO, RUSSELL H., DAVID M. SANBONMATSU, MARTHA C. POWELL, AND FRANK R. KARDES (1986). "On the Automatic Activation of Attitudes," *Journal of Personality and Social Psychology*, 50 (February), 229–238.

FAZIO, RUSSELL H., AND CAROL WILLIAMS (1986). "Attitude Accessibility as a Moderator of the Attitude-Perception and Attitude-Behavior Relations: An Investigation of the 1984 Presidential Election," *Journal of Personality and Social Psychology*, 51 (September), 505–514.

FAZIO, RUSSELL H., AND MARK P. ZANNA (1978). "Attitudinal Qualities Relating to the Strength of the Attitude-Behavior Relationship," *Journal of Experimental Social Psychology*, 14 (July), 398–408.

FELDMAN, JACK M., AND JOHN G. LYNCH, JR. (1988). "Self-Generated Validity and Other Effects of Measurement on Belief, Attitude, Intention, and Behavior," *Journal of Applied Psychology*, 73 (August), 421–435.

FEUSTEL, TIMOTHY C., RICHARD M. SHIFFRIN, AND AITA SALASOO (1983). "Episodic and Lexical Contributions to the Repetition Effect in Word Identification," *Journal of Experimental Psychology: General*, 112 (September), 309–346.

FINN, ADAM (1988). "Print Ad Recognition Readership Scores: An Information Processing Perspective," *Journal of Marketing Research*, 25 (May), 168–177.

FISCHHOFF, BARUCH, PAUL SLOVIC, AND SARAH LICHTENSTEIN (1978). "Fault Trees: Sensitivity of Estimated Failure Probabilities to Problem Representation," *Journal of Experimental Psychology: Human Perception and Performance*, 4 (May), 330–344.

FISCHOFF, BARUCH, PAUL SLOVIC, AND SARAH LICHTENSTEIN (1980). "Knowing What You Want: Measuring Labile Values," in *Cognitive Processes in Choice and Decision Behavior*, ed.

Thomas S. Wallsten. Hillsdale, NJ: Erlbaum, 117–141.

FISHBEIN, MARTIN, AND ICEK AJZEN (1975). *Belief, Attitude, Intention, and Behavior: An Introduction to Theory and Research*. Reading, MA: Addison-Wesley.

FISKE, SUSAN T., AND MARK A. PAVELCHAK (1986). "Category-Based Versus Piecemeal-Based Affective Responses: Developments in Schema-Triggered Affect," in *The Handbook of Motivation and Cognition: Foundations of Social Behavior*, eds. Richard M. Sorrentino and E. Tory Higgins. New York: Guilford Press, 167–203.

FOLKES, VALERIE S. (1988). "The Availability Heuristic and Perceived Risk," *Journal of Consumer Research*, 15 (June), 13–23.

FREEDMAN, J. L., AND ELIZABETH F. LOFTUS (1971). "Retrieval of Words from Long-Term Memory," *Journal of Verbal Learning and Verbal Behavior*, 10, 107–115.

FRIENDLY, MICHAEL L. (1979). "Methods for Finding Graphic Representations of Associative Memory Structures," in *Memory Organization and Structure*, ed. C. R. Puff. New York: Academic Press, 85–129.

FUNDER, DAVID C. (1987). "Errors and Mistakes: Evaluating the Accuracy of Social Judgment," *Psychological Bulletin*, 101 (January), 75–90.

GARDNER, MERYL PAULA (1983). "Advertising Effects on Attributes Recalled and Criteria Used for Brand Evaluations," *Journal of Consumer Research*, 10 (December), 310–318.

GIBSON, LAWRENCE D. (1983). "Not Recall," *Journal of Advertising Research*, 23 (February/March), 39–46.

GILOVICH, THOMAS (1981). "Seeing the Past in the Present: The Effect of Associations to Familiar Events on Judgments and Decisions," *Journal of Personality and Social Psychology*, 40 (May), 797–808.

GORDON, PETER C., AND KEITH J. HOLYOAK (1983). "Implicit Learning and Generalization of the 'Mere Exposure' Effect," *Journal of Personality and Social Psychology*, 45 (September), 492–500.

GRASS, ROBERT C., AND WALLACE H. WALLACE (1969). "Satiation Effects of TV Commercials," *Journal of Advertising Research*, 9 (September), 3–8.

GREENWALD, ANTHONY G. (1968). "Cognitive Learning, Cognitive Response to Persuasion and Attitude Change," in *Psychological Foundation of At-*

titudes, eds. Anthony G. Greenwald, Timothy C. Brock, and Thomas M. Ostrom. New York: Academic Press, 147–170.

GRUENWALD, PAUL J., AND GREGORY R. LOCKHEAD (1980). "The Free Recall of Category Examples," *Journal of Experimental Psychology: Human Learning and Memory,* 6 (May), 225–240.

HALEY, RUSSELL I., AND PETER B. CASE (1979). "Testing Thirteen Attitude Scales For Agreement and Brand Discrimination," *Journal of Marketing,* 43 (Fall), 20–32.

HANNAH, DARLENE B., AND BRIAN STERNTHAL (1984). "Detecting and Explaining the Sleeper Effect," *Journal of Consumer Research,* 11 (September), 632–642.

HARRIS, RICHARD J. (1977). "Comprehension of Pragmatic Implications in Advertising," *Journal of Applied Psychology,* 62 (October), 603–608.

HARRIS, RICHARD J., AND GREGORY E. MONACO (1978). "Psychology of Pragmatic Implication: Information Processing Between the Lines," *Journal of Experimental Psychology: General,* 107 (March), 1–22.

HARRIS, RICHARD J., R. ROSS TESKE, AND MARTHA J. GINNS (1975). "Memory for Pragmatic Implications from Courtroom Testimony," *Bulletin of the Psychonomic Society,* 6 (November), 494–496.

HASHER, LYNN, DAVID GOLDSTEIN, AND THOMAS TOPPINO (1977). "Frequency and the Conference of Referential Validity," *Journal of Verbal Learning and Verbal Behavior,* 16 (February), 107–112.

HASTIE, REID, AND BERNADETTE PARK (1986). "The Relationship Between Memory and Judgment Depends on Whether the Judgment Task is Memory-Based or On-Line," *Psychological Review,* 93 (June), 258–268.

HAUGTVEDT, CURTIS P. (1989). "Persistence and Resistance of Communication-Induced Attitude Changes," *Proceedings of the Society for Consumer Psychology,* ed. David W. Schumann. Washington, DC: American Psychological Association, 111–113.

HAUSER, JOHN R. (1978). "Testing the Accuracy, Usefulness, and Significance of Probabilistic Models: An Information-Theoretic Approach," *Operations Research,* 26 (May/June), 406–421.

HAUSER, JOHN R. (1986). "Agendas and Consumer Choice," *Journal of Marketing Research,* 23 (August), 199–212.

HAUSER, JOHN R., AND BIRGER WERNERFELT (1990). "An Evaluation Cost Model of Consideration Sets," *Journal of Consumer Research,* 16 (March). (in press).

HELGESON, JAMES G., AND SHARON E. BEATTY (1987). "Price Expectation and Price Recall Error: An Empirical Study," *Journal of Consumer Research,* 14 (December), 379–386.

HERR, PAUL M. (1989). "Priming Price: Prior Knowledge and Context Effects," *Journal of Consumer Research,* 16 (June), 67–75.

HERR, PAUL M., STEVEN J. SHERMAN, AND RUSSELL H. FAZIO (1983). "On the Consequences of Priming: Assimilation and Contrast Effects," *Journal of Experimental Psychology,* 19 (July), 323–340.

HIGGINS, E. TORY, AND GILLIAN KING (1984). "Accessibility of Social Constructs: Information-Processing Consequences of Individual and Contextual Variability," in *Personality, Cognition and Social Interaction,* eds. Nancy Cantor and John F. Kihlstrom. Hillsdale, NJ: Erlbaum, 69–121.

HIGGINS, E. TORY, AND LIORA LURIE (1983). "Context, Categorization, and Recall: The 'Change-of-Standard' Effect," *Cognitive Psychology,* 15 (October), 525–547.

HIGGINS, TORY E., AND WILLIAM S. RHOLES (1978). "Saying is Believing: Effects of Message Modification on Memory and Liking for the Person Described," *Journal of Experimental Social Psychology,* 14 (July), 363–378.

HIGGINS, E. TORY, WILLIAM S. RHOLES, AND CARL R. JONES (1977). "Category Accessibility and Impression Formation," *Journal of Experimental Social Psychology,* 13 (March), 141–154.

HIRSCHMAN, ELIZABETH C., AND MORRIS B. HOLBROOK (1982). "Hedonic Consumption: Emerging Concepts, Methods, and Propositions," *Journal of Marketing,* 46 (Fall), 92–101.

HOCH, STEPHEN J. (1984a). "Hypothesis Testing and Consumer Behavior: If It Works, Don't Mess With It," in *Advances in Consumer Research,* Vol. 11, ed. Thomas C. Kinnear. Provo, UT: Association for Consumer Research, 478–483.

HOCH, STEPHEN J. (1984b). "Availability and Interference in Predictive Judgment," *Journal of Experimental Psychology: Learning, Memory, and Cognition,* 10 (October), 649–662.

HOCH, STEPHEN J., AND JOHN DEIGHTON (1989). "Managing What Consumers Learn From Experience," *Journal of Marketing,* 53 (April), 1–20.

HOCH, STEPHEN J., AND YOUNG-WON HA (1986). "Consumer Learning: Advertising and the Ambiguity of Product Experience," *Journal of Consumer Research*, 13 (September), 221–233.

HONG, SUNG-TAI, AND ROBERT S. WYER, JR. (1989). "Effects of Country-of-Origin and Product-Attribute Information on Product Evaluation: An Information Processing Prospective," *Journal of Consumer Research*, 16 (September), 175–187.

HOUSTON, MICHAEL J., TERRY L. CHILDERS, AND SUSAN E. HECKLER (1987). "Picture-Word Consistency and the Elaborative Processing of Advertisements," *Journal of Marketing Research*, 24 (November), 359–369.

HOUSTON, DAVID A., AND RUSSELL H. FAZIO (1989). "Biased Processing as a Function of Attitude Accessibility: Making Objective Judgments Subjectively," *Social Cognition*, 7 (Spring), 51–66.

HOWARD, JOHN A., AND JAGDISH N. SHETH (1969). *The Theory of Buyer Behavior*, New York: Wiley.

HOYER, WAYNE D. (1984). "An Examination of Consumer Decision Making for a Common Repeat Purchase Product," *Journal of Consumer Research*, 11 (December), 822–829.

HUBER, JOEL, JOHN W. PAYNE, AND CHRISTOPHER PUTO (1982). "Adding Asymmetrically Dominated Alternatives: Violations of Regularity and the Similarity Hypothesis," *Journal of Consumer Research*, 9 (June), 90–98.

HUMPHREYS, MICHAEL S., JOHN D. BAIN, AND RAY PIKE (1989), "Different Ways to Cue a Coherent Memory System: A Theory for Episodic, Semantic, and Procedural Tasks," *Psychological Review*, 96 (April), 208–233.

HUTCHINSON, J. WESLEY (1983). "Expertise and the Structure of Free Recall," in *Advances in Consumer Research*, Vol. 10, eds. R. P. Bagozzi and A. M. Tybout. Ann Arbor, MI: Association for Consumer Research, 585–589.

HUTCHINSON, J. WESLEY, MURALI K. MANTRALA, AND KALYAN RAMAN (1990). "Finding Choice Alternatives in Memory: Stochastic Models of Brand Name Recall," Paper Presented at the TIMS Marketing Science Conference, Champaign, IL.

INDOW, TAROW, AND KAWORU TOGANO (1970). "On Retrieving Sequence From Long Term Memory," *Psychology Review*, 77 (July), 317–331.

JACOBY, JACOB, AND WAYNE D. HOYER (1982). "Viewer Miscomprehension of Televised Communication: Selected Findings," *Journal of Marketing*, 46 (Fall), 12–26.

JACOBY, JACOB, AND WAYNE D. HOYER (1989), "The Comprehension/Miscomprehension of Print Communication: Selected Findings," *Journal of Consumer Research*, 15 (March), 434–443.

JACOBY, JACOB, AND CONSTANCE B. SMALL (1975). "The FDA Approach to Defining Misleading Advertising," *Journal of Marketing*, 39 (October), 65–73.

JACOBY, JACOB, TRACY TROUTMAN, ALFRED KUSS, AND DAVID MAZURSKY (1986). "Experience and Expertise in Complex Decision Making," in *Advances in Consumer Research*, Vol. 13, ed. Richard J. Lutz. Provo, UT: Association for Consumer Research, 469–475.

JACOBY, LARRY L. (1983a). "Perceptual Enhancement: Persistent Effects of an Experience," *Journal of Experimental Psychology: Learning, Memory, and Cognition*, 9 (January), 21–38.

JACOBY, LARRY L. (1983b). "Remembering the Data: Analyzing Interactive Processes in Reading," *Journal of Verbal Learning and Verbal Behavior*, 22 (October), 485–508.

JACOBY, LARRY L., AND BROOKS, LEE R. (1984). "Nonanalytic Cognition: Memory, Perception, and Concept Learning," in *The Psychology of Learning and Motivation*, Vol. 18, ed. G. H. Bower. New York: Academic Press, 379–421.

JANISZEWSKI, CHRIS (1990). "The Influence of Non-attended Material on the Processing of Advertising Claims," *Journal of Marketing Research*. (in press).

JOHN, DEBORAH ROEDDER, CAROL A. SCOTT, AND JAMES R. BETTMAN (1986). "Sampling Data for Covariation Assessment: The Effects of Prior Beliefs on Search Patterns," *Journal of Consumer Research*, 13 (June), 38–47.

JOHNSON, ERIC J., JOHN W. PAYNE, AND JAMES R. BETTMAN (1988). "Information Displays and Preference Reversals," *Organizational Behavior and Human Decision Processes*, 42 (August), 1–21.

JOHNSON, ERIC J., AND J. EDWARD RUSSO (1981). "Product Familiarity and Learning New Information," in *Advances in Consumer Research*, Vol. 8, ed. Kent B. Monroe. Ann Arbor, MI: Association for Consumer Research.

JOHNSON, ERIC J., AND J. EDWARD RUSSO (1984). "Product Familiarity and Learning New Information," *Journal of Consumer Research,* 11 (June), 542–550.

JOHNSON, MARCIA K., CAROL L. RAYE, HUGH J. FOLEY, AND MARY ANN FOLEY (1981). "Cognitive Operations and Decision Bias in Reality Monitoring," *American Journal of Psychology,* 94 (March), 37–64.

JOHNSON, MICHAEL D. (1984). "Consumer Choice Strategies for Comparing Noncomparable Alternatives," *Journal of Consumer Research,* 11 (December), 741–753.

JOHNSON, RONALD E. (1970). "Recall of Prose as a Function of the Structural Importance of the Linguistic Unit," *Journal of Verbal Learning and Verbal Behavior,* 9 (February), 12–20.

JOHNSTON, WILLIAM A., VERONICA J. DARK, AND LARRY L. JACOBY (1985). "Perceptual Fluency and Recognition Judgments," *Journal of Experimental Psychology: Learning, Memory and Cognition,* 11 (January), 3–11.

JUDD, CHARLES M., AND JAMES A. KULIK (1980). "Schematic Effects of Social Attitudes on Information Processing and Recall," *Journal of Personality and Social Psychology,* 38 (April), 569–578.

KAHN, BARBARA, WILLIAM L. MOORE, AND RASHI GLAZER (1987). "Experiments in Constrained Choice," *Journal of Consumer Research,* 14 (June), 96–113.

KARDES, FRANK R. (1986). "Effects of Initial Product Judgments on Subsequent Memory-Based Judgments," *Journal of Consumer Research,* 13 (June), 1–11.

KASSARJIAN, HAROLD H. (1978). "Presidential Address," in *Advances in Consumer Research,* Vol. 5, ed. H. Keith Hunt. Chicago: Association for Consumer Research, 13–14.

KASSARJIAN, HAROLD H. (1982). "The Development of Consumer Behavior Theory," in *Advances in Consumer Research,* Vol. 9, ed. Andrew A. Mitchell. Provo, UT: Association for Consumer Research, 12–17.

KASSARJIAN, HAROLD H. (1986). "Consumer Research: Some Recollections and a Commentary," in *Advances in Consumer Research,* Vol. 13, ed. Richard J. Lutz. Provo, UT: Association of Consumer Research, 6–8.

KELLER, KEVIN LANE (1987). "Memory Factors in Advertising: The Effect of Advertising Retrieval Cues on Brand Evaluations," *Journal of Consumer Research,* 14 (December), 316–333.

KELLER, KEVIN LANE (1988). "Memory and Evaluation Effects in Competitive Advertising Environments," Research Paper No. 1012 (September), Graduate School of Business, Stanford University, Stanford, CA.

KELLER, KEVIN LANE (1989). "Cue Compatibility and Framing in Advertising," Research Paper No. 1051 (July), Graduate School of Business, Stanford University, Stanford, CA.

KINTSCH, WALTER, AND TEUN A. VAN DYK (1978). "Toward a Model of Text Comprehension and Production," *Psychological Review,* 85 (September), 363–394.

KISELIUS, JOLITA, AND BRIAN STERNTHAL (1984). "Detecting and Explaining Vividness Effects in Attitudinal Judgments," *Journal of Marketing Research,* 21 (February), 54–64.

KISELIUS, JOLITA, AND BRIAN STERNTHAL (1986). "Examining the Vividness Controversy: An Availability-Valence Interpretation," *Journal of Consumer Research,* 12 (March), 418–431.

KLEIN, NOREEN M., AND STEWART W. BITHER (1987). "An Investigation of Utility-Directed Cutoff Selection," *Journal of Consumer Research,* 14 (September), 240–256.

KORIAT, ASHER, SARAH LICHTENSTEIN, AND BARUCH FISCHHOFF (1980). "Reasons for Confidence," *Journal of Experimental Psychology: Human Learning and Memory,* 6 (March), 107–118.

LANGER, ELLEN J. (1989). "Minding Matters: The consequences of Mindlessness-Mindfulness," in *Advances in Experimental Psychology,* Vol. 22, ed. Leonard Berkowitz. New York: Academic Press, 137–173.

LAVIDGE, ROBERT J., AND GARY A. STEINER (1961). "A Model for Predictive Measurement of Advertising Effectiveness," *Journal of Marketing,* 25 (October), 59–62.

LESSNE, GREG G., AND NICHOLAS M. DIDOW JR. (1987). "Innoculation Theory and Resistance to Persuasion in Marketing," *Psychology and Marketing,* 4 (Summer), 157–165.

LEVIN, IRWIN P., AND GARY J. GAETH (1988). "How Consumers are Affected by the Framing of Attribute Information Before and After Consuming the Product," *Journal of Consumer Research,* 15 (December), 374–378.

LICHTENSTEIN, EDWARD H., AND WILLIAM F. BREWER (1980). "Memory for Goal-Directed Events," *Cognitive Psychology,* 12 (July), 412–445.

LICHTENSTEIN, MERYL, AND THOMAS K. SRULL (1985). "Conceptual and Methodological Issues in Examining the Relationship Between Consumer Memory and Judgment," in *Psychological Processes and Advertising Effects: Theory, Research, and Application,* eds. Linda F. Alwitt and Andrew A. Mitchell. Hillsdale, NJ: Erlbaum 113–128.

LICHTENSTEIN, MERYL, AND THOMAS K. SRULL (1987). "Processing Objectives as a Determinant of the Relationship Between Recall and Judgment," *Journal of Experimental Psychology,* 23 (March), 93–118.

LICHTENSTEIN, SARAH, PAUL SLOVIC, BARUCH FISCHHOFF, MARK LAYMAN, AND BARBARA COMBS (1978) "Judged Frequency of Lethal Events," *Journal of Experimental Psychology: Human Learning and Memory,* 4 (November), 551–578.

LINGLE, JOHN H., MARK W. ALTOM, AND DOUGLAS L. MEDIN (1984). "Of Cabbages and Kings: Assessing the Extensibility of Natural Object Concept Models to Social Things," in *Handbook of Social Cognition,* Vol. 1, eds. Robert S. Wyer and Thomas K. Srull. Hillsdale, NJ: Erlbaum, 71–118.

LINGLE, JOHN H., JANET M. DUKERICH, AND THOMAS M. OSTROM (1983). "Accessing Information in Memory-Based Judgments: Incongruity Versus Negativity in Retrieval Selectivity," *Journal of Personality and Social Psychology,* 44 (February), 262–272.

LINGLE, JOHN H., NEHEMIA GEVA, THOMAS M. OSTROM, MICHAEL R. LEIPPE, AND MICHAEL H. BAUMGARDNER (1979). "Thematic Effects of Person Judgments on Impression Organization," *Journal of Personality and Social Psychology,* 37 (May), 674–687.

LINGLE, JOHN H., AND THOMAS M. OSTROM (1979). "Retrieval Selectivity in Memory-Based Impression Judgments," *Journal of Personality and Social Psychology,* 37 (February), 180–194.

LOKEN, BARBARA (1984). "Attitude Processing Strategies," *Journal of Experimental Social Psychology,* 20 (May), 272–296.

LOKEN, BARBARA, AND RONALD HOVERSTAD (1985). "Relationships Between Information Recall and Subsequent Attitudes: Some Exploratory Findings," *Journal of Consumer Research,* 12 (September), 155–168.

LOKEN, BARBARA, IVAN ROSS, AND RONALD L. HINKLE (1986). "Consumer 'Confusion' of Origin and Brand Similarity Perceptions," *Journal of Public Policy & Marketing,* 5, 195–211.

LUCE, R. DUNCAN (1963). "Detection and Recognition," in *Handbook of Mathematical Psychology,* eds.

R. Duncan Luce, R. R. Bush, and Eugene Galanter. New York: Wiley, 103–189.

LUTZ, KATHY A., AND RICHARD J. LUTZ (1977). "Effects of Interactive Imagery on Learning: Application to Advertising," *Journal of Applied Psychology,* 62 (August), 493–498.

LYNCH, JOHN G. JR., HOWARD MARMORSTEIN, AND MICHAEL F. WEIGOLD (1988). "Choices from Sets Including Remembered Brands: Use of Recalled Attributes and Prior Overall Evaluations," *Journal of Consumer Research,* 15 (September), 225–233.

LYNCH, JOHN G., JR., AND THOMAS K. SRULL (1982). "Memory and Attentional Factors in Consumer Choice: Concepts and Research Methods," *Journal of Consumer Research,* 9 (June), 18–37.

MACKENZIE, SCOTT B. (1986). "The Role of Attention in Mediating the Effect of Advertising on Attribute Importance," *Journal of Consumer Research,* 13 (September), 174–195.

MACINNIS, DEBORAH J., AND LINDA L. PRICE (1987). "The Role of Imagery in Information Processing," *Journal of Consumer Research,* 13 (March), 520–533.

MAZURSKY, DAVID, AND YAACOV SCHUL (1988). "The Effects of Advertisement Encoding on the Failure to Discount Information: Implications for the Sleeper Effect," *Journal of Consumer Research,* 15 (June), 24–36.

MCALISTER, LEIGH, AND EDGAR PESSEMIER (1982). "Variety Seeking Behavior: An Interdisciplinary View," *Journal of Consumer Research,* 9 (December), 311–322.

MCCLOSKEY, MICHAEL, AND SAM GLUCKSBERG (1979). "Decision Processes in Verifying Category Membership Statements: Implications for Models of Semantic Memory," *Cognitive Psychology,* 11 (January), 1–37.

MCGILL, ANN L., AND PUNAM ANAND (1989). "The Effect of Vivid Attributes on the Evaluation of Alternatives: The Role of Differential Attention and Cognitive Elaboration," *Journal of Consumer Research,* 16 (September), 188–196.

MCGUIRE, WILLIAM J. (1968). "Personality and Susceptibility to Social Influence," in *Handbook of Personality Theory and Research,* ed. Edgar F. Borgatta and William W. Lambert. Chicago: Rand McNally.

MEDIN, DOUGLAS L., AND MARGUERITE M. SCHAFFER (1978). "Context Theory of Classification Learning," *Psychology Review,* 85 (May), 207–238.

MILLAR, MURRAY G., AND ABRAHAM TESSER (1986). "Effects of Affective and Cognitive Focus on the Attitude-Behavior Relation," *Journal of Personality and Social Psychology,* 51 (August), 270–276.

MILLER, GEORGE A. (1956). "The Magical Number Seven, Plus or Minus Two: Some Limits on Our Capacity for Processing Information," *Psychological Review,* 63 (March), 81–97.

MOORE, DANNY L., AND J. WESLEY HUTCHINSON (1983). "The Effects of Ad Affect on Advertising Effectiveness," in *Advances in Consumer Research,* Vol. 10, ed. Richard P. Bagozzi and Alice M. Tybout. Ann Arbor, MI: Association for Consumer Research, 536–531.

MOORE, DANNY L., AND J. WESLEY HUTCHINSON (1985). "The Influence of Affective Reactions to Advertising: Direct and Indirect Mechanisms of Attitude Change," in *Psychological Processes and Advertising Effects: Theory, Research and Application,* eds. Linda Alwitt and Andrew A. Mitchell. Hillsdale, NJ: Erlbaum, 65–87.

MORTON, JOHN (1969). "The Interaction of Information in Word Recognition," *Psychological Review,* 76 (March), 165–178.

MORTON, JOHN (1979). "Facilitation in Word Recognition: Experiments Causing Change in the Logogen Model," in *Processing of Visible Language,* Vol. 1, eds. Paul A. Kolers, Merald E. Wrolstad, and Herman Bouma. New York: Plenum, 259–268.

MURPHY, GREGORY L. (1982). "Cue Validity and Levels of Categorization," *Psychology Bulletin,* 91 (January), 174–177.

MURPHY, GREGORY L., AND HIRAM H. BROWNELL (1985). "Category Differentiation in Object Recognition: Typicality Constraints on the Basic Category Advantage," *Journal of Experimental Psychology: Learning, Memory, and Cognition,* 11 (January), 70–84.

MURPHY, GREGORY L., AND DOUGLAS L. MEDIN (1985). "The Role of Theories in Conceptual Coherence," *Psychological Review,* 92 (July), 289–316.

MURPHY, GREGORY L., AND EDWARD E. SMITH (1982). "Basic Level Superiority in Picture Categorization," *Journal of Verbal Learning and Verbal Behavior,* 21 (February), 1–20.

MURRELL, GRAHAM A., AND JOHN MORTON (1974). "Word Recognition and Morphemic

Structure," *Journal of Experimental Psychology,* 102 (June), 963–968.

MYERS, JAMES H., AND MARK I. ALPERT (1968). "Determinant Buying Attitudes: Meaning and Measurement," *Journal of Marketing,* 32 (October), 13–20.

NARAYANA, CHEM L., AND RAM J. MARKIN (1975). "Consumer Behavior and Product Performance: An Alternative Conceptualization," *Journal of Marketing,* 39 (October), 1–6.

NEDUNGADI, PRAKASH, AND J. WESLEY HUTCHINSON (1985). "The Prototypicality of Brands: Relationships with Brand Awareness, Preference, and Usage," in *Advances in Consumer Research,* Vol. 12, eds. Elizabeth C. Hirschman and Morris B. Holbrook. Provo, UT: Association for Consumer Research, 498–503.

NEDUNGADI, PRAKASH (1989), "Recall and Consumer Consideration Sets: Influencing Choice Without Altering Brand Evaluations," Unpublished Working Paper, University of Toronto, Toronto, Ont.

NEWMAN, JOSEPH W. (1977). "Consumer External Search: Amount and Determinants," in *Consumer and Industrial Buying Behavior,* eds. Arch Woodside, Jagdish Sheth, and Peter Bennett. New York: Elsevier, 79–84.

NICKERSON, RAYMOND S. (1984). "Retrieval Inhibition from Part-Set Cuing: A Persisting Enigma in Memory Research," *Memory & Cognition* 12 (November), 531–522.

NISBETT, RICHARD E., DAVID H. KRANTZ, CHRISTOPHER JEPSON, AND ZIVA KUNDA (1983). "The Use of Statistical Heuristics in Everyday Inductive Reasoning," *Psychological Review,* 90 (October), 339–363.

NISBETT, RICHARD, AND TIMOTHY DECAMP WILSON (1977). "The Halo Effect: Evidence for Unconscious Alteration of Judgments," *Journal of Personality and Social Psychology,* 35 (April), 250–256.

NOSOFSKY, ROBERT M. (1984). "Choice, Similarity, and the Context Theory of Classification," *Journal of Experimental Psychology: Learning, Memory, and Cognition,* 10 (January), 104–114.

NOSOFSKY, ROBERT M. (1986). "Attention, Similarity, and the Identification-Categorization Relationship," *Journal of Experimental Psychology: General,* 115 (March), 39–57.

NOSOFSKY, ROBERT M., STEVEN E. CLARK, AND HYUN JUNG SHIN (1989). "Rules and Exemplars in Categorization, Identification, and Recognition," *Journal of Experimental Psychology: Learning, Memory, and Cognition,* 15 (2), 282–304.

OBERMILLER, CARL (1985). "Varieties of Mere Exposure: The Effects of Processing Style and Repetition on Affective Response," *Journal of Consumer Research,* 12 (June), 17–30.

OLSHAVSKY, RICHARD W., AND DONALD H. GRANBOIS (1979). "Consumer Decision Making — Fact or Fiction?" *Journal of Consumer Research,* 6 (September), 93–100.

PARK, C. WHAN, EASWAR S. IYER, AND DANIEL C. SMITH (1989). "The Effects of Situational Factors on In-Store Grocery Shopping Behavior: The Role of Store Environment and Time Available for Shopping," *Journal of Consumer Research,* 15 (March), 422–433.

PAYNE, JOHN W. (1976). "Task Complexity and Contingent Processing in Decision Making: An Information Search and Protocol Analysis," *Organizational Behavior and Human Performance,* 16 (August), 366–387.

PAYNE, JOHN W. (1982). "Contingent Decision Behavior," *Psychological Bulletin,* 92 (September), 382–402.

PAYNE, JOHN W., JAMES R. BETTMAN, AND ERIC J. JOHNSON (1988). "Adaptive Strategy Selection in Decision Making," *Journal of Experimental Psychology: Learning Memory and Cognition,* 14 (July), 534–552.

PETTY, RICHARD E., AND JOHN T. CACIOPPO (1984). "Source Factors and the Elaboration Likelihood Model of Persuasion," in *Advances in Consumer Research,* Vol. 11, ed. Thomas C. Kinnear. Provo, UT: Association for Consumer Research, 668–672.

PETTY, RICHARD E., CACIOPPO, JOHN T., AND DAVID SCHUMANN (1983). "Central and Peripheral Routes to Advertising Effectiveness: The Moderating Role of Involvement," *Journal of Consumer Research,* 10 (September), 135–146.

PRATKANIS, ANTHONY R., ANTHONY G. GREENWALD, MICHAEL R. LEIPPE, AND MICHAEL H. BAUMGARDNER (1988). "In Search of Reliable Persuasion Effects: III. The Sleeper Effect is Dead. Long Live the Sleeper Effect," *Journal of Personality and Social Psychology,* 54 (February), 203–218.

PUNJ, GIRISH N., AND RICHARD STAELIN (1983). "A Model of Consumer Information Search Behavior for New Automobiles," *Journal of Consumer Research,* 9 (March), 366–380.

RAAIJMAKERS, JEROEN G. W., AND RICHARD M. SHIFFRIN (1981). "Search of Associative Memory," *Psychological Review,* 88 (March), 93–134.

RATNESHWAR, S., DAVID G. MICK, AND GAIL REITINGER (1990). "Selective Attention in Consumer Information Processing: The Role of Chronically Accessible Attributes," in *Advances in Consumer Research,* 17. (in press).

RATNESHWAR S., AND ALLAN D. SHOCKER (1988). "The Application of Prototypes and Categorization Theory in Marketing: Some Problems and Alternative Perspectives," in *Advances in Consumer Research,* Vol. 15, ed. Michael J. Houston, 280–285.

RATNESHWAR, S., AND ALLAN D. SHOCKER (1989). "Substitution in Use and the Cognitive Structure of Product Categories," Working Paper, University of Florida, Gainesville, FL.

RAY, MICHAEL L., ALAN G. SAWYER, MICHAEL L. ROTHSCHILD, ROGER M. HEELER, EDWARD C. STRONG, AND J. B. REED (1973). "Marketing Communication and the Hierarchy-of-Effects," in *New Models for Mass Communication Research,* ed. P. Clarke. Beverly Hills, CA: Sage, 147–176.

REECE, BONNIE B. (1984). "Children's Ability to Identify Retail Stores From Advertising Slogans," in *Advances in Consumer Research,* Vol. 11, ed. Thomas C. Kinnear. Provo, UT: Association for Consumer Research, 320–323.

REILLY, MICHAEL, AND THOMAS L. PARKINSON (1985). "Individual Correlates of Evoked Set Size for Consumer Package Goods," in *Advances in Consumer Research,* Vol. 12, eds. Morris B. Holbrook and Elizabeth C. Hirshman. Provo, UT: Association for Consumer Research, 492–495.

REYES, ROBERT M., WILLIAM C. THOMPSON, AND GORDON H. BOWER (1980). "Judgmental Biases Resulting from Differing Availabilities of Arguments," *Journal of Personality and Social Psychology,* 39 (July), 2–12.

RISKEY, DWIGHT R. (1979), "Verbal Memory Processes in Impression Formation," *Journal of Experimental Psychology: Human Learning and Memory,* 5 (May), 271–281.

ROSCH, ELEANOR (1978), "Principles of Categorization," in *Cognition and Categorization,* eds. Eleanor Rosch and Barbara B. Lloyd. Hillsdale, NJ: Erlbaum, 27–48.

ROSCH, ELEANOR, AND CAROLYN B. MERVIS (1975). "Family Resemblances: Studies in the Internal Structure of Categories," *Cognitive Psychology,* 7 (October), 573–605.

ROSCH, ELEANOR, CAROLYN B. MERVIS, WAYNE D. GRAY, DAVID M. JOHNSON, AND PENNY BOYES-BRAEM (1976). "Basic Objects in Natural Categories," *Cognitive Psychology,* 8 (July), 382–439.

ROSENBERG, SEYMORE, AND ANDREA SEDLAK (1972). "Structural Representations of Implicit Personality Theory," in *Advances in Consumer Research,* Vol. 7, ed. Jerry Olson. Ann Arbor, MI: Association for Consumer Research, 417–422.

ROSS, HAROLD L., JR. (1982). "Recall Versus Persuasion: An Answer," *Journal of Advertising Research,* 22 (February/March), 13–16.

ROSSITER, JOHN R., AND LARRY PERCY (1987). *Advertising and Promotion Management.* New York: McGraw-Hill.

ROTH, EMILIE M., AND EDWARD J. SHOBEN (1983). "The Effect of Context on the Structure of Categories," *Cognitive Psychology,* 15 (July), 346–378.

SALASOO, AITA, RICHARD M. SHIFFRIN, AND TIMOTHY C. FEUSTEL (1985). "Building Permanent Memory Codes: Codification and Repetition Effects in Word Identification," *Journal of Experimental Psychology: General,* 114 (March), 50–77.

SAWYER, ALAN G. (1976). "The Need to Measure Attitudes and Beliefs Over Time: The Case of Deceptive and Corrective Advertising," in *Marketing: 1776–1976 and Beyond,* ed. Kenneth L. Bernhardt. Chicago: American Marketing Association, 380–385.

SAWYER, ALAN G. (1973). "The Effects of Repetition of Refutational and Supportive Advertising Appeals," *Journal of Marketing Research,* 10 (February), 23–33.

SAWYER, ALAN G., AND SCOTT WARD (1979). "Carry-Over Effects in Advertising," *Research in Marketing,* 2, 259–314.

SCHMIDT, DANIEL E., AND RICHARD C. SHERMAN (1984). "Memory for Persuasive Messages: A Test of a Schema-Copy-Plus-Tag Model," *Journal of Personality and Social Psychology,* 47 (July), 17–25.

SHEDLER, JONATHAN, AND MELVIN MANIS (1986). "Can the Availability Heuristic Explain Vividness Effects," *Journal of Personality and Social Psychology,* 51 (July), 26–36.

SHEPARD, ROGER N. (1958). "Stimulus and Response Generalization: Deduction of the Generalization Gradient from a Trace Model," *Psychological Review,* 65, 242–265.

SHEPARD, ROGER N. (1987). "Toward a Universal Law of Generalization for Psychological Science," *Science,* 237 (September), 1317–1323.

SHEPARD, ROGER N., AND JIE-JIE CHANG (1963). "Stimulus Generalization in the Learning of Classifications," *Journal of Experimental Psychology,* 65, 94–102.

SHEPARD, ROGER N., C. I. HOVLAND, AND H. M. JENKINS (1961). "Learning and Memorization of Classifications," *Psychological Monographs,* 75, Whole No. 517.

SHERMAN, STEVEN J., KARIN AHLM, LEONARD BERMAN, AND STEVEN LYNN (1978). "Contrast Effects and Their Relationship to Subsequent Behavior," *Journal of Experimental Social Psychology,* 14 (July), 340–350.

SHERMAN, STEVEN J., KIM S. ZEHNER, JAMES JOHNSON, AND EWARD R. HIRT (1983). "Social Explanation: The Role of Timing, Set, and Recall on Subjective Likelihood Estimates," *Journal of Personality and Social Psychology,* 44 (June), 1127–1143.

SILK, ALAN J., AND GLEN L. URBAN (1978). "Pre-Test Market Evaluation of New Package Goods: A Model and Measurement Methodology," *Journal of Marketing Research,* 15 (May), 171–191.

SINGH, SURENDRA N., MICHAEL J. ROTHSCHILD, AND GILBERT A. CHURCHILL (1988). "Recognition Versus Recall as Measures of Television Commercial Forgetting," *Journal of Marketing Research,* 25 (February), 72–80.

SLOVIC, PAUL, AND DOUGLAS MACPHILLAMY (1974). "Dimensional Commensurability and Cue Utilization in Comparative Judgment," *Organizational Behavior and Human Performance,* 11 (April), 179–194.

SMITH, DONALD A., AND ARTHUR C. GRAESSER (1981). "Memory for Actions in Scripted Activities as a Function of Typicality, Retention Interval, and Retrieval Task," *Memory & Cognition,* 9 (November), 550–559.

SMITH, EDWARD E., AND DOUGLAS L. MEDIN (1981). *Categories and Concepts.* Cambridge, MA: Harvard University Press.

SMITH, EDWARD E., EDWARD J. SHOBEN, AND LANCE J. RIPS (1974). "Structure and Process in Semantic Memory: A Feature Model for Semantic Decision," *Psychological Review,* 81 (May), 214–241.

SMITH, J. E. K. (1980). "Models of Identification," in *Attention and Performance,* Vol. 8, ed. R. Nickerson. Hillsdale, NJ: Erlbaum, 129–158.

SMITH, ROBERT E., AND WILLIAM R. SWINYARD (1983). "Attitude-Behavior Consistency: The Impact of Product Trial Versus Advertising," *Journal of Marketing Research,* 20 (August), 257–267.

SRIVASTAVA, RAJENDRA K., MARK I. ALPERT, AND ALLAN D. SHOCKER (1984). "A Customer-Oriented Approach for Determining Market Structures," *Journal of Marketing,* 48 (Spring), 32–45.

SRULL, THOMAS K., MERYL LICHTENSTEIN, AND MYRON ROTHBART (1985). "Associative Storage and Retrieval Processes in Person Memory," *Journal of Experimental Psychology: Learning, Memory and Cognition,* 11 (April), 316–345.

SRULL, THOMAS K., AND ROBERT S. WYER, JR. (1980). "Category Accessibility and Social Perception: Some Implications for the Study of Person Memory and Interpersonal Judgments," *Journal of Personality and Social Psychology,* 38 (June), 841–856.

SUJAN, MITA (1985). "Consumer Knowledge: Effects on Evaluation Strategies Mediating Consumer Judgments," *Journal of Consumer Research,* 12 (June), 31–46.

SUJAN, MITA, AND JAMES R. BETTMAN (1989). "The Effects of Brand Positioning Strategies on Consumer's Brand and Category Perceptions: Some Insights from Schema Research," *Journal of Marketing Research,* 26 (November), 454–467.

SUJAN, MITA, AND CHRISTINE DEKLEVA (1987). "Product Categorization and Inference Making: Some Implications for Comparative Advertising," *Journal of Consumer Research,* 14 (December), 372–378.

TULVING, ENDEL (1983). *Elements of Episodic Memory.* Oxford: Clarendon Press.

TULVING, ENDEL (1984). "Precis of *Elements of Episodic Memory,*" *Behavioral and Brain Sciences,* 7 (June), 257–268.

TULVING, ENDEL (1985). "How Many Memory Systems Are There?" *American Psychologist,* 40 (April), 385–398.

TULVING, ENDEL, DANIEL L. SCHACTER, AND HEATHER STARK (1982). "Priming Effects in Word-Fragment Completion are Independent of Recognition Memory," *Journal of Experimental Psychology: Learning, Memory, and Cognition,* 8 (July), 336–342.

TVERSKY, AMOS (1972). "Elimination By Aspects: A Theory of Choice," *Psychological Review,* 79 (July), 281–299.

TVERSKY, AMOS (1977). "Features of Similarity," *Psychological Review,* 84 (July), 327–352.

TVERSKY, AMOS, AND SHMUEL SATTATH (1979). "Preference Trees," *Psychological Review,* 86 (November), 542–573.

TVERSKY, BARBARA, AND KATHLEEN HEMENWAY (1984). "Objects, Parts, and Categories," *Journal of Experimental Psychology: General,* 113 (June), 169–193.

TYBOUT, ALICE M., BRIAN STERNTHAL, AND BOBBY CALDER (1983). "Information Availability as a Determinant of Multiple Request Effectiveness," *Journal of Marketing Research,* 20 (August), 280–290.

URBAN, GLEN L. (1975). "PERCEPTOR: A Model for Product Positioning," *Management Science,* 21 (April), 858–871.

VOSS, JAMES F., GREGG T. VESONDER, AND GEORGE J. SPILLICH (1980). "Text Generation and Recall by High-Knowledge and Low-Knowledge Individuals," *Journal of Verbal Learning & Verbal Behavior,* 19 (December), 651–657.

WARD, JAMES, AND BARBARA LOKEN (1986). "The Quintessential Snack Food: Measurement of Product Prototypes," in *Advances in Consumer Research,* Vol. 13, ed. Richard J. Lutz. Provo UT: Association for Consumer Research, 126–131.

WATTS, WILLIAM A., AND WILLIAM J. MCGUIRE (1964). "Persistence of Induced Opinion Change and Retention of the Inducing Message Contents," *Journal of Abnormal and Social Psychology,* 48 (3), 233–241.

WEBER, RENEE, AND JENNIFER CROCKER (1983). "Cognitive Processes in the Revision of Stereotypic Belief," *Journal of Personality and Social Psychology,* 45 (November), 961–977.

WICKER, ALAN W. (1969). "Attitudes vs. Actions: The Relationship of Verbal and Overt Behavioral Responses to Attitude Objects," *Journal of Social Issues,* 25 (Autumn), 41–78.

WILKINSON, J. B., J. BARRY MASON, AND CHRISTIE H. PAKSOY (1982). "Assessing the Impact of Short-Term Supermarket Variables," *Journal of Marketing Research,* 19 (February), 72–86.

WILSON, TIMOTHY D., DANA S. DUNN, DOLORES KRAFT, AND DOUGLAS J. LISLE (1989). "Introspection, Attitude Change, and Attitude-Behavior Consistency: The Distuptive Effects of Explaining Why We Feel the Way We Do," in *Advances in Experimental Social Psychology,* 22, ed.

Leonard Berkowitz. New York: Academic Press, 287–343.

WIND, YORAM, AND MICHAEL DEVITA (1976). "On the Relationship Between Knowledge and Preference," in *Marketing: 1776–1976 and Beyond,* ed. Kenneth L. Bernhardt. Chicago: American Marketing Association, 153–157.

WITHERSPOON, DAWN, AND LORRAINE G. ALLAN (1985). "The Effect of a Prior Presentation on Temporal Judgments in a Perceptual Identification Task," *Memory and Cognition,* 13 (March), 101–111.

WRIGHT, PETER (1975). "Consumer Choice Strategies: Simplifying vs. Optimizing," *Journal of Marketing Research,* 12 (February), 60–67.

WRIGHT, PETER (1980). "Message-Evoked Thoughts: Persuasion Research Using Thought Verbalizations," *Journal of Consumer Research,* 7 (September), 151–175.

WRIGHT, PETER, AND PETER D. RIP (1980). "Product Class Advertising Effects on First Time Buyers' Decision Strategies," *Journal of Consumer Research,* 7 (September), 176–188.

WRIGHT, PETER, AND BARTON WEITZ (1977). "Time Horizon Effects on Product Evaluation Strategies," *Journal of Marketing Research,* 14 (November), 429–443.

WYER, ROBERT S., JR., AND THOMAS K. SRULL (1986). "Human Cognition in Its Social Context," *Psychological Review,* 93 (July), 322–359.

ZAJONC, ROBERT B. (1980). "Feeling and Thinking: Preferences Need No Inferences," *American Psychologist,* 35, 151–175.

ZAJONC, ROBERT B., AND HAZEL MARCUS (1982). "Affective and Cognitive Factors in Preferences," *Journal of Consumer Research,* 9 (September), 123–131.

CONSUMER DECISION MAKING*

2

James R. Bettman
Duke University

Eric J. Johnson
Wharton School, University of Pennsylvania

John W. Payne
Duke University

This chapter reviews theories and research on consumer decision making. We characterize the properties of the consumer decision-making task and the consumer information environment. The limited information processing capabilities of consumers are addressed, and the choice heuristics used by consumers to cope with difficult decisions are described. Conceptual frameworks for understanding contingent consumer decision making and a review of relevant research on contingent processing are presented. Finally, methods for studying consumer decision making are discussed, and future research opportunities are outlined.

INTRODUCTION

Consumers constantly make decisions regarding the choice, purchase, and use of products and services. These decisions are of great import not only for the consumers themselves, but also for marketers and policymakers. These decisions are often difficult. Consumers are often faced with a large number of alternatives, which are constantly changing due to new technologies and competitive pressures. There is often a great deal of information available from many sources (e.g., advertisements, packages, brochures, salespeople, and friends). Moreover, the consumer is often not completely certain about how a product might perform. Finally, the consumer is often faced with difficult value trade-offs, such as price versus safety in the purchase of an automobile.

This multifaceted nature of the consumer decision-making task has generated a number of important research questions. Such ques-

*This chapter was partially supported by a contract from the Perceptual Science Programs, Office of Naval Research, and by a grant from the National Science Foundation.

tions as how consumers develop and use strategies for making decisions, how different amounts of prior knowledge influence consumer choice processes, how consumers adapt to different decision settings, and how consumers categorize products have spawned major streams of research.

Our goal in this chapter is to provide an introduction to these and other research areas that are related to consumer decisions. We hope not only to arouse interest in consumer decision making as a research focus, but also to suggest approaches and directions for new research. To keep the scope of the chapter manageable, we focus mostly on consumer choice; consumer judgments and inferences receive more limited attention.

We begin by outlining the properties of the consumer's decision task and ask what makes these decisions difficult? We categorize different types of consumer decisions and examine the implications of such distinctions for consumers. Next we consider the resources that consumers can bring to bear on such tasks. In particular, we discuss the properties of consumer memory, knowledge, and the *heuristics* — simplified strategies or rules of thumb — used to make choices. Given the potential mismatch between a difficult decision task and limited processing capabilities, we next look at how consumers cope. We argue that consumers adapt and change the strategies they use depending upon the demands made by the specific decision they face. After explaining this concept of contingent decision making and outlining two conceptual frameworks that could explain such contingent processing, several areas of research on consumer decision making are briefly reviewed. Finally, we describe research methods useful for studying consumer decisions and present some areas for future research on consumer decision making.

THE CONSUMER DECISION MAKING TASK

What defines a consumer's task? How can we characterize a consumer's choice as easy or difficult? To answer this question, we will provide an initial *task analysis* (Newell and Simon 1972) for consumer choice. First, we must examine the elements that compose a choice: alternatives, attributes of value, and uncertainties. We then look at how that information is available in the environment, both in terms of content (what is available) and structure (how it is organized). Finally, we look at other factors that may influence how a consumer responds to a choice task. In this section, we present a simplified overview of the factors that define a consumer's choice task and that affect a consumer's response to that task. In the subsequent section on contingent consumer decision making, we discuss such factors in more detail.

A typical consumer choice consists of a set of alternatives, each described by several attributes. Consider, for example, selecting an automobile. Each car has different mileage, attractiveness, passenger capacity, and so forth. The values of some of these attributes may be known with reasonable certainty (e.g., an alternative automobile's engine size). However, the value of other attributes is uncertain, such as the reliability or durability of a newly introduced car. For many choices, the types of attributes considered are similar across the available alternatives (e.g., choosing among different brands of automobiles). However, recent research (e.g., Johnson 1984) has emphasized that in some cases different attributes may apply to different alternatives. Given an amount of money to spend, one might choose, for example, between a vacation, described by attributes such as the number of days of sunshine and the quality of food, and a new dishwasher, described by its effectiveness in cleaning pans. Such choices have been called "noncomparable."

The difficulty of a consumer's choice depends directly upon such elements. For example, choice difficulty generally will increase (1) as the number of alternatives and attributes increases, (2) if some specific attribute values are difficult to process, (3) if there is a great deal of uncertainty about the values of many attributes, and (4) as the number of shared attributes becomes smaller.

The Consumer Information Environment

The difficulty of the consumer's decision is influenced not only by the elements of the task, but also by how information is provided in the environment. First, information is available in advertisements, on packages, via in-store displays, or in brochures. Information is also indirectly conveyed by the price and by the type of store in which the product is sold. The consumer may also draw upon his or her own prior experience; the consumer may obtain information from friends, family, or salespeople, or read about products in product-rating publications or specialty magazines (e.g., high fidelity or photography magazines). And a consumer may observe products being used by others. Finally, policymakers may mandate the provision of certain types of information, such as mileage ratings for automobiles or annual percentage rates for consumer credit. Note that, at any given moment, such information can be placed into two categories: that available in the consumer's memory and that found in the external environment. As we will discuss, this distinction can have an impact on how consumers make decisions.

The organization of information also affects the difficulty of a consumer's task. For example, advertisements usually discuss one brand at a time and only present a favorable subset of the available information about that brand. Additional information about that brand or information about competing brands is typically acquired at different times, when other advertisements or sources of information are encountered. In such an environment, where information is received sequentially rather than simultaneously, some methods for making a decision become very difficult (Bettman 1982). If we were to ask a consumer to recall the values of all brands in a product category on a particular attribute and to pick the best, the consumer would probably be unable to do so. That process would be trivial, however, if a table summarizing the values of the brands' attributes were available, such as the tables presented in *Consumer Reports*. The match between properties

of the consumer's information environment and the specific methods or strategies the consumer might use to make a choice in that environment is a major focus of this chapter.

A related distinction has been suggested by Lynch and Srull (1982), who categorized decisions as either *stimulus-based, memory-based,* or *mixed*. A decision where all the relevant information is externally available (e.g., in a summary table, in a catalog, or on several packages) is called a stimulus-based decision. In contrast, if a decision must be made using only information available in memory, it is a memory-based decision. Mixed decisions, where information in memory and information externally available are used, are probably most prevalent. Whether a choice is stimulus-based, memory-based, or mixed will influence the way consumers make choices. If choices are made based only upon information in memory, for example, they will be influenced by the characteristics of memory: information may be incomplete, inferences may be made about missing information, and the information that can be recalled may be a function of the many factors which influence retrieval from memory. As a result, consumers might not be able to employ some strategies that require complete and comparable information for all the alternatives. However, if faced with an stimulus-based display listing all the alternatives, such complete strategies could then be used. Whereas much early research on consumer decision making focused on stimulus-based choices, new work on memory-based and mixed choice (e.g., Biehal and Chakvavarti 1983) has opened up this exciting research area.

Given that information is present in memory and/or in the external environment, consumers must somehow integrate this information to make a decision. Specific strategies for combining information are discussed below. It is important, however, to realize that consumers can use two general approaches: (1) utilize an existing strategy, perhaps one that has been used previously for the same or a similar decision, and (2) construct a new strategy on the spot, exploiting whatever structure characterizes the existing information (e.g., eliminating an attribute from further consideration if all the available alternatives have the same or very similar values on that attribute). Such dynamic decision processes, where a strategy is developed on-line, represent an exciting area for recent research (e.g., Payne, Bettman, and Johnson, in press).

Other Factors Characterizing Consumer Decision Tasks

A variety of other factors characterize consumer decision tasks and affect how consumers respond to those tasks. One major factor is the importance of the task. For most consumers, there is an enormous difference between choosing a brand of mayonnaise and buying an automobile. In the former case, the decision is often routine, has relatively few consequences, and is made almost automatically, with little effort. In the latter case, the consequences are much greater, and the consumer will often devote a great deal of effort, searching large amounts of information, soliciting advice, and agonizing over difficult trade-offs. Many theories of consumer choice postulate three different types of decision process: a simple, habitual process, a process with moderate processing, and a process with extensive processing (e.g., Howard and Sheth 1969; Hansen 1972; Howard 1977; Engel, Blackwell, and Kollat 1978; and Bettman 1979).

Aspects of the choice task, such as time pressures (Wright 1974; Wright and Weitz 1977); characteristics of the alternatives themselves, such as the variation in importance weights for the attributes (Payne, Bettman, and Johnson 1988); individual differences in ability or knowledge; and social factors can also influence how consumers respond to a decision task. More details on these factors and others are provided later in the section on contingent decision making.

How Consumers Cope with Difficult Decision Tasks

We have described above the types of decision tasks faced by consumers and have argued that these tasks can often become quite difficult.

How do consumers cope with such difficulty? One approach to consumer decision making, favored by economists, argues that consumers are exquisitely rational beings. This perfect rationality model assumes that a consumer obtains complete information on the alternatives, makes trade-offs that allow him or her to compute utilities for every alternative, and selects the alternative that maximizes utility. Any limitations in processing capacities are ignored or assumed to be easily circumvented. The key research question from the economic perspective is understanding the values that different consumers use to make choices.

An alternative, and more realistic, perspective is that of *bounded rationality* (Simon 1955). Simon argues that decision makers have limitations on their abilities for processing information. Hence, decision makers cannot be perfectly rational in the sense outlined above. Rather, decision makers attempt to do as well as they can given the limitations to which they are subject. Simon's major conceptual contribution is the notion that information processing considerations play a major role in understanding decision making. From this perspective, the key research question is understanding the processing strategies consumers use to solve difficult choice problems with their limited processing capacity. In the next section, we discuss the consumer's processing abilities and limitations in more detail. (See also the chapters in this volume by Shimp and by Alba, Hutchinson, and Lynch).

THE CONSUMER AS A LIMITED INFORMATION PROCESSOR

Over the past thirty years, psychologists have greatly expanded our knowledge of the human information processing system.

One of the most important theoretical postulates in current psychology is to describe behavior (e.g., a consumer choosing a product) in terms of a small number of memories and processes (strategies) involving the acquisition, storage, retrieval, and utilization of information (for reviews, see Haugeland 1981; Newell and Simon 1972; Bettman 1979; Cowan 1988).

The set of memories and processes that interact with the environment to produce behavior can be divided into three major subsystems: (1) the perceptual system; (2) the motor system; and (3) the cognitive system (Card, Moran, and Newell 1983). The perceptual system consists of sensors (receptors), such as the eyes and ears and the associated buffer memories. It translates sensations from the physical world (i.e., visual or aural input) into a symbolic code that can be processed more fully by the cognitive system. The motor system, on the other hand, translates thought into action by activating patterns of voluntary muscles. Much research has been done to understand the components of these two subsystems. Some of that work is relevant to consumer decision making. For example, the amount of information a reader can take in with a single eye fixation has been shown to be a joint function of the perceptual difficulty of the material (e.g., the spacing of letters) and the skill of the reader. However, we will focus on the work concerning the properties of the cognitive system that is most relevant to consumer decision making.

Human Memory

In discussing the cognitive system, most researchers have found it useful to distinguish between two types of memories: (1) Working Memory, and (2) Long-Term Memory. Working Memory contains the information under current consideration. Long-Term Memory (LTM) holds (i.e., stores) the individual's mass of available knowledge, including both facts and procedures for doing things. We will briefly review what is known about both memories. It should be noted that this distinction does not necessarily imply that there are two physically distinct memories. Working Memory may simply be the currently activated portion of Long-Term Memory. It is the different functioning of these two types of memories that is the crucial distinction.

Working Memory. Working Memory can combine information from both the environment, as produced by the perceptual system, and information drawn (i.e., retrieved) from Long-Term Memory. For example, in solving an arithmetic problem, one uses both the given information (e.g., the numbers) and the procedural information (e.g., the rules of addition) retrieved from Long-Term Memory. Working Memory, which is often termed Short-Term Memory, also contains the intermediate products of thinking. That term captures the important fact that items of information in Working Memory are quickly lost if not actively rehearsed.

The central constraint on Working Memory is its limited capacity. That is, only a few items of information can be considered at any one time. How few? The standard answer to this question is seven items of information, plus or minus two (Miller 1956), although some researchers have suggested that roughly four to five items is a more accurate estimate (Simon 1974). This capacity limitation is easily shown using a memory span task. The task requires that a person recall a sequence of items in their correct order. For example, imagine that the following letters were read to you, one per second, and you were then asked to recall them in the correct order:

B-W-A-M-I-C-S-I-A-C-B-T.

Most of us would find that a very difficult task. A shorter list, such as M-C-A-S, would be easier. Seven to nine letters is the limit for most of us. The number of items of information recalled, however, can be increased by recoding the information to form "chunks." What constitutes a chunk of information is somewhat ill-defined, but it might be best characterized as any piece of information that is represented as a single, meaningful item or that has some unitary representation in long-term memory. To illustrate, consider reordering the previous 12 letter sequence like this:

T-W-A-I-B-M-C-I-A-C-B-S.

For most people in this culture, the twelve letters now can be formed into four chunks—TWA, IBM, CIA, CBS—that are easy to recall. This increase in recall due to chunking can be dramatic. In one instance, a student was trained to recall eighty-one digits (Chase and Ericsson 1981). The student, an avid runner, was able to chunk the numbers into a much smaller set of items by relating the sequence of numbers to running times.

Another example of the limitations of Working Memory is provided by mental multiplication: Try multiplying two 4-digit numbers. Even if the numbers themselves are easily remembered (e.g., 1776 and 1492), the need to remember intermediate products will overwhelm most people's Working Memory.

Such limitations of Working Memory are likely to affect consumer decision making. For example, a consumer probably cannot remember a long shopping list; however, if such a list could be chunked into ingredients for two or three dishes, it would be easier to recall. Likewise, remembering prices for several brands in a category and doing mental arithmetic using those prices is likely to be difficult and prone to errors (Friedman 1966).

More generally, Working Memory capacity limitations impose limits on how much information it is reasonable to expect a consumer will be able to process in any given amount of time. While current research (Biehal and Chakravarti 1982, 1983, 1986) has shown that both memory organization and information format can affect choice processes, limitations in Working Memory suggest that transforming information from one form to another may be difficult. Given the cognitive effort involved, Bettman and Kakkar (1977) have shown that people often do not transform information, but instead process it in the form given. This has been termed the *concreteness principle* (Slovic 1972), and it is one of the reasons why the same information presented in different formats can have a different impact on a person's decision. Consumer behavior examples of information format effects will be discussed at several points later in this chapter.

A second consequence of a limited Working Memory is the use of heuristics to process information (Haugeland 1981; Card, Moran, and Newell 1983). Heuristics are procedures for systematically simplifying the search through the available information about a problem. That is, heuristics function by disregarding some of the available information. Heuristics improve a person's chances of making a reasonably good decision given the limitations in processing capacity, while leaving some possibility of a "mistake." The use of heuristic strategies to solve problems and make decisions is one of the general principles of human information processing. Newell and Simon (1981) have argued that the use of heuristic search is at the heart of intelligence. As noted above, the use of particular heuristics can be premeditated, or strategies may be simply constructed or realized on the spot, given a set of resources and task contingencies. Specific heuristics for decision making are described in more detail later.

Long-Term Memory. Unlike Working Memory, Long-Term Memory's capacity is generally thought of as infinite. That is, for all practical purposes there are not limits to the amount of information that can be stored in Long-Term Memory. It has also been suggested that once information has been transferred from Working Memory into Long-Term Memory it is never lost. Obviously, however, we do "forget" information. What is suggested is that forgetting really is just the person's inability to retrieve the information from Long-Term Memory at a particular point in time. At a different time, new retrieval cues or strategies may allow the person to remember information that was previously viewed as forgotten.

Because of its capacity, Long-Term Memory is sometimes viewed as an external memory, just like a library, encyclopedia, or management information system (see Simon, 1981, for an elaboration of this view). Problem solving and decision making would then involve a search for information in both the external perceptual environment and in the memory environment, with information from one environment often guiding the search in the other (see, for example, Simonson, Huber, and Payne 1988).

In spite of its unlimited capacity, not all information that is perceived, that is, placed in Working Memory, is transferred to or stored in Long-Term Memory. In part, this is due to the amount of time it takes to transfer an item of information to Long-Term Memory. Writing (the storage of) an item of information into Long-Term Memory takes about seven seconds of processing effort. In contrast, it has been estimated that retrieval from Long-Term Memory is orders of magnitude faster than writing to Long-Term Memory (Card, Moran, and Newell 1983). As noted by Card, Moran, and Newell (1983, p. 4), "this asymmetry puts great importance on the limited capacity of Working Memory, since it is not possible in tasks of short duration to transfer very much

knowledge to Long-Term Memory as a working convenience."

Capacity and read (retrieval) and write times are just some of the features of Long-Term Memory. We do not have the space to adequately summarize this vast literature. However, we should note two important issues addressed in the literature: (1) how information is encoded in memory, and (2) how it is retrieved. Most current models of long-term storage posit that information is represented in terms of a network of semantic associations. That is, information is processed and encoded in the form of separate concepts and the associations among those concepts. It is also thought that information is often represented hierarchically. An example of this form of representation for bleach with some encoded information about its hazards is provided in Figure 2.1. Note that in this example the concept of

FIGURE 2.1   Semantic Network for the Concept Bleach

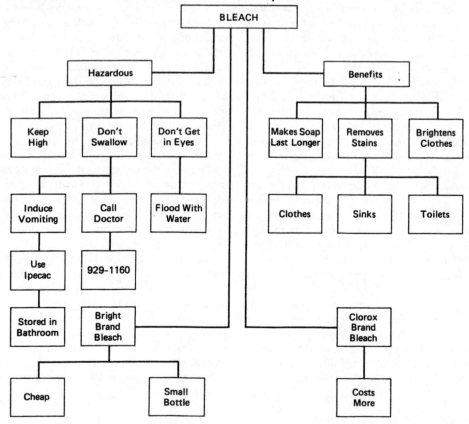

hazard is encoded with the generic concept "bleach" instead of being associated with the two specific brands, Bright Bleach and Clorox. If this were the case, then the consumer would not perceive different hazard levels for the two brands. Consequently, the hazardous nature of the product category should not influence the consumer's decision between the two brands, for this specific example. If a policymaker wanted this consumer to choose among brands on the basis of hazard, the coding of the information must be changed so that specific hazard levels are associated with each brand.

Given the importance of the encoding of information by consumers on how they ultimately use this stored information in making a decision, it is necessary to understand better the factors that affect the encoding process. One important feature is that the acquisition of new knowledge appears to be greatly facilitated by the existence of previously acquired relevant knowledge that can be used to form associations. This suggests, for example, that use of both a common format and a common set of concepts in labeling hazardous chemicals across products would facilitate a consumer's ability to successfully encode hazard information about a new brand once the format had been learned through prior experience with other labels. Put differently, the learned structure will enhance future encoding of new information that fits into that existing memory structure.

Retrieval within a memory network is often modeled by a process of spreading activation (Anderson 1983). Once a concept is activated, say by seeing a product on a billboard, activation flows from that concept tot he others which are linked to it in memory. Concepts that are more closely tied to the activated concept receive more activation and are more likely to be recalled. In Figure 2.1, activation of the concept of bleach is likely to cause recall of the concept of possible hazards, potential benefits of bleach, and the two brands, Bright Bleach and Clorox. Other concepts related to this category only because they are also hazards, such as air disasters, are less likely to be recalled. For decision making, the consequences of these models are largely unexplored, but this suggests that memory-based decisions may depend largely upon what is activated in memory, which, in turn, can depend greatly upon recent experience, the relations between concepts in memory, and external cues. For instance, Keller (1987) shows how cues available on the package (e.g., a picture of the boy Mikey on Life cereal packages) can activate information stored in memory from previous advertising exposures.

Implications of Consumer Processing Limitations

The brief summary just presented has indicated that consumers have limited capacities to process information. These conclusions are contrary to the typical perfect rationality assumptions that consumers are extensive information processors and that providing more information is always helpful. Rather, consumers may use simplifying heuristics to limit processing. Thus, merely making information available may not be sufficient. Instead one must distinguish between the *availability* and the *processability* of information (Russo, Krieser, and Miyashita 1975). Processability refers to the ease with which information can be comprehended and used. In general, information must be both available and easily processable to be utilized.

Processability of information is in part a function of the way the information is presented. That is, presenting information that is well organized and in formats that facilitate processing can increase usage of that information. Processability is not only a function of how information is provided, however; the kind of processing to be done is also important (Bettman 1979). Consumers may use different processing strategies depending upon the task. Some of the more common decision strategies are described below. Thus, a major goal in the design of information systems for consumers is to take advantage of the power of heuristics while minimizing their potential for errors. This means that effective consumer information should be designed with awareness that most people will adopt simplifying strategies for processing that information. The use of more accurate heuristics can be encouraged by designing information displays so that strategies which tend to be more accurate are simpler to implement. The basic concept is that mental processing capacity should be viewed as a scarce resource (Simon 1978). To the extent that the mental effort associated with that processing can be reduced, people will tend to process more of the available information.

CHOICE HEURISTICS

The decision-making strategies described in this section are defined in terms of a typical choice problem, consisting of a set of alternatives, each described by values on several attributes. For each attribute, there may also be an importance weight and a cutoff value specifying a minimal acceptable level for that attribute (see Klein and Bither, 1987, for a model of cutoff selection).

Before considering the specific heuristics, some general aspects of consumer decision processes should be addressed briefly. First, these heuristics can either be used alone or in combination with other heuristics. Some typical combinations are discussed subsequently after the individual heuristics have been presented. Second, as noted previously, heuristics can be either constructed on the spot or their use could be planned a priori. Third, heuristics differ in both how much effort they require to use and how accurate they are likely to be. For example, a heuristic that only considered information on one attribute (e.g., the lexicographic heuristic) might require less effort and be less accurate for some types of decisions than a heuristic which examined a larger proportion of the available information. Following the descriptions of the heuristics and their properties, we will provide a framework for determining which heuristics will be used in a particular choice situation.

The Weighted Additive (WADD) Rule. Normative procedures for dealing with decision problems generally prescribe processes involving the consideration of all the relevant problem information. For example, the weighted additive (WADD) rule considers the values of each alternative on *all* the relevant attributes and considers *all* the relative importances of the attributes to the decision maker. Furthermore, a rule like WADD involves substantial computational processing of the information. For instance, the WADD rule develops a weighted value for each attribute by multiplying the weight times the attribute value and summing over all attributes to arrive at an overall evaluation of an alternative. It is assumed that the alternative with the highest overall evaluation is chosen. While people sometimes make decisions in ways consistent with such a normative procedure, more often people appear to make decisions using simpler decision processes (heuristics).

A number of heuristics used to solve decision problems have been identified (Svenson 1979). Some of the more common heuristics are described subsequently. Each heuristic represents a different method for simplifying decision making by limiting the amount of information that is processed and/or by making how that information is processed easier.

The Satisficing (SAT) Heuristic. Satisficing is one of the oldest heuristics identified in the literature (Simon 1955). With this strategy, alternatives are considered one at a time, in the order they occur in the set. The value of each attribute of an alternative is considered to see whether it meets a predetermined cutoff level. If any attribute value is below the cutoff, then that alternative is rejected. The first alternative that has values which meet the cutoff requirements for all attributes is chosen. If no alternatives pass all the cutoffs, the cutoff level can be relaxed and the process repeated, or an alternative can be randomly selected. An implication of the satisficing heuristic is that choice will be a function of the order in which consumers evaluate products. That is, if Brand A and Brand B both pass the cutoff levels, then whether A or B is chosen will depend on whether A or B is evaluated first. There will be no comparison of the relative merit of Brand A as compared with Brand B.

The Lexicographic (LEX) Heuristic. The lexicographic procedure determines the most important attribute, and then examines the values of all alternatives on that attribute. The alternative with the best value on the most important attribute is selected. If two alternatives are tied, that is, are equivalent on the key attribute, the second most important attribute is then considered, and so on, until the tie is broken. An example from consumer choice of the LEX procedure might be choosing the cheapest brand. Sometimes the LEX strategy includes the notion of a just-noticeable difference (JND). If several alternatives are within a JND of the best alternative on the most important attribute, they are considered to be tied (Tversky 1969). This version of the LEX rule is sometimes called lexicographic-semiorder (LEXSEMI).

The Elimination-by-Aspects (EBA) Heuristic. First described by Tversky (1972), an EBA strategy begins by determining the most important attribute. Then, the cutoff level for that attribute is retrieved, and all alternatives with values for that attribute below the cutoff level are eliminated. The process continues with the second most important attribute, then the third, and so on, until one alternative remains. Interestingly, the example Tversky used to motivate this heuristic involved an advertisement for computer training schools in San Francisco. The advertisement presented a series of arguments about why all other schools should be eliminated on the basis of various aspects until only the advertised school remained.

The Majority of Confirming Dimensions (MCD) Heuristic. This heuristic, described by Russo and Dosher (1983), involves processing pairs of alternatives. The values for each of the two alternatives are compared on each attribute, and the alternative with a majority of winning (better) attribute values is retained. The retained alternative is then compared with the next alternative among the set of alternatives. The process of pairwise comparison repeats until all alternatives have been evaluated and the final winning alternative identified.

The Frequency of Good and Bad Features (FRQ) Heuristic. Alba and Marmorstein (1987) suggest that consumers may evaluate or choose alternatives based simply upon counts of the good or bad features the alternatives possess. To implement this heuristic, consumers would need to develop cutoff levels for specifying good and bad features. Then the consumer would count the number of such features. Depending upon whether the consumer focussed on good features, bad features, or both, different variants of the heuristic would arise.

The Equal Weight (EQW) Heuristic. This processing strategy examines all the alternatives and all the attribute values for each alternative. However, the equal weight strategy simplifies decision making by ignoring information about the relative importance or probability of each attribute. A value is obtained for each alternative by simply summing the values of the attributes for each alternative. Hence this heuristic is a special case of the weighted additive rule. The equal weight rule has been advocated as a highly accurate simplification of the decision-making process for both risky (Thorngate, 1980) and nonrisky choice (Dawes 1979; Einhorn and Hogarth 1975).

Combined Heuristics. In some instances, consumers may use combined or phased strategies. Typically, such combined strategies have an initial phase where poor alternatives are eliminated, and then a second phase examining the remaining alternatives in more detail (Payne 1976). One such combined heuristic is an elimination-by-aspects plus weighted additive strategy. EBA would be used to reduce the number of alternatives to some small number (e.g., two or three), and then a weighted additive rule would be used to select among those remaining alternatives.

Other Heuristics. In the area of consumer choice, several even simpler heuristics have been proposed. A frequent strategy for choice of this type is the habitual heuristic: choose what one chose last time. A related heuristic, suggested by Wright (1975), is *affect referral*. The consumer simply elicits a previously formed evaluation for each alternative from memory and selects the most highly evaluated alternative. No detailed attribute information is considered.

General Properties of Choice Heuristics

The strategies we have just discussed are only some of those proposed to describe choice behavior. These strategies have come from a number of disciplines and have been described using very different kinds of formalisms. As a result, in order to compare and contrast strategies for choice, researchers have often described them using fairly broad and global characteristics (Bettman 1979).

Compensatory versus Noncompensatory. One of the most important distinctions among rules is the extent of compensatory as compared to noncompensatory processing. Some rules (e.g., the lexicographic rule) are noncompensatory, since excellent values on less important attributes cannot compensate for a poor value on the most important attribute. Rules such as weighted additive or equal weight are compensatory, on the other hand, since high values on some attributes can compensate for low values on others. Hogarth (1987) has suggested that people find making explicit trade-offs emotionally uncomfortable. Thus, consumers may avoid strategies that are compensatory not only because they are difficult to execute (require great cognitive effort), but also because they require the explicit resolving of difficult value trade-offs.

Consistent versus Selective Processing. A related aspect of choice heuristics is the degree to which the amount of processing is consistent or selective across alternatives or attributes. That is, is the same amount of information examined for each alternative or attribute, or does the amount vary? In general, it has been assumed that more consistent processing across alternatives is indicative of a more compensatory decision strategy (Payne 1976). Consistent processing sometimes involves examination of all information for every alternative and attribute.

A more variable (selective) processing pattern, on the other hand, is seen as indicating a strategy of eliminating alternatives or attributes on the basis of only a partial processing of information, without considering whether additional information might compensate for a poor value.

Amount of Processing. A third general processing characteristic is the total amount of processing carried out. Whether processing is consistent or not, the total amount of information examined can vary, leading to an examination that can be quite cursory to very exhaustive. For some strategies, such as EBA, lexicographic, and satisficing, the total amount of information processed is contingent upon the particular values of the alternatives and the cutoff levels.

Alternative-based versus Attribute-based Processing. A fourth aspect of processing concerns whether the search and processing of alternatives proceeds across or within attributes. The former (across attribute processing) is often called holistic, alternative-based, or brand-based processing. The latter (within attribute processing) is called dimensional or attribute-based processing. In alternative-based processing, multiple attributes of a single alternative are considered before information about a second alternative is processed. In contrast, in attribute-based processing, the values of several alternatives on a single attribute are processed before information about a second attribute is processed. Russo and Dosher (1983) suggest that attribute-based processing is cognitively easier.

Quantitative versus Qualitative Reasoning. Note that heuristics also differ in terms of the degree of quantitative versus qualitative reasoning used. Some heuristics include quantitative reasoning operations. For example, the equal weight method involves a summing of values, and the frequency heuristic requires counts. The weighted adding rule, a normative strategy, includes the even more quantitative operation of multiplying two values. In contrast, most of the reasoning contained in the other heuristics described above is more qualitative in nature. That is, most of the operations for a heuristic such as EBA involve simple comparisons of values. Hegarty, Just, and Morrison (1988) have recently explored strategy differences in making inferences about mechanical systems that involve a similar distinction between qualitative and quantitative reasoning.

Formation of Evaluations. Finally, the heuristics differ in terms of whether or not an evaluation for each alternative is formed. In the equal weight or weighted additive rules, for example, each alternative is given a score that represents its overall evaluation. On. the other hand, rules such as lexicographic or EBA eliminate some alternatives and select others without directly forming an overall evaluation.

The various heuristics described previously represent different combinations of these general properties. Table 2.1 characterizes each heuristic in terms of five of these properties. Amount of information processed is not included in the table because it is variable for many of the strategies.

Implementation of Heuristics

By now the reader might ask if any of these rules describes how consumers make decisions. While we can categorize specific heuristics using distinctions like those previously described, an obvious question is exactly how these heuristics might be implemented. Do people actually use any one heuristic to make a given decision? As noted earlier, an important distinction can be made between two ways in which choice processes might be implemented. On one hand, consumers may have a set of strategies or rules stored in memory and then invoke these rules in their entirety when needed. This might be called a *stored rule* method for implementing choice. A second conception, a *constructive method,* states that rules of thumb are developed at the time of choice using fragments or elements of rules stored in memory (Bettman 1979; Bettman and Park 1980 a,b). These fragments or elements may be beliefs about alternatives; evaluations; simple rules of thumb involving subsets of beliefs (e.g., "Compare these products on Attribute A to see if they differ very much"); rules for integrating beliefs (e.g., "Count how many attributes Alternative X is best on" or "Average those ratings"); rules for assigning weights (e.g., "If performance is comparable across brands, weight price heavily"); or, perhaps, even computational rules. Presumably the elements used will be a function of what is available in the particular choice situation and how easy various pieces of information are to process (e.g., a "Compare prices" element may not be used if unit prices are not given and different brands have different-size packages). The basic idea behind the distinction between the stored rule methods and constructive methods for implementing heuristics is that in some cases completed heuristics or rules do not exist in memory, but must be built up from subparts. Biehal and Charkravarti (1986) argue that simple processing operations

TABLE 2.1 Properties of Choice Heuristics

Heuristics	Compensatory (C) versus Noncompensatory (N)	Consistent (C) versus Selective (S)	Attribute-based (AT) versus Alternative-based (AL)	Quantitative (QN) versus Qualitative (QL)	Evaluation Formed? (Yes or No)
WADD	C	C	AL	QN	Y
EQW	C	C	AL	QN	Y
EBA	N	S	AT	QL	N
SAT	N	S	AL	QL	N
LEX	N	S	AT	QL	N
MCD	C	C	AT	QN	Y
FRQ	C	C	AL	QN	Y

Note: WADD = weighted additive; EQW = equal weight; EBA = elimination-by-aspects; SAT = satisficing; LEX = lexicographic; MCD = majority of confirming dimensions; FRQ = frequency of good and bad features.

such as those described earlier may be the level at which consumers store their information processing repertoire in memory.

The consumer may have only a general plan to guide the construction of a heuristic in a particular situation. Thus choice heuristics might vary from one situation to the next if a constructive method is used, depending on how the elements available were put together. A heuristic may then be the strategy realized as individual elements are brought to bear, depending upon the properties of the task. Stored rules will tend to be used in situations in which there is a good deal of prior experience, and constructive processes in situations in which there is little prior knowledge or experience.

A concept related to the idea of constructive decision processing is that of "editing" (Kahneman and Tversky 1979). Editing involves the use of combinations of simple operations, like the cancellation of outcomes which are identical across alternatives or the elimination of dominated alternatives to simplify decision problems. For example, a consumer may notice that all the refrigerators available in a particular store have frost-free operation and an ice maker. When considering those alternatives, the consumer will probably pay little attention to those features.

As initially formulated (Kahneman and Tversky 1979; Goldstein and Einhorn 1987), editing processes were assumed to come first, with alternatives edited and the simplified options evaluated. Alternatively, we have argued that editing is more opportunistic (Payne, Bettman and Johnson 1990). Editing may occur throughout a choice whenever individuals notice some structure in the choice environment that can be exploited. Hence, editing may be seen as part of a constructive method of decision processing. An implication of this viewpoint is that the regularities in the task environment (if any) which are noted and exploited can profoundly affect the course of the decision process. A related implication is that the resultant decision process and choice may be highly sensitive to the structure of the decision task. These concepts of constructive decision making and editing represent exciting topics for new research on consumer decision making.

CONTINGENT CONSUMER DECISION MAKING

The Concept of Contingent Decision Making

While we have discussed many different decision-making strategies, we have not specified the conditions where one rule or another would be used. As noted above, many factors can influence which strategy is used. Three major classes of such factors are shown in Figure 2.2: characteristics of the decision problems, characteristics of the person, and characteristics of the social context.

Characteristics of the Decision Problem. Increasingly, it seems that the use of a rule is contingent on the variables that describe the decision problem (Payne 1982). For example, when faced with a decision problem involving only two or three alternatives, people generally use compensatory types of decision strategies.

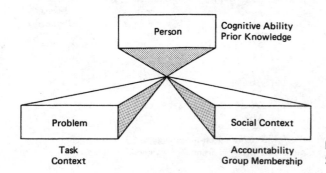

FIGURE 2.2   Contingent Strategy Selection

When faced with more complex (multiple alternative) decision tasks, people tend to use noncompensatory strategies such as elimination-by-aspects (Payne 1976; Lussier and Olshavsky 1979).

The response of decision makers to time pressure is another example of contingent decision making. Several studies indicate that reducing the time available to make decisions causes people to shift attention (Ben Zur and Breznitz 1981; Svenson, Edland, and Karlson, 1985; Wright 1974; Wright and Weitz 1977). A general hypothesis underlying much of the work on time pressure is that increased time constraints lead to efforts by the decision maker to simplify the task (Wright 1974). One approach, acceleration (Ben Zur and Breznitz 1981), would simply be to process the same information more rapidly. Selectively focussing on the use of only the more important information under time pressure (the idea of "filtration," see Miller 1960) is another way the task might be simplified. Finally, one might shift strategies in order to cope with time pressure. Payne, Bettman, and Johnson (1988) report results indicating that people do accelerate their processing, focus on a subset of information, and finally, under severe time pressure, change their decision strategies.

Number of alternatives and time pressure represent *task variables,* which are associated with general characteristics of the decision problem and are not dependent on the particular values of the alternatives (Payne 1982). *Context variables,* on the other hand, are associated with the particular values of the alternatives. Context variables have also been shown to impact decision behavior. Several studies, for example, have shown that choice probabilities can be strongly influenced by the similarity of alternatives in a decision set (Restle 1961; Tversky 1972). Issues of similarity and choice have played a major role in consideration of new product introduction strategies and the problem of "cannibalization" in product lines (e.g., Batsell and Polking 1985). Another context variable that has been shown to affect choice is the presence of certain types of dominated alternatives (Huber, Payne, Puto 1982).

Characteristics of the Person. Individual differences can also influence contingent decision behavior. Both ability and knowledge differences can have major effects. For example, decision makers who find arithmetic operations relatively difficult may use heuristics requiring qualitative reasoning more frequently than individuals for whom arithmetic operations are comparatively easy (Bettman, Johnson, and Payne 1990). There is also a good deal of evidence that prior knowledge and expertise can affect how information is processed (e.g., Brucks 1985), inferences (e.g., Ford and Smith 1987), and memory (e.g., Hutchinson 1983).

Characteristics of the Social Context. Decisions are not made in a social vacuum; rather, many social factors can influence decision making. For example, even if an individual is making a decision, he or she may feel accountable to others, such as family members. Such feelings of accountability can lead to choice heuristics that focus on how easy a decision is to justify to others. For example, Simonson (1989) shows that the need to justify leads consumers to choose options that provide easy rationales or justifications. In addition to the implicit influence of accountability, many consumer decisions explicitly involve multiple individuals, such as different family members or different members of an individual purchasing unit. Clearly, there is an important difference between deciding for yourself (satisfying your own goals) and deciding jointly with a spouse, a child, or a boss, where your goals and theirs may conflict (Park 1982). There are important issues of coordination, organization, and information flow involved in multiperson decision making.

Problem, person, and social context factors provide an outline of the major aspects affecting contingent consumer decision making. We have provided only a brief overview of each of these three aspects thus far. Next we will consider alternative conceptual frameworks for understanding contingent consumer decision making. Then we will consider empirical research on decision problem and person-related factors in more detail. We do not provide a more detailed discussion of social context influences because of the paucity of available research.

Conceptual Frameworks for Contingent Decision Making

Given the substantial evidence for contingent decision behavior, a natural question is why decision makers, given a particular task, select one particular decision strategy instead of another. There are two major conceptual frameworks that have been proposed to account for contingent decision making: the cost/benefit and perceptual.

The Cost/Benefit Framework. One possible reason that a decision maker decides to use a particular decision strategy in a specific task environment is that rule usage is the result of a cost/benefit analysis. The idea is that any decision strategy has certain benefits associated with its use and also has certain costs. The benefits would include the probability that the strategy will lead to a "correct" decision, the speed of making the decision, and its justifiability. Costs might include the information acquisition and the computational effort involved in using the strategy. Decision rule (heuristic) selection would then involve consideration of both the costs and benefits associated with each possible strategy. Strategy selection is the result of a compromise between the desire to make a correct decision and the desire to minimize effort (Beach and Mitchell 1978, Johnson and Payne 1985; Klayman 1983; Russo and Dosher 1983; Shugan 1980).

A view of strategy selection as involving benefits and costs has several appealing aspects. The assumption of calculated rationality on the part of the decision maker (March 1978) can be maintained once the costs of the decision process itself are included in the assessment of rationality. In addition, the perspective of costs and benefits can potentially explain contingent decision behavior, because the costs and benefits of decision strategies will vary between tasks. Such factors as the importance of the choice or the need to justify the choice will affect how the trade-off between costs and benefits will be set in selecting a strategy. (See Simonson, 1989, for a demonstration of the sensitivity of consumer choices to the need to justify decisions.)

In our own work, we have taken a cost/benefit perspective which considers cognitive effort as the major component of cost and the accuracy of choice as the principal component of benefit. Effort is measured by decomposing strategies into a common set of component elementary information processes (e.g., reads, comparisons, and additions). (See Newell and Simon, 1972, and Chase, 1978.) Counts of these component processes are a measure of effort. Both simulation work and experimental results have demonstrated that this approach can explain contingent decision making (Johnson and Payne 1985; Payne, Bettman, and Johnson 1988, in press; Bettman, Johnson, and Payne, 1990). Simulations were used to characterize the expected levels of accuracy and effort for various heuristics in a variety of decision task environments. Based upon the results of such simulations, conclusions could be drawn about the performance of the heuristics. For example, in an environment with a good deal of dispersion in attribute importance weights (i.e., some weights are high and others low), such heuristics as elimination-by-aspects and lexicographic maintain fairly high levels of accuracy with substantial savings in effort. Experimental studies with human subjects showed that they switched to such attribute-based strategies for problems with greater dispersion in importance weights.

The previous discussion may seem to imply that consumers come to a decision situation with a repertoire of strategies, that they assess costs and benefits, and then choose a strategy. While such global, a priori analysis of costs and benefits may occur in some situations, it is very important to note that it is also possible for consumers to construct heuristics on the spot based upon cost/benefit trade-offs. That is, consumers may make more local, momentary, contingency-driven cost/benefit assessments that result in a realized or constructed heuristic. For example, a consumer may start to compare alternatives on a particular attribute and discover that the values are all very similar. Then he or she may decide to look at another attribute but find that it is difficult to understand. Such spur of the moment shifts in processing direction can be based upon cost/benefit considerations, even though the consumer is building or realizing a heuristic rather than using one selected a priori. Recent research by Klein and Yadav (1989) seems more consistent with such a local, "bottom-up" approach to cost/benefit considerations than with a "top-down," a priori approach.

A Perceptual Framework. Tversky and Kahneman (1981) prefer to explain contingent decision making in terms of basic principles governing human perception. They have shown, for example, how simple changes in the wording of a decision problem can reverse preferences because of the differences in response to gains and losses. For example, in one problem you are asked to imagine that the United States is faced with the outbreak of a certain Asian disease that is expected to kill 600 people. You are asked to indicate your preference between two alternative programs to combat the disease. In one wording of this problem, the first alternative is said to result in 200 people being saved. The second alternative is said to save 600 people with a probability of 1/3 and no people with a probability of 2/3. Most people prefer the first alternative. In a rewording of the problem, the first alternative is said to result in the death of 400 people. The second alternative gives a probability of 1/3 that none will die and a probability of 2/3 that 600 people will die. Most people in this case prefer the second alternative. Why the reversal in preference? Tversky and Kahneman argued that the first wording causes people to code the possible outcomes as gains, and the second wording causes the outcomes to be coded as losses. Furthermore, because people are often risk averse for gains and risk-seeking for losses, one observes the reversal in choice between two problems that are *formally identical.*

Similarly, Puto (1987) demonstrates in an industrial buying situation that decision makers' choices from the same set of alternatives are greatly influenced depending on whether individuals view the choices as offering potential gains or losses. He achieves this difference in views by manipulating the individual's reference point for the expected price of the item to be purchased.

Kahneman and Tversky (1979) argue that our perceptual apparatus is attuned to changes rather than absolute magnitudes. Hence, outcomes will tend to be coded as gains or losses relative to some reference point. Likewise, Tversky and Kahneman argue that different ways of framing a problem can lead to different choices or preferences in the same way that taking different perspectives can influence perceptual appearances. For example, Levin and Gaeth (1988) show that labeling beef as 75 percent lean leads to more favorable evaluations than labeling it as 25 percent fat, particularly before tasting the beef. There are several other instances in the consumer decision making literature where perceptual interpretations seem to be more compelling or more correct than cost/benefit notions (e.g., Bettman and Sujan 1987; Johnson 1988) or where cost/benefit predictions are not borne out (e.g., Klein 1983).

The perceptual framework clearly complements the cost/benefit framework because it is difficult to see how simple wording changes alone (e.g., as seen in "lives saved" versus "lives lost" in Tversky and Kahneman 1981) change either cognitive effort or the desire for accuracy. On the other hand, it is not clear how the perceptual framework would handle contingent behavior due to the number of alternatives, for example, yet that phenomenon fits nicely into a cost/benefit framework.

One major opportunity for integrating cost/benefit and perceptual frameworks may be to develop the notions of editing discussed previously. That is, in the course of constructing a heuristic, consumer decision makers may cycle between noticing aspects or characteristics of the choice set (e.g., extreme values across alternatives) and deciding how to exploit those aspects. Perceptual frameworks may be most relevant for the noticing process, whereas cost/benefit notions may be more relevant for determining what to do to take advantage of what has been noticed. That is, some task and context effects may operate perceptually, by influencing the likelihood with which various cognitions come to mind. This distinction is similar to that between interrupts and reactions or responses to those interrupts proposed by Bettman (1979). Interrupts may be more perceptually based, while reactions to the interrupts may be determined to a greater extent by cost/benefit concerns. A second opportunity for integrating the two frameworks would be to consider that individuals' assessments of costs and benefits for any heuristic may be greatly influenced by perceptual concerns such as how information is presented or how the problem is framed.

RESEARCH ON CONTINGENT CONSUMER DECISION MAKING

While we have both introduced the concept of contingent decision making and described frameworks for understanding contingent choices, we have only provided a cursory look at empirical findings. In the next sections, we review several factors that seem to affect consumer choice processes, using, where possible, examples from consumer research. We organize our review using the classification scheme presented earlier: problem factors, with two major subcategories of task variables and context variables; and person factors, with the two major subcategories of prior knowledge and ability.

Problem Factors: Task Variables

Problem Size. Many consumer researchers have found that increasing the number of alternatives causes consumers to use strategies that lead to early elimination of a number of alternatives (Payne 1976; Lussier and Olshavsky 1979; Johnson and Meyer 1984). Consumers use compensatory strategies to a greater extent for small numbers of alternatives and noncompensatory strategies for large numbers. Inter-

estingly, changes in the number of dimensions or attributes do not appear to change the underlying decision strategies but may increase selective processing of the attributes (Payne 1976; Lussier and Olshavsky 1979; Olshavsky 1979).

If the consumer faces increases in both the number of alternatives and attributes, a natural question arises: Is there a point at which the consumer can be given too much information? This research topic has been of major and long-standing interest in consumer research. Both marketers and policymakers are greatly interested in the possibility that consumers may make less accurate decisions with more information. If there were deleterious effects on consumers' processing or choices as the amount of available information increased, then policies that required additional information to be given to consumers, such as new warnings, might perversely have an impact opposite to that intended.

The initial research on information load by Jacoby and his colleagues (Jacoby, Speller, and Kohn 1974 a,b) purported to show that consumers were overloaded by large amounts of information. Their conclusion was that consumers made poorer decisions with more information. This conclusion was quickly disputed by several researchers (Russo 1974; Wilkie 1974; Summers 1974), who noted that choice accuracy actually increased as more attributes were added. Accuracy only decreased when the number of alternatives was increased. Malhotra (1982) and Keller and Staelin (1987) have also shown decreases in accuracy of choices with increases in information load, but there is still controversy surrounding the interpretation of these findings (Keller and Staelin 1989; Meyer and Johnson 1989). For example, Meyer and Johnson point out that a major problem with this research area is identifying what constitutes a good decision. Most research uses subjects' ratings of attribute importance to determine the best alternative, and such ratings are subject to error. Because this error often covaries with the amount of information, defining an accurate choice in these studies seems extremely problematic. Hence, the information load issue remains an important unresolved question in consumer decision research. One possible direction for such research would be to examine how consumers *select* their information load by deciding what information to examine. Such heuristics for selectivity could then be examined to determine if systematic effects on decision making result from their use.

Time Pressure. As we have described above, individuals appear to accelerate their processing, become more selective, and change strategies when time pressure becomes severe (Payne, Bettman, and Johnson 1988). Payne, Bettman, and Johnson (1988) also found that attribute-based heuristics such as EBA or lexicographic heuristics tended to be more robust under severe time pressure. When time pressure is severe, it appears that quickly examining at least some information on every alternative is an effective approach to coping. Wright (1974) and Wright and Weitz (1977) provided evidence for an additional effect of time pressure. They argued that decision makers simplify the task by placing greater weight on negative information about the alternatives, and they reported results consistent with this contention.

Response Mode. Many theories of decision making assume that preferences should not depend upon the methods used to assess them. This assumption, called *procedure invariance* (Tversky, Sattath and Slovic 1988), seems not to hold. Instead, different assessment methods show a marked influence on the nature of preferences. For example, Mowen and Gentry (1980) found that preferences between pairs of new product projects could be reversed depending upon whether the decision maker chose one project from the pair or assigned a price for the rights to each product. Such preference reversals are commonly found in a variety of contexts (Slovic and Lichtenstein 1983; Tversky, Slovic and Kahneman, 1990). A general principle seems to be that inputs are weighted more heavily the more compatible they are with the output (Tversky, Sattath, and Slovic 1988).

The studies showing response-mode contin-

gent processing are of great importance to marketing research. As Tversky et al. (1988) note, the classical economic view of preferences assumes that consumers have well-defined preference orders. When asked how much they like one product versus another, it is assumed that consumers read that preference from some master store of information about personal values. The problem for the marketing researcher is, therefore, simply one of efficiently measuring those preferences or values. The demonstrations of response mode effects, however, suggest another view of preferences. In many situations, it may be that preferences are actually constructed during the elicitation process, rather than just reported. Thus, observed preferences are likely to reflect both a consumer's underlying values and the heuristics or fragments of decision rules used to construct the required response in a particular situation. This suggests that the marketing researcher's task of measuring consumer values will be even more complicated than generally accepted. Using a judgment response to measure a consumer's values, for example, may not be predictively accurate when the consumer actually makes choices among products. Marketing researchers will need to understand how a variety of seemingly minor changes in the task and context of consumer decisions will impact observed preferences.

Types of Decision Task. Several studies have examined the effects of different types of decision tasks on the resultant processes. For example, Biehal and Chakravarti (1982) placed subjects in conditions where they either learned information and then made choices or made choices and were then asked to recall the information. Subjects who learned the information first tended to organize that information in memory by brand, and they showed a greater tendency to process information by brand when they made choices that the subjects who make choices first. The subjects who made choices first, on the other hand, processed more by attribute and showed much greater attribute organization in memory than the subjects who learned the information first. The choice-first subjects also showed much better recall for the chosen brand than for the rejected brands. (These results are also found in Johnson and Russo 1981, 1984.)

Biehal and Chakravarti (1983) also show how the interactions between memory and choice influence choices made over time. They examine a situation where subjects first either learn information or make a choice. Information on new alternatives and new attributes is then added, and a second choice is made. The added attribute information makes one of the original alternatives more attractive. The results show that if a choice is made first, the decreased memory for rejected alternatives makes it harder to reevaluate an alternative that had been rejected, even if that alternative would be attractive if processed. In conjunction, the Biehal and Chakravarti studies make important points about how memory and attentional processes constrain choice and about how the task has an influence on when memory and attentional factors come into play.

Johnson and Russo (1981, 1984) studied the effects of the type of decision task (judgment task or choice task) on memory. Work in behavioral decision theory has emphasized that judgment and choice are not equivalent (Einhorn and Hogarth 1981). In a judgment task, the subject makes an overall evaluation of each alternative, while in a choice task, he or she picks the most preferred alternative. A judgment task encourages a complete examination of all of the information for each alternative, whereas a choice task allows the subject to be much more selective (e.g., some alternatives may be virtually ignored if they have a bad value on one attribute). Johnson and Russo show that prior knowledge is positively related to memory for information about the alternatives for a judgment task, but that the subjects with the greatest prior knowledge show decreased memory for information about current alternatives in the choice task. If subjects process all information, as in the judgment task, then greater knowledge aids memory. However, in the choice task, subjects with greater knowledge appear to process information more

selectively, and hence remember less (for related results see Bettman and Park 1980). Thus, memory and choice show interactions in both directions. What is in memory can influence future choice processes, and current choice processes can affect subsequent memory. Brucks (1985) also shows that experts appear to search more selectively and more efficiently than novices.

Lynch, Marmorstein, and Weigold (1988) have investigated choices where some or all of the alternatives had to be retrieved from memory. They show that consumers will use information in memory to make a choice if it is accessible and if it is perceived to be more diagnostic than other accessible information (Feldman and Lynch 1988).

Information Format. We have stressed that how information displays are organized can have a major impact on consumer decision making. A nice illustration of this is provided by Russo (1977). He showed that the use of unit price information increased when the information was presented to shoppers in the form of a sorted list where the available brands are ranked by increasing unit price. This list, when it appeared on the supermarket shelf, resulted in consumers saving about 2 percent, on average, as compared with consumers using a normal unit price display with separate tags for each item. Russo argues that the list display works because it makes price comparisons easier. Consumer decision making is aided in this case by making information easier to process. Attempts to duplicate this success using nutritional information have met with mixed results (Muller 1984; Russo, Staelin, Nolan, Russell, and Metcalf 1986).

Bettman and Kakkar (1977) demonstrate another display effect. They found that information acquisition proceeds in a fashion consistent with the display format. For example, if a display encouraged alternative-based processing, more alternative-based processing was observed. Biehal and Chakravarti (1982) have shown, however, that memory organization can interact with format to determine processing. For example, prior brand-based organization of information in memory attenuates the effects of attribute-based formats in their research.

Problem Factors: Context Variables

Similarity. Recall that context effects refer to factors describing a particular set of alternatives, such as similarity (Payne 1982). Huber, Payne, and Puto (1982), Huber and Puto (1983), and Huber (1983) find that adding a dominated alternative to the set can increase choice of the alternative which is dominant, a violation of the principle of regularity fundamental to many formal choice models. (See Ratneshwar, Shocker, and Stewart, 1987, for another viewpoint on this research.) Huber and Puto (1983) and Huber (1983) extend these findings to nondominated alternatives and document the existence of an attraction effect (i.e., a new item can lead to increased choice of similar items) as well as the normal substitution effects (i.e., a new item takes choice from those items to which it is most similar). These findings provide important new constraints that viable choice models must meet.

As alternatives become less similar, the variance in the attributes across alternatives increases. Researchers have examined whether the importance weights given an attribute depend on this variation in scores. Meyer and Eagle (1982) report that weights did shift as a function of variance: Attributes with greater variance received more weight. In contrast, Curry and Menasco (1983) find that weights do not depend on the variation in scores. The difference in results may be partially due to Curry and Menasco's use of a judgment task, whereas Meyer and Eagle get their strongest results by using a choice task. More research is clearly warranted. Chakravarti and Lynch (1983) provide a conceptual framework for such research on context effects.

Correlated Attributes. A concept closely related to similarity is the correlation of the attribute scores across alternatives. If the alternatives are similar, the attributes will be positively correlated; if they are very dissimilar, the attributes are negatively correlated. Interattribute correlation is also related to dominance, because, when the number of attributes is small, removing dominated alternatives from choice sets results in a negative correlation between the attributes for the remaining alternatives (Curry and Faulds 1986; Krieger and Green 1988). Several normative models assume that consumers make choices from sets in which dominated alternatives are removed (e.g., Hauser and Gaskin 1984; Shugan 1987).

Several authors have speculated that the case where attributes are negatively correlated might be a particularly interesting variation in context. The major reason is that many simplified heuristics, when compared with a weighted additive model, become less accurate under these conditions (Newman 1977; McClelland 1978; Einhorn, Kleinmuntz, and Kleinmuntz 1979). Thus, a cost/benefit perspective would suggest that consumers might shift away from heuristics when faced with such choice sets. Research in this area is just beginning, but Johnson, Meyer, and Ghose (1989) report that their subjects did not appear to shift strategies when faced with negatively correlated attributes. One possible reason for this result is that the perception of correlation is notoriously inaccurate (Crocker 1981), suggesting that this may be one important context effect which is difficult for decision makers to detect.

Comparable versus Noncomparable Choices. Until the early 1980s, consumer choice research had concentrated almost exclusively on examining decision processes for comparable alternatives, such as the process of selecting among several brands of microwave ovens. Johnson (1984, 1986) for the first time examined how consumers may evaluate and choose among noncomparable alternatives (e.g., things to buy with a bonus). For example, the consumer might try to decide whether to take a vacation trip, to buy a new television set, or to buy several new outfits of clothing. Johnson (1984) shows that as alternatives become more noncomparable, consumers represent attributes at higher levels of abstraction (e.g., necessity or enjoyment), so as to allow comparisons within attributes. At some point, however, consumers shift to a strategy where they form overall evaluations for each alternative and then compare the overall evaluations. Bettman and Sujan (1987) further showed that one fundamental distinction between noncomparable and comparable alternatives is knowledge of goals and goal-relevant attributes for making choices, rather than any inherent difference in the types of choices. When a goal was provided, decision processes for noncomparable alternatives more closely resembled the decision processes that consumers use when choosing between comparable alternatives. Thus, one aspect of knowledge—knowledge of goals—explained differences in decision processes between the two types of alternative sets.

The Quality of the Alternatives Available. Another important context factor that might affect consumer choices is the overall quality of the set of available alternatives. That is, choices may differ depending upon whether the options are mostly good or mostly bad. While this factor has not yet been studied in consumer choice contexts, Payne, Laughhunn, and Crum (1980, 1981) have shown that choices between pairs of investment options differ contingent upon whether the potential outcomes are above or below the decision maker's aspiration level. The issues of aspiration levels, reference points, or target values are part of the more general question of the framing of consumer decisions.

Person Factors

Prior Knowledge. The degree of previous knowledge that a consumer brings to a choice task can have substantial impact on the resultant process. For example, Fiske (1982) and Fiske and Pavelchak (1986) have proposed that individuals may evaluate stimuli in two basic modes. In piecemeal processing, the evaluation of a stimulus is the combination of the evaluations of the individual elements or attributes of that stimulus. In category-based processing, if a stimulus is successfully categorized in an existing category, the evaluation associated with

that category is associated with the stimulus. Fiske and Pavelchak hypothesize a two-stage process. If the first categorization stage succeeds, then category-based evaluation processing ensues. If categorization fails, piecemeal processing is invoked.

This categorization approach has been examined by Sujan (1985) in a consumer setting. Sujan shows that when the information in a print advertisement matches expectations, there is evidence of category-based processing: faster impression times, more category verbalizations, and fewer attribute verbalizations. When the information does not match expectations, there is evidence of piecemeal processing. These effects are more pronounced for experts than for novices in the product category used (cameras). Thus, there is some very interesting evidence that prior knowledge can affect the basic type of evaluative processing being carried out.

Another aspect of consumer decision making that may depend upon prior knowledge is making inferences. If a consumer does not know the value of a particular attribute for some alternative, he or she may infer that attribute's value from other available information. Meyer (1981) developed a model that accounts for consumer uncertainty about attribute values and assumes that consumers make inferences if no information is available. His results showed that consumers infer a discounted value for a missing attribute value (i.e., a value which is less than the average value of that attribute across other alternatives). Huber and McCann (1982), Yates, Jagacinski, and Faber (1978), and Johnson and Levin (1985) obtained similar results. Ford and Smith (1987) find that consumers' inferences about a missing value for a given brand are influenced more by information about other attributes of that brand than by information about the same attribute for other competing brands.

A final area in which the relationship between prior knowledge and decision processes has been examined is children's judgments. Roedder (1981, 1982) and John and Whitney (1986) argue that one must consider whether the processing deficits observed in children are due to the lack of ability or to the lack of learning the appropriate strategy. Her work indicates that lack of knowledge of procedures for comparing alternatives may be the basis of poor judgments (e.g., inconsistent attitude-behavior judgments) made by children (Roedder, Sternthal, and Calder 1983). This finding suggests education affecting the relevant knowledge base (e.g., decision-making strategies) may be a remedy for improving judgments among children. Note that these results imply that knowledge base, rather than age, may be most crucial in affecting children's processing. Other research supports this notion, showing that children can process more effectively than adults for categories where children have greater knowledge (e.g., Lindberg 1980).

Several of the results described above imply that characterizing consumer expertise and its effects could be an extremely important contribution. The early search for the supposedly more powerful problem—solving heuristics of experts has yielded to the study of the different knowledge structures of experts (Chi 1983). It is felt that the content and organization of knowledge is the crucial factor underlying expertise. For example, Hutchinson (1983) shows that subjects with higher expertise tend to group items more by their functional equivalencies than by their surface similarities. Alba and Hutchinson (1987) provide an extremely thorough review and a set of propositions about consumer expertise that may be very useful in achieving research progress in this area.

Information Processing Abilities. Several studies have demonstrated that individuals' information processing abilities are related to consumer choice processes. For example, Capon and Davis (1984) find that measures which tap systematic combination abilities (Inhelder and Piaget 1958) are correlated with more complex patterns of information acquisition and integration. Capon and Burke (1980) report that subjects lower in socioeconomic status acquired less information and used less attribute-based processing in their choice processes than subjects higher in socioeconomic status. Finally, Bettman, Johnson, and Payne (1990)

provide preliminary evidence that a decision maker will use strategies to a lesser extent if those strategies utilize operations which that individual finds difficult.

Implications of Contingent Decision Making

The contingent perspective on consumer decision making outlined above has a variety of implications. In particular, such a perspective is extremely valuable for designing consumer information environments. As an example, one straightforward implication of an accuracy/effort conceptualization of contingent consumer decision making is that reductions in the effort required to use more accurate strategies will increase the usage of such strategies. This principle has been applied in studies that have attempted to reduce the required effort by manipulating information format. The change in formats can encourage or discourage certain forms of processing by making information easier to process. Recall a classic example of this approach, presented earlier, provided by Russo (1977). Russo was able to provide unit price information in a list format, which facilitated both processing and usage of that information. In general, the principle of increasing the use of more optimal strategies by making such strategies easier to use has important implications for policymakers wishing to provide information to the public (Bettman, Payne, and Staelin 1986).

Another example is provided by Payne, Bettman, and Staelin (1986), who note that particular formats and methods for organizing information can greatly influence the ease with which various types of processing can be carried out. Thus, the congruence between format and type of processing is crucial. It should be noted that there are two basic approaches to congruence. The first is reactive. That is, one can attempt to determine how consumers are currently processing information and develop formats to make existing types of processing easier. A second approach, particularly relevant for policy, is more proactive. The policymaker determines how consumers should process information (e.g., by making more comparisons across brands) and designs formats that facilitate such processing. As we noted before, there is some evidence that consumers tend to process information in the format in which it is provided rather than transforming it (Bettman and Kakker 1977). Therefore, the policymaker or marketer may be able to facilitate certain types of processing through judicious designs for information provision. For example, Bettman, Payne, and Staelin (1986) formulate general principles relevant for designing labels to present information about product hazards: (1) make important information more salient by using color and/or type size, (2) use a common organization for information on all labels, (3) design this common organization hierarchically and in a manner compatible with the scheme used by most consumers to store information about the product, (4) use symbols that quickly convey the concept, (5) collect information on benefits in one place on the label, (6) collect information on risks in one place on the label, (7) organize the label so that the information on benefits and risks are in close proximity, (8) provide information in a relative or comparative format, and (9) consider in-store comparative lists in addition to labels.

These examples illustrate the principle of *passive decision support* (Johnson, Payne, and Bettman 1988). In contrast to more active approaches, which replace human cognitive processes to aid decisions, better decisions can be encouraged by designing displays in ways that possibly encourage more accurate strategies by making them easier to execute. Such reduction in execution effort can be achieved, for example, by using formats that make operations such as comparisons easier or by making individual pieces of data easier to process.

To summarize, research has shown that consumers have limited information processing capacity. As a consequence, consumers often use heuristics in making decisions. A wide variety of heuristic decision strategies have been identified and characterized. The use of a particular heuristic in making a particular decision appears to be highly contingent on a number of

variables related to task, context, and individual differences. From the perspective of a consumer researcher, the contingent nature of consumer decision behavior presents an exciting challenge. No single model appears adequate to predict and explain consumer decision processes. Instead, a researcher interested in better understanding consumer decision making must be prepared to investigate at a detailed level how specific types of consumers respond to a variety of decision situations. In the next section, we examine some of the methods that are useful for studying consumer decision processes.

METHODS FOR STUDYING CONSUMER DECISION MAKING

Input-Output Approaches

There are two basic classes of methods for studying consumer decision making: input-output methods and process-tracing approaches. Input-output methods do not attempt to directly measure the decision process. Instead, an underlying decision process is postulated, and factors are selected which should affect that process in certain ways. Then an experiment would be carried out that manipulated those factors (the input) and measured the result of the process (the output). If the effects were as predicted, the researcher might claim that the experiment provided support for the hypothesized process, even though no attempt was made to observe that process. Russo's (1977) information format study is of this type. The observed monetary savings by consumers are consistent with the hypothesis that the new unit price format led consumers to process the unit price information to a greater extent. However, there is no direct evidence for this process.

Process-Tracing Approaches

In process-tracing approaches, the researcher attempts to measure the ongoing decision process more directly without disturbing that process. The basic idea is to increase the density of observations about decision processes in a time-ordered fashion. We will discuss three major process-tracing methods: verbal protocols, information acquisition approaches, and, to a lesser extent, chronometric methods.

Verbal Protocols. Protocol analysis has been used in several consumer research studies (e.g., Bettman 1970; Payne 1976; Bettman and Park 1980a; Biehal and Chakravarti 1982a,b; 1983; 1986; 1988; Rosen and Olshavsky 1987; Park, Iyer, and Smith 1989). In using this method, the subject is instructed to think out loud as he or she is actually performing the task of interest, for instance, shopping or choosing among alternatives. This verbal record is termed a protocol. It may be distinguished from introspection or retrospective reports in that the subject is asked to verbalize thoughts as they occur in the course of problem solving. The protocol data are then used to gain insights into the processes being used. The major advantage of the method is that a great deal of data on internal events may be made available for inspection. Without these data available, details of the heuristics may be lost. Protocol data are then used to develop a model of the processes used by consumers in making judgments or choices. Bettman and Park (1980a,b) developed an extensive scheme for coding protocols. Their scheme was used and expanded upon by Biehal and Chakravarti (1982a,b; 1983; 1986; 1989).

There are disadvantages to protocol analysis, however. The collection of protocol data in the volume necessary for model inference is extremely time-consuming. Thus small samples have typically been used. In addition, the quality of the data has been questioned. Subjects' protocols may not reflect what they are actually doing. The protocols could reflect biases or self-censoring of protocols as they are being reported, or they may simply show that subjects are unable to retrospectively verbalize internal processes (Nisbett and Wilson 1977). It is particularly difficult to obtain verbalization of currently occurring thoughts, instead of retrospective rationales, when protocols are taken during shopping trips for items about which the subject has some prior knowledge and experience.

Also, protocol output is not obtained for all processing performed. There may not be output corresponding to all internal states (Lindsay and Norman 1972, pp. 517–520). Subjects may select which processing to verbalize based upon what they believe is important, and not verbalize precisely that data most valuable to the researcher (Frijda 1967). While selectivity in verbal reporting may be an issue, several researchers have provided convincing evidence that decision makers do have self-insight (e.g., Ericsson and Simon 1984; Wright and Rip 1984). For further discussion of these issues, see Lynch and Srull (1982) and Biehal and Chakravarti (1989).

The process of providing protocols may also affect the choice processing being carried out. Ericsson and Simon (1984) report many studies finding no effects of taking protocols on decision processes. In studies of consumer decision making, however, there are mixed results when the validity of verbal protocols has been examined. Smead, Wilcox, and Wilkes (1981) and Biehal and Chakravarti (1983) report no significant difference between protocol and no-protocol conditions for some measures. However, Biehal and Chakeravarti (1989) present results showing differences in the extent of alternative-based processing and problem framing due to verbal protocols. Hence, while verbal protocols can provide valuable data regarding choice processes, the researcher must be cautious and attempt to control any effects of taking protocols. (See Biehal and Chakravarti, 1989, and Russo, Johnson, and Stephens, 1989, for suggestions.)

Information Acquisition Approaches. Initial attempts to monitor the sequence of information acquired (e.g., Jacoby 1975; Payne 1976) employed an information display board, essentially a matrix array (often with brands as rows and attributes as columns). Information cards were available in each cell of the matrix, giving the value for the particular attribute and brand appearing in that row and column (e.g., the price for Brand X). The subject was asked to choose a brand after examining as many cards as desired, one at a time. The sequence of cards selected and the amount of information acquired became the major data provided by the method. This detailed record of the sequence of information examined was made available by directly controlling the selection process for information. This technique has been updated by using computer displays.

The major disadvantages of such information monitoring approaches concern the nature of the task. First, it is a relatively obtrusive process, with subjects perhaps biasing their information-seeking behavior since it is so obviously under observation. Second, internal processing is not studied directly, but only external information-seeking responses (i.e., which information is selected) are examined. Not all internal processing may be revealed explicitly in the information-seeking sequence. There is no observation of a possible search of internal memory that may take place in parallel with external search through the matrix. The time spent during an information acquisition may be some indication of the amount of internal processing, however. Third, the typical matrix structure of the information presentation makes it equally easy for a consumer to process by brand or by attribute. This is not similar to many actual consumer tasks in which information is often organized by brand (e.g., on supermarket shelves and in commercials), which hinders attribute processing. A matrix display also helps structure the decision problem for decision makers, which prevents the researcher from studying how consumers develop a structure for themselves.

This last problem has been addressed by a recently developed information search program (Brucks 1988). Brucks stored information about the attributes of several alternatives in a computer database. Subjects were able to access this database through a user interface that simulates a shopping situation. The alternatives and attributes are not presented in a matrix structure—in fact, the names of the attributes are not presented at all on the display. Rather, using their own words (which can be interpreted by artificial intelligence programs or unobtrusive human intervention), subjects make inquiries about the attributes of the alternatives of interest.

Analysis of eye movements has also been used to study information acquisition (e.g., Russo and Rosen 1975; Russo and Dosher 1983; Van Raaij, 1977). In using this method, the choice objects are displayed either on a screen in front of the subject, in tabular format (Russo and Dosher 1983; Russo and Rosen 1975), or perhaps as separate packages (Van Raaij 1977). The sequence of eye movements used by the subject in examining the choice objects is then recorded by a specialized apparatus. Often this entails some restrictions: Subjects' heads may be immobilized to prevent large head movements, or subjects who wear contact lenses or eyeglasses may not participate. Similarly the visual display must guard against the subjects' use of peripheral vision by providing relatively large separations between items.

The resulting eye movement data provide a very detailed and dense trace of the information search, and eye movements may be relatively more difficult for subjects to censor than verbal protocols. Eye movement data may be more useful in conditions when protocols may fail, such as when studying processes which occur rapidly or which involve nonverbal representations or automated processes (Ericsson and Simon 1984). In addition, eye movements have a major advantage over information display boards, because the eye movement requires much less effort than physically retrieving a card. Comparison between eye movement recording and information display boards show that eye movements show both more acquisitions and more reacquisitions (Russo 1978).

Eye movement data also have unresolved problems. First, collecting such data is very time-consuming, expensive, and usually uses small sample sizes. Also, since the apparatus often is quite obtrusive, subjects are obviously quite aware that their eye movements are being monitored (although more recently developed eye movement systems do not require restriction of the head). Second, the choice stimuli used in eye movement studies have often been simplistic arrays because of the desire by researchers to localize eye movements. More detailed and complex visual stimuli, such as standard product shelf displays, have been examined using videotaping procedures, but these provide information only about the aggregate characteristics of the looking behavior (Russo 1978). Finally, the fixations are information-seeking responses, and they do not necessarily reveal the details of internal processing (see Russo, 1978, for more details on this method).

A middle ground between eye movement recording and information display boards is provided by a computer-based information display that employs a mouse to control information acquisition (Johnson, Payne, Schkade, and Bettman 1988). This acquisition system measures both the sequence and timing of information gathering in several different types of task environments. Because the mouse is a relatively effortless response, Johnson et al. argue that it approximates the detail provided by eye movements with much less cost. While the computer displays are still quite structured, environments other than brand by attribute matrices and responses other than choice can be used.

Chronometric Analysis. Analysis of response times, or chronometric analysis, has been used to study consumer choice (e.g., Johnson and Russo 1978; Gardner, Mitchell, and Russo 1978; Sujan 1985). The basic data collected in using this approach are the times taken to complete a response, usually measured as the time between the presentation of a stimulus and the response to that stimulus. Note that in a sense this is a form of input-output analysis where the output is total time. Measurement of such times can be carried out with varying degrees of sophistication, ranging from the use of tachistoscopes to the use of stop watches (Russo 1978). The assumption is usually made that this time directly reflects the amount of processing effort used in completing the task. By comparing the mean response times over different experimental conditions, it is hoped that one can learn

about the information processing characterizing such tasks.

Various types of insights can be obtained from analyses of response times. Several authors have used such analyses to study the structure of memory (e.g., Johnson and Russo 1978). Other applications have included testing models of cognitive effort in decision processes (Bettman, Johnson, and Payne 1990) and attempting to distinguish exemplar-based versus rule-based processing in categorization (Cohen and Basu 1987). Lynch (1981) discusses how response times can be used to determine the sequence of cognitive processes in judgment.

A major advantage of response time analysis is that it can be used to study covert and rapid processes such as memory search. Other methods do not seem as generally powerful in exposing such memory phenomena. Some have argued that, although response time measures are very useful for studying such brief processes, they may be less useful for longer tasks (Russo 1978). The longer the duration of the task, the greater the chance that factors not manipulated by the experimenter may affect response times.

Response time analysis is a technically demanding approach that has certain disadvantages. Perhaps the most problematical is the trade-off between speed and accuracy. In almost all tasks, subjects can choose to sacrifice accuracy to attain greater speed, or they may take more time in order to improve accuracy. A discussion and an example of the problems created by the speed-accuracy trade-off are cogently presented by Pachella (1974). The usual technique for dealing with this trade-off is to attempt to have subjects perform at the same accuracy level in all experimental tasks. This strategy may be difficult to implement in consumer research settings in which there may often be no objectively correct response against which subjects' responses can be compared (Gardner, Mitchell, and Russo 1978).

A second disadvantage is that response time measures are very much aggregate measures, and, as such, may be difficult to interpret; that is, knowing only how long a process took does not directly lead to insights about the components of the process. Initial theorizing about the process is essential for designing experiments using response time analysis if there is to be some hope of obtaining insights (Gardner, Mitchell, and Russo 1978). Finally, response time analysis can be an obtrusive method, with subjects usually aware that their response times are being measured. This is particularly true for cases where speed-accuracy trade-off instructions are used.

We have barely scratched the surface with this necessarily brief discussion of methods for studying consumer decision making. These approaches are described in more detail in Carroll and Johnson (in press) and in Ford, Schmitt, Schechtman, Hults, and Doherty (1989). It should be clear, however, that no one method is perfect. Each method has its own biases and disadvantages. Combinations of methods in which several complementary approaches are used in the same study seem to hold the greatest promise. Since the various methods have different strengths and weaknesses, multimethod approaches let us separate the effects of the research method from those associated with the phenomenon under study.

FUTURE RESEARCH OPPORTUNITIES

We have argued that consumers, faced with potentially complex decisions, use a variety of heuristics to simplify their task. As a result of processing limitations, consumers are contingent processors, using different strategies for different decision environments. Two conceptual frameworks for understanding such adaptivity were presented, and the research supporting the contingent approach was outlined. Finally, we examined methods for studying consumer decisions and some implications of these methods.

Consumer decision making remains rich in possibilities for future research. One particularly important area for study is the notion of constructive decision processes and editing. We know very little about how consumers notice properties of choice environments and adapt to

such properties on the spur of the moment. Studies of how the focus of consumers' attention varies as a function of attribute values, display formats, and other factors could shed light on these noticing processes. Monitoring information acquisition sequences and taking verbal protocols may help to uncover how consumers decide to react to what they notice. A related issue of great importance is how consumers assess how well they are doing. While consumers may have reasonable perceptions of the effort they are expending, how perceptions of accuracy are developed is an open and crucial question (Klein and Yadav 1989).

A related topic of substantial interest is how decision makers represent alternatives. Thaler and Johnson (1989), for example, demonstrate that how decision makers represent prior gains and losses can dramatically influence choices. Such questions as whether consumers view cents-off coupons and sales as an original price and a discount or as a final net price are examples of the sorts of representation issues that might be addressed. Another example of a representational issue in consumer choice is Loewenstein's (1988) research on frames of mind in intertemporal decisions they face (e.g., whether a purchase at a particular point in time or as a two-stage decision that involves first the decision to purchase followed by a deliberation concerning when to purchase) may impact on the optimality of consumer choices. Such questions as impulse buying behavior and the negotiation processes used in reaching purchase settlements may reflect intertemporal framing effects. More generally, framing issues like those above are at the core of attempting to apply the perceptual framework to contingent decision making.

Since prior knowledge influences many consumer decision processes, consumer expertise represents another major area for research. In particular, conceptualizing and measuring different aspects of consumer knowledge (see Brucks, 1985, for one attempt) and studying how such knowledge influences decision processes is a promising direction for research. Another sort of individual difference variable that seems worthy of more research is the idea of differences in need for cognition (Cacioppo and Petty 1982). The degree of need for cognition should be related to amount of information search and perhaps to the types of heuristics preferred.

Several potentially important areas within consumer decision making have seen virtually no research to date. For example, connections could be made from the literature on risky decision making to consumer choice. For example, to our knowledge no one has yet attempted to integrate notions from Kahneman and Tversky's (1979) prospect theory with the ideas about heuristics and contingent decision making presented in this chapter. More generally, the roles of such constructs as risk (as defined by theorists of risky choice) and ambiguity in consumer choice have not been explored fully. (See Kahn and Sarin, 1988, for an initial effort to consider ambiguity.)

Another area that has seen very little research is incentives. What effects do incentives have on decision processes? According to the cost/benefit approach, incentives should affect the trade-off between costs and benefits. Simonson (1989) reports results of having to justify choices to others, but there is room for much more research in the area of incentives. One potentially fruitful focus for such research may be the distinction between working harder versus working smarter. Tversky and Kahneman (1986), for example, argue that incentives work by focussing attention and prolonging deliberation. That is, incentives cause people to work harder but not necessarily smarter. However, if people do not change strategies but just work harder, this may have the paradoxical effect of increasing error in decisions through increased effort applied to executing a flawed strategy (Arkes, Dawes, and Christensen 1986). Finally, any shift in strategy due to incentives would seem to require awareness of alternative strategies. In some cases, incentives may have limited impact due to a lack of awareness of any better decision strategy than the one currently being used. Thus, an important direction for research on consumer decision making is to understand better when and how incentives will impact processing and choice.

Research on multiperson decision processes is also a wide-open area for research. Virtually nothing has been done in terms of process-tracing studies of group decisions. How information is shared and how inputs from various individuals are coordinated represent important and fascinating research areas.

Many of the research issues noted in this chapter place severe demands on methodology, since more detailed process-tracing analyses seem appropriate. As a result, research that refines or develops new process-tracing techniques is crucial. In particular, methods that allow consumers highly flexible and rapid access to information and keep a trace of the sequence and timing of such access seem necessary. Current information acquisition methodologies may be too slow and/or inflexible to examine issues of editing or constructive choice processes, for example.

Another research methodology issue, with more applied aspects, concerns the effects of different response modes on the elicitation of consumer preferences (see Johnson and Meyer 1984). As noted earlier, different response modes can affect stated preferences in systematic ways. Research characterizing the impact of such response modes are rating, ranking, and pick *n* on the processes consumers use to examine and evaluate alternatives could be very useful.

This set of opportunities for future research is of course very selective. Any of the areas discussed earlier in this chapter provide fascinating prospects for future research. We have attempted to highlight some of the more exciting possibilities in this section. We hope that this chapter helps to make those opportunities, new theories, and new methodologies salient and that it helps to stimulate exciting new research.

REFERENCES

ALBA, J. W., & HUTCHINSON, J. W. (1987). Dimensions of consumer expertise. *Journal of Consumer Research, 13,* 411–454.

ALBA, J. W., & MARMORSTEIN, H. (1987). The

effects of frequency knowledge on consumer decision making. *Journal of Consumer Research, 14,* 14–26.

ANDERSON, J. R. (1983). *The architecture of cognition.* Cambridge, MA: Harvard University Press.

ARKES, H. R., DAWES, R. M., & CHRISTENSEN, C. (1986). Factors influencing the use of a decision rule in a probabilistic task. *Organizational Behavior and Human Decision Processes, 37,* 93–110.

BATSELL, R. R., & POLKING, J. C. (1985). A new class of market share models. *Marketing Science, 4,* 177–198.

BEACH, L. R., & MITCHELL, T. R. (1978). A contingency model for the selection of decision strategies. *Academy of Management Review, 3,* 439–449.

BEN ZUR, H., & BREZNITZ, S. J. (1981). The effects of time pressure on risky choice behavior. *Acta Psychologica, 47,* 89–104.

BETTMAN, J. R. (1970). Information processing models of consumer behavior. *Journal of Marketing Research, 7,* 370–376.

BETTMAN, J. R. (1979). *An information processing theory of consumer choice.* Reading, MA: Addison-Wesley.

BETTMAN, J. R. (1982). A functional analysis of the role of overall evaluation of alternatives in choice processes. In A. Mitchell (Ed.), *Advances in Consumer Research,* Vol. 9. Ann Arbor, MI: Association for Consumer Research, 87–93.

BETTMAN, J. R., JOHNSON, E. J., & PAYNE, J. W. (1990). A componential analysis of cognitive effort in choice. *Organizational Behavior and Human Decision Processes.*

BETTMAN, J. R. & KAKKAR, P. (1977). Effects of information presentation format on consumer information acquisition strategies. *Journal of Consumer Research, 3,* 233–240.

BETTMAN, J. R., & PARK, C. W. (1980a). Effects of prior knowledge, experience, and phase of the choice process on consumer decision processes: A protocol analysis. *Journal of Consumer Research, 7,* 234–248.

BETTMAN, J. R., & PARK, C. W. (1980b). Implications of a constructive view of choice for analysis of protocol data: A coding scheme for elements of choice processes. In J. C. Olson (Ed.), *Advances in Consumer Research,* Vol. 7. Ann Arbor, MI: Association for Consumer Research, 148–153.

BETTMAN, J. R., PAYNE, J. W., & STAELIN, R. (1986). Cognitive considerations in designing ef-

fective labels for presenting risk information. *Journal of Marketing and Public Policy, 5,* 1–28.

BETTMAN, J. R., & SUJAN, M. (1987). Effects of framing on evaluation of comparable and noncomparable alternatives by expert and novice consumers. *Journal of Consumer Research, 14,* 141–154.

BIEHAL, G. J., & CHAKRAVARTI, D. (1982a). Information presentation format and learning goals as determinants of consumers' memory retrieval and choice processes. *Journal of Consumer Research, 8,* 431–441.

BIEHAL, G. J., & CHAKRAVARTI, D. (1982b). Experiences with the Bettman-Park verbal protocol coding scheme. *Journal of Consumer Research, 8,* 442–448.

BIEHAL, G. J., & CHAKRAVARTI, D. (1983). Information accessibility as a moderator of consumer choice. *Journal of Consumer Research, 10,* 1–14.

BIEHAL, G. J., & CHAKRAVARTI, D. (1986). Consumers' use of memory and external information in choice: Macro and micro processing perspectives. *Journal of Consumer Research, 12,* 382–405.

BIEHAL, G. J., & CHAKRAVARTI, D. (1989). The effects of concurrent verbalization on choice processing. *Journal of Marketing Research, 26,* 84–96.

BRUCKS, M. (1985). The effects of product class knowledge on information search behavior. *Journal of Consumer Research, 12,* 1–16.

BRUCKS, M. (1988). Search monitor: An approach for computer-controlled experiments involving consumer information search. *Journal of Consumer Research, 15,* 117–121.

CACIOPPO, J. T., & PETTY, R. E. (1982). The need for cognition. *Journal of Personality and Social Psychology, 42,* 116–131.

CAPON, N., & BURKE, M. (1980). Individual, product class, and task-related factors in consumer information processing. *Journal of Consumer Research, 7,* 314–326.

CAPON, N., & DAVIS, R. (1984). Basic cognitive ability measures as predictors of consumer information processing strategies. *Journal of Consumer Research, 11,* 551–563.

CARD, S. K., MORAN, T. P., & NEWELL, A. (1983). *The psychology of human-computer interaction.* Hillsdale, NJ: Erlbaum.

CARROLL, J. S., & JOHNSON, E. J. (in press). *Doing decision research: Methods for understanding how decisions are made.* Beverly Hills, CA: Sage.

CHAKRAVARTI, D., & LYNCH, J. G. (1983). A

framework for examining context effects on consumer judgment and choice. In R. P. Bagozzi and Alice M. Tybout (Eds.), *Advances in Consumer Research,* Vol. 10. Ann Arbor, MI: Association of Consumer Research, 289–297.

CHASE, W. G. (1978). Elementary information processes. In W. K. Estes (Ed.), *Handbook of Learning and Cognitive Processes,* Vol. 5. Hillsdale, NJ: Erlbaum.

CHASE, W. G., & ERICSSON, K. A. (1981). Skilled memory. In J. R. Anderson (Ed.), *Cognitive skills and their acquisition.* Hillsdale, NJ: Erlbaum.

CHI, M. T. H. (1983). The role of knowledge on problem solving and consumer choice behavior. In R. P. Bagozzi and Alice M. Tybout (Eds.), *Advances in Consumer Research,* Vol. 10. Ann Arbor, MI: Association for Consumer Research, 569–571.

COHEN, J. B., & BASU, K. (1987). Alternative models of categorization: Toward a contingent processing framework. *Journal of Consumer Research, 13,* 455–472.

COWAN, N. (1988). Evolving conceptions of memory storage, selective attention, and their mutual constraints within the human information-processing system. *Psychological Bulletin, 104,* 163–191.

CROCKER, J. (1981). Judgment of covariation by social perceivers. *Psychological Bulletin, 90,* 272–292.

CURRY, D. J., & FAULDS, D. J. (1986). Indexing product quality: Issues, theory, and results. *Journal of Consumer Research, 13,* 134–145.

CURRY, D. J., & MENASCO, M. B. (1983). On the separability of weights and scale values: Issues and empirical results. *Journal of Consumer Research, 10,* 83–92.

DAWES, R. M. (1979). The robust beauty of improper linear models in decision making. *American Psychologist, 34,* 571–582.

EINHORN, H. H., & HOGARTH, R. M. (1975). Unit weighting schemes for decision making. *Organizational Behavior and Human Performance, 13,* 171–192.

EINHORN, H. J., & HOGARTH, R. M. (1981). Behavioral decision theory: Processes of judgment and choice. *Annual Review of Psychology, 32,* 53–88.

EINHORN, H. J., KLEINMUNTZ, D. N., & KLEINMUNTZ, B. (1979). Linear regression and process-tracing models of judgment. *Psychological Review, 86,* 465–485.

ENGEL, J. F., BLACKWELL, R. D., & KOLLAT, D. T. (1978). *Consumer Behavior,* 3rd ed. Hinsdale, IL: Dryden.

ERICSSON, K. A., & SIMON, H. A. (1984). *Protocol analysis: Verbal reports as data.* Cambridge, MA: MIT Press.

FELDMAN, J. M., & LYNCH, J. G. (1988). Self-generated validity and other effects of measurement on belief, attitude, intention, and behavior. *Journal of Applied Psychology, 73,* 421–435.

FISKE, S. T. (1982). Schema-triggered affect: Applications to social perception. In M. S. Clark and S. T. Fiske (Eds.), *Affect and Cognition: The 17th Annual Carnegie Symposium on Cognition.* Hillsdale, NJ: Erlbaum.

FISKE, S. T., & PAVELCHAK, M. A. (1986). Category-based versus piecemeal-based effective responses: Developments in schema-triggered affect. In R. M. Sorrentino and E. T. Higgins (Eds.), *The Handbook of Motivation and Cognition: Foundations of Social Behavior.* New York: Guilford.

FORD, G. T., & SMITH, R. A. (1987). Inferential beliefs in consumer evaluations: An assessment of alternative processing strategies. *Journal of Consumer Research, 14,* 363–371.

FORD, J. K., SCHMITT, W., SCHECHTMAN, S. L., HULTS, B. M., & DOHERTY, M. L. (1989). Process tracing methods: Contributions, problems, and neglected research questions. *Organizational Behavioral and Human Decision Processes, 43,* 75–117.

FRIEDMAN, M. P. (1966). Consumer confusion in the selection of supermarket products. *Journal of Applied Psychology, 50,* 529–534.

FRIJDA, N. (1967). Problems of computer simulation. *Behavioral Science, 12,* 59–67.

GARDNER, M. P., MITCHELL, A. A., & RUSSO, J. E. (1978). Chronometric analysis: An introduction and an application to low involvement perception of advertisements. In H. K. Hunt (Ed.), *Advances in Consumer Research,* Vol. 5. Chicago: Association for Consumer Research, 581–589.

HANSEN, F. (1972). *Consumer choice behavior: A cognitive theory.* New York: The Free Press.

HAUGELAND, J. (ED.) (1981). *Mind design.* Cambridge, MA: MIT Press.

HAUSER, J. R., & GASKIN, S. P. (1984). Application of the "Defender" consumer model. *Marketing Science, 3,* 327–351.

HEGARTY, M., JUST, M. A., & MORRISON, I. R.

(1988). Mental models of mechanical systems: Individual differences in qualitative and quantitative reasoning. *Cognitive Psychology, 20,* 191–236.

HOGARTH, R. M. (1987). *Judgment and choice: The psychology of decision.* New York: Wiley.

HOWARD, J. A. (1977). *Consumer behavior: Application of theory.* New York: McGraw-Hill.

HOWARD, J. A., & SHETH, J. N. (1969). *The Theory of Buyer Behavior.* New York: Wiley.

HUBER, J. (1983). The effect of set composition on item choice: Separating attraction, edge aversion, and substitution effects. In R. P. Bagozzi and Alice M. Tybout (Eds.), *Advances in Consumer Research,* Vol. 10. Ann Arbor, MI: Association for Consumer Research, 298–304.

HUBER, J., & McCANN, J. (1982). The impact of inferential beliefs on product evaluations. *Journal of Marketing Research, 19,* 324–333.

HUBER, J., PAYNE, J. W., & PUTO, C. (1982). Adding asymmetrically dominated alternatives: Violations of regularity and the similarity hypothesis. *Journal of Consumer Research, 9,* 90–98.

HUBER, J., & PUTO, C. P. (1983). Market boundaries and product choice: Illustrating attraction and substitution effects. *Journal of Consumer Research, 10,* 31–44.

HUTCHINSON, J. W. (1983). Expertise and the structure of free recall. In R. P. Bagozzi and Alice M. Tybout (Eds.), *Advances in Consumer Research,* Vol. 10. Ann Arbor, MI: Association for Consumer Research, 585–589.

INHELDER, B., & PIAGET, J. (1958). *The growth of logical thinking from childhood to adolescence.* New York: Basic Books.

ISEN, A. M. (1984). The influence of positive affect on decision making and cognitive organization. In T. C. Kinnear (Ed.), *Advances in Consumer Research,* Vol. 11. Ann Arbor, MI: Association for Consumer Research, 534–37.

JACOBY, J. (1975). Perspectives on a consumer information processing research program. *Communication Research, 2,* 203–215.

JACOBY, J., SPELLER, D. E., & KOHN, C. A. (1974a). Brand choice behavior as a function of information load. *Journal of Marketing Research, 11,* 63–69.

JACOBY, J., SPELLER, D. E., & KOHN, C. A. (1974b). Brand choice behavior as a function of information load: Replication and extension. *Journal of Consumer Research, 1,* 33–42.

JOHN, D. R., & WHITNEY, J. C. (1986). The devel-

opment of consumer knowledge in children: A cognitive structure approach. *Journal of Consumer Research, 12,* 406–417.

JOHNSON, E. J. (1979). Deciding how to decide: The effort of making a decision. Unpublished manuscript, University of Chicago, Chicago, IL.

JOHNSON, E. J., & MEYER, R. J. (1984). Compensatory choice models of noncompensatory processes: The effect of varying context. *Journal of Consumer Research, 11,* 528–541.

JOHNSON, E. J., MEYER, R. M., & GHOSE, S. (1989). When choice models fail: Compensatory representations in negatively correlated environments. *Journal of Marketing Research, 26,* 255–270.

JOHNSON, E. J., & PAYNE, J. W. (1985). Effort and accuracy in choice. *Management Science, 31,* 395–414.

JOHNSON, E. J., PAYNE, J. W., & BETTMAN, J. R. (1988). Information displays and preference reversals. *Organizational Behavior and Human Decision Processes, 42,* 1–21.

JOHNSON, E. J., PAYNE, J. W., SCHKADE, D. A., & BETTMAN, J. R. (1988). Monitoring information processing and decisions: The mouselab system. Unpublished manuscript, Center for Decision Studies, Fuqua School of Business, Duke University, Durham, NC.

JOHNSON, E. J., & RUSSO, J. E. (1978). The organization of product information in memory identified by recall times. In H. K. Hunt (Ed.), *Advances in Consumer Research,* Vol. 5. Chicago: Association for Consumer Research, 79–86.

JOHNSON, E. J., & RUSSO, J. E. (1981). Product familiarity and learning new information. In K. Monroe (Ed.), *Advances in consumer research,* Vol. 8. Ann Arbor, MI: Association for Consumer Research, 151–155.

JOHNSON, E. J., & RUSSO, J. E. (1984). Product familiarity and learning new information. *Journal of Consumer Research, 11,* 542–550.

JOHNSON, M. D. (1984). Consumer choice strategies for comparing noncomparable alternatives. *Journal of Consumer Research, 11,* 741–753.

JOHNSON, M. D. (1986). Modeling choice strategies for noncomparable alternatives. *Marketing Science, 5,* 37–54.

JOHNSON, M. D. (1988). Comparability and hierarchical processing in multialternative choice. *Journal of Consumer Research, 15,* 303–314.

JOHNSON, R. D., & LEVIN, I. P. (1985). More than meets the eye: The effect of missing information on purchase evaluations. *Journal of Consumer Research, 12,* 169–177.

KAHN, B. E., & SARIN, R. K. (1988). Modeling ambiguity in decisions under uncertainty. *Journal of Consumer Research, 15,* 265–272.

KAHNEMAN, D., & TVERSKY, A. (1979). Prospect theory: An analysis of decision making under risk. *Econometrica, 47,* 263–291.

KELLER, K. L. (1987). Memory factors in advertising: The effect of advertising retrieval cues on brand evaluations. *Journal of Consumer Research, 14,* 316–333.

KELLER, K. L., & STAELIN, R. (1987). Effects of quality and quantity of information on decision effectiveness. *Journal of Consumer Research, 14,* 200–213.

KELLER, K. L., & STAELIN, R. (1989). Assessing biases in measuring decision effectiveness and information overload. *Journal of Consumer Research, 15,* 504–508.

KLAYMAN, J. (1983). Analysis of predecisional information search patterns. In P. C. Humphreys, O. Svenson, and A. Vari (Eds.), *Analyzing and aiding decision processes.* Amsterdam: North Holland.

KLEIN, N. M. (1983). Utility and decision strategies: A second look at the rational decision maker. *Organizational Behavior and Human Performance, 31,* 1–25.

KLEIN, N. M., & BITHER, S. W. (1987). An investigation of utility-directed cutoff selection. *Journal of Consumer Research, 14,* 240–256.

KLEIN, N. M., & YADAV, M. S. (1989). Context effects on effort and accuracy in choice: An inquiry into adaptive decision making. *Journal of Consumer Research, 15,* 411–421.

KRIEGER, A. M., & GREEN, P. E. (1988). On the generation of Pareto optimal, conjoint profiles from orthogonal main effects plans. Working paper, Wharton School, University of Pennsylvania, Philadelphia, PA.

LEVIN, I. P., & GAETH, G. J. (1988). How consumers are affected by the framing of attribute information before and after consuming the product. *Journal of Consumer Research, 15,* 374–378.

LEVIN, I. P., & JOHNSON, R. D. (1984). Estimating price-quality trade-offs using comparative judgments. *Journal of Consumer Research, 11,* 593–600.

LINDBERG, M. A. (1980). Is knowledge base development a necessary and sufficient condition for memory development? *Journal of Experimental Child Psychology, 30,* 401–410.

LINDSAY, P. H., & NORMAN, D. A. (1972). *Human Information Processing.* New York: Academic Press.

LOEWENSTEIN, G. F. (1988). Frames of mind in intertemporal choice. *Management Science, 34,* 200–214.

LUSSIER, D. A., & OLSHAVSKY, R. W. (1979). Task complexity and contingent processing in brand choice. *Journal of Consumer Research, 6,* 154–165.

LYNCH, J. G. (1981). A method for determining the sequencing of cognitive processes in judgment: Order effects on reaction time. In Kent B. Monroe (Ed.), *Advances in Consumer Research,* Vol. 8. Ann Arbor, MI: Association for Consumer Research, 134–139.

LYNCH, J. G., & SRULL, T. K. (1982). Memory and attentional factors in consumer choice: Concepts and research methods. *Journal of Consumer Research, 9,* 18–37.

LYNCH, J. G., MARMORSTEIN, H., & WEIGOLD, M. F. (1988). Choices from sets including remembered brands: Use of recalled attributes and prior overall evaluations. *Journal of Consumer Research, 15,* 169–184.

MALHOTRA, N. K. (1982). Information load and consumer decision making. *Journal of Consumer Research, 8,* 419–430.

MARCH, J. G. (1978). Bounded rationality, ambiguity, and the engineering of choice. *Bell Journal of Economics, 9,* 587–608.

McCLELLAND, G. H. (1978). Equal versus differential weighting for multiattribute decisions. Unpublished manuscript, University of Colorado, Boulder, CO.

MEYER, R. J. (1981). A model of multiattribute judgments under attribute uncertainty and information constraint. *Journal of Marketing Research, 18,* 428–441.

MEYER, R. J., & JOHNSON, E. J. (1989). Information overload and the nonrobustness of linear models: A comment on Keller and Staelin. *Journal of Consumer Research, 15,* 498–503.

MEYER, R. J., & EAGLE, T. C. (1982). Context-induced parameter instability in a disaggregate-stochastic model of store choice. *Journal of Marketing Research, 19,* 62–71.

MILLER, G. A. (1956). The magical number seven, plus or minus two: Some limits on our capacity for processing information. *Psychology Review, 63,* 81–97.

MILLER, J. G. (1960). Information input overload and psychopathology. *American Journal of Psychiatry, 116,* 695–704.

MOWEN, J. C., & GENTRY, J. W. (1980). Investigation of the preference-reversal phenomenon in a new product introduction task. *Journal of Applied Psychology, 65,* 715–722.

MULLER, T. C. (1984). Buyer response to variations in product information load. *Journal of Applied Psychology, 69,* 300–306.

NEWELL, A., & SIMON, H. A. (1972). *Human problem solving.* Englewood Cliffs, NJ: Prentice-Hall.

NEWELL, A., & SIMON, H. A. (1981). Computer science as empirical inquiry: Symbols and search. In J. Haugeland (Ed.), *Mind design.* Cambridge, MA: MIT Press.

NEWMAN, J. R. (1977). Differential weighting in multiattribute utility measurement: Where it should and where it does make a difference. *Organizational Behavior and Human Performance, 20,* 312–325.

NISBETT, R. E., & WILSON, T. D. (1977). Telling more than we can know: Verbal reports on mental processes. *Psychological Review, 84,* 231–259.

OLSHAVSKY, R. W. (1979). Task complexity and contingent processing in decision making: A replication and extension. *Organizational Behavior and Human Performance, 24,* 300–316.

PACHELLA, R. G. (1974). The interpretation of reaction time in information processing research. In B. H. Kantowitz (Ed.), *Human information processing: Tutorials in performance and cognition.* Hillsdale, NJ: Erlbaum.

PARK, C. W. (1982). Joint decisions in home purchasing: A muddling-through process. *Journal of Consumer Research, 9,* 151–162.

PARK, C. W., IYER, E. S., & SMITH, D. C. (1989). The effects of situational factors on in-store grocery shopping behavior: The role of store environment and time available for shopping. *Journal of Consumer Research, 15,* 422–433.

PAYNE, J. W. (1976). Task complexity and contingent processing in decision making: An information search and protocol analysis. *Organizational Behavior and Human Performance, 16,* 366–387.

PAYNE, J. W. (1982). Contingent decision behavior. *Psychological Bulletin, 92,* 382–402.

PAYNE, J. W., BETTMAN, J. R., & JOHNSON, E. J. (1988). Adaptive strategy selection in decision making. *Journal of Experimental Psychology: Learning, Memory, and Cognition, 14,* 534–552.

PAYNE, J. W., BETTMAN, J. R., & JOHNSON, E. J. (in press). The adaptive decision maker: Effort and accuracy in choice. In R. M. Hogarth (Ed.), *Insights in decision making: Theory and applications— A tribute to Hillel J. Einhorn.* Chicago: University of Chicago Press.

PAYNE, J. W., LAUGHHUNN, D. J., & CRUM, R. (1980). Translation of gambles and aspiration level effects in risky choice behavior. *Management Science, 26,* 1039–1060.

PAYNE, J. W., LAUGHHUNN, D. J., & CRUM, R. (1981). Further tests of aspiration level effects in risky choice behavior. *Management Science, 27,* 953–958.

PUTO, C. P. (1987). The framing of buying decisions. *Journal of Consumer Research, 14,* 301–316.

RATNESHWAR, S., SHOCKER, A. D., & STEWART, D. W. (1987). Toward understanding the attraction effect: The implications of product stimulus meaningfulness and familiartiy. *Journal of Consumer Research, 13,* 520–533.

REED, S. K. (1982). *Cognition: Theory and application.* Monterey, CA: Brooks/Cole.

RESTLE, F. (1961). *Psychology of judgment and choice: A theoretical essay.* New York: Wiley.

ROEDDER, D. L. (1981). Age differences in children's responses to television advertising: An information processing approach. *Journal of Consumer Research, 8,* 144–153. ˙

ROEDDER, D. L. (1982). Understanding and overcoming children's processing deficits. In A. Mitchell (Ed.), *Advances in Consumer Research,* Vol. 9. Ann Arbor, MI: Association for Consumer Research, 148–152.

ROEDDER, D. L., STERNTHAL, B., & CALDER, B. J. (1983). Attitude-behavior consistency in children's responses to television advertising. *Journal of Marketing Research, 20,* 337–349.

ROSEN, D. L., & OLSHAVSKY, R. W. (1987). A protocol analysis of brand choice strategies involving recommendations. *Journal of Consumer Research, 14,* 440–444.

RUSSO, J. E. (1974). More information is better: A reevaluation of Jacoby, Speller, and Kohn. *Journal of Consumer Research, 1,* 68–72.

RUSSO, J. E. (1977). The value of unit price information. *Journal of Marketing Research, 14,* 193–201.

RUSSO, J. E (1978). Eye fixations can save the world: Critical evaluation and comparison between eye fixations and other information processing methodologies. In H. K. Hunt (Ed.),

Advances in Consumer Research, Vol. 5. Ann Arbor, MI: Association for Consumer Research, 561–570.

RUSSO, J. E., & DOSHER, B. A. (1983). Strategies for multiattribute binary choice. *Journal of Experimental Psychology: Learning, Memory, and Cognition, 9*, 676–696.

RUSSO, J. E., JOHNSON, E. J., & STEPHENS, D. M. (1989). The validity of verbal protocols. *Memory & Cognition, 17*, 759–769.

RUSSO, J. E., KRIESER, G., & MIYASHITA, S. (1975). An effective display of unit price information. *Journal of Marketing, 39*, 11–19.

RUSSO, J. E., & ROSEN, L. D. (1975). An eye fixation analysis of multialternative choice. *Memory and Cognition, 3*, 267–276.

RUSSO, J. E., STAELIN, R., NOLAN, C. A., RUSSELL, G. J., & METCALF, B. L. (1986). Nutrition information in the supermarket. *Journal of Consumer Research, 13*, 48–70.

SHUGAN, S. M. (1980). The cost of thinking. *Journal of Consumer Research, 7*, 99–111.

SHUGAN, S. M. (1987). Estimating brand positioning maps using supermarket scanning data. *Journal of Marketing Research, 24*, 1–18.

SIMON, H. A. (1955). A behavioral model of rational choice. *Quarterly Journal of Economics, 69* 99–118.

SIMON, H. A. (1974). How big is a chunk? *Science, 183*, 482–488.

SIMON, H. A. (1978). Rationality as a process and product of thought. *American Economic Review, 68*, 1–16.

SIMON, H. A. (1981). *The sciences of the artificial* (2nd ed.). Cambridge, MA: MIT Press.

SIMONSON, I. (1989). Choice based on reasons: The case of attraction and compromise effects. *Journal of Consumer Research, 16*, 158–174.

SIMONSON, I., HUBER, J., & PAYNE, J. (1988). The relationship between prior brand knowledge and information acquisition order. *Journal of Consumer Research, 14*, 566–578.

SLOVIC, P. (1972). From Shakespeare to Simon: Speculations and some evidence about man's ability to process information. *Oregon Research Institute Bulletin, 12* (3).

SLOVIC, P., & LICHTENSTEIN, S. (1983). Preference reversals: A broader perspective. *American Economic Review, 73*, 596–605.

SMEAD, R. J., WILCOX, J. B., & WILKES, R. E. (1981). How valid are product descriptions and protocols in choice experiments? *Journal of Consumer Research, 8*, 37–42.

SUJAN, M. (1985). Consumer knowledge: Effects on evaluation strategies mediating consumer judgments. *Journal of Consumer Research, 12*, 16–31.

SUMMERS, J. O. (1974). Less information is better? *Journal of Marketing Research, 11*, 467–468.

SVENSON, O. (1979). Process descriptions of decision making. *Organizational Behavior and Human Performance, 23*, 86–112.

SVENSON, O., EDLAND, A., & KARLSSON, G. (1985). The effect of numerical and verbal information and time stress on judgments of the attractiveness of decision alternatives. In L. B. Methlie and R. Sprague (Eds.), *Knowledge Representation for Decision Support Systems*. Amsterdam: North Holland, 133–144.

THALER, R. H., & JOHNSON, E. J. (1989). The effect of prior outcomes on risky choice. Unpublished working paper, Cornell University, Ithaca, NY.

THORNGATE, W. (1980). Efficient decision heuristics. *Behavioral Science, 25*, 219–225.

TVERSKY, A. (1969). Intransitivity of preferences. *Psychological Review, 76*, 31–48.

TVERSKY, A. (1972). Elimination by aspects: A theory of choice. Psychological Review, 79, 281–299.

TVERSKY, A., & KAHNEMAN, D. (1981). The framing of decision and the psychology of choice. *Science, 211*, 453–458.

TVERSKY, A., & KAHNEMAN, D. (1986). Rational choice and the framing of decisions. *Journal of Business, 59*, 251–S278.

TVERSKY, A., & SATTATH, S., & SLOVIC, P. (1988). Contingent weighting in judgment and choice. *Psychological Review, 95*, 371–384.

TVERSKY, A., SLOVIC, P., & KAHNEMAN, D. (1990). The determinants of preference reversal. *American Economic Review, 80*, 204–217.

VAN RAAIJ, W. F. (1977). *Consumer choice behavior: An information processing approach*. Voorschoten, Netherlands: VAM.

WILKIE, W. L. (1974). Analysis of effects of information load. *Journal of Marketing Research, 11*, 462–466.

WRIGHT, P. L. (1974). The harassed decision maker: Time pressures, distractions, and the use of evidence. *Journal of Applied Psychology, 59*, 555–561.

WRIGHT, P. L. (1975). Consumer choice strategies: Simplifying vs. optimizing. *Journal of Marketing Research, 11,* 60–67.

WRIGHT, P. L., & RIP, P. D. (1981). Retrospective reports on the causes of decisions. *Journal of Personality and Social Psychology, 60,* 601–614.

WRIGHT, P. L., AND WEITZ, B. (1977). Time horizon effects on product evaluation strategies. *Journal of Marketing Research, 14,* 429–443.

YATES, J. F., JAGACINSKI, C. M., & FABER, M. D. (1978). Evaluation of partially described multiattribute options. *Organizational Behavior and Human Performance, 21,* 240–251.

PROBABILISTIC MODELS OF CONSUMER CHOICE BEHAVIOR

3

Robert J. Meyer
University of Pennsylvania

Barbara E. Kahn *
University of Pennsylvania

In this chapter, we review recent developments in the literature on models of individual discrete choice. These models seek to represent the process that individuals use to integrate information about a set of alternatives when making a choice of a single preferred option. We focus on the major theoretical model forms and discuss some of the most important generalizations. These generalizations include the effects on choice of similarity and dominance among items in a choice set and temporal dependencies among choices. We conclude by suggesting an agenda for future work in the area.

INTRODUCTION

Much of the modern research on consumer decision making is based on a simple conjecture: Human cognitive operations, no matter how complex, can be represented by mathematical analogs. While the validity of this conjecture is certainly not foregone, its implica-

tions have attracted the interest of researchers across numerous disciplines. Specifically, if correct, the conjecture implies the possibility of building models that would allow one to forecast choices consumers would make from a set of options, and perhaps, to alter the outcome of those choices.

Over the past twenty years the possibility of such "consumer engineering" has served to spawn a large literature of mathematical models of consumer judgment and choice. Since 1980, for example, there have been over 200 articles published on the subject in the

*This chapter was written while the authors were at U.C.L.A. We thank Richard Batsell, Lee Cooper, Sunil Gupta, Donald Lehmann, Jordan Louviere, William Moore, and David Schmittlein for their comments and suggestions on an earlier draft of the chapter.

literature of marketing,[1] and this reflects only a small fraction of the total literature on the subject that has appeared across disciplines. Indeed, the work has proliferated to such a degree that the field of quantitative models of behavior is probably best thought of as a discipline in its own right.

In this chapter we provide a review of recent developments in one aspect of this discipline, models of individual discrete choice. These are models that seek to represent the process by which individuals integrate information about a set of alternatives when making a choice of a single preferred option. Within the study of consumer behavior, these models are usually used to describe the choice of a brand from a competitive set of brands.

We should stress that our survey is by no means meant to be exhaustive. Because a complete review of even the most recent developments in individual choice modeling is beyond the scope of a single review article, our focus will be limited. We provide a discussion of the major theoretical model forms that are used to represent consumer choices from sets of options, and we look at the major generalizations of these model forms that have appeared in the recent literature. The specific generalizations we focus on are choice models which recognize the effects of the similarity and dominance among items in a choice set on evaluation processes, and models which recognize temporal dependencies in choice. Excluded from our review will be discussion of statistical issues in the estimation of these models and their application in managerial settings. For a review of these topics we refer the reader to recent texts by Ben-Akiva and Lermann (1985), Cooper and Nakanishi (1988), Hensher and Johnson (1981), and Train (1986), as well as to review articles by Amemiya (1981), Corstjens and Gautschi (1983) and Wrigley, Longley, and Dunn (1984; 1988). In addition, we also exclude from discussion work in a number of areas that have strong traditional ties to the literature of probabilistic choice models; in particular, the literatures of multiattribute attitude models (e.g., Green and Wind 1973; Louviere 1988), models of purchase quantity and timing (e.g., Ehrenberg 1959; Massy, Montgomery, and Morrison 1970; Neslin, Henderson, and Quelch 1985), and models of group choice (e.g., Corfman and Lehmann 1987; Davis 1976; Webster and Wind 1972).

We begin by offering a general taxonomy of the literature on choice models, which will be useful in both organizing our subsequent discussion and in identifying major future research directions. We will then review the dominant theoretical paradigm in the study of individual discrete choice, economic random utility theory. We then survey attempts to generalize this model in two directions: models that recognize a dependency of preferences on the external appearance of the set of choice options, and models that recognize a dependency among a sequence of choice (dynamic models). We conclude with a discussion of research challenges facing the area.

The Literature on Individual Choice Models

The contemporary literature of consumer choice models does not have a simple genealogy. While several taxonomies have been suggested (e.g., Corstjens and Gautschi 1983; McFadden 1986), they belie the complex history of many of the key ideas in the area, and the disagreements which often exist about the relationship among these concepts. Much of this lack of clarity stems from the multidisciplinary nature of research in the area; modeling ideas are often developed in parallel by several authors in several disciplines. In addition, ideas have sometimes been proposed and then left idle in one discipline, only to be rediscovered and developed further in another discipline. As a result, models that are seen as the general form of one class of representations by one author are often seen as the special case

---

[1]This compilation spans entries in the *Journal of Consumer Research*, the *Journal of Marketing*, the *Journal of Marketing Research*, *Marketing Science*, conference proceedings in Marketing, and original book compilations.

of another class by another author.[2] The field is thus best viewed as a collage of works rather than an organized system; it reflects the independent efforts of researchers in different disciplines, unified by a common interest in how individuals make choices from sets of options.

The central tenet of our view of the field is that there exists two intellectual traditions of models (see Figure 3.1), each reflecting different views of the ability of humans to process information. At one extreme is the view that individuals make choices by considering all relevant information available to the decision maker at the time of choice, and that individuals choose that option which maximizes some utility function defined across this information set. Central to the basic forms of such models is an assumption that preferences for items can be defined independently from the set of options under consideration, and that any errors which

exist in the measurement of preferences are also independent of the consideration set. Termed *simply scalable* choice models, they are illustrated by the choice models of Luce (1959), the Multinominal Logit (McFadden 1981), and the Independent Probit (Domenich and McFadden 1975).

At the other extreme is the view that individuals are inherently limited in their ability to process information, and thus they make choices through simplified heuristics, which do not use all the information available at the time of choice. Central to these models is the assumption that preferences are inherently context dependent. Specifically, these models assume that the likelihood an option will be chosen is a function of both the attractiveness of its features and the extent to which these features are shared by other options under consideration. Work in the area is best associated with the attribute elimination models of Restle (1959), Tversky (1972), and Tversky and Sattath (1979). These models, although rich in explanatory power, are often difficult to estimate empirically.

Perhaps paradoxically, although each para-

---

[2]To illustrate, as an economist, McFadden (1981) has described the multinominal logit model as following in a line of microeconomic theories of choice. In contrast, Yellott (1978) has described the same model as a descendent of psychological theories of comparative judgment developed in the late 1920s.

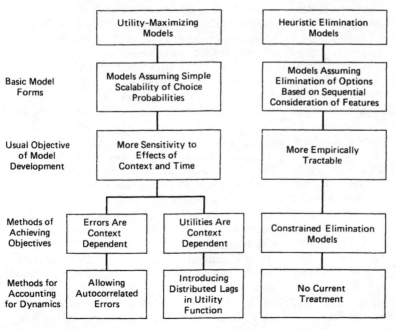

FIGURE 3.1 A Taxonomy of Theoretical Choice Model Forms

digm starts with quite different views of decision making, research within each area has been characterized by movement to a common ground; specifically, research in utility-maximization models centers on attempts to make them sensitive to the effects of choice context, while research in heuristic elimination models centers on attempts to make them empirically tractable.

Within the paradigm of utility-maximization models, two general approaches to relax assumptions of context independence have emerged. One stream of work retains the assumption that utilities can be defined independently of context, but relaxes the assumption of independence among errors in the measurement of utilities. These representations are best illustrated by McFadden's (1979) Generalized Extreme Value model and Hausman and Wise's (1978) Covariance Probit model. The other major approach relaxes the assumption that utilities can be defined independently of context, but retains the assumption that errors are independent. Such representations are illustrated by the differential cross-effects choice models of Batsell and Polking (1985) and Cooper and Nakanishi (1988). The two streams have also been extended to the treatment of temporal context; dynamics have been handled both through the addition of lagged effects in the utilities of options (while assuming that errors are not time dependent), and by allowing time dependencies in measurement errors.

Research on heuristic elimination models has tended to search for ways to approximate a general sequential choice model, Elimination-by-Aspects (EBA) (proposed by Tversky (1972)), by simpler forms which are more easily estimable. In contrast, only limited work has been directed to adding greater generality to the EBA models, such as by allowing them to account for learning.

In this chapter we will review in greater detail both the structure of the basic model forms within each of these paradigms and their recent refinements. Because the utility-maximization models form the dominant paradigm in modern choice analysis, they will form the central focal point of the chapter. Our discus-

sion of heuristic-based models will appear as it is usually positioned in the literature, as a discussion of an alternative approach to modeling the effects of item similarity on choice probabilities (e.g., Corstjens and Gautschi 1983).

THE ECONOMIC THEORY OF INDIVIDUAL CHOICE

The Consumer as a Random Utility Maximizer

Most models of consumer choice are based on a simple behavioral postulate: When faced with a set of options, consumers choose that option that is thought to deliver the highest level of perceived gratification or utility. As noted by McFadden (1981; 1986), this postulate is essentially tautological; if an individual chooses an option, it must be that which was anticipated to be the best among the array of alternatives, at least according to some criterion.

Although there exist a number of formal theories of how consumers seek to maximize utility within a given choice setting, by far the most often cited is that first attributed to Thurstone (1927) in psychology, and later generalized in economics by McFadden (1974). When faced with a choice, a consumer is presumed to view each option as a bundle of attributes. The consumer is then thought to form an overall evaluation of each option by combining perceptions of the option's attributes through a cognitive "integration rule" or utility function. The chosen alternative is then that option for which this overall evaluation is the highest.

Due to temporal variation in tastes and unmeasured influences on choice, however, it is assumed that these utilities are not fully observable by the analyst. Rather, the utility of each option is considered a random variable, defined by a distribution of possible values. Models that yield estimates of the probability that each option will be chosen based on assumptions about the form of these distributions are termed *random utility models*.

This formal modeling process can be described as follows: Let X_i be a vector of the measured attributes of choice option i, and let $V_i(X_i)$ be a preference mapping which links the vector X_i to a summary indicator of the overall utility or value of i. Although V may be any multiattribute function, in most applications it is assumed to be a linear combination of the set of observed attributes of i:

$$V_i (X_i) = b_i + \sum_{k=1}^{m} b_k x_{ik} , \qquad (3.1)$$

where x_{ik} is the observed value of option i on attribute k (such as its price), $k = 1, \ldots, m$, and b_i and $b_k, k = 1, \ldots, m$ are scaling parameters. Expression (3.1) is the most well-known representation of measurable utility used in random utility models (cf. Hensher and Johnson 1981). It presumes an intercept b_i which is unique to each alternative, and a set of generic attribute effects $b_k, k = 1, \ldots, m$. The alternative-specific intercept is designed to capture the systematic constant component in the attractiveness of option i not captured by the attribute vector X_i. As such, it plays a role similar to a "subject-specific" blocking effect in a repeated-measures analysis of variance (Hensher and Johnson 1981).

We might note that there is no a priori reason for constraining the attribute effect coefficients to be equal across alternatives except for reasons of parsimony. Cooper (1988), Cooper and Nakanishi (1988), and Train (1986), for example, note that in many contexts the effect of variations in attribute values will differ across alternatives, implying alternative-specific attribute effect coefficients. Similarly, in many instances overall impressions will not be an additive combination of attribute values (e.g., Anderson 1981, Louviere 1988). In this case expression (3.1) might be expanded to included higher-order cross products among attributes (e.g., Lynch 1985, Louviere and Meyer 1980).

We presume that $V(X_i)$ is an imperfect indicator of the true utility an individual assigns to option i at the time of choice, U_i. Specifically,

U_i is assumed to be linked to $V(X_i)$ through an independent disturbance ϵ_i, such that

$$U_i = V_i(X_i) + \epsilon_i , \qquad (3.2)$$

where ϵ_i reflects the observed tastes of the individual with respect to i. And $V_i(X_i)$ is termed the *strict utility* of i, while ϵ_i is the *random utility* (McFadden 1981).

Given a choice set A, the likelihood that a decision maker will choose option i from this set $[Pr(i/A)]$ is thus the likelihood that the latent variable U_i is the highest at the time of choice. Formally,

$$Pr(i|A) = Pr(U_i > U_j) \, \forall \, j \in A, j \neq i .$$

This expression, in turn may be rewritten in terms of (3.1) as:

$$Pr(i|A) = Pr([V_i(X_i) + \epsilon_i] > [V_j(X_j) + \epsilon_j]), \, \forall \, j \in A, j \neq i .$$

or, more conveniently,

$$Pr(i|A) = Pr([\epsilon_j < V_i(X_i) - V_j(X_j) + \epsilon_i]) \, \forall \, j \in A, \, j \neq i . \qquad (3.3)$$

The probability that i is chosen is then obtained by making an assumption about the form of the distribution of the random variables ϵ_i and ϵ_j, and integrating (3.3) over a continuum of possible values of ϵ_i. Specifically,

$$Pr(i|A) =$$
$$\int_{-\infty}^{+\infty} Pr(\epsilon_i = \epsilon)(Pr(\epsilon_j < V_i(X_i) \qquad (3.4)$$
$$- V_j(X_j)$$
$$+ \epsilon)d\epsilon) \, \forall \, j \in A, j \neq i ,$$

where ϵ is a constant of integration (cf. Hensher and Johnson 1981).

The most common assumption made about ϵ_i and ϵ_j is that they have independently and identically distributed Type I Extreme Value distributions; that is,

$$Pr(\epsilon_i \leq \epsilon) = e^{-\epsilon^{-\epsilon}}.$$

Under this assumption, integration of (3.4) yields the closed-form probability model,

$$Pr(i|A) = \frac{e^{V(X_i)}}{\sum_{j \in A} e^{V(X_j)}}, \qquad (3.5)$$

which is the well-known multinominal logit model of choice (Hensher and Johnson 1981; McFadden 1981; Schmittlein 1986; Yellott 1977).

Of course, other assumptions can (and have) been made about the distribution of ϵ_i and ϵ_j, however none yield probability expressions which are as computationally tractable as the logit. In his early work on comparative judgment, Thurstone (1927), for example, posited a normal distribution for the random components, an assumption which yields the binary probit model (Ben-Akiva and Lerman 1985). The primary limitation of the assumption of normality, however, is that it does not offer a closed-form solution for the probability of choice, and extensions to cases with more than two alternatives have proved computationally difficult (an issue we will elaborate on later).

Because of its simplicity, the multinomial logit has emerged as the most widely used form of individual choice model. Applications have been diverse, including the study of consumer's choices of packaged goods (e.g., Cooper 1988; Currim, Meyer, and Le 1988; Guadagni and Little 1983; Gupta 1988; Malhotra 1984), travel mode choice and automobile ownership (Ben-Akiva and Lerman 1985; Gensch and Recker 1978; Train 1986), and college choice (Punj and Staelin 1979), to cite just a few examples. In all of these instances the model is shown to provide a good account of the relationship between the attributes of sets of alternatives and the choices made from these sets.

Adding to the appeal of the mutinominal logit is that it is linked to a number of other well-known models for discrete data anlysis, such as the models suggested by Bradley and Terry (1957) in statistics and Luce (1959) in psychology for the scaling of paired-comparison data, and the models used for the analysis of market share data in marketing (e.g.,

Nakanishi and Cooper 1974; Ghosh, Neslin, and Shoemaker 1984). Because Luce's model is perhaps the best known of these variations, choice models which can be written in the form of expression (3.5) are often generically referred to as "Luce Models" (e.g., Yellott 1977).

The Random Utility Models as a Representation of Population Choice Behavior

Although random utility models such as the multinomial logit are most conveniently presented as representations of an individual's choice from a set of options, in practice they are more often used as models of aggregate behavior. In principle, this application is straightforward: When viewed as a model of population behavior, the strict utility function $V(X_i)$ of the multinomial logit is an indicator of the tastes of a "representative" member of the population, and the random utility ϵ_i reflects random individual variation about this mean (Hensher 1984; McFadden 1981).

In most settings, however, such application will be complicated by the presence of systematic variations in tastes across the population; for example, older consumers may have different loyalties than younger consumers, and consumers with higher incomes may be less price elastic. There exist two standard approaches for handling such variation: The analyst can either expand the strict utility function to include a battery of characteristics for each individual (e.g., Fisher and Nagin 1981), or models can be estimated for differing consumer segments, each homogeneous with respect to a set of consumer characteristics (e.g., Currim 1981; Gensch 1985). The assumption in both of these cases is that while tastes may vary systematically across consumers with differing characteristics, within groups heterogeneity is a double exponentially distributed random error.

While these approaches to dealing with taste variation will usually be adequate in most settings, they are less tenable in cases where the analyst has limited access to useful sociodemographic/economic measures, or residual taste variation is not well described by a symmetric probability density function. To address this problem several authors have explored the use of compound probability models of choice: individual choice probabilities are characterized by a simple choice model (such as the multinomial logit), and variation in probabilities is characterized by a distribution that allows for a flexible representation of taste variation, such as a beta distribution (e.g., Dunn and Wrigley 1985; 1987). A good pedagogic introduction to this approach to modeling aggregate choice behavior is provided by Massy, Montgomery, and Morrison (1970), with more recent applications in the context of random utility models being provided by Wrigley, Longley, and Dunn (1988), Jones and Zufryden (1980), and Steckel and Vanhonacker (1988).

MODELS RECOGNIZING THE EFFECTS OF THE ITEM SIMILARITY AND DOMINANCE ON CHOICE PROBABILITIES

Despite its frequent applications as a model of both individual and aggregate behavior, the multinomial logit model of choice has been criticized for offering an overly restrictive view of the process that underlies choice. Although proponents point out that the model is often an extremely robust predictor of choice even when its underlying assumptions—such as the independence of the random components of utility—are violated (e.g., Louviere and Woodworth 1983), critics have claimed that the model does not provide an accurate description of the *process* which underlies choice, except in highly limited contexts.

At the heart of most criticism is the model's assumption that the process by which options are evaluated and chosen is independent of the external appearance of the option set. On one hand, this assumption of independence is perhaps the simple logit's greatest asset; if the assumption holds, one can, in principle, estimate a model in one context and use it to predict the choices individuals will make in any other. On the other hand, it is an assumption that many

have argued will rarely, if ever, be empirically verified. Specifically, there is extensive behavioral evidence that choice processes tend to be constructed only *after* the composition of a choice set is first considered by consumers (e.g., Bettman 1987; Payne 1983).

The limitations of the context independence assumption are perhaps most readily seen by considering the model's predictions about how choice probabilities will be redistributed given the introduction of a new option to the choice set that is highly similar to one of the existing options. One of the key properties of models of the form of expression (3.5) is that the ratio of the choice probabilities of any two options is invariant under changes in the composition of the choice set in which both appear. This result is called the "constant ratio rule," or the "independence of irrelevant alternatives" (IIA) property (McFadden 1981). Its central implication is that if a new option is added to a choice set, the shares of existing options will always decrease in direct proportion to the size of their original shares.

Debreu (1960) is usually credited with offering the best known counter-example to this prediction. Although there have been many variants of the original Debreu discussion, all share the following basic structure: An individual is initially faced with a choice between two dissimilar choice alternatives, such as between ordering lamb or fish entree from a menu. A new option is then made available which is nearly identical to one of the originals except for an unimportant difference, say a new lamb entree with slightly different seasoning. The intuitive effect of this new option would seem clear: Because the new option does little to resolve the basic dilemma of whether to order lamb or fish for dinner, if it has any effect at all, it will be to diminish the probability of ordering the original lamb entree, while leaving the probability of ordering the fish largely unchanged. Unfortunately, this intuition would not be reflected in the predictions of a simple logit model; the constant ratio rule dictates that the new option would "draw" from each option in proportion to their original (binary) probabilities of being chosen. Hence, if the individual was initially indifferent between the fish and lamb entrees, the new lamb entree would draw shares equally from both options.

Since the early 1970s a major thrust of research in mathematical choice modeling has been to develop representations of choice that provide more intuitively plausible accounts of how changes in the relative similarity of options in a choice set affect choice probabilities. These modeling efforts can generally be categorized as following one of three strategies for generalization:

1. Models which assume that choices are not made by a utility-maximization process, but rather by a feature elimination process;
2. Models which retain the assumption that strict utility functions can be defined independently of the particular set of options under consideration, but which allow dependencies among the measurement errors; and
3. Models which retain the assumption that measurement errors are independent among options, but which allow the strict utility function to be dependent upon the consideration set.

We will briefly review each of these strategies.

Feature Elimination Models

Process-tracing studies of human choice offer a dramatically different portrait of the process by which decisions are made than that presumed by most random utility models. When individuals are asked to "think aloud" when making choices (e.g., Bettman 1971; Hayes-Roth and Hayes-Roth 1979), when eye movements are traced (e.g., Russo and Dosher 1983), and when patterns of information search are monitored (e.g., Bettman 1981; Johnson, Meyer, and Goshe 1988; Payne 1976), there is little evidence that individuals form independent assessments of the overall value of each in a set of options, and then select that with the highest value, even in highly simplistic settings (Russo and Dosher 1983). Rather, the process of choice seems better characterized by the ap-

plication of a sequence of discrete elimination heuristics, in which only a limited subset of the total amount of information in a choice set is considered at any one time. In such processes the external appearance of the choice set is an integral part of choice; the criteria used for eliminating options and the ultimate likelihood that an option will be chosen appears driven by the perceived structure of the entire option set.

Restle (1959) was the first to propose a model characterizing choice as a process of sequential eliminations. More recent work in the area, however, has tended to be dominated by Tversky's (1972) *elimination-by-aspects* (EBA), a generalization of Restle's original model.

The psychological process which underlies the EBA model is straightforward. When faced with a choice, the individual is hypothesized to view each alternative in the set as a collection of measurable attributes or features. Each of these features are shared by at least one, but not all, alternatives in a choice set. The individual then selects one of these features for consideration with a probability proportional to its relative desirability among all features. Options which share this feature are retained for further consideration, while all others are eliminated. If there is more than one option in the surviving set, a second feature is selected by the same probabilistic process as before, with the tournament continuing until only one option remains.

For example, consider the choice of an entree from a menu. If "spiciness" were the most important single aspect in the set, then whether an entree was spicy or mild would have the highest probability of being the first criterion used for evaluation. Assuming "spiciness" was the first aspect, then all entrees which were not spicy would be eliminated. Given the remaining alternatives, another aspect, say "lamb" would be selected and all alternatives which were not made of lamb would be eliminated. This would continue until one entree was left.

The EBA model can be formally stated as follows. Let $T = \{x, y, z, \ldots \}$ be the total set of options faced by the decision maker, and let A, B, C denote the nonempty subsets of T. Let $P(x|A_\alpha)$ be the probability of choosing alternative x from that subset of options offered in A which share aspect or feature α. Next, let A' be a set of aspects that belong to at least one alternative in A (note A' is the set of aspects and A_α is a set of alternatives). Finally let x' be a set of aspects of x, $x' = \{\alpha, \beta, \ldots\}$ and $u(\alpha)$ be a scale value defining the desirability of feature α. EBA is defined in terms of the recursive formula,

$$P(x|A) = \frac{\sum_{\alpha \in x'} u(\alpha) P(x|A\alpha)}{\sum_{\beta \in A'} u(\beta)}, \qquad (3.6)$$

where $u(\beta)$ is a scale value defining the desirability of feature β which may or may not be possessed by option x. Equation (3.6) may also be rewritten:

$$\frac{\sum_{\alpha \in x'} u(\alpha) P(x|A\alpha)}{\sum_{y \in A} (\sum_{\alpha \in y'} u(\alpha) P(y|A\alpha))}. \qquad (3.7)$$

Expression (3.7) illustrates one of EBA's central properties: It collapses to a model of the simple logit form (expression 3.5) when either each option is defined in terms of unique features or when the conditional probabilities of choice given a feature are equal across options. In such cases (3.7) simplifies to:

$$P(x|A) = \frac{V(x)}{\sum_{y \in A} V(y)}, \qquad (3.8)$$

where

$$V(x) = \sum_{\alpha \in x'} u(\alpha). \qquad (3.9)$$

A key property of the EBA model is that the "features" used to eliminate options are not necessarily measured by the analyst prior to choice. Rather, the objective is to conduct an *internal* analysis of preferences, where the analyst's objective is to derive a set of psychological scales for options which best reproduce an observed set of choices or judgments (cf. Carroll 1972; Cooper and Nakanishi 1983). This contrasts with the *external* analysis pro-

vided by the logit model, where the observed set of choices is linked to a set of externally derived scales, such as measures of the prices of options and their perceived attractiveness.

The central appeal of the EBA model is that it provides a highly flexible theoretical scaling model for choice data in contexts where options can be assumed to be "screened" through a sequential consideration of features. The major drawback is difficulty of estimation: Given a set of n options, the EBA model requires the estimation of $2^n - 3$ scaling parameters, which, in turn, require estimates of the conditional probabilities of choice within all possible $(2^n - 1)$ nondegenerate subsets of alternatives in a choice set of interest (Tversky 1972). Because this data requirement rapidly becomes excessive with increases in set size, published applications have been limited to small illustrative examples (e.g., Tversky 1972), and we are aware of no attempts to apply the model to "normally available" econometric data.

In an attempt to overcome this estimation problem, Tversky and Sattath (1979) suggested that computational tractability could be improved if the analyst imposed a prior hierarchical structure. The logic behind the approach is that number of scaling parameters required to reproduce a set of choice probabilities is driven by the complexity one assumes for the underlying choice process. For example, if expression (3.8) can be assumed to hold for a set of choice data (i.e., a simple Luce model holds), only n (rather than $2^n - 3$) parameters would need to be estimated; that is, one scale parameter for each option. The intermediate case is where choice is assumed to follow a hierarchical agenda, in which case $2n - 3$ parameters would be sufficient (Tversky and Sattath 1979). Based on this notion, Tversky and Sattath developed a modeling procedure and estimation algorithm called PRETREE, which allows the calibration of a hierarchical-elimination choice model mirroring EBA, but with fewer parameters and correspondingly less stringent data demands.

There have been a number of published applications of PRETREE, all reporting reasonable success in recovering the parameters of a feature-based hierarchical choice process from paired-comparison data (e.g., Kahn, Moore, and Glazer 1987; Moore, Lehmann, and Pessemier 1986). These investigations, however, also suggest some caveats (e.g., Lehmann and Moore 1985). Preeminent among these is the difficulty of identifying the "correct" decision tree in a given setting; the fit and form of the final choice tree is often sensitive to how it is initially "seeded," hence repeated applications of the estimation algorithm are required in most settings. A central consequence of this limitation is that it becomes difficult to apply the procedure at the individual level, which inhibits investigations into heterogeneity in decision rules within a sample.

Recent Developments in Hierarchical Elimination Models. Given the strong intuitive appeal of viewing choice as a process of sequential elimination, a number of authors have sought alternatives to the EBA and PRETREE models in an attempt to overcome their discussed drawbacks. Efforts have focused in three general areas:

1. those which have explored alternative approaches to the estimation of feature-elimination models;
2. those which have attempted to extend feature-elimination models to the case of continuous attributes; and
3. those which have sought means for the estimation of models at a disaggregate level without a need to prespecify a decision sequence.

Illustrative of work in this first area are the efforts of Lehmann and Moore (1985), who explore the possibility of using a hierarchy of logit models as a tool for developing feature models similar to those yielded by PRETREE (we will elaborate on this procedure shortly). Likewise, DeSarbo and De Soete (1984), DeSarbo, De Soete, Carroll, and Ramaswamy (1987), and Rao and Sabavala (1981) have explored the possibility of inferring hierarchical feature models through the use of hierarchical clustering algorithms — a possibility which was also explored by Tversky and Sattath (1979). Manrai and Sinha (1989) and Rotondo

(1986) have considered the problem of extending feature-elimination models to cases where options are described by continuous attribute dimensions rather than by discrete features. In Manrai and Sinha's (1989) approach, termed *Elimination-by-Cutoffs* (EBC), options are initially rank-ordered with respect to their scores on each of a number of prescribed dimensions. Options are chosen by sequentially eliminating alternatives that share a common maximum preference distance from another option in the set; for example, the first elimination stage might be to eliminate all alternatives which are no more than k rating points better than the worst option in the set on a dimension. The limitation of the current version of EBC, however, is that attribute scales have to be defined by the user prior to analysis, and that it does not allow recognition of similarity effects accruing to groups of options possessing unique discrete features, such as the example of choices among dinner entrees.

The problem of estimating hierarchical models of choice that recognize individual differences in elimination strategies has proven to be more elusive. Gensch and Svestka (1984), for example, provide an algorithm which provides a lexicographic screening of options at the individual level; however, it requires as input individuals' rankings of the relative importance of product attributes, as well as their ratings of the attractiveness of each option on these attributes. More recently, Currim, Meyer, and Le (1988) and Greene and Smith (1988) have illustrated how tree-structured regression procedures such as AID and CART (Breiman, Olshen, and Stone 1983) can be used to derive hierarchical models of binary choice at an individual level from normally available consumer panel data, without requiring assumptions about the form of the decision hierarchy. Unfortunately, because the decision trees yielded by such procedures are derived from an analysis of independent choice rather than proximities (such as in PRETREE or hierarchical clustering), they may not be directly interpreted as implying competitive groupings within an option set — the normative role of partitions in PRETREE models. Nevertheless, if the trees turn out to be a reasonably close match with those yielded by more complex methods, they would provide an efficient solution to the problem of assessing the pattern of heterogeneity in choice structures that exists in a sample.

Random Utility Models Relaxing the Assumption of Error Independence

Within the framework of random utility models the task of developing models that do not possess the IIA assumption would seem straightforward: because IIA follows from an assumption that the random comments of utility are independent across options, non-IIA models can, in principle, be derived simply by allowing a more flexible distribution of errors. The behavioral rationale for similarity effects that underlies such a modeling approach would be quite different than that presumed by feature-elimination models. The consumer would be thought to be attempting to maximize utility across a set of options, and similarity would be presumed to be driven by unobserved influences on utility that are correlated across subsets of options. For example, when choosing among entrees on a menu, unmeasured factors which detract from or contribute to the attractiveness of, say, one fish entree would be presumed to affect all fish entrees. The consequences is a dependence of the choice probabilities for any one option on its similarity with other options in the set—the same context effects the EBA model captures by assuming choices are made through a sequential elimination process.[3]

There are two major classes of random utility models which are derived from an assumption of a potential dependence among the unobserved components of utility: Generalized Extreme Value Models and Generalized Probit Models. We will briefly review each in turn.

The Generalized Extreme Value Model. The Generalized Extreme Value (GEV) Model (McFadden 1979) is a family of logit-like models which follows from the assumption that the components of utility in the general random utility model given in expression (3.4) have a multivariate extreme value distribution. The "standard" GEV (Amemiya 1981) model can be stated as follows: Assume that at the time of choice the decision maker initially partitions the total set of available options into n subsets A_p, $p = 1, \ldots, n$, of similar alternatives such that the IIA property of the basic logit holds within these sets but not necessarily between these sets. The GEV model asserts that the probability that an individual will choose option i which is an element of subgroup q, P_{iq} is given by:

$$P_{iq} = \frac{e^{V(X_{iq})/\lambda q}[\sum_{j \epsilon q} e^{V(X_{jq})/\lambda q}](\lambda q - 1)}{\sum_{p=1}^{n}[\sum_{j \epsilon p} e^{V(X_{jp})/\lambda p}](\lambda_p - 1)} , \quad (3.10)$$

where $V(X^{iq})$ is the strict utility of option i in subset q as in expression (3.2), and λ_p is an inverse measure of the correlation among the unobserved components of utility within subset p. An important property of (3.10) is that in the case where unobserved components are all uncorrelated ($\lambda_q = 1$ for all p), (3.10) reverts to a simple (independent) multinomial logit.

Although seemingly complex, the probability given by Expression (10.3) turns out to have a rather simple intuition, and it has a straightforward computational form. Specifically, the expression implies a decision tree in which the probability that a given option is chosen is the product of a series of conditional probabilities that the sets to which it belongs are chosen and then that the option is chosen from those sets.

Train (1986) offers the following intuition for this result: Imagine that we decompose the strict utility associated with any option $(V(X_{iq}))$

---

[3]Several authors have pointed out that when a random utility model is used as a model of aggregate choice, violations of IIA can also be viewed as a problem of unobserved heterogeneity in preferences in a population. Specifically, one could presume there exist subsets of consumers who are attracted to similar types of options, such that when one consumer becomes attracted to an option of a given type, the aggregate attractiveness of all options of that type increases.

into two components: those attributes which are shared by all options in subset q and those which are unique to each option. For example, if a subset under study is the set of all fish entrees on a menu, the first component would be those attributes shared by fish entrees (e.g., seafood), and the second component would be made up of attributes which discriminate among the entrees (e.g., fish varieties and seasonings). Formally,

$$V(X_i) = W(X_{\cdot q}) + \theta_q Y(X_{iq}), \qquad (3.11)$$

where $W(X_{\cdot q})$ is a utility mapping defined over the attributes common to all options in set q, $Y(X_{iq})$ is a utility mapping defined over the attributes which vary across options within set q, and θ_q is a scaling constant.

This decomposition allows us to separate the probability in (3.6) into the product of the marginal probability that subset q (for example, seafood) is chosen from the total set of $p = 1, \ldots, n$ subsets (for example, all food groups) times the conditional probability that option i (for example, a particular seafood entree) is chosen given q. Specifically,

$$P_{iq} = P(A_q) \cdot P(i|A_q),$$

where $P(A_q)$ and $P(i|A_q)$ are simple multinomial logit models of the probability of choosing subset q from all subsets and choosing option i given a choice of subset q, respectively. In particular,

$$Pr(A_q) = \frac{e^{W(X_{\cdot q}) + \theta_q I_q}}{\sum_p e^{W(X_{\cdot p}) + \theta_p I_p}},$$

$$Pr(i|A_q) = \frac{e^{Y(X_{iq})}}{\sum_{i \epsilon q} e^{Y(X_{iq})}}, \qquad (3.12)$$

where

$$I_q = \sum_{i \epsilon q} e^{Y(X_{i\cdot})}.$$

Expression (3.12) is the probability that subset q will be chosen from all subsets. The term I_q, which appears in (3.12) is the sum of all the strict utilities of the options in subset q and is termed the "inclusive value" of the subset. It is the inclusive value which causes the GEV model to be referred to as a "nested logit"; choice is modeled as a sequence of logit models, in which the utilities derived from a model of conditional choice are nested within the model of marginal choice.

The two-stage GEV or nested logit model described here easily generalizes to the case of multiple stages of subset selection, such as an individual first partitioning the set of menu items into "spicy" versus "nonspicy" items, then meat types within each seasoning group, and so forth. In the multiple-stage situation, the modeling process is a straightforward one: The analyst first estimates a model for the choice of an item within a given subset (for example, the entree from the set of spicy meat dishes). The sum of the calibrated strict utilities for all of the items in that subset then serves as an explanatory variable in a higher-level model of choice among subsets, with such a model being augmented by attributes which vary across subsets [the vector $W(X_{\cdot q})$]

The GEV model captures one of the simplest ways in which the appearance of a choice set affects choice probabilities, and provides an intuitively plausible means of accounting for the Debreu counter-example to the simple logit discussed previously. Because when GEV choice options are partitioned into discrete groups with differential degrees of substitutability, new alternatives to a set will not uniformly affect existing options. Specifically, the effect of a new option depends upon the number of existing options which exist in the subgroup to which it is assigned; the less "new" it brings to the overall choice set, the smaller its incremental share.

We should stress that while the GEV and EBA model discussed earlier both characterize choice as a hierarchical process, the behavioral process which underlies them is quite different. Specifically, the GEV model characterizes a full-information, "bottom-up," decision process, in which choices among subsets of options at one stage explicitly consider the utilities of all alternatives which might be available at later stages. The EBA and related models, in contrast, characterize a limited-information, "top down," decision process, in which elimination decisions at one stage do *not* consider the value of options available in later stages. Despite this difference, GEV and the EBA model might nevertheless be viewed as parallel developments: In the same way that the EBA model generalizes the psychology-based Luce model to the case of sequential considerations of product features, GEV generalizes the economic-based multinomial logit model to the sequential consideration of subsets of options.

Because of its strong intuitive appeal and relative ease of estimation, the GEV model has been applied to contexts where analysts have a priori reasons to suspect that the IIA assumption of the basic logit may be empirically untenable (e.g., Dubin 1986; Guadagni 1983). For example, Onaka and Clark (1984) and McFadden (1979) report applications of the model in studies of residential choice. In these models the individual is first postulated to choose a neighborhood, then residence within a neighborhood. Likewise, Brown (as presented in Hensher and Johnson 1981) reports an application to the study of choice of vacations; here, the individual is modeled as first deciding upon the duration of the vacation, then selecting a destination conditional upon duration.

Despite these successes, the GEV model has some limitations that have caused it to be viewed as only a partial solution to the problem of modeling choice where the IIA assumption is likely to be violated. The three most salient limitations are the following:

1. the need to prespecify how choice options are partitioned prior to choice and, in the case of multiple-stage GEV model, the order in which subset decisions are made;
2. the continued assumption that within subsets, the IIA assumption holds; and
3. the assumption that sequential consideration process itself is independent of context.

The first of these is usually the most troublesome. In the absence of any prior knowledge about how an individual partitions the option

set, the analyst must proceed by trial and error, estimate a GEV model for one possible decision structure, note its fit, and then compare this fit to that derived for others (e.g., McFadden 1986). While this process is perhaps only an inconvenience in instances where the number of possible structures is small, it becomes burdensome when there are numerous partitioning possibilities, such as in cases where there is the possibility of heterogeneity in decision structures across segments of decision makers.

Although progress is being made towards the development of methods that would allow the partitioning structure of an option to be set prior to estimation of the GEV model (e.g., Currim, Meyer, and Le 1988), these still fail to relieve the second and third limitations, which are far more fundamental. In many instances the IIA assumption will continue to be untenable within option sets in a way which eludes discrete partitioning of these options. For example, when building a model of choices from a menu, one might presume that an individual first partitions the menu into "fish" and "meat" entrees, then, perhaps, into different types of fish and meat (e.g., "steak" or "lamb"). While each final set will thus be homogeneous with respect to these features, it will always be heterogeneous with respect to any remaining features, such as "spiciness" and "price." As such, there will always be the possibility of clusters of items which are more similar than others (unless, of course, the final set contains only one or two options). Finally, while the model's predictions are "context sensitive," the functional form itself is not: It assumes that both the partitioning of options and the order in which subgroups are considered is invariant under changes in the option set. If individuals formulate their eliminations strategies in a strategic fashion depending upon the characteristics of a choice set, the model thus becomes of limited value as an empirical tool.

The Multinomial Probit Model

The multinomial probit model represents the second major class of models that relaxes the IIA property of the simple multinomial logit by allowing dependencies among the unobserved components of utility. As we mentioned briefly at the outset, the probit is the form of random utility model which arises when the unobserved components of utility in choice are assumed to have a multivariate normal rather than extreme value distribution. Formally, following expression (3.4), the multinomial probit (MNP) model can be expressed as follows:

$$P(i|A) = \int_{-\infty}^{+\infty} d\epsilon_i (\pi j \neq i)$$

$$\int_{-\infty}^{V(X_i) - V(X_j) + \epsilon_i} \qquad (3.13)$$

$$d\epsilon_j \phi_N(\epsilon_1, \ldots, \epsilon_N; \Sigma),$$

where ϕ_N is an N-dimensional multivariate normal density with variance covariance matrix Σ. The off-diagonal elements of Σ capture pairwise dependencies which may exist among the unobserved components of utility.

The central advantage of the MNP model is that it provides the analyst with a much greater degree of flexibility in capturing differing patterns of substitution among options than the GEV model. Specifically, the GEV model's parsimony comes from its assumption that unobserved taste variation can be modeled by a multivariate extreme value (MEV) distribution. A drawback of the MEV, however, is that it is not does yield an arbitrary covariance matrix; as such, the GEV model captures only a prespecified pattern of substitution among options (which are prescribed by a posited hierarchical structure). In contrast, because the covariance matrix of a multivariate normal is flexible, the MNP model can, in principle, be used to represent any pattern of substitution among options.

Because of these potential advantages, the MNP model attracted considerable interest as soon as software for its estimation became available (e.g., Daganzo 1979; Hausman and Wise 1979), and cross-method comparisons with the GEV model indicated that it might be a preferable modeling approach in settings where a hierarchical structure is difficult to pre-

specify (e.g., Currim 1982). Applications of the procedure continue (e.g., Johnson and Hensher 1982; Kamakura and Srivastava 1985, 1986), although on a more limited scale than the GEV approaches.

The primary limitation of the model, which has inhibited broader application, is that the model poses perhaps the most formidable estimation problems of all the generalized forms that we have discussed. Because the model does not provide a closed-form solution for the probability of choice, estimation is cumbersome, and currently available packages (e.g., Daganzo 1979) provide only approximate solutions for the parameters. Most critically, the accuracy of this approximation has been a point of major controversy in the literature, particularly when the model is applied to choice problems involving more than three alternatives (e.g., Horowitz 1980; Wrigley 1985). As such, serious further consideration of the multinomial probit is probably best put on hold until reliable methods of estimation are devised.

Accounting for Context Effects within the Simple Logit Form

While generalized distribution models such as the GEV and feature elimination models attract a considerable amount of interest among researchers in the area of formal choice models, they also attract a large number of criticisms. The most important is that even the simple forms pose formidable estimation problems in practice, and this tends to outweigh the advantage of offering a more general description of choice (e.g., Batsell and Polking 1985). In light of these concerns, a number of researchers have developed choice models that were not subject to the IIA property, yet retained the computational simplicity of the basic multinomial logit model. The essence of their approach is to allow the strict utility argument of the multinomial logit to be dependent upon the set of options under consideration.

The psychological rationale for such models is that while the "true" cause of context effects may be the tendency of individuals to make choices in a staged, contingent fashion, within any single choice there may be instability in the sequential structure (e.g., options eliminated and then readmitted for consideration) such that the most parsimonious description may well be a simultaneous consideration model, such as the simple Luce model (Tversky 1972). While context variations would still be presumed to affect choice probabilities, the influence would be on the perceived overall attractiveness of each option, not on altering the basic choice process (the approach taken by deterministic hierarchical models, such as PRETREE or GEV).

Although most such "generalized logit models" have been presented as ad hoc formulations (e.g., Gaudry and Dagenais 1979), they can also be viewed as approximate choice probabilities which arise by assuming a stochastic elimination process, such as in Tversky's elimination-by-aspects (EBA) model. To illustrate, recall that the EBA model, given earlier in expression (3.6), can be written in the form (3.7) reproduced here:

$$P(x|A) = \frac{\Sigma_{\alpha \epsilon x'} u(\alpha) P(x|A_\alpha)}{\Sigma_{y \epsilon A}(\Sigma_{\alpha \epsilon y'} u(\alpha) P(y|A_\alpha))} , \quad (3.14)$$

where, as before $P(x|A)$ is probability that option x is selected from choice set A, $u(\alpha)$ is the utility or weight associated with feature α and A_α is that subset of options of A which share this feature. If we multiply the numerator and the denominator by

$$\frac{\Sigma_{\alpha \epsilon y'} u(\alpha)}{\Sigma_{\alpha \epsilon y'} u(\alpha)} ,$$

(3.14) may be rewritten in the form

$$P(x|A) = \frac{\Sigma_{\alpha \epsilon x'} u(\alpha) K_x}{\Sigma_{y \epsilon A} (\Sigma_{\alpha \epsilon y'} u(\alpha)) K_y} , \quad (3.15)$$

where

$$K_y = \frac{\Sigma_{\alpha \epsilon y'} u(\alpha) P(y|A_\alpha)}{\Sigma_{\alpha \epsilon y'} u(\alpha)} . \quad (3.16)$$

Expression (3.15) provides an important result: Choice probabilities consistent with EBA can be derived from a simple logit or Luce model in which the overall utility of some option is defined by an independent sum of its attribute worths, multiplied by a scaling factor (K_y). Any model which takes on the general form of (3.15) with a consistent scaling of K_y thus yields choice probabilities consistent with EBA.

We should stress, of course, that simply rewriting the EBA model in terms of (3.15) does not make the representation any easier to estimate, since the definition of K_y provided in expression (3.16) remains recursive. Nevertheless, inspection of (3.16) suggests that scaling factor K_y has some rather simple properties which may render approximation straightforward:

1. it is theoretically bounded by 0 (when the features of any one option are shared by an infinite number of other options) and 1;
2. it increases as the number of shared aspects of x decreases; and
3. it achieves the upper bound of 1 in the limiting case where all aspects = α are unique to each option (when $P(y|A_\alpha) = 1$ for all α).

Hence, K_y might be seen as a measure of the distinctiveness of option y in the choice set A; when all options are unique and hence are equally substitutable ($K_y = K$ for all y), (3.15) reduces to a simple logit or Luce model. In general, however, adding new options to a set will affect existing options differentially, depending on their similarity to the new option.

Adjusted logit models can be seen as rescalings of the strict utility argument in the mutinomial logit in a fashion similar to (3.15), but with a more easily estimable function for the scaling factor K_x. For example, the first effort in this area was that by Gaudry and Dagenais (1979), who proposed the generalized logit model,

$$Pr(i|A) = \frac{e^{V(X_i)} + \theta_i \Sigma_{j \epsilon A} e^{V(X_j)}}{(1 + \Sigma_{j \epsilon A} \theta_j) \Sigma_{j \epsilon A} e^{V(X_j)}} , \quad (3.17)$$

where θ_i was a nonnegative parameter reflecting the degree to which the strict utility of option i would be affected by the introduction of a new option to the choice set. They called the representation the "DOGIT" model, to capture the idea that it is a logit model which "dodges" the assumption of the independence of irrelevant alternatives.

Although the DOGIT model was widely discussed in the literature at the time of its introduction and was used in at least some applications (e.g., Gaudry and Willis 1979), it still offers only a limited solution to the problem of generalizing the basic logit model. Specifically, the substitution parameter θ is not modeled as a direct function of the similarity of the attributes of options (hence it is not generalizable beyond a specific estimation context), and the model remained computationally complex.

In an effort to overcome these limitations, Batsell (1981), Huber and Sewall (1982), and Meyer and Eagle (1982), and others, suggested similar generalized logit models which directly mirror the form given in expression (3.15). Although the specific proposals vary somewhat, the basic suggestion is that expression (3.15) is equivalent to the adjusted logit model

$$Pr(i|A) = \frac{e^{V(X_i)}\,\theta_i}{\sum_{j \epsilon A} e^{V(X_j)}\,\theta_j} \, , \qquad (3.18)$$

where, following (3.16), θ_i is a 0-1 bounded inverse measure of the similarity of option i to all other options in the choice set. Here θ_i is either treated as a single scaling constant to be inferred from observed choice data, or parameterized separately, with θ_i being computed from attribute measures.[4]

A related development by Cooper and Nakanishi (1983a) suggests that distinctiveness effects might be modeled at the level of the individual attribute. Specifically, they describe a family of "zeta-score" models of choice, where the strict utility of an option is modeled as a weighted sum of a set of distinctiveness measures for individual attributes. Specifically, they suggest that a useful measure of the distinctiveness of attribute k of option i in choice set A is the "zeta-score" index,

$$\zeta ikA = \begin{cases} (1 + z_{ikA}^2)^{\frac{1}{2}} \; if \; z_{ikA} \geq 0 \\ (1 + z_{ikA}^2)^{-\frac{1}{2}} \; if \; z_{ikA} < 0 \, , \end{cases}$$

where z_{ikA}^2 is the standardized value or z-score of attribute k of i in set A. In general, attribute scores near the mean in a choice set will have zeta scores near 1, those which are low outliers will have zeta scores approaching zero, and those which are high outliers will have zeta scores greater than one. The overall probability of choice is then derived by estimating a standard multinomial logit model, in which the strict utility argument is defined in terms of zeta scores rather than raw attribute values.

Cooper and Nakanishi have reported a number of applications of choice models defined in terms of zeta scores (see Cooper and Nakanishi, 1988, for a review), and report that in almost all instances the transformation provides modeling fits equal to or better than those provided by models estimated by raw attribute values. In other words, in most cases distinctiveness in attributes helps to explain choices. A limitation of zeta-score models, however, is that they model distinctiveness only as it surfaces in ob-

---

[4]To illustrate, Meyer and Eagle (1982) suggest that a simple consistent proxy for θ_i might be the average Pearson product-moment correlations between options across attributes; in particular,

$$\theta_i = \left(\frac{1}{N} \sum_{\substack{j=1 \\ j \neq i}}^{N} |\frac{r_{ij} - 1}{2}|\right)^{\beta} \, ,$$

where r_{ij} is correlation between the observed attributes of

options i and j. Batsell (1982), in contrast, suggests the weighted similarity measure:

$$\theta_i = exp \left(\frac{1}{N} \sum_{\substack{j=1 \\ j \neq i}}^{N} \left(\sum_{k=1}^{m} w_k|x_{ik} - x_{jk}|\right)\right) \, ,$$

where $k = 1, \ldots m$ subscripts a series of m attributes, defined by the measures x_{ik}, and weighted by the parameters w_k.

served attributes of options; hence, violations of IIA which accrue to correlations among measured attributes (such as attributes of appearance) would not be overcome by the model. In such cases the model would have to be augmented by empirical "correction factors."

The most general class of generalized logit models that have been explored are those which modify the strict utility term in a basic logit through a battery of factors representing the pattern of substitution which exists among individual options in a set (e.g., Batsell and Polking 1985; Carpenter, Cooper, Hanssens, and Midgley 1988; Cooper 1988). Termed *competitive-effect models,* they provide a variance decomposition of the single "similarity factor," θ_i, contained in the simple adjusted logit model, expression (3.18). Specifically, the proposed model forms can be shown to be equivalent to letting θ_i be a linear or multilinear combination of competitor-specific parameters, each measuring the degree of substitutability provided by a particular competing option in the choice set.

To illustrate, imagine that we define θ_i in expression (3.18) in terms of the additive decomposition,

$$\theta_i = exp \left(\sum_{\substack{j \in A \\ j \neq i}} b_j \right.$$

$$\left. + \sum_{\substack{j \in A \\ j \neq i}} \sum_{k=1}^{m} b_{jk} \, x_{jk} \right) , \quad (3.19)$$

where x_{ik} is the observed score of option i on attribute k, and each b is a parameter to be estimated. In addition, assume that the strict utility of option i $V(X_i)$ is also additive in form, as in expression (3.1):

$$Vi(Xi) = b_i + \sum_{k=1}^{m} b_k \, x_{ik} .$$

Substituting these expressions for $V(i)$ and θ_i in

(3.18) the following generalized choice model immediately follows:

$$Pr(i|A) = \frac{e^{V(X_i|A)}}{\sum_{j \in A} e^{V(X_j|A)}} , \quad (3.20)$$

where

$$V(i|A) = \sum_{j \in A} b_j$$

$$+ \sum_{j \in A} \sum_{k=1}^{m} b_{jk} \, x_{jk} . \quad (3.21)$$

More complex competitive decompositions might, of course, be postulated. Batsell and Polking (1985) and Louviere and Woodworth (1983), for example, note that in some contexts multilinear or higher-order interactive decompositions will be needed to fully characterize the pattern of substitution in a choice setting. The most extreme case is that where the effect of one option on another is fully conditional upon the remaining options in the set (an interaction of order n).

The central appeal of decompositions is that they provide a detailed look at the way in which changes in the composition of a choice set affects the likelihood that a given option will be chosen. Competitor-specific parameters, for example, measure the extent to which the mean likelihood of choosing option i will be affected by the presence or absence of another option j in the choice set, controlling for the observed attributes of i and j. Likewise, the competitor attribute effect measures of the extent to which i's choice share will be differentially affected by competitors' attribute changes (Cooper and Nakanishi 1988). Hence, in addition to providing a predictive model of choice, the parameters of the model might be the focus of separate analyses in their own right. Cooper (1988), for example, has illustrated how the coefficients of competitive-effects models can be used to infer maps of the structure of competition within a product class.

The major drawback of competitive-effect models is their lack of parsimony; the large number of parameters lend interpretability problems to the model, and complete model forms are not always estimable given normally available data (see, e.g., Currim, Meyer, and Le 1988; Carpenter, Cooper, Hanssens, and Midgley 1988).[5] In addition, the model parameters simply serve to describe competitive effects, not explain them. As such, the models are of limited usefulness in contexts where new options are being added to a set, or when there are changes in the characteristics of options which have the potential of altering the competitive relationship among options. Nevertheless, that the models potentially allow one to model complex substitution patterns among options within an analytic framework of a simple logit model has caused them to be widely seen as the state of the art in mathematical choice modeling.

Context Effects on Choice: What Current Models Can and Cannot Explain

The Effects of Item Similarity and Dominance. The models discussed all recognize that the process by which an individual chooses an option from a set will be sensitive to the external appearance of that set. These efforts, however, have been generally designed to capture only one type of context effect, the so-called Debreu counter-example to IIA, or the phenomenon that items which are more similar in a choice set compete more closely (given a fixed set of choices) than those which are more distinctive. After twenty years of work toward this goal, it can reasonably be concluded that a range of satisfactory solutions has been obtained. There exist three major families of models which capture such similarity effects, each offering a possible approach. If similarities among a set of items seem best described in

terms of a set of hierarchical partitions, such as in cases where the decision maker faces a large number of choice options, the GEV model provides a straightforward, and usually easily estimable, modeling solution. If a hierarchical representation is difficult to specify or appears theoretically inappropriate, an adjusted logit model can be specified. Finally, if the analyst is modeling choice among a small set of options and the source of violations of IIA are thought best attributed to correlations among the unobserved components of utility, the multinomial probit model is a plausible option.

Unfortunately, there exist a broader range of empirically observed context effects which have proven more difficult to model. For example, Huber and Puto (1983) note that the effect of item similarity can actually, at times, be a complex one. While existing non-IIA models tend to predict that as two options become more similar their choice shares should also become similar, the opposite may be the case in reality; because similar options are also more easily comparable, their choice shares may in fact *diverge* if it becomes apparent that one has a decisive edge on an attribute. In particular, given two options which are identical on all attributes except for one, intuition suggests that the option which is inferior on this remaining option will have little rational probability of being chosen. While this "dominance" effect is theoretically captured in feature-based models such as EBA and PRETREE, it is not captured in algebraic multiattribute models, such as GEV, the adjusted logit, or MNP.[6]

Some potential solutions have been offered for how the simple logit model might be gener-

---

[5]Louviere and Woodworth (1983) point out that the multicollinearity problems which plague econometric applications of competitive-effect models are less of a barrier in laboratory applications of the model, in which data is drawn from experimentally designed choice sets.

[6]The GEV, or nested logit model, can capture the effect of dominance if the choice model in each stage is composed on only one attribute, or if the nested logit process is the same as PRETREE. Our critique centers on the more general case where choice model at each stage is composed of multiple attributes. To illustrate, if two options are identical on two attributes and the choice probabilities are 0.5, ML estimates of the attribute parameters will also be equal (or indeterminant). If one option then became a slight bit better on one attribute, intuition suggests that probabilities would go to 1 and 0 for each option, but equal weights on the attributes would predict choice probabilities remaining near 0.5.

alized to account for dominance effects, however none seem truly satisfactory. For example, Meyer and Eagle (1982) suggested that the dominance effect might be modeled by presuming a "weight-shifting" process in multiattribute evaluations: When making a choice between two options, the amount of weight given to a particular attribute in choice will depend on the amount of variance displayed by that attribute relative to the variability displayed by other attributes. As options become increasingly similar on a set of dimensions, choice thus becomes increasingly driven by the subset of attributes which continue to differ across options. Hence, as intuition would suggest, given a choice between two alternatives which differ on only one attribute, choice probabilities polarize to one and zero. Meyer and Eagle apply this model to a study of binary store choice and find good explanatory ability. Unfortunately, a drawback of the approach is that it is not parsimoniously generalized to multinomial choice contexts; more critically, estimation requires choice probabilities for all possible paired comparisons of options with a given choice setting.

A more perplexing effect of item similarity has been noted in a series of studies by Huber, Payne, and Puto (1982), Huber and Puto (1983), and Ratneshwar, Shocker, and Stewart (1987). They report that when an option which is identical to another on several dimensions, but worse on one, is added to a choice set — an alternative which is normatively irrelevant — it actually serves to *increase* the choice share of the option which dominates it. They characterize this as part of a general "attraction effect," in which the joint likelihood of purchasing a group of similar items in a choice set tends to be greater than would be expected based on their independent preferences alone.

Kahn, Moore and Glazer (1987) and Kahn and Lehmann (1989) suggest that the phenomenon is perhaps most plausibly explained as a "portfolio effect": when asked to choose among groups of items from which one will eventually be selected, individuals exhibit a tendency toward selecting that group with the largest number of elements, presumably because it is thought to give them most flexibility when a final choice is made. When there are differential patterns of similarity in a choice set, options naturally fall into similar subgroups. Individuals may be analogously lured toward initially focussing on the set with the largest number of elements, and then choosing the most preferred option from the subset.

Choice Set Formation. The "attraction effect" may be a consequence of a much broader problem facing applications of current choice models: How does the process by which individuals form evoked sets, or the subset of options which are seriously evaluated at the time of choice, affect the final choice outcome? The pragmatic consequence of ignoring the consideration process (as is almost universally done in field applications of logit-type choice models) is that model parameters have limited psychological meaning: While attribute coefficients are theoretically measures of the effect of variations in an attribute on the strict utility of a choice option, this is not the case if only a subset of the individuals under study were considering the option at the time of choice. Hence, in general, attribute effect parameters will be biased downward from the "true" value which would be obtained if the model was specified only for actively considered subsets of options. As an illustration, in applications of aggregate market-share models analysts often report findings of low attribute elasticities for small market share brands (e.g., Cooper 1988). While one might interpret this result as meaning that such brands are purchased by a small group of "loyal" buyers, another, perhaps more plausible, explanation is that it is an artifact of estimating an aggregate model over a heterogeneous buyer group, most of which never consider the smaller brands, with those who do consider the smaller brands actually being highly attribute sensitive. While this distinction would seemingly be an important one from a managerial perspective, it is confounded in current models.

How to specify choice sets at an individual level has long been a major stumbling block in applications of formal choice models (cf. Fotheringham 1989). Heuristic solutions that have been proposed include defining the relevant choice set as that set of options which have been chosen at least once during a time interval (e.g., Hensher and Johnson 1981), or, if survey information is available, directly asking consumers for their "usual" set of considered options (e.g., Silk and Urban 1979). Models which allow an analyst to predict *variation* in considerations sets from occasion to occasion, however, have proven more elusive. The only such model we are aware of that has been implemented is that proposed by Gensch (1987), who uses his MLH algorithm (discussed earlier) to conduct a hierarchical screening which determines the "best" n options on a given choice occasion (in his application n is arbitarily 4). He then calibrates a multinomial logit model under the assumption that these n options form the relevant consideration set.

The paradox of Gensch's approach, however, is that it assumes that all options are considered (at least initially) in the hierarchical screening. Hauser and Wernerfelt (1988), Meyer (1980), and Richards (1982) have proposed that this difficulty be circumvented by modeling the choice set formation process as a Bayesian search problem, in which options enter the choice set when their hypothesized utility exceeds some reservation level (an idea we will elaborate on later when we discuss learning processes).

Other Effects of Context. Finally, there exist a number of other, more subtle, ways in which choice context has been observed to affect the process of choice. Johnson and Meyer (1984), for example, note that the parameters of choice models tend to become increasingly skewed as the size of the consideration set grows; in particular, with larger choice sets, choice tends to be driven by observed variation on a smaller number of attributes. Similarly, Eagle (1985), Lynch and Hutchinson (1984), and Meyer and Louviere (1982) have found evidence for a general effect of attribute variance: Individuals tend to attend more closely to attributes which exhibit greater variability in a choice set. Although such effects are usually not represented

within applied choice models, they are more easily overcome than dominance, attraction, and choice set effects noted earlier. Specifically, as illustrated by Borgers and Timmermans (1987) and by Meyer and Louviere (1982), given choice experiments in which set size and variance are manipulated, these effects can be directly recognized as interactive effects in the strict utility function of a traditional logit.

CHOICE DYNAMICS

The individual choice models described previously are inherently static models. While they can — and often are — estimated by observing a sequence of choices made over time (e.g., Elrod 1988), such applications are based on an assumption which is questionable in practice: the assumption that choices on one occasion are independent of those made on subsequent occasions. Violations of this assumption arise frequently: Tastes may systematically change as a consequence of learning or habit formation (e.g., Kuehn 1962, Jeuland 1978) or as an explicit desire among individuals to seek variety in choice (e.g., McAlister and Pessemier 1982, McAlister 1982), or both (Bawa forthcoming, Kahn, Kalwani and Morrison 1986).

Over the years there has been extensive modeling research which has explored the nature of temporal effects on choice. The work has proceeded in two ways. The first direction has been to develop model forms for choices made over time among options which are familiar to the decision makers. These models, which generally have focussed on the effects of loyal/habitual or variety-seeking behavior, have traditionally not incorporated explanatory variables, but rather have tried to provide parsimonious constructs for measuring the degree to which past choice behavior influences current choice behavior. Researchers have begun to extend these simple models to include explanatory market variables which further explain the patterns of switching over time (e.g., Carpenter and Lehmann 1985; Zufryden 1986).

The second direction has been to develop

model forms for choices made in situations when full information is initially not available for all items in the choice set. In these cases, temporal dependencies result from individuals learning the attributes of options over time through choice.

Models Which Measure the Effects of Temporal Dependencies

There are three families of models that have been used to measure temporal effects on brand choice: Markov models (primarily first-order), linear learning models, and the incorporation of a term which is the weighted average of past purchases into the simple multinomial logit model. All three of these types of modeling efforts have been used to measure both brand loyal and variety-seeking or switching behavior.

Markov Models. For first-order Markov models the probability of purchasing a brand is dependent upon the purchase which was made at the previous purchase occasion. These conditional probabilities are generally represented in a transition matrix. To illustrate, consider a market where there are two choice options, Brand 1 and Brand 0. In a first-order Markov model the conditional probabilities of a purchase of i at time $t + 1$ given a purchase of j at time t, $P(i|j)$, is given by the matrix:

$$
\begin{array}{c}
\\
\\
\text{Brand Purchased at } t
\end{array}
\begin{array}{cc}
\multicolumn{2}{c}{\begin{array}{c}\text{Brand Purchased}\\ \text{at } t + 1\end{array}}\\
\begin{array}{cc}1 & \quad 0\end{array}\\
\begin{array}{c}1\\0\end{array}
\left[
\begin{array}{cc}
P(1|1) & P(0|1)\\
P(1|0) & P(0|0)
\end{array}
\right]
\end{array}
$$

This model could be extended to the study of markets with multiple brands, either by assuming that Brand 0 represents all other brands and Brand 1 represents the brand of interest (e.g., Massy, Montgomery, and Morrison 1970), or by extending the matrix to n brands (e.g., Givon 1984).

If the two rows of this transition matrix have equal entries, then there are no temporal dependencies. In that case, $P(1|1) = P(1|0) = P(1)$ and choice behavior is said to be zero-order, which implies that the probability of purchase for a brand on each trial is independent of any past purchase behavior (Kahn, Kalwani, and Wright 1986).[7] In contrast, if the two rows are not equal, there is evidence for temporal dependency. For example, if the probability of choosing a brand increases if the brand has been chosen before, when $(P1|1)$ is greater than $P(1)$), then there is evidence of brand loyal behavior. On the other hand, if the probability of choosing a brand decreases if the brand has been chosen before, when $(P(1|1)$ is less than $P(1))$, this would reflect variety-seeking behavior (e.g., Givon 1984, McAlister, and Pessemier 1982; McAlister 1982; Jeuland 1978). The exact modeling specification for these two types of conditional probabilities, of course, is open to speculation. We will review proposed approaches to each.

Markov Models for Brand Loyal Behavior. One of the first researchers to use a first-order Markov model to measure brand loyalty was Lipstein (1959). Although he did not offer any specific model, he suggested that the repeat purchase probabilities, for example, $P(1|1)$ and $P(0|0)$, be used as indices of loyalty. Telser (1962) was one of the first researchers to investigate the relationship between a marketing variable, price, and patterns of brand choice switching over time. He specified a linear relationship between the transition probabilities and the difference between the price of the brand considered and the average price of all other brands.

Morrison (1966) explicitly modeled brand loyal behavior in a first-order Markov model. He developed two first-order Markov models: the Brand Loyal model and the Last Purchase Loyal model. In the Brand Loyal model an individual with a high probability of remaining

---

[7]The simple multinomial logit models described earlier were zero-order models of behavior as they did not recognize the effect of past purchase history on current history.

with Brand 1 would also have a higher probability of choosing brand 1 after a purchase of Brand 0. Morrison modeled this probability as follows:[8]

$$P(1|1) = p$$

$$P(1|0) = kp$$

where:

p = distributed beta across the population
k = a positive constant which is the same for all individuals

In the Last Purchase Loyal model an individual is more loyal to the brand last purchased than any brand in particular. Morrison modeled this dependency as follows:

$$P(1|1) = p$$

$$P(1|0) = 1 - kp$$

where:

p = distributed beta across the population
k = a positive constant which is the same for all individuals

Although Morrison's models allow for behavior on one choice occasion to influence behavior on another, his models do not provide a convenient way of measuring the strength of this influence. Jeuland (1979) has extended Morrison's representations to include a specific parameter to measure inertia or loyal behavior. In his extension, the probability of repeat purchasing brand i is increased by a fraction of the maximum possible increase if brand i was purchased at the previous purchase occasion. His model is characterized as follows:

$$P(1|1) = \theta + I(1 - \theta)$$

$$P(0|0) = (1 - \theta) + I\theta$$

where:

θ = zero-order probability of purchasing brand 1
I = an inertia parameter which varies from 0 to 1

In this model, the parameter I captures the degree of dependency from one choice occasion to the next. If I equals one then the choice on one occasion completely determines the choice on the next occasion; if I equals zero then the choice process reduces the zero-order.

Markov Models for Variety-Seeking Behavior. Jeuland's model provides a way to parsimoniously measure the degree of loyalty or inertia represented from one choice occasion to the next. The next logical step is to use this type of methodology to investigate the "opposite" of brand loyal behavior, or variety-seeking behavior, in which choosing the brand on one occasion decreases the probability of choosing the same brand on the next occasion. Givon (1984) did exactly that. He used the Markov model to measure variety-seeking behavior as well as loyal behavior. In this model, the choice made on the last purchase occasion can either increase the probability of choosing the same brand on this occasion (i.e., loyal behavior), decrease the probability of choosing the same brand on this occasion (i.e., variety-seeking behavior) or have no effect (i.e., zero-order behavior).

He defines a parameter VS which ranges from -1 to 1. When VS is positive then brand loyal behavior is occurring, when VS is negative then variety-seeking behavior is occurring, and, finally, when VS is zero, then zero-order behavior is occurring. Although Givon defines his model for n brands, the simple 2-brand conditional probabilities are as follows:

$$P(1|1) = (|VS| - VS)/2 + (1 - |VS|)\theta$$

$$P(1|0) = (|VS| + VS)/2 + (1 - |VS|)\theta$$

where:

θ = preference for brand 1
VS = measure of the effect of last period's choice on this period choice

---

[8]Note that in all first-order matrices $P(1|1)$ and $P(1|0)$ = 1 and $P(1|0)$ and $P(0|0)$ = 1, so the entire matrix is characterized by just defining one entry on each row of the matrix.

Kahn, Kalwani, and Morrison (1986) used Givon's and Jeuland's models to form the basis of a taxonomy that integrates brand loyalty and variety-seeking research into one framework. In addition to the two first-order models, they also defined four second-order Markov models. In these models, the probability of choosing a brand on the current occasion depended on the choices made on the past two occasions. By adding the second order models, Kahn et al. could describe a large spectrum of choice behavior which depended on previous choices made. Bawa (forthcoming) also considers higher-order behavior. He shows how the preference function for a brand behaves nonmontonically as repeat purchasing or switching take place.

Markov Models of Brand Switching That Incorporate Explanatory Variables

Although the above stochastic models provide a framework of parameters for measuring the degree of dependency of the current choice on the last period or last two period choices, they do not provide any help in determining why that dependency exists. Some attempt has been made to explain this dependency within the Markov model. Lattin and McAlister (1985) and Feinberg, Kahn, and McAlister (1989) use measures of the similarity between brands to help explain the patterns of dependencies associated with variety-seeking behavior. Specifically, for markets in which there is reason to believe that consumers are influenced by a desire to seek variety in choice, Lattin and McAlister and Feinberg, Kahn, and McAlister offer the following model of the conditional probability that some option i will be chosen given a previous choice of a different option j:

$$p_{i|j} = \frac{\pi_i - V(S_{ij})}{1 - V\sum_k S_{kj}}, \qquad (3.22)$$

where π_i is a measure of the overall attractiveness of brand i, S_{ij} is a measure of the value of the product features shared by both i and j (a measure of similarity), and V is a (0,1) bounded scaling factor measuring the consumer's need

for variety in choice. This model has a straightforward interpretation: It hypothesizes if a consumer has a strong need for variety, the likelihood that he or she will buy brand i after previously buying brand j increases with the independent attractiveness of $i(\pi_i)$, its distinctiveness vis-à-vis brand j, and its distinctiveness vis-à-vis all other competing options. Aspects which are unique to an alternative thus have a positive impact on the conditional probability of choosing that alternative. Although their model is restricted to the study of variety-seeking tendencies, clearly similarity could also be used to help explain the dependencies for a brand loyal consumer as well. In an analogous fashion, Kahn and Raju (1990) propose a model which extends the Markov framework to include the effects of frequency of promotion on variety-seeking and loyal behavior.

Other researchers have looked at a broader range of explanatory variables to investigate the effect on choice of brands over time. These researchers have used the simple multinomial logit model discussed earlier to model the transition probabilities of the Markov model. For example, Carpenter and Lehmann (1985) used a multinomial logit model to express the conditional probabilities as a function of marketing mix variables, product features, and their interactions. In their model, individuals are grouped to form segments according to their last purchase. For example, consider a segment j, defined as the set of consumers who purchased brand j in time t. Assume that for this segment switching to brand i of a set of M brands yields measurable utility $v_{i|j}$. The probability of switching from brand j at time t to brand i at time $t + 1$, $p_{i|j}$ (which is equivalent to the conditional probability entry in a Markov matrix) is then modeled as:

$$P_{i|j} = e^{v_{i|j}} \left/ \sum_{k\in M} e^{v_{i|k}} \right.$$

Carpenter and Lehmann express $v_{i|j}$, the utility of switching to product i from j, as a function of the attributes and marketing activities of both products. They have tested their model on consumer nondurable data and have shown how price promotion, advertising, and brand name strength affect both loyal and switching behavior.

In a similar manner, Jones and Zufryden (1980) and Zufryden (1980, 1981) model the transition probabilities within a two-brand Markov model as a binomial logit model. Within this formulation, Zufryden could relate purchase-explanatory variables (e.g., product features, pricing, consumer characteristics, etc.) to switching probabilities. Zufryden (1986) then extended his earlier model to consider multibrand market situations.

Linear Learning Models. Another type of modeling form that has been used to represent the dependencies of past choices on the current choice is the linear learning model. This model, originally proposed in psychology by Bush and Mosteller (1955), represents the probability of purchasing a brand at time t as a linear function of whether or not the brand is purchased on occasion $t - 1$. The parameters of the linear relationship are a function of the past purchase history. In this way, the model is both first-order, because it directly depends on the purchase made on the last occasion, and infinite order, because the coefficients of the linear relationship are derived from all previous choices.

Kuehn (1962) was the first to apply the linear learning model to study the study of temporal buying patterns, with other applications reported by Aaker (1970), Carman (1966), Massy (1970), and McConnell (1968). In these applications it is assumed that if a brand was purchased on purchase occasion t then the probability of purchasing the brand on occasion $t + 1$ would increase. If the brand was rejected on occasion t then the probability of purchasing it on $t + 1$ would decrease. The two influences are captured through two linear relationships: a purchase operator and a rejection operator. The acceptance operator is given by:

$$p_{t+1} = \alpha + \beta + \lambda p_t,$$

and the rejection operator is given by:

$$p_{t+1} = \alpha + \lambda p_t,$$

where α, β, and λ are nonnegative parameters determined from the purchase history, and are subject to the constraint $(\alpha + \beta + \lambda) \leq 1$. Srinivasan and Kesavan (1976) note that in the special case where $\alpha = 0$ and $(\beta + \lambda) = 1$, the linear learning model becomes equivalent to an exponential smoothing model, in which the probability of a brand's choice at one point in time is modeled as the weighted sum of previous choice outcomes, with recent outcomes being weighted most heavily.

Although the linear model has often proven to be a useful descriptive device (e.g., Srinivasan and Kesavan 1976), it has been subject to two sets of criticisms. First, as originally formulated, the model offers a representation of an *individual* consumer's learning process, hence it can be applied to the study of aggregates only under the assumption that individuals in a sample are homogeneous in their learning processes—an assumption which will often be empirically untenable. This problem has been addressed first by Jones (1970) with a model which was difficult to estimate and, subsequently, by Givon and Horsky (1978, 1979). Givon and Horsky (1978) developed a heterogeneous linear learning model which allowed consideration of an entire population and nested a first-order Markov model and a zero-order model as well. A second criticism, suggested by Aaker (1970), is that even in cases where heterogeneity in parameters is not a concern the model may still fail if yet another assumption is violated: that of stationarity in parameters over time. Specifically, in some settings the likelihood that an individual will switch to an option may vary over time in response to both changes in the set of choice alternatives (for example, one option being made more attractive due to a lowering of its price, or due to new options being introduced), as well as changes in the decision maker's tastes (e.g., a desire to seek variety). These sorts of influences, however, are not explicitly recognized by the model.

Unlike the Markov models, the linear learning model has not been readopted by researchers in the 1980s aside from a few attempts to use it to measure variety-seeking behavior by reversing the rejection and acceptance operators (e.g., Sharma and Durand 1980). Instead models of learning have been advanced based on theories of risk aversion, as will be discussed in a later section.

Exploring the Effect of Past Choices in the Multinomial Logit Model.

Although as mentioned earlier, the simple multinomial logit model is a zero-order model, it can be extended to represent dynamic choice behavior by introducing distributed lags of previous purchases in the indirect utility function of the logit (e.g., Guadagni 1983, Guadagni and Little 1983, Gupta 1988, Meyer and Cooper 1986). For example, Guadagni and Little (1983) incorporate "brand loyalty" and "size loyalty" in their multinomial logit analysis of coffee purchases by nesting an exponential smoothing model of previous brand and previous size purchases. Specifically, they include an independent variable in their strict utility function which they called "loyalty" and which is defined as follows:

$$x_k^i(n) = \alpha_b x_k^i(n-1) + (1 - \alpha_b)z$$

where:

$$z = \begin{cases} 1 \text{ if customer i bought brand } k \\ \quad \text{on purchase occasion (n-1)} \\ 0 \text{ otherwise} \end{cases},$$

$x_k^i(n)$ = loyalty for brand k for nth purchase of customer i

α_b = carryover constant

This modeling approach also closely parallels one proposed by Keon (1979). He suggested that, over a series of successive choice occasions, choice patterns will be driven by three elements: (1) the relative zero-order desirability of a product's attribute mix relative to others, (2) the tendency for the attractiveness of a brand to be "forgotten" given the absence of a purchase, and (3) the tendency for consumers to become bored or satiated with a brand given a purchase. Brand loyalty would be modeled by a dominance of the forgetting effect: while the purchase of a brand at one point in time would not enhance its attractiveness per se, it would enhance its relative attractiveness by the gradual reversion of the perceived attractiveness of the options to a neutral level. On the other hand, variety-seeking behavior would be modeled by a dominance of the satiation effect.

Lattin (1987) developed a "balance model" of choice behavior, which uses the multinomial logit form and includes a variable accounting for the effects of past choices on the current choice. Lattin assumes that the utility for a brand is the sum of the utilities provided by the characteristics or attributes constituting the brand. He then further assumes that the utility derived from these product characteristics depends on its salient quality in memory. The "salience" refers to the lingering impact of the characteristics after consumption. The salience of the characteristics can have either a negative (i.e., variety-seeking type behavior) or a positive effect (i.e., brand loyal behavior). The form Lattin used for item salience is identical to the exponential smoothing model used by Guadagni and Little (1983) as their construct of loyalty; however, in Lattin's model the specification permits variety-seeking as well as loyal behavior in the choice of brands and attributes.

Summary: Models Recognizing Temporal Dependencies.

Although different in form, Markov models, linear learning models, and multinomial logit models, which include "loyalty" variables, share a common objective: They each are attempts to parametrize or measure the degree to which brand choices made in one period affect the brand choices in subsequent periods. For example, in Kahn, Kalwani, and Morrison (1986), the models provided an estimate of the degree to which the previous choice reinforced (or negatively reinforced) the choice made on the next period. In the linear learning models these measures were provided by the coefficients in the linear model. Finally, in the models similar to Guadagni and Little's (1983) model, the coefficient of the "loyalty" or "salience" terms measures the importance of previous brand choices on the current choice.

While these models of loyalty and variety-seeking behavior recognize the systematic dependencies among choices over time, the effects are limited to those of habituation and/or satiation and not to *changes* in information about the option set.

An increasing number of authors have argued that full-information assumptions may be violated in a number of consumer buying situations. (e.g., Ford and Smith 1987; Levin and Johnson 1985). In many cases, such as in new product decisions, because consumers have limited experience in consuming differing options, choices will be driven by consumers' hypotheses about the utilities of each option, which may bear little resemblance to the "true" utilities these options might hold given a greater range of experiences by the consumers. As a consequence, consumer choices will invariably involve at least some level of uncertainty, with this uncertainty varying over time as a consequence of both individuals becoming more familiar with the option set, and changes in the option set itself.

Models of Dynamic Choice Under Uncertainty

Several authors have recently offered suggestions for how impression-formation models might be generalized to account for the effects of attribute uncertainty and learning, with Meyer and Sathi (1985) and Roberts and Urban (1987) offering extensions to the study of choice from competitive sets. Although their formulations differ somewhat in structure, both draw their roots from economic expected utility theory.

The basic approach is as follows: As in static choice theory under certainty, we begin with the assumption that individuals choose that option which is thought to deliver the highest level of utility at the time of choice. Because the decision maker is uncertain as to what this value may be given a choice, however, he or she is treated as an expected utility maximizer; that is, the decision maker selects the option which holds the highest expectation given a distribution of possible values.

As before, it is assumed that overall impressions of choice options can be modeled in terms of a multiattribute function of their attributes. In this case, however, it is assumed that these attribute values are not known with certainty prior to choice; rather, they are random variables, each characterized by a distribution of possible values. The expected utility of given option i, EU_i, is thus represented as a multiattribute function of the expected utility of each attribute, as in the linear-additive form,

$$EV_i = \sum_{k=1}^{m} b_{ik} \, EU(x_{ik}) \; ,$$

where $EU(x_{ik})$ is the expected utility of the random variable x_{ik}, which is the actual value of the kth attribute of option i.

Roberts and Urban (1987) derive a normative expression for $EU(x_{ik})$ by assuming that individuals are risk averse in decisions under uncertainty, and treat x_{ik} as a random draw from a normal distribution with mean $\bar{x}_{ik}$ and variance σ_{ik}^2. Specifically, following Keeney and Raiffa (1976) they propose:

$$EU(x_{ik}) = \bar{x}_{ik} - \frac{r}{2} \, \sigma_{ik}^2 \; , \qquad (3.23)$$

where r is a measure of the decision maker's attitude toward risk. Expression (3.23) has a simple intuition: When faced with the task of evaluating an uncertain choice option, impressions are formed by integrating a set of risk-adjusted expectations for the value of each attribute. If the risk parameter r is positive, implying risk aversion, the model captures a well-known finding in studies of choice under limited information: Increasing uncertainty in attribute values (increases in the variance σ_{ik}^2) leads to diminished expected utilities (e.g., Ford and Smith 1987; Meyer 1981). Hence, given a choice between a certain option with a known attribute value and an uncertain option with the same mean, most will prefer the certain option (e.g., Huber and McCann 1983; Levin and Johnson 1985; Yakanishi and Hill 1979).

A limitation of expression (3.23) as an empirical device, however, is that its predictions may not perfectly correspond to actual subjective expected utilities provided by individuals. Specifically, while individuals may form expectations through some notion of central tendency and dispersion, it may not necessarily correspond to the simple difference given in expression (3.22). To account for a broader range of processing rules, Meyer and Sathi (1985) suggest the following alternative definition of EU_i:

$$EU\ (x_{ik})\ =\ k_1 u_{\bar{x}}(\bar{x}_{ik})\ +\ k_2 u_D\ (D_{ik})$$
$$+\ k_3 u_{\bar{x}}(\bar{x}_{ik}) u_D(D_{ik})\ ,$$
(3.24)

where D_{ik} is a measure of the perceived dispersion around the mean expected attribute level $\bar{x}_{ik}$, $u_{\bar{x}}(\cdot)$ and $u_D(\cdot)$ are utility mappings, and K_1, K_2, and K_3 are normalized scaling constants. Like expression (3.23), (3.24) also captures a negative effect of uncertainty in the case where $u_D(\cdot)$ decreases with increases in perceived dispersion D_{ik}. The argued advantage of (3.24) is that it allows greater flexibility in the scaling of means and dispersions, and allows for nonadditive integration rules.

Ford and Smith (1987), Levin and Johnson (1985), and Meyer (1982, 1985) have also explored generalizations of mean/variance models, similar to expressions (3.23) and (3.24), that recognize the possibility of cross-attribute inferences (for more extensive discussion see Chapter 11 by van Raaij in this volume). Specifically, the expected utility of a given attribute is modeled as a function of not only the mean and variance of that attribute, but also as a weighted sum of the observed value of other, certain, attributes. In this case the weights correspond to the perceived covariance between the certain and uncertain attributes.[9]

Central to these developments is the notion that expected values are subject to change

---

[9]Meyer (1985) derives a normative cross-attribute inference model by assuming that individuals view attribute values as drawn from an *m*-dimensional multivariate normal distribution with covariance matrix σ. The forms presented by Ford and Smith (1987), Levin and Johnson (1985), and Meyer (1982) are structurally similar, although are not derived from a normative perspective.

through learning. Specifically, a choice on one occasion will likely serve to alter the decision maker's inferences about the utility of the chosen option for the next occasion by yielding a more certain estimate of its expected utility. Both Meyer and Sathi (1985) and Roberts and Urban (1987) posit Bayesian-like updating models for this process, in which the means and variances underlying a given expected utility are modeled as a weighted average of a "no information" baseline or prior and a full-information value.

By successively substituting the updating models into a model of expected value, generalized evaluation models are provided which enable simple choice models (such as the multinomial logit) to be applied to contexts in which consumers initially have limited information about the attributes of options but in which the information is updated over time. Applications of models of this sort have been made in laboratory studies of choice and learning (e.g., Meyer and Sathi 1985), and in the real-world application of changing consumer preferences for new automobiles (Roberts and Urban 1987).

Search and the Formation of Choice Sets. Although the above family of models appears to be a reasonable first step in modeling choice dynamics given limited information about options, they hold an important limitation: As noted by Horsky and Raban (1988), the models are limited to characterizing "rational" choice under uncertainty in the limited case where the decision maker seeks to maximize utility for the immediate choice occasion, and does not consider its impact on the *stream* of utilities gained from future choices. Where this assumption is most problematic is in instances where a particular choice is viewed as part of an information-gathering or search process.

A convenient example is selections among restaurants: A primary rationale for trying out a new restaurant may not be that it is thought to deliver the highest utility among all restaurants for a given evening, but rather that one's total future utility gained from dining out will be enhanced if it can be added to the future "choice set."

While search effects have been discussed to some degree in the choice modeling literature (e.g., Richards 1982), there is no emerging consensus as to how they might best be represented. The most direct approach would simply be to assume that search effects are manifested in the risk-attitude parameter of a mean/variance model, as in expression (3.22). If the individual is actively seeking to expand his or her choice set, he or she should exhibit a preference for less certain over more certain options. The drawback of this modeling approach, however, is that search strategies and risk attitudes are conceptually quite different constructs; an individual may be generally risk averse, yet still find it desirable to seek out unfamiliar options as an "investment" in the future utility stream. By failing to separate them, one may observe considerable temporal variance in apparent risk attitudes.

Horsky and Raban (1988) model product choice over time as a "multiarmed bandit" problem, in which the individual makes sequential choices from a set of options, each characterized by a distribution of utility values.[10] This presumes that the decision maker's objective on each choice occasion is to maximize a total stream of utilities across a series of choices. The consequence of the model is a prediction about patterns of switching among options similar to that often reported in studies of temporal choice under uncertainty (e.g. Meyer and Sathi 1985); over time, individuals should first act as risk seekers, actively trying out new options, but then progressively act as risk avoiders, repeatedly selecting that limited subset which delivers the "safest" level of utility.

Recent Issues in Modeling Choice Dynamics

As an increasing number of authors have turned to the problem of estimating models of consumer choice on time-series data, the array

of problems posed in such applications has become increasingly apparent. In the previous discussion we focussed on current solutions to the three most well-understood issues in dynamics: brand loyalty, variety-seeking, and attribute learning. These are, however, only a subset of the possible sources of dependency in choice.

For example, several authors (Bass and Pilon 1981, Kahn and Louie 1990, Winer 1983) have noted that there will often be temporal dependencies in attribute effects that are distinct from temporal dependencies in choices. Perhaps the most well known is the effect of advertising: The effect of brand advertising on the choice observed at time t may be a weighted cumulative function of the number of exposures to that advertisement, as well as the time since exposure. In such cases, the problem of correctly specifying a distributed lag model in exposures becomes paramount, and often not easily solvable (e.g., Carpenter, Cooper, Hanssens, and Midgley 1989).

A somewhat different potential temporal effect is that of price variation. Winer (1983), for example, reports that consumers often judge the expensiveness of a brand not simply relative to the prices of competitors (as would be presumed by a traditional multinominal logit model), but also with reference to its "expected" price, or at the price it would "normally" be sold. Exactly how consumers form such expectations is currently an issue of some debate. Winer (1983), for example, offers evidence that expectations can be modeled as a simple adaptive expectations model, in which expectations are represented as a weighted average of previously observed prices. While the adaptive expectations model is intuitively appealing, its weakness is that it becomes inappropriate in cases where consumers base expectations on longer-term trends and periodicities in a price series, such as anticipating monthly discounts.

Finally, perhaps the most difficult technical problem which has surfaced in attempts to apply discrete choice models to the study of behavior over time is that of temporal dependencies among the unobserved components of utility. While time-series methods for the treat-

---

[10]"Armed bandit problems" refer to a family of sequential sampling problems in which a gambler faces a set of slot machines, and his or her goal is to determine that with the highest average or total payoff.

ment of autocorrelated errors given continuous dependent variables are well developed, this is not the case for discrete multinomial models, such as the multinomial logit (e.g., Heckman 1981). There have been two recent efforts to remedy this shortcoming; Heckman (1981) and Sugita (1986) have proposed probit models for the analysis of binary (two alternative) panel data, in which the unobserved components of utility over time are presumed to be characterized by a multivariate normal distribution. Unfortunately, the models are currently not easily estimable, and we are aware of few applications beyond those reported in the original works. The current "solution" to such problems is either thus one of incorporating a rich enough array of temporal variables in the strict utility function so as to minimize the potential for autocorrelation, or to estimate models on aggregated choice shares, where standard least-squares procedures can be exploited (e.g., Carpenter, et al. 1989).

FUTURE RESEARCH

Toward a Theory of Consumer Choice Models

The evolution of the literature in mathematical models of consumer choice reflects a dialogue between two quite different research motivations: that of developing simple and accurate tools for predicting the outcome of individual choices, and that of providing an accurate psychological explanation for these choices. On one hand, these motivations are often conflicting; efforts toward simpler models have often come at the cost of psychological richness, while efforts toward models which are rich in psychological detail have come at the cost of the ease of implementation. On the other hand, this conflict would seem to have been a useful one: by pointing out the psychological limitations of simple choice models our ability to predict choice has been systematically enhanced, and by insistence on developing theories with well-defined mathematical structures has yielded more rigorous theories of behavior.

In light of this diversity in models and modeling approaches, will these streams of thought ever converge to a "unified" mathematical theory of consumer choice? Our answer to this is both yes and no. It seems unlikely that there will ever be a mathematical theory of consumer choice which pervades work in the field, in the same way that, say, the theory of rational choice dominates modern economics. Because there will always be diversity in the objectives of modeling, there will always be diversity in the theoretical model forms which best satisfy those objectives. However, it *does* seem plausible to suggest that we will converge to agreement about a taxonomy of models which offer successive gradations of explanations of consumer choice behavior, and that we will agree to an understanding of the types of contexts in which each is most appropriate.

Given such a direction, perhaps the single greatest future research need is something resembling a meta theory of models. Although the field is replete with tools for capturing a wide range of choice policies, we currently have little understanding of why different models are appropriate in different contexts, and we have limited ability to predict which model will be appropriate a priori. As such, choice modelers are often tied into the role of being passive descriptors; we can describe past choices, but we can forecast only when there is reason to believe that decision policies will remain invariant over time and/or across contexts.

If a meta theory of choice models is to emerge, it would seem to require consideration of three separate influences:

1. statistical factors which influence the robustness of choice data to alternative specifications of choice models;
2. an understanding of how consumers alter their choice processes in response to observed changes in the appearance of the set of options; and
3. an understanding of how consumers alter their choice processes as a result of learning, satiation, or inertia over time.

The first consideration reflects findings that the robustness of a choice model to specification error often depends on the pattern of correlation which exists among attributes in a choice set (Curry and Faulds 1985; Johnson, Meyer, and Goshe 1989; Newman 1977). Specifically, when predicting choices made from sets where attributes are orthogonal or positively correlated across options, simple random utility models seem to provide a good account of the data, even when the underlying process is known to be one based on hierarchical elimination (cf. Johnson, Meyer, and Goshe 1989). In contrast, when attributes are negatively correlated (such as might arise if the consumer makes a choice from efficient sets of options, or choice sets which are screened for dominated alternatives), similar process misspecifications can dramatically hurt model performance. The implication is, therefore, that concern over fitting the "right" choice model may begin with a simple consideration of the correlational structure of the environment; the more forgiving the environment, the less one needs to worry about instability in processes.

Given that correct specification *is* a critical issue in a given modeling setting, a natural concern is whether changes in the set of options might induce changes in the way choices are made, implying a constant need to reconsider the propriety of a given estimated model form. Ideally, we would like to be in a position of predicting such effects a priori; in particular, we need models which characterize how consumers "decide how to decide."

The dominant current conjecture about how consumers formulate strategies for choice is that such strategies are the result of intuitive cost/benefit calculations. Specifically, consumers are presumed to learn the ability of differing choice strategies to yield "optimal" outcomes, and to learn the robustness of differing rules to changes in the decision environment. (See Chapter 2 by Bettman, Johnson, and Payne in this volume for a more extensive discussion.) In any given context the consumer is thus thought to select that rule which yields the highest expected outcome at the lowest cognitive effort. General normative treatments of this problem have been offered by Johnson and Payne (1985) and Shugan (1979), with norma-

tive solutions for optimal elimination strategies offered by Grether and Wilde (1984) and Huber and Klein (1989).

Empirical tests of cost/benefit models of strategy selection have yielded mixed results. On one hand, strong apparent support for cost/benefit models of strategy selection has surfaced in a number of studies of the effect of choice set size on choice rules (e.g., Johnson and Meyer 1984; Johnson, Meyer, and Goshe 1989; Payne 1976, 1983; Payne, Bettman, and Johnson 1988). If consumers choose strategies through intuitive cost/benefit calculations, increases in choice set size should be associated with increases in the use of heuristic elimination rules, owing to increases in information load. Experimental results have consistently supported this prediction: As choice set sizes increase, consumers alter information search strategies in a way consistent with a switch from compensatory to noncompensatory rules, and this is manifested in changes in the parameters of discrete choice models (cf. Johnson and Meyer 1984). In addition, there is also evidence that consumers utilize more stringent cutoff criteria when using elimination rules (resulting in a shorter decision time) as the cost of deliberation increases, and when the risk of ending up with a suboptimal final choice decreases—something again consistent with cost/benefit models (e.g., Grether and Wilde 1984; Huber and Klein 1988).

On the other hand, support for more subtle features of context, such as the pattern of correlation among attributes, affecting rule selection has been more limited. For example, Johnson, Meyer, and Goshe (1989) conjectured that if consumers choose decision rules through intuitive cost/benefit calculations, the use of noncompensatory elimination heuristics should increase as interattribute correlations become more positive (due to the increased ability of simple heuristics to mimic compensatory combination rules). In a separate study, Klein and Yadav (1989) made the same prediction about the effect of interattribute correlations, although offering a somewhat different rationale for why positive correlations should be associated with increased use of eliminations strategies: because positive correlations imply the presence of dominated options, we should observe increased use of elimination strategies as a result of consumers screening these dominant options from consideration prior to a final choice. Neither study, however, found a sensitivity of choice strategies to interattribute correlation. A similar lack of support for the effects of correlation have also been reported in a study of how consumers set cutoffs in heuristic elimination strategies reported by Huber and Klein (1988).

Another possible direction work in "deciding how to decide" might take is to link the study of rule choice to the growing literature on judgment under ambiguity or vagueness (e.g., Einhorn and Hogarth 1985; Kahn and Sarin 1990). The rationale for this link is that rule selection clearly involves uncertainty; in general, the consumer will *not* know beforehand exactly how much effort will be involved executing a particular strategy, or what the payoffs of a particular strategy will be. Unfortunately, such uncertainty is not explicitly recognized in current cost/benefit models of strategy selection. An intriguing potential future area for research would thus be to investigate how consumers make rule selections, given varying levels of uncertainty about the likelihood that a given rule is, indeed, optimal and given the cost of using different rules.

Although we are unaware of investigators who have explored this issue, Kahn and Meyer (1990) have reported on a related investigation into how consumers choose decision weights in multiattribute judgment problems under uncertainty. Their central finding is that consumers act as if they are risk averse in weight selection — uncertainty about the weight of attributes which serve to enhance an already acceptable level of utility for a product (e.g., add-ons to a television) tend to be underweighted, whereas attributes which serve to preserve acceptable levels of utility for a product (e.g., insurance) tend to be overweighted. An interesting conjecture for future research is whether risk or vagueness aversion is also manifested in selections of choice rules. One possibility is that, *ceteris paribus,* the less certain consumers

are about the attributes of options in a choice set, the less likely they are to use simplified (and risky) heuristic elimination rules.

Finally, if a theory of choice models is to emerge, perhaps the most difficult problem to address is that of understanding learning, or of understanding how choice strategies change over time as consumers gain experience in a decision environment. Although we discussed work which addresses how consumers develop beliefs about the attributes of products, research on how consumers learn how to make choices is more limited. The absence of such work would seem particularly critical in new technology contexts; in such contexts, the key uncertainty facing consumers is how to integrate new technological improvements or attributes during the course of making a choice. As such, one might expect considerable variability in choice processes over time.

A recent body of research which might suggest a template for future work on the learning of choice rules is the literatures on multiple-cue learning (e.g., Castellan 1977; Klayman 1986). This literature examines the ability of individuals to learn algebraic combination rules through induction. Although we are aware of no work which has examined the learning of rules for choosing from discrete sets of options, findings in the learning of judgment rules may hold parallels. For example, Meyer (1987) found that given limited experience in a product category consumers tended to make evaluative judgments by noting how similar a given option was to his or her mental prototype of a "good" option in that product category. Early in learning judgments seem to be made in a noncompensatory (nonadditive) fashion, but over time these judgments became increasingly compensatory. An interesting area for future work would be to extend this domain of study to the acquisition of choice rules.

Other Future Directions

Perhaps more than any other literature in consumer research, the field of choice modeling is faced with the problem of reconciling the three great disciplinary traditions which underlie the field: psychology, economics, and applied marketing. Because of this position, researchers in the area face the seemingly impossible task of developing models that possess the rich explanatory power of psychological theories of decision making and possess the axiomatic rigor of economic theories, yet are amenable to widespread application in field settings. While the development of a meta theory of the field may be the most important long-term goal, there are also a large number of critical short-term problems which focus on achieving this reconciliation among the various disciplinary traditions.

One such direction is to develop stronger links between the literature of choice models and the broader range of consumer choice application problems. One example is that of consumer planning, or sequential decisions (e.g., Urban and Hauser 1987). This is a context where heuristic models might demonstrate their greatest value; a good illustration of such an application was offered by Hayes-Roth and Hayes-Roth (1978), who described a prototype heuristic model of how individuals plan sequences of activities under time constraints. While, in theory, one could represent this same planning process as a nested string of random utility models (each characterizing an activity choice), the approach would be excessively cumbersome, particularly given multiple decisions.

The largest existing barrier to a wider use of heuristic choice models as an approach to modeling sequential decisions, however, is the difficulty of utilizing traditional inferential techniques to infer models. If the analyst has no prior hypothesis about how a consumer conducts plans, the recovery of a unique hierarchical plan requires the observation of a factorial array of contingent plans (e.g., "given that you did A in time $t - 1$ and B in time $t - 2$, what would you do in time t?"). Because this data requirement becomes excessive with increasing numbers of planned activities, such models have traditionally relied on consumers' own accounts of their planning processes (as revealed though verbal protocols) as a basis for estimation. Modeling techniques that minimize the reliance on introspective accounts would thus seem to be an important area for future development. Currim, Meyer, and Le's (1988) and Smith, Clark, and Cotton's (1984) exploration of the use of algorithms to infer heuristic choice rules illustrates one possible direction.

Other related domains of consumer decisions are those of purchase timing and quantity selection. Although choice models of this type have begun to appear (e.g., Gupta 1988), they are largely at an embryonic stage. The largest difficulty facing the formulation of such models is that consideration sets are often difficult to specify, and normative models of how such decisions *should* be made seem implausible as descriptive devices. For example, consider the deceptively simple problem of modeling the number of units of a desired good that a consumer will choose to buy when that good is on sale at a supermarket. While one could model the choice as one among several possible quantities, each having a utility level (e.g., Gupta 1988), such a model would fail to capture the rather complex thought processes which *should* underlie such a decision. Specifically, purchase quantities should be driven by an explicit consideration of how a given purchase quantity will impact later decisions, such as one's ability to stock up on an even lower price which may occur later. An important focus of future research would be to explore the development of parsimonious models which capture such considerations.

Future research would also seem usefully directed toward the problem of group choice, or choices which are driven by a negotiation process. Although there exists a large and growing literature of models of group decision making (e.g., Davis 1976; Corfman and Lehmann 1987; Webster and Wind 1972), it has tended to remain separate from that of individual choice theory. An interesting area for future work would be to assess the extent to which many of the results on individual choice, such as the effects of context, are also manifested in group decisions, and whether parsimonious means for estimating group choice models can be developed.

Finally, efforts should also be directed toward expanding the domain of outside disciplinary traditions from which insights about choice behavior are drawn. As we have noted, the existing literature in formal choice models is dominated by work drawn from two areas: mathematical psychology and microeconomics. While one presumes that these ties will continue to be pervasive, the recent literature offers examples of how other areas can be useful for offering insights into modeling structures and methods. Illustrations include the work by Roberts and Urban (1987) and Horsky and Rabin (1988), who use theoretical models of sequential decision making developed in economics and statistics to suggest models for new product forecasting. Similarly, Greene and Smith's (1988) work on hierarchical model estimation draws its roots from inference algorithms first used to build expert systems in artificial intelligence. We presume that the future literature will provide an even richer array of examples.

REFERENCES

AAKER, DAVID A. (1970). "A New Method for Evaluating Stochastic Models of Brand Choice," *Journal of Marketing Research,* VII, 300–306.

AMEMIYA, TAKESHI (1981). "Qualitative Response Models: A Survey," *Journal of Economic Literature,* 19 (December), 1483–1536.

ANDERSON, NORMAN H. (1981). *Foundations of Information Integration Theory.* New York: Academic Press.

BATSELL, RICHARD R., and POLKING, JOHN C. (1985). "A New Class of Market Share Models," *Marketing Science,* 4 (Summer), 177–198.

BATSELL, RICHARD R. (1982). "A Multiattribute Extension of the Luce Model Which Simultaneously Scales Utility and Substitutability," in J. Huber (Ed.), *The Effect of Item Similarity on Choice Probabilities.* Durham, NC: Fuqua School of Business, Duke University, 4–23.

BAWA, KAPIL (forthcoming). "Modeling Inertia and Variety-Seeking Tendencies in Brand Choice Behavior," *Marketing Science.*

BEN-AKIVA, MOSHE, and LERMAN, STEVEN (1985). *Discrete Choice Analysis: Theory and Application to Predicting Travel Demand.* Cambridge, MA: MIT Press.

BETTMAN, JAMES R. (1971). "Information Processing Models of Consumer Behavior," *Journal of Marketing Research,* 7 (August), 370–376.

BETTMAN, JAMES R. (1981). *An Information Processing Theory of Consumer Choice.* Reading, MA: Addison-Wesley.

BETTMAN, JAMES R. (1987). "Process of Adaptivity in Decision Making," in M.J. Houston (Ed.), *Advances in Consumer Research,* 15, 1–4.

BORGERS, ALOYS, and TIMMERMANS, HARRY. "A Context-Sensitive Model of Spatial Choice Behavior," in R. G. Golledge and H. Timmermans (Eds.), *Behavioral Modelling in Geography and Planning.* London: Croom-Helm, 159–178.

BRADLEY, RALPH A., and TERRY, M. E. (1952). "Rand Analysis of Incomplete Block Designs, I: The Method of Paired Comparisons," *Biometrika,* 39, 324–345.

BREIMAN, LEO, FRIEDMAN, JEROME, OLSHEN, RICHARD, and STONE, CHARLES (1984). *Classification and Regression Trees.* Monterey, CA: Wadsworth and Brooks.

BUSH, ROBERT R., and MOSTELLER, FREDERICK (1955). *Stochastic Models for Learning.* New York: Wiley.

CARMAN, JAMES M. (1966). "Brand Switching and Linear Learning Models," *Journal of Advertising Research,* 6 (June), 23–31.

CARPENTER, GREGORY S., COOPER, LEE G., HANSSENS, DOMINIQUE M., and MIDGLEY, DAVID F. (1989). "Modeling Asymmetric Competition," *Marketing Science,* 7 (Fall), 393–412.

CARPENTER, GREGORY S., and LEHMANN, DONALD R. (1985). "A Model of Marketing Mix, Brand Switching, and Competition," *Journal of Marketing Research,* 22 (August), 318–329.

CARROLL, J. DOUGLAS (1972). "Individual Differences and Multidimensional Scaling," in R. N. Shepard, A. K. Rommey, and S. Nerlove (Eds.), *Multidimensional Scaling: Theory and Applications in the Social Sciences, Vol. 1: Theory.* New York: Seminar Press, 105–155.

CASTELLAN, J. JOHN (1977). "Decision Making with Multiple Probabilistic Cues," in N. John Castellan, N. B. Pisoni, and G. R. Potts (Eds.), *Cognitive Theory,* Vol. 2. Hillsdale, NJ: Erlbaum.

CHAKRAVARTI, DIPANKAR, and LYNCH, JOHN G. (1983). "A Framework for Exploring Context Effects on Consumer Judgment and Choice," in

R. Bagozzi and A. Tybout (Eds.), *Advances in Consumer Research*, 10, 289–297.

COOPER, LEE G., and NAKANISHI, MASAO (1983a). "Standardizing Variables in Multiplicative Choice Models," *Journal of Consumer Research*, 10, (June), 96–108.

COOPER, LEE G., and NAKANISHI, MASAO (1988). *Market Share Analysis: Evaluating Competitive Marketing Effectiveness*. New York: Kluwer.

COOPER, LEE G. (1988). "Competitive Maps: The Structure Underlying Asymmetric Cross Elasticities," *Management Science*, 34 (June), 707–723.

COOPER, LEE G., and NAKANISKI, MASAO (1983b). "Two Logit Models for External Analysis of Preferences," *Psychometrika*, 48 (December), 607–620.

CORFMAN, KIM P., and LEHMANN, DONALD R. (1987). "Models of Cooperative Group Decision-Making and Relative Influence," *Journal of Consumer Research*, 14 (June), 1–13.

CORSTJENS, MARCEL L., and GAUTSCHI, DAVID A. (1983). "Formal Choice Models in Marketing," *Marketing Science*, 2 (Winter), 19–56.

CURRIM, IMRAN S. (1981). "Using Segmentation Approaches for Better Prediction and Understanding from Consumer Mode Choice Models," *Journal of Marketing Research*, 18 (August), 301–309.

CURRIM, IMRAN S. (1982). "Predictive Testing of Consumer Choice Models Not Subject to Independence of Irrelevant Alternatives," *Journal of Marketing Research*, 19 (May), 308–322.

CURRIM, IMRAN S., MEYER, ROBERT J., and LE, NHAN (1988). "Disaggregate Tree-Structured Modeling of Consumer Choice Data," *Journal of Marketing Research*, 25 (August), 253–265.

CURRY, DAVID, and FAULDS, DAVID (1985). "Indexing Product Quality: Issues, Theory, and Results," *Journal of Consumer Research*, 31(1), 134–145.

DAGANZO, CARLOS (1979). *Multinomial Probit: The Theory and Applications to Demand Forecasting*. New York: Academic Press.

DALAL, S. R., and KLEIN, R. W. (1988). "A Flexible Class of Discrete Choice Models," *Marketing Science*, 7 (Summer), 232–251.

DAVIS, HARRY L. (1976). "Decision Making within the Household," *Journal of Consumer Research*, 2 (March), 241–260.

DAWES, ROBYN M., and CORRIGAN, BERNARD (1974). "Linear Models in Decision Making," *Psychological Bulletin*, 81(2), 95–106.

DEBREU, G. (1960). "Review of R.D. Luce, Individual Choice Behavior: A Theoretical Analysis," *American Economic Review*, 50, 186–188.

DESARBO, WAYNE S., DE SOETE, GEERT, CARROLL, J. DOUGLAS, and RAMASWAMY, V. (1987). "A New Stochastic Ultrametric Unfolding Methodology for Assessing Competitive Market Structure and Deriving Market Segments," Working Paper, Wharton School of Business, University of Pennsylvania, Philadelphia, PA.

DESARBO, WAYNE S., and DE SOETE, GEERT (1984). "On the Use of Hierarchical Clustering for the Analysis of Nonsymmetric Proximities," *Journal of Consumer Research*, 11 (June), 601–610.

DOMENCICH, T., and McFADDEN, D. (1975). *Urban Travel Demand: A Behavioral Analysis*. Amsterdam: North Holland.

DUBIN, JEFFREY. "A Nested Logit Model of Space and Water Heat System Choice," *Marketing Science*, 5 (Spring), 112–124.

DUNN, RICHARD, READER, S., and WRIGLEY, NEIL (1987). "A Non-Parametric Approach to the Incorporation of Heterogeneity into Repeated Polytomous Choice Models of Urban Shopping Behavior," *Transportation Research A*, 21, 327–345.

DUNN, RICHARD, and WRIGLEY, NEIL (1985). "Beta-Logistic Models of Urban Shopping Behavior," *Geographical Analysis*, 17, 95–113.

EAGLE, THOMAS C. (1984). "Parameter Instability in Disaggregate Retail Choice Models: Experimental Evidence," *Journal of Retailing*, 60, 101–123.

EHRENBERG, A. S. C. (1959). "The Pattern of Consumer Purchases," *Applied Statistics*, 8, 26–41.

EINHORN, HILLEL, and HOGARTH, ROBIN (1985). "Ambiguity and Uncertainty in Probabilistic Inference," *Psychological Review*, 92, 433–461.

ELROD, TERRY (1988). "Choice Map: Inferring a Product Map from Panel Data," *Marketing Science*, 7 (Winter), 21–40.

FOTHERINGHMAN, A. STEWART (1988). "Consumer Store Choice and Choice Set Definition," *Marketing Science*, 7 (Summer), 299–310.

FEINBERG, FRED, KAHN, BARBARA, and McALISTER, LEIGH (1990). "Market Share Response when Consumers Seek Variety," Working Paper, Fuqua School of Business, Duke University, Durham, NC.

FISCHER, GREGORY, and NAGIN, DANIEL (1981). "Fixed Versus Random Coefficient Quantal Choice Models," in C. F. Manski and D. McFadden (Eds.), *Structural Analysis of Discrete Data with Econometric Applications.* Cambridge, MA: MIT Press, 273–304.

FORD, GARY T., and SMITH RUTH ANN (1987). "Inferential Beliefs in Consumer Evaluations: An Assessment of Alternative Processing Strategies," *Journal of Consumer Research,* 14 (December), 363–371.

GAUDRY, M. J. I., and WILLS, MICHAEL J. (1979). "Testing the Dogit Model With Aggregate Time-Series and Cross-Sectional Travel Data," *Transportation Research B,* 13, 155–166.

GAUDRY, MARC J. I., and DAGENAIS, M. G. (1979). "The Dogit Model," *Transportation Research B,* 12, 105–111.

GENSCH, DENNIS, and SVESTKA, J. (1984). "A Maximum-Likelihood Hierarchical Disaggregate Model for Predicting Choices of Individuals," *Journal of Mathematical Psychology,* 28 (June), 160–178.

GENSCH, DENNIS, and RECKER, WILFRIED W. (1979). "The Multinomial, Multiattribute Logit Choice Model," *Journal of Marketing Research,* 16 (February), 124–132.

GENSCH, DENNIS H. (1987a). "A Two-Stage Disaggregate Attribute Choice Model," *Marketing Science,* 6 (Summer), 223–240.

GENSCH, DENNIS H. (1985). "Empirically Testing a Disaggregate Choice Model for Segments," *Journal of Marketing Research,* 22 (November), 462–467.

GHOSH, AVIJIT, NESLIN, SCOTT, and SHOEMAKER, ROBERT (1984). "A Comparison of Market Share Models and Estimation Procedures," *Journal of Marketing Research,* 21 (May), 202–210.

GIVON, MOSHE, U. (1984). "Variety-Seeking Through Brand Switching," *Marketing Science,* 3 (Winter), 1–22.

GIVON, MOSHE U., and HORSKY, DAN (1978). "Market Share Models as Approximators of Aggregated Heterogeneous Brand Choice Behavior," *Management Science,* 24 (September), 1404–1416.

GIVON, MOSHE U., and HORSKY, DAN (1979). "Application of a Composite Stochastic Model of Brand Choice," *Journal of Marketing Research,* XVI (May), 158–167.

GREEN, PAUL, and WIND, YORAM (1973). *Multiattribute Decisions in Marketing: A Measurement Approach,"* Hinsdale, IL: Dryden Press.

GREENE, DAVID P., and SMITH, STEPHEN F. (1988). "A Genetic System for Learning Models of Consumer Choice," *IEEE Transactions,* 217–223.

GRETHER, and WILDE, LOUIS (1984). "An Analysis of Conjunctive Choice: Theory and Experiments," *Journal of Consumer Research,* 10 (March), 373–385.

GUADAGNI, PETER M., and LITTLE, JOHN D. C. (1983). "A Logit Model of Brand Choice Calibrated on Scanner Data," *Marketing Science,* 2 (Summer), 203–238.

GUADAGNI, PETER M. (1983). "A Nested Logit Model of Product Choice and Purchase Incidence," in F. S. Zufryden (Ed.), *Advances and Practices of Marketing Science 1983.* Providence, RI: Institute of Management Sciences.

GUPTA, SUNIL S. (1988). "Impact of Sales Promotions on What, When, and How Much to Buy," *Journal of Marketing Research,* XXV (November).

HAUSER, JOHN, and URBAN, GLEN L. (1986). "The Value Priority Hypotheses for Consumer Budget Plans," *Journal of Consumer Research,* 12 (March), 446–462.

HAUSMANN, J., and WISE, D. (1978). "A Conditional Probit Model for Qualitative Choice: Discrete Decisions Recognizing Interdependence and Heterogeneous Preferences," *Econometrica,* 46(2), 403–426.

HAYES-ROTH, BARBARA, and HAYES-ROTH, FREDERICK (1979). "A Cognitive Model of Planning," *Cognitive Science,* 3, 275–310.

HECKMAN, JAMES J. (1981). "Statistical Models for Discrete Panel Data," in C. F. Manski and D. McFadden (Eds.), *Structural Analysis of Discrete Data with Econometric Applications.* Cambridge, MA: MIT Press, 114–178.

HENSHER, DAVID A. (1984). "Achieving Representativeness of the Observable Component of the Indirect Utility Function in Logit Choice Models: An Empirical Revelation," *Journal of Business,* 265–280.

HENSHER, DAVID A., and JOHNSON, LESTER W. (1981). *Applied Discrete-Choice Modelling.* New York: Wiley.

HOROWITZ, JOEL (1980). "The Accuracy of the Multinomial Logit as an Approximation to the Multinomial Probit Model of Travel Demand," *Transportation Research B,* 14, 331–341.

HORSKY, DAN, and RABAN, YOEL (1988). "A Bayesian Updating Model of Dynamic Brand Choice Behavior." Paper presented at the meetings of the Marketing Science Conference, Seattle, WA.

HUBER, JOEL, and KLEIN, NOREEN (1988). "Choosing Which to Choose: A Model of Cutoff Selection in a Two-Stage Decision Process," Working Paper, Fuqua School of Business, Duke University, Durham, NC.

HUBER, JOEL, and MCCANN, JOHN (1982). "The Impact of Inferential Beliefs on Product Evaluations," *Journal of Marketing Research,* 19 (August), 324–333.

HUBER, JOEL, PAYNE, JOHN W., and PUTO, CHRISTOPHER (1982). "Adding Asymmetrically Dominated Alternatives: Violations of Regularity and the Similarity Hypothesis," *Journal of Consumer Research,* 9 (June), 90–98.

HUBER, JOEL, and PUTO, CHRISTOPHER (1983). "Marketing Boundaries and Product Choice: Illustrating Attraction and Substitution Effects," *Journal of Consumer Research,* 10 (June), 31–44.

HUBER, JOEL, and SEWALL, MURPHY (1982). "Market Structure From Indices of Competitive Substitutability," in A. Shocker and R. Srivastava (Eds.), *Analytic Approaches to Product and Market Planning: The Second Conference.* Boston, MA: Marketing Science Institute, 7–16.

HUTCHINSON, J. WESLEY (1983). "On the Locus of Range Effects in Judgment and Choice," in R. P. Bagozzi and A. Tybout (Eds.), *Advances in Consumer Research,* 10, 305–308.

HUTCHINSON, J. WESLEY (1986). "Discrete Attribute Models of Brand Switching," *Marketing Science,* 5 (Fall), 350–371.

JEULAND, ABEL P. (1979). "Brand Choice Inertia as One Aspect of the Notion of Brand Loyalty," *Management Science,* 25 (7), 671–682.

JEULAND, ABEL P. (1978). "Brand Preferences Over Time: A Partially Deterministic Operationization of the Notion of Variety-Seeking," in Subhash Jain (Ed.), *AMA Research Frontiers in Marketing: Dialogues and Directions,* Educators' Proceedings, Series No. 43, Chicago, IL: American Marketing Association, 33–37.

JOHNSON, RICHARD D., and LEVIN, IRWIN P. (1985). "More Than Meets the Eye: The Effect of Missing Information on Purchase Evaluations," *Journal of Consumer Research,* 12 (September), 169–177.

JOHNSON, ERIC J., and MEYER, ROBERT J. (1984). "Compensatory Choice Models of Noncompensatory Choice Processes: The Effect of Varying Context," *Journal of Consumer Research,* 11 (June), 528–541.

JOHNSON, ERIC J., MEYER, ROBERT J., and GHOSE, SANJOY (1989). "When Choice Models Fail: Compensatory Models in Negatively-Correlated Environments," *Journal of Marketing Research,* 26 (August).

JOHNSON, ERIC J., and PAYNE, JOHN W. (1985). "Effort and Accuracy in Choice," *Management Science,* 30, 1213–1231.

JOHNSON, LESTER, and HENSHER, DAVID (1982), "Application of Multinomial Probit to a Two-Period Panel Data Set," *Transportation Research A,* 16 (5–6), 457–464.

JONES, J. MORGAN (1970). "A Comparison of Three Models of Brand Choice," *Journal of Marketing Research,* VII (November), 466–73.

JONES, J. MORGAN, and ZUFRYDEN, FRED (1980). "Adding Explanatory Variables to a Consumer Purchase Behavior Model: An Exploratory Study," *Journal of Marketing Research,* 17 (August), 323–334.

KAHN, BARBARA E., KALWANI, MANOHAR U., and MORRISON, DONALD G. (1986). "Measuring Variety-Seeking and Reinforcement Behaviors Using Panel Data," *Journal of Marketing Research,* XXIII (May), 89–100.

KAHN, BARBARA E., and LEHMANN, DONALD R. (1989). "Modeling Choice Among Menus," Working Paper, Anderson Graduate School of Management, University of California, Los Angeles, CA.

KAHN, BARBARA E., and LOUIE, THERESE (1990). "The Effects of Retractions of Price Promotions on Brand Choice Behavior for Variety-Seeking and Lost-Purchase-Loyal Consumers," *Journal of Marketing Research XXVII* (August).

KAHN, BARBARA E., and MEYER, ROBERT J. (1990). "A Model of Multiattribute Attribute Judgments Under Attribute Weight Uncertainty," *Journal of Consumer Research* (December 1990.)

KAHN, BARBARA E., MOORE, WILLIAM L., and GLAZER, RASHI (1987). "Experiments in Constrained Choice," *Journal of Consumer Research,* 14 (June), 96–113.

KAHN, BARBARA E., MORRISON, DONALD, and WRIGHT, GORDON P. (1986). "Aggregating Individual Purchases to the Household Level," *Marketing Science* 5 (Summer), 260–268.

KAHN, BARBARA E., and RAJU, JAGMOHAN (1989). "A Stochastic Model of the Effects of Frequency of Promotions on Brand Choice," Working Paper, Anderson Graduate School of Management, University of California, Los Angeles, CA.

KAHN, BARBARA E. and SARIN, RAKESH K. (1990). "Modeling Ambiguity in Decisions Under Uncertainty," *Journal of Consumer Research,* 15 (September), 265–273.

KAMAKURA, WAGNER A., and SRIVASTAVA, RAJENDRA K. (1985). "Predicting Choice Shares Under Conditions of Brand Interdependence," *Journal of Marketing Research,* 21 (November), 420–433.

KAMAKURA, WAGNER A., and SRIVASTAVA, RAJENDRA K. (1986). "An Ideal-Point Probabilistic Choice Model for Heterogeneous Preferences," *Marketing Science,* 5 (Summer), 199–218.

KEENEY, RALPH, and RAIFFA, HOWARD (1976). *Decisions With Multiple Objectives: Preferences and Value Tradeoffs.* New York: Wiley.

KLAYMAN, JEOSHUA (1986). "Experimentation, Observation, and Learning in Probabilistic Environments," Working Paper No. 117, Center for Decision Research, Graduate School of Business, University of Chicago, Chicago, IL.

KLEIN, NOREEN and YADAV, MANJIT S. (1989). "Context Effects on Effort and Accuracy in Choice: An Enquiry into Adaptive Decision Making," *Journal of Consumer Research,* 15 (March), 411–421.

KRISHNAN, D S., and BECKMAN, M. J. (1979). "Dynamic Discrete Choice Models, With an Application in Transportation," *Decision Sciences,* 10, 218–231.

KUEHN, A. A. (1962). "Consumer Brand Choice – A Learning Process?" *Journal of Advertising Research,* Vol. II, 10–17.

LATTIN, JAMES M. (1987). "A Model of Balanced Choice Behavior," *Marketing Science,* 6 (Winter), 48–65.

LATTIN, JAMES M., and MCALISTER, LEIGH (1985). "Using a Variety-Seeking Model to Identify Substitute and Complimentary Relationships Among Competing Products," *Journal of Marketing Research,* 22 (August), 330–339.

LEHMANN, DONALD, and MOORE, WILLIAM L. (1989). "A Combined Simply Scalable and Tree-Based Preference Model," Working Paper, Graduate School of Business, Columbia University, New York, NY.

LIPSTEIN, BENJAMIN (1959). "The Dynamics of Brand Loyalty and Brand Switching," Proceed-

ings, Fifth Annual Conference of the Advertising Research Foundation, New York, NY.

LOUVIERE, JORDAN J., and WOODWORTH, GEORGE (1983). "Design and Analysis of Simulated Consumer Choice or Allocation Experiments: An Approach Based on Aggregate Data," *Journal of Marketing Research,* 20 (November), 350–367.

LOUVIERE, JORDAN J., and MEYER, ROBERT J. (1981). "A Composite Attitude-Behavior Model of Traveler Decision Making," *Transportation Research,* 5, 411–420.

LOUVIERE, JORDAN J. (1988). *Metric Conjoint Analysis,* New York: Sage.

LOUVIERE, JORDAN J. (1981). "On the Identification of the Functional Form of the Utility Expression and Its Relationship to Discrete Choice," in D. A. Hensher and L. Johnson (Eds.), *Applied Discrete-Choice Modeling.* London: Croom-Helm, 385–416.

LUCE, R. DUNCAN (1977). "The Choice Axiom After Twenty Years," *Journal of Mathematical Psychology,* 15, 215–233.

LUCE, R. DUNCAN (1959). *Individual Choice Behavior.* New York: Wiley.

LYNCH, JOHN G. (1985). "Uniqueness Issues in the Decompositional Modeling of Multiattribute Overall Evaluations: An Information Integration Perspective," *Journal of Marketing Research,* 22 (February), 1–19.

MALHOTRA, NARESH K. (1984). "The Use of Linear Logit Models in Marketing Research," *Journal of Marketing Research,* 21 (February), 20–31.

MANRAI, AJAY K., and SINHA, PRABHAKANT (1989). "Elimination by Cutoffs," *Marketing Science,* 8 (Spring), 133–152.

MASSY, WILLIAM F., MONTGOMERY, DAVID B., and MORRISON, DONALD G. (1970). *Stochastic Models of Buying Behavior.* Cambridge, MA: MIT Press.

MCALISTER, LEIGH (1982). "A Dynamic Attribute Satiation Model of Variety-Seeking Behavior," *Journal of Consumer Research,* 9 (September), 141–151.

MCALISTER, LEIGH, and PESSEMIER, EDGAR (1982). "Variety Seeking Behavior: An Interdisciplinary Review," *Journal of Consumer Research,* 9 (December), 311–322.

McCONNELL (1968). "Repeat-Purchasing Estimation and the Linear Learning Model," *Journal of Marketing Research,* 3 (August), 304–306.

McFADDEN, DANIEL (1986). "The Choice Theory Approach to Marketing Research," *Marketing Science,* 5 (Fall), 275–297.

McFADDEN, DANIEL (1981). "Econometric Models of Probabilistic Choice," in C. F. Manski and D. McFadden (Eds.), *Structural Analysis of Discrete Data with Econometric Applications.* Cambridge, MA: MIT Press, 198–272.

McFADDEN, DANIEL (1979). "Modeling the Choice of Residential Location," *Transportation Research Record,* 673, 72–78.

MEYER, ROBERT J. (1981). "A Model of Multiattribute Judgment Under Attribute Uncertainty and Informational Constraint," *Journal of Marketing Research,* 18 (November), 428–441.

MEYER, ROBERT J. (1982). "A Descriptive Model of Consumer Information Search Behavior," *Marketing Science,* 1 (Winter), 93–121.

MEYER, ROBERT J. (1985). "On The Representation and Measurement of Consumer Choice Under Limited Information," in R. Lutz (Ed.), *Marketing Communications: Proceedings of the Winter Educators' Conference.* Chicago: American Marketing Association.

MEYER, ROBERT J., and COOPER, LEE G. (1988). "A Longitudinal Choice Analysis of Consumer Response to a Product Innovation," in R. G. Golledge and H. Timmermans (Eds.), *Behavioral Modelling in Geography and Planning.* London: Croom-Helm, 424–450.

MEYER, ROBERT J., and EAGLE, THOMAS C. (1982). "Context-Induced Parameter Instability in a Disaggregate-Stochastic Model of Store Choice," *Journal of Marketing Research,* 19 (February), 62–71.

MEYER, ROBERT J., and LOUVIERE, JORDAN J. (1981). "Multiattribute Parameter Shifting: An Approach to Modeling Context and Dominance Effects in Individual Choice Behavior," in J. Huber (Ed.), *The Effect of Item Similarity on Choice Probabilities.* Durham, NC: Fuqua School of Business, Duke University.

MEYER, ROBERT J., and SATHI, ARVIND (1985). "A Multiattribute Model of Consumer Choice During Product Learning," *Marketing Science,* 4 (Winter), 41–61.

MOORE, WILLIAM L., LEHMANN, DONALD R., and PESSEMIER, EDGAR A. (1986). "Hierarchical Representations of Market Structure and Choice Processes Through Preference Trees," *Journal of Business Research,* 14, 371–386.

MOORE, WILLIAM L., LEHMANN, DONALD R., and PESSEMIER, EDGAR A. (1989). "A Paired Comparison Nested Logit Model of Individual Preference Structures," *Journal of Marketing Research,* 26 (November), 420–428.

MORRISON, DONALD G. (1966). "Testing Brand Switching Models," *Journal of Marketing Research,* III (November), 401–409.

NAKANISHI, MASAO, and COOPER, LEE G. (1974). "Parameter Estimation for a Multiplicative Interaction Model–Least Squares Approach," *Journal of Marketing Research,* 11 (August), 303–311.

NESLIN, SCOTT A., HENDERSON, CAROLINA, and QUELCH, JOHN (1985). "Consumer Promotions and the Acceleration of Product Purchases," *Marketing Science,* 4 (Summer), 147–165.

NEWMAN, J. ROBERT (1977). "Differential Weighting in Multiattribute Utility Theory: Where it Should and Where is Does Make a Difference," *Organizational Behavior and Human Performance,* 20 (December), 312–325.

ONAKA, J., and CLARK, WILLIAM A. V. (1983). "A Disaggregate Model of Residential Mobility and Housing Choice," *Geographical Analysis,* 15, 287–304.

PAYNE, JOHN W. (1983). "Contingent Decision Behavior," *Psychological Bulletin,* 92 (September), 382–402.

PAYNE, JOHN W. (1976). "Task Complexity and Contingent Processing in Decision Making: An Information Search and Protocol Analysis," *Organizational Behavior and Human Performance,* 16 (August), 366–387.

PAYNE, JOHN W., BETTMAN, JAMES R., and JOHNSON, ERIC J. (1988). "Adaptive Strategy Selection in Decision Making," *Journal of Experimental Psychology: Human Learning, Memory, and Cognition.*

PUNJ, GIRISH, and STAELIN, RICHARD (1978). "The Choice Process for Graduate Business Schools, *Journal of Marketing Research,* 25 (November), 588–598.

RAO, VITHALA R., and SABAVALA, DARIUS JAL (1981). "Inference of Hierarchical Choice Processes from Panel Data," *Journal of Consumer Research,* 8 (June), 85–96.

RATNESHWAR, SRINIVASAN, SHOCKER, ALLAN D., and STEWART, DAVID W. (1987). "Toward an Understanding of the Attraction Effect: The Implications of Product Stimulus Meaningfulness and Familiarity," *Journal of Consumer Research,* 13 (March), 520–533.

RECKER, WILLIAM W., and GOLOB, THOMAS F. (1979). "A Noncompensatory Model of Transportation Behavior Based on a Sequential Consideration of Attributes," *Transportation Research B*, 13, 269–280.

RICHARDS, ANTHONY (1982). "Search Models and Choice Set Generation." *Transportation Research A*, 16, 403–419.

ROBERTS, JOHN H., and URBAN, GLEN (1988). "Modeling Multiattribute Utility, Risk, and Belief Dynamics for New Consumer Durable Brand Choice," *Management Science*, 34 (February), 167–185.

ROTONDO, JOHN (1986). "Price as an Aspect of Choice in EBA," *Marketing Science*, 5 (Fall), 391–402.

RUSSO, JAY E., and DOSHER, BARBARA E. (1983). "Strategies for Multiattribute Binary Choice," *Journal of Experimental Psychology: Learning, Memory, and Cognition*, 9 (October), 676–696.

SCHMITTLEIN, DAVID C. (1986). "Which Preference Distributions Lead to Luce's Choice Model?" Working Paper, Department of Marketing, The Wharton School of Business, University of Pennsylvania, Philadelphia, PA.

SHARMA, SUBHASH, and DURAND, RICHARD (1980). "Using the Linear Learning Model to Represent Variety-Seeking Behavior," American Marketing Association Educators' Conference Proceedings, Series NO. 46, 148–151.

SILK, ALVIN J., and URBAN, GLEN (1978). "Pre-Test Market Evaluation of New Packaged Goods: A Model and Measurement Methodology," *Journal of Marketing Research*, 15 (May), 171–191.

SRINIVASAN, V., and KESAVAN, R. (1976). "An Alternate Interpretation of the Linear Learning Model of Brand Choice," *Journal of Consumer Research*, 3 (September), 76–83.

STECKEL, JOEL H., and VANHONACKER, WILFRIED R. (1988). "A Heterogeneous Conditional Logit Model of Choice," *Journal of Business and Economic Statistics*, 6 (July), 391–398.

SUGITO, YOSHIHIRO (1986). *A Dynamic Probit Model of Brand Choice: Model Development and Application to Consumer Dealing*, Unpublished Ph.D dissertation, Anderson Graduate School of Management, University of California, Los Angeles, CA.

TELSER, LESTER G. (1962). "The Demand for Consumer Goods as Estimated from Consumer Panel Data," *Review of Economics and Statistics*, 44, 471–499.

THURSTONE, L. L. (1927). "A Law of Comparative Judgment," *Psychological Review*, 34, 273–286.

THURSTONE, L. L. (1959). *The Measurement of Values*. Chicago: University of Chicago Press.

TRAIN, KENNETH (1986). *Qualitative Choice Analysis*. Cambridge, MA: MIT Press.

TVERSKY, AMOS, and SATTATH, SHUMEL (1979). "Preference Trees," *Psychological Review*, 86 (November) 542–573.

TVERSKY, AMOS (1972). "Elimination By Aspects: A Theory of Choice," *Psychological Review*, 79 (4), 281–299.

WEBSTER, FREDERICK E., and WIND, YORHAM (1972). "A General Model of Organizational Buying Behavior," *Journal of Marketing*, 36 (April), 12–19.

WINER, RUSSELL S. (1986). "A Reference Price Model of Brand Choice for Frequently Purchased Products," *Journal of Consumer Research*, 13 (September), 250–256.

WRIGLEY, NEIL, LONGLEY, PAUL, and DUNN, RICHARD (1984). "Some Recent Developments in the Specification, Estimation, and Testing of Discrete Choice Models," in *Categorical Data Analysis for Geographers and Environmental Scientists*. London: Longman.

WRIGLEY, NEIL, LONGLEY, PAUL, and DUNN, RICHARD (1988). "Some Recent Developments in the Specification, Estimation, and Testing of Discrete Choice Models," in R. G. Golledge and H. Timmermans (Eds.), *Behavioral Modelling in Geography and Planning*. London: Croom-Helm, 96–123.

YAMAGISHI, TOSHIO, and HILL, CHARLES T. (1983). "Initial Impression Versus Missing Information as Explanations for the Set-Size Effect," *Journal of Personality and Social Psychological*, 44 (5), 942–951.

YELLOTT, J. I. (1977). "The Relationship Between Luce's Choice Axiom, Thurstone's Theory of Comparative Judgment, and the Double Exponential Distribution," *Journal of Mathematical Psychology*, 15, 109–144.

ZUFRYDEN, FRED S. (1980). "A Multivariate Stochastic Model of Brand Choice and Market Behavior," in J. Sheth, (Ed.), *Research in Marketing*, Vol. 3. Greenwich, CT: JAI Press, 273–303.

ZUFRYDEN, FRED S. (1981). "A Logit-Markovian Model of Consumer Purchase Behavior Based on Explanatory Variables," *Decision Sciences*, 12, (October), 645–660.

ZUFRYDEN, FRED S. (1986). "Multibrand Transition Probabilities as a Function of Explanatory Variables: Estimation by a Least-Squares Based Approach," *Journal of Marketing Research*, XXIII (May), 177–183.

THE ROLE OF PSYCHOPHYSIOLOGY IN CONSUMER RESEARCH

4

Richard P. Bagozzi
The University of Michigan

The purpose of this chapter is to (1) develop a conceptual framework for using physiological measures in consumer research, (2) review and critique relevant empirical research, and (3) set an agenda for future research. To set the tone, three basic psychophysiological prototypes are described consisting of cognitive processes as antecedents of physiological responses, affective processes as antecedents of psychological responses, and physiological responses as antecedents of psychological processes. Next, the nature of psychophysiological inference is considered. Particular focus is given to the meaning of arousal, the definitions of key terms, measurement issues, and a framework for representing the relationships between psychological and physiological variables. Following this the central studies in the literature are scrutinized. This is done for both research in psychology and research in consumer behavior. The chapter then ends with a presentation of several fundamental areas that must be addressed if progress is to be made in the use of physiological measures in consumer research.

INTRODUCTION

Physiological measures were used in consumer research as early as the 1920s, when professor of psychology A. R. Gilliland and his students at Northwestern University applied the psychogalvanometer to evaluate responses to advertisements (Wesley 1978). Yet despite many such applications by other practitioners in the ensuing years, interest in physiological measures by academic consumer researchers has been marked by cycles involving both strong interest and then ambivalence. The cycle typically begins with high hopes that physiological procedures will constitute universal and potentially infallible methods for assessing the efficacy of alternative marketing stimuli. The cycle ends, temporarily, in frustration and disillusionment when it is learned how difficult it is to apply physiological instrumentation and how complex it is to interpret the resulting data. The love/hate relationship with physiological measurement resumes when a new generation of researchers comes to see physiological procedures as an *elixir vitae* for its measurement problems. Only the providers of commercial marketing research seem able to maintain a high level of enthusiasm for, and use of, physiological measurements (Hopkins 1987).

There is a touch of irony in the mixed reception received by physiological procedures in consumer research, for a number of real advantages can be identified with their use. Physiological measures can be taken as indicators or markers of psychological processes in real time (i.e., as the processes actually occur). They reflect real manifestations of mental, hormonal, and/or motor activities that are intimately associated with information processing, emotional reactions, decision making and choice, and nonvolitional actions. Self-reports, in contrast, are generally retrospective and involve a translation or self-interpretation of one's own mental or behavioral symptoms. The perceived expectations, actual or imagined, of a person, group, or institution with whom one interacts in relation to the elicitation of the self-reports, or with whom one has interacted in the past, or by whom one might ultimately be influenced in the future, can also affect self-reports in ways at odds with the actual inner states of the subjects. At the same time, consumers are not always able to be aware of their thoughts and feelings, are often unable to retrieve them reliably from memory, are apt to frequently alter their remembrances and interpretations of events and experiences through unconscious construction processes, and are even motivated on occasion to conceal or distort their self-reports. Physiological measures offer the opportunity to circumvent most of these problems, and they provide additional advantages that will be discussed later.

Be that as it may, what then accounts for the ambivalent reactions to physiological measures so often noted among researchers? It is easy to dismiss this vacillation as primarily a techno-

logical issue rooted in the need for sophisticated electronic equipment, knowledgeable technicians, and special computer software for controlling data collection and transforming observations into a usable form. However, this author believes that the lack of real progress in consumer research with the use of physiological measures stems more from the point of view followed by researchers to date than from any technological complexities that exist. Indeed, it is a premise of this review that if we are to break out of the unproductive cycle noted previously we must shift emphasis away from measurement in its narrow sense and stress the interplay between theory and method in its broadest sense (e.g., Bagozzi 1984).

To do this requires that we come to see physiological measurement as an addition to, or an augmenter of, the experimental method and that our inquiries progress to an integration of this method with the tests and explorations of psychological and social psychological theories in consumer research. Consumer research to date has tended to focus more on the physiological *measurement* of responses in isolation rather than examining the *theoretical linkages* between physiological data and psychological constructs.

One goal of this review will be to develop a conceptual framework for using physiological measures in consumer research that is grounded in recent developments in psychophysiology, a new and burgeoning subfield in psychology (e.g., Cacioppo and Petty 1983b; Cacioppo and Tassinary, in press, a; Coles, Dorchin, and Proges 1986; Wagner and Manstead 1989). The review will begin with a definition and statement of the role and significance of psychophysiology. Next, three prototypes will be presented as fruitful exemplars for future consumer research. Following this, the logic of psychophysiological inference will be explored. A second goal of this chapter will be to review relevant empirical research. Because the use of physiological measurements in consumer research has been both sparse and, with few exceptions (e.g., Cacioppo and Petty 1982c; Olson and Ray 1983), ungrounded in psychological theory, an effort will be made to select key studies from the literature of psychology that have direct pertinence for consumer researchers. In addition, recent studies in the consumer research literature, as well as some from the past, will be considered. But because thorough reviews have already appeared in the past decade (e.g., Klebba 1985; Stewart and Furse 1982), no attempt is made to be exhaustive. The chapter closes with an agenda for future research.

PSYCHOPHYSIOLOGY

Psychophysiology is "the scientific study of social, psychological, and behavioral phenomena . . . as related to and revealed through physiological principles and events in humans" (Cacioppo and Tassinary, in press, b). Psychophysiological inquiry most often consists of the manipulation of social or psychological variables, the monitoring of physiological responses as dependent variables, and the interpretation of the results in the light of specific hypotheses designed to test processes underlying the interactions between people or the mental or emotional responses occurring within an individual (e.g., Furedy 1983). Less frequently, physiological events have been manipulated as independent variables and psychological processes or behaviors measured as dependent variables (e.g., Cacioppo 1979). We will discuss both forms of inquiry later when we examine the three psychophysiological prototypes suggested for consumer research.

Psychophysiology has a long history, dating back at least to the time of Alexander the Great, when Erasistratos used signs of sudden sweating, an irregular pulse rate, and stammering speech to diagnose the "love-sickness" of a boy for his stepmother (e.g., Mesulam and Perry 1972). Galen, a Roman physician in the second century A.D., proposed perhaps the first developed theory of psychophysiology (Brazier 1959). He postulated that human behavior was under the control of the flow of various fluids in the body ("humors"), which in turn were driven by organs and passed, in part, through the nerves. The theory was based on an hydraulic

analogue and set the tone for scientific discourse for nearly 1,500 years. Important landmarks in the post-Galen period, which corrected his work and went beyond it, include research on the heart and blood flow by Harvey (c. 1628), on electricity and muscle movement by Galvani (c. 1790), and on skin resistance by Vigouroux (c. 1880) and by Fere (c. 1888). The ideas of Darwin (c. 1870) on the origins and expression of emotions and James (c. 1880) on the psychology of emotions were also instrumental in developing psychophysiology. For a fuller accounting of the evolution of psychophysiology see the works of Bloom, Lazerson, and Hofstadtes (1985) and Brazier (1959).

The early twentieth century witnessed numerous progenitors of modern psychophysiology (e.g., Smith 1922; Syz 1926–1927). But psychophysiology as a scientific field of study is credited with beginning in the 1960s, when the journal *Psychophysiology* (1964) first began publication (Cacioppo and Tassinary, in press, b). So the field is in one sense quite new. Indeed, it has only been in the decade of the 1980s that the intellectual, methodological, and empirical dimensions of the field have been integrated. For example, in an impressive sequence of commentaries by Cacioppo and colleagues, as well as through the impact of their program of research on attitudes and social cognition (e.g., Cacioppo and Petty 1979a, 1981a; Cacioppo, Petty, Losch, and Kim 1986; Cacioppo, Petty, and Marshall-Goodell 1984; Cacioppo, Petty, and Morris 1985; Cacioppo, Petty, and Quintanor 1982), the philosophy of the principles of scientific inference (e.g., Popper 1968), measurement theory (Coombs, Dawes, and Tversky 1970), and the methodological axioms of experimental design (e.g., Cacioppo and Petty 1986, pp. 654–658; Campbell and Stanley 1963) have been combined in important ways with the technology of physiological measurement (e.g., Cacioppo and Dorfman 1987; Fridlund and Cacioppo 1986) and the test of physiological theories to yield a new foundation for psychophysiology (e.g., Cacioppo and Petty 1982a, 1983a; Cacioppo and Tassinary 1989, a, b; Cacioppo, Petty, and Tassinary 1989; Petty and Cacioppo 1983). It is largely this perspective that this review, supplemented by other points of view, draws upon.

To understand psychophysiological research, it is useful to obtain at least an introductory background in physiology, in psychophysiological recording procedures, in the design of psychological experiments, and in the substantive area pertaining to one's research interests. Obviously it is impossible to provide such a background here. An excellent, short introduction to psychophysiological principles, including discussions of physiology and its relation to psychophysiological responses, can be found in Cacioppo and Petty (1983a). A very readable presentation of measurement procedures in psychophysiology can be found in Stern, Ray, and Davis (1980). A deeper background is recommended for one interested in following the literature and can be pursued by beginning with the more detailed readings in Ackles, Jennings, and Coles (1985), Cacioppo and Tassinary (in press, a), Coles, Donchin, and Porges (1986), Gale and Edwards (1983), Martin and Venables (1980), Solomon and Phillips (1987), and Wagner and Manstead (1989).

THREE BASIC PSYCHOPHYSIOLOGICAL PROTOTYPES

Psychophysiology has developed in a number of directions and can be characterized by particular functional themes. For example, cognitive psychophysiology deals with the relationship between information processing and physiological processes. "The basic assumption of the cognitive psychophysiological approach is that cognitive activity is implemented in the nervous system by means of physiological changes" (Coles, Gratton, and Gehring 1987, p. 13). Social psychophysiology involves "the use of noninvasive procedures to study the relationships between actual or perceived physiological events and the verbal or behavioral effects of human association" (Cacioppo and Petty 1983a, p. 3; see also Cacioppo and Petty 1986; Cacioppo, Petty, and Tassinary 1989). Among

other areas, social psychophysiology has focussed upon persuasive communication, affective responses, cognitive dissonance, and social facilitation. Other functional themes exist as well, such as clinical psychophysiology and developmental psychophysiology.

For purposes of discussion, it is useful to develop three distinctions that cut across the functional themes found in the literature of psychology. The distinctions are based on the ordering of independent and dependent variables, and they entail: cognitive processes as antecedents of physiological responses, affective processes as antecedents of physiological responses, and physiological events as antecedents of cognitive and affective processes. No attempt is made to be inclusive by using these categories. It is only claimed that these three distinctions serve as useful prototypes for the study of many theoretical and applied problems found in consumer research.

Cognitive Processes as Antecedents

For over a decade consumer research has been dominated by the information processing paradigm wherein consumer responses to marketing stimuli are explained through particular cognitive processes intervening between stimuli and responses (e.g., Bettman 1979a; Wright and Rip 1980). One typical approach is to manipulate environmental information (e.g., the number of brands or product attributes, the presentation of information organized by brand or type of attribute, the time available for deliberations, and the level of involvement) and then monitor self-report cognitive responses (e.g., information search, judgments) and/or behavior (e.g., choices, response time). In the simplest case, experimental and control conditions are created such that a hypothesized process is thought to be present in the former and absent in the latter. Together with a theoretical rationale for the hypothesis, the strategic design of conditions to rule out alternative hypotheses, and the recording of appropriate indicators of information processing, it is possible to obtain evidence for or against the hypothesis.

The logic for psychophysiological inquiry in such contexts follows a similar form except that physiological markers are used in place of or in addition to self-report and behavioral measures. Coles, Gratton, and Gehring (1987), express the rationale as follows:

First, we have a hypothetical construct that explains the relationship between an experimental manipulation and overt behavior. Second, we have a theoretical statement about the relationship between the hypothetical construct and a physiological measure. Third, this leads to a prediction about the relationship between the measure and overt behavior. (p. 14)

To explore the cognitive-processes-as-antecedents prototype in greater depth, let us consider how the investigation of cognitive theories expressed as stages of processing might be examined. Many theories in consumer research are predicated on sequential stages of cognitive activity such as Bettman's (1979b) information processing model of consumer choice or the hierarchy of effects model (e.g., Ray 1974).

As an illustration, we will consider a study of the continuous flow model of human information processing by Coles, Gratton, Bashore, Eriksen, and Donchin (1985). The continuous flow model proposes that each stage in a system of stages (termed *elementary processors*) produces a continuous output, which is available as input to concurrent and subsequent stages (e.g., Eriksen and Schultz 1979). This is in contrast to the traditional model of human information processing, which assumes that stages operate serially (e.g., Donders 1969; Sternberg 1969). In the serial stage model, information from an antecedent stage must be processed completely before it can be operated upon by a succeeding stage. By comparison, the continuous flow model maintains that, as information is first monitored visually, it begins to accumulate and induce an initial or partial activation in one or more other stages. Whether these stages will become fully activated or not depends on the internal criteria idiosyncratic to each stage, as well as to the response competition existing among the stages under partial activation.

Consider the simple squeeze task experiment, where people are required to respond to the presentation of the target letter "H" by squeezing a dynomometer with their left hand and to respond to the target letter "S" by squeezing a dynomometer with their right. A serial stage model to account for performance on this task might assume the following: evaluation → decision → response execution. That is, the stimulus is first evaluated, the results of the evaluation then enter a decision stage whereupon the proper response is identified, and finally the judgment is transferred to a response execution stage prior to an actual squeezing of the appropriate apparatus. Response time (RT) measures for choice tasks have often been used to test hypotheses pertaining to serial stage models.

To explain performance in the squeeze task experiment, at least three mechanisms have been proposed within the framework of the continuous flow model:

First, there is a process of *stimulus evaluation* that continuously feeds information about the stimulus to associated response activated systems. Second, there is a process of response competition by which concurrently activated responses inhibit each other. Third, a process of *aspecific priming* or a mechanism of a *variable response criterion* affects the amount of stimulus-related response activation required for overt response execution. (Coles et al. 1985, p. 531)

Because responses are hypothesized to be activated continuously during the stimulus evaluation process, RT measures cannot be used effectively as markers of the underlying process in the continuous flow model. Coles et al., therefore, used a component of event-related brain potential (ERP) as a relevant marker. In particular, the latency of the P300 response was recorded, which is a background indicator of cortical brain activity as measured by the electroencephalogram (EEG). Previous research indicates that P300 latency is a measure of relative evaluation time and is largely insensitive to manipulations of response-related processes (e.g., McCarthy and Donchin 1981). Coles et al. (1985) also employed measures of electromyogram (EMG) and analog dynamometer outputs as indicators of response priming and response competition effects. These measures were designed so as to pick up changes in electrical potential associated with slight muscle movements stimulated under partial activation.

Three manipulations were performed. In the noise/compatibility manipulation, the target letter was presented in the center of a five-letter array flanked either by noise letters the same as the target (e.g., SS *S* SS), called compatible noise condition, or by noise letters implying the opposite response (e.g., SS *H* SS), called incompatible noise condition. One hypothesis was that more frequent partial activation should occur in the incompatible than in the compatible noise conditions. This is a consequence of the greater implied response competition resulting from partial activation of multiple response processors. Notice that this manipulation provides a direct test of the mechanism underlying the oft observed differences in RT found in response competition experiments.

In the warning manipulation, a tone was sounded 1,000 ms prior to presentation of the letter arrays (in one half of trial blocks). The tone thus alerted some subjects of the impending array but, of course, provided no information as to the nature of the array. The hypothesis was that the tone would facilitate motor preparation (i.e., response-related processes) but not affect evaluation processes.

Finally, in the blocking manipulation, the level of noise in a series of trials was either constant (i.e., always compatible or always incompatible) or variable. The constant conditions thus created cases where a complete evaluation of the stimulus arrays was not necessary for successful response execution. That is, because the target letter in the constant conditions was either always the same as the noise, and therefore did not have to be localized, or always distinct from noise, and thus stood out continually, less time for stimulus evaluation was required when compared to the variable condition. This manipulation, then, affects evaluation processes directly.

The results tended to confirm the hypotheses. Overall, the evidence supported the continual activation of response processes. These processes were found to be under control of stimulus evaluation and aspecific priming. Information flows continually from evaluation processes to activate response processors. In addition, responses can be paired independently of stimulus evaluation. Further, competition resulting from partial activation of alternative response processors delays motor reactions. These findings support the continuous flow model but are difficult to explain from a discrete serial processing perspective. However, Miller's (1982, 1983) hybrid parallel-discrete model may be able to accommodate the results, but it was not explored in detail by Coles et al. (1985).

It should be pointed out that the experimental design employed by Coles et al. (1985) provides conditions where RT and P300 latency are associated and dissociated. Hence, rather specific hypotheses and hypotheses particularly relevant to the continuous flow model were tested. Moreover, a relatively strong test of hypotheses was provided in that rival explanations had been controlled for and ruled out. Notice further that more than one psychophysiological measure, rather than a single reaction, was used to investigate the pattern of physiological responses. This, too, enriches the quality of the hypotheses tested and increases our confidence in the interpretation of the meaning of these responses. More will be said on this issue later. Finally, it should be mentioned that the basis for the connections between information processing steps and psychophysiological measures received special attention by Coles et al. (1985). The authors not only drew upon previous research to bolster the rationale for their predictions, but also they made linkages to a number of similar experiments and pointed out additional predictions implied by their conceptionalization of the continuous flow model and their experimental design and use of RT and psychophysiological measures (c.f. Coles et al. 1987, p. 14). It is in these senses that their experiment serves as an exemplar for research in consumer information processing.

Affective Processes as Antecedents

There are two senses in which consumer researchers might be interested in affective processes as antecedents of psychophysiological responses. The first involves the discovery of a consumer's attitude toward marketing stimuli such as advertisements, spokespersons, messages, packages, brands, or slogans. The second entails the study of intervening processes between the presentation of marketing stimuli and attitude formation/change and/or behavioral responses. This latter sense is similar to the cognitive-processes-as-antecedents prototype except that affective or attitudinal processes replace cognitive processes as the focus of inquiry. Actually, a fine line typically exists between the cognitive and the affective/attitudinal processes, and the distinction is maintained here more for organizational purposes than for anything else. As we shall see, to take one particular example, cognitive elaboration can be the focus of, or the explanatory vehicle for, attitudinal processes (e.g., Petty and Cacioppo 1986 a,b).

Attitudes toward Marketing Stimuli. This has been, perhaps, the dominant rationale for pursuing physiological measurement in consumer research to date. Nevertheless, much of extant consumer research has been ungrounded in psychological theory, has tended to ignore the linkages between psychological constructs and physiological responses, or has exhibited ambiguous interpretations. As a consequence, we have chosen an experiment from the psychology literature by Cacioppo and Petty (1979a) as our exemplar. Because their experiment investigated reactions to persuasive communications, it is directly relevant to consumer research.

Cacioppo and Petty (1979a, Experiment 2) recorded EMG activity over selected facial muscles of people in order to see if the measures could distinguish between positive and nega-tive reactions to a persuasive communication. Three locations were monitored; corrugator supercilium (eyebrow area), depressor angulus oris (side of chin area), and zygomatic major (cheek area) muscle sites. People were divided into two groups and were exposed to either a proattitudinal or counterattitudinal communication (a control group was also included). The results showed that exposure to the proattitudinal message exhibited less corrugator, more depressor, and more zygomatic activity than the corresponding reactions to the counterattitudinal message. In other words, the pattern of muscle activity (which, incidentally, was imperceptible to the naked eye) could be used to distinguish between positive and negative affective states. Cacioppo, Petty, and Marshall-Goodell (1984) also found that EMG activity differentiated agreeable from disagreeable reactions toward imagined readings of editorials.

Cacioppo and Petty's (1979a) study is noteworthy because it is one of the first psychophysiological investigations to unambiguously identify the *polarity* of affective states. Earlier research using electrodermal activity has been unable to ascertain the direction of affective reactions, and research on pupillary responses has been contradictory. Similarly, contemporary work on the relationship between heart rate and the direction of affect has been inconclusive, though promising. Only research surfacing on hemispheric asymmetry seems as encouraging as EMG research for discriminating positive and negative reactions. We will review this research in more detail later in this chapter.

To ascertain the *intensity,* as well as polarity, of affective reactions, Cacioppo, Petty, Losch, and Kim (1986) investigated people's responses to slides of scenery that were either mildly exciting or upsetting to view (e.g., a mountain cliff or a bruised torso), or mildly relaxing or boring to view (e.g., an ocean beach or a polluted roadway). Reactions were measured as EMG activity monitored on the corrugator supercilia, zygomatic major, orbicular oris (mouth area), orbicularis oculus (eye area) and medial frontalis (forehead area) muscle sites on the left side of the face. The findings revealed that, not only did facial EMG activity differentiate the polarity of affective responses, but the intensity of responses was discriminable as well. Moreover, given their experimental design, Cacioppo et al. (1986) were able to rule out the possibility that their results were due to either a general increase in arousal, per se, or specific muscle tensing in response to the mere presentation of slides. Thus the findings could be interpreted as showing evidence for measuring the polarity and intensity of affective responses. Although Cacioppo et al. (1986, p. 266) cautioned that "people are capable of suppressing, falsifying, and distorting their facial expressions" and that facial EMG responses are transient and do not necessarily coincide with one's global attitude toward an object, we can envision the potential of the procedure for measuring responses to the attributes of attitudinal objects, and, thereby, the procedure may serve to provide input for product design decisions, for example.

Tests of Intervening Processes. Another exemplar is the use of psychophysiological reactions as indicators of mediating activities between exposure to marketing stimuli and attitudinal responses. To illustrate, consider an experiment by Cacioppo, Petty, and Quintanor (1982, Experiment 1), wherein men were exposed to either proattitudinal or counterattitudinal messages while alpha EEG activity was monitored over the left and right parietal areas. Alpha responses are high amplitude brain waves in the 8–12 Hz range and reflect processing activity that often occurs asymmetrically in the two hemispheres of the brain (e.g., Niedermeyer 1982; Olson and Ray 1983). Based on research showing that the right hemisphere is more active under conditions of both positive and negative emotion (e.g., Davidson, Schwartz, Sharon, Bennett, and Goleman 1979), it was hypothesized that greater activation of the right hemisphere should lead to more affectively polarized cognitive responses. Specifically, a proattitudinal message should stimulate more affectively positive cognitive responses, whereas a counterattitudinal message should lead to more affectively negative cognitive responses for those individuals exhibiting greater right-hemispheric processing.

After hearing either a proattitudinal or counterattitudinal message, subjects were given two and one-half minutes to list any thoughts or ideas that came to mind as they listened to the message. The measure of affective polarization consisted of the number of favorable minus unfavorable thoughts for the proattitudinal message and the number of unfavorable minus favorable thoughts for the counterattitudinal message. Using a median split to form subject blocks of high and low abundance of hemispheric alpha activity, Cacioppo et al. (1982) found that subjects produced more affectively polarized thoughts in the high-relative activation group. The findings were replicated using different message topics and exposing subjects to both proattitudinal and counterattitudinal messages (Cacioppo et al. 1982, Experiment 2).

This study, then, provides insight into the nature of thinking processes generated during exposure to persuasive communications. People generating more affectively polarized cognitive responses than others exhibited greater right hemispheric alpha activity. One implication is that the amount and direction of attitude change can be explained by differential cognitive responses and their integration. In addition to message processing, Cacioppo and Petty (1986, pp. 670–673) suggest that psychophysiological measures can be used to investigate the role of cognitive dissonance in attitude change.

Physiological Events as Antecedents

Rather than considering physiological responses as measures of reactions to marketing stimuli or markers of cognitive or affective processes explaining consumer reactions to marketing stimuli, we might be interested in exploring the implications of physiological events on cognitive, attitudinal, or behavioral reactions, per se. One way that this has frequently been done is to create a state of *general,* nonfocused arousal and to see the impact on psychological functioning. We will consider both the nature and limitations of this approach as well as its relatively successful applications (e.g., Kroeber-Riel 1979; Sanbonmatsu and Kardes 1988) later in the review. Most research investigating general arousal has taken place in contexts wherein people are aware of their arousal. For now, we wish to focus on a study inducing a *specific* physiological change, heart rate acceleration, of which subjects were unaware (Cacioppo 1979).

Building on research by Lacey and Lacey (1974) showing that phasic heart rate (HR) acceleration is associated with cognitive elaboration, Cacioppo (1979) induced cardiac acceleration and observed the effects on relatively complex mental tasks. Subjects were outpatients in a cardiac clinic and had implanted pacemakers. By placing a capped or uncapped magnet over a reed in the subject's pacemaker, it was possible to produce an acceleration in HR to 88 bpm from the constant floor setting of 72 bpm, which was normally maintained when natural activity produced a rate below this level. Subjects were unable to detect the manipulated acceleration.

In Experiment 1, subjects in both the 72 and 88 bpm conditions were asked to attend to sentences pertaining to a certain theme while they listened to a 17-minute excerpt from a clinical interview. They then completed a reading comprehension test and were asked to recall sentences. The hypothesis was based on previous research (e.g., Lacey, Kagan, Lacey, and Moss 1963), that accelerated HR would facilitate cognitive elaboration and thereby improve reading comprehension and recall. The results showed that accelerated HR significantly improved reading comprehension but did not significantly improve recall, although the findings were in the proper direction for the sentence-generation task. Hence, the exogenously induced psychophysiological response, HR, facilitated cognitive processing.

In Experiment 2, a subject's HR was again either accelerated to 88 bpm or not allowed to fall below 72 bpm while they read counterattitudinal messages. The messages were approximately 400 words in length and were personally relevant (e.g., stating that all social security

and medicare programs should be eliminated) to the subjects, who were elderly persons. After reading each message, subjects were given two and one-half minutes to verbally generate all thoughts they had while reading the messages and to express their agreement with (i.e., attitude toward) the recommendations. The findings showed that significantly more counterarguments were generated when the messages were read under accelerated HR than basal HR conditions. Again, the evidence shows that psychophysiological events, in this case HR acceleration, can enhance cognitive elaboration. Finally, although no effect was found on the level of agreement with the advocated policies, agreement was significantly and negatively correlated with the number of counterarguments ($r = -0.46$).

Cacioppo's (1979) study is exemplary because it demonstrates that physiological events can affect mental processes in predictable ways. Further, his research avoids the ambiguities associated with past research into the effects of general arousal. Finally, his results have implications for affective and attitude change. That is, physiological changes, in this case ones undetected by respondents, might serve as indirect causes of affective and attitude change to the extent that they inhibit or facilitate cognitive elaboration (e.g., the generation of counterarguments or support arguments). In another study examining the effects of HR acceleration, Cacioppo, Sandman, and Walker (1978) found that more counterarguments and more negative attitudes were generated toward counterattitudinal messages under accelerated than under either basal or decelerated HR conditions. However, because subjects were aware of their accelerated heart rate and given the induction used, which was based on a conditioned, self-administration, it is not possible to be certain of the precise direction of causality among physiological, cognitive, and attitudinal reactions. Nevertheless, in conjunction with Cacioppo's (1979) exogenously stimulated HR study, this study points to a very promising subject area and methodology for research into the processes underlying affective and attitude change in consumer research.

Summary

The three prototypes discussed herein are of course not the only exemplars for consideration. We might be interested in more complex sequences of effects such as marketing stimulus → physiological event → cognitive processes → affective responses → behavior; or, to take another case, marketing stimulus → cognitive processes → physiological arousal → attitude change → behavior. Nevertheless, most such sequences, and others one might envision, can be seen to be composed of extensions or combinations of the three prototypes considered herein. It is premature, given the state of the art and our knowledge of the role of psychophysiology in consumer behavior today, to pursue these more complex possibilities here.

Early in this review we mentioned a number of advantages to the use of physiological measures in consumer research. These reflected (1) the closeness of physiological measures to the mental and affective processes fundamental to consumer inquiry, (2) the potential for avoiding concealment or distortion of true consumer reactions, and (3) the ability to monitor thoughts and feelings of which one is unaware, which cannot be easily retrieved, and/or which would become transformed or altered in subsequent verbal translations or elicitations. To these, we might add that psychophysiological inquiry in consumer research can provide insights into the effects of physiological events on information processing, attitudes, and choices; the determinants of physiological responses to marketing stimuli; the construct validity of paper-and-pencil indicators, experimental manipulations, and other traditional measures in consumer research; the design of marketing policy variables such as product features and advertising copy, as well as other applied issues; and the development and testing of consumer theories, as well as the generation of new theories.

PSYCHOPHYSIOLOGICAL INFERENCE

Before we provide a more comprehensive review of psychophysiological research in psychology and in consumer research, it will prove useful to step back and consider the nature of psychophysiological inference in some detail. A fundamental question that must be addressed is the relationship between a psychological state and a physiological response. The relationship is not simply a matter of measurement or operational definitions. Nor is it a purely conventional or conceptual issue. Rather, the relationship is steeped in theoretical (i.e., substantive), methodological (i.e., procedural and inferential), and observational criteria. In this sense, the issues parallel those in other areas of the social sciences wherein theories are constructed, observations strategically chosen, hypotheses tested, and interpretations made in some more or less integrated manner, that is, according to the philosophy of science criteria (Bagozzi 1984). However, the complexity involved when using psychophysiological measures is increased when compared with traditional paper-and-pencil or participant-observer methods because of the nature of the procedures used to make measurements, the meaning of these measurements, and the need typically to integrate or reconcile these measures with psychological theory and self-reports.

To put the discussion is perspective, consider the narrow, but related, issue of what exactly is a physiological response. We might think that a pounding heart or a sweating palm is an "emotional" response. But is it? A lot depends on what we mean by emotion. Theories of emotion vary considerably as to which of the following variables are part of emotion: cognitive processes, subjective feelings, autonomic nervous system reactions, somatic nervous system reactions, central nervous system responses, and gross motor actions (e.g., Cotton 1981; Ekman, Levenson, and Friesen 1983; Izard 1977; Lazarus 1982; Leventhal 1980; Leventhal and Mosbach 1983; Maslach 1979;

Marshall and Zimbardo 1979; Schachter and Singer 1962, 1979; Zajonc 1980a, 1984). At the same time, many antecedents can produce the same physiological response. For example, in addition to emotionality, the electrodermal response (EDR) associated with sweating can be produced by an orienting response (OR) or a defense response (DR), which need not reflect emotional content (Cacioppo and Sandman 1981; Hare, 1973). A pounding heart could suggest emotionality. But it could also imply the execution of information processing tasks (e.g., Jennings 1986). Nor is the meaning of a physiological response necessarily solved by examining its effects. We saw earlier that the manipulation of HR can influence cognitive elaboration without necessarily influencing affect. Moreover, even if a physiological response could be shown to produce an emotional reaction, we cannot automatically infer that the converse is true. Neither can we conclude necessarily that the physiological response is an emotion or part of an emotion. Finally, a number of measurement issues make the interpretation of any physiological response problematic. Some of these are technological concerns, such as the need to take into account random measurement error, to control for systematic error (e.g., a variable environment external to the experimental manipulation), and to consider variability and idiosyncracies in subjects. Others relate to the complexities involved in multiple operationalism and its relation to issues of construct validity.

In this section, therefore, we will consider a number of conceptual, measurement, and empirical issues related to the use and interpretation of physiological measures. Following this, a framework will be presented for thinking about the relationship between psychological variables/processes and physiological responses.

What Is Arousal?

Physiological arousal is a general term originally used to denote a global state of activity of the human organism ranging from low (e.g., sleeping) to high (e.g., strong agitation). Some of the terms used often to mean the same thing as *arousal* are *activation, inner tension, alertness, excitation,* and *energy mobilization* (e.g., Cacioppo and Petty 1983a; Kroeber-Riel 1979). Early on psychologists tended to conceive of arousal as a diffuse, *unidimensional* concept that nevertheless could be measured by any one of a number of physiological responses (e.g., Duffy 1957, 1962; Malmo 1959). Some consumer researchers have even gone so far as to equate virtually all physiological responses as equivalent measures of this unitary conceptualization of arousal: "You have here a choice of perhaps fifty different measures, which to a great extent are all measuring the same thing, arousal. . . . The question of which of many different measures of arousal to use is to some extent irrelevant; i.e., . . . they all are measuring the same thing" (Krugman 1981, p. 2).

The unidimensional view of arousal has been attacked on a number of fronts. As an example, consider autonomic measures of sexual arousal while men subjects watch slides of nude females:

If we were to measure vasomotor activity . . . we would probably not detect any changes and might conclude that our subjects were not becoming aroused; however, if we recorded heart rate, we might come to a different conclusion . . . sexual arousal (while looking at nudes) . . . is primarily a parasympathetic response, while vasomotor activity . . . is governed by the sympathetic nervous system. Heart rate is controlled by both the parasympathetic and sympathetic systems; thus, we should expect to see some heart rate changes . . . (Stern et al. 1980. pp. 54–55)

This illustration suggests that different physiological responses do not necessarily indicate the same arousal state; in this instance, responses from two different divisions of the same system, the autonomic nervous system (ANS), fail to converge.

Actually, Lacey (1967) proposed that, instead of a single form of arousal, there are in fact three: cortical, autonomic, and behavioral. Hence, not only might different responses within a particular form of arousal fail to covary and, therefore, falsely suggest that the single continuum view of arousal is too simplistic, but also responses across forms may differ as well. Indeed, some responses may even go in opposite directions instead of positively covarying or remaining independent. Lacey (1967) termed this phenomenon, *directional fractionation*. Again to take an example,

Picture the following scene . . . A soldier is on guard duty . . . in enemy territory, and it is late at night. Suddenly there is a noise approaching in the darkness. What happens to the arousal level of the soldier? If we measured his EEG, we would conclude that he showed cortical arousal. If we measured skin conductance and heart rate as autonomic indices, however, we would probably find that his skin conductance increased but his heart rate decreased . . . and if we observe the soldier's behavior, we see that he is probably standing very still, looking toward the source of the noise and trying to determine if it is . . . friend or foe. (Stern et al. 1980, p. 56)

Directional fractionation makes it difficult to support an unidimensional view of arousal, since one must reconcile some evidence suggesting greater arousal with other evidence pointing to less arousal. Furthermore, the case for the use of *any one* measure as an indicator of arousal is weakened. We will return to this issue shortly.

In sum, the notion of *generalized arousal* is too imprecise a concept to be of much theoretical utility. But what about *specific physiological responses?* These can be meaningful, as suggested by many of the studies cited previously in conjunction with the three prototypes for consumer research. Nevertheless, some cautions are in order when interpreting research based on single measures of physiological states.

To highlight the central issues, consider once again EDR. Early work pointed to the possibility that intense emotional stimuli lead to increased EDR. This was shown, for example, for responses to pro or con attitude statements (e.g., Dickson and McGinnies 1966) and reactions to people of different races (e.g., Rankin and Campbell 1955). On the basis of this and similar research, can we conclude that EDR is a measure of affect or attitudes? Not necessarily. Based in part on the experimental designs used

in such research and the natural reactions people have to the kinds of stimuli employed, Cacioppo and Sandman (1981) argued that many studies using EDR could be reinterpreted as reflecting the basic human OR (orienting response) to novel stimuli rather than as an attitudinal reaction.

An *orienting response,* popularly referred to as a "what-is-it?" reaction, is an adaptive response helping people deal with novel situations. It is typically composed of the following articulation of bodily responses (Lynn 1966): increases in the sensitivity of sense organs, increases in motor responses (e.g., turning one's head), changes in EEG, increases in EDR, changes in the focussing of muscle readiness, changes in differential blood flow and respiration rates, and decreases in HR. Aside from the fact that the OR is a pattern of multiple physiological responses, an issue to be considered later, it should be pointed out that these responses are largely automatic and do not involve deeper or conscious information processing. Attitudinal processes are not automatic in the sense that the OR is, or at least they entail thinking processes such as cognitive elaboration or retrieval of information. If one wishes to use specific physiological responses as indicators of attitudinal or cognitive processes, it is important to control for or rule out the OR as a rival explanation for these responses. At the same time, it should be acknowledged that the OR can be interpreted within the context of other psychological responses, such as those found in Berlyne's (1960) theories. The OR may thus be of interest as one of a number of phenomena in some substantive research. Potential problems with an OR response can sometimes be mitigated by use of familiar stimuli or repeated exposures to induce habituation.

Similarly, the *defense response* can influence physiological measures and complicate the interpretation of findings. The DR protects an individual from very intense stimulation and differs from the OR in the following physiological reactions (Stern et al. 1980, p. 59): decreases in the sensitivity of sense organs, increases in attempts to physically move away from the stimulus, decreases in HR, and constriction of the blood flow in the periphery and head (for the OR, blood flow vessels dilate in the head). The DR is similar to the OR with respect to the remainder of physiological responses noted previously. Thus, it is important, in studies of information processing and attitudes, to strategically design the research so as to isolate the processes under study and not to confound them with a DR.

Still another response potentially contaminating psychophysiological inquiry is the related process of *attention,* which of course occurs for non-novel, less intense, and nonthreatening stimuli as well as for more extreme cases. It is often difficult to disentangle attentional processes from subsequent information processing, and some researchers focussing on the latter may have unwittingly witnessed evidence for experimental effects based on the former. We will return to this issue later when we review research on the interaction between cognitive processes and physiological events. For now, to take a specific example, note that early research seemingly demonstrating a relation between HR acceleration and information processing may have reflected more the direction of attention to cognitive processing than have provided strong evidence for specific information processing activities (e.g., Jennings 1986). Because attention processes are so intimately intertwined with cognitive and affective responses, it is important to consider their role when examining complex psychological hypotheses in consumer research.

We have seen that the notion of general arousal does not go very far and that care must be taken when interpreting specific physiological indices. Let us now address the use of *multiple physiological responses.* There are at least two reasons for using multiple responses in addition to the desire to avoid the ambiguities noted earlier. One reason is that multiple responses permit an investigation of construct validity, and in particular, convergent and discriminant validity (e.g., Campbell and Fiske 1959). Related to this is a second rationale. Many, if not most, marketing stimuli produce a pattern or constellation of effects in consumers, not a single, unitary reaction such as general arousal. At the same time, many consumer behaviors are themselves composed of, or are produced by, multidimensional elements. Attitudes, affect, emotions, decision making, and other psychological processes are themselves either defined complexly or are emergent constructs based on many elementary psychological and/or physiological states or processes. For these reasons, it is frequently necessary to examine *patterns* of physiological responses (and, in addition, integrate these with psychological and, in interpersonal research, social variables).

More broadly, we need to be concerned with *stimulus-response specificity* (e.g., Lacey 1967), which is the general principle that certain stimuli tend to bring about the same pattern of responses in most people. Stimulus-response specificity has also been referred to in the literature as stimulus response stereotypy. For example, research over the past twenty years or so shows that reactions to stimuli inducing fear are different from those creating anger (e.g., Schwartz 1986, p. 366). With fear one generally sees greater systolic blood pressure, less diastolic blood pressure, more peaks in muscle tension, a lower magnitude in muscle tension, a higher magnitude in skin conductance, and less of a rise in skin conductance than one sees with anger. When one recognizes that fear and anger are but two of perhaps as many as eight kinds or components of emotion (e.g., Izard 1977), and that blood pressure, muscle tension, and skin conductance are but three of many possible physiological responses, it can be appreciated how difficult it is to draw conclusions about the meaning of psychological processes and physiological measures and their relationships to each other.

One difficulty is that psychological processes occur both at different levels of abstraction and different levels of complexity within any level of abstraction. When we speak of emotional behavior, a very abstract phenomenon, for example, it is difficult to be as precise as one can be when speaking about sadness, a less abstract component or special case of emotion. And even more precise statements can be made of manifestations of sadness such as indicated by changes in HR, blood pressure, self-reports, and other reactions. At the same time, so-called emergent constructs, such as depression, a combination of sadness and anger (e.g., Izard 1972), will exhibit different patterns of physiological responses than other constructs at the same or at higher or lower levels of abstraction. As a consequence, we need to pay particular attention to the conceptualization of any psychological construct under consideration and its relationship to its measures. The most valid research using these constructs will require examination of patterns of multiple physiological and verbal responses.

The role of patterns of responses is of course crucial for more specific hypotheses of phenomena at relatively lower levels of abstraction than emotions. Consider, for example, the pioneering study by Cacioppo and Petty (1979a) who, in addition to the hypotheses noted earlier, investigated the effects of forewarning subjects about the topic and position of a persuasive communication that was allegedly to be heard later in the experiment. After the forewarning, subjects were asked to take 60 seconds to "collect their thoughts." Immediately prior to and following the forewarning and the instructions to collect thoughts, HR, breathing rate, EMG over the perioral and trapezius muscles, and cephalic pulse amplitudes were monitored. The results showed that HR, breathing rate, and perioral EMG were heightened, indicating thinking processes, but the trapezius muscle EMG and cephalic pulse amplitudes did not change, ruling out general arousal as the cause of the observed changes. Cacioppo and Petty also manipulated the discrepancy between the initial attitudes of subjects and the recommendation in the persuasive communication. The manipulation affected the number of favorable and unfavorable thoughts listed, as well as the agreement with the recommendation, but it did not influence any of the physiological measures. Thus, the findings suggest that, when exposed to persuasive messages, the stages of issue-relevant thinking and attitudinal responses exhibit distinct patterns of physiological reactions. We will explore further the significance of examining response patterns when we review selected studies later in the chapter.

Measurement Issues

A number of other factors need to be considered when interpreting physiological responses, including individual response stereotypy, habituation, the law of initial values, cognitive sets, and the analysis of recordings. These factors are not strictly measurement issues, but because they relate to measurement and for the sake of presentational purposes, they are briefly discussed here.

Individual response stereotypy has been defined as "the tendency for the same person to display the same profile of physiological response to a wide variety of eliciting situations and stimuli" (Cacioppo and Petty 1983a, p. 20). Note also that some researchers additionally use the term to refer to the idiosyncratic nature of physiological responses across individuals to the same stimulus (e.g., Stern et al. 1980, pp. 65–66). Cacioppo and Petty point out that individual response stereotypy discloses itself as a "response hierarchy":

This means that, for any one individual, stimuli consistently elicit the greatest change in responding from one effector (e.g., a change in heart rate), the second greatest change in responding from some other effector (e.g., electrodermal changes), and so on. Thus, which effector responds most, second most, and so forth, to stimuli varies across individuals. (Cacioppo and Petty 1983a, p. 20)

Because of individual response stereotypy, researchers often have to take special precautions in the design of studies, the recording of responses, and/or the analysis of data. For instance, some hypotheses may be more fruitfully studied through within-subjects, as opposed to between-subjects, designs. A number of stimuli arranged as a gradient, as opposed to a single stimulus, might have to be employed. Repeated presentations of stimuli over time may be necessary. Techniques for normalizing data by respondents, stimuli, or both may be needed. Certain physiological responses may be critical to employ, others important to avoid, depending on what is to be investigated. Special instrumentation and procedures may be required, and so on. Note also that large individual differences exist with respect to reactions to drugs and other stimuli, and these differences reflect what is known as differential *autonomic balance* (Wenger 1972).

Habituation is "the cessation or diminution of responding that occurs to the repeated presentation of the same stimulus" (Stern et al. 1980, p. 56). It is an inverse function of the intensity, uniqueness, and complexity of a stimulus and varies according to whether or not the subject is required to perform a behavioral response. It is a direct function of the rate of presentation of a stimulus and its duration. Further, a person's initial affective state (e.g., anxiety) and expectations can influence habituation. All of these factors, then, can affect the recording of physiological responses and complicate the interpretation of findings. To control both for the effects of habituation and the occurrence of random noise, psychophysiological studies are typically conducted in surroundings where light, temperature, humidity, and noise are controlled and where disruptions are avoided.

A related issue concerns the initial physiological state of any particular subject under study. Because people differ with respect to their own internal homeostatic states and, at the same time, come to the experimental setting with different degrees of arousal, it is necessary to provide an *adaptation period* at the start of any experiment to allow the subject to relax and become accustomed to the setting and to permit physiological responses to have the opportunity to subside. This is also a time when recording equipment is applied and calibrated.

The *law of initial values* states that "the response to a stimulus is smaller (and eventually, inverted) the higher the prestimulus level of activity in the effector (e.g., cardiovascular) system" (Cacioppo and Petty 1983a, p. 22; see also Wilder 1967). Thus the level and even the direction of physiological response to an experimental manipulation can be influenced by the subjects' homeostatic states prior to exposure to the manipulation. The law of initial values, it should be noted, varies considerably by subject and physiological response mode. In addition

to randomization of subjects to conditions and the use of adaptation periods, two methods of statistical control have been proposed to neutralize the effects of the law of initial values, both based on the analysis of covariance (e.g., Stern et al. 1980, pp. 63–64). Further, range-corrected difference scores (Johnson and Lubin 1972) and time series analyses (Lykken, Rose, Luther, and Maley 1966) have been used to compensate for the effects.

Cognitive sets are individual difference variables that frequently affect and complicate the interpretation of physiological measures. Physiological responses can be affected by expectations, subjective judgments, attitudes, and fears, among other psychological reactions. To the extent that such reactions inadvertently accompany a manipulation, they can contaminate its meaning. Cognitive sets are difficult to anticipate but need to be controlled.

A final issue and a very broad one relates to the analysis of physiological recordings. A myriad of analyses can be performed on common measures from any physiological recording apparatus. For instance, five EEG waveforms are often of interest — alpha, beta, gamma, delta, and theta. Each exhibits distinct forms and responses. With respect to spontaneous EEG, analysts may be concerned with amplitudes of waves, increases or decreases in responses, the distribution of responses at different locations, and extraneous sources of noise. With respect to ERP, one might be concerned with single trial responses or averages, amplitudes of individual waveform components, latency of components, periodicity, and even the slopes of responses. With respect to electrodermal activity, one might be concerned with amplitudes, latency, recovery time, and frequency of responses, each of which poses both choices among options and problems. All other physiological responses have their own idiosyncracies and challenges to measurement. It is not possible to do justice here to the measurement issues, and the reader is referred to Coles et al. (1986) and Stern et al. (1980) for discussions of these issues. For a discussion of the role of microcomputers in psychophysiological research, see Tassinary, Marshall-Goodell, and Cacioppo (1985).

A Framework Rooted in the Philosophy of Science

To come to grips with the meaning of the relationship between psychological variables and physiological responses, we must consider the nature of *psychophysiological inference* in greater depth. Cacioppo and Tassinary (in press, b) develop a way of thinking about psychophysiological inference, which we discuss below, that is based on the logic of proper inference drawing and is designed to explicitly avoid the fallacy known as affirmation of the consequent. Specifically, knowledge that a statement is true about a causal sequence, such as A leads to B, does not imply that the converse, B leads to A, is true.

For example, let us assume that we performed a study showing that the manipulation of message argument quality in a persuasive communication leads to attitude change. The manipulation is presumed to affect the generation of cognitive responses, and this is taken as the explanation for attitude change. A manipulation check verifies the differential generation of counterarguments. Assume further that it is known also from previous research that the direct manipulation of HR produces attitude change. Can we therefore conclude that greater cognitive elaboration will be accompanied by an acceleration in HR? No, at least not on the basis of the results of the first study and the use, through analogy, of the findings of the second. We need a direct manipulation of HR or cognitive responses and a monitoring of the complement under controlled conditions to have confidence in such a conclusion. Reasoning .by analogy on the basis of two studies containing a common dependent variable (i.e., attitude change) does not validly permit drawing conclusions with respect to the association between the psychological and physiological variables underlying the different manipulations in the two studies. To draw a conclusion on such a basis is known as *affirmation of the consequent.*

The Relationship between Psychological and Physiological Variables. In the final analysis, most psychophysiological research is predicated on the validity of one of two possible forms of inference. Form A consists of the experimental manipulation of psychological variables and the monitoring of physiological responses as indicators of those variables. Here we perform observations in the physiological domain so as to make inferences about events or processes in the psychological domain. An example of this form of psychophysiological inference is the study by Cacioppo et al. (1982) investigating the generation of polarized cognitive responses to persuasive communications and using differential EEG activity in the left and right hemispheres of the brain. Form B occurs when physiological states are manipulated and psychological and/or behavioral variables are measured as outcomes of changes in physiological states. The objective here is to make inferences about the effects of physiological changes on psychological processes. Cacioppo's (1979) study of the impact of HR acceleration on cognitive elaboration is an example of this form of psychophysiological inference.

To explore psychophysiological inference in greater depth, let us expand upon Form A (a parallel development could be provided for Form B by reversing the variables and relationships but is not pursued herein for the sake of brevity). Following Cacioppo and Tassinary (in press, b), we will use Ψ to designate the psychological domain where one or more psychological processes are of concern, and Φ to refer to the physiological domain where one or more responses are of interest. Figure 4.1 shows five possible outcomes bearing upon psychophysiological inference, where the lower case, encircled ψ's and ϕ's stand for individual psychological and physiological variables, respectively, and the line segments represent associations between variables across domains.

Consider first the null relation. In Case a, a

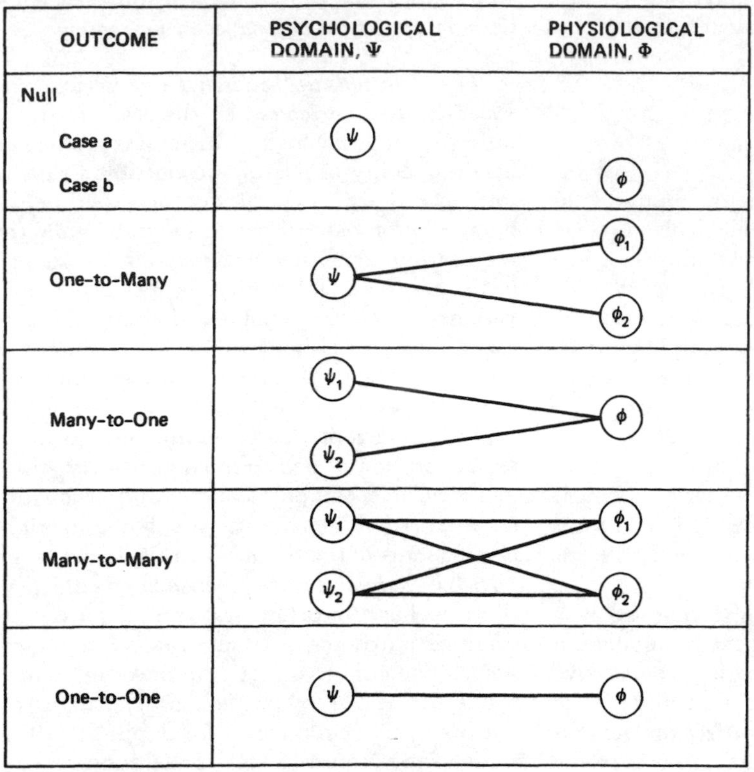

OUTCOME	PSYCHOLOGICAL DOMAIN, Ψ	PHYSIOLOGICAL DOMAIN, Φ
Null Case a Case b	ψ	ϕ
One-to-Many	ψ	ϕ_1 ϕ_2
Many-to-One	ψ_1 ψ_2	ϕ
Many-to-Many	ψ_1 ψ_2	ϕ_1 ϕ_2
One-to-One	ψ	ϕ

FIGURE 4.1 Five Possible Outcomes in Psychophysiological Inference. (Ψs and Φs are psychological variables, respectively, and line segments connecting variables across domains are inference relations.)

psychological event is manipulated but no simple physiological response is linked to it. Unless a nonphysiological measure from another domain (e.g., behavioral response such as physical movement or an actual choice outcome) is connected to the psychological event, no meaning can be given to it, and it cannot function in an explicit test of hypotheses. (It could, however, under certain circumstances, serve as a primitive term or variable in an untestable premise, say, for the purposes of developing an axiomatic theory.) In Case b, a physiological response is measured but no psychological event corresponds to it. One particular instance of this is a spontaneous ANS response; another is a physiological reaction associated with an inadvertent movement such as produced by a cough or exaggerated deep breath (e.g., Stern et al. 1980, pp. 50–51). Null occurrences of this

sort, of course, have no valid meaning as reflections of psychological processes.

A one-to-many relation exists when a psychological variable has two or more physiological referents. For example, the generation of more affectively polarized cognitive responses might be accompanied by greater facial EMG and right hemispheric EEG activity. The one-to-many relation is a desirable one, both from the perspective of measurement theory (e.g., Coombs et al. 1970, pp. 351–371) and from the perspective of construct validity procedures which require multiple operationalizations. In contrast, a many-to-one relation occurs when two or more psychological variables lead to the same physiological response. For instance, both the OR and DR are characterized by constriction of peripheral vasomotor activity. Notice that it is impossible, then, to differentiate between the OR and DR strictly on the basis of the direction of peripheral vasomotor activity. This illustrates the limitation of the many-to-one relation and reiterates the need to look at response patterns of physiological recordings.

The many-to-many relation happens when two or more psychological events are associated with two or more physiological responses and vice versa. For example, cognitive elaboration and affective responses might both be associated with EMG activity and HR acceleration. However, unless one can either control for causal sequences among the psychological events or find physiological responses relating to only one of the psychological variables in a set under consideration, the interpretation of the many-to-many relations is tenuous.

Finally, a one-to-one relation exists when one psychological event is linked to one physiological response and vice versa. Perhaps uncommon in practice, the one-to-one relation provides strong grounds for psychophysiological inference and, like the one-to-many relation, exhibits desirable measurement theory properties (e.g., Coombs et al. 1970, pp. 351–371).

Cacioppo and Tassinary (in press, b) proposes that psychophysiological inferences can be improved in cases of ambiguity (e.g., many-to-many relations) by redefining the linkages between psychological events and physiological responses through the skillful interpretation of particular spatial and temporal distinctions. To illustrate this, consider the example shown in Figure 4.2 from Cacioppo and Tassinary (in press, b). In the top panel of Figure 4.2, we have the case of the many-to-many relation in that the OR, DR, and startle response (SR) are each associated with skin conductance responses (SCR) and heart rate responses (HRR).

To disentangle the ambiguity, Cacioppo and Tassinary first consider whether any contemporaneous refinements can be made in the SCR and HRR recordings. The goal is to find one or more subsets of physiological measures, each of which can be replaced uniquely with a single

grouping of responses to yield a one-to-one relation with a psychological variable. As shown in the middle panel of Figure 4.2, by scrutinizing accelerative and decelerative HRR separately, it is possible to reduce the many-to-many relations to a single one-to-one relation and a single many-to-one relation. The OR is associated with increased SCR and decelerative HRR, while both the SR and DR exhibit increased SCR and accelerative HRR. Of course, the many-to-one relation still makes it impossible to differentiate between the SR and DR.

Cacioppo and Tassinary then propose that further refinements might be made by strategically examining the unfolding of physiological responses over time. Again the objective is to find one or more subsets of physiological measures, each of which can be replaced uniquely with a single grouping of responses to yield a one-to-one relation with a psychological variable. Specifically, the differentiation shown in the bottom panel of Figure 4.2 was derived. Here, accelerative HRR is further decomposed to produce a one-to-one relation between the SR and increased SCR and abrupt accelerative HRR, and a one-to-one relation between the DR and increased SCR and the temporarily accelerative HRR, respectively. The distinctions are based on research showing that "HR acceleration peaks and returns to normal within approximately two seconds in the case of startle, but does not begin to rise for several seconds and peaks much later following the stimulus in the case of the defense response" (Cacioppo and Tassinary, in press b, p. 30; see also Turpin 1986).

In sum, psychophysiological inference can be enhanced to the extent that one-to-one relations can be specified. Any refinement might entail a contemporaneous decomposition, a temporal decomposition, or both. Note that in the example shown in Figure 4.2 each one-to-one relation exists between a single psychological event and a subset of physiological responses that are uniquely associated with that event. Some of the physiological measures

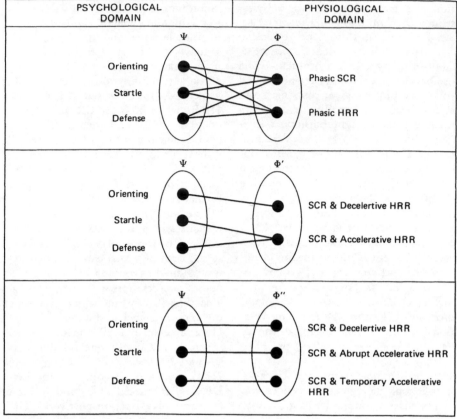

SCR = Skin Conductance Response
HRR = Heart Rate Response

FIGURE 4.2 An Example of Redefining a Many-to-Many Relation to Reflect One-to-One Relations. (Source: Reprinted from Cacioppo and Tassinary, in press.)

might be related nominally, ordinarily, or in an interval or ratio scale manner with the psychological event, depending on the application. Notice, too, that some physiological responses (see the SCR in Figure 4.2) can be associated with more than one psychological event, yet still contribute useful information to the specification of a one-to-one relation. Presumably this occurs either because the physiological measure differs as a matter of degree across psychological events or qualitatively differentiates the events from other events not represented in the psychological domain under study.

A General Framework. Figure 4.3 presents a general conceptualization for representing the relationship between psychological and physiological variables. For purposes of discussion, let us assume that the stimulus is an experimental manipulation of message argument quality, and we desire to study psychological responses to this manipulation such as cognitive elaboration. One type of measurement of cognitive elaboration is shown, that is, verbal reports from a thought listing procedure. Note that cognitive elaboration is represented here as a theoretical construct which, in turn, is con-

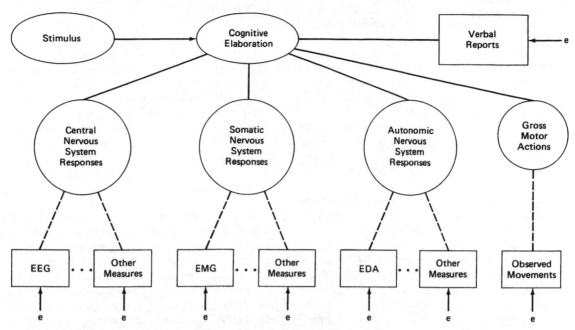

FIGURE 4.3 A General Framework for Representing Psychological and Physiological Variables, their Measures, and the Relationships among Them. (Circles, and ellipses represent theoretical constructs, boxes are measurements, the large arrow signifies an experimental manipulation, solid lines depict theoretical relations among constructs, lines with multiple breaks denots measurement relations, and the small arrows and accompanying e's reflect random measurement error.)

nected to four other categories of theoretical constructs: central nervous system (CNS) responses, somatic nervous system (SNS) responses, autonomic nervous system (ANS) responses, and gross motor actions. The linkages among theoretical constructs are shown as solid lines and represent hypotheses as implied by an underlying theory or theories. For example, cognitive responses might be linked to the CNS and the SNS through a comprehensive theory of emotion. The boxes in Figure 4.3 depict specific measurements and are, in turn, connected formally to their respective theoretical constructs through measurement relations. For instance, within the context of a theory accounting for cognitive responses and emotional reactions, facial muscles might become innervated through the CNS and muscles in the legs

and arms through the SNS. These could be measured by EMG activity. In addition to theoretical and measurement relations, Figure 4.3 shows each measurement to be a function of measurement error.

The general framework presented in Figure 4.3 roughly parallels modern extensions of classical test score theory and the philosophy of science criteria for representing correspondence rules and theoretical propositions (e.g., Bagozzi 1984). For the sake of simplicity, we have only shown one example measure for each theoretical construct, but many are, of course, possible. For instance, one might use multiple measures of the cardiovascular system such as HR, blood pressure, and plethysmography. Or, within a particular measurement procedure, one might scrutinize multiple indicators of activity, for example, multiple facial cites for EMG activity or alpha, beta, and theta brain waves from the EEG.

In Figure 4.3, we have shown the CNS, SNS, and ANS responses as parallel constructs from which we desire to draw inferences concerning cognitive elaboration. In some applications, as guided by theory, other relations among cognitive elaboration and the remaining theoretical constructs might be of interest. For example, cognitive elaboration might be hypothesized to precede or influence the SNS and gross motor responses (or vice versa). Interactions among the CNS, SNS, and ANS might be hypothesized. Or higher-order relations among the theoretical constructs might be studied, such as the overall governance of the CNS on subsidiary cognitive responses, SNS, and ANS activity. Moreover, it is conceivable that the CNS, SNS, and ANS could be organized as subsystems of the nervous system and related to psychological variables, as theory might dictate.

Another issue to mention, with respect to the general framework, is that other psychological constructs can be represented as theoretical variables linked to cognitive elaboration and/or physiological and motor responses. Thus, one might wish to specify attitudes as a function of the integration of cognitive responses, to take one particular example. Attitudes might, in addition, be linked to one or more physiological constructs as well as to verbal measures. These extensions are not shown in Figure 4.3

The general framework is an idealization which nevertheless focuses attention on the theoretical connections between psychological and physiological variables. Measurement is of course important in the framework, but it plays a subordinate role to the substance of what is being investigated and the conceptual meaning of constructs. Significantly, the framework stresses the need for a formal integration of theoretical, methodological, and observational criteria in any substantive investigation. Although not explicitly expressed in the language used herein, many of the exemplars discussed earlier can be reconceptualized along the lines outlined in Figure 4.3

KEY STUDIES IN THE LITERATURE

In this section, we will briefly highlight important research in the psychological and marketing literatures. Again, no attempt is made to be exhaustive. Moreover, the exemplars and other relevant studies mentioned earlier in this chapter are not repeated here in the interests of brevity. Selected areas of the literature that are relevant for consumer research are viewed.

Psychology

Cognitive Processes. Consider first the use of physiological changes as markers of memory and thought. Early research pointed to the association of HR deceleration with the intake of information and the association of HR acceleration with both cognitive elaboration and the rejection of information (e.g., Lacey and Lacey 1974). By rejection of information, researchers meant negative affect toward information, which, nevertheless, was accompanied by increased processing (e.g., Hare, Wood, Britain, and Frozelle 1971). A spate of research supported the association of HR deceleration with information intake (e.g., Carroll and Anastasiades 1978; Tursky, Schwartz, and Crider 1970) and HR acceleration with such information-processing tasks as decision making and response selection (e.g., Coles and Duncan-Johnson 1975), cognitive imaging (e.g., Schwartz and Higgins 1971), and mental arithmetic, solving anagrams, memorizing, retention, and logical reasoning (e.g., Cacioppo and Sandman 1978; Jennings and Hall 1980).

Some uncertainty still exists as to the nature of the mental processes associated with HR, however. With respect to HR acceleration, the affective-rejection hypothesis has been replaced with a more perceptual or cognitive interpretation, asserting that one's control of information input is associated with HR acceleration. This has been termed *motivated inattention* (e.g., Lacey and Lacey 1978). Jennings (1975) investigated whether HR acceleration is either a marker of memory processes or points to motivated inattention. His research supported the interpretation that cognitive manipulations augment but do not initiate HR acceleration.

A key question is whether HR acceleration reflects general information processing, specific cognitive activities, or simply the allocation of attention to competing tasks. Jennings (1986) summarizes the research findings in this regard across a wide range of studies as follows:

Cardiac deceleration appears to be related to anticipation and detection to information input, and cardiac acceleration seems related to further processing of that information (i.e., storage, transformation). There is little evidence to suggest that cardiac acceleration is related to a specific cognitive process. . . . Rather, heart rate acceleration seems related to the directing of attention to cognitive processing, to the exclusion of further input. Furthermore, cardiac acceleration during information processing appears unrelated to graduations of reported arousal. (Jennings 1986, p. 296)

Another noteworthy body of research using physiological measures as markers of mental processes is Cacioppo and Petty's program of research into the extent of cognitive elaboration. The extent of cognitive elaboration refers to the *amount* of effortful thinking devoted to the processing of information, such as in response to a persuasive communication, and should be contrasted to research investigating the *nature* of cognitive elaboration, such as the polarity of cognitive responses and attitude formation.

Cacioppo and Petty (1979b; 1981a) investigated, among other questions, whether covert oral EMG responses can indicate the extent of semantic processing. In their first study, subjects were asked to perform two judgments on stimuli presented visually: (1) whether or not adjectives relating to traits were self-descriptive, and (2) whether or not adjectives were printed in uppercase letters. While subjects made judgments by pressing buttons marked yes or no, EMG readings were taken of activity adjacent to the lips, among other measurements. The findings showed that more EMG activity occurred when judgments of self-reference were made than when judgments were made as to which type of letters were employed (Cacioppo and Petty 1979b). This was inter-

preted as suggesting deeper information processing during the self-referent than during the letter-assessment tasks.

In their second study, Cacioppo and Petty (1981a) used aural stimuli and asked subjects to perform five tasks: volume discrimination ("Is the following word spoken louder than this question?"), rhyme judgments ("Does the following word rhyme with _____?"), association assessment ("Is the following word similar in meaning to _____?"), evaluations ("Is the following word 'good'?"), and self-reference appraisals ("Is the following word self-descriptive?"). Notice that the five tasks are ordered according to the extent of processing from low to high. The results of a recognition test indeed suggested that the depth of processing increased from low to high (i.e., more semantic processing is required by the tasks at the high end as compared with the low end of the continuum, which should facilitate recognition). The findings for the lip EMG measurements revealed that self-reference and evaluation judgments had the highest readings, which were, in fact, at a higher level than the prestimulus baseline. The volume discrimination, rhyme, and association judgments, however, generated low EMG activity and were even below the level of the prestimulus baseline. Thus it appears that covert oral EMG activity indicates the extent of cognitive elaboration. As an aside, it is interesting to note that Cacioppo and Petty found that HR acceleration did not differ across the tasks. Oral EMG measures may be more sensitive to cognitive processes than HR measures. At least this was the case in their studies of linguistic elaboration.

In addition to the use of EMG measures as markers of semantic processing of linguistic symbols, Cacioppo and Petty (1979a) used the EMG to examine the extent of cognitive elaboration in the context of persuasive communications. Specifically, the authors were interested in discovering whether or not cognitive preparation would be greater when people are led to expect a counterattitudinal message versus either a proattitudinal or an unidentified message. A forewarning of an impending counterattitudinal message for involving issues that might threaten one's attitudes should lead to more extensive cognitive elaboration than either a proattitudinal or unidentified message. Using covert oral EMG measures, Cacioppo and Petty, indeed, found that greater increases in activity occurred for the counterattitudinal as opposed to the proattitudinal and unidentified conditions. These results also demonstrate that EMG activity can indicate the extent of cognitive elaboration.

So far we have reviewed a number of important studies using physiological responses as markers of cognitive processes. We turn now to research investigating the facilitative or inhibitory effects of physiological states on psychological processes. We have already reviewed the classic study in this genre earlier in this chapter, namely Cacioppo's (1979) examination of the effects of directly induced HR acceleration on cognitive elaboration. Because the remaining research in this area has focussed primarily on the effects of general arousal on memory and thought, we should reiterate the limitations of this concept as discussed earlier when interpreting this research.

Kleinsmith and Kaplan (1963) set the tone for research in this area by finding that general arousal (measured as changes in skin conductance) has differential effects on memory. In particular, it was found that arousal facilitated long-term memory, presumably by promoting a consolidation of information, and inhibited short-term memory, allegedly because information consolidation processes made memory traces unavailable in the short-run. A number of studies have replicated these findings, but tests of the underlying consolidation mechanism or of alternative mechanisms have proven ambiguous (e.g., Craik and Blankstein 1975; Eysenck 1976; Smith and Broadbent 1981).

A final study to note is an investigation by Revelle, Humphreys, Simon, and Gilliland (1980). Unlike previous research into the effects of general arousal, which typically used either single measures of arousal, such as skin conductance, or which failed to measure arousal at all (e.g., because stimuli presumed to be arousing, such as loud noises, were manipulated), Revelle et al. (1980) looked at three converging

determinants of arousal: introversion-extraversion, caffeine, and time of day (morning versus evening). Instead of finding a single state of arousal based on these determinants, however, Revelle et al. found a number of complex interactions that necessitated rather ad hoc interpretations of arousal, depending on the levels and combinations of the three operations. Eysenck and Folkard (1980) question Revelle et al.'s interpretation on the basis of other physiological data at odds with Revelle et al.'s concept of arousal. Nevertheless the attempt by Revelle et al. to search for converging operationalizations of arousal is laudatory and points to a need for a more complex conceptualization of general arousal. Future research will, it is hoped, be directed at a new theory of general arousal and its measurement, as well as at the use of specific physiological responses in psychophysiological research.

Affective and Social Processes. Let's first consider research investigating *affective and attitudinal processes*. In addition to those noted hereafter, the reader is again reminded of the studies described earlier in this review as exemplars and as examples of psychophysiological inference.

Cognitive dissonance arises when a person performs an action that he or she realizes is discrepant or inconsistent with his or her attitude toward a target behavior or object (e.g., Festinger 1957; Wicklund and Brehm 1976). Dissonance occurs frequently in consumer contexts, such as when a person buys an expensive product, experiences many attributes and consequences of product use (some of which are found lacking), confronts information suggesting that unbought alternatives are in some ways superior, and, in general, is therefore motivated to seek information reducing dissonance (for a review of cognitive dissonance effects in consumer research, see Cumming and Venkatesan 1976).

A key feature of the theory of cognitive dissonance is the hypothesized presence of accompanying physiological reactions (e.g., Fazio and Cooper 1983). In one of the few published studies examining physiological responses to dissonance, Gerard (1967) observed that blood vessels in the hands of ten of twelve subjects constricted when they were asked to choose between two attractive paintings (a dissonant action), whereas only one of twelve subjects experienced similar constriction when asked to choose between an attractive and a relatively unattractive painting (a relatively dissonant-free action). The interpretation of these findings as providing evidence for dissonance is weakened, however, because it is impossible to rule out attention or orienting reactions as rival hypotheses (Cacioppo and Petty 1986). Finally, Croyle and Cooper (1983) found some evidence suggesting that high versus low dissonance is accompanied by higher levels of spontaneous skin conductance responses (SCRs). Overall, given the frequency of dissonant reactions in everyday consumer behavior contexts, we would expect that the use of psychophysiological approaches offers considerable promise for the future, particularly as a basis for inferring cognitive and affective processes in response to dissonance inducing consumption acts.

Some renewed interest is occurring in consumer behavior with respect to classical conditioning (see chapter 5 in this volume). Psychophysiology may provide complementary input here. For example, physiological responses can be classically conditioned to words or other stimuli, and these might elicit the same reactions to similar words or objects (e.g., Acker and Edwards 1964). The phenomenon is termed *semantic generalization* and will be returned to later when we discuss research in consumer behavior. Tursky and Jamner (1983) discuss the use of classical conditioning for the study of beliefs. Cacioppo and Petty (1983a, p. 64) caution that physiological measures that are relatively insensitive to influence by cognitive factors may be necessary to be employed in studies investigating classical conditioning effects if one is to produce unambiguous findings.

Another area of research into affective and attitudinal processes can be found in the stream of inquiry investigating EMG recordings. In an early study, Schwartz, Fair, Salt, Mandel, and Klerman (1976) found differential responding of covert facial muscles to happy versus sad events. Specifically, it was found that, when imagining happy events, lower mean amplitudes of integrated EMG activity resulted for the corrugator supercilium muscles and, when imagining sad events, higher mean amplitudes resulted for the depressor annulus oris and zygomatic major muscles. Cacioppo, Petty, and Marshall-Goodell (1984) investigated the effects of adopting either an agreeable or disagreeable attitudinal set while subjects either read neutral text or imagined reading an editorial. The data showed that covert affective processing was associated with the innervation of a particular pattern of facial muscles (e.g., corrugator supercilium, zygomatic major) but not muscles in the forearm or the obicularis oris muscle area of the face. This study is noteworthy not only for its clever analysis of the spatial and temporal patterns of muscle activity but also for its innovative measurement procedures and statistical analyses.

The EMG has also been used extensively to measure higher-order psychological constructs. Schwartz (1986) summarizes the results of his program of research into the study of emotion and EMG activity as follows:

1. Different patterns of facial muscle activity accompany the generation of happy, sad, and angry imagery, and these patterns are not typically noticeable in the overt face.

2. Instructions to re-experience or "feel" the specific emotions result in greater EMG changes in relevant muscles than instructions to "think" about the situations.

3. The biggest facial EMG difference between depressed and nondepressed subjects occurs when subjects imagine what they do in a "typical day," with nondepressed subjects generating miniature happy facial EMG pattern and depressed subjects generating a miniature mixed sadness-anger facial EMG pattern.

4. Females (compared to males) tend to:
   a. Generate facial EMG patterns of greater magnitude (relative to rest) during affective imagery, and report a corresponding stronger subjective experience to the affective imagery.
   b. Show greater within-subject correlations between the experience of particular emotions and relevant facial muscles.

c. Show somewhat higher corrugator levels during rest (possibly reflecting more sadness and/or concern) and lower masseter levels during rest (possibly reflecting less anger).

d. Generate larger facial EMG patterns when instructed to voluntarily produce overt expressions reflecting different emotions. (p. 363)

It should be stressed that these conclusions are tentative, as the research to date does not unambiguously provide support to the degree one would like. Interestingly, Schwartz (1986, p. 364) notes that "self-reports [of subjective experience] are *preceded* by the generation of unique patterns of facial muscle activity that vary both in pattern and intensity with the subsequent self-reports." He speculates that self-reports and covert EMG activity are "two different aspects of the same, underlying neuropsychological system." This is consistent with the framework presented earlier for representing psychological processes and physiological responses and their measures.

A final area of inquiry into affective processes we wish to mention concerns research into the CNS. A number of studies have examined the relationship between hemispheric lateralization and the experience of positive and negative emotions. One hypothesis is that, for right-handed people, positive emotions are accompanied by greater activity in the left hemisphere and negative emotions are accompanied by greater activity in the right hemisphere (e.g., Davidson 1984). The opposite is believed to occur for left-handed people. Some support for this conjecture has been found by Sirota and Schwartz (1982) using EMG recordings and by Ahern and Schwartz (1979) using eye-movement procedures. More complex interpretations of emotional reactions have also been proposed. For instance, it has been suggested that emotional stimuli are processed holistically in an initial phase, which occurs in the right parietal region of the brain, and this is then followed by the aforementioned lateral specialization for both the interpretation and expression of positive and negative emotions, respectively (Schwartz 1986, p. 371). Davidson and Fox

(1982) found support for this sequence of intra- and interhemispheric processing in their study of the responses of ten-month-old female infants to happy or sad faces of an actress displayed on a video tape.

The last area of the psychology literature that we will examine deals with *social processes*. Consider first the responses of people to the overt facial expression of emotions by others. Vaughan and Lanzetta (1980) found that subjects exhibited higher amplitudes of mean integrated EMG activity, as recorded over the medial frontalis, masseter, and orbicularis oculus muscles, after viewing the grimacing of a confederate. Similarly, Englis, Vaughan, and Lanzetta (1982) found that subjects who participated in a stock market game with a confederate showed higher amplitudes of mean integrated EMG over the corrugator supercilium, masseter, and obicularis oculus muscles when the confederate and subjects shared outcomes and the confederate revealed a pained rather than a happy face. The reverse profile was found when the confederate and subjects had asymmetrical outcomes. In sum, these studies demonstrate that EMG responses can mark the affective reactions of people to the facial expression of emotions by others.

It has been observed that the presence of people while one performs a task increases performance in easy tasks and decreases performance in difficult tasks (e.g., Zajonc 1965; c.f. Geen and Gange 1977). This phenomenon has come to be known as *social facilitation*, although, as noted, inhibitory effects occur under certain conditions. One explanation for social facilitation is that the presence of people induces arousal and general drive and this, in turn, leads to the selection of the motor response most readily available such as the one most easily performed or the one previously learned (Zajonc 1980b). Geen (1977) measured palmar sweating of subjects as they solved anagrams under various conditions. The greatest amount of sweating occurred when an experimenter watched subjects and they were led to believe that their performance was being evaluated; the least sweating occurred when no observer was present. Consistent with the social facilitation hypothesis, anagrams were solved fastest in the unobserved and slowest in the observed conditions. The increase in palmar sweating, a crude measure of ANS activity, was taken as an indicator of arousal. Similarly, Geen (1979) found that subjects who received failure feedback on a preliminary task and then were asked to participate in a difficult paired-associates task performed more poorly and demonstrated more spontaneous skin resistance responses when observed than when unobserved. For an in-depth interpretation of the research in social facilitation, see Cacioppo and Petty (1986, pp. 658–664), who propose that two stages underlie the phenomenon: threat assessment, followed by effortful striving. Cacioppo and Petty suggest that, rather than generalized drive, heightened sympathetic activity occurs when others are present in a task situation and this then determines how hard one strives to perform a behavior. Unfortunately, very little use of physiological measures has been done in the social facilitation context (c.f. Geen and Bushman 1989).

Cacioppo and Petty (1986) propose that social processes can be fruitfully studied as a sequence of subprocesses and that physiological measures can be used to mark these subprocesses. They describe two general procedures for investigating social processes in this regard, namely, the substantive method and the additive-factors method (Cacioppo and Petty 1986, pp. 654–658). Because it is beyond the scope of this review to consider these here, the reader is referred to their original work. Other research into the use of psychophysiological measures in the study of social processes include work on prosocial behavior (e.g., Salovey and Rosenhan 1989) and interpersonal relations (e.g., Notarius and Herrick 1989), but these will not be considered further herein.

Consumer Research

Because most psychophysiological studies in consumer research have used only single physiological measures, we will organize the following discussion around individual measurement procedures. It should be mentioned further that much of the research has not employed physiological measures as markers of underlying cognitive or affective processes, per se, but has instead either focussed on the use of the procedures to distinguish between alternative marketing stimuli (e.g., different advertising copy) or examined the effects of general arousal on consumer responses. Many studies found in the consumer behavior literature failed to provide sufficient details of the designs and methodologies used and, therefore, preclude replications and make interpretations of findings difficult. No consumer research studies were found using either HR or EMG measurements, despite the growing literature in psychology using these procedures and their obvious relevance for studying consumer behavior. Only a sampling of the relevant research is included herein.

Pupillography. Pupillary dilation and constriction have been touted as measures of positive and negative affect, respectively, thus suggesting utility as bidirectional physiological indicators and offering an advantage over unidirectional responses such as EDA. Some of the earliest research was conducted by Hess and colleagues who found that pupil size was associated with the "interest value" of pictures (Hess and Polt 1960), extent of mental activity associated with problem solving (Hess and Polt 1964), and "private attitudes" toward pictures of food and other stimuli (Hess 1965). More directly in consumer research, Hess (1968) claims that pupil responses correlate with different print and television ad executions, as well as the sales of different designs of watches, watch bands, and silverware. Similarly, Krugman (1964) presents evidence showing that pupillary responses correlated with the sales of greeting cards and silverware. Krugman (1965) also found that the procedures discriminated among various television ads. Halpern (1967) discovered that pupillary responses were sensitive to the explanation of a convenience feature in a new package design. Finally, van Bortel (1968) found that pupillary responses predicted postcard returns related to ads for encyclopedias, but not to actual sales.

A severe limitation with respect to published research in consumer behavior using pupillary responses is that the descriptions of the research designs have been so incompletely stated that it is difficult to make an informed assessment of the literature. As a consequence, we will limit discussion here to shortcomings of research into pupillary response that have been pointed out in the psychology literature. Note also that in the literature researchers have not always found evidence for both an association between dilation and positive stimuli and an association between constriction and negative stimuli (e.g., Janisse 1977; White and Maltzman 1978).

Two broad criticisms of pupillary response research can be noted (Cacioppo and Petty 1983a). The first is methodological and concerns the observation that sufficient controls have not always been undertaken. For example, changes in pupil size have been monitored without allowing for proper baseline assessments. Or nonpsychological factors capable of affecting pupil size have not always been eliminated or corrected for. Tryon (1975), for instance, documents twenty-three separate stimuli affecting pupil size such as the lid-closure reflex, light and darkness reflexes, alcohol, sexual preference, wavelength, age, and binocular summation effects.

More telling is the criticism that previous research may have shown evidence for psychological processes other than those presumably being investigated. One such psychological process that is a prime candidate is the OR (e.g., Cacioppo and Sandman 1981). Another is the allocation of attention so often found in information processing tasks, which is difficult to separate from other cognitive and affective responses (e.g., Kahneman 1973).

In sum, while pupillary responses seem to offer promise on the surface, little evidence exists demonstrating their utility in psychological or consumer research. This is not to say that fruitful research will not be forthcoming. We only wish to stress that careful designs and measurement procedures will need to be integrated with sound theory. One area that may offer opportunities, in addition to the use of pupillary responses as indicators of attitudinal reactions, is the use of pupillary response as a marker of short-term activation during information processing tasks (e.g., Beatty 1982; Beatty and Wagoner 1978).

Electrooculography. Electrooculography, the measurement of eye movements, has been used to study information processing (e.g., Oster and Stern 1980) and hemispheric activity in the brain (e.g., Ehrlichman and Weinberger 1978). Although there are at least twelve types of eye movements studied by researchers (e.g., Tursky 1974), we will only briefly mention three measures herein: fixation points, saccades, and smooth pursuit movements. *Fixation points* refer to discrete units of information in a visual field which a person momentarily focuses upon. A *saccadic eye movement* is a fast, voluntary jump from one fixation point to another. A *smooth pursuit movement* is a slow scan of information in a moving visual field and is thought to be involuntary. The measurement of eye movements is rather complicated and many procedures exist (e.g., Young and Sheena 1975).

Very little electrooculographic research has been conducted in consumer behavior. One focus of inquiry has been the transfer of information from the sensory register to short term memory, where the frequency of eye fixations serves as an index of this activity. Witt (1977), in an unpublished study referenced by Kroeber-Riel (1979), investigated the effect of more versus less nudity in print ads on the frequency of eye fixations. Greater arousal led to significantly more eye fixations on the pictorial stimuli but had no effect upon attention to textual information. Witt also discovered that frequency of fixations was correlated with recall. Morrison and Dainoff (1972) found somewhat similar results in their study of print ads but used the amount of time that the elements were looked at in the ads as their dependent variable. This is a rather crude measure and may not be highly correlated with frequency of fixation and saccadic eye movements. Similarly, Treistman and Gregg (1979) examined various eye movement responses to catalog ads for cosmetics, and they reported that average viewing time discriminated between high and low performing ads. Finally, Krugman (1971) found that the extent of visual scanning was associated with greater recall of television ads.

Voice Pitch Analysis. Changes in one's voice are thought to reflect stress (Hollien 1981) and even indicate emotional commitment (Brickman 1980). In particular, muscular contractions in the larynx respond to emotional changes and result in changes in pitch (e.g., Williams and Stevens 1972). Nevertheless, the particular mechanism underlying these changes and the specific physiological responses and their associations with emotion are little understood (e.g., Atkinson 1978). Academic research in consumer behavior has been sparse (c.f. Grant and Allman 1988).

Nelson and Schwartz (1979) report that voice pitch analysis of reactions to ads predicted those products with the highest market shares, whereas verbal measures did not. However, the incomplete description of the methodology and analyses prevent one from making firm conclusions. Brickman (1976) found that voice pitch analysis could be used to assess the favorability of consumers toward brands of dog food as well as to assess market shares of the products. Moreover, he used the procedure successfully to investigate new product concepts and prototype packages (Brickman 1980). Nevertheless, numerous methodological shortcomings of the studies have been noted, again making interpretations difficult (e.g., Nighswonger and Martin 1981).

Overall, voice pitch analysis, while intriguing and attractive for its simplicity and relatively inexpensive apparatus, has not proven as yet to be an effective procedure for psychophysiological research. Various methodological and conceptual problems remain unresolved (e.g., Martin and Nighswonger 1981; Nighswonger and Martin 1981).

Electrodermal Activity. The sympathetic nervous system, a division of the ANS, controls the sweat glands, which in turn are related complexly to arousal and emotionality. By measuring the ability of the skin (such as skin on the palm) to conduct electricity, one can get an indication of certain psychological responses.

We have already touched upon the measurement of EDA earlier in the chapter with respect to the measurement of attitudes. In consumer research, a long history of inquiry into EDA can be found. Early studies measuring skin resistance with the psychogalvanometer to study advertising copy were often unsuccessful (e.g., Caffyn 1964; Kohan 1968). On the other hand, Bose and Ghosh (1974) report a positive association between galvanic skin response and rank-order preferences for magazine ads (cited in Watson and Gratchel 1979). Likewise, Barg (1977) found that pictorial ads differing in the level of erotic activation as measured by EDA led subsequently to higher recall of the "schematic structure of the ads" 20 minutes and 24 hours after exposure (cited in Kroeber-Riel 1979).

Bagozzi (1990a,b) investigated the effect of arousal on attitude processes and structure. In the first study (Bagozzi 1990a), arousal was found to influence the halo effect. Specifically, arousal reduced the halo effect for negative beliefs, enhanced it for positive beliefs, and eliminated it for all beliefs treated as an aggregate. A spreading activation semantic network model of memory was used to describe the effects. In the second study, arousal was found to increase the consolidation of attitudes represented as affective and cognitive evaluations of an action. Moreover, arousal inhibited the association of negative beliefs and attitudes toward the act and increased the association of positive beliefs and attitudes toward the act. With respect to the integration of beliefs and evaluations of the consequences of the act, arousal decreased the association of attitude toward the act and the summation of beliefs times evaluations for negative consequences and increased the association of attitude toward the act and the summation of beliefs times evaluations for positive consequences. A theoretical rationale was employed based on the spreading activation semantic network model of memory. Overall, the findings show that arousal affects the organization of beliefs and evaluations and their relationship to global attitudes.

The use of EDA as a measure of arousal is based on the relatively well-developed theory of psychophysiological processing (e.g., Kroeber-Riel 1979; Venables and Christie 1980). Nevertheless, it is important to recognize that the OR can produce similar EDA responses as affective reactions (e.g., Fletcher 1971; Cacioppo and Sandman 1981), as can the DR and SR. Indeed, it is likely that many factors can affect EDA in addition to arousal, and care should be taken when designing studies and interpreting results. To mention only one area, we can point out that EDA may respond to behavioral inhibition that is distinct from arousal (e.g., Fowles 1980).

Brain Waves. Electrocortical activity, or brain waves, can be measured with a polygraph machine and supporting equipment. Three different approaches have been taken in contemporary EEG research: EEG as an indicator of arousal, emotionality, and information processing (e.g., Olson and Ray 1983, pp. 8–14).

One of the first studies in consumer research was reported by Krugman (1971) who monitored the brain waves of one woman while she looked at a magazine and then watched television. Brain wave activity over a wide frequency band was recorded as the subject viewed a cosmetic print ad and three 60-second television ads repeated three times. Based on results showing that the print ad generated greater beta activity (a fast wave response) and less delta and theta activity (a slow wave response) than did the television ads, Krugman (1971) concluded that print ads are a high-involvement and television ads a low-involvement medium.

Three other studies examined EEG responses to ads: Appel, Weinstein, and Weinstein (1979), Weinstein, Appel, and Weinstein (1980), and Gallup and Robinson (1980). Because each of these has serious limitations and/or was not published and therefore is difficult to

assess, they will not be described herein. Olson and Ray (1980, pp. 17–30) provide thorough descriptions and critiques.

In the only published study found using the EEG to test hypotheses with respect to psychological processes in consumer research, Cacioppo and Petty (1982) found that subjects experiencing greater right hemispheric activation while listening to a persuasive communication (measured as the ratio of right minus left to right plus left hemispheric alpha activity) produced more affectively polarized thoughts about the message (see also Cacioppo et al. 1982). This study points to an important use of EEG in consumer research, namely, the measurement of cognitive elaboration and attitudes. However, for a revealing exchange suggesting the need for careful thought and execution in any EEG endeavor see Weinstein, Weinstein, and Drozdenko (1984), Stewart (1984, 1985), Weinstein, Drozdenko, and Weinstein (1985), and Cacioppo and Petty (1985).

Cardiovascular Responses. Physiological activity associated with the heart and nervous system can be measured as electrical activity (heart rate) with an EKG, as changes in blood pressure, and as vasomotor activity such as blood volume and pulse volume (e.g., Stern et al. 1980). The only study using cardiovascular responses that could be found in the consumer behavior literature is the one by Sanbonmatsu and Kardes (1988). Sanbonmatsu and Kardes had subjects step up and down on a 7 inch block for 7 minutes in order to induce arousal, which was measured both by systolic blood pressure and self-reports. High and moderate arousal levels were created by varying the starting point of subsequent manipulations by using either a 3 or 7 minute waiting period. Following this, subjects were exposed to booklets containing six ads. Depending on the condition to which one was assigned, subjects either read strong or weak arguments and experienced either a celebrity or noncelebrity endorser. It was hypothesized and found that (1) endorser status had a greater impact on brand attitudes under high, rather than moderate, arousal levels, and that

(2) argument strength had a greater influence on brand attitudes under moderate, rather than high, arousal levels. The rationale is based on the elaboration likelihood model (Petty and Cacioppo 1986a,b), which suggests that high arousal reduces the amount of information processing capacity and, thus, peripheral cues (e.g., the status of the endorser) are processed more readily, whereas message argument processing is inhibited. The reverse is true when relatively less arousal is present. That is, more processing capacity is available for interpreting arguments, and argument content, therefore, has relatively more input to attitudes than peripheral cues.

In sum it can be said that, although very little published research exists in the consumer behavior literature, considerable opportunity abounds for using psychophysiological concepts and methods. As researchers become more familiar with the procedures and see how psychophysiology can aid in hypothesis testing, it is hoped they will embrace the approach with the enthusiasm that so far has largely been reserved for the commercial world (e.g., Abbondanza 1985; Hopkins 1987).

THE FUTURE

Psychophysiological inquiry clearly lags in the field of consumer research, but the dynamism found in the psychology literature promises to spill over into our field. At least seven areas are in need of attention, however, if the promise of psychophysiology in consumer research is to be fulfilled. Let us briefly consider these.

Area No. 1. Consumer researchers should attempt to use physiological responses as indicators of cognitive and affective processes. This is not to imply that researchers should abandon the use of physiological measures as a way to evaluate alternative marketing stimuli or to investigate the effects of physiological changes on psychological and social processes. The opportunity for useful research still exists in these areas to be sure. Rather, the recommendation is made that researchers devote special atten-

tion to the use of physiological measures, along with traditional measures, to test hypotheses about underlying information processing, decision making, and affective processes. These must be grounded in sound theory derived from psychology.

Area No. 2. Whenever possible, multiple physiological (and self-report) measures should be employed. Ideally, these should be taken within and across different physiological systems. At the same time, researchers should strive to discover patterns of responses, not simply employ multiple measures examined in isolation.

Area No. 3. Given that general arousal is a pervasive factor in everyday consumer behavior, work is needed to develop a more valid conceptualization of the phenomenon. This should be accompanied by construct validity and empirical research as well.

Area No. 4. Another requisite for advancement is the need to directly manipulate specific physiological responses and relate these theoretically and empirically to particular psychological processes. The induction of specific bodily responses will ultimately supplant general arousal in importance as consumer research matures. In addition to specific physiological responses, researchers may find that combinations of two or more concomitant reactions may have utility as a research tool.

Area No. 5. Although molecular phenomena (e.g., cognitive elaboration, attitudes) will undoubtedly constitute the mainstay of consumer research in the future, efforts should be directed as well toward the study of more molar phenomena and their relation to physiological responses. Social processes (e.g., interpersonal influence) are one class of molar behaviors for future study. Emergent phenomena, such as higher order emotions, should also be studied. For example, Schwartz, Weinberger, and Singer (1981) found unique patterns of physiological responses (using HR and systolic and diastolic blood pressure) for happiness, sadness, anger, fear, control, and relaxation conditions when subjects imagined these emotions. After a period of exercise, the pattern of physiological responses changed as a function of arousal. It is likely that higher order or emergent psychological processes are the most phenomenological and managerially relevant constructs in consumer research, and we are likely to see increased attention devoted to their study in the years ahead.

Area No. 6. All areas of inquiry, molar and molecular, would benefit from greater attention paid to the theoretical specification of psychological and physiological constructs, their measurements, and the linkages among constructs and between constructs and measurements. The integration of physiological variables with verbal responses and gross motor responses should facilitate the development and the testing of theories of consumer behavior. Researchers should keep abreast of the philosophy of science and advances in measurement theory as they apply to psychophysiological inquiry.

Area No. 7. Finally, special care is needed with respect to experimental design issues, the control of extraneous factors, proper selection and use of sophisticated recording equipment, and the analysis and interpretation of complex, often voluminous, data.

The future looks bright. But considerable effort will be required to put psychophysiological ideas and methods to work in consumer research.

REFERENCES

ABBONDANZA, J. M. (1985). "The Applications of Biobehavioral Measures in Market Research," paper presented at the Attitude Research Conference, American Marketing Association, Lake Tahoe, NV.

ACKER, I. E., and A. E. EDWARDS (1964). "Transfer of Vasoconstriction Over a Bipolar Meaning Dimension," *Journal of Experimental Psychology*, 67, 1–6.

ACKLES, P. K., J. R. JENNINGS, and M. G. H. COLES (1985). *Advances in Psychophysiology*, Vol. 1. Greenwich, CT: JAI Press.

AHERN, G. L., and G. E. SCHWARTZ (1979). "Dif-

ferential Lateralization for Positive versus Negative Emotion," *Neuropsychologia*, 17, 693–697.

APPEL, V. S. WEINSTEIN, and C. WEINSTEIN (1979). "Brain Activity and Recall of TV Advertising," *Journal of Advertising Research*, 19, 7–15.

ARCH, D. C. (1979). "Pupil Dilation Measures in Consumer Research: Application and Limitation," *Advances in Consumer Research*, 6, 166–168.

ATKINSON, J. E. (1978). "Correlation Analysis of the Physiological Factors Controlling Fundamental Voice Frequency," *Journal of the Acoustical Society of America*, 63, 211–222.

BAGOZZI, R. P. (1984). "A Prospectus for Theory Construction in Marketing," *Journal of Marketing*, 48, 11–29.

BAGOZZI, R. P. (1990a). "The Role of Arousal in the Creation and Control of the Halo Effect in Attitude Models," unpublished working paper, The University of Michigan, Ann Arbor, MI.

BAGOZZI, R. P. (1990b). "An Investigation of the Effects of Arousal on Attitude Structure," unpublished working paper, The University of Michigan, Ann Arbor, MI.

BARG, C. (1977). "Measurement and Effects of Psychological Activation Through Advertising," unpublished Ph.D. dissertation, the University of the Saarlands, Federal Republic of Germany.

BEATTY, J. (1982). "Task-evoked Pupillary Responses, Processing Load, and the Structure of Processing Resources," *Psychological Bulletin*, 91, 276–292.

BEATTY, J., and B. L. WAGONER (1978). "Pupillometric Signs of the Brain Activation vary with Levels of Cognitive Processing," *Science*, 199, 1216–1218.

BERLYNE, D. E. (1960). *Conflict, Arousal and Curiosity,* New York: McGraw-Hill.

BETTMAN, J. R. (1979a). "Memory Factors in Consumer Choice: A Review," *Journal of Marketing*, 43, 37–53.

BETTMAN, J. R. (1979b). *An Information Processing Theory of Consumer Choice.* Reading, MA: Addison-Wesley.

BLOOM, F. E., A. LAZERSON, and L. HOFSTADTER (1985). *Brain, Mind, and Behavior.* New York: Freeman.

BOSE, S. and A. GHOSH (1974). "Efficacy of Psychologalvanoscopic Readings to Rank Appealing Advertisements Concurrent to Preferences of Ad's Readers," *Indian Journal of Applied Psychology*, 11, 7–11.

BRAZIER, M. A. (1959). "The Historical Development of Neurophysiology," in J. Field (Ed.), *Handbook of Physiology Section I: Neurophysiology,* Vol. 1. Washington, DC: American Physiology Society, 1–58.

BRICKMAN, G. A. (1976). "Voice Analysis," *Journal of Advertising Research,* 16, 43–48.

BRICKMAN, G. A. (1980). "Use of Voice-Pitch Analysis," *Journal of Advertising Research,* 20, 69–73.

CACIOPPO, J. T. (1979). "Effects of Exogenous Changes in Heart Rate on Facilitation of Thought and Resistance to Persuasion," *Journal of Personality and Social Psychology,* 37, 489–498.

CACIOPPO, J. T. (1982). "Social Psychophysiology: A Classic Perspective and Contemporary Approach," *Psychophysiology,* 19, 241–251.

CACIOPPO, J. T., and D. D. DORFMAN (1987). "Waveform Moment Analysis in Psychophysiological Research," *Psychological Bulletin,* 102, 421–438.

CACIOPPO, J. T., and R. E. PETTY (1979a). "Attitudes and Cognitive Response: An Electrophysiological Approach," *Journal of Personality and Social Psychology,* 37, 2181–2199.

CACIOPPO, J. T., and R. E. PETTY (1979b). "Lip and Nonpreferred Forearm EMG Activity as a Function of Orienting Task," *Journal of Biological Psychology,* 9, 103–113.

CACIOPPO, J. T., and R. E. PETTY (1981a). "Electromyograms as Measures of Extent and Affectivity of Information Processing," *American Psychologist,* 36, 441–456.

CACIOPPO, J. T., and R. E. PETTY (1981b). "Electromyographic Specificity During Covert Information Processing," *Psychophysiology,* 18, 518–523.

CACIOPPO, J. T., and R. E. PETTY (1982a). "A Biosocial Model of Attitude Change: Signs, Symptoms, and Undetected Physiological Responses," in J. T. Cacioppo and R. E. Petty (Eds.), *Perspectives in Cardiovascular Psychophysiology.* New York: Guilford Press, 151–188.

CACIOPPO, J. T., and R. E. PETTY (Eds.) (1982b). *Perspectives in Cardiovascular Psychophysiology.* New York: Guilford Press.

CACIOPPO, J. T., and R. E. PETTY (1982c). "The Relationship Between Differential Hemispheric Alpha Abundance and the Affective Polarization of Thoughts About an Attitude Issue," in K. B. Monroe (Ed.), *Advances in Consumer Research,* Vol. 10. Ann Arbor, MI: Association for Consumer Research, 156–160.

CACIOPPO, J. T., and R. E. PETTY (1983a). "Foundations of Social Psychophysiology," in J. T. Cacioppo and R. E. Petty (Eds.), *Social Psychophysiology.* New York: Guilford Press, 3–36.

CACIOPPO, J. T., and R. E. PETTY (Eds.) (1983b). *Social Psychophysiology: A Sourcebook.* New York: Guilford Press.

CACIOPPO, J. T., and R. E. PETTY (1985). "Physiological Responses and Advertising Effects: Is the Cup Half Full or Half Empty?" *Psychology and Marketing,* 2, 115–126.

CACIOPPO, J. T., and R. E. PETTY (1986). "Social Processes," in M. G. H. Coles, E. Donchin, and S. Porges (Eds.), *Psychophysiology: Systems, Processes, and Applications.* New York: Guilford Press, 646–679.

CACIOPPO, J. T., R. E. PETTY, and T. R. GEEN (1989). "Attitude Structure and Function: From the Tripartite to the Homeostatis Model of Attitudes," in A. R. Pratkanis, S. J. Breckler, and A. G. Greenwold (Eds.), *Attitude Structure and Function.* Hillsdale, NJ: Erlbaum, 485–510.

CACIOPPO, J. T., R. E. PETTY, M. E. LOSCH, and H. S. KIM (1986). "Electromyographic Activity Over Facial Muscle Regions Can Differentiate the Valence Intensity of Affective Reaction," *Journal of Personality and Social Psychology,* 50, 260–268.

CACIOPPO, J. T., R. E. PETTY, and B. MARSHALL-GOODELL (1984). "Electromyographic Specificity During Simple Physical and Attitudinal Tasks: Location and Topographical Features of Integrated EMG Responses," *Biological Psychology,* 18, 85–121.

CACIOPPO, J. T., R. E. PETTY, and K. J. MORRIS (1985). "Semantic, Evaluative, and Self-Referent Processing: Memory, Cognitive Effort, and Somatovisceral Activity," *Psychophysiology,* 22, 371–384.

CACIOPPO, J. T., R. E. PETTY, and L. QUINTANOR (1982). "Individual Differences in Relative Hemispheric Alpha Abundance and Cognitive Responses to Persuasive Communications," *Journal of Personality and Social Psychology,* 43, 623–636.

CACIOPPO, J. T., R. E. PETTY, and L. G. TASSINARY (1989). "Social Psychophysiology: A New Look," in L. Berkowitz (Ed.), *Advances in Experimental Social Psychology,* Vol. 22. New York: Academic Press, 39–91.

CACIOPPO, J. T., and C. A. SANDMAN (1981). "Psychophysiological Functioning, Cognitive Responding, and Attitudes," in R. E. Petty, T. M. Ostrom, and T. C. Brock (Eds.), *Cognitive Re-*

sponses in Persuasion. Hillsdale, NJ: Erlbaum, 81–104.

CACIOPPO, J. T., C. A. SANDMAN, and B. B. WALKER (1978). "The Effects of Operant Heart Rate Conditioning on Cognitive Elaboration and Attitude Change," *Psychophysiology*, 15, 330–338.

CACIOPPO, J. T., and L. G. TASSINARY (Eds.) (in press, a). *Principles of Psychophysiology: Physical, Social, and Inferential Elements*. Cambridge: Cambridge University Press.

CACIOPPO, J. T., and L. G. TASSINARY (Eds.) (in press, b). "Psychophysiology and Psychophysiological Inference," in J. T. Cacioppo and L. G. Tassinary (Eds.), *Principles of Psychophysiology: Physical, Social, and Inferential Elements*. Cambridge: Cambridge University Press.

CACIOPPO, J. T., and L. G. TASSINARY (1989). "The Concept of Attitude: A Psychophysiological Analysis," in H. L. Wagner and A. S. R. Manstead (Eds.), *Handbook of Psychophysiology: Emotion and Social Behavior*. Chichester, England: Wiley, 307–344.

CAFFYN, J. M. (1964). "Psychological Laboratory Techniques in Copy Research," *Journal of Advertising Research*, 4, 45–50.

CAMPBELL, D. T., and D. W. FISKE (1959). "Convergent and Discriminant Validation by the Multitrait-Multimethod Matrix," *Psychological Bulletin*, 56, 81–105.

CAMPBELL, D. T., and J. C. STANLEY (1963). *Experimental and Quasi-Experimental Designs for Research*. Chicago: Rand McNally.

CARROLL, D., and P. ANASTASIADES (1978). "The Behavioral Significance of Heart Rate: The Lacey's Hypothesis," *Biological Psychology*, 1, 249–275.

COLES, M. G. H., E. DONCHIN, and S. PORGES (1986). *Psychophysiology: Systems, Processes, and Applications*. New York: Guilford Press.

COLES, M. G. H., G. GRATTON, and W. J. GEHRING (1987). "Theory in Cognitive Psychophysiology," *Journal of Psychophysiology*, 1, 13–16.

COLES, M. G. H., G. GRATTON, T. R. BASHORE, C. W. ERIKSEN, and E. DONCHIN (1985). "A Psychophysiological Investigation of the Continuous Flow Model of Human Information Processing," *Journal of Experimental Psychology: Human Perception and Performance*, 11, 529–553.

COOMBS, C. H., R. M. DAWES, and A. TVERSKY (1970). *Mathematical Psychology: An Elementary Introduction*. Englewood Cliffs, NJ: Prentice-Hall.

COTTON, J. L. (1981). "A Review of Research on Schachter's Theory of Emotion and the Misattribution of Arousal," *European Journal of Social Psychology*, 11, 365–397.

CROYLE, R. T., and J. COOPER (1983). "Dissonance Arousal: Physiological Evidence," *Journal of Personality and Social Psychology*, 45, 782–791.

CUMMING, W. H., and M. VENKATESAN (1976). "Cognitive Dissonance and Consumer Behavior: A Review of the Evidence," *Journal of Marketing Research*, 13, 303–308.

DAVIDSON, R. J. (1984). "Affective, Cognitive, and Hemispheric Specialization," in C. E. Izard, J. Kagan, and R. Zajonc (Eds.), *Emotion, Cognition, and Behavior*. New York: Cambridge University Press.

DAVIDSON, R. J., and N. A. FOX (1982). "Asymmetrical Brain Activity Discriminates Between Positive versus Negative Affecting Stimuli in 10-month-old Human Infants," *Science*, 218, 1235–1236.

DAVIDSON, R. J., G. E. SCHWARTZ, C. SHARON, J. BENNETT, and D. J. GOLEMAN (1979). "Frontal versus Parietal EEG Asymmetry During Positive and Negative Affect," *Psychophysiology*, 16, 202–203.

DICKSON, H. W., and E. MCGINNIES (1966). "Affectivity in the Arousal of Attitudes as Measured by Galvanic Skin Responses," *American Journal of Psychology*, 79, 584–587.

DUFFY, E. (1957). "The Psychological Significance of the Concept of 'Arousal' or 'Activation,'" *Psychological Review*, 64, 265–275.

DUFFY, E. (1962). *Activation and Behavior*. New York: Wiley.

EHRLICHMAN, H., and A. WEINBERGER (1978). "Lateral Eye Movements and Hemispheric Asymmetry: A Critical Review," *Psychological Bulletin*, 1080–1101.

EKMAN, P., R. W. LEVENSON, and W. V. FRIESEN (1983). "Autonomic Nervous System Activity Distinguishes Among Emotions," *Science*, 221, 1208–1210.

ENGLIS, B. G., K. D. VAUGHAN, and J. T. LANZETTA (1982). "Conditioning of Counteremphatic Emotional Responses," *Journal of Experimental Social Psychology*, 18, 375–391.

ERIKSEN, C. W., and D. W. SCHULTZ (1979). "Information Processing in Visual Search: A Continuous Flow Conception and Experimental Results," *Perception and Psychophysics*, 25, 249–263.

EYSENCK, M. W. AND S. FOLKARD (1980). "Personality, Time of Day, and Caffeine: Some Theoretical and Conceptual Problems in Revelle et al.," *Journal of Experimental Psychology*, 109, 33–41.

FAZIO, R. H., and J. COOPER (1983). "Arousal in the Dissonance Process," in J. T. Cacioppo and R. E. Petty (Eds.), *Social Psychophysiology: A Sourcebook*. New York: Guilford Press.

FAZIO, R. H., D. M. SANBONMATSU, M. C. POWELL, and F. R. KARDES (1986). "On the Automatic Activation of Attitudes," *Journal of Personality and Social Psychology*, 50, 229–238.

FESTINGER, L. (1957). *A Theory of Cognitive Dissonance*. Stanford, CA: Stanford University Press.

FLETCHER, J. E. (1971). "The Orienting Response as an Index of Mass Communication Effect," *Psychophysiology*, 8, 699–703.

FOWLES, D. C. (1980). "The Three Arousal Model: Implications of Gray's Two-factor Learning Theory for Heart Rate, Electrodermal Activity, and Psychopathy," *Psychophysiology*, 17, 87–104.

FRIDLUND, A. J., and J. T. CACIOPPO (1986). "Guidelines for Human Electromyographic Research," *Psychophysiology*, 23, 567–589.

FUREDY, J. J. (1983). "Operational, Analogical, and Genuine Definitions of Psychophysiology," *International Journal of Psychophysiology*, 1, 13–19.

GALE, A., and J. A. EDWARDS (1983). *Physiological Correlates of Human Behavior, Vol. 1: Basic Issues*. London: Academic Press.

GALLUP and ROBINSON STUDY (1980). Described in Olson and Ray (1983).

GARRITZ, L. I. (1977). "Electromyography: A Review of the Current Status of Subvocal Speech Research," *Memory and Cognition*, 5, 615–622.

GEEN, R. G. (1977). "Affects of Anticipation of Positive and Negative Outcomes on Audience Anxiety," *Journal of Consulting and Clinical Psychology*, 45, 715–716.

GEEN, R. G. (1979). "Affects of Being Observed on Learning Following Success and Failure Experiences," *Motivation and Emotion*, 3, 355–371.

GEEN, R. G., and B. J. BUSHMAN (1989). "The Arousing Effect of Social Presence," in H. Wagner and A. Manstead (Eds.), *Handbook of Social Psychophysiology*. Chichester, England: Wiley, 261–281.

GEEN, R. G., and J. J. GANGE (1977). "Drive Theory of Social Facilitation: Twelve Years of Theory and Research," *Psychological Bulletin*, 84, 1267–1288.

GERARD, H. B. (1967). "Choice Difficulty, Dissonance, and the Decision Sequence," *Journal of Personality*, 35, 91–108.

GRANT, J., and D. E. ALLMAN (1988). "Voice Stress Analyzer is a Marketing Research Tool," *Marketing News*, January 4, 22.

HALPERN, S. (1967). "Application of Pupil Response to Before and After Experiments, *Journal of Marketing Research*, 4, 320–321.

HANSEN, F. (1981). "Hemispheric Lateralization: Implications for Understanding Consumer Behavior," *Journal of Consumer Research*, 8, 23–25.

HARE, R. D. (1973). "Orienting and Defensive Responses to Visual Stimuli," *Psychophysiology*, 10, 453–464.

HESS, E. H. (1965). "Attitude and Pupil Size," *Scientific American*, 212, 46–54.

HESS, E. H., and J. M. POLT (1960). "Pupil Size as Related to Interest Value of Visual Stimuli," *Science*, 132, 349–350.

HIRSCHMAN, R., and M. CLARK (1983). "Bogus Physiological Feedback," in J. T. Cacioppo and R. E. Petty (Eds.), *Social Psychophysiology*. New York: Guilford Press, 177–214.

HOLLIEN, H. (1981). "Vocal Indicators of Psychological Stress," *Annals, New York Academy of Science*, 47–72.

HOPKINS, R. (1987). "Consumer 'Act-Good' Responses in Pre-Tests and Subsequent Sales," in J. H. Leigh and C. R. Martin (Eds.), *Current Issues and Research in Advertising*. Ann Arbor, MI: The University of Michigan, 1–38.

IZARD, C. E. (1972). *Patterns of Emotions*. New York: Academic Press.

IZARD, C. E. (1977). *Human Emotions*. New York: Plenum.

JANISSE, M. P. (1977). *Pupillometry: The Psychology of the Pupillary Response*, Washington, DC: Hemisphere.

JENNINGS, RICHARD J. (1986). "Memory, Thought, and Bodily Response," in M. G. H. Coles, E. Donclin, and S. W. Porges (Eds.), *Psychophysiology: Systems, Processes, and Applications*. New York: Guilford Press: 290–308.

JOHNSON, L. C., and A. LUBIN (1972). "On Planning Psychophysiology Experiments: Design, Measurement, and Analysis," in M. S. Greenfield and R. A. Sternback (Eds.), *Handbook of Psychophysiology*. New York: Holt, Rinehart & Winston.

KAHNEMAN, D. (1973). *Attention and Effort.* Englewood Cliffs, NJ: Prentice-Hall.

KLEBBA, J. M. (1985). "Physiological Measures of Research: A Review of Brain Activity, Electrodermal Response, Pupil Dilation, and Voice Analysis Methods and Studies," in J. H. Leigh and C. R. Martin, Jr. (Eds.), *Current Issues and Research in Advertising,* Vol. 1. Ann Arbor, MI: University of Michigan Graduate School of Business Administration, 53–76.

KOHAN, X. (1968). "A Physiological Measure of Commercial Effectiveness," *Journal of Advertising Research,* 8, 46–48.

KROEBER-RIEL, W. (1979). "Activation Research: Psychobiological Approaches in Consumer Research," *Journal of Consumer Research,* 5, 240–250.

KRUGMAN, H. E. (1964). "Some Applications of Pupil Measurement," *Journal of Marketing Research,* 1, 15–19.

KRUGMAN, H. E. (1965). "A Comparison of Physical and Verbal Responses to Television Commercials," *Public Opinion Quarterly,* 29, 323–325.

KRUGMAN, H. E. (1971). "Brain Wave Measures of Media Involvement," *Journal of Advertising Research,* 11, 3–9.

KRUGMAN, H. E. (1981). "The Effective Use of Physiological Measurement in Advertising Research," unpublished working paper presented at the 12th Annual Attitude Research Conference, American Marketing Association, Hot Springs, VA.

LACEY, B. C., and J. I. LACEY (1974). "Studies of Heart Rate and Other Bodily Processes in Sensorimotor Behavior," in P. A. Obrist, A. H. Black, U. J. Berner, and L. V. DiCara (Eds.), *Cardiovascular Psychophysiology: Current Issues in Response Mechanisms, Biofeedback and Methodology.* Chicago: Aldine-Atherton.

LACEY, J. I. (1967). "Somatic Response Patterning and Stress: Some Revisions of Activation Theory," in M. H. Appley and R. Trumbull (Eds.), *Psychological Stress.* New York: Appleton-Century-Crofts.

LAZARUS, R. L. (1982). "Thoughts on the Relations Between Emotion and Cognition," *American Psychologist,* 37, 1019–1024.

LEVENTHAL, H. (1980). "Toward a Comprehensive Theory of Emotion," in L. Berkowitz (Ed.), *Advances in Experimental Social Psychology,* 13, 139–207.

LEVENTHAL, H., and P. MOSBACH (1983). "The Perceptual-Motor Theory of Emotion," in J. T.

Cacioppo and R. E. Petty (Eds.), *Social Psychophysiology: A Sourcebook.* New York: Guilford Press.

LYKKEN, D. T., R. ROSE, B. LUTHER, and M. MALEY (1966). "Correcting Psychophysiological Measures for Individual Differences in Range," *Psychological Bulletin,* 66, 481–484.

LYNN, R. (1966). *Attention, Arousal, and the Orientation Reaction.* Oxford: Pergamon Press.

MALMO, R. B. (1959). "Activation: A Neuropsychological Dimension," *Psychological Review,* 66, 367–386.

MARSHALL, G. D., and P. G. ZIMBARDO (1979). "Affective Consequences of Inadequately Explained Physiological Arousal," *Journal of Personality and Social Psychology,* 37, 970–988.

MARTIN, C. R., JR., and N. J. NIGHSWONGER (1981). "Voice Analysis in Advertising Research: Two Additional Concerns," in H. Keith Hunt (Ed.), *Advertising in a New Age.* New York: American Academy of Advertising, 64–67.

MASLACH, C. (1979). "Negative Emotional Biasing of Unexplained Arousal," *Journal of Personality and Social Psychology,* 37, 953–969.

McCARTHY, G., and E. DONCHIN (1981). "A Metric for Thought: A Comparison of P300 Latency and Reaction Time," *Science,* 211, 77–80.

MERSULUM, M., and J. PERRY (1972). "The Diagnosis of Love-Sickness: Experimental Psychophysiology without the Polygraph," *Psychophysiology,* 9, 546–551.

METALIS, S. A., and E. H. HESS (1982). "Pupillary Response/Semantic Differential Scale Relationships," *Journal of Research in Personality,* 16, 201–216.

MILLER, J. (1982). "Discrete versus Continuous Stage Models of Human Information Processing: In Search of Partial Output," *Journal of Experimental Psychology: Human Perception and Performance,* 8, 273–296.

MILLER, J. (1983). "Can Response Preparation Begin Before Stimulus Recognition Finishes?" *Journal of Experimental Psychology: Human Perception and Performance,* 9, 161–192.

MORRISON, B. J., and M. J. DAINOFF (1972). "Advertisement Complexity and Looking Time," *Journal of Marketing Research,* 9, 396–400.

NELSON, R. A., and D. SWARTZ (1979). "Voice Pitch Analysis," *Journal of Advertising Research,* 19, 55–59.

NIEDERMEYER, E. (1982). "The Normal EEG of the

Waking Adult," in E. Niedermeyer and F. Lopes Da Silva (Eds.), *Electroencephalography*. Baltimore, MD and Munich, FRG: Urban and Schwarzenberg.

NIGHSWONGER, N. J., and C. R. MARTIN, JR. (1981). "On Using Voice Analysis in Marketing Research," *Journal of Marketing Research*, 18, 350–355.

NOTARIUS, C. I., and L. R. HERRICK (1989). "The Psychophysiology of Dyadic Interaction," in H. Wagner and A. Manstead, (Eds.), *Handbook of Psychophysiology*. Chichester, England: Wiley, 393–419.

OBRIST, P. A. (1982). "Cardiac-Behavioral Interactions: A Critical Appraisal," in J. T. Cacioppo and R. E. Petty (Eds.), *Perspectives in Cardiovascular Psychophysiology*. New York: Guilford Press.

OLSON, J. C., and W. J. RAY (1983). "Using Brainwave Measures to Assess Advertising Effects," Report No. 83-108, Marketing Science Institute, Cambridge, MA.

OSTER, P. J., and J. A. STERN (1980). "Electro-oculography," in I. Martin and P. H. Venables (Eds.), *Techniques in Psychophysiology*. London: Wiley.

PETTY, R. E., and J. T. CACIOPPO (1983). "The Role of Bodily Responses in Attitude Measurement and Change," in J. T. Cacioppo and R. E. Petty (Eds), *Social Psychophysiology: A Sourcebook*. New York: Guilford Press, 51–101.

PETTY, R. E., and J. T. CACIOPPO (1986a). *Communication and Persuasion: Central and Peripheral Routes to Persuasion*. New York: Springer-Verlag.

PETTY, R. E., and J. T. CACIOPPO (1986b). "The Elaboration Likelihood Model of Persuasion," in L. Berkowitz (Ed.), *Advances in Experimental Social Psychology*, Vol. 19. New York: Academic Press, 123–205.

POPPER, K. R. (1968). *The Logic of Scientific Discovery*. New York: Harper and Row.

RAGOT, R. (1984). "Perceptual and Motor Space Representation: An Event-Related Potential Study," *Psychophysiology*, 21, 159–170.

RANKIN, R. E., and D. T. CAMPBELL (1955). "Galvanic Skin Response to Negro and White Experimenters," *Journal of Abnormal and Social Psychology*, 51, 30–33.

RAY, M. L. (1974). "Consumer Initial Processing: Definitions, Issues, and Applications," in G. D. Hughes and M. L. Ray (Eds.), *Buyer/Consumer Information Processing*. Chapel Hill, NC: University of North Carolina Press, 145–156.

RAY, W. J., and J. C. OLSON (1983). "Perspectives on Psychophysiological Assessment of Psychological Responses to Advertising," in L. Percy and A. G. Woodside (Eds.), *Advertising and Consumer Psychology*. Lexington, MA: Lexington Books, 253–269.

REVELLE, W., M.S. HUMPHREYS, L. SIMON, and K. GILLILAND, (1980). "The Interactive Effect of Personality, Time of Day, and Caffeine: A Test of the Arousal Model," *Journal of Experimental Psychology* 108, 1–31.

ROTHSCHILD, M. L. (1982). "Summary of Brain Wave Data as an Advertising Diagnostic," *Advances in Consumer Research*, 9, 184.

SALOVEY, P., and D. L. ROSENHAN (1989). "Mood States and Prosocial Behavior," in H. Wagner and A. Manstead, (Eds.), *Handbook of Social Psychophysiology*. Chichester, England: Wiley, 371–391.

SANBONMATSU, D. M., and F. R. KARDES (1988). "The Effects of Physiological Arousal on Information Processing and Persuasion," *Journal of Consumer Research*, 15, 379–385.

SCHACHTER, S., and J. SINGER (1962). "Cognitive, Social, and Physiological Determinants of Emotional State," *Psychological Review*, 65, 379–399.

SCHACHTER, S., and J. SINGER (1979). "Comments on the Maslach and Marshall-Zimbardo Experiments," *Journal of Personality and Social Psychology*, 37, 989–995.

SCHEIER, M. F., C. S. CARVER, and K. A. MATTHEWS (1983). "Attentional Factors in the Perception of Bodily States," in J. T. Cacioppo and R. E. Petty (Eds.), *Social Psychophysiology*. New York: Guilford Press: 510–542.

SCHWARTZ, G. E. (1986). "Emotion and Psychophysiological Organization: A Systems Approach," in M. G. H. Coles, E. Donchin, and S. W. Porges (Eds.), *Psychophysiology: Systems, Processes, and Applications*. New York: Guilford Press: 354–377.

SCHWARTZ, G. E., P. L. FAIR, P. SALT, M. R. MANDEL, and G. L. KLERMAN (1976). "Facial Muscle Patterning to Affective Imagery in Depressed and Nondepressed Subjects," *Science*, 192, 489–491.

SCHWARTZ, G. E., and D. A. WEINBERGER (1980). "Patterns of Emotional Responses to Affective Situations: Relations Among Happiness, Sadness, Anger, Fear, Depression and Anxiety," *Motivation and Emotion*, 4, 175–191.

SCHWARTZ, G. E., D. A. WEINBERGER, and J. A.

SINGER (1981). "Cardiovascular Differentiation of Happiness, Sadness, Anger, and Fear Following Imagery and Exercise," *Psychosomatic Medicine,* 43, 343–364.

SHAPIRO, D., and J. L. REEVES II (1982). "Modification of Physiological and Subjective Responses to Stress Through Heart Rate Biofeedback," in J. T. Cacioppo and R. E. Petty (Eds.), *Perspectives in Cardiovascular Psychophysiology.* New York: Guilford Press.

SINGH, S. N., and G. A. CHURCHILL, JR. (1987). "Arousal and Advertising Effectiveness," *Journal of Advertising,* 16, 4–10, 40.

SIROTA, A. D., and G. E. SCHWARTZ (1982). "Facial Muscle Patterning and Lateralization During Elation and Depression Imagery," *Journal of Abnormal Psychology,* 91, 25–34.

SMITH, W. (1922). *The Measurement of Emotion.* London: Kegan Paul.

SOKOLOV, A. N. (1963). *Perception and the Conditional Reflex.* Oxford: Pergamon.

SOLOMON, E. P., and G. A. PHILLIPS (1987). *Understanding Human Anatomy and Physiology.* Philadelphia: Saunders.

STAFFORD, J. E., A. E. BIRDWELL, and C. E. VON TASSEL (1970). "Integrated Advertising—White Backlash?" *Journal of Advertising Research,* 10, 15–20.

STERN, R. M., W. J. RAY, and C. M. DAVIS (1980). *Psychophysiological Recording.* New York: Oxford University Press.

STERNBERG, S. (1969). "The Discovery of Processing Stages: Extensions of Donder's Method," in W. G. Koster (Ed.), *Attention and Performance II.* Amsterdam: North Holland, 276–315.

STEWART, D. W. (1984). "Physiological Measurement of Advertising Effects," *Psychology and Marketing,* 1, 43–48.

STEWART, D. W. (1985). "Differences Between Basic Research and the Validation of Specific Measures: A Reply to Weinstein, et al.," *Psychology and Marketing,* 2, 41–49.

STEWART, D. W., and D. H. FURSE (1982). "Applying Psychophysiological Measures to Marketing and Advertising Research Problems," in J. H. Leigh and C. R. Martin (Eds.), *Current Issues and Research in Advertising,* Ann Arbor, MI: University of Michigan Press, 1–38.

SYZ, H. (1926–1927). "Observations on Unreliability of Subjective Reports of Emotional Reactions," *British Journal of Psychology,* 17, 119–126.

TASSINARY, L. G., B. S. MARSHALL-GOODELL, and J. T. CACIOPPO (1985). "Microcomputers in Social Psychophysiological Research: An Overview," *Behavior Research Methods, Instruments, & Computers,* 17, 532–536.

TREISTMAN, J., and J. P. GREGG (1979). "Visual, Verbal, and Sales Response to Print Ads," *Journal of Advertising Research,* 19, 41–47.

TRYON, W. W. (1975). "Pupillometry: A Survey of Sources of Variation," *Psychophysiology,* 12, 90–93.

TUCKER, D. M., C. E. STENSLIE, R. S. ROTH, and S. L. SHEARER (1981). "Right Frontal Lobe Activation and Right Hemisphere Performance Decrement During a Depressed Mood," *Achives of General Psychiatry,* 38, 169–174.

TURPIN, G. (1986). "Effects of Stimulus Intensity on Autonomic Responding: The Problem of Differentiating Orienting and Defense Reflexes," *Psychophysiology,* 23, 1–14.

TURSKY, B. T. (1974). "Recording of Human Eye Movement," in R. F. Thompson and M. M. Patterson (Eds.), *Bioelectric Recording Techniques.* New York: Academic Press.

TURSKY, B., and L. JAMNER (1983). "Evaluation of Social and Political Beliefs: A Psychophysiological Approach," in J. T. Cacioppo and R. E. Petty (Eds.), *Social Psychophysiology: A Sourcebook.* New York: Guilford Press.

VAUGHAN, K. D., and J. T. LANZETTA (1980). "Vicarious Instigation and Conditioning of Facial Expression in Autonomic Responses to a Model's Display of Pain," *Journal of Personality and Social Psychology,* 38, 909–923.

VENABLES, P. H., and M. J. CHRISTIE (1980). "Electrodermal Activity," in I. Martin and P. H. Venables (Eds.), *Techniques in Psychophysiology,* New York: Wiley, 3–67.

WAGNER, H. L., and A. MANSTEAD (Eds.) (1989). *Handbook of Psychophysiology: Emotion and Social Behavior.* Chichester, England: Wiley.

WATSON, P. J., and R. J. GATCHEL (1979). "Autonomic Measures of Advertising," *Journal of Advertising Research,* 19, 15–26.

WENGER, M. A. (1972). "Automic Balance," in N. S. Greenfield and R. A. Sternbach (Eds.), *Handbook of Psychophysiology.* New York: Holt, Rinehart & Winston.

WEINSTEIN, S. (1982). "A Review of Brain Hemisphere Research," *Journal of Advertising Research,* 22, 59–63.

WEINSTEIN, S., V. APPEL, and C. WEINSTEIN

(1980). "Brain-activity Responses to Magazine and Television Advertising," *Journal of Advertising Research,* 20, 57–63.

WEINSTEIN, S., R. DROZDENKO, and C. WEINSTEIN (1985). "Brain Wave Analysis in Advertising Research: Validation from Basic Research and Independent Replications," *Psychology and Marketing,* 2.

WEINSTEIN, S., C. WEINSTEIN, and R. DROZDENKO (1984). "Brain Wave Analysis: An Electroencephalographic Technique Used for Evaluating the Communication-effect of Advertising," *Psychology and Marketing,* 1, 17–42.

WESLEY, W. A. (1978). "The Use of the Psychogalvanometer in Testing the Effectiveness of Advertising," paper presented at the 16th Annual Advertising Research Conference, New York Chapter of the American Marketing Association. Available from the Walt Wesley Company, 348 W. Sierra Madre Blvd., Sierra Madre, CA 91024.

WESLEY, W. A. (1981). "Validation Studies Indicating a Relationship Between The Wesley 'Arousal' Method (WAM) and Sales," unpublished manuscript, available from the Walt Wesley Company, 348 W. Sierra Madre Blvd., Sierra Madre, CA 91024.

WHITE, G. L., and I. MALTZMAN (1978). "Pupillary Activity While Listening to Verbal Passages," *Journal of Research in Personality,* 12, 361–369.

WICKLUND, R. A., and J. W. BREHM (1976). *Perspectives on Cognitive Dissonance.* Hillsdale, NJ: Erlbaum.

WILDER, J. (1967). *Stimulus and Response: The Law of Initial Value.* Bristol, England: Wright.

WILLIAMS, C., and K. STEVENS (1972). "Emotions and Speech: Some Acoustical Correlates," *Journal of the Acoustical Society of America,* 52, 238–250.

WITT, D. (1977). "Emotional Advertising: The Relationship Between Eye-Movement Patterns and Memory—Empirical Study with the Eye-Movement Monitor," unpublished Ph.D. dissertation, University of the Saarlands, Federal Republic of Germany.

WRIGHT, P., and P. D. RIP (1980). "Product Class Advertising Effects on First-time Buyers' Decision Strategies," *Journal of Consumer Research,* 7, 176–188.

YANIV, I., and D. E. MEYER (1987). "Activation and Metacognition of Inaccessible Stored Information: Potential Bases for Incubation Effects in Problem Solving," *Journal of Experimental Psychology: Learning, Memory, and Cognition,* 13, 187–205.

YOUNG, L., and D. SHEENA (1975). "Survey of Eye Movement Recording Methods," *Behavior of Research Methods and Instrumentation,* 7, 397–429.

ZAJONC, R. B. (1965). "Social Facilitation," *Science,* 149, 269–274.

ZAJONC, R. B. (1980a). "Feeling and Thinking: Preferences Need No Inferences," *American Psychologist,* 35, 151–175.

ZAJONC, R. B. (1980b). "Compresence," in P. B. Paulis (Ed.), *Psychology of Group Influence.* Hillsdale, NJ: Erlbaum.

ZAJONC, R. B. (1984). "On the Primacy of Affect," *American Psychologist,* 39, 117–123.

NEO-PAVLOVIAN CONDITIONING AND ITS IMPLICATIONS FOR CONSUMER THEORY AND RESEARCH

5

Terence A. Shimp*

University of South Carolina

In recent years consumer researchers have begun to show considerable interest in classical conditioning, also referred to as Pavlovian or respondent conditioning. This chapter's primary objectives are to provide an updated view of classical conditioning and to show how the modern (neo-Pavlovian) theory of classic conditioning is a fully cognitive one that has a meaningful nexus with better known research streams in consumer behavior. Requirements for conducting true classical conditioning experiments are discussed; major consumer behavior applications of classical conditioning are reviewed; and opportunities for further research are examined.

INTRODUCTION

Pavlovian conditioning—also known as classical or respondent conditioning—has interested consumer researchers for years. Although much remains to be learned about classical conditioning in a consumer behavior context,

impressive strides are being made. Nord and Peter's (1980) treatment of the behavior modification perspective likely played some role in encouraging Gorn's (1982) seminal demonstration of classical conditioning in a consumer behavior context. This work encouraged subsequent empirical efforts and probably also played some role in influencing two nonconsumer researchers, McSweeney and Bierley (1984), to submit their outstanding review article to the *Journal of Consumer Research*. That article introduced many of us to the complexities and intricacies of classical conditioning,

*My sincere appreciation goes out to the following friends and colleagues for helpful comments and suggestions on earlier drafts: Chris Allen, Gerry Gorn, Hal Kassarjian, Tom Madden, Paul Peter, Tom Robertson, Elnora Stuart, and Joe Urbany.

prompted additional empirical activity, and guided discussions of conditioning in consumer behavior texts (e.g., Engel, Blackwell, and Miniard 1986; Mowen 1987).[1]

Despite these advances, the general coverage of classical conditioning is not substantially different than what appeared more than two decades ago in the first major consumer behavior text (Engel, Kollat, and Blackwell 1968). Significant developments in the theory of classical conditioning have not entered consumer behavior on a wide scale basis. However, we can take comfort in knowing that our discipline is no different than the rest of psychology. Robert Rescorla, a noted conditioning scholar, chastised his colleagues in a self-descriptive review article titled "Pavlovian Conditioning: It's Not What You Think It Is" (Rescorla 1988).

It is true; the modern view of Pavlovian conditioning is dramatically different than what most of us thought. The conventional—though, as will be shown, outdated—view is that classical conditioning is a simple, primitive, non-complex, automatic, passive form of low-involvement learning. This chapter will build the case that there is much more to conditioning than this; indeed, more descriptive chapter titles might have been: "How Can Something So Apparently Simple Be So Complex?" or "Classical Conditioning: A Chimera?" The chapter's primary objectives are to provide an updated view of classical conditioning and to show how the modern perspective might direct more sophisticated research.

GENERAL LEARNING THEORY AND CONSUMER BEHAVIOR

Classical conditioning is part of the learning-theory tradition in psychology. Since the days of the psychologist John Hall, learning has been considered to represent changes in response tendencies resulting from experience. Modern learning theorists offer definitions of learning such as "an enduring change in the mechanisms of behavior that results from experience with environmental events" (Domjan and Burkhard 1986, p. 12). Learning is seen as a process of adaptation whereby an individual alters goal-directed behavior in response to changing environmental conditions (Holyoak, Koh, and Nisbett 1989). In the marketplace, learning occurs when consumers adapt their beliefs to make sense of new data (Hoch and Deighton 1989). Learning includes the learning of attitudes and other cognitive elements as well as the learning of overt behavioral responses. The learning of attitudes is the area in which classical conditioning likely has the most to offer consumer researchers.

General learning theory in psychology and treatments of the subject in the consumer literature (e.g., Engel, Blackwell, and Miniard 1986; Hawkins, Best, and Coney 1986; Ray 1973; Wilkie 1986) distinguish two major types of learning: (1) the cognitive orientation and (2) what is variously called the stimulus-response, the behavioral, or the associative orientation. This latter orientation includes Pavlovian (classical, respondent conditioning) and instrumental (operant) conditioning.

Cognitive Learning

The cognitive orientation, which is closely aligned with the consumer information processing model of consumer behavior, views learning as an active process whereby the consumer forms hypotheses about consumption alternatives, acquires and encodes information, and integrates the new information with preexisting beliefs (Alba and Hutchinson 1987; Bettman 1979; Hoch and Deighton 1989). Several chapters in this volume deal directly or indirectly with the cognitive tradition and nothing more will be said here about cognitive learning.

Associative Learning

Associative learning takes place when humans or lower animals draw connections be-

---

[1]The present chapter is devoted exclusively to Pavlovian conditioning; all references to conditioning are to be taken as referring to Pavlovian (classical) conditioning and not to operant (instrumental) conditioning.

tween environmental events (Petty and Cacioppo 1981). Contained within the associative framework are instrumental (operant) as well as Pavlovian conditioning, but only the latter is discussed in this chapter. (For treatments of the instrumental (operant) conditioning tradition and its implications for consumer behavior, see Foxall 1986; Nord and Peter 1980; Peter and Nord 1982; and Rothchild and Gaidis 1981).

Classical associative learning has as its kernel idea the rather vague notion of an association. Philosophers and psychologists have long disputed the concept of association. Many researchers consider an association as nothing more than the linkage or connection between two concepts (cf. Murdock 1985). Others regard an association as the fusing or blending of two ideas. "There is no 'link' or 'connection' at all. Instead, the two separate items are combined to form a larger unit that has no immediate resemblance to either item alone" (Murdock 1985, p. 470).

Technical distinction noted, it is beyond the purpose of the present undertaking to pursue the issue of whether an association is a connection or a fusion of concepts. The fact, regardless, is that both consumer researchers and marketing practitioners regard associative learning to be a significant aspect of consumer behavior. For example, a Coca-Cola executive exclaimed: "Pavlov took a neutral object and by associating it with a meaningful object, made it a symbol of something else . . . that is what we try to do in modern advertising" (cited in Peter and Olson 1987; Wilkie 1986). A recent advertising campaign for a branded produce product, Foxy lettuce, used model and actress Brooke Shields in television spots and magazine ads. In justifying the choice of Ms. Shields, the creative director for the advertising agency exclaimed: "Once the association is made between the product and the beauty angle, any woman who walks into the supermarket would prefer to pick up Foxy [lettuce]" (Meyers 1989). Other examples of associational marketing efforts are universal.

Classical Conditioning: A Mechanism for Associative Learning

Associative learning via classical conditioning involves the organism's learning of an association between a conditioned stimulus (CS) and a biological salient (e.g., food, fragrance) or symbolically salient (e.g., patriotic monuments) unconditioned stimulus (US). In a consumer behavior context, conditioned stimuli are brands, products, stores, and other consumption objects, whereas unconditioned stimuli include celebrities and entertainers (such as Brooke Shields in the Foxy lettuce example), music, and well-known consumption symbols that have acquired meaning for consumers through higher-order learning. Through their association, the CS comes to elicit a conditioned response (CR) that may or may not be similar to the unconditioned response (UR) that is evoked by the US itself.

TRADITIONAL VERSUS MODERN PERSPECTIVES ON PAVLOVIAN CONDITIONING

The foregoing discussion has provided a general overview of Pavlovian conditioning. In this section I elaborate on issues only alluded to previously and compare in detail the traditional view of conditioning with the neo-Pavlovian, or cognitive, perspective. Bear in mind that what is referred to as the traditional view is the model that still dominates thinking throughout psychology and consumer behavior (cf. Rescorla 1988).

Traditional View of Pavlovian Conditioning

Pavlovian (classical) conditioning traditionally has been regarded as a dumb sort of learning (Davies, Davies, and Bennett 1982, p. 663) involving a reflexive, automatic, and noncognitive process by which an animal or human learns (Bettman 1979, p. 270). When the classical conditioning paradigm was exported to the United States from Russia, this noncognitive, reflexive conception of Pavlovian conditioning "fit well with the flourishing behavioristic zeitgeist" (Dawson, Schell, Beers, and Kelly 1982, p. 274). However, as will be shown shortly, the modern view of Pavlovian conditioning has supplanted the reflexive conception with a fully cognitive account.

S-R Relations and Reflexes. The traditional view holds that conditioning represents the establishment of new reflexes, or stimulus-response (S-R) connections, resulting from frequent pairings of conditioned and unconditioned stimuli. Classical conditioning, according to this view, is seen as little more than "a kind of low-level mechanical process in which the control over a response is passed from one stimulus to another" (Rescorla 1988, p. 152). The conditioned stimulus is viewed, in other words, as a mechanism for evoking the same response as elicited by the unconditioned stimulus itself (see Figure 5.1). This perspective applied to consumer behavior would suggest, for example, that if a particular musical arrangement emotionally excites the listener, then a brand paired with that music should similarly excite the consumer.

Consumer scholars have incorporated this approach as evidenced by the following sampling of views:[2]

[T]he process of classically conditioning an organism nearly always involves a stimulus that reflexively elicits some type of response. (Mowen 1987, p. 179)

Classical conditioning assumes that consumers are passive beings who react with predictable responses to stimuli after a number of trials. (Schiffman and Kanuk 1987, p. 240)

[Classical conditioning learning] seems to occur

---

[2]I hasten to note that my intent is not to be contemptuous of individual authors or to embarrass anyone. Many of these scholars will have been exposed to the same literature I have read in recent years and would now present a more sophisticated perspective on classical conditioning.

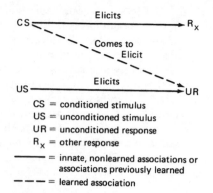

CS = conditioned stimulus
US = unconditioned stimulus
UR = unconditioned response
R_X = other response
——— = innate, nonlearned associations or associations previously learned
– – – = learned association

FIGURE 5.1 Traditional View of Classical Conditioning Process

in an almost automatic fashion. (Wilkie 1986, p. 422)

[Classical conditioned learners are] essentially passive, since they do not consciously control the emission of the response. (Robertson, Zielinski, and Ward 1984, p. 193)

[Classical affective conditioning] is . . . a relatively passive and automatic learning process. (Rossiter and Percy 1983, p. 117)

[T]here appears to be an emerging consensus that classical conditioning is especially germane in passive/uninvolving consumption contexts . . . (Allen and Madden 1985, p. 301)

[Classical conditioning is] probably most common in low-involvement situations. (Hawkins, Best, and Coney 1986, p. 348)

The widespread view that classical conditioning is a passive, reflexive form of learning that is relevant only to low-involvement consumption behavior is somewhat odd, however, when one considers that most of what is known about conditioning has been borrowed from research with lower animal life (e.g., Pavlov's widely cited dog experiments). It would seem in the phylogenic scheme of things that dogs attempting to acquire food, rats trying to avoid being shocked, and rabbits making every effort to avoid having air blown in their eyes are anything but uninvolved!

Separation of Theoretical Traditions. Philosophical reasons and matters of metaphysical ideal provide a further account for why the traditional view of Pavlovian conditioning continues to hold sway. Modern conditioning theory can be said to fall somewhere in the "seams" between the behaviorist and the cognitive traditions.[3] Some scholars oppose this fusion of originally bifurcated ontologies and argue for the complete separation of behaviorist and cognitive traditions when studying social phenomena. For example, Kahle, Beatty, and Kennedy (1987, p. 411) assert: " 'Cognitive classical conditioning' is an inherently contradictory phrase."

The Modern View

Pavlovian conditioning has undergone a revolution during the past two decades to the point where the approach now taken by many researchers is a thoroughgoingly cognitive one (Furedy, Riley, and Fredrikson 1983, p. 126; see also Holland 1984). The modern view holds that Pavlovian conditioning involves the learning of *relations among events in the environment,* or, in other words, conditioning is cognitive associative learning (Dawson, Schell, Beers, and Kelly 1982, p. 275). Classically conditioned learning, according to the modern view, is not the acquisition of new reflexes but the acquisition of new knowledge about the world (Mackintosh 1983, p. 10).

Mere Contiguity Is Insufficient. Until at least the mid-1960s, conditioning theorists believed that simple contiguity, that is, the mere pairing of conditioned and unconditioned stimuli, was the key factor determining the level of associative learning (cf. Granger and Schlimmer 1986). Although contiguity of CS and US remains important to modern views of conditioning, contiguity per se is neither necessary nor sufficient. The modern view "emphasizes the

---

[3]The "seam" metaphor was coined by Anderson (1986, p. 165) in his discussion of programmatic dominance and ontological barriers involved in crossing research traditions. Allen and Janiszewski (1989) picked up on this metaphor and characterized attitudinal conditioning as being in the "seam" somewhere between cognitivism and behaviorism.

information that one stimulus gives about another . . . [and recognizes] that arranging for two well-processed events to be contiguous need not produce an association between them; nor does the failure to arrange contiguity preclude associative learning" (Rescorla 1988, p. 152). In response to what he believes are serious misconceptions of the theory, Rescorla (1988, p. 154), remonstrates:

Pavlovian conditioning is not a stupid process by which the organism willy-nilly forms associations between any two stimuli that happen to co-occur. Rather, the organism is better seen as an information seeker using logical and perceptual relations among events, along with its own preconceptions, to form a sophisticated representation of its world. . . . If one thinks of Pavlovian conditioning as developing between a CS and a US under just those circumstances that would lead a scientist to conclude that the CS causes the US, one has a surprisingly successful heuristic for remembering the facts of what it takes to produce Pavlovian associative learning. . . .

Contingency Relations and S-S Learning. It is the covariation between CS and US and not simply their nearness in time and space that determines the likelihood and strength of classical conditioning (Hugdahl 1987, p. 148). Contingency relations, or CS-US event relations, are not tantamount to mere pairings between the CS and US. Rather, contingency is established when an animal or human learns that the probability of the US occurring, given that the CS has occurred, is greater over trials than the probability of the US occurring given that the CS has not occurred. Symbolically, a contingent relation exists when $p(US|CS) > p(US|\text{not } CS)$. The CS comes to predict the US, or, alternatively, a signal relation between the conditioned and unconditioned stimuli is established such that the CS signals the forthcoming US (Domjan and Burkhard 1986, p. 56).

A major contribution to the Pavlovian research tradition was provided by the invention of the truly random control group (Rescorla 1967). This control procedure gave researchers an unambiguous control mechanism for empirically implementing the concept of contingency relations. In a truly random control group the CS and US are presented to subjects for the identical numbers of times they occur in the experimental conditioning group, but no contingency whatsoever exists between CS and US. Consequently, any differences in conditioned responses between experimental and control groups is attributable to the contingent relation established and not to alternative accounts, such as the mere frequency of CS presentations.

The Richness of Conditioned Learning. It should be clear that although contingency relations are fundamental to classical associative learning, conditioned learning cannot be fully explained by temporal relations between conditioned and unconditioned stimuli. The role of experience, expectations, and context factors are crucial additional considerations.

Rescorla and Wagner (1972) feature the importance of expectations in their well-known mathematical model of associative learning. The model postulates that learning depends on expectations and surprisingness. When a US is not somewhat unexpected, it is unable to startle the experimental subject sufficiently enough so that the subject may denote the requisite mental energy for learning the CS-US association. Learning will continue as long as an unconditioned stimulus remains somewhat surprising but will cease when it becomes fully expected.

Racapitulation

Pavlovian conditioning involves more than simply learning the relations between CSs and USs. Rather, much in the same way that cognitive psychologists represent the complex and interconnected nature of memory, modern Pavlovians realize that learned associations are rich, often complex, and may involve relations among multiple objects and events.

Returning to the earlier Foxy lettuce example, learned associations between that brand (the CS) and Brooke Shields (the US) include representations of other associations that the

consumer has previously learned. Prior to viewing television spots for Foxy lettuce, a consumer may already consider lettuce to be a healthy food and know that Brooke Shields is an educated person (receiving a Princeton degree), who leads a vegetarian lifestyle, is well paid for her sex appeal (e.g., her past role in promoting Calvin Klein jeans), yet reflects an aura of innocent youthfulness. Hence, any learned association between Foxy lettuce and Brooke Shields includes a number of potentially complex and rich representations that go beyond these two stimuli per se. The marketers of Foxy lettuce obviously hope that members of the target audience will associate that product with healthiness, beauty, and perhaps even intelligence.

THE NATURE AND FUNCTION OF CLASSICAL CONDITIONING IN CONSUMER BEHAVIOR

The foregoing discussion is based largely on research and theorizing by experimental psychologists who have never "run" a human subject. This is not to say that the theory is inapplicable to consumers; it is to suggest, however, that leaps of faith, perhaps heroic ones, would be required to accept carte blanche everything to this point as directly relevant to consumer behavior.[4] Nevertheless, I wish in this section to show how the modern conditioning model is appropriate to consumer behavior and why conditioned learning is functionally important. It first will be helpful to examine the nature of the conditioned response that is most relevant to consumer theory and research.

---

[4]Though research and theorizing about learning in lower animals may not be directly applicable to humans, it would seem equally incorrect to think that findings with animals have no relevance to human behavior. Indeed, recent evidence suggests that animals are more intelligent and more cognitive than humans have given them credit for. Many scientists are beginning to refute the idea that animal behavior consists entirely of reflexes. "There is too much hard evidence that animals live by their wits" (Cowley 1988, p. 59).

The Nature of the Conditioned Response

The word *response* suggests that what is conditioned in classical conditioning is overt behavior, a physical response. This, however, would be an inappropriate interpretation. How associations are learned should be treated as distinct from the issue of how associations are translated into performance: "The two questions are distinct, and attempts to ignore the distinction have provided bad answers to both questions" (Mackintosh 1983, p. 19).

The British conditioning researchers Levey and Martin (1975, 1983; Martin and Levey 1978, 1985, 1987) also reject performance as the criterion for assessing conditioned response and argue that what is conditioned is an evaluative response and not overt behavior per se. These researchers go so far as to claim that the evaluative response, and not overt behavior, is the response that is both necessary and sufficient for conditioned learning in all levels of animal life.

The Evaluative Response. For well over a decade Levey and Martin have argued that conditioning occurs only if the evaluative response is first elicited. These researchers contend that the evaluative response is both necessary and sufficient for classical conditioning because it enables all living beings to adapt to the temporal structure and to anticipate which environmental events are beneficial or harmful (Martin and Levey 1987, p. 64). In their most recent specification of the evaluative response, Martin and Levey (1987, p. 62) state:

The evaluative response is postulated as a characteristic internal reaction to environmental stimuli in terms of the evaluation of good/bad, liked/disliked, pleasant/unpleasant. It is subjective in the sense that it is unique to the individual and refers to the individual's own internal state; nonspecific in that it is not attributable to a particular sensory modality. It is seen as a mechanism which provides the necessary link between immediate and final (unknowable) consequences with the requirement that immediate consequences must anticipate eventual consequences more often than not to ensure survival.

It will be noted that this conceptualization is essentially the same as what consumer researchers refer to as attitudinal conditioning, emotional conditioning, or affective conditioning. Martin and Levey (1987) themselves note the similarity of their concept to Zajonc's (1980; Zajonc and Marcus 1982) ideas on the primacy of affect, ideas which are well known to consumer researchers. Allen and Madden's (1985) idea of "feeling state" and Chattopadhyay and Alba's (1988) description of "global evaluation" are essentially equivalent to Martin and Levey's evaluative-response concept. Hence, although the term *evaluative response* is new, the concept it embodies represents the type of pre–overt-behavior response that is most widely accepted by consumer scholars and the form of response most relevant to applications of classical conditioning in consumer behavior.

A Functional Perspective

The primary role of classical conditioning is to condition an evaluative response, or what consumer researchers may feel more comfortable calling global affect or attitude. The relationship between attitude and evaluation is firmly established in attitude theory. For example, Fazio and his colleagues view attitude as a simple association between a given object and a given evaluation (Fazio, Sanbonmatsu, Powell, and Kardes 1986, p. 230). They use evaluation in a broad sense, ranging from very "hot" affect (the attitude object is associated with a strong emotional response) to a very "cold," cognitively based judgment of one's affect (i.e., feelings of favorability or unfavorability toward the object).

Attitudes involving strong associations are highly functional in the sense that they free the individual from the effort required for deliberate reasoning and guide behavior in a fairly automatic fashion (Fazio et al. 1986). Further, any variable which strengthens the object-evaluation association has a corresponding impact on attitude accessibility and attitude-behavior consistency (Fazio, Powell, and Herr 1983, p. 725; see also Fazio, Chen, McDonel, and Sherman 1982; Fazio and Williams 1986).

These views have significant implications for the role and function of classical conditioning inasmuch as associations between an attitude object and evaluations can be established via conditioning procedures. As the associations increase in strength through repeated pairings, they can be automatically activated and influence behavioral choice at the point of purchase.

In a more general sense, the primary function of attitudes is adaptation (cf. Kahle 1984, p. 38), which is precisely what Pavlovian conditioning represents: "an adaptive mechanism by which organisms adjust to relatively short-term variations in their environment, specifically, relations among events" (Holland 1984, p. 130). Classical conditioning provides an efficient learning mechanism for responding to environmental events and serves to minimize information processing prior to initiating appropriate responses (Davies 1987; Levey and Martin 1983).

Alloy and Tabachnik (1984, p. 112), in discussing covariation judgments in general rather than conditioning per se, offer additional support for the functional role of classical conditioning when they state: "Information about the relationships or covariations between events in the world [i.e., the modern view of Pavlovian conditioning] provides people and animals with a means of explaining the past, controlling the present, and predicting the future, thereby maximizing the likelihood that they can obtain desired outcomes and avoid aversive ones."

EMPIRICAL EVIDENCE

A number of consumer behavior publications in recent years have offered classical conditioning as one possible account for their results (especially studies in the attitude-toward-the-ad tradition). However, only a few experiments have been positioned specifically as tests of Pavlovian conditioning. These direct-test studies are reviewed in this section.

Prelude

Before proceeding to this review, it will be helpful to examine what exactly a classical con-ditioning study entails and the type of research procedures required to obtain a measurable and strong conditioned response. It also will be useful to scrutinize several studies that are erroneously labeled or misconstrued as classical conditioning research, but which technically are not.

Conditions for Conditioning Experiments. As summarized in Table 5.1, a true classical conditioning experiment with human subjects must minimally satisfy five conditions.

First, the experiment must include a *discrete conditioned stimulus;* in consumer research, the CS typically is a product or brand. Second, there must be a *clearly identifiable unconditioned stimulus,* such as music, humor, attractive people, scenery, or any other stimulus that is biologically nonneutral or which has acquired symbolic or affective significance via prior learning. Third, *CS and US must be paired* in some systematic fashion. Pairing can be accomplished by presenting the stimuli simultaneously, the CS first followed by the US (forward conditioning), or the US followed by the CS (backward conditioning). Greater learning (i.e., enhanced associative strength between CS and US) is to be expected with increasing the numbers of trials. A fourth condition is that *a measure of conditioned response be taken at the end of conditioning trials.* Attitudinal or behavioral responses typically are used in consumer research. Finally, the measure of conditioned response to the CS *must be taken in the absence of the unconditioned stimulus;* that is, the US must *not* be present or in force at the time the CR is measured. To do otherwise would create a confounding whereby it would be unclear whether

TABLE 5.1 Minimal Conditions for a True Classical Conditioning Experiment

Condition	Description
1.	A discrete conditioned stimulus (CS)
2.	An identifiable unconditioned stimulus (US)
3.	Systematic pairing of CS and US
4.	Conditioned response (CR) measured at end of conditioning trials
5.	Unconditioned stimulus absent when CR is measured

the measured response is due to the CS or the US. The following analogy clarifies this point: Consider one of Pavlov's classic experiments using meat powder as the US and a metronome as the CS. After repeated pairings of CS and US, dogs were conditioned to salivate to the moving metronome in the absence of the meat powder. Pavlov, had he kept the meat powder present at the time of calibrating the number of drops of spittle, would not have been able to unambiguously determine whether the response was an unconditioned response (i.e., the natural response to the biologically appetizing meat powder) or a conditioned response to the previously neutral metronome. In like fashion, measures of conditioned responses in consumer research must be taken when the US is physically dissociated from the measurement context.

Mislabeled Studies. The above points can be better understood by examining several consumer behavior studies that sometimes are regarded as evidence of classical conditioning but which actually do not satisfy all of the conditions specified.

Milliman (1982, 1986) performed two interesting field studies to determine the impact of background music on shopping time and supermarket sales (1982) and on dining time and restaurant sales (1986). Both studies offer fascinating results showing that music has salutary effects. Yet, although perhaps interpretable within a general behavioral modification framework (Nord and Peter 1980) or in terms of mood effects (Allen and Madden 1985), these studies should not be taken as tests of classical conditioning.[5] This is because Milliman's studies did not satisfy Condition 3 (Table 5.1), which requires the arranging of a systematic temporal ordering between music and any specific CS. In other words, although Milliman demonstrated that playing slow-tempo music in a supermarket and restaurant increased the length of stay and expenditures in both outlets,

classically conditioned responses could not have accounted for the effects because no particular CS was systematically associated with the background music. Moreover, the Milliman studies could not possibly have measured a conditioned response in the absence of music (Condition 5), since the music was played continually.

Another published study that is erroneously interpreted in terms of classical conditioning examined the role of credit-card stimuli on spending behavior. Feinberg (1986) conducted four experiments using credit-card paraphernalia as the unconditioned stimulus. In Experiment 1, student subjects were seated at a table with a looseleaf book that contained pictures of seven consumer products. Credit-card stimuli (MasterCard insignias and replicas of Master-Cards) were presented for half the subjects and absent for the other half. Subjects were simply asked to indicate the amount of money they would spend for each of the seven items. Results indicated that subjects anticipated spending significantly more for each of the seven items when the credit card stimuli were present. Experiment 2 used a slightly different procedure but replicated the prior results in showing that the presence of credit-card stimuli enhanced the magnitude of estimated spending and reduced the decision time required to arrive at a spending estimate. Experiments 3 and 4 altered the conditioned stimulus by replacing the consumer products used in the previous experiments with the United Way charity. In Experiment 3 subjects estimated how much they would donate to this charity if asked to make a donation. It was learned that donation plans were significantly higher for subjects who made their estimate in the presence of credit-card stimuli. Experiment 4 measured actual rather than estimated donations, and found that student subjects gave significantly more and took significantly less time to make a decision when credit-card stimuli were present.

To recapitulate, all four of Feinberg's experiments involved two groups: (1) an experimental group that attended consumer products or the United Way charity in the context of credit-card stimuli, and (2) a no-treatment control group that attended the same information in

---

[5] Milliman himself has not characterized his studies in a Pavlovian framework, but I have heard colleagues refer to the Milliman work as supporting a classical conditioning interpretation.

the absence of credit-card stimuli. The consistent and strong differences between the two groups are dramatic in showing the impact a single marketing stimulus can have. However, these results do not evidence classical conditioning because the credit-card stimuli were present in all four experiments at the time measures of the conditioned response were taken (in violation of Condition 5). Hence, in the experimental groups, subjects' spending plans and actual donation behavior were a function of the MasterCard stimuli per se and not of any learned association. Apparently, what Feinberg's results tell us is that people's spending behavior is less inhibited when paying with a credit card than when paying with cash. Although this is an interesting and important finding, classical conditioning is not the theoretical mechanism that accounts for it.

Feinberg is not the only consumer researcher to have misinterpreted their results. Gresham and Shimp (1985) tested the role of attitude toward the ad and claimed to use a classical conditioning perspective to examine the mechanism linking Aad with brand attitude. Two factors dictate against treating this study as a true, rigorous test of classical conditioning: First, research materials were commercials for fifteen mature grocery brands. Because these brands are nonnovel and anything but affectively neutral, attitude conditioning should not have been expected.[6] Second, because actual (though off-the-air) commercials were used, there was no way to control for the order of CS-US presentation and no systematic pairing of a discrete CS with an identifiable US (thus violating Condition 3). Though Gresham and Shimp's findings have meaningful implications for the general relationship between advertising and brand attitudes, they should not be interpreted as directly relevant to mainstream classical conditioning research.

The point of the foregoing discussion is to caution against the temptation to treat any

marketing action (and corresponding consumer response) as interpretable within the parameters of Pavlovian conditioning. This would be a crude, Procrustean, and meaningless treatment. In doing so, classical conditioning would be applicable to everything, but capable of explaining nothing.

True Conditioning Studies

Seven consumer behavior publications are true Pavlovian conditioning studies according to the conditions laid out in Table 5.1. Bare essentials of each study are described as a backdrop for evaluating how well each study has satisfied "optimality requirements" for effecting conditioned responses. Optimal conditioning (i.e., increasing the association strength between CS and US toward asymtotic levels) generally requires the use of (1) forward conditioning procedures, (2) multiple trials (i.e., repeated pairings of CS with US), (3) CSs and USs that belong together, (4) CSs that are novel and unfamiliar, and (5) USs that are biologically or symbolically salient.[7] Table 5.2 guides the review by summarizing pertinent details.

Gorn (1982). In Experiment 1, Gorn presented subjects with slides of a writing pen (the CS) with simultaneous playings of background music. The experimental design created four stimulus combinations: (1) liked music (i.e., music from the movie "Grease" serving as the positive US) accompanying the presentation of a light blue pen, (2) liked music with a beige pen, (3) unliked music (i.e., classical Indian music) with a light blue pen, and (4) unliked music with a beige pen. Subjects were processed in a classroom setting. Following exposure to the pen/music combinations, subjects were given an opportunity to select a pen, either light blue or beige, as a gift for having participated in the study. Congruent with conditioning expectations, 79 percent of the sub-

---

[6]In a "reverse-English" sense the study does provide support for Pavlovian conditioning in that conditioning should not have occurred, and it did not—only one of 15 tested brands satisfied all of the requirements specified for demonstrating a conditioning effect.

[7]For further discussion on these points, the reader is encouraged to read the review article by McSweeney and Bierley (1984) and the empirical undertakings by Bierley, McSweeney, and Vannieuwkerk (1985) and Stuart, Shimp, and Engle (1987).

TABLE 5.2   Features of Classical Conditioning Studies in Consumer Behavior

Gorn (1982):

Subjects:	Mixed-sex university students
Subject processing:	Large groups
Research design:	Between-subject factorial
Number of experiments:	Two
Cond. Stim. (CS):	Blue and beige writing pens
CS familiarity:	High familiarity
Uncond. stim. (US):	Music
US familiarity:	High (low) familiarity for "Grease" (Indian classical)
CS-US belongingness	Problematic
Pairing sequence:	Simultaneous
Number of trials:	One
Conditioned response:	Product choice

Allen and Madden (1985):

Subjects:	Female university students
Subject processing:	Individually
Research design:	Between-subject factorial
Number of experiments:	One
Cond. stim. (CS):	Green and black writing pens
CS familiarity:	High familiarity
Uncond. stim. (US):	Humor
US familiarity:	High familiarity
CS-US belongingness	Problematic
Pairing sequence:	Simultaneous
Number of trials:	One
Conditioned response:	Product choice and "buy-back"

Bierley et al. (1985):

Subjects:	Mixed-sex university students
Subject processing:	Small groups
Research design:	Mixed factorial
Number of experiments:	One
Cond. stim. (CS):	Red, blue, yellow objects
CS familiarity:	High familiarity
Uncond. stim. (US):	Music from "Star Wars"
US familiarity:	High familiarity
CS-US belongingness	Problematic
Pairing sequence:	Forward and random control
Number of trials:	28
Conditioned response:	Magnitude estimate of preference

Macklin (1986):

Subjects:	Mixed-sex preschoolers
Subject processing:	Small groups
Research design:	Between-subjects factorial
Number of experiments:	One
Cond. stim. (CS):	Orange and yellow pencils
CS familiarity:	High familiarity
Uncond. stim. (US):	Cartoon character "Smurf"
US familiarity:	High familiarity
CS-US belongingness	Problematic
Pairing sequence:	Forward, simultaneous, and random control
Number of trials:	Three
Conditioned response:	Product choice and "buy-back"

Stuart et al. (1987):

Subjects:	Mixed-sex university students
Subject processing:	Small groups
Research design:	Between-subject factorial
Number of experiments:	Four
Cond. stim. (CS):	Brand L Toothpaste
CS familiarity:	Familiar product; unfamiliar brand
Uncond. stim. (US):	Four water scenes
US familiarity:	Relatively unfamiliar
CS-US belongingness	Problematic
Pairing sequence:	Forward, backward, simultaneous, and random control
Number of trials:	1, 3, 10, and 20
Conditioned response:	Evaluative response

Allen and Janiszewski (1989):

Subjects:	Mixed-sex university students
Subject processing:	Individually
Research design:	Between-subject factorial
Number of experiments:	Two
Cond. stim. (CS):	Norwegian words
CS familiarity:	Unfamiliar words
Uncond. stim. (US):	Positive verbal feedback
US familiarity:	Familiar
CS-US belongingness	Good fit
Pairing sequence:	Forward and random control
Number of trials:	10
Conditioned response:	Evaluative response

Kellaris and Cox (1989):

Subjects:	Mixed-sex university students
Subject processing:	Large groups
Research design:	Between-subject factorial
Number of experiments:	Three
Cond. stim. (CS):	White and yellow pens
CS familiarity:	Highly familiar
Uncond. stim. (US):	Music
US familiarity:	Liked music, familiar; disliked, unfamiliar
CS-US belongingness	Problematic
Pairing sequence:	Simultaneous
Number of trials:	One
Conditioned response:	Product choice

---

jects picked the pen color associated with the liked music, whereas only 30 percent picked the pen color associated with the disliked music. In a second experiment Gorn established that consumers in a decision-making mode are more likely to rely on product information than upon background cues, whereas consumers in a non-decision making situation utilize background cues more fully.

Gorn's experiments are noteworthy for several reasons. His is the first major study in consumer research positioned directly as a test of classical conditioning. Perhaps most interesting of all is that Gorn obtained evidence of conditioning using non-optimum procedures.[8] Specifically, Gorn's experiments were characterized by the following: (1) The research employed a single-trial pairing of CS and US; (2) the CS and US appeared simultaneously

---

[8]This statement is not made with critical intent; rather it is merely a statement of fact based on a better understanding of the conditioning mechanism in consumer research obtained after Gorn's important first step.

rather than in the superior CS-then-US order; (3) there was no compelling reason why music and writing pens "belong together"; (4) the unconditioned stimulus in the positive-affect condition (i.e., "Grease" music) was a familiar stimulus, which diminishes the likelihood that the CS would have established a unique new predictiveness relation with the music, since subjects would likely have had associational linkages already in memory between the "Grease" music and potentially numerous other extra-experimental concepts; and (5) a behavioral-choice criterion was a stringent requirement in light of earlier discussion about overt responses being a demanding, and perhaps even inappropriate, measure for the conditioned response. Gorn's findings are all the more remarkable in light of these considerations.

Allen and Madden (1985).[9] These researchers performed a systematic replication of Gorn's first experiment. Three major changes distinguish this study from Gorn's: (1) Subjects were processed individually, rather than in groups due to concern that Gorn's results may have been contaminated by subjects talking about the experiment between classes; (2) humor served as the US, as compared with Gorn's use of music; and (3) a systematic postexperimental inquiry was conducted, along the lines of the funneling procedure recommended by Page (1969), to assess the potential presence of awareness bias and demand artifact.

Using a 2 (pen color) $\times$ 2 (humor source) design, female subjects viewed one of two writing-pen colors (green or black) while listening to humorous episodes from either of two famous comedians, Bill Cosby or Redd Foxx. Cosby's humor represented a composite positively valenced US, whereas Foxx's antifemale,

---

[9]An experiment by Kroeber-Riel (1984) actually was the first published study following Gorn's article. Kroeber-Riel claims to have conditioned emotional responses toward "Hoba" soap (and I have no reason to question his claim) by associating this German brand with US pictures conveying emotional events: eroticism, exotic landscapes, etc. I have chosen not to comment further on Kroebel-Riel's findings, because the publication details in the *ACR Proceedings* are too sketchy to make an informed assessment.

sexist humor was chosen to represent a negatively valenced US. Dependent variables included (1) pen selection (both pen colors were included in a single box from which subjects selected one) and (2) a buy-back measure, whereby the experimenter offered to repurchase a subject's chosen pen for $0.25 or, if they refused to sell at that price, for $0.50. The pen-color–selection results indicated no significant difference between the percentage of subjects selecting either green or black pens as a function of whether pen color was paired with pleasant or unpleasant humor. On the buy-back measure, a greater percentage of the Foxx subjects (27 percent) sold their pens back compared to only 7 percent of the Cosby subjects ($p < 0.05$).

Allen and Madden interpret these results as not supporting Gorn's findings. They claim their results contradict Gorn's and raise concerns about the generalizability of his findings. They correctly point out that the two studies differ procedurally and that caution is necessary in drawing inferences from one study to the other. The same deviations from optimal-conditioning procedures characteristic of Gorn's research apply also to Allen and Madden's experiment. Briefly, they used a single conditioning trial, familiar USs, a simultaneous-conditioning procedure, behavioral measures of conditioned response, and questionable CS-US belongingness. Also, their small sample size (15 per cell) is likely to be underpowered for picking up the relatively small effects typical of behavioral research (less than 10–15 percent; cf. Peterson, Albaum, and Beltramini 1985). These study limitations are noted without critical intent. The contribution of Allen and Madden's research transcends their empirical showing and is to be found in their provocative suggestions for blending conditioning research with other research streams (e.g., mood research).

Bierley, McSweeney, and Vannieuwkerk (1985). This study used music from *Star Wars* as the US and twelve colored geometric shapes (red, blue, and yellow circles, squares, triangles, and rectangles) as conditioned stimuli.

One hundred subjects were assigned randomly in groups of thirty each to two conditioning groups and in groups of twenty each to two control groups. In Group 1 ("red predictive"), red geometric shapes were consistently followed by music in a forward-conditioning fashion; blue shapes were followed by music on half of their presentations, and yellow shapes were never followed by music. In Group 2 ("yellow predictive"), yellow shapes were always followed by music (forward conditioning), blue shapes were followed by music for half of the presentations, and red shapes were never followed by music. Group 3 ("truly random control"), received the same numbers of red, blue, and yellow shapes as presented to Groups 1 and 2 and heard music from *Star Wars*, but the geometric figures and music were presented randomly with respect to each other. Group 4 ("CS-only control") saw the colored shapes but never listened to music.

The procedure involved eighty-four trials — twenty-eight trials for each of the three colors. Each CS was on the screen for 5 seconds. Music (US), when scheduled, was presented for 10 seconds. The intertrial interval averaged 45 seconds, with a minimum interval of 10 seconds, which Bierley et al. consider to be a "fairly long" intertrial interval.[10] Magnitude estimation was used to measure preference for the CSs. Although results were mixed, there was some support for a conditioning prediction: Both red and yellow geometric shapes were more preferred when they were presented before *Star Wars* music as compared with when the shapes' appearance was systematically unrelated to the music. That is, in support of Rescorla's (1967) contingency relation proposition presented earlier in the chapter, preference was significantly higher when the contingency (i.e.,

conditional probability) between the US and CS was one than when it was zero.

This study's primary contribution arises by demonstrating to consumer researchers the use of experimental procedures that have been shown in previous research to enhance the likelihood of detecting classical conditioning. Bierley et al. overcome most all the limitations associated with the Gorn and the Allen and Madden studies. But even this study's procedures are not ideal for maximizing the conditioned response. As with the USs in the previously described studies, *Star Wars* music is a familiar stimulus, which implies that less conditioning probably occurred than would have had an original, novel (i.e., nonfamiliar) music arrangement been used. Also problematic is whether the *Star Wars* music is an appropriate stimulus for conditioning preferences for colored geometric shapes.

Macklin (1986). Macklin researched preschoolers by manipulating the temporal relation between a CS (orange and yellow pencils) and a US (the cartoon character Smurf). The conditioned and unconditioned stimuli were arranged in three orders: simultaneous conditioning, forward conditioning, and truly random control. The CS (pencils) and US (Smurf) were presented to the preschool subjects as 9" × 12" laminated posters. The experiment involved three exposures (trials) to the pictures; each exposure lasted 5 seconds, and the exposures were approximately equally spaced during a 20-minute session. The key dependent variable was pencil selection. The experimenter presented the orange and yellow pencils side by side and permitted subjects to select one. No significant relationship was detected between pencil-color selection and color of pencil subjects were exposed to; that is, pencil selection was not influenced by the color of pencil "advertised" contiguously with the positively valenced US, the Smurf.

This study's failure to support a conditioning explanation must be qualified in terms of several limitations Macklin herself has acknowledged: (1) The sample size was underpowered (only fourteen subjects per treatment condi-

---

[10]The intertrial interval is the length of time separating one conditioning trial from the next. Bierley et al. probably were extrapolating from animal research or from autonomic/skeletal conditioning research with humans, and not from attitudinal conditioning research, when characterizing their intertrial interval as "fairly long." Clearly, the optimum intertrial interval varies from research situation to situation and remains an empirical question.

tion); (2) the length of total time presentation and number of trials (three) may not have been optimal — the total time of presentation was possibly too long, creating fatigue, or the number of trials may not have been sufficient for the children to learn the association between pencil color and the Smurf's appearance; (3) the conditioning procedures were non-opitmal due to both a US-preexposure effect (the Smurf is a familiar stimulus) and a CS-preexposure effect (orange and yellow pencils are familiar, non-novel stimuli).

Stuart, Shimp, and Engle (1987). These researchers performed four experiments to test different classical conditioning characteristics. In all experiments attractive water scenes (a mountain waterfall, sunset over water, a boat mast against the sky, and a lavender-hued island) represented a composite US, and Brand L toothpaste served as the conditioned stimulus. A hypothetical brand, toward which subjects had initially neutral feelings, was chosen over a familiar brand to optimize the opportunity for attitudinal conditioning. The ordering of the various slides was systematically manipulated to structure foward- and backward-conditioning groups and truly random and CS-only control groups.

Experiment 1 manipulated the number of trial presentations at four levels — one, three, ten, and twenty pairings of conditioned and unconditioned stimuli. Subjects exposed to the conditioning trials exhibited significantly more positive attitudes toward the CS, Brand L toothpaste, at all trial levels than the corresponding random control groups. The amount of conditioning did not, however, significantly increase with progressive increases in the number of CS-US trial pairings. Experiment 2 tested the so-called CS-preexposure, or latent inhibition, effect. A latent inhibition group received a number of preexposures to Brand L toothpaste presented by itself *prior to* its being paired with the US scenes. This preexposure was expected to retard the development of a conditioned response, and, in fact, this is what the data reflected. A third experiment evaluated forward versus backward conditioning

and found that backward conditioning was, as expected, inferior to forward conditioning although there was some evidence for backward conditioning.[11] Experiment 4 used slightly different procedures but basically replicated earlier results in showing the superiority of forward over backward conditioning in influencing attitudes toward Brand L toothpaste and the superiority of both over a nonconditioning random-control procedure.

Several aspects of these experiments are noteworthy in context of the brief evolution of classical conditioning studies in consumer behavior. First, having benefited from predecessor studies, Stuart et al.'s use of rigorous conditioning procedures and appropriate control groups permits unambiguous conclusions regarding the conditionability of attitudes toward consumption objects. Second, with the possible exception that water scenes (the composite US) may not have been entirely relevant for the conditioned product, toothpaste, the experiments arranged appropriate conditions for classical conditioning to occur. Specifically, the CS was a novel, unfamiliar stimulus toward which subjects had no established schemas, no preexisting attitudes, and no previously established associations with other concepts; moreover, the US composite was established via pretesting to represent a relatively novel set of visual scenes. These conditions increased the likelihood that a contingent relation between CS and US would be established, and that the favorable evaluation of the US scenes would serve to condition a favorable evaluative response to the hypothetical toothpaste brand.

Allen and Janiszewski (1989). Allen and Janiszewski (1989) performed two experiments to condition evaluative responses to five neutral Norwegian words (e.g., *Nedpa, Glatt*). A cre-

---

[11]In forward conditioning the CS precedes the occurrence of the US in all trials, whereas the reverse is true in backward conditioning. Forward conditioning generally has been shown to be superior to backward conditioning in effecting a conditioned response. This is because learning results from a relatively pallid, neutral stimulus (the CS) signalling the imminent occurrence of a biologically or symbolically salient stimulus (the US), and not vice versa.

ative computerized word game led subjects to think their task was to determine for each of fifty trials whether a particular five-letter Norwegian word could be spelled from a string of twelve random letters that was presented briefly on the computer screen just before the Norwegian word appeared. For each trial, subjects entered a yes or no response into the computer to indicate whether the word would be spelled with the twelve letters. The computer then responded with either no feedback or positive feedback (e.g., "nice job," "well done") according to a prerecorded schedule that was independent of whether the subject's response was correct or incorrect. That is, subjects' responses to each of the five words received positive feedback 100 percent, 80 percent, 50 percent, 20 percent or 0 percent of the time. At the completion of the fifty trials (10 per word), subjects' evaluations of the five Norwegian words were measured.

Allen and Janiszewski's results (especially Experiment 1) evidenced attitudinal conditioning. However, the most important facet of this research is the showing that contingency awareness is a necessary precondition for attitudinal conditioning. These researchers provide an excellent discussion on the role of subject awareness of the CS-US contingency as an alternative account for conditioning results.

Kellaris and Cox (1989). These researchers conducted three experiments that systematically replicated Gorn's (1982) seminal study. Experiment 1 modified Gorn's procedure by (1) varying the type of music that served as the unconditioned stimulus, (2) changing the color of the pens used as conditioned stimuli, (3) using a less obtrusive measure of pen-choice behavior (the conditioned response), and (4) applying a cover story that was less demand-artifact prompting than the cover used by Gorn. Results yielded no evidence for conditioned behavior; that is, subjects who were exposed to the liked music were no more likely to select the "advertised" pen than those exposed to the unliked music. A subsequent experiment modified the music selection to more closely parallel the type of music used in Gorn's experi-

ments, but again the results revealed no evidence of classically conditioned behavior.

In another experiment, Kellaris and Cox tested the possibility that Gorn's results may have evidenced demand artifact rather than classically conditioned behavior. The experiment was actually a nonexperiment that reenacted Gorn's procedure by merely describing, rather than administering the treatments, to subjects. Results from this nonexperiment supported Gorn's original findings: subjects who were asked to imagine themselves listening to "a very pleasant, likable piece of upbeat music taken from a popular film" were significantly more likely to select the advertised pen color than were subjects who imagined listening to "a rather unpleasant piece of Indian classical music that most people would dislike."

These results pose some vexing problems in making sense out of Gorn's earlier findings. Were Gorn's findings purely artifactual, as Kellaris and Cox suggest, or is it possible that even the slightest change in conditioning procedures can alter the outcome? This can never be known, but I would caution against jumping to the conclusion that Gorn's original results were due solely to demand artifacts. Kellaris and Cox's nonexperiment is not convincing proof inasmuch as this procedure has been criticized on grounds that it tends to produce a special mental set that is unique to role-playing subjects (Kruglanski 1975).

RESEARCH OPPORTUNITIES AND DIRECTIONS

Classical conditioning research in consumer behavior is very much in the introduction stage of a potentially gainful life cycle. Very little is known about conditioning the evaluative response. Yet, because classical conditioning principles are widely used by marketing practitioners, if only on an intuitive basis, the formal study of conditioning has much to contribute toward understanding how consumers process information and form attitudes. Moreover, as discussed subsequently, Pavlovian conditioning has natural nexus with various theoretical streams in consumer psychology and can both contribute to and benefit from interactions with these research programs.

Pavlovian conditioning is not, however, the simple, automatic, reflex-form of learning it historically was thought to be. The neo-Pavlovian view embraces a cognitive interpretation of conditioning and accordingly demands a sophisticated research approach. Studying conditioning requires consideration of factors other than the mere sequencing of conditioned and unconditioned stimuli. I would argue that meaningful conditioning research in consumer behavior must take into consideration five general classes of factors: (1) consumer (subject) characteristics, (2) stimulus characteristics (i.e., CS, US, and the relationship between them), (3) background or context factors, (4) the nature of the conditioned response, and (5) "mechanical" experimental conditions (such as the number of trials and the length of intertrial intervals).

Consumer (Subject) Characteristics

Human subjects are inherently more or less conditionable based on personal characteristics related to the specific nature of the stimuli involved in a conditioning experiment. Failure to consider subject characteristics ensures something less than a complete understanding of how classical conditioning operates.

For example, in experiments where stimuli are predominantly visual (e.g., Stuart et al. 1987), it would be appropriate to include as covariates visual imaging ability and processing style (Childers and Houston 1984). It might be expected that subjects scoring relatively high on the visualizer component may be more readily conditioned than verbalizers. When music is used as the unconditioned stimulus, especially a familiar musical arrangement, it would be appropriate to use memory probes to determine whether the music already has acquired a rich repertoire of associations. Subjects who associate the music with other objects and events probably are not good candidates for learning new associations in a conditioning experiment.

Another important line of research involves the measurement of subject awareness. It has been argued that subject awareness of the CS-US contingency is necessary for conditioning attitudinal or other responses, but the exact mediational role of awareness remains unknown. As Bierley et al. (1985, p. 323) note: "The role of awareness in conditioning cannot be conclusively assessed until a measure of awareness is developed that can unambiguously classify subjects as aware or unaware, and that is independent of their performance on the conditioning task." Verbal self-report measures of awareness are problematic for at least two reasons: (1) They typically dichotomize responses as aware or unaware but miss fine gradations in degree of awareness; and (2) they are unable to identify cognitive processes during the CS-US interval that cannot be verbalized (cf. Dawson et al. 1983, p. 276). Future research directed at developing superior measures of awareness would be invaluable.

Stimulus Characteristics

Decisions concerning the choice of conditioned and unconditioned stimuli are critical to the outcomes of conditioning experiments. It is firmly established that the amount and rapidity of conditioning increase with increases in the salience of the US and intensity of the CS (Rescorla and Wagner 1972), and that conditioning is retarded when either the CS or US is nonnovel or familiar (cf. Domjan and Burkard 1986; Mackintosh 1983; McSweeney and Bierley 1984).

These requirements create dilemmas for consumer researchers, especially in the choice of USs. On the one hand, we would like to use well-known cultural symbols as USs (e.g., popular music, celebrities) because they appear frequently in actual marketing communications. Yet because of their popularity and celebrity, it is problematic whether such stimuli are appropriate for conditioning evaluative responses. Familiar USs are subject to what is termed the *US preexposure effect*. That is, when familiar stimuli become habituated, people stop paying attention and responding to them. "Familiarity breeds not contempt, but indifference" (Swartz 1989, p. 72).

In the consumer behavior literature, McSweeney and Bierley (1984, p. 624) have claimed that familiar stimuli should not be used as USs because they are expected to retard or even prevent a conditioned response. As it turns out, this suggestion may be erroneous. Clearly, advertisers' widespread usage of popular songs and famous athletic and entertainment personalities suggests that marketing communicators are not concerned with the potentially deleterious effects of employing what amount to familiar USs in their advertisements. On theoretical grounds, the US preexposure effect need not always retard or prevent classical conditioning from taking place. Interestingly, when a US is learned (preexposed) in a different context than the context in which conditioning takes place, there is evidence that conditioning in the new context will not be retarded (Randich and Lolordo 1979; Swartz 1989, p. 73).

The possibility that habituation in one context may not carryover to other contexts (and thus that familiar stimuli are not necessarily a deficit) supports advertising practice but challenges McSweeney and Bierley's (1984) claim to the contrary. This is the type of situation that is ideal for experimental inquiry. It is easy to imagine an experiment that preexposes subjects to what is to become the unconditioned stimulus in a subsequent classical conditioning experiment. Following the preexposure episode, part of the subjects (Group 1) would be exposed to conditioning trials with the preexposed stimulus as US and a consumption object, such as a new brand, as the CS. Remaining preexposed subjects (Group 2) would be subjected to conditioning trials in a context different from the preexposure context. If the habituation effect is noncontext specific, then neither Group 1 nor 2 should exhibit a conditioned response. However, if habituation is context specific, Group 2 but not Group 1 should manifest a conditioned response.

That past consumer research has obtained mixed results when testing for conditioned effects is partially explained by differences in the familiarity of USs. For example, Gorn's (1982) use of classic Indian music was truly an unfamiliar stimulus in comparison with the familiar "Grease" music. Comparatively, Allen and Madden's (1985) use of Bill Cosby and Redd Foxx humorous episodes were much closer to being equally familiar USs. Thus, whereas Gorn could have expected rapid negative conditioning to the unfamiliar Indian music but no rapid positive conditioning to the familiar "Grease" music, Allen and Madden could not have expected rapid conditioning to either of the two familiar comedians. Macklin (1986) also could not have expected rapid conditioning of her preschoolers to the three-trial contingency between pencils and the familiar cartoon character, Smurf. Similarly, Bierley et al. (1985) should not have expected rapid conditioning to the well-known *Star Wars* music arrangement. This probably explains why they felt it necessary to employ 28 separate trials for each color.

In making the preceding comments, I am, of course, assuming that experimental results with animals apply equally to human attitudinal conditioning. This assumption might be unwarranted. The only way that consumer researchers will know whether familiar, nonnovel stimuli are indeed inferior to unfamiliar stimuli as USs is by pitting one type of stimuli against the other in the same research program. That is, researchers need to hold constant the CS, the numbers of trial presentations, and so forth, while altering the relative degree of US familiarity. Of course, the same applies on the CS side of the conditioning equation. Holding constant the USs, the numbers of trials, and so forth, one can then test whether new, unfamiliar brands do indeed condition more rapidly and more strongly than established brands.

Another major area for research involves the issue of CS-US relevance/belongingness. At present it is not known what makes unconditioned and conditioned stimuli relevant to each other (Domjan and Burkhard 1986), but intuition would suggest some likely possibilities for applied consumer research. For example, Stuart et al.'s (1987) water scenes were somewhat relevant for toothpaste and perhaps for products such as soft drinks and beach equipment, but would likely be much less relevant for, say, electronic appliances. Interestingly, Macklin's (1986) use of the blue-hued cartoon character Smurf may have exhibited greater belongingness had she attempted to condition preference for blue pencils rather than for orange and yellow pencils. In other words, the superficial similarity between a blue-hued Smurf (US) and blue-colored pencils may have resulted in more rapid conditioning for the preschool children that Macklin studied.

The point of the preceding comments is that researchers need to carefully pretest CSs and USs for "fit" rather than simply assuming that one is appropriate for the other. This is more easily said than done in that no guidance is available from basic researchers in specifying the properties that make USs and CSs belong with one another. However, intuition suggests a variety of senses in which conditioned and unconditioned stimuli might fit together. USs and CSs that share common physical properties (color, size, shape, etc.) would be expected to belong together in at least a superficial sense. Probably more important for consumer research, USs and CSs should share some common symbolic trait. For example, certain types of music naturally go with some products and retail outlets—classical music with an antique store; new-wave music with premium ice cream, luxury household items, and other consumption artifacts purchased by young professionals.

Context Factors

It was long believed that the mere contiguity between CS and US was responsible for conditioning. That erroneous idea has since been discarded. Background conditions and context factors surrounding a conditioning experiment are now known to influence associative learning. "Context stimuli can have such large effects on resultant associative strength that they cannot satisfactorily be ignored by a nontrivial theory of classical conditioning" (Sutton and Barto 1981, p. 149).

This suggests that all contextual factors,

such as experimental setting and the atmospherics, might all play some role in influencing the strength of attitudinal conditioning detected by consumer researchers. Introducing background factors in conditioning research will enable a richer understanding of the conditions under which classical conditioning is most effective and will have potential implications for marketing practice. Advertisers and retail merchandisers regularly use background factors to evoke positive moods and create favorable feeling states.

The Nature of the Conditioned Response

Consumer researchers have used product choice or measures of attitudes to assess the magnitude of conditioned response. It was earlier argued in describing the work of Martin and Levey that the evaluative response is the response of preference. The basic argument was that the evaluative response enables animals and humans to cope with their environments, and that by learning what is good and bad organisms know which objects to approach and which to avoid. This, of course, is the function of Pavlovian conditioning. Animals and humans not only learn Pavlovian CS-US relations, but they develop conditioned responses (CRs) that do them some good (Swartz 1989, p. 66).

"Mechanical" Experimental Conditions

The number of CS-US trials, the length of intertrial interval, the amount of time given each stimulus presentation, and the overall length of stimulus exposure are important considerations when conducting conditioning experiments. Unfortunately, there are no guiding principles in providing answers for each of these determinations. "It's an empirical question" is the only possible retort in response to practical questions such as: "How many trials should be used?" "How long should each trial last?" "How long should the intertrial interval be?"

Each research program needs to experiment with these mechanical factors until a workable set of conditions is identified. This is where conditioning research gets tedious. The right CS-US combination might be chosen, but a conditioned response (as evidenced, say, by a significant difference between the conditioned group's mean and the control group's mean) may not be detected because the number of trials is insufficient or the intertrial interval is not enough. Yet, if consumer researchers are to truly commit to sophisticated classical conditioning studies, false starts and travails will have to be experienced in the process.

Classical Conditioning's Nexus with Other Research Streams

A natural tendency is to compartmentalize theoretical frameworks and to disregard the interrelations that invariably exist. This certainly characterizes treatment of the conditioning model in the consumer behavior literature. There exist, however, a number of linkages between classical conditioning and other frameworks of interest to consumer scholars. Some of these linkages have been identified (e.g., Nord and Peter 1980), others have not. The general point to be made is that conditioning has something to contribute to each of the following areas and probably much to gain by being incorporated within a general consumer-behavior–process framework rather than being looked upon, often pejoratively, as little more than an empirical procedure used by animal researchers.

The Elaboration Likelihood Model. One of the areas where a specific linkage already has been identified is the general ELM theory of attitude formation/change proposed by Petty and Cacioppo (1981). This theory, in its most fundamental form, proposes that when people are motivated and able to process information—that is, when the elaboration likelihood is high—they will focus on message arguments and experience positive attitude change if the arguments are cogent. However, when people are unable or unmotivated to process message arguments, they may nonetheless be persuaded

by peripheral features of the message presentation (music, models, etc.). Hence, persuasion is seen as involving a continuum ranging from central to peripheral possibilities, and attitude change is postulated to be more enduring as the message processing strategy moves toward the central end of the persuasion continuum. According to Petty and Cacioppo, attitude impact affected by classical conditioning occurs via the peripheral route to persuasion. Attitude formation resulting from classical conditioning is relatively fleeting in the absence of continuous pairings of the attitude object and the unconditioned stimulus that is responsible for the attitude.

Attitude toward the Ad. Mitchell and Olson (1981) and Shimp (1981) both proposed classical conditioning as a mechanism by which attitude toward the ad (Aad) might exert causal influence on attitude toward a brand. Rossiter and Percy (1978), though not referring to Aad per se, actually had made the same prediction earlier, as had Silk and Vavra (1974) before them. Others (e.g., Allen and Madden 1985; Edell and Burke 1984; Gardner 1985; Lutz 1985; MacKenzie, Lutz, and Belch 1986; and Mitchell 1986) have directly or indirectly implicated the role of classical conditioning in the attitude-toward-the-ad model. Edell and Burke (1984, p. 646) have proposed what probably is the most precise and speculative prediction regarding the role of conditioning as it relates to the Aad model:

If classical conditioning is the underlying process by which Aad affects Ab [brand attitude], we should expect Aad and Ab to be uncorrelated initially, but become increasingly positively correlated as the number of ad exposures increases. Then, as the period of no exposure to the ad increases, the correlation between Aad and Ab should decrease due to extinction. Additionally, classical conditioning theory requires that the valence of the unconditioned response (Aad) remain constant regardless of the number of times the ad is seen. Thus, the Aad "score" should not change systematically.

Visual Imaging. Although relatively little is known about consumers' processing of visual information, in recent years there has been a significant increase in attention devoted to visualization, imagery, and related matters (e.g., Childers and Houston 1984; Edell and Staelin 1983; Kisielius and Sternthal 1984, 1986; Lutz and Lutz 1977; Mitchell and Olson 1981; Mitchell 1986; Rossiter and Percy 1978, 1983). Rossiter and Percy (1978) propose that visual imaging mediates the role of both visual and verbal stimuli via a process they call visual reinforcement. They see visual reinforcement operating somewhat analogously to the verbal reinforcement established by Staats and Staats (e.g., 1957, 1958). Their position is that because visual stimuli are much easier to process than verbal stimuli they should also generate the same type of affective learning as accomplished in Staats and Staat's research. Classical conditioning is the proposed mechanism via which visualization affects attitudes.

Hedonic Consumption and Cultural Meaning. Hedonic and experiential consumption (Hirschman and Holbrook 1982; Holbrook and Hirschman 1982), and McCracken's (1986, 1987) cultural-meaning concept all give tribute to the role of nonverbal factors in influencing consumers' understanding and evaluation of consumption objects.[12] Classical conditioning relates to all these conceptualizations by providing one account of how products are infused with cultural meaning.

Covariation Assessment. Routine covariation assessments (e.g., Do bigger stores charge lower prices? Are country of origin and product quality related?) doubtlessly play an important role in influencing choice behavior. Consumer researchers (e.g., Bettman, John, and Scott 1986; John, Scott, and Bettman 1986) recently have studied covariation judgments to identify whether covariation assessments are driven more by prior beliefs or more by incoming data. Alloy and Tabachnik (1984) have argued that the relative influence of prior beliefs and data depends upon their comparative strength

and accessibility, with stronger and more accessible elements (beliefs or data) dominating judgment.

Though initial consumer behavior results (especially, the work of Bettman et al. 1986) have not completely supported Alloy and Tabachnik's predictions, there is much yet to be studied, and classical conditioning offers one approach to these studies. The Pavlovian model would predict, for example, that conditioning an attitude toward a nonnovel stimulus (e.g., a brand name for which the individual already possesses a well-formed schema) would be difficult if not impossible. Stated in covariation-assessment terms, attitudinal judgments for well-known brands would be driven more by prior beliefs than by incoming data. Classical conditioning offers an experimental paradigm for conducting covariation research and an alternative theoretical framework for interpreting covariation-judgment results.

Causal Inference. Consumers' causal inferences (e.g., Why did the product fail? Did the salesperson influence me to purchase a product I really didn't need? Why is this item on sale?) represent an important topic for research. Attribution theory is the primary theoretical framework for studying causal inferences (Folkes 1988), but it is not the only useful framework. Shanks and Dickinson (1988) develop a case and present empirical support in arguing that the factors critical for classical associative learning affect causal judgments.

Summary. The foregoing discussion has intended to provide some appreciation of how classical conditioning is related to more mainstream areas of consumer theory and research. Obviously, the suggestion is not that classical conditioning should subsume these other perspectives. Rather, as indicated at the outset, there is a natural and unfortunate tendency to treat different theoretical orientations as unrelated. It is hoped that this section has shown that classical conditioning provides a useful perspective for understanding the functioning of other theories that are used in explaining consumer behavior.

---

[12]This is not to suggest that these perspectives exclude verbal considerations, but rather that they place greater importance on nonverbal considerations than does the prevailing consumer information processing orientation.

CONCLUSION

Meaningful advances in better understanding classical conditioning and its role in consumer behavior were accomplished during the 1980s. However, in response to a question such as "Just precisely what do we know?" the only possible answer at this time would have to be "Not very much." The foregoing claims — of advances on the one hand, but limited knowledge on the other — may appear inconsistent. They really are not. The advances I refer to are more in the realm of better understanding what classical conditioning is and how rigorous research should be conducted, and less in terms of specific empirical findings. Two facts are undeniable: First, there has been limited empirical activity; and, second, research has been widely disparate in terms of the approaches taken and the conditioning issues examined.

Many opportunities exist for doing meaningful classical conditioning research. I have identified some of the areas where research is needed. There no doubt are a variety of other areas worthy of investigation. Regardless of the approach taken, I am absolutely certain of one conclusion: Results from individual conditioning experiments are meaningless by themselves. A host of factors play a role in influencing the likelihood and magnitude of conditioned responses. As such, it is folly to pose questions such as the following: "Do Allen and Madden's (1985) results establish the nonexistence of attitudinal conditioning?" "Does Macklin's (1986) research show that preschoolers' product preferences cannot be influenced by classical conditioning?" "Have Stuart et al. (1987) proven that forward conditioning is superior to backward conditioning in an advertising context?" "Are Kellaris and Cox's (1989) results correct and Gorn's (1982) flawed?" Answers to these and a magnitude of other interesting questions will come about only after intensive, programmatic research.

One final consideration is the matter of appropriate experimental context and stimuli for classical conditioning research. The issue is one of whether research should be done with real advertisements or with other marketing communication stimuli, and conducted in real contexts or in laboratories using necessarily simplified stimuli. I opt for the latter and argue that developing an understanding of how classical conditioning operates in a consumer context requires tightly controlled experiments along the lines of the animal research conducted by experimental psychologists. The problem with testing, say, actual television commercials is that one can never be sure whether the results are attributable to conditioning effects or to other processes. We are much better served by conducting careful laboratory experiments, which individually may say little but collectively provide a sense of how marketing stimuli operate and how consumers process and respond to these efforts.

REFERENCES

ALBA, JOSEPH W., and J. WESLEY HUTCHINSON (1987). "Dimensions of Consumer Expertise," *Journal of Consumer Research,* 13 (March), 411–454.

ALLEN, CHRIS T., and CHRIS A. JANISZEWSKI (1989). "Assessing the Role of Contingency Awareness in Attitudinal Conditioning with Implications for Advertising Research, *Journal of Marketing Research,* 26 (February), 30–43.

ALLEN, CHRIS T., and THOMAS J. MADDEN (1985). "A Closer Look at Classical Conditioning," *Journal of Consumer Research,* 12 (December), 301–315.

ALLOY, LAUREN B., and NAOMI TABACHNIK (1984). "Assessment of Covariation by Humans and Animals: The Joint Influence of Prior Expectations and Current Situational Information," *Psychological Review,* 91, No. 1, 112–149.

ANDERSON, PAUL F. (1986). "On Method in Consumer Research: A Critical Relativist Perspective," *Journal of Consumer Research,* 13 (September), 155–174.

BETTMAN, JAMES R. (1979). *An Information Processing Theory of Consumer Choice.* Reading, MA: Addison-Wesley.

BETTMAN, JAMES R., DEBORAH ROEDDER JOHN, and CAROL A. SCOTT (1986). "Covariation Assessment by Consumers, *Journal of Consumer Research,* 13 (December), 316–326.

BIERLEY, CALVIN, FRANCES K. MCSWEENEY, and RENEE VANNIEUWKERK (1985). "Classical Conditioning of Preferences for Stimuli," *Journal of Consumer Research,* 12 (December), 316–323.

CHATTOPADHYAY, AMITAVA, and JOSEPH W. ALBA (1988). "The Situational Importance of Recall and Inference in Consumer Decision Making," *Journal of Consumer Research,* 15 (June), 1–12.

CHILDERS, TERRY L., and MICHAEL J. HOUSTON (1984). "Conditions for a Picture-Superiority Effect on Consumer Memory, *Journal of Consumer Research,* 11 (September), 643–654.

COWLEY, GEOFFREY (1988). "The Wisdom of Animals," *Newsweek,* May 23, 52–59.

DAVEY, GRAHAM C. L. (1987a). *Cognitive Processes and Pavlovian Conditioning in Humans.* Chichester, England: Wiley, ix–x.

DAVEY, GRAHAM C. L. (1987b). "An Integration of Human and Animal Models of Pavlovian Conditioning: Associations, Cognitions, and Attributions," in G. Davey (Ed.), *Cognitive Processes and Pavlovian Conditioning in Humans.* Chichester: Wiley, 83–114.

DAVIES, PETER (1987). "Conditioning and Perception," in G. Davey (Ed.), *Cognitive Processes and Pavlovian Conditioning in Humans.* Chichester: Wiley, 183–210.

DAVIES, PETER, GEOFFREY L. DAVIES, SPENCER BENNETT (1982). "An Effective Paradigm for Conditioning Visual Perception in Human Subjects," *Perception,* 11, 663–669.

DAWSON, MICHAEL E., ANNEL M. SCHELL, JAMES R. BEERS, and ANDREW KELLY (1982). "Allocation of Cognitive Processing Capacity During Human Autonomic Classical Conditioning," *Journal of Experimental Psychology: General,* III (September), 273–295.

DOMJAN, MICHAEL, and BARBARA BURKHARD (1986). *The Principles of Learning & Behavior.* Monterey, CA: Brooks/Cole.

EDELL, JULIE A., and MARIAN C. BURKE (1984). "The Moderating Effect of Attitude Toward an Ad on Ad Effectiveness Under Different Processing Conditions," in Thomas C. Kinnear (Ed.), *Advances in Consumer Research,* Vol. 11. Provo, UT: Association for Consumer Research, 644–649.

EDELL, JULIE, A., and RICHARD STAELIN (1983). "The Information Processing of Pictures in Print Advertisements," *Journal of Consumer Research,* 10 (June), 45–61.

ENGEL, JAMES F., ROGER D. BLACKWELL, and PAUL W. MINIARD (1986). *Consumer Behavior.* Chicago: Dryden Press.

ENGEL, JAMES F., DAVID T. KOLLAT, ROGER D. BLACKWELL (1968). *Consumer Behavior.* New York: Holt, Rinehart & Winston.

FAZIO, RUSSELL H., JEAW-MEI CHEN, ELIZABETH C. McDONEL, and STEVEN J. SHERMAN (1982). "Attitude Accessibility, Attitude-Behavior Consistency, and the Strength of the Object-Evaluation Association," *Journal of Experimental Social Psychology,* 18, 339–357.

FAZIO, RUSSELL H., MARTHA C. POWELL, and PAUL M. HERR (1983). "Toward a Process Model of the Attitude-Behavior Relation: Accessing One's Attitude Upon Mere Observation of the Attitude Object," *Journal of Personality and Social Psychology,* 44, No. 4, 723–735.

FAZIO, RUSSELL H., DAVID M. SANBONMATSU, MARTHA C. POWELL, and FRANK R. KARDES (1986). "On the Automatic Activation of Attitudes," *Journal of Personality and Social Psychology,* 50, No. 2, 229–238.

FAZIO, RUSSELL H., and CAROL J. WILLIAMS (1986). "Attitude Accessibility as a Moderator of the Attitude-Perception and Attitude-Behavior Relations: An Investigation of the 1984 Presidential Election," *Journal of Personality and Social Psychology,* 51, No. 3, 505–514.

FEINBERG, RICHARD A. (1986). "Credit Cards as Spending Facilitating Stimuli: A Conditioning Interpretation," *Journal of Consumer Research,* 13 (December), 348–356.

FISHBEIN, MARTIN, and ICEK AJZEN (1975). *Belief, Attitude, Intention and Behavior: An Introduction to Theory and Research.* Reading, MA: Addison-Wesley.

FOLKES, VALERIE S. (1988). "Recent Attribution Research in Consumer Behavior: A Review and New Directions," *Journal of Consumer Research,* 14 (March), 548–565.

FOXALL, GORDON R. (1986). "The Role of Radical Behaviorism in the Explanation of Consumer Choice," in Richard J. Lutz (Ed.), *Advances in Consumer Research,* Vol. 13. Provo, UT: Association for Consumer Research, 187–191.

FUREDY, JOHN J., DIANE M. RILEY, and MATS FREDRIKSON (1983). "Pavlovian Extinction, Phobias, and the Limits of the Cognitive Paradigm," *Pavlovian Journal of Biological Science,* 17 (July–September), 126–135.

GARDNER, MERYL PAULA (1985). "Does Attitude Toward the Ad Affect Brand Attitude Under a Brand Evaluation Set?" *Journal of Marketing Research,* 22 (May), 192–198.

GORN, GERALD J. (1982). "The Effects of Music in Advertising on Choice Behavior: A Classical Conditioning Approach," *Journal of Marketing,* 46 (Winter), 94-101.

GRANGER, RICHARD H. JR., and JEFFREY C. SCHLIMMER (1986). "The Computation of Contingency in Classical Conditioning," in Gordon H. Bower (Ed.), *The Psychology of Learning and Motivation: Advances in Research and Theory,* Vol. 20. Orlando, FL: Harcourt Brace Jovanovich.

GRESHAM, LARRY G., and TERENCE A. SHIMP (1985). "Attitude Toward the Advertisement and Brand Attitudes: A Classical Conditioning Perspective," *Journal of Advertising,* 14, No. 1, 10-17.

HAWKINS, DEL I., ROGER J. BEST, and KENNETH A. CONEY (1986). *Consumer Behavior: Implications for Marketing Strategy.* Plano, TX: Business Publications.

HIRSCHMAN, ELIZABETH C., and MORRIS B. HOLBROOK (1982). "Hedonic Consumption: Emerging Concepts, Methods and Propositions," *Journal of Marketing,* 46 (Summer), 92-101.

HOCH, STEPHEN J., and JOHN DEIGHTON (1989). "Managing What Consumers Learn," *Journal of Marketing,* 53 (April 1989), 1-20.

HOLBROOK, MORRIS B., and ELIZABETH C. HIRSCHMAN (1982). "The Experiential Aspects of Consumption: Consumer Fantasies, Feelings, and Fun," *Journal of Consumer Research,* 9 (September), 132-140.

HOLYOAK, KEITH J., KYUNGHEE KOH, and RICHARD E. NISBETT (1989). "A Theory of Conditioning: Inductive Learning Within Rule-Based Default Hierarchies," *Psychological Review,* 96 (No. 2), 315-340.

HOLLAND, PETER C. (1984). "Origins of Behavior in Pavlovian Conditioning," in G. H. Bower (Ed.), *The Psychology of Learning and Motivation,* Vol. 18. Orlando, FL: Harcourt Brace Jovanovich, 129-174.

HUGDAHL, KENNETH (1987). "Pavlovian Conditioning and Hemispheric Asymmetry: A Perspective," in G. Davey (Ed.), *Cognitive Processes and Pavlovian Conditioning in Humans.* Chicester, England: Wiley, 147-182.

JOHN, DEBORAH ROEDDER, CAROL A. SCOTT, and JAMES R. BETTMAN (1986). "Sampling Data for Covariation Assessment: The Effect of Prior Beliefs on Search Patterns," *Journal of Consumer Research,* 13 (June), 38-47.

KAHLE, LYNN R. (1984). *Attitudes and Social Adaptation: A Person-Situation Interaction Approach.* Oxford: Pergamon Press.

KAHLE, LYNN R., SHARON E. BEATTY, and PATRICIA KENNEDY (1987), "Comment of Classically Conditioning Human Consumers, in Melanie Wallendorf and Paul F. Anderson (Eds.), *Advances in Consumer Research,* 14, Provo, UT: Association for Consumer Research, 411-414.

KELLARIS, JAMES J., and ANTHONY D. COX (1989). "The Effects of Background Music in Advertising: A Reassessment," *Journal of Consumer Research,* 16 (June), 113-118.

KISIELIUS, JOLITA, and BRIAN STERNTHAL (1984). "Detecting and Explaining Vividness Effects in Attitudinal Judgments," *Journal of Marketing Research,* 21 (February), 54-64.

KISIELIUS, JOLITA, and BRIAN STERNTHAL (1986). "Examining the Vividness Controversy: An Availability-Valence Interpretation," *Journal of Consumer Research,* 12 (March), 418-431.

KROEBER-RIEL, WERNER (1984). "Emotional Product Differentiation by Classical Conditioning," in Thomas C. Kinnear (Ed.), *Advances in Consumer Research,* Vol. 11. Provot, UT: Association for Consumer Research, 538-543.

KRUGLANSKI, A. W. (1975). "The Human Subject in the Psychology Experiment: Fact and Artifact," in L. Berkowitz (Ed.), *Advances in Experimental Social Psychology,* Vol. 8. Orlando, FL: Academic Press, 101-147.

LEVEY, A. B., and IRENE MARTIN (1975). "Classical Conditioning of Human 'Evaluative' Responses," *Behavioural Research and Therapy,* Vol. 13, 221-226.

LEVEY, A. B., and IRENE MARTIN (1983). "Part I. Cognitions, Evaluations and Conditioning: Rules of Sequence and Rules of Consequence," *Advances in Behavioural Research and Therapy,* 4, 181-195.

LUTZ, KATHY A., and RICHARD J. LUTZ (1977). "Effects of Interactive Imagery on Learning: Applications to Advertising," *Journal of Applied Psychology,* 62 (August), 493-498.

LUTZ, RICHARD J. (1985). "Affective and Cognitive Antecedents of Attitude Toward the Ad: A Conceptual Framework," in Linda F. Alwitt and Andrew A. Mitchell (Eds.), *Psychological Processes and Advertising Effects: Theory, Research and Applications.* Hillsdale, NJ: Erlbaum, 45-63.

MACKENZIE, SCOTT B., RICHARD J. LUTZ, and GEORGE E. BELCH (1986). "The Role of Attitude Toward the Ad as a Mediator of Advertising Effectiveness: A Test of Competing Explanations," *Journal of Marketing Research,* 23 (May), 130–143.

MACKINTOSH, N. J. (1983). *Conditioning and Associative Learning.* New York: Oxford University Press.

MACKLIN, M. CAROLE (1986). "Classical Conditioning Effects in Product/Character Pairings Presented to Children," in Richard J. Lutz (Ed.), *Advances in Consumer Research,* Vol. 13. Provo, UT: Association for Consumer Research, 198–203.

MARTIN, IRENE, and A. B. LEVEY (1978). "Evaluative Conditioning," *Advances in Behavioural Research and Therapy,* 1, 57–101.

MARTIN, IRENE, and A. B. LEVEY (1985). "Conditioning, Evaluations and Cognitions: An Axis of Integration," *Behavioural Research and Therapy,* 23, No. 2, 167–175.

MARTIN, IRENE, and A. B. LEVEY (1987). "Learning What Will Happen Next: Conditioning, Evaluation, and Cognitive Processes," in G. Davey (Ed.), *Cognitive Processes and Pavlovian Conditioning in Humans.* Chichester, England: Wiley, 57–81.

MCCRACKEN, GRANT (1986). "Culture and Consumption: A Theoretical Account of the Structure and Movement of the Cultural Meaning of Consumer Goods, *Journal of Consumer Research,* 13 (June), 71–84.

MCCRACKEN, GRANT (1987). "Advertising: Meaning or Information," in Melanie Wallendorf and Paul F. Anderson (Eds.), *Advances in Consumer Research,* Vol. 14, Provo, UT: Association for Consumer Research, 121–124.

MCSWEENEY, FRANCES K., and CALVIN BIERLEY (1984). "Recent Developments in Classical Conditioning," *Journal of Consumer Research,* 11 (September), 619–631.

MEYERS, JANET (1989). "Foxy Lady, Lettuce: Brooke Pitches Lettuce," *Advertising Age,* May 8, 3.

MILLIMAN, RONALD E. (1982). "Using Background Music to Affect the Behavior of Supermarket Shoppers," *Journal of Marketing,* 46 (Summer), 86–91.

MILLIMAN, RONALD E. (1986). "The Influence of Background Music on the Behavior of Restaurant Patrons," *Journal of Consumer Research,* 13, 286–289.

MITCHELL, ANDREW A. (1986). "The Effect of Verbal and Visual Components of Advertisements on Brand Attitudes and Attitude Toward the Adver-

tisement," *Journal of Consumer Research,* 13 (June), 12–24.

MITCHELL, ANDREW A., and JERRY C. OLSON (1981). "Are Product Attribute Beliefs the Only Mediator of Advertising Effects on Brand Attitude?" *Journal of Marketing Research,* 18 (August), 318–332.

MOWEN, JOHN C. (1987). *Consumer Behavior.* New York: Macmillan.

MURDOCK, BENNETT B., JR. (1985). "The Contributions of Hermann Ebbinghaus," *Journal of Experimental Psychology: Learning, Memory, and Cognition,* Vol. 11, No. 3, 469–471.

NORD, WALTER R., and J. PAUL PETER (1980). "A Behavior Modification Perspective on Marketing," *Journal of Marketing,* 44 (Spring), 36–47.

PAGE, MONTE M. (1969). "Social Psychology of a Classical Conditioning of Attitudes Experiment," *Journal of Personality and Social Psychology,* 11, No. 2, 177–186.

PETER, J. PAUL, and WALTER R. NORD (1982). "A Clarification and Extension of Operant Conditioning Principles in Marketing," *Journal of Marketing,* 46 (Summer), 102–107.

PETER, J. PAUL, and JERRY C. OLSON (1987). *Consumer Behavior: Marketing Strategy Perspectives.* Homewood, IL: Irwin.

PETERSON, ROBERT A., GERALD ALBAUM, and RICHARD F. BELTRAMINI (1985). "A Meta-Analysis of Effect Sizes in Consumer Behavior Experiments, *Journal of Consumer Research,* 12 (June), 97–103.

PETTY, RICHARD E., and JOHN T. CACIOPPO (1981). *Attitudes and Persuasion: Classic and Contemporary Approaches.* Dubuque, IA: Brown.

RANDICH, ALAN, and VINCENT M. LOLORDO (1979). "Associative and Nonassociative Theories of the US Preexposure Phenomenon: Implications for Pavlovian Conditioning," *Psychological Bulletin,* 86 (3), 523–548.

RAY, MICHAEL L. (1973). "Psychological Theories and Interpretations of Learning," in Scott Ward and Thomas S. Robertson (Eds.), *Consumer Behavior: Theoretical Sources.* Englewood Cliffs, NJ: Prentice-Hall, 45–117.

RAZRAN, GREGORY (1971). *Mind in Evolution.* New York: Houghton-Mifflin.

RESCORLA, ROBERT A. (1967). "Pavlovian Conditioning and Its Proper Control Procedures," *Psychological Bulletin,* Vol. 74, No. 1, 71–80.

RESCORLA, ROBERT A. (1988). "Pavlovian Conditioning: It's Not What You Think It Is," *American Psychologist,* 43 (March), 151–160.

RESCORLA, ROBERT A., and ALLAN R. WAGNER (1972). "A Theory of Pavlovian Conditioning: Variations in the Effectiveness of Reinforcement and Nonreinforcement," in A. H. Black and W. K. Prokasy (Eds.), *Classical Conditioning II: Current Research and Theory.* New York: Apple-Century-Crofts.

ROBERTSON, THOMAS S., JOAN ZIELINSKI, and SCOTT WARD (1984). *Consumer Behavior.* Glenview, IL: Scott, Foresman.

ROSSITER, JOHN R., and LARRY PERCY (1978). "Visual Imaging Ability as a Mediatory of Advertising Response," in H. Keith Hunt (Ed.), *Advances in Consumer Research,* Vol. 5. Ann Arbor, MI: Association for Consumer Research, 621–629.

ROSSITER, JOHN R., and LARRY PERCY (1983). "Visual Communication in Advertising," in Richard J. Harris (Ed.), *Information Processing Research in Advertising.* Hillsdale, NJ: Erlbaum.

ROTHSCHILD, MICHAEL L., and WILLIAM C. GAIDIS (1981). "Behavioral Learning Theory: Its Relevance to Marketing and Promotions," *Journal of Marketing,* 45 (Spring), 70–78.

SCHIFFMAN, LEON G., and LESLIE LAZAR KANUK (1987). *Consumer Behavior.* Englewood Cliffs, NJ: Prentice-Hall.

SHANKS, DAVID R., and ANTHONY DICKINSON (1988). "Associative Accounts of Causality Judgment," in Gordon H. Bower (Ed.), *The Psychology of Learning and Motivation,* Vol. 21. San Diego: Academic Press, 229–261.

SHIMP, TERENCE A. (1981). "Attitude Toward the Ad as a Mediator of Consumer Brand Choice," *Journal of Advertising,* 10 (2), 9–15.

SILK, ALVIN J., and TERRY G. VAVRA (1974). "The Influences of Advertising's Affective Qualities on Consumer Response," in G. David Hughes and Michael L. Ray (Eds.), *Buyer/Consumer Information Processing.* Chapel Hill, NC: University of North Carolina Press.

STAATS, CAROLYN K., and ARTHUR W. STAATS (1957). "Meaning Established by Classical Conditioning," *Journal of Experimental Psychology,* 54, 74–80.

STAATS, ARTHUR W., and CAROLYN K. STAATS (1958). "Attitudes Established by Classical Conditioning," *Journal of Abnormal and Social Psychology,* 57, 37–40.

STUART, ELNORA W., TERENCE A. SHIMP, and RANDALL W. ENGLE (1987). "Classical Conditioning of Consumer Attitudes: Four Experiments in an Advertising Context," *Journal of Consumer Research,* 14 (December), 334–349.

SUTTON, RICHARD S., and ANDREW G. BARTO (1981). "Toward a Modern Theory of Adaptive Networks: Expectation and Prediction," *Psychological Review,* Vol. 88, No. 2, 135–170.

SWARTZ, BARRY (1989). *Psychology of Learning and Behavior.* New York: Norton.

WILKIE, WILLIAM L. (1986). *Consumer Behavior.* New York: Wiley.

ZAJONC, ROBERT B. (1980). "Feeling and Thinking: Preferences Need No Inferences," *American Psychologist,* 35, 151–175.

ZAJONC, ROBERT B., and HAZEL MARKUS (1982). "Affective and Cognitive Factors in Preferences," *Journal of Consumer Research,* 9 (September), 123–131.

6

AFFECT AND CONSUMER BEHAVIOR *

Joel B. Cohen
University of Florida

Charles S. Areni
University of Florida

The influence of affect on consumers' psychological functioning and behavior is quite pervasive, though it is often undramatic and sometimes subtle enough to be unrecognized. The chapter begins with a brief historical perspective on the nature of psychological inquiry involving affect. Next, it identifies and describes streams of research in various subdisciplines of psychology that address the content of affect and its relationship to cognition, motivation, and behavior. A comprehensive review of the relevant consumer behavior literature follows. The concluding section presents a conceptual model emphasizing the multistage interaction between affect and the cognitive system in response to an external stimulus such as an advertisement.

HISTORICAL PERSPECTIVES ON AFFECT

In their reviews of philosophies and theories of internal influences on behavior, Hilgard (1980) and Isen and Hastorf (1982) note the reoccurring theme of the tripartite conceptualization or

trilogy of the mind. This thesis is traceable to the works of Plato and Aristotle, who identified three aspects of the human spirit: thoughts, feelings, and desires. A rough physiological parallel was drawn in which thoughts were associated with the head, feelings with the chest, and desires with the belly and organs of regeneration (Shute 1976; Allport 1967).

Leibnitz (1714) and Kant (1781) were among the first to formally treat cognition, affect, and conation as fundamentally mentalistic activities involving separate faculties. Physi-

*The preparation of this chapter was supported by the Center for Consumer Research and a summer research grant from the College of Business Administration at the University of Florida.

ological correlates became a matter of debate: Gall (1758–1828), for example, assigned each of the three components to specific regions of the brain. In the modern era, conceptualizations of the trilogy moved away from the identification of separate structures and instead emphasized the interaction between the three systems. For example, McDougall (1923) offers the following description:

> . . . it is generally admitted that all mental activity has these three aspects, cognitive, conative, and affective; and when we apply one of these three adjectives to any phase of mental process, we mean merely that the aspect named is the most prominent of the three at the moment. Each cycle of activity has this triple aspect; though each tends to pass through these phases in which cognition, conation, and affection are in turn most prominent. (p. 266)

While such thinking suggests the development of dynamic models—which integrate affective, cognitive, and conative processes—as Isen and Hastorf (1982) note, this integration has not occurred. Instead, twentieth century psychology has been dominated by a search for principles to explain the occurrence and extinction of behavior (conation) or the acquisition and change of people's mental representations and judgments (cognition). Affect has frequently been assigned a subordinate role—for example, as a functional aspect of goal-directed behavior and performance feedback (hence blended into conation) or as a component of evaluation (hence blended into cognition). Often it was simply ignored or its disruptive influence on more orderly cognitive operations minimized, lest insights into more important areas of human functioning be compromised.

Why has affect failed to gain prominence in the psychological *Zeitgeist*? Isen and Hastorf (1982) suggest that this may, in part, be due to the influence of research methods on the development of theory. If reliance is placed on observational methods, the status of intervening variables is ambiguous at best. If reliance is placed on verbal reports, the limitations of the cognitive system in capturing and recording affective processes (e.g., of different types, in-

tensities, and durations) produce an overly restrictive and potentially misleading account of such activity. While valid and reliable measurement has been a problem across the full range of the psychological spectrum, measurement and identification of affective states and processes has been particularly difficult, and this has doubtless discouraged many people from working in the area. Yet despite these formidable methodological obstacles, interest in affect is increasing in several areas of psychology as well as in consumer behavior.

Recently, social psychologists have given added attention to the effects affective states have on various cognitive processes (Isen et al. 1978; Isen and Shalker 1982; Bower, Gilligan, and Monteiro 1981). Some of the more interesting findings are that affective states influence people's: (1) recall, (2) evaluative judgments, (3) free associations, (4) categorizations of novel and familiar stimuli, (5) decision rules in choice tasks, and (6) negotiation strategies in bargaining tasks.

A particular challenge for those seeking an expanded role for affect has been to link differences in the content and intensity of experienced affect to underlying physiological responses. While many physiological indicators have failed to produce consistent evidence for specific affective states (e.g., heart rate, blood pressure, respiratory rate, artery dilation and contraction, and electrical skin resistance), more adequate conceptualization of such relationships and the development of more sophisticated measurement (e.g., electromyographs [EMGs] for measuring unobservable muscular activity) have revitalized interest in psychophysiological approaches. Accordingly, we devote a section of the chapter to physiological approaches to the study of affect. Chapter 4 by Richard P. Bagozzi provides an expanded treatment of physiological concepts and research.

Considerable added interest in affect within consumer behavior comes from researchers who are interested in how advertising works. A typical TV commercial might use sexy models, smiling babies, provocative sunsets, and other "peripheral" components to create a positive affective state, often without the degree of attention likely to cause more active processing of such information. This positive affective state might then produce a heightened and favorable reaction to other elements in the commercial (i.e., the brand). Much attention is now being paid to the conditions under which this would occur and to providing an adequate explanation of the underlying process.

Cognition-centered models of persuasion, which held center stage for many years, are now being modified to better incorporate the role of affective processes. While such models explicitly address *attitude formation* and change, they do not adequately account for the added contribution of affective responses. Nor do they distinguish a consumer's *evaluation* of a brand or ad from affect caused by, attributed to, or directed to each of these.

DISENTANGLING ATTITUDINAL AND AFFECTIVE CONCEPTS

We believe it is important to distinguish between attitude and affect and to clarify the relationship between them (see Cohen 1990). As suggested earlier, one way in which affect was assigned a more subordinate theoretical role was to give it an overly cognitive conceptualization. As a prime example, in the attitude literature affect was typically treated as either the evaluative component of a tripartite belief system (together with knowledge and intentions) or as synonymous with attitude (see a related discussion by Holbrook 1986). To avoid the conceptual and operational ambiguity that results from this treatment of affect, "*attitude*" can be conceptualized as an *evaluative judgment,* and *affect* could be reserved for a *valenced feeling state.*

Indeed, within contemporary treatments of consumer behavior, *attitude* is often operationalized via bipolar evaluative scales such as like-dislike and good-bad. Implied, therefore, is a cognitive element that results, deliberately or not, from some type of object identification (i.e., as a member of an evaluative category) or comparison with a criterion (e.g., some personal goal, norm, or frame of reference). *Affect*—once freed from its ambiguous status in the consumer attitude literature—would then be understood to have some unique properties (Cohen 1990; see also Batra and Ray 1983).

First, we would understand it to be a response involving at least a minimal state of arousal. As is elaborated subsequently, this arousal is often linked to the motivational relevance of a particular stimulus and can be thought of as generating at least general action tendencies in the organism (Plutchik 1980a). Second, affect's status in the cognitive domain would involve more than a simple object/person evaluation. Affect would result in a tag or "marker" used to both label and record the aforementioned state. In this sense, then, it is a trace of an emotional response to an entity with which we have come into psychological contact (Bower 1981). Its necessary antecedent is some "affective state" strong enough to leave an *affective trace* (Cohen 1990). It is worth noting that while the affect itself may be transitory, it may be possible to retrieve the memory trace of that experience over a considerable period of time. In general, however, an attitude is likely to be more enduring, probably as a result of a greater degree of processing and elaboration at inception and greater functional relevance (giving rise to more retrieval opportunities that should strengthen the association).

An argument against adopting one term to refer to both evaluative cognitions and affective traces is that many evaluative cognitions are "cold" things; outcomes of object/person assessment processes (e.g., Ajzen and Fishbein 1980) or remembrances of things learned. *Affective traces,* on the other hand, are often the residue of highly involving emotional states. By restricting the term *affective trace* to cognitive elements that serve as tags for experienced states of affect, their instantiation implies more than merely retrieval of information. In particular, when the memory of such an episode is brought to mind it may well have the capacity of eliciting the same feeling or emotion (though not always to the same degree). One of the most frequently used mood induction techniques is simply to ask people to bring to mind such a recollection. Retrieval of evaluative cognitions associated with some person, object or event, on the other hand, is little different from the retrieval of any other kind of information. Accordingly, we see no reason to blur these important distinctions for the sake of semantic expediency.

The Distinction between Affect, Emotion, and Mood

The term *affect* is probably best employed as a general descriptor of a valenced feeling state. Emotion and mood can be thought of as specific examples of such states. The distinction most commonly made between moods and emotions is that emotions are more intense and stimulus specific than moods (Clark and Isen 1982; Isen 1984; Gardner 1985). In addition, research suggests that emotions lead to a focusing of attention on the instigating stimulus (Easterbrook 1959; Gilligan and Bower 1984) and a disruption of ongoing goal-directed activity (Simon 1967; Clark and Isen 1982). Moods, on the other hand, may be elicited and maintained without conscious awareness of the feeling state, its cause, or its influence on current activities.

Together these differences suggest that moods might be viewed as "milder" instances of emotions. These less intense affective states (moods) may result when an environmental stimulus is only peripherally related to the motivational system. In these instances the individual may be unaware of the state and may continue to pursue his present objective without interruption.

Highly involving stimuli, on the other hand, elicit more intense and arousing affective states (i.e., emotions) that demand attention. Ongoing activity is interrupted and, in some cases, behavior in response to the affect-eliciting stimulus occurs involuntarily. After such a motivationally relevant stimulus has been dealt with, the affective state begins to subside. The individual shifts attention away from the stimulus and begins focusing on the other tasks and objectives of the day. However a residue of the earlier experienced emotion may still function

as a mood. Thus, if someone spills a drink on my new shirt at lunch I may get angry (i.e., experience the emotion). Well after lunch, though my attention is directed elsewhere, I may continue to be in a bad mood and remain so for the rest of the day. I may even put the mood outside of awareness, and yet it may influence my ability to carry out various tasks.

It may be helpful to work through an example to see how these affective and evaluative variables interact. Say a consumer goes to a large department store to look for a television set. Let us take the simplest case first. In the store the consumer may notice many products on route to the department selling television sets. Because the television set purchase dominates the consumer's mind (and even though the names of other products on display could probably be retrieved from memory later on), the likelihood of an affective response to any of these products is low. Not only is no *affect* created, but in the absence of any reason to evaluate these products there is probably no change in any preexisting *attitude* toward any of them.

Now, let us say that the store has put some changes into place between the consumer's last visit and the present visit. The lighting has been made softer, pleasant music has been added, displays have been made a little less cluttered. While hurrying to look at televisions, our consumer experiences positive feelings in response to his or her surroundings and *may* even be vaguely aware of that. When the television salesperson approaches, our consumer smiles and makes a cheerful remark. Later, over dinner, the consumer recalls feeling good in the store and attributes these feelings to a plausible focal object (e.g., the store rather than the time of day). The resulting inference is that it is a pretty good store, and so the consumer forms an intention to go back there to look for a new coffee maker.

What has happened in this example? According to our taxonomy, we would say that the consumer's experience in the store created a positive *mood* state. Further, through a coding process that probably requires little conscious processing (see Bargh 1984; Mandler 1982), an *affective trace* resulting from the mood state was formed. Such a trace—which can be thought of as the informational aspect of affect—is potentially retrievable, depending on the circumstances. But, in the absence of some greater amount of thought, there should be no *attitude change* toward the store, and this was the case until an evaluative frame of reference was applied to the store. The remembered pleasant feeling (affective trace) was then attributed to the store, thereby producing an effect not unlike retrieving a positive evaluation. This resulted in a more favorable *attitude* toward the store.

There remains, however, an important difference between retrieving an affective trace and retrieving an evaluative judgment, and this could dramatically effect the above outcome. Since the retrieved affective trace represents "pure feeling" (i.e., it lacks an evaluative or judgmental basis), the individual may attempt to infer "reasons" for being able to recall a positive feeling toward the store, perhaps because of a desire to explain or understand the basis for it. Further, if the retrieved affective trace is sufficiently positive (or negative), the person may actually "reexperience" some of the same feelings. Should this occur an even stronger and more highly valenced attitude is likely to result. Of course, were the consumer to attribute this retrieved affective trace and any resulting affect to some dispositional factor or other occurrences, there may be no attitude change toward the store at all. In summary, while the creation of an affective state of any intensity should produce its own affective trace, only strong associative bonding to something present at the time, or further inferential processes at the time of retrieval, will definitely lead to the formation or change of attitude.

A far more direct route to attitude formation and change is through evaluative cognitions that result from judgments made about the strengths and weaknesses of particular objects (e.g., with respect to one's needs and goals). So, any and all aspects of the department store that were important to the person might have been assessed, evaluative cognitions formed, and some overall attitudinal judgment made. In such a case there is no reason why *affect* should either lead to or result from these cognitive operations. This represents, then, an evaluative rather than an affective process.

Cohen (1990) offers the following account to further illustrate the distinctions we are drawing between affect and attitude, especially as concerns the "transfer" of affect to a product.

When I was growing up, a bunch of us used to play a "serious" game of baseball in the sweltering summer's heat. There happened to be a gas station with a Coke machine near the ball field. For some inexplicable reason, this machine happened to keep the bottles of Coca-Cola at what must have been the perfect temperature. There could not have been a better Coca-Cola anywhere in the world! When we were thoroughly exhausted, we would head for the gas station and put our money in that marvelous machine. I used to imagine the taste of that Coke from the middle of the baseball game on. My cognitive response to drinking the Coke was very direct and very primitive: the affective trace and the affect itself seemed almost indistinguishable. Yet, of course, I can be prompted to recall my feeling state without actually reexperiencing its full intensity.

He speculates as to the functional significance of such affective traces: could they serve as "markers" for the specific "purpose" of helping us identify the source of our satisfaction (to aid in finding our way back to it)?

This example also illustrates that the linkage between an affective trace and an attitude is more complex than we would at first imagine. The author doubts this experience led him to a more favorable attitude toward Coca-Cola. Perhaps the specific type of soft drink was not a particularly salient part of the stimulus field (as evidenced by the fact that the soft drink machine dominates his mental picture of the scene). Or, perhaps in subsequent thought he attributed his positive feeling to reduction of thirst and the ideal temperature of the soft drink.

Both of these fundamental perceptual and inferential mechanisms are likely to be important in most consumer contexts in which affect is experienced (e.g., product usage, responses to "emotional" advertising). This suggests that much more needs to be understood about the interaction of affective and cognitive processes before we should feel confident about predicting the attitudinal consequences of particular types of affect induction.

As a final example of the complex interaction between affect and evaluation, consider the following. Suppose an advertisement is used to elicit a rather intense affective state in the hope it will be attributed to the brand. While affective states of greater intensity may have the greater potential impact on attitudes, much may depend on factors perceived to be responsible. Should the affect be attributed to a heavy-handed and manipulative attempt at persuasion, as in a fear-arousing ad, the attitudinal implications of such attributions might be considerably different than would be assumed based on the initial affective state. A weaker and more diffuse affective state could well produce a more positive product attitude.

EMOTION AS A DISRUPTIVE INFLUENCE

In the early portion of this century, particularly during the reign of behaviorism, several "conflict" theories, which viewed emotions as primarily dysfunctional, emerged in the literature. Building on the ideas of Plato and Aristotle, these theories centered on competition between rational (cognitive) and irrational (affective) forces. Watson (1929), one of the founders of the behavioristic tradition, once wrote that " . . . the shock of an emotional stimulus throws the organism for the moment at least into a chaotic state" (p. 216).

Dewey (1894; see also Angier 1924), in an attempt to unite the physiological perspective of James (1890) with the evolutionary perspective of Darwin (1872) [discussed subsequently in greater detail], developed an "attitudinally" based theory of emotions. Here, attitudes were given a rather conative definition as summaries of possible behaviors in a particular situation (e.g., a type of habit family hierarchy). A given context was thought to possess features that activate attitudes relating previous behavior episodes to the stimulus. However, the "appropriate" behaviors may vary from situation to situation so the attitudinal impulse may not lead to complete satisfaction. When there is a conflict

between an attitudinal reaction and the appropriate end state, emotion arises. Not surprisingly, this conceptualization led Dewey to focus on negative rather than positive emotional states.

Darrow (1935) extended Dewey's notions by offering a more central, neurologically defined basis for emotion. Research had demonstrated that emotional responses dominate an animal's behavior once its cerebral cortex is separated from various subcortical mechanisms. However, the capacity for emotion is destroyed when subcortical structures, such as the hypothalamus, are removed. Darrow thus concluded that one of the primary functions of the cerebral cortex is to maintain an inhibitory control over subcortical mechanisms central to the elicitation of emotion. This inhibitory control is generally maintained, he asserted, except in situations whose stimulus patterns are in conflict with those typically associated with physical safety, comfort, social dignity, and so forth. In these situations the inhibitory control of the cerebral cortex is interrupted and emotion is activated. Darrow saw implications of this interruption beyond ". . . the mere production of conflicting motor impulses" (p. 572). He viewed incoordination, the failure of verbal skills, and an inability to access necessary information as potential consequences of heightened emotional activation.

Although some of the basic tenets of these and other conflict theories of emotion are a basis of more recent research in psychology (Easterbrook 1959; Tucker and Newman 1981; Gilligan and Bower 1984) and consumer behavior (Park and Young 1986; Pavelchak, Antil, and Munch 1988; Sanbonmatsu and Kardes 1988), they seem appropriate mostly for negative *and* highly arousing affective states.

PHYSIOLOGICAL APPROACHES TO THE STUDY OF AFFECT

A Simplified Model

Most modern physiological theories of affect link it to neurological activation in various regions of the autonomic (ANS) and central nervous systems (CNS).[1] More specifically, the neurological activation we refer to as affect results from a complex sequence of interactions among the cerebral cortex, the limbic system, and the hypothalamus. A basic, if oversimplified, sensory input–behavioral output model is useful for reviewing the research literature (Strongman 1987).

First, sensory input is transmitted along the central nervous system to the cerebral cortex, where a number of cognitive operations are carried out to enable the person to interpret and assess the sensory input. This assessment is transmitted to the limbic system, producing activation that the hypothalamus can translate into requisite muscular and visceral (i.e., respiratory, cardiovascular) responses via the endocrine system and the autonomic and central nervous systems. Muscular responses, particularly in the facial region, are associated with the "expressive responses" thought to be basic components of emotion in a number of conceptual theories (Tomkins 1962, Izard 1977; Plutchik 1980a). According to the model, these activations produce "reverberations" in the cerebral cortex that, along with the organism's appraisal of its external environment, influence the human experience of emotion (James 1890; Bindra 1969: Leventhal 1980).

Cardiovascular and Respiratory Response Patterns

Several areas of research focus on physiological response patterns in the visceral and

muscular systems.[2] This research attempts to distinguish affective responses, such as fear and anger, in terms of blood pressure, arterial dilation/constriction, respiratory rate, muscle tension, electrical skin resistance, and so forth. In early theories these responses were thought to be central to the content of affect. James (1890), for example stated that " . . . bodily changes flow directly from the perception of the exciting fact . . . our feeling of these changes as they occur is the emotion." Thus, he postulated a direct relationship between sensory input and visceral responses (i.e., the sensory input was thought to *contain* information for the visceral system). Modern physiological treatments of affect emphasize neurological activation in various regions of the ANS and CNS and assign more of a peripheral role to visceral responses. Nonetheless, empirical work in this area continues to be of interest to researchers seeking noncognitive measures/indicators of affective responses.

Much current work in this area stems from an early study by Ax (1953). He employed a bogus polygraph test to elicit either anger (by delivering mild, "accidental" shocks) or fear (by acting alarmed about a dangerous malfunctioning of the machine) in subjects. Significant differences between anger and fear on various physiological measures were observed. For example, whereas heart rate and systolic blood pressure increased equally, diastolic blood pressure increased more during anger. Later, Schachter (1957) found that fear produced dilation of certain groups of arteries, whereas anger caused considerable constriction in various muscular regions. This provided an explanation for Ax's observed difference in diastolic blood pressure.

Averill's (1969) subjects viewed a happiness-inducing, sadness-inducing, or neutral film.

---

[1]The function of the ANS is to monitor the internal adjustments of the organism, while the CNS enables the individual to adapt to its environment by organizing, storing, and transforming information brought to it. The central nervous system (CNS) is essentially the part of the nervous system enclosed in the bony structure of the skull and backbone. The autonomic nervous system (ANS) contains the many nerves leading from the brain and spinal cord out to various endocrine glands, the heart and blood vessels, and the smooth muscles of the body. It is responsible for changes in heart rate and blood pressure, as well as for the distribution of blood to the exterior muscles and digestive tract, thus preparing the body for activities that place different demands on the heart and various muscle groups.

---

[2]There is a separate program of research that focuses on the more central neurological structures involved in the elicitation of affect. Such studies typically employ surgical methods on less cerebrally developed animals, or they involve electrical and chemical stimulation of various regions of the nervous system. Because they are not as directly relevant to consumer behavior, they will not be covered in this review.

Those in the mirth condition differed from control-group subjects and sadness-condition subjects predominantly in their increased respiration rate. There were only insignificant differences with respect to cardiovascular responses. Subjects in the sadness condition, on the other hand, differed from control-group subjects and mirth-condition subjects *predominantly* in cardiovascular responses. They exhibited increased blood pressure with a disproportionate increase in diastolic pressure.

Schwartz, Weinberg, and Singer (1981) manipulated affective state by having subjects imagine a past life experience associated with either happiness, sadness, anger, fear, or relaxation. Control-group subjects imagined an emotionally irrelevant experience. This manipulation was then followed by an exercise session in which subjects walked steps. Various respiratory and cardiovascular responses were then measured.

The results were intriguing. The different affect "imaginings" produced different patterns of cardiovascular activity with respect to blood pressure: The ratio of systolic pressure to diastolic pressure was significantly higher for fear subjects and lower for anger subjects. Most interesting, multiple regression analysis revealed that the affective-state manipulation outperformed diastolic pressure and heart rate as a predictor of systolic blood pressure, even after the exercise sessions. Together these findings suggest that certain affective states may have *identifiable* correlates in the visceral system.

Recent variations on this research have investigated the reverse direction of influence between visceral arousal and affect. Berger and Owen (1983) review psychosomatic medicine studies that attempt to establish causal links between vigorous exercise and reported affective states. Building on joggers' frequent reports that running reduces feelings of anxiety and depression (Morgan 1979; Brown, Ramirez, and Taub 1978; Graham 1981), Berger and Owen (1983) employed a before-after design comparing subjects meeting for a swimming class with subjects meeting for a lecture-oriented health sciences class. They found that swimmers reported significantly greater reductions in tension-anxiety, depression-dejection, anger-hostility, and confusion-bewilderment and greater gains in vigor-activity than the lecture audience. There is, however, a great deal of difficulty in establishing a direct causal link between exercise (i.e., visceral arousal) and affect with such a paradigm. For example, the sense of accomplishment that follows a hard workout may also be a mediator of the observed effects.

Strongman (1987) suggests that while such research indicates that visceral responses are important in the study of affect, they may only be "vague reflections" (i.e., reverberations) of the more central aspects of affect. In many physiologically based theories affect is viewed as neurological activation originating in various cortical and subcortical regions of the brain designed to elicit specific expressive-motor responses. In the broader adaptive theories to be discussed in a subsequent section, affective states involve, in addition, the presence (or recollection) of motivationally relevant stimuli and a resulting behavioral impulse that is functional for satisfying a given motivation. This broader perspective implies that the most central aspects of affective states are those that lie directly on the stimulus-activation-behavior chain. Thus, visceral responses are assigned a more peripheral role.

Brain Wave Activity and Hemispheric Lateralization

Contemporary treatments are somewhat less clear about the centrality of activity in the cerebral cortex. As indicated by the general input-output model, the cerebral cortex influences which affective state is elicited (through its "appraisal" of the external environment) and how that affective state is experienced (through its "interpretation" of internal activity). From an adaptive perspective, the previous functions, particularly environmental appraisal, suggest that cerebral activity is an integral component of affect (i.e., it has an impact along the stimulus-activation-behavior chain). However, assessing the centrality of cerebral activity physiologically is difficult due to the complexity of the relationship between the cerebral cortex and the subcortical structures implicated in the activation of affect.

Much of the research in this section is based on either the measurement or inhibition of activity in various regions of the cerebral cortex. This cerebral activity takes the form of electrical fluctuations of extremely low amplitude (Schwartz 1978). These fluxes can be recorded by attaching electrodes to various regions of the scalp. If the activity of a single neural area must be isolated, then *microelectrodes* must be used. These instruments are extremely delicate and their construction requires great care (Greenfield and Sternbach 1972). It is easier and more common for researchers to measure gross electrical recordings from large populations of neurons with electrodes taking the form of gold or silver discs that are pasted to the scalp. The resulting recording (termed an electroencephalogram or EEG) appears oscillatory and wavelike. Using EEGs, researchers attempt to associate a continuous pattern of brain wave activity with ongoing cognitive activity. A second procedure that is commonly employed with neurologically damaged subjects involves the creation of brain lesions. This involves the temporary or permanent arrest of neural tissue through physical, chemical, or electrical means with the goal of observing the debilitative effects of the lesions on specific cognitive functions. Using either procedure the interpretation of experimental results assumes that the measured (affected) region is central to the ongoing (inhibited) cognitive activity. But, as Carpenter (1984) points out, an experimenter might observe that a lesion in Region X results in an inhibition in Function Y. While it might be tempting to conclude that Function Y is localized in Region X, Function Y might actually be located in Region Z, which merely has connecting neural fibers running through Region X. This limitation makes research in this area difficult to interpret.

The theoretical basis for adopting a hemispheric perspective on affective processes emanates from the cognitive specialization of each hemisphere.[3] Specifically, the left hemisphere has been shown to be well adapted for analytic and verbal processing, whereas the right hemisphere appears more suited for holistic and global conceptual and organizational functions. Safer and Leventhal (1977) point out that many contemporary theories of emotion emphasize the integration of visceral and sensory information into a consummate subjective experience. They argue, therefore, that the right hemisphere's holistic, organizational orientation makes it more suitable for processing emotional information. Experiments involving abnormal subjects tend to support this conjecture.

Subjects with brain lesions in the right hemisphere exhibit difficulty in processing affective information. For example, Heilman, Scholes, and Watson (1975) asked subjects with lesions in either the left or right hemisphere to judge the content of sentences and the mood of the speaker. Both groups did well on content, but right-lesioned subjects had difficulty judging emotion. Similarly, Tucker, Watson, and Heilman (1976) showed that right-lesioned subjects could not interpret the emotional tone of oral stimuli. In addition, Ross and Mesulam (1979) demonstrated that right-lesioned subjects have difficulty in expressing emotion through tone of voice inflections. Research with neurologically sound subjects has also produced some intriguing results. Schwartz, Davidson, and Maer (1975) and Tucker et al. (1977) found that *verbally* presented emotional material increased the frequency of movement in the *left eye*. Activity on the left side of the face is controlled by the right hemisphere. Thus, the observed eye movement suggests greater involvement of the right hemisphere in processing emotional material. Safer and Leventhal (1977) asked subjects to judge the message content and emotional tone of verbal material presented to either the left or right ear. Subjects' judgments of emotional tone were consistently more accu-

---

[3]Much of the following discussion is adapted from a more comprehensive review of this literature by Tucker (1981).

rate when the material was presented to the left, thus suggesting the superiority of the right hemisphere in processing the material. However, Tucker (1981) reports several studies which suggest that the roles of various regions of the cerebral cortex may be far more complex, involving frontal/anterior as well as left/right hemispheric distinctions.

Though many studies implicate the right hemisphere as the primary processing center for affective information, Tucker (1981) suggests a *lateralized valence* hypothesis in which positive (negative) affect is processed in the right (left) hemisphere. A number of studies with neurologically sound as well as impaired subjects tend to be consistent with this view. For example, Harmon and Ray (1977) monitored unimpaired subjects' hemispheric activity as they recalled either positive or negative life experiences. They found that brain wave activity increased predominantly in the right (left) hemisphere for positive (negative) experiences. Unfortunately, other researchers looking at facial muscle responses report hemisphere-valence relationships that appear to be opposite (e.g., Schwartz, Ahern and Brown 1979). Clearly, then, these issues are complex. For example, positive affect often is associated with pleasant experiences that may not demand the type of critical analysis and thought (primarily a left-hemisphere function) needed to understand and cope with negatively experienced affective states. As a result, it is often difficult to separate hemispheric cognitive specialization from lateralized valence interpretations. Those seeking straightforward hemispheric approaches to the study of affective responses in consumer behavior are likely to be disappointed.

Facial Muscle Activity

Facial muscle activity is given special status because of the central role of "expressive" behaviors in many contemporary theories of affect. Interest in this topic stems from Darwin's (1872) interpretation of facial expressions as communicators of motivationally relevant information between lower animals. Smith (1989) reports considerable support for the ability of distinct facial expressions to convey at least six emotions (happiness, sadness, surprise, disgust, anger, fear) and, possibly, shame and contempt as well. Further, there is general agreement on the particular combinations of muscle components that convey these expressions. This perspective is supported by studies that reveal uniform interpretations of facial expressions across individuals. For example, Schlosberg (1952) asked subjects to view a set of pictures of a male face exhibiting various affect-related expressions. They were then asked to rate the pictures on pleasant-unpleasant and attention-rejection dimensions and to array them in order according to similarity. The results showed convergence between the two tasks. That is, the similarity ordering of pictures could essentially be "wrapped around" the ratings of the pictures in the two dimensional space. These results were replicated with a set of pictures of a female face. Ekman and Friesen (1986) have provided evidence that these interpretations hold for people of different cultures.

Facial expressions occupy a central role in Tomkins' (1962) and Izard's (1977) theories of emotion together with neurological activation patterns and cognitive appraisal properties. These three components interact such that motivationally relevant *appraisals of the environment* will automatically lead to specific patterns of neurological activation as well as appropriate facial expressions. However, this chain of influence can begin with either of the components, as will be illustrated.

The facial feedback hypothesis is derived from Tomkins' (1962) and Izard's (1977) conception of interactions among three components of emotion: neurological activation, cognitive appraisal, and facial expression. In its strongest form this hypothesis asserts that if there is no expression of a particular emotion the person would not experience that emotion. The notion is that the neurological feedback from a facial expression that resembles one commonly generated by a particular affective state will tend to elicit a similar affective response " . . . in a rapid, reflexive fashion" (Izard 1977). However, both Tomkins and Izard are somewhat ambiguous as to what constitutes an adequate simulation of an emotional expression. Tourangeau and Ellsworth (1979) interpreted this to be any expression, however artificially created, that an observer could reliably associate with a specific emotion. In their experiment 128 student subjects were instructed to hold specific facial expressions (of fear, sadness, or neutrality) or they were given no instructions. They were then exposed to a film designed to elicit fear, sadness or no emotion. During exposure their facial expressions were coded independently by three judges. After completion of the film, subjects verbally reported their emotional state. Although film content produced a significant effect, the facial manipulations, by themselves, did not influence reported emotion. Even a weaker form of the facial feedback hypothesis, that facial expression and reported emotion should be positively correlated, was rejected.

Izard (1981), Tomkins (1981a), and Hager and Ekman (1981) criticized the Tourangeau and Ellsworth experiment on a number of theoretical and methodological points. First, neurological feedback from the artificially created expressions may be significantly different from that of spontaneous emotional expressions. Ekman, Hager and Friesen (1981) have provided evidence to support this view. They found that the facial asymmetry of emotional expressions differed in frequency and sidedness (left versus right emphasis) depending on whether they were natural or artificial. As Ellsworth and Tourangeau (1981) responded, however, if a "real" emotion is necessary for an adequate simulation, then the facial feedback hypothesis (in which the facial expression by itself elicits the affective response) seems untestable. Second, the observational technique employed for coding facial expressions may not have been sensitive enough to record the facial action components most central to the elicitation of emotion. Ekman, Friesen, and Ancoli (1980) replicated Tourangeau and Ellsworth's no instruction

(i.e., film only) condition, but they found a significant correlation between facial expression and reported emotion (between 0.21 and 0.60), using a more sophisticated coding scheme (see Ekman and Friesen 1976). Judges were able to reliably distinguish subjects exposed to a disgust-eliciting film from those exposed to either an anger- or fear-eliciting film.

The dialogue between Tourangeau and Ellsworth and their critics points out the limitations of observational techniques in detecting facial muscle activity. Cacioppo and Petty (1979) replicated a study by Love (1972) in which independent judges could detect no differences in facial expression when *observing* audiences exposed to either a proattitudinal or counterattitudinal appeal. Measures of electromyographic (EMG) activity did, however, detect significantly different responses in particular facial regions. Cacioppo et al. (1986) indicate that the most consistent EMG finding is greater activity in the muscles which draw the eyebrows together for negative affective responses and the mouth up and back for positive affective responses. The results of Ekman and his colleagues suggest that EMGs may be capable of making even finer distinctions between specific positive (i.e., joy versus love) and negative (i.e., fear versus anger) emotional states. Despite these potential improvements in measurement, Zuckerman et al. (1981) point out that *demand effects* seem particularly likely if subjects guess the true purpose of an artificial facial manipulation (i.e., subjects who are asked to move the corners of their mouth outward and upward may determine that they are now "smiling" and connect it to the subsequent evaluation tasks, questions about mood, etc.).

In order to overcome this shortcoming researchers have designed increasingly clever cover stories and manipulations to ensure that subjects' cognitive activity is irrelevant to the experimental hypothesis. Strack et al. (1988) led subjects to believe that the researchers were interested in people's ability to perform various tasks with parts of their body they would not normally use: They suggested a link to the problems that handicapped people face. Subjects were induced to hold and write with a pen using either their lips only or their teeth only. The "lips" manipulation caused subjects' eyebrows to contract and be drawn together (the negative affect condition), whereas the "teeth" manipulation caused subjects to stretch and raise the corners of their mouths (the positive affect condition). In the critical task, subjects — while holding the pen in their mouths — rated the funniness of a set of newspaper cartoons on a semantic differential scale. As predicted, subjects in the lips only condition rated the cartoons as being less funny than did subjects in the teeth only condition. Moreover, task difficulty was ruled out as an alternative explanation for the results.

Although some of the relationships are not strong, results such as those of Strack et al. (1988) provided general support for Tomkin's (1962) and Izard's (1977) ideas. One other provocative finding is that cells in a specific area of the temporal lobe in monkeys respond only to faces (Perrett, Rolls, and Caan 1982), which suggests not only the importance of facial expression but the development of highly specialized response mechanisms. Also, compared with cardiovascular and respiratory responses, facial muscular activity may stand on more of a direct line in a stimulus-activation-behavior chain, possibly becoming a component of certain adaptive behaviors (James 1890; Cannon 1927; Arnold 1960; Bindra 1969; Plutchik 1980).[4] Although it is assigned a peripheral role (as is all nonneurological activity) by Strongman (1987), facial muscle activity is diagnostic of certain affective responses.

AFFECT AS SUBJECTIVE EXPERIENCE

Much of the present effort to describe the experience of emotion can be traced to the work of James (1890). In his view, emotional states are

experienced differently because each generates a specific pattern of arousal in the visceral system which the cognitive system is then able to interpret. By contrast, in Schachter's (1964) "nonspecific arousal" theory, an emotional state is a function of a general state of arousal and a particularly important cognitive appraisal process. Subjective experience is essentially determined by the cognitive appraisal of an *external stimulus event*. For example, Schachter and Singer (1962) demonstrated that subjects injected with epinephrine (an arousal-inducing drug) exhibited either anger or elation depending on the emotional state displayed by a confederate with whom they were asked to wait. However, subsequent attempts to replicate these results were disappointing (see Leventhal 1980). While it is generally accepted that Schachter and Singer overstated the role of cognitive appraisal in the experience of affect (e.g., assuming an undifferentiated state of arousal as their starting point), their work did much to spark interest in the more cognitive aspects of emotion. Recent efforts have focused on the identification of underlying perceptual components that best account for the more highly differentiated and subtle nuances making up our array of emotional experiences.

Whereas self-introspection of emotional experience was the dominant method of the early theorists, contemporary approaches employ experimental paradigms and utilize standardized measurement systems (e.g., semantic differential scales) coupled with multivariate statistical methods to determine the underlying structure. Subjects are asked to rate or organize a set of affective adjectives on a number of scales or with respect to some criteria. Various statistical methods for reducing dimensionality are then employed to determine the underlying dimensions. Each affective adjective can be given coordinates in the reduced space that emerges.

One of the most well-developed representational systems is the circumplex model of Russell (1980). Subjects would typically rate a set of affective adjectives on a number of semantic differential scales. They then ordered the adjectives in a circular pattern according to similarity. Finally, they rated each pair of terms

---

[4]As suggested earlier, although a *general* state of arousal is adaptive for preparing an organism to respond to its environment (e.g, McDougall 1927; Bindra 1969) the direct relevance of *specific patterns* of visceral response (e.g., the ratio of systolic to diastolic blood pressure) is difficult to determine.

on the basis of overall similarity. Principal components analysis of such semantic differential data generated an easily interpretable two dimensional solution (pleasant-unpleasant, sleepiness-arousal), which corresponded to a multidimensional scaling of similarity data and the adjective circle produced by the ordering task.[5]

In general, empirical support for pleasant-unpleasant (P-U) and sleepiness-arousal (S-A) dimensions is abundant (Block 1957; Mehrabian and Russell 1974; Daly, Lancee, and Polivy 1983). However, in other respects the evidence is not highly consistent. For example, when Plutchik's (1980a) subjects performed the circular-ordering task described previously, the emotions anger and fear appeared as polar opposites, while in Russell's model they were very close in proximity.

A second type of inconsistency involves the number of interpretable dimensions in the resulting model. Daly et al. (1983) report that most studies produce Wundt's P-U and S-A dimensions and a third dimension that receives different interpretations across studies. However, Smith and Ellsworth (1985) generated an eight-dimensional solution that not only included the P-U dimension, but also contained dimensions regarding the degree of (1) attention, (2) control, (3) certainty, (4) effort, (5) self-agency (responsibility), (6) perceived obstacle, and (7) importance.

While procedural and measurement differences across studies contribute to these observed inconsistencies, Smith and Ellsworth (1985) suggest that the overriding cause is the content of the stimulus set. First, stimulus set size has direct implications for multidimensional scaling techniques. For a given loss function (i.e., amount of allowable error) larger set sizes lead to higher dimensional solutions (Shepard 1962). More important, the content and variability of the stimulus set greatly influence the final solution.

Consider the differences in adjective proximity between Plutchik's (1980a) and Russell's

(1980) circular models. These disparities can be given an intuitive explanation by examining the affective adjectives employed in each study. Plutchik employed eight primary emotion terms. Consistent with his psychoevolutionary theory (to be discussed later), these terms had strong *motivational significance* (e.g., acceptance, anticipation). Russell, on the other hand, utilized 28 affect terms. Many of these terms were more related to *experienced physiological states* (e.g., aroused, sleepy). Not surprisingly, Plutchik found anger and fear to be polar opposites. This is certainly compatible with a general approach(anger)-avoidance(fear) motivational taxonomy. However, as experienced physiological states, anger and fear may seem quite similar (e.g., unpleasant, arousing, etc.). Consistent with this conjecture, Russell's model placed them in close proximity (see also Havlena and Holbrook 1986).

In light of these inconsistent findings, Smith and Ellsworth (1985) emphasize the importance of a theoretical basis for the choice of the stimulus set. Since the objective of *their* empirical investigation was to pull apart the dimensions involved in cognitive appraisal (an integral component in many theories of emotion; Schachter 1959; Arnold 1960; Averill 1983), they deliberately chose emotion terms and rating scales that would comprehensively address the cognitive aspects of emotional experience.

Shaver et al. (1987), proceeding from prototype categorization concepts, produced a *hierarchical* taxonomy of emotional terms. A cluster analysis of subjects' similarity ratings of 135 emotion terms yielded three distinct *levels* of emotional groupings. The first level comprised a basic positive versus negative differentiation. At the next level, five distinct clusters (love, joy, anger, sadness, fear) emerged. At the most sensitive level of discrimination there were 24 clusters (affection, lust, longing, cheerfulness, zest, contentment, pride, optimism, enthrallment, relief, irritation, exasperation, rage, disgust, envy, torment, suffering, sadness, disappointment, shame, neglect, sympathy, horror, nervousness). Shaver et al. contend that such hierarchical representations may contain information about the relationships among various

----

[5]The principal components analysis also produced a three-dimensional solution, but one of the dimensions was extremely difficult to interpret.

emotions that is lost in the more traditional dimensional depictions. Hierarchical analyses may also suggest hypotheses regarding the dynamics of emotional appraisal.

For those who choose to work in this area, it is important to recognize the contingency between the content of the stimulus set and the resulting solution space and to choose their stimulus set so as to unveil the portion of the puzzle in which they are most interested. It seems apparent, then, that there is no simple "best" representation of emotional experience.

TOWARD A UNIFYING THEORETICAL PERSPECTIVE

In addition to examining the various aspects of emotion (i.e., physiological responses, facial expressions, subjective experience) separately, researchers have begun to explore the relationships among them.

As indicated earlier, Darwin (1872) was among the first to emphasize the link between emotions and "habitual" behaviors. As part of the basic instinctual system, emotions were related closely to environmental assessments in generating nondeliberative behavioral tendencies to help the organism adapt to its environment. (Darwin distinguished humans from other animals by noting their ability to invoke the cognitive system in order to "override" these tendencies. However, as we shall see later, he felt that the cognitive system was powerless to interrupt "hard wired" reflex responses.) He also noted that, across species, specific facial patterns were associated with given affective states. This led him to conclude that such facial expressions must be functional for communicating the emotional state of the animal to others in the immediate environment. The basic tenets of his work provide a foundation for the more recent theories of Arnold (1960), Izard (1977), De Rivera (1977, 1984), and Plutchik (1980a).

Arnold's (1960) conception of emotions centers on Darwin's notion of appraisal. It rests on the three premises that (1) emotions are integrally related to the motivational system,

(2) emotions require the (deliberate or automatic) appraisal of an environmental stimulus relative to the motivational system, and (3) emotions may or may not generate corresponding behavioral tendencies. There is, here, an important enhancement in the role of cognitive processes, as compared with the view that the cognitive system would function primarily to *negate* behavioral tendencies engendered by affective responses. Furthermore, Arnold suggests that even intense affective responses *require* cognitive appraisal in order to generate a behavioral response, and further cognitive appraisal mediates the affective response itself.

In many situations, of course, the relationship between an environmental stimulus and the organism is simple and seems to be determined almost automatically (or at least outside conscious awareness). In other cases, the motivational relevance of a stimulus is complex and nonobvious and requires greater deliberation before the appropriate appraisal and resulting affective response can occur. There is often no direct link between the affective state and behavior.

Arnold labels emotions that generate behavioral tendencies *contending* emotions, while those without a behavioral component are termed *impulse* emotions. To produce a taxonomy of emotional states, she then introduces three additional distinctions: (1) valence of the stimulus (positive or negative), (2) presence of the stimulus (present or absent), and (3) attainability of the stimulus (easy or difficult). This four-dimensional framework was used to classify and distinguish twelve basic emotions (love, hate, wanting, aversion, joy, sorrow, hope, despair, daring, fear, anger, and rejection).

De Rivera (1977, 1984) offers a structural model similar to Arnold's, except for his conception of continuous cognitive appraisal dimensions rather than discrete appraisal features. Each of the three appraisal dimensions emanates from the notion of a self/other dyad. The first describes appraisals as being either *self* or *other* focused. The second dimension defines the point of reference for a given appraisal as being either *relative* to a particular self or *absolute* (i.e., the same for all selves) in nature. Finally, consistent with other dimensional models (Wundt 1896; Schlosberg 1952; Block 1957; Russell 1980; Plutchik 1980), there is a *positive-negative* dimension.

De Rivera interprets 24 emotions in terms of the resulting three dimensional space. So, for instance, *anger* results from an *absolute, negative* appraisal that is *other* directed. Although this structural translation is useful for interpreting the emotional content of interpersonal relations (see for example, De Rivera 1984), there are troublesome conceptual inconsistencies. As an example, fear and anger are distinguished along the absolute(anger)/relative(fear) dimension. Yet, it is easy to imagine objects (i.e., a guillotine) that almost universally produce fear as well as anger-eliciting objects (i.e., a hated enemy) that are quite specific to the self.

Other frameworks lend greater precision to Arnold's useful distinction between automatic and deliberative appraisals (Lazarus 1982; 1984; Mandler 1976; Leventhal 1980; Buck 1985). For example, Leventhal proposes three distinct levels of cognitive appraisal. Expressive motor appraisals occur immediately in response to sensory information sent to isolated neurological centers. These appraisals automatically generate motor (i.e., expressive) activity and, through a "feed forward" mechanism, influence subsequent stages of processing. The next level of appraisal results when the sensory input matches some perceptual schema in memory. These schema are formed over time to allow the organism to generalize emotional responses across perceptually similar stimuli. This information modifies an expressive response through automatic processes and influences the final stage in the sequence through a second feed forward mechanism. This last level of processing involves cognitive appraisal and deliberation, which provides the organism with a great deal of flexibility in order to respond to an unfamiliar but motivationally relevant stimulus.

In Buck's (1985) *prime theory,* motivation and emotion are viewed as different aspects of a single system. Motivation represents the potential for activation (much like potential energy in

physics) whereas "emotion involves the means by which that potential is realized or read out, when activated by challenging stimuli." In this view, we might ignore emotional information, for example when experienced (i.e., readout) as contentment when we are satisfied. Nevertheless, emotion is constantly occurring, predisposing responses important for adaptation. Primes are "special-purpose systems" serving functions that are as basic as simple neural system responses (e.g, reflexes, fixed action patterns). They also encompass internal bodily disturbances (e.g., the need for food, water, temperature regulation, and sleep) as well as acquired drives and "hard-wired" primary affect. The capacity to experience these affective responses is innate, but appraisal and modes of response involve interactions with general purpose systems of learning and cognition. Finally, primes also serve highly flexible motivational systems, such as those involved in exploratory and achievement pursuits.

Buck identifies three basic forms of emotional "readouts" that motivational primes produce when activated. These readouts combine to determine the organism's experience of the state. The first readout incorporates internally and externally generated visceral and skeletal responses. The second involves feedback from the organism's overt expressive behavior (such as facial expressions) which have evolved as part of species specific signalling and coordination needs. The third results from the cognitive experience of the emotional state, possibly originating in the right hemisphere and then becoming an object for analytic cognition and decision making. Like Leventhal, Buck allows for interaction between the three forms of readouts. He stresses the centrality of cognitive appraisal in differentiating emotional states. In this respect his perspective is not unlike that of Schachter (1964; Schachter and Singer 1962).

Recent elaborations of the cognitive appraisal perspective have focused on individuals' deliberate appraisals of motivationally meaningful events. For example, Averill (1983) found that subjects related experiences of anger to a discrepancy in judgment between themselves and the instigating target regarding the justifiability, deliberateness, and avoidability of a particular act. Weiner (1986) extends this type of analysis to a wider spectrum of emotional states. In his taxonomy, specific emotions (i.e., anger, fear, joy, etc.) arise as a result of attributions an individual makes regarding the cause (internal-external), controllability (high-low), and stability (high-low) of a motivationally relevant outcome.

While notions of adaptivity are apparent in the theories of Darwin and Arnold, they are only partially delineated. Darwin discusses it only in general terms and through examples, and Arnold simply classifies functional behaviors according to several general features (i.e., positive/negative, present/absent, attainable/unattainable). Plutchik's (1980a, 1980b) "psychoevolutionary" perspective is more specific about the adaptive purposes served by affective states in helping a person deal with the environment. He identifies basic motivations/functions (protection, destruction, incorporation, rejection, reproduction, reintegration, orientation, and exploration) and links them to specific emotions (fear, anger, joy, love, sadness, startle, and anticipation).

This functional view of emotions allows them to be described as stimulus-event–cognition–feeling–behavior sequences. For example, a threat by an enemy (a stimulus-event) might lead to the realization that there is danger (a cognitive appraisal), which then elicits fear (a feeling), which then leads the organism to retreat (a behavior). This entire sequence of events serves the function/motivation of protection. Readers interested in a particularly comprehensive, functionally oriented perspective are encouraged to examine Plutchik's work in more detail.

Tomkins (1962, 1981b) and Izard (1977) view emotions as the cornerstone of the primary motivational system in human beings. Emotions are conceptualized as having physiological, evaluative/motivational, and facial expression components. In these theories, then, facial expressions are assigned a more integral role in defining the meaning of an emotion. They not only communicate the motivational state of the organism to other individuals but provide feedback to the organism to allow it to interpret the affective state.

Three general principles are particularly important in Izard's work. The *principle of differential emotions* suggests that the nine basic emotions (interest-excitement, enjoyment-joy, surprise-startle, distress-anguish, anger-rage, disgust-revulsion, contempt-scorn, fear-terror, and shame-humiliation) can be differentiated according to their physiological content, evaluative implication, and facial expression. While other physiological correlates have been heavily researched (as discussed in earlier sections), Izard's treatment is more integrative—and more ambitious—than most.

The *principle of interacting emotion components* asserts that the physiological, evaluative, and facial expressive components interact as if they were in a continuous feedback loop. This principle provides a basis for interpreting much of the empirical research reviewed previously.

For example, Schachter's (1964; Schachter and Singer, 1962) assertion that an unexplained state of arousal elicits "evaluative needs" in the individual suggests feedback from the physiological component to the evaluative and expressive components. Also, as elaborated previously, the facial feedback hypothesis proposes feedback from the expressive component to the evaluative and physiological components.

The principle of interacting emotion components implies that feedback between the three components is an ongoing phenomenon when affect is elicited. Consistent with this notion, Smith (1989) proceeds from the assumption that physiological activity and appraisal of the adaptive significance of the environment are linked so as to promote both preparation for coping and communication to others. He investigated the possibility that specific muscle groups convey information about the person's cognitive appraisal of the situation. In particular, based on observations by Darwin (1872) and the work of Ekman and Friesen (1976) and Smith and Ellsworth (1985), he predicted that heart rate and eyebrow contraction activity (frowning) would be greater for appraisals involving anticipated effort and other (rather than self) agency. In his experiment subjects connected to an EMG measuring device and a pulse monitor imagined various emotion-related scenarios. Both heart rate and eyebrow activity were significantly related to ratings of anticipated effort. However, neither heart rate nor eyebrow activity was significantly correlated with ratings of other agency.

Finally, the *principle of interacting systems* postulates that activities in the affective system influence the functions of the cognitive and conative systems, which, through another feedback loop, may influence subsequent activities in the affective system. Izard's broad "systems" view of affect brings us full circle to the trilogy with which we began our discussion of the history of research on affect. There has been considerable progress to report. Not only do we have a much better understanding of affective processes, but we are beginning to develop a more comprehensive picture of how the three systems interact — and we have a good deal yet to report concerning affect-cognition interactions. We share Izard's view, however, that a truly comprehensive model involving affect must have dynamic properties that parallel ongoing behavior. We will return to this in a subsequent section when we present a proposed model of this type.

RESEARCH ON AFFECT IN CONSUMER BEHAVIOR

In an attempt to organize a rather diffuse literature,[6] we have adopted the three-part framework shown in Figure 6.1. The figure assumes a flow from the manipulated or measured antecedent variables to a set of cognitive and behavioral consequences and provides illustrative lists of variables that have drawn research attention.

---

[6]Much of the research reviewed in this section is incorporated in a more comprehensive treatment of the attitude and affect literatures by Cohen (1990).

Arrows are used to specify research paths which encompass affect.

We shall restrict our attention to research that treats "affect" as a valenced feeling state which generates affective traces (rather than "affect" as an evaluative cognition). Thus, studies that do not attempt to either manipulate or measure the effects of some affective process and which only use the term "affect" to refer to a strictly attitudinal assessment are not discussed. By and large this work is quite recent, so many of the relationships portrayed in the figure have yet to be examined. Relationships illustrated in Figure 6.1 using bidirectional arrows are to be thought of as dynamic in that the potential for mutual influence over a short period of time is assumed to be high. As discussed earlier, affective states give rise to affective traces. Affective states are shown to respond directly to all antecedent variables as well as cognitive and behavioral consequences. The latter variables are linked via a feedback loop so that, for example, behavior during the prepurchase stage can affect both cognitive structure and processes leading to subsequent behavior. Affective traces, of course, can be retrieved from memory independent of feeling states, similar to other cognitive elements. We do not illustrate this straightforward retrieval process; however we specifically incorporate a feedback loop to indicate that such traces may be modified by subsequent cognitive activities. Finally, while affective states can impact directly on both cognitive and behavioral outcomes, affective traces must first be interpreted by the cognitive system before they can influence subsequent behavior.

Primary research attention has been directed to advertising and situationally induced *moods* rather than more central motivational factors and stronger *emotions*. With respect to advertising, there appear to be plenty of "warm" effects, but the ability of advertising to generate more intense drivelike responses seems quite limited.

The ability of purchase settings, consumption experiences, and want satisfaction episodes to elicit affectively charged states is just beginning to come under systematic study, even though the creation of affect has long been regarded as important to marketing success. In-

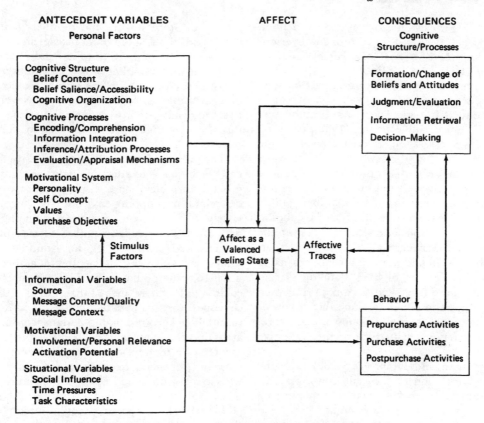

ANTECEDENT VARIABLES　　　　AFFECT　　　　CONSEQUENCES

Personal Factors

Cognitive
Structure/Processes

Cognitive Structure
　Belief Content
　Belief Salience/Accessibility
　Cognitive Organization

Cognitive Processes
　Encoding/Comprehension
　Information Integration
　Inference/Attribution Processes
　Evaluation/Appraisal Mechanisms

Motivational System
　Personality
　Self Concept
　Values
　Purchase Objectives

Formation/Change of
Beliefs and Attitudes

Judgment/Evaluation

Information Retrieval

Decision-Making

Stimulus
Factors

Affect as a
Valenced
Feeling State

Affective
Traces

Informational Variables
　Source
　Message Content/Quality
　Message Context

Motivational Variables
　Involvement/Personal Relevance
　Activation Potential

Situational Variables
　Social Influence
　Time Pressures
　Task Characteristics

Behavior

Prepurchase Activities

Purchase Activities

Postpurchase Activities

FIGURE 6.1　Research on Affect in Consumer Behavior

deed many accounts of marketing and advertising's view of the consumer point out that as far back as the 1930s (based largely on psychoanalytic theories) emotional appeals became "the order of the day, reflecting a new view of consumers as emotional beings . . ." (Robertson, Zielinski, and Ward 1984, p. 13). The "emotional appeal" of various "background" factors of the purchase setting is frequently referred to in the marketing literature. For example, Kotler (1974) has advocated that considerable attention be paid to the ambient environment within which products are purchased in the conviction that variations in overall design and "atmospherics" can play a major role in shaping attitudes and behavior. Still, systematic research on the effects of feeling states (induced or otherwise) in consumer behavior was almost nonexistent until quite recently.

Affective Responses to Product Purchase and Use

Clearly some products have greater "affect potential" as a function of the degree to which they are linked to important goals and values (e.g., Laurent and Kepferer 1985; Zaichkowsky 1985; Belk 1988). Of course, most such products also have greater "information processing potential" (Celsi and Olson 1988). It is important, therefore, to distinguish between the affect-laden outcomes of a decision and the affective dimensions of the decision-making process itself. To the extent that a "special relationship" exists between a consumer and a product (e.g., "As soon as I saw that car I fell in love with it."), some research to be discussed later suggests that affective processes may influence the nature of the evaluation process — perhaps making the evaluation process less deliberate and analytical and more prone to overlook weaknesses both before and after purchase. (Alas, perhaps love *is* blind!)

An external factor likely to impact on both affective states and related evaluative outcomes is the context in which purchase decisions are made. Donovan and Rossiter (1982), using interviewers to assess the affective tone of a set of stores, found that they would provide more favorable self-reported purchase intentions when they also rated the environment as *both* pleasant and arousing. As Gardner (1985) points out, some bias may be created by obtaining both sets of subjective assessments from the same people. Gardner and Siomkos (1986) attempted to simulate store atmospherics using written descriptions high in both detail and evaluative tone (e.g., dirty, dingy) and then asked subjects to either imagine themselves or others in either a high- or low-image store. Store descriptions elicited consistent evaluative ratings.

Hirschman and Holbrook (1982) raise the provocative notion of "hedonic consumption," according to which the goal of experiencing emotive stimulation becomes an important end state for consumers, quite apart from enjoyment of the product purchased. Thus, shopping environments that are made more enjoyable, exciting, and multisensory may become not only more desirable for their own sake, they may also "inject" positive affect into the product evaluation and decision-making process. The aesthetic aspects of products, advertisements, and so forth, and the sensory experience itself, with its varied emotional texture, are advocated as topics for study. Hill and Gardner (1987) discussed the role of moods in triggering the buying process, particularly in directing consumers to products associated with salient or desired mood states.

In one study (Sherman and Smith 1987), the moods of eighty-nine shoppers at different clothing and specialty stores were assessed using the Mehrabian-Russell scale. Factor analysis identified three distinct factors; pleasure-displeasure, arousal-excitement, and alertness, which were significantly correlated with ratings of store image, the number of items purchased, the amount of money spent, and the time spent shopping. Since the results are correlational we do not know to what extent mood "caused" such effects or was simply a reflection of a favorable shopping experience. Nevertheless, the results are interesting and indicate that this is a potentially promising area for further research.

The precise effects of different affective tones and mechanisms of affect induction (e.g., background variables, store displays, salespeople's behaviors) in shopping environments may have widely different consequences depending, in part, on the extent and nature of consumers' attributional processes. If, for example, consumers are well aware of the attempt and attribute it to a manipulative purpose, the outcome could well be the reverse of that intended. Ethical issues may likewise be involved if, say, as a result of background manipulations, consumers are induced to alter their deliberative processes, spend more money, and so forth. There is almost no published research in consumer contexts to draw on in addressing these and related issues. One exception is the work by Milliman (1982; 1986). In the first study, supermarket shoppers over a two-month period were exposed to either no music, music at 60 beats per minute, or music at 108 beats per minute (with a wide variation of musical selections in each condition). All were played at the level of background music, and awareness was consistently fairly low over treatments. It was demonstrated that walking speed was 17 percent faster in the fast-paced music condition compared with the slow-paced music condition. No music shoppers were about midway between these). *And,* most important, the slower walking consumers spent about 38 percent more money! Milliman (1986) also found that playing slow-tempo background music in a restaurant led customers to stay longer and consume a greater amount of alcoholic beverages. They did not consume more food, possibly merely slowing down the rate of consumption in response to the induced mood.

Defining *impulse buying* in terms of a combination of high activation, little intellectual control, and largely automatic behavior actuated by the situation, Weinberg and Gottwald (1982) obtained a nonreactive record of mimical expressions as well as a subsequent self-report of emotional content, strength, and direction on the part of secretly filmed consumers shopping for decals. These filmed sequences of 15 selected buyers and nonbuyers (who were subsequently advised that they had been filmed, gave their consent, and were then interviewed) were shown to 35 subjects who were uninformed as to whether or not a purchase had been made by each. Emotional qualities (e.g., surprise, boredom, anger, enthusiasm, doubt), together with strength (e.g., stimulating, exciting), and direction (e.g., pleasant, inspiring) were assessed by both observers and participants using scale items, and a comparable factor structure emerged.

Buyers assessed themselves as more amused, delighted, and enthusiastic than nonbuyers. Buyers also saw themselves as less astonished and indifferent, and, in general, naive observers agreed with these assessments. With regard to activation, the authors concluded that buyers were significantly more emotional (based both on self-assessments and observed behavior). Linking these results back to impulsive behavior, however, is somewhat tenuous since the relationship between particular scale items and the concept of impulsiveness, per se, is not particularly clear. In addition, the study does not allow us to determine when these emotional states were experienced, and many of the results are consistent with post-purchase emotions.

Rook and several coauthors (Rook and Hock, 1985: Rook 1987; Gardner and Rook 1988) offer insights and exploratory analyses of how impulse purchases are experienced in terms of both precipitating contextual factors and subsequent feelings of pleasure and excitement, as well as in terms of anxiety and guilt. The use of product purchases such as self-gifts and unplanned (and possibly "unnecessary") purchases to repair negative moods as well as to bolster self-esteem is an interesting facet of consumer behavior.

Just as affect differs from attitude, such post-purchase feeling states are different from judged satisfaction (e.g., Oliver and De Sarbo 1988: Tse and Wilton 1988). A consumer survey by Westbrook (1980) examines the moderating role of both generalized attitudes (e.g., overall life satisfaction, optimism) and transient affective states (e.g., elation-depression) coincident with product experience on ratings of product satisfaction. Some support for the role of the former (but not the latter) factors was obtained. Using retrospective aided recall of positive and negative affective experiences (as assessed by Izard's, 1977, self-administered inventory), Westbrook (1987) reports affective implications of postpurchase automobile and CATV judgments and behavior. It is, however, difficult to disentangle the interplay among outcome appraisal, satisfaction, and affect in this type of research design.

Affective Responses to Advertising

The most frequently studied of the external factors thought to affect the consumer's cognitive and motivational systems, is, of course, advertising. In this research domain affective feeling states are thought to result from both the advertisement (i.e., its appeal and execution) and the program context (e.g., the television program, the magazine) in which it is embedded.

The consumer's cognitive structure and the degree to which the advertisement matches prior expectations may together play an important role in determining affective response. Little work has been done to examine the affective impact of departures from expectations, although a recent study by Meyers-Levy and Tybout (1989) builds on Mandler's (1982) discussion of schema-incongruity effects and examines resulting product evaluations (see also Fiske and Pavelchak 1986; Sujan 1985). Advertising appeals and executions focusing on such themes as "add some excitement" or "simplify your life" may have relevance for the seemingly intractable delineation of an "optimum stimulation level" (Raju 1980; Joachimsthaler and Lastovicka 1984; Wahlers and Etzel 1985). Zinkhan and Martin (1983) assessed consumers' cognitive complexity with respect to calculators and exposed them to ads differing in the clarity of their internal structure (as assessed by the individuals' ability to provide deleted words). Using self-report scales to tap "affective response" (e.g., enjoyment, likability), the authors found that the more cognitively complex the viewer was the more the complex ad was preferred (i.e., the content of the ad would then appear to become more predictable). They suggest that the advice often given to "keep it simple" in advertising might not always be correct.

Program Context. Programs in which advertisements are embedded can affect encoding and elaboration of message content as well as receptivity to its recommendations. Affective responses to the advertisement should also be influenced by the affective state the consumer brings into the situation and the expectations and predispositions that are likely to play some role in comprehending and in interpreting the advertising. A survey study by Schultz (1979) involving marketing managers and media directors of leading advertising companies and agencies suggests that such context effects are of growing concern to practitioners. Conventional wisdom suggests that both the affect induced by the program context and its consistency with the affective tone of the advertisement should be important, but this has been a matter of some disagreement within advertising circles (e.g., Yuspeh 1979). Many practitioners are leery of programmatic material that is too arousing, too apt to create negative feelings or outlooks, or too likely to encourage a critical response orientation. Instead they would rather have consumers feeling generally positive.

An early and frequently cited study by Axelrod (1963) supports this point of view, though the programmatic material (documentary film footage of Nazi war crimes) is almost certainly "stronger stuff" than most TV fare. The film was successful in inducing the expected mood, and it also influenced viewers' beliefs that the use of various products would prompt a generally similar affective state (e.g., depression), thus leading attitudes toward the products to

shift in a consistent manner. One question, of course, is whether subjects merely responded the way they felt they *should*, given the nature of the film.

Alternative mechanisms that might explain the influence of a program-induced mood on reactions to TV commercials are (1) the priming of mood congruent material related to the commercial, (2) a less cognitively mediated transfer of affect resulting from mere temporal association, and (3) consistency-induced judgments regarding attributes of the program and commercial (particularly if judgments are not made "on-line" but on the basis of subsequent information retrieval). Goldberg and Gorn (1987) embedded informational and emotional ads in either happy or sad TV programs. Those viewing the *happy programs* were happier, evaluated the commercials as more effective and had improved recall of the commercials (though there was no program effect on intention to purchase). Subjects also felt happier watching the emotional commercials, evaluated them as more effective and indicated a higher intention to purchase. Program valence influenced the subjects' moods more as they watched the emotional commercials, but there was no significant interaction between the mood induced by the program and the type of commercial with regard to the perceived effectiveness of the commercials or intentions to purchase. Whether similar results would occur for products for which informational appeals might be expected and preferred awaits further study.

Positive feelings did not have a facilitating effect on recall for those viewing Super Bowl XX in the winning city (presumably a pleasurable experience) as compared with those in the losing city and a neutral city (Pavelchak, Antil, and Munch 1988). The latter viewers recalled more ads, with winners recalling the fewest number. Day-after interviewing confirmed that reported pleasure and arousal had remained high in the winning city and had dropped off in both of the other cities (perhaps because the score was not close and the game was not exciting). While positive feelings did not apparently enhance encoding of the advertising material, emotional intensity/arousal may have inhibited it by narrowing attention to the contextual stimuli responsible for the emotional experience. Another possibility is that the program was distracting. It may have competed more effectively for viewers' attention in the winning and, to a lesser extent, in the losing city than it did in the neutral city, where presumably there was less carry over of game-related thoughts when the commercials appeared.

Singh and Churchill (1987) provide a general theoretical interpretation of context effects with their "excitation transfer" explanation. Here, arousal (defined as energy which enhances psychological and motor activity), is implicated as a mediating variable. The excitation transfer hypothesis stems from Schachter and Singer's (1962) examination of the effects of a misattribution of a state of arousal (to be reviewed in greater detail later), and it had earlier been applied to communication-mediated aggressive behavior (Zillman 1971). Basically, individuals are thought to misattribute the arousal generated by TV programming to the embedded advertisements, thus producing attitudinal effects. Although this interpretation has some general intuitive appeal, the conditions that would lead people to misattribute such arousal are not obvious, and the relevance of this explanation for advertising context effects needs to be established.

Thinking versus Emotional Advertising. Friestad and Thorson (1986), in addressing this distinction, produced favorable long-term memory and evaluative effects through a single exposure to emotional ads. The authors define an "emotional message" as "a vehicle that creates over-time flow of feelings that people report as emotional experience" (p. 111). This is a departure from earlier definitions that emphasized the *type* of information/appeal being used, the viewer's mood, or judgments of liking for the ad. A key premise of the authors' approach is that an experience that occurs in the presence of emotional arousal leaves much stronger episodic traces. These may become integrated into product-related semantic memory, this being much more likely under higher involvement, personal relevance, and "on-line" (i.e., same-

time) judgment conditions. Subjects were either instructed to watch and evaluate promotional messages (as to personal relevance) in the semantic processing condition, or they were simply asked to watch the material carefully (episodic conditions). They were each exposed to five emotional and five neutral commercials embedded in several program segments. Two months later subjects were telephoned and interviewed, and it was found that the emotional messages generated a higher level of free recall (number of messages, brand names, executional elements), with episodic instructions providing a weak but consistent advantage. In contrast to Golden and Johnson (1983), who found that emotional ads in four product categories were not as well liked as ads relying on objective (i.e., "thinking") appeals, the emotional messages were significantly better liked and had a higher perceived influence. (Golden and Johnson's (1983) "emotional" ads tended to rely on music and dramatic display to create a mood, and hence they may have been different in several respects.)

Friestad and Thorson acknowledge the difficulty of establishing the equivalence of emotional and neutral messages on other dimensions that could make the latter less accessible. Doing so is pivotal if we are to better understand the process that is producing these effects. For example, is the emotional aspect more responsible for the recall differences than the potentially greater distinctiveness or interest value of those messages? Also, while episodic and semantic memory differences may be involved, the semantic memory instructions introduced an additional task which may have drawn the subjects' attention away from the message elements themselves and toward an evaluation of them. Nevertheless, the conceptualization and results are very interesting and provide a strong challenge to the conventional wisdom that "feeling" ads are likely to fare worse than "thinking" ads in recall tests (the standard of the copy-testing industry being day-after recall), possibly because "thinking" ads and recall tests may both emphasize left-brain activity (Zielski 1982; Puto and Wells 1984).

Emotional ads often give a dominant role to

music and pictures as stimulus properties likely to generate an affective response (e.g., Kroeber Riel 1984a; Mitchell 1986). Anand et al. (1988) found that subjects' evaluations of musical (verbal) passages were more favorable when the stimuli were presented to the left (right) ear. Though each hemisphere receives information from both ears, the primary input is contralateral. Accordingly, the authors suggested that the results were due to the specialization of the right (left) hemisphere for processing musical (verbal) stimuli.

In the Puto and Wells (1984) twofold classification system, informational ads are perceived to present factual, relevant information in a verifiable format. Transformational advertising, on the other hand, associates the experience of using the product with "a unique set of psychological characteristics." Thus, the experience of using the product is likely to be made "richer, warmer, more exciting, and/or more enjoyable" than it would otherwise be by the advertisement. The authors see this "transformational" designation as comparable to "affect-based," but they also require such ads to cause consumers to relate the affective properties to the experience of owning or using the product. Further, they advance the proposition that the "generalized emotion" resulting from transformational advertising will have a number of selective effects on recall (e.g., recall of similar feelings) and experience generation (e.g., producing similar feelings). Any advertisement may represent a combination of informational and transformational approaches. The authors report initial work to develop an inventory composed of informational and transformational scale items that can be used in assigning ads to these categories or rating their adequacy on each dimension.

Getting Through versus Being Liked. Robertson, Zielinski, and Ward (1984, p. 229) report that advertisers, in general, operate with two conflicting theories with regard to the affective aspects of messages. The first they term the "law of extremes," which states that "whether consumers like or dislike an advertisement is less important than the intensity with which

they perceive it." The "superiority of the pleasant" view however, is simply that "pleasant stimuli are more effective than unpleasant stimuli." The latter hypothesis is loosely modeled after various conditioning principles, whereas the former takes particular account of the importance of getting through the clutter of competing advertisements and registering the strongest possible associations between the product category, a brand's name, and its key features (some support for this view can be found in a study by Silk and Vavra 1974).

There is also some belief that the affective tone of the message and the content of the message may become disassociated in consumers' minds with the passage of time (a type of "sleeper effect"; see Moore and Hutchinson 1983 for a particularly relevant discussion). This suggests that intensity might matter more than positivity. In addition, certain "negative" affective states (usually created by elements of the message but possibly by the surrounding context) may, in fact, if not overly threatening, promote greater attention to and interest in the product (e.g., fear and anxiety-based increases in sensitivity to the "problem" the product is attempting to "solve"). More generally, however, it is clear that advertisers seek to create positive moods, which they hope will somehow "rub off" onto their products and either persist until purchase or be reintroduced by similar cues at the point of purchase (Shimp 1981).

Affect and Attitude toward the Ad(A_{ad}). Increasingly, models offered to explain the nature of A_{ad} specify affective as well as cognitive *responses* to the ad and identify both cognitive and affective *antecedents*. Attitude toward the ad is sometimes defined (e.g., Lutz 1985) in predispositional terms. as "an affective reaction to the ad generated at the time of exposure." Lutz adds that a strong A_{ad}, while situationally bound, can have not only a direct effect on *immediate* consumer responses (e.g., toward the brand advertised) but also a continuing indirect effect on the consumer's behavior.

Cognitive antecedents of A_{ad} include perceived credibility, beliefs regarding advertising execution (along dimensions such as informativeness, entertainment, and vigor), and more general attitudes toward the advertiser and advertising. In Lutz's model, affect enters the model separately, primarily as a result of the consumer's mood at the time of exposure. Mood is itself a function of both personal factors and the context into which the ad has been placed (e.g., program material, the number of ads presented). Lutz's analysis seems to imply that this "transfer" of affect from the advertisement to the product will occur primarily in situations in which the consumer's involvement is low and when little cognitive capacity is being directed to the ad. However, the analysis may be too restrictive in relegating affect to low-involvement status. Stronger affective responses may occur when involvement is heightened, such as by the personal implications of the message or by reactions to the methods of persuasion being used.

MacKenzie, Lutz, and Belch (1986) evaluated four views of how A_{ad} mediates advertising effectiveness:

1. The effect transfer hypothesis—a one-way causal flow from A_{ad} to A_b, possibly as a result of low involvement, peripheral processing of ad execution elements, classical conditioning, or mood congruency.
2. The dual mediation view—in addition to direct affect transfer, a favorable A_{ad} may also produce a greater likelihood of accepting message claims.
3. The reciprocal mediation hypothesis—a two-way flow between A_{ad} and A_b, possibly as a result of people's preference for a balanced liking relationship.
4. The independent influences hypothesis—where A_{ad} and A_b are independent determinants of purchase intention.

Cognitive responses to ads were assigned to ad cognition categories (e.g., source bolstering, negative ad execution) or brand cognition categories (e.g., counterargument, support argument), and A_{ad} and A_b were measured in terms of overall favorable or unfavorable reactions to each. The dual-mediation version of a structural equation model was judged superior under ad pretest conditions.

Park and Young (1986) demonstrated that the relationship between A_{ad} and A_b may depend upon the nature of the "information" processed in an ad. Their processing set instructions led high-involvement subjects to focus either on performance attributes ("cognitive involvement") or image aspects ("affective involvement") of a shampoo commercial. Directing attention to performance attributes was reflected in their greater effect on A_b. But this was reduced (to the level of A_{ad}) when background music—which was not well integrated into the commercial and may have been distracting—was added. Directing attention to the commercial's emotional appeal and image led to a much stronger contribution of A_{ad} than the performance attributes under both the music and no-music conditions. However the overall explanatory power of the combined factors was low. A low product relevance/distraction (i.e., low-involvement) processing instruction produced effects comparable to that of affective involvement.

Much more work remains to be done to establish the basis of any automatic or reasoned "transfer of affect" or evaluation from A_{ad} to A_b. Gardner (1985b) provides an insightful analysis of how one's reactions to ad execution (e.g., generation of positive feelings; production of nonproduct benefit associations, such as brand image and quality connotations; communication of product use experiences) may not only affect A_{ad} but A_b, even under a brand processing set. Her study found an A_{ad} effect on A_b whether people were evaluating linguistic style or the brands advertised. By itself, of course, an incremental contribution of A_{ad} beyond that of measured brand beliefs says little about what A_{ad} may have been capturing.

Stayman and Aakar (1988) tested the proposition that specific feeling responses (in this case warmth, amusement, and irritation) can affect attitudes toward an advertised product apart from A_{ad}. Using 4, 8, and 12 exposure levels and two ads for each feeling type, subjects viewed four programs over a two-week period. A_{ad} influenced postexposure brand attitude beyond prior brand attitude, and at lower exposure levels for the warm and humorous executions there was a direct effect of ad-induced feelings on brand attitudes. One limitation is the retrospective reporting of feelings about the ad and overall liking for the ad rather than an on-line assessment. Also, to the extent the A_{ad} measure primarily captures reasoned assessments of the ad, other dimensions of ad appraisal or response (e.g., general liking) may be reflected in overall product ratings. Research on this topic must confront difficult measurement problems in order to validly attribute brand evaluation outcomes to particular causal factors.

Assessing Affective Responses to Advertising

Since consumers' affective responses to advertising are undoubtedly more differentiated and subtle than are likely to be captured on simple directional measures (e.g., happy-sad), a variety of alternatives have been employed including Izard's Differential Emotions Scale (Allen, Machleit, and Marine 1988) and a variety of factor analyzed lists of emotional self-descriptors (Hill and Mazis 1986; Edell and Burke 1987; Zinkhan and Fornell 1985). While there are likely to be specific dimensions of affective response that are of interest to advertising researchers (e.g., Leavitt 1970; Schlinger 1979; Moore and Hutchinson 1983; Gresham and Shimp 1985; Friestad and Thorson 1986; Batra and Ray 1986), it would also be useful to link measurement to underlying theories of emotion (e.g., Holbrook and Batra 1987; Allen, Machleit, and Marine 1988) and to emphasize the discriminatory power and validity of each measure (e.g., Aaker, Stayman, and Hagerty 1986).

Advertising agencies have relied on the types of subjective experience measures exemplified by the Viewer Response Profile (Schlinger 1979; see also Aaker and Bruzzone 1981). Generally, a large number of statements from people who have been exposed to various television commercials are accumulated and then reduced (e.g., using factor analysis) to underlying response themes. Many of these recurrent themes have emotional content and are used to construct self-report scale items to be used in assessing subsequent commercials. For example, Gresham and Shimp (1985) measured emotional responses to advertisements using seven item dimensions (e.g., happy, affectionate, sad).

Retrospective response protocols have become somewhat popular in this tradition as a way of overcoming the intrusiveness and reactivity thought to be associated with concurrent protocols (either written or verbal). Hill and Mazis (1986), for example, exposed subjects to either emotional or factual advertising inserted during breaks in a television movie. They attempted to match two versions of three separate commercials on length and other aspects. After viewing the commercials, written protocols were obtained and coded into several categories including positive affect (e.g., feeling good) and negative affect (e.g., feeling angry). In addition, subjects rated each commercial using 45 adjectives taken from Leavitt's (1970) factor analysis of responses to television commercials (e.g., amusing, sensual, dislike). The authors found that emotional advertisements produced more affective comments, but no clear pattern emerged in counterarguments or source-bolstering statements. While scales used to report overall evaluation of the ads (e.g., good-bad, like-dislike) did not discriminate between the factual and emotional ads, the execution-related adjectives (e.g., sensual, energetic) did somewhat better. The considerable heterogeneity that exists within factual and emotional ads makes it desirable to further refine this categorization scheme.

Batra and Ray (1986) distinguished between affective responses and cognitive responses to advertising on the basis that the former are not evaluative but reflect advertising-evoked moods and feelings. After reviewing previous work on affect typologies, they developed a nine category coding scheme for cognitive responses, six of which are primarily cognitive (support arguments, execution discounting, etc.) and three of which are considered affective response categories (surgency/elation, deactivation [e.g., soothing, relaxing], and social affection [e.g., warm, tender]). After exposing subjects to a variety of "affective" and "rational" ad executions under conditions designed to produce high variance (e.g., involvement level, prior knowledge, response opportunity), the authors encouraged self-reports of both thoughts and feelings (not "playback," but such things as statements about agreement-disagreement, what the ad reminded them about, and how it made them feel). Satisfactory interjudge agreement in coding was obtained, and roughly 12 percent of the responses were placed into one of the three affective categories. There was a significant, though small, incremental impact of these responses in predicting attitudes toward the ad. The authors also suggest that the process their measures allow them to study is apparently quite open to conscious awareness and, therefore, is different from the "affect transfer" mechanisms thought to be linked to classical conditioning.

Holbrook and Batra (1987) examine the manner in which intervening emotional reactions mediate the relationship between advertising content and attitudes toward the ad or brand. Each set of variables (e.g., advertising content, emotional reactions) was determined by judges' ratings of each ad along selected inventories of items (i.e., 66 advertising content items and 94 items representing 29 emotional indices). A separate set of judges was used to rate the ads on each set of variables. Principal components analysis reduced the 66 ad content items to those dimensions described as emotional, threatening, mundane, sexy, cerebral, and personal. The 93 emotional response items were reduced to the dimensions of pleasure, arousal, and dominance (as in Mehrabian and Russell 1974; Russell 1978, 1980). Interjudge reliability for the emotional response ratings was quite low (.52) suggesting that conceiving emotional responses to be invariant properties of the stimulus may be inappropriate. Many advertising content dimensions seemed to be correlated with their emotional dimension counterparts. The causal flow of the model through attitude toward the ad was generally supported, with the emotional dimensions mediating the effect of the content dimensions. The relationship of these variables to attitude toward the brand seems somewhat more complex.

The importance of task instructions and perceptions on subjects' responses to advertising was nicely demonstrated by Madden, Allen, and Twibble (1988), as otherwise quite positive affective responses to a humorous ad were suppressed by an evaluative set, and evaluations of the ad tended to be unfavorable. Under nonadvertising-focussed viewing conditions, evaluative responses to the humorous/nonhumorous ads did not differ, but subjects reported much more favorable affect when subsequently asked how the humorous commercial made them feel (using a 15-adjective scaled response format). The authors demonstrate the importance of distinguishing between attitudinal (i.e., evaluative) responses to ads and reported feeling states.

Edell and Burke (1987) examine the distinction between the way consumers describe and judge an ad and the feelings that the ad generates in consumers. They build upon the Puto and Wells (1984) characterization of ads as being informational or transformational. Ads defined as being in the latter category connect the experience of the ad so tightly to the brand that feelings evoked by the ad invariably come to mind when the brand is considered. Feelings, then, were hypothesized to be more important (relative to semantic judgments) for ads that were high in transformation (as opposed to information). A 69-item inventory of feelings was factor analyzed to form scales described as upbeat feelings, negative feelings, and warm feelings. When combined with three semantic judgment scales (evaluation, activity, gentleness) in a regression, feelings were found to contribute significantly to predictions of both attitude toward the ad and attitude toward the brand, though no consistent differences emerged between the two different types of ads (i.e., transformational versus informational). A second study again demonstrated that the self-rated feelings/reactions to the ad contributed significantly to relevant attitudes and judgments about the ad and brand when these were unfamiliar to subjects. The reliability of both indices and their intercorrelations were reported in Burke and Edell (1989). They again found an incremental contribution of the "feeling" factors to A_{ad} and A_b as well as brand attribute evaluations (even after the ads were seen repeatedly and after a four-week delay). The latter seemingly were mediated by the direct relationship between the feeling indices and the judgment scales.

While relationships among particular feelings, judgments, and attitudes that are suggested by structural models are interesting, they are based on correlations among response scales whose validity and link to manipulated feeling states deserve careful attention. It is possible to question whether gains in prediction come about because of the addition of a separate class of variables (i.e., feelings) or because, more simply, they capture a set of somewhat different dimensions of judgment. There is far from a consensus that verbal protocols (and the instructional sets used to gather them), scaled self-reports, and the like represent an adequate system of measurement for affective responses. They may not successfully isolate affect from evaluation and inference processes, or tap more immediate, transitory, and less easily verbalizable feelings states. As a result they may not be sufficiently diagnostic.

Physiological measures are an alternative (Rothschild et al. 1988). However, as Aaker, Stayman, and Hagerty (1986) point out, physiological measures are not only difficult to administer, but they cannot be easily linked to specific feeling states (and they may not tap "warm," mood-like states as successfully as "hot," emotional responses). Several concurrent "dial-turning" methodologies have been employed in advertising research, and while these have the advantage of more precise tracking of the onset of feeling states, they have had only a bidirectional orientation (i.e., positive-negative) and may also confound feeling and evaluation. Aaker, Stayman, and Hagerty (1986) have developed a "warmth monitor," essentially a paper-and-pencil instrument in which respondents move down the paper at a constant rate of speed while viewing a commercial, indicating the absence of warmth by moving the pencil to the left and progressively greater warmth (i.e., warmhearted/tender, emotional/moist eyes) by moving it to the right. Some evidence for the reliability and convergent validity of the instrument (with respect to postexposure scale ratings) was obtained. In addition, subjects viewing several commercials produced warmth-monitor scores that were significantly correlated with a standard measure of skin resistance for ads judged by a different sample to be warm but *not* for ads judged to be humorous, informative, or irritating. On the other hand, some evidence that subjects may tend to assign higher warmth-monitor scores to more generally positive executions was obtained in a subsequent study. Trends both between ads (of the same versus different warmth) and within ads (of varying warmth segments) were generally consistent with predictions (including contrast and adaptation effects), and warmth-monitor scores were also correlated with attitude toward the ad and purchase likelihood. The authors suggest that similar instruments might be developed to tap other feeling states, although the methodology seems limited to one dimension at a time.

Measures that combine direction and intensity of affect (e.g., pleasant-unpleasant *and* arousal/excitement-sleepiness/relaxation) so as to register "total" positive affect and, separately, "total" negative affect (e.g., Watson, Clark and Tellegen 1988: Watson and Tellegen 1985) reflect a general consensus that affect can be summarized along these two dimensions. However, some unpleasant feelings are associated with a *lack* of excitement (e.g., depression), whereas positive affect and arousal tend to be correlated. Accordingly, it seems advisable to separate direction and intensity of affect. A recently developed "affect grid" (Russell, Weiss, and Mendelsohn 1989) does this using an easy to administer visual map. Initial validation and use of this instrument in mood research has been encouraging, and it deserves examination by consumer researchers. As an undisguised, self-report measure it is, however, subject to the usual cautions regarding both access to feelings and willingness to report them.

In general, the measurement difficulties involved in assessing diverse feeling states continue to plague researchers. Neither an adequate taxonomy nor an adequate understanding of the relationships among moods, emotions, arousal, and generalized affect can be said to exist. This is further complicated by the differing levels of analysis (i.e., physiological to attributional) at which research on these constructs is being conducted (Coyne 1982). There may also be important effects of more diffuse feeling states that are at a reduced level of awareness and for which no target (or causal agent) is clearly perceived.

THE UNRESOLVED ISSUE OF AFFECT ACQUISITION

Since most products and brands presumably start out as fairly "neutral" stimuli, the issue of whether or not and how affect becomes "attached" to them is of considerable interest. Pleasant and unpleasant experiences with a product, the vicarious experience that results from observing others using a product, and the association of a product with affect-eliciting people, objects, and events all have the potential to generate affect and produce affective traces. In some cases such affect seems clearly to belong directly to the product (i.e., product-mediated affect). At other times it seems to have flowed to the product from some discernible external source (i.e., externally originated affect). A systematic treatment of product-mediated affect would involve the various ways the purchase and use of products can generate affect (including functional, self-enhancement, social facilitation, and expressive sources of gratification; the role of expectancy-confirmation and other comparative appraisal processes, etc.). Since this would take us very far afield (and well into the domains of motivation and learning) we are restricting our focus to the "transfer mechanisms" involved in affect acquisition. A broader view of learning processes in consumer behavior is presented in Chapter 5 by Terrence A. Shimp.

Affect and Repeated Exposure

In general, repeated exposure increases the strength of association among elements presented together. Accordingly, the strength of association may increase for objects and affective states either experienced directly by the person or observed in others present at the time (e.g., friends or characters portrayed in movies or television commercials). Indeed, familiarity alone, rather than fostering contempt, may instead produce more favorable feelings and evaluations. This phenomenon is termed the *mere exposure* effect (Zajonc 1968). By contrast, unfamiliar objects, people, and situations increase our uncertainty and may tend to make us apprehensive. In some adaptive sense, the ability to withdraw focal attention from stimuli that initially were less predictable is desirable and may produce positive affect. Certain conditions (e.g., research settings) may heighten the favorability of old stimuli relative to new stimuli (see Obermiller 1985). This occurs because people feel more certain (and less anxious) when they can recognize a previously presented item. But, this effect may disappear when the new stimuli are easier to identify as new.

There has been some debate as to whether or not the positive affect generated by familiarity requires the *conscious* recognition of a stimulus. Zajonc (1968) found that subjects preferred previously presented stimuli to novel ones even though they could not accurately recognize them. However, Anand, Holbrook and Stephens (1988) found that a similar effect was moderated by the recognition of the previously presented stimuli (i.e., correctly recognized stimuli were better liked).

Zajonc's conclusion that affect is independent of (or precedes) cognition because it does not depend on recognition appears to be unwarranted (see Zajonc 1980 and a response by Lazarus 1982). In an insightful discussion of perceptual processes, Marcel (1983) differentiates between cognitive *processes* — which operate automatically and outside of awareness through a sequence of information processing and analysis stages — and their *records* or traces. While records of *sensory analyses* may be inaccessible, records which match concepts that are themselves available in memory are capable of being retrieved. This implies that stimulus identification occurs at a relatively advanced stage in the perceptual process (i.e., after extraction of sensory and feature information). Accordingly, failure to recognize a previously presented — and now liked — stimulus does not imply either an absence of cognition or a primacy of affective processes. Rather, recognition failure seems more a function of a perceptual record that was difficult to identify because matching concepts were then inaccessible in memory (as they would be for an unfamiliar stimulus) and/ or because the time or opportunity necessary to identify such a stimulus was restricted (as they were in many mere exposure studies, such as when attention was divided among several tasks).

Interestingly, Buck's (1985) third level "read out" of a person's emotional experience is termed *syncretic cognition*. By this term he intends to refer to a type of holistic "knowledge by acquaintance," as opposed to knowledge by description that characterizes analytic thought. The notion that feelings are a starting point for cognition was advanced by James (1890) and is developed more fully in the present day treatment by Zajonc (1980). Following Buck's analysis, though it is doubtful that affective responses truly precede all cognition, such "feelings" and "affective responses" may precede easily verbalizable thoughts and analytic reasoning. In his view, considerable right-hemisphere processing is likely to have taken place up to the point of holistic representation, and this might extend to object identification and categorization via nonanalytic mechanisms (Cohen and Basu 1987).

Though there has been little "hard evidence" brought to bear on mere exposure in the consumer behavior literature, a number of papers have discussed the possibility that affect as well as positive or negative evaluations may arise out of repeated exposures to products and advertising. Zajonc and Markus (1982) distinguish between preferences as combined utilities (resulting from components or features of prod-

ucts) and preferences resulting from "affective supports," which appear to include such things as parental reinforcement and social identification. In the latter case, so argue Zajonc and Markus, not only affective reactions but *preferences* may precede cognitive appraisal. Preferences, however, go beyond mere liking for a product and are even less likely to be precognitive, since they imply a type of comparison process related to either some criterion or some other products or both. Obermiller (1985), manipulating the number of exposures to melodies, reports "no evidence for the notion that affective responses occurred independently of cognitive mediation." Evaluation, using bipolar-adjective scales, constituted the key dependent measure. Repeated exposures, he argues, may reduce uncertainty as well as providing additional opportunities for the development of positive associations.

As noted in a comment to Zajonc and Markus (1982), the precise point at which "cognition" enters the picture in any affective process depends to a considerable extent on what one includes in a definition of "cognition" (Tsal 1985). The analysis we presented previously is generally consistent with Tsal's view. Both suggest that the generation of an affective trace is an unconscious process resulting from some motivational or mood state (of which we *may* be aware). Further, the attribution of such affect or its trace to a causal agent or property of a stimulus is a subsequent process that depends initially on the accessibility of a matching concept for the causal agent.

Affect and Classical Conditioning

The dominant explanation for affect acquisition (from an external source) has been classical conditioning (McSweeney and Bierley 1984; Gresham and Shimp 1985; Kroeber-Riel 1984b). The general acceptance of the idea that classical conditioning is responsible for many such effects, particularly in advertising, is well documented by Allen and Madden (1985). Careful research on the nature of this process within the advertising context has only recently begun to appear in the literature, although "higher-order" classical conditioning of both evaluative meaning (e.g., Staats and Staats 1957) and affect (e.g., Zanna, Kiesler, and Pilkonis 1970) has been studied for some time in the attitude research area. One problem has always been the difficulty of ruling out an "experimenter demand" interpretation of the results because the hypothesis under study is frequently easy to grasp and subjects may understand that it is their task to comply with these expectations. Indeed, in some studies only subjects who are aware of the contingencies *and* the demands show evidence of conditioning. Procedures used by Zanna et al. help to overcome some of the usual criticisms and demonstrate not only heightened arousal and altered evaluations of the conditioned words but also generalization to semantically related words. Yet, demonstrating that this is truly an automatic and unconscious process presents vast difficulties.

Gorn (1982) has done much to spark interest in classical conditioning within consumer behavior. By pairing slides of one of two colors of the same pen with either liked or disliked music (to be used "in a commercial for a pen"), he found that subjects' pen preferences, indexed by choices, could be influenced. Further, this conditioning effect required only one trial, a fact which has led some to question whether or not classical conditioning was responsible for the effect (i.e., even with a strong unconditioned stimulus a number of trials are typically needed). Perhaps helpful business students were trying to give the advertiser feedback — via their pen choices — as to the wisdom of using the liked and disliked music. Bierley et al. (1985) also argue that a "true" classical conditioning procedure must establish that increased familiarity coupled with contiguity of stimuli does not produce the effect. Rather, it must establish that people exposed to the conditioned stimulus (i.e., the pen) *followed* by the unconditioned stimulus (i.e., the music) should demonstrate superiority over subjects who are presented the two stimuli *randomly* in time. The established "predictiveness" of the conditioned stimulus, in this view, is necessary to differentiate classical conditioning from simpler familiarity effects

(McSweeney and Bierley 1984). Gorn believes that his use of disliked music (in one condition) provides a sufficient check on the possibility that familiarity might have been responsible for the effect on subjects' pen choices (i.e., he posits that such effects would lead to more positive attitudes as a function of increased familiarity regardless of the valence of the unconditioned stimulus).

Replicating Gorn's use of colors and music, Bierley et al. (1985) used a "predictiveness" design (with a random-order control group) in which each noncontrol subject was exposed to a set of 84 red, blue, and yellow geometric figures, each followed or not by music from the movie *Star Wars*. (For red predictiveness subjects, every red figure was followed by music, half of the blue figures were followed by music, and the yellow figures were never followed by music). Instructions to subjects included, it should be noted, asking them to attempt to *predict* the onset of music. After separating out basic color preference differences, reliable but small combined conditioning effects were found in subjects' ratings of the set of conditioned stimuli (in the case cited, excitatory/positive for red and inhibitory/negative for yellow). A very weak generalization effect to new geometric forms of the same colors was observed. In general, though, the results are somewhat discouraging in their applicability to the "noisy" reality of advertising, since 28 consecutive predictive trials were needed to establish even a weak effect. The authors note, however, that only mild affect may have been produced by the unconditioned stimulus, severely limiting the strength of the conditioning. Finally, though the authors made some attempt to rule out an awareness-demand explanation (by asking subjects about the basis for their music predictions and their understanding of the purpose of the experiment), they unnecessarily complicated this issue by, in fact, making subjects aware of the predictive link between the slides and the music. Level of awareness, adequacy of awareness-assessment procedures, and potential self-report biases, therefore, are troublesome issues for this study.

Allen and Madden's (1985) careful review of

this topic leads them to regard the conditioning of evaluative meaning as quite different from the conditioning of affect. The latter, they also argue, may be less susceptible to criticism on "awareness" grounds since "as the cognitive complexity of the conditioned response increases, one might anticipate more confounding from conscious, deliberate mental processes" (p. 303). In a partial replication and extension of Gorn's (1982) study, Allen and Madden exposed subjects to humorous program segments (which had received widely different ratings on a set of evaluative scales) while viewing a slide for one of two pens differing only in color. Described as a test of different "styles of humor" being considered as a part of a radio advertising campaign for the pen, subjects next rated the comic material (just as Gorn's subjects had evaluated the music), provided a retrospective thought listing, and were then encouraged to take one pen from a box filled with a mixture of both colors (recorded after the subjects left the room). Whereas Gorn's subjects had been run in large groups, and hence a subject's choice might have been visible to other subjects, Allen and Madden processed their subjects individually to minimize the possibility of social influence. Allen and Madden's subjects did not display the anticipated conditioning effect: Roughly two-thirds picked the color pen displayed on the slide, regardless of whether it was paired with the pleasant or unpleasant comic material. The data suggest, however, that the manipulation designed to create an unpleasant program segment was not successful. Further, the stimuli may well vary along other dimensions that may produce unwanted effects.

In a series of four experiments, Stuart, Shimp, and Engle (1987) present the most comprehensive investigation of classical conditioning yet carried out using advertising stimuli. Their research employs sophisticated control procedures (i.e., random presentation and conditioned stimulus-only control groups) in an effort to rule out "mere exposure" effects and to assess the effects of forward, simultaneous, and backward pairing of the unconditioned and conditioned stimuli. The stimuli were slides of fictitious brands for various products (CS) and slides of outdoor scenes (US), which were determined to be affectively positive or neutral in pretests. The number of learning trials was manipulated at 1, 3, 10, and 20. Significant conditioning effects were obtained for various attitudinal measures in all contiguous conditions, but there was only a slight (and nonsignificant) enhancement as a function of the number of trials. The implication was that a substantial amount of conditioning occurred after just one trial. The authors demonstrate latent inhibition—by producing more modest conditioning effects when the CS was presented alone several times before the conditioning trials began—and backward conditioning, through small but significant effects when the conditioned stimulus followed the unconditioned stimulus in the trials.

In evaluating this study one must be concerned, as always, with possible demand effects. While the authors combined filler trials involving dummy brands and affectively neutral outdoor slides with irrelevant questionnaire items to alleviate such influences, their direct assessment of these effects involved only an open-ended questionnaire, asking subjects what they thought the experiment was about. Though 48 percent of the subjects seemed generally aware of the CS-US contingency, an analysis of the data using only the remaining subjects continued to support the hypotheses, and an analysis of variance using awareness as a factor suggested that it played only a minor role. However, the depth of the "awareness" probe can be questioned. Such concerns point to a need for the development of a "middle range" awareness assessment tool for future research.

Several replications of Gorn's study were carried out by Kellaris and Cox (1989), but in no case could product preferences be conditioned through a single exposure to liked or disliked music. They provide some evidence that Gorn's procedure of having subjects go to different sides of the room to pick their desired pen color may have signaled the relationship between pen color and the judgment task.

Allen and Janiszewski (1989) focused specifically on awareness as a causal factor in the conditioning process. They also wished to impede hypothesis guessing while at the same time adhering to recognized conditioning principles. The latter objective was achieved through an ingenious paradigm influenced by the work of McSweeney and Bierley (1984). The cover story described the experiment as an attempt to identify the kinds of foreign words susceptible to "spurious meaning development." Subjects played a game which involved the unscrambling of a series of letters to determine if previously learned Norwegian words could be spelled from them. This task was made virtually impossible by restricting exposure to the letter string to three seconds. Following a manipulation employed by Isen and her associates (1978), differential success rates (US) accompanied each word (CS). The success rate of each word differed between groups, allowing for both a within and between groups test for conditioning effects. The dependent measures of interest were word evaluations and ratings of the word as a cologne brand name.

Both contingency and demand (i.e., hypothesis) awareness were assessed through a battery of ten questions ranging in depth from an open-ended item to an item which stated the hypothesis interrogatively and asked for a yes or no response. When subjects coded as being demand aware were removed from the analysis, the results continued to support a conditioning hypothesis. However, no effects were obtained for subjects classified as being completely unaware. This suggests that contingency awareness may play a critical role in the conditioning process.

A second experiment was conducted to provide evidence for contingency awareness as a causal factor. Here contingency and demand awareness were manipulated experimentally through pretrial instructions to subjects. The ten question assessment tool provided evidence that these manipulations were successful. The results were exactly as expected. Subjects in the unaware (no directions) condition exhibited no conditioning effect for either dependent variable; those in the contingent-aware condition exhibited conditioning effects for the word evaluations only, and the demand aware subjects

showed conditioning effects for both word evaluations and brand name ratings. This study thus provides strong evidence for contingency awareness as a causal factor in the conditioning process. An implication of such data is that "higher order conditioning" involves learning and "testing" predictive hypotheses, and that substantial cognitive mediation is likely.

Gorn (1982) had also investigated the moderating effects of purchase involvement by having half of his subjects in a second experiment devote thought to a choice between a three pen packet (displayed in conjunction with the well-liked music) and its different-colored equivalent (for which a planned informational commercial was described). After an hour time delay, all subjects were allowed to choose a pen, and a strong reversal was obtained. Subjects selected the pen for which product information was presented when *choice* was salient at the time of exposure, but selected the pen associated with well-liked music in the nonchoice condition. Allen and Madden (1985) chose to examine the issue of active cognitive evaluation through the use of a postchoice "buy-back" measure in which subjects were offered the option to sell the pen back (using the ploy, "our sponsor would also like to get some idea of what you think a pen like this is worth"). Somewhat surprisingly, given their weak choice results, subjects in the pleasant humor condition *were* less inclined to sell the pens back. A conditioning explanation for this in the absence of an effect on choice is problematic. The authors speculate that subjects placed into a pleasant mood might generate more positive thoughts about the pens, making them more resistant to a buy-back attempt, but, especially given the lack of such an effect on choice, why this should occur is not obvious.

The classical conditioning explanation for the transfer of affect from some aspect of an advertisement to a product, at this juncture at least, faces some formidable obstacles. Applying the underlying process to domains that are far beyond the traditionally studied autonomic and skeletal nervous systems has proven troublesome. Nonautomatic and conscious mechanisms may well be implicated despite every methodological precaution. If one departs from a rigorous theoretical treatment of conditioning to deal with the complex advertising domain (e.g., nonneutral and informationally rich products as conditioned stimuli, informationally and affectively complex unconditioned stimuli), one may be able to do little more than demonstrate the relevance of basic association concepts. Rossiter and Percy (1980), for example, had earlier sought to conceptualize *any* increase in evaluation of a product as an outcome of associating unconditioned (i.e., favorably regarded) product attributes, as well as visual and auditory imagery, with it, thus leading to a positive emotional response to the product.

Allen and Madden (1985) recommend further research on two competing positions, "affective-conditioning" and "mood." The former is assumed to operate by a "direct or noncognitively mediated transfer of pleasant (or unpleasant) feelings" from the advertisement to the brand, and the latter is assumed to operate through "prompting and biasing cognitive activity" rather than some automatic transfer of affect. While the first position does not appear to contain a compelling explanation of the process, it seems to be equated with the operational stricture of finding *no* evidence of cognitive mediation. This is a subtle point as cognitive mediation occurs at different stages: first, as awareness of the unconditioned stimulus, and, second, in linking the unconditioned stimulus to the conditioned stimulus (see Allen and Janiszewski 1989). The authors go on to suggest that these two processes might be unravelled through the use of "noncognitive" measures (e.g., choice, amount consumed). While such measures may be useful in reducing demandlike effects (depending on the study's design), the processes producing overt behavior of this type cannot be *assumed* to be carried out in the absence of considerable cognitive activity, as the authors suggest, unless there is literally nothing to be learned, no other connections to be strengthened, and no inferences to be drawn from increasing familiarity (see, for example, Alba and Marmorstein 1987). Some of the cognitive activity involved in both conditioning and mood explanations is (as discussed earlier)

both preattentive and nondeliberative (Marcel 1983). The point at which the "cognitive" and "noncognitive" distinction is being drawn seems, at this stage at least, to be more a matter of judgment than something more conceptually rigorous.

We have, it seems, almost returned to the point at which we began in attempting to understand the "affect transfer" process. The phenomenon has virtually become its own explanation. Allen and Madden (1985) may, however, be on the right track in thinking that we should approach the problem by delineating possible mechanisms (e.g., familiarity, association, mood-produced biases) leading to affect formation and to subsequent evaluatively based judgments and behavior. Adopting a pluralistic orientation may be the best way to attack the problem. Learning more about each mechanism (i.e., when it occurs, its limits) is something we can do, and if some are more difficult than others to pin down it may still not mean that the account is "wrong."

THE INFLUENCE OF AFFECT ON COGNITION

To this point, our review has examined the role of external stimuli and cognitive processes in generating affect. Now we turn to the work of a number of researchers in social psychology and consumer behavior who have begun to examine the influence of *affective* states on various *cognitive* processes.

Affect and Attribution

Perhaps the most basic way in which affect influences cognition is during the emotion/affect appraisal process. Schachter (1959), as discussed earlier, postulated that an unexplained state of arousal produces "evaluative needs" When a reasonable explanation (or attribution) for the arousal is found, the individual experiences a mood state appropriate to that explanation. In a subsequent experiment (Schachter and Singer 1962), he injected subjects with either epinephrine (an arousal-causing drug) or a placebo. Several cover stories were employed, so that subjects receiving the epinephrine either expected or did not expect to feel arousal. Only subjects in the latter conditions were expected to experience evaluative needs. After the injection subjects were sent to a waiting room in which a confederate was instructed to exhibit either angry or elated behavior in front of the subject. Subjects in the epinephrine-unexpected arousal conditions exhibited and reported being more angry (angry confederate condition) or more elated (happy confederate condition) than subjects in the placebo or expected-arousal conditions. The joint role of externally induced arousal and attributional processes can be seen in a study by Cantor, Bryant, and Zillman (1974). After inducing arousal through physical exercise, subjects observed erotic pictures either immediately or after four or ten minute delays. When the arousal could be attributed to the exercise (the immediate condition) or after the exercise-induced arousal had significantly diminished (ten minute condition), the pictures were judged to be less erotic than they were after the short delay. Presumably, the latter subjects felt greater arousal and judged the proximal stimulus to be a plausible cause.

As discussed earlier, the role and placement of cognitive appraisal within the emotional response process is a matter of considerable debate (i.e., cognitive appraisal may not be important until an already differentiated emotional response has occurred). Weiner (1982, 1986) presents a particularly comprehensive treatment of the attributional process. In the strongest version of this attributional approach, emotions are largely postattributional, under the assumption that the cause of a feeling state needs to be identified before the emotion is labeled. Attributional processes give rise to important distinctions among feelings and therefore contribute not only to the richness of human experience but also to actions that result from such interpretations. Weiner's research indicates that the way an affective response to some outcome is labeled (and therefore experienced) should be related to inferences regarding

locus (internal to the person or caused by some external factor), *stability* (constant over time or changing), and *controllability* (subject to volitional alteration or not). Positive feelings might be interpreted as pride (not relief) if they are associated with your good performance (rather than a too easy task), your competence (rather than a combination of effort and good fortune), and actions for which *you* made key choices and accepted responsibility (rather than when you are simply following directions). To take another example, sadness may result in feelings of guilt if one attributes a distressing outcome to a failure to behave responsibly. Such thought processes may also produce affect that differs qualitatively from that experienced earlier.

When arousal cannot be attributed to one particular external factor — say things have "simply gone wrong" in carrying out some task — it may color subsequent affective responses to a range of stimuli. This might happen because the people and objects in the immediate environment are perceived to be associated with the affective state (e.g., contributing factors, obstacles) or through an internal attribution. In the latter case, feelings of frustration or guilt (in an opposite situation, joy and pride) may arise and seem to be able to affect one's mood for some period of time. To better account for the role of cognition in such circumstances, Ortony, Clore, and Collins (1988) have provided a more fine-grained analysis of the contribution that cognition makes to emotion — particularly what distinguishes our valenced reactions to events and their causes. They discuss "attribution emotions" in terms of praiseworthiness judgments of causal agents (i.e., approving/disapproving). They add "event-based emotions" (i.e., judgments regarding the desirability of the outcomes) and "attraction emotions" (i.e., judgments regarding the appealingness of the activity). The type and intensity of the emotional reaction is seen as a combined function of such judgments.

Such analyses are likely to be important in consumer appraisals of affect resulting from interactions with marketing variables or which are part of the consumption experience. To the extent the affect is of fairly low intensity and its origin is unidentified, attributional processes can influence both the consumer's labeling of the affective state and his or her subsequent attitudes and behavior. The implications of such a process for consumer behavior extend from the in-store context (e.g., pleasant moods generated by soft music, lighting, and display techniques) to advertising. Say, for example, a commercial is placed at the beginning of a particularly entertaining program, especially if the commercial contrasts in mood from the lead-in program, it is *possible* to misattribute one's awareness of positive feelings to the commercial or even the product (see the earlier discussion of Singh and Churchill 1987).

Given the importance of cognitive processes such as attributional reasoning in mood interpretation, it seems clear that consumer researchers need to pay particular attention to how mood is manipulated. While more exotic means have been used (e.g., hypnotic suggestion), most mood induction uses some variant of exposure to positive or negative stimuli (e.g., lists of words or pictures), directed retrieval of affectively colored personal experiences, the unexpected receipt of a material reward (e.g., money left where the subject will encounter it), and manipulated success or failure (see Gardner 1985). As Hill and Ward (1989) illustrate, the affective implications of positive performance feedback as opposed to a chance occurrence may be quite different. Not only may self-efficacy and luck produce somewhat different affective states, these states may have different impacts on the task under study. For example, when success led to higher personal self-efficacy, subjects tended to put more effort into a decision-making task. Perhaps people who perceive themselves to be on a lucky streak may act more intuitively than they would normally. This analysis suggests that researchers might wish to consider more differentiated aspects of mood than simply whether it is positive or negative, and that multiple and divergent means of mood induction should be used to validate research findings.

Controlled versus Automatic Processes

Earlier we discussed cognitive appraisals as having both automatic and deliberative aspects, and we have now linked the latter to the kinds of inferential mechanisms that are central to attribution theory. Such attributions might also be part of a deliberate attempt to alter one's emotional state. A person may attempt to "reassess" the cause of some affect-producing outcome in order to enhance self-esteem or to simply "feet better" about things (e.g., "It was the other person's fault; there was nothing I could do.").

While affect is often viewed as a *response* to a motivationally relevant stimulus (McDougall 1923; Arnold 1960; Bindra 1968: Plutchik 1980a), Isen (1984b) suggests that the generation of affect may *elicit* subsequent motivations to either "maintain" or "repair" the existing mood state. For example, individuals in negative affective states, not wishing to remain in such states, may attempt to bring information to mind that will "repair" their mood. These processes are somewhat related to Holbrook and Hirschman's (1982) notion of "hedonic consumption": in that consumers shop, in part, to feel good. So, a shopping trip to an attractive new mall may be valuable for its own sake. In addition, an individual in a bad mood may purchase an arrangement of flowers or some new clothing in order to feel better. Or, a person in a good mood may decide to take the family to the movies or to dinner partly in an attempt to maintain the mood for the rest of the evening. Both mood maintenance and repair exert a positive bias on goal-directed behavior and (as we will see subsequently) on the cognitive activity that supports it.

More basic, automatic processes through which mood states can bias cognitive activity have been studied by Bower (Bower, Gilligan, and Monteiro 1981; Bower and Cohen 1982), who builds on the notion of selective attention to mood congruent stimulus material. This research has shown that subjects better remember material that is congruent with their mood state at the time of *encoding*. Their subjects read a narrative containing both positive and negative information while they were in either a positive or negative mood. A subsequent recall task revealed that subjects recalled more of the mood congruent material (see also Forgas and Bower 1987).

Isen et al. (1978), in Experiment 2, produced selective *retrieval* effects in a paradigm similar to that of Bower et al. (1981). They randomly assigned subjects to either succeed (positive affect) or fail (negative affect) at a computer game. Subjects were then asked to learn a list of words containing positive, negative, and neutral adjectives. At a later time, they again succeeded or failed at the computer game and were then asked to recall as many of the words as possible. The results showed that subjects in a positive mood during *retrieval* recalled more of the positive-trait words, whereas subjects in a negative mood recalled more of the negative words.[7] Unlike Bower's research, no effect for mood at encoding was obtained. More research is needed to fully understand the conditions that enhance mood-congruent memory effects at both encoding and retrieval, although we will have a little more to say about this later on.

Isen et al. (1978), in Experiment 1, have also shown that mood states can bias subjects' evaluations. Half of those shopping in a store were given a small gift (positive affect) by an experimenter posing as a company representative. The other half of the subjects simply were not approached (neutral affect). Then a second experimenter, blind to the mood manipulation, asked subjects to evaluate the performance of various products they owned, and those in the positive affect condition reported higher levels of performance.

In a related set of studies, Isen and Shalker (1982) either gave subjects positive or negative feedback on a bogus problem-solving skills test or caused positive-mood condition subjects to find a dime in their cubicle just before they began a subsequent experimental task. Subjects then rated slides determined by a pretest to be either positive, negative, or ambiguous on overall pleasantness. As expected, though mood induction was quite different, subjects in the two positive-mood conditions gave higher ratings than control subjects who, in turn, gave higher ratings than those in the negative-feedback condition. This effect was more pronounced when the stimuli were ambiguous.

Bower (1981) and Isen (1984b) have explained these and other similar results by positing that affect can serve to prime certain concepts, schemas, or categories in memory. Bower's explanation follows from the spreading activation memory model of Anderson and Bower (1973). Briefly, that model assumes that when a concept is processed or attended to, a memory node is activated and the activation spreads out from that node along a network. This activation decreases in intensity as it moves away from the original node. The longer a concept is attended to the longer the corresponding node is activated. Finally, some nodes require more thought to "fire" than do others.[8]

Bower (1981) raises the possibility that a particular emotional node (e.g., anger) may become linked to *all* events/nodes eliciting that particular affective response, rather than merely serving as a cue for a *specific* unpleasant event. Cue overload theory (Keppel and Un-

---

[7]Selective retrieval of negative information has been difficult to replicate (see Isen 1985). This, in part, led Isen to develop the notions of mood maintenance and mood repair. Note that this latter process should inhibit the selective retrieval of negative information (i.e., individuals *try* to think positive thoughts to eliminate their negative mood).

[8]Research by Johnson and Tversky (1983) raises some questions about the adequacy of the spreading activation explanation. While the induction of a negative-mood state (via a report of a tragic event) increased subjects' estimates of the frequency of other undesirable events, this effect was *independent* of event *similarity*. If similar events should be strongly associated in memory, then—according to the distance metaphor of the spreading activation model—the activation generated by the report should have spread to these "closely" associated events with greater intensity, making them more salient and increasing subjects' estimates of their frequency. This was not the case.

derwood 1962; Loess 1964), however, suggests that all-inclusive nodes are ineffective when activated as recall cues, probably because the large number of competing responses produces interference and lowers the likelihood that any specific response will occur. Bower's suggestion—that the "availability of emotion congruent interpretations" is enhanced by the activation of an emotional state and its corresponding node—is more in accord with our processing-oriented explanation for encoding effects on subsequent information retrieval. When affective states are induced or made salient, emotion congruent stimuli may receive more elaboration at encoding than will neutral stimuli. The enhanced network of associations that results is likely to facilitate retrieval, especially when this produces greater stimulus differentiation and enrichment.

In order to explain the well-documented mood congruity effects at retrieval (particularly for positive mood), Isen (1984b) begins with the premise that information about experienced affective states is stored in memory along with other aspects of the stimulus/event. For example, if a child always has a good time when he goes to watch the home baseball team play, then the concept *makes me feel good* should be associated with *home baseball team* in memory. In this view, an experienced affective state activates concepts in memory having similar valence in much the same way as "cognitive" cues at retrieval facilitate the recall of associated concepts.

Identifying the specific mechanisms through which mood at retrieval influences recall of information will require a great deal of further research. Why should a positive feeling state add significantly to the likelihood of recalling positively evaluated product attributes? As a relatively undifferentiated affective state, mood, by itself, should not constitute a strong retrieval cue, especially for semantically unrelated items. Such a positive mood may have stronger links to positive episodic traces than to more neutral items, yet our life histories are filled with potentially interfering positive episodic traces. Though Isen does not bring any particular model of memory to bear on this

general explanation, one possibility is that the activated concepts function *in parallel*. Thus, when Isen et al. (1978) put people into a positive mood and asked them to evaluate a product they owned, a "search" commenced *as well* from a positive affective trace. Thus *positive* product features and experiences may have been somewhat more easily accessed, leading to a resulting "bias" in overall evaluations.

Another possibility is that the affective state is not an effective enough retrieval cue to activate a particular memory trace. However, a particular category or portion of a memory network corresponding to a type of affective experience might be primed by a similar feeling state. If this were the case, then items could be sampled from within the appropriately primed category, partially transforming the recall task into an easier recognition task in which item familiarity could play a vital role. This depiction raises several methodological concerns. We should probably attempt to rule out recency (via increased familiarity) as a main contributor to the observed mood effect. This could pose a particular problem if a subject becomes aware that the instigation of a particular mood must bear some relationship to the recall task he or she is about to undertake. This awareness could lead to the ad hoc construction of a category of similarly toned items (emphasizing those that have been recently experienced). Then, the aforementioned recognition or familiarity test could be applied to the items generated by the category prime. Since this type of problem-solving behavior would be an experimental artifact, it would lead us to overstate the prevalence and impact of mood as a retrieval cue. Evidence that supports the beneficial effect of positive mood states on retrieval of not only positive but evaluatively neutral items would not be as readily explainable through a category-priming/familiarity mechanism.

Affect and Higher-Order Cognitive Processes

Isen (1984a) has demonstrated additional effects of mood states beyond recall and evaluation. She cites work by Boucher and Osgood

(1969), which suggests that positive material in memory is more extensive and diverse than neutral or negative material. If this is the case, then the selective cuing power of positive affective states should bring more varied and comprehensive information to bear on a given task. Several empirical investigations support this contention. Isen and Daubman (1984) demonstrated that subjects in a positive mood created broader, more inclusive categories when asked to complete a sorting task. Subjects were able to identify more relationships between the stimuli when they were in a positive mood. In a rating task, subjects in a positive mood rated atypical instances as being more representative of a category than did their neutral-mood counterparts. Isen et al. (1985) showed that subjects experiencing positive affect gave more unusual responses to a free association task. Also, subjects in a positive affective state took less time and used more simplified decisions rules in a mock automobile-selection task (Isen 1984b).

Isen, Daubman, and Nowicki (1987) established that the induction of a positive-mood state facilitates problem solving for both spatial and verbal tasks. In the spatial task, subjects were given a box of tacks, a candle, and a book of matches and asked to attach the candle to the (corkboard) wall in such a way that it would burn without dripping wax on the floor. Significantly more of the subjects in the positive-affect condition (manipulated through divergent methods) solved the problem — by using the box as a candle holder — in the ten minute time limit. For the verbal task, subjects had to identify a concept that linked three seemingly unrelated words. Again, subjects in the positive-mood conditions correctly identified more of the concepts than subjects in the neutral or negative conditions.

Gardner & Hill (1988) investigated the possibility that, depending on a person's mood state, an informational *or* an experiential decision strategy might be preferred. Following a mood manipulation, subjects in the positive (negative) mood condition were more likely to choose an experiential (informational) strategy. A more favorable *subsequent* mood was also found for positive (negative) mood subjects who

selected an experiential (informational) strategy. Those in a positive mood may have been more prone to act on some overall assessment or even on a hunch (and these might also do little to alter the existing mood) than those in a negative mood, who seemed to prefer a more careful assessment strategy (which might also be more likely to alter the existing mood, not to mention leading to greater success).

Research showing that affect often facilitates cognitive processing is a far cry from more traditional notions. Recall that Plato and Aristotle viewed thought and feelings as being in conflict with one another and that Watson (1929) viewed affect as interrupting otherwise organized cognitive processes. While this may be the case for intense and arousing affective states, current research clearly established that the two systems interact in more subtle ways. Even manipulating arousal per se via an exercise task (so that it is unconfounded with content) appears to have complex effects on message processing (Sanbonmatsu and Kardes 1988). The greater persuasiveness Sanbonmatsu and Kardes found under high arousal may have been due to a deflection of attention from message elaboration to arousal-produced internal cues. Under such conditions, peripheral elements of the message (i.e., celebrity status) could play a significant role in message acceptance. That arguments were judged to be stronger in celebrity conditions, but only when arousal was high, supports that interpretation.

Effects of Mood on Encoding and Retrieval of Ads

Srull (1983) induced either positive or negative moods by asking subjects to recall everything possible from an appropriately affectively toned event in their lives. Subjects then read either two positive, two negative, or two neutral ads, all of which were unfamiliar and informationally complex but varied in presenting valenced attribute evaluations. After an irrelevant task, they were asked to recall as much information as possible. In one study intense moods, regardless of valence, led to better recall, and, unexpectedly, mood-incongruent ads were better recalled. In a second study, ratings of the products advertised were more favorable if subjects were in a positive mood and were less favorable if subjects were in a negative mood, but only if mood were consistent with the evaluative implications of the ad. In a third study, subjects returned after 24 hours and were randomly put into a positive, negative, or neutral mood for a second time. Unexpectedly, there were assimilation effects on product ratings at encoding but contrast effects (only for mood-incongruent ads) at the time of judgment.

Experiment 4 provides some insight into the process that may have produced these results. Subjects in a positive mood at retrieval were better able to retrieve negative than positive attributes. However, subjects in a negative mood at retrieval were more likely to retrieve positive attributes. No such differences were found for mood state at encoding, and there were no significant *recognition* memory differences across conditions. Srull speculates that mood at retrieval may cue a large number of additional (and irrelevant) *cue-consistent* events. Such a "set size" effect might undermine the cue's effectiveness in retrieving the specific mood-consistent attributes of the product relative to the more distinctive *cue-inconsistent* attributes. He cautions, however, that such cue-overload effects may even reverse over time with lower levels of recall since *some* cue-inconsistent retrieval may still be likely.

Lawson (1985) presents data that are more consistent with a mood-congruent retrieval effect and argues that mood at retrieval may be able to prime mood-congruent information in memory. Using a mood-induction procedure similar to Srull (1983), Lawson found that sad subjects recalled more negative than positive attributes and happy subjects recalled roughly equal amounts of both. There was no tendency for either group to retrieve more of the information from reports differing in the proportion of positive and negative attributes. Subjects were required to rate a set of products twice in terms of desirability, and their postmood induction ratings revealed a change in the direction of mood-consistent evaluations. Such procedures may, however, sensitize subjects to "expected"

consequences of mood states, though Lawson reports little apparent subject awareness from his debriefing session. The author suggests that mood effects on recall are likely to be modest at best and to vary as a function of the deliberativeness of internal information search as well as the nature and extent of processing during encoding.

Isen (1989), going beyond the notion of mood-congruent message elaboration (Bower 1981), has recently suggested that positive affective states may enhance the processing of the verbal content of an ad. This could result in greater elaboration (and hence better recall) as well as heightened message comprehension, particularly if the assertions are somewhat complex. Research will be needed to determine just how robust such effects might be and to provide greater insight into the mechanisms responsible. For example, does moderate arousal have a generally facilitative effect on attention and encoding, perhaps analogous to involvement?

Mood and Evaluative Judgment

In a series of three experiments, Calder and Gruder (1988) manipulated both positive and negative emotional states (anger, satisfaction, fear, and disgust) by using hypnotic induction as well as subjects' retrieval of strong emotional experiences. These induced emotional states influenced subjects' selection/use of associated objective information (from a larger set of positive and negative items contained in a "restaurant review") in such a way that subsequent attitudes toward the object became more highly valenced and there was some enhancement in subjects' recall of information having similar affective content. One interesting finding was that attitudes became more negative when the activated emotional state and the information content were similar (i.e., the manipulated anger and the reported anger in the restaurant script) than when they were different (i.e., a combination of anger and disgust). More complex relationships among emotions were suggested by the data: Disgust seems to be more strongly associated with anger than vice versa and fear may inhibit anger, producing a less negative evaluative response to an object. The authors interpret their work in terms of network models (Bower and Cohen 1982) and production rules, although this research does not constitute a strong test of any particular conceptualization of memory. It does, however, represent one of the few studies that chart the interaction among affective states, affective traces, and subsequent cognitive and evaluative processes (as displayed in Figure 6.1).

Srull (1987) demonstrated that subjects placed into a positive mood at retrieval provided more favorable product evaluations when they had not formed a product evaluation earlier, but instead *computed* their evaluation based on information from memory. All subjects had been in a neutral mood during exposure to product information 48 hours earlier. Apparently, mood at retrieval colored their evaluations, though the precise mechanism is unclear (e.g., selective retrieval, selective attention, or weighting of features). Srull also suggests that this type of effect is more likely for consumers who are less familiar with a product since they would be more apt to form an evaluation at the time of retrieval rather than relying on already existing evaluations.

Srull (1984) differentiates between evaluations resulting from a retrieval process (i.e., bringing to mind earlier formed overall judgments) and those resulting from a computational process (i.e., bringing to mind information, probably at the attribute level, and combining it into an overall judgment). The person's goals or processing objectives during encoding (i.e., evaluation versus comprehension/incidental learning) will likely determine whether or not an overall evaluation is formed at that time and is subsequently available in memory. One implication of this conceptualization is that the relationship between the overall evaluation of a product and recall of evaluative attribute information may not always be very strong (e.g., when overall evaluations were based on information that is no longer easily accessible). A second implication is that affective states during encoding should have an effect on overall evaluations if these are formed at the time of encoding, but not if such evalua-

tions are computed at a subsequent time. These effects were found in a study using a similar mood-induction procedure as that used by Srull (1983), but varying subjects' processing objectives at the time of exposure to a complex informational advertisement. Thus, some subjects formed an evaluation of the product "on-line" and others rated the advertisement on product-neutral factors (e.g., how grammatical it was). No effects on attribute recall were found; however, the correlations between recall and judgment were higher when the judgments were made after a short delay rather than on-line (since presumably retrieval of the preformed judgment in the latter condition is independent of attribute recall). Affective states influenced product judgments for those subjects whose evaluations were formed at the time of encoding but not for those who "computed" them later. The effect was shown for both positive and negative moods.

Looking at the expert-novice distinction in greater depth, Srull (1987) found that mood at the time of encoding had a stronger effect on the judgments of self-designated automobile "nonexperts" than on "experts." He suggests that these effects may be due to novices searching for an algorithm to combine the information contained in an advertisement, whereas experts may have well-developed computational rules. Presumably, mood states exert greater influence in the former case. It is also true, however, that experts are likely to be considerably more certain of what their evaluations of the automobile advertised should be, and, therefore, they could be less sensitive to *any* influence attempts (i.e., informational or mood-based). Nonexperts might be more inclined to respond to any situational cue and possibly to be more susceptible to demand effects as a result. A caution (see also Srull 1987) may apply to studies manipulating mood and requesting judgments at about the same time. It is possible that mood will influence how subjects use evaluative scales quite apart from the separate question of mood effects on substantive evaluative processes and judgments. This is an important distinction and deserves careful treatment in this type of research.

Mitchell (1986) calls into question the robustness of the "on-line" only mood effect, believing that affective traces should become linked to the product during encoding regardless of whether a brand attitude is formed at the same time. Such traces would then be available in memory and retrieved at a time of subsequent judgment.

Srull (1987), however, presents additional evidence that only subjects asked to form a product evaluation on-line benefited from the effects of the mood state at encoding. Why the presumably favorable mood-state associations had little or no impact some 48 hours later for subjects who were *only then* asked to evaluate the product (and who were put into a neutral mood at the time) is not entirely clear. Is there some initial difference in encoding between affective traces and other cognitive traces that results in weakened or less accessible memory links for the former? A further possibility is that experiencing a different mood at retrieval could create a response competition or interference effect. Also, the greater difficulty of the delayed recall and evaluation task may tend to invoke a more deliberative and analytic product evaluation, one in which peripheral factors such as mood play a smaller role (Cohen and Basu 1987). So, at this point, we have the basic presumption raised by Mitchell (1986) that these affective traces should be available, and we need to understand under what conditions they are either made less accessible or fail to have a noticeable impact.

Though the effect is elusive at best, we probably should not dismiss the possibility that a comparable mood state at the time of judgment might be more likely to cue the earlier encoded affective trace if the ad generated a *strikingly similar* mood at encoding. Response interference, however, is likely to be sufficiently high for most affective states to render such state-dependent effects infrequent or of marginal significance.[9]

We are now starting to assemble a fairly impressive body of evidence as to the facilitating effects of positive-feeling states and dispositions on cognitive *processes* themselves, with resulting effects on creativity, risk taking, and evaluative judgments. The full implications of the motivational processes, which Isen (1984b) refers to as mood maintenance (for positive moods) and mood repair (for negative moods), are yet to be explored within consumer behavior. This should be an especially fertile area for research, involving not only memory and related cognitive processes but consumer decision making more generally.

A DYNAMIC MODEL OF AFFECT IN CONSUMER BEHAVIOR

We have stressed the differences between *valenced feeling states* (i.e., affect) and *evaluative cognitions* (i.e, attitude), assigning the former to the affective system and the latter to the cognitive system. Much of the chapter has examined research bearing on interaction between the cognitive and affective systems. The work of Isen (1984), Bower (1981), and their colleagues, for example, demonstrates that valenced feeling states, once elicited, can influence subsequent cognitive activity. Some of the work discussed earlier (e.g., Lazarus 1984; Arnold 1960) stresses the necessity of cognitive appraisal in the generation of affect. These appraisals may be automatic and immediate in some situations and deliberate and elaborative in others.

To this point, then, we have developed the notion of two distinct yet interacting systems. By and large, however, the research we have reviewed offers only a static, one-step view of the interaction between the affective and cognitive systems. Yet, as Lazarus (1984) notes, in many stimulus situations the sequence of thought, feeling, and behavior is far more complex as psychological processes continue to un-

---

[9]Bower, Monteiro, and Gilligan (1978) reported "state dependent learning" effects in which subjects better recalled a list of words when their mood during the recall task was similar to their mood at the time they learned the list. Yet other investigations (e.g., Isen et al. 1978; Bower et al. 1981) have failed to produce these effects; and when Bower and Mayer (1985) reported a similar failure, they questioned the robustness of the effect.

fold and give rise to subsequent levels of activity. In order to develop a more dynamic conceptualization, we must find some way to break apart this continuing flow of influence between the affective and cognitive systems into meaningful phases.

Earlier we summarized work by Leventhal (1980) and Buck (1985), which provides a helpful starting point.[10] Leventhal described three levels of cognitive appraisal: The first is an automatic response to sensory information, the second results from a match between the sensory input and some memory schema, and the third involves higher-level appraisal and deliberation. Each level essentially feeds its outcome forward to the next level of appraisal. Buck's system involves three readouts of emotional expression: the first from visceral and skeletal responses as part of largely automatic processes involved in adaptation and homeostasis, the second from external expression (particularly facial expression), and the third from cognitive experience and possible subsequent analysis of the emotional state. The third of these is of greater applicability to the issues that concern us; although for emotional responses of sufficient strength, the role of proprioceptive and autonomic feedback on subsequent cognition may be important.

Hoffman (1986) discussed three distinct "modes" of affect elicitation. The first is described as a physical-sensory mode. Included here are "hard wired" unconditioned responses, conditioned responses to once neutral stimuli, and responses to the facial expressions of others. The second mode is in response to the "match" between a stimulus and an affectively charged schema. Thus, an individual expecting to meet an old friend experiences joy if the person entering the room matches an old friend schema and disappointment if he or she does not. The third mode is a type of affective response that is the result of higher-order cognitive processing. These responses involve either the deliberate categorization of an unfamiliar stimulus or the conscious appraisal (i.e., assessing consequences, inferring causes, etc.) of a stimulus event. The model is then extended to allow sequential affect elicitation and interaction among the three modes.

Hoffman's model, particularly the assumptions of sequential elicitation and interaction, is consistent with a dynamic view of affect and cognition in which interactions among the three types of affective responses are mediated by identifiable cognitive activity. As with any arbitrary delineation of stages of cognitive and affective activity, this model is better applied to some problems than others. In order to be most usefully applied to the study of consumer behavior, we believe there needs to be more of a focus on affective responses to *gradations of meaning* (e.g., product identification, symbolic expression, personal implications). To prevent the model from becoming unwieldy, this might have to be at the expense of discriminating between truly "primitive" affective responses and affective responses to such things as confirmed expectations.

The model described in the next section is discussed, first, in terms of conceptual distinctions between three phases of affective-cognitive interaction. Next, the dynamic and interactive aspects of the model are presented in the form of a set of propositions. Finally, the model is applied to an advertising example in order to better illustrate its use.

Phases of Affective-Cognitive Interaction

Each of the three phases can be distinguished by the type of cognitive activity that precedes the elicitation of affect. The initial affective response occurs when there is a match between some sensory input — processed to a representational form that the person is capable of associating with already stored representations — and an affectively charged concept (i.e., one having an associated affective trace) in memory. The link between the affective trace and the concept is so well learned that the response

---

[10]While the theories of Tomkins (1962), Izard (1977), and Leventhal (1980) identify distinct "mechanisms" of affect elicitation, such differentiations are links to physiological processes, making direct application to consumer behavior extremely difficult.

is elicited without awareness of the meaning of the stimulus—its memory representation need only be activated. At that moment, then, the person is (at most) aware only of an external stimulus and a label for it. So, it seems to the person that nothing other than the perception of the stimulus is responsible for the experience of affect. The stimulus may be identified as a color, or a direction of movement, or as something as complex as a luxury car—as long as it exists as a single, unified memory representation.

As an example of such a phase one, *concept representation* affective response, consider the elicitation of fear in response to flashing red and blue lights. This affective response, of course, had to be learned, and so it was *initially* mediated by semantic processing of the stimulus (i.e., identifying it as an emergency vehicle). Over time, however, its association with tragic events became so strong that negative affect came to be elicited automatically as a result of a more basic stimulus-recognition process. This is now a concept representation affective response because no additional concepts need to be activated for the response to occur. The individual will be unaware of a *reason* (e.g., danger—an additional concept) for the affective response unless thought is devoted to this *after* the affect has been elicited.

A phase two affective response requires some recognition of stimulus "meaning" (i.e., the individual is aware of some basis for the response). This level of knowledge requires the activation of at least one categorical or featural implication beyond object representation (i.e., it [verb]s _____; it's for _____; it has a _____). So at least two concepts—designated as an "idea"—must be activated, and either or both may have affect associated with them (e.g., a brand and an attribute). Accordingly, the second phase affective response will be described as an *idea representation* affective response. Perhaps an example will be useful for illustrating the distinctions being made between concept representation and idea representation affective responses.

Darwin (1872) described attending an exhibit of various reptiles and amphibians. He was startled by a pit viper, which struck the side of a glass cage just a few inches from his head. Though he did not explicitly pursue this line of thought, it is interesting to consider which aspects of the stimulus elicited Darwin's affective response. Was he reacting to a "snake that bites" (idea representation) or merely a "sudden movement" (concept representation)? In the latter case one might imagine that a harmless animal (i.e., a frog) could have elicited a similar phase one response. The affective response to the concept of a sudden movement may almost be "hard wired" in the sense that we really do not think about why we react to it . . . we just do. At the second phase of the process, however, the differential meaning of the two objects should produce substantially different affective responses. The idea representation for a pit viper might include concepts such as "poisonous" and "dangerous," whereas the frog schema might include such concepts as "slimy" and "harmless."

Whereas second phase idea representation responses result from a largely automatic process—through which the affective traces associated with elicited concepts produce an affective state—the third phase of affective response results from an *elaborative interpretation*. Third phase responses occur when the individual *deliberately* investigates or generates (i.e., infers) associations between the stimulus and other concepts in memory as part of a process of assigning further meaning to it.

An important implication of the model is that affective responses to a stimulus are often multilayered. First phase responses are immediate and automatic and are not accompanied by conscious awareness, apart from the possible (but not necessary) conscious recognition of the stimulus.[11] Second phase responses stem not only from the affective trace associated with the identified stimulus but also from the network of concepts (and their affective traces) made sa-

---

[11]As discussed earlier, the stimulus identification process must extract enough information to connect the stimulus to an affectively charged concept (i.e., one having an affective trace). However, conscious recognition further requires that the record produced by this identification process be accessed and achieve awareness.

lient when the initial concept is activated. Some of these prior associated concepts may have considerable motivational significance. However, phase two affective responses are still automatic (i.e., they depend on the strength of prior learning) and occur rapidly. As with phase one responses, the *process* itself is unconscious; however, associated concepts that are themselves more accessible are likely to come into conscious awareness.

If phase three is reached, the situation changes in some important ways. Whether it is the meaning of an activated concept, its unexpectedness, or the nature and intensity of the affect previously generated—for some reason the person engages in a process designed to bring additional knowledge to bear. One purpose would be to better *understand* earlier, automatically produced outputs. Another would be to *control* or guide subsequent outputs. Processing, therefore, becomes deliberate and directed, as potentially relevant information and personal implications of the stimulus (as well as one's earlier responses to it) are considered and interpreted. In our example, noting that you are surrounded by people who have seen you flinch, the frog scenario might generate an affective response associated with embarrassment. The pit viper—which at phase two may have produced more negative affect—may here generate a more positive affective response associated with "relief" as you consider what might have been.

While we refer to these as phase three affective responses, this category of *elaborative interpretation* affective responses is not meant to imply a single response at one instant in time. Rather, these refer to a pattern of differentiated affective responses, sharpened by cognitive activity at advanced stages of processing. They are grouped together using this label because we believe such responses have enough in common—and are so clearly different from earlier phase responses—that it may prove useful to conceptualize the overall process in this manner.

To illustrate the multilayered interaction across the three phases, consider the student who notes the look of disappointment in a teacher's face when handling back an exam. This generates phase one negative affect (i.e., in response to the recognized facial expression). Upon seeing the "F" prominently displayed on the paper—the meaning of which is all too clear—the negative affect is likely to both sharpen (i.e., become more differentiated) and intensify. However, this phase two affective response is likely to be modified if, for example, the poor performance is attributed to a lack of effort (i.e., feelings associated with guilt), on the one hand, or to the severity of the exam (i.e., feelings associated with anger toward the instructor) on the other.

The following propositions summarize these multiple levels of interaction between the affective and cognitive systems and specify the relationship between each phase of affective response and evaluative responses (i.e., attitudes):

1. Each phase is elicited sequentially.
2. The higher the phase that is reached, the more differentiated the experienced affective state (see also Leventhal 1980, 1982).
3. Each phase may differ in valence, intensity and subjective experience from those that precede/follow it.
4. Affect experienced at subsequent stages is more accessible, more easily verbalizable and more strongly related to evaluations and judgments about the instigating stimulus (see also Hoffman 1986; Greenwald and Leavitt 1984).

A schematic depiction of the proposed model appears in Figure 6-2.

Applying the Model in an Advertising Context

In order to illustrate some of the key properties of the model, consider an advertising campaign run by the Michelin Tire Company. The beginning of a television commercial shows happy toddlers in diapers playing with a Michelin tire. The audio portion begins with a background conversation between two adults, while the video portion remains focused on the children and the tire throughout the commercial.

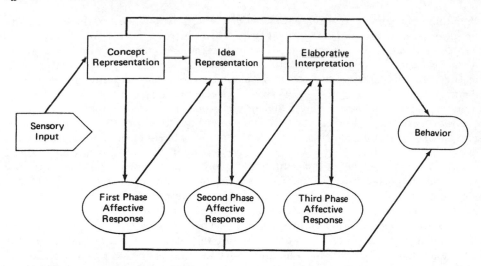

FIGURE 6.2 A Dynamic Model of Affective Response

One of the adults speaks highly of the quality and peace of mind that comes from owning Michelin tires, while the other argues that they are too expensive. Then, the first adult becomes identifiable as the parent of the child playing with the Michelin tire. The second adult again makes reference to the high price, but the parent suggests that love for the child makes the extra safety of Michelin tires worth their price.

How would affective responses to this commercial be explained using the concepts from our model? The happy babies in the commercial should elicit an immediate, almost automatic affective response. Viewers may even find themselves smiling. This "primitive" affective response occurs without consideration of the meaning of any element of the ad. It may be more related to the facial pattern of the smiling baby's face, or the happy baby may have virtually become an "unconditioned stimulus" for the generation of affect. Thus, we look upon the initial affective reaction to the commercial as a *concept representation* affective response.

The meaning of this commercial is easily evoked from the memory network activated by the concepts conveyed in the commercial: Michelin tires provide safety for one's family. The affective response (e.g., pleasure, joy) to

this *idea representation* is a phase-two affective response.

This affective response is likely to persist as the audience continues processing the message. The idea of a safe tire might also be thought about in relation to the higher price of the tire, and one's need for such tire may be considered more fully. The affective responses evoked at this point are indicative of phase three, *elaborative interpretation* affective responses. Because it is more difficult to predict the kinds of elaborative interpretations people will make (depending on their prior knowledge, involvement, inferential processes, etc.), the affective responses during this phase should be much more varied. If, for example, viewers have young children but do not have Michelin steel-belted radial tires, they may experience guilt (a negative affective response). Such guilt, however, might actually produce a *positive* attitude toward the product. If, on the other hand, the guilt is thought to result from an unfair and manipulative attempt by the advertiser to get consumers to buy the product, a very different elaborative interpretation response — anger — might result. This would probably lead to a negative attitude toward the source of the message and possibly toward the product itself.

Looking at Figure 6–2, the upper panel de-

ines the principal information-processing ac-
ivity occurring at each phase. The panel indicates that outcomes of each phase can prompt
further processing of the stimulus, as well as
produce unique affective responses. Although
the model is not intended to focus on overt
behavior, different behaviors can result from
both the meanings given to sensory input and
the affective responses to the meanings generated at each phase.

Affect experienced earlier can bias affect experienced during the next phase by priming
concepts that will be used to identify and interpret stimulus information. So, for example, if
the phase-one affective response to the concept
"happy baby" is decidedly positive, this may
prime concepts that, at least for the moment,
reduce the likelihood of a negative or hostile
reaction to the cost of the product or the type of
appeal used.

Feedback arrows *within* phases two and three
indicate that experienced affective states may
be assigned additional meaning at each of these
stages of processing. So, for example, if a positive affective state — experienced as "joy" during
a phase-two response to the Michelin commercial — produced and made salient the corresponding affective trace (i.e., for joy), it might
alter the idea extracted from the commercial.
Specifically, if the concepts "tire," "safe," and
"joy" were activated together, Michelin's idea
representation might include being a "nice" or
even a "happy" tire (provided that "happy" was
part of the memory network associated with
"joy," and hence was activated by it).[12] The
same feedback process occurs at phase three,
but to a greater degree: Affective responses interpreted as "guilt" may produce feelings of
"shame," but in attempting to deal with the
negative affect focused on the self, an interpretation might be made that shifts the blame to
the advertiser, resulting in feelings of "anger."

As proposition four indicates, affect experi-

enced and identified/interpreted at a *subsequent*
stage will dominate earlier affective responses,
in part because it is likely to be less diffuse,
more enduring, and meaningfully experienced,
and because it should be better integrated into
the cognitive system.

While the three phase model obviously simplifies a very complex interaction between the
affective and cognitive systems, it seems useful
as a starting point. The model reflects growing
insight into the interdependent nature of affect
and cognition and the realization that they need
to be studied together in some systematic manner if we are to better understand how people
function in complex environments. Accordingly, we will end this discussion by advocating
research to examine the sequential flows of influence highlighted by this type of model as a
way to better understand the significance of
affective responses in consumer contexts.

REFERENCES

AAKER, D. A., and BRUZZONE, D. E. (1981).
Viewer perceptions of prime-time television advertising, *Journal of Advertising Research*, 21, 15–23.

AAKER, D. A., STAYMAN, D. M., and HAGERTY,
M. R. (1986). Warmth in advertising: measure-
ment, impact, and sequence effects, *Journal of
Consumer Research*, 12, 365–381.

AJZEN, I., and FISHBEIN, M. (1980). *Understanding
attitudes and predicting social behavior*. Englewood
Cliffs, NJ: Prentice-Hall.

ALBA, J. W., and MARMORSTEIN, H. (1987). The
effects of frequency knowledge on consumer decision making, *Journal of Consumer Research*, 14,
14–25.

ALLEN, C. T., and JANISZEWSKI, C. A. (1989).
Assessing the role of contingency awareness in
attitudinal conditioning with implications for advertising research, *Journal of Marketing Research*,
26, 30–43.

ALLEN, C. T., and MADDEN, T. J. (1985). A closer
look at classical conditioning, *Journal of Consumer
Research*, 12, 301–315.

ALLPORT, G. W. (1967). The historical background
of modern social psychology. In G. Lindsey & E.
Aronson (Eds.), *Handbook of Social Psychology*, 1,
Reading, MA: Addison-Wesley.

---

[12]It is interesting to consider a similar commercial that
did not elicit such warm feelings. What would the difference
be? While the idea of a safe tire is no doubt a terrific selling
point, the tire seems somehow more "distant" — technically
superior perhaps — but you might not take particular pleasure in buying it.

ANAND, P., HOLBROOK, M. B., and STEVENS, D. (1988). The formation of affective judgments: the cognitive-affective model versus the independence hypothesis, *Journal of Consumer Research*, 15, 386–391.

ANDERSON, J. R., and BOWER, G. H. (1973). *Human Associative Memory.* Washington, DC: Winton.

ANGIER, R. P. (1927). The conflict theory of emotion, *American Journal of Psychology*, 39, 390–401.

ARNOLD, M. B. (1960). *Emotion and Personality*, Vol. 1. New York: Columbia University Press.

AVERILL, J. R. (1969). Autonomic response patterns during sadness and mirth, *Psychophysiology*, 5, 399–414.

AVERILL, J. R. (1983). Studies on anger and aggression: implications for theories of emotion, *American Psychologist*, November, 1145–1159.

AX, A. F. (1953). The physiological differentiation of fear and anger in humans, *Psychosomatic Medicine*, 15, 433–442.

AXELROD, J. N. (1963). Induced moods and attitudes toward product, *Journal of Advertising Research*, 3, 19–24.

BARGH, J. A. (1984). Automatic and conscious processing of social information. In R. S. Wyer, Jr. and T. K. Srull (Eds.), *Handbook of Social Cognition*, Vol. 3. Hillsdale, NJ: Erlbaum, 1–43.

BATRA, R., and RAY, M. L. (1983). Advertising situations: the implications of differential involvement and accompanying affect responses. In R. J. Harris (Ed.), *Information processing research in advertising.* Hillsdale, NJ: Erlbaum, 127–151.

BATRA, R., and RAY, M. L. (1986). Affective responses mediating acceptance of advertising, *Journal of Consumer Research*, 13, 234–249.

BELK, R. W. (1988). Possessions and the extended-self, *Journal of Consumer Research*, 15: 139–168.

BERGER, B. G., and OWEN, D. R. (1983). Mood alteration with swimming: swimmers really do "feel better," *Psychosomatic Medicine*, 45, 425–431.

BIERLEY, C., McSWEENEY, F. K., and VAN-NIEUWKERK, R. (1985). Classical conditioning of preferences for stimuli, *Journal of Consumer Research*, 12, 316–323.

BINDRA, D. (1969). A unified interpretation of emotion and motivation, *Annual Review of the New York Academy of Sciences*, 159, 1071–1083.

BLOCK, J. (1957). Studies in the phenomenology of emotions, *Journal of Abnormal and Social Psychology*, 64, 358–363.

BOUCHER, J., and OSGOOD, C. E. (1969). The Pollyanna hypothesis, *Journal of Verbal Learning and Verbal Behavior*, 8, 1–8.

BOWER, G. H. (1981). Mood and memory, *American Psychologist*, 36, 129–148.

BOWER, G. H., GILLIGAN, S. G., and MONTEIRO, K. P. (1981). Selectivity of learning caused by affective states, *Journal of Experimental Psychology: General*, 110, 451–473.

BOWER, G. H., and COHEN, P. R. (1982). Emotional influences in memory and thinking. In S. Fiske and M. Clark (Eds.), *Affect and social cognition.* Hillsdale, NJ: Erlbaum, 291–331.

BROWN, R. S., RAMIREZ, D. E., and TAUB, J. M. (1978). The prescription of exercise for depressions, *Physician Sportsmed*, 6, 34–37, 40–41, 44–45.

BUCK, R. (1985). Prime theory: an integrated view of motivation and emotion, *Psychological Review*, 92, 389–413.

CACIOPPO, J. T., and PETTY, R. E. (1979). Attitudes and cognitive response: an electrophysiological approach, *Journal of Personality and Social Psychology*, 37, 2181–2199.

CACIOPPO, J. T., PETTY, R. E., LOSCH, M. E., and KIM, H. S. (1986). Electromyographic activity over facial muscle regions can differentiate the valence and intensity of affective reactions, *Journal of Personality and Social Psychology*, 50, 260–268.

CALDER, B. J., and GRUDER, C. L. (1988). A network activation theory of attitudinal affect. Unpublished manuscript. Northwestern University, Evanston, IL.

CANNON, W. B. (1927). The James-Lange theory of emotion: a critical examination and an alternative theory, *American Journal of Psychology*, 39, 106–124.

CANTOR, J. R., BRYANT, J., and ZILLMAN, D. (1974). Enhancement of humor appreciation by transferred excitation, *Journal of Personality and Social Psychology*, 30, 812–821.

CARPENTER, R. S. H. (1984). *Neurophysiology.* London: University Park Press.

CELSI, R. L., OLSON, J. C. (1988). The role of involvement in attention and comprehension processes, *Journal of Consumer Research*, 15, 210–224.

CLARK, M. S., and ISEN, A. M. (1982). Toward understanding the relationship between feeling states and social behavior. In A. Hastorf and A. M. Isen (Eds.), *Cognitive Social Psychology.* Amsterdam: Elsevier/North Holland, 73–108.

COHEN, J. B. (1990). Attitude, affect and consumer behavior. In B. S. Moore and A. M. Isen (Eds.), *Affect and Social Behavior.* New York: Cambridge University Press. 152–206.

COHEN, J. B., and BASU, K. (1987). Alternative models of categorization: toward a contingent processing framework, *Journal of Consumer Research,* 13, 455–472.

COYNE, J. C. (1982). Putting humpty dumpty back together: cognition, emotion and motivation reconsidered, *Advances in Consumer Research,* 9, 153–155.

DALY, E. M., LANCEE, W. J., and POLIVY, J. (1983). A conical model for the taxonomy of emotional experience. *Journal of Personality and Social Psychology,* 45, 443–457.

DARROW, C. W. (1935). Emotion as relative functional decortication: the role of conflict, *Psychological Review,* 42, 566–578.

DARWIN, C. R. (1872). *The Expression of Emotions in Man and Animals.* London: Murray.

DE RIVERA, J. (1977). *A Structural Theory of the Emotions.* New York: International Universities Press.

DE RIVERA, J. (1984). Development and the full range of emotional experience. In C. Z. Malatesta and C. E. Izard (Eds.), *Emotion in Adult Development.* Beverly Hills: Sage.

DEWEY, J. (1894). The theory of emotion: I. emotional attitudes, *Psychological Review,* 1, 553–569.

DEWEY, J. (1895). The theory of emotion: II. the significance of emotions, *Psychological Review,* 2, 13–32.

DONOVAN, R. J., and ROSSITER, J. R. (1982). Store atmospherics: an environmental psychology approach, *Journal of Retailing,* 58, 34–57.

EASTERBROOK, J. A. (1959). The effect of emotion on cue utilization and the organization of behavior, *Psychological Review,* 66, 183–221.

EDELL, J. A., and BURKE, M. C. (1987). The power of feelings in understanding advertising effects. *Journal of Consumer Research,* 14, 421–433.

EKMAN, P., and FRIESEN, W. V. (1986). A new pan-cultural facial expression of emotion, *Motivation and Emotion,* 10, 159–168.

EKMAN, P., FREISEN, W. V., and ANCOLI, S. (1980). Facial signs of emotional experience, *Journal of Personality and Social Psychology,* 39, 1125–1134.

ELLSWORTH, P. C., and TOURANGEAU, R. (1981). On our failure to disconfirm what nobody ever said, *Journal of Personality and Social Psychology,* 40, 363–369.

FISKE, S. T., and PAVELCHAK, M. A. (1986). Category-based versus piecemeal-based affective responses: developments in schema-triggered affect. In Richard M. Sorrentino and E. Tory Higgins (Eds.), *Handbook of Motivation and Cognition.* New York: Guilford Press, 167–203.

FORGAS, J. P., and BOWER, G. H. (1987). Mood effects on person-perception judgments, *Journal of Personality and Social Psychology,* 53, 53–60.

FRIEDSTAD, M., and THORSON, E. (1986). Emotion-eliciting advertising: effect on long-term memory and judgment, *Advances in Consumer Research,* 13, 111–115.

GARDNER, M. P. (1985). Mood states and consumer behavior: a critical review, *Journal of Consumer Research,* 12, 281–300.

GARDNER, M. P., and HILL, R. P. (1988). Consumer's mood states: antecedents and consequences of experiential versus informational strategies for brand choice, *Psychology & Marketing,* 5, 169–182.

GARDNER, M. P., and ROOK, D. W. (1988). Effects of impulse purchases on consumers' affective states, *Advances in Consumer Research,* 15:127–130.

GARDNER, M. P., and SIMOKOS, G. J. (1986). Toward a methodology for assessing effects of in-store atmospherics, *Advances in Consumer Research,* 13, 27–31.

GILLIGAN, S. G., and BOWER, G. H. (1984). Cognitive consequences of emotional arousal. In C. Izard et al. (Eds.), *Emotion, Cognition and Behavior.* New York: Cambridge University Press, 547–488.

GOLDBERG, M. E., and G. J. GORN (1987). Happy and sad TV programs: how they affect reactions to commercials, *Journal of Consumer Research,* 14, 387–403.

GOLDEN, L. L., and JOHNSON, K. A. (1983). The impact of sensory preference and thinking versus feeling appeals on advertising effectiveness, *Advances in Consumer Research,* 10, 203–208.

GORN, G. J. (1982). The effects of music in advertising on choice behavior: a classical conditioning approach, *Journal of Marketing,* 46, 94–101.

GRAHAM, F. W. (1981). The anxiety of the runner: terminal helplessness. In M. H. Sachs and M. L. Sachs (Eds.), *Psychology of Running.* Champaign, IL: Human Kinetics, 149–156.

GREENFIELD, N. S., and STERNBACH, R. A. (1972).

Handbook of Psychophysiology. New York: Holt, Rinehart & Winston.

GREENWALD, A. G., and LEAVITT, C. (1984). Audience involvement in advertising: four levels, *Journal of Consumer Research,* 11, 581–592.

GRESHAM, L. G., and SHIMP, T. A. (1985). Attitude toward the advertisement and brand attitudes: a classical conditioning perspective, *Journal of Advertising,* 14, 10–17.

HAGER, J. C., and EKMAN, P. (1981). Methodological problems in Tourangeau and Ellsworth's study of facial expression and experience of emotion, *Journal of Personality and Social Psychology,* 40, 358–362.

HARMON, D. W., and RAY, W. J. (1977). Hemispheric activity during affective verbal stimuli: an EEG study, *Neuropsychologia,* 15, 457–460.

HAVLENA, W. J., and HOLBROOK, M.B. (1986). The varieties of consumption experience: comparing two typologies of emotion in consumer behavior, *Journal of Consumer Research,* 13, 394–404.

HILGARD, E. R. (1980). The trilogy of the mind: cognition, affection and conation, *Journal of History of Behavioral Sciences,* 16, 107–117.

HILL, R. P., and GARDNER, M. P. (1987). The buying process: effects of and on consumer mood states, *Advances in Consumer Research,* 14, 408–410.

HILL, R. P., and MAZIS, M. B. (1986). Measuring emotional responses to advertising, *Advances in Consumer Research,* 13, 164–169.

HILL, R. P., and WARD, J. C. (1989). Mood manipulation in marketing research: An examination of potential confounding effects, *Journal of Marketing Research,* 97–104.

HIRSCHMAN, E. C., and HOLBROOK, M. B. (1982). Hedonic consumption: emerging concepts, methods and propositions, *Journal of Marketing,* 46, 92–101.

HOFFMAN, M. L. (1986). Affect, cognition and motivation. In R. M. Sorrentino and E. T. Higgins (Eds.), *Handbook of Motivation and Cognition.* New York: Guilford Press, 244–280.

HOLBROOK, M. B. (1986). Emotion in the consumption experience: Toward a new model of the human consumer. In R. A. Peterson, W. D. Hoyer, and W. R. Wilson (Eds.), *The Role of Affect in Consumer Behavior.* Lexington, MA; D. C. Heath.

HOLBROOK, M. B., and HIRSCHMAN, E.C. (1982). The experiential aspects of consumption: consumer fantasies, feelings and fun, *Journal of Consumer Research,* 9, 132–140.

HOLBROOK, M. B., and BATRA, R. (1987). Assessing the role of emotions as mediators of consumer responses to advertising, *Journal of Consumer Research,* 14, 404–420.

ISEN, A. M. (1984a). The influence of positive affect on decision making and cognitive organization, *Advances in Consumer Research,* 11, 534–537.

ISEN, A. M. (1984b). Toward understanding the role of affect in cognition. In R. S. Wyer, Jr. and T. K. Srull (Eds.), *Handbook of social cognition.* Hillsdale, NJ: Erlbaum, 179–236.

ISEN, A. M. (1989). Some ways in which affect influences cognitive processes: implications for advertising and consumer behavior. In A. M. Tybout and P. Cafferata (Eds.), *Advertising and Consumer Psychology.* New York: Lexington Books. 91–117.

ISEN, A. M., SHALKER, T. E., CLARK, M., and KARP. L. (1978). Affect, accessibility of material in memory, and behavior: A cognitive loop? *Journal of Personality and Social Psychology,* 36, 1–12.

ISEN, A. M., and HASTORF, A. H. (1982). Some perspectives on cognitive social psychology. In A. H. Hastorf and A. M. Isen (Eds.), *Cognitive Social Psychology.* New York: Elsevier, North-Holland, 1–31.

ISEN, A. M., and SHALKER, T. (1982). The effect of feeling state on evaluation of positive, neutral and negative stimuli: when you "accentuate the positive," do you "eliminate the negative"? *Social Psychology Quarterly,* 45, 58–63.

ISEN, A. M., and DAUBMAN, K. A. (1984). The influence of affect on categorization. *Journal of Personality and Social Psychology,* 47, 1206–1217.

ISEN, A. M., DAUBMAN, K. A., and NOWICKI, G. P. (1987). Positive affect facilitates creative problem solving, *Journal of Personality and Social Psychology,* 52, 1122–1131.

ISEN, A. M., JOHNSON, M. M. S., MERTZ, E., and ROBINSON, G. F. (1985). The influence of positive affect on the unusualness of word associations, *Journal of Personality and Social Psychology,* 48, 1–14.

IZARD, C. E. (1977). *Human Emotions.* New York: Plenum Press.

IZARD, C. E. (1981). Differential emotions theory and the facial feedback hypothesis of emotion activation: comments on Tourangeau and Ellsworth's "The role of facial response in the experience of emotion," *Journal of Personality and Social Psychology,* 40, 350–354.

JAMES, W. (1890). *Principles of Psychology.* New York: Holt.

JANISZEWSKI, C. (1988). Preconscious processing effects: the independence of attitude formation and conscious thought, *Journal of Consumer Research,* 15, 199–209.

JOACHIMSTHALER, E., LASTOVICKA, J. L. (1984). Optimal stimulation level–exploratory behavior models. *Journal of Consumer Research,* 11, 830–835.

KALLARIS, J. J., and COX, A. D. (1989). The effects of background music in advertising: a reassessment. *Journal of Consumer Research,* 16, 113–118.

KEPPEL, G., and UNDERWOOD, B. J. (1962). Proactive inhibition in short-term retention of single terms. *Journal of Verbal Learning and Verbal Behavior,* 1, 153–161.

KOTLER, P. (1974). Atmospherics as a marketing tool, *Journal of Retailing,* 49, 48–64.

KROEBER-RIEL, W. (1984a). Effects of emotional pictorial elements in ads analyzed by means of eye movement monitoring, *Advances in Consumer Research,* 11, 591–596.

KROEBER-RIEL, W. (1984b). Emotional product differentiation by classical conditioning. *Advances in Consumer Research,* 11, 538–543.

LAURENT, G., KAPFERER, J. N. (1985). Measuring consumer involvement profiles, *Journal of Marketing Research,* 22, 41–53.

LAWSON, R. (1985). The effects of mood on retrieving consumer product information, *Advances in Consumer Research,* 12, 399–403.

LAZARUS, R. S. (1982). Thoughts on the relations between emotion and cognition, *American Psychologist,* 35, 1019–1024.

LAZARUS, R. S. (1984). On the primacy of cognition. *American Psychologist,* 39, 124–129.

LEAVITT, C. (1970). A multidimensional set of rating scales for television commercials, *Journal of Applied Psychology,* 54, 427–429.

LEVENTHAL, H. (1980). Toward a comprehensive theory of emotion, *Advances in Experimental Social Psychology,* 13, 139–207.

LEVENTHAL, H. (1982). The integration of emotion and cognition: a view from the perceptual-motor theory of emotion. In M. S. Clark and S. T. Fiske (Eds.), *Affect and Cognition: the 17th Annual Carnegie Symposium.* Hillsdale, NJ: Erlbaum, 121–149.

LOESS, H. (1964). Proactive inhibition in short-term memory, *Journal of Verbal Learning and Verbal Behavior,* 3, 362–368.

LOVE, R. E. (1972). Unobtrusive measurement of cognitive reactions to persuasive communications. Unpublished doctoral dissertation. Ohio State University, Columbus, OH.

LUTZ, R. J. (1985). Affective and cognitive antecedents of attitude toward the ad: a conceptual framework. In L. F. Alwitt and A. A. Mitchell (Eds.), *Psychological Processes and Advertising Effects: Theory, Research, and Application.* Hillsdale, NJ: Erlbaum.

MADDEN, T. J., ALLEN, C. T., and TWIBLE, J. L. (1988). Attitude toward the ad: an assessment of diverse measurement indices under different processing "sets." *Journal of Marketing Research,* 25, 242–252.

MANDLER, G. (1976). *Mind and Emotion.* Malabar, FL: Krieger.

MANDLER, G. (1982). The structure of value: accounting for taste. In M. S. Clark and S. T. Fiske, *Affect and cognition: the 17th annual Carnegie symposium.* Hillsdale, NJ: Erlbaum, 3–36.

MARCEL, A. J. (1983). Conscious and unconscious perception: an approach to the relations between phenomenal experience and perceptual processes. *Cognitive Psychology,* 15, 238–300.

McDOUGALL, W. (1923). *Outline of Psychology.* New York: Scribner.

McSWEENEY, F. K., and BIERLEY, C. (1984). Recent developments in classical conditioning, *Journal of Consumer Research,* 11, 619–631.

MEHRABIAN, A., and RUSSELL, J. A. (1974). *An approach to environmental psychology.* Cambridge, MA: MIT press.

MEYERS-LEVY, G., and TYBOUT, A. M. (1989). Schema Congruity as a basis for product evaluation, *Journal Consumer Research,* 16, 39–54.

MILLIMAN, R. E. (1982). Using background music to affect the behavior of supermarket shoppers, *Journal of Marketing,* 46, 86–91.

MILLIMAN, R. E. (1986). The influence of background music on the behavior of restaurant patrons, *Journal of Consumer Research,* 13, 286–289.

MITCHELL, A. A. (1986). The effect of verbal and visual components of advertising on brand attitudes and attitude toward advertisement, *Journal of Consumer Research,* 13, 12–24.

MOORE, D. L., and HUTCHINSON, J. W. (1983).

The effects of ad affect on advertising effectiveness, *Advances in Consumer Research,* 10, 526-531.

MOORE, D. L., and HUTCHINSON, J.W. (1985). The influence of affective reactions to advertising: direct and indirect mechanisms of change. In L. F. Alwitt and A. A. Mitchell (Eds.), *Psychological Processes and Advertising Effects: Theory, Research, and Application.* Hillsdale, NJ: Erlbaum.

MORGAN, W. P. (1979). Anxiety reduction following acute physical activity, *Psychiatry Annual,* 9, 141-147.

OBERMILLER, C. (1985). Varieties of mere exposure: the effects of processing style and repetition on affective response, *Journal of Consumer Research,* 12, 17-30.

OLIVER, R. L., DeSARBO, W. S. (1988). Response determinants in satisfaction judgments, *Journal of Consumer Research,* 14, 495-507.

ORTONY, A., CLORE, G. L., and COLLINS, A. (1988). *The Cognitive Structure of Emotions.* New York: Cambridge University Press.

PARK, C. W., and YOUNG, S. M. (1986). Consumer response to television commercials: the impact of involvement and background music on brand attitude formation, *Journal of Marketing Research,* 23, 11-24.

PERRETT, D. L., ROLLS, E. T., AND CAAN, W. (1982). Visual neurone's responsive to faces in the monkey temporal cortex, *Experimental Brain Research,* 47, 329-342.

PETTY, R. E., CACIOPPO, J. T., SEDIKIDES, C., and STRATHMAN, A. J. (1988). Affect and Persuasion, *American Behavioral Scientist,* 31, 355-371.

PLUTCHIK, R. (1980a). *Emotion: A Psychoevolutionary Synthesis.* New York: Harper & Row.

PLUTCHIK, R. (1980b). A language for the emotions, *Psychology Today* (February), 68-78.

PUTO, C. P., and WELLS, W. D. (1984). Informational and transformational advertising: the differential effects of time. *Advances in Consumer Research,* 11, 638-643.

RAJU, P. S. (1980). Optimum stimulation level: its relationship to personality, demographics and exploratory behavior, *Journal of Consumer Research,* 7, 272-282.

ROBERTSON, T. S., ZIELINSKI, J., and WARD, S. (1984). *Consumer Behavior.* Glenview, IL: Scott, Foresman.

ROOK, D. W. (1987). The buying impulse, *Journal of Consumer Research,* 14, 189-199.

ROOK, D. W., and HOCH, S. J. (1985). Consuming impulses, *Advances in Consumer Research,* 12, 23-27.

ROSS, E. D., and MESULAM, M. M. (1979). Dominant language functions of the right hemisphere? Prosody and emotional gesturing, *Archives of Neurology,* 36, 144-148.

ROSSITER, J. R., and PERCY, L. (1980). Attitude change through visual imagery in advertising, *Journal of Advertising,* 9, 10-16.

ROTHSCHILD, M. L., HYUN, Y. J., REEVES, B., THORSON, E., and GOLDSTEIN, R. (1988). Hemispherically lateralized EEG as a response to television commercials, *Journal of Consumer Research,* 15, 185-198.

RUSSELL, J. A. (1978). Evidence of convergent validity on the dimensions of affect, *Journal of Personality and Social Psychology,* 36, 1152-1168.

RUSSELL, J. A. (1980). A circumplex model of affect, *Journal of Personality and Social Psychology,* 39, 1161-1178.

RUSSELL, J. A., WEISS, A., and MENDELSOHN, G. A. (1989). Affect grid: A single-item scale of pleasure and arousal, *Journal of Personality and Social Psychology,* 57, 493-502.

SANBONMATSU, D. M., and KARDES, F. R. (1988). The effects of physiological arousal on information processing and persuasion, *Journal of Consumer Research,* 15:379-385.

SAFER, M. A., and LEVENTHAL, H. (1977). Ear differences in evaluating emotional tone of voice and verbal content, *Journal of Experimental Psychology: Human Perception and Performance,* 3, 75-82.

SCHACHTER, S. (1957). Pain, fear and anger in hypertensives and a psychophysiologic study, *Psychosomatic Medicine,* 19, 17-29.

SCHACHTER, S. (1959). *The Psychology of Affiliation.* Stanford, CA: Stanford University Press.

SCHACHTER, S. (1964). The interaction of cognitive and physiological determinants of emotion state. In L. Berkowitz (Eds.), *Advances in Experimental Social Psychology.* New York: Academic Press.

SCHACTER, S., and SINGER, J. E. (1962). Cognitive, social and physiological determinants of emotional state, *Psychological Review,* 69, 379-399.

SCHLINGER, M. J. (1979). A profile of responses to commercials, *Journal of Advertising Research,* 19, 37-46.

SCHLOSBERG, H. (1952). The description of facial expressions in terms of two dimensions, *Journal of Experimental Psychology,* 44, 229-237.

SCHULTZ, D. E. (1979). Media research users want, *Journal of Advertising Research,* 19, 13–17.

SCHWARTZ, G. E., AHERN, G. L., and BROWN, S. (1979). Lateralized facial muscle response to positive and negative emotional stimuli, *Psychophysiology,* 16, 6, 561–571.

SCHWARTZ, G. E., DAVIDSON, R. J., and MAER, F. (1975). Right hemisphere lateralization for emotion in the human brain, *Science,* 190, 286–288.

SCHWARTZ, G. E., WEINBERGER, D.A., and SINGER, J.A. (1981). Cardiovascular differentiation of happiness, sadness, anger, and fear following imagery and exercise, *Psychosomatic Medicine,* 43, 343–362.

SCHWARTZ, M. (1978). *Physiological Psychology.* Englewood Cliffs, NJ: Prentice-Hall.

SHAVER, P., SCHWARTZ, J., KIRSON, D., and O'CONNOR, C. (1987). Emotion knowledge: further exploration of a prototype approach, *Journal of Personality and Social Psychology,* 52, 1061–1086.

SHEPARD, R. N. (1962). The analysis of proximities: multidimensional scaling with an unknown distance function. I., *Psychometrika,* 27, 125–140.

SHERMAN, E., and SMITH, R. B. (1987). Mood states of shoppers and store image: promising interactions and possible behavioral effects, *Advances in Consumer Research,* 251–254.

SHIMP, T. A. (1981). Attitude toward the ad as a mediator of consumer brand choice, *Journal of Advertising,* 10(2), 9–15.

SHUTE, R. (1976). *On the History of the Process by Which the Aristotelian Writings Arrived at Their Present Form.* New York: Arno Press.

SILK, A. J., and VAVRA, T. G. (1974). The influence of advertising's affective qualities on consumer response. In D. Hughes and M. L. Ray (Eds.), *Buyer/Consumer Information Processing.* Chapel Hill, NC: University of North Carolina Press, 157–186.

SIMON, H.A. (1967). Motivational and emotional controls of cognition, *Psychological Review,* 74, 29–39.

SINGH, S. N., and CHURCHILL, G. A., JR. (1987). Arousal and advertising effectiveness, *Journal of Advertising,* 16, 4–10.

SMITH, C. A. (1989). Dimensions of appraisal and physiological response in emotion, *Journal of Personality and Social Psychology,* 56, 339–353.

SMITH, C. A., and ELLSWORTH, P. C. (1985). Patterns of cognitive appraisal in emotion, *Journal of Personality and Social Psychology,* 48, 813–838.

SRULL, T. K. (1983). Affect and memory: the impact of affective reactions in advertising on the representation of product information in memory, *Advances in Consumer Research,* 10, 520–525.

SRULL, T. (1984). The effects of subjective affective states on memory and judgment, *Advances in Consumer Research,* 11, 530–533.

SRULL, T. K. (1987). Memory, mood, and consumer judgment, *Advances in Consumer Research,* 14, 404–407.

STAATS, A. W., and STAATS, C. K. (1958). Attitudes established by classical conditioning. *Journal of Abnormal and Social Psychology,* 57, 37–40.

STRACK, F., MARTIN, L. L., and STEPPER, S. (1988). Inhibiting and facilitating conditions of the human smile: a nonobtrusive test of the facial feedback hypothesis, *Journal of Personality and Social Psychology,* 54, 768–777.

STRONGMAN, K. T. (1987). *The Psychology of Emotion.* New York: Wiley.

STUART,, E. W., SHIMP, T. A., and ENGLE, R. W. (1987). Classical conditioning of consumer attitudes: four experiments in an advertising context, *Journal of Consumer Research,* 14, 334–349.

TOMKINS, S. S. (1965). Affect and the psychology of knowledge. In S. S. Tomkins and C. E. Izard (Eds.), *Affect, Cognition and Personality.* New York: Springer.

TOMKINS, S. S. (1981a). The role of facial response in the experience of emotion: a reply to Tourangeau and Ellsworth, *Journal of Personality & Social Psychology,* 40, 355–357.

TOMKINS, S. S. (1981b). The quest for primary motives: biography and autobiography of an idea, *Journal of Personality and Social Psychology,* 41, 306–329.

TOURANGEAU, R., and ELLSWORTH, P. C. (1979). The role of facial response in the experience, *Journal of Personality & Social Psychology,* 37, 1519–1531.

TSAL, Y. (1985). On the relationship between cognitive and affective processes: a critique of Zajonc and Markus, *Journal of Consumer Research,* 12, 358–362.

TSE, D. K., and WILTON, P. C. (1988). Models of consumer satisfaction information: an extension, *Journal of Marketing Research,* 15, 204–212.

TUCKER, D. M. (1981). Lateral brain function, emotion, and conceptualization, *Psychological Bulletin,* 89, 19–46.

TUCKER, D. M., and NEWMAN, J. P. (1981). Verbal versus imaginal cognitive strategies in the inhibition of emotional arousal, *Cognitive Therapy and Research*, 5, 197–202.

TUCKER, D. M., WATSON, R. G., and HEILMAN, K. M. (1976). Affective discrimination and evocation in patients with right parietal disease, *Neurology*, 26, 354.

TUCKER, D. M., ROTH, R. S., ARNESON, B. A., and BUCKINGHAM, V. (1977). Right hemisphere activation during stress, *Neuropsychologia*, 15, 697–700.

WAHLERS, R. G., and ETZEL, M. J. (1985). A consumer response to incongruity between optimal stimulation and lifestyle satisfaction, *Advances in Consumer Research*, 12, 97–101.

WATSON, J. B. (1908). *The Philosophy of Kant Explained*. Glasgow: Maclehose and Sons.

WATSON, J. B. (1929). *Psychology: From the Standpoint of a Behaviorist*. Philadelphia and London: Lippincott.

WATSON, D., CLARK, L. A., and TELLEGEN, A. (1988). Development and validation of brief measures of positive and negative affect: The PANAS scales, *Journal of Personality and Social Psychology*, 54, 1063–1070.

WATSON, D., and TELLEGEN, A. (1985). Toward a consensual structure of mood, *Psychological Bulletin*, 98, 219–235.

WEINBERG, P., and GOTTWALD, W. (1982). Impulsive consumer buying as a result of emotions, *Journal of Business Research*, 10, 43–57.

WEINER, B. (1982). The emotional consequences of causal attributions. In M. Clark and S. T. Fiske (Eds.), *Affect and Cognition: 17th Annual Carnegie Symposium on Cognition*. Hillsdale, NJ: Erlbaum, 185–209.

WEINER, B. (1986). Attribution, emotion, and action. In R. M. Sorrentino and E. T. Higgins (Eds.), *Handbook of Motivation and Cognition*. New York: Guilford Press, 281–312.

WESTBROOK, R. A. (1980). Intrapersonal affective influences on consumer satisfaction with products, *Journal of Consumer Research*, 7, 49–54.

WESTBROOK, R. A. (1987). Product/consumption-based affective responses and postpurchase processes, *Journal of Marketing Research*, 24, 258–270.

WUNDT, W. (1896). *Outlines of Psychology*, Leipzig: Germany, Wilhelm Engleman.

YUSPEH, S. (1979). The medium versus the message. In G. Hafer (Ed.), *A Look Back, A Look Ahead: Proceedings of the 10th National Attitude Research Conference*. Chicago: American Marketing Association, 109–138.

ZAICHKOWSKY, J. L. (1985). Measuring the involvement construct. *Journal of Consumer Research*, 12, 341–352.

ZAJONC, R. B. (1968). Attitudinal effects of mere exposure, *Journal of Personality and Social Psychology Monograph*, 9, (2, Part 2), 1–28.

ZAJONC, R. B. (1980). Feeling and thinking: preferences need no inferences, *American Psychologist*, 35, 151–175.

ZAJONC, R. B., and MARKUS, H. (1982). Affective and cognitive factors in preferences, *Journal of Consumer Research*, 9, 123–131.

ZANNA, M. P., KIESLER, C. A., and PILKONIS, P. A. (1970). Positive and negative attitudinal affect established by classical conditioning, *Journal of Personality and Social Psychology*, 14, 321–328.

ZIELSKI, H. A. (1982). Does day after recall penalize "feeling" ads? *Journal of Advertising Research*, 22, 19–22.

ZILLMAN, D. (1971). Excitation transfer in communication-mediated aggressive behavior, *Journal of Experimental Social Psychology*, 7, 419–434.

ZINKHAN, G. M., and MARTIN, C. R., JR. (1983). Message characteristics and audience characteristics: predictors of advertising response, *Advances in Consumer Research*, 10, 27–31.

ZUCKERMAN, M., KLORMAN, R., LARRANCE, D. T., and SPIEGEL, N. H. (1981). Facial, autonomic, and subjective components of emotion: the facial feedback hypothesis versus the externalizer-internalizer distinction, *Journal of Personality and Social Psychology*, 41, 929–944.

THEORIES OF ATTITUDE CHANGE

Richard E. Petty
Ohio State University

Rao H. Unnava
Ohio State University

Alan J. Strathman*
Ohio State University

This chapter reviews many of the major theoretical approaches used to understand the processes responsible for attitude change, and it employs the Elaboration Likelihood Model of persuasion as an organizing framework. Theories that rely on effortful cognitive mediation of persuasion are described, as well as those theories that posit less cognitively taxing heuristics and other peripheral strategies.

INTRODUCTION

A critical assumption of most current attempts to understand consumer behavior is that people make decisions about such things as the make of car they will purchase, the supermarket at which they will shop, and where they will take

*We are grateful to Curt Haugtvedt, Jeff Kasmer, John Myers, David Schumann, and Bas Verplanken for providing comments on a previous version of this chapter. Preparation of this chapter was facilitated by NSF grant BNS 84-18038.

their next vacation, based, in large part, on their overall *attitudes* toward those entities (see Ajzen and Fishbein 1980; Bettman 1986; Day 1973; Kassarjian 1982; Petty and Cacioppo 1983). In recognition of the importance of the attitude construct to marketing, Aaker and Myers (1987) noted that "brand attitude is the pillar on which the sales and profit fortunes of a giant corporation rest" (p. 160).

After a period of considerable conflict among researchers regarding the definition of attitudes (see McGuire 1969) and their role in influencing behavior (see Wicker 1969), there is now a consensus that it is useful to view attitudes as global and relatively enduring (i.e., stored in long-term memory) *evaluations* of objects, issues, or persons (e.g., Ajzen 1987; Cooper and Croyle 1984; Fazio 1986). These evaluations can be based on behavioral, cognitive, and affective information and experiences, and they are capable of guiding behavioral, cognitive, and affective responses (Petty and Cacioppo 1986b; Zanna and Rempel 1988). That is, a person may come to like a new product only after being induced to purchase it, or after finding the claims in a magazine ad to be compelling, or after feeling pleasure in response to the background music in a commercial for the product. Similarly, if a person already evaluates a product positively, he or she may engage in the behavior of recommending it to friends, may process new ads for the product in a biased fashion, or may feel disgust when his or her favorite store discontinues the product line.

After intense exploration of the cognitive and behavioral underpinnings of attitudes during the 1960s and 1970s, the 1980s brought a renewed interest in the affective bases of attitudes (e.g., Abelson, Kinder, Peters, and Fiske 1982; Breckler 1984; Cacioppo and Petty 1982a; Cafferata and Tybout 1989; Edell and Burke 1984; Holbrook and Batra 1987; Peterson, Hoyer and Wilson 1986; Petty, Cacioppo, Sedikides, and Strathman 1988). Also the last decade also brought about an increasing appreciation of the idea that not all attitudes are created equally. That is, attitudes may come about through a variety of processes that imbue them with a multiplicity of characteristics and render them capable of inducing a diversity of consequences (e.g., Chaiken 1987; Fazio and Zanna 1981; Petty and Cacioppo 1981; Sherman 1987). For example, attitudes that result from direct experience with an attitude object tend to be more accessible in memory and directive of behavior than similar attitudes formed without such experience (Fazio 1986). In this chapter we focus on the processes responsible for *changes* in attitudes and the characteristics and consequences of these changes.[1] Furthermore, our focus is on the theories that presently generate the bulk of contemporary empirical work on attitude change (for excellent previous reviews, see Insko 1967; Kiesler, Collins, and Miller 1969).

In reviewing the various theories of attitude change that had developed over the previous five decades, Petty and Cacioppo (1981) concluded that, even though the many different theories had different names, postulates, and particular effects and variables that they specialized in explaining, these theories could be thought of as emphasizing just two relatively distinct "routes to persuasion." The first, or *central route,* focussed on the information that a person had about the central merits of the object under consideration. Some of the central route approaches postulated that comprehending and learning the information about the object was critical for persuasion (e.g., Hovland, Janis, and Kelley 1953; McGuire 1968), whereas others focussed more on the evaluation, elaboration, and integration of the information (e.g., Anderson 1981; Fishbein and Ajzen 1975; Petty, Ostrom, and Brock 1981). In contrast, the *peripheral route* approaches emphasized attitude changes that were brought about with-

---

[1]Although some researchers make a qualitative distinction between situations involving attitude formation (i.e., when "new" attitudes are involved) and those involving attitude change (i.e., when "old" attitudes are challenged), we do not. This is not because we fail to recognize that there are typically different aspects of the two situations. For example, in attitude formation, one is dealing with issues about which people have little or no prior *knowledge* or prior *commitment,* have done little or no prior *thinking,* and have little or no *behavioral experience,* etc. However, attitude *change* situations differ from each other in these respects as well (e.g., some attitude change situations involve attitudes based on high prior knowledge, some on low or no knowledge). Thus, we view it as more parsimonious to view any persuasion situation as falling along a continuum composed of dimensions such as those above. At the low end of the continuum on several dimensions would be those situations that have traditionally been viewed as involving attitude formation. Thus, the attitude formation versus attitude change distinction can be viewed as a quantitative rather than a qualitative one.

out the person thinking about information central to the merits of the attitude issue. Thus, the peripheral approaches dealt with changes resulting from rewards, punishments, and affective experiences that were associated directly with the attitude object (e.g., Staats and Staats 1958), changes resulting from simple inferences that people drew about the appropriate attitude to adopt based on their own behavior (e.g., Bem 1967), or changes brought about by other simple cues in the persuasion environment, such as the expertise of the source of the message (e.g., Chaiken 1980). We will review the current status of the major central and peripheral approaches to persuasion in this chapter.

In their *Elaboration Likelihood Model* (ELM) of persuasion, Petty and Cacioppo (1980; 1981; 1986b) proposed that the central and peripheral routes anchor an elaboration likelihood continuum. The processes emphasized by the central route theories should be largely responsible for attitude change on the high-elaboration end of this continuum (i.e., when a person's motivation and ability to scrutinize issue-relevant information is high). The peripheral route processes should become more dominant as one moves down the continuum (i.e., when either motivation or the ability to process is attenuated). Furthermore, there should be differential consequences of the route to persuasion. The antecedents and consequences of the two routes to persuasion are depicted in Figure 7.1. Because the ELM provides a general context from which other persuasion theories may be understood, we begin our review of current theories with it and will use it to organize the chapter.

THE ELABORATION LIKELIHOOD MODEL OF PERSUASION

The ELM represents an attempt to integrate the many seemingly conflicting findings in the persuasion literature under one conceptual umbrella by specifying a finite number of ways in which source, message, and other variables have an impact on attitude change (Petty and Cacioppo 1981; 1986a). The ELM is based on the notion that people want to form correct attitudes (i.e., those that will prove useful in functioning in the environment) as a result of exposure to a persuasive communication, but that there are a variety of ways in which a reasonable position may be adopted.

The most effortful procedure for evaluating an advocacy involves drawing upon prior experience and knowledge to carefully scrutinize and elaborate the issue-relevant arguments in the persuasive communication along the dimensions that are perceived central to the merits of the attitude object. According to the ELM, attitudes formed or changed by this *central route* are postulated to be relatively persistent, predictive of behavior, and resistant to change, until they are challenged by cogent contrary information along the dimension or dimensions perceived central to the merits of the attitude object.

The ELM recognizes that it is neither adaptive nor possible for people to exert considerable mental effort in processing all of the persuasive communications to which they are exposed (cf. Miller, Maruyama, Beaber, and Valone 1976; Robertson 1971). Indeed, people often act as "lazy organisms" (McGuire 1969) or "cognitive misers" (Taylor 1981). This does not mean that people never form attitudes when motivation and/or ability to scrutinize a message are low, but rather that attitudes are more likely to be changed as a result of relatively simple associations (as in classical conditioning induced by pleasant music; Staats and Staats 1958), on-line inferences (as in the self-perception mandate, "I bought it, so I must like it"; Bem 1972), well-learned heuristics retrieved from memory (as in "experts are generally correct"; Chaiken 1980, 1987; Cialdini 1987), or category-based processing (as in "it's from a *discount store,* so it must be cheap"; Fiske and Pavelchak 1986; Sujan 1985) in these situations. Attitudes formed or changed by these *peripheral route* processes are postulated to be relatively less persistent, resistant, and predic-

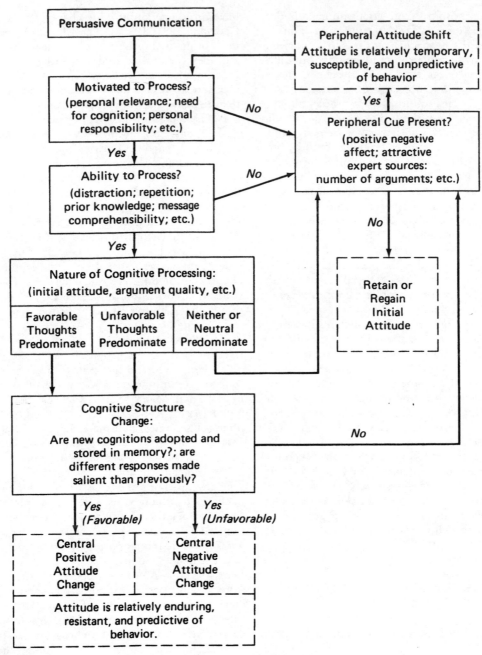

FIGURE 7.1 The Elaboration Likelihood Model of Persuasion
(Schematic depiction of the central and peripheral routes to persuasion.
This diagram depicts the possible endpoints on the elaboration likelihood
continuum. Source: Adapted from Petty 1977; Petty and Cacioppo 1981a,
1986.)

tive of long-term behavior than those based on the central route processes.[2]

This discussion highlights two ways in which variables can have an impact on persuasion. Variables (e.g., an attractive endorser) can serve as persuasive *arguments,* providing information as to the central merits of an object or issue, or they can serve as peripheral *cues,* allowing favorable or unfavorable attitude formation in the absence of a diligent consideration of the true merits of the object or issue. In addition, however, variables can have an impact on persuasion by influencing the *extent* of argument elaboration (i.e., the extent to which the person is motivated and able to evaluate the merits of the issue-relevant information presented) and the *direction* of elaboration (i.e., whether the thoughts elicited are relatively favorable or un-

favorable). When conditions foster people's motivation and ability to engage in issue-relevant thinking, the "elaboration likelihood" is said to be high. Sometimes this elaboration occurs in a relatively objective manner, but sometimes the elaboration is biased. In contrast, when the elaboration likelihood is low, any attitude change that takes place is more likely to be the result of responding to peripheral cues in the persuasion context. In short, the elaboration likelihood moderates the route to persuasion.

Motivation versus Ability

The ELM holds that there are many variables capable of affecting elaboration and influencing the route to persuasion. Some variables affect a person's *motivation* to process issue-relevant arguments, whereas others affect their *ability* or opportunity to process these arguments. Some variables are part of the persuasion *situation,* whereas others are part of the *individual.* Some variables affect processing in a relatively *objective* manner, whereas others influence elaboration in a *biased* fashion. Table 7.1 illustrates variables falling into each cell of the $2 \times 2 \times 2$ matrix.

Perhaps the most important variable affecting a person's motivation to process a message is the perceived personal relevance of the communication. When the personal importance of a message is high, people are motivated to scrutinize the information presented (Leippe and Elkin 1987; Petty and Cacioppo 1979b, 1990). In an advertising context, this means that when relevance is high, people may spend more time processing an ad and its claims, generate more

[2]One of the earliest theories that explicitly acknowledged the different processes underlying attitude expression was Kelman's (1958) three process model. Kelman tied the type of persuasion largely to the source of the message—expert sources produced *internalization* (a permanent type of change based on personal acceptance of the message conclusion as one's own); attractive sources produced *identification* (change that was tied to a continued association with a desirable referent); powerful sources produced *compliance* (change that was expressed only under the continued threat of rewards and punishments controlled by the source). Kelman's distinction of the different types of change is a useful one even though as we explain in this chapter, the determinants of those changes have proven to be much more complicated than he initially suspected. The term "internalization" may be useful when referring to changes induced by the central route. The term "identification," however, refers to only one process by which attitudes may be changed by the peripheral route. The term "compliance" doesn't refer to real change at all, but only that expressed when the person is under appropriate scrutiny.

TABLE 7.1 Categorization and Examples of Individual and Situational Factors Affecting the Extent and Bias of Message Processing

	MOTIVATIONAL FACTORS		*ABILITY FACTORS*	
	Situational	*Individual*	*Situational*	*Individual*
RELATIVELY OBJECTIVE PROCESSING	induced personal relevance	need for cognition	external distraction	general intelligence
RELATIVE BIASED PROCESSING	forewarning of intent to persuade	open/closed mindedness	instructed head movements	attitude-congruent knowledge

product-relevant thoughts and inferences, and spontaneously draw more conclusions about the product (Celsi and Olson 1988; Kardes 1988). When perceived relevance is high, the extent of the attitude change is dependent upon the *quality* of the claims in an advertisement (Burnkrant and Unnava 1989). When personal relevance is low, argument scrutiny is reduced and attitudes may be affected more by variables serving as peripheral cues, such as the celebrity status of the product endorsers or the attractiveness of the pictures in the ad (Miniard, Bhatla, and Rose 1988; Petty, Cacioppo, and Schumann 1983). For example, in two studies on message repetition, Schumann, Petty, and Clemons (1990) found that under high relevance conditions, product attitudes were influenced by providing new product arguments in the repeated ads, but that when relevance was low, attitudes were influenced by introducing new peripheral ad features (e.g., new headlines, pictures, etc.) over multiple exposures.[3]

It is important to note that variables other than personal relevance can also affect the motivation to process a message. For example, people are more motivated to scrutinize information when they are solely responsible for doing so (Petty, Harkins, and Williams 1980), or when they are individually accountable (Tetlock 1983). Increasing the number of message sources has been shown to increase information

processing activity (e.g., Harkins and Petty 1981, 1987; Moore and Reardon 1987), as has the use of rhetorical questions when issue-relevance is low (Burnkrant and Howard 1984; Petty, Cacioppo, and Heesacker 1981; Swasy and Munch 1985). In contrast, messages that are overly quantitative may increase reliance on peripheral strategies because people are less motivated or able to process them (Yalch and Yalch 1984). Messages that are moderately inconsistent with an existing attitude schema may enhance processing over schema-consistent messages because the former may pose some threat that needs to be understood or some incongruity that needs to be resolved (Cacioppo and Petty 1979; Mandler 1982; Meyers-Levy and Tybout 1989).

In addition, there are individual differences in motivation to think about persuasive communications (Cacioppo and Petty 1982b). People who enjoy thinking (high in "need for cognition") tend to form attitudes on the basis of the quality of the arguments in a message, thereby following the central route to persuasion (Cacioppo, Petty, and Morris 1983). People who do not enjoy thinking are more reliant on simple peripheral cues in the persuasion context (Axsom, Yates, and Chaiken 1987; Cacioppo and Petty 1984; Haugtvedt, Petty, Cacioppo, and Steidley 1988). Also, some variables affect a person's motivation to think in a relatively objective manner, but others affect motivation in a relatively biased fashion. For example, when people are forewarned of a speaker's persuasive intent, they become motivated to *counterargue* the message in order to defend their initial positions rather than process the message objectively (Petty and Cacioppo 1979a). On the other hand, two-sided messages may inhibit counterarguing compared with one-sided messages, since they make the source appear less biased (Kamins and Assael 1987).

Among the important variables affecting a person's *ability* to process issue-relevant arguments is message repetition. Moderate message repetition provides more opportunities for argument scrutiny (e.g., Cacioppo and Petty 1979; Gorn and Goldberg 1980; Rethans, Swasy, and Marks 1986), which will prove ben-

---

[3]Current work on personal relevance stems from previous work in social psychology on ego involvement conducted within the context of social judgment theory (Sherif and Sherif 1967; for a review see Johnson and Eagly 1989) and work within consumer psychology on involvement stemming from Krugman's (1965) hierarchy of effects model. These frameworks made different predictions about the effects of "involvement," and neither the predictions nor the underlying rationale for them have received consistent empirical support (see Barry 1987). Many specific definitions and models of "involvement" have appeared in the literature since these early studies. Some definitions and models of involvement are quite narrow, but some would encompass nearly every factor that affected any type of information processing activity (cf. Greenwald and Leavitt 1984). In this chapter, we talk about specific variables (e.g., personal relevance, knowledge, etc.) that affect a person's motivation or ability to process the merits of an attitude object, rather than dwell on the many definitions and meanings of the "involvement" concept.

eficial for persuasion as long as the arguments are strong and tedium is not induced (Batra and Ray 1986; Cacioppo and Petty 1989; Cox and Cox 1988). Distraction, however, reduces argument elaboration, which can be beneficial when the message would have been easily counterargued (Petty, Wells, and Brock 1976). People are also generally better able to process messages that appear in print than those that are controlled externally (e.g., radio and TV; Chaiken and Eagly 1976; Wright 1980). On the other hand, placing time pressures on processing increases reliance on simple cues (e.g., Kruglanski and Freund 1983).

Some variables, such as distraction, affect ability in a relatively objective manner, but others bias one's ability. For example, since people tend to have more information in favor of their attitudes than against them, increasing knowledge tends to make them more able to counterargue opposing communications and bolster congruent ones (e.g., Lord, Lepper, and Ross 1979). Knowledge is only effective, however, to the extent that it is accessible. For example, in one study, children's prior knowledge about the misleading aspects of commercials helped them resist an advertisement only when the knowledge was primed with a test shortly before the ad presentation (Brucks, Armstrong, and Goldberg 1988). When attitude consistent knowledge is low or inaccessible, people are less able to counterargue (e.g., Burke, DeSarbo, Oliver, and Robertson 1988) and more reliant on simple cues (cf. Alba and Hutchinson 1987). For example, in one study, increasing the number of claims about a bicycle increased persuasion for people who had little knowledge about bikes even though the claims were weak. For bicycle experts, however, the message became less effective as more weak claims were added (Alba and Marmorstein 1987; see also, Wood, Kallgren, and Priesler 1985; Wood and Kallgren 1988).

Finally, it is important to note that in most communication settings, a confluence of factors determines the nature of information processing rather than one variable acting in isolation. When multiple variables are involved, interaction effects are possible. For example,

rhetorical questions tend to increase thinking when motivation would normally be low, but are distracting when motivation is high (Munch and Swasy 1988; Petty, Cacioppo, and Heesacker 1981; Swasy and Munch 1985). The next decade is likely to see more research on the interacting effects of variables affecting motivation and ability to process ads.

Multiple Roles for Variables

As noted above, the ELM holds that variables can serve in one of several distinct capacities in persuasion situations: The variable can serve as an argument, it can serve as a cue, or it can affect the extent or nature of information processing. One of the powerful, albeit complicating, features of the ELM is that any one variable can serve in multiple roles, though in different situations. For example, consider the question of how the "price" of a product is related to product evaluations (e.g., Leavitt 1954; Rao and Monroe 1988). Imagine that people are first exposed to ads for a $10 widget, and then a $50 widget. Each ad contains four different arguments that are equally strong. Which widget will be rated as better, and why? Person A who is completely unfamiliar with widgets rates the $50 widget as superior by employing the rule of thumb, "the more it costs, the better it must be." Person B, who is a widget expert, also rates the $50 widget as better, but this judgment is based on the expert's knowledge that the price of widgets is carefully controlled by the government to reflect quality. Person C, who is only moderately familiar with widgets, rates the $50 widget as better because the price information caused him to think about the other arguments in the ad. Since Person C knew that most widgets sell for $8 to $12, Person C was very curious about the $50 widget, processed the strong arguments carefully, and became convinced. In short, for Person A, price served as a peripheral cue; for Person B it served as a product-relevant argument; and for Person C it served as a motivator of thought.

The fact that variables can have the same impact on judgments via different processes makes it essential that the conditions under which each process operates are identified. Research on this problem is just beginning, but existing literature already suggests the conditions under which source factors can serve in each of the three roles postulated by the ELM. In one study, for instance, people who were high and low in their need for cognition (Cacioppo and Petty 1982b) were exposed to an advertisement for an electric typewriter featuring either attractive or unattractive endorsers (Haugtvedt et al. 1988). Subjects who were low in need for cognition were influenced by the simple cue of attractiveness, but people who characteristically enjoyed thinking were not. In this study, the attractiveness of the endorsers was completely tangential to the merits of the attitude object — a typewriter.

For other objects, however, source attractiveness could provide information that is central to an evaluation of merit. In these situations, source attractiveness should be an important determinant of attitudes when the elaboration likelihood is high. In a study relevant to this notion, subjects were exposed to an advertisement for a new shampoo product that featured either two attractive or two unattractive endorsers (Petty and Cacioppo 1980). In addition, the motivation of subjects to process the ad was manipulated. Unlike the previously discussed typewriter study, in this research the attractiveness of the endorsers *is* potentially relevant to determining the merits of the product (e.g., "the shampoo will make my hair look like that of the endorsers"), and source attractiveness had an impact on attitudes toward the shampoo under high-relevance as well as under low-relevance conditions. This is the expected result if attractiveness served as a pertinent product argument when the elaboration likelihood was high, but served as a peripheral cue when elaboration likelihood was low (cf. Kahle and Homer 1985).

Finally, source attractiveness should also be capable of affecting the extent of argument processing. In one study, for example, subjects evaluated strong or weak essays attributed to attractive or unattractive sources (Puckett,

Petty, Cacioppo, and Fisher 1983). In this study, the relevance of the message was neither particularly high nor low, and the major finding was that the arguments were more carefully processed when they were associated with the attractive sources.

In sum, these studies have shown that under conditions of relatively low elaboration likelihood, increased source attractiveness, if it has any impact at all, serves as a peripheral cue, enhancing attitudes regardless of whether a message contains strong or weak arguments. Under conditions of relatively high elaboration likelihood, source attractiveness is less important as a peripheral cue, and may serve as a persuasive argument if it provides information central to the merits of the attitude object. Finally, under conditions of moderate elaboration likelihood, source attractiveness affects the extent of argument elaboration.

When the elaboration likelihood is high (e.g., having high personal relevance, high knowledge, a simple message in print, having no distractions, etc.), people typically know what they want, and are able to evaluate the merits of the arguments presented, and they do so. Simple peripheral cues have relatively little impact on these evaluations. However, when the elaboration likelihood is low, people know what they do not want or they are not able to evaluate the merits of the arguments presented, or they do not even consider exerting effort to process the message. Thus, if any evaluation is formed, it is likely to be the result of relatively simple associations or inferences. When the elaboration likelihood is moderate (e.g., uncertain personal relevance, moderate knowledge, moderate complexity, etc.), however, people may be unsure as to whether the message warrants or needs scrutiny, and as to whether or not they are capable of providing this analysis. In these situations, they may examine the persuasion context for indications (e.g., is the source credible?) as to whether or not they should attempt to process the message.

A number of studies have examined the impact of variables at two levels of elaboration likelihood (high and low), and these studies have provided evidence for the trade-off between argument processing and cue effects postulated by the ELM (see review by Petty and Cacioppo 1986a). For example, Sanbonmatsu and Kardes (1988) exposed subjects to ads immediately after exercise (low elaboration likelihood) or after being allowed to rest (high elaboration likelihood). Immediately after exercise, attitudes were influenced by peripheral cues in the ad (endorsement by a celebrity), but not by the quality of the claims. After resting, however, attitudes were affected by the quality of the claims, but not by the peripheral cues.

Two experiments have examined the effects of a variable across three distinct levels of elaboration likelihood (Moore, Hausknecht, and Thamodaran 1986; Pechmann and Estaban 1990) and have provided support for the ELM predictions outlined above (see Petty, Kasmer, Haugtvedt, and Cacioppo 1987). For example, Moore et al. (Experiment 3) found that when a message was presented at a very rapid pace so that it was quite difficult to process, people were greatly influenced by the expertise of the product endorser, but the quality of the arguments for the product had little effect. When the message was presented at a normal pace and was quite easy to process, the quality of arguments in the ad made a difference, but the expertise of the endorser was reduced in importance compared with the fast-message presentation. Finally, when the message was presented at a moderately fast pace and processing was possible but challenging, the expertise of the endorser determined how much processing occurred — the expert source induced more thinking than the nonexpert source.[4]

Now that we have outlined the ELM, we will use it as an organizing framework for the remainder of the chapter.

---

[4]Although a number of studies have provided support for the basic postulates of the ELM, more work is needed on the specific variables that serve as arguments, cues, and determinants of thought in the various consumer behavior contexts (cf. Bitner and Obermiller 1985).

CENTRAL ROUTE APPROACHES TO PERSUASION

Message Learning Approach

One of the most influential programs of research on attitude change was that undertaken by Carl Hovland and his colleagues at Yale University in the years following World War II (Hovland 1957; Hovland, Janis, and Kelley 1953; Hovland and Janis 1959). The Yale group studied how source, message, recipient, and channel factors affected the comprehension, acceptance, and retention of the arguments in a persuasive communication. Although no formal theory tied together the many experiments conducted by this group, they often attempted to explain the results obtained in terms of general learning principles. As McGuire (1968) explained, the use of the message learning approach involves "predicting how any independent variable in the communication situation (such as order of presentation, source credibility, . . . etc.) will be related to attitude change by analyzing that variable's likely impact on learning the message contents" (p. 179). Also, the model assumed that the better the initial learning of the message, the longer the attitude change induced by it would persist.

Argument Recall and Persuasion. Unfortunately, relatively little evidence was produced that either initial persuasion or its persistence was dependent upon a person's ability to learn and remember the arguments in the persuasive communication (for reviews see Cook and Flay 1978; McGuire 1969). There are several reasons for this. First, mere learning and recall of arguments should not be positively related to persuasion if a person finds the arguments to be weak or specious. As McGuire (1968) postulated, persuasion should depend upon "yielding" to the message in addition to "receiving" it. Current memory theorists deal with this issue by proposing that attitudes are based on the evaluative implications of the arguments recalled (e.g., Kardes 1986; Keller 1987; Lynch, Marmorstein, and Weigold 1988). That is, the same piece of information recalled might be positively viewed by one person, but negatively viewed by another. When recalled information is weighted by a person's idiosyncratic evaluations of it, attitude-recall relationships can be increased (e.g., Chattopadhyay and Alba 1988).

Second, argument learning and recall might not relate to persuasion even if perceptions of argument quality were controlled because a person might not find all of the arguments equally relevant for assessing the validity of the message, or equally diagnostic in allowing a comparison among alternatives (Feldman and Lynch 1988). If a person is processing a message as it is received and is evaluating the information it contains, it is likely that an attitude will emerge following the communication. To the extent that both relevant and irrelevant arguments are equally accessible immediately following message exposure, but considering that only relevant arguments enter into the attitude, an inconsistency between recall and persuasion could occur. Even if memory for relevant over irrelevant arguments increased with time, a low correlation between atttitudes and message recall could still occur at a delayed testing if some determinants of which arguments are recalled (such as novelty), are independent of the determinants of which arguments are impactful (e.g., relevance).

On the other hand, if a person is not forming an attitude as a message is received, but must express an opinion at a later point in time, then the judgment should be dependent on the implications of the information that can be recalled if that information is perceived relevant at the time of judgment. Researchers who have distinguished between attitudes formed during information exposure (spontaneous or on-line judgments) and attitudes formed subsequent to message exposure, have shown that the latter type of judgment has a greater relationship to the information recalled (Bargh and Thein 1985; Hastie and Park 1986; Lichtenstein and Srull 1985; Loken and Hoverstad, 1985). One way to increase the likelihood that product in-

formation from an advertisement will be recalled at the time of purchase is to place retrieval cues on the product package (Keller 1987).

In persuasion situations, factors that increase a person's motivation (e.g., personal relevance) and ability (e.g., prior knowledge) to process information at the time of ad exposure should increase the likelihood of "on-line" judgments, and thereby attenuate the correlation between attitudes and arguments recalled from the message. For example, one study found that the product attitudes of individuals low in need for cognition were related to the number of arguments from an advertisement that could be recalled, but the attitudes of individuals high in need for cognition were unrelated to message recall (Haugtvedt, Petty, and Cacioppo 1990).[5] Conversely, the research we have outlined above suggests some circumstances in which message recall should be correlated with attitudes. Such correlation should occur when (1) the elaboration likelihood at the time of message exposure is low, so that attitudes are not formed on-line, (2) an unexpected judgment is required following message exposure, and (3) no peripheral cues are available or attended to by the recipient that yield an attitude which can be accessed or formed at the time of judgment. Although these conditions may seem restrictive and are not typical of those created in the laboratory, they are probably more common in consumer contexts where people may not form an attitude at the time of ad exposure, but rather attempt to piece together an opinion at the time of product choice.[6]

---

[5]Attitudes formed under high-elaboration conditions are more accessible than attitudes formed under low-elaboration conditions (Rennier 1988). This finding is consistent with the view that high-elaboration conditions are more likely to produce spontaneous (one line) attitude formation than low-elaboration conditions (Fazio 1989).

[6]Some theorists have attributed the low attitude-recall link to poor measurement of message recall (e.g., Eagly and Chaiken 1984). Improved measurement is desirable and should improve the overall magnitude of the correlations observed, but, more important, even perfect measurement techniques should not increase the number of *situations* in which the recall-persuasion relation holds.

Augmenting and Discounting Cues. Another important reason why message recall may be unrelated to persuasion is that, as we noted in our discussion of the ELM, factors other than message arguments have a role in producing attitude change. The Yale group explicitly acknowledged the potential impact of "peripheral cues" in their work on the "sleeper effect." A sleeper effect is said to occur when a message that is accompanied initially by a negative cue (e.g., a low credible source) increases in effectiveness over time (see Cook, Gruder, Hennigan, and Flay 1979; Pratkanis, Greenwald, Leippe, and Baumgardner 1988). To account for this effect, Kelman and Hovland (1953) proposed that in addition to message arguments, various cues could have an impact on attitude change. These cues were thought to add to the effects of the persuasive message. Thus, if a message alone would produce 3 units of change, the addition of an augmenting cue (e.g., a trustworthy source) might add an additional 3 units of change. Similarly, the addition of a discounting cue might produce an effect of −3, or when it is added to the +3 of the message, the net result is that no (zero) initial change would occur.

Of considerable importance, the cue and message were viewed as *independent* and were postulated to have different decay functions. Given this formulation, Cook et al. (1979) proposed that a sleeper effect would be produced if a person were exposed to a message with a discounting cue and the following conditions were met: (1) the message alone had a strong positive impact, (2) the discounting cue was sufficiently negative to suppress the positive impact of the message, and (3) the decay function for cue and arguments was such that the discounting cue was dissociated from the message conclusion more quickly than the conclusion was dissociated from the message arguments. Under these conditions it is possible for the positive residue of the message to have outlasted the negative effect of the cue, leading to increased agreement with the message conclusion over time.

The postulated conditions leading to a sleeper effect are unique and have several implications. In particular, the discounting cue formulation requires that the effects of a low credible source and of strong message arguments operate jointly and additively. Yet, the ELM holds that there is typically a trade-off between the operation of source factors and the impact of message arguments, or an interaction between them. When the elaboration likelihood is high, arguments should be the primary determinant of persuasion, but when the elaboration likelihood is low, source and other cues should dominate. When the elaboration likelihood is moderate, the nature of the source could determine the extent of argument processing.

Interestingly, in the 20 years following the Kelman and Hovland study, so few sleeper effect studies had appeared in the literature that some researchers declared that the effect did not exist (Gillig and Greenwald 1974). One key to producing a sleeper effect is to construct a situation in which both a strong negative cue *and* strong arguments have an initial impact. As noted previously, however, this should be difficult to produce because of the trade-off between the two, or because of an interaction between them (e.g., if the source is initially presented as untrustworthy, people may choose to ignore the message, thereby overturning one of the critical conditions for the effect). A clever solution to this dilemma is to have subjects process the message so that the strength of the arguments is realized, and *following this* present a discounting cue that causes subjects to doubt the validity of the message. This is the procedure employed in the successful sleeper effect studies by Kelman and Hovland (1953), Cook et al. (1979), and Mazursky and Schul (1988). In a compelling series of studies, Pratkanis and colleagues (1988) showed that presenting the discounting cue after the message may be critical for obtaining a reliable sleeper effect.[7]

In sum, after a period in which persuasion theorists generally dismissed recall and learning processes from the list of persuasion mediators,

---

[7]In some research it is difficult to determine if a true sleeper effect was obtained or whether the increase in persuasion over time is a result of decay of "boomerang" (e.g., Hannah and Sternthal 1984).

current research has documented conclusively that there is a specific role for a memory-based approach. In addition to work on the conditions under which argument recall will be related to attitudes, current work on learning and memory processes in persuasion is focussing on questions such as (1) the situational and contextual determinants of what information will be recalled (e.g., Kisielius and Sternthal 1984, 1986; MacKenzie 1986; Schul and Burnstein 1983; Sherer and Rogers 1984; Weldon and Malpass 1981), (2) how arguments are represented in memory (e.g., Schmidt and Sherman 1984); and (3) individual differences in message recall (e.g., Cacioppo, Petty, and Morris 1983; Reardon and Rosen 1984).

Self-Persuasion Approaches

Cognitive Response Approach. The cognitive response approach was developed as an explicit attempt to salvage a learning view of persuasion when it had been challenged by numerous findings of low attitude recall correlations. Greenwald (1968) proposed that it was not the specific arguments in a message which were paired with the message conclusion in memory, as the Yale group had suggested, but rather, that it was a person's idiosyncratic *cognitive responses* or reactions to the message arguments which were paired with the conclusion and responsible for persuasion (see also, Brock 1967). To the extent that a person's thoughts in response to the message were favorable, persuasion would result, but to the extent that they were unfavorable (e.g., counterarguments), resistance or even a boomerang effect was likely (Petty, Ostrom, and Brock 1981). Greewald further proposed that persistence of persuasion depended upon the decay function for cognitive responses rather than decay of message arguments per se. (See Kisielus and Sternthal's (1986) "availability-valence hypothesis" for a similar notion.)

The cognitive response approach has generated a considerable body of evidence consistent with the view that in certain situations people spontaneously produce cognitive responses during message presentation, and that these thoughts are good predictors of postmessage

attitudes and beliefs (e.g., Hastak and Olson 1989; see reviews by Eagly and Chaiken 1984; Perloff and Brock 1980; Petty and Cacioppo 1986a). In a typical study, message recipients list or verbally report their thoughts either during or after the message and it is found that (1) physiological activity indicative of information processing (e.g., speech EMG) is elevated when cognitive responding is presumed to occur; (2) thought profiles show the same pattern as the attitude measure in response to some manipulation (e.g., the manipulation produces increased persuasion and increased favorable thoughts and/or decreased unfavorable thoughts); (3) the polarity of these thoughts (e.g., positive minus negative thoughts) is a good predictor of the postmessage attitude, and (4) when the effects of some manipulation on thoughts is removed, then the effect of the manipulation on attitudes is removed, but the reverse does not occur (for reviews see Cacioppo & Petty 1981a, 1981b; Wright 1980).

In addition to simply categorizing thoughts as to whether or not they are favorable toward the advocacy, other coding procedures have been developed (e.g., recipient-generated or externally originated thoughts, as in Greenwald 1968; cognitive versus affective reactions, as in Batra and Ray 1985; source versus message thoughts, as in Chaiken 1980; Wright 1980; self-oriented or non-self thoughts, as in Shavitt and Brock 1986; and others). The ELM holds that it is important to distinguish between cognitive responses that are based on argument scrutiny (e.g., counterarguments) and cognitive responses that are based on peripheral cues (e.g., source derogations). The former category of thoughts is a better predictor of attitudes when the elaboration likelihood is high, but the latter is more predictive when the elaboration likelihood is low (e.g., Wright 1974; Chaiken 1980; Petty and Cacioppo 1979b, 1984a).

Current work on cognitive responses to advertising continues to explore the extent to which issue-relevant elaboration is determined by motivational and ability factors (e.g., Celsi and Olson 1988; Sujan and Dekleva 1987), the role of cognitive responses as mediators of belief structure and brand attitudes (e.g., Hastak and

Olson 1989), and the specific cognitive responses that are most predictive of attitudes. For example, Chattopadhyay and Alba (1988) compared the predictive utility of cognitive responses to ads that were "single fact interpretations" (50 mpg translated into "good gas mileage") with "abstractions" (50 mpg translated into "economical"). They found that the latter accounted for more variance in attitudes after traditional assessments of support and counterargumentation were taken out.

Role-playing Research. Just as a person's thoughts in response to a persuasive message can determine the extent and direction of attitude change, so too can a person's thoughts in the *absence* of any explicit external message. The powerful and persisting effect of completely self-generated messages was shown in early research on "role-playing" (e.g., Janis and King 1954; Watts 1967, see also Higgins and McCann 1984). In this research, people were typically asked to generate messages on certain topics (e.g., the dangers of smoking), and the subsequent attitudes of these people were compared with those in a control group who had either passively listened to the communication or who had received no message. A consistent result was that active generation of a message was a successful strategy for producing attitude change, and these changes persisted longer than changes based on passive exposure to a communication (e.g., Elms 1966; see also Huesmann, Eron, Klein, Brice, and Fischer 1983). In addition, some research showed that people found their own arguments to be more original than those generated by others, and self-generated arguments were also more memorable (Greenwald and Albert 1968; Slamecka and Graf 1978).

Generating Explanations and Imagining Events. In another more recent stream of experiments, the effects of asking people to generate explanations for some proposition or to imagine the occurrence of some event have been examined. For example, in one study, students were presented with detailed case histories that led them to explain why high (or low) riskiness was associated with being a good fire-

man (Anderson, Lepper, and Ross 1980). Those led to think about why high riskiness predicted success in firefighting continued to believe in this relationship, whereas those led to think about the opposite continued to believe in it even after it became clear that the case histories upon which the explanations were based were completely false.

Similarly, people who are asked to imagine hypothetical events (e.g., that Ohio State will beat UCLA in the Rose Bowl) come to believe that these events have a higher likelihood of occurring (e.g., Sherman, Cialdini, Schwartzman, and Reynolds 1985). Consistent with the earlier work on "role-playing," the work on generating explanations and imagining events has shown consistently that self-generation is a powerful way to change beliefs, and that these beliefs are remarkably impervious to change (see also, Lepper, Ross, and Lau 1986; Sherman, Zehner, Johnson, and Hirt 1983).

Research on Mere Thought. Finally, in an extensive series of studies, Tesser (1978) and his colleagues have examined the effects of merely asking someone to think about an issue, object, or person. For example, in one early study Sadler and Tesser (1973) introduced subjects to a likable or dislikable partner (via a tape recording). Some of the subjects were instructed to think about the partner, whereas others were distracted from doing so. The thinking manipulation polarized judgments of the partner. Specifically, enhanced thinking was associated with more favorable evaluations of the likable partner, but less favorable ratings of the dislikable partner.

Current research indicates that both moderation and polarization may result from mere thought. Specifically, the polarization effect requires that subjects have a well-integrated schema to guide processing and that they are motivated to employ this issue-relevant knowledge (Chaiken and Yates 1985; Tesser and Leone 1977). In the absence of these conditions, such as when motivation to think is low or when the issue-relevant information in memory represents independent dimensions of knowledge rather than a highly interconnected (correlated) system of beliefs, mere thought can lead to attitude moderation (e.g., Judd and Lusk 1984; Linville 1982; Millar and Tesser 1986b).

In sum, the cognitive response approach and research on self-generated attitude and belief change has demonstrated quite conclusively that active thought processes often accompany attitude change, and that self-generated change can be quite enduring. The cognitive response approach in particular was critical in identifying variables that both increase and decrease the likelihood of thinking when a person is confronted by a persuasive message.

Expectancy-Value Approach

The message learning approach and the self-persuasion approach focus on the information that is responsible for persuasion. The former approach highlights the information provided to the message recipient by the source of the communication, whereas the latter approach emphasizes the information and inferences that recipients generate either on their own, or in response to the externally provided information. Neither approach, however, has much to say about the particular features of the information that are critical for influencing attitudes.

Expectancy-value theorists analyze attitudes by focussing on the extent to which people expect the attitude issue to be related to important values or produce positive and negative consequences (e.g., Peak 1955; Rosenberg 1956; see reviews by Bagozzi 1984, 1985). In one influential expectancy-value model, Fishbein and Ajzen (1975) and Ajzen and Fishbein (1980) hold that the attributes (or consequences) associated with an attitude object are evaluated along two dimensions. First, a person considers the *likelihood* that an attribute or consequence is associated with the object, and, second, the person considers the *desirability* of that attribute or consequence. Although some questions have been raised about the necessity of one or the other of these components, a monumental body of research supports the idea that attitudes toward objects, issues, and people are more favorable the more that likely desirable conse-

quences (or attributes) and unlikely undesirable consequences are associated with them (for reviews see Ajzen and Fishbein 1980; Fishbein 1980; Fishbein and Ajzen 1975; Pieters 1988; Wilkie and Pessimier 1973).

The major implication of this theory for attitude change is that a persuasive message will be effective to the extent that it produces a change in either the likelihood or the desirability component of the attribute (cf. Areni and Lutz 1988). For example, consider a person who prior to message exposure believes that Detergent X has a 0.7 chance of getting his clothes clean (a consequence valued at +8 on a 10-point scale). The message will produce a more positive attitude toward Detergent X to the extent that either the likelihood is increased beyond 0.7, or the value of clean clothes is increased beyond +8. Given the wide applicability of Fishbein and Ajzen's approach and the extensive number of studies documenting the link between attitudes and the likelihood and desirability components of beliefs, it is perhaps surprising that relatively little work on attitude *change* has been guided explicitly by this framework. Nevertheless, existing research supports the view that advertisements may influence attitudes by changing either the evaluation or the likelihood component of beliefs (e.g., Lutz 1975; MacKenzie 1986). Also, as might be expected given the thoughtful processing assumed by this approach, research indicates that the expectancy-value framework may account for less variance in attitudes when topic-relevant knowledge is low (e.g., Lutz 1977; Olson, Toy, and Dover 1978).

Functional Approaches

In their theory of reasoned action, Fishbein and Ajzen speculate that five to seven attributes or consequences are critical in determining a person's overall attitude. It is not clear, however, which particular attributes will be the most important. Functional theories of persuasion focus on the specific needs or functions that attitudes serve for a person and are therefore relevant for understanding the underlying dimensions of the attitude that are necessary to change (see Lutz 1981). Katz (1960) and others (e.g., Smith, Bruner, and White 1956) have distinguished various functions that attitudes might serve for a person. For example, some attitudes protect people from threatening truths about themselves or serve to enhance their own self-image ("ego-defensive function"). Other attitudes serve to give expression to important values ("value-expressive function") or to help people understand the world around them ("knowledge function"). Still other attitudes may be formed in order to gain explicit rewards and/or to avoid punishments ("utilitarian function").

After an extended period of neglect, persuasion researchers are beginning to show renewed interest in functional theories. Researchers initially lost interest in these theories because it was not possible to assess what specific functions attitudes held for people. At present, several solutions to this problem have been suggested. One solution is to propose that there are categories of people for whom a wide variety of attitudes serve the same function (e.g., Prentice 1987). For example, Snyder and DeBono (1985) hypothesized that the self-monitoring scale (Snyder 1974) could be used to differentiate the functional basis of attitudes for different groups of people. According to Snyder (1979), people high in "self-monitoring" typically strive to be the type of person called for by each unique situation, whereas the behavior of people low in self-monitoring is guided more by their own internal dispositions.

Snyder and DeBono hypothesized that the attitudes of low self-monitors would serve primarily a "value-expressive function," whereas the attitudes of high self-monitors would serve primarily a "social adjustive function" (e.g., adopting attitudes that provide rewards from valued peers). Consistent with this reasoning, in several studies high self-monitors were found to be more susceptible to arguments addressing social adjustment concerns (e.g., the image associated with a consumer product), whereas low self-monitors were more susceptible to arguments addressing value-expressive concerns (e.g., the quality of a consumer product; Snyder and DeBono 1987, 1989; see also De-

Bono 1987). DeBono and Harnish (1988) have also employed a functional analysis to predict which sources would affect information processing for high and low self-monitors. Specifically, they proposed and found evidence for the view that an attractive source would engender more interest and enhance message processing for the image-oriented high self-monitors, but that an expert source would enhance processing for the more value-expressive low self-monitors.

An alternative to the personality approach to functional theory is to propose that many issues and objects serve a common function for a wide variety of people (e.g., Shavitt, 1989). For example, attitudes toward air-conditioners probably serve a utilitarian function for most people and thus would be more susceptible to utilitarian rather than ego-defensive arguments. Herek (1987), in a third approach, has employed the thought-listing procedure to analyze on an individual level the functional bases of attitudes.

Despite the promising new directions in functional theory, some pitfalls remain. The Herek (1987) procedure allows functions to be assessed post hoc, which is useful for *understanding* the basis of individuals' attitudes and designing individual persuasion treatments, but is less amenable to a mass communication context unless the functional basis of an attitude is widespread. The Shavitt (1989) proposition that functions are inherent in attitude objects seems applicable to only a limited domain of attitude entities. The personality strategy of Snyder and DeBono (1989) could be quite useful if evidence shows that other personality variables are linked consistently to particular functions (e.g., for high authoritarians, attitudes serve an ego-defensive function; Snyder and DeBono 1989).

Dissonance Theory

Just as functional theories hold that attitudes serve important needs for individuals, dissonance theory holds that attitudes may often be in the service of maintaining a need for *consistency* among the elements in a cognitive system (Festinger 1957). In Festinger's original formulation of dissonance theory, two elements in a cognitive system (e.g., a belief and an attitude; an attitude and a behavior) were said to be *consonant* if one followed from the other (e.g., I bought a Chevrolet; it was rated highly in *Consumer Reports*), and *dissonant* if one implied the opposite of the other (e.g., I bought a Chevrolet; it was rated poorly). Of course, two elements could also be *irrelevant* to each other (I bought a Chevrolet; the sky is blue). Festinger proposed that the psychological state of dissonance was aversive and that people would be motivated to reduce it. One of the more interesting dissonance situations occurs when a person's behavior is in conflict with his or her attitudes or beliefs because behavior is usually difficult to undo. According to the theory, however, dissonance may be reduced by bringing beliefs and attitudes into line with the behavior.

Although the most studied dissonance paradigm involves the "forced compliance" situation in which people are induced to engage in behavior that is counter to their initial attitudes and beliefs (e.g., Festinger and Carlsmith 1959), the dissonance paradigm most relevant to consumer attitudes involves the consequences of choice among alternatives (Petty and Cacioppo 1984b). As a result of virtually any decision, a person must accept the negative features and consequences of the chosen alternative, and must forgo the positive features and consequences of the rejected alternative. Considerable research supports the proposition that as a result of a choice among alternatives, people will come to view the selected alternative as more desirable, and/or view the rejected alternative as less attractive (Wicklund and Brehm 1976).

For example, in one early study, Brehm (1956) told female students that various manufacturers were interested in determining consumer reactions to certain products. The women rated the desirability of a wide variety of products (e.g., a stopwatch, a portable radio), and then were given a choice of two products to take home with them in payment for their participation. In the control condition, the women were given a product by the investigator and thus made no decision on their own. After the

selection or gift of a product, the women read some reports about some of the products and then were asked to rate them again. As expected by dissonance theory, the women who were responsible for their own choices came to overvalue the chosen product and undervalue the rejected product. The women in the control group did not show a reevaluation of the product that they had been given. Similar results have been obtained in other research on evaluations of products (e.g., Holloway 1967; LoScuito and Perloff 1967; Sheth 1970).

Following the early work on choice, current research has shown that the spreading apart of chosen and rejected alternatives is greatest when (1) the two alternatives are close in their rated desirability but have dissimilar features (Wicklund and Brehm 1976), (2) the choice is irreversible (Brehm and Cohen 1962), (3) there is sufficient time to think about the choice (Frey, Kumpf, Irle and Gneich 1984), and (4) the expected consequences of the choice are imminent (Gerard and White 1983).

Although the work on choice among alternatives has produced a reasonably coherent pattern of results, other aspects of dissonance theory were more controversial (e.g., Chapanis and Chapanis 1964), and several competing formulations were proposed (e.g., Bem 1967). Although it is now clear that many of the behaviors described by Festinger induce in people an "unpleasant tension," (see Fazio and Cooper 1983), current research has begun to focus more on understanding the precise cause of that tension. For example, some have questioned Festinger's view that *inconsistency* per se produces tension in many people. Rather, some argue that people must believe that by their behavior they have freely chosen to bring about some foreseeable negative consequence (e.g., Cooper and Fazio 1984; Scher and Cooper 1989), or that the inconsistency involves a critical aspect of oneself or a threat to one's positive self-concept (e.g., Aronson 1968; Greenwald and Ronis 1978; Steele 1988). Of course, bringing about negative consequences is inconsistent with most peoples' views of themselves as rational, caring individuals. Festinger originally hypothesized that inconsistency among personally important elements would induce more dissonance than inconsistency among more trivial elements. Thus, some have speculated that Festinger was correct in asserting that inconsistency per se was dissonance arousing, but that many (e.g., non–self-relevant) inconsistencies produce trivial (undetectable) amounts of dissonance (e.g., Berkowitz and Devine 1989).

Although dissonance theory continues to generate interest in social psychology (Cooper and Fazio 1989), it does not presently generate much research on consumer behavior. Nevertheless, it is now quite clear that dissonance can lead to increased cognitive activity designed to reduce a cognitive conflict. Dissonance may result in a reanalysis of the reasons why a person engaged in a certain behavior or made a certain choice, and it may cause a person to rethink the merits of an attitude object. The end result of this reassessment can be a change in attitude toward the object.[8]

PERIPHERAL ROUTE APPROACHES

Each of the central route approaches described previously assumed that attitude change resulted from people actively considering the merits of some position. People were proposed to be learning and elaborating arguments, or to be self-generating reasons to explain or justify some outcome or behavior. In some theories the processing appeared to be relatively objective (e.g., the message learning model),

---

[8]In contrast to dissonance theory, "balance theory" (Heider 1958) holds that inconsistency pressures may sometimes lead to attitude change by a simple inference process rather than because of a reanalysis of the merits of the attitude object. In particular, the theory holds that balance occurs when people agree with people they like, or disagree with people that they dislike. This theory accounts for why a person would come to like a product more after it is endorsed by a favorite sports star. The theory holds that imbalance (e.g., disagreeing with someone you like) leads to attitude change toward the product (or the product endorser) in the direction of balance (see Insko 1981, 1984 for an extended discussion). A related formulation, congruity theory, holds that attitudes toward *both* source and object change to restore "congruity" (Osgood and Tannenbaum 1955).

whereas in others the processing was clearly biased (e.g., the theory of cognitive dissonance), but in each case, learning, analyzing, and/or generating reasons to hold a position were central to the theory. The class of theories that we discuss next do not share this assumption. Instead, these theories suggest that people often prefer to conserve their cognitive resources. We begin with theories that emphasize inference and heuristic processes in persuasion, and we conclude with theories that emphasize the association of affect with attitude objects.

Inference Approaches

Attribution Theory. The 1970s brought an explosion of interest within psychology in examining how people came to understand the causes of their own and others' behavior. The gist of this attributional approach was that people made inferences about the underlying characteristics of themselves and others from the behaviors that they observed and the situational constraints imposed on these behaviors (e.g., Jones and Davis 1965; Kelley 1967).

In a provocative paper, Bem (1965) suggested that people sometimes have no special knowledge of their own internal states and simply infer their attitudes in a manner similar to that by which they infer the attitudes of others. In his *self-perception theory,* Bem reasoned that just as people would assume that the behavior of others and the context in which it occurs provides information about the presumed attitudes of these people, so, too, would a person's own behavior provide information about the person's own attitude (Bem 1972).

The *overjustification effect* is one phenomenon that is explained nicely by Bem's formulation. This effect occurs when a person is provided with more than sufficient reward for engaging in an action that is already highly regarded (e.g., Lepper, Greene, and Nisbett 1973). To the extent that the person comes to attribute the action to the external reward rather than to the intrinsic enjoyment of the behavior, attitudes toward the behavior will become less favorable (Deci 1975; cf. Crano, Gorenflo, and Shakelford 1988). Thus, if people are provided with continuous extrinsic rewards for using a product that they already like, they may come to devalue the product when the external rewards stop. They may devalue the product to the extent that they view their product-relevant behavior as caused by the rewards rather than by the true merits of the product. Consistent with this reasoning, Scott and Yalch (1978) found that external rewards for trying a new product could undermine liking for it.

According to the ELM, people should be more likely to rely on this relatively simple inference process when well-defined attitudes are not very accessible, or the elaboration likelihood is low (see Tybout and Scott 1983). In a study relevant to this idea, Wood (1982) examined the power of self-perception processes for people who had relatively high versus low knowledge and experience with the issue of environmental preservation. Subjects committed themselves to deliver a speech that was consistent with their attitudes after learning that they would receive either $5 or nothing for the task. Following this, they expressed their opinions on the issue. The major result was that for subjects with low knowledge and experience, the $5 incentive undermined their positive attitudes (e.g., "I must have made the proenvironmental statements for the money"), but for high-knowledge subjects, the incentive had no effect (see also Chaiken and Baldwin 1981).

Given the relatively simple inference on which attitudes are based according to self-perception theory, one would expect attitudes formed by these means to have characteristics more similar to peripheral than central route attitudes. Consistent with this notion, Taylor (1975) found that when attitudes were formed by a self-perception process, the attitudes were not predictive of subsequent behavior.

However, some research has shown that attitudes formed on the basis of a review of past behavior can have characteristics similar to attitudes formed via the central route (e.g., Fazio, Herr, and Olney 1984; Kiesler and Sakamura 1966; Zanna, Olson, and Fazio 1981). The ELM holds that the critical issue for examining the consequences of attitude change is not whether the change is based on behavioral in-

formation or some other type of information (e.g., affective). According to the ELM, the crucial factor concerns how the behavioral (or other) information is processed. For example, consider two people who initially rate Detergent X as +3, but then, after being reminded that they washed their clothes with this detergent last week, report attitudes of +4. What are the likely consequences of the attitude change induced by this behavioral information? The ELM holds that in order to answer this it is important to distinguish the diligent consideration of issue-relevant behavioral information (e.g., the last time I washed my clothes with Detergent X they came out clean and smelling fresh, therefore I like Detergent X) from the use of behavior as a simple cue (I used Detergent X to wash my clothes, therefore I must like Detergent X). It is the latter type of inference that is typical of self-perception. Whenever people are asked to reflect upon their behavior, it is possible that many issue-relevant thoughts and feelings that are central to the merits of the issue or object under consideration will be invoked and involved in attitude change. If so, the change produced will not be the result of the relatively simple self-perception inference.

Finally, we note that the attribution approach has also been useful in understanding how people make inferences about relatively simple cues. For example, Eagly, Chaiken, and Wood (1981) have argued that people often approach a persuasion situation with some expectation regarding the communicator's position. This expectation is formed from premessage cues regarding the communicator's traits and situational pressures. For example, a bank president might be expected to advocate opening a savings account in his or her bank. If the expectation is confirmed by the communicator's presentation, little persuasion will occur if the recipient attributes the message to the traits and pressures that initially generated the expectation. However, when the premessage expectation is disconfirmed, persuasion will be increased if the disconfirmation makes the speaker appear more credible (e.g., Eagly, Wood, and Chaiken 1978; Smith and Hunt 1978). Similarly, when the external incentives (e.g., money) for a celebrity product endorsement are made salient, the endorsement is less effective than when an external attribution is not possible (for a review, see Folkes 1988). It is important to note that the attributional framework holds that attitude change may occur without the person evaluating the actual merits of the object. Instead, an inference may be made about why a communicator took a particular stance, and the nature of this inference determines the effectiveness of the message.[9]

The Heuristic Model. Like the attributional framework developed by Eagly and her colleagues, the heuristic model of persuasion represents an explicit attempt to explain *why* certain peripheral cues, such as source expertise or message length, have the impact that they do. However, the heuristic model, as outlined by Chaiken (1980, 1987) focuses on heuristics retrieved from memory rather than decision rules generated on-line. That is, Chaiken proposes that in contrast to "systematic" (or central route) processing, many source cues, message cues, and other cues are processed by means of simple schemas or cognitive heuristics that people have learned on the basis of past experience and observation. To the extent that various persuasion rules of thumb are available in memory, they may be retrieved to evaluate persuasive communications.

For example, because of either prior personal experience or explicit training, people may come to process the peripheral cue of the number of message arguments by invoking the heuristic "the more arguments in favor of something, the more valid it is" (a length implies strength heuristic; Alba and Marmorstein 1987; Petty and Cacioppo 1984a; Wood et al. 1985). If this heuristic is available in memory and accessed during exposure to a persuasive communication, it should make agreement more likely than if the heuristic was not accessed.

---

[9]Of course, if attributional reasoning was employed in the service of evaluating the specific attributes of a product rather than in providing a simple inference about the communicator, then the resulting attitude would have more in common with central than with peripheral route persuasion.

In four explicit tests of the heuristic model, Chaiken (1987) and her colleagues attempted to make certain decision rules more accessible, and then track their influence on attitudes following message exposure. Although the individual studies produced weak results, the general pattern supported the utility of the heuristic model. For example, in one study subjects in the experimental condition memorized eight phrases relevant to the length implies strength heuristic (e.g., "the more the merrier"), whereas control subjects memorized eight irrelevant phrases. Subsequently, subjects received a message from a speaker who claimed to have either two or ten reasons in support of mandatory comprehensive exams for seniors. Subjects in the study were also divided into those who were high versus low in their need for cognition (Cacioppo and Petty 1982b). The only group to be influenced significantly by the claim of ten reasons (as opposed to two reasons) was composed of low need for cognition subjects who had been primed with the relevant phrases. Cialdini (1987) has analyzed a variety of heuristics that are effective in modifying consumer attitudes and behavior (e.g., "scarcity heuristic"—if there are only a few left, it must be good).

Approaches Emphasizing Affect

The self-perception and heuristic models focus on simple cognitive inferences that can modify attitudes. Next, we discuss theoretical approaches emphasizing the role of affective processes in attitude change.

Classical Conditioning. One of the most direct means of associating "affect" with objects, issues, or people is through classical conditioning. In brief, conditioning occurs when an initially neutral stimulus (the conditioned stimulus, CS) is associated with another stimulus (the unconditioned stimulus, US), which is connected directly or through prior conditioning to some response (the unconditioned response, UR). By pairing the US with the CS, the CS becomes able to elicit a conditioned response (CR) that is similar to the UR. For example, the taste of a banana split elicits a pleasant consummatory response in most people. Over time, the mere sight of a banana split will elicit a similar pleasant response. Then, the sight of a banana split may be paired with the name of a restaurant in an advertisement to produce pleasant feelings toward the restaurant (for relevant reviews, see McSweeney and Bierley 1984; Petty, Cacioppo, and Kasmer 1988; and Gardner 1985).

Considerable psychological research has shown that attitudes can be affected by pairing initially neutral objects with stimuli about which people already feel positive or negative. For example, peoples' evaluations of words (e.g., Staats and Staats 1958), other people (e.g., Griffit 1970), political slogans (e.g., Razran 1940), products (e.g., Gresham and Shimp 1985), and persuasive communications (e.g., Rogers 1983) have been modified by pairing them with such affect producing stimuli as unpleasant odors and temperatures, the onset and cessation of electrical shock, harsh sounds, and elating or depressing films (e.g., Gouaux 1971; Staats, Staats, and Crawford 1962; Zanna, Kiesler, and Pilkonis 1970).

Similar work on consumer behavior has shown that the use of pleasant pictures in ads can produce favorable product attitudes even if the pictures are irrelevant to the product (e.g., Mitchell and Olson 1981), though it is not clear that conditioning is responsible for these effects. Although some studies have been unsuccessful in producing conditioning effects with advertising stimuli (especially when there is only one conditioning trial; e.g., Allen and Madden 1985; Kellaris and Cox 1989), other research has proven supportive (e.g., Bierley, McSweeney, and Vannieuwkerk 1985; Kroeber-Riel 1983). For example, in a series of studies, Stuart, Shimp, and Engle (1987) paired brand names with pleasant pictures (e.g., a mountain waterfall) or with neutral ones several times. To control for contingency awareness and demand effects (see Page 1974), subjects were divided into those who were and were not aware of the contingency between brand name and picture. Although in one study 48 percent of subjects reported awareness of the

contingency, the conditioning effect was present for both the aware and the unaware group.

According to the ELM, people should be especially susceptible to the simple transfer of affect from one stimulus to another when the likelihood of object-relevant thinking is rather low. In a pertinent study, Gorn (1982) investigated the power of a simple affective cue to modify attitudes toward a product when the likelihood of elaboration of an advertisement for the product was low. Before viewing any ads, subjects in the high-elaboration condition were told that their task was to advise an advertising agency as to whether or not they should purchase time on television for their ads, and that they would be able to choose a brand of pen from among the pens advertised in the segment that they would judge. The low-elaboration subjects did not expect to advise the ad agency and did not expect to make a choice among pens. All subjects were exposed to two ads for a pen. One ad presented strong attributes about the pen (e.g., never smudges), whereas the other ad featured pleasant music rather than relevant information. About one hour after ad exposure, subjects were given a choice between the two advertised brands. The low-elaboration subjects favored the pen advertised with pleasant music, whereas the high-elaboration subjects favored the pen advertised with the relevant information (see also, Batra and Ray 1985; Srull 1983).

Mere Exposure. Another procedure for modifying attitudes through simple affective means was identified by Zajonc (1968) in his work on "mere exposure." In this research, Zajonc and his colleagues have shown consistently that "when objects are presented to the individual on repeated occasions, the mere exposure is capable of making the individual's attitude toward these objects more positive" (Zajonc and Markus 1982, p. 125). An early explanation for the mere-exposure effect was provided by Titchener (1910) who proposed that familiar objects led people to experience a "glow of warmth, a sense of ownership, a feeling of intimacy" (p. 411).

The most recent work on this phenomenon

indicates that simple repetition of objects can lead to more positive evaluations even when people do not recognize that the objects are familiar. For example, in one study Kunst-Wilson and Zajonc (1980) visually presented polygon images to subjects a number of times under viewing conditions that resulted in chance reports of recognition. During a later session, subjects were shown pairs of polygons under ideal viewing conditions. In each pair, one shape was one that had been seen in the earlier session, but the other shape was new. Subjects were asked which shape they liked better and which one they had seen before. Even though subjects were unable to recognize beyond chance which of the polygons was new and which was old, they showed a significant preference for the old over the new shapes.

Mere exposure effects have been shown in a number of studies using a variety of stimuli. In addition to the polygons, such stimuli as tones, nonsense syllables, Chinese ideograms, photographs of faces, and foreign words have been used (e.g., Matlin 1970; Wilson 1979; Zajonc 1968). More interesting, what these stimuli have in common is that they tend to be meaningless and are relatively unlikely to elicit spontaneous elaboration. In fact, the simple affective process induced by mere exposure appears to be more successful in influencing attitudes when processing of the repeated stimuli is minimal (cf. Obermiller 1985). When more meaningful stimuli have been repeated, such as words or sentences, mere-exposure effects have been less common. Instead, when processing occurs with repetition, the increased exposures enhance the dominant cognitive response to the stimulus. Thus, attitudes toward negative words (e.g., "hate") and weak message arguments become more unfavorable, but attitudes toward positive words (e.g., "love") and strong arguments become more favorable, at least until the point of tedium is reached (e.g., Cacioppo and Petty 1985; 1989; Grush 1976; Sawyer 1981).

Alternative Approaches to Affect. Previous approaches to the role of affect in persuasion, such as classical conditioning and mere expo-

sure, have tended to show that affective processes are most likely to influence attitudes for low-knowledge, low-relevance, and/or initially meaningless attitude objects or issues. This does not mean, however, that affect will influence attitudes only when the elaboration likelihood is low. According to the ELM, when the likelihood of issue-relevant thinking is low, affect will serve largely as a peripheral cue, providing meaning to the attitude object by a simple association process. As the likelihood of elaboration increases, affect (like other variables) may take on different roles.

Specifically, when the elaboration likelihood is more moderate, affect (like source attractiveness, Puckett et al. 1983; and credibility, Moore et al. 1986) has been shown to have an impact on the extent of argument elaboration. In particular, people who have been placed in a positive mood have shown less inclination to process message arguments than people in a neutral mood (Bless et al. 1990; Mackie and Worth 1989; Worth and Mackie 1987). At this point it is not clear if positive affect engages more cognitive capacity than neutral mood (reducing the ability to process) or whether people in a positive mood are less motivated to process the arguments since thinking about the message might attenuate the good mood.[10]

When the elaboration likelihood is high and people are processing the message arguments already, the ELM holds that affective states may bias information processing activity or bias the interpretation of arguments (Petty, Cacioppo and Kasmer 1988). For example, if a message recipient experiences fear during a message on cigarette smoking, this might influence the person's perception of the severity of the threat of smoking on their health or the

---

[10]It is also possible that the affect manipulations used in the research engaged subjects' thoughts, which distracted them momentarily from processing the message. For example, in one study, subjects viewing a commercial in the context of a sad TV program generated more thoughts about the program and fewer about the product than subjects viewing the same commercial in the context of a happy TV program (Goldberg and Gorn 1987). It is important to rule out these "distraction" effects before the impact of the manipulations can be attributed to affect per se.

subjective likelihood of the negative consequences postulated (Johnson and Tversky 1983; Rogers 1983; Schwarz, Servay, and Kumpf 1985). When people are actively processing a message, affect could serve as a retrieval cue for material in memory, influencing what comes to mind, and coloring the ongoing information processing activity (Bower 1981; Isen 1984).

In research on the effects of advertising, current work is focussed on the manner by which the feelings invoked by a commercial or a television program affect attitudes toward the advertisement and the featured brand. Some research has supported the view that the effect of feeling on brand attitudes is mediated largely by attitudes toward the advertisement (e.g., Holbrook and Batra 1987), but other studies suggest that feelings can have a more direct effect on brand attitudes and beliefs (e.g., Edell and Burke 1987). As noted previously, the ELM would expect that both direct and indirect effects are possible depending upon the elaboration likelihood conditions. For example, Stayman and Aaker (1988) found that the direct effect of feelings on brand attitudes was greater at low-repetition levels rather than high-repetition levels since more cognitive activity presumably occurs with repeated exposure.[11]

---

[11]Just as brand attitudes can be based directly on affective or cognitive factors, so too can attitudes toward the ad (e.g., Burke and Edell 1986; Madden, Allen, and Twible 1988; Shimp 1981). For example, Miniard, Bhatla, and Rose (1988) showed that under high-involvement conditions, attitude toward the ad could be based in part on an evaluation of the quality of the arguments about the brand contained in the ad. The quality of arguments used in an ad is central to an evaluation of the ad and is central to an evaluation of the brand, and, thus, argument quality affected both ad and brand attitudes under high-involvement conditions. On the other hand, ad features such as the quality of pictures employed is central to an evaluation of the ad, but typically peripheral to an evaluation of the brand. Consistent with this reasoning, picture quality affected ad but not brand attitudes under high-involvement conditions. As expected, under low-involvement conditions, picture quality affected both brand and ad attitudes, but argument quality affected neither. (See also Mitchell 1986 and Hastak and Olson 1989 for evidence that, under some circumstances, ad attitudes partially mediate the effects of argument quality on brand attitudes.)

Similarly, the affect elicited by a television program should be capable of modifying attitudes via the central or peripheral routes. In one study, for example, motivation to process an ad for a pen was varied in the context of a television program that elicited relatively positive or negative affect (Shumann 1986). Although attitudes toward the pen were affected similarly under high- and low-motivation conditions, thoughts about the product were influenced by the affect manipulation only when motivation was high. This result is consistent with the idea that affect modified attitudes via the peripheral route when the likelihood of thinking was low, but via the central route when ad elaboration was high (for further discussion see Petty, Gleicher, and Baker, in press).

CHARACTERISTICS AND CONSEQUENCES OF ATTITUDES PRODUCED BY DIFFERENT ROUTES TO PERSUASION

Our review of the major theories of persuasion suggested a variety of processes by which attitudes might be changed. In addition, we have used the ELM to suggest some of the general conditions under which each of the various processes would be more likely to operate. For example, consider the decade-long controversy regarding the viability of dissonance theory versus self-perception theory. Both conceptualizations predicted the same pattern of attitude results in many situations, though for difference reasons (Greenwald 1975). As noted earlier, self-perception theory focussed on a relatively simple cognitive inference as the basis of change, whereas dissonance theory postulated a more cognitively active process of rationalization. Thus, the dissonance process should be more likely when conditions foster a high likelihood of elaboration (i.e., conditions of high personal relevance, consequences, responsibility, prior knowledge, etc.) rather than a low likelihood of elaboration. Research is generally supportive of this view (e.g., Fazio, Zanna, and Cooper 1977; Cooper and Fazio 1984). On the other hand, self-perception processes should be more likely to operate when the elaboration likelihood is rather low (i.e., conditions of low personal relevance, consequences, responsibility, prior knowledge, etc.). This, too, has received empirical support (e.g., Chaiken and Baldwin 1981; Taylor 1975; Wood 1982).

In this section we turn briefly to some of the important characteristics and consequences of attitudes induced by different processes. In particular, we focus on the temporal persistence of attitude changes, the resistance of attitude changes to counterpersuasion, and the ability of attitudes to predict behavior.

Persistence of Attitude Change

Persistence of persuasion refers to the extent to which attitude changes endure over time. In a comprehensive review of the experimental work on attitude persistence in 1978, Cook and Flay concluded quite pessimistically that most of the laboratory studies on attitude change tended to find very little persistence of persuasion. In the years since this influential paper, it has become more clear when attitude changes will persist and when they will not.

In particular, current research is compatible with the view that when attitude changes are based on extensive issue-relevant thinking, they tend to persist. That is, conditions that foster peoples' motivation and ability to engage in issue-relevant cognitive activity at the time of message exposure are associated with increased persistence of persuasion. Thus, for example, research has shown that increased persistence is associated with the self-generation of messages (e.g., Watts 1967), the use of interesting or involving communication topics (e.g., Chaiken 1980; Ronis et al. 1977), the provision of increased time to think about a message (e.g., Mitnick and McGinnies 1958), an increase in message repetition (e.g., Johnson and Watkins 1971), and the reduction of distraction (e.g., Watts and Holt 1979). Also, people who characteristically enjoy thinking (high need for cognition) show greater persistence of attitude change than people who do not (Haugtvedt and Petty 1989). It is important to note that simple

cues may be associated with persistent attitudes if the cues remain salient over time. This may be accomplished by repeated pairings of the cue and attitude object so that the cue remains relatively accessible (e.g., Weber 1972) or by reintroducing the cue at the time of attitude assessment, such as when a product package is examined (e.g., Kelman and Hovland 1953).

Resistence to Counterpersuasion

Resistance refers to the extent to which attitude changes are capable of surviving an attack from contrary information. The stronger the attack they can withstand, the more resistant are the attitudes. In a consumer context, contrary information may come from subsequent reports that question an initially favorable attitude (e.g., from *Consumer Reports*), from competing advertising, and from unfavorable product trial experiences.

Although attitude persistence and resistance tend to co-occur, their potential independence is shown conclusively in McGuire's (1964) work on cultural truisms. Truisms such as "you should brush your teeth after every meal," tend to be highly persistent in a vacuum, but very susceptible to influence when challenged. As McGuire notes, people have very little practice in defending these beliefs because they have never been attacked. These beliefs were likely formed with little issue-relevant thinking at a time during childhood when extensive thinking was relatively unlikely. Instead, the truisms were probably presented repeatedly by powerful, likable, and expert sources. As noted earlier, the continual pairing of a belief with positive cues may produce a relatively persistent attitude, but these attitudes may not prove resistant when attacked.

That the resistance of attitudes can be improved by motivating and enabling people to defend their positions is shown clearly in McGuire's (1964) important early work on *inoculation theory*. Using a biological analogy, McGuire suggested that just as people can be made more resistant to a disease by giving them a mild form of the germ, people can also be made more resistant to discrepant messages by inoculating their initial attitudes. The inoculation treatment consists of exposing people to a few pieces of counterattitudinal information prior to the threatening communication and showing them how to refute this information. This presumably produces subsequent resistance because the inoculation poses a threat that motivates and enables people to develop bolstering arguments for their somewhat weakened attitudes (e.g., McGuire and Papageorgis 1961). In a relevant consumer study on resistance, Kamins and Assael (1987) exposed subjects to a negative product trial experience after they were exposed to a one-sided or two-sided advertisement for the product. Consistent with McGuire's model and previous research on one-sided versus two-sided messages (e.g., Lumsdaine and Janis 1953), the two-sided ad led to greater protection against the subsequent negative trial experience.

Although there is relatively little work on the specific qualities that render attitude changes resistant to counterattack, current research suggests that attitudes tend to be resistant when they are accessible, when they are supported by a network of relevant beliefs, and when people are motivated to use these beliefs to defend their positions (e.g., Wood 1982). Thus, when attitudes are formed via direct experience (e.g., Wu and Shaffer 1987), or via the central route (e.g., Haugtvedt 1989), or when the processing conditions motivate a negatively biased elaboration of the message (e.g., Petty and Cacioppo 1979a), resistance is likely.

Attitude-Behavior Consistency

Perhaps the most important quality of attitudes for those interested in understanding consumer behavior concerns the ability of attitudes to predict peoples' actions. A number of situational and dispositional factors have been shown to enhance the consistency of attitudes with behaviors. For example, attitudes have been found to be more predictive of behavior when (1) the persons tested are of a certain personality type (e.g., are low in "self-monitoring," Snyder and Swann 1976; or high in "need for cognition," Cacioppo, Petty, Kao, and

Rodriguez 1986), (2) the attitudes in question are consistent with underlying beliefs (e.g., Norman 1975); (3) the attitudes are based on high rather than low amounts of issue-relevant knowledge and/or personal experience (e.g., Davidson, Yantis, Norwood, and Montano 1985; Fazio and Zanna 1981; Smith and Swinyard 1983), (4) the attitudes were likely formed as a result of issue-relevant thinking (e.g., Petty, Cacioppo, and Schumann 1983; Verplanken 1989), (5) the cues in the situation indicate that the person's attitude is relevant to the behavior (e.g., Borgida and Campbell 1982) and others (for reviews see Ajzen 1989; and Pieters 1988).

A number of methodological considerations have also proven to be important if attitudes are to predict behaviors. In particular, the attitude and behavior should be measured at the same level of correspondence (e.g., general attitudes predict multiact criteria, specific attitudes predict single behaviors; Ajzen and Fishbein 1977; Bagozzi 1981). Also, the attitude and behavioral measures should be assessed at about the same time (e.g., Davidson and Jaccard 1979) and under similar conditions (e.g., Millar and Tesser 1986a). If people are asked to think about the basis of their attitudes just prior to attitude measurement, attitude-behavior consistency may be reduced if thinking produces an expressed attitude that is not representative of the true one (Wilson, Dunn, Kraft, and Lisle 1989). It is also important to note that behavioral prediction in general can be improved by including factors other than attitudes (e.g., societal and personal norms, Ajzen and Fishbein 1977; habits, Triandis 1977; and perceived control, Ajzen 1988) in one's model.

Two general models of the process by which attitudes guide behavior have achieved considerable attention. First, in Ajzen and Fishbein's (1980) "theory of reasoned action," the assumption is that "people consider the implications of their actions before they decide to engage or not engage in a given behavior" (p. 5). Specifically, a person forms intentions to perform or not perform behaviors, and these intentions are based on the person's attitude toward the behavior as well as his or her perception of the opinions of significant others (norms). The model focuses on the relatively thoughtful processing involved in considering the personal costs and benefits of engaging in a behavior. This may involve (1) the formation of attitudes, norms, and intentions just prior to the behavior, (2) the formation of intentions based on previously stored attitudes and norms, or, at a minimum, (3) the accessing of a previously stored intention prior to the behavior.[12] Although a number of studies have raised challenges to some of the specifics of the Fishbein and Ajzen model (e.g., Bentler and Speckart 1979; Miniard and Cohen 1983; Ryan 1978; Shimp and Kavas 1984), the theory has proven remarkably successful in accounting for a wide variety of behaviors (for reviews, see Cialdini et al. 1981; Cooper and Croyle 1984; Chaiken and Stangor 1987). A recent meta-analysis of studies relevant to the theory concluded that the model "has strong predictive utility, even when utilized to investigate situations and activities that do not fall within the boundary conditions originally specified for the model" (Sheppard, Hartwick, and Warshaw 1988, p. 338). Nevertheless, the model performed better in some situations than in others. For example, the model performed better when the attempt was to predict a specific behavior (e.g., applying for a home loan) rather than a general goal (e.g., owning a house); and it was better when the behavior involved a choice from among alternatives rather than a single action. Sheppard et al. (1988) suggest that the latter effect may hold because a choice among alternatives invokes greater involvement and thought than a single option.

In contrast to the theory of *reasoned* action, Fazio (1986) has proposed that much behavior is rather spontaneous and that attitudes guide behavior by a relatively automatic process (cf. Wright 1975). Specifically, Fazio argues that attitudes can guide behavior without any delib-

erate reflection or reasoning if (1) the attitude is accessed spontaneously by the mere presence of the attitude object, and (2) the attitude colors perception of the object so that if the attitude is favorable (or unfavorable), the qualities of the object appear more favorable (or unfavorable). Considerable evidence suggests that both of these processes can occur, and to the extent that both conditions are present, behavior is likely to be consistent with the attitude (see the review by Fazio 1989). For example, in one study, people with highly accessible attitudes toward a consumer product were more likely to select it when given the opportunity than were people with identical but less accessible attitudes (Fazio, Powell, and Williams 1989). When attitude accessibility was low, people were more likely to select a product based on the salience of its position in an array (i.e., near products were selected more often than distant ones).

The notion that accessibility is an important moderator of attitude-behavior relations is an important one with the potential for integrating a considerable number of research findings. For example, many of the variables found to moderate attitude-behavior consistency might be explained by the accessibility notion. Thus, low self-monitors have more accessible attitudes than high self-monitors (Kardes, Sanbonmatsu, Voss, and Fazio 1986), and attitudes formed by the central route and via direct experience are more accessible than attitudes formed by the peripheral route (Rennier 1988) and those based only on indirect experience (Fazio and Zanna 1981).

Recently, Fazio (1990) has proposed a more general model to account for both the reasoned and spontaneous processes outlined above. This framework (the MODE model) outlines the conditions under which each process is likely to occur. Not surprising, perhaps, the conditions are similar to those that determine which route to persuasion will be followed. For example, Fazio notes that both motivational and ability factors will be important in determining the means by which attitudes guide behavior. Thus, for behavioral decisions that are high in personal consequences, attitudes are likely to guide behavior by a reasoned process,

---

[12]In an extension of the model into a "theory of planned behavior," Ajzen (1988) argues that people also consider the likelihood that they will have the necessary skills and opportunities to engage in the behavior. This factor is also important in Warshaw's (1980) behavioral expectation model.

but when consequences are low, spontaneous attitude activation should be more important. Similarly, as the time allowed for a decision is reduced, the importance of spontaneous attitude activation processes should be increased over more deliberative ones.

SUMMARY AND CONCLUSIONS

Our goal in this chapter has been to outline current theories of attitude change as they relate to understanding consumer choices. Although there were many early attempts to apply basic psychological research to understanding advertising and consumer preferences (Strong 1925; Cox 1960), basic and applied research programs often proceeded in isolation from each other, and a large body of conflicting research findings appeared in both the psychology and consumer behavior literatures. Over the past two decades there has been a growing consensus regarding the appropriate use of theory and methods among basic and applied researchers, and much has been learned about the underlying determinants and consequences of attitude change.

In this chapter we have argued that it is useful to divide the theoretical processes responsible for attitude change into those that emphasize central and those that emphasize peripheral routes to persuasion. This framework allows understanding and prediction of what variables affect attitudes and in what general situations. It also permits understanding and prediction of the consequences of attitude change. We have emphasized that all attitudes (e.g., whether toward an ad or a brand) can be based on cognitive, affective, and behavioral information, and that any one variable can have an impact on persuasion by invoking different processes in different situations. Finally, we noted that attitudes that appear identical when measured can be quite different in their underlying basis or structure and thus can be quite different in their temporal persistence, resistance, or in their ability to predict behavior.

Although much progress has been made in understanding the processes responsible for attitude change, much work remains to be done. We hope that the next decade will bring advances in several areas. First, greater appreciation is needed for the view that any one variable is capable of multiple roles in the persuasion process. At present, most studies still focus on the "one true" process by which a variable has an impact on attitudes. For example, in a recent paper Hong and Wyer (1989) discussed several ways in which the "country-of-origin" (C-O) of a product might have an impact on attitudes toward the product. That is, the country-of-origin could (1) act as an informational argument like any other, (2) serve as a simple peripheral cue for inferring product quality, (3) activate concepts and knowledge that bias information processing, and (4) affect the extent of processing of the attribute information provided. But Hong and Wyer appeared to assume that just one process would turn out to be the correct one. Although their research suggested that the C-O of a product enhanced elaboration of the other attributes presented (especially when subjects were not otherwise motivated to elaborate), our view is that different situations could be constructed in which C-O would serve in other roles. For example, if the attribute information were too complex to elaborate, or were presented too rapidly, or if subjects were distracted from processing, then C-O might serve as a simple peripheral cue. Research is only just beginning on the multiple roles for variables and the situations in which variables switch roles. Thus, much work needs to be done.

A second area of research that warrants increased attention concerns the consequences of attitudes changed by different means. Although considerable work has examined the extent to which existing attitudes are predictive of behavior (e.g., Ajzen and Fishbein 1980), relatively little work has been conducted on the ability of newly formed or changed attitudes to predict behavior. Similarly, research on the ability of new attitudes to persist over time and resist pressure from countervailing messages is needed. In addition to the conceptual significance of this work, investigations of the consequences of attitudes changed by different means has much practical significance. That is, it may no longer be sufficient to judge the effectiveness of experimental treatments (or advertising campaigns) solely by the *amount* of attitude change that they produce. A campaign that produces 2 units of change that persist over time may be more desirable than one that produces 6 units of change that decay rapidly.

A third area that is likely to engage the interest of researchers concerns the emotional bases of attitudes. Although important work on the cognitive foundations of attitudes and the cognitive structure of opinions will undoubtedly continue (cf. Pratkanis, Breckler, and Greenwald 1989), the next decade will likely bring new ways of conceptualizing and investigating the role of affect in persuasion. What roles can affect play in persuasion and what processes can it elicit? What are the consequences of affective versus cognitive versus behavioral persuasion? Under what circumstances and for which people and products is each type of persuasion most effective?

The accumulated research on attitude change clearly indicates that the processes of persuasion are diverse and complex, but need not be mysterious. We expect that the next decade will bring greater appreciation for the complexity and pervasiveness of attitudinal phenomena and will continue the integrative advances that are a joint product of both basic and applied research.

REFERENCES

AAKER, D. A., and MYERS, J. G. (1987). *Advertising Management* (3rd ed.). Englewood Cliffs, NJ: Prentice-Hall.

ABELSON, R. P., KINDER, D. R., PETERS, M. D., and FISKE, S. T. (1982). Affective and semantic components in political person perception. *Journal of Personality and Social Psychology, 42,* 619-630.

AJZEN, I. (1987). Attitudes, traits and actions: Dispositional prediction of behavior in personality and social psychology. In L. Berkowitz (Ed.), *Advances in Experimental Social Psychology* (Vol. 20, pp. 1-62). New York: Academic Press.

AJZEN, I. (1988). *Attitudes, Personality, and Behavior.* Chicago: Dorsey Press.

AJZEN, I. (1989). Attitude structure and behavior. In A. R. Pratkanis, S. J. Breckler, and A. G. Greenwald (Eds.), *Attitude Structure and Function* (pp. 241-274). Hillsdale, NJ: Erlbaum.

AJZEN, I., and FISHBEIN, M. (1977). Attitude-behavior relations: A theoretical analysis and review of empirical research. *Psychological Bulletin, 84,* 888-918.

AJZEN, I., and FISHBEIN, M. (1980). *Understanding Attitudes and Predicting Social Behavior.* Englewood Cliffs, NJ: Prentice-Hall.

ALBA, J. W., and HUTCHINSON, J. W. (1987). Dimensions of consumer expertise. *Journal of Consumer Research, 13,* 411-454.

ALBA, J. W., and MARMORSTEIN, H. (1987). The effects of frequency knowledge on consumer decision making. *Journal of Consumer Research, 14,* 14-25.

ALLEN, C. T., and MADDEN, T. J. (1985). A closer look at classical conditioning. *Journal of Consumer Research, 12,* 301-315.

ANDERSON, C. A., LEPPER, M. R., and ROSS, L. (1980). Perseverance of social theories: The role of explanation in the persistence of discredited information. *Journal of Personality and Social Psychology, 39,* 1037-1049.

ANDERSON, N. H. (1981). *Foundations of Information Integration Theory.* New York: Academic Press.

ARENI, C. S., and LUTZ, R. J. (1988). The role of argument quality in the elaboration likelihood model. *Advances in Consumer Research, 15,* 197-203.

ARONSON, E. (1968). Dissonance theory: Progress and problems. In R. Abelson, E. Aronson, W. J. McGuire, T. M. Newcomb, M. J. Rosenberg, and P. H. Tannenbaum (Eds.), *Theories of Cognitive Consistency: A Sourcebook* (pp. 5-27). Chicago: Rand-McNally.

ARONSON, E. (1989). Analysis, synthesis and the treasuring of the old. *Personality and Social Psychology Bulletin, 15,* 508-512.

AXSOM, D., YATES, S., and CHAIKEN, S. (1987). Audience response as a heuristic cue in persuasion. *Journal of Personality and Social Psychology, 53,* 30-40.

BAGOZZI, R. P. (1981). Attitudes, intentions, and behavior: A test of some key hypotheses. *Journal of Personality and Social Psychology, 41,* 607-627.

BAGOZZI, R. P. (1984). Expectancy-value attitude models: An analysis of critical measurement issues. *International Journal of Research in Marketing, 1,* 295–310.

BAGOZZI, R. P. (1985). Expectancy-value attitude models: An analysis of critical theoretical issues. *International Journal of Research in Marketing, 2,* 43–60.

BARGH, J. A., and THEIN, R. D. (1985). Individual construct accessibility, person memory, and the recall-judgment link: The case of information overload. *Journal of Personality and Social Psychology, 49,* 1129–1146.

BARRY, T. E. (1987). The development of the hierarchy of effects: An historical perspective. *Current Issues and Research in Advertising, 10,* 251–295.

BATRA, R., and RAY, M. L. (1985). How advertising works at contact. In L. F. Alwitt, A. A. Mitchell (Eds.), *Psychological Processes and Advertising Effects: Theory, Research, and Application* (pp. 13–43). Hillsdale, NJ: Erlbaum.

BATRA, R., and RAY, M. L. (1986). Situational effects of advertising repetition: The moderating influence of motivation, ability, and opportunity to respond. *Journal of Consumer Research, 12,* 432–445.

BEM, D. J. (1965). An experimental analysis of self-perception. *Journal of Experimental Social Psychology, 1,* 199–218.

BEM, D. J. (1967). Self-perception: An alternative interpretation of cognitive dissonance phenomena. *Psychological Review, 74,* 183–200.

BEM, D. J. (1972). Self-perception theory. In L. Berkowitz (Ed.), *Advances in Experimental Social Psychology* (Vol. 6, pp. 1–62). New York: Academic Press.

BENTLER, P. M., and SPECKART, G. (1979). Models of attitude-behavior relations. *Psychological Review, 86,* 452–464.

BERKOWITZ, L., and DEVINE, P. G. (1989). Research traditions, analysis, and synthesis in social psychological theories. *Personality and Social Psychology Bulletin, 15,* 493–507.

BETTMAN, J. R. (1986). Consumer psychology. *Annual Review of Psychology, 37,* 257–289.

BIERLEY, C., MCSWEENEY, F. K., and VANNIEUWKERK, R. (1985). Classical conditioning of preferences for stimuli. *Journal of Consumer Research, 12,* 316–323.

BITTNER, M. J., and OBERMILLER, C. (1985). The Elaboration Likelihood Model: Limitations and extensions in marketing. *Advances in Consumer Research, 12,* 420–425.

BLESS, H., BOHNER, G., SCHWARZ, N., and STRACK, F. (1990). Mood and persuasion: A cognitive response analysis. *Personality and Social Psychology Bulletin, 17,* 332–346.

BORGIDA, E., and CAMPBELL, B. (1982). Belief relevance and attitude-behavior consistency: The moderating role of personal experience. *Journal of Personality and Social Psychology, 42,* 239–247.

BOWER, G. H. (1981). Mood and memory. *American Psychologist, 36,* 129–148.

BRECKLER S. J. (1984). Empirical validation of affect, behavior, and cognition as distinct components of attitude. *Journal of Personality and Social Psychology, 47,* 1191–1205.

BREHM, J. W. (1956). Postdecision changes in the desirability of alternatives. *Journal of Abnormal and Social Psychology, 54,* 89–102.

BREHM, J. W., and COHEN, A. R. (1962). *Explorations in Cognitive Dissonance.* New York: Wiley.

BROCK, T. C. (1967). Communication discrepancy and intent to persuade as determinants of counterargument production. *Journal of Experimental Social Psychology, 3,* 296–309.

BRUCKS, M., ARMSTRONG, G. M., and GOLDBERG, M. E. (1988). Children's use of cognitive defenses against television advertising: A cognitive response approach. *Journal of Consumer Research, 14,* 471–482.

BURKE, M. C., and EDELL, J. A. (1986). Ad reactions over time: Capturing changes in the real world. *Journal of Consumer Research, 13,* 114–118.

BURKE, R. R., DESARBO, W. S., OLIVER, R. L., and ROBERTSON, T. S. (1988). Deception by implication: An experimental investigation. *Journal of Consumer Research, 14,* 482–494.

BURNKRANT, R. E., and HOWARD, D. J. (1984). Effects of the use of introductory rhetorical questions versus statements on information processing. *Journal of Personality and Social Psychology, 47,* 1218–1230.

BURNKRANT, R. E., and UNNAVA, H. R. (1989). Self-referencing: A strategy for increasing processing of message content. *Personality and Social Psychology Bulletin, 15,* 628–638.

CACIOPPO, J. T., and PETTY, R. E. (1979). Effects of message repetition and position on cognitive response, recall and persuasion. *Journal of Personality and Social Psychology, 37,* 97–109.

CACIOPPO, J. T., and PETTY, R. E. (1981a). Electromyograms as measures of extent and affectivity of information processing. *American Psychologist, 36,* 441–456.

CACIOPPO, J. T., and PETTY, R. E. (1981b). Social psychological procedures for cognitive response assessment: The thought listing technique. In T. Merluzzi, C. Glass, and M. Genest (Eds.), *Cognitive Assessment.* New York: Guilford Press.

CACIOPPO, J. T., and PETTY, R. E. (1982a). A biosocial model of attitude change. In J. T. Cacioppo and R. E. Petty (Eds.), *Perspectives in Cardiovascular Psychophysiology* (pp. 151–188). New York: Guilford Press.

CACIOPPO, J. T., and PETTY, R. E. (1982b). The need for cognition. *Journal of Personality and Social Psychology, 42,* 116–131.

CACIOPPO, J. T., and PETTY, R. E. (1984). The need for cognition: Relationship to attitudinal processes. In R. McGlynn, J. Maddux, C. Stoltenberg, and J. H. Harvey (Eds.), *Social Perception in Clinical and Counseling Psychology* (pp. 113–140). Lubbock, TX: Texas Tech University Press.

CACIOPPO, J. T., and PETTY, R. E. (1985). Central and peripheral routes to persuasion: The role of message repetition. In L. F. Alwitt and A. A. Mitchell (Eds.), *Psychological Processes and Advertising Effects: Theory, Research, and Application* (pp. 91–111). Hillsdale, NJ: Erlbaum.

CACIOPPO, J. T., and PETTY, R. E. (1989). Effects of message repetition on argument processing, recall, and persuasion. *Basic and Applied Social Psychology, 10,* 3–12.

CACIOPPO, J. T., PETTY, R. E., KAO, C. F., and RODRIQUEZ, R. (1986). Central and peripheral routes to persuasion: An individual difference perspective. *Journal of Personality and Social Psychology, 51,* 1032–1043.

CACIOPPO, J. T., PETTY, R. E., and MORRIS, K. J. (1983). Effects of need for cognition on message evaluation, recall, and persuasion. *Journal of Personality and Social Psychology, 45,* 805–818.

CACIOPPO, J. T., PETTY, R. E., and TASSINARY, L. (1989). Social psychophysiology: A new look. In L. Berkowitz (Ed.), *Advances in Experimental Social Psychology* (Vol. 22, pp. 39–91). New York: Academic Press.

CAFFERATA, P., and TYBOUT, A. M. (Eds.) (1989). *Cognitive and Affective Responses to Advertising.* Lexington, MA: D. C. Heath.

CELSI, R. L., and OLSON, J. C. (1988). The role of involvement in attention and comprehension processes. *Journal of Consumer Research, 15,* 210–224.

CHAIKEN, S. (1980). Heuristic versus systematic information processing and the use of source versus message cues in persuasion. *Journal of Personality and Social Psychology, 39,* 752–766.

CHAIKEN, S. (1987). The heuristic model of persuasion. In M. P. Zanna, J. M. Olson, and C. P. Herman (Eds.), *Social Influence: The Ontario Symposium* (Vol. 5, pp. 3–49). Hillsdale, NJ: Erlbaum.

CHAIKEN, S., and BALDWIN, M. W. (1981). Affective-cognitive consistency and the effect of salient behavioral information on the self-perception of attitudes. *Journal of Personality and Social Psychology, 41,* 1–12.

CHAIKEN, S., and EAGLY, A. H. (1976). Communication modality as a determinant of message persuasiveness and message comprehensibility. *Journal of Personality and Social Psychology, 34,* 605–614.

CHAIKEN, S., and STANGOR, C. (1987). Attitude and attitude change. *Annual Review of Psychology, 38,* 575–630.

CHAIKEN, S., and YATES, S. (1985). Affective-cognitive consistency and thought-induced attitude polarization. *Journal of Personality and Social Psychology, 49,* 1470–1481.

CHAPANIS, N., and CHAPANIS, A. (1964). Cognitive dissonance: Five years later. *Psychological Bulletin, 61,* 1–22.

CHATTOPADHYAY, A., and ALBA, J. W. (1988). The situational importance of recall and inference in consumer decision making. *Journal of Consumer Research, 15,* 1–12.

CIALDINI, R. B. (1987). Compliance principles of compliance professionals: Psychologists of necessity. In M. P. Zanna, J. M. Olson, and C. P. Herman (Eds.), *Social Influence: The Ontario Symposium* (Vol. 5, pp. 165–184). Hillsdale, NJ: Erlbaum.

CIALDINI, R. B., PETTY, R. E., and CACIOPPO, J. T. (1981). Attitude and attitude change. *Annual Review of Psychology, 32,* 357–404.

COOK, T. D., and FLAY, B. R. (1978). The persistence of experimentally induced attitude change. In L. Berkowitz (Ed.), *Advances in Experimental Social Psychology* (Vol. 11, pp. 1–57). New York: Academic Press.

COOK, T. D., GRUDER, C. L., HENNIGAN, K. M., and FLAY, B. R. (1979). History of the sleeper effect: Some logical pitfalls in accepting the null hypothesis. *Psychological Bulletin, 86,* 662–679.

COOPER, J., and CROYLE, R. T. (1984). Attitudes and attitude change. *Annual Review of Psychology, 35,* 395–426.

COOPER, J., and FAZIO, R.H. (1984). A new look at dissonance theory. In L. Berkowitz (Ed.), *Advances in Experimental Social Psychology* (Vol. 17, pp. 229–265). New York: Academic Press.

COOPER, J., and FAZIO, R. H. (1989). Research traditions, analysis, and synthesis: Building a faulty case around misinterpreted theory. *Personality and Social Psychology Bulletin, 15,* 519–529.

COX, D. (1960). Clues for advertising strategies. *Harvard Business Review.*

COX, D. S., and COX, A. D. (1988). What does familiarity breed: Complexity as a moderator of repetition effects in advertisement evaluation. *Journal of Consumer Research, 15,* 111–116.

CRANO, W. D., GORENFLO, D. W., and SHAKELFORD, S. L. (1988). Overjustification, assumed consensus, and attitude change. *Journal of Personality and Social Psychology, 55,* 12–22.

DAVIDSON, A. R., and JACCARD, J. J. (1979). Variables that moderate the attitude-behavior relation: Results of a longitudinal survey. *Journal of Personality and Social Psychology, 37,* 1364–1376.

DAVIDSON, A. R., YANTIS, S., NORWOOD, M., and MONTANO, D. E. (1985). Amount of information about the attitude object and attitude behavior consistency. *Journal of Personality and Social Psychology, 49,* 1184–1198.

DAY, G. S. (1973). Theories of attitude change. In S. Ward and T. Robertson (Eds.), *Consumer Behavior: Theoretical Perspectives* (pp. 304–353). Englewood Cliffs, NJ: Prentice-Hall.

DeBONO, K. G. (1987). Investigating the social-adjustive and value-expressive functions of attitudes: Implications for persuasion processes. *Journal of Personality and Social Psychology, 52,* 279–287.

DeBONO, K. G., and HARNISH, R. J. (1988). Source expertise, source attractiveness and the processing of persuasive information: A functional approach. *Journal of Personality and Social Psychology, 55,* 541–546.

DECI, E. L. (1975). *Intrinsic Motivation.* New York: Plenum Press.

EAGLY, A. H., and CHAIKEN, S. (1984). Cognitive theories of persuasion. In L. Berkowitz (Ed.), *Advances in Experimental Social Psychology* (Vol. 17, pp. 268–359). New York: Academic Press.

EAGLY, A. H., CHAIKEN, S., and WOOD, W.

(1981). An attributional analysis of persuasion. In J. H. Harvey, W. J. Ickes, and R. F. Kidd (Eds.), *New Directions in Attribution Research* (Vol. 3, pp. 37–62). Hillsdale, NJ: Erlbaum.

EAGLY, A. H., WOOD, W., and CHAIKEN, S. (1978). Causal inferences about communicators and their effect on opinion change. *Journal of Personality and Social Psychology, 36,* 424–435.

EDELL, J. A., and BURKE, M. C. (1984). The moderating effect of attitude toward an ad on ad effectiveness under different processing conditions. *Advances in Consumer Research, 11,* 644–649.

EDELL, J. A., and BURKE, M. C. (1987). The power of feelings in understanding advertising effects. *Journal of Consumer Research, 14,* 421–432.

ELMS, A. C. (1966). Influence of fantasy ability on attitude change through role playing. *Journal of Personality and Social Psychology, 4,* 36–43.

FAZIO, R. H. (1986). How do attitudes guide behavior? In R. M. Sorrentino, and E. T. Higgins (Eds.), *The Handbook of Motivation and Cognition: Foundation of Social Behavior* (pp. 204–243). New York: Guilford Press.

FAZIO, R. H. (1989). On the power and function of attitudes: The role of attitude accessibility. In A. R. Pratkanis, S. J. Breckler, and A. G. Greenwald (Eds.), *Attitude Structure and Function.* Hillsdale, NJ: Erlbaum.

FAZIO, R.H. (1990). Multiple processes by which attitudes guide behavior: The MODE model as an integrative framework. In M. P. Zanna (Ed.), *Advances in Experimental Social Psychology* (Vol. 23, pp. 75–109). New York: Academic Press.

FAZIO, R. H., and COOPER, J. (1983). Arousal in the dissonance process. In J. T. Cacioppo and R. E. Petty (Eds.), *Social Psychophysiology: A Sourcebook* (pp. 122–151). New York: Guilford Press.

FAZIO, R. H., HERR, P. M., and OLNEY, T. J. (1984). Attitude accessibility following a self-perception process. *Journal of Personality and Social Psychology, 47,* 277–286.

FAZIO, R. H., POWELL, M. C., and WILLIAMS, C. J. (1989). The role of attitude accessibility in the attitude-to-behavior process. *Journal of Consumer Research, 16,* 280–288.

FAZIO, R. H., and ZANNA, M. P. (1981). Direct experience and attitude-behavior consistency. In L. Berkowitz (Ed.), *Advances in Experimental Social Psychology* (Vol. 14, pp. 162–202). New York: Academic Press.

FAZIO, R. H., ZANNA, M. P., and COOPER, J.

(1977). Dissonance and self-perception: An integrative view of each theory's proper domain of application. *Journal of Experimental Social Psychology, 13,* 464–479.

FELDMAN, J., and LYNCH, J. G. (1988). Self-generated validity and other effects of measurement on belief, attitude, intention, and behavior. *Journal of Applied Psychology, 73,* 421–435.

FESTINGER, L. (1957). *A Theory of Cognitive Dissonance.* Stanford, CA: Stanford University Press.

FESTINGER, L., and CARLSMITH, J. M. (1959). Cognitive consequences of forced compliance. *Journal of Abnormal and Social Psychology, 58,* 203–210.

FISHBEIN, M. (1980). A theory of reasoned action: Some applications and implications. In H. Howe, and M. Page (Eds.), *Nebraska Symposium on Motivation* (Vol. 27, pp. 65–116). Lincoln, NE: University of Nebraska Press.

FISHBEIN, M., and AJZEN, I. (1975). *Belief, Attitude, Intention and Behavior: An Introduction to Theory and Research.* Reading, MA: Addison-Wesley.

FISKE, S. T., and PAVELCHAK, M. A. (1986). Category-based versus piecemeal-based affective responses: Developments in schema triggered affect. In R. M. Sorrentino and E. Tory Higgins (Eds.), *The Handbook of Motivation and Cognition* (pp. 167–203). New York: Guilford Press.

FOLKES, V. S. (1988). Recent attribution research in consumer behavior: A review and new directions. *Journal of Consumer Research, 14,* 548–565.

FREY, D., KUMPF, M., IRLE, M., and GNIECH, C. (1984). Reevaluation of decision alternatives dependent upon the reversibility of a decision and the passage of time. *European Journal of Social Psychology, 14,* 447–450.

GARDNER, M. P. (1985). Mood states and consumer behavior: A critical review. *Journal of Consumer Research, 12,* 281–300.

GERARD, H. B., and WHITE, G. L. (1983). Postdecisional reevaluation of choice alternatives. *Personality and Social Psychology Bulletin, 9,* 365–369.

GILLIG, P. M., and GREENWALD, A. G. (1974). Is it time to lay the sleeper effect to rest? *Journal of Personality and Social Psychology, 29,* 132–139.

GOLDBERG, M. E., and GORN, G.J. (1987). Happy and sad TV programs: How they affect reactions to commercials. *Journal of Consumer Research, 14,* 387–403.

GORN, G. (1982). The effects of music in advertising on choice behavior: A classical conditioning approach. *Journal of Marketing, 46,* 94–101.

GORN, G. J., and GOLDBERG, M. E. (1980). Children's responses to repetitive television commercials. *Journal of Consumer Research, 6,* 421–424.

GOUAUX, C. (1971). Induced affective states and interpersonal attraction. *Journal of Personality and Social Psychology, 20,* 37–43.

GREENWALD, A. G. (1968). Cognitive learning, cognitive response to persuasion, and attitude change. In A. G. Greenwald, T. C. Brock, and T. M. Ostrom (Eds.), *Psychological Foundations of Attitudes* (pp. 147–170). New York: Academic Press.

GREENWALD, A. G. (1975). On the inconclusiveness of "crucial" cognitive tests of dissonance versus self-perception theories. *Journal of Experimental Social Psychology, 11,* 490–499.

GREENWALD, A. G., and ALBERT, R. (1968). Acceptance and recall of improvised arguments. *Journal of Personality and Social Psychology, 8,* 31–34.

GREENWALD, A. G., and LEAVITT, C. (1984). Audience involvement in advertising: Four levels. *Journal of Consumer Research, 11,* 581–592.

GREENWALD, A. G., and RONIS, D. L. (1978). Twenty years of cognitive dissonance: Case study of the evolution of a theory. *Psychological Review, 85,* 53–57.

GRESHAM, L. G., and SHIMP, T. A. (1985). Attitude toward the advertisement and brand attitude: A classical conditioning perspective. *Journal of Advertising, 14,* 10–17.

GRIFFIT, W. B. (1970). Environmental effects on interpersonal behavior: Ambient effective temperature and attraction. *Journal of Personality and Social Psychology, 15,* 240–244.

GRUSH, J. E. (1976). Attitude formation and mere exposure phenomena: A nonartifactual explanation of empirical findings. *Journal of Personality and Social Psychology, 33,* 281–290.

HANNAH, D., and STERNTHAL, B. (1984). Detecting and explaining the sleeper effect. *Journal of Consumer Research, 11,* 632–642.

HARKINS, S. G., and PETTY, R. E. (1981). The effects of source magnification on cognitive effort and attitudes: An information-processing view. *Journal of Personality and Social Psychology, 40,* 401–413.

HARKINS, S. G., and PETTY, R. E. (1987). Information utility and the multiple source effect. *Journal of Personality and Social Psychology, 52,* 260–268.

HASTAK, M., and OLSON, J.C. (1989). Assessing the role of brand-related cognitive responses as mediators of communication effects on cognitive structure. *Journal of Consumer Research, 15,* 444–456.

HASTIE, R., and PARK, B. (1986). The relationship between memory and judgment depends on whether the judgment task is memory-based or on-line. *Psychological Review, 93,* 258–268.

HAUGTVEDT, C. P. (1989). Persistence and resistance of communication-induced attitude changes. In D. Schumann (Ed.), *Proceedings of the Society for Consumer Psychology (1988).* Knoxville, TN: Society for Consumer Psychology.

HAUGTVEDT, C., PETTY, R. E., and CACIOPPO, J. T. (1990). Need for cognition: An individual difference approach to understanding consumer attitude change and persistence. Working paper, Ohio State University, Columbus, OH.

HAUGTVEDT, C., PETTY, R. E., CACIOPPO, J. T., and STEIDLEY, T. (1988). Personality and ad effectiveness: Exploring the utility of need for cognition. *Advances in Consumer Research, 15,* 209–212.

HEIDER, F. (1958). *The Psychology of Interpersonal Relations.* New York: Wiley.

HEREK, G. M. (1987). Can functions be measured? A new perspective on the functional approach to attitudes. *Social Psychology Quarterly, 50,* 285–303.

HIGGINS, E. T., and McCANN, C. D. (1984). Social encoding and subsequent attitudes, impressions, and memory: "Context-driven" and motivational aspects of processing. *Journal of Personality and Social Psychology, 47,* 26–39.

HOLBROOK, M. B., and BATRA, R. (1987). Assessing the role of emotions as mediators of consumer response to advertising. *Journal of Consumer Research, 14,* 404–420.

HOLLOWAY, R. J. (1967). An experiment on consumer dissonance. *Journal of Marketing, 31,* 39–43.

HONG, S., and WYER, R. S. (1989). Effects of country of origin and product-attribute information on product evaluation: An information processing perspective. *Journal of Consumer Research, 16,* 175–187.

HOVLAND, C. I. (Ed.) (1957). *Order of Presentation in Persuasion.* New Haven, CT: Yale University Press.

HOVLAND, C. I., and JANIS, I. L. (Eds.) (1959). *Personality and Persuasibility.* New Haven, CT: Yale University Press.

HOVLAND, C. I., JANIS, I. L., and KELLEY, H. H. (1953). *Communication and Persuasion: Psychological Studies of Opinion Change.* New Haven, CT: Yale University Press.

HUESMANN, L. P., ERON, L. D., KLEIN, R., BRICE, P., and FISCHER, P. (1983). Mitigating the imitation of aggressive behaviors by changing children's attitudes about media violence. *Journal of Personality and Social Psychology, 44,* 899–910.

INSKO, C. A. (1967). *Theories of Attitude Change.* New York: Appleton-Century-Crofts.

INSKO, C. A. (1981). Balance theory and phenomenology. In R. E. Petty, T. M. Ostrom, and T. C. Brock (Eds.), *Cognitive Responses in Persuasion.* Hillsdale, NJ: Erlbaum.

INSKO, C. A. (1984). Balance theory, the Jordan paradigm, and the Wiest tetrahedron. In L. Berkowitz (Ed.), *Advances in Experimental Social Psychology* (Vol. 18, pp. 89–141). New York: Academic Press.

ISEN, A. M. (1984). Toward understanding the role of affect in cognition. In R. Wyer, and T. Srull (Eds.), *Handbook of Social Cognition* (Vol. 3, pp. 174–236). Hillsdale, NJ: Erlbaum.

JANIS, I. L., and KING, B. T. (1954). The influence of role-playing on opinion change. *Journal of Abnormal and Social Psychology, 49,* 211–218.

JOHNSON, B. T., and EAGLY, A. H. (1989). Effects of involvement on persuasion: A meta-analysis. *Psychological Bulletin, 106,* 290–314.

JOHNSON, E., and TVERSKY, A. (1983). Affect, generalization, and the perception of risk. *Journal of Personality and Social Psychology, 45,* 20–31.

JOHNSON, H. H., and WATKINS, T. A. (1971). The effect of message repetitions on immediate and delayed attitude change. *Psychonomic Science, 22,* 101–103.

JONES, E. E., and DAVIS, K. E. (1965). From acts to dispositions: The attribution process in person perception. In L. Berkowitz (Ed.), *Advances in Experimental Social Psychology* (Vol. 2, pp. 219–266). New York: Academic Press.

JUDD, C. M., and LUSK, C. M. (1984). Knowledge structures and evaluative judgments: Effects of structural variables on judgmental extremity. *Journal of Personality and Social Psychology, 46,* 1193–1207.

KAHLE, L. R., and HOMER, P. M. (1985). Physical attractiveness of the celebrity endorser: A social adaptation perspective. *Journal of Consumer Research, 11,* 954–961.

KALLGREN, C. A., and WOOD, W. (1986). Access to attitude-relevant information in memory as a determinant of attitude-behavior consistency. *Journal of Experimental Social Psychology, 22*, 328–338.

KAMINS, M. A., and ASSAEL, H. (1987). Two-sided versus one-sided appeals: A cognitive perspective on argumentation, source derogation, and the effect of disconfirming trial on belief change. *Journal of Marketing Research, 24*, 29–39.

KARDES, F. R. (1986). Effects of initial product judgments on subsequent memory-based judgments. *Journal of Consumer Research, 13*, 1–11.

KARDES, F. R. (1988). Spontaneous inference processes in advertising: The effects of conclusion omission and involvement on persuasion. *Journal of Consumer Research, 15*, 225–233.

KARDES, F. R., SANBONMATSU, D. M., VOSS, R. T., and FAZIO, R. H. (1986). Self-monitoring and attitude accessibility. *Personality and Social Psychology Bulletin, 12*, 468–474.

KASSARJIAN, H. (1982). Consumer psychology. *Annual Review of Psychology, 33*, 619–649.

KATZ, D. (1960). The functional approach to the study of attitudes. *Public Opinion Quarterly, 24*, 315–320.

KELLARIS, J. L., and COX, A. D. (1989). The effects of background music in advertising: A reassessment. *Journal of Consumer Research, 16*, 113–118.

KELLER, K. L. (1987). Memory factors in advertising: The effect of advertising retrieval cues on brand evaluations. *Journal of Consumer Research, 14*, 316–333.

KELLEY, H. H. (1967). Attribution theory in social psychology. In D. Levine (Ed.), *Nebraska Symposium on Motivation* (Vol. 15, pp. 192–241). Lincoln, NE: University of Nebraska Press.

KELMAN, H. C. (1958). Compliance, identification, and internalization: Three processes of attitude change. *Journal of Conflict Resolution, 2*, 51–60.

KELMAN, H. C., and HOVLAND, C. I. (1953). Reinstatement of the communicator in delayed measurement of opinion change. *Journal of Abnormal and Social Psychology, 48*, 327–335.

KIESLER, C. A., COLLINS, B. E. and MILLER, N. (1969). *Attitude change: A Critical Analysis of Theoretical Approaches.* New York: Wiley.

KIESLER, C. A., and SAKAMURA, J. (1966). A test of a model for commitment. *Journal of Personality and Social Psychology, 3*, 349–353.

KISIELIUS, J., and STERNTHAL, B. (1984). Detecting and explaining vividness effects in attitudinal judgments. *Journal of Marketing Research, 21*, 54–64.

KISIELIUS, J., and STERNTHAL, B. (1986). Examining the vividness controversy: An availability-valence interpretation. *Journal of Consumer Research, 12*, 418–431.

KROEBER-RIEL, W. (1984). Emotional product differentiation by classical conditioning. *Advances in Consumer Research, 11*, 538–543.

KRUGLANSKI, A. W., and FREUND, T. (1983). The freezing and unfreezing of lay-inferences: Effects on impressional primacy, ethnic stereotyping, and numerical anchoring. *Journal of Experimental Social Psychology, 19*, 448–468.

KRUGMAN, H. (1965). The impact of television advertising: Learning without involvement. *Public Opinion Quarterly, 29*, 349–356.

KUNST-WILSON, W. R., and ZAJONC, R. B. (1980). Affective discrimination of stimuli that cannot be recognized. *Science, 207*, 557–558.

LEAVITT, H. (1954). A note on some experimental findings about the meaning of price. *Journal of Business, 27*, 205–210.

LEIPPE, M. R., and ELKIN, R. A. (1987). When motives clash: Issue-involvement and response-involvement as determinants of persuasion. *Journal of Personality and Social Psychology, 52*, 269–278.

LEPPER, M. R., GREENE, D., and NISBETT, R. E. (1973). Undermining children's intrinsic interest with extrinsic reward: A test of "overjustification" hypothesis. *Journal of Personality and Social Psychology, 28*, 129–137.

LEPPER, M. R., ROSS, L., and LAU, R. R. (1986). Persistence of inaccurate beliefs about the self: Perseverance effects in the classroom. *Journal of Personality and Social Psychology, 50*, 482–491.

LICHTENSTEIN, M., and SRULL, T. K. (1985). Conceptual and methodological issues in examining the relationship between consumer memory and judgment. In L. F. Alwitt, and A. A. Mitchell (Eds.), *Psychological Processes and Advertising Effects: Theory, Research and Application* (pp. 113–128). Hillsdale, NJ: Erlbaum.

LINVILLE, P. W. (1982). The complexity-extremity effect and age-based stereotyping. *Journal of Personality and Social Psychology, 42*, 193–211.

LOKEN, B., and HOVERSTAD, R. (1985). Relationships between information recall and subsequent attitudes: Some exploratory findings. *Journal of Consumer Research, 12*, 155–168.

LORD, C. G., LEPPER, M. R., and ROSS, L. (1979). Biased assimilation and attitude polarization: The effects of prior theories on subsequently considered evidence. *Journal of Personality and Social Psychology, 37,* 2098–2109.

LoSciuto, L., and Perloff, R. M. (1967). Influence of product preference on dissonance reduction. *Journal of Marketing Research, 4,* 286–290.

LUMSDAINE, A. A., and JANIS, I. L. (1953). Resistance to "counterpropaganda" produced by one-sided and two-sided "propaganda" presentations. *Public Opinion Quarterly, 17,* 311–318.

LUTZ, R. J. (1975). Changing brand attitudes through modification of cognitive structures. *Journal of Consumer Research, 1,* 49–59.

LUTZ, R. J. (1977). An experimental investigation of causal relations among cognitions, affect, and behavioral intention. *Journal of Consumer Research, 3,* 197–208.

LUTZ, R. J. (1978). Rejoinder. *Journal of Consumer Research, 4,* 266–271.

LUTZ, R. J. (1981). A functional theory framework for designing and pretesting advertising themes. In R. J. Lutz (Ed.), *Contemporary Perspectives in Consumer Research* (pp. 295–304). Boston: Kent.

LYNCH, J. G., MARMORSTEIN, H., and WEIGOLD, M. F. (1988). Remembered brands: Use of recalled attributes and prior overall evaluations. *Journal of Consumer Research, 15,* 169–184.

MACKENZIE, S. B. (1986). The role of attention in mediating the effect of advertising on attribute importance. *Journal of Consumer Research, 13,* 174–195.

MACKENZIE, S. B., LUTZ, R. J., and BELCH, G. E. (1986). The role of attitude toward the ad as a mediator of advertising effectiveness: A test of competing explanations. *Journal of Marketing Research, 23,* 130–143.

MACKIE, D. M., and WORTH, L. T. (1989). Processing deficits and the mediation of positive affect in persuasion. *Journal of Personality and Social Psychology, 57,* 27–40.

MADDEN, T. J., ALLEN, C. T., and TWIBLE, J. L. (1988). Attitude toward the ad: An assessment of diverse measurement indices under different processing sets. *Journal of Marketing Research, 25,* 242–252.

MANDLER, G. (1982). The structure of value: Accounting for taste. In M. S. Clark and S. T. Fiske (Eds.), *Affect and Cognition: The 17th Annual Carnegie Symposium.* Hillsdale, NJ: Erlbaum.

MATLIN, M. W. (1970). Response competition as a mediating factor in the frequency-affect relationship. *Journal of Personality and Social Psychology, 16,* 536–552.

MAZURSKY, D., and SCHUL, Y. (1988). The effects of advertisement encoding on the failure to discount information: Implications for the sleeper effect. *Journal of Consumer Research, 15,* 24–36.

McGUIRE, W. J. (1964). Inducing resistance to persuasion: Some contemporary approaches. In L. Berkowitz (Ed.), *Advances in Experimental Social Psychology* (Vol. 1, pp. 191–229). New York: Academic Press.

McGUIRE, W. J. (1968). Personality and attitude change: An information-processing theory. In A. G. Greenwald, T. C. Brock, and T. M. Ostrom (Eds.), *Psychological Foundations of Attitudes* (pp. 171–196). New York: Academic Press.

McGUIRE, W. J. (1969). The nature of attitudes and attitude change. In G. Lindzey, and E. Aronson (Eds.), *The Handbook of Social Psychology* (2nd ed.) (Vol. 3, pp. 136–314). Reading, MA: Addison-Wesley.

McGUIRE, W. J., and PAPAGEORGIS, D. (1961). The relative efficacy of various types of prior belief-defense in producing immunity against persuasion. *Journal of Abnormal and Social Psychology, 62,* 327–337.

McSWEENEY, F. K., and BIERLY, C. (1984). Recent developments in classical conditioning. *Journal of Consumer Research, 11,* 619–631.

MILLAR, M. G., and TESSER, A. (1986a). Effects of affective and cognitive focus on the attitude-behavior relationship. *Journal of Personality and Social Psychology, 51,* 270–276.

MILLAR, M. G., and TESSER, A. (1986b). Thought-induced attitude change: The effects of schema complexity and commitment. *Journal of Personality and Social Psychology, 51,* 259–269.

MILLER, N., MARUYAMA, G., BEABER, R. J., and VALONE, K. (1976). Speed of speech and persuasion. *Journal of Personality and Social Psychology, 34,* 615–624.

MINIARD, P. W., BHATLA, S., and ROSE, R. L. (1988). On the formation and relationship of ad and brand attitudes: An experimental and causal analysis. Working Paper Series, WP5-88-21, College of Business, Ohio State University, Columbus, OH.

MINIARD, P. W., and COHEN, J. B. (1983). Modeling personal and normative influences on behavior. *Journal of Consumer Research, 10,* 169–180.

MITCHELL, A. A. (1986). The effect of verbal and visual components of advertisements on brand attitudes and attitude toward the advertisement. *Journal of Consumer Research, 13,* 12–24.

MITCHELL, A. A., and OLSON, J. C. (1981). Are product attribute beliefs the only mediator of advertising effects on brand attitude? *Journal of Marketing Research, 18,* 318–332.

MITNICK, L., and McGINNIES, E. (1958). Influencing enthnocentrism in small discussion groups through a film communication. *Journal of Abnormal and Social Psychology, 56,* 82–92.

MOORE, D. L., and REARDON, R. (1987). Source magnification: The role of multiple sources in the processing of advertising appeals. *Journal of Marketing Research, 24,* 412–417.

MOORE, D. L., HAUSKNECHT, D., and THAMODARAN, K. (1986). Time compression, response opportunity, and persuasion. *Journal of Consumer Research, 13,* 85–99.

MUNCH, J. M., and SWASY, J. L. (1988). Rhetorical question, summarization frequency, and argument strength effects on recall. *Journal of Consumer Research, 15,* 69–76.

MYERS-LEVY, J., and TYBOUT, A. (1989). Schema-congruity as a basis for product evaluation. *Journal of Consumer Research, 16,* 39–54.

NORMAN, R. (1975). Affective-cognitive consistency, attitudes, conformity and behavior. *Journal of Personality and Social Psychology, 32,* 83–91.

OBERMILLER, C. (1985). Varieties of mere exposure: The effects of processing style and repetition on affective response. *Journal of Consumer Research, 12,* 17–30.

OLSON, J. C., and DOVER, P. A. (1979). Disconfirmation of consumer expectations through product trial. *Journal of Applied Psychology, 64,* 179–189.

OLSON, J. C., TOY, D. R., and DOVER, P. A. (1978). Mediating effects of cognitive responses to advertising on cognitive structure. *Advances in Consumer Research, 5,* 72–92.

OLSON, J. C., TOY, D. R., and DOVER, P. A. (1982). Do cognitive responses mediate the effects of advertising content on cognitive structure? *Journal of Consumer Research, 9,* 245–262.

OSGOOD, C. E., and TANNENBAUM, P. H. (1955). The principle of congruity in the prediction of attitude change. *Psychological Review, 62,* 42–55.

PAGE, M. M. (1974). Demand characteristics and the classical conditioning of attitudes experiment. *Journal of Personality and Social Psychology, 30,* 468–476.

PEAK, H. (1955). Attitude and motivation. In M. R. Jones (Ed.), *Nebraska Symposium on Motivation* (Vol. 3). Lincoln, NE: University of Nebraska Press.

PECHMANN, C., and ESTABAN, G. (1990). How comparative claims affect the route to persuasion. Unpublished manuscript. University of California, Irvine, CA.

PERLOFF, R. M., and BROCK, T. C. (1980). And thinking makes it so: Cognitive responses to persuasion. In M. E. Roloff, and G. R. Miller (Eds.), *Persuasion: New Directions in Theory and Research.* Beverly Hills, CA: Sage.

PETERSON, R. A., HOYER, W. D., and WILSON, W. R. (Eds.) (1986). *The Role of Affect in Consumer Behavior: Emerging Theories and Applications.* Lexington, MA: D. C. Heath.

PETTY, R. E., and CACIOPPO, J. T. (1977). Forewarning, cognitive responding, and resistance to persuasion. *Journal of Personality and Social Psychology, 35,* 645–655.

PETTY, R. E., and CACIOPPO, J. T. (1979a). Effects of forewarning of persuasive intent and involvement on cognitive responses and persuasion. *Personality and Social Psychology Bulletin, 5,* 173–176.

PETTY, R. E., and CACIOPPO, J. T. (1979b). Issue involvement can increase or decrease persuasion by enhancing message-relevant cognitive responses. *Journal of Personality and Social Psychology, 37,* 1915–1926.

PETTY, R. E., and CACIOPPO, J. T. (1980). Effects of issue involvement on attitudes in an advertising context. In G. Gorn and M. Goldberg (Eds.), *Proceedings of the division 23 program* (pp. 75–79). Montreal: American Psychological Association.

PETTY, R. E., and CACIOPPO, J. T. (1981). *Attitudes and Persuasion: Classic and Contemporary Approaches.* Dubuque, IA: Wm. C. Brown.

PETTY, R. E., and CACIOPPO, J. T. (1983). Central and peripheral routes to persuasion: Application to advertising. In L. Percy, and A. G. Woodside (Eds.), *Advertising and Consumer Psychology* (pp. 3–23). Lexington, MA: Lexington Books.

PETTY, R. E., and CACIOPPO, J. T. (1984a). The effects of involvement on responses to argument quantity and quality: Central and peripheral routes to persuasion. *Journal of Personality and Social Psychology, 46,* 69–81.

PETTY, R. E., and CACIOPPO, J. T. (1984b). Motivational factors in consumer response to advertisements. In R. G. Geen, W. W. Beatty, and R. M. Arkin (Eds.), *Human Motivation: Physiological, Behavioral, and Social Approaches* (pp. 418–454). Boston: Allyn and Bacon.

PETTY, R. E., and CACIOPPO, J. T. (1986a). *Communication and Persuasion: Central and Peripheral Routes to Attitude Change.* New York: Springer/Verlag.

PETTY, R. E., and CACIOPPO, J. T. (1986b). The elaboration likelihood model of persuasion. In L. Berkowitz (Ed.), *Advances in Experimental Social Psychology* (Vol. 19, pp. 123–205). New York: Academic Press.

PETTY, R. E., and CACIOPPO, J. T. (1990). Involvement and persuasion: Tradition versus integration. *Psychological Bulletin, 107,* 367–374.

PETTY, R. E., CACIOPPO, J. T., and GOLDMAN, R. (1981). Personal involvement as a determinant of argument based persuasion. *Journal of Personality and Social Psychology, 41,* 847–855.

PETTY, R. E., CACIOPPO, J. T., and HEESACKER, M. (1981). The use of rhetorical questions in persuasion: A cognitive response analysis. *Journal of Personality and Social Psychology, 40,* 432–440.

PETTY, R. E., CACIOPPO, J. T., and KASMER, J. A. (1988). The role of affect in the elaboration likelihood model of persuasion. In L. Donohew, H. E. Sypher, and E. T. Higgins (Eds.), *Communication, Social Cognition, and Affect* (pp. 117–146). Hillsdale, NJ: Erlbaum.

PETTY, R. E., CACIOPPO, J. T., and SCHUMANN, D. W. (1983). Central and peripheral routes to advertising effectiveness: The moderating role of involvement. *Journal of Consumer Research, 10,* 134–148.

PETTY, R. E., CACIOPPO, J. T., SEDIKIDES, C., and STRATHMAN, A. J. (1988). Affect and persuasion: A contemporary perspective. *American Behavioral Scientist, 31,* 355–371.

PETTY, R. E., GLEICHER, F., and BAKER, S. (in press). Multiple roles for affect in persuasion. In J. Forgas (Ed.), *Affect and Judgment.* London: Pergamon.

PETTY, R. E., HARKINS, S. G., and WILLIAMS, K. D. (1980). The effects of group diffusion of cognitive effort on attitudes: An information-processing view. *Journal of Personality and Social Psychology, 38,* 81–92.

PETTY, R. E., KASMER, J. A., HAUGTVEDT, C. P.,

and CACIOPPO, J. T. (1987). Source and message factors in persuasion: A reply to Stiff's critique of the Elaboration Likelihood Model. *Communication Monographs, 54, 233–249.*

PETTY, R. E., OSTROM, T. M., and BROCK, T. C. (1981). Historical foundations of the cognitive response approach to attitudes and persuasion. In R. E. Petty, T. M. Ostrom, and T. C. Brock (Eds.), *Cognitive Responses in Persuasion* (pp. 1–29). Hillsdale, NJ: Erlbaum.

PETTY, R. E., WELLS, G. L., and BROCK, T. C. (1976). Distraction can enhance or reduce yielding to propaganda: Thought disruption versus effort justification. *Journal of Personality and Social Psychology, 34,* 874–884.

PIETERS, R. G. M. (1988). Attitude-behavior relationships. In W. F. Van Raaij, G. M. Van Veldhoven, and K. Warneryd (Eds.), *Handbook of Economic Psychology* (pp. 147–204). Dordrecht: Kluwer Academic.

PRATKANIS, A. R., BRECKLER, S. J., and GREENWALD, A. G. (Eds.) (1989). *Attitude Structure and Function.* Hillsdale, NJ: Erlbaum.

PRATKANIS, A. R., GREENWALD, A. G., LEIPPE, M. R., and BAUMGARDNER, M. H. (1988). In search of reliable persuasion effects: III. The sleeper effect is dead. Long live the sleeper effect. *Journal of Personality and Social Psychology, 54,* 203–218.

PRENTICE, D. A. (1987). Psychological correspondence of possessions, attitudes, and values. *Journal of Personality and Social Psychology, 53,* 993–1003.

PUCKETT, J., PETTY, R. E., CACIOPPO, J. T., and FISHER, D. (1983). The relative impact of age and attractiveness stereotypes on persuasion. *Journal of Gerontology, 38,* 340–343.

RAO, A. R., and MONROE, K. B. (1988). The moderating effect of prior knowledge on cue utilization in product evaluations. *Journal of Consumer Research, 15,* 253–264.

RAZRAN, G. H. S. (1940). Conditioned response changes in rating and appraising sociopolitical slogans. *Psychological Bulletin, 37,* 481.

REARDON, R., and ROSEN, S. (1984). Psychological differentiation and the evaluation of juridic information: Cognitive and affective consequences. *Journal of Research in Personality, 18,* 195–211.

REGAN, D. T., and FAZIO, R. H. (1977). On the consistency between attitudes and behavior: Look to the method of attitude formation. *Journal of Experimental Social Psychology, 13,* 28–45.

RENNIER, G. A. (1988). The strength of the object-evaluation association, the attitude-behavior relationship and the elaboration likelihood model of persuasion. Unpublished doctoral dissertation, University of Missouri-Columbia, Columbia, MO.

RETHANS, A. J., SWASY, J. L., and MARKS, L. J. (1986). Effects of television commercial repetition, receiver knowledge, and commercial length: A test of the two-factor model. *Journal of Marketing Research, 23,* 50–61.

ROBERTSON, T. (1971). *Innovation and the Consumer.* New York: Holt, Rinehart & Winston.

ROGERS, R. W. (1983). Cognitive and psychological processes in fear appeals and attitude change: A revised theory of protection motivation. In J. T. Cacioppo, and R. E. Petty (Eds.), *Social Psychophysiology: A sourcebook* (pp. 153–176). New York: Guilford Press.

RONIS, D. L., BAUMGARDNER, M., LEIPPE, M., CACIOPPO, J. T., and GREENWALD, A. G. (1977). In search of reliable persuasion effects: I. A single session procedure for studying persistence of persuasion. *Journal of Personality and Social Psychology, 35,* 548–569.

ROSENBERG, M. J. (1956). Cognitive structure and attitudinal affect. *Journal of Abnormal and Social Psychology, 53,* 367–372.

RYAN, M. J. (1978). An examination of an alternative form of the behavioral intention model's normative component. *Advances in Consumer Research, 5,* 283–289.

SADLER, O., and TESSER, A. (1973). Some effects of salience and time upon interpersonal hostility and attraction during social isolation. *Sociometry, 36,* 99–112.

SANBONMATSU, D. M., and KARDES, F. R. (1988). The effects of physiological arousal on information processing and persuasion. *Journal of Consumer Research, 15,* 379–385.

SAWYER, A. G. (1981). Repetition, cognitive responses, and persuasion. In R. E. Petty, T. M. Ostrom, and T. C. Brock (Eds.), *Cognitive Responses in Persuasion* (pp. 237–262). Hillsdale, NJ: Erlbaum.

SCHER, S. J., and COOPER, J. (1989). Motivational basis of dissonance: The singular role of behavioral consequences. *Journal of Personality and Social Psychology, 56,* 899–906.

SCHMIDT, D. F., and SHERMAN, R. C. (1984). Memory for persuasive messages: A test of a schema-copy-plus-tag model. *Journal of Personality and Social Psychology, 47,* 17–25.

SCHUL, Y., and BURNSTEIN, E. (1983). The informational basis of social judgments: Memory for informative and uninformative arguments. *Journal of Experimental Social Psychology, 19,* 422–433.

SCHUMANN, D. W. (1986). Exploring the program/commercial relationship: How does attitude toward the program affect attitude toward the advertised products? Unpublished doctoral dissertation, University of Missouri-Columbia, Columbia, MO.

SCHUMANN, D. W., PETTY, R. E., and CLEMONS, D. S. (1990). Predicting the effectiveness of different strategies of advertising variation: A test of the repetition variation hypotheses. *Journal of Consumer Research, 17.*

SCHWARZ, N., SERVAY, W., and KUMPF, M. (1985). Attribution of arousal as a mediator of fear-arousing communications. *Journal of Applied Social Psychology, 15,* 178–188.

SCOTT, C. A., and YALCH, R. F. (1978). A test of the self-perception explanation of the effects of rewards on intrinsic interest. *Journal of Experimental Social Psychology, 14,* 180–192.

SHAVITT, S. (1989). Operationalizing the functional theories of attitudes. In A. R. Pratkanis, S. J. Breckler, and A. G. Greenwald (Eds.), *Attitude Structure and Function* (pp. 311–338). Hillsdale, NJ: Erlbaum.

SHAVITT, S., and BROCK, T. C. (1986). Self-relevant responses in commercial persuasion. In J. Olson and K. Sentis (Eds.), *Advertising and Consumer Psychology* (pp. 149–171). New York: Praeger.

SHELTON, M. L., and ROGERS, R. W. (1981). Fear-arousing and empathy-arousing appeals to help: The pathos of persuasion. *Journal of Abnormal and Social Psychology, 11,* 366–378.

SHEPPARD, B. H., HARTWICK, J., and WARSHAW, P. R. (1988). The theory of reasoned action: A meta-analysis of past research with recommendations for modifications and future research. *Journal of Consumer Research, 15,* 325–343.

SHERER, M., and ROGERS, R. W. (1984). The role of vivid information in fear appeals and attitude change. *Journal of Research in Personality, 18,* 321–334.

SHERIF, M., and SHERIF, C. W. (1967). Attitude as

the individual's own categories: The social judgment-involvement approach to attitude and attitude change. In C. W. Sherif and M. Sherif (Eds.), *Attitude, Ego-Involvement, and Change*. New York: Wiley.

SHERMAN, S. J. (1987). Cognitive processes in the formation, change, and expression of attitude. In M. P. Zanna, J. M. Olson, and C. Peter Herman (Eds.), *Social Influence: The Ontario Symposium*. Hillsdale, NJ: Erlbaum.

SHERMAN, S. J., CIALDINI, R. B., SCHWARTZMAN, D. F., and REYNOLDS, K. D. (1985). Imagining can heighten or lower the perceived likelihood of contracting a disease: The mediating effect of ease of imagery. *Personality and Social Psychology Bulletin, 11,* 118–127.

SHERMAN, S. J., ZEHNER, K. S., JOHNSON, J., and HIRT, E. R. (1983). Social explanation: The role of timing, set, and recall on subjective likelihood estimates. *Journal of Personality and Social Psychology, 44,* 1127–1143.

SHETH, J. N. (1970). Are there differences in dissonance reduction behavior between students and housewives? *Journal of Marketing Research, 7,* 243–245.

SHIMP, T. A. (1981). Attitude toward the ad as a mediator of consumer brand choice. *Journal of Advertising, 10,* 9–15.

SHIMP, T. A., and KAVAS, A. (1984). The theory of reasoned action applied to coupon usage. *Journal of Consumer Research, 11,* 795–809.

SLAMECKA, N. J., and GRAF, P. (1978). The generation effect: Delineation of a phenomenon. *Journal of Experimental Psychology: Human Learning and Memory, 4,* 592–604.

SMITH, M. B., BRUNER, J. S., and WHITE, R. W. (1956). *Opinions and Personality*. New York: Wiley.

SMITH, R. E., and HUNT, S. D. (1978). Attributional processes and effects in promotional situations. *Journal of Consumer Research, 5,* 149–158.

SMITH, R. E., and SWINYARD, W. R. (1983). Attitude-behavior consistency: The impact of product trial versus advertising. *Journal of Marketing Research, 20,* 257–267.

SNYDER, M. (1974). The self-monitoring of expressive behavior. *Journal of Personality and Social Psychology, 30,* 526–537.

SNYDER, M. (1979). Self-monitoring processes. In L. Berkowitz (Ed.), *Advances in Experimental Social Psychology* (Vol. 12, pp. 85–128). New York: Academic Press.

SNYDER, M., and DEBONO, K. G. (1985). Appeals to image and claims about quality: Understanding the psychology of advertising. *Journal of Personality and Social Psychology, 49,* 586–597.

SNYDER, M., and DEBONO, K. G. (1987). A functional approach to attitudes and persuasion. In M. P. Zanna, J. M. Olson, and C. P. Herman (Eds.), *Social Influence, The Ontario Symposium* (Vol. 5, pp. 107–125). Hillsdale, NJ: Erlbaum.

SNYDER, M., and DEBONO, K. G. (1989). Understanding the functions of attitudes: Lessons from personality and social behavior. In A. R. Pratkanis, S. J. Breckler, and A. G. Greenwald (Eds.), *Attitude Structure and Function* (pp. 339–360). Hillsdale, NJ: Erlbaum.

SNYDER, M., and SWANN, W. B., JR. (1976). When actions reflect attitudes: The politics of impression management. *Journal of Personality and Social Psychology, 34,* 1034–1042.

SRULL, T. K. (1983). The role of prior knowledge in the acquisition, retention, and use of new information. *Advances in Consumer Research, 10,* 572–576.

STAATS, A. W., and STAATS, C. K. (1958). Attitudes established by classical conditioning. *Journal of Abnormal and Social Psychology, 57,* 37–40.

STAATS, A. W., STAATS, C. K., and CRAWFORD, H. L. (1962). First-order conditioning of meaning and the parallel conditioning of a GSR. *Journal of General Psychology, 67,* 159–167.

STAYMAN, D. M., and AAKER, D. A. (1988). Are all the effects of ad-induced feelings mediated by Aad? *Journal of Consumer Research, 15,* 368–373.

STEELE, C. M. (1988). The psychology of self-affirmation: Sustaining the integrity of the self. In L. Berkowitz (Ed.), *Advances in Experimental Social Psychology* (Vol. 21, pp. 261–302). New York: Academic Press.

STRONG, E. K. (1925). *The Psychology of Selling and Advertising*. New York: McGraw-Hill.

STUART, E. W., SHIMP, T. A., and ENGLE, R. W. (1987). Classical conditioning of consumer attitudes: Four experiments in an advertising context. *Journal of Consumer Research, 14,* 334–349.

SUJAN, M. (1985). Consumer knowledge: Effects on evaluation strategies mediating consumer judgments. *Journal of Consumer Research, 12,* 1–16.

SUJAN, M., and DEKLEVA, C. (1987). Product categorization and inference making: Some implications for comparison advertising. *Journal of Consumer Research, 14,* 372–378.

SWASY, J. L., and MUNCH, J. M. (1985). Examining the target of receiver elaborations: Rhetorical question effects on source processing and persuasion. *Journal of Consumer Research, 11,* 877–886.

TAYLOR, S. E. (1975). On inferring one's attitudes from one's behavior: Some delimiting conditions. *Journal of Personality and Social Psychology, 31,* 126–131.

TAYLOR, S. E. (1981). The interface of cognitive and social psychology. In J. H. Harvey (Ed.), *Cognition, Social Behavior, and the Environment.* Hillsdale, NJ, Erlbaum.

TESSER, A. (1978). Self-generated attitude change. In L. Berkowitz (Ed.), *Advances in Experimental Social Psychology* (Vol. 11, pp. 289–338). New York: Academic Press.

TESSER, A., and LEONE, C. (1977). Cognitive schemas and thought as determinants of attitude change. *Journal of Experimental Social Psychology, 13,* 340–356.

TETLOCK, P. (1983). Accountability and complexity of thought. *Journal of Personality and Social Psychology, 45,* 74–83.

TITCHENER, E. B. (1910). *Textbook of Psychology.* New York: Macmillan.

TRIANDIS, H. C. (1977). *Interpersonal Behavior.* Monterey, CA: Brooks/Cole.

TYBOUT, A. M., and SCOTT, C. A. (1983). Availability of well-defined internal knowledge and the attitude formation process: Information aggregation versus self-perception. *Journal of Personality and Social Psychology, 44,* 474–491.

URBANY, J. E., BEARDEN, W. O., and WEILBAKER, D. C. (1988). The effect of plausible and exaggerated reference prices on consumer perceptions and price search. *Journal of Consumer Research, 15,* 95–110.

VERPLANKEN, B. (1989). Involvement and need for cognition as moderators of beliefs-attitude-intention consistency. *British Journal of Social Psychology, 28,* 115–122.

WARSHAW, P. R. (1980). A new model for predicting behavioral intentions: An alternative to Fishbein. *Journal of Marketing Research, 17,* 153–172.

WATTS, W. A. (1967). Relative persistence of opinion change induced by active compared to passive participation. *Journal of Personality and Social Psychology, 5,* 4–15.

WATTS, W. A., and HOLT, L. E. (1979). Persistence of opinion change induced under conditions of forewarning and distraction. *Journal of Personality and Social Psychology, 37,* 778–789.

WEBER, S. J. (1972). Opinion change is a function of the associative learning of content and source factors. Unpublished doctoral dissertation, Northwestern University, Evanston, IL.

WELDON, D. E., and MALPASS, R. S. (1981). Effects of attitudinal, cognitive and situational variables on recall of biased communications. *Journal of Personality and Social Psychology, 40,* 39–52.

WICKER, A. W. (1969). Attitudes versus actions: The relationship of verbal and overt behavioral responses to attitude objects. *Journal of Social Issues, 25,* 41–78.

WICKLUND, R. A., and BREHM, J. W. (1976). *Perspectives on Cognitive Dissonance.* Hillsdale, NJ: Erlbaum.

WILKIE, W. L., and PESSEMIER, A. (1973). Issues in marketing's use of multi-attribute. *Journal of Marketing Research, 10,* 428–441.

WILSON, W. R. (1979). Feeling more that we can know: Exposure effects without learning. *Journal of Personality and Social Psychology, 37,* 811–821.

WILSON, T. D., DUNN, D. S., KRAFT, D., and LISLE, D. J. (1989). Introspection, attitude change, and attitude-behavior consistency: The descriptive effects of explaining why we feel the way we do. In L. Berkowitz (Ed.), *Advances in Experimental Social Psychology* (Vol. 22, pp. 297–343), New York: Academic Press.

WOOD, W. (1982). Retrieval of attitude-relevant information from memory: Effects on susceptibility to persuasion and on intrinsic motivation. *Journal of Personality and Social Psychology, 42,* 798–810.

WOOD, W., and KALLGREN, C. A. (1988). Communicator attributes and persuasion-recipients' access to attitude-relevant information in memory. *Personality and Social Psychology Bulletin, 14,* 172–182.

WOOD, W., KALLGREN, C. A., and PRIESLER, R. M. (1985). Access to attitude-relevant information in memory as a determinant of persuasion: The role of message attributes. *Journal of Experimental Social Psychology, 21,* 73–85.

WORTH, L. T., and MACKIE, D. M. (1987). Cognitive mediation of positive affect in persuasion. *Social Cognition, 5,* 76–94.

WRIGHT, P. L. (1974). Analyzing media effects on advertising responses. *Public Opinion Quarterly, 38,* 192–205.

WRIGHT, P. L. (1975). Consumer choice strategies: Simplifying vs. optimizing. *Journal of Marketing Research, 12,* 60–67.

WRIGHT, P. L. (1980). Message evoked thoughts: Persuasion research using thought verbalizations. *Journal of Consumer Research, 7,* 151–175.

WU, C., and SHAFFER, D. R. (1987). Susceptibility to persuasive appeals as a function of source credibility and prior experience with the attitude object. *Journal of Personality and Social Psychology, 52,* 677–688.

YALCH, R. F., and YALCH, R. (1984). The effect of numbers on the route to persuasion. *Journal of Consumer Research, 11,* 522–527.

ZAJONC, R. B. (1968). Attitudinal effects of mere exposure. *Journal of Personality and Social Psychology Monograph Supplement, 9,* 1–27.

ZAJONC, R. B., and MARKUS, H. (1982). Affective and cognitive factors in preferences. *Journal of Consumer Research, 9,* 123–131

ZANNA, M. P., KIESLER, C. A., and PILKONIS, P. A. (1970). Positive and negative attitudinal affect established by classical conditioning. *Journal of Personality and Social Psychology, 14,* 321–328.

ZANNA, M. P., OLSON, J. M., and FAZIO, R. H. (1981). Self-perception and attitude-behavior consistency. *Personality and Social Psychology Bulletin, 7,* 252–256.

ZANNA, M. P., and REMPEL, J. K. (1988). Attitudes: A new look at an old concept. In D. Bar-Tal, and A. Kruglanski (Eds.), *The Social Psychology of Knowledge.* New York: Cambridge University Press.

8

SOCIAL COGNITION: CONSUMERS' INFERENCES ABOUT THE SELF AND OTHERS*

Valerie S. Folkes
University of Southern California

Tina Kiesler
University of Southern California

In this chapter we examine how cognitive processes influence ways in which consumers think about the self, other consumers, marketers, and the goods and services they choose, buy, use, and discard. Topics covered include the self and other schemas, stereotyping, causal attribution, social comparison theory, inferences about the commonality of one's beliefs, and self-fulfilling prophesies in social interaction.

INTRODUCTION

Understanding the cognitive processes underlying individual behavior has been a central concern since consumer behavior was first established as a distinct discipline. Of all the contexts in which investigators study cognitive structures and their consequences, one of the most important involves perceptions and judgments of the self, the social world, and the relationship between the self and others. How consumers think about themselves and their social world influences their behavior in the marketplace — what they think about other consumers, those who sell and service products, and the goods and services that they choose.

Consider the wide variety of phenomena that are relevant to consumer behavior. When purchasing, using, and disposing of products, consumers must organize incoming information about themselves and others. A consumer might purchase a pick-up truck because it fits a self-concept of being a practical person, but might fear being classified by others as a "red neck." The individual makes inferences about how, when, and what kinds of others buy certain products. For instance, employers glean information about job candidates from their

*The authors appreciate the helpful comments of Henrianne Sanft, James Bettman, C. W. Park, and David Stewart on an earlier draft of this chapter.

hobbies and the attire they wear to the interview. Further, for joint-buying decisions consumers must take into account the other's preferences and share their knowledge and understanding of the buying situation. A spouse may try to predict whether the partner will like a particular film, food, or furnishing. When interacting with others, consumers have expectations about how the others will behave, which then serve to influence the nature of the interaction. Tourists who think the British are formal, the Parisians rude, or the Italians gregarious may interact with them in a manner that perpetuates those perceptions. Finally, consumers evaluate their skills and opinions partly by comparing themselves with others. For instance, children assess their skills at electronic video games by comparing their scores with their friends' scores.

In this chapter we examine how cognitive processes influence ways in which consumers reason about the self and social information. Because a great deal of social cognition research involves an understanding of how individuals make decisions, it may be helpful to identify how the topic discussed in this chapter differs from that in Chapter 2, "Consumer Decision Making," by Bettman, Johnson, and Payne. Although the topics discussed in these two chapters overlap, information processing approaches to individual consumer decision making have generally emphasized the task at hand and have had a more situation specific and immediate focus. The variables of interest are typically characteristics of the decision-making task (e.g., information format, information overload), product attributes (e.g., price, quality), and task-related characteristics of the decision maker (e.g., expertise, involvement). Most of the literature examines single consumer decision-making situations rather than consumers' strategies for making multiple decisions over time.

Rather than a purchase focus, this chapter has a more consumer-centered or person-centered focus in that we stress the consumer's sense of self and social knowledge. Whereas the goal remains understanding behavior through the mind of the consumer, we take a broader perspective, accentuating the larger meaning of product purchase and ownership for a sense of self and of who others are. Thus, the main issues of interest in this chapter are as follows:

1. In regard to the self-concept, how does product ownership contribute to a notion of who one is? Conversely, how does a sense of who one is shape what one purchases?

2. In stereotyping and categorizing others, how does selling or owning a product contribute to a notion of who another person is? How do stereotypes about others influence judgments of the products used or endorsed by others?

3. How do consumers make causal inferences about themselves and others in the marketplace and about product performance?

4. What kinds of inferences about the self does one make from knowledge of others' attitudes towards products and their abilities in using products?

5. How does knowledge about oneself influence inferences about others' product decisions?

6. How do consumers' inferences about others before and during social interactions influence the nature of those interactions?

We begin a discussion of these issues by examining cognitive structures and then move on to a review of research examining the content of self and social judgments. Self-perception has traditionally been a subarea of social cognition partly because we develop a sense of who we are from perceptions of how others see us (e.g., Cooley 1902; Mead 1934). Cognitive structures, such as the self-schema and the self-concept, are discussed as a means of understanding mechanisms by which consumers think about themselves. Schemas also are important means of structuring information about others. The value of such concepts as role schemas, categories, and stereotypes to consumer behavior are examined.

In addition to discussing the way information about the self and others is structured, this chapter examines the contents of self-perceptions and social perceptions, focusing on how such cognitive mechanisms as memory and attention influence the kinds of judgments consumers make. Biases in cause and effect judgments for one's own and others' behaviors are discussed, as well as how consumers arrive at causes and the consequences of their attributions. Consumers use others as an important source of knowledge about themselves and about how, why, and what to buy, use, and discard in the way of goods and services. We concentrate on the most common theoretical approach to understanding what motivates the search for information about others, social comparison theory. This leads to a discussion of the nature of social judgments and some types of inferences about others that are more likely to emerge due to various cognitive processes. Consumers also use knowledge about the self to make inferences about others. We discuss the prevalence of such inferences and the extent to which such inferences lead to errors in judgments about others. Finally, the chapter examines the cognitive antecedents and consequences of interaction with others in the marketplace, emphasizing the role of self-fulfilling prophesies.

KNOWLEDGE AND BELIEFS ABOUT THE SELF

To understand the influence of social factors in a consumer setting it is important to understand the nature of social perceptions. How are social perceptions represented as cognitions and how do those cognitions influence consumer inference and consumption?

Historical Background

Asch's (1946) series of studies on person perception provided the basis for further studies regarding the representation of social cognitions. He examined the ways in which people integrate multiple pieces of information about another to come up with an overall impression of the person. Asch found that the meaning of information depends upon the context. Each piece of information is not evaluated in isolation and then combined to form an overall evaluation. Rather, people look at the information given, infer the meaning of the information from the informational context in which it is

provided, and evaluate another person based on the "gestalt." For instance, a new person in town may be interested in finding a responsible doctor. Upon asking for friends' opinions he or she is told that one doctor is intelligent, skillful, industrious, warm, determined, practical, and cautious. Another doctor is described as intelligent, skillful, industrious, cold, determined, practical, and cautious. The descriptions differ only in one trait: warm or cold. Yet, the nature of that one trait may influence the meaning of the other traits. In fact, Asch gave subjects these same two lists and asked them to form an impression of the person described. He found that people formed very different impressions of the person depending upon which of the two lists they based their impression on. The "warm" person, for instance, was more likely to be seen as wise and generous, whereas the "cold" person was described as calculating. It is likely that a consumer who is searching for someone to provide a service, such as the person looking for a new doctor, will prefer a wise and generous individual over a calculating person.

This view can be contrasted with the more stimulus-oriented approach to perception that has been espoused by Norman Anderson. Anderson's (1970) cognitive algebra approach to object and person perception posits that each perceived trait of another is evaluated independently, and that trait evaluations are combined (by adding or averaging) in a summary judgment. Troutman and Shanteau (1976) have used this paradigm to assess how consumers make judgments of product quality. Couples who were expecting children were asked to make quality judgments for infant car seats, diapers, and pediatric services based on product/quality attribute information. Their results indicate that when given this information, consumers tend to combine attribute information by averaging the attribute ratings rather than by adding the attribute ratings. Likewise, support has been found for a cognitive algebra interpretation of multiattribute attitude formation for products (e.g., Bettman, Capon, and Lutz 1975).

However, evidence indicates that consumers

often go beyond the information given when utilizing information in a social context. Thus, a gestalt view of person perception may be a more realistic portrayal of social perception than the cognitive algebra view. For instance, Haire (1950) found that consumers formed very different impressions of women shoppers based merely on the purchase of one nondurable product, coffee. Compared with a purchaser of drip ground coffee, a woman who purchased instant coffee was more likely to be seen as lazy, a spendthrift, and a woman who fails to plan purchases and schedules (in short, she was not perceived to be a very good homemaker). Since then a variety of products have been found to influence the impressions that others form of the user (for reviews see Belk, Bahn, and Mayer 1982; and Holman 1981)—from the automobile one chooses to drive (Wells et al. 1957) to the lipstick a woman wears (McKeachie 1952).

The ability to go beyond the information given when forming impressions of others has been found to occur with children as well as adults. In particular, consumption-based cues have been influential as a basis for impressions of others in a consumer context. For instance, Belk, Bahn, and Mayer (1982) found that the type of house or car owned by another person influenced the inferences of second-grade children (although it did not significantly influence the inferences of preschoolers). By the sixth grade, children shared well-developed ideas about the types of people who own different types of houses and cars. These shared perceptions of groups of people are often referred to as stereotypes. College students showed the greatest degree of stereotyping based on consumption cues (compared with preschoolers, second and sixth-grade children, and older adults). These studies make clear that consumers, even at a very young age, form inferences of others based on very little information.

Research in this area has served to describe the variety of inferences consumers make from consumption cues. The research emphasis has now shifted in an effort to gain a more general understanding of the cognitive processes involved.

Categorization

It is now evident that people readily categorize people into various person "types" (e.g., salesperson, friend, professor, student) and that these structures serve as the basis for the inference process. Although there are many views regarding the process by which people are categorized (for a review see Cohen and Basu 1987), a well-accepted view holds that we compare another person with a category prototype (Rosch and Mervis 1975; see Cantor and Mischel 1979 in particular for a discussion of person prototypes). A prototype may not be descriptive of an actual category member, but rather it is an abstraction based on experience with members of a category. If a person is sufficiently similar to the category prototype (based on shared features), then he or she is likely to be perceived as a member of that category.

One individual may be a member of a number of categories. For example, Mary may be your friend, a professor, and a smart shopper. Sometimes a situation will make her membership in one category more salient than her membership in other categories. If one is a student in her class then the most salient category may be professor. The student is most likely to remember information about her intellect, professional experience, and presentation skills, and the student will be likely to use this information in forming inferences about her. For instance, the student may infer that Mary reads a lot and enjoys philosophical conversation. If one is planning on going shopping with Mary, then the smart-shopper category becomes more salient. The extent of Mary's knowledge about local boutiques, her preferred style of clothing, and her negotiating skills may be better remembered in this situation and may be more likely to be used as a basis for inferences about her than her professional marketing experience (or other information that is perceived to be more relevant to one's knowledge about professors). The salient category at the time will influence one's expectations, and thus one's inferences, regarding her behavior.

In the previous example, the various roles

Mary fulfilled made different categories salient. Perceptually salient consumer goods may provide another important means of classifying others. People are motivated to categorize others because it provides a means of simplifying one's world; categorization itself is simplified when one can classify others merely by viewing their possessions. Goods that can be publicly displayed, such as a person's home, clothing, or car, permit an easy means of classifying that person. Thus, categorization processes can help explain the findings reported earlier that even young children have stereotypes about others based on home and car ownership (Belk et al. 1982). The marketplace also facilitates classification by branding (e.g., designer jeans). Consumers themselves provide others with the means of visual classification of themselves by displaying more permanent and overt evidence of otherwise transient or covert purchases (e.g., T-shirts attesting to participation in a marathon, matchbooks from expensive restaurants, travel souvenirs).

In addition to such simplistic means of classifying others, more complex inferences can be involved. The belief that the other person has exercised choice in engaging in a behavior provides a basis for categorization. For example, the driver of a *rented* bright red car is less likely to be classified as an extrovert than the driver who owns a bright red car. Thus, causal inferences for individual behavior should influence categorization (Jones and Davis 1965; Kelley 1972).

There is considerable room for future research examining how a label is applied to a consumer. Once a person has been categorized (or labeled) as a particular type, inferences may be made about the person based on a schema that is associated with that label.

Person and Self-Schemas

A *schema* has been defined as a generic knowledge structure, stored in memory, that consists of relevant attributes of some stimulus domain as well as interrelations among those attributes (Crocker, Fiske, and Taylor 1984; Fiske and Linville 1980; Fiske and Taylor 1984; Hastie 1981; Taylor and Crocker 1981). One may possess schemas for types of people (including the self), social roles (e.g., salesperson, customer, female), or events (e.g., parties). Schemas for events in which a temporal sequence is expected are often called *scripts* (e.g., shopping, eating at a restaurant). For example, beliefs that instant coffee purchasers are lazy were apparently part of consumers' schemas some time ago (Haire, 1950).

Basically, the schema is an organized pattern of expectations (Bettman 1979) for a stimulus domain. These expectations are abstracted from information obtained through knowledge and experience. For example, a person may acquire expectations about car salespeople from past interactions with them, through hearing anecdotes from others, from watching late-night television advertisements for automobiles, and so on. Once a person has categorized another as a certain type of person, then the knowledge and expectations one has developed over time (the schema) regarding that type of person (e.g., car salespeople) will selectively influence the information that a person encodes about the other. The schema will also selectively influence the manner in which the information is given meaning and the inferences that are consequently made from the other's behavior.

Person Schemas. We willingly categorize others into different "types" of people. Research indicates that the information we remember about others differs significantly when people are given a different label for the person. We tend to remember the information that is consistent with the schema, and we usually recall less of the inconsistent and schema-irrelevant information (keep in mind that what is inconsistent and irrelevant is dependent upon the category; Zadny and Gerard 1974). For instance, let us say that a consumer walks onto a car lot with the intention to purchase a car. She is met by a friendly but aggressive individual who introduces himself and offers his assistance. He shows the consumer a number of cars that might meet her needs, but he suggests one in particular. Although that car received very favorable consumer-satisfaction ratings, it also happens to be one of the more expensive cars on the lot. When the consumer verbalizes her reservations about the car, he tells her that it is in great demand and that he might be able to get her a little better deal, but she will have to buy the car that day to get the deal.

If the consumer in the previous example has a schema for car salespeople in which she perceives them to be primarily commission oriented (versus customer, or service, oriented), she may be more likely to recall that the salesman was aggressive and that he suggested one car in particular that happened to be one of the more expensive cars on the lot. That the salesperson was also friendly, that he showed the consumer a number of cars, and that the car he recommended received very favorable consumer-satisfaction ratings may not be well remembered. She may even "misremember" items that are schema consistent but were never presented (e.g, Cantor and Mischel 1977). If encoded, the meaning of ambiguous aspects of the interaction may be construed as consistent with the schema (e.g., Higgins and Rholes 1978)—the friendliness of the salesperson, for example, may be perceived to be insincerity instead of genuine warmhearted candor. Furthermore, she may make schema-consistent inferences that go beyond the given information (Fiske 1982). For instance, in accordance with her general commission-oriented schema for car salespeople, she may infer, among other things, that this particular salesperson is also pushy, a fast-talker, and concerned primarily with the commission he will acquire from the sale (rather than in meeting the needs of the consumer).

The tendency to attend to information that is consistent with one's schema, to encode information in a schema-consistent manner, and to make schema-consistent inferences may perpetuate incorrect or biased perceptions. However, in some situations consumers do seem to utilize information that is incongruent with their schema. Further when such information is integrated with one's existing schema it may result in a revision of the schema (e.g, Crocker and Weber 1983; Weber and Crocker 1983).

Some evidence suggests that information

that is incongruent with one's schema receives more attention (Brewer, Dull, and Lui 1981; Hastie 1980) and results in better recall (Bower, Black, and Turner, 1979; Hastie 1980; Hastie and Kumar 1979; Srull 1981; and others) than congruent or irrelevant information. This effect has been found to be more prevalent when people are instructed to form an impression of another than when they are told merely to remember information about the other (Hamilton, Katz, and Leirer 1980). Thus, when people must find meaning in information, they are more apt to process schema-incongruent information. However, the greater attention that incongruent information receives and its greater memorability does not necessarily mean that it is integrated into one's impression of another (e.g., Dreben, Fiske, and Hastie 1979). The enhanced recall may instead be due to consumers' greater processing of the information in an effort to understand its presence. The presence of incongruent information is often unexpected and thus it may instigate a causal analysis. Only when consumers cannot attribute the information to an external or situational cause will they then turn to dispositional causes and integrate the incongruent information into their impression of another individual (cf. Crocker, Hannah, and Weber 1983).

Self-Schemas. A self-schema may be thought of as a more specific instance of a person schema. The self-schema consists of a system of knowledge structures organized in memory (Markus 1977; Markus and Sentis 1982; Markus and Smith 1981). Each interrelated schema contains self-relevant information that is associated with a particular aspect of the individual. Thus one's self-representations regarding personality characteristics, as well as one's abilities, physical attributes, preferences, sex-role identification, and anything else perceived to be relevant to the self, are linked in a cognitive system associated with the concept of self.

The particular characteristics that constitute a consumer's self-schema may have important implications for behavior. For instance, self-relevance is thought to be an important determinant of consumer involvement (Greenwald and Leavitt 1984; Mitchell 1979; Rothschild 1984). Whereas consumers experience low levels of involvement in many decision situations (Kassarjian 1978), they are more likely to be cognitively active in decisions that are personally relevant. Often this means that consumers form attitudes toward alternatives that mediate their behavior (Krugman 1965; Ray 1973).

The Self-Schema, Personal Relevance, and Attitude Change.

In a review of the effects of involvement on persuasion, Johnson and Eagly (1989) suggest that the influence of involvement on attitude change depends on the aspect of one's self-concept that is activated by the involvement. They propose three types of involvement. When one's enduring values are at stake, value-relevant involvement is activated and tends to inhibit persuasion. This type of involvement has been emphasized by numerous consumer researchers (e.g., Houston and Rothschild 1978; Zaichowsky 1985). When the issue under consideration is one of personal importance then outcome involvement (also called issue involvement by Petty and Cacioppo 1979) is activated. Outcome involvement in consumer research seems to incorporate product interest and importance (e.g., Bloch and Richins 1983; Mitchell 1979). Under these conditions, high-involvement subjects tend to be more persuaded than low-involvement subjects by strong arguments, and less persuaded by weak arguments (e.g., Petty and Cacioppo 1979). Finally, when one is concerned about making a favorable impression on others, impression-relevant involvement is established, and high-involvement subjects tend to be slightly less persuaded than low-involvement subjects. This sort of involvement seems to be tapped by consumer researchers when they examine social risk (e.g., Laurent and Kapferer 1985).

The results of the Johnson and Eagly meta-analysis indicate that the influence of involvement upon attitude change depends upon the aspect of the self-schema that serves as a basis for the involvement. Thus, the self-schema may not only serve to define the self, but it may also determine the vigor with which a consumer experiences the marketplace.

The Acquisition and Consequences of Self-Schemas.

Aspects of the individual that are central to one's self-definition are more strongly held than other, less central, aspects of the self. As a certain aspect becomes important to one's self-evaluation, one develops a self-schema in that domain and the individual becomes schematic with respect to that aspect. Accordingly, individuals are aschematic on dimensions that are not perceived to be relevant to the self. People are schematic on dimensions that are important to them (e.g., independence), about which they rate themselves as extreme (e.g., very independent), and about which they believe the opposite is not true (e.g., not at all dependent) (Markus 1977). So, for example, a consumer who thinks it is important to be thrifty, who perceives himself as very thrifty, and who believes that he is not extravagant is schematic for thriftiness.

The development and activation of self-schemata in memory may be at least partially determined by context. For instance, distinctive aspects of the self relative to other people in the environment may be used as cues to instantiate a schema, or a dimension of the self-concept, that will be used to process and integrate self-relevant information. Evidence of the impact of contextual cuing of self-schemata comes from research on self-descriptions. When asked to describe themselves, people are more likely to mention attributes that make them distinctive in a given context (e.g., McGuire and Padawer-Singer 1976). For instance, an overweight person may be more likely to use this dimension of the self as a basis for information processing when in the company of thin people than when not. As a salient dimension of the self, a consumer's weight may then influence his grocery purchases, his restaurant (and menu) selections, and perhaps even his self-esteem. The more a particular self-schema is used, the stronger it becomes in memory and the more available it becomes for future use (Hayes-Roth 1977).

People who are schematic on a particular dimension (e.g., independence) will make "that's me" type of judgments faster for words that are related to their self-schema than for other words (Markus 1977). For example, a consumer with a self-schema for independence might respond faster to the word "individualistic" when seen in a sales message than to the word "sophisticated." Compared with aschematics people who are schematic on a dimension are also able to readily state more examples of schema-consistent (e.g., independent) behaviors, they believe that they are more likely to engage in schema-consistent actions in the future, and they are also more resistant to accepting information about themselves that implies a deviation from the schema (e.g., that they are not independent). The easy availability and processing of schema-consistent information and the resistance to schema-inconsistent information help a consumer maintain unified perceptions of the self, but also has the potential to bias self-perceptions in a schema-consistent manner.

Differences between Self-Schemata and Person Schemata. Our self-schemata differ from our schemata for others in a number of ways. For one, we know more about ourselves than we know about others. Thus our self-schemata are more complex than our schemata for other people (Linville 1982). We can more easily process and assimilate information (especially large amounts of information) about the self than about others.

Knowledge about the self may also be more affect-laden than our knowledge of others (see Greenwald and Pratkanis 1984). This may have a variety of implications for advertising and sales. Emotional messages, for instance, may be more influential than rational messages when the self is the main consideration in a purchase. Sales personnel may be more persuasive when highlighting the affective consequences, rather than utilitarian benefits, of a potential purchase when the customer is likely to be the ultimate consumer of the product.

Further, there is evidence suggesting that knowledge about the self is stored in a verbal form whereas knowledge about others is often stored in visual form (Lord 1980). This makes

sense given that we "see" others behave but we are generally actors, rather than observers, of our own behavior. Again, this may have implications for advertising and persuasion. Radio, for instance, may be a more effective medium for messages directed to the self as the primary consumer of a product. On the other hand, imagery-eliciting strategies (cf. Lutz and Lutz 1978; see also McInnis and Price 1987 for a review) may be less effective in situations in which the consumer must think about the product with reference to the self (image-enhancing products, for instance).

The Contribution of Self Schemas to Previous Consumer Research on the Self. The schema approach to the self can be contrasted with the self concept approach. Consumer researchers have focused on the extent to which the self concept is congruent with consumption behavior. For instance, the relationship between self-concept and product preference has been widely researched in consumer behavior (for a review see Sirgy 1982). The focus has been on the extent to which a match in product image or brand image and self-image (often defined in terms of personality characteristics) determines product preference (e.g., Dolich 1969; Grubb and Hupp 1968).

Although there is general support for the notion that self-image and product-image congruity is correlated with consumer choice, the strength of the relationship depends on the operationalization of self-concept. For instance, the relationship is strongest when the self is defined as one's own perceptions of the self (often referred to as the actual self). Some research support also exists for a strong relationship when the self is defined as how one would like others to perceive one (ideal self). However, when self is defined as how one presents the self to others (the social self) the relationship is not supported. Perhaps the strength of the relationship is due to the centrality of the these "selves" within one's self schema.

Whereas the previous view implies that a consumer will search for consistency between his or her own self-concept and his or her product choices, Belk (1988) has recently taken a broader view of the self by conceptualizing the "extended" self in terms of one's possessions. Unlike previous self-concept research, he does not limit possessions to consumer purchases. Rather, the term also encompasses items such as pets, friends, family, and even one's ideas. Further, multiple levels of the self can account for one's identification with family, community, or other groups. Defining the self in terms of possessions has a variety of implications for consumer behavior. For example, consumers may choose to experience products or services vicariously through friends and family members that are perceived to be part of the self. Further, consumers may try to extend the life of those possessions that are most meaningful to them. Perhaps they will care for them more or service them more often, and they may go as far as to hold on to them beyond their useful life span.

The concept of self/product image congruity and Belk's view of the extended self are useful in that they can allow for the multidimensionality and context-dependent nature of the self with respect to product and possession preference. Both of these views indicate that different possessions may highlight different aspects (the real self, the ideal self, and so on) of one's self. However, they are largely atheoretical, often merely identifying product categories or possessions in which preference (or "possession") is linked with self-image. The schema concept provides the cognitive underpinnings to explain how that self-knowledge is represented and how it might influence information processing, judgment, and product choice.

The Self-Perceptions of Aschematics. Whereas schematics might form judgments and behave in a manner consistent with their well-defined perceptions of the self, aschematics do not have well-defined schemas from which to base their inferences and behavior. Bem's (1972) self-perception theory may serve to explain perceptions and behaviors of aschematics. Bem claims that people examine their own actions much like an observer would—they look at the behavior and then make inferences about the actor based on the behavior. If external constraints or incentives exist (e.g., coupons) then one's attitudes and behavior are attributed to those external factors rather than to the self (e.g., Hansen 1980; Scott and Yalch 1980). Research by Tybout and Scott (1983) indicates that this process may be mediated by well-defined knowledge. They found that an extrinsic reward for choosing a soft drink undermined liking for the product only when well-defined internal data (based on a taste test) was absent. Then individuals observed their own behavior and judged their attitudes from it, consistent with Bem's predictions.

Self-labeling effects have also been explained as a self-perception phenomenon. Consistent with Bem's theory, labeling a consumer as a certain type of person often leads to behavior consistent with the label (e.g., Allen 1982; Allen and Dillon 1982; Reingen and Bearden 1983). Tybout and Yalch (1980) provide evidence that indicates that this process might work for aschematics but that a label influences the behavior of schematics only when it is consistent with their self-schemas. Further, the effects of the label were only short-term, perhaps indicating that the label influenced behavior only as long as the label or schema was accessible in memory.

Role Schemas and Stereotypes

Considerable research suggests that often we categorize people by the social roles in which we see them. For instance, consumers categorize salespeople based on their role as a salesperson because that role is quite salient to them (rather than their hidden role as a neighbor, or as an athlete), and salespeople may be likely to categorize consumers in the same way. Roles are thought to be the "basic" level of categorization in person categories (Cantor and Mischel 1979). The basic level of categorization is the level at which within-category similarity is maximized and between-category similarity is minimized. Items and people are quickly identified at this level. Thus, the social role in which a person is seen is quite likely to be the category level at which one is identified. The schema associated with that category label may then be used as the basis for inference.

Perhaps due to the quick and easy identifiability of social roles, consumers may come to share expectations and beliefs about people in those roles, and stereotypes may develop based on role identity. *Stereotypes* are generalized beliefs about the personal attributes of a group of people (Ashmore and Del Boca 1981). Perhaps due to our (often incorrect) belief that group members are similar (see the section on the ingroup bias), we readily impose our generalized beliefs about groups onto individual members of groups.

It is likely that any one individual will have many different social roles (e.g., consumer, parent, male, doctor, gourmet), some of which are achieved through training and experience (e.g., doctor, gourmet) and others that are ascribed (e.g., male) and thus may fit into many different role schemas. The appropriate schema, and thus expectations for behavior, depends upon the situation in which the person is perceived. Often the role schema that is used is the role which is most salient or distinctive at the time (Taylor 1981). Thus a male in a store full of females will be distinctive based on his gender role, and he (as well as others) will be most likely to use a schema for males as a basis for inference rather than schemas for other possible but less distinctive roles (e.g., as a parent). The same male in a store filled predominantly with men will not be distinctive based on his gender role. In that case, a different schema may be instantiated depending upon the role that is distinctive (e.g., if he is with children then the parent schema may be used).

Gender Schemas and Stereotypes. Gender stereotypes, in particular, have been a topic of interest in consumer behavior. On the assumption that the media create and reinforce sex-role stereotypes, a number of researchers have examined the portrayal of men and women in advertising. Based on their review of this literature, Courtney and Whipple (1983, p. 24) conclude:

Women and men in society today clearly are different from their portrayed images in advertising. As sex-roles continue to change and expand at a faster rate than the advertisers' response, the image of the sexes in advertising is not keeping pace with the change. In fact, the image reflects the status quo of a time gone by.

Although gender stereotyping in advertising has decreased since the 1960s, the decline has been slight (Courtney and Whipple 1983). Compared with the mid-1970s, women are now less frequently shown as dependent upon men and are more frequently depicted as career-oriented (Lysonski 1983). However, differences still exist. Women are still shown primarily in the home and men are more often shown in business settings (see Courtney and Whipple 1983). When women are portrayed as workers, they are often shown in traditional female occupations. Women are more likely to be young (under 35 years of age) and are often represented as product users rather than as product authorities. They are also often portrayed as recipients of advice, which is often provided by men (Gilly 1988).

Furthermore, the stereotypical depiction of women in advertisements occurs internationally, as Gilly (1988) found in her content analysis of television commercials in Australia, Mexico, and the United States; however, the manifestation of the stereotype differs by country. Although, greater differences were found in the portrayal of men and women in Mexican and American advertisements than in Australian advertisements, ads in all three countries portrayed women as young more often than men, showed women as less independent than men, and were more likely to use men's voices as voice-overs. Mexican and American ads are more likely to have women appear in ads for men's products than vice versa. Also, in the Mexican and American ads men are more likely to be depicted as employed, and men are portrayed more often as product authorities and women as product users. In the American ads women were more likely to be the recipients of advice (from men), whereas in Mexican ads they were more likely to be recipients of help (from men). Although it is obvious that stereotypical depictions of the sexes exist in the media, the influence of advertising's use of these stereotypes upon consumption behavior is less obvious and is also quite difficult to measure.

Of concern is the perpetuation of these stereotypes by the media. Stereotyping in television commercials may have a particular impact, not only because Americans spend so much time watching TV but also because their involvement level is often low. Low-involvement stimuli engender less cognitive response from the message recipient and thus there is less screening of the message content (Krugman 1965).

Regardless of the source of gender stereotypes, gender does seem to be a pervasive role in which people are identified. Qualls (1987) has examined the influence of sex roles on judgments in household decision making. Using causal modeling, he has shown that the traditional sex-role orientation (versus a more modern view) of husbands and wives is significantly related to household influence and the manner in which decision conflicts are resolved. It is not, however, significantly related to agreement between husband and wife regarding rank ordering of product features, nor is it significantly related to the actual decision outcome—in Quall's study, the selection of a house. These findings highlight the complexity of the effects of sex roles on family decision making.

One's own gender identification may also influence the way in which marketing stimuli are encoded and processed. For instance, Schmitt, Leclerc, and Dube-Rioux (1988) have examined the way gender-related information is encoded and processed from advertisements and product alternatives. They distinguished a person's sex-type from their gender. Sex type was measured, via Bem's Sex Role Inventory (Bem 1974), by one's self-evaluations on a series of gender-related traits. Those who rated themselves high on either masculine or feminine traits were classified as gender-schematic, whereas those who rated themselves high on both traits (androgynous) or rated themselves low on both traits were gender-aschematic. Bem's gender-schema theory (1981, 1985) posits that gender-schematic individuals encode and organize incoming information in terms of their gender schema, whereas gender-aschematic individuals use other nongender-related di-

mensions to encode and organize information. Research in psychology indicates that one's sex type is often a better indicator of information processing than gender per se (Bem 1981). Yet, Schmitt et al. did not find significant sex-type effects, but they did receive strong sex effects. Further research needs to ascertain the differences in the consumer setting that may have led to their surprising results.

Schemer Schemas. Before discussing the roles that consumers perceive marketers to play, it is important to note that consumers do have general theories regarding the persuasive intentions of marketers. Wright (1986) refers to these sets of assumptions as schemer schemas. A consumer may possess a number of (sub) schemas to explain marketers' intentions. For instance one may have a set of theories regarding others' intentions based on their bargaining tactics, the way in which a message is framed, the format in which a message is communicated, or the type of message used, among other things. Likewise, marketers (the schemers) may have schemas for consumers' reactions to their persuasive attempts.

There is some evidence to suggest that general schemer schemas may develop at a young age and that the existence of a schemer schema influences the response process. For instance, most research indicates that by the age of eight, children have an understanding that the intention of advertising is to sell a product (Robertson and Rossiter 1974; Ward 1972; Ward, Reale, and Levinson 1972; Ward, Wackman, and Wartella 1977). Sanft's research indicates that this understanding is not necessarily aged-based but is acquired through knowledge (Sanft 1986, 1987). When provided with the knowledge (schema) that the intention of advertising is to sell a product, children as young as four years of age can understand and respond accordingly. Children who realize that advertisers' aim is to sell them a product are less likely to want the advertised products (Robertson and Rossiter 1974; Sanft 1987).

Salesperson Schemas. Evidence indicates that consumers also have schemas for salespeople based on the product they sell (Kiesler, 1990; Sujan, Bettman, and Sujan 1986). More specifically, the type of product leads consumers to form expectations regarding the personality and behavior of the salesperson. Think back to the car salesperson example given earlier. The customer may have assumed that the salesperson would be pushy, aggressive, and fast talking merely because he worked as a car salesperson (and those attributes are consistent with her schema for car salespeople). These expectations are then likely to influence the outcome of the consumer's interaction with the salesperson.

If the salesperson seems to be typical of the category then consumers' product judgments are unaffected by the salesperson's product arguments (Sujan et al. 1986). Apparently "typical" salespeople are easily categorized and inferences are made about them and the product they endorse based on the consumer's schema. Atypical salespeople cannot be categorized with confidence and, therefore, inferences are formed from a more "piece-meal" evaluation of the information rather than based on a schema. That is, instead of relying upon a schema as a basis for inference, consumers rely more upon the specific data given as a basis for their inferences. Consistent with this, Sujan et al. found that when salespersons are atypical of the category, their arguments have an influence on consumers' product judgments such that strong arguments result in higher-product evaluations than weak arguments.

Customer Schemas. Not only do role schemas influence our expectations for others' behavior, but we often expect to be treated in a manner consistent with our own role. For example, Surprenant and Solomon (1987) found that consumers evaluate service institutions and personnel positively when the personnel treat them as individuals who have specific needs to be met by the service. However, when they are treated as individuals outside of their role of customer (such as when small talk is instigated by the service personnel), their evaluations of the service institution are negatively affected. These findings suggest that as consumers we have a set of expectations for *others'* behavior

when they interact with us in our role as customers, and that we prefer that they behave in a manner consistent with those expectations.

Overview

In sum, categories, schemas and stereotypes are central to our understanding of consumer behavior. In contrast to early research, which described the inferences consumers make of others based on the consumption of particular products or services, more recent research examines the cognitive processes that account for the inferences. Clearly, the categorization process plays a crucial role. In an effort to simplify their world, consumers categorize people into person "types." Inferences about the self and others are then made based on one's schema associated with the category label. The schema concept can be used to explain how information might be encoded and used by consumers, and how the meaning and use of information may differ by context.

The schema concept can also account for biases in a consumer's perceptions about the self and about others. For instance, biases may occur because of overreliance on a particularly accessible schema (due to contextual cueing). When it comes to perceptions of others, Markus and Smith (1981) posit a world in which the self forms the basis from which we interpret all aspects of the world. Other stimuli (people, issues, activities, etc.) are evaluated according to their relevance to the self, indicating that evaluations may be made along schema-relevant dimensions, if possible. Further, we are more familiar with the self and tend to access information about the self more than any other individual. Thus biases may result in the inferences we make about the self relative to others.

Role schemas are of particular relevance to consumer behavior. Expectations are formed and inferences are likely to be made about people based on the role that is most salient, whether it be one's role as a salesperson, an advertiser, a female (or male), or a customer.

CAUSAL INFERENCES
ABOUT THE SELF AND OTHERS

One type of schema that has received considerable attention is the cause and effect schema. People give meaning to the world around them and are able to predict and control events by making causal inferences. Consumer researchers have examined biases in the types of causes people infer, as well as the antecedents and consequences of causal attributions.

Antecedents of Causal Attributions

Many consumer researchers have been interested in how people arrive at causal attributions (see Folkes 1988a, and Mizerski, Golden and Kernan 1979 for reviews). The single most influential theorist guiding this work has been Kelley (1972, 1973). Developing ideas first proposed by Heider (1958), Kelley suggested that people observe how causes and effects covary to arrive at their attributions. Information about whether an effect is consistent over time or modality, whether or not the effect occurs for others (the degree of consensus), and the extent to which the effect is distinctive can identify the source of the cause as being the situation, the stimulus, or the person.

For example, a consumer might wonder why a car dealer offers a particularly good price on a car (Lichtenstein and Bearden 1986). The consumer might infer that the dealer wants to reduce inventory, that the car has poor styling, or that the dealer wants to attract new customers. Information about consistency (e.g., whether the dealer always or rarely offers good prices), consensus (e.g., whether all dealers offer a good price or just this one dealer), and distinctiveness (e.g., whether the dealer offers a good price on all models or just one model) helps the consumer explain the dealer's behavior.

People often do not have the motivation or ability to collect information about consistency, consensus, and distinctiveness. Instead, they often rely on preexisting hypotheses, suppositions, and expectations about how causes are related (e.g., Kelley 1972, 1973). Consumer researchers have been particularly interested in beliefs about motivations for endorsing and selling products. When consumers infer that a product endorsement could arise from other than a sincere liking for the product, they are less persuaded to buy the product (see also Chapter 7 on attitudes by Petty, Unnava, and Stratham).

Consumers use a variety of cues to infer the reasons for an endorser's actions. A small extrinsic incentive for endorsement suggests intrinsic liking for the product more than does a large incentive. Frank Sinatra is a more persuasive endorser for Chrysler when he is known to have been paid $1, as compared to when no payment amount has been specified (Sparkman 1982). Providing negative information about the product makes a communicator seem less biased. Thus, for example, two-sided appeals lead to less source derogation than do one-sided appeals (Kamins and Assael 1987). Consumers infer that firms spend excessive amounts in advertising products because they are confident of the product's quality (Kirmani and Wright 1989).

Because consumers have many ways of arriving at causal inferences, we can expect people to differ in their explanations for the same event. In a later section, we will discuss research that explores how various antecedents of causal attributions create predictable biases. But first, we turn to the structure of causes.

The Structure of Causes

Considering the myriad causes that can be used to explain events, there is considerable value in having a means of classifying them. One basic distinction focuses on the locus of causality; causes can be internal or external (Weiner 1986). For example, a consumer can make a good purchase because of internal reasons (e.g., the consumer's diligence in finding merchandise on sale) or external reasons (e.g., the store mismarked the price). Classifying causes by locus is useful because internal and external causes are linked to affective and cognitive consequences.

Locus is related to esteem affects (Weiner 1986). Thus, the consumer should feel greater pride when a good purchase is due to internal reasons rather than to external reasons (Schindler 1988, 1989). Oliver and DeSarbo (1988) found that locus influenced postpurchase satisfaction. Investors were thought to experience less satisfaction from successful stock purchases resulting from external causes (the broker's research and recommendation) than when due to internal causes (the investor's research).

Locus also influences beliefs about who should solve product problems; problems arising from consumers' actions should be solved by consumers, whereas problems arising from the firm's actions should be solved by the firm (Folkes 1984). When product failure is attributed to the seller, people believe that refunds and apologies are owed. Similarly, those who identified the public as causing the energy crisis of the mid-1970s felt the general public should also solve the problem, whereas those who pointed to the oil companies as the cause thought that the government should pressure the oil companies to find a solution (Belk, Painter, and Semenik 1981).

A second dimension that can be used to classify causes is controllability (Weiner 1986). When an individual "could have done otherwise" then the cause is controllable, but when the situation forces an action then the cause is uncontrollable. Controllability seems to influence the evaluation of product hazards. Voluntarily assumed risks are perceived as more acceptable than risks imposed by firms (Rethans and Albaum 1980).

Some affective reactions are linked with controllability as well as locus (Weiner 1986). When products fail for reasons that are controllable by firms, consumers feel angry and are more likely to complain about the problem to the firm and to other consumers (Curren and Folkes 1987; Folkes, Koletsky, and Graham 1987). For example, airline delays that are due to poor airline management lead passengers to feel more anger, to complain more, and to be less willing to fly the airline again than do airline delays that are due to air traffic controllers' actions.

Causes can also be classified by their temporal stability according to whether they are temporary and changeable or more permanent and stable (Weiner 1986). Stability influences expectancies. When compared with stable causes, unstable causes lead to less confidence that the same outcome will recur. Thus, when products fail for unstable reasons (e.g., airline delays due to a mechanical glitch), consumers are less certain that the product will fail in the future. When products fail for stable causes (e.g., airline delays due to poor maintenance), then future failures seem more certain (Folkes 1984).

In sum, causes can be classified by their locus, controllability, and stability. Although other types of classification systems are conceivable, an advantage of this typology is that links between dimensions and consumer reactions have been documented. Further, the locus dimension is a typical way to describe self-serving attribution biases.

Attributional Biases

Consumers' self-perceptions bias their judgments such that consumers often see themselves more positively and their role to be more valuable, important, or influential than is actually the case. This tendency is manifested in three types of biases: the self-serving bias, the self-centered bias, and the in-group bias.

Self-serving Attributions. Considerable research has demonstrated a self-serving bias in explanations for success and failure for reviews (see Bradley 1978, Miller and Ross 1975; Ross and Fletcher 1985). People tend to see their successes as due to their own abilities and efforts, but their failures as due to external factors, such as bad luck or task difficulty. Studies of consumers show some evidence for these patterns. When making attributions for the same product failure, consumers tend to blame sellers (i.e., buyers blame car mechanics for auto breakdowns and blame clothing manufacturers for apparel problems), whereas those who sell the products show the reverse pattern (i.e., car mechanics blame drivers for auto breakdowns and clothing sellers blame the purchaser for apparel problems) (Folkes and Kotsos 1986).

The affective consequences of such self-serving atttributional patterns are often emphasized as determinants of the bias. The "smart shopper" who perceives her good buy is due to her own persistence or ingenuity feels an exhilaration that does not accompany savings due to a salesperson's error (Schindler 1988, 1989). Similarly, blaming others for product dissatisfaction permits one to direct anger outward, toward the firm, rather than toward oneself (Folkes 1984; Folkes, Koletsky, and Graham 1987).

Nevertheless, the self-serving bias can also be explained using more cognitive mechanisms. In the study just described in which buyers and sellers showed different patterns of blame for product failure, they also had different beliefs about how commonly other consumers experienced product failure (Folkes and Kotsos 1986). Buyers thought that products failed more commonly than did sellers. This may be because consumers are more likely to complain about problems to each other than to the sellers (TARP 1981). Furthermore, consumers do not complain to the sellers for all product problems, so sellers may underestimate the extent to which consumers experience product defects. Thus, when confronted with the relatively rare complaint, the seller may attribute the problem to something unusual about the purchaser (e.g., a careless user, a fabricated complaint) rather than to a product defect. Thus, different information about product problems, rather than hedonic needs, may account for these buyer-seller discrepancies in explaining product performance.

An additional argument for a cognitive explanation of a self-serving bias is that such a bias is consistent with most consumers' self-schemas. In general, people intend and expect successful outcomes for themselves (e.g., good purchases), so attributing negative outcomes to situational factors is an inference that provides consistency in self-judgments (Miller and Ross 1975). In short, biases in attributions for one's outcomes may not be merely hedonicly motivated but also may

"make sense" in light of current knowledge and beliefs about the self.

At this point there is some consensus that both cognitive and hedonic factors can be involved in the self-serving bias and may sometimes be closely intertwined (Tetlock and Levi 1982). For example, ego protective concerns seem to motivate people to recruit evidence from memory to support self-enhancing self-concepts (Kunda and Sanitioso 1989). Thus, a consumer faced with product failure may recall incidents when manufacturers produced shoddy goods, rather than those occasions when the consumer's carelessness caused a product problem. Memory search for disconfirming incidents would be less strongly motivated.

Attributing Responsibility for Group Decisions. In contrast to the previous bias' focus on self-judgments during individual consumer judgment and decision making, other biases in self-judgments are more social and have particular relevance to household and other multiperson decision making. The self-centered bias in group judgments refers to the individual's tendency to overestimate one's own responsibility for a group outcome or decision. For example, when spouses were asked to estimate their responsibility for various household tasks (e.g., planning leisure activities, child care), individuals gave themselves more credit for positive activities than did their spouses (Ross 1981). Consistent with the self-serving bias described previously, the self-centered bias was weaker for negative activities (e.g., initiating conflicts) than for positive activities (e.g, making purchase decisions). Spouses thought that their partners shared their perceptions of each other's role and often were quite distressed at discovering a discrepancy.

Park (1982) found comparable results in that couples showed little agreement about their relative influence in housing purchases. The only exception occurred when roles were clearly differentiated as to which spouse was better able to evaluate a particular dimension of the house purchase. For example, when both believed the husband was clearly more expert at evaluating insulation, the spouses also agreed about the husband's greater influence. Evidence of the self-centered bias also appears in studies using children. Teenagers overestimate their influence on family decision making, as compared with their parents' estimates (Belch, Belch and Ceresino 1985; Foxman, Tansuhaj, and Ekstrom 1989).

Cognitive processes can at least partially account for the self-centered bias in group judgments. One's own actions may be more accessible for retrieval from memory. In family decision making in particular, decisions may often be made under conditions of distraction and with limited resources available for cognitive processing (e.g., Park 1982). Thus one might be less aware of others' contributions. In group decision making in general, the individual's attention is often directed toward one's own actions (Ross 1981). Additionally, people probably ruminate about their own actions more than about others' actions, and they have more information about their own thoughts and strategies than do others. Further, group members may not fully appreciate that a joint decision is not merely the sum of one's own and the other's inputs. Because of the synergism involved in most group decisions, an "emergent" or interactive contribution must be included besides just one's own contributions and the contributions of another or others. For example, spouses may each claim individual responsibility for devising purchase criteria that emerge from joint discussion without recognizing the interactive component. A fruitful approach to household decision making is exploring such cognitive processes.

The In-Group Bias. The in-group bias refers to one's biased perceptions regarding the groups to which one belongs (in-groups) as opposed to perceptions of groups to which they do not belong (out-groups). In contrast, the self-centered bias pertains to one's inflated judgments of self-contribution as compared with the contribution of others *within* one's group. Consumers belong to a variety of groups, both formal (e.g., churches, fraternities, clubs) and informal (e.g., one's peer group) (Stafford 1966).

The strength of attachment to these groups can vary. At the extreme, the consumer identifies with the group so strongly that the group's attitudes and consumption behaviors are internalized (Kelman 1960). As an example, think of the adolescent who adopts the distinctive apparel, speech, and mannerisms of the peer group. On the other hand, consumers may feel little attraction toward the group but may conform to others' behavior patterns because the group has the power to reward or punish the individual (e.g., Venkatesan 1966). In light of these influences on consumption behavior, two issues of interest to consumer researchers are (1) the consumer's attraction to, and evaluation of the group and (2) the consumer's perceived similarity toward the group.

In-group bias research generally employs a methodology where subjects believe they are assigned to groups based on some criterion (their taste in art, for example), when in fact they are randomly assigned to groups by the experimenter. As a consequence of this group assignment, subjects tend to evaluate in-group members more favorably than out-group members (for reviews see Brewer 1979 and Wilder 1981). This phenomenon is illustrated by the "ultimate attribution error": Causes for socially desirable behaviors are attributed to the in-group's internal, dispositional causes, whereas similar behaviors by out-group members are more likely to be attributed to situational causes (Pettigrew 1979). Thus, consumers should be likely to give different explanations for products purchased or made by the in-group than for products purchased or made by the out-group. For example, U.S. consumers may believe that American-made products excel due to the in-group's dispositional tendencies (e.g., American ingenuity), whereas good products from other countries may be attributed to situational factors (e.g., the Japanese are successful because they erect strong trade barriers and receive government subsidies). Along this line, trade negotiators with China attributed successful business negotiations primarily to causes internal to the Americans (e.g., the team's preparation, patience, and sincerity) but failures to external causes (e.g., cultural differences) (Tung, 1982).

Memory effects seem to partially account for biases in evaluation of, and perceived similarity toward, in-groups and out-groups. Although people tend to recall about the same amount of positive information about in-groups and out-groups, they tend to recall more negative attributes about out-groups than is actually the case. But they also recall fewer negative attributes about in-groups than is actually the case (Howard and Rothbart 1980). When the self is used as a basis for comparison, people tend to show better recall of information indicating in-group similarity relative to the self, and they tend to show better recall of information indicating out-group dissimilarities relative to the self. People also tend to show more recognition errors of information indicating in-group similarities and out-group dissimilarities relative to the self (Wilder 1981). Not only do people tend to remember group information in a biased manner, but when allowed to search for information about others, they prefer information that may confirm their biases, thus perpetuating the bias (Wilder and Allen 1978).

Because the previous findings employed a methodology where subjects were randomly assigned to groups, these findings indicate that the mere act of group assignment serves as a basis for self-categorization, from which perceptions of group members are formed and behavior is interpreted. Sometimes consumers do have such loose group affiliations, such as when loyal Coca-Cola drinkers banded together to protest Coke's strategy of removing the original Coke (now Classic Coke) from the market in favor of New Coke. However, situations in which consumers have a greater degree of knowledge about the groups to which they belong are perhaps more relevant to consumer behavior. The previously discussed studies cannot address the influence that one's accumulated knowledge and experience about groups will have on evaluations of members of those groups. Some insights on this topic can be found in Linville's research.

In her research, Linville has used members of groups based on attributes such as age, gender, and race. Her research indicates that people have a more complex cognitive structure for their own group than for other groups (Linville 1982), presumably because they have had more contact with the in-group members over a variety of situations. Their greater awareness of the variety of abilities, opinions, and behaviors of in-group members leads to a better ability to perceive distinctions between in-group members than between out-group members. In-group members also perceive greater variance in the characteristics and behaviors of in-group than out-group members (Linville, Fischer, and Salovey 1989). For example, teenagers may assume more variability in fellow teenagers' product preferences but assume the elderly display more homogeneity in their preferences. Similarly, the elderly may assume more variability in their age peers' preferences than in those of teenagers (see also the previous section in this chapter on stereotyping and categorization). One consequence of a more complex knowledge structure for in-groups is that one's evaluations of in-group members will be less extreme than their evaluations of out-group members (Linville 1982; Linville and Jones 1980). Perhaps extreme and negative reactions to out-groups motivate consumers to avoid products associated with the out-group more than has been suggested by previous consumer behavior studies, which have emphasized the in-group's influence.

Some implications of the complexity of knowledge upon perceptions are highlighted by a study by Deshpande, Hoyer, and Donthu (1986). They discuss the fact that marketers tend to assume homogeneity within subcultures of consumers, and they illustrate their point in regard to the Hispanic subculture. Given that the majority of marketers in the United States are not Hispanic, Hispanics can be considered an out-group. They are often identified by surname, country of origin, and a few other easily identifiable variables. As an out-group, marketers might assume that they are quite homogeneous (at least relative to one's in-group) and so treat them in a stereotypical manner. Deshpande et al. show that they are, in fact, much more heterogeneous than marketers assume.

Positive Self-Illusions. The phenomena just discussed, the self-serving bias, self-centered bias, and the in-group bias may also be seen as examples of a more general tendency to hold positive self-illusions. People see themselves as better than the average person on many traits and abilities (see Taylor and Brown 1988, for a review). They also have exaggerated beliefs in their personal control over events, even when events are heavily determined by chance. Consider, for example, the difficulty compulsive spenders, and those with other addictions, have in admitting they lack control over their behavior (e.g., Faber and O'Guinn 1989; Krych 1989). Finally, people hold overly optimistic views of their future (Taylor and Brown 1988). These tendencies seem to arise partly because social feedback tends to be supportive, whereas negative feedback is withheld. Thus, social interaction helps to maintain and develop a positive self-schema. Further, as noted in reference to the self-serving bias, information is selectively interpreted and recalled to be consistent with prior positive conceptions or self-schemas. Such devices as excuses and denial are instrumental when people must deal with negative information and so "negotiate" a new "personal reality" (Snyder and Higgins 1988).

These optimistic self-appraisals have important implications for consumer behavior that should be explored in future research. Positive beliefs about one's self-efficacy lead one to persist longer in the face of failure, to cognitively construct or to simulate success scenarios, including actions leading to success, and to hold higher expectations (for a review, see Bandura 1989). Thus, consumers may be surprisingly vulnerable to appeals to aspirations that the objective observer would find unrealistic. This may account for frequent discrepancies between peoples' prepurchase predictions about how often they will use products and actual usage patterns. One has only to consider the number of unused food processors in the kitchens of aspiring gourmet chefs, dusty exercise equipment in the home gyms of would-be athletes, and so on, to marvel at consumers' costly inability to match aspirations with actual behavior.

Other implications of optimistic self-appraisals are that, compared to what objective standards might suggest, consumers may be overconfident of their own product expertise and not fully appreciate others' expertise, at least relative to the self. Consumers would be unlikely to read product instructions if they overestimated their abilities. Further, products positioned as aids for those lacking skills or remedial products would elicit less consumer interest than objective assessments of consumer abilities would indicate. For example, because people believe they are more skillful than the average driver (Svenson 1981), they will be more likely to dismiss products promoting improved driving because they see these products as being irrelevant to their own driving.

Overview

Consumers make causal inferences about why products perform as they do, why they themselves like products, why communicators endorse or criticize products, and about a variety of other events in the marketplace. Studies have examined the cognitive processes by which causes are inferred, the systematic biases that result from cognitive and motivational factors, and the consequences of various causal inferences on consumers' behavior. Because research on the antecedents and consequences of causal inferences has been extensively reviewed elsewhere (Folkes 1988a), we have emphasized attributional biases here.

The consumer's sense of who he or she is, and how one differs from or is similar to others, guides one's behavior in the marketplace. In general, research shows a tendency for people to view themselves through rose-colored glasses, whether evaluating their own outcomes, their abilities, their contributions to group decisions, or their group's performance relative to others. These biases in causal attributions have important implications for a number of consumer behaviors including consumer complaining behavior, household decision making, and perceptions of country of origin for products. Research up to this point has focused on demonstrating the biases; important work needs to be done on examining when and why they occur.

SOCIAL COMPARISON THEORY AND INFERENCES ABOUT THE SELF AND OTHERS

The previous theoretical approaches discussed here — schemas and causal attributions — share certain basic assumptions and constructs but are not single, unified theories. In contrast, we now turn to a particular theory of social cognition, social comparison theory. Not surprisingly, it is narrower in its domain of interest compared with the two earlier topics, focussing on social inferences that relate the self to others. The impetus for early investigations of this theory arose partly from group dynamics and conformity studies that explored group members' influences on individual consumers (e.g., Burnkrant and Cousineau 1975; Moschis 1976; Park and Lessig 1977). These studies pointed out that others are often used as a reference point for arriving at and for evaluating one's beliefs about the world.

Social Comparison and Self-Evaluation

Whereas the self-serving biases discussed previously might imply a consumer enveloped in a narcissistic world of his or her own with little contact with social reality, in fact others provide an important source of information about one's opinions and abilities. Extensive research over more than thirty years has examined the process by which individuals compare themselves to others to arrive at self-evaluations. According to social comparison theory (Festinger 1954), people have a drive to evaluate their opinions and abilities. Consumers want to know if their evaluations of products are correct (e.g., Have I selected the most prestigious store? Is this repair shop reliable? Is this

style out-of-date?) And they want to know the extent of their abilities (e.g., Can I be considered an art connoisseur, a gourmet chef, a smart shopper?).

Because many of these evaluations cannot be objectively determined, people turn to comparisons with relevant others. "An opinion, a belief, an attitude is 'correct,' 'valid,' and 'proper' to the extent that it is shared by a group of people with similar beliefs, opinions, and attitudes" (Festinger 1950, p. 272). For example, discussions with peers and one's spouse as well as observation of others have been shown as important influences on men's suit purchases (Midgely 1983). Consistent with social comparison theory, interpersonal influences were stronger when the uncertainty of a socially risky apparel style was involved.

Choice of Comparison Others

Social comparison research has examined how people compare themselves with others and what motivates this comparison. Festinger emphasized the information seeking or self-evaluative benefit of social comparison. Clearly, there is utility in possessing an accurate assessment of oneself. Selecting similar others as standards of comparison rather than dissimilar others provides more precise information (e.g., the amateur violinist is better able to gauge his or her abilities by comparing the self with other amateurs than with a virtuoso).

In a refinement of the theory, others have noted that similarity must be specific to relevant dimensions (Goethals and Darley 1977). For example, when a student wonders whether he has purchased the correct attire for a wedding, he would choose as comparisons those with relevant characteristics (e.g., the attire selected by those of similar age, sex, and social status) rather than irrelevant characteristics (e.g., those of similar eye color or skill at tennis). Comparisons are more likely to be made on dimensions for which one is schematic (Miller 1984). For example individuals schematic on gender are more likely to compare themselves with those of a similar gender, relative to those aschematic on gender. Whether people actually think of others in terms of multiple distinct dimensions, such as age, sex, and status, seems unlikely. Instead, broad categorizations of others as similar to the self probably are salient depending on the comparison to be made.

Downward Comparisons

More recent social comparison research has explored the hedonic needs, as opposed to informational needs, that can influence ability evaluations (for a review, see Wood 1989). Comparisons with similar others may be informative but can lead one to feel insecure, guilty, or deviant should they be unfavorable. The threat to one's self-esteem leads to preferences for downward comparisons (Brickman and Bulman 1977; Pyszczynski, Greenberg, and LaPrelle 1985; Wills 1981). Consumers will arrive at a more favorable evaluation and feel better about themselves if they compare themselves against those with lesser abilities. For example, to minimize loss of self-esteem, a consumer who makes an unwise purchase might select for comparison other consumers who chose even more foolishly. In attribution theory terms, downward comparisons provide consensus information that is more likely to lead to external attributions for negative events (e.g., to infer that others would also have made a poor purchase).

However, downward evaluation seems to be accompanied by upward affiliation (Taylor and Lobel 1989). Contact with more expert or skilled others provides information about how to improve one's lot, as well as the inspiration to do it. Thus, upward affiliation may facilitate diffusion of innovation.

Cognitive Processes in Comparisons

Social comparisons may be more pervasive and automatic than Festinger originally proposed (Wood 1989). Rather than a completely selective process, the choosing of others for comparison may at times be based upon those who are salient or highly available in memory

and so present themselves in memory as a source of comparison information. For example, students have more frequent social contacts with similar others than do housewives and so seem to be more susceptible to social comparisons with their peers (Park and Lessig 1977). Frequent advertising may make certain comparisons to others highly available for retrieval from memory, particularly when they fit the criteria of being similar to the target on relevant characteristics. For example, the heavy television viewer may be more susceptible to making dissatisfying comparisons with the exciting and affluent lifestyles commonly portrayed in the media (cf. O'Guinn and Faber 1987).

On the other hand, there is some evidence for discrimination in the selection of comparison others, to the point where individuals sometimes create or cognitively construct others (Wood, Taylor, and Lichtman 1985). Thus, a consumer might simulate or imagine others who suffer worse outcomes in order to feel better about the self. For example, consumers who are disadvantaged in terms of material goods may console themselves by imaging others with fewer valuable possessions.

Overview

Social comparison theory has emphasized the social world as a source of self-evaluation for many abilities and opinions. It is one of the more durable of social cognition theories. Numerous advances in the late 1980s have further broadened and strengthened the theory. Such developments as greater understanding of the cognitive mechanisms involved in comparison, increased precision regarding who is chosen as a comparison other and recognition of the multiple goals that influence the need for comparison have increased the theory's usefulness for understanding consumers.

Further, as a theory of consumer behavior, social comparison theory has advantages over reference group theory, another common approach to the relationship between a consumer and others. A reference group refers to those to whom an individual turns as a standard for behavior (Hyman 1942). Thus, a middle-class consumer might model the opinions and purchasing habits of other middle-class consumers in the belief that these are appropriate and desirable. The notion of the reference group, as used in consumer behavior, is more descriptive, classifying types of reference groups (e.g., aspirational, dissociative), but inadequately indicating how people choose reference groups or why and when particular groups are chosen. Social comparison theory's greater specificity on these issues yields greater predictive ability.

INFERENCES ABOUT THE EXTENT TO WHICH OTHERS SHARE ONE'S OPINIONS

Social comparison theory deals with how individuals use *others'* opinions to evaluate *one's own* opinions. We now turn to research examining related issues, but with a different focus. Some of the research investigates the use of *one's own* opinion as a basis for inferring *others'* opinions. Other research in this section investigates belief similarities, like social comparison theory, but emphasizes effects of being in the majority or minority.

These types of social inferences are quite pertinent to consumer behavior. Beliefs about others' opinions are an important component in many fundamental theories and concepts in consumer behavior, such as the theory of reasoned action (Ajzen and Fishbein 1980; Shimp and Kavas 1984), perceived social risk (Jacoby and Kaplan 1972), and conformity and compliance (Bearden and Etzel 1982; Burnkrant and Cousineau 1975). Moreover, inferring the extent to which others share one's own opinions is particularly important for specific kinds of consumer behaviors. Household decision making proceeds more smoothly if the family members are able to discern others' preferences and opinions. Certainly, skill at bargaining and negotiation is related to using tactics based on accurate inferences about the other's preferences (e.g., Dwyer, Schurr, and Oh 1987; Evans and Beltramini 1987; Weitz 1978). Another consumer behavior in which accurate assessment of others' opinions has obvious importance is gift giving. Gifts are sometimes chosen with the intent of changing the recipient in a manner fitting the giver's desires (Belk 1978; McCracken 1986). Yet, the recipient's delight with the gift should increase as it corresponds with the recipient's preference. Research investigating the extent to which others share one's opinions falls into three interrelated areas: the false consensus effect, the pluralistic ignorance effect, and the majority versus minority group conformity effect. Unlike the previous sections in this chapter, no single theoretical approach unifies the consideration of these phenomena.

A False Consensus about Others' Beliefs?

Many researchers have proposed that people falsely assume consensus for their beliefs, inferring more similarity than is warranted between the self and others (e.g., Marks and Miller 1987; Mullen et al. 1985). As noted earlier, individuals perceive more similarity with other members of the in-group than with out-group members, and they also perceive more attitudinal variability within their group and more homogeneity for the out-group. False consensus differs from the in-group bias in that false consensus refers to the general tendency to overestimate *how many* others agree with one's opinions and behavior, regardless of their group affiliation.

Early research examined various sources of false consensus, whether due to informational or motivational biases. Affective enhancement serves as a motivation to believe that others share one's beliefs. Commonly held preferences and consumption habits bolster one's ego by assuring one that they are appropriate and correct (cf. social comparison theory). For example, nonconservationists can justify their irresponsible behavior by believing that most others also waste energy (Van der Pligt 1984, 1985). Smokers overestimate the number of other smokers, perhaps to reassure themselves that it is not so deviant a behavior (Sherman et al. 1983).

Despite these studies emphasizing the motivational determinants of false consensus, more research has found informational determinants for the effect (see reviews by Marks and Miller 1987; Mullen et al. 1985). For example, using one's own beliefs to infer those of others may be a fairly rational process of what is termed "anchoring and adjustment" (e.g., Hoch 1987). When one has limited information about others' opinions, it makes sense to use one's own opinions as a starting point or anchor for prediction. Then one might adjust for those factors that should lead to differences.

Hoch and his colleagues have found evidence for this sort of process in husband-wife decision making. Further, contrary to what many "false consensus" researchers have maintained, people often increase their accuracy when they assume similarity between themselves and others. When asked to predict their spouses' liking for various new products, the husband and wife seemed to anchor predictions for their partner on their own preferences (Davis, Hoch, and Ragsdale 1986). Then they adjusted their predictions to account for their partner's differences in preferences. However, in most cases spouses would have performed better had they taken their own preferences into account more when predicting partners' preferences. Thus, the "error" made in inferring the spouse's preferences was not in projecting one's own opinion on to the other but in the extent to which they adjusted for how they thought the partner would respond. The discrepancy occurred because spouses tend to be similar to each other and because each spouse did not seem to know which dimensions would predict differences between their own and their partner's choices.

Similar results were found by Hoch (1987) when examining students' ability to predict opinions held by spouses, peers, and the general population. The opinions tested included political (e.g., "communism is the greatest peril in the world today"), consumer (e.g., "I like to pay cash for everything I buy"), and lifestyle (e.g., "I am a homebody") items. Subjects used their own opinions to infer the opinions of others, particularly for peers (fellow MBA students) and spouses. But most subjects could have improved their predictive accuracy had

they weighed their own opinions more heavily. People seem to recognize that others are different from the self, but have difficulty identifying the relevant differences. Low-predictive accuracy was also found in a similar study by Hoch (1988). Even marketing professionals who were considered experts in estimating consumer opinion proved no more accurate than the students, apparently for the same reasons. In summary, the motivational basis for, and even the existence of a *false* consensus for belief similarity has been called into question.

Pluralistic Ignorance

Insufficient weighing of one's own beliefs in predicting others' opinions and behaviors is not an entirely new observation, but it has been thought to occur in a more limited circumstance that has been described as pluralistic ignorance. *Pluralistic ignorance* occurs when people assume that their own (usually socially undesirable) behaviors or traits are not shared by others (Miller and McFarland 1987). Because open communication about the socially undesirable behavior or opinion is inhibited, people may not realize it is widespread. This phenomenon is particularly relevant for consumers' purchases of "unmentionables." For example, certain physical ailments (e.g., incontinence among the elderly) are quite common but often go untreated partly because the individual does not realize that many others also share the problem. Consequently, they feel stigmatized when buying products that deal with the condition. Advertising may help correct such misperceptions by explicitly informing consumers about the prevalence of their experiences (e.g., by stating the number of people who have dandruff). An additional benefit of advertising is that consumers may infer from frequent ads in the mass media that problems are more common than they thought (see also Chapter 10 on Mass Communication by O'Guinn and Faber). For example, television ads for alcoholic treatment centers may imply that drinking problems are common.

A major source of pluralistic ignorance seems to be the belief that fear of embarrassment has a more potent effect on one's own behavior than on others (Miller and McFarland 1987). That is, consumers may underestimate the consequences of social risk in product purchase for others as compared with the self. There is evidence to confirm that social inhibition is common. A recent survey of a cross section of adults found that 68 percent of the sample "do not like to have others notice and comment on my appearance." And 83 percent said they "do not like to be the center of attention" (Harris 1987).

Whereas individuals often go to great lengths to avoid a potentially humiliating course of action, they may underestimate the number of others who also experience such social inhibition (Miller and McFarland 1987). For example, one reason consumers do not complain to retailers about product problems is fear of being embarrassed (Richins 1982; Richins and Verhage 1985). Because people generally try to hide their embarrassment and feel uncomfortable discussing embarrassing incidents, consumers are likely to assume that others experience less chagrin in these situations and, therefore, that firms receive more feedback about defective and problem products than they actually do.

Consequences of Being in the Majority or Minority

Pluralistic ignorance focuses on one's mistaken belief that one holds a deviant position. More generally, beliefs about the extent of agreement with one's position, whether one holds minority or majority positions, have interesting cognitive consequences (Nemeth 1988). When one feels that one holds a minority opinion, awareness of the majority opinion may focus attention on that opinion under the assumption that it is more likely to be correct. Further, the tensions that often accompany perception of deviance can hinder information processing. For example, disagreeing with the majority of other household members about a product purchase can lead to stress and poor decision making. In contrast, exposure to a minority opinion when one believes oneself to

be in the majority can stimulate consideration of more alternative positions—in addition to the minority position one has been exposed to. For example, dissent over a group purchase decision can lead those in the majority to consider other alternatives, beyond the one proposed by the minority member. Thus, the outcome of group consumer decision making may actually be improved if members hold divergent views, although the level of conflict may make the process more aversive.

Overview

The phenomena discussed in this section are concerned with inferences about others' opinions and, particularly, with the commonality of one's own opinions. It is not so surprising that people err when judging others' opinions. The issues of interest in this line of research are why does this happen and what effect does this have. Cognitive processes can illuminate the answers to these questions (e.g., cognitive processes of anchoring and adjustment are used to judge others' opinions).

Although cognitive processes have been hypothesized as playing important roles in the phenomena discussed in this section, we should not forget that the nature of social interaction is also important. Norms of conflict avoidance restrain the expression of different opinions and so leave people uncertain about what others think. Social inhibition prevents sharing opinions, and this can lead to pluralistic ignorance. Others' disapproval contributes to the tension experienced by minority opinion holders. Such social interaction variables deserve more attention in the consumer behavior literature.

COGNITION AND SOCIAL INTERACTION

Many of the consumer behaviors discussed in the previous sections are social in that they involve mental representations of others and the relationship between the self and others. Consumer behavior becomes even more complex when social interaction is involved. Doubtless this complexity partially accounts for the fact that consumers' social interactions are infrequently studied, even though interactions between people are often necessary before culminating in an exchange. Consumers interact with service providers, salespeople, complaint handlers, market researchers, and other consumers when they acquire information about products, use products, and make joint decisions about products.

Anticipating Interaction

Let us first consider the most basic aspect of interaction, anticipating a social exchange. Planning to make a purchase can lead a consumer to foresee interaction with a salesperson or service provider, as when the consumer intends to hire an accountant, painter, plumber, or other service provider. Simply anticipating a social exchange influences the consumer's behavior. Compared with when no interaction is expected, anticipated interaction leads one to better recall information provided in advance about the person, to make causal attributions for the other's behavior, and to like the other more (Berscheid, Graziano, Monson, and Dermer 1976; Devine, Sedikides, and Fuhrman 1989; Srull and Brand 1983). One is also more likely to utilize incongruous information about the other (Erber and Fiske 1984).

Considering these effects, it is not surprising that people often modify their opinions when anticipating social interaction. People who believe that their beliefs are about to be attacked sometimes change and tend toward agreement with the attacker (McGuire and Millman 1965). This anticipatory belief change has been attributed to impression management concerns. The individual expects to be persuaded but wants to appear to have agreed with the message all along. Thus, knowing that a salesperson or another consumer will criticize one's product preference may lead a consumer to change opinions in order to be in line with that yet to be expressed criticism.

More generally, simply anticipating having to justify one's product preference to others of unknown opinions influences the kinds of prod-

uct choices a consumer makes (Simonson 1989). Consumers expecting to account for their brand choice take into consideration whether or not a compelling argument can be made for their selection. Specifically, given a choice of brands that varied on an array of attributes, subjects expressed a preference for the brand whose attributes would be easier to justify to others when their choice would be made public, but they expressed different preferences when their choice was to be anonymous. Decision rules varied depending on the presence of an audience and the particular product. These self-presentational concerns have led Simonson to conclude that "the more complex decision processes of accountable decision makers do not necessarily lead to better decisions" (p. 172). This is in contrast to Tetlock's (1985) contention that accountable decisions lead to improved decision making because the decision maker engages in "preemptive self-criticism."

Self-Fulfilling Prophesies in Interaction

Prior expectancies (or schemas) about the salesperson or service provider can also influence the nature of the interaction. Research into self-fulfilling prophesies suggests that people behave consistently with their expectations, and these behaviors elicit responses that tend to confirm what they expect. For example, when people believe in advance that others like them, their subsequent interaction is quite different than if they believe others dislike them (Curtis and Miller 1986). They engage in more self-disclosure, use a more pleasant tone of voice, disagree less, and withhold expressions of dissimilarity. These findings suggest that consumers who expect a certain type of behavior (e.g., friendly service from an establishment) may be more likely to elicit just that sort of behavior from the seller. Similarly, in negotiation, those who bargain with a competitive orientation elicit a competitive response from the other, even if the other has a more cooperative orientation (Kelley and Stahelski 1979).

Schurr and Ozanne (1985) manipulated perceptions of a negotiator's trustworthiness and found that these differences persisted even after an interactive bargaining session. Thus, behavioral evidence that contradicted the manipulation did not eradicate the initial set given to the negotiators. For those instances when the others' behaviors do not confirm expectations, people pay more attention to those behaviors that do confirm expectations, unless they are motivated to form an accurate impression (Neuberg and Fiske 1987).

A particularly interesting aspect of such self-fulfilling prophesies is that people do not seem to recognize that by acting in such a biased manner, they elicit behaviors from the other that confirm their expectancies. That is, they do not take into account their own influence when forming impressions of others. For example, when a person is induced to act in a self-promoting (versus modest) manner, the corresponding behavior is elicited from a partner (Baumeister, Hutton, and Tice 1989). However, the partner's behavior is not interpreted as a result of one's own self-promotion (or modesty). Similarly, a hostile consumer may elicit correspondingly hostile behavior from a service provider, complaint handler, or salesperson, without realizing that his or her own behavior provoked such a reaction. Self-fulfilling prophesies may be partially due to the consumer's often limited cognitive resources when interacting with others. The information processing capacity devoted to managing one's self-presentation reduces the capacity available for other cognitive tasks. Thus, one is less able to process information occurring during the interchange (Baumeister et al. 1989).

Changing Cognitions after Social Interaction

The act of communicating with another about an issue can change one's initial beliefs. When a communicator tailors a message to fit the listener's bias, the communicator's memory of the original material may become distorted so that it is more consistent with the message (Higgins and Rholes 1978). Thus, even when word-of-mouth communication about a prod-

uct is unidirectional (as in the two-step flow opinion leader model), the act of tailoring one's message can alter one's initial opinion. For example, people are more likely to relay negative impressions by word-of-mouth about products than positive impressions (Arndt 1967; Mizerski 1982). Conversations about product failure may make these experiences more available in memory and so overestimated in frequency (Folkes 1988b).

Overview

Social interaction is almost always influenced by self-presentational and impression management concerns, so that consumers adjust their behaviors to fit assumptions about those with whom they interact. Different approaches are likely when a consumer believes that the complaint handler will try to pin the blame for a product problem on the customer, when the consumer anticipates a hard sell from a salesperson, when the consumer assumes the survey researcher will disapprove of the consumer's expression of certain attitudes, and so on. One interesting aspect of interactions is that they necessitate people making inferences about others, often simultaneously throughout the communication process. Whereas consumers may generally be quite conscious of tailoring their behaviors to fit different situations, they may be oblivious to the ways such cognitive factors as information overload and memory biases influence, and are influenced by, social interaction. This is a fruitful area for future research.

CONCLUSION AND GENERAL DIRECTIONS FOR FUTURE RESEARCH

For consumer behavior an understanding of the cognitive processes underlying how one classifies, evaluates, and judges the self and others is essential. After all, the marketplace revolves around the transaction — the exchange of values between two parties (Hunt 1983, Kotler 1972). The flow of goods from one person to another cannot proceed without a conception of who one is and the meaning of one's own and others' behaviors. The topics discussed in this chapter illustrate the value of comprehending how consumers perceive themselves and others. Research on self-schemas, role schemas, social comparison theory, and biases in judgments about the self and others has shed light on numerous other topics of concern to consumer researchers, including advertising, sales messages, sales promotion techniques, the diffusion of innovations, household decision making, consumer complaining behavior, bargaining, and negotiation.

At various points in this chapter we have suggested specific hypotheses that might be tested, as well as issues that have received little attention in the consumer behavior literature. In addition, some broader recommendations for future research can be seen. One general research direction lies in a closer examination of the dynamic role of the self in consumer behavior. Although consumer researchers have recognized the influence that individual-level factors (e.g., personality and self-concept) have on consumer behavior, researchers have virtually ignored the influence that one's judgments or decisions may in turn have on the development of a consumer's self-schema.

Another general direction for research lies in recognizing and identifying the multiple goals underlying an individual's consumption behavior. Examples of possible directions for research can be seen in this chapter's discussion of (1) self-serving biases (i.e., the contrast between ego-protective needs versus the informational needs used to explain one's outcomes), (2) social comparison theory (i.e., the contrast between comparing oneself against similar others to accurately evaluate oneself versus downward comparisons for self-esteem maximization), and (3) the false consensus effect (i.e., the contrast between assuming others share one's opinions to bolster one's ego versus using a cognitive process of anchoring and adjustment to infer others' opinions). The particular goal pursued by the consumer is often primed by the context,

and this has important implications for consumer behavior. For instance, Skowronski and Carlston (1989) found that people weigh information differentially depending on the valence and type of social judgment to be made.

The field would also benefit by greater awareness of the literature discussing person perception, impression formation, and interpersonal processes. The inferences one makes about others will influence the course of their interaction. When the exchange of goods in the marketplace involves services rather than objects, social processes are undeniably central. Consumers form impressions of service providers, categorize the individuals providing the service, and modify their self-presentations in anticipation of and during interaction with service personnel.

Further, consumer researchers may not have fully considered the extent to which social cognition comes into play. For example, country of origin research certainly involves the examination of social inference processes, yet investigations of this topic have generally been limited to an attitude framework (e.g., Johansson, Douglas, and Nonaka 1985). People may even derive social meaning from seemingly nonsocial entities in the marketplace. Consumers appear to attribute human qualities, such as intentions and personality dispositions, to products and firms, especially when encouraged by brand names and logos.

This brief overview of some future research directions gives a sense of the many intriguing issues that need to be addressed. At the core of these complex issues is the search for how consumers give meaning to their own and others' actions in the marketplace. Consumer researchers have used such concepts as schemas and causal attributions to illuminate the content of such cognitions and the processes involved. Considerable progress has been made in terms of defining the content of consumers' perceptions, the processes used to infer the meaning of one's own and others' behaviors in the marketplace, and the biases displayed in consumers' inferences.

REFERENCES

AJZEN, ICEK, and MARTIN FISHBEIN (1980). *Understanding Attitudes and Predicting Social Behavior,* Englewood Cliffs, NJ: Prentice-Hall.

ALLEN, CHRIS T. (1982). "Self-Perception Based Strategies for Stimulating Energy Conservation," *Journal of Consumer Research,* 8 (March), 381-390.

ALLEN, CHRIS T., and WILLIAM R. DILLON (1983). "Self-Perception Development and Consumer Choice Criteria: Is There A Linkage?" in *Advances in Consumer Research,* Vol. 10, Eds. Richard P. Bagozzi and Alice M. Tybout. Ann Arbor, MI: Association for Consumer Research, 45-50.

ANDERSON, NORMAN H. (1970). "Functional Measurement and Psychophysical Judgment," *Psychological Review,* 77 (May), 153-170.

ARNDT, JOHAN (1967). "Role of Product-Related Conversation in the Diffusion of a New Product," *Journal of Marketing Research,* 4 (August), 291-295.

ASCH, SOLOMON E. (1946). "Forming Impressions of Personality," *Journal of Abnormal and Social Psychology,* 41 (July), 258-290.

ASHMORE, RICHARD D., and FRANCES K. DEL BOCA (1981). "Conceptual Approaches to Stereotypes and Stereotyping," in *Cognitive Processes in Stereotyping and Intergroup Behavior,* Ed. David L. Hamilton. Hillsdale, NJ: Erlbaum, 1-35.

BANDURA, ALBERT (1989). "Human Agency in Social Cognition Theory," *American Psychologist,* 9 (September), 1175-1184.

BAUMEISTER, ROY F., DEBRA G. HUTTON, and DIANNE M. TICE (1989). "Cognitive Processes During Deliberate Self-Presentation: How Self-Presenters Alter and Misinterpret the Behavior of their Interaction Partners," *Journal of Experimental Social Psychology,* 25 (January), 59-78.

BEARDEN, WILLIAM O., and MICHAEL J. ETZEL (1982). "Reference Group Influence on Product and Brand Purchase Decisions," *Journal of Consumer Research,* 9 (September), 183-194.

BELCH, GEORGE, MICHAEL A. BELCH, and GAYLE CERESINO (1985). "Parental and Teenage Child Influences in Family Decision Making," *Journal of Business Research,* 13 (April), 163-176.

BELK, RUSSELL B. (1978). "Gift Giving Behavior," in *Research in Marketing,* Vol. 2., Ed. Jagdish Sheth. Greenwich CT: JAI Press, 95-126.

BELK, RUSSELL B. (1988). "Possessions and the Extended Self," *Journal of Consumer Research,* 15 (September), 139-168.

BELK, RUSSELL B., KENNETH D. BAHN, and ROBERT N. MAYER (1982). "Developmental Recognition of Consumption Symbolism" *Journal of Consumer Research,* 9 (June), 4-17.

BELK, RUSSELL B., JOHN PAINTER, and RICHARD SEMENIK (1981). "Preferred Solutions to the Energy Crisis as a Function of Causal Attributions," *Journal of Consumer Research,* 8 (December), 306-312.

BEM, DARYL (1972). "Self Perception Theory," in *Advances in Experimental Social Psychology,* Vol. 6, Ed. Leonard Berkowitz. New York: Academic Press.

BEM, SANDRA L. (1974). "The Measurement of Psychological Androgyny," *Journal of Consulting and Clinical Psychology,* 42 (April), 155-162.

BEM, SANDRA L. (1981). "Gender Schema Theory: A Cognitive Account of Sex Typing," *Psychological Review,* 88 (July), 354-364.

BEM, SANDRA L. (1985). "Androgyny and Gender Schema Theory: A Conceptual and Empirical Integration," in *Nebraska Symposium on Motivation: Psychology and Gender,* Ed. Theo B. Sonderegger. Lincoln, NE: University of Nebraska Press, 179-226.

BERSCHEID, ELLEN, WILLIAM GRAZIANO, THOMAS MONSON, and MARSHALL DERMER (1976). "Outcome Dependency: Attention, Attribution and Attraction," *Journal of Personality and Social Psychology,* 34 (November), 978-989.

BETTMAN, JAMES (1979). *An Information Processing Theory of Consumer Choice.* Reading, MA: Addison-Wesley.

BETTMAN, JAMES, B. NOEL CAPON, and RICHARD J. LUTZ (1975). 'Cognitive Algebra in Multi-Attribute Attitude Models," *Journal of Marketing Research,* 12 (May), 151-164.

BLOCH, PETER, and MARSHA RICHINS (1982). "A Theoretical Model for the Study of Product Importance Perceptions," *Journal of Marketing,* 47 (Summer), 69-81.

BOWER, GORDON H., JOHN B. BLACK, and TERENCE J. TURNER (1979). "Scripts in Memory for Text," *Cognitive Psychology,* 11, 177-220.

BRADLEY, GIFFORD WEARY (1978). "Self-Serving Biases in the Attribution Process: A Re-Examination of the Fact or Fiction Question," *Journal of*

Personality and Social Psychology, 36 (January), 56–71.

BREWER, MARILYN B. (1979). "In-Group Bias in the Minimal Intergroup Situation: A Cognitive-Motivational Analysis," *Psychological Bulletin,* 86 (2), 307–324.

BREWER, MARILYN B., VALERIE DULL, and LAYTON LUI (1981). "Perceptions of the Elderly: Stereotypes as Prototypes," *Journal of Personality and Social Psychology,* 41 (April), 656–670.

BRICKMAN, PHILLIP, and RONNIE J. BULMAN (1977). "Pleasure and Pain in Social Comparison," in *Social Comparison Processes: Theoretical and Empirical Perspectives,* Eds. J. M. Suls and R. L. Miller. Washington, DC: Hemisphere.

BURNKRANT, ROBERT E., and ALAIN COUSINEAU (1975). "Informational and Normative Social Influences in Buyer Behavior," *Journal of Consumer Research,* 2 (December), 206–215.

CANTOR, NANCY, and WALTER MISCHEL (1977). "Traits as Prototypes: Effects on Recognition Memory," *Journal of Personality and Social Psychology,* 35 (January), 38–48.

CANTOR, NANCY, and WALTER MISCHEL (1979). "Prototypes in Person Perception," *Advances in Experimental Social Psychology,* 12, 3–52.

COHEN, JOEL B., and KUNAL BASU (1987). "Alternative Models of Categorization: Toward a Contingent Processing Framework," *Journal of Consumer Research,* 13 (March), 455–472.

COOLEY, CHARLES H. (1902). *Human Nature and the Social Order.* Glencoe, IL: Free Press.

COURTNEY, ALICE E., and THOMAS W. WHIPPLE (1983). *Sex Stereotyping in Advertising.* Toronto: Lexington Books.

CROCKER, JENNIFER, SUSAN T. FISKE, and SHELLEY E. TAYLOR (1984). "Schematic Bases of Belief Change," in *Attitudinal Judgment,* Ed. J. Richard Eiser. New York: Springer-Verlag, 197–226.

CROCKER, JENNIFER, DARLENE B. HANNAH, and RENEE WEBER (1983). "Person Memory and Causal Attributions," *Journal of Personality and Social Psychology,* 44 (January), 55–66.

CROCKER, JENNIFER, and RENEE WEBER (1983). "Cognitive Structure and Stereotype Change," in *Advances in Consumer Research,* Vol. 10, Eds. Richard P. Bagozzi and Alice M. Tybout. Ann Arbor, MI: Association for Consumer Research, 459–463.

CURTIS, REBECCA C., and KIM MILLER (1986). "Believing Another Likes or Dislikes You: Behav-

ior Making the Beliefs Come True," *Journal of Personality and Social Psychology,* 51 (August), 284–290.

DAVIS, HARRY L., STEPHEN J. HOCH, and E. K. EASTON RAGSDALE (1986). "An Anchoring and Adjustment Model of Spousal Predictions," *Journal of Consumer Research,* 13 (June), 25–37.

DESHPANDE, ROHIT, WAYNE D. HOYER, and NAVEEN DONTHU (1986). "The Intensity of Ethnic Affiliation: A Study of the Sociology of Hispanic Consumption," *Journal of Consumer Research,* 13 (September), 214–220.

DEVINE, PATRICIA G., CONSTANTINE SEDIKIDES, and ROBERT W. FUHRMAN (1989). "Goals in Social Information Processing: The Case of Anticipated Interaction," *Journal of Personality and Social Psychology,* 56 (May), 680–690.

DOLICH, IRA J. (1969). "Congruence Relationships Between Self Images and Product Brands," *Journal of Marketing Research,* 6 (February), 80–85.

DREBEN, ELIZABETH K., SUSAN T. FISKE, and REID HASTIE (1970). "The Independence of Evaluative and Item Information: Impression and Recall Order Effects in Behavior-based Impression Formation," *Journal of Personality and Social Psychology,* 37 (October), 1758–1768.

DWYER, F. ROBERT, PAUL H. SCHURR, and SEJO OH (1987). "Developing Buyer-Seller Relationships," *Journal of Marketing,* 51 (April), 11–27.

ERBER, RALPH, and SUSAN T. FISKE (1984). "Outcome Dependency and Attention to Inconsistent Information," *Journal of Personality and Social Psychology,* 47 (October), 709–726.

EVANS, KENNETH R., and RICHARD BELTRAMINI (1987). "A Theoretical Model of Consumer Negotiated Pricing: An Orientation Perspective," *Journal of Marketing,* 51 (April), 58–73.

FABER, RONALD J., and THOMAS O'GUINN (1989). "Classifying Compulsive Consumers: Advances in the Development of a Diagnostic Tool," in *Advances in Consumer Research,* Vol. 16, Ed. Thomas J. Srull. Provo, UT: Association for Consumer Research, 738–744.

FESTINGER, LEON (1954). "A Theory of Social Comparison Processes," *Human Relations,* 7. 117–140.

FESTINGER, LEON (1950). "Informal Social Communication," *Psychological Review,* 57, 271–282.

FISKE, SUSAN T. (1982). "Schema-Triggered Affect: Applications to Social Perception," in *Affect and Cognition: The 17th Annual Carnegie Symposium on*

Cognition, Eds. Margaret S. Clark and Susan T. Fiske. Hillsdale, NJ: Erlbaum, 55–78.

FISKE, SUSAN T., and PATRICIA W. LINVILLE (1980). "What Does the Schema Concept Buy Us?" *Personality and Social Psychology Bulletin,* 6 (December), 543–557.

FISKE, SUSAN T., and SHELLEY E. TAYLOR (1984). *Social Cognition,* Reading, MA: Addison-Wesley, 139–181.

FOLKES, VALERIE S. (1984). "Consumer Reactions to Product Failure: An Attributional Approach," *Journal of Consumer Research,* 10 (March), 398–409.

FOLKES, VALERIE S. (1988a). "Recent Attribution Research in Consumer Behavior: A Review and New Directions," *Journal of Consumer Research,* 14 (March), 548–565.

FOLKES, VALERIE S. (1988b). "The Availability Heuristic and Perceived Risk," *Journal of Consumer Research,* 15 (June), 13–23.

FOLKES, VALERIE S., and BARBARA KOTSOS (1986). "Buyers' and Sellers' Explanations for Product Failure: Who Done It," *Journal of Marketing,* 50 (April), 74–80.

FOLKES, VALERIE S., SUSAN KOLETSKY, and JOHN GRAHAM (1987). "A Field Study of Causal Inferences and Consumer Reaction: The View from the Airport," *Journal of Consumer Research,* 13 (March), 534–539.

FOXMAN, ELLEN R., PATRIYA S. TANSUHAJ, and KARIN M. EKSTROM (1989). "Family Members' Perceptions of Adolescents' Influence in Family Decision Making," *Journal of Consumer Research,* 15 (March), 482–490.

GILLY, MARY C. (1988). "Sex Roles in Advertising: A Comparison of Television Advertisements in Australia, Mexico and the United States," *Journal of Marketing,* 52 (April), 75–85.

GOETHALS, GEORGE R., and JOHN M. DARLEY (1977). "Social Comparison Theory: An Attributional Approach," in *Social Comparison Processes: Theoretical and Empirical Perspectives,* Eds. J. M. Suls and R. L. Miller. Washington, DC: Hemisphere.

GREENWALD, ANTHONY G., and CLARK LEAVITT (1984). "Audience Involvement in Advertising: Four Levels," *Journal of Consumer Research,* 11 (June), 581–592.

GREENWALD, ANTHONY G., and ANTHONY R. PRATKANIS (1984). "The Self," in *Handbook of Social Cognition,* Vol. 3, Eds. Robert S. Wyer, Jr.,

and Thomas K. Srull. Hillsdale, NJ: Erlbaum, 129–178.

GRUBB, E. L., and G. HUPP (1968). "Perception of Self, Generalized Stereotypes, and Brand Selection," *Journal of Marketing Research,* 5 (February), 58–63.

HAIRE, MASON (1950). "Projective Techniques in Marketing Research," *Journal of Marketing,* 14 (April), 649–656.

HAMILTON, DAVID L., LAWRENCE B. KATZ, and VON O. LEIRER (1980). "Organization Processes in Impression Formation," in *Person Memory: The Cognitive Basis of Social Perception,* Eds. Reid Hastie, Thomas M. Ostrom, Ebbe B. Ebbesen, Robert S. Wyer, Jr., David L. Hamilton, and Donal E. Carlston. Hillsdale, NJ: Erlbaum, 121–153.

HANSEN, ROBERT A. (1980). "A Self-Perception Interpretation of the Effect of Monetary and Nonmonetary Incentives on Mail Survey Respondent Behavior," *Journal of Marketing Research,* 17 (February), 77–83.

HARRIS, LOUIS (1987). *Inside America.* New York: Vintage Books.

HASTIE, REID (1980). "Memory for Behavioral Information that Confirms or Contradicts a Personality Impression," in *Person Memory: The Cognitive Basis of Social Perceptions,* Eds. Reid Hastie, Thomas M. Ostrom, Ebbe B. Ebbesen, Robert S. Wyer, Jr., David L. Hamilton, and Donal E. Carlston. Hillsdale, NJ: Erlbaum, 155–177.

HASTIE, REID (1981). "Schematic Principles in Human Memory," in *Social Cognition: The Ontario Symposium,* Vol. 1., Eds. E. Tory Higgins, C. Peter Herman, and Mark P. Zanna. Hillsdale, NJ: Erlbaum, 39–88.

HASTIE, REID, and PUROHIT KUMAR (1979). "Person Memory: Personality Traits as Organizing Principles in Memory for Behaviors," *Journal of Personality and Social Psychology,* 37 (January), 27–38.

HAYES-ROTH, B. (1977). "Evolution of Cognitive Structures and Processes," *Psychological Review,* 84, 260–278.

HEIDER, FRITZ (1958). *The Psychology of Interpersonal Relations.* New York: Wiley.

HIGGINS, E. TORY, and WILLIAM S. RHOLES (1978). "Saying is Believing: Effect of Message Modification on Memory and Liking for the Person Described," *Journal of Experimental Social Psychology,* 14 (July), 363–378.

HOCH, STEPHEN (1987). "Perceived Consensus and Predictive Accuracy: The Pros and Cons of Projection," *Journal of Personality and Social Psychology,* 53 (August), 221–234.

HOCH, STEPHEN (1988). "Who Do We Know: Predicting the Interests and Opinions of The American Consumer," *Journal of Consumer Research,* 15 (December), 315–324.

HOLMAN, REBECCA H. (1981). "Product Use as Communication: A Fresh Appraisal of a Venerable Topic," in *Review of Marketing,* Eds. Ben M. Enis and Kenneth J. Roering. Chicago, IL: American Marketing Association, 106–119.

HOUSTON, MICHAEL, and MICHAEL ROTHSCHILD (1978). "Conceptual and Methodological Perspectives on Involvement," in *American Marketing Association 1978 Educators' Proceedings,* Ed. Subhash C. Jain. Chicago, IL: American Marketing Association, 184–187.

HOWARD, JOHN W. and MYRON ROTHBART (1980). "Social Categorization and Memory for In-group and Out-group Behavior," *Journal of Personality and Social Psychology,* 38, 301–310.

HUNT, SHELBY D. (1983). *Marketing Theory: The Philosophy of Marketing Science,* Homewood, IL: Irwin.

HYMAN, H. H. (1942). "The Psychology of Status," *Archives of Psychology,* 38, No. 269.

JACOBY, JACOB, and LEON B. KAPLAN (1972). "The Components of Perceived Risk," in *Proceedings of the Third Annual Conference of the Association for Consumer Research,* Ed. M. Venkatesan. College Park, MD: Association for Consumer Research, 382–392.

JOHANSSON, JOHNY K., SUSAN P. DOUGLAS, and IKUJIRO NONAKA (1985). "Assessing the Impact of Country of Origin on Product Evaluations: A New Methodological Perspective," *Journal of Marketing Research,* 22 (November), 388–396.

JOHNSON, BLAIR T., and ALICE H. EAGLY (1989). "Effects of Involvement on Persuasion: A Meta Analysis," *Psychological Bulletin,* 106 (2), 290–314.

JONES, EDWARD E., and KEITH DAVIS (1965). "From Acts to Dispositions: The Attribution Process in Person Perception," in *Advances in Experimental Social Psychology,* Ed. Leonard Berkowitz. New York: Academic Press, 219–266.

KAMINS, MICHAEL A., and HENRY ASSAEL (1987). "Two-Sided Versus One-Sided Appeals: A Cognitive Perspective on Argumentation, Source Derogation, and the Effect of Disconfirming Trial on Belief Change," *Journal of Marketing Research,* 24 (February), 29–39.

KASSARJIAN, HAROLD H. (1978). "Presidential Address, 1977: Anthropomorphism and Parsimony," in *Advances in Consumer Research,* Vol. 5, Ed. H. Keith Hunt. Ann Arbor, MI: Association for Consumer Research, xiii–xiv.

KELLEY, HAROLD H. (1972). "Causal Schemata and the Attribution Process," *Attribution: Perceiving the Causes of Behavior,* Eds. Edward E. Jones, David E. Kanouse, Harold H. Kelley, Richard E. Nisbett, Stuart Valins, and Bernard Weiner. Morristown, NJ: General Learning Press, 151–174.

KELLEY, HAROLD H. (1973). "The Process of Causal Attribution," *American Psychologist,* 28 (February), 107–128.

KELLEY, HAROLD H., and ANTHONY J. STAHELSKI (1970). "Social Interaction Basis of Cooperators' and Competitors' Beliefs About Others," *Journal of Personality and Social Psychology,* 16 (September), 66–91.

KELMAN, HERBERT (1960). "Compliance, Identification, and Internalization: Three Processes of Attitude Change," *Journal of Conflict Resolution,* 2, 51–60.

KIESLER, TINA (1990). "The Influence of Schema Cues and Incongruent Information on Perceptions of Salespeople," unpublished dissertation, University of California, Los Angeles, CA.

KIRMANI, AMNA, and PETER WRIGHT (1989). "Money Talks: Perceived Advertising Expense and Expected Product Quality," *Journal of Consumer Research,* 16 (December), 344–353.

KOTLER, PHILIP (1972). "A Generic Concept of Marketing," *Journal of Marketing,* 36 (April), 46–54.

KRUGMAN, HERBERT E. (1965). "The Impact of Television Advertising: Learning without Involvement," *Public Opinion Quarterly,* 29 (Fall), 349–356.

KRYCH, RAYMOND (1989). "Abnormal Consumer Behavior: A Model of Addictive Behaviors," in *Advances in Consumer Research,* Vol. 16. Ed. Thomas K. Srull. Provo, UT: Association for Consumer Research, 745–748.

KULIK, JAMES A. (1983). "Confirmatory Attribution and the Perpetuation of Social Beliefs," *Journal of Personality and Social Psychology,* 44 (June), 1171–1181.

KUNDA, ZIVA, and RASYID SANITIOSO (1989). "Motivated Changes in the Self-Concept," *Journal of Experimental Social Psychology,* 25 (May), 272–285.

LAURENT, GILLES, and JEAN-NOEL KAPFERER (1985). "Measuring Consumer Involvement Profiles," *Journal of Marketing Research,* 22 (February, 41-53.

LICHTENSTEIN, DONALD R., and WILLIAM O. BEARDEN (1986). "Measurement and Structure of Kelley's Covariance Theory," *Journal of Consumer Research,* 13 (September), 290-296.

LINVILLE, PATRICIA W. (1982). "The Complexity-Extremity Effect and Age-Based Stereotyping," *Journal of Personality and Social Psychology,* 42 (February), 192-211.

LINVILLE, PATRICIA W., GREGORY W. FISCHER, and PETER SALOVEY (1989). "Perceived Distributions of the Characteristics of In-Group and Out-Group Members: Empirical Evidence and a Computer Simulation," *Journal of Personality and Social Psychology,* 57 (August), 165-188.

LINVILLE, PATRICIA W., and EDWARD E. JONES (1980). "Polarized Appraisals of Out-Group Members," *Journal of Personality and Social Psychology,* 38 (May), 689-703.

LORD, CHARLES G. (1980). "Schemas and Images as Memory Aids: Two Modes of Processing Social Information," *Journal of Personality and Social Psychology,* 38 (February), 257-269.

LUTZ, KATHY A., and RICHARD J. LUTZ (1978). "Imagery-Eliciting Strategies: Review and Implications of Research," in *Advances in Consumer Research,* Vol. 5, Ed. H. Keith Hunt, Ann Arbor, MI: Association for Consumer Research, 611-620.

LYSONSKI, STEVEN (1983). "Female and Male Portrayals in Magazine Advertisements: A Re-Examination," *Akron Business Review,* 14 (Summer), 45-50.

MACINNIS, DEBORAH J., and LINDA L. PRICE (1987). "The Role of Imagery in Information Processing: Review and Extensions," *Journal of Consumer Research,* 13 (March), 473-491.

MARKS, GARY, and NORMAN MILLER (1987). "Ten Years of Research on the False-Consensus Effect: An Empirical and Theoretical Review," *Psychological Bulletin,* 102 (July), 72-90.

MARKUS, HAZEL (1977). "Self-Schemata and Processing Information about the Self," *Journal of Personality and Social Psychology,* 35 (February), 63-78.

MARKUS, HAZEL, and KEITH SENTIS (1982). "The Self in Social Information Processing," in *Psychological Perspectives on the Self,* Ed. Jerry Suls. Hillsdale, NJ: Erlbaum, 41-70.

MARKUS, HAZEL, and JEANNE SMITH (1981). "The Influence of Self-Schemas on the Perception of Others," in *Personality, Cognition and Social Interaction,* Eds. Nancy Cantor and John F. Kihlstrom. Hillsdale, NJ: Erlbaum Associates, Inc. Publishers, 233-262.

MCCRACKEN, GRANT (1986). "Culture and Consumption: A Theoretical Account of the Structure and Movement of the Cultural Meaning of Consumer Goods," *Journal of Consumer Research,* 13 (June), 71-84.

MCGUIRE, WILLIAM J., and SUSAN MILLMAN (1965). "Anticipatory Belief Lowering Following Forewarning of a Persuasive Attack," *Journal of Personality and Social Psychology,* 2 (October), 471-479.

MCGUIRE, WILLIAM J., and ALICE PADAWER-SINGER (1976). "Trait Salience in the Spontaneous Self-Concept," *Journal of Personality and Social Psychology,* 33 (June), 743-754.

MCKEACHIE, WILLIAM J. (1952). "Lipstick as a Determinant of First Impression of Personality: An Experiment for the General Psychology Course," *Journal of Social Psychology,* 36, 241-244.

MEAD, GEORGE H. (1934). *Mind, Self and Society.* Chicago: University of Chicago Press.

MIDGLEY, DAVID F. (1983). "Patterns of Interpersonal Information Seeking for the Purchase of a Symbolic Product," *Journal of Marketing Research,* 20 (February), 74-83.

MILLER, CAROL T. (1984). "Self-Schemas, Gender and Social Comparisons: A Clarification of the Related Attributes Hypothesis," *Journal of Personality and Social Psychology,* 46 (June), 1222-1229.

MILLER, DALE T., and CATHY MCFARLAND (1987). "Pluralistic Ignorance: When Similarity is Interpreted as Dissimilarity," *Journal of Personality and Social Psychology,* 53 (August), 298-305.

MILLER, DALE T., and MICHAEL ROSS (1975). "Self-Serving Biases in the Attribution of Causality: Fact or Fiction?" *Psychological Bulletin,* 28, 213-225.

MITCHELL, ANDREW (1979). "Involvement: A Potentially Important Mediator of Consumer Research," in *Advances in Consumer Research,* Vol. 6. Ed. William L. Wilkie. Ann Arbor, MI: Association for Consumer Research, 191-196.

MIZERSKI, RICHARD W. (1982). "An Attribution Explanation of the Disproportionate Influence of Unfavorable Information," *Journal of Consumer Research,* 9 (December), 301-310.

MIZERSKI, RICHARD W., LINDA L. GOLDEN, and JEROME B. KERNAN (1979). "The Attribution Process in Consumer Decision Making," *Journal of Consumer Research*, 6 (September), 123–140.

MOSCHIS, GEORGE P. (1976). "Social Comparison and Informal Group Influence," *Journal of Marketing Research*, 13 (August), 237–244.

MULLEN, BRIAN, JENNIFER L. ATKINS, DEBBIE S. CHAMPION, CECELIA EDWARDS, DANA HARDY, JOHN E. STORY, and MARY VANDERKLOK (1985). "The False Consensus Effect: A Meta-Analysis of 115 Hypothesis Tests," *Journal of Experimental Social Psychology*, 21 (May), 262–259.

NEMETH, CHARLON JEANNE (1988). "Differential Contributions of Majority and Minority Influences," *Psychological Review*, 93 (January), 23–32.

NEUBERG, STEVEN, and SUSAN FISKE (1987). "Motivational Influences on Impression Formation: Outcome Dependency, Accuracy-Driven Attention and Individuating Processes," *Journal of Personality and Social Psychology*, 53 (September), 431–449.

O'GUINN, THOMAS C., and RONALD J. FABER (1987). "Mass Mediated Consumer Socialization: Non-Utilitarian and Dysfunctional Outcomes," in *Advances in Consumer Research*, Eds. Melanie Wallendorf and Paul Anderson. Provo, UT: Association for Consumer Research, 473–477.

OLIVER, RICHARD L., and WAYNE S. DESARBO (1988). "Response Determinants in Satisfaction Judgments," *Journal of Consumer Research*, 14 (March), 495–507.

PARK, C. WHAN (1982). "Joint Decisions in Home Purchasing: A Muddling Through Process," *Journal of Consumer Research*, 9 (September), 151–162.

PARK, C. WHAN, and V. PARKER LESSIG (1977). "Students and Housewives: Differences in Susceptibility to Reference Group Influence," *Journal of Consumer Research*, 4 (September), 102–110.

PETTIGREW, THOMAS F. (1979). "The Ultimate Attribution Error: Extending Allport's Cognitive Analysis of Prejudice," *Personality and Social Psychology Bulletin*, 5 (October), 461–476.

PETTY, RICHARD E., and JOHN T. CACIOPPO (1979). "Issue Involvement Can Increase or Decrease Persuasion by Enhancing Message-Relevant Cognitive Responses," *Journal of Personality and Social Psychology*, 37 (October), 1915–1926.

PYSZCZYNSKI, TOM, JEFF GREENBERG, and JOHN LAPRELLE (1985). "Social Comparison After Success and Failure: Biased Search for Information Consistent with a Self-Serving Conclusion," *Journal of Experimental Social Psychology*, 21, 195–211.

QUALLS, WILLIAM J. (1987). "Household Decision Behavior: The Impact of Husbands' and Wives' Sex Role Orientation," *Journal of Consumer Research*, 14 (September), 264–279.

RAY, MICHAEL L. (1973). "Psychological Theories and Interpretations of Learning," in *Consumer Behavior: Theoretical Perspectives*, Eds. Scott Ward and Thomas S. Robertson. Englewood Cliffs, NJ: Prentice-Hall, 45–117.

REINGEN, PETER H., and WILLIAM O. BEARDEN (1983). "Salience of Behavior and the Effects of Labeling," in *Advances in Consumer Research*, Vol. 10, Eds. Richard P. Bagozzi and Alice M. Tybout. Ann Arbor, MI: Association for Consumer Research, 51–55.

RICHINS, MARSHA L. (1982). "An Investigation of Consumers' Attitudes Toward Complaining," in *Advances in Consumer Research*, Vol. 9, Ed. Andrew Mitchell. Ann Arbor, MI: Association for Consumer Research, 502–506.

RICHINS, MARSHA L., and BRONISLOW J. VERHAGE (1985). "Cross Cultural Differences in Consumer Attitudes and their Implications for Complaint Management," *International Journal of Research in Marketing*, 2, 197–206.

ROBERTSON, THOMAS S., and JOHN R. ROSSITER (1974). "Children and Commercial Persuasion: An Attribution Theory Analysis," *Journal of Consumer Research*, 1 (June), 13–20.

ROSCH, ELEANOR, and CAROLYN B. MERVIS (1975). "Family Resemblances: Studies in the Internal Structure of Time Categories," *Cognitive Psychology*, 7 (October), 573–605.

ROSS, MICHAEL (1981). "Self-Centered Biases in Attributions of Responsibility: Antecedents and Consequences," in *Social Cognition: The Ontario Symposium*, Vol. I, Eds. E. Tory Higgins, C. Peter Herman, and Mark P. Zanna, Hillsdale, NJ: Erlbaum, 305–321.

ROSS, MICHAEL, and GARTH, J. O. FLETCHER (1985). "Attribution and Social Perception," in *Handbook of Social Psychology*, Vol. II, 3rd ed., Eds. Gardner Lindzey and Elliot Aronson. New York: Random House, 73–122.

ROTHSCHILD, MICHAEL L. (1984). "Perspectives in Involvement: Current Problems and Future Directions," in *Advances in Consumer Research*, Vol. 11, Ed. Tom Kinnear. Ann Arbor, MI: Association for Consumer Research, 216–217.

SANFT, HENRIANNE (1986). "The Role of Knowledge in The Effects of Television Advertising on Children," in *Advances in Consumer Research*, Vol. 13, Ed. Richard J. Lutz. Provo, UT: Association for Consumer Research, 147–152.

SANFT, HENRIANNE (1987). "Children's Processing of Advertising: Mediating Variables and Measurement Issues," unpublished dissertation, Carnegie-Mellon University, Pittsburgh, PA.

SCHINDLER, ROBERT M. (1988). "The Role of Ego-Expressive Factors in the Consumer's Satisfaction with Price," *Journal of Consumer Satisfaction, Dissatisfaction and Complaining Behavior*, 1, 34–39.

SCHINDLER, ROBERT M. (1989). "The Excitement of Getting a Bargain: Some Hypotheses Concerning the Origins and Effects of Smart-Shopper Feelings," *Advances in Consumer Research*, Vol. 16, Ed. Thomas K. Srull. Provo, UT: Association for Consumer Research, 447–453.

SCHMITT, BERND H., FRANCE LECLERC, and LAURETTE DUBE-RIOUX (1988). "Sex Typing and Consumer Behavior: A Test of Gender Schema Theory," *Journal of Consumer Research*, 15 (June), 122–128.

SCHURR, PAUL H., and JULIE L. OZANNE (1985). "Influences on Exchange Processes: Buyers' Preconception of a Seller's Trustworthiness and Bargaining Toughness," *Journal of Consumer Research*, 11 (March), 939–953.

SCOTT, CAROL, and RICHARD F. YALCH (1980). "Consumer Response to Initial Product Trial: A Bayesian Analysis," *Journal of Consumer Research*, 7 (June), 32–41.

SHERMAN, STEVEN J., CLARK C. PRESSON, LAURIE CHASSIN, ERIC CORTY, and RICHARD OLSHAVSKY (1983). "The False Consensus Effect in Estimates of Smoking Prevalence: Underlying Mechanisms," *Personality and Social Psychology Bulletin*, 9 (June), 197–207.

SHIMP, TERENCE A., and ALICAN KAVAS (1984). "The Theory of Reasoned Action Applied to Coupon Usage," *Journal of Consumer Research*, 11 (December), 795–810.

SIMONSON, ITAMAR (1989). "Choice Based on Persons: The Case of Attraction and Compromise Effects," *Journal of Consumer Research*, 16 (September), 158–174.

SIRGY, JOSEPH M. (1982). "Self-Concept in Consumer Behavior: A Critical Review," *Journal of Consumer Behavior*, 9 (December), 287–300.

SKOWRONSKI, JOHN J., and DONALD CARLSTON

(1989). "Negativity and Extremity Biases in Impression Formation: A Review of Explanations," *Psychological Bulletin*, 65 (January), 131–142.

SNYDER, CHARLES R., and RAYMOND L. HIGGINS (1988). "Excuses: Their Effective Role in the Negotiation of Reality," *Psychological Bulletin*, 104 (July), 23–35.

SPARKMAN, RICHARD, M., JR. (1982). "The Discounting Principle in the Perception of Advertising," in *Advances in Consumer Research*, Vol. 9, Ed. Andrew Mitchell. Ann Arbor, MI: Association for Consumer Research, 277–280.

SRULL, THOMAS K. (1981). "Person Memory: Some Tests of Associative Storage and Retrieval Models," *Journal of Experimental Psychology: Human Learning and Memory*, 7 (November), 440–463.

SRULL, THOMAS K., and JULIANNE F. BRAND (1983). "Memory for Information About Persons: The Effect of Encoding Operations Upon Subsequent Retrieval," *Journal of Verbal Learning and Verbal Behavior*, 22, 219–230.

STAFFORD, JAMES E. (1966). "Effects of Group Influence on Consumer Brand Preferences," *Journal of Marketing Research*, 3 (February), 68–72.

SUJAN, MITA, JAMES R. BETTMAN, and HARISH SUJAN (1986). "Effects of Consumer Expectations on Information Processing in Selling Encounters," *Journal of Marketing Research*, 23 (November), 346–353.

SURPRENANT, CAROL F., and MICHAEL R. SOLOMON (1987). "Predictability and Personalization in the Service Encounter," *Journal of Marketing*, 51 (April), 86–96.

SVENSON, O. (1981). "Are We All Less Risky and More Skillful Than Our Fellow Drivers?" *Acta Psychologica*, 47, 143–148.

TAYLOR, SHELLEY E. (1981)."A Categorization Approach to Stereotyping," in *Cognitive Processes in Stereotyping and Intergroup Behavior*, Ed. David L. Hamilton. Hillsdale, NJ: Erlbaum, 83–114.

TAYLOR, SHELLEY E., and JENNIFER CROCKER (1981). "Schematic Bases of Social Information Processing," in *Social Cognition: The Ontario Symposium* Vol. 1, Eds. E. Tory Higgins, C. Peter Herman, and Mark T. Zanna. Hillsdale, NJ: Erlbaum, 89–134.

TAYLOR SHELLEY, E., and JONATHON BROWN (1988). "Illusion and Well-Being: A Social Psychological Perspective on Mental Health," *Psychological Bulletin*, 103 (March), 193–210.

TAYLOR, SHELLEY, E., and MARCI LOBEL (1989).

"Social Comparison Activity Under Threat: Downward Evaluation and Upward Contacts," *Psychological Review*, 96 (October), 569–575.

TECHNICAL ASSISTANCE RESEARCH PROGRAMS (1981). *Measuring the Grapevine: Consumer Response and Word-of-Mouth,* Washington, DC: Tarp.

TETLOCK, PHILLIP (1985). "Accountability: The Neglected Social Context of Judgment and Choice," *Research in Organizational Behavior,* 7, 297–332.

TETLOCK, PHILLIP, and ARIEL LEVI (1982). "Attribution Bias: On the Inconclusiveness of the Cognition-Motivation Debate," *Journal of Experimental Social Psychology,* 18 (January), 68–88.

TROUTMAN, C. MICHAEL, and JAMES SHANTEAU (1976). "Do Consumers Evaluate Products by Adding or Averaging Attribute Information?" *Journal of Consumer Research,* 3 (September), 101–106.

TUNG, ROSALIE L. (1982). "U.S.-China Trade Negotiations: Practices, Procedures and Outcomes," *Journal of International Business Studies,* (Fall), 25–37.

TYBOUT, ALICE M., and CAROL A. SCOTT (1983). "Availability of Well-Defined Internal Knowledge and the Attitude Formation Process: Information Aggregation Versus Self-Perception," *Journal of Personality and Social Psychology,* 44 (March), 474–491.

TYBOUT, ALICE M., and RICHARD F. YALCH (1980). "The Effect of Experience: A Matter of Salience?" *Journal of Consumer Research,* 6 (March), 406–413.

VAN DER PLIGT, JOOP (1984). "Attributions, False Consensus and Valence: Two Field Studies," *Journal of Personality and Social Psychology,* 46 (January), 57–68.

VAN DER PLIGT, JOOP (1985). "Energy Conservation: Two Easy Ways Out," *Journal of Applied Social Psychology,* 15 (1), 3–15.

VENKATESAN, M. (1966). "Consumer Behavior: Conformity and Independence," *Journal of Marketing Research,* 3 (November), 384–387.

WARD, SCOTT (1972). "Children's Reactions to Commercials," *Journal of Advertising Research,* 12 (April), 37–45.

WARD, SCOTT, GREG REALE, and DAVID LEVINSON (1972). "Children's Perceptions, Explanations and Judgments of Television Advertising: A

Further Exploration," in *Television and Social Behavior, Vol. 4: Television in Day-to-Day Life,* Eds. E. A. Rubinstein, G. A. Comstock, and J. P. Murray. Washington, DC: U.S. Department of Health, Education, and Welfare.

WARD, SCOTT, DANIEL B. WACKMAN, and ELLEN WARTELLA (1977). *How Children Learn to Buy.* Beverly Hills, CA: Sage.

WEBER, RENEE, and JENNIFER CROCKER (1983). "Cognitive Processes in the Revision of Stereotypic Beliefs," *Journal of Personality and Social Psychology,* 45 (November), 961–977.

WEINER, BERNARD (1986). *An Attributional Theory of Motivation and Emotion.* New York: Springer-Verlag.

WEITZ, BARTON (1978). "The Relationship Between Salesperson Performance and Understanding of Customer Decision Making," *Journal of Marketing Research,* 15 (November), 501–516.

WELLS, WILLIAM D., FRANK J. ANDRUILI, FEDELE J. GOI, and STUART SEADER (1957). "An Adjective Checklist for the Study on 'Product Personality,'" *Journal of Applied Psychology,* 41 (5), 317–319.

WILDER, DAVID A. (1981). "Perceiving Persons as a Group: Categorization and Intergroup Relations," in *Cognitive Processes in Stereotyping and Intergroup Behavior,* Ed. David L. Hamilton. Hillsdale, NJ: Erlbaum, 213–257.

WILDER, DAVID A., and VERNON L. ALLEN (1978). "Group Membership and Preference for Information About Other Persons," *Personality and Social Psychology Bulletin,* 4 (Winter), 106–110.

WILLS, THOMAS (1981). "Downward Comparison Principles in Social Psychology," *Psychological Bulletin,* 90, 245–71.

WOOD, JOANNE (1989). "Theory and Research Concerning Social Comparisons of Personal Attributes," *Psychological Bulletin,* 106 (September), 231–248.

WOOD, JOANNE, SHELLEY E. TAYLOR, and ROSEMARY LICHTMAN (1985). "Social Comparison in Adjustment to Breast Cancer," *Journal of Personality and Social Psychology,* 49 (May), 1169–1183.

WRIGHT, PETER (1986). "Schemer Schema: Consumers' Intuitive Theories About Marketers' Influence Tactics," in *Advances in Consumer Research,* Vol. 13, Ed. Richard J. Lutz. Provo, UT: Association for Consumer Research, 1–3.

ZADNY, JERRY, and HAROLD B. GERARD (1974). "Attributed Intentions and Informational Selectivity," *Journal of Experimental Social Psychology,* 10 (January), 34–52.

ZAICHKOWSKY, JUDITH LYNNE (1985). "Measuring the Involvement Construct," *Journal of Consumer Research,* 12 (December), 341–352.

INNOVATIVE DECISION PROCESSES

9

Hubert Gatignon
*University of Pennsylvania**

Thomas S. Robertson
University of Pennsylvania

This chapter poses a number of research questions within the domain of innovative decision processes. The objective is to enrich the existing diffusion paradigm by suggesting new research directions from cognitive decision theory, network analysis, and marketing and competitive strategy.

INTRODUCTION

The topic of innovative decision processes has a rich heritage in the social and behavioral sciences. Within a number of domains, there is a concern with the processes of adoption and diffusion of innovations—whether new ideas, practices, technologies, or products. Research on the adopters of innovation ranges from farmers (Rogers 1983) to physicians (Coleman, Katz, and Menzel 1966), to industrial firms (Mansfield 1961), to educational institutions (Lawton and Lawton 1979; Stern, Craig, La

Greca, and Salem 1976), to complex organizations (Zaltman, Duncan, and Holbek 1973; Kimberly and Evaniska 1981), to consumers (Robertson 1971).

The domain within which we shall focus is *consumer* acceptance of innovation, that is, the *ultimate* consumer, rather than other organizational units in the chain of production or distribution. Nevertheless, much of the theory, modeling, methodology, and empirical findings on diffusion of innovation are multidisciplinary. As such, we shall draw extensively not only on the consumer behavior and marketing literatures, but also on the relevant literatures within economics, sociology, geography, management strategy, and organizational behavior.

Our objectives in this chapter are to present

*This chapter was written while Hubert Gatignon was a Visiting Professor at the European Institute for Advanced Studies in Management (Belgium).

a summary and research agenda concerning innovative decision processes. However, given the relatively recent literature review of Gatignon and Robertson (1985), we do not intend to repeat the propositional inventory that they propose but, instead, to develop some research topics that we believe hold significant promise. These topics are selected based on their importance in the consumer domain and based on their research potential.

THE CONSUMER DIFFUSION PARADIGM

Figure 9.1 represents the various elements of the framework proposed by Gatignon and Robertson (1985) to depict the consumer diffusion paradigm. The solid lines between the boxes correspond to causal relationships posited by the theory. Only the main effects are represented in Figure 9.1 in order to maintain clarity. The dotted line represents relationships that are presumed to exist but are not directly linked to diffusion. For example, the marketing strategy for the launch of an innovation is affected by the competitors' activities (Gatignon, Weitz, and Bansal 1989). Similarly, competi-

tors do not remain passive when confronted by a competitive innovation, but react in order to maintain their relative position (Gatignon, Anderson, and Helsen 1989).

The major elements of the diffusion research paradigm are the following:

1. the innovation and its characteristics
2. the social system within which the innovation diffuses
3. the diffusion process that occurs
4. the adoption process at the individual consumer level
5. the personal influence that is transmitted
6. personal characteristics of innovators and other adopters
7. the marketing strategy for the innovation
8. competitive activities within the product category

Each element of the diffusion research paradigm will be briefly defined. Then, theories designed to expand the state of the art of diffusion research are discussed for five of these elements. The three elements which we shall not pursue—the social system, the diffusion process, and the personal characteristics of adopters—represent the most heavily researched areas in marketing and in other disci-

FIGURE 9.1 The Main Relationships of the Consumer Diffusion Paradigm

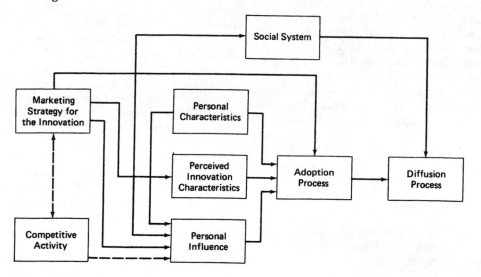

plines studying diffusion processes. Therefore, we have chosen to suggest potential research initiatives and particular approaches where the incremental gains in understanding diffusion of innovation are likely to be highest. Thus, the selected topics covered in the remainder of this chapter represent our notion of research priorities regarding innovative decision processes.

The Innovation and Its Characteristics

An innovation is a new product or service that is perceived by consumers to have effects upon established consumption patterns. A continuum of innovation exists from continuous to discontinuous, depending on the effects on consumption patterns. It would be expected that the type of innovation and its characteristics will have a major bearing on innovative decision processes and the speed and nature of diffusion.

The perceived characteristics of an innovation are an essential aspect of the adoption and diffusion of innovations, as demonstrated by research in rural sociology (Feder 1982; Fliegel and Kivlin 1966) and in organizational behavior (Zaltman et al. 1973). The scheme proposed by Rogers (1983) to evaluate innovations dominates research in this area. Undoubtedly, relative advantage, compatibility, feasibility, observability, and complexity are related to the likelihood and speed of adoption. However, these characteristics might not be the most appropriate for understanding the adoption of consumer innovations, or for explaining the adoption decision-making process.

In this chapter, we focus on the need for more precise conceptual and operational definitions of what constitutes an innovation. Much of the inconsistency in diffusion findings may be due to the lack of constancy in definitions. Additionally, research on a broader conceptualization of innovation attributes is suggested.

The Social System

In some of the classic research on innovative decision processes, the context of the research is the *social system,* by which is meant a set of people with a shared sense of commonality who tend to interact over time. Thus, rural sociological research generally has taken the local farming community as the social system. In a similar vein, research on physicians has taken the local community of doctors (Coleman, Katz, and Menzel 1966) as the social system. Even industrial research has tended to be within the social system composed of the participants of a particular industry (Mansfield 1961).

Consumer research on innovative decision processes has sometimes taken the individual social system as the context for research, particularly in tracing personal influence patterns (Arndt 1967; Brown and Reingen 1987). On balance, however, most consumer research is not limited to the social system, but is conducted within a market segment of consumers, which crosses multiple social systems. Indeed, this is compatible with most forms of consumer marketing, which do not identify nor direct activities to individual social systems. By contrast, a considerable amount of industrial marketing is within the context of a specific industry's social system.

We may think of a *market segment* as a *set of social systems.* The assumption is that there is some sense of commonality that links consumers to the social system and, indirectly, to the broader market segment. This may be a particularly reasonable assumption for some product category innovations, such as symbolic innovations, such as in fashion and design, (Hirschman 1981), which seem to require social system endorsement for their diffusion.

The social system would also seem to be of importance in the diffusion of many technologies that exhibit *network externalities;* that is, the utility of the innovation is proportional to the number of other consumers purchasing the innovation (Katz and Shapiro 1985). This is particularly the case in communications and information systems' technologies, including VCRs, personal computers, and FAX machines. The diffusion of such technologies is very much dependent on whether other social system members with whom one would communicate also acquire the technology.

The social system and its level of homogeneity are critical to most conceptualizations and models of diffusion, including the Bass (1969) model. The contagion effect assumes the transmission of influence among peers, yielding a logistic curve. The absence of social influence — that is, the low incidence of contagion effects for some consumer innovations — suggests that the social system is not a meaningful level of analysis in examining diffusion for all products.

The values and norms of the social system have a major effect on the innovation's diffusion potential within that social system. The implication is that diffusion patterns may vary by social system and that the diffusion process for the total market may be composed of multiple diffusion curves. Wind, Robertson, and Fraser (1982), for example, in research on the diffusion of CT-scanners, found varying diffusion patterns for hospitals when comparing government hospitals with nonprofit/nongovernment hospitals.

Three major social system characteristics affect the diffusion process. The first is the values and norms of the social system. However, these are not static and, therefore, a second factor is the system's normative evolution, for example, toward greater acceptance of technology. Third, homogeneity of the social system encourages faster diffusion by maximizing interpersonal content. These factors are elaborated in the earlier work of Gatignon and Robertson (1985).

The Diffusion Process

The *diffusion process* is concerned with the aggregate adoption curve over time for the innovation, that is, the rate of penetration of the innovation within the social system or market segment. However, given that the potential population may vary over time — due to changes in the strategy of the innovating firm or due to competitors' responses, for example — the study of the penetration rate per se can be misleading.

The typical characteristics used as dependent variables in the study of the diffusion of an innovation are (1) the shape or pattern of the aggregate adoption curve (the number of adop-

ters over time), (2) the rate of adoption at specific periods, and (3) the size of the potential market (the number of potential adopters) over time. Although diffusion theory has been concerned essentially with first purchases, repeat purchase behavior affects the product life cycle (Midgley 1981; Dolan and Jeuland 1981). Postpurchase behavior offers opportunities for expanding the diffusion research base.

The Adoption Process

The *adoption process* concerns the decision sequence that consumers use to determine whether or not to adopt the innovation. These innovative decision processes are at the core of diffusion theory. Research, however, has been content to rely on the traditional learning-oriented "hierarchy of effects" model and has ignored information-processing theory and behavioral decision theory approaches to innovative decision processes. In this chapter we suggest that the decision process may vary for innovative stimuli when compared with familiar stimuli and that innovators may process information differently than noninnovators. The adoption process would seem to be a fertile area for new research directions.

Personal Influence

Personal influence is a basic underlying component of diffusion theory and diffusion models. Recent research, however, has been sparse, and the diffusion literature continues to rely heavily on the primitive two-step model of Katz and Lazarsfeld (1955) and the concept of opinion leadership.

A number of factors condition the extent and impact of personal influence: (1) the relevance of the information for the decision-making process of the potential adopter; (2) the role played by information from members of the social system versus the value of complementarity of other sources of information; (3) the direction of the information (i.e., an information-seeking direction as opposed to an information-giving direction); (4) the motivation or intent of the information exchange; (5) the form (visual or verbal) of the communication; (6) the sign (positive or negative) of the information; (7) the characteristics of the information provider, and (8) the origin (homophilous or heterophilous) of the information.

In the present chapter, we suggest some possible directions to enrich the research base concerning personal influence. In particular, we rely on an exchange theory model of personal influence that focuses on the motivations for both information-seeking and information-giving behavior. The source and message characteristics that enhance the exchange of influence are also elaborated.

Personal Characteristics of Adopters

Much of the research on consumer diffusion is concerned with ascertaining the *personal characteristics* of innovators for market segmentation purposes. Although some variables appear to discriminate innovators from later adopters or nonadopters (such as a higher income, of higher level education, a younger age, a greater social mobility, a positive attitude towards risk, a greater social participation, and a higher degree of opinion leadership), these results are not entirely consistent across product categories (Robertson, Zielinski, and Ward 1984). The prevalent and consistent finding, however, is one of heavy product category usage and experience among innovators.

The conclusion on this issue, however, might not be definitive. Indeed, this research has traditionally been based on a definition of innovators that does not coincide with today's prevailing understanding of what constitutes an innovator. Midgley and Dowling (1978) propose that a definition of innovativeness be based on two criteria: (1) the degree of receptivity to new ideas, and (2) the degree to which the consumer's decision process is independent of the influence of other members of the social system. This distinction, which is consistent with Bass's (1969) notion of innovators and imitators, might be the basis for a reevaluation of the influence of personal characteristics on the innovation adoption decision process. How-

ever, we will not pursue this topic, even though it may be a key new direction.

Marketing Strategy for the Innovation

The innovative decision process literature has ignored the strategy pursued by the change agent, that is, the strategy of the firm marketing the innovation. It seems rather obvious that the speed, shape, and extent of the diffusion of consumer innovations is determined, in part, by the launch strategy pursued by the firm. This is recognized in recent modeling efforts, which incorporate marketing mix variables into diffusion models (Mahajan and Muller 1979; Mahajan and Peterson 1979).

The role and impact of marketing strategy is an important untapped research area. One of our objectives in this chapter is to suggest a framework for assessing the contribution of marketing strategy and to encourage future research that explicitly tests the effects of varying marketing strategy alternatives.

Competitive Activities

Most innovations are marketed by more than one supplier. Yet, past research has neglected the competitive environment that affects consumer decision processes and adoption decisions. This is probably due to diffusion research's heritage in rural sociology and the focus on primary rather than secondary demand.

The case of the monopolist's marketing activity implicit in most diffusion research, with a single change agent, should be generalized to the competitive setting where multiple suppliers provide the same innovation with differentiated products or brands. Robertson and Gatignon (1986) provide a framework for understanding how competition affects the organizational diffusion of innovations. This framework can be adapted, in part, for evaluating the impact and role of competition in the diffusion of consumer innovations and may provide direction for future research on assessing the role of competitive factors on innovative decision processes.

Synopsis

Given this basic description of the elements of the diffusion paradigm, we now turn to some detailed discussions elaborating those areas of research that we view as high priorities for future inquiry. It is our thesis that innovative decision processes will remain a robust topic of research because of the importance of new technologies, new services, and new products in global markets. We further believe that research can continue to contribute to an understanding of how and why innovations diffuse.

THE INNOVATION AND ITS CHARACTERISTICS

Research that has investigated the effects of innovation characteristics on the adoption of consumer innovations generally has endorsed Rogers' (1983) scheme evaluating innovations along the dimensions of relative advantage, compatibility, triability, observability, and complexity. Consumer behavior researchers have tended to consider perceptions, rather than "objective" measures, along these dimensions (Labay and Kinnear 1981). An additional dimension of perceived risk has been shown by Ostlund (1974) to be a significant factor explaining adoption.

A recent initiative in this stream of research is provided by Srivastava et al. (1985) who relate innovation characteristics to the parameters of the Bass diffusion model. The coefficient of "innovation," that is, the propensity to adopt at any given point in time but without being influenced by previous adopters, is related to characteristics of the product. The study also demonstrates that the extent of interpersonal influence (internal to the social system) varies depending on the innovation.

Following this approach, future research might contribute by analyzing how innovative decision processes vary depending on innovation characteristics. In particular, some innovations by their very nature may generate a low-involvement adoption process (Zaikowsky 1985). However, it still remains to be determined how the characteristics of an innovation might contribute to explaining the information search and processing modes used by potential adopters.

A major dilemma in future research derives from the fact that the relevant dimensions of an innovation are not well specified. In particular, there is little theoretical basis for specifying which aspects of the innovation lead to adoption without social influence, and which aspects of the innovation result in adoption conditional on social interaction. It is our view that more attention should be paid to the concept of the innovation itself.

Innovation in the consumer diffusion literature is a rather ill-defined concept. In fact, most research does not explicitly define the innovation construct, and the operational definition is sometimes not explicitly made either. The underlying assumption seems to be that the innovation construct is undimensional and that the meaning has broad convergence.

A content analysis of the leading marketing and consumer behavior journals for the 1984–1988 period indicates that approximately fifteen articles could be considered within the diffusion of innovation research stream. Of these, only two focus explicitly on the meaning of the innovation.[1] Most research simply assumes that whatever is being studied is an innovation. These research studies on innovation dealt with such products as packaged goods, personal computers, and solar energy systems.

When reference is made to the concept of the innovation, the most common citations are to the work of Rogers (1983), Robertson (1971), and Hirschman (1981). The work of Rogers represents the classic statement of diffusion theory and its constructs, beginning with his 1962 book *Diffusion of Innovations*, which is now in its third edition. Rogers defines an innovation as ". . . an idea, practice, or object that is perceived as new by an individual or other unit of adoption" (1983, p. 11). There are considerable

---

[1]This informal content analysis examined the 1984–1988 issues of the *Journal of Consumer Research,* the *Journal of Marketing Research, Marketing Science,* and the *Journal of Marketing.*

difficulties in operationalizing this definition, since it depends on the perception of each individual. Says Rogers, "If the idea seems new to the individual, it is an innovation" (p. 11).

The Robertson (1971) conceptualization suggests that the critical determinant of an innovation is its effect upon established patterns of consumption. An innovation continuum is proposed that classifies innovations as to how "continuous or discontinuous" their effects are on established consumption processes. Robertson further suggests that it might be useful to think in terms of continuous innovations (the minimal consumption pattern effects), dynamically continuous innovations (the intermediate level consumption pattern effects), and discontinuous innovations (the creation of new consumption patterns).

This conceptualization advances beyond the simple dichotomy of whether something is, or is not, an innovation. Compatible with Rogers, it continues to rely on potential adopter perception. Although the operational definition is not explicit, the determination of how continuous or discontinuous an innovation is depends on "majority consumer opinion" (p. 7). From a marketing perspective, therefore, there is value in the idea that an innovation may be defined by market segment judgment, and not simply that an idea may be an innovation if it is new to a particular individual.

The notion of continuity/discontinuity is useful in classifying technological innovation as well, as elaborated by Tushman and Anderson (1986). The historically based analysis suggests that new technologies represent a stream of evolutionary new products or processes "punctuated by discontinuous change" (p. 440), which creates new product classes or process substitution. Indeed, if our purpose were not to limit the discussion to consumer innovations, we could pursue alternative definitions of innovations, such as those developed by Calantoni and Cooper (1981) for industrial innovations, or Damanpour (1988) for administrative and technological innovations.

Hirschman (1981) has proposed that innovations can be classified on two dimensions — symbolic and technological. The symbolic dimension suggests a new social meaning. The technological dimension suggests tangible features that are new to the product category. The combination of dimensions results in a matrix such that innovations can be classified by quadrant. An innovation high on both the symbolic and technological dimensions (compact disc players, for example) would seem to have a different meaning and might well follow a different adoption process than one high on symbolism and low on technology (fashion, for example) or low on symbolism and high on technology (medical instrumentation, for example). A product would not seem to constitute an innovation if it were low on both symbolic and technological attributes. Indeed, there may well be other dimensions that should be incorporated in defining innovation. The relationship between the Hirschman and Robertson frameworks has been explored by Hirschman, who suggests that technological innovations have a greater capability to be discontinuous, whereas symbolic innovations are more likely to be continuous in matching consumers' existing patterns of experience.

Hirschman (1980) has also proposed that innovativeness may be manifested not only in the adoption of new products but also in the innovative use of existing products. This concept of use innovativeness — using an "old" product in a novel way — has been pursued by Price and Ridgeway (1983) who have developed a scale for its measurement that is highly reliable. In addition, Foxall (1988) has looked at a form of use innovativeness in terms of the "adapter" (versus innovator) category of cognitive style. Adapters tend to use present products in an adaptive manner, whereas innovators try new products.

An obvious need in diffusion research is for explicit conceptual and operational definitions of what constitutes an innovation. More interesting, meaning is left implicit not only in consumer research, but in important work in other areas as well. Von Hippel, for example, in his important work on the sources of innovation (in which he finds that customers are often the major source), never concretely defines innovation (Von Hippel 1986, 1988).

An example of a concrete definition of innovation is provided in the organizational diffusion research stream. Here, Souder (1987), after reviewing the literature in this area, proposes that the term "innovation" refers to "a high-risk idea that is new to the sponsoring organization, and which the organization believes has high profit potential or other favorable commercial impacts for them" (p. 3). He then proceeds to operationalize these terms.

We may or may not agree with the definition, but there is value in knowing exactly what is being measured and whether results can be related to other results as a function of the comparability of the definitions. Indeed, Downs and Mohr (1976), in research within organizational diffusions, have lamented the "troubling instability" of diffusion results, and they have cited that at least one important reason for this is the "varying operationalizations of innovation" that are pursued by researchers (pp. 700–701).

The classification of a product as an innovation may also depend on the change agent's capabilities in proving the advantages to potential adopters and broadening the base of potential adopters by refining the innovation. Gold (1981) makes the point that most innovations undergo numerous changes to increase their attractiveness. Furthermore, changes in diffusion rates ". . . may be due in large measure to the extent of technological changes in the innovations being studied rather than to changes in the receptiveness of prospective adopters . . ." (p. 248). Gold, like other scholars, therefore, places the delineation of a product as an innovation in the eyes of the perceiver, but he further suggests that this delineation may change as the product evolves. Indeed, in many product categories the innovative product does improve over time, which expands the potential market.

The role of innovation characteristics in the study of innovative decision processes is an underresearched and potentially fertile area for future study. An initial need is for a more rigorous conceptual framework for classifying innovations based on consumer perceptions. A factor analytic approach might be a logical first step. Given some confidence in the conceptual classification, research could proceed to examine the effects of innovation characteristics on adoption and diffusion and to test the value of alternative marketing and competitive strategies in influencing the rate and level of diffusion.

In the hopes of advancing consumer research on innovative decision processes based on an explicit definition of innovation, we propose the following:

An *innovation* is a new product or service that is perceived by consumers within a market segment to have effects upon established consumption patterns. A continuum of innovation exists from continuous (having minor effects on consumption patterns) to discontinuous (creating new consumption patterns).

Additionally, we offer Table 9.1 as a summary set of dimensions for classifying innovations. Some of these have been pursued in research and some have not. Their relevance may vary by product category. Research is very

TABLE 9.1 Dimensions Affecting the Speed of Diffusion

Dimensions	Relationship to Speed of Diffusion
• The value of innovation	
—Relative advantage	+
• The cost of the innovation	
—Purchase costs	−
—Switching costs	−
• The uncertainty of the innovation	
—Standardization	+
—Expected length of life cycle	+
• The level of social relevance	
—Observability	+
—Social value	+
• Customer learning requirements	
—Complexity	−
—Compatability	+
—Trial	+
• Marketing program design	
—Expenditures on advertising and sales	+
—Appropriate positioning and segmentation	+
—Ability to generate social influence	+
—Ability to generate trial	+

much needed to broaden and test this or similar frameworks and to derive an empirically based set of factors for evaluating innovations and projecting the likely adoption and diffusion processes that will result.

Although it is not our intent to expound specific findings or propositions, some brief discussion of the variables and expectations listed in Table 9.1 might be helpful.

Value of the Innovation. As conceptualized by Rogers, relative advantage is positively associated with the speed of diffusion. This hardly requires justification, although relative advantage is probably a multidimensional concept and its measurement is not so obvious.

Costs. It seems to us that costs are a major determinant of diffusion speed. A contribution to the research would be to show the relationships and interactions of different types of costs and rates of diffusion. *Purchase costs* are one obvious dimension. However, *switching costs* may sometimes be very important. One explanation for the slower diffusion of dishwashers, in contrast to microwaves, for example, is the kitchen renovation, or switching costs, that must be incurred.

Uncertainty. In general, uncertainty about the innovation slows diffusion. Multiple conceptions of uncertainty are part of the literature (Milliken 1987), but we would suggest, in particular, that uncertainty as to *standardization* and *length of the life cycle* are highly salient. If consumers are uncertain as to technology standards (VHS versus Beta, cassette versus 8-track, IBM versus non-IBM), this will slow diffusion until a single standard emerges. Similarly, if consumers think that the technology is evolving too rapidly and that the risk of obsolescence is high, this will also slow diffusion.

Customer Learning Requirements. Here are encompassed three of Rogers's dimensions — *complexity, compatibility,* and *trial likelihood.* It is our opinion that these are mainly related to consumer learning requirements. In general, high consumer learning needs are related to a slower diffusion rate, and a major change agent objective may be to lower the learning require-

ment or to provide training or support. Products that are complex, incompatible with existing consumption patterns, and difficult to try are simply not going to diffuse very quickly.

Social Relevance. The social component of an innovation is critical to generating imitation and rapid follow-on diffusion. One dimension affecting social relevance is *observability,* which is generally correlated with a logistic diffusion pattern. Less operational is the *social value* of an innovation, that is, essentially whether it has some level of social cachet which generates social imitation.

Marketing Program Design. It is stretching a point to suggest that the marketing program is a characteristic of the innovation. Yet the firm's marketing actions help define the innovation and affect the rate of diffusion, interdependent with the other dimensions suggested previously. In general, we expect that the diffusion rate will be enhanced to the extent that the firm allocates greater *expenditures to marketing and sales,* appropriately *positions and segments,* undertakes programs to *generate social influence,* and pursues *trial* (or sampling) programs. We shall return to the role of marketing on diffusion later in this chapter.

In concluding this section on the concept of the innovation, we would suggest that research is needed within the consumer diffusion realm on defining exactly what is an innovation. Additionally, a significant contribution could be made by developing a model of innovation dimensions and showing their effects on adoption and diffusion patterns. We have suggested some dimensions for consideration and their likely effects on the rate of diffusion. It is also necessary to conduct research as to how different innovation profiles (sets of dimensions) engender varying information-processing modes.

THE ADOPTION PROCESS

Our purpose in this section is not to elaborate on the traditional views of the adoption process. This is well-trodden territory and not particularly fertile as a source of inspiration for research. Instead, we wish to draw upon an information-processing perspective and to suggest new ideas based on this view. First, however, we must briefly review the extant notion of adoption.

The adoption process usually is characterized in the diffusion literature as some form of the "hierarchy of effects" model. In the first edition of *Diffusion of Innovation,* Rogers (1962) conceptualized the process as awareness-interest-evaluation-trial-adoption. In his third edition, Rogers' (1983) revised model encompassed knowledge-persuasion-decision-implementation-confirmation.

It is useful to focus on postadoption and satisfaction. This suggests that adoption should be measured not only by initial commitment but also by width (the number of applications or different uses) and depth (the amount of usage) of adoption. Width and depth may be predictive of purchasing additional units, enhanced products, or complementary products (such as peripherals or software for computers, or programming for VCRs).

Consumers who do not adopt the innovation at a particular time are typically considered "nonadopters." However, those nonadopters may be either "postponers" or "rejectors." Decision postponers are unwilling to commit at a given point in time. They are undecided as to whether they should adopt the innovation and need more information than they currently possess or more information-processing time. Rejectors, in contrast, have processed the information that they required to make a decision and have concluded not to adopt.

Although much of the diffusion literature has a proinnovation bias (Rogers 1976), there may be product categories or market segments where innovation resistance is predominant. Sheth (1981) suggests that the two key factors explaining innovation resistance are habit strength toward the existing product and the perceived risk associated with the innovation. More recently Ram (1987) and Ram and Sheth (1989) have developed a set of propositions concerning factors associated with consumer resistance to innovation. Gatignon and Robertson (1989) show that the decision to reject is not

explained by the same factors that explain adoption: rejection is not the mirror image of adoption but a different type of behavior. Future research could contribute by specifying factors uniquely tied to innovation resistance.

In any conceptualization of the adoption process, it is essential to separate trial and adoption. This is especially necessary for repeat purchase products. Indeed, most diffusion models, both academic and commercial, recognize this distinction (Mahajan and Wind 1986). New product forecasts are highly dependent on decomposing emerging sales into trial and repeat purchase components.

The typical characterizations of the adoption process, such as those of Rogers, exhibit a "learning" bias, that is, consumers progress through a deliberate purchase hierarchy. This may often be a useful schematic, but many adoption decisions may not resemble this learning sequence. A useful distinction is between the "hierarchy of effects" model and a "low involvement" model with limited cognitive processing (Zaichkowsky 1985). It would seem that there are multiple forms that the adoption process might take, depending on the levels of cognitive processing generated. The amount of information search and processing would seem to depend on consumer knowledge, uncertainty, and the importance of the adoption decision to the consumer.

Information Processing for Innovations

There would appear to be differences in information processing for innovative versus familiar products. These differences will depend on how novel or innovative the product is, such that discontinuous innovations (high novelty) will be characterized by distinct decision processes versus continuous innovations (low novelty).

Lynch and Srull (1982), in their elaborate review of the memory literature, have documented that novel or unexpected information is more likely to gain attention, to be processed more extensively, and to be better recalled (p. 32). This is referred to as the "von Restorff effects," whereby novel information produces enhanced recall. Lynch and Srull also conclude that novel information captures attention and enhances recall at the expense of other information in the decision process, due to the individual's limited attention and processing capacities. This might suggest not only that new products have a positive perceptual and retrieval bias, but that new attributes of a product may also benefit from such a bias to the degree that they are perceived as "novel."

A documented finding over time is that the usage of information sources varies by stage of the decision process. The generalized finding is that impersonal sources are more prevalent early in the decision process and that personal sources are more prevalent later in the decision process (Robertson 1971; Bettman 1979). This is due to the increased availability of personal sources as diffusion progresses and to a preference for personal sources (which are seen as more "objective"). This result depends on the product category, however, since personal sources involve greater information seeking and "exchange" costs, and the consumer may be reluctant to incur such costs for reasonably unimportant product categories. The role of exchange costs will be discussed later in the chapter in the section on personal influence.

Innovators and Information Processing

There is a surprising lack of research that examines the information processing of innovators versus noninnovators. Yet, we might expect divergence in amount, source, content, and style of processing.

A perspective on cognitive style and its relationship to innovativeness is that of Foxall and Haskins (1986) and Foxall (1988). One finding, based on administration of the Kirton Adaption-Innovation Inventory of cognitive style, is that innovators exhibit differences in cognitive style, such as a propensity toward less observation, planning, and deliberation. Furthermore, differences in cognitive style are exhibited depending on the continuity or discontinuity of the innovation. This may represent a promising future research approach.

The most promising literature that we might relate to innovative decision making focuses on *expertise*. An interesting set of findings relates expertise to information-processing characteristics (Sujan 1985; Johnson and Russo 1984; Brucks 1985; Park and Lessig 1981; Alba and Hutchinson 1987). This is the essential question: What is the relationship between expertise and innovativeness? Or, are innovators more knowledgeable about the product category than noninnovators?

The literature that we draw upon tends to use a number of related constructs—"expertise," "knowledge," "familiarity." Alba and Hutchinson (1987) have recently made the useful distinction that "knowledge" should be thought of in terms of a "familiarity" component, which are the product-related experiences of the consumer, and an "expertise" component, which are the abilities to perform product-related tasks. It is in the latter sense that we shall mainly think of expertise, although the two concepts are closely related since expertise draws upon familiarity.

Another useful distinction is between objective and subjective expertise. Park and Lessig (1981) and Brucks (1985), for example, distinguish between how much the consumer knows about the product (objective) versus how much the consumer thinks he or she knows about the product (subjective). The lack of congruence between the two measures may lead to some interesting results.

Although the relationship between expertise and innovativeness has not been explicitly probed, there are strong suggestions that innovators are higher on product-category expertise. This may be inferred from the heavy product-category usage of innovators and their higher levels of opinion leadership.

A considerable volume of research across product categories reveals that innovators are heavy users within the product category and may have significant experience in related product categories. This finding encompasses personal computers and computer services

(Danko and MacLachlan 1983; Dickerson and Gentry 1983), food and personal care products (Frank, Massy, and Morrison 1964; Taylor 1977), appliances (Robertson 1971), and pharmaceuticals (Coleman, Katz, and Menzel 1957). Although product category usage is not necessarily the same as knowledge, we would expect the two to be reasonably correlated. Indeed, expertise measures sometimes have usage and ownership as components (Park and Lessig 1981).

The diffusion literature is also replete with studies showing that innovators are higher on opinion leadership (Rogers 1983). Again this is not the same as knowledge, but peers who acknowledge this opinion leadership by seeking advice apparently believe that innovators have more information and expertise to share.

Expertise Effects

High expertise, in contrast to low expertise, is associated with differences in decision heuristics.[2] Based on the extant literature, particularly Alba and Hutchinson's (1987) excellent review, a number of expectations can be suggested.

Memory and Cognitive Structure. Experts have better developed (more complex) product category cognitive structures. They develop more abstract levels of categorization and deeper levels of categorization. Category structure is also less stereotypical. Experts are able to rely more on memory in evaluating new stimuli. Additionally, they are more able to notice relative differences and to separate schemata, inconsistent facts, and product attributes. Higher levels of prior knowledge may also reduce information load during the encoding of new stimuli, which may result in greater learning (Alba and Hutchinson 1987, p. 437).

The implications for innovativeness would seem to be that experts are better able to recognize and cope with atypicality and to compare

diverse stimuli. Many innovations combine product-category attributes in novel and unfamiliar ways. Experts are better able to abstract and to rely on schemata in order to reach more informed judgments and to engage in evaluation.

It may also be that if novelty is a desired attribute (a preference for innovativeness), experts are better able to discriminate true novelty within a set of product category stimuli. As suggested by Alba and Hutchinson, experts are more capable at recognizing nonprototypicality, as, for example, in the separation of current fashion innovations (p. 416). Experts are also more adept at identifying similarity (Murphy and Wright 1984).

Information Search and Processing. Expert consumers utilize their product-category knowledge to engage in more efficient information search (Johnson and Russo 1984). Brucks (1985) has found that experts seek information about a greater number of product attributes but seek less information about inappropriate alternatives. Expertise seems to enhance a consumer's ability to encode information and to utilize more efficient decision heuristics (Johnson and Russo 1984; Alba and Hutchinson 1987). Experts also seem to process information more deeply and to be better problem solvers.

A study that might be particularly related to innovative stimuli is that of Sujan (1985). She pursues an interesting condition that occurs when product information is "discrepant" from category knowledge, which tends to be the case for innovative products. Her findings are that experts engage in more analytical or piecemeal-based processing and take longer to reach a judgment. Novices tend to use more category-based processing.

The expectation is that experts are more able to scan the environment for new product solutions and to more efficiently and accurately reach judgments as to the value of new products. We might also expect that they are more skilled in using retrieval cues (Keller 1987). The logical result is that they should be in a more advantageous position to quickly adopt

---

[2]Although we are assuming monotonic relationships, this may not always be the case (for example, Park and Lessig 1981).

superior new product alternatives. Indeed, the absence of knowledgeable consumers severely hampers market ability to evaluate innovations and to forecast adoption. In such cases Wilton and Pessemier (1981) have proposed building consumer knowledge in order to be able to assess the probability of adoption.

Future research on adoption could contribute to our understanding by probing the expertise-innovativeness relationship more deeply. Under what conditions is the relationship strongest? How is the relationship a function of various factors? What is the role of self-confidence and the perception of uncertainty? Do innovators possess high levels of both objective and subjective knowledge? It might be speculated that they have particularly high levels of self-confidence and subjective knowledge.

Information Source and Valence

Innovators, by their very nature, rely more on impersonal sources of information (particularly mass media and advertising), since credible personal sources do not emerge until later in the diffusion process. Indeed, Midgley (1977) and others have defined innovators as those who make adoption decisions "independently of the communicated experience of others" (p. 49). In Bass's (1969) terms, innovators act independently rather than being influenced by social imitation.

Our previous discussion of the expertise literature would suggest that innovators are more capable processors of limited and incomplete information. Impersonal sources of information sent by marketers to innovators also require an ability to cope with biased (one-sided) information. Alba and Hutchinson (1987) suggest that "prior knowledge prevents consumers from accepting the erroneous pragmatic implications of advertising . . ." (p. 428). Innovators also have been shown in research to have greater exposure to print media (Robertson, Zielinski, and Ward 1984, p. 390).

Innovators may also gain readier access to diversified information because of their attitude toward information heterogeneity. Innovators are more likely to utilize heterophilous informa-

tion sources beyond the boundaries of their social system and are less dependent on homophilous sources internal to the social system. Research generally demonstrates that innovators are more cosmopolitan and more integrated into external networks of information (Kimberly 1978; Rogers 1983). Recent research at a country by country level shows that cosmopolitanism (of the population), measured by such variables as international travel, mail, and telephone usage, is positively related to the propensity to innovate in the area of consumer durable goods (Gatignon, Eliashberg, and Robertson 1989).

Response to negative information as part of the adoption process may also separate innovators from noninnovators. The dominant finding is that of a negativity bias; that is, negative information outweighs positive information (Kalish and Lilien 1986; Leonard-Barton 1985; Mahajan, Muller, and Kerin 1984; Mizerski 1982; Richins 1983). However, innovators seem to prefer higher levels of cognitive complexity and may have a greater tolerance for ambiguity (Shaffer and Hendrick 1974). As such, they may even be receptive to certain levels of negative information.

If innovators have a greater tolerance for ambiguity, they may be less subject to the confirmatory bias that exists in information processing. In a sense, they should be more willing to engage in hypothesis testing rather than hypothesis confirmation. The level of processing in general, and the level of processing of negative information in particular, should also increase as the uncertainty surrounding the innovation increases (Ross 1989).

Synopsis on Adoption Process

A rich literature has emerged within consumer behavior examining the information search and processing of consumers. This topic has generally been ignored in research on innovative decision processes, yet it offers an intriguing set of hypotheses for studying the adoption process. We have tried to suggest some expectations regarding search and processing heuristics and outcomes for novel stimuli. We believe that these expectations constitute an interesting research direction for studying innovative decision processes.

PERSONAL INFLUENCE

The role of personal influence is central to the innovative decision process literature. The major areas addressed concern the identification of the information providers, the flows of information within a set of individuals forming a network, the amount and type of information provided, and the influence of that information on receivers. There are other areas where research is needed: the intent of the informant, the direction of the information, whether the acceptance of personal influence emanates from conformity or from information-seeking behavior, and the form of the influence (visual or verbal).

In this section we shall present a framework that offers a unified approach to four questions related to the areas of personal influence research mentioned above:

1. What is the role of personal influence? In particular, why do individuals seek information from other individuals and why are those other individuals willing to provide information?

2. What is the extent of personal influence and the value of different sources? There are multiple sources of personal influence; for example, from adopters, from knowledgeable persons that have not adopted, or from distribution channel sources. These sources might not be expected to have the same degree of influence on a given consumer.

3. Why does negative influence appear to be more powerful than positive influence? The attributional explanation proposed by Mizerski (1982) provides an attempt to answer that question. Nevertheless, this explanation should be complemented by other theories in order to explore this issue more fully. In particular, the role of dissatisfied adopters, who might discontinue the use of the innovation, must be further investigated, following Richins (1983), possibly using recent advances in the theoretical bases of dissatisfaction (Oliver 1989).

4. How can we measure the degree of personal contact and resulting influence? Most research in this

area has concentrated on the identification of opinion leaders (Wilkening 1952; Summers 1970; Baumgarten 1974), in particular using the analysis of networks (Stern, Craig, LaGreca, and Salem 1976; Johnson-Brown, and Reingen 1987). This has permitted testing some hypotheses concerning the characterization of opinion leaders and the type of information provided as a function of location in the network (e.g., Reingen and Kernan 1986; Brown and Reingen 1987). Further research is needed to develop a methodology applicable to a larger population of potential innovators and to assess the impact of communication. In particular, it will be interesting to measure how this impact varies according to the frequency of interpersonal communication, according to the type of information provided, and according to the characteristics of the source of information.

In assessing these four research questions, we conclude that the role and motivation for interpersonal communication has been a highly underresearched topic. An exchange theory model is now presented in the hopes of generating a theoretical basis for a new stream of research in this area.

A Conceptual Model of Personal Influence[3]

The objectives of this model are to explain the motivations of information givers and to provide reasons for recipients to search or accept information from other people. The model uses the social exchange theory (Homans 1961; Blau 1964, 1974), with the central concept being one of reciprocity, which postulates that social interactions will continue only if mutually rewarding.

Figure 9.2 proposes a version of this model. On the left side are listed factors motivating and inhibiting an individual to provide information to other individuals, either on his/her own initiative or after receiving a request. The right side of Figure 9.2 represents the receiver side.

---

[3]This section is adapted from Gatignon, Hubert, and Thomas S. Robertson (1986). "An Exchange Theory Model of Interpersonal Communications," in Richard J. Lutz (Ed.), *Advances in Consumer Research*, 13, 629–632.

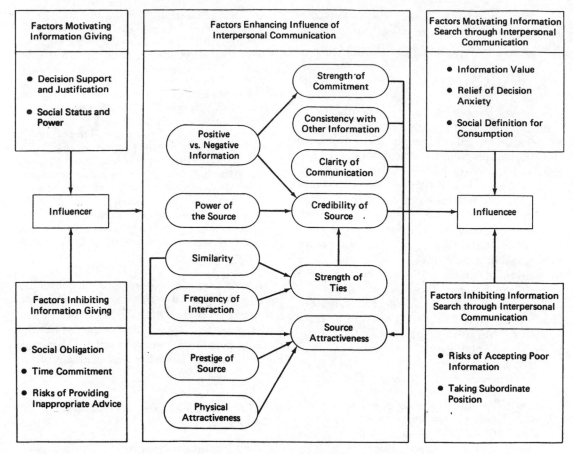

FIGURE 9.2 An Exchange Theory Model of Interpersonal Influence

Here, the factors are divided into those motivating and inhibiting the receiver to search for information and those motivating and inhibiting the receiver to accept the information without having requested the information through a search procedure. The box in the middle represents moderating factors that explain the degree to which the communication is likely to be effective or not. These factors are directly related to the communication research paradigm. It is important to note, however, that this communication process occurs only if there is a reciprocity as generated from the factors on both sides of the figure.

Information Giving

The transmission of influence is a function of a cost/benefit analysis by the potential influencer. This analysis is rarely explicit, as in economic transactions, but is subject to the same rules of utility maximization as found in economic decisions. Indeed, Blau (1974) has suggested that diminishing marginal utilities apply, in that, if an influencer is constantly asked for information, the social value of being asked declines over time. Similarly, from the point of view of the influence receiver, initial advice is worth more than later advice (diminishing marginal utility), assuming equivalent information content.

The potential rewards from assuming the influencer role relate to decision support and justification and to social status and power. The potential costs include the social obligation incurred, the time commitments made to information giving, and the risks of providing inappropriate advice.

A major incentive for assuming the influencer role is to gain support and justification for a purchase decision. In a sense, the information giver may be seeking legitimation from friends in order to overcome cognitive dissonance. Previous research has tended to show that information giving is at its height immediately following purchase, and declines with the passage of time.

A second major benefit from information giving is social status and power. The act of information giving places the influencer in a superior position. By providing information, the giver makes a claim for recognition and status. Influence receivers, in turn, incur obligations and must demonstrate gratitude for information received or provide other services in return.

Much as influence receivers incur a social cost for receiving information, influencers may also incur a social cost "for being listened to." If the influencer has been given free rein to demonstrate knowledge in one domain of consumption, it might be expected that he or she should reciprocate by receiving knowledge in another domain of consumption. Alternatively, any social relationship that is one-sided will be unstable, since the costs of information for the receiver will be too high. This will lead to resentment at constantly being in a subordinate position and eventually to a breakdown in communication.

There are also time-commitment costs associated with information giving. These costs may be high in a work environment, as studied by Blau, where "experts" may be accessed unduly and information giving may come to be burdensome. It is conceivable that this could

also occur in certain high-technology areas of consumer behavior. Rogers, Daly, and Wu (1982), for example, found that the most likely influencers (persuaders) for personal computers had the highest levels of experience/expertise. Such individuals would seem least likely to receive purchase-decision justification benefits and might be less interested in social status benefits. If so, the costs of continually providing personal-computer advice could quickly exceed the rewards.

Finally, there are risks associated with the provision of information. These risks include the probability of inappropriate advice for a particular recipient and the resulting problems if recipients hold the influencer accountable. These risks may be assessed to be high for friends whose utility functions are unclear or for new technologies where long-run performance is unclear.

Information Seeking (Active and Passive)

The reception of information is also governed by cost/benefit analysis. The potential rewards relate to the value of the information, the relief of decision anxiety, and the social legitimation provided. The potential costs include the risk of poor information and the assumption of a subordinate position.

The most obvious benefit of soliciting information is the value which it provides for decision making. Information from personal sources may be of particular value if objective nonsocial information is lacking or is conflicting. It may also be perceived that interpersonal communication is less biased than change-advocate information, such as advertising or sales personnel.

Interpersonal communication may also relieve decision anxiety. The recipient may be able to gain confidence from the prior experience of peers or may be able to avoid extensive information seeking and processing by relying on personal influence. In particular, the information provided might be in the form of a conclusion about what decision to take, which allows the information seeker to avoid the processing of large amounts of information. Even if information processing is not substantially reduced, Blau (1974) has suggested a decision value in simply being able to "think out loud" with a peer.

Information seeking from friends may also be important in defining group standards for the recipient. This suggests that various consumption domains are socially defined, as in fashion and automobiles. The individual may check with relevant others in order to determine the appropriateness of certain consumption decisions. Such information seeking, or social checking, will be most prevalent when the individual has a high level of identification with the group or a great desire for assimilation within the group.

As in all information seeking, the information gained may be poor, that is, erroneous, biased, or incomplete. The decision value of personal sources for many products may be overstated due to the small experiential base that informal opinion leaders generally possess. This again raises the interesting question of the relationship between opinion leadership and expertise. In consumer research on stereos, Jacoby and Hoyer (1980) found a strong positive correlation between opinion leadership and expertise. In research on home computers, Rogers, Daley, and Wu (1982) found that the opinion leaders most likely to persuade later adopters were those who were most experienced and had the greatest expertise. In research within a professional group (dentists), Leonard-Barton (1985) focussed on national experts rather than local opinion leaders, implicitly suggesting that friendship-based opinion leadership may not correlate highly with expertise in this professional domain. The Leonard-Barton research is useful also in focussing on negative influence, whereas most research on interpersonal communication focuses on positive recommendations.

Information seekers also incur the cost of assuming a subordinate position. Individuals may have different levels of tolerance for taking this position, but for almost all consumers it will be intolerable in the long term unless reciprocity occurs. Such reciprocity could result from taking the opinion leadership role in another consumption domain or from more general patterns of social exchange and reciprocity, not necessarily tied to consumption.

Factors Enhancing the Influence of Personal Communication

The relative influence of interpersonal information exchange is moderated by the set of factors specified in the center of Figure 9.2. The essence of these factors is that the potential for influence is a function of the level of motivation in information search combined with the level of incentive in information giving. The degree of influence depends on the perceived attributes of the source and the perceived nature of the communication message.

Perceived Source Characteristics. Two aspects of the source explain the extent to which an individual influences others. The first aspect deals with source credibility and the second with source attractiveness. Both notions have been developed in communication theory. However, the individual nature of interpersonal communication adds new elements to the theory beyond those that are typically pursued in the mass communication context. In general, the degree of interpersonal influence increases as the source is perceived to be more attractive and as source credibility increases.

- The attractiveness of a source is determined by the individual's prestige, his or her similarity to the receiver, and physical attractiveness. The mechanism by which attractiveness enhances interpersonal influence is based on the greater attention paid to the communications (Sternthal and Craig 1982).

- The source credibility literature borrows from cognitive theories. A highly credible source is typically more persuasive than a less credible source (Brock 1964) because the high credibility of the source inhibits counterargumentation (Sternthal,

Dholakia, and Leavitt 1978).[4] This corresponds also to the implications of a Bayesian model of information integration (Gatignon 1984). The two main determinants of credibility are the power of the source and the strength of ties between the source and the influence.

- The communication literature has concentrated on the power of the source as the major determinant of source credibility (Aaker and Myers 1982). The main type of power that has been studied is the expertise level of the source. It is clearly an essential determinant of source credibility, since the uncertainty associated with information declines as expertise increases. However, even if the source is an expert, the information must be communicated at a technical level that can be understood by the recipient. Therefore, personal influence will be more readily accepted if the information is communicated at the technical level at which the potential recipient is knowledgeable and comfortable.

  Other types of power, such as coercive power, can also moderate the degree of influence of interpersonal communication, such as the communication between parents and children or between group members (including those of a family) where certain levels of coerciveness can exist. This type of power might not lead to a greater credibility of the source, but can determine the extent to which the information will be used by the recipient.

- Further determinants of the credibility of a source can be derived from the concept of the *strength of ties* (Granovetter 1973, 1983). The strength of an interpersonal tie is defined as the "combination of the amount of time, the emotional intensity, the intimacy (mutual confiding), and the reciprocal sources which characterize the tie" (Granovetter 1973, p. 1261). The stronger the tie and, therefore, the greater the emotional intensity and intimacy between two individuals, the greater the credibility of each of these individuals to each other. According to Granovetter, the strength of

the interpersonal tie is greater between individuals who are similar and between individuals who interact frequently. Consequently, personal influence will be more readily accepted from sources who are perceived to be similar to the recipient. Also, personal influence will be more readily accepted from sources who interact frequently with the recipient.

These concepts of similarity and frequency of interaction, are, in fact, indicators of a more general level of social integration, which provides an individual with access to information available within the social system. More specifically, the credibility of the source depends on the past experience that a recipient has had with the advice and information given by the source. Therefore, personal influence will be more readily accepted from sources who have low variance in their previous recommendations. In other words, potential recipients will extrapolate from their previous experience and the accuracy of prior recommendations by the source (Barone and Byrne 1984).

Communication Characteristics. A message contains information; however, there is uncertainty as to what the information really means. The degree of uncertainty, or the degree of confidence associated with a unit of information, acts as a weight determining the degree of persuasiveness of the message. There are three main determinants of the uncertainty associated with a message: the clarity of the message, the consistency with other information, and the strength of the source commitment.

- Personal influence will be more readily accepted if the message sent by the source is high in clarity. High in clarity refers here to the lack of ambiguity in the communication, or the absence of noise in the communication (Shannon and Weaver 1949). As indicated earlier, in terms of the power of the source, technical expertise is not sufficient for information to be used by the recipient. Adapting the message so that the information is communicated at the technical level at which the recipient is knowledgeable and comfortable leads to a clearer message and, therefore, to a lower uncertainty associated with the message.

- The degree to which information from one source is compatible with other information that the receiver has is a determinant of influence potential.

---

[4]Sternthal, Dholakia, and Leavitt (1978) have hypothesized an interaction of source credibility with prior opinions: A less credible source would be more persuasive if the receiver's prior opinion is positive because it would generate a greater support argumentation in the receiver's cognitive responses. It is, however, unlikely that this would occur as the result of an information-seeking activity because the information seeker is unlikely to seek information from a low-credibility source.

The consistency of the information with other information enhances the acceptance of the information by the receiver (Howell and Burnett 1978). In fact, the recipient will evaluate new information against prior opinion and the strength of (or uncertainty associated with) this opinion (Wyer 1974). The consistency of new and old information is important since previous information creates expectations and individuals react differently to confirmation or disconfirmation of their expectations (Oliver 1989).

- The uncertainty attached to the message depends on the strength with which the information giver has committed himself or herself to the recommended behavior. The greater the commitment that the influencer has made to the recommended behavior (such as purchasing the innovation), the greater the social imitation.

Synopsis on Personal Influence

In this section we have proposed a conceptual framework that integrates both the recipient's and the information giver's perspectives. This joint view offers a potential to broaden the research base on interpersonal influence by considering the objective nature of the phenomenon. In addition, interactions due to factors that moderate the effectiveness of personal communication have been discussed. This model remains untested and its components could be analyzed in subsets, offering different research opportunities.

THE MARKETING STRATEGY FOR THE INNOVATION

The marketing strategy of the supplier of the innovation has been usually ignored in the literature on innovative decision processes. The exception is in the literature on the derivation of diffusion models, where the objective is to provide normative guidelines for the marketing of new products. These models have incorporated price, advertising, and salesforce marketing mix variables. For example, in regard to advertising expenditures, although some restrictions apply, the general trends over the diffusion

process are (1) if advertising affects the propensity to innovate, advertising expenditures should decrease over time; and (2) if advertising affects the propensity to imitate, advertising expenditures should increase over time (Dockner and Jorgensen 1988).

Few attempts have been made to test empirically the specification of diffusion models as to how these marketing activities influence sales over time (Simon and Sebastian 1987; Horsky and Simon 1983; Bass 1980; Lilien, Rao, and Kalish 1981). Empirical testing of multiple model specifications, however, is difficult (Simon and Sebastian 1987). Therefore, individual level theoretical explanations are necessary to justify model specifications. This calls for a research agenda that explains the role of different marketing mix variables on an individual's decision to purchase an innovation and on the timing of that decision. More specifically, the evolution of the role of marketing mix variables over the product life cycle must be understood in order to assess the appropriate marketing strategies to pursue and their likely impact on consumers over the life cycle of an innovation.

The marketing strategy of the innovation, however, is not limited to the marketing mix variables after the brand is introduced into the market. Significant effort may be devoted to the marketing of innovations before the actual market launch. In fact, many marketing activities precede the introduction of an innovation. Eliashberg and Robertson (1988) have provided some evidence that the preannouncement strategy that marketers design for different audiences depends on the characteristics of the innovation and of the firm as a participant in the competitive environment.

Preannouncements and Market Pioneer Advantages

A strategic option confronting the firm may be whether or not to preannounce a new product, that is, whether or not to make an announcement in advance of its intended action before test marketing or market introduction. The anticipated gain might be seen as providing a preemptive move against a competitor or as building consumer demand in advance. Research by Eliashberg and Robertson (1988) showed that firms preannounced new products in about one-half of their case studies, and that the audiences for the preannouncements (in declining order of importance) were the company's salesforce, its customers, its distributors, its employees, and eventually its competitors. Strategically, the value of preannouncing is tied to concerns about the shortening of product life cycles, the narrowing of market windows, and the advantages of being a market pioneer.

Shorter product life cycles challenge the firm to achieve market penetration quickly. The objective is to achieve steeper acceleration of the product life cycle in order to build a sales base before further technological change dilutes the product's potential. Preannouncing may hasten the take-off point in the typical logistic diffusion pattern.

The concept of a "market window" also suggests the need for rapid diffusion. Abell (1978) has proposed the notion that there are often limited periods when the fit between the market's needs and the firm's competencies are at an optimum. In product categories subject to rapid competitive change, the market window may be "open" only briefly before it begins to "close" due to competitive preemption. Preannouncing new products may be a viable course of action in competitive situations characterized by such narrow market window opportunities.

The value associated with being a "market pioneer" further suggests that preannouncing should be considered. Research documents that market pioneers gain lasting market share advantage. Urban et al. (1986), using Assessor (simulated test market) data for 47 brands of frequently purchased goods, found that the second firm to enter a market could expect to do only 71 percent as well in market share as the market pioneer, and that the third firm to enter could expect to do only 58 percent as well. Robinson and Fornell (1985), in a PIMS analysis of the consumer goods businesses, found that market pioneers achieved a 29 percent average market share versus a 17 percent share

for early followers and a 12 percent share for late entrants. In terms equivalent to Urban et al. (1986), this would mean that the early follower could expect to do only 59 percent as well as the market pioneer and the late entrant only 41 percent as well. Robinson (1988) has also documented the value of market pioneering in industrial products. Market pioneers tend to achieve substantially higher market shares—19 percent versus 21 percent for early followers, and 15 percent for late entrants. This means that the early follower can expect to do only 76 percent as well as the market pioneer and the late entrant only 51 percent as well as the pioneer.

The sources of market pioneer advantage are based on the erection of barriers to entry to the disadvantage of later entrants—if the pioneering product successfully fulfills customer needs. These barriers are likely to be built among consumers and within the channel of distribution.

Consumer advantage emanates from the ability of the pioneer to achieve awareness, trial, and brand loyalty before other firms enter. If the new product is successful in fulfilling customer needs, trial levels may decline substantially for later entrants. Indeed, research has shown the tenacity of brand loyalties over considerable periods of time (Whitten 1979). Carpenter and Nakamoto (1989) show that consumers develop preference for the pioneer because it becomes a reference for "ideal" values attributes and for the weights that attach to the product attributes. In addition, the pioneer has the ability to choose the most profitable market segments (Schmalansee 1982) and to engage in preemptive positioning (Carpenter 1987). The market pioneer may also take advantage of the insights provided by lead users, who are positioned at the front of market trends (Von Hippel 1988). Market pioneers, furthermore, may gain access to the most efficient distribution channels (Robinson and Fornell 1985), and they may achieve greater experience and scale advantages (Lane 1980; Judd 1985).

Nevertheless, there are major risks in preannouncing as well. It may simply encourage competitive reaction, rather than achieve the intended preemption effect. Preannouncements may also cannibalize sales from existing products. Furthermore, there may be the risk of an inability to deliver as promised.

Robertson and Eliashberg (1989) have proposed a conceptual model of whether or not to preannounce (Figure 9.3). The major components of the conceptualization are *competitive structure* and *customer behavior*. The specific variables to be taken into account and the conditions under which preannouncing is beneficial are listed for each component.

COMPETITIVE STRUCTURE

1. The firm has low market dominance in the product category where the new entry will occur. This suggests that cannibalization will be minimized due to the low share in the product category.

2. The firm is small in absolute size. This suggests little risk of "market overhanging" or antitrust allegations.

3. The competitive environment lacks rivalry. This suggests that reaction from competitors may be less likely.

CONSUMER BEHAVIOR

1. Switching costs to adopt the new product are high. Preannouncing may allow consumers to engage in advance planning in order to minimize switching costs.

2. Customer learning requirements are high. This suggests the value of building knowledge in advance of the introduction of the product into the market.

3. The product has a lengthy purchase decision process. This suggests the value of preannouncing in order to initiate consideration within the tenure of the purchase decision process.

FIGURE 9.3 **Whether to Preannounce** (Source: Robertson and Eliashberg (1989).)

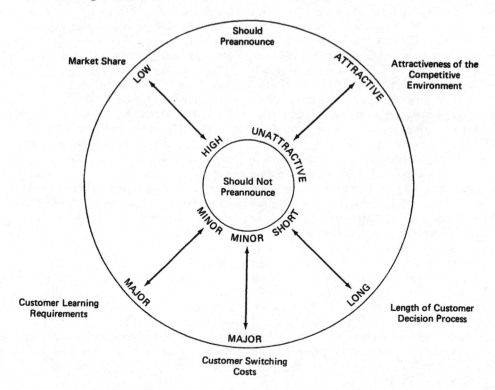

The graphic in Figure 9.3 summarizes these variables. The larger the circle, the stronger the recommendation that the firm should preannounce a new product. The smaller the circle, the stronger the recommendation that the firm should not preannounce a new product. Firms that either preannounced or did not preannounce consistent with this conceptualization achieved higher market share gains for their new product after introduction than firms which took preannouncing or non-preannouncing actions inconsistent with the recommendations of the conceptualization.

Research by Eliashberg and Robertson (1988) provides some support for this conceptualization. The actual incidence of preannouncing is associated with lack of market dominance, small size, and a competitive environment that is characterized by a lack of rivalry. High consumer switching costs are also associated with preannouncing. High learning requirements are also found, although this finding is insignificant.

Marketing Mix Strategy Over the Product Life Cycle

The mix of marketing variables changes over the product life cycle and, therefore, affects the diffusion curve of the innovation over time. Diffusion models have attempted to incorporate marketing mix activity. However, there is great difficulty, in practice, in selecting a model based on empirical evidence (such as likelihood tests). This is due, in part, to the overidentification of the model and, in part, to the multicollinearity introduced in the design matrix of predictor variables. Although Simon and Sebastian (1987) conclude that the model specification should be based on theoretical explanations of the role played by marketing mix variables, little theory has been advanced as to how the marketing process evolves over the product life cycle. Our goal now is to review the literature around a conceptual framework attempting to explain the selective role of marketing mix variables over the product life cycle.

What is the role of marketing mix variables in influencing the adoption decision process?

The basic issues identified by Simon and Sebastian (1987) concern (1) determining what aspects of the decision process are being affected by each marketing variable, (2) determining how long it takes for the marketing activity to affect the process, and (3) determining how long the effects last (i.e., seeing if there is a timing or a lagging effect)? These issues can be examined by analyzing the critical elements of the adoption/diffusion process.

The adoption process is driven by three basic concepts:

1. awareness, which is a condition for adoption;
2. willingness to pay the market price, which depends on
   a) the utility or relative advantage of the innovation taking into account price, and
   b) the uncertainty associated with that utility; and
3. the availability of the product.

Development of Awareness. Awareness about the availability of the innovation and its attributes (used by consumers to form a priori judgments) is communicated through marketer-controlled sources, such as advertising, and sometimes through personal sales or the distribution system. Awareness is also developed by word-of-mouth from consumers who are adopters, or at least who are already aware of the innovation, even if they have not adopted it yet.

Given the probabilistic nature of advertising exposure and the number of repetitions required for advertising to be effective, the impact of advertising on awareness is not immediate, but instead follows a dynamic process over time (Strong 1977; Zielske 1959; Zielske and Henry 1980). In order for word-of-mouth to operate, contacts with other individuals who have adopted or are considering the product need to be made. These contacts are effective, however, only if the adopter or considerer transmits useful information (Ozga 1960). The distribution system may be another source of information for developing new product awareness. Indeed, for innovations where a push strategy is used, the extent of the acceptance of the innovation by the trade is a primary factor in explaining the innovation's diffusion among consumers (Jones and Ritz 1987). In fact, depending on the image of the distribution outlets used, the awareness development process might be accomplished at different rates.

Willingness to Pay. The perceived utility of the innovation relative to price and the distribution of the perceived utility across consumers help to explain diffusion. In general, an individual who has developed awareness will adopt if the perceived value is greater than the price (Kalish 1985). Price can then be considered as a factor driving the market size at a given point in time because of its economic interpretation as a reservation price level. Therefore, when price decreases, more individuals are willing to pay for the product. Although critical, this is the sole direct role played by price, unless price is also used by consumers as a signal of quality. This might, however, be more appropriate for brand choice rather than for the decision to adopt or not adopt the product.

The consumer must compare the price of the innovation relative to its perceived value. The consumer must be persuaded, therefore, of the value of the innovation. The value of an innovation clearly differs across individuals and is sometimes uncertain. However, advertising plays an undeniable role in communicating information (even if biased) to the consumer and in building an image of the product for the consumer. These informative and persuasive efforts result in advertising affecting the market size. Given the communication efforts necessary for advertising to be persuasive (in particular via repetition), the value of an innovation, and consequently the market size at a given point in time, are not solely affected by the current period's advertising but also by past advertising. In a related vein, for example, Lilien, Rao, and Kalish (1981) demonstrate the cumulative effects of detailing efforts for pharmaceutical innovations.

Furthermore, previous adopters provide feedback to those consumers who have not yet adopted. This feedback is either positive or negative, depending on the experience of adopters (Midgley 1976), although cognitive dissonance might reduce the amount of negative information provided by adopters. Indeed, given the availability of distribution, the main reason for nonadoption by individuals who are aware of the innovation is that these individuals find the value too low for the price.

The degree of influence of adopters on nonadopters depends on factors (including marketing mix variables) that affect (1) the degree to which interpersonal contacts occur, (2) the probability of relevant information being passed during the interpersonal contact, (3) the quantity and nature of information transmitted, and (4) the persuasive power of this information. Regarding this last factor, a great persuasive power (a) reduces the information receiver's uncertainties and (b) enables the arguments presented to change the information receiver's perceptions or to develop proactive opinions about the product. Price, in particular, may be related to the extent of interpersonal influence due to its saliency. High-priced products are more likely to encourage a learning hierarchy, whereby information is gathered to evaluate the product. This would suggest, therefore, that high-priced products are more likely to be the subject of discussion between adopters and nonadopters.

Another factor affecting perceived value may be the sheer size of the adopter group. If broad adoption is of value to the innovation, then the size of the existing market, measured by current adopters, affects the potential market at the next time period. This is the case when network externalities are operative, as in the telecommunication or computer industries, where the demand for a product might depend on the wide adoption of a related product (or standard). In this case, the market potential—as determined by the perceived value of the innovation—is a function of the current level of diffusion. At the opposite extreme are products whose value is purely a function of social leadership. The benefits of the innovation diminish as the penetration level increases. This is often the case for fashion items. As the innovation's market acceptance reaches high levels, it has sown the seeds of its own demise.

Finally, distributors might play an important role in conveying information regarding the benefits of the innovation. Distributors and retailers have contact with potential customers and, therefore, can influence the adoption decision. This push strategy is particularly effective when the product is complex and the consumer has considerable information needs that must be met by the channel of distribution. More interesting, channels often evolve to mass channels over the life cycle of the product as the information needs of later adopters decrease because of the availability of information from earlier adopters.

This discussion has dealt with the necessity for the consumer to be persuaded of the value or utility of the innovation. The consumer, however, is not always certain of this utility. Uncertainty is typically reduced by positive information. Consumers might derive information from advertising, from adopters, or from the channel of distribution. A particular type of information from adopters is knowledge of the sheer number of previous adopters, which can be interpreted by potential adopters as a measure of the quality of the product. In fact, in Kalish's theoretical model (1985), uncertainty is the driving force in the diffusion process (beyond the diffusion mechanism, which drives awareness), because of the specification of the certainty equivalent of the value of the innovation, which is directly related to the number of adopters. This information is similar to the "social pressure" described by Horsky and Simon (1983), which derives from information provided by the fact that the group of nonadopters is becoming smaller and smaller. This information can be interpreted by consumers as a signal of the "quality" of the innovation. In addition, the information provided by adopters about product attributes and benefits is available at lower costs because of the greater ease with which adopters can be reached as the innovation diffuses in the population.

Finally, and particularly for products which require service after purchase, the number of distribution outlets can be both an indicator of quality and a risk-decreasing factor. In general, any type of information should rationally make the consumer more confident in the updated evaluation of the innovation, since information should lead to uncertainty reduction. Behaviorally, this is not always the case. Indeed, some types of information might generate doubts as to the real value of the innovation. This might depend on whether the information confirms or disconfirms expectations (Oliver 1989).

More generally, expectations about price and future product enhancements should play a decisive role in the timing decision of the adoption (Winer and Oliver 1987). Even when the value of the innovation is greater than the price, a consumer might decide to wait because prices are expected to become lower, or because the product is expected to be improved. The future expectations can play an essential role in the case of technological innovations, where a standard has not yet developed in the industry.

Availability of the Innovation. Finally, given that the consumer is receptive to adopting the innovation, it must be available. Production should be sufficient and distribution must be compatible with consumer shopping patterns. The production level is actually a policy variable, which interacts with other marketing mix policies (Jain, Mahajan, and Muller 1988). If the supply is restricted because of the production policy of the manufacturer, consumers might postpone purchase or might lose interest. This is particularly true if there are perfect or imperfect substitute products that the consumer might decide to adopt instead. Lack of availability could also influence the consumer's perceptions about the innovation.

Distribution level is a critical marketing factor in the diffusion of a consumer product innovation (Jones and Ritz 1987). This variable is very often ignored in diffusion research and models, and product availability is presumed. However, due to forecasting errors, this variable cannot always be controlled by the manufacturer. It is indispensable to understand, therefore, what makes distributors agree to carry an innovation. Factors that can affect distributor receptivity include (1) the sales force effort behind the innovation and the types of contractual terms given to distributors (the amount of selling push), (2) the level of awareness in the population (the amount of consumer pull exerting pressure on the distribution system), and (3) the level of distributor interest generated by an imitation process of other distributors (Jones and Ritz 1987).

It should be noted that advertising influences the distribution level indirectly through the consumer pull factor. Related factors that influence distributor decisions concern their expectations in terms of price margins and product turnover, that is, the speed of future adoptions. Although these factors are not, strictly speaking, related to consumer behavior, they influence the behavioral adoption outcome and must be considered explicitly in empirical field studies of consumer behavior.

Synopsis of Marketing Activities

We have developed a conceptual framework for understanding how marketing mix variables influence the diffusion process. In particular, we have suggested a number of potential areas for future behavioral research. These include the following:

- The role of new product preannouncements used to lower consumer switching costs and to enhance learning;
- the development of market pioneer advantages at the consumer level;
- the role of advertising in building consumer awareness of the innovation;
- the impact of repetition and of the timing of advertising messages in developing consumer awareness over time;
- the role of distribution outlets in developing brand awareness;
- the persuasive effects of advertising for innova-

tions (aimed at consumers with little a priori knowledge);
- the cumulative effects of persuasive communication efforts;
- the types of information transmitted by adopters, in contrast to knowledgeable nonadopters, and their respective behavioral motivations;
- the informational value (social pressure) of the number of current adopters;
- the role of network externalities in the diffusion of innovations;
- the type of information provided by distributors to consumers in contrast to the type of information provided by advertising;
- the influence of product characteristics (e.g., product complexity or learning requirements) on the effectiveness of difficult information sources;
- the role of adopter uncertainty in assessing the value of an innovation and how this uncertainty changes due to advertising, word-of-mouth, penetration level, or distribution level;
- the formation and the role of expectations about future prices and product technology improvements on adoption intent; and
- the effects of the nonavailability of the innovation on consumers who have decided to adopt.

These issues are crucial in the specification of models of diffusion, which have important managerial implications as discussed earlier. In addition, a better understanding of these marketing variables in the diffusion process can be critical in resolving the issue of why and how marketing mix elasticities change over the product life cycle. Although there have been attempts to study changes in price elasticity (Simon 1979; Liu and Hansens 1981) and advertising elasticity (Arora 1979; Parsons 1975) over time, there is little theory as to the causes of these changes. The previous discussion suggests five main reasons for changes in elasticities: (1) changes in consumer sensitivity to marketing variables due to exogenous factors, (2) the distribution of marketing mix elasticities in the population, (3) changes in the competitive situation, (4) learning requirements and processes that evolve over time, and (5) effects due to the saturation of the market.

COMPETITIVE ACTIVITIES

Competition may have a considerable effect on the diffusion of an innovation. Most innovations, unless they are highly discontinuous, are introduced into an existing product category competitive environment. The positioning of the product and the design of the marketing program must take into account the existing set of brands on the market. The condition of interdependency is negatively related to the level of discontinuity of the innovation.

In a competitive environment, multiple innovation entries to the market are likely to occur. Such entries may expand the total market potential, although they often limit the market share of the firm that first introduced the innovation. Competitive entry tends to take one of two forms: imitation or differentiation.

In an *imitation* strategy, the later entrant generally matches the positioning and strategy of the innovating firm. Although the market pioneer can be expected to retain dominant share (as discussed earlier) considerable interdependency now exists, especially in pricing. In many product categories where imitation occurs, imitating firms will seek to replicate the positioning of the innovator and to gain market share with a lower price. The net effect may be to expand the market if there is reasonable price sensitivity, or if the imitating firm helps expand the market by using advertising or additional distribution resources.

In a *differentiation* strategy, the later entrant attempts to replicate the innovation but to also add additional benefits. This strategy may then lead to an additional round of product enhancement by the market pioneer. This may be evidenced by the competition between Apple and IBM in the personal computer market. The net effect of additional innovations as enhancements may be to increase the market potential. Additionally, the later entrant may undertake advertising and distribution strategies that expand the size of the market or speed the diffusion process. The net effect of IBM's entry into the personal computer market behind Apple has been to expand the market size, in part because of IBM's resource commitment to advertising and distribution, as well as to the multiple rounds of product enhancement that have occurred.

Competitive Interdependency

The extent of competitive interdependency is a function of the level of product differentiation that an innovation is able to achieve. Each firm enters the market with varying degrees of product differentiation and each competitor designs its own competitive marketing strategy. This strategy is competitive in the sense that the firm's decision set is based on competitors' strategies. It is also competitive in that the objective is to obtain or maintain a competitive advantage over competitors.

Although the concept of competitiveness just described concerns the rivalry behavior (interdependency) of competitors, typical measures of competitiveness are structural in nature and measure such factors as the number of competitors, the concentration ratios, and the mobility barriers that competitors are able to erect (Porter 1980). These measures of competitiveness and the firms' strategies are interrelated and affect the adoption behavior of consumers. First of all, competitive structures and rivalry push prices down (Eliashberg and Jeuland 1986). When a new firm enters the market, optimal prices often go down. Consequently, consumers are willing to purchase the product earlier (i.e., more individuals are under their reservation price). Similarly, for advertising competitive reaction leads to an escalation of expenditures. These competitive effects of advertising may mainly affect market share or may benefit primary demand. However, at early stages of the diffusion process, additional resources devoted to communication of the innovation (even as it relates to specific brand attributes) improve consumer knowledge about the product and, therefore, help develop the market potential and enhance the speed with which this potential is realized.

Network Externalities

Network externalities occur when the adoption of an innovation depends (positively) on the extent to which prior adoption has occurred. Network externalities are typical of consumer products involving technological innovations, such as home computers, compact discs, video discs, high-definition television, satellite television, or video text home terminals (such as the French Minitel). The benefits to the consumer, who is considering the adoption of such innovations, when there is a high level of prior adoption, relate to the probabilities of standards having emerged and the availability of programming, software, and so forth.

When considering network externalities, some interesting questions that have been addressed concern the degree of product differentiation that is optimal among competitors and the pricing of these competing products (Katz and Shapiro 1985, 1986; Leruth 1988). Little behavioral research, however, exists concerning the innovative decision process involved when consumers are facing such a competitive array, with differentiated brands presenting varying levels of standardization.

An interesting conceptual domain may be the pursuit of research that focuses on consumer decision behavior for innovations under varying conditions of network externalities. The major reasons for the positive effects of network externalities might be the increased benefits that consumers perceive and the reduced uncertainty concerning the expectation of technological stability. However, the concept of network externalities could benefit from greater precision, since it may take several forms.

Synopsis on Competitive Activities

In summary, innovative adoption decisions are not made independently of competitive activities. Instead, substitutes and alternatives — current or expected — are generally available to consumers considering the acquisition of innovations. This context is composed not only of substitute products, but also of other interrelated innovations, with interdependent processes of diffusion. Whereas these issues have led to recent work in the management and strategy literature, consumer research should analyze the behavioral processes underlying the adoption and diffusion of competing and related innovations.

CONCLUSIONS

Our intent in this review of innovation decision processes has not been to be exhaustive, but rather to suggest some promising research directions. As every research stream develops and matures, a dominant conceptual paradigm evolves. Much of the impetus for research on innovative decision processes can be attributed to the Rogers paradigm, originally proposed in 1962, and based on earlier work of the 1950s in rural sociology. As valuable as this paradigm is, however, it also has some limitations. In particular, the dominant diffusion of innovation paradigm ignores marketing strategy and competitive activities. Yet these initiatives may considerably affect the process of diffusion, including the very nature of the innovation and its perception by consumers as a function of marketing strategy positioning and target market selection.

Additionally, the extant paradigm was developed before cognitive decision theory and has a strong learning theory bias in its view of the adoption process. A major research opportunity can be found in taking an information search and decision orientation toward consumer processing of innovative stimuli.

This chapter has posed a number of research questions within the domain of innovative decision processes. The objective has been to encourage a program of research that might enrich the conceptual foundations of diffusion theory. The end goal, of course, would be that marketers and other change agents have a better developed body of knowledge from which to draw in order to effectively and efficiently disseminate innovative ideas, practices, products, and services.

REFERENCES

AAKER, DAVID and JOHN G. MYERS (1982). *Advertising Management*. Englewood Cliffs, NJ: Prentice-Hall.

ABELL, DEREK F. (1978). "Strategic Windows," *Journal of Marketing*, 42 (July), 21–26.

ALBA, JOSEPH W., and J. WESLEY HUTCHINSON (1987). "Dimensions of Consumer Expertise," *Journal of Consumer Research*, 13 (March), 411–454.

ARNDT, JOHAN (1967). "Role of Product-Related Conversations in the Diffusion of a New Product," *Journal of Marketing Research*, 4 (August), 291–295.

ARORA, RAJINDAS (1979). "How Promotion Elasticities Change," *Journal of Advertising Research*, 19 (June), 57–62.

BARON, ROBERT A., and DONN BYRNE (1984). *Social Psychology: Understanding Human Interaction*, Boston, MA: Allyn and Bacon.

BASS, FRANK M. (1969). "A New Product Growth Model for Consumer Durables," *Management Science*, 15 (January), 215–227.

BASS, FRANK M. (1980). "The Relationship Between Diffusion Rates, Experience Curves, and Demand Elasticities for Consumer Durable Technological Innovations," *Journal of Business*, 53, 3 (July), 551–567.

BAUMGARTEN, STEVEN A. (1974). "The Innovative Communicator in the Diffusion Process," *Journal of Marketing Research*, 12 (February), 12–18.

BETTMAN, JAMES R. (1979). *An Information Processing Theory of Consumer Choice*, Reading, MA: Addison-Wesley.

BETTMAN, JAMES R., and MITA SUJAN (1987). "Effects of Framing on Evaluation of Comparable and Noncomparable Alternatives by Expert and Novice Consumers," *Journal of Consumer Research*, 14 (September), 141–154.

BLAU, PETER M. (1964). *Exchange and Power in Social Life*. New York, NY: Wiley.

BLAU, PETER M. (1974). *On the Nature of Organizations*. New York, NY: Wiley.

BROCK, T. (1964). "Communication-Recipient Similarity and Decision Change," *Journal of Personality and Social Psychology*, 1, 650–654.

BROWN, JACQUELINE JOHNSON, and PETER H. REINGEN (1987). "Social Ties and Word-of-Mouth Referral Behavior," *Journal of Consumer Research*, 14 (December), 350–362.

BRUCKS, MERRIE (1985). "The Effects of Product Class Knowledge on Information Search Behavior," *Journal of Consumer Research*, 12 (June), 1–16.

CALANTONE, ROGER, and ROBERT G. COOPER (1981). "New Product Scenarios: Projects for Success," *Journal of Marketing*, 45 (Spring), 48–60.

CARPENTER, GREGORY S. (1987). "Market Pioneering and Competitive Positioning Strategy," *Annales Des Telecommunications*, 42 (November/December), 699–709.

CARPENTER, GREGORY S., and KENT NAKOMOTO (1989). "Consumer Preference Formation and Pioneering Advantage," *Journal of Marketing Research*, 26, 3 (August), 285–298.

COLEMAN, JAMES S., ELIHU KATZ, and HERBERT MENZEL (1957). "The Diffusion of an Innovation Among Physicians," *Sociometry*, 20, 4 (December), 253–270.

COLEMAN, JAMES S., ELIHU KATZ, and HERBERT MENZEL (1966). *Medical Innovation: A Diffusion Study*, Indianapolis, IN: Bobbs-Merrill.

CZEPIEL, JOHN A. (1975). "Patterns of Inter-Organizational Communications and the Diffusion of a Major Technological Innovation in a Competitive Industrial Community," *Academy of Management Journal*, 18 (March), 6–24.

CZEPIEL, JOHN A. (1975). "Word-of-Mouth Processes in the Diffusion of a Major Technological Innovation," *Journal of Marketing Research*, 11 (May), 172–180.

DAMANPOUR, FARIBORZ (1988). "Innovation Type, Radicalness, and the Adoption Process," *Communication Research*, 15 (October), 545–567.

DANKO, WILLIAM D., and JAMES M. MACLACHLAN (1983). "Research to Accelerate the Diffusion of a New Invention," *Journal of Advertising Research*, 23 (June/July), 39–43.

DICKERSON, MARY DEE, and JAMES W. GENTRY (1983). "Characteristics of Adopters and Non-Adopters of Home Computers," *Journal of Consumer Research*, 10 (September), 225–235.

DOCKNER, ENGLEBERT, and STEFFEN JORGENSEN (1988). "Optimal Advertising Policies for Diffusion Models of New Product Innovation in Monopolistic Situations," *Management Science*, 34, 1 (January), 119–130.

DOLAN, ROBERT J., and ABEL P. JEULAND (1981). "Experience Curves and Dynamic Demand Models: Implications for Optimal Pricing Strategies," *Journal of Marketing*, 45 (Winter), 52–62.

DOWNS, G. W., and L. B. MOHR (1976). "Conceptual Issues in the Study of Innovations," *Administrative Science Quarterly*, 21, 4, 700–714.

ELIASHBERG, JEHOSHUA, and KRISTIAAN HELSEN (1988). "Cross-Country Diffusion Processes and Market Entry Timing," Working Paper No. 87-039, The Wharton School, University of Pennsylvania, Philadelphia, PA.

ELIASHBERG, JEHOSHUA and ABEL P. JEULAND (1986). "The Impact of Competitive Entry in a Developing Market Upon Dynamic Pricing Strategies," *Marketing Science*, 5, 20–36.

ELIASHBERG, JEHOSHUA, and THOMAS S. ROBERTSON (1988). "New Product Preannouncing Behavior: A Market Signaling Study," *Journal of Marketing Research*, 25, 3 (August), 282–292.

FEDER, G. (1982). "Adoption of Interrelated Agricultural Innovations: Complementarity and the Impacts of Risk, Scale, and Credit," *American Journal of Agricultural Economics*, 64, 1, 94–101.

FLIEGEL, FREDERICK C., and JOSEPH E. KIVLIN (1966). "Attributes of Innovations as Factors in Diffusion," *American Journal of Sociology*, 72 (November), 235–248.

FOXALL, GORDON R. (1988). "Consumer Innovativeness: Novelty-Seeking, Creativity and Cognitive Style," in *Research in Consumer Behavior*, Vol. 3. Greenwich, CT: JAI Press.

FOXALL, GORDON R., and CHRISTOPHER G. HASKINS (1986). "Cognitive Style and Consumer Innovativeness," *Marketing Intelligence and Planning*," 4, 1, 26–46.

FRANK, RONALD E., WILLIAM F. MASSY, and DONALD G. MORRISON (1964). "The Determinants of Innovative Behavior with Respect to a Branded, Frequently Purchased Food Product," in L. George Smith, Ed., *Proceedings of the American Marketing Association*. Chicago, IL: American Marketing Association, 312–323.

GATIGNON, HUBERT (1984). "Toward A Methodology for Measuring Advertising Copy Effects," *Marketing Science*, 3, 4 (Fall), 308–326.

GATIGNON, HUBERT, ERIN ANDERSON, and KRISTIAAN HELSEN (1989). "Competitive Reaction to Market Entry: Explaining Interfirm Differences," *Journal of Marketing Research*, 26, 1 (February), 44–55.

GATIGNON, HUBERT, JEHOSHUA ELIASHBERG, and THOMAS S. ROBERTSON (1989). "Modeling Multinational Diffusion Patterns: An Efficient Methodology," *Marketing Science*, .

GATIGNON, HUBERT, and THOMAS S. ROBERTSON (1985). "A Propositional Inventory for New Diffusion Research," *Journal of Consumer Research*, 11, 4 (March), 859–867.

GATIGNON, HUBERT, and THOMAS S. ROBERTSON (1986a), "Integration of Consumer Diffusion Theory and Diffusion Models: New Research Directions," in Vijay Mahajan and Yoram Wind, Eds., *Innovation Diffusion Models of New Product Acceptance*. Cambridge, MA: Ballinger, 37–60.

GATIGNON, HUBERT, and THOMAS S. ROBERTSON (1986b). "An Exchange Theory Model of Interpersonal Communications," in Richard J. Lutz, Ed., *Advances in Consumer Research*, Vol. 13, 629–632.

GATIGNON, HUBERT, and THOMAS S. ROBERTSON (1988). "The Role of Uncertainty in the Diffusion of High Technology Innovations: An Experimental Study," Working Paper, The Wharton School, University of Pennsylvania, Philadelphia, PA.

GATIGNON, HUBERT, and THOMAS S. ROBERTSON (1989). "Technology Diffusion: An Empirical Test of Competitive Effects," *Journal of Marketing*, 53, 1 (January), 35–49.

GATIGNON, HUBERT, BARTON A. WEITZ, and PRADEEP BANSAL (1989). "Brand Introduction Strategies and Competitive Environments," Working Paper, The Wharton School, University of Pennsylvania, Philadelphia, PA.

GOLD, BELA (1981). "Technological Diffusion in Industry: Research Needs and Shortcomings," *Journal of Industrial Economics*, 29 (March), 247–269.

GRANOVETTER, MARK S. (1973). "The Strength of Weak Ties," *American Journal of Sociology*, 78, 6, 1360–1380.

GRANOVETTER, MARK S. (1983). "The Strength of Weak Ties: A Network Theory Revisited," *Sociological Theory*, 1, 201–233.

HIRSCHMAN, ELIZABETH C. (1980). "Innovativeness, Novelty Seeking, and Consumer Creativity," *Journal of Consumer Research*, 7, 283–295.

HIRSCHMAN, ELIZABETH C. (1981). "Technology and Symbolism as Sources for the Generation of Innovations," in Andrew A. Mitchell, Ed., *Advances in Consumer Research*, Vol. 9. St. Louis, MO: Association for Consumer Research, 537–541.

HOMANS, GEORGE C. (1961). *Social Behavior: Its Elementary Forms*. New York: Harcourt Brace Jovanovich.

HORSKY, DAN and LEONARD S. SIMON (1983).

"Advertising and the Diffusion of New Products," *Marketing Science,* 2 (Winter), 1–10.

HOWELL, WILLIAM C., and SARAH A. BURNETT (1978). "Uncertainty Measurement: A Cognitive Taxonomy," *Organizational Behavior and Human Performance,* 22, 45–68.

JACOBY, JACOB, and WAYNE D. HOYER (1980). "What If Opinion Leaders Didn't Really Know More? A Question of Nomological Validity," in Kent B. Monroe, Ed., *Advances in Consumer Research,* Vol. 8. Chicago, IL: Association for Consumer Research, 299–302.

JAIN, DIPAK, VIJAY MAHAJAN, and EITAN MULLER (1988). "Innovation Diffusion in the Presence of Supply Restrictions," Working Paper, Southern Methodist University, Dallas, TX.

JOHNSON, ERIC J., and J. EDWARD RUSSO (1984). "Product Familiarity and Learning New Information," *Journal of Consumer Research,* 11 (June), 542–550.

JONES, J. MORGAN, and CHRISTOPHER RITZ (1987). "Incorporating Distribution Into New Product Diffusion Models," Working Paper, University of North Carolina, Durham, NC.

JUDD, K. (1985). "Credible Spatial Preemption," *Rand Journal of Economics,* 16, (Summer), 153–165.

KALISH, SHLOMO (1985). "A New Product Adoption Model with Price, Advertising, and Uncertainty," *Management Science,* 31, 12 (December), 1569–1585.

KALISH, SHLOMO, and GARY L. LILIEN (1986). "A Market Entry Timing Model for New Technologies," *Management Science,* 32 (February), 194–205.

KATZ, ELIHU, and PAUL F. LAZARSFELD (1955). *Personal Influence.* New York: Free Press.

KATZ, MICHAEL L., and CARL SHAPIRO (1985). "Network Externalities, Competition and Compatibility," *American Economic Review,* 94, 4, 424–440.

KATZ, MICHAEL L., and CARL SHAPIRO (1986). "Technology Adoption in the Presence of Network Externalities," *Journal of Political Economy,* 94, 4, 822–841.

KELLER, KEVIN LANE (1987). "Memory Factors in Advertising: The Effect of Advertising Retrieval Cues on Brand Evaluations," *Journal of Consumer Research,* 14 (December), 316–333.

KIMBERLY, JOHN R. (1978). "Hospital Adoption of Innovation: The Role of Integration Into External Informational Environments," *Journal of Health & Social Behavior,* 12 (December), 361–373.

KIMBERLY, JOHN R., and MICHAEL J. EVANISKO (1981). "Organizational Innovation: The Influence of Individual, Organizational, and Contextual Factors on Hospital Adoption of Technological and Administrative Innovations," *Academy of Management Journal,* 24, 4, 689–713.

KRUGMAN, HERBERT E. (1965). "The Impact of Television Advertising: Learning Without Involvement," *Public Opinion Quarterly,* 29 (Fall), 349–356.

LABAY, DUNCAN G., and THOMAS C. KINNEAR (1981). "Exploring the Consumer Decision Process in the Adoption of Solar Energy Systems," *Journal of Consumer Research,* 8, 3, 271–278.

LANE, W. J. (1980). "Product Differentiation in a Market with Sequential Entry," *Bell Journal of Economics,* 11 (Spring), 237–259.

LAWTON, S. B., and W. H. LAWTON (1979). "An Autocatalytic Model for the Diffusion of Educational Innovations," *Education Administration Quarterly,* 15, 1 (Winter), 19–43.

LEONARD-BARTON, DOROTHY (1985). "Experts as Negative Opinion Leaders in the Diffusion of a Technological Innovation," *Journal of Consumer Research,* 11 (March), 914–926.

LERUTH, LUC (1988). "Compatibility and Externalities in Competing Networks," Unpublished Doctoral Dissertation, Universite Libre de Bruxelles, Brussels, Belgium.

LILIEN, GARY L., AMBAR G. RAO, and SHLOMO KALISH (1981). "Bayesian Estimation and Control of Detailing Effort in a Repeat Purchase Environment," *Management Science,* 27, 5 (May), 493–507.

LIU, L. M., and DOMINIQUE M. HANSSENS (1981). "A Bayesian Approach to Time-Varying Cross-Section Regression Models," *Journal of Econometrics,* 15, 341–356.

LYNCH, JOHN G. JR., and THOMAS K. SRULL (1982). "Memory and Attentional Factors in Consumer Choice: Concepts and Research Methods," *Journal of Consumer Research,* 9 (June), 18–36.

MAHAJAN, VIJAY, and EITAN MULLER (1979). "Innovation Diffusion and New Product Growth Models in Marketing," *Journal of Marketing,* 43, 4, 55–68.

MAHAJAN, VIJAY, EITAN MULLER, and ROBERT A. KERIN (1984). "Introduction Strategy for New

Products with Positive and Negative Word-of-Mouth," *Management Science,* 30 (December), 1389-1404.

MAHAJAN, VIJAY, and ROBERT A. PETERSON (1979). "First-Purchase Diffusion Models of New-Product Acceptance," *Technological Forecasting and Social Change,* 15, 127-146.

MAHAJAN, VIJAY, and YORAM WIND (1986). *Innovation Diffusion Models of New Product Acceptance.* Cambridge, MA: Ballinger.

MANSFIELD, E. (1961). "Technological Change and the Rate of Imitation," *Econometrica,* 29, 741-766.

MEYER, ROBERT J. (1981). "A Model of Multiattribute Judgments Under Attribute Uncertainty and Informational Constraint," *Journal of Marketing Research,* 18 (November), 428-441.

MEYER, ROBERT J. (1985). "A Multiattribute Model of Consumer Choice During Product Learning," *Marketing Science,* 4, 1, 41-61.

MIDGLEY, DAVID F. (1976). "A Simple Mathematical Theory of Innovative Behavior," *Journal of Consumer Research,* 3 (June), 31-41.

MIDGLEY, DAVID F. (1977). *Innovation and New Product Marketing.* New York, NY: Wiley.

MIDGLEY, DAVID F. (1981). "Toward a Theory of the Product Life Cycle: Explaining Diversity," *Journal of Marketing,* 45 (Fall), 109-115.

MIDGLEY, DAVID F., and GRAHAME R. DOWLING (1978). "Innovativeness: The Concept and Its Measurement," *Journal of Consumer Research,* 4 (March), 229-242.

MILLIKEN, FRANCES J. (1987). "Three Types of Perceived Uncertainty About the Environment: State, Effect, and Response Uncertainty," *Academy of Management Review,* 12, 1, 133-143.

MITCHELL, DEBORAH J. (1988). "Mind Over Matter: The Role of Mental Imagery in Evaluation," Working Paper, The Wharton School, University of Pennsylvania, Philadelphia, PA.

MIZERSKI, RICHARD W. (1982). "An Attributional Explanation of the Disproportionate Influence of Unfavorable Information," *Journal of Consumer Research,* 9 (December), 301-310.

MURPHY, GREGORY L., and JACK C. WRIGHT (1984). "Changes in Conceptual Structure with Expertise: Differences Between Real-World Experts and Novices," *Journal of Experimental Psychology,* 10, 1, 144-155.

NEWMAN, JOSEPH W., and RICHARD STAELIN

(1973). "Information Sources of Durable Goods," *Journal of Advertising Research,* 13, 2 (April), 19-29.

OLIVER, RICHARD L. (1977). "Effects of Expectation and Disconfirmation on Postexposure Product Evaluations: An Alternative Interpretation," *Journal of Applied Psychology,* 62, 4, 480-486.

OLIVER, RICHARD L. (1989). "Processing of the Satisfaction Response in Consumption: A Suggested Framework and Research Propositions," *Journal of Consumer Satisfaction, Dissatisfaction and Complaining Behavior.* Vol. 2, 1-16.

OLSHAVSKY, RICHARD W. (1980). "Time and the Rate of Adoption of Innovations," *Journal of Consumer Research,* 6 (March), 425-428.

OSTLUND, LYMAN E. (1974). "Perceived Innovation Attributes as Predictors and Innovativeness," *Journal of Consumer Research,* 1 (June), 23-29.

OZGA, S. A. (1960). "Imperfect Markets Through Lack of Knowledge," *Quarterly Journal of Economics,* 74 (February), 29-52.

PARK, C. WHAN, and V. PARKER LESSIG (1981). "Familiarity and Its Impact on Consumer Decision Biases and Heuristics," *Journal of Consumer Research,* 8 (September), 223-230.

PARSONS, LEONARD J. (1975). "The Product Life Cycle and Time Varying Advertising Elasticities," *Journal of Marketing Research,* 12, 3 (November), 476-480.

PRICE, LINDA L., and NANCY M. RIDGWAY (1983). "Development of a Scale to Measure Use Innovativeness," in Richard P. Bagozzi and Alice M. Tybout, Eds., *Advances in Consumer Research,* 10, 679-684.

PORTER, MICHAEL E. (1980). *Competitive Strategy: Techniques for Analyzing Industries and Competitors.* New York: Free Press.

RAM, S. (1987). "A Model of Innovation Resistance," in Melanie Wallendorf and Paul Anderson, Eds., *Advances in Consumer Research,* Vol. 14. Provo, UT: Association for Consumer Research.

RAM, S., and JAGDISH N. SHETH (1989). "Consumer Resistance to Innovations: The Marketing Problem and Its Solutions," *Journal of Consumer Marketing,* 6, 2, 5-14.

RAY, MICHAEL L. (1973). "Marketing Communication and the Hierarchy of Effects," in Peter Clarke, Ed., *New Models for Mass Communication Research,* Vol. 2. Beverly Hills, CA: Sage, 147-176.

REINGEN, PETER H., and JEROME B. KERNAN (1986). "Analysis of Referral Networks in Marketing: Methods and Illustration," *Journal of Marketing Research,* 23 (November), 370–378.

RICHINS, MARSHA L. (1983). "Negative Word-of-Mouth by Dissatisfied Consumers: A Pilot Study," *Journal of Marketing,* 47 (Winter), 68–78.

ROBERTSON, THOMAS S. (1967). "Determinants of Innovative Behavior," in Reed Moyer, Ed., *Proceedings of the American Marketing Association.* Chicago: American Marketing Association, 328–332.

ROBERTSON, THOMAS S. (1971). *Innovative Behavior and Communication.* New York: Holt, Rhinehart & Winston.

ROBERTSON, THOMAS S. (1976). "Low-Commitment Consumer Behavior," *Journal of Advertising Research,* 16 (April), 19–24.

ROBERTSON, THOMAS S., and JEHOSHUA ELIASHBERG (1989). "New Product Preannouncing: Industry Practice and Market Share Effects," Working Paper, Wharton School, University of Pennsylvania, Philadelphia, PA.

ROBERTSON, THOMAS S., and HUBERT GATIGNON (1986). "Competitive Effects on Technology Diffusion," *Journal of Marketing,* 50, 3 (July), 1–12.

ROBERTSON, THOMAS S., and JOHN H. MYERS (1969). "Personality Correlates of Opinion Leadership and Innovative Buying Behavior," *Journal of Marketing Research,* 6, 164–168.

ROBERTSON, THOMAS S., and JOHN H. MYERS (1970). "Personality Correlates of Innovative Buying Behavior: A Reply," *Journal of Marketing Research,* 4, 260.

ROBERTSON, THOMAS S., JOAN ZIELINSKI, and SCOTT WARD (1984). *Consumer Behavior.* Glenview, IL: Scott, Foresman.

ROBINSON, WILLIAM T. (1988). "Sources of Market Pioneer Advantages: The Case of Industrial Goods Industries," *Journal of Marketing Research,* 25 (February), 87–94.

ROBINSON, WILLIAM T., and CLAES FORNELL (1985). "Sources of Market Pioneer Advantages in Consumer Goods Industries," *Journal of Marketing Research,* 22 (August), 305–317.

ROGERS, EVERETT M. (1962 and 1983). *The Diffusion of Innovations.* New York: Free Press.

ROGERS, EVERETT M. (1976). "New Product Adoption and Diffusion," *Journal of Consumer Research,* 2 (March), 290–301.

ROGERS, EVERETT M., HUGH M. DALEY, and THOMAS D. WU (1982). *The Diffusion of Home Computers: An Exploratory Study.* Stanford, CA: Institute for Communication Research, Stanford University.

ROSEN, DENNIS L., and RICHARD L. OLSHAVSKY (1987). "The Dual Role of Informational Social Influence: Implications for Marketing Management," *Journal of Business Research,* 15, 123–144.

ROSS, WILLIAM (1989). "The Effect of Ambiguity on Strategic Marketing Decision Making," Working Paper, The Wharton School, University of Pennsylvania, Philadelphia, PA.

SCHAFFER, DAVID R., and CLYDE HENDRICK (1974). "Dogmatism and Tolerance for Ambiguity as Determinants of Differential Reactions to Cognitive Inconsistency," *Journal of Personality and Social Psychology,* 29, 5, 601–608.

SCHMALENSEE, RICHARD (1982). "Product Differentiation Advantages of Pioneering Brands," *American Economic Review,* 72 (June), 349–365.

SHANNON, CLAUDE E., and WARREN WEAVER (1949). *The Mathematical Theory of Communication.* Urbana, IL: University of Illinois Press.

SHETH, JAGDISH N. (1981). "Psychology of Innovation Resistance," *Research in Marketing,* 4, 273–282.

SIMON, HERMANN (1979). "Dynamics of Price Elasticity and Brand Life Cycles: An Empirical Study," *Journal of Marketing Research,* 16, 4 (November), 439–452.

SIMON, HERMANN, and KARL-HEINZ SEBASTIAN (1987). "Diffusion and Advertising: The German Telephone Campaign," *Management Science,* 33, 4 (April), 451–466.

SOUDER, WILLIAM E. (1987). *Managing New Product Innovations.* Lexington, MA: D.C. Heath.

SRIVASTAVA, R. K., V. MAHAJAN, S. N. RAMASWAMI, and J. CHERIAN (1985). "A Multiattribute Diffusion Model for Adoption of Investment Alternatives for Consumers," *Technological Forecasting and Social Change,"* 28 (December), 325–333.

STERN, LOUIS W., C. SAMUEL CRAIG, ANTHONY J. LA GRECA, and RICHARD G. SALEM (1976). "The Effect of Sociometric Location on the Adoption of an Innovation Within a University Faculty," *Sociology of Education,* 49 (January), 90–96.

STERNTHAL, BRIAN, and C. SAMUEL CRAIG (1982). *Consumer Behavior: An Information Processing Perspective.* Englewood Cliffs, NJ: Prentice-Hall.

STERNTHAL, BRIAN, RUBY DHOLAKIA, and CLARK LEAVITT (1978). "The Persuasive Effect of

Source Credibility: Tests of Cognitive Response," *Journal of Consumer Research,* 4 (March), 252–260.

STRONG, EDWARD C. (1977). "The Spacing and Timing of Advertising," *Journal of Advertising Research,* 17, 6 (December), 25–31.

SUJAN, MITA (1985). "Consumer Knowledge: Effects On Evaluation Strategies Mediating Consumer Judgments," *Journal of Consumer Research,* 12 (June), 31–46.

SUMMERS, JOHN O. (1970). "The Identity of Women's Clothing Fashion Opinion Leaders," *Journal of Marketing Research,* 7 (May), 178–185.

TAYLOR, JAMES W. (1987). "A Striking Characteristic of Innovators," *Journal of Marketing Research,* 14 (February), 104–107.

TUSHMAN, MICHAEL L., and PHILIP ANDERSON (1986). "Technological Discontinuities and Organizational Environments," *Administrative Science Quarterly,* 31 (September), 439–465.

URBAN, GLEN L., THERESA CARTER, STEVEN GASKIN, and ZOFIA MUCHA (1986). "Market Share Rewards to Pioneering Brands: An Empirical Analysis and Strategic Implications," *Management Science,* 32 (June), 645–659.

VON HIPPEL, ERIC (1986). "Lead Users: A Source of Novel Product Concepts," *Management Science,* 32, 7 (July), 791–805.

VON HIPPEL, ERIC (1988). *The Sources of Innovation.* New York: Oxford University Press.

WHITTEN, I. T. (1979). *Brand Performance in the Cigarette Industry and the Advantage of Early Entry: 1913–73,* Staff Report to the Federal Trade Commission. Washington, DC: U.S. Government Printing Office.

WILKENING, EUGENE A. (1952). "Informal Leaders and Innovators in Farm Practices," *Rural Sociology,* 17 (September), 272–275.

WILTON, PETER C., and EDGAR A. PESSEMIER (1981). "Forecasting the Ultimate Acceptance of An Innovation: The Effects of Information," *Journal of Consumer Research,* 8 (September), 162–171.

WIND, YORAM, THOMAS S. ROBERTSON and CYNTHIA FRASER (1982). "Industrial Product Diffusion by Market Segment," *Industrial Marketing Management,* 11, 1–8.

WINER, RUSSELL S., and RICHARD L. OLIVER (1987). "A Framework for the Formation and Structure of Consumer Expectations: Review and Proposition," *Journal of Economic Psychology,* 8 (December), 469–499.

WRIGHT, PETER (1974). "The Harassed Decision Maker: Time Pressures, Distractions, and the Use of Evidence," *Journal of Applied Psychology,* 59, 5, 555–561.

WYER, ROBERT S. (1974). *Cognitive Organization and Change: An Information Processing Approach.* Hillsdale, NJ: Erlbaum.

ZAICHOWSKY, JUDITH LYNNE (1985). "Measuring the Involvement Construct," *Journal of Consumer Research,* 12 (December), 341–352.

ZALTMAN, GERALD, ROBERT DUNCAN, and JONNY HOLBEK (1973). *Innovations and Organizations.* New York: Wiley.

ZIELSKE, HUBERT A. (1959). "The Remembering and Forgetting of Advertising," *Journal of Marketing,* 23, 1 (January), 239–243.

ZIELSKE, HUBERT A., and WALTER A. HENRY (1980). "Remember and Forgetting Television Ads," *Journal of Advertising Research,* 20, 2 (April), 7–13.

10

MASS COMMUNICATION AND CONSUMER BEHAVIOR

Thomas C. O'Guinn*
University of Illinois

Ronald J. Faber
University of Minnesota

This chapter presents a review of selected areas of research in mass communication. It begins with a brief history of the field's dominant metatheories, and then presents discussions of seven research areas that seem particularly promising and relevant to those studying consumer behavior. These include theories related to media choice decisions and the effects of media use. In several instances, explicit connections are drawn to extant work in consumer behavior research. In other places, this relationship may be inferred by the reader.

INTRODUCTION

Since its inception in the 1920s and 30s, the discipline of mass communication research has frequently been characterized as a field in search of an identity (Paisley 1972; Roberts and Bachen 1981). This identity crisis arises because the influence of the mass media is so ubiquitous and intertwined with other aspects of modern human existence that it is difficult to explicate or extract their unique properties. For this very basic reason, mass communication has most often been treated as a variable or a factor that is important in explaining some other phenomena, rather than as a distinct set of processes and effects unto itself. Wilbur Schramm may have stated it best when he wrote:

The field of communication research has sometimes been likened to an oasis in the desert, where many trails cross, and many travelers pass but only a few tarry. Because communication is a —perhaps the— basic social process, every discipline concerned with human behavior and society must pay it some attention; and therefore a large part of all the studies we

*The authors would like to acknowledge the assistance of Professors Albert Tims, John McCarty, Tim Meyer, Sharon Shavitt, George Moschis, and L. J. Shrum.

think of as constituting communication research have been done as a part of psychology, sociology, anthropology, political science, or economics (Schramm 1967).

As a result, most reviews of mass communication research are organized by content areas, such as politics, violence, erotica, prosocial behaviors, health, news, and consumer information; or by specific groups of people, such as children, the elderly, women, or minorities; or by using some aspects of both (cf. Comstock et al., 1978; Harris 1989; Roberts and Bachen 1981).

In contrast, this chapter is organized around theoretical models and paradigms. It begins with a brief review of the major changes in metatheoretical perspective that have thus far guided the field, and then presents some current theory and research into the processes, uses, and effects of the mass media. This chapter is not offered as a complete review of the field since several areas often classified as mass communication research have already been discussed in other chapters of this book (see for example the chapters on attitude change and innovative decision processes). Some additional areas are outside the particular social science perspective taken here. Rather, we will present areas of inquiry in mass communication effects that currently seem relevant, appropriate, and promising for our understanding of both mass communication and consumer behavior. Although some explicit connections to consumer behavior will be made, the basic approach taken here is to present an overview of communication research and theory and to allow the reader to determine how it may best be integrated and applied to his or her specific area of interest.

A METATHEORETICAL PERSPECTIVE OF THE EFFECTS OF THE MEDIA

The history of mass communications effects research can be divided into four periods, each reflecting a change in beliefs about how the media affect their audience (see Figure 10.1).

These periods are known by the theories or models that dominated them: the bullet theory, the limited effects model, the transactional model and the powerful effects model.

Bullet Theory

Initial interest in the influence of the mass media arose following World War I with the publication of books such as *Propaganda Techniques in the World War* (Lasswell 1927) and *Words That Won the War* (Mock and Larson 1939). These and other similar works stressed the powerful and direct impact the mass media could have in changing public attitudes. Although the focus of these books was on techniques used to change attitudes regarding the war, these authors suggested that similar techniques could be applied to other types of persuasive communications, including advertising. The basic premise of these works was that by manipulating specific symbols and information, the media could directly change people's attitudes, beliefs, and behaviors. This rather simple model indicated that the prime concern in mass communication was the message. If the right message was designed and delivered, it was assumed that people would immediately change their views to conform with its intent.

Public concern about the powerful impact of the mass media continued to spread throughout the 1930s. This was fueled by several events that seemed to confirm the bullet theory. The rise of the Nazi movement in Germany (and even to some extent in the United States) was due partly to the effective use of media propaganda. The spread of information about the stock market crash via the mass media was seen as contributing to the mass panic that followed. Finally, the mass hysteria resulting from Orson Wells famed "War of the Worlds" broadcast fully established a widespread belief in the bullet theory.

As a result of the concern about the powerful influence of the media, the Institute for Propaganda Analysis was formed in 1937. This was the first formal organization devoted to the study of media effects. It was predominantly concerned, however, with educating people

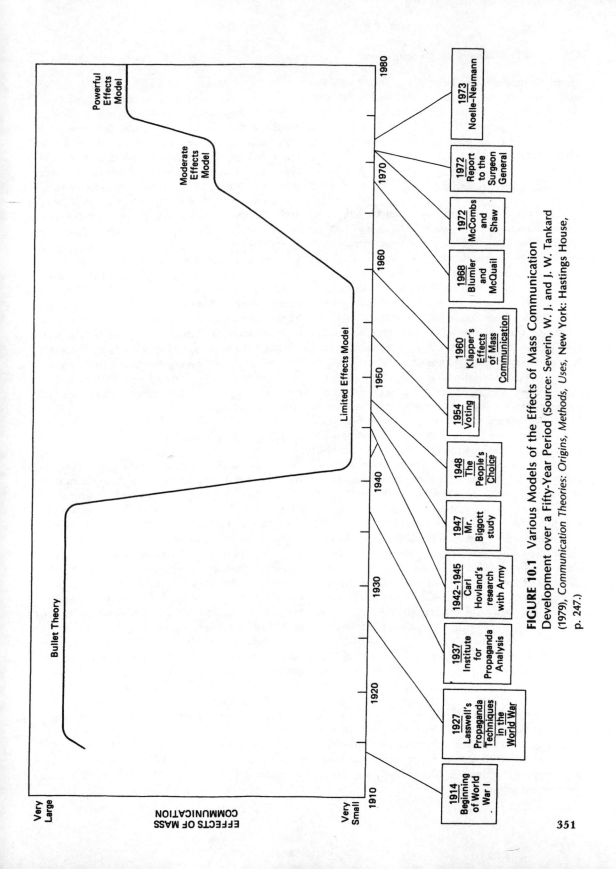

FIGURE 10.1 Various Models of the Effects of Mass Communication Development over a Fifty-Year Period (Source: Severin, W. J. and J. W. Tankard (1979), *Communication Theories: Origins, Methods, Uses,* New York: Hastings House, p. 247.)

about propaganda techniques rather than formally testing the tenets of the bullet theory. Actual research based on the bullet theory beliefs did not occur until the 1940s and resulted in a very different view of the influence of the mass media.

Limited Effects Model

Two major programs of research led to a reformulation of beliefs about the impact of the media. The first of these came from work done for the U.S. Army during World War II. The army established a unit of top social scientists to develop films to train and motivate American soldiers. Exposure to these films was found to help impart knowledge to inductees, but they were not very successful in changing attitudes toward the enemy or in motivating soldiers for fighting (Severin and Tankard 1979). Toward the end of the war, the focus shifted to developing effective messages designed to get German soldiers to surrender. Although interviews with POWs suggested that 60–80 percent of the German troops were exposed to this propaganda, it rarely had any effect on them. By the end of the war, a message stressing good treatment for POWs and giving detailed instructions on how to surrender was found to be influential, but only among troops that already had low group cohesion (Shils and Janowitz 1948).

Research into the media's impact in political campaigns also challenged the bullet theory. Panel studies conducted during the 1940s found that rather than seeing large amounts of change in voter preference as would be expected if the media had powerful effects, people tended to have highly stable preferences over the course of elections (Berelson, Lazersfeld, and McPhee 1954; Lazersfeld, Berelson, and Gaudet 1948).

These research programs, along with a few attempts to use mass communication to change attitudes and behaviors (Cooper and Jahoda 1947; Hyman and Sheatsley 1947), led to a reformulation of beliefs about the effect of the mass media. Instead of being seen as a powerful influence on attitudes, the media were now seen as having only limited effects, typically reinforcing already existing beliefs.

This new perspective was best articulated by Klapper (1960), who argued that the media are generally neither a necessary nor a sufficient condition for creating attitudinal or behavioral change in an audience. Instead, there are a large number of other mediating factors that typically serve to reduce or modify the media's influence. These factors include selectivity variables (selective attention, selective exposure, and selective perception), prior attitudes and beliefs, and other forms of influence (such as interpersonal communication). Accordingly, it seemed that the audience would most likely ignore or even counterargue inconsistent information provided by the media. Therefore, the media were thought to serve more as reinforcers of existing beliefs rather than as instruments of attitude change. It was only in the rare instance when all the mediating factors are either inoperative or supportive of a mass media presentation that one could expect mass mediated messages to result in significant changes in attitude and behavior.

Transactional Model

The popular acceptance of the limited effects model led at least one investigator to claim that the field of communication research appeared to be dead (Berelson 1959). Responding to this, Katz (1959) suggested that the lack of development in the field was perhaps due to an error in focus. Communication research had been concerned with examining "what the media did to people," rather than with looking at "what people did with the media." This change in perspective suggested the need to look at many previously underexamined factors to develop a more complete model of media influence, one which viewed mediated communication as negotiated meaning or transaction. Thus, this broader view of media effects has been referred to as the "transactional model" (Bauer 1964).

Out of this transactional model came an interest in the role of specific types of mass communication content, such as violence (Comstock and Rubinstein 1972; Liebert 1972), advertising (Ward 1974; Ward and Wackman 1973), political communication (Chaffee 1975), prosocial content (Friedrich and Stein 1975), and the specific characteristics of the source, the message, the medium, and the receiver (McGuire 1973). These studies found that the mass media did produce observable effects when one considered additional mediating variables (e.g., age, developmental stage, interest, etc.) or when different types of dependent variables were examined (e.g., attention, knowledge, perceptions, and the acquisition of novel behaviors and response contingencies). Research in these areas seemed to breathe new life into the field. The transactional model gave rise to many of the specific theories and paradigms that now dominate mass communication research.

From a consumer behavior standpoint, perhaps the most important outcome of the transactional approach was Krugman's development of the construct of involvement (Krugman 1965; 1966). Krugman (1965) argued that Klapper's view of limited effects might be due to our exclusively viewing "effects" as attitude changes regarding important issues. However, since people were less involved with media content such as found in television advertising, such messages might not create overt attitudinal changes, but rather lead to subtle shifts in cognitive structure. Ray (1973) further developed this notion by contrasting the hierarchy of effects occurring under conditions of low and high involvement. Later, Petty and Cacioppo (1981) conceptualized two routes to persuasion dependent on the extent of cognitive elaboration. Involvement and related constructs consistent with the transactional paradigm have become quite prominent in both consumer behavior and mass communication research over the last decade.

Powerful Effects

The belief that the media exert powerful effects on the audience has reemerged in mass communication research. However, unlike the bullet theory which assumed that these effects would occur as a result of one-time exposure, the current view is that it is the long-term consistency and ubiquity of media messages that give rise to these effects. As McLeod and Chaffee (1972) stated:

It is hard for us to realize how little of our information comes from direct experience with the physical environment, and how much of it comes only indirectly, from other people and the mass media. Our complex communication systems enable us to overcome the time and space limitations that confined our ancestors, but they leave us with a greater dependence on others for shaping our ideas about how things are in the world. While becoming aware of places and events far from the direct experience of our daily lives, we have given up much of our capacity to confirm what we think we know. . . . It appears that much of the information obtained from others is given the status of *reality,* as if it were no less valid than if it had been a direct observation of physical reality. The personal and tentative nature of our information may be forgotten as the material becomes absorbed into our cognitive structure. This tendency to treat information as reality is reinforced by the fact that a large proportion of unverified information is shared by others around us. That is, they seem to have the same information and ideas we do, and we may find ourselves agreeing that everyone "ought to" see things the way we do. (pp. 50–51)

It is this long-term alteration in our beliefs about the world that form the basis of several recent theories and models of mass communication. The remainder of this chapter presents some of these theories and models in greater depth. Two of these (uses and gratifications, and arousal) emphasize why people use specific media and content. The others (agenda setting, cultivation, socialization, knowledge gap, and formal features) are more directly concerned with the outcome of media use and how differences in audience and content characteristics influence media effects.

USES AND GRATIFICATIONS

Uses and gratifications represents an important paradigm in mass communications research. It attempts to link motivations for media use with the effects of media exposure. More specifically, it has been characterized as being concerned with (1) the social and psychological

origins of (2) needs, which generate (3) expectations of (4) the mass media or other sources,
which lead to (5) differential patterns of media
exposure (or engagement in other activities),
resulting in (6) need gratifications and (7) other
consequences, perhaps mostly unintended
ones" (Katz, Blumler, and Gurevitch 1974, p.
20). A model of this paradigm is presented in
Figure 10.2. The emergence of the uses and
gratifications paradigm has historical importance because it moved research attention to the
individual, and away from the field's singular
obsession with the message. It focused instead
on the consumer of mass media. Still, its critics
claim that it is so broadly conceived as to be
unwieldy, poorly specified, imprecise, and in
some sense so intuitive as to be trivial. Blumler
(1979, p. 11) concluded that there "is no such
thing as *a* or *the* uses and gratifications theory,
although there are plenty of theor*ies* about uses
and gratifications phenomena." It may very
well be that the very thing that makes it attractive, its extremely broad focus encompassing

social and psychological needs, media use, and
the outcomes of this use, may also make it
unwieldy and inelegant.

The Development of Uses and Gratifications Research

Research in uses and gratifications has been
characterized as occurring in three distinct evolutionary stages (Katz et al. 1974; Palmgreen et
al. 1985). The first stage occurred during the
1940s and 1950s with studies that simply described different audience uses or motivations
for exposure to the same content. For example.
Herzog (1941) found that regular listeners to
radio soap operas tuned in for distinctly different reasons. These reasons included emotional
release ("for a good cry"), escape (to avoid
drudgery or for excitement), and advice. Other
studies during this time found that people also
had many different reasons for reading newspapers (Berelson 1949), listening to classical

FIGURE 10.2 Visualized Paradigm for Uses and Gratifications
Research (Source: Rosengren, K. E. (1974), "Uses and Gratifications: A
Paradigm Outlined," in J. G. Blumler and E. Katz (eds.) *The Uses of Mass
Communications: Current Perspectives on Gratifications Research,* Beverly Hills:
Sage, p. 271.)

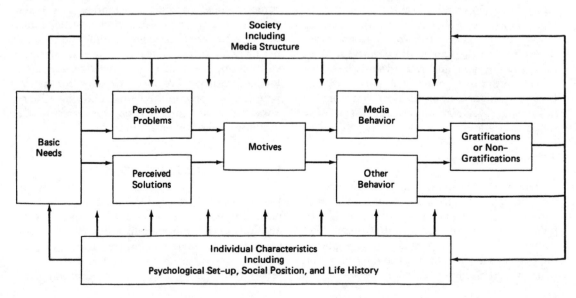

music (Suchman 1942), and reading children's comics (Wolfe and Fiske 1949).

Uses and gratifications research faded during the 1950s and 1960s, but reemerged in the 1970s. During this second stage, many studies attempted to develop categories or typologies of the various uses people had for different media or content (Brown, Cramond, and Wilde 1974; Greenberg 1974; Rubin 1981). Looking across several studies, McQuail, Blumler, and Brown (1972) proposed that motivations could be reduced down to four basic categories — diversion, personal relationships, personal identity, and surveillance. Diversion included motivations such as escaping from a personal problem or daily routines and experiencing an emotional release. Personal relationship motives ranged from facilitating interpersonal conversations (using the media as a source of topics and information) to replacing them (using the media to provide companionship). Personal identity motives encompass reality exploration, value reinforcement, and problem solving. The desire to acquire news and information comprise the surveillance motives.

Criticisms

During its resurgence in the 1970s, the uses and gratifications approach attracted the attention of a number of critics. They pointed out problems with some of the basic tenets of the model as well as some limitations caused by weaknesses in its then current state of development.

Critics pointed out that uses and gratifications is a functional model because it assumes people recognize their needs and use the media to satisfy them (to return to balance). It is thus seen as possessing an inherently conservative bias stressing maintenance of a system rather than change (Anderson and Meyer 1975; Carey and Kreiling 1974; Elliot 1974).

Another criticism is the assumption of an active audience (Blumler 1979; Swanson 1979). Initial conceptions of audience activity focussed on the belief that people were aware of the needs and the gratifications with which the media could provide them, and that they were

active in their effort to match these needs with desired gratifications (Katz et al. 1974; McQuail et al. 1972). Some studies of audience behavior, however, have challenged this belief. For example, examinations of audience duplication have found that while program preferences cluster nicely into category types, actual viewing behavior does not (Goodhardt, Collins, and Ehrenberg 1975). Instead, behavior is more dependent on time availability, overall program rating, and the channel of the program previously viewed. Findings like this have been used to question whether people are actively choosing program content based on needs. It should be pointed out, however, that consistency in content choice might not be expected if multiple needs are operating and the predominance of any one need was constantly shifting.

Another problem with this model was that it often failed to specify how its components were related (Anderson and Meyer 1975; Swanson 1978). Empirical efforts at this time focused on developing typologies of uses, and on relating perceived needs to specific media and content usage, leaving many important linkages unexplored and unexplained. These included the relationship of social and psychological needs with audience motivations and actual behaviors, and the relationship between different motivations and both intended and unintended effects. Even in areas that were investigated, the results often failed to provide clear understanding. One critic summed the results of uses and gratifications research as showing that "almost any message construct can serve almost any use or provide almost any gratification to almost any sort of person in almost any circumstance" (Swanson 1978, p. 12).

Perhaps the most valid and troublesome criticism of uses and gratifications was its lack of conceptual clarity. Terms were often used interchangeably. No clear distinction existed among critical concepts such as use, need, motivation, and gratification. This also raised the question of whether respondents could distinguish the needs or motivations for media use from the gratifications received.

Some authors (Becker 1979; Palmgreen and

Rayburn 1985) have proposed the need to study not just uses, but also the reasons for actively not engaging in some types of media consumption (such reasons are termed *avoidances*). Becker (1979) has argued that avoidances are not just the opposite of uses, but are conceptually distinct. Empirically, he has shown that avoidances can explain variance in political effects beyond that attributable to gratifications.

Current Research

The most recent stage of development in uses and gratifications has made some progress in addressing the various criticisms levied against it. One way in which this is being done is by reconsidering the assumption of an active audience. While no one has suggested abandoning this assumption, it has been reinterpreted in several ways. Swanson (1979) suggested that activity be considered as an attribute of processing media content rather than as something only operative at the selection stage. Several authors have recommended that activity be treated as a variable and subjected to empirical testing (Blumler 1979; Levy 1978; Windahl 1981).

Levy and Windahl (1984) have posited that there could be three different types of activity (selectivity, involvement, and use), each of which can occur at three distinct time periods (before exposure, during exposure, and after exposure). Measures of some of these different forms of activity have been shown to improve prediction of the gratifications sought and/or obtained (Levy and Windahl 1984; Rubin and Perse 1987). Although all forms of activity are unlikely to be related to all parts of the model, measuring various types of activity that are theoretically related to different outcome measures appears to be a promising direction for uses and gratifications research.

Recent efforts to merge uses and gratifications with expectancy-value theory (cf. Ajzen and Fishbein 1980) from the attitude literature have served to provide an improved conceptualization of terms and a theoretical model which is able to investigate more of the linkages

in the paradigm (Galloway and Meek 1981; Palmgreen and Rayburn 1984; 1985; Rayburn and Palmgreen 1984). A clear distinction is now made between gratification sought (the motivations for media use) and gratifications obtained (the results of media consumption). Utilizing an expectancy-value framework, gratifications sought are conceived as the product of affective evaluations of a particular outcome of media use and the belief that a medium or type of content will provide that outcome (Palmgreen and Rayburn 1985). Gratifications obtained are also hypothesized to be related to beliefs about the outcome of media use, but unlike gratifications sought, are unrelated to the evaluation of these outcomes. Measures of association between gratifications sought and obtained support the belief that they are related but separate concepts, generally yielding correlations in the 0.40 to 0.60 range (Palmgreen et al. 1985).

The expectancy-value model also helps to explain the relationship between gratifications sought and avoidances. Gratifications sought result whenever the product of beliefs and evaluations is positive. However, in some situations, we may believe a medium or vehicle possesses a particular attribute, but we negatively evaluate that attribute. For example, a person may believe that watching the evening news will provide information about world affairs, but that same person may find politics and world affairs boring (a negative evaluation). The result would be that this person would likely avoid exposure to the evening news. Of course, the well-discussed problem with expectancy value research remains; it is most useful when the temporal separation of attitude and behavior are minimal, thus severely limiting application.

Efforts have also been made to improve the specification of linkages between variables. Gratifications sought are hypothesized to be the product of specific attribute-media beliefs and evaluations. Gratifications sought along with other variables (such as the desires of coviewers) are expected to predict media consumption which, in turn, influences the perceived gratifications obtained. Gratifications obtained are then assumed to form a feedback loop that, along with expectations derived from other sources (comments by others, advertising, reviews, etc.), will help to further refine beliefs about media usage.

A few studies have attempted to provide a greater explanation of how social structure variables can influence needs. Some have found that low levels of interpersonal contact and integration into peer groups lead to using the media for escape and for parasocial interaction (Johnstone 1974; Rosengren and Windahl 1977). More recent studies, using ethnographic methods, have found that interactions among peers and family members influence needs and uses of the media (Lull 1980; Roe 1983). Still other studies have hypothesized and found that needs arising at different life cycle stages can be met through media use, and that these needs combined with perceived knowledge lead to differential effects of media exposure (Faber, Brown, and McLeod 1979; Kline, Miller, and Morrison 1974). Cultural needs may be another structural variable that can influence media use. Research on ethnic media use has found that choice of media is influenced by demographic variables (Lopez and Enos 1973; Dunn 1975); level of acculturation (Kim 1977; O'Guinn and Meyer 1984); and role expectations (Faber, O'Guinn, and Meyer 1986).

Research has also examined how different motivations can lead to different outcomes of media use. Blumler has proposed that specific types of motivations should be related to specific dependent variables. He hypothesized that cognitive motivations should facilitate information gain; that personal identity motives should create reinforcement effects, and that escape or diversion motives should increase the perceived reality of media portrayals and thus enhance social reality effects.

Research has generally supported Blumler's first hypothesis. Several studies of political elections and news usage have found that surveillance motives are most strongly related to knowledge gain (Garramone 1983; McLeod and Becker 1974; McLeod, Luetscher, and McDonald 1980). Unfortunately, no research has examined Blumler's second hypothesis re-

garding personal identity. His third prediction, which states that the perceived reality of content would be enhanced by escapist motivations, has not found empirical support. Escapist motives have been unrelated or only weakly related to perceived reality (Palmgreen et al. 1985; Rubin 1985). However, this may be due to a questionable assumption underlying this hypothesis. The assumption is that the greatest impact on perceived reality occurs when counterarguing is low. An alternative explanation for mediated perceived reality is that its impact is greatest when the total amount of information one has about a topic and/or the information available from memory are limited and consistent with media portrayals. This would help to explain why the motivation most strongly associated with perceived reality effects is a desire to learn about life (Greenberg 1974; Rubin 1981).

Applications of Uses and Gratifications to Consumer Behavior

The uses and gratifications paradigm suggests that there may be several reasons why people would attend to advertisements. Most research on advertising use has focused solely on consumers' need for information prior to purchases and their desire to reduce post-purchase dissonance. However, as Bloch et al. (1986) have pointed out, attention to ads can also occur outside of a purchase situation. They refer to this as *ongoing search*. In examining the motivations behind ongoing search they found that recreational and hedonic motivations were more important than informational ones. Thus, people may attend to ads not just to gain information, but also for surveillance, for entertainment, and for alleviating boredom.

The development of a typology of uses of advertisements might be useful in explaining differences in how people process advertising content, in showing what they desire and retain from ads, and in describing how these ads influence purchase behavior. Research with adolescents has found that social utility and interpersonal discussion motives influenced the amount and type of product information desired (Moschis 1980) and that social utility reasons for watching TV commercials was positively related to materialism and social motivations for consumption, but negatively related to economic motivations (Moschis and Churchill 1978). Bloch et al. (1986) found that participating in ongoing search was positively related to product expenditures for adults even after controlling for the level of involvement with a product category.

The application of a uses and gratifications approach in consumer behavior is not limited to just advertising. It may also be extended to examine the use of special interest magazines, retail browsing, and interpersonal discussions about product classes (Bloch et al. 1986). It might also be helpful in investigating purchase criteria used in different situations and the meaning possessions have for people. Decision criteria and the types of attributes and benefits desired from products may well differ depending on whether the item is purchased to fulfill a need, as a gift for another, as a self-gift, or according to the usage situation. Gratifications obtained from possessions may also differ based on the social and psychological origins of needs. For example, research has found intergenerational differences in what people consider to be meaningful possessions (Belk 1985). Andreasen (1984) has also found changes in brand preferences and more openness to new information about products during periods of change in life status. He has suggested that these life changes may directly influence consumer wants and needs as well as indirectly influence brand preference through the creation of stress. These phenomena might profitably be examined from a uses and gratifications perspective. Additionally, the uses and gratifications paradigm might be used to compare gratifications sought in purchase decisions with the gratifications obtained from these purchases.

One of the attractive things about uses and gratification is that it conceives of the consumer as something more than the unwitting recipient of advertising, or even as an individual actively seeking information supplied by the marketer. It sees consumers as having many different agenda, and as using advertising for many purposes other than those intended by advertisiers — perhaps as entertainment, or diversion, or in order to derive any numbers of gratifications. Even the advertiser's and the consumer's notions of what constitutes information may be wildly different. Work by Haefner and Haefner (1990) supports this through their content analysis of tape recorded conversations between viewers in a natural setting. This is important because sometimes consumer behavior models imply that the consumer and the marketer have similar goals, with one being a supplier of wanted information and the other being a seeker. The assumption that what is offered and what is sought is roughly the same is challenged by the uses and gratifications model.

The Future of Uses and Gratifications

Within communications, uses and gratifications theory appears to be moving in a generally more positive direction. Efforts to more precisely define terms, standardize the types of gratifications examined, strengthen the theoretical underpinnings, improve predictive ability, and tie gratifications sought to differential effects are all welcome advances. However, more work needs to be done in developing expectations about how specific motivations will influence specific outcomes.

Although work in this field started with explorations of a wide range of media content, current research has paid excessive attention to news and public affairs content. One possible outcome of this is to overemphasize audience activity, rational behavior, information-based effects, and intended consequences. It should be remembered that the vast majority of media use in the United States is entertainment based. This is likely to involve very different motivations for use and a greater potential for unintended consequences. More studies are needed that focus on media and content used predominantly for enjoyment, such as entertainment TV programming, sports, comics, movies, music, and novels. Research on other informational content, such as advertising, self-improvement books and tapes, and other forms of nonfiction material would also be useful in generating a more complete picture of media uses and gratifications. Finally, it appears that the uses and gratifications perspective can move beyond its focus on media to provide a framework for examining other behaviors, including consumption.

Continued methodological improvements in uses and gratifications are also needed. More sophisticated empirical models need to be used to test larger portions of the uses and gratifications model. Larger models will allow us to see how environmental and psychological needs influence media use both directly and through the differing gratifications sought, and how these factors influence the outcomes of media use. Additionally, panel studies may allow researchers to determine how media use and the effects of that use provide feedback to change or reinforce gratifications sought.

An increase in the use of methods other than surveys is also needed. Qualitative studies (cf. Lull 1980, 1985; Radway 1984; Roe 1983) can help develop a more complete understanding of the uses of various media or content. Experimental methods (cf. Garramone 1983; Zillmann, Hezel, and Medoff 1980) can be profitably employed to test specific hypotheses about how motivations influence media choice or about the outcomes of use. By bringing multiple methodologies to the study of uses and gratifications, we should be able to enhance significantly our understanding of how and why people use the media, and how it impacts their behavior as consumers.

AROUSAL, MOOD, AND MEDIA CHOICE

A model similar to uses and gratifications, but based primarily on affective rather than cognitive factors, has been advanced by Zillmann and his colleagues (Zillmann 1982; Zillmann and Bryant 1985, 1986). They propose that television program choices are often used to maintain positive emotional states or to change negative affective states to more desirable ones.

Desirable states of arousal differ across individuals (Zuckerman 1979), and within individuals across time. One's preferred state of arousal serves as a comparison by which to judge current levels as either desirable or undesirable. If a current state is judged positively, the individual will want to maintain that state, and this will typically involve continuing current activities. If the current state is judged negatively, the individual should be motivated to change their arousal level. Television use is one of many ways in which this might be done. Although television viewing is often seen as a sedentary and mindless activity, research has shown that it can both decrease and increase arousal, depending on the type of content viewed. Nonviolent nature films have been shown to reduce excitedness (Levi 1965), whereas programs like comedies, action dramas, and game shows produce small increases in arousal (Zillmann and Bryant 1985). Specific content attributes such as high levels of violence, fear-provoking content, tense action in sports or quiz shows, and sexual themes can further increase television's arousal potential (Donnerstein and Hallam 1978; Zillmann, Hoyt, and Day 1974; Zillmann and Bryant 1985). Therefore, viewers are seen as capable of mediating and motivated to mediate undesirable excitatory levels through their content choices.

Although the ability and desire to change excitatory states through television viewing exists, this model, unlike uses and gratifications, does not assume that people purposefully or rationally make such choices. Instead, it assumes that most program choices are made rather haphazardly. Typically, one decides to watch television and then flips through the channels, making instantaneous appraisals, in order to find a desirable program. These appraisals are based more on initial affective reactions than deliberate decisions. These affective reactions are at least partially determined by current and preferred levels of arousal. If the initial reaction is one that moves the individual toward a desired arousal end state, then the viewer will be more likely to watch. If not, the person will likely continue to search. To test this affective model of program selection it is necessary to determine two things: (1) if television content is capable of influencing arousal levels, and (2) if people with different initial levels of arousal make different program choices. Research has found some support for both of these hypotheses.

Media's Effect on Arousal

Self-report data has indicated that people use television to both increase arousal (to alleviate boredom; to enhance excitement) and decrease arousal (to relax; to forget about problems; to calm down) (Greenberg 1974). Physiological measures have also shown that television viewing can change adrenalin levels, blood pressure, heart rate, and genital reactions (Bryant and Zillmann 1984; Levi 1965; Reifler et al. 1971).

Some question, however, remains as to why television content changes arousal level. One hypothesis is that content with positive hedonic valence can reduce negative affective states. Research using pleasant music (Day 1980), erotica (Zillmann and Sapolsky 1977), and cartoons (Baron and Ball 1974) have found that these pleasant stimuli improve the mood of people placed in a negative affective state. However, not all positively valenced material reduces negative feelings. For example, hostile comedy was unable to reduce anger although nonhostile comedy could (Berkowitz 1970). Positively valenced, but strongly arousing erotica not only failed to reduce negative affect, it actually intensified it (Zillmann and Bryant 1985).

An alternative explanation is that activities such as television watching that interrupt ruminating or thinking about the cause of a negative emotional state serve to reduce arousal level (Bandura 1965; Zillmann 1979). Bryant and Zillmann (1977) found that highly involving programming was much more effective than less involving programming in reducing the level of anger that had been experimentally induced in subjects. Further support for this second explanation comes from findings indicating that highly involving content will not reduce negative affect if it is too similar to the

cause of the initial mood state. Violent drama and sports and hostile comedy have been found to be relatively unsuccessful in reducing aggression and anger in provoked subjects, even though these material were rated as being highly absorbing (Berkowitz 1970; Bryant and Zillmann 1977; Zillmann and Johnson 1973). If content is likely to remind viewers of the cause of their anger, they will continue to think about their own feelings and mood change is unlikely.

It appears that at least some of the time viewing both pleasant stimuli and content that interrupts thinking about personal problems can improve mood (Zillmann and Sapolsky, 1977; Zillmann 1982). Perhaps the best explanation, then, is that valence, arousal, and involvement all contribute independently to changes in affective state. At least one study has found that both valence and arousal had a main effect on aggression, but when valence and arousal levels leading to opposite effects were combined, they canceled each other out (Zillmann, et al. 1981).

Arousal and Program Selection

Given that television viewing appears capable of changing arousal level, the next question is whether people actually choose programs most likely to accomplish this. Several studies have shown that people placed in negative mood states (highly stressed, bored, or angry) select programs that are capable of changing them (Bryant and Zillmann 1984; Christ and Medoff 1984; Zillmann et al. 1980). Even children as young as four and five appear able to use exposure to television content to alter negative moods (Masters, Ford, and Arend 1983).

Although most studies experimentally alter arousal levels or mood states, one study found naturally occurring mood states also affect selective exposure to television. Based on research showing variations in mood related to the hormonal changes during women's menstrual cycles, Meadowcroft and Zillmann (1987) hypothesized that program choices should vary at different menstrual phases. As predicted, premenstrual and menstrual women preferred more comedies than women in the midpoint of the menstrual cycle.

If arousal and emotional state affect program choice, learning theory would suggest this might result in consistent program preferences over time. Supporting this belief, Tims et al. (1986) found a significant positive relationship between a sensation-seeking trait and a preference for sports and adult (R or X rated) films. They also found negative correlations between a sensation-seeking trait and a preference for situation comedies, dramas, and game shows.

Not all research findings are, however, consistent with Zillmann's selective exposure hypotheses. Both field and laboratory studies have found evidence that people prefer violent and arousing films to an even greater extent after exposure to fear-provoking events (Boyanowski 1977; Boyanowski, Newtson, and Walster 1974). Using cognitive considerations, Wakshlag et al. (1983) explain this apparent inconsistency by arguing that people choose to see content showing the successful resolution of unpleasant events in order to reduce fear and arousal.

Another problem for Zillmann's theory of selective exposure is that there are frequently observed gender differences (Zillmann and Bryant 1985). These differences emerge most often in the selection of violent programming during states of induced anger. During periods of anger or aggressive feelings, women tend to avoid exposure to violent content, whereas men tend to seek out this type of content (Fenigstein 1979; Zillmann and Bryant 1985). These gender differences may reflect socialization differences between men and women. Men may deal with anger through fantasies of retaliation that can be enhanced by watching violent programming, whereas women may have, to a greater extent, been socialized to avoid both violent action and thoughts.

Arousal and Media Enjoyment

It has been suggested that both arousal and empathy for various characters can also influence how much people enjoy programming (Zillmann 1980, 1985; Zillmann and Bryant 1986). While both factors appear to be important in this context, work on arousal seems to offer the greatest potential. To explain enjoy-

ment of suspenseful content, Zillmann (1971) reformulated Berlyne's arousal-jag model. Berlyne (1960) had posited that pleasure arises from the removal of adverse arousal. Subsequent research, however, found that enjoyment was sometimes accompanied by an increase in arousal rather than the hypothesized decrease (Berlyne 1967). To account for this, Zillmann advanced the notion of excitation-transfer (1971). It is somewhat similar to, but conceptually distinct, from Schacter and Singer's (1962) work on emotion as labeled arousal.

Excitation-transfer is based on the fact that arousal takes time to dissipate. Thus, arousal from one antecedent event may combine with newly experienced arousal from another to yield an "overly intense" level. The summation of this arousal is then attributed solely to the more recently experienced or more easily recognized event. In this way, excitation transfer could help explain why engaging in certain socially restricted activities seems more enjoyable when the fear of being caught is present. Enjoyment of suspenseful content can, therefore, be seen as dependent on three things: (1) the amount of residual excitement generated by the suspense; (2) the length of time this residual excitement lasts (typically this is a relatively short time); and (3) the degree of excitement generated by the resolution of the suspense.

Research has found support for the notion of excitation-transfer using both verbal and behavioral dependent measures. Prior sexual arousal enhanced reported enjoyment of both humor and music (Cantor, Bryant, and Zillmann 1974; Cantor and Zillmann 1973). Behaviorally, more retaliatory aggression following provocation has been found after viewing a highly arousing but nonaggressive erotic film than after seeing a violent, but less arousing film (Cantor et al, 1978; Zillmann 1971).

Applications in Consumer Behavior

Research on media arousal has several implications for consumer behavior. Perhaps the most apparent is in terms of advertising. The excitation-transfer paradigm could be applied to research in the placement of commercials in television programming, and in the successful use of fear and other emotional appeals. It provides a different explanation for why emotional reactions to ads differ depending on the emotion evoked by a prior ad. Aaker, Stayman, and Hagerty (1986), for example, used a contrast effect to explain why people rated a commercial as warmer when it followed a humorous rather than an irritating ad. However, the same result may have occurred because of greater transfer from these more "exciting" ads than from other "warm" ads. Given other work showing that emotional reactions to ads can affect belief formations and the nature of subsequent processing of ads (Edell and Burke 1987), excitation-transfer may be an important concept in explaining the role of feelings in ads.

Other aspects of the work of Zillmann and his colleagues might be usefully integrated into the literature on the impact of prior programs and commercials on target commercials. Several studies have found that films and TV programs can induce mood states in viewers and that these mood states influence evaluations of products and subsequent commercials (Axelrod 1963; Goldberg and Gorn 1987; Singh and Churchill 1987). Srull (1983) found that greater levels of arousal (either positive or negative) leads to greater recall from ads. However, other researchers have found just the opposite effect with neutral levels of arousal leading to the highest levels of recall (Pavelchak et al. 1988). Still other researchers have focused on valence of mood states rather than arousal level and found that viewing positively valenced programs leads to greater recall and more positive evaluations of commercials than the viewing of negatively valenced content (Goldberg and Gorn 1987).

Future advertising studies might utilize Zillmann's work in expanding their model to include the effect of antecedent states that lead to program selection on advertising recall and evaluations. These studies should examine both arousal and valence as well as other important elements, such as the involvement level with both the program and commercial content. Finally, some research suggests that the processing and evaluation strategies used by viewers

may differ under different arousal conditions. Sanbonmatsu and Kardes (1988) found that highly aroused subjects evaluated ads on the basis of peripheral cues, whereas moderately aroused viewers were more influenced by the strength of the arguments in the ad.

One of the greatest challenges facing contemporary advertising is how to break through an increasingly formidable level of clutter. In the early to mid-1980s the use of highly affective messages was thought to be an effective solution, but now with so many advertisers using the same strategy, the problem is further exacerbated. Merely producing "emotional" advertising is insufficient; one now has to break through the affective clutter. Ads created in isolation, do not run in isolation. Consumers are confronted with emotional appeal after emotional appeal, all embedded within programming content which is not always affectively neutral. For this reason, concern over where a commercial comes in a given commercial break and the effects of the surrounding "emotional context" is becoming a much more relevant and practical issue.

Although Zillmann's work has only examined TV viewing, it can easily be applied to other media and other behaviors as well. Results from Zillmann's program of research have been applied to help explain how arousal can influence compulsive buyers (O'Guinn and Faber 1989), and it may also be useful in further research on impulse buying and recreational shopping. Furthermore, with more attention being given to in-store selling via environmental factors, a better understanding of arousal and attributed affect is relevant to retailers as well. The research may also be applicable to the further study of the relationship between attitudes toward ads and attitudes toward brands (Lutz, MacKenzie, and Belch 1983).

Problems and Future Needs

A potentially useful area for further research would be to focus on additional types of affective functions that the media might serve. Zillmann (1980) has stated that enjoyment is related to liked characters succeeding and disliked characters failing. More research on the second half of this hypothesis may be particularly interesting in light of the success of soap operas in both daytime and prime time. Some of the most popular characters in soap operas are villains. Does their popularity rest on seeing these villains defeated? An alternative view may be that social inhibitions prevent people from experiencing the type of anger or hate that can be appropriately felt toward a TV villain. These shows may serve as a socially acceptable outlet for what might otherwise be unacceptable feelings. Similarly, there may be some desire to understand how these villains feel. One small scale study found that when asked which character they would most like to be for a day, soap opera viewers almost unanimously chose villains (Faber 1983). The reason given for this choice was frequently to have the opportunity to feel what it would be like to do evil deeds and get away with it.

The biggest problem with Zillmann's arousal/affect model is that media programs are not simple stimuli. There are many different components of a television program that have the potential to increase or decrease a viewer's arousal level. Many unexpected findings in arousal studies have capitalized on this by employing post hoc explanations based on different program attributes. The result is that now it is almost impossible to fail to explain virtually any finding from an arousal perspective.

A viewer who chooses not to watch TV may do so because he or she is either already in a positive mood or is too annoyed. If a person does watch TV, a program may be chosen or rejected based on (1) the type of genre (comedy, drama, quiz show, etc.), (2) a specific attribute of the content (level of hostility, type of humor, quality of the script), (3) the involvement or distraction potential of the program, and (4) the arousal potential of the formal features used (number of cuts, pacing, background music, etc.). Additionally, each of these factors along with other attributes, such as the viewers' feelings toward the characters, can affect program enjoyment as well as other effects of viewing. Therefore, among the most critical needs for future research is the further isolation of the

factors in programming that create or dissipate arousal, and how these factors interact with one another.

AGENDA-SETTING

The limited effects perspective led to the belief that media messages serve predominantly to reinforce existing attitudes rather than to change them. However, many researchers felt this view underestimated the impact of the media. As a result, they began to examine other potential outcomes of media exposure, such as knowledge gain. One such program of research was the formal testing of the agenda-setting hypothesis.

Agenda-setting refers to the ability of the mass media to influence the public's perception of the importance of different issues. The distinction between attitude change and agenda-setting research may have been stated most succinctly by Cohen (1963, p. 13) who said.

. . . [the press] may not be successful much of the time in telling people what to think, but it is stunningly successful in telling its readers what to think about.

Although the notion of agenda-setting is often traced back to Walter Lippman (1922), its first formal test was conducted by McCombs and Shaw (1972). They compared the frequency of media news stories about different issues in the 1968 presidential election with the importance assigned to these issues by undecided voters. The correlation between the media's emphasis on major news stories and the undecided voters' perceptions of issue importance was 0.97; and the correlation between minor news stories the same voter's perceptions of issue importance was 0.98.

Although McCombs and Shaw's original study found extremely strong correlations, this does not establish causation. It may well be that the issues the public considers important dictate what the media cover. The media may simply be good marketers, giving the public what it wants. To try to establish causal ordering, researchers have used time-lag correlation (Shaw and McCombs 1977; Tipton et al. 1975), time series analysis (Funkhouser 1973; MacKuen 1981), and experimental research (Iyengar and Kinder 1987). The results of these studies are not unanimous, but the majority support the agenda-setting hypothesis.

Methodological Issues in Agenda-setting Research

In order to determine if an agenda-setting effect is occurring, most studies compare a content analysis of the media's agenda with survey data assessing the public's agenda. However, the specific operationalization of these agenda have differed significantly from one study to the next.

To assess the media's agenda, some studies simply count the number of stories about an issue. Others, believing that the amount of space or time devoted to a story will also influence perceptions, weigh the number of stories by their column inches or length of air time. Since location in the newscast or newspaper may also affect the audience's perceptions, still other studies limit the pages they code or account for location in some other way.

Other differences across agenda-setting studies include the types of issues covered (local versus national), the time frame of the issue (long-term versus short-term issues), and the level of generality at which the issue is being examined (interest rates versus all economic issues). Although it has been argued that the media do not differ greatly in the issues they cover (Fan and Tims 1989), some agenda-setting differences by media have been found (McClure and Patterson 1976; McCombs 1981; Palmgreen and Clarke 1977).

Both print and television have been shown to influence the public's agenda, but comparative studies generally find print to be the more effective (McClure and Patterson 1976; Tipton et al. 1975; Shaw and McCombs 1977). However, media effectiveness in agenda-setting appears to be conditional on several other factors. Television can be particularly effective when the stories reported are dramatic, pictorially

vivid, but relatively simple events (McClure and Patterson 1976). Newspapers exert a stronger influence on personal agendas when dealing with local issues, but television is more effective in the case of national news (Palmgreen and Clarke 1977). In research on political campaigns, newspapers were found to exert a greater agenda-setting influence early in the campaign, but television overtakes it in the later stages of the race (Shaw and McCombs 1977; Weaver et al. 1981). Based on these findings, it has been argued that newspapers exert a more consistent long-term effect on agenda-setting, whereas television is more likely to play a "spotlighting" role, exerting short-term influence on a few key issues (McCombs 1981).

Several studies have assumed that there will be a time lag between the media's reporting of issues and their impact on the public's agenda, and have attempted to empirically determine the optimal amount of time for this lag. Stone and McCombs (1981), looking across six issues, determine the optimal lag period was four months. Winter and Eyal (1981) found the typical lag varied between zero and eight weeks. However, experimental studies have found an immediate effect on personal agendas (Iyengar and Kinder 1987). These differences may be partially due to differences in exposure levels in field versus lab studies as well as to differences in levels of analysis. Survey data typically employ a systems level of analysis examining changes in salience across large groups of viewers. In this situation, a multistep flow model of communication may operate, whereby some people are directly influenced by media presentations while others are affected indirectly through personal communication with people who have seen or heard about the story. This multistep flow of information takes time to occur. It is also likely to be affected by the same factors that influence diffusion of knowledge rates (e.g., conflict, local versus national issues, and the amount of interpersonal discussion). Experimental studies, on the other hand, utilize an individual level of analysis where changes in issue salience are due solely to media presentations and therefore should be more instantaneous.

Expansion of the Agenda-setting Hypothesis

The initial agenda-setting hypothesis is a rather simple idea concerned only with the media's agenda and the public's perception of issue salience. By considering variables that limit or expand the agenda-setting effect, however, it moves from the realm of a single hypothesis to a broader theory (McCombs 1981). Differences in agenda-setting effects have been noted for different types of issues. More dramatic events are rated by the public as being more important than would be predicted by just their frequency of appearance in the media (MacKuen and Coombs 1981). It has also been suggested that the greater the conflict associated with an issue, the greater the agenda-setting effect (McCombs and Gilbert 1986).

Another issue characteristic that has been suggested as an important contingent condition is the level of issue obtrusiveness. Unobtrusive issues are those that people do not have much personal knowledge about, whereas obtrusive issues are ones that people experience directly in their own lives (Winter and Eyal 1981; Zucker 1978). For obtrusive issues like inflation and, perhaps, crime, for which people have direct personal experience, it stands to reason that the impact of the media would be less. For unobtrusive issues like foreign affairs, where people have no direct experience, agenda-settings effects should be greatest. Empirical comparison of obtrusive and unobtrusive issues have supported this expectation (Weaver et al. 1981; Winter and Eyal 1981; Zucker 1978).

While evidence supports the impact of issue obtrusiveness as an important contingent variable, it might better be viewed as a characteristic of the receiver rather than of an issue. Issues like crime, unemployment, and pollution may be unobtrusive to some people, but obtrusive issues for others. This is similar to the conceptualization problems experienced by consumer behavior researchers in dealing with involvement (cf. Cohen 1983; Zaichkowsky 1986). If we view obtrusiveness as a characteristic of the audience member, then agenda-setting effects might best be predicted by considering individ-

ual difference variables such as interest level, existing knowledge, and need for orientation.

Need for orientation may be a particularly useful measure. It is conceived of as a typology based on two dimensions: relevance and uncertainty. We might predict the greatest agenda-setting effects at moderate levels of need for orientation, when people are sufficiently motivated to attend to media issues, but relatively unfamiliar with these issues (McCombs and Weaver 1985). Supporting this belief, McLeod et al. (1974) found a stronger agenda-setting effect among less interested voters than among highly interested ones, but the strongest agenda-setting effect was found for undecided voters.

As research on these contingent conditions continues, agenda-setting may move from the status of a single hypothesis to a larger theory. Agenda-setting also needs to expand in regard to the type of content studied. The vast majority of studies have looked at issue salience emerging from news and public affairs programming, but agenda-setting may also result from viewing entertainment programs. Miller and Quarles (1984) found that viewers of the television movie *The Day After* perceived issues dealing with nuclear war and weapons as more important than either a previewing sample or a group of nonviewers. Evidence also indicates that media presentations may affect image salience as well as issue salience (Weaver 1982; Weaver et al. 1981).

Experimental Evidence for Agenda-setting

Although most agenda-setting studies have relied on content analyses and public opinion surveys, one excellent program of research has employed experimental studies (Iyengar and Kinder 1987). Over a ten year period, 14 experiments were conducted using two basic types of designs to systematically examine the agenda-setting capability of television news.

In sequential design studies, subjects participated every day for one week. Each day they viewed a national news telecast that had been edited to emphasize a particular issue. Agenda-setting effects were measured by comparing open and closed-ended importance ratings of issues taken before and after the week of viewing with those of a control group. The other type of design, referred to as assemblage studies, showed people only one newscast, which was described as a composite of news stories over the past year, and used a posttest only design to measure effects. While assemblage studies are even more removed from the typical viewing situation than sequential studies, they allowed for more precise control of the news content.

Across studies, a wide number of different issues have been examined, with the number of stories about target issues varying from as many as six per newscast to as few as one each day. In virtually every test, agenda-setting effects emerged. In the few cases that failed to show significant effects, it was typically because people rated the issue so highly before exposure that a ceiling effect occurred. Follow-up studies found that the agenda-setting effect persisted just as strongly one week later.

Expanding Agenda-Setting to Attitude Change

Large-scale studies have leant support to the belief that media coverage affects the aggregate movement of public opinion. Page et al. (1987) compared an extensive coding of network television news with results from national public opinion studies. After controlling for the first order autoregressive structure of public opinion change, they found that media coverage of the preceding month had accounted for a high percentage of change in public opinion.

In a series of studies, similar results have been found using the ideodynamic theory of the influence of media messages (Fan 1988). Ideodynamic theory utilizes a mathematical model that accounts for:

(1) the rate at which new messages enter the social system via the news media; (2) the persuasive influences of messages contained in news stories; (3) the decay in those influences over time; (4) the propor-

tion of population at a given point in time likely to be affected by the persuasive influences identified in the message environment (Fan and Tims 1989, p. 153).

Typically, research employing the ideodynamic model uses stories on the Associated Press wire to represent all stories appearing in the system. A sample of these stories is chosen and filtered for paragraphs containing key words. The text is then scored to represent either favorable or unfavorable messages called *infons* about the issue under study. Infons represent pressure on public sentiment (either positive or negative). Infons entering the system every 24 hours are calculated to indicate predicted movement in public opinion. Utilizing several assumptions (i.e., message pressure only affects those opposed to the message) and additional concepts (e.g., decay rate, issue volatility), this model then predicts expected changes in aggregate public opinion. Studies across a wide range of issues including defense spending, Contra aid, the spread of AIDS, presidential preference during an election, and consumer confidence in the economy have found that the model predicts changes in public sentiment over time exceptionally well (Fan 1988; Fan and Tims 1989; Tims, Fan and Freeman 1989). Figure 10.3 demonstrates the results of this model in the case of consumer sentiment about the economy.

It appears that communication research has now come full circle, from first believing the media changed attitudes, to believing it only changed issue salience, to now believing it can change attitudes. The biggest difference is that now attitude change is conceived of as occurring as a result of changes in issue salience or attribute availability rather than as a result of gross changes in total evaluations.

Agenda-setting and Consumer Behavior

In terms of consumer behavior, examples of agenda-setting seem plentiful. In getting us to think about things such as cholesterol and oat bran, the mass media set an important social agenda in which consumers behave. The proc-

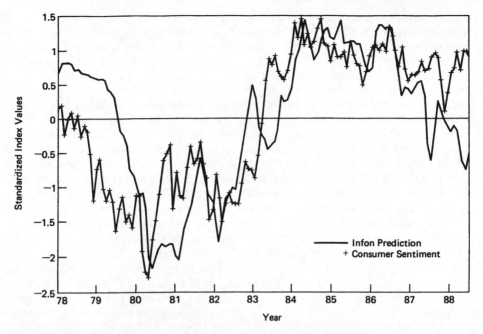

FIGURE 10.3 Ideodynamic Prediction and CSI (Source: Tims, A. R., Fan, D. P. and Freeman, J. R. "The Cultivation of Consumer Confidence: A Longitudinal Analysis of News Media Influence on Consumer Sentiment," in T. K. Srull (ed.) Advances in Consumer Research, Vol XVI, Association for Consumer Research, Provo: UT.)

ess that drives that macro social-psychological phenomenon should not be ignored by consumer behavior researchers. Work by researchers such as Fan et al. (1989) on consumer sentiment and the expression of social attitudes in consumer behavior seem immediately applicable.

Agenda-setting assumes that frequency of exposure serves as a cue that influences viewer's perception of the salience of issues. Given this, it seems likely that saliency of attributes within issues could similarly be changed. Empirical studies looking at attributes of economic (Benton and Frazier 1976) and environmental (Cohen 1975) issues have found that the media's agenda-setting ability is as strong for attributes as it is for issues. This effect on attributes, and the subsequent impact on overall evaluations and decision making, tie agenda-setting to several important areas of consumer behavior.

From a consumer behavior viewpoint,

changes in attribute salience are particularly important. Some attitude formulations suggest that one way advertisers can change brand attitudes is to increase the salience of an attribute consumers believe their brand possesses (Lutz 1975; Millar and Tesser 1986; Shavitt and Fazio 1990; Wilson and Dunn 1986). Research identifying factors that influence agenda-setting may, therefore, be useful in explaining how and in what situations advertisers may be able to change consumers' attribute salience perceptions. This phenomenon may be most immediately observable in the case of health-related attributes, such as the oat bran products being prominently discussed in the mass media.

Recent studies in agenda-setting and consumer behavior also share an interest in the effects of availability and accessibility. The more frequently the media cover an issue or attribute, the more that item is updated in memory and thus made more accessible. This issue or attribute might reasonably, therefore, play a more important role in attitude evaluations. Iyengar and Kinder (1987) found that people exposed to specific types of issues in the news were more likely to use these types of issues in assessing the president's overall job performance. Similarly, research in consumer behavior has found that making specific knowledge, attributes, or decision criteria more available can alter brand evaluations (Bettman and Sujan 1987; Folkes 1988; Levin and Gaeth 1988). Additionally, in both agenda-setting and consumer behavior research on the availability of information and decision criteria (Folkes 1988; Kisielius and Sternthal 1986; MacKeun and Coombs 1981), message factors such as the vividness of information have been found to be important.

CULTIVATION

Drama is life with the dull bits cut out.
— Alfred Hitchcock

Television dominates the symbolic environment of modern life. (Gerbner et al. 1980a, p. 14)

Since the mid 1970s George Gerbner and colleagues have been developing and refining the theory of cultivation. Despite some well publicized problems and limitations (see Hirsh 1980), cultivation has emerged as a significant theory in the study of mass communication. It holds that television viewing significantly assists in creating or cultivating a view of reality that is biased toward the highly formulaic and stylized narrative content of television. The more one views, the greater the likelihood one will perceive the real world to be similar to the way things are on television. Cultivation theory represents a significant departure from much of the traditional mass communications effects research in that it abandoned the assumption that individuals acquire and utilize information in a predominately purposive manner. Instead, cultivation assumes a rather passive absorption of available information. Summary beliefs about the social environment are built or "con-

structed" *a la* Berger and Luckman (1966) with bits of information coming from a number of sources. Television is a largely narrative, dramatic medium, in which viewers willfully suspend their disbelief, often in a very passive cognitive state (Ray 1973) for an average of four hours per day (Comstock et al. 1978). Cultivation theorists reason that television figures prominently in the individual's construction of summary beliefs about the nature of social things. The cultivation effect is most likely when direct experience is limited. Given the generally homogeneous composition of American social environs, what the average middle-class white knows about African-Americans or the urban poor, for example, may be more a function of exposure to stereotypical media portrayals than anything else. Even more disturbing is that viewers may not question the veracity or depth of this knowledge. One effect of learning via television may be that one has something of a false sense of one's knowledge.

The television set has become a key member of the family, the one who tells most of the stories most of the time. Its massive flow of stories showing what things are, how things work, and what to do about them has become the common socializer of our times. These stories form a coherent if "mythical" world in every home. (Gerbner et al. 1980a, p. 14).

Methodology

Cultivation theory emerged out of sociological and anthropological traditions focusing primarily on group differences. Like agenda-setting, cultivation research is generally composed of two distinct research stages. First, there is message systems analysis (MSA). This involves content analyses of segments of selected television programming and the coding of critical pieces of action. Gerbner and his colleagues have been involved in conducting detailed content analyses of week-long samples of network television since the late 1960s. Their analyses record the frequency with which different types of people and events appear or occur in the television world.

Message system analysis has found that the composition of the television world is significantly different from that of the "real world." For example, there are three times as many men on television as women (Gerbner et al. 1980a), and television is overpopulated by characters who are 25 to 45 years old. Further, it is underpopulated with regard to young and old people (Gerbner et al. 1980b; 1980c). Occupationally, professionals, especially doctors and lawyers, and people in the law enforcement occupations predominate on television (Gerbner et al. 1980a). Studies of the events occurring on television have often focused on violence and found that threats and physical force are extremely common. Approximately two-thirds of the male characters and almost one-half of the female characters are involved in violent acts (Gerbner et al. 1980a).

Although most message system analyses have simply documented the occurrence of people and events on television, a few studies have gone beyond this to establish characteristics associated with different types of characters. For example, the elderly on television are shown as lacking common sense, and they are shown as being eccentric and prone to failure (Arnoff 1974; Gerbner et al. 1980c). Other studies have reported the level of job satisfaction associated with commonly portrayed occupations (Jeffries-Fox and Signiorelli 1979) and the degree of success and happiness associated with characters of different demographic groups (Gerbner et al. 1980b). Thus, message system analysis provides an assessment of the "facts" and associated characterizations that television provides about the world and the people populating it.

The second stage of research needed to document the cultivation effect is to show that the television content that is at variance with real life has a greater influence on heavy viewers than on light viewers. This is often referred to as cultivation analysis. Cultivation analysis uses survey instruments to compare heavy and light television viewers' estimates of the occurrences of various types of people or events in the real world. The survey questions posed are a function of the earlier MSA.

Cultivation analysis has found some support for the belief that heavy viewers of television are more likely than light viewers to have incorrect beliefs about the world that are biased in the direction of television portrayals. For example, heavy viewers have been found to overestimate the prevalence of violence in the world and their chances of being a victim of a crime (Doob and McDonald 1979; Gerbner et al. 1977, 1978). A review of findings indicates that this is true for both child and adult viewers (Hawkins and Pingree 1982). Other studies have found that heavy viewers are also more likely to have greater faith in doctors (Volgy and Schwarz 1980); have more negative attitudes toward the elderly (Gerbner et al. 1980a); hold more sexist attitudes (Morgan 1980; Volgy and Schwarz 1980); and overestimate the stability of the nuclear family (Pingree et al. 1979).

Mainstreaming and Resonance

There have been two significant modifications to cultivation theory: "mainstreaming" and "resonance" by Gerbner et al. (1980a). Cultivation assumes that the media act to both change and reinforce perceptions depending on how media depictions compare with the individual's own perceptions of his or her social environment. Different demographic groups (based on income, education, sex, socioeconomic status, etc.) are likely to have had different life experiences, which will lead to different perceptions of social reality. However, over time, heavy television viewers from these different groups will develop similar social perceptions. This effect is referred to as "mainstreaming." Mainstreaming occurs when heavy viewers from different demographic groups change their views to more closely reflect the television world, and are metaphorically swept into the "mainstream."

Yet for some groups, television reality may closely match their own real world experiences. In this case, television would serve to simply reinforce existing social perceptions. If an individual's environment was consonant with the television world, Gerbner et al. (1980a) claim we should see evidence of "resonance." In other words, the television world would resonate with the individual's own experiences, thus producing a "double dose." Thus, we should see more pronounced effects of heavy exposure to televised violence in neighborhoods that are in reality more violent. Heavy television viewers in such neighborhoods should see their neighborhoods as significantly more violent than do light viewers living in the same neighborhood.

Criticism

There are at least a half dozen criticisms of cultivation research based on both theoretical and methodological grounds. One common criticism is that because of the addition of mainstreaming and resonance, cultivation is no longer falsifiable. Any result can be interpreted as supportive of the extended theory. This criticism, however, rests on the premise that mainstreaming and resonance are exact opposites existing in the same domain and operating at the exact same level. This is really not the case. Mainstreaming reflects a general orientation due to membership in socioeconomic, ethnic, and other social or cultural groups. It is a macro-level variable, whereas resonance is a micro-level variable that really captures salience in a more narrow, situationally defined sense. The two components, as is true in a traditional attitude model, may affect the final summary attitude in opposing directions. They represent different domains and different levels. The problem, however, has been exacerbated by Gerbner et al.'s research procedures, since they typically operationalize and report results in a manner that implies that they are representing equal and opposing forces, operating at the same level. It is, therefore, easy to understand the presence of confusion on this point.

From our present vantage, the arguments for mainstreaming seem to rest on somewhat firmer theoretical ground than do those for resonance. If anything, the mass media represent an homogenizing force. Further, the extant literature suggests that cultivation like effects should be strongest in the absence of knowledge obtained via direct experience. Real-life experiences should overwhelm mediated ones and not

result in a large incremental shift in perceptions or a "double dose." Rubin, Perse, and Taylor (1988) demonstrated the importance of demographic differences in perceived reality outcomes. Actually, one might expect a ceiling effect in this case; those who directly experience violence, for example, may already be at such a high level of agreement with a statement such as "fear of crime is a very serious personal problem," that measurement of incremental change due to exposure to televised violence may be unlikely.

Another criticism of cultivation is that it fails to provide any psychological process or dynamic. It is basically a black box theory. It implies the importance of notions like availability, accessibility, the frequency, and the passivity of viewing, but offers little elaborated theory. A clear understanding of how cultivation works would greatly help to overcome several criticisms. For example, some critics claim there is the possibility of reverse causality. People who see the world as violent, for instance, may simply have a greater preference for violent programming. We cannot say for certain that it is not the case, but current thinking in socialization and communication research would argue against that interpretation. Still, it would be naive to believe that effects occur in only one direction; the actual process is most likely recursive and dynamic.

One of the most common criticisms of cultivation is the assertion that its effects are spurious or are due to other sociological confounds or covariates. For example, television viewing is negatively correlated with years of education, income, and socioeconomic status (SES). Although Gerbner et al. employ these as control variables, they have generally been employed one at a time. When all are used simultaneously the cultivation effects are often diminished and sometimes even eliminated (Hawkins and Pingree 1982; Hirsch 1980). This is, of course, a traditional problem in all sociological studies. Covariability among such variables being what it is, the odds of completely partialling out an effect are high. It would appear that control variables should be used simultaneously, but not indiscriminantly. They must have some clear theoretical relationship to the effect under study in order to be meaningfully applied.

Another criticism questions the belief that viewing is both habitual and undifferentiated. This is the basis for assuming that total viewing is an appropriate predictor of effects. Hawkins and Pingree (1981) find that viewing is more varied and less habitual than Gerbner et al. suggest, but that the cultivation effect is actually stronger when nested within the type of programming typically viewed. For example, a cultivated violence effect is even more likely among regular viewers of action dramas than among people who are heavy viewers overall.

A final criticism is that the coding of television content is simplistic and misses the true symbolic nature of the television narrative. This is no doubt true; complex and rich behavior has often been reduced to unambiguous codifiable bits by cultivation researchers. While this may partially be the result of traditional trade-offs between reliability and validity, certainly coding could be made to incorporate much more of the symbolic richness available in the visual narrative.

Despite all of these criticisms, Pearl et al. (1982), reviewing the cultivation literature for the National Institute of Mental Health, offered the following conclusion:

Television may be only one of many influences playing a part in the shaping of social reality, but it has come to play a role that is generally regarded as significant. (Pearl et al. 1982, Vol. 1, p. 63)

This view seems fairly consistent with the field's general assessment. While, Gerbner et al.'s specific theory of mass media cultivation is not without flaw, it has generated considerable interest in the mass media's role in constructing social reality.

Alternative and Complementary Theories

Other theories may contribute to understanding how the cultivation effect works. Research on the availability heuristic (Kahneman and Tversky 1982; Tversky and Kahneman 1973), as well as related work in social cognition, indicates that information more easily retrieved from memory may be disproportionately represented in judgments regarding the occurrence of events or the frequency of things. Numerous factors have been suggested as facilitating retrieval, including distinctiveness, novelty, affective valence, and frequency and recency of exposure (see Folkes 1988; Wyer and Srull 1989). It could be that, when television viewers are asked to estimate the incidence of something such as the likelihood of being the victim of a violent crime, those relevant cognitive structures which have been significantly influenced in their construction by television exposure are more easily accessed. Given that media portrayals may be affectively charged, distinctive, and both recently and frequently encountered, they may be more accessible. This has been observed at least in one study where mass media exposure was positively correlated with overestimating the frequency of certain lethal events prominently displayed in the media (Lichtenstein et al. 1978). This is, of course, the same prediction made by the cultivation theory, except that in this case the availability heuristic was offered as the explanatory dynamic.

Other work in social cognition, as well as other research which looks at the unique properties of television, may also help explain cultivation effects. Research on the vividness of media images (Janis 1980), imagability's relationship to accessibility (Kisielius and Sternthall 1986; Gregory, Cialdini, and Carpenter 1982; McGill and Anand 1989: Nisbett and Ross 1980; Sherman et al. 1985), television and fantasy (Singer and Singer 1981), and the psychological properties of the narrative (Brewer and Lichtenstein 1982) could all contribute to a greater understanding of mass-mediated social reality effects. Particularly relevant is the work of Tyler and his colleagues (Tyler 1980; 1984; Tyler and Cook 1984) on the effect of directly and indirectly experienced events on beliefs about personal risk as well as base-rate assessments (e.g., perceptions of how dangerous the neighborhood is in general). This distinction between personal-level risk assessment and general base-rate assessment provides a very important distinction that may help explain some of the inconsistencies in the extant cultivation literature.

Consumer Behavior and Cultivation

Clearly the world of television involves consumption. Television characters buy, sell, own, display and, in a multitude of ways, consume. Material things are used as visual shorthand to tell the audience important things about TV characters and their values. The effects of long-term exposure to these symbol laden portrayals are predicted by cultivation theory. Yet, the processes and effects of this ubiquitous source of social construction have yet to be systematically examined to any significant degree. While it is true that some have written about the role of advertisements in creating symbolic and cultural beliefs in consumers (Mick 1986; McCracken 1986; Levy 1959), the programs between the ads have largely been ignored by consumer researchers.

Exposure to the "world" of consumption as portrayed on television has the potential to influence our perceptions of the incidence and importance of things. Things like swimming pools, expensive cars, hot tubs, and servants may just be set dressing to television producers, but their ubiquitous over-representation may have some lasting long-term effects on individuals' normative beliefs, attitudes, and perhaps even their values. If unchallenged these perceptions may become part of enduring cognitive structures. These pictures in our heads, vague as they might be on closer examination, may drive a great deal of consumer behavior, at least in terms of the origin and persistence of normative beliefs.

There have been only a few published studies that have directly investigated consumer cultivation. Fox and Phillber (1978) examined the impact of television viewing on perceptions of affluence in the United States. However, their measure of TV viewing was a very questionable one. It simply asked people to indicate the number of evenings in an aver-

age week they watched one hour or more of television. A person who watched one hour every evening would be treated as a heavy viewer even though they would be well below the national average in the total amount of television viewed. Using this measure, they found a significant relationship between amount of viewing and perceptions of affluence, but this relationship disappeared when control variables were applied.

A study of Israeli viewers of American programs found that respondents overestimated not only the percentage of Americans owning various household items but also the average earnings of American families (Weimann 1984). Heavy viewers overestimated these things to a greater extent than light viewers. In addition, by testing different causal models, it was found that the data were best explained by a model in which control variables influenced the amount of viewing but not the cultivation effects directly, thus indicating that the amount of viewing does have a direct effect on cultivation. The generalizability of this study to American viewers, however, is problematic, especially since the control variables did not include any measure of direct experience with American households.

Lee (1988) and Lee and O'Guinn (1989) have studied cultivation among Taiwanese immigrants to the United States. By taking measures in Taiwan and at several levels of years the Taiwanese had lived within the United States, these researchers were able to use a cross-sectional design to study the process by which immigrants learned about the role and value of consumption objects. Their findings indicate that media exposure significantly alters the paths of consumer acculturation. In a related work, Shrum, O'Guinn, and Faber (1990) found significant correlations in the amount of television viewed by college students and their estimates of material abundance after controlling for several likely confounding variables (e.g., grade point average, income of the student's family, and materialism). These correlations were most apparent when measured within program type (i.e., news, game shows, action/adventure, and situation comedy). Most were in the r = 0.20 to r = 0.40 range. Further, significant differences in normative beliefs were observed between men and women. For example, when asked to estimate the percentage of couples making less than $25,000 a year, for male respondents, the correlation between the number of hours of situation comedies viewed per week and their percentage estimates was -0.23 ($p < 0.05$), whereas for women it was $+0.21$ ($p < 0.05$). These results suggest that men and women may actually take away very different perceptions of economic and consumption related norms when exposed to the same television content. Faber, O'Guinn, and Shrum (1990) combined survey methodology with diaries to further explicate cultivation effects nested within specific program-viewing preferences.

Some researchers have attempted to address cultivation effects on a social cognition level. O'Guinn and Shrum (1990) developed a study that measured reaction times to various normative belief stimuli. They reasoned that if the things television overrepresents do indeed dominate the cognitive structures of heavy television viewers, then these various perceptual stimuli should be more accessible in memory. Results showed heavy viewers of television, when asked to make estimates of the incidence of various consumer goods or activities, responded significantly faster than light viewers.

Cultivation effects could also result from the way consumer decision making is portrayed on television. Research has shown that decisions on television tend to infrequently consider important purchase decisions such as if finances are available or if there are alternative choices (Faber 1978; Way 1982). Additionally, on television few sources of information are considered and decisions are made within a very short time frame (typically within one day) (Faber 1978). Therefore, we may find that heavy viewers of television are less deliberate and thorough in their purchase decision making.

In developing a complete theory or model of the impact of cultivation on consumer behavior we need to go beyond frequency estimates. Cultivation may also significantly contribute to the "affective socialization" of consumers that Riesman and Roseborough (1955) spoke of 35 years ago. Although products would have symbolic meaning in the absence of television, this medium is one of the most effective transmitters of that symbolic code in a mass-mediated consumer culture. This has significant implications for our understanding of the origin and persistence of consumers' beliefs about the ownership of material things according to social class, what members of other ethnicities or social classes are like, and the happiness associated with having, displaying, and consuming things.

Final Note on Cultivation Effects

It should be pointed out that most studies on cultivation effects find that television has only a weak or moderate effect on beliefs, especially after controlling for other variables. Similar levels of effect are likely in the study of the cultivation of consumption beliefs. However, this should not necessarily be taken as an indication that the media have only weak effects. Even light viewers of television are likely to be effected by the images and values of television either directly through viewing or indirectly through interactions with others. Given the similarity of content from place to place and the prevalence of television in American life, assessments of its effects are likely to produce much less variance across individuals than other sources of socialization (Chaffee 1976; Gerbner et al. 1986). Thus, we must assume that some of the influence of television may well be masked by its ubiquitous effect.

Cultivation analysis provides one way to examine some of the potential effects of the mass media on consumer socialization and enculturation throughout the life span. Many of the findings may be strongest for children and adolescents who have limited real-life experiences. However, cultivation may also occur for adults, both in situations where their real-life experiences are limited, and through mainstreaming when direct experience is more common. There are many factors that may play important roles in mitigating the effect of cultivation and the development of a comprehensive model may still be in the distance. Cultivated beliefs may be unchallenged, unelaborated, and vague representations of the social world rather than thought-out solutions and evaluations. However, given the pervasiveness of television and other mass media, it appears to be worthwhile for consumer researchers to further utilize and develop models that incorporate the role entertainment media can play in fostering perceptions of consumption reality and how these perceptions ultimately influence consumer attitudes, values, and behaviors.

SOCIALIZATION

One of the areas (along with the diffusion of innovations and persuasion) where the fields of communication and consumer behavior have overlapped most is in the study of socialization. Yet, there are important differences in perspective. In communications, consumer socialization is only one of several types of role socialization studied. Additionally, communication researchers tend to consider program and editorial content almost to the exclusion of advertising, whereas just the opposite is true in the study of consumer behavior.

Traditionally, socialization has focused only on the young. However, researchers in both communications and consumer behavior have proposed that socialization is an ongoing process and should be examined throughout the life cycle. Although we strongly support these calls for a life cycle perspective, the vast majority of research has been limited to children and adolescents, with a smaller literature beginning to develop about the elderly.

Children and Adolescents

While not always cast as "socialization" studies per se, many investigations of children and adolescents are precisely that; they are studies of how children acquire various norms, values, and behaviors. These include studies examining such topics as aggression, prosocial behaviors, political knowledge, and advertising.

Considering all of these studies, we can conclude that, independent of other factors, exposure to television produces observable differences in the beliefs, attitudes, and behaviors of children and adolescents. However, it is rarely if ever the case that television portrayals are truly independent of other factors. Thus, we are left with the very important question of deciding what factors will determine the individuals who will be influenced by what content in which situations. An equally difficult problem in socialization studies is determining the relative importance of various socialization agents. The media's role is frequently affected by both the topic being investigated and by other sources of socialization, especially parents, who may or may not choose to provide or exercise any influence. In addition, when other sources are absent, the media may fill the void.

Consumer Socialization

Consumer socialization was an important topic in communication research during the 1970s. Research during that period focused on issues such as children's ability to distinguish television ads from programs and to determine the purpose of commercials (Robertson and Rossiter 1974; Ward, Wackman, and Wartella 1977); the effect of advertising on children's requests, parental yielding, and family harmony (Ward and Wackman 1973; Goldberg and Gorn 1978; Robertson 1980; Robertson et al. 1989); the extent and effect of parental mediation (Corder-Bolz and O'Bryant 1978; Robertson 1980); and appropriate methods for assessing these and other effects (Donohue, Henke, and Donohue 1980). Much of this research was fueled (and funded) by the public policy implications it had for proposed legislation effecting the production of commercials. However, after the FTC hearings on television advertising aimed at children ended in 1979 with the decision not to impose any restrictions, the interest of communication researchers seemed to wane. Although occasional studies still appear in communication journals (i.e., Kunkel 1988; Robertson et al. 1989), most research on children and advertising now appears in consumer behavior journals.

Early work on television advertising aimed at children was concerned with children's acquisition of discrete information-processing skills (Robertson and Rossiter 1974; Ward and Wackman 1973; Ward, Wackman and Wartella 1977). These authors demonstrated differences in the acquisition and utilization of consumer information by children of different cognitive developmental levels. This focus continues in the work of Roedder-John and Whitney (1986), Macklin (1987), and Brucks et al. (1988). Early studies were also concerned with the issue of coviewing and parental mediation. Initial work found that relatively few parents watched much television with their children, even fewer discussed the ads they saw, and what limited mediation exists is strongest for younger children (Dorr 1986; Robertson 1980). Robertson et al. (1989) have extended research on parent child interaction and conflict to a cross-cultural context, separating what appears to be pan-cultural from what seems culture bound.

Contemporary consumer behavior research in children and advertising remains predominately concerned with the abilities of the child from an information-processing standpoint. Underlying this orientation is a concern with the child's vulnerability. How capable are children of various ages at interpreting and utilizing advertising? Macklin (1987), for example, demonstrated via nonverbal tasks that a significant minority (at least 20 percent) of five-year-olds understood the informational function of television ads. Yet, as she points out, such findings are insufficient evidence to assure ourselves that children really understand the ad from the seller's perspective, or its true persuasive intent. Roedder-John and Whitney (1986) suggest that merely increasing the amount of information directed to children less than five years old is not a suitable remedy or safeguard due to the limited cognitive script development of preschool children. Also consistent with this are the findings of Brucks, Armstrong, and Goldberg (1988), which demonstrated that fourth graders do not generate a significant number of counterarguments without the aid of direct cuing of "advertising knowledge," or

knowledge of the manner and workings of advertising. Since ads do not typically offer much information, it seems reasonable to conclude that preschoolers are a more vulnerable audience as a function of less developed information-processing skills.

Research in this area should be extended to include the various photographic and video production techniques used in commercials and the ability of children at different developmental levels to understand them. This is the objective of some of the work in "formal features" suggesting that developmental level influences children's "media literacy" (Meyer 1983; Salomon 1979). Thus, young children may be particularly vulnerable to certain film or video conventions that they are unable to understand.

Socialization to Other Roles

Communications researchers have also looked at several other types of role socialization. Role socialization involving occupation (Abel et al. 1980), family (Buerkel-Rothfuss et al. 1981; Greenberg 1982), gender (Henderson and Greenberg 1980; Miller and Reeves 1976), politics (Atkin 1981; Chaffee et al. 1970), and age (Gerbner et al. 1980b; Graney 1975) have been prominent. Work in these areas indicates that television typically supplements and enhances information derived from other socialization agents rather than functioning as the primary agent. However, there are some important exceptions. These seem to occur when the attitude objects are most remote (Greenberg 1972; Hornick, Gonzales, and Gould 1980). For example, since most children encounter a fairly narrow range of occupations first hand, their knowledge about many professions comes solely from television portrayals. Evidence suggests that exposure to these portrayals can alter both children's perceptions and occupational aspirations (DeFleur and DeFleur 1967). While some of these beliefs will be significantly attenuated by subsequent information as the child's world expands with age and experience, initial decisions based on media portrayals may have important lasting effects (Leifer and Lesser 1976).

Interaction of Family and Media

The family plays a critical role in understanding socialization from the media since it serves both as an alternative source of learning and forms the environment in which much of television is viewed. This has led to several approaches to studying the interaction between the family and television (Moschis 1987). One important approach involves the study of family communication patterns or FCP (McLeod and Chaffee 1972; Moschis 1985).

The FCP model rests on the existence of two critical dimensions or orientations of families: concept-orientation and socio-orientation. Concept-orientation refers to the degree to which parents stress the value and importance of objects and ideas, thus encouraging the expression of one's own ideas and thoughts. Socio-orientation is the extent to which parents stress social relationships, thus encouraging social harmony, deference, and tranquility. High and low levels of these two dimensions are crossed to yield the two-by-two FCP typology.

Communications researchers have observed interesting differences between FCP groups. Typically these are in terms of information-seeking behaviors or their correlates, such as school performance, media use, political socialization, and consumer skills (Chaffee et al. 1971; Moschis 1985; Tims 1986). Generally, children from homes with high levels of concept-orientation are shown to outperform or fare better than other children. One reason for this difference may be evident in a study by Messaris and Kerr (1983), which found that high concept-orientation was predictive of mothers discussing the moral issues raised by television programs, amplifying or providing in greater detail the content, and telling their children that various aspects of TV are just "make believe." In contrast, mothers in high socio-orientation families were far more likely to tell their children of the "true to life" nature of televised portrayals, particularly with regard to misfortune and evil.

It may be that critical differences in family structure, such as those captured by the FCP typology, are necessary to really understand inherently complex socialization processes, including consumer socialization. However, to be truly useful, a greater understanding of what FCP represents and how it operates is necessary. In one of the more theoretically developed studies, Tims (1986) presents work supportive of a model in which value orientations are shown to predict FCP, which in turn, predicts differences in political norms. More efforts like this are needed. Future research might profitably examine if FCP influences the way social reality is constructed, and the degree to which media portrayals are accepted as substitutes for direct experience.

Researchers must be careful to understand that FCP orientation is not static. Like individual difference factors, it interacts with many things, including situational factors and cognitive developmental level (Meadowcroft 1986). Still, the inclusion of FCP in media socialization studies is appealing since the family forms the environment in which exposure and interpretation of media content occurs. In consumer behavior, FCP has been found to contribute to explaining socialization outcomes in adolescent consumers (Moschis 1985; 1987; Moschis, Moore, and Smith 1984).

A different approach to studying the family media interaction is apparent in the works of a few prominent ethnographers (Lindloff et al. 1988; Lull 1980, 1988). Lull (1980) conducted a three year ethnographic study of over 200 families from varying demographic, geographic, and socioeconomic classes. He and his team interviewed informants and observed and participated in normal family activities (including eating, cooking, doing chores, watching television) from mid-afternoon to bedtime for two to seven days per family. Families initially knew only that the investigators were interest in "family life." As the work progressed certain patterns began to emerge and were then systematically examined. Lull's analysis yielded a typology known as the "social uses of television."

The social uses typology has two major divisions: structural and relational. The structural uses of television are seen when television is used as companionship for household chores, background noise, or as a behavioral regulator signaling the time for meals or bed. Relational uses, on the other hand, are seen in "the ways in which audience members use television to create practical social arrangements" (Lull 1980, p. 202). Lull's four types of relational uses are displayed in Figure 10.4. While a full accounting is beyond the scope of this chapter, it is worth noting that all four of these uses apply quite nicely to the study of mass-mediated socialization. However, they suggest a much more subtle and extensive type of socialization than is typically reported in the literature. For example, Lull documented and detailed how children use television characters as known-in-common referents for starting conversations and for explaining real world experiences to cohorts as well as parents and teachers. Consider this example of sex-role socialization:

. . . adolescent girls competed to correctly identify wardrobe fashions from various historical periods during a program which featured this topic. The girls tried to identify the periods before the announcer on the program did so. Correct identification gave status to the girl who guessed right, validating her as an expert on women's fashions and placing her in an esteemed position in the eyes of her peers. (Lull 1980, p. 226)

Lull's work serves as an example of what a good ethnography can provide apart from what might be accessible via other methods. It is able to reveal important relationships embedded within the delicate nexus of individuals, family, and the media with a sensitivity that does not obliterate the very thing it is trying to understand. The work of other authors on the impact of video technology, particularly the VCR, on socialization further demonstrates the use of ethnographies in this area (Lindloff et al. 1988; Levy 1989).

FIGURE 10.4 Social Uses of Television

Structural

Environmental
(Background noise; companionship; entertainment)

Regulative
(punctuation of time and activity; talk patterns)

Relational

Communication Facilitation
(experience illustration; common ground; conversational entrance; anxiety reduction; agenda for talk; value clarification)

Affiliation/Avoidance
(physical; verbal contact/neglect; family solidarity; family relaxant; conflict reduction; relationship maintenance)

Social Learning
(decision-making; behavior modeling; problem solving; value transmission; legitimization; information dissemination; substitute schooling)

Competence/Dominance
(role enactment; role reinforcement; substitute role portrayal; intellectual validation; authority exercise; gatekeeping; argument facilitation)

Source: Lull, James (1980). "Social Uses of Television," *International Communication Association and Human Communication Research,* 6, 3, (Spring), 197–209.

Adulthood

Adulthood has often been ignored as a period of study for researchers interested in socialization. This may be partially because most developmental theories posit the onset of the highest level of stage growth to occur during adolescence or early adulthood (Ginsburg and Opper 1969; Kohlberg 1969). If a person has not achieved the highest stage by that point, it is generally believed that future growth is unlikely (Kohlberg 1969). Media and consumer behavior research has also reinforced the belief that little change occurs during adulthood. Himmelweit and Swift (1976) found that the best predictor of adults' TV preferences was what they watched during adolescence. Similarly, brand preference in adulthood has been found to be strongly related to preferences held during adolescence (Guest 1955).

Another possible reason for ignoring socialization during adulthood is that, unlike with children and adolescents, when changes do occur they are unlikely to happen at the same age for all adults. Instead, changes during adulthood are likely to emerge because of major life changes for the individual. One example that has been studied is the moving of an individual from one culture to another. Researchers examining acculturation (a special case of socialization) have found important differences in adults' media preferences, brand and product usages, and preferences due to acculturation level (Deshpande, Hoyer and Donthu 1989; Faber et al. 1987; Lee 1988; O'Guinn and Meyer 1984; Wallendorf and Reilly 1983). Unfortunately, most acculturation studies have been cross-sectional investigations rather than longitudinal studies, which are needed to more directly examine the impact of acculturation in adulthood (McCarty 1989).

Other changes in life status, such as marriage, having children, divorce and geographical moves, have also been hypothesized to create new socialization needs in adults (Andreasen 1984; Faber et al. 1979). These life status changes have been found to be related to greater changes in brand preferences (Andreasen 1984) and media use (Dimmick et al. 1979).

The aging process itself may create differences among adults. Belk (1985) examining materialism across three generations found that the middle group scored highest on materialism and that the oldest group were the least materialistic. Although several possible reasons can account for this, it may reflect changes in value orientation as people get older.

Finally, changes in societal concerns may lead to socialization effects during adulthood. Concern about issues such as AIDS and healthy lifestyles, combined with large scale media campaigns, have led adults to develop new skills, knowledge, attitudes, and values (Solomon 1982). Greater attention to these forms of socialization during adulthood are needed to develop a true life-span socialization perspective.

The Elderly

Like children and adolescents, several things happen during late adulthood that make members of this age group a special audience. For many, the social world constricts as they retire from work, and contacts with colleagues, friends, and relatives decline. Often associated with this is the social-psychological process of "disengagement" (Cumming and Henry 1961; Smith and Moschis 1985). A decrement in mental-processing ability may also occur. Changes in both physical condition and lifestyle lead to significant changes in consumption patterns and needs.

At the very time that many elderly consumers are disengaging from the social world, television viewing for this group increases significantly (Real et al. 1980; Rubin and Rubin 1982). Television may become a surrogate for missing relatives and friends (Graney 1975). Ironically, the elderly are often negatively stereotyped on television (Gerbner et al. 1980b). This means that while more and more of the world is accessed via television for the group, it portrays this audience in a fairly pejorative manner. This poses several research questions.

First, one has to wonder about the effect on self-concept. Does frequent exposure to negative portrayals contribute to a diminished self-concept in the elderly? Does this result in efforts along some compensatory lines, including consumption? Second, as with any social role, one has to learn what it means to be elderly. The media may play a vital role in defining this role, including information regarding appropriate or desirable goods and services (Smith et al. 1985; 1986). Finally, given that this audience has special needs, they may be at greater risk of being deceived or misled by advertising.

Roedder-John and Cole (1986) suggests that among the elderly there is a combination of both slower processing speed and poorer memory strategy usage. Gaeth and Heath (1987) do not find any significant difference between young and old adult consumers in susceptibility to deceptive advertising when responding from memory, but when the ads were actually present the elderly consumers fared less well than their younger counterparts. Of course as the authors pointed out, these differences may be attributable to cohort effects, or differences in life experiences rather than processing differences.

Implications for Future Research

Back in 1974, Ward, after providing an historical account of the evolution of the concept of consumer socialization, set out several relevant concerns and suggested a research agenda. After a promising start, there has been a disappointingly small number of studies published in this area. Most of those have been limited to the study of children and television advertising. Future research in consumer socialization needs to expand in several ways.

First, programming may be an even more important source of learning about consumption than advertising. Information about consumer values and behaviors is embedded within the narrative of programs as incidental, but symbolic material. This type of media content may greatly impact the affective or value expressive side of socialization. Further, programming material may be processed by the consumer differently than ads since there is no explicit attempt to persuade.

The view of mass-mediated socialization needs to be expanded to include less direct, less utilitarian, and less functional outcomes. Rather than starting with the premise that socialization agents teach children the things necessary to be good and "effective" consumers (Ward 1980), we should ask what beliefs, attitudes, values, and behaviors are suggested by media content and theories, and we should then systematically test for them as a function of exposure. This would expand the types of dependent variables examined and suggest the application of much more sophisticated models, where variables such as the needs of the viewer are considered. Functional attitude theories (see Shavitt 1989) and uses and gratifications may provide useful approaches to integrating needs with consumer socialization.

The range of socialization research also needs to move beyond adolescence to encompass a true life-cycle perspective. It should also be noted that much of socialization is anticipatory, occurring in advance of some expected change in life status or role. People may thus pay particular attention to incidental program content that provides information about problems or roles they expect to encounter. Faber, Brown, and McLeod (1979), for example, show how television may be used to help prepare for and resolve specific problems encountered during adolescent development, such as dealing with a changing body image, asserting independence from family, and making career choices. Study of this type of mass-mediated socialization could obviously be extended to consumer behavior.

Finally, research in consumer socialization should be conducted on many fronts with multiple methodologies. Ward (1980), for instance, has called for the use of more naturalistic methods. Still, no single methodology, or even discipline, is capable of fully explaining the manner in which the media act as socialization agents. However, with all of these changes, we may begin to recognize the true impact of the media as powerful consumer socialization agents.

KNOWLEDGE GAP

Some mass communication researchers have concerned themselves with communication inequities or "knowledge gaps." They hold that even broadly available general information is not evenly distributed throughout society, and that, therefore, there are information-rich and information-poor. The knowledge gap hypothesis goes beyond this important, but rather axiomatic assertion (Dervin 1980; Gaziano 1983), holding that heavy media coverage not only fails to eliminate information disparities, it actually *increases* them. Tichenor et al. (1970) formalized this hypothesis:

As the infusion of mass media information into a social system increases, segments of the population with higher socioeconomic status tend to acquire this information at a faster rate than the lower status segments, so that the gap in knowledge between these segments tends to increase rather than decrease. (Tichenor et al. 1970. p. 160)

At the most basic level, there is little doubt that knowledge gaps exist. They exist in many domains, even where mass media coverage has been heavy (Donohue, Olien, and Tichenor 1987; Gaziano 1984; Tichenor, Donohue, and Olien 1980). Those with more education and income appear more knowledgeable about national and international news events, political issues, and various types of health information than the poor and less educated (Dervin 1980; Gaziano 1983). Furthermore, they may derive greater benefits from mass media educational efforts. There is also evidence for the existence of a class of chronically uninformed people whom Hyman and Sheatsley (1947) termed the "know nothings."

Many explanations for why these gaps should exist have been suggested. They have been attributed to individual factors such as poorer information-processing skills and background knowledge among the less educated. Also, there are structural variables, such as less functional access and exposure to the more information-rich print media (Dervin 1980), that keep people information poor. Still others point to motivational factors (Donohue et al. 1975; Ettema and Kline 1977; Ettema, Brown, and Luepker 1983). Some people (especially the poor) may perceive less utility, and thus have less interest, in accessing and acquiring certain types of information from the mass media than other people do. This may be exacerbated by media content. In an age where information, including news, is marketed, what the media offer as information is partially determined by what they believe their customers want. Perhaps, as Dervin (1980) argues in her criticism of "traditional" knowledge gap research, we should spend less time looking for "audience deficiencies," and instead turn our attention to the "source deficiencies" of the media.

Widening Gaps

There is evidence of a positive association between the amount of coverage of an issue and increasing knowledge differentials among individuals with high and low levels of education and high and low levels of income (Gaziano 1984; Moore 1987), but this is countered by an even larger body of work that finds either no

change or a narrowing gap between these groups with increased issue coverage in the media (Gaziano 1988). Several factors may account for this. First, some studies employed dependent measures that tapped discreet bits of knowledge, not depth of knowledge (Spitzer and Denzin 1965). As Ettema and Kline (1977) point out, this can create a ceiling effect prohibiting the possibility of a widening gap. Second, "knowledge" is usually defined by the researcher. Dervin (1980) suggests that taking a more emic approach might yield very different results. Finally, there may be important factors that help determine when gaps will or will not increase. While conflict, need, and interest have occasionally been utilized, better and more consistent measures of these and other factors, such as issue salience and complexity, are needed. A study by Moore (1987) illustrates the importance of some of these factors. During the 1987 New Hampshire gubernatorial campaign, Moore found that in the case of a simple "for or against" tax issue, a preexisting knowledge gap was eliminated by campaign coverage. However, in the case of an equally covered, but more complex, nuclear energy related tax issue (CWIP), knowledge difference between educational groups' increased significantly (see Figure 10.5). It is possible that given enough time even gaps such as these would disappear. However, in an election or other situation in which time is a critical factor, the luxury of waiting for homogenous and more complete diffusion is not afforded.

Future Research

The mere existence of information inequities is important to those interested in consumer behavior. If, in addition, the information rich are getting richer, and the poor are getting poorer, as a function of mass media, it does not strike an optimistic note for the existence of an informed democracy, for improved public health throughout society from the use of educational campaigns, or even for the assumption that there are informed consumers. In areas of consumer protection and satisfaction, it may very well be that this is another way in which

Knowledge of the Respondents at the Beginning and
at the end of the campaign

	Beginning of Campaign	End of Campaign	Percent of Voters w/ Increased Knowledge
Know Which Candidate Closest to Own Position on Tax Issue	40%	66%	+26%
Know Which Candidate Closest to Own Position on CWIP* Issue	36%	62%	+26%

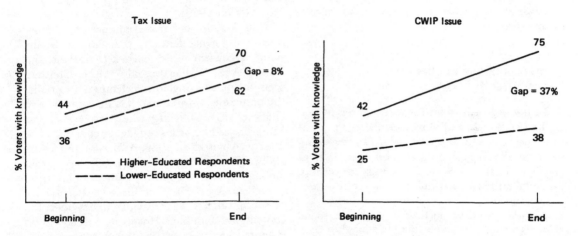

FIGURE 10.5 Knowledge of the Respondents at the Beginning and
at the End of the Campaign (Source: Moore, D. W. (1987), "Political
Campaigns and the Knowledge Gap Hypothesis," *Public Opinion Quarterly*,
51, pp. 186–200.
*Construction Work in Progress at the controversial Seabrook nuclear
power plant.)

"the poor pay more" (Caplovitz 1963). It would therefore seem important to further examine what factors may enhance, and, conversely, what factor could reduce, knowledge gaps in the wake of informational campaigns. This would be particularly valuable to those interested in health marketing and public informational campaigns, where detailed knowledge is needed and where differences between SES groups are more likely.

FORMAL FEATURES

Although small and fairly obscure by comparison to the major research traditions in mass communication, formal features research merits discussion. Making it distinct is its focus on the *form* rather than the content of televised messages. As such it comes closest to empirically testing McLuhan's (1964) now famous, "the medium is the message" pronouncement.

Studying the language and conventions of moving pictures (edits, fades, dissolves, slow motion, music, flashbacks, laugh tracks, etc.) may yield insight into the psychological processes underlying their use, interpretation, and effect upon audience members.

Although interest in the relationship between motion pictures and various psychological processes dates back almost to the turn of the century (Munsterberg 1915), surprisingly little research has been conducted. Almost all work on formal features was done with child subjects and from a developmental framework (Meyer 1983; Salomon 1979). While this is an appropriate application, it has been an unnecessary limitation.

Attention, Comprehension, and Affect

Much of formal features research has looked at the relationship of various features to attention and message comprehension. In reviewing work in the area, Rice, Huston, and Wright (1983), cite five consistent findings concerning formal features and visual attention in children.

1. Auditory features, such as lively music, sound effects, children's voices (but not adult dialogue), peculiar voices, nonspeech vocalizations, and frequent changes of speaker attract and hold children's attention.
2. Conventional visual features, such as cuts, zooms, and pans have less influence, but visual effects do attract children's attention.
3. In most studies, high levels of physical activity or action elicit and maintain children's attention.
4. Changes in scene, characters, themes, or auditory events are especially effective in eliciting attention, though they are less important for maintaining it once the child is looking.
5. Features that lose children's attention include complex speeches, long zooms, song and dance, men's voices, and live animals.

Evidence indicates that auditory features are superior to visual ones in terms of eliciting and holding children's attention (Rolandelli, Wright, and Huston 1982). Children seem to "monitor" television programming while not looking directly at the set, relying on auditory cues (Rice et al. 1983; Tower et al. 1979). By a fairly early age, children appear able to use formal features to predict changes in upcoming content and recognize which messages are "for them" (Alwitt et al. 1980; Anderson and Lorch 1983). Recent research with adults using EEGs (Reeves et al. 1985) and EKGs (Lang 1987; 1988) to measure attention find that formal features like cuts, scene changes, and movement also serve to regain adult viewers' attention. However, some visual features can have a detrimental effect on attention (Walker and Von Gotten 1989).

Comprehension can be enhanced by the use of salient formal features that emphasize the point or content to be learned (Anderson and Lorch 1983; Calvert et al. 1982). Children seem adept at using formal features to predict the occurrence of understandable content, and children cease viewing when irrelevant, less comprehensible, or less engaging content is imminent (Alwitt et al. 1980; Anderson and Lorch 1983). Thorson and Lang (1988) found that among adults recall and recognition of information occurring during and directly after the use of special effects was enhanced, provided the content was familiar. However, special effects inhibited learning for unfamiliar content.

Some research suggests that certain formal features (i.e., fast action, rapid editing) may increase arousal and thus affect emotional response (Huston et al. 1981; Bryant, Zillmann, and Brown 1983; McGhee 1980). Unfortunately, this is an area where form and content are so thoroughly intertwined in existing stimulus material (i.e., horror films), that exact causality is usually difficult to ascertain.

Another formal feature that might have significant emotional consequences on viewers is visual point of view (POV). Point of view shots demonstrate a particular character's perspective for the audience, thus increasing emotional reaction by creating a greater empathetic link between viewers and the narrative character. Spiesman et al. (1964), manipulating point of view in film footage of an incision being made on a man's penis during a primitive puberty rite, found that POV had a significant impact on the subjects' affective responses. Storms (1973) manipulated point of view with video-taped presentations to study their effect on at-tributional processes.

Formal features would appear to be an es-sential area of research for those interested in emotion and advertising. Camera angles, cuts, POV, and special effects appear to be capable of creating affective reactions in viewers. How-ever, research in this area has been slowed by the difficulty in isolating one factor at a time while keeping all others equal. This may change with the work currently being done by Reeves and others. Using technological ad-vances in the ability to edit stimuli to reflect changes in formal features should greatly en-hance future research in this area.

Social Behavior

At least a couple of studies suggest that con-tent containing formal features that are typ-ically associated with violent content (rapid cuts, fast pacing) can lead to aggressive behav-ior even in the absence of violent portrayals (Huston-Stein et al. 1981; Greer et al. 1982). In Greer et al. (1982) advertisements with varying levels of salient formal features (action, pace, special effects), but no aggression or violence were cut into the commercial breaks of nonag-gressive programs. As predicted, children ex-posed to commercials with these salient formal features exhibited more aggressive play than children exposed to commercials with different formal features or those in a control group. Thus, children may associate certain formal features normally present in violent program-ming with violence, and when they are pre-sented with violence cued toys, they may mani-fest this behavior. Of course, rival hypotheses cannot be ruled out. It may be that arousal caused by these formal features leads directly to an increase in aggressive acts or that the toys themselves are a source of demand.

Formal features may also contribute to so-cialization outcomes such as sex-role stereotyp-ing. It has been observed, for example, that commercials for male sex-typed toys "are made with high action, rapid cuts, and loud noise, whereas feminine sex-typed toys are advertised with fades, dissolves, and soft music" (Rice, Huston, and Wright 1983, p. 25). Greer et al. (1981) and Leary and Huston (1983) have shown that children as young as five and six understand these features as cues for either girl- or boy-relevant toys.

Consumer Behavior and Formal Features

The vast majority of consumer behavior re-search on ad elements deal with static print ads as opposed to the features associated with *mov-ing* pictures in television advertisements. As a result little is known about how consumers re-spond to the formal features of television ads.

Consumer behavior researchers working with print ads have found visual information to be generally superior in terms of recognition and recall. This is especially true when there is a close association between the visual and ver-bal message (Childers and Houston 1984; Lutz and Lutz 1977). However, involvement seems to be a significant mediating variable. When involvement is low, visual information is domi-nant; when it is high, verbal information be-comes much more of a factor (Edell 1988).

A major theoretical question underlying much of the visual/verbal research is the extent to which verbal and visual information is pro-cessed separately, or in a distinctly different manner. While there is some support for a dual processing model, the question remains open. Shanteau (1988), for example, in his work in impression formation finds "no fundamental difference between verbal and visual informa-tion" (1988, p. 45), and thus sees no compelling evidence for the existence of such a model.

The one formal feature of television receiv-ing some attention by consumer researchers is music. Gorn (1982) demonstrated that music can influence product preference. Park and Young (1986), however, noted that music in a television ad interfered with subjects' ability to attend to product messages. The relationship between formal features and various types of content may be particularly complex. For instance, Drew and Grimes (1987) found that audio-visual redundancy enhanced the learning of aural information from news stories, but detracted from the learning of visual information. This suggests that audio information, at least in the case of television viewing, may be superior in redundant situations: Pictures enhance the understanding of words, but words may interfere with the learning of visual information.

Overall, given the intriguing notions of Munsterberg (1915) and McLuhan (1964), it is disappointing to see how little work has been done in formal features. Although there is beginning to be some interest in drama and the properties of the narrative (Deighton, Romer, and McQueen 1989; Wells 1988), many fundamental questions remain unaddressed. How is the visual language of moving pictures learned, processed, and interpreted? What can the manner of processing and interpretation tell us about the way the mind deals with pictorial language? How are visual inferences made, and how do they affect decision processes? How do consumers make inferences from visual codes? What happens when moving pictures and sounds vary in congruence? Is the cognitive development of children who grow up with these visual narrative systems different from those who grow up without this exposure? These are but a few of the research questions suggested by formal features research. So far, our attention in consumer behavior has been almost exclusively on the static image, and our research has been excessively language bound. It is hoped that future work on television advertising effects will begin to incorporate more complex models that will include formal features.

THE FUTURE

We have witnessed a great deal of change in the mass communication effects literature during the past 15 to 20 years. The dominant metatheoretical approach is returning to a belief that the media can have powerful effects. Powerful effects, however, are no longer conceived of as being immediate and obvious, but are now seen as subtle influences occurring over long periods of time. The power of the media is due to its pervasive place in society and will be greatest when other sources of information are less prevalent. We are now recognizing that relatively little of what we know comes from direct experience, and that the opportunity for the media to be influential is much greater than previously realized.

It is also interesting to note that although several theoretical perspectives suggestive of powerful effects emerged independently, they are essentially complementary, sharing several commonalities. Given this, we believe that it is only a matter of time until future work in mass communications effects begins to integrate these different theories and develops a unified theory of media effects.

Uses and gratifications and arousal/affect models of media selection seem capable of being integrated into a larger theory of media choice that includes both cognitive and affective influences. Zillmann's arousal model stresses choice based on immediate needs, whereas uses and gratifications pays greater attention to more stable and long lasting desires. However, it likely that a complete model would include both current psychological states and long-term predispositions. Although Zillmann's belief, which states that media selection is based on instantaneous evaluations of the match between needs and potential gratifications, seems to better account for most television viewing, it is hard to deny that some part of selection is dependent on elaborated thought and preexisting knowledge. Thus, both models appear to be complementary, and together they offer a fuller account of media choice than either model does alone.

Both uses and gratifications and Zillmann's arousal model recognize that the reason for choosing a particular content fare may influence the outcome of viewing. Thus their integration may well be part of a larger model that also inc'udes several of the effects theories. Agenda-setting and cultivation both rely on media content to predict changes in perceptions. In fact, the biggest difference between them may be the type of content they typically examine. Although knowledge gap theory posits greater differences among viewers as a result of exposure, whereas other models suggest greater homogeneity, this may be largely a function of the fact that the knowledge gap theory applies to detailed knowledge, whereas most of the other theories are concerned with perceptions and impressions. The inclusion of important mediating variables may also help to reconcile these different perspectives. Variables such as conflict, need, and interest have been found to mediate knowledge gaps as well as to promote learning in several other models.

Methodological Changes

In the last few years, some communication scholars have begun to question the basic assumptions underlying traditional communication research methods. For example, "constructionists" question if there is sufficient commonality among individual group members to utilize aggregate measures, and even if there is, they doubt that the key aspects of this commonality will be discernible to researchers (Anderson 1981). Although most of the field still accepts these assumptions, there is some growing concern regarding this second point. Dorr (1986) for example, expressed this concern when describing children's television research:

Most [studies] employ samples of content that researchers believe represent messages in a particular area (e.g., aggression, geography, arithmetic, sex roles). The material is shown to children and their responses in the same area, again as defined by researchers, are measured. It is delivered meaning, as constructed by researchers, that is studied assuming it is similar to the meaning children themselves construct for the content. The meaning of the outcome measures is also defined by researchers not children. To the extent that researchers and children share a common culture and common means of making sense of experience, these research practices are defensible. (p. 69)

It may be that researcher-defined problems and audience experiences are not always the same thing. In a sense, we are confronted by the classic emic-etic dilemma common in cross-cultural research. To understand the effect of the media, the researcher needs to know the essential parameters of the viewer's world: from the raw cognitive-processing abilities to the subtle workings of the filters (family, peers, school, etc.) through which this information is passed. They may also have to start viewing mass-mediated human communication as involving meaning which is not only shared but negotiated and accommodated (Anderson and Meyer 1988).

To overcome this problem we will need to use new methodologies alongside existing ones. A multiplicity of methods are beginning to be used to investigate communication effects. One direction has been towards more in-depth research. Depth is being achieved in terms of more extensive data collection via ethnographies (e.g., Lull 1980; Radway 1984) in terms of time through greater use of longitudinal designs for surveys and content analyses (e.g., Gerbner et al. 1986; Graney 1975), and in terms of quantity of data examined by employing improved computer software and mathematical models to examine media content and its influence on public opinion (e.g., Fan 1988).

We are also beginning to see more experiments used creatively to supplement survey research (e.g., Iyengar and Kinder 1987; Garramone 1983: Zillmann 1982). Advances in physiological measure and in the technological hardware and software used in experimental designs (Reeves, Thorson, and Schluder 1986; Rothschild et al. 1986; Thorson and Snyder 1984) offer additional hope of better understanding how various types of televised content may affect individuals, especially in terms of attention, arousal, emotion, information processing, and social cognition.

Calls for methodological pluralism have come from many places and at many times in communication research (Hovland 1959; Iyengar and Kinder 1987; Zillmann 1985). However, all too often researchers using different methods have ended up doing research unrelated to and unappreciated by others. To truly expand our understanding of communication-related phenomenon will require utilizing multiple methods to investigate similar issues.

Communication Research and Consumer Behavior

In a 1987 review, Ward discussed three perspectives that communication research can bring to consumer behavior. These are the communication effects perspective, the information-processing perspective, and the transactional perspective, which emphasizes interpersonal communication. On a more micro level, we feel the potential for the integration and synthesis of communication and consumer behavior may be even greater. We have presented brief discussions of seven research areas in communication. Each of these areas has much to offer the study of consumer behavior.

Cultivation theory offers a way to examine the origins and persistence of social beliefs. It seeks to uncover how we know what we think we know and to explore the passive side of information acquisition. It also challenges our comfortable assumptions concerning the veracity of our social beliefs by pointing out that what we think we know is often distorted as a function of exposure to the mass media. It seeks to better understand our beliefs about what other people, particularly those outside our direct purveyance, think and do. Cultivation also helps to explain how we establish our concepts of normative beliefs regarding behaviors and possessions. What do most people have in their homes? What do they value? How do they shop? What makes them happy? For many of us, the answers to these questions are likely to be affected by the presentations we repeatedly see in the media.

Agenda-setting and cultivation research ask similar questions. They suggest that the mass media may be most influential in telling us what to think about. However this, in turn, may affect evaluation criteria and influence attitude change. The particular economic indicators discussed in the news may make these measures particularly salient. In turn, they may be the ones that influence our buying or investing behaviors. In advertising, agenda-setting may contribute to explaining when attribute-based ads can change the concerns the public considers in making brand decisions. Agenda-set-

ting also suggests that it might behoove advertisers to better understand the manner in which the social agenda is set in order to recognize and capitalize on changing trends and fads.

Although agenda-setting suggests people learn from media exposure, knowledge gap research illustrates that inequities in the diffusion of public information can result. It poses the disturbing hypothesis that increased consumer information may only be better for the more educated and fortunate. This challenges one of our fondest assumptions of an informed public. Researchers in consumer behavior that are concerned about public policy and persuasive information for the public good (focusing on such issues as wearing seat belts; decreasing energy consumption; decreasing the consumption of cholesterol, fats, alcohol, or drugs, increasing organ donations, encouraging the use of condoms, etc.) should find work on the existence of knowledge gaps, and the factors that exacerbate or reduce them, of particular relevance.

Formal features and excitation transfer deal more with the properties of messages and their more immediate effects. Formal features research could be vital to understanding just how television commercials operate. We know very little about how the language of the moving visual is acquired, processed, and effectively manipulated. Formal features may extend work on the visual/verbal differences in information processing. Research into excitation transfer could help explain the impact of previous ads or programming content on target messages, as well as explain how prior states influence later emotional reactions in buying situations.

The uses and gratifications paradigm emphasizes the critical need for consumer behavior researchers to keep in mind how motivation influences behavior and cognition. Interest in this area coincides with a renaissance of functional attitude theory in psychology (Shavitt 1989). In both cases it has been problems of operationalization that have frustrated greater implementation.

Finally, in the study of socialization, communication research illustrates the need to utilize alternative methods and to consider the impact of the family in determining the role of mass-mediated consumer socialization. Cultivation research also suggests the need to broaden the list of outcome measures in consumer socialization to include the more subtle and the less utilitarian and purposeful results.

It appears that communication theory and research can contribute greatly to better understanding of the manner in which people behave as consumers. Similarly, consumer behavior research can assist the development of communication theory. This overlap of interests and concerns demonstrates that each discipline can only benefit from greater familiarity with the other.

REFERENCES

AAKER, DAVID A., DOUGLAS M. STAYMAN, and MICHAEL R. HAGERTY (1986). "Warmth in Advertising: Measurement, Impact, and Sequence Effects," *Journal of Consumer Research,* 12, 365–381.

ABEL, J., B. FONTES, BRADLEY GREENBERG, and CHARLES ATKIN (1980). "The Impact of Television on Children's Occupational Role Learning," unpublished report, East Lansing, MI: Michigan State University.

AJZEN, ICEK, and MARTIN FISHBEIN (1980). *Understanding Attitudes and Predicting Social Behavior.* Englewood Cliffs, NJ: Prentice-Hall.

ALWITT, LINDA F., D. R. ANDERSON, E. P. LORCH, and S. E. LEVIN (1980). "Preschool Children's Attention to Attributes of Television," *Human Communication Research,* 7, 52–67.

ANDERSON, D. R., and E. P. LORCH (1983). "Looking at Television: Action or Reaction?," in J. Bryant and D. R. Anderson (Eds.), *Children's Understanding of Television: Research on Attention and Comprehension.* New York: Academic Press.

ANDERSON, JAMES A. (1981). "Research on Children and Television: A Critique," *Journal of Broadcasting,* 25 (4), 395–400.

ANDERSON, JAMES A., and TIMOTHY P. MEYER (1975). "Functionalism and the Mass Media," *Journal of Broadcasting,* 19, 11–22.

ANDERSON, JAMES A., and TIMOTHY D. MEYER (1988). *Mediated Communication: A Social Action Perspective,* Newbury Park, CA: Sage.

ANDREASEN, ALAN R. (1984). "Life Status Changes and Changes in Consumer Preferences and Satisfaction," *Journal of Consumer Research,* 11 (December), 784–794.

ARNOFF, CRAIG (1974). "Old Age in Prime Time," *Journal of Communication,* 24 (1), 86–87.

ATKIN, CHARLES A. (1981). "Communication and Political Socialization," in D. D. Nimmo and K. R. Sanders (Eds.), *Handbook of Political Communication,* Beverly Hills, CA: Sage, 299–328.

AXELROD, JOEL (1963). "Induced Moods and Attitudes Toward Products," *Journal of Advertising Research,* 3 (2), 19–24.

BANDURA, A. (1965). "Vicarious Processes: A Case of No-Trial Learning," in L. Berkowitz (Ed.), *Advances in Experimental Social Psychology,* Vol. 2. New York: Academic Press.

BARON, R. A., and R. L. BALL (1974). "The Aggression-Inhibiting Influence of Nonhostile Humor," *Journal of Experimental Social Psychology,* 10, 23–33.

BAUER, RAYMOND A. (1964). "The Obstinate Audience: The Influence Process from the Point of View of Social Communication," *American Psychologist,* 19, 319–328.

BECKER, LEE B. (1979). "Measurement of Gratifications," *Communication Research,* 6, 54–73.

BELK, RUSSELL W. (1985). "Materialism: Trait Aspects of Living in the Material World," *Journal of Consumer Research,* 12 (December), 265–280.

BENTON, M., and P. J. FRAZIER (1976). "The Agenda-Setting Function of Mass Media at Three Levels of Information Molding," *Communication Research,* 3, 261–274.

BERELSON, BERNARD R. (1949). "What 'Missing the Newspaper' Means," in Paul F. Lazarsfeld and Frank N. Stanton (Eds.), *Communication Research 1948–1949.* New York: Harper, 111–129.

BERELSON, BERNARD R. (1959). "The State of Communication Research," *Public Opinion Quarterly,* 23, 1–6.

BERELSON, BERNARD R., PAUL F. LAZERSFELD, and WILLIAM N. MCPHEE (1954). *Voting: A Study of Opinion Formulation in a Presidential Campaign.* Chicago: University of Chicago Press.

BERKOWITZ, L. (1970). "Aggressive Humor as a Stimulus to Aggressive Responses," *Journal of Personality and Social Psychology,* 16, 710–717.

BERLYNE, D. E. (1960). *Conflict, Arousal, and Curiosity.* New York: McGraw-Hill.

BERYLNE, D. E. (1967). "Arousal and Reinforcement," in D. Levine (Ed.), *Nebraska Symposium on*

Motivation, Vol. XV. Lincoln, NE: University of Nebraska Press.

BERGER, PETER L., and THOMAS LUCKMAN (1966). *The Social Construction of Reality*. Garden City, NY: Doubleday.

BETTMAN, JAMES R., and MITA SUJAN (1987). "Effects of Framing on Evaluation of Comparable and Noncomparable Alternatives by Expert and Novice Consumers," *Journal of Consumer Research*, 14 (September), 141–154.

BLOCH, PETER H., DANIEL L. SHERRELL, and NANCY M. RIDGEWAY (1986). "Consumer Search: An Extended Framework," *Journal of Consumer Research*, 13 (June), 119–126.

BLUMLER, JAY G. (1979). "The Role of Theory in Uses and Gratifications Studies," *Communication Research*, 6, 9–36.

BOYANOWSKI, E. O. (1977). "Film Preference Under Conditions of Threat," *Communication Research*, 4, 133–145.

BOYANOWSKI, E. O., D. NEWTSON, and E. WALSTER (1974). "Film Preference Following a Murder," *Communication Research*, 1, 32–43.

BROWN, J. R., J. K. CRAMOND, and R. J. WILDE (1974). "Displacement Effects of Television and the Child's Functional Orientation to Media," in J. G. Blumler and E. Katz (Eds.), *The Uses of Mass Communications: Current Perspectives on Gratifications Research*. Beverly Hills, CA: Sage, 93–112.

BREWER, WILLIAM F., and E. H. LICHTENSTEIN (1982). "Stories are to Entertain: A Structural Affect Theory of Stories," *Journal of Pragmatics*, 6, 473–486.

BRYANT, J., and D. ZILLMANN (1977). "The Mediating Effect of the Intervention Potential of Communications on Displaced Aggressiveness and Retaliatory Behavior," in B. D. Ruben (Ed.), *Communication Yearbook 1*. New Brunswick, NJ: Transaction Press.

BRYANT, J., and D. ZILLMANN (1984). "Using Television to Alleviate Boredom and Stress: Selective Exposure as a Function of Induced Excitational States," *Journal of Broadcasting*, 28, 1–20.

BRYANT, J., D. ZILLMANN, and D. BROWN (1983). "Entertainment Features in Children's Educational Television: Effects on Attention and Information Acquisition," in J. Bryant and D. R. Anderson (Eds.), *Children's Understanding of Television: Research on Attention and Comprehension*. New York: Academic Press.

BRUCKS, MERRIE, GARY M. ARMSTRONG, and MARVIN E. GOLDBERG (1988). "Children's Use of Cognitive Defenses Against Television Advertising: A Cognitive Response Approach," *Journal of Consumer Research*, 14 (4), 471–482.

BUERKEL-ROTHFUSS, NANCY L., and SANDRA MAYES (1981). "Soap Opera Viewing: The Cultivation Effect," *Journal of Communication*, 31, 108–115.

CALVERT, S. L., A. C. HUSTON, B. A. WATKINS, and J. C. WRIGHT (1982). "The Relation Between Selective Attention to Television Forms and Children's Comprehension of Content," *Child Development*. 43, 601–610.

CANTOR, J. R., J. BRYANT, and D. ZILLMANN (1974). "Enhancement of Humor Appreciation by Transferred Excitation," *Journal of Personality and Social Psychology*, 30, 812–821.

CANTOR, J. R., and D. ZILLMANN (1973). "The Effect of Affective State and Emotional Arousal on Music Appreciation," *Journal of General Psychology*, 89, 97–108.

CANTOR, J. R., ZILLMANN, D., and EINSIEDEL, E. F. (1978). "Female Responses to Provocation After Exposure to Aggressive and Erotic Films," *Communication Research*, 5, 395–411.

CAPLOVITZ, D. (1963). *The Poor Pay More*. New York: Free Press.

CAREY, JAMES, W., and A. L. KREILING (1974). "Popular Culture Uses and Gratifications: Notes Toward an Accommodation," in J. G. Blumler and E. Katz (Eds.), *The Uses of Mass Communications: Current Perspectives on Gratifications Research*. Beverly Hills, CA: Sage.

CHAFFEE, STEVEN (1975). *Political Communication: Issues and Strategies for Research*. Beverly Hills, CA: Sage.

CHAFFEE, STEVEN (1976). "Comparing Television to Other Agencies of Socialization," unpublished manuscript, University of Wisconsin, Madison, WI.

CHAFFEE, STEVEN H., JACK McLEOD, and CHARLES A. ATKIN (1971). "Parental Influences on Adolescent Media Use," *American Behavioral Scientist*, 14, 323–340.

CHAFFEE, STEVEN H., SCOTT WARD, and LEONARD P. TIPTON (1970). "Mass Communication and Political Socialization," *Journalism Quarterly*, 47, 647–659.

CHILDERS, TERRY, and MICHAEL HOUSTON (1984). "Conditions for a Picture Superiority Effect on Consumer Memory," *Journal of Consumer Research,* 11, 643–654.

CHRIST, W. G., and N. J. MEDOFF (1984). "Affective State and Selective Exposure to and Use of Television," *Journal of Broadcasting,* 28, 51–63.

COHEN, B. C. (1963). *The Press and Foreign Policy.* Princeton, NJ: Princeton University Press.

COHEN, D. (1975). "A Report on a Non-Election Agenda-Setting Study," paper presented at the Association for Education in Journalism Conference, Ottawa, Ont., Canada.

COHEN, JOEL B. (1983). "Involvement and You: 1,000 Great Ideas," in R. P. Bagozzi and A. M. Tybout (Eds.), *Advances in Consumer Research,* Vol. 10. Ann Arbor, MI: Association for Consumer Research, 325–328.

COMSTOCK, GEORGE, STEVEN CHAFFEE, NATHAN KATZMAN, MAXWELL MCCOMBS, and DONALD ROBERTS (1978). *Television and Human Behavior.* New York: Columbia University Press.

COMSTOCK, GEORGE, and ELI RUBINSTEIN (1972). *Television and Social Behavior, Vol. III: Television and Adolescent Aggressiveness.* Washington, DC: U.S. Government Printing Office.

COOPER, EUNICE, and MARIE JAHODA (1947). "The Evasion of Propaganda: How Prejudiced People Respond to Anti-Prejudice Propaganda," *Journal of Psychology,* 23, 15–25.

CORDER-BOLZ, CHARLES R., and SHIRLEY O'BRYANT (1978). "Teacher vs. Program," *Journal of Communication,* 28 (Winter), 97–103.

CUMMING, ELAINE, and W. HENRY (1961). *Growing Old: The Process of Disengagement.* New York: Basic Books.

DAY, K. D. (1980). "The Effect of Music Differing in Excitatory Potential and Hedonic Valence on Provoked Aggression," unpublished doctoral dissertation, Indiana University, Bloomington, IN.

DEFLEUR, MELVIN, and L. DEFLEUR (1967). "The Relative Contribution of Television as a Learning Source of Children's Occupational Knowledge," *American Sociological Review,* 32, 777–789.

DEIGHTON, JOHN, DANIEL ROMER, and JOSH MC-QUEEN (1989). "Using Drama to Persuade," *Journal of Consumer Research,* 16 (3), 335–343.

DESHPANDE, ROHIT, WAYNE D. HOYER, and NAVEEN DONTHU (1986). "The Intensity of Ethnic Affiliation," *Journal of Consumer Research,* 13 (2), 155–173.

DERVIN, BRENDA (1980). "Communication Gaps and Inequities: Moving Toward a Reconceptualization," in B. Dervin and M. J. Voit (Eds.), *Progress in Communication Science VII.* Norwood, NJ: Ablex, 73–112.

DIMMICK, JOHN W., THOMAS A. MCCAIN, and W. THEODORE BOLTON (1979). "Media Use and the Life Span: Notes on Theory and Method," *American Behavioral Scientist,* 23, (September/October), 7–31.

DONNERSTEIN, E., and J. HALLAM (1978). "Facilitating Effects of Erotica on Aggression Against Women," *Journal of Personality and Social Psychology,* 36, 1270–1277.

DONOHUE, THOMAS, LUCY HENKE, and WILLIAM A. DONOHUE (1980). "Do Kids Know What TV Commercials Intend?" *Journal of Advertising Research,* 20 (5), 51–57.

DONOHUE, GEORGE, C. N. OLIEN, and PHILLIP J. TICHENOR (1987). "Media Access and Knowledge Gaps," *Critical Studies in Mass Communication,* 4, 87–92.

DONOHUE, GEORGE, P. J. TICHENOR, and C. N. OLIEN (1975). "Mass Media and the Knowledge Gap: A Hypothesis Reconsidered," *Communication Research,* 2, 3–23.

DOOB, ANTHONY, and GLEN MCDONALD (1979). "Television Viewing and Fear of Victimization: Is the Relationship Causal?" *Journal of Personality and Social Psychology,* 37, 170–179.

DORR, AIMEE (1986). *Television and Children: A Special Medium for a Special Audience.* Beverly Hills, CA: Sage.

DREW, DAN G., and THOMAS GRIMES (1987). "Audio-Visual Redundancy and TV News Recall," *Communication Research,* 14, 4 (August), 452–461.

DUNN, E. (1975). "Mexican-American Media Behavior: A Factor Analysis," *Journal of Broadcasting,* 19, 3–11.

EDELL, JULIE A. (1988). "Nonverbal Effects in Ads: A Review and Synthesis," in Sidney Hecker and David W. Stewart (Eds.), *Nonverbal Communication in Advertising.* Lexington, MA: Lexington Books, 11–28.

EDELL, JULIE A., and MARIAN C. BURKE (1987). "The Power of Feelings in Understanding Advertising Effects," *Journal of Consumer Research,* 14, 421–433.

ELLIOTT. P. (1974). "Uses and Gratifications Research: A Critique and a Sociological Alternative," in J. G. Blumler and E. Katz (Eds.), *The Uses of Mass Communications: Current Perspective on Gratifications Research.* Beverly Hills, CA: Sage.

ETTEMA, J. S., J. W. BROWN, and R. V. LUEPKER (1983). "Knowledge Gap Effects in a Health Information Campaign," *Public Opinion Quarterly,* 47, 516–527.

ETTEMA, J. S., and F. G. KLINE (1977). "Deficits, Differences, and Ceilings: Contingent Conditions for Understanding the Knowledge Gap," *Communication Research,* 4, 179–202.

FABER, RONALD (1978). "Decision Making on Television: A Content Analysis," unpublished manuscript, University of Wisconsin, Madison, WI.

FABER, RONALD J. (1983). "Exploring Evil and Other Functions: A Depth Analysis of the Uses and Gratifications of Soap Opera Viewing," unpublished manuscript, University of Texas, Austin, TX.

FABER, RONALD J., JANE D. BROWN, and JACK M. McLEOD (1979). "Coming of Age in the Global Village: Television and the Resolution of Adolescent Developmental Tasks," in E. Wartella (Ed.), *Children Communicating: Media and the Development of Thought, Speech and Understanding,* Beverly Hills, CA: Sage.

FABER, RONALD J., THOMAS C. O'GUINN, and JOHN A. McCARTY (1987). "Ethnicity, Acculturation and the Importance of Product Attributes," *Psychology and Marketing,* 4 (2), 121–134.

FABER, RONALD J., THOMAS C. O'GUINN, and TIMOTHY P. MEYER (1986). "Diversity in the Ethnic Media Audience: A Study of Spanish Language Broadcast Preference in the U.S.," *International Journal of Intercultural Relations,* 10, 347–359.

FABER, RONALD J., THOMAS C. O'GUINN, and L. J. SHRUM (1990). "Consumer Cultivation: Contrasting Direct and Indirect Experience," working paper, Urbana, IL: University of Illinois.

FAN, D. P. (1988). *Predictions of Public Opinion From the Mass Media.* Westport, CT: The Greenwood Press.

FAN, D. P., and A. R. TIMS (1989). "The Impact of the News Media on Public Opinion: American Presidential Elections," *International Journal of Public Opinion Research,* 1, 151–163.

FENIGSTEIN, A. (1979). "Does Aggression Cause a Preference for Viewing Media Violence?" *Journal of Personality and Social Psychology,* 37, 2307–2317.

FOLKES, VALERIE (1988). "The Availability Heuristic and Perceived Risk," *Journal of Consumer Research,* 15; 1 (June), 113–23.

FOX, STEPHEN, and WILLIAM PHILLBER (1978).

"Television Viewing and The Perception of Affluence," *Sociological Quarterly,* 19, 103–112.

FRIEDRICH, L., and A. STEIN (1975). "Prosocial Television and Young Children: The Effects of Verbal Labeling and Role Playing on Learning and Behavior," *Child Development,* 46, 27–38.

FUNKHOUSER, G. R. (1973). "The Issues of the Sixties: An Exploratory Study in the Dynamics of Public Opinion," *Public Opinion Quarterly,* 37, 62–75.

GALLOWAY, J. J., and MEEK, F. L. (1981). "Audience Uses and Gratifications: An Expectancy Model," *Communication Research,* 8, 435–450.

GAETH, GARY J., AND TIMOTHY B. HEATH (1987). "The Cognitive Processing of Misleading Advertising in Young and Old Adults," *Journal of Consumer Research,* 14, 1, 43–54.

GAZIANO, CECILE (1983). "The Knowledge Gap: An Analytical Review of Media Effects," *Communication Research,* 10, 41, 447–486.

GAZIANO, CECILE (1984). "Neighborhood Newspapers, Citizen Groups and Public Affairs Knowledge Gaps," *Journalism Quarterly,* 61, 556–566, 599.

GAZIANO, CECILE (1988). "Community Knowledge Gaps," *Critical Studies in Mass Communication,* 5 (September), 351–357.

GARRAMONE, GINA (1983). "Issue Versus Image Orientation and Effects of Political Advertising," *Communication Research,* 10, 59–76.

GERBNER, GEORGE, LARRY GROSS, MICHAEL ELLEY, MARILYN JACKSON-BEECK, SUZANNE JEFFRIES-FOX, and NANCY SIGNIORELLI (1977). "TV Violence Profile No. 8," *Journal of Communication,* Vol. 27, 171–180.

GERBNER, GEORGE, LARRY GROSS, MICHAEL ELLEY, MARILYN JACKSON-BEECK, SUZANNE JEFFRIES-FOX, and NANCY SIGNIORELLI (1978). Violence Profile No. 9, *Journal of Communication,* 28, 176–207.

GERBNER, GEORGE, LARRY GROSS, MICHAEL MORGAN, and NANCY SIGNIORELLI (1980a). "The 'Mainstreaming of America,'" Violence Profile No. 11, *Journal of Communication,* 30, 10–29.

GERBNER, GEORGE, LARRY GROSS, MICHAEL MORGAN, and NANCY SIGNIORELLI (1980b). "Aging with Television: Images on Television Drama and Conceptions of Social Reality," *Journal of Communication,* 30, 37–47.

GERBNER, GEORGE, LARRY GROSS, MICHAEL

MORGAN, and NANCY SIGNIORELLI (1980c). "Aging With Television: Images on Television Drama and Conceptions of Social Reality," Report to the Office of Human Development, Department of Health, Education and Welfare, Washington, DC.

GERBNER, GEORGE, LARRY GROSS, MICHAEL MORGAN, and NANCY SIGNIORELLI (1986). "Living with Television: The Dynamics of the Cultivation Process," in Jennings Bryant, and Dolf Zillmann (Eds.), *Perspectives on Media Effects.* Hillsdale, NJ: Erlbaum.

GINSBURG, HERBERT, and SYLVIA OPPER (1969). *Piaget's Theory of Intellectual Development.* Englewood Cliffs, NJ: Prentice-Hall.

GOLDBERG, MARVIN E., and GERALD J. GORN (1978). "Some Unintended Consequences of TV Advertising to Children," *Journal of Consumer Research,* 5 (June), 22–29.

GOLDBERG, MARVIN E., and GERALD J. GORN (1987). "Happy and Sad TV Programs: How They Affect Reactions to Commercials," *Journal of Consumer Research,* 14 (December), 387–403.

GOODHARDT, G. J., M. A. COLLINS, and A. S. C. EHRENBERG (1975). *The Television Audience: Patterns of Viewing.* Lexington, MA: D. C. Heath.

GORN, GERALD J. (1982). "The Effects of Music in Advertising on Choice Behavior: A Classical Conditioning Approach," *Journal of Marketing,* 46 (Winter), 94–101.

GRANEY, M. (1975). "Communication Uses and the Social Activity Constant," *Communication Research,* 2, 347–366.

GREENBERG, BRADLEY S. (1974). "Gratifications of Television Viewing and Their Correlates for British Children," in J. G. Blumler and E. Katz (Eds.), *The Uses of Mass Communications: Current Perspectives on Gratifications Research.* Beverly Hills: Sage.

GREENBERG, BRADLEY S. (1982). "Television and Role Socialization: An Overview," in D. Pearl, L. Bouthilet and J. Lazar, *Television and Behavior: Ten Years of Scientific Progress and Implications for the Eighties,* Vol. 2. Washington, DC: U.S. Government Printing Office.

GREER, D., A. C. HUSTON, R. L. WELCH, J. C. WRIGHT, and R. P. ROSS (1981, April). "Children's Comprehension of Television Forms with Masculine and Feminine Connotations," paper presented at biennial meeting, Society for Research in Child Development, Boston.

GREER, D., R. POTTS, J. C. WRIGHT, and A. HUSTON-STEIN (1982). "The Effects of Television Commercial Form and Commercial Placement on Children's Attention and Social Behavior," *Child Development,* 53, 611–619.

GREGORY, W. LARRY, ROBERT B. CIALDINI, and KATHLEEN M. CARPENTER (1982). "Self-Relevant Scenarios as Mediators of Likelihood Estimates and Compliance: Does Imagining Make It So?" *Journal of Personality and Social Psychology,* 43, 89–99.

GUEST, LESTER (1955). "Brand Loyalty—Twelve Years Later," *Journal of Applied Psychology,* 39, 405–408.

HAEFNER, MARGET J., and JAMES E. HAEFNER (1990). "Dyad Conversational Content While Viewing Television Commercials Imbedded in Programs, Working Paper, Urbana: University of Illinois.

HARRIS, RICHARD J. (1989). *Cognitive Psychology of Mass Communication.* Hillsdale, NJ: Erlbaum.

HAWKINS, ROBERT P., and SUZANNE PINGREE (1981). "Uniform Messages and Habitual Viewing: Unnecessary Assumptions in Social Reality Effects," *Human Communication Research,* 7, 4 (Summer), 291–301.

HAWKINS, ROBERT P., and SUZANNE PINGREE (1982). "Television's Influence on Social Reality," in D. Pearl, L. Bouthilet, and J. Lazar (Eds.), *Television and Behavior: Ten Years of Scientific Progress and Implications for the Eighties,* Technical Reports. Washington, DC: U.S. Government Printing Office, 224–247.

HENDERSON, L., and BRADLEY GREENBERG (1980). "Sex Typing of Common Behaviors on Television," in B. Greenberg (Ed.), *Life on Television.* Norwood, NJ: Ablex.

HERZOG, HERTA (1941). "On Borrowed Experience: An Analysis of Listening to Daytime Sketches," *Studies in Philosophy and Social Science,* 9, 65–95.

HIMMELWEIT, HILDE, and BETTY SWIFT (1976). "Continuities and Discontinuities in Media Usage and Taste: A Longitudinal Study," *Journal of Social Issues,* 32, 133–156.

HIRSH, PAUL (1980). "The 'Scary World' of the Nonviewer and Other Anomalies: A Re-Analysis of Gerbner et al.'s Findings of Cultivation Analysis," *Communication Research,* 7, 403–456.

HORNICK, ROBERT, M. GONZALES, and J. GOULD (1980, May). "Susceptibility to Media Effects," paper presented to the International Communication Association, Acapulco, Mexico.

HOVLAND, CARL I. (1959). "Reconciling Conflicting Results Derived from Experimental and Survey Studies of Attitude Change," *American Psychologist,* 14, 8–17.

HUSTON, A. C., J. C. WRIGHT, E. WARTELLA, M. L. RICE, B. A. WATKINS, T. CAMPBELL, and R. POTTS (1981). "Communicating More Than Content: Formal Features of Children's Television Programs," *Journal of Communication,* 31, 3, 32–48.

HUSTON-STEIN, A., S. FOX, D. GREER, B. A. WATKINS, and J. WHITAKER (1981). "The Effects of Action and Violence in Television Programs on the Social Behavior and Imaginative Play of Preschool Children," *Journal of Genetic Psychology,* 138, 183–191.

HYMAN, H., and P. SHEATSLEY (1947). "Some Reasons Why Information Campaigns Fail," *Public Opinion Quarterly,* 11, 412–423.

IYENGAR, SHANTO, and DONALD R. KINDER (1987). *News that Matters: Television and American Opinion.* Chicago: University of Chicago Press.

JANIS, I. (1980). "The Influence of Television on Personal Decision Making," in S. Whitney and R. Abels (Eds.), *Television and Social Behavior: Beyond Violence and Children.* Hillsdale, NJ: Erlbaum, 161–189.

JEFFRIES-FOX, SUZANNE, and NANCY SIGNIORELLI (1979). "Television and Children's Conceptions of Occupations," in Herbert S. Dordick (Ed.), *Proceedings of the Sixth Annual Telecommunications Policy Research Conference.* Lexington, MA: D. C. Heath.

JOHNSTONE, J. W. C. (1974). "Social Integration and Mass Media Use Among Adolescents: A Case Study," in J. G. Blumler and E. Katz (Eds.), *The Uses of Mass Communications: Current Perspectives on Gratifications Research.* Beverly Hills, CA: Sage.

KAHNEMAN, D., and AMOS TVERSKY (1982). *Judgment Under Uncertainty: Heuristic and Biases.* New York: Cambridge University Press.

KATZ, ELIHU (1959). "Mass Communication Research and the Study of Popular Culture: An Editorial Note on a Possible Future for the Journal," *Studies in Public Communication,* 2, 1–6.

KATZ, ELIHU, JAY G. BLUMLER, and MICHAEL GUREVITCH (1974). "Utilization of Mass Communication by the Individual," in Jay G. Blumler and Elihu Katz (Eds.), *The Uses of Mass Communication.* Beverly Hills, CA: Sage, 19–32.

KIM, Y. (1977). "Communication Patterns of Foreign Immigrants in the Process of Acculturation," *Human Communication Research,* 4, 66–77.

KISIELIUS, JOLITA, and BRIAN STERNTHAL (1986). "Examining the Vividness Controversy: An Availability-Valence Interpretation," *Journal of Consumer Research,* 12 (March), 418–431.

KLAPPER, JOSEPH T. (1960). *The Effects of Mass Communication.* New York: The Free Press.

KLINE, F. GERALD, PETER V. MILLER, and ANDREW J. MORRISON (1974). "Adolescent and Family Planning Information: An Exploration of Audience Needs and Media Effects," in J. G. Blumler and E. Katz (Eds.), *The Uses of Mass Communications: Current Perspectives on Gratifications Research.* Beverly Hills, CA: Sage.

KOHLBERG, LAWRENCE (1969). "Stage and Sequence: The Cognitive-Developmental Approach to Socialization," in D. A. Gostin (Ed.), *Handbook of Socialization Theory and Research.* Chicago: Rand McNally, 347–480.

KRUGMAN, HERBERT E. (1965). "The Impact of Television Advertising: Learning Without Involvement" *Public Opinion Quarterly,* 29, 349–356.

KRUGMAN, HERBERT E. (1966). "The Measurement of Advertising Involvement," *Public Opinion Quarterly,* 30 (4), 583–596.

KUNKEL, DALE (1988). "Children and Host-Selling Television Commercials," *Communication Research,* 15 (1), 71–101.

LANG, ANNIE (1987). "The Effects of the Formal Features of Television on Viewers' Attention and Arousal: Cardiac Response, Attention and Arousal." Unpublished doctoral dissertation, University of Wisconsin, Madison, WI.

LANG, ANNIE (1988). "Involuntary Attention and Physiological Arousal Evoked by Formal Features and Mild Emotion in TV Commercials," paper presented at the International Communication Association, New Orleans, LA.

LASSWELL, HAROLD W. (1927). *Propaganda Techniques in the World War.* New York: Peter Smith.

LAZERSFELD, PAUL, BERNARD BERELSON, and HAZEL GAUDET (1948). *The People's Choice.* New York: Columbia University Press.

LEARY, A., and A. C. HUSTON (1983, April). "The Influence of Television Production Features with Masculine and Feminine Features on Children's Comprehension and Play Behavior," paper presented at biennial meeting, Society for Research in Child Development. Detroit, MI.

LEE, WEI-NA (1988). *Becoming an American Consumer: A Cross-Cultural Study of Consumer Acculturation Among Taiwanese, Taiwanese in the U.S., and Americans,* unpublished doctoral dissertation, University of Illinois, Urbana, IL.

LEE, WEI-NA, and THOMAS C. O'GUINN (in preparation), "The Consumer Acculturation of Taiwanese Immigrants," University of Texas, Austin, TX.

LEIFER, AIMEE D., and GERALD S. LESSER (1976). *The Development of Career Awareness in Young Children.* Washington, DC: National Institute of Education.

LEVI, L. (1965). "The Urinary Output of Adrenalin and Noradrenalin During Pleasant and Unpleasant Emotional States: A Preliminary Report," *Psychosomatic Medicine,* 27, 80–85.

LEVIN, IRWIN P., and GARY J. GAETH (1988). "How Consumers Are Affected by the Framing of Attribute Information Before and After Consuming the Product," *Journal of Consumer Research,* 15 (December), 374–378.

LEVY, MARK R. (1989). *The VCR Age.* Newbury Park, CA: Sage.

LEVY, MARK R. (1978). "The Audience Experience with Television News," *Journalism Monographs,* 55.

LEVY, MARK R., and SVEN WINDAHL (1984). "Audience Activity and Gratifications: A Conceptual Clarification and Exploration," *Communication Research,* 11, 51–78.

LEVY, SIDNEY (1959). "Symbols for Sale," *Harvard Business Review,* 37, 117–124.

LICHTENSTEIN, SARAH, PAUL SLOVIC, BARUCH BISCHOFF, MARK LAYMAN, and BARBARA COOMBS (1978). "Judged Frequency of Lethal Events," *Journal of Experimental Psychology: Human Learning and Memory,* 6 (November), 551–578.

LIEBERT, ROBERT M. (1972). "Television and Social Learning: Some Relationships Between Viewing Violence and Behaving Aggressively," in G. Comstock and E. Rubinstein, *Television and Social Behavior, Vol. III: Television and Adolescent Aggressiveness.* Washington, DC: U.S. Government Printing Office, 1–42.

LINDLOFF, THOMAS R., MILTON J. SHATZER, and DANIEL WILKINSON (1988). "Accommodation of Video and Television in the American Family," in J. Lull (Ed.), *World Families Watch Television.* Newbury Park, CA: Sage.

LIPPMAN, W. (1922). *Public Opinion.* New York: Macmillan.

LOPEZ, R., and D. ENOS (1973). "Spanish-Language-Only Television in Los Angeles County," *Aztlan Chicano Journal of the Social Sciences and the Arts,* 4, 284–313.

LULL, JAMES (1988). "Constructing Rituals of Extension Through Family Television Viewing," in *World Families Watch Television.* Newbury Park, CA: Sage.

LULL, JAMES (1985). "The Naturalistic Study of Media Use and Youth Culture," in K. E. Rosengren, L. A. Wenner, and P. Palmgreen (Eds.), *Media Gratifications Research: Current Perspectives.* Beverly Hills, CA: Sage.

LULL, JAMES (1980). "The Social Uses of Television," *Human Communication Research,* 6, 197–209.

LUTZ, RICHARD J. (1975). "Changing Brand Attitudes through Modification of Cognitive Structure," *Journal of Consumer Research,* 1 (March), 49–59.

LUTZ, RICHARD J., SCOTT B. MACKENZIE, and GEORGE E. BELCH (1983). "Attitude Toward the Ad as a Mediator of Advertising Effectiveness," in *Proceedings of the 1983 Winter Educators' Conference.* Chicago: American Marketing Association, 70–75.

LUTZ, K. A., and RICHARD J. LUTZ (1977). "Effects of Interactive Imagery on Learning: Applications to Advertising," *Journal of Applied Psychology,* 62, 493–498.

MACKUEN, M. (1981). "Social Communication and the Mass Policy Agenda," in M. MacKuen and S. Coombs (Eds.), *More than News: Media Power in Public Affairs.* Beverly Hills, CA: Sage, 19–144.

MACKUEN, M., and S. COOMBS (1981). *More than News: Media Power in Public Affairs.* Beverly Hills, CA: Sage.

MACKLIN, M. CAROLE (1987). "Preschoolers' Understanding of the Informational Function of Television Advertising," *Journal of Consumer Research,* 14 (2), 229–239.

MASTERS, J. C., M. E. FORD, and R. A. AREND (1983). "Children's Strategies for Controlling Affective Responses to Aversive Social Experiences," *Motivation and Emotion,* 7, 103–116.

MCCLURE, R. D., and T. E. PATTERSON (1976). "Setting the Political Agenda: Print vs. Network News," *Journal of Communication,* 26, 23–28.

MCCARTY, JOHN A. (1989). "Current Theory and Research on Cross-cultural Factors in Consumer Behavior," in Thomas K. Srull (Ed.), *Advances in Consumer Research,* Vol. 16. Provo, UT: Association for Consumer Research, 127–129.

McCombs, M. E. (1981). "The Agenda-Setting Approach," in D. D. Nimmo and K. R. Sanders (Eds.), *Handbook of Political Communication.* Beverly Hills, CA: Sage, 121–140.

McCombs, M. E., and S. Gilbert (1986). "News Influence on Our Pictures of the World," in J. Bryant and D. Zillmann (Eds.), *Perspectives on Media Effects.* Hillsdale, NJ: Erlbaum, 303–324.

McCombs, M. E., and D. L. Shaw (1972). "The Agenda Setting Function of the Mass Media," *Public Opinion Quarterly, 36,* 176–187.

McCombs, M. E., and D. Weaver (1985). "Toward a Merger of Gratifications and Agenda-Setting Research," in K. E. Rosengren, A. Wenner, and P. Palmgreen (Eds.), *Media Gratifications Research: Current Perspectives.* Beverly Hills, CA: Sage.

McCracken, Grant (1986). "Culture and Consumption: A Theoretical Account of the Structure and Movement of the Cultural Meaning of Consumer Goods," *Journal of Consumer Research, 13,* 71–84.

McGhee, Paul E. (1980). "Toward the Integration of Entertainment and Educational Functions of Television: The Role of Humor," in P. H. Tannenbaum (Ed.), *The Entertainment Function of Television.* Hillsdale, NJ: Erlbaum.

McGill, Ann L., and Punam Anand (1989). "The Effect of Vivid Attributes on the Evaluation of Alternatives: The Role of Differential Attention and Cognitive Elaboration," *Journal of Consumer Research, 16, 2,* 188–196.

McGuire, William (1973). "Persuasion, Resistance, and Attitude Change," in I. de Sola Pool and W. Schramm (Eds.), *Handbook of Communication.* Chicago: Rand McNally, 216–252.

McLeod, Jack M., and Lee B. Becker (1974). "Testing the Validity of Gratification Measures Through Political Effects Analysis," in J. G. Blumler and E. Katz (Eds.), *The Uses of Mass Communications: Current Perspectives on Gratifications Research.* Beverly Hills, CA: Sage.

McLeod, Jack M., Lee B. Becker, and J. E. Byrnes (1974). "Another Look at the Agenda Setting Function of the Press," *Communication Research, 1,* 131–166.

McLeod, Jack M., and Steven R. Chaffee (1972). "The Construction of Social Reality," in James T. Tedeschi (Ed.), *The Social Influence Process.* Chicago: Aldine Atherton, 50–99.

McLeod, Jack M., William D. Luetscher, and

Daniel G. McDonald (1980). "Beyond Mere Exposure: Media Orientations and their Impact on Political Processes," paper presented at the Association for Education in Journalism Conference, Boston.

McLuhan, Marshall (1964). *Understanding Media: The Extensions of Man.* New York: McGraw-Hill.

McQuail, D., Jay G. Blumler, and J. R. Brown (1972). "The Television Audience: A Revised Perspective," in D. McQuail (Ed.), *Sociology of Mass Communications.* Middlesex, England: Penguin, 135–165.

Meadowcroft, Jeanne M. (1986). "Family Communication Patterns and Political Development: The Child's Role," *Communication Research, 13, 4* (October, 603–624.

Meadowcroft, J., and D. Zillmann (1987). "Women's Comedy Preferences During the Menstrual Cycle," *Communication Research, 14,* 204–218.

Messaris, Paul, and Dennis Kerr (1983). "Mothers' Comments About TV: Relation to Family Communication Patterns," *Communication Research, 10, 2* (April), 175–194.

Meyer, Manfred (Ed.) (1983). *Children and the Formal Features of Television: Approaches and Findings of Experimental and Formative Research.* New York: K. G. Saur.

Mick, David G. (1986). "Consumer Research and Semiotics: Exploring the Morphology of Signs, Symbols and Significance," *Journal of Consumer Research, 13,* 196–213.

Millar, M. G., and A. Tesser (1986). "Effects of Affective and Cognitive Focus on the Attitude Behavior Relation," *Journal of Personality and Social Psychology, 51,* 270–276.

Miller, M. Mark, and J. P. Quarles (1984). "Dramatic Television and Agenda Setting: The Case of *The Day After,*" paper presented to the Association for Education in Journalism and Mass Communication, Gainesville, FL.

Miller, M. Mark, and Byron Reeves (1976). "Dramatic TV Content and Children's Sex Role Stereotypes," *Journal of Broadcasting, 20,* 35–50.

Mock, J. R., and C. Larson (1939). *Words That Won the War.* Princeton, NJ: Princeton University Press.

Moore, D. W. (1987). "Political Campaigns and the Knowledge Gap Hypothesis," *Public Opinion Quarterly, 51,* 186–200.

Morgan, Michael (1980 "*Longitudinal Patterns of*

Television Viewing and Adolescent Role Socialization," unpublished doctoral dissertation, Annenberg School of Communication, University of Pennsylvania, Philadelphia, PA.

MOSCHIS, GEORGE P. (1987). *Consumer Socialization: A Life-Cycle Perspective.* Lexington, Mass: Lexington Books.

MOSCHIS, GEORGE P. (1985). "The Role of Family Communication in Consumer Socialization of Children and Adolescents," *Journal of Consumer Research,* 11 (4), 898–913.

MOSCHIS, GEORGE P. (1980). "Consumer Information Use: Individual versus Social Predictors," *Communication Research,* 7 (2), 139–160.

MOSCHIS, GEORGE P., and GILBERT A. CHURCHILL, JR. (1978). "Consumer Socialization: A Theoretical and Empirical Analysis," *Journal of Marketing Research,* 15 (November), 599–609.

MOSCHIS, GEORGE P., ROY MOORE, and RUTH SMITH (1984). "The Impact of Family Communication on Adolescent Consumer Socialization," in Thomas C. Kinnear (Ed.), *Advances in Consumer Research.* Provo, UT: Association for Consumer Research, 314–319.

MUNSTERBERG, HUGO (1915). *The Photoplay: A Psychological Study,* reprint (1970), New York: Dover.

NISBETT, RICHARD E., and LEE ROSS (1980). *Human Inference Strategies and Shortcomings of Social Judgment.* Englewood Cliffs, NJ: Prentice-Hall.

O'GUINN, THOMAS C., and RONALD J. FABER (1989). "Affect in Compulsive Buying," paper presented at the Association for Consumer Research Conference, New Orleans, LA.

O'GUINN, THOMAS C., RONALD J. FABER, and L. J. SHRUM (1990), "The Social Construction of Consumer Reality: A Cultivation Analysis, working paper," University of Illinois, Urbana, IL.

O'GUINN, THOMAS C. and TIMOTHY P. MEYER (1984). "Segmenting the Hispanic Market: The Use of Spanish-Language Radio," *Journal of Advertising Research,* 23, 9–16.

O'GUINN, THOMAS C., and L. J. SHRUM (1990, July). "Biases in Normative Consumer Beliefs Related to Television Exposure," paper presented at the International Association for Research in Economic Psychology, Exeter, England.

PAGE, B., R. SHAPIRO, and G. DEMPSEY (1987). "What Moves Public Opinion?" *American Political Science Review,* 81, 23–43.

PAISLEY, WILLIAM (1972). *"Communication Research as*

a Behavioral Discipline," unpublished manuscript, Stanford University, Institute for Communication Research, Palo Alto, CA.

PALMGREEN, P., and P. CLARKE (1977). "Agenda-Setting with Local and National Issues," *Communication Research,* 4, 435–452.

PALMGREEN, PHILIP, and J. D. RAYBURN (1982). "Gratifications Sought and Media Exposure: An Expectancy Value Model," *Communication Research,* 9, 561–580.

PALMGREEN, PHILIP, LAWRENCE A. WENNER, and KARL E. ROSENGREN (1985). "Uses and Gratifications Research: The Past Ten Years," in K. E. Rosengren, L. A. Wenner, and P. Palmgreen (Eds), *Media Gratifications Research: Current Perspectives.* Beverly Hills, CA: Sage.

PARK, C. WHAN, and S. MARK YOUNG (1986). "Consumer Response to Television Commercials: The Impact of Involvement and Background Music on Brand Attitude Formation," *Journal of Marketing Research,* 23, (February), 11–24.

PAVELCHAK, MARK A., JOHN H. ANTIL, and JAMES M. MUNCH (1988). "The Super Bowl: An Investigation into the Relationship Among Program Context, Emotional Experience, and Ad Recall," *Journal of Consumer Research,* 15 (3), 360–367.

PEARL, D., L. BOUTHILET, and J. LAZAR (EDS.) (1982). *Television and Behavior: Ten Years of Scientific Progress and Implications for the Eighties,* Vol. 1. Washington, DC: U.S. Government Printing Office.

PETTY, RICHARD, and JOHN T. CACIOPPO (1981). *Attitudes and Persuasion: Classic and Contemporary Approaches.* Dubuque, IA: William C. Brown.

PINGREE, SUZANNE, SANDRA STARRETT, and ROBERT HAWKINS (1979). "Soap Opera Viewers and Social Reality," unpublished manuscript, Women's Studies Program, University of Wisconsin, Madison, WI.

RADWAY, J. (1984). "Interpretive Communities and Variables Literacies: The Functions of Romance Reading," *Daedalus,* 113, 49–71.

RAY, MICHAEL L. (1973). "Marketing Communication and the Hierarchy-of-Effects," in P. Clarke (Ed.), *New Models for Mass Communication Research,* Beverly Hills, CA: Sage, 147–176.

RAYBURN, J. D., and PHILIP PALMGREEN (1984). "Merging Uses and Gratifications and Expectancy Value Theory," *Communication Research,* 11, 537–562.

REAL, M. R., N. ANDERSON, and M. HARRINGTON (1980). "Television Access for Older Adults," *Journal of Communication* 30 (Winter), 74–76.

REEVES, BYRON, ESTHER THORSON, MICHAEL ROTHSCHILD, DANIEL MCDONALD, J. HIRSCH, and R. GOLDSTEIN (1985). "Attention to Television: Intrastimulus Effects of Movement and Scene Changes on Alpha Variation Over Time," *International Journal of Neuroscience*, 25. Sweden, 241–255.

REEVES, BYRON, ESTHER THORSON, and JOAN SCHLUDER (1986). "Attention to Television: Psychological Theories and Chronometric Measures," in J. Bryant and D. Zillmann (Eds.), *Perspectives on Media Effects*. Hillsdale, NJ: Erlbaum, 303–324.

REIFLER, C. B., J. HOWARD, M. A. LIPTON, M. B. LIPTZIN, and D. E. WIDMANN (1971). "Pornography: An Experimental Study of Effects," *American Journal of Psychiatry*, 128, 575–582.

RICE, MABEL, ALTHEA HUSTON, and JOHN C. WRIGHT (1983). "The Forms of Television: Effects of Children's Attention, Comprehension, and Social Behavior," in Manfed Meyer (Ed.), *Children and the Formal Features of Television*. New York: K. G. Saur, 21–55.

RIESMAN, DAVID, and H. ROSEBOROUGH (1955). "Careers and Consumer Behavior," in L. Clark (Ed.), *Consumer Behavior Vol. II: The Life Cycle and Consumer Behavior*. New York: New York University Press.

ROBERTS, DONALD F., and CHRISTINE M. BACHEN (1981). "Mass Communication Effects," *Annual Review of Psychology*, 32, 307–356.

ROBERTSON, THOMAS (1980). "Television Advertising and Parent-Child Relations," in Adler, Ricard P., Gerald S. Lesser, Laurene Krasny Meringoff, Thomas S. Robertson, John Rossiter, and Scott Ward (1980). *The Effects of Television Advertising on Children*. Lexington, MA: Lexington.

ROBERTSON, THOMAS S., and JOHN R. ROSSITER (1974). "Children and Commercial Persuasion: An Attribution Theory Analysis," *Journal of Consumer Research*, 1, 13–20.

ROBERTSON, THOMAS S., SCOTT WARD, HUBERT GATIGNON, and DONNA KLEES (1989). "Advertising and Children: A Cross-Cultural Study," *Communication Research*, 16, 4 (August), 459–485.

ROE, K. (1983). "The Influence of Video Technology in Adolescence." Media Panel Report 27, Vaxjo University College and Lund University.

ROEDDER-JOHN, DEBORAH, and CATHERINE COLE (1986). "Age Differences in Information Processing: Understanding Deficits in Young and Elderly Consumers" *Journal of Consumer Research*, 13 (3), 297–315.

ROEDDER-JOHN, DEBORAH, and JOHN C. WHITNEY, JR. (1986). "The Development of Consumer Knowledge in Children: A Cognitive Structure Approach," *Journal of Consumer Research*, 12 (4), 406–417.

ROLANDELLI, D. R., J. C. WRIGHT, and A. C. HUSTON (1982, April). "Auditory Attention to Television" A New Research Methodology," paper presented at Biennial Meeting, Southwest Society for Research in Human Development, Galveston, TX.

ROSENGREN, KARL E. (1974). "Uses and Gratifications: A Paradigm Outline," in J. G. Blumler and Elihu Katz (Eds.), *Uses of Mass Communications: Current Perspective on Gratifications Research*. Beverly Hills, CA: Sage, 269–286.

ROSENGREN, KARL E., and SVEN WINDAHL (1977). "Mass Media Uses: Cause and Effects," *Communications: International Journal of Communication Research*, 3, 336–351.

ROTHSCHILD, MICHAEL, ESTHER THORSON, BYRON REEVES, JUDITH E. HIRSCH, and ROBERT GOLDSTEINE (1986). "EEG Activity and the Processing of Television Commercials," *Communication Research*, 13 (2), 182–220.

RUBIN, ALAN M. (1985). "Uses, Gratifications, and Media Effects Research," in J. Bryant and D. Zillmann (Eds.), *Perspectives on Media Effects*. Hillsdale, NJ: Erlbaum.

RUBIN, ALAN M. (1981). "An Examination of Television Viewing Motives," *Communication Research*, 8, 141–165.

RUBIN, ALAN M., and ELIZABETH M. PERSE (1987). "Audience Activity and Television News Gratifications," *Communication Research*, 14, 58–84.

RUBIN, ALAN M., and REBECCA B. RUBIN (1982). "Contextual Age and Television Use," *Human Communication Research*, 8, 228–244.

RUBIN, ALAN M., ELIZABETH M. PERSE and DONALD S. TAYLOR (1988), "A Methodological Examination of Cultivation," *Communication Research*, 15:2, 107–134.

SALOMAN, GAVRIEL (1979). *Interaction of Media, Cognition and Learning*. San Francisco: Jossey Bass.

SANBONMATSU, DAVID M., and FRANK R. KARDES (1988). "The Effect of Physiological Arousal on Information Processing and Persuasion," *Journal of Consumer Research*, 15 (3), 379–395.

SCHACTER, STANLEY, and JEROME E. SINGER (1962). "Cognitive, Social and Psychological Determinents of Emotional State," *Psychological Review*, 69, 379–399.

SCHRAMM, WILBUR (1967). "Human Communication as a Field of Behavioral Science," unpublished manuscript, Stanford University, Institute for Communication Research, Palo Alto, CA.

SEVERIN, WERNER J., and JAMES W. TANKARD (1979). *Communication Theories*. New York: Hastings House.

SHANTEAU, JAMES (1988). "Consumer Impression Formation: The Integration of Visual and Verbal Information," in Sidney Becker and David W. Stewart (Eds.), *Nonverbal Communication in Advertising*. Lexington, MA: Lexington Books, 43–58.

SHAVITT, SHARON (1989). "Operationalizing Functional Theories of Attitude," in A. Pratkanis, R. Anthony, Steven J. Breckler, and A. G. Greenwald, (Eds.), *Attitude Structure and Function*. Hillsdale, NJ: Erlbaum, 311–337.

SHAVITT, SHARON, and RUSSELL H. FAZIO (1990). "Effects of Attribute Salience on the Consistency of Product Evaluations and Purchase Predictions," in M. Goldberg, G. Gorn, and R. Pollay (Eds.), *Advances in Consumer Research*, Vol. 17. Provo, UT: Association for Consumer Research.

SHAW, D. L., and M. E. McCOMBS (1977). *"The Emergence of American Political Issues,"* St. Paul, MN: West Publishing.

SHERMAN, STEVEN J., ROBERT B. CIALDINI, DONNA F. SCHWARTZMAN, and KIM D. REYNOLDS (1985). *Personality and Social Psychology Bulletin*, 11:1 (March), 118–127.

SHILS, EDWARD A., and MORRIS JANOWITZ (1948). "Cohesion and Disintegration in the Wehrmacht," *Public Opinion Quarterly*, 12, 300–306; 308–315.

SHRUM, L. J., THOMAS C. O'GUINN, and RONALD J. FABER (1990, June). "Television and the Social Reality of Consumption," paper presented at International Communication Association, Dublin, Ireland.

SINGER, JEROME L., and DOROTHY G. SINGER (1981). *Television, Imagination and Aggression: A Study of Preschoolers*. Hillsdale, NJ: Erlbaum.

SINGH, SURENDRA N., and GILBERT A. CHURCHILL (1987). "Arousal and Advertising Effectiveness," *Journal of Advertising*, 16 (1), 4–10.

SMITH, RUTH BELK, and GEORGE P. MOSCHIS (1985). "Consumer Socialization of the Elderly: An Exploratory Study," in Thomas C. Kinnear (Ed.), *Advances in Consumer Research*. Ann Arbor, MI: Association for Consumer Research, 548–552.

SMITH, RUTH BELK, GEORGE P. MOSCHIS, and ROY L. MOORE (1985). "Some Advertising Influences on the Elderly Consumer: Implications for Theoretical Considerations," *Current Issues and Research in Advertising*. Ann Arbor, MI: University of Michigan.

SMITH, RUTH BELK, GEORGE P. MOSCHIS, and ROY L. MOORE (1986). "Social Effects of Advertising and Personal Communications on the Elderly Consumer," in J. M. Sheth (Ed.), *Research in Marketing*. Greenwich, CT: JAI Press.

SOLOMON, DOUGLAS S. (1982). "Health Campaigns on Television," in D. Pearl, L. Bouthilet, and J. Lazar (Eds.), *Television and Behavior: Ten Years of Scientific Progress and Implications for the Eighties*, Vol. 2. Washington, DC: U.S. Government Printing Office, 308–321.

SPEISMAN, J. C., R. S. LAZARUS, A. MORDKOFF, and L. DAVISON (1964). "Experimental Reduction of Stress Based on Ego Defense Theory," *Journal of Abnormal and Social Psychology*, 68, 367–380.

SPITZER, S. P., and NORMAN K. DENZIN (1965). "Levels of Knowledge in Emergent Crisis," *Social Forces*, 44, 234–237.

SRULL, THOMAS K. (1983). "Affect and Memory: The Impact of Affective Reactions in Advertising on the Representation of Product Information in Memory," in Richard P. Bagozzi and Alice M. Tybout (Eds.), *Advances in Consumer Research*. Provo, UT: Association for Consumer Research, 520–525.

SRULL, THOMAS K., and ROBERT S. WYER (1979). "The Role of Category Accessibility in the Interpretation of Information About Persons: Some Determinants and Implications," *Journal of Person-*

ality and Social Psychology, 37 (October), 1660–1672.

SRULL, THOMAS K., and ROBERT S. WYER (1980). "Category Accessibility and Social Perception: Some Implications for the Study of Person Memory and Interpersonal Judgments," *Journal of Personality and Social Psychology,* 38 (June), 841–856.

STONE, G. C., and M. E. McCOMBS (1981). "Tracing the Time Lag in Agenda-Setting," *Journalism Quarterly,* 58, 51–55.

STORMS, M. D. (1973). "Videotape and the Attribution Process: Reversing Actors' and Observers' Points of View," *Journal of Personality and Social Psychology,* 27, 165–175.

SUCHMAN, E. (1942). "An Invitation to Music," in Paul F. Lazersfeld and Frank N. Stanton (Eds.), *Radio Research—1941.* New York: Duell, Sloan & Pearce.

SWANSON, D. L. (1979). "The Continuing Evolution of the Uses and Gratifications Approach," *Communication Research,* 6, 3–7.

SWANSON, D. L. (1978). "The Uses and Gratifications Approach to Mass Communication Research: An Assessment and Proposal," paper presented at the International Communication Association Conference, Chicago.

THORSON, ESTHER, and ANNIE LANG (1988, May). "The Effects of Videographic Complexity on Memory for Television Information," paper presented to the International Communication Association, New Orleans, LA.

THORSON, ESTHER, and R. SNYDER (1984). "Viewer Recall of Television Commercials: Prediction from the Propositional Structure of Commercial Scripts," *Journal of Marketing Research,* 21, 127–136.

TICHENOR, P. J., GEORGE A. DONOHUE, and C. N. OLIEN (1970). "Mass Media Flow and Differential Growth of Knowledge," in P. Clarke (Ed.), *New Models for Mass Communication Research,* Beverly Hills, CA: Sage, 45–80.

TICHENOR, P. J., GEORGE A. DONOHUE, and C. N. OLIEN (1980). *Community Conflict and the Press,* Beverly Hills, CA: Sage.

TIMS, ALBERT R. (1986). "Family Political Communication and Social Values," *Communication Research,* 13, 1 (January), 5–17.

TIMS, A. R., D. P. FAN, and J. R. FREEMAN (1989). "The Cultivation of Consumer Confidence: A Longitudinal Analysis of News Media Influence on Consumer Sentiment," in T. Srull (Ed.), *Advances in Consumer Research.* Provo, UT: Association for Consumer Research.

TIMS, ALBERT R., JACOB J. WAKSHLAG, MARY C. BROIHIER, and CARMEN MANNING-MILLER (1986). "Sensation Seeking, Entertainment and Television Program Preferences," paper presented at the International Communication Association Conference, Chicago.

TIPTON, L. P., R. D. HANEY, and J. B. BASEHEART (1975). "Media Agenda-Setting in City and State Election Campaigns," *Journalism Quarterly,* 52, 15–22.

TOWER, R. B., D. G. SINGER, J. L. SINGER, and H. BIGGS (1979). "Differential Effects of Television Programming on Preschoolers' Cognition, Imagination and Social Play," *American Journal of Orthopsychiatry,* 49, 265–281.

TVERSKY, AMOS, and D. KAHNEMAN (1973). "Availability: A Heuristic for Judging Frequency and Probability," *Cognitive Psychology,* 5 (September), 207–232.

TYLER, TOM R. (1980). "Impact of Directly and Indirectly Experienced Events: The Origin of Crime-Related Judgments and Behaviors," *Journal of Personality and Social Psychology,* 39, 1, 13–28.

TYLER, TOM R. (1984). "Assessing the Risk of Crime Victimization: The Integration of Personal Victimization Experience and Socially Transmitted Information," *Journal of Social Issues,* 40, 1, 27–38.

TYLER, TOM R., and FAY LOMAX COOK (1984). "The Mass Media and Judgments of Risk: Distinguishing Impact on Personal and Societal Level Judgments," *Journal of Personality and Social Psychology,* 47, 4, 693–708.

VOLGY, THOMAS, and JOHN SCHWARZ (1980). "Television Entertainment Programming and Sociopolitical Attitudes," *Journalism Quarterly,* 57, 150–155.

WAKSHLAG, J., V. VIAL, and R. TAMBORINI (1983). "Selecting Crime Drama and Apprehension About Crime" *Human Communication Research,* 10, 227–242.

WALKER, W., and M. VON GOTTEN (1989). "Explaining Related Recall Outcomes: New Answers from a Better Model," *Journal of Advertising Research,* 29, 11–21.

WALLENDORF, MELANIE, and MICHAEL D. REILLY (1983). "Ethnic Migration, Assimilation and Consumption," *Journal of Consumer Research,* 10 (December), 293–302.

WARD, SCOTT (1974). "Consumer Socialization," *Journal of Consumer Research*, 1, 1–13.

WARD, SCOTT (1980). "The Effect of Television Advertising on Consumer Socialization," in Richard P. Adler, Gerald S. Lesser, Laurene Krasny Meringoff, Thomas S. Robertson, John Rossiter, and Scott Ward (Eds.), *The Effects of Television Advertising on Children*. Lexington, MA: Lexington Books.

WARD, SCOTT (1987). "Consumer Behavior," in Charles R. Berger and Steven H. Chaffee (Eds.), *Handbook of Communication Science*. Beverly Hills, CA: Sage.

WARD, SCOTT, and DANIEL WACKMAN (1973). "Children's Information Processing of Television Advertising," in P. Clarke (Ed.), *New Models for Mass Communication Research*. Beverly Hills, CA: Sage, 119–146.

WARD, SCOTT, DANIEL WACKMAN, and ELLEN WARTELLA (1977). *How Children Learn to Buy: The Development of Consumer Information Processing Skills*. Beverly Hills, CA: Sage.

WAY, WENDY (1982). "The Consumer Content of Prime-Time Television: Implications for Consumer Educators," paper presented to the American Council on Consumer Interests, Washington, D.C. (April).

WEAVER, D. (1982). "Media Agenda-Setting and Media Manipulation," in D. C. Whitney, E. Wartella, and S. Windahl (Eds.), *Mass Communication Review Yearbook*, Vol. 3. Beverly Hills, CA: Sage, 537–554.

WEAVER, D., D. GRABER, M. E. McCOMBS, and C. EYAL (1981). *Media Agenda-Setting in a Presidential Election: Issues, Images, Interest*. New York: Praeger.

WEIMANN, GABRIEL (1984). "Images of Life in America: The Impact of American T.V. in Israel," *International Journal of Intercultural Relations*, 8, 185–197.

WELLS, WILLIAM D. (1988). "Lectures and Dramas," in Pat Cafferata and Alice Tybout (Eds.), *Cognitive and Affective Responses to Advertising*. Lexington, MA: D. C. Heath.

WILSON, T. D., and DUNN, D. S. (1986). "Effects of Introspection on Attitude-Behavior Consistency: Analyzing Reasons versus Focusing on Feelings," *Journal of Experimental Social Psychology*, 47, 5–16.

WINDAHL, SVEN (1981). "Uses and Gratifications at the Crossroads," in G. C. Wilhoit and H. de Bock (Eds.), *Mass Communication Review Yearbook*. Beverly Hills, CA: Sage.

WINTER, J. P., and C. EYAL (1981). "Agenda-Setting for the Civil Rights Issue," *Public Opinion Quarterly*, 46, 376–383.

WOLFE, K. M., and M. FISKE (1949). "Why Children Read Comics," in Paul F. Lazersfeld and Frank N. Stanton (Eds.), *Communication Research, 1948–1949*. New York: Harper and Row.

WYER, ROBERT S., and THOMAS K. SRULL (1989). *Memory and Cognition in Its Social Context*. Hillsdale, NJ: Erlbaum.

ZAICHKOWSKY, JUDITH L. (1986). "Conceptualizing Involvement," *Journal of Advertising*, 15 (2), 4–14.

ZILLMANN, DOLF (1971). "Excitation Transfer in Communication-Mediated Aggressive Behavior," *Journal of Experimental Social Psychology*, 7, 419–434.

ZILLMANN, D. (1979). *Hostility and Aggression*. Hillsdale, NJ: Erlbaum.

ZILLMANN, D. (1980). "Anatomy of Suspense," in P. H. Tannenbaum (Ed.), *The Entertainment Function of Television*. Hillsdale, NJ: Erlbaum, 133–163.

ZILLMANN, D. (1982). "Television Viewing and Arousal," in D. Pearl, L. Bouthilet, and J. Lazar (Eds.), *Television and Behavior: Ten Years of Scientific Progress and Implications for the Eighties, Vol. 2*, Washington, DC: U.S. Government Printing Press, 53–67.

ZILLMANN, D. (1985). "The Experimental Exploration of Gratifications from Media Entertainment," in K. E. Rosengren, L. A. Wenner, and P. Palmgreen (Eds.), *Media Gratifications Research: Current Perspectives*. Beverly Hills, CA: Sage, 225–239.

ZILLMANN, D., and J. BRYANT (1985). "Affect, Mood and Emotion as Determinants of Selective Exposure," in D. Zillmann and J. Bryant (Eds.), *Selective Exposure to Communication*. Hillsdale, NJ: Erlbaum, 157–190.

ZILLMANN, D., and J. BRYANT (1986). "Exploring the Entertainment Experience," in J. Bryant and D. Zillmann (Eds.), *Perspectives on Media Effects*. Hillsdale, NJ: Erlbaum, 303–324.

ZILLMANN, D., J. BRYANT, P. W. COMISKY, and N. J. MEDOFF (1981). "Excitation and Hedonic Valence in the Effect of Erotica on Motivated Intermale Aggression," *European Journal of Social Psychology*, 11, 233–252.

ZILLMANN, DOLF, R. HEZEL, and N. MEDOFF (1980). "The Effects of Affective States on Selective Exposure to Television Entertainment," *Journal of Applied Social Psychology,* 10, 323–339.

ZILLMANN, D., J. HOYT, and K. D. DAY (1974). "Strength and Duration of the Effect of Aggressive, Violent and Erotic Communication on Subsequent Aggressive Behavior," *Communication Research,* 1, 286–306.

ZILLMANN, D., and R. C. JOHNSON (1973). "Motivated Aggressiveness Perpetuated by Exposure to Aggressive Films and Reduced by Exposure to Nonaggressive Films," *Journal of Research in Personality,* 7, 261–276.

ZILLMANN, D., and B. S. SAPOLSKY (1977). "What Mediates the Effect of Mild Erotica on Annoyance and Hostile Behavior in Males?" *Journal of Personality and Social Psychology,* 35, 587–596.

ZUCKER, H. G. (1978). "The Variable Nature of News Media Influence," in B. D. Ruben (Ed.), *Communication Yearbook 2,* New Brunswick, NJ: Transaction Books.

ZUCKERMAN, M. (1979). *Sensation Seeking: Beyond the Optimal Level of Arousal.* Hillsdale, NJ: Erlbaum.

THE FORMATION AND USE
OF EXPECTATIONS IN CONSUMER
DECISION MAKING

11

W. Fred van Raaij
Erasmus University

In this chapter the literature on the formation, revision, and retrieval of expectations is reviewed. Expectations are formed as an outcome of the cognitive processes of inference, attribution, and cue combination. Expectations are revised through extrapolation and the use of new information. Expectations are retrieved as an input for the processes of (dis)confirmation and (dis)satisfaction. Expectations play a crucial role in the (generic) decision to spend or to save, and in the (specific) choice between alternatives with uncertain outcomes. In this chapter, economic psychology and consumer behavior are both used as perspectives.

INTRODUCTION

Expectations

Expectations play a crucial role in many economic decisions: in the business decision to invest, in the consumer generic decision to spend or to save, and in the consumer specific decision on which brand or type of product to buy. Economic decisions are often made under conditions of uncertainty about future income, prices, interest rates, inflation, and economic and political conditions. What can we expect from a product in terms of performance, durability, and dependability? What service should one expect at a restaurant or at an automobile dealership? Information processing about the likelihood of future events and the formation and revision of expectations helps guide decision making and behavior. Although both investors and consumers try to reduce uncertainties about the future, they will never be absolutely certain whether or not they made the right decision and spent their money in the optimal way.

Expectations refer to the future. People are

interested to know the consequences of their behavior. They form expectations about product performance and are dissatisfied if these expectations are not confirmed. Expectations also refer to the present. A doctor, observing the patient's symptoms, expects a certain illness. Thus, one may form expectations about the present conditions based on observable cues. Oliver and Winer (1987) provide an overview of the formation and structure of consumer expectations.

According to the psychologist Tolman (1932), people learn "expectations," that is, beliefs that a given response will be followed by some event. These events can be either positive or negative reinforcers. Thus, people learn to perform behaviors that are positively reinforced. Tolman's expectations are part of a theory of learning that is called operant conditioning. It is an example of *intentional expectations,* that is, expectations that are at least partially under one's own control. Goal setting, aspirations, and plans are activities that are expected to lead to certain outcomes. These outcomes are at least partly dependent on one's own performance.

Contingent expectations refer to future contingencies over which a person has no control. Expectations about inflation, unemployment, interest rates, and earthquakes are contingent. One cannot change these events by one's own efforts as an individual. One should thus adapt to these expectations.

From the approach of Tolman and others, expectancy-value theory has been developed. The best known expectancy-value models are the subjective expected utility (SEU) model of behavioral decision theory (Edwards 1954), and the attitude models of Rosenberg (1956) and Fishbein and Ajzen (1975).

The economist Shackle (1952, p. 2) perceives the formation of an expectation as an act of creating imaginary situations, associating them with future dates, and assigning scaled measures indicating the degree of belief that these situations will become true. From a social science perspective Georgescu-Roegen (1958, p. 12) defines an *expectation* as "the state of mind of an individual with respect to an assertion, a

coming event, or any other matter on which absolute knowledge does not necessarily exist."

The organizational behavior researcher Vroom (1964, p. 17) defines an *expectancy* as "a momentary belief concerning the likelihood that a particular act will be followed by a particular outcome." Vroom connects expectancies to outcomes of acts. In the expectancy-value tradition, an expectancy is a perceived probability that a certain outcome will occur.

Note that in the previous definitions the term *expectation* is distinguished from *expectancy.* Newcomb (1972) notes that the term *expectancy* emphasizes a psychological state, some sort of preparatory adjustment to anticipated events or situations. The term *expectation* commonly refers to the content of what is expected. In Newcomb's terminology, the term *expectancy* in the expectancy-value model should be *expectation.* However, most authors do not make this distinction and use these terms interchangeably. The term *expectation* will be used in this chapter.

Expectations are also used by some authors in referring to social norms of behavior and the roles of others. These expectations have no temporal and no obvious economic dimension. We will not discuss this type of expectations in this chapter.

Thus, in the previous definitions the fundamental aspects of an expectation are *uncertainty,* either risk or ambiguity, and a *temporal dimension,* that is, uncertainty about future events or situations. An expectation is often stated as a probability of a future event or as a confidence interval in which the value of a future event will lie.

Risk and Uncertainty

Einhorn and Hogarth (1985) distinguish risk and uncertainty. Under *risk,* the probability distribution of an outcome is known. The basic risk paradigm (MacCrimmon and Wehrung 1987) is the choice between a sure outcome and a risky outcome, not knowing what is going to occur. Under *ambiguity,* the probability distribution is unknown; one may only exclude some probability or attach some probability to probability distributions. Ambiguity is thus a "second-order" uncertainty. In the extreme case of ignorance, no probability distributions can be excluded and all outcomes are still possible.

Within the *uncertainty* dimension, Einhorn and Hogarth (1985) propose five components:

1. the expected attribute or product outcome level
2. its probability of occurrence,
3. the certainty/uncertainty with which this probability is held (ambiguity),
4. the unknown attribute or outcome levels not anticipated, and
5. the ambiguity surrounding unanticipated levels.

Expectations have a cognitive and an affective dimension. The emphasis in research is on the cognitive component, although people attach affective meanings to their cognitions. People tend to overestimate the probability of favorable outcomes and to underestimate the probability of unfavorable ones, at least when they are in a happy mood (Johnson and Tversky 1983). The reverse may be true if a person is in a sad mood. Then the probability of favorable outcomes is underestimated, whereas the probability of unfavorable outcomes tend to be overestimated. This should be investigated. On the one hand, people in a sad mood tend to adapt their expectations to become consistent with reality. On the other hand, people prefer a happy mood and try to change their mood in a positive direction, especially after observing that a mood change is possible (Pieters and van Raaij 1988).

The interaction between expectation and affect may have two directions. A positive affect leads to more optimistic expectations. Favorable expectations, in turn, may be accompanied by positive affect (and thus become even more favorable).

We now proceed with the discussion of the formation of expectations, the revision of expectations when new information becomes known, and the retrieval (decoding) of expectations. We examine the action consequences of expectations such as satisfaction or dissatisfaction.

THE FORMATION OF EXPECTATIONS

Introduction

Tolman (1932) was one of the first psychologists to study expectations. His concept of expectations refers to beliefs that behaviors will be followed by positively or negatively valenced events. The sources of expectations are memories of actual experiences, perceptions of current stimuli, inferences drawn from related experiences (such as the trial of other objects), and information from others. Tolman, in the prewar period, did not mention the mass media (advertising) as a source of information. These expectations are formed by trial-and-error learning over time. In fact, expectations are constantly constructed for what should come next. In our perceptions, we are continually constructing, testing, and revising hypotheses about what is being perceived and what may be expected. Such a system is very efficient: If events are proceeding in accordance with our expectations, only limited information processing needs to be carried out. If the expectations are disconfirmed, more information processing is needed in order to revise our expectations.

Katona (1975), studying aggregate consumer expectations, distinguished two forms of learning (pp. 147–149): learning by memorizing (repetition), and learning by problem solving and understanding. Sources of information are personal experiences, the experiences of others, and the mass media. Some expectations are learned by repetition and reinforcement, and are extrapolated from the past. The "psychological field" remains relatively stable under these conditions. Problem solving, on the other hand, results in understanding and insights into the relationships of factors. As a consequence, we may arrive at expectations that are not simply extrapolations from the past. The "psychological field" may then be reconstructed. An example of this is the perception of inflation. If inflationary expectations were formed in no other way than by repetition, their strength would depend on the frequency of past experiences. The longer an inflationary period lasted, the greater would be the expected price increase. Under problem-solving conditions, external factors, such as the outbreak of a war, can make people think about the possible consequences, and thus raise their inflationary expectations. Consumers might be erroneous in their causal thinking, but if many consumers believe a situation to be a certain way, it influences the levels of sales and savings. In the extreme case, expectations may be self-fulfilling. If a prediction of a recession is widely publicized and induces consumers to postpone their purchases, the result can be that the prediction will become true.

Katona (1975) indicated the importance of mass media in the formation of expectations. Pruitt, Reilly, and Hoffer (1988) investigated the effect of media presentation on the formation of economic presentations. In their study, the *Washington Post* presentation resulted in more accurate expectations regarding short-term future unemployment than did the presentations of CBS television and the *Wall Street Journal*. The authors provided an explanation of this difference based on the length and the ambiguity of the latter's reports. Not only the facts as such, but also the presentation format or framing (Kahneman and Tversky 1979) affects the formation of accurate expectations.

In attitude theory (Fishbein and Ajzen 1975) "belief" is a central concept. In the history of attitude theory, *beliefs* related first to the attributes of objects, later to the attributes of acts with regard to the object, and more recently to the consequences of behavior with regard to the object. Attitude theory has developed from an ontological into a teleological perspective, and it has returned, in fact, to Tolman's (1932) original conceptualization. People engage in behavior expecting positive and negative consequences of their actions. For each action a "balance sheet" with positive and negative consequences could be developed. Actions with a higher expected profit are preferred over actions with lower profit and over actions with a loss. Conclusions from the "balance sheet" are formed with a linear-compensatory rule.

Several types of beliefs, and thus expecta-

tions, exist. Fishbein and Ajzen (1975) distinguish descriptive, informational, and inferential beliefs. *Descriptive beliefs* result from direct experience with the object. These beliefs are often held with much certainty and do predict behavior relatively well (Fazio and Zanna 1981). Consumers having experience with a product know what to expect of it. The process of forming descriptive beliefs is a form of associative or verbal learning; that is, it is a process of forming stimulus-response bonds.

Beliefs formed by accepting the information provided by outside sources (e.g., the mass media) are termed *informational beliefs*. The degree of certainty with which an informational belief is held depends on source characteristics, such as the reliability, expertise, and power of the information source. Information sources can be categorized as social (parents, peers, friends), commercial (salespersons, advertising), or neutral (newspapers, magazines, government reports, consumer organizations). Advertising for new products purposefully attempts to create favorable informational beliefs (expectations) among consumers.

Beliefs that go beyond direct experience and information from others and from the mass media are called *inferential beliefs*. Some reasoning, knowledge of relations, and information processing is needed to form an inferential belief. For instance, consumers may expect a high quality product, knowing the high price or the brand name of the product. The process of forming inferential beliefs is a reasoning process, using such processes as causal attribution, cue utilization, and logical reasoning. Allison and Uhl (1964) found that consumers, knowing the brand name of a beer, had different perceptions of the taste than consumers tasting unbranded beers. Thus, just knowing the brand name leads to different taste perceptions.

Several ways exist to form beliefs (expectations) about the consequences of behavior and about present and future events. The main processes of expectation formation are the processes of causal attribution, cue utilization, and heuristics.

Causal Attribution

In an attribution process a person tries to find the most likely cause of an event or a behavior, mainly by excluding less likely causes. Classes of causes are the person or the agent (internal attribution), the object or target (external attribution), or the situation or contingency (circumstantial attribution). With several measures over time, the covariation principle (with the criteria being distinctiveness, consistency, and consensus) guides the person to infer the most likely cause (McArthur 1972; van Raaij 1987). High distinctiveness means that the effect occurs only with one particular target and not with other targets. High consistency is the repetition of the same effect over time. High consensus is the same causal attribution made by other observers.

The causal attribution effects are summarized in Table 11.1

With multiple measures from a single observation, the configuration principle helps to find the most plausible cause of the event or the behavior (van Raaij, 1987). Generally, internal and external causes are distinguished. Internal causes are the volitional disposition or attitude of the agent (intentional expectations). External causes pertain to pressure or force applied to the agent by others or by the situation (contingent expectations).

Jones and Davis (1965) distinguish internal versus external attributions. With an internal attribution one infers an intrinsic motivation ("intention") of the person, for example, a salesperson, to tell his or her real opinion. The

person can then be trusted. With an external attribution to the situation or convention the person will tell what is expected of him or her in that situation, and cannot be trusted to tell the truth. If a salesperson gives negative information about the company's products, this cannot be attributed to convention or role, and, therefore, it must be attributed to his or her intention. Jones and Davis (1965) call this a noncommon effect. Consumer usually look for noncommon effects, that is, cues to test the trustworthiness of salespeople.

Knowing the most likely cause is valuable for predicting the future and knowing what to expect from the person, the agent, or the target. Kelley and Michela (1980) describe the consequences of attributions, for example, the expectations one could derive from causal attributions. Distinctiveness and consistency provide the best basis for veridical attributions. Distinctiveness occurs if the behavior cannot be attributed to a permanent attribute of the actor, or to convention. Consistency is a repetition of the effect over time. Consensus occurs if a number of independent observers come to the same causal attribution.

Cue Utilization

Cue utilization is another way to form expectations. Often one has to make inferences about a person or a situation based on items of information: "cues." Stockbrokers have cues at their disposal, such as the Dow-Jones average, the volume of trade, the gain or loss of market share of a company. Based on these cues the stockbroker forms expectations about the future value of a certain stock. A causal, or at least a correlational, relationship is then assumed with the variable to help make predictions. Inferential beliefs are predicted with a considerable accuracy on the basis of a weighted linear combination of cues ("multiple regression model"). Although the linear model does a good job predicting inferential beliefs, it does not necessarily describe the process with which persons arrive at inferential beliefs.

Cue utilization in consumer behavior has

TABLE 11.1 Causal Attributions for Three Criteria

Criteria		Frequent Attribution	Infrequent Attribution
distinctiveness	high	target	agent
	low	agent	target
consistency	high	agent or target	circumstance
	low	circumstance	agent or target
consensus	high	target	agent
	low	agent	target

Source: van Raaij, 1987.

been studied by Olson and Jacoby (1972) and Schellinck (1983). In their work, a cue is similar to an attribute. Cue utilization is also an aspect of the "peripheral route" to persuasion in the Elaboration Likelihood Model (Petty and Cacioppo 1986). In this model, a cue is a superficial aspect of a message, such as a form or a spokesperson, used instead of arguments to reach quick conclusions. Forming an expectation based on these cues is often called a heuristic.

Heuristics

The previous models of expectation formation assume a more or less systematic way of information processing through causal attribution, cue weighing, and combination. An exception is the reasoning based on cues. Human beings are less than perfect information processors. People are biased and, therefore, tend to use heuristics to collect information and to form expectations. A heuristic is a simple and often biased form of information acquisition and reasoning. Two classes of heuristics will be distinguished: representativeness and availability (Tversky and Kahneman 1974).

The *representativeness* heuristic may be formulated as the expected probability that Event B originates from Process A, for example, that inflation will result from a policy measure. Process A is seen as representative for Event B. Gamblers may believe that after observing a long run of red on the roulette wheel, black is now due (gambler's fallacy). Knowing the values of A, people estimate the (correlational or causal) relationship between A and B in order to estimate the future value of B.

Humans, however, tend to underutilize base-rate information and trends, and to overestimate the value of the vivid example of a specific case. For instance, to know the quality of a football team the win-loss record is good information. Watching a particular game is a poorer indicator of the team's quality. Nevertheless, many people give more weight to one vivid observation than to abstract statistics.

The *availability* heuristic (Tversky and Kahneman 1973) pertains to the number of cases one is able to bring to mind. The expecta-

tion of a probability or frequency of an Event B will be higher, if one can easily observe, find, or imagine examples of B. After reading about traffic accidents in the newspapers, people will often have a higher expectation of a traffic accident than they had before reading the newspapers. Or, after experiencing or observing a car accident, people estimate the probability of accidents as higher than without this experience.

Expectations that already exist in mind, tend to bias new stimuli in the direction of the existing expectations (anchoring). Existing knowledge structures serve as internalized frames of reference in which to encode incoming stimuli. An expectation is an important frame of reference (Craik and Lockhart 1972). Consumers may have a reference price in mind, and from this reference price (frame) they perceive (and recall) actual prices. New incoming information may not only change existing expectations insufficiently, but also an existing expectational frame may bias the perception of incoming new information. People are not only biased in their perception of new information, but also they are underutilizing this new information in changing their existing expectations. People learn less from new information than is good for them. Research with the Bayesian perspective also points towards this conservative tendency in changing beliefs and expectations.

Regret

Most models of expectation formation pertain to expected future gains or reduced losses of selected alternatives. *Regret theory* is one of the few models to consider foregone opportunities or opportunity costs. Regret theory assumes that people have two kinds of expectations, "what is to be" and "what might have been" (Loomes and Sugden 1982).

Opportunity costs do not appear in the probability distribution of the selected final outcome, because they were precluded by the chosen alternative. They become part of the expectation, however, because they often diminish the value of the selected alternative. The selected alternative should be discounted for the opportunity costs. Cognitive dissonance theory, however, predicts that people will rather increase the evaluation of the chosen alternative and decrease the evaluation of the rejected alternatives (Festinger 1957). By doing this, they reduce their perceived opportunity costs.

Regret relates to nonselected alternatives and foregone opportunities. At the time of the decision, alternatives may be unknown and unanticipated, but they will become known later. Expectations about computer usage, biogenetics, new medications are necessarily ambiguous. The loss of environmental value is, for instance, often only realized after the motorway has b⬛⬛⬛

Co⬛

In ⬛ ⬛ns play an im⬛ ⬛ to the consu⬛ ⬛eted or discre⬛ ⬛to buy. Buyir⬛ ⬛ing are influe⬛ ⬛ingness factor⬛ ⬛ined by expec⬛ ⬛evelopment⬛ ⬛ncome, futur⬛ ⬛yment, and ⬛ ⬛sumers with ⬛ ⬛d more on di⬛ ⬛d tend to sa⬛ ⬛sumers with ⬛ ⬛tend to spend⬛ ⬛more.

Katona distinguishes two components in the expectation formation process. The first is the direct experience of consumers, such as in shopping, and the indirect experience, received through the mass media, from which the consumers acquire information on inflation levels, interest rates, wars and threats of wars, the business cycle, and government policies. Direct experience leads to descriptive beliefs, whereas indirect experience leads to informational beliefs. The second component is problem solving. With a change in the environment consumers have to adapt their expectations. Katona (1975) calls the process of expectation formation "social learning" by which he means problem solving and the combining information from several sources into a meaningful

picture of the most likely economic conditions of the future.

Consumer Expectations

Meyer (1981) was among the first to model how consumer expectations of uncertain or unknown product attributes are formed. The expectations of the attributes are weighted functions of the subjective mean, its variance, and their interaction. The subjective mean of an unknown attribute is a function of a weighted average of similar attributes of other products in the same category. Thus, similar to Tolman (1932), the expectation of a product's attribute level is formed as a combination of the attribute levels derived from similar products (in the same product class). In the same way, the expectation of the variance of a product's attribute level is formed as a combination of the variance of the attribute levels derived from similar products.

In Meyer's (1981) approach, missing product information is inferred from the information available from other similar (competitive) products. This is an "other product" approach. Another strategy is to infer missing information from the other attributes of the same (partially described) product. Highly correlated attributes may influence inferences as well. This is the "same product" approach. Ford and Smith (1987) found a greater effect of the "same product" approach than of the "other product" approach.

In a model similar to that of Meyer (1981), Woodruff, Cadotte, and Jenkins (1983) state that attribute expectations are based on norms derived from the performance of one product over time or from the average performance of several similar products in the product class. Consumers may expect less from a cheap product than from an expensive one. Consumers are assumed to have a latitude of acceptance around the average product performance. The range of consumer expectations is thus less dispersed than the range of actual product performance levels.

Hagerty and Aaker (1984) propose a model of consumer information search based on the notion that consumers will maximize their expected values of sample information. They indicate that the attribute variance is determined by the dispersion of attributes over products and the consumer's familiarity with the product class.

Bettman (1979) states that consumers place the new information they receive in a context based on both past and current events, and that they then form expectations about the future. New information about a brand is placed in the context of the past experience with the brand, the state of the technology, the performance of similar brands in the product class; and then expectations are developed about the performance of the brand.

Oliver (1977, 1980) describes the expectation formation process as based on the product itself, through prior experience and current information, through the retail context, such as dealings with salespeople, and through individual consumer characteristics, such as their persuasibility.

Thus, the formation of expectations of uncertain or unknown product attributes is based on the levels of similar known attributes from the past, on other attributes of the same product, or on attributes of other products in the category. It is expected that the degree of attribute intercorrelation determines which strategy a consumer will select. With highly correlated attributes, the "same product" approach is more likely. With low correlations, the "other product" approach is more likely. Contextual information may also play a role for consumers in inferring the value of unknown information.

THE REVISION OF EXPECTATIONS

Introduction

Expectations are studied in economics and in psychology, and they are thus an important part of economic psychology. Economists generally assume that expectations are extrapolated from existing time series. Keynes (1936) assumed a revision process composed of past actual values, past expectations, and an un-

specified updating process. Hicks (1939) included noneconomic, psychological factors as inputs to a price expectation revision process. Psychologists are more interested in the processes of the revision of expectations: How people process incoming (external) information and integrate this new information with the existing information in memory.

In the economic approach, a more or less rational way of revising expectations is assumed using a certain rule. This does not necessarily describe the actual process of revision, but it does at least predict the outcome of the process. Economic models are outcome oriented. In the psychological approach, a learning or reasoning process is often assumed. Psychological models are more process oriented.

The Economic Approach

Under the influence of econometric modeling, extrapolative expectational models were developed. Expectations in these models were simple extrapolations of time series. Cagan (1956) adopted a simple error-learning hypothesis: *adaptive expectations*. Error learning for price expectations is as follows: " . . . the expected rate of change in prices is revised per period of time in proportion to the difference between the actual rate of change in prices and the rate of change that was expected" (p. 37). Adaptive expectations are thus similar to autoregressive and distributed-lag expectations.

The following rules of expectation revision can be distinguished (Blomqvist 1983), and these rules have been employed in the study of inflationary expectations.

1. The *adaptive expectations* rule has been used most often. The rule states that the new expectation is a weighted average of the actual level now and the expectation formed at a preceding point in time:

$$p^e_t = ap_t + (1 - a) p^e_{t-1} \qquad (11.1)$$

in which p^e_t is the expectation formed at time t, and p_t is the actual level now.

2. The *extrapolative expectations* rule is based on the assumption that the recent rate is extrapolated, taking the most recent changes into account:

$$p^e_t = p_t + b(p_t - p_{t-i}) \qquad (11.2)$$

in which i denotes the time period over which the change is taken into account.

3. The *adjusted long-run expectations* rule is based on the idea that the short-run expectations are derived starting from long-run expectations (seen as the "normal" expectations), adjusted for recent changes:

$$p^e_t = P^e_t + c(P^e_t - p_t) \qquad (11.3)$$

in which P denotes the long-run expectations.

4. The *augmented* rule includes other information besides just the variable to be estimated. The "rational expectations" model (Muth 1961; explained subsequently) includes all relevant information of other variables in order to estimate the variable under study. The augmented rule can be considered to be quasi-rational.

Blomqvist (1983) finds in a study in Finland that uninformed (lay) subjects tend to use the adaptive expectations rule, whereas informed subjects (economists) more often use the extrapolative rule to estimate future levels of inflation. The dispersion was also greater with the uninformed group.

Nerlove (1983) states that, when economic outcomes are not undergoing a structural change, one will generally find a univariate time series relationship between a variable and its own past. Expectations are then seen as adaptive, extrapolative, or adjusted; and discontinuous changes cannot be predicted. With the augmented rule and the rational expectations hypothesis a discontinuous change can be predicted.

Rational Expectations

Muth (1961) formulated his "rational expectations hypothesis" in the following way: " . . . expectations, since they are informed predictions of future events, are essentially the same as the predictions of the relevant economic theory" (p. 316). Muth thus believed that consumers and business people are lay economists discovering and using economic theories. Consumers and other economic agents form and revise their expectations based on all the relevant information available. The rational expectations hypothesis may be used to derive hypotheses for empirical testing, especially at the macro/aggregate level. It is however unlikely that it describes the process of expectation formation of individual consumers and entrepreneurs. Shaw (1987) states that it is impossible for the average consumer to know the "true" economic theory, when even professional economists disagree about what is the true theory.

The rational expectations hypothesis has been revised to include a learning mechanism. Learning leads to convergence and to rational expectations. This assumes that the economic agents know the true economic model, but are uncertain about the values of the parameters during the learning phase. Economic agents behave like computer algorithms converging to the true values. An application of the rational expectations hypothesis in consumer behavior is found in the work of Winer (1986).

Friedman (1977) introduced the "semi-rational" model of expectation revision. The expectations depend on an optimal learning process. The expected values are a weighed average of adaptive and rational expectations. Over time, the expectations converge to the rational expectations.

Evaluation of the Economic Approach

The economic approach to expectation revision is narrow in scope, with a simple description of the processes that are employed by economic agents: adjustment and convergence to the true value. In the economic approach, the outcomes of these processes are more important than the processes themselves. Bacharach (1986, p. 175) complained:

What is missing is a satisfactory Theory of Belief for individual economic agents. A Theory of Belief deals with the way the economic agent comes by beliefs, comes to abandon them; the weight he gives to the testimony of the authorities, the strength of his beliefs, the different categories of his beliefs, his expectations about the future values, certainly, but also the theories of the economy and the proverbs about the economy he believes . . .

Thus Bacharach notes the absence of a cognitive theory of expectation formation. The "theory of the economy and the proverbs about the economy" point toward causal maps of economic relations, as people believe these to exist.

In the adaptive expectations models usually the trend in the time series is estimated by the subjects. It is expected that changes either persist or regress to a previous level, depending on the attributions that are made to explain the recent changes. Andreassen (1987) studied the expectations people have of the stock market. The mass media, playing an important role in making these expectations, tend to stress causes for changes other than just chance, and this leads their audience to make less regressive changes in their expectations.

The Psychological Approach

In psychology, the revision of expectations is studied as a process of information processing. Examples are multiple cue learning, concept formation, formal inference models, and the Bayesian revision of probabilities. In these models, prior expectations are revised based on new information. In some cases, the new information is feedback information on actions based on the prior information. The revision of expectations may thus be an ongoing process for the individual.

Multiple Cue Learning

In multiple cue learning, persons have a set of cues at their disposal describing some object with which they order to make an inferential judgment about the object. After each judgment the subject is given feedback as to the accuracy of the judgment. In Brunswik's "lens model" (1956), cues provide information on an objective "distal" criterion variable. It is possible to compute a correlation between the person's prediction and the actual criterion. This correlation, the "achievement index," reflects the accuracy of the judgment. When persons are given feedback as to the accuracy of their judgments, they progressively learn to place more appropriate weights on the various cues. Hammond and Summers (1972) have shown that accuracy is influenced not only by the appropriate weighing of the cues, but also by the way these weights are used by the person. Not only *obtaining* knowledge from the outside world, but also *using* this knowledge appropriately increases the accuracy of the judgment.

The basic approach in *concept formation* is similar to multiple cue learning. Here too, concept formation consists of learning the attributes of a concept and learning the rule for combining these attributes. The person's task in a concept formation study is to discover the attributes and the combination rule that define a given concept (Johnson 1972). As in multiple cue learning, feedback leads to successive revisions until the concept is correctly identified.

Formal Inference

Formal inference models are often not descriptive but normative models of reasoning. Syllogistic reasoning and probability models exist and may be used as a criterion to evaluate the actual human performance of belief formation. A syllogism consists of three belief statements, two premises and one conclusion, as seen in the following example:

Premise 1: Detergents will pollute the environment.
Premise 2: Brand X is a detergent.
Conclusion: Brand X will pollute the environment.

Subjective probabilities largely follow the laws of objective probabilities (Wyer 1970). For instance, the conjunctive probability that both A and B are true, is given by:

$$p(A \cap B) = p(A|B) \cdot p(B)$$
$$= p(B|A) \cdot p(A), \qquad (11.4)$$

where $p\,(A \cap B)$ is the conjunctive probability of A and B; $p(A|B)$ and $p(B|A)$ are the conditional probabilities of A, given B is true, respectively, B, given A is true; $p(A)$ and $p(B)$ are the probabilities of A and B, respectively.

Bayes' Theorem

Bayes' theorem deals explicitly with the revision of beliefs in the light of new information. Note that Bayes' theorem is a normative model describing the optimal revisions of probabilities. The theorem deals with the revision of beliefs or hypotheses (H) on the basis of new information or data (D):

$$p(H|D) = p(H) \cdot p(D|H)/p(D). \quad (11.5)$$

For instance, a person might estimate the prior probability of rain during a vacation in England to be $p(H) = 0.30$. The prior probability of sunshine is $p(D) = 0.40$. The probability of sunshine, given a rainy vacation, is $p(D|H) = 0.10$. Then $p(H|D) = 0.075$. The probability of rain should thus be reduced from 0.30 to 0.075, knowing the probability of sunshine, given a rainy vacation. In this case, $p(H|D)$ could be compared with the actual estimation of rain given the new information D on sunshine.

A large number of studies have shown that Bayes' theorem is a reasonably good descriptive model of human information processing (Slovic and Lichtenstein 1971). Brickman (1972) studied the reactions to disconfirmed expectancies, that is, how persons revise their probabilities consistent with Bayes' theorem. He gave some subjects information about their grades that was discrepant with their expectations, and other subjects information that was consistent with their expectations. He found that unexpected (discrepant) information produced smaller revisions than expected (consistent) information. Disconfirmation of expectations did not result in reluctance to accept the information, but it was used to revise the information, although in a somewhat conservative manner. Bayes' theorem constitutes a model of a "rational" person using new information in an optimal way.

Adjustment

In the revision of expectations, as in the formation of expectations, people tend to be biased and to use heuristics. Using new information, *adjustments* of a prior value to a new value are typically insufficient. Anchoring occurs if a starting value determines the final expectation. High starting values tend to result in higher estimates than low starting values (Tversky and Kahneman 1974). Consumers may use the price of their present car as an anchor for the evaluation of other cars. If their present car is cheap, this low starting value will lead to lower estimates of car prices than if their present car is expensive.

Adjustment of expectations may occur through personal experience. For instance, consumers may form expectations of a product based on advertising information. Actual product performance may then lead to satisfaction or dissatisfaction, and then to adjustment of prior expectations for the next purchase.

As we have seen before, expectations that already exist in mind, tend to bias new stimuli in the direction of the existing expectations. This impedes learning from new information. An expectation is an important frame of reference (or schema) from which to judge new information (Craik and Lockhart 1972).

RETRIEVAL OF EXPECTATIONS

Introduction

Although expectations have to be retrieved from memory in order to be revised, and although the revision of expectations has been discussed previously, it is useful to devote a separate section to the retrieval of expectations from memory. Retrieved expectation may be used as an input to other processes, such as the expectation-disconfirmation processes leading to satisfaction or dissatisfaction.

Active and Passive Expectations

Kahneman and Tversky (1982a) developed a typology of the degree of activity needed for retrieval (called "arousal" by the authors) of the expectations. The first category, *active expectations,* is easily available in memory. People think about active expectations frequently and they have a high level of consciousness and involvement and may be instrumental in the purchase of products.

The other category, *passive expectations* does not result in active information processing. One type of passive expectations is part of a schema and resides permanently and passively in memory (e.g., inflationary expectations after years of increasing price levels). Passive expectations exist as generally true beliefs and are probably not processed until disconfirmed. Disconfirmation may even be necessary for these expectations to become salient. Kahneman and Tversky (1982ab) call the process of activation of expectations "priming." Passive expectations become more important after having been primed. The other type of passive expectations are temporary. Temporary passive expectations remain only in memory for a brief time period (e.g., the expectation that the store will be open and the liquor will be available).

The mood of the individual may affect the retrieval of expectations. In one study by Bower and Cohen (1982), subjects were asked to estimate on a 0-to-100 scale the "objective" probability of possible future events. Americans were asked, for instance, to estimate the probability that within the next three years they would take a vacation in Europe, or the probability that within the next ten years there would be a major disaster at a nuclear power plant in California. Experimentally, either a happy or a depressed mood had been induced in the subjects. Analyses of the probability estimates showed that happy subjects elevated their probability estimates of positive future events, for example, the vacation trip to Europe, and reduced their estimates of negative future events, for example, the nuclear power plant disaster. Exactly the opposite results were obtained for depressed subjects.

Johnson and Tversky (1983) gave subjects a newspaper report of a tragic event in order to induce a negative mood in them. Subjects in such a depressed mood gave higher estimates of the risks of undesirable events, not necessarily related to the newspaper report. Conversely, an account of a happy event induced a positive mood and also decreased the likelihood estimates (expectations) of undesirable events. The mood state thus influences the retrieval or reconstruction of expectations in the sense that people in an unhappy mood give higher expectations of undesirable events than people in a happy mood.

Consumers often store positive and negative aspects of products and services in their memory. Consumers in a good mood tend to retrieve more positive expectations about a product or a service than consumers in a bad mood — the mood congruency hypothesis (Bower 1981) or the accessibility hypothesis (Isen, Shalker, Clark, and Karp 1978). Consumers in a good mood are willing to take more risk and are thus more easily convinced to buy the particular product or service. Consumers in a bad mood form more negative expectations, take less risk, and are thus less likely to buy. Katona (1975) found that a positive (optimistic) mood or sentiment (in the aggregate sense) enhances spending, especially on durables, luxury services, and consumer credit, and a positive mood tends to decrease consumer saving.

Intentional and Contingent Expectations

In the introduction to this chapter the distinction was made between intentional and contingent expectations. *Intentional expectations* are under one's control, for example, plans, goals, and aspirations. Expectations related to events under one's control have direct feedback effects. One has to revise the expectations based on the actions performed. Controllability is a continuous dimension. *Contingent expectations* refer to events that are outside one's control. Reasons for lack of control (MacCrimmon and Wehrung 1987) are insufficient resources, insufficient information, and lack of time. The latter two insufficiencies may be solved by hiring an "ex" to provide the information, on which the The actions of petitors, cogely outside oare contingeunpredictabned by naturakes and torn

Hindsi

Kahneman and Miller (1986) discuss the role of *norms* in expectations. Norms follow a sequence of backward processing, whereby the present defines the past. An evoking present stimulus is reinforced by selectively retrieved elements from memory. The model assumes that people have ambiguous and even inconsistent expectations passively stored in memory. New information activates the consistent expectations. The present may be more decisive than the past in estimating future values. This phenomenorelated to "hindsight" or the "I knew it all alct (Fischhoff 1975), in which people bmore correctthey actuallypectation aion, in whichhave adjustedse of norm acs retrieved fuous expectati

Disconfirmation

As stated previously with the priming process, expectations are often activated through disconfirmation. If an actively or passively held expectation is disconfirmed, dissatisfaction arises. If the performance of a product does not meet prior expectations, dissatisfaction will result. If the actual product performance exceeds or equals the prior expectations, satisfaction will result. The expectation-disconfirmation model assumes that satisfaction is the outcome

of a four-step process (Oliver 1980). First, prepurchase expectations are formed. Then, the actual performance of a product or service is evaluated. As a third step, expectations are compared with performance, and confirmed or disconfirmed. The degree of (dis)confirmation determines the level of satisfaction or dissatisfaction. Satisfaction may have several dissimilar forms. If a disconfirmation of an unfavorable expectation occurs, relief will be the result. If a confirmation of a favorable expectation occurs, pleasure will be the result.

The fourth step is the behavior with regard to the product: To buy it again or not. Swan and Trawick (1981) apply this model to study expectations and satisfaction with restaurant service and find support for the major hypothesis that satisfaction increases as positive disconfirmation (the actual service exceeding the expectations) increases.

AGGREGATE CONSUMER EXPECTATIONS

Introduction

Keynes (1936) lists consumer expectations as one of the factors influencing the "propensity to consume."

Whilst it may affect considerably a particular individual's propensity to consume, it is likely to average out for the community as a whole. Moreover, it is a matter about which there is too much uncertainty for it to exert much influence. (p. 95)

This might have been true in the pre-World War II era, but today consumer expectations tend to be uniform and tend to spread rather than cancel out (Katona 1975). Expectations are often more than just extrapolations from the past. Expectations, together with the level and changes of income, influence individual and mass behavior, consumer spending, saving, and credit. In this section, the Index of Consumer Sentiment, as a measure of aggregate expectations, will be described.

Consumer Expectations

Household discretionary income, the ability to buy, needs to be augmented by consumer sentiment, the willingness to buy, in order to explain and to predict consumer expenditure. Katona (1975) argued that the expectation of one's personal financial progress, the expectation about the business cycle, and the expectation about the market situation influence buying and saving decisions, especially for durable goods, vacations, and recreation. The purchase of durables, credit, and mortgages involves risk in the future loan payments one now has to make and in the money taken away from savings used as a buffer against risks. These non-discretionary expenditures can be postponed or canceled, and are thus more affected by consumer expectations than the purchase of groceries and the payment of mortgages, insurance premiums, medical bills, and other contractual obligations.

In 1952 Katona constructed the Index of Consumer Sentiment (ICS), consisting of five questions, asked to consumers in regular surveys. This ICS has been used in regular surveys to the present day. Two questions relate to personal finances: whether the subject feels the household is financially better off, worse off, or in the same situation as a year earlier; and whether the subject expects to be better off, worse off, or the same a year hence. Two questions concern business cycle trends: whether the next twelve months and whether the next five years will bring good or bad times for the economy as a whole. A fifth question regarding market conditions asks whether it is a good or a bad time to buy durable goods. The ICS is a simple average of the scores on these five survey questions. The five questions can be classified as evaluations of the present situation and expectations about the future. As can be seen from Table 11.2, three survey questions pertain to expectations and two to evaluations of the present situation. The questions are scored as follows: the proportions of optimistic responses (P_o) and pessimistic responses (P_n) are computed for each question in each survey. An index is computed for each question: $100 + P_o$

TABLE 11.2   Survey Questions of the Index of Consumer Sentiment

	Evaluation	*Expectation*
personal finances	better off compared with year ago?	better off a year hence?
business cycle		better business conditions a year/ 5 years hence?
market conditions	good time to buy?	

$- P_n$. The ICS is the mean of the five index scores.

The ICS predicts aggregate consumer spending (especially on new cars), saving, and borrowing rather well. Mueller (1963) concludes that the ICS in combination with income data contains information not obtainable from financial and business-cycle indicators. Adams (1964) finds that the ICS and/or the separate survey questions perform especially well in time series, but not so well in cross-section data. Buying intentions do not improve the prediction, once income and ICS questions are present in the regression equations.

McNeil (1974) describes a federal program to predict consumer expenditure with longitudinal "purchase expectations" (intentions) data. At the onset of this program it was argued that purchase intentions are closer in time to the actual purchase than consumer attitudes and expectations. This is true for individual buyers in a longitudinal test. For aggregate time-series data, however, attitudes and expectations perform better than intentions to predict consumer expenditure. The program thus failed and was discontinued in 1973. One should be cautious using cross-section results to infer time-series performance. This is also known as the time-series cross-section paradox (Adams 1965; van Raaij 1984).

The surveys to assess consumer sentiment consist of evaluation and expectation questions, with regard to the present and to future conditions, respectively. Strümpel, Kuss, and Curtin (1979) distinguish two subindexes, one for the present situation and one for the future. The evaluation of the future is generally somewhat more favorable than the evaluation of the present. People seem to be rather optimistic, in spite of the present situation. The patterns of the subindexes are, however, rather similar as leading indicators of the business cycle.

Katona (1975, p. 185) describes a segment of the population: the "better-better group" of households who feel better off than four years ago and also expect to be better off one or four years hence. For them, and for other segments such as "worse-worse," "same-worse," and "worse-same," expectations correspond to past experiences. This resembles the extrapolative expectations rule (Cagan 1956). However, the experience of an increasing income and improvements in the standard of living are not the only cause for optimism for some people. Katona (1975, pp. 187–189) mentions three other considerations: (1) a general shift for some people from blue-collar to white-collar jobs, who then reach their peak income later in life, (2) an increase for these people in their educational attainment, and (3) notions shared by these people about progress that reflect their personal achievement, attributing success to internal causes (van Raaij 1986).

Principal components analysis of the survey questions reveals high correlations between evaluations of the present and expectations toward the future (van Raaij and Gianotten 1990). One component is related to personal finances, the other to the economy as a whole (the business cycle). This supports the idea that expectations are grounded on evaluations of the present and are not held separately from experiences and evaluations. Only Strümpel et al. (1979) found separate factors for the present and the future. In the 1970s, Dutch consumers were more optimistic about their own finances than about the economy as a whole. Yet after the recession of 1980–1984, a reversed pattern has been observed: the optimism about the economy as a whole is greater than the optimism about one's personal finances.

As a consequence of optimistic expectations consumers tend to spend and to save more. Katona and Mueller (1968) found that consumers, expecting income gains, made both anticipatory and concurrent expenditures on discretionary items, especially on durables. An upward income trend is associated with the highly valued material goals people have: the acquisition of durable goods and the accumulation of savings.

CONCLUSIONS

Most economic behavior, including consumer behavior, is governed by expectations about the future. Individual economic actors have to make decisions about alternatives with uncertain outcomes, and they have to judge the consequences of their present choices. At an aggregate level, consumer expectations, as a climate of opinion, influence consumer spending, saving, and borrowing. Not only economic possibilities, such as available income or the supply of goods, determine purchase, but also consumer willingness to spend, based on expectations, increasingly determine consumer expenditure. Given income and an available supply, consumer expectations and confidence about the retailer, the brand, and the producer will become more and more crucial for transactions.

Human beings are not perfect in information processing or in the formation and revision of expectations. Information is uncertain and ambiguous. Nevertheless, most individuals try to reduce this uncertainty and to form impressions about what may happen and how the future will be. These inference processes, and the degree that the outcomes govern behavior will be of the utmost relevance in the years to come. In detail, more research is needed on (1) the inference processes in forming expectations, (2) the relations between the evaluation of the present and expectations about the future, (3) how economic actors perceive trends, (4) the degree to which expectations are seen to be intentional and under one's control, (5) how expectations influence behavior, and (6) how performance and behavior may influence expectations.

This sounds like a ten-year research program, but it is worth the efforts. The results will be relevant for marketing, advertising, consumer affairs, and governmental consumer and economic policy.

REFERENCES

ADAMS, F. G. (1964). Consumer attitudes, buying plans and purchases of durable goods: A principal components time series approach, *Review of Economics and Statistics, 46,* 347–355.

ADAMS, F. G. (1965). Prediction with consumer attitudes: The time series cross section paradox, *Review of Economics and Statistics, 47,* 367–378.

ADAMS, F. G., and E. W. GREEN (1965). Explaining and predicting aggregative consumer attitudes, *International Economic Review, 6,* 275–293.

ANDREASSEN, P.B. (1987). On the social psychology of the stock market: Aggregate attributional effects and the regressiveness of prediction, *Journal of Personality and Social Psychology, 53,* 490–496.

BACHARACH, M. O. L. (1986). "The problems of agents' beliefs in economic theory," in M. Baranzini and R. Scazzieri (Eds.), *Foundations of Economics.* Oxford: Basil Blackwell.

BETTMAN, J. R. (1979). *An Information Processing Theory of Consumer Choice.* Reading, MA: Addison-Wesley.

BETTMAN, J. R., M. SUJAN, and H. SUJAN (1986). Effects of consumer expectations on information processing in selling encounters, *Journal of Marketing Research, 23,* 346–353.

BLOMQVIST, H. C. (1983). On the formation of inflationary expectations: Some empirical evidence from Finland, 1979–1980, *Journal of Economic Psychology, 4,* 249–266.

BOWER, G. H. (1981). Mood and memory, *American Psychologist, 36,* 129–148.

BOWER, G. H., and P. R. COHEN (1982). "Emotional influences in memory and thinking: Data and theory," in M. S. Clark and S. T. Fiske (Eds.), *Affect and Cognition.* Hillsdale, NJ: Erlbaum, 291–331.

BRICKMAN, P. (1972). Rational and nonrational elements in reactions to disconfirmation of performance expectancies, *Journal of Experimental Social Psychology, 8,* 112–123.

BRUNSWIK, E. (1956). *Perception and the Representative Design of Experiments.* Berkeley, CA: University of California Press.

CAGAN, P. (1956). "The monetary dynamics of hyperinflation," in M. Friedman (Ed.), *Studies in the Quantity Theory of Money.* Chicago: University of Chicago Press.

CRAIK, F. I. M., and R. S. LOCKHART (1972). Levels of processing: A framework for memory research, *Journal of Verbal Learning and Verbal Behavior, 11,* 671–684.

EDWARDS, W. (1954). The theory of decision making, *Psychological Bulletin, 51,* 380–417.

EINHORN, H. J., and R. M. HOGARTH (1985). Ambiguity and uncertainty in probabilistic inference, *Psychological Bulletin, 92,* 433–461.

FAZIO, R. H., and M. P. ZANNA (1981). "Direct experience and attitude-behavior consistency," in L. Berkowitz (Ed.), *Advances in Experimental Social Psychology,* Vol. 14. New York: Academic Press, 162–202.

FEATHER, N. T. (1982). "Actions in relation to expected consequences: An overview of a research program," in N. T. Feather (Ed.), *Expectations and Actions: Expectancy-Value Models in Psychology.* Hillsdale, NJ: Erlbaum, 53–95.

FESTINGER, L. (1957). *A Theory of Cognitive Dissonance.* New York: Harper & Row.

FISCHHOFF, B. (1975). Hindsight ≠ foresight: The effects of outcome knowledge on judgment under uncertainty, *Journal of Experimental Psychology: Human Perception and Performance, 1,* 288–299.

FISHBEIN, M., and I. AJZEN (1975). *Belief, Attitude, Intention, and Behavior.* Reading, MA: Addison-Wesley.

FORD, G. T., and R. A. SMITH (1987). Inferential beliefs in consumer evaluations: An assessment of alternative processing strategies, *Journal of Consumer Research, 14,* 363–371.

FRIEDMAN, B. (1979). Optimal expectations and the extreme information assumptions of "rational expectations" macro models, *Journal of Monetary Economics, 5,* 23–41.

FRIEND, I., and F. G. ADAMS (1964). The predictive ability of consumer attitudes, stock prices, and nonattitudinal variables, *Journal of the American Statistical Association, 59,* 987–1005.

GEORGESCU-ROEGEN, N. (1958). "The nature of expectations and uncertainty," in M. J. Bowman (Ed.), *Expectations, Uncertainty, and Business Behavior.* New York: Social Science Research Council, 11–29.

GOERING, P. A. (1985). Effects of product trial on consumer expectations, demand, and prices, *Journal of Consumer Research, 12,* 74–82.

HAGERTY, M. R., and D. A. AAKER (1984). A normative model of consumer information processing, *Marketing Science, 3,* 227–246.

HAMMOND, K. R., and D. A. SUMMERS (1972). Cognitive control, *Psychological Review, 79,* 58–67.

HELGESON, J. G., and S. E. BEATTY (1987). Price expectations and price recall error: An empirical study, *Journal of Consumer Research, 14,* 379–386.

HICKS, J. R. (1939). *Value and Capital.* Oxford: Oxford University Press.

ISEN, A. M., T. E. SHALKER, M. S. CLARK, and L. KARP (1978). Positive affect, accessibility of material in memory and behavior: A cognitive loop? *Journal of Personality and Social Psychology, 36,* 1–12.

JACOBY, J., and J. C. OLSON (1972). An extended expectancy model of consumer comparison processes, *Advances in Consumer Research,* Vol. 1, 319–333.

JOHNSON, D. M. (1972). *A Systematic Introduction to the Psychology of Thinking.* New York: Harper & Row.

JOHNSON, E., and A. TVERSKY (1983). Affect, generalization and the perception of risk, *Journal of Personality and Social Psychology, 45,* 20–31.

JONES, E. E., and K. E. DAVIS (1965). "From acts to dispositions," in L. Berkowitz (Ed.), *Advances in Experimental Social Psychology,* Vol. 2, New York: Academic Press, 219–266.

JONUNG, L. (1986). Uncertainty about inflationary perceptions and expectations, *Journal of Economic Psychology, 7,* 315–325.

KAHNEMAN, D., and D. T. MILLER (1986). Norm theory: Comparing reality to its alternatives, *Psychological Review, 93,* 136–153.

KAHNEMAN, D., and A. TVERSKY (1979). Prospect theory: An analysis of decision under risk, *Econometrica, 47,* 263–291.

KAHNEMAN, D., and A. TVERSKY (1982a). Variants of uncertainty, *Cognition, 11,* 143–157.

KAHNEMAN, D., and A. TVERSKY (1982b). The psychology of preferences, *Scientific American, 246,* 136–141.

KATONA, G. (1975). *Psychological Economics.* New York: Elsevier.

KATONA, G., and E. MUELLER (1968). *Consumer Response to Income Increases.* Washington, DC: Brookings Institution.

KELLEY, H. H., and J. L. MICHELA (1980). Attribution theory and research, *Annual Review of Psychology, 31,* 457–501.

KEYNES, J. M. (1936). *The Central Theory of Employment, Interest and Money.* London: McMillan.

LOOMES, G., and R. SUGDEN (1982). Regret theory: An alternative theory of rational choice under uncertainty, *The Economic Journal, 92,* 805–824.

MCARTHUR, L. A. (1972). The how and what of why: Some determinants and consequences of causal attribution: *Journal of Personality and Social Psychology, 22,* 171–193.

MACCRIMMON, K. R., and D. A. WEHRUNG (1987). *Taking Risks, The Management of Uncertainty.* New York: The Free Press.

MCNEIL, J. (1974). Federal programs to measure consumer purchase expectations, 1946–1973: A post-mortem, *Journal of Consumer Research, 1,* 1–15.

MEYER, R. J. (1981). A model of multiattribute judgments under attribute uncertainty and informational constraint, *Journal of Marketing Research, 18,* 428–441.

MUELLER, E. (1963). Ten years of consumer attitude surveys: Their forecasting record, *Journal of the American Statistical Association, 58,* 899–917.

MUTH, J. F. (1961). Rational expectations and the theory of price movements, *Econometrica, 29,* 315–335.

NERLOVE, M. (1983). Expectations, plans and realizations in theory and practice, *Econometrica, 51,* 1251–1279.

NEWCOMB, T. M. (1972). "Expectations as a social psychological concept," in B. Strümpel, J. N. Morgan, and E. Zahn (Eds.), *Human Behavior in Economic Affairs.* Amsterdam: Elsevier, 109–118.

OLIVER, R. L. (1977). Effect of expectation and disconfirmation on post-exposure product evaluations: An alternative explanation, *Journal of Applied Psychology, 62,* 480–486.

OLIVER, R. L. (1980). A cognitive model of the antecedents and consequences of satisfaction decisions, *Journal of Marketing Research, 17,* 460–469.

OLIVER, R. L., and R. S. WINER (1987). A framework for the formation and structure of consumer expectations: Review and propositions, *Journal of Economic Psychology, 8,* 469–499.

OLSHAVSKY, R. W., and J. A. MILLER (1972). Consumer expectations, product performance, and perceived product quality, *Journal of Marketing Research, 9,* 19–21.

OLSON, J. C., and P. DOVER (1979). Disconfirmation of consumer expectations through product trial, *Journal of Applied Psychology, 64,* 179–189.

OLSON, J. C., and J. JACOBY (1972). "Cue utilization in quality perception processes," in M. Venkatesan (Ed.), *Proceedings Association of Consumer Research*, 167–179.

PETTY, R. E., and J. T. CACIOPPO (1986). "The elaboration likelihood model of persuasion," in L. Berkowitz (Ed.), *Advances in Experimental Social Psychology*, Vol. 18. New York: Academic Press, 123–205.

PIETERS, R. G. M., and W. F. VAN RAAIJ (1988). Functions and management of affect: Applications to economic behavior, *Journal of Economic Psychology*, 9, 251–282.

PRUITT, S. W., R. J. REILLY, and G. E. HOFFER (1988). The effect of media presentation on the formation of economic expectations: Some initial evidence, *Journal of Economic Psychology*, 9, 315–325.

ROSENBERG, M. J. (1956). Cognitive structure and attitudinal affect, *Journal of Abnormal and Social Psychology*, 53, 367–372.

SCHELLINCK, D. A. (1983). Cue choice as a function of time pressure and perceived risk, *Advances in Consumer Research*, 10, 470–475.

SCHMALENSEE, R. (1976). An experimental study of expectation formation, *Econometrica*, 44, 17–41.

SHACKLE, G. L. S. (1952). *Expectation in Economics*. Cambridge: Cambridge University Press, 2nd edition.

SHAPIRO, H. T. (1972). "The Index of Consumer Sentiment and economic forecasting: A reappraisal," in B. Strümpel, J. N. Morgan, and E. Zahn (Eds.), *Human Behavior in Economic Affairs*. Amsterdam: Elsevier, 373–396.

SHAW, G. K. (1987). Rational expectations, *Bulletin of Economic Research*, 39, 187–209.

SHEFFRIN, S. M. (1983). *Rational Expectations*. Cambridge: Cambridge University Press.

SLOVIC, P., and S. LICHTENSTEIN (1971). Comparison of Bayesian and regression approaches to the study of information processing in judgment, *Organizational Behavior and Human Performance*, 6, 649–744.

STRÜMPEL, B., A. KUSS, and R. CURTIN (1979). The use and potential of consumer anticipations data in the member countries of the European Community, working paper, Berlin: Free University.

SWAN, J. E., and I. F. TRAWICK (1981). Disconfirmation of expectations and satisfaction with a retail service, *Journal of Retailing*, 57, 49–67.

TOLMAN, E. C. (1932). *Purposive Behavior in Animals and Men*. New York: Appleton-Century-Crofts.

TVERSKY, A., and D. KAHNEMAN (1973). Avail-ability: A heuristic for judging frequency and probability, *Cognitive Psychology*, 4, 207–232.

TVERSKY, A., and D. KAHNEMAN (1974). Judgment under uncertainty: Heuristics and biases, *Science*, 185, 1124–1131.

TVERSKY, A., and D. KAHNEMAN (1982). "Evidential impact of base rates," in D. Kahneman, P. Slovic, and A. Tversky (Eds.), *Judgment under Uncertainty: Heuristics and Biases*. Cambridge: Cambridge University Press, 153–160.

VANDEN ABEELE, P. (1983). The Index of Consumer Sentiment: Predictability and predictive power in the EEC, *Journal of Economic Psychology*, 3, 1–17.

VANDEN ABEELE, P. (1988). "Economic agents' expectations in a psychological perspective," in W. F. van Raaij et al. (Eds.), *Handbook of Economic Psychology*. Dordrecht, The Netherlands: Kluwer Academic, 478–515.

VAN RAAIJ, W. F. (1984). Micro and macro economic psychology, *Journal of Economic Psychology*, 5, 385–401.

VAN RAAIJ, W. F. (1987). "Causal attributions in economic behavior," in A. J. MacFadyen and H. W. MacFadyen (Eds.), *Economic Psychology: Intersections in Theory and Application*. Amsterdam, The Netherlands: North-Holland, 353–379.

VAN RAAIJ, W. F. (1988). "Information processing and decision making. Cognitive aspects of economic behavior," in W. F. van Raaij et al. (Eds.), *Handbook of Economic Psychology*. Dordrecht, The Netherlands: Kluwer Academic, 74–106.

VAN RAAIJ, W. F., and H. J. GIANOTTEN (1990). Consumer confidence, expenditure, saving, and credit, *Journal of Economic Psychology*, 11, (in press).

VROOM, V. H. (1964). *Work and Motivation*. New York: Wiley.

WEBLEY, P., and R. SPEARS (1986). Economic preferences and inflationary expectations, *Journal of Economic Psychology*, 7, 359–369.

WYER, R. S., JR. (1970). Quantitative prediction of belief and opinion change: A further test of a subjective probability model, *Journal of Personality and Social Psychology*, 16, 559–570.

WINER, R. S. (1986). A reference price model of brand choice for frequently purchased products, *Journal of Consumer Research*, 13, 250–256.

WOODRUFF, R. B., E. R. CADOTTE, and R. L. JENKINS (1983). Modeling consumer satisfaction processes using experience-based norms, *Journal of Marketing Research*, 20, 296–304.

12

ORGANIZATIONAL BUYING BEHAVIOR*

Scott Ward
University of Pennsylvania

Frederick E. Webster, Jr.
Dartmouth University

Organizational buying behavior refers to decision-making processes in formal organizations. Research in this area has traditionally focussed on supplier choice, but more recent research has examined intrafirm and interfirm processes affecting a variety of outcomes.

The early comprehensive paradigms attempted to model broad classes of influences on vendor selection. More recently, researchers have attempted to capture the international nature of organizational buying behavior, and have broadened the scope of their interests beyond vendor selection to issues, such as formation of strategic alliances between firms, and the outcomes of the focussed aspects of organizational buying behavior, such as dyadic communication between vendors and buyers. This chapter surveys the state of knowledge from research based on early models and on more recent interaction paradigms. In addition, methodological and measurement issues are discussed.

INTRODUCTION

If one judges by the length of time an area has attracted research attention, the study of organizational buying behavior is relatively ma-

ture—at least in the field of consumer behavior research. Early studies portrayed a "rational buyer" characteristic of industrial purchasing (Copeland 1924), reflecting economic theories fashionable at the time, but many researchers in the field would point to behavioral science inquiries as the starting point of "modern" research in the field [e.g., Cyert and March's classic, *A Behavioral Theory of the Firm* (1963), as

*The authors wish to thank Victor Cook and David Wilson for their thoughtful and useful comments on early drafts of this chapter.

well as the work of Cyert, Simon, and Trow 1956; Sills 1957; Blau 1955; and Etzioni 1961]. On the other hand, if the "maturity" of a research area is measured more by theoretical elegance and the depth of related empirical research, the field of organizational buying behavior is far from maturity.

Kassarjian (1986) observes that research in consumer behavior follows a "product life cycle" curve, with early, ground-breaking conceptualizations followed by considerably more narrow "fine tuning" empirical investigations and by studies focussing on methodological and measurement issues. His characterization is mostly true for this field: early models of organizational buying behavior were followed by a spate of studies that focussed on particular aspects of models, such as measurement and methodological issues, elaboration of subparts of the model, or, in some cases, attempts to validate models. However, the process of model generation continues today. In the last two decades, no fewer than two dozen models have appeared, ranging from reasonably complete paradigms to more limited conceptualizations. The proliferation of model generation has outpaced follow-up research to test the models: A mismatch exists between the generation of conceptualizations and the production of research findings based on them.

For all of these reasons, the field is far from a set of "middle-range" theories[1] that can satisfactorily explain the phenomena of organizational buying behavior. Our position is that such middle-range theories are the goal of research in this area. Moreover, we believe that near-term progress will not lie in developing more broad conceptualizations, but interested researchers need not fear that they will be relegated to "fine tuning" either. Rather, research that reorganizes existing findings and concepts, and operationalizes, tests, and extends existing work, will be useful in attaining the goal of a coherent set of middle-range theories of organizational buying behavior.

Our predilection for middle-range theories reflects our belief that attempts to develop simple, broad theories or models, which characterized early work in this field, have formed a useful basis for research in recent years, as we will see. However, we are disturbed that much more recent research has jumped to measurement issues—"fine tuning"—before more limited models and theories have emerged to satisfactorily explain aspects of the overall phenomenon. Middle-range theories seek to explain circumscribed aspects of larger processes. For example, middle-range theories might focus on intrafirm influence processes that determine sourcing decisions. Such a research topic focuses on a particular aspect of overall organizational buying behavior (intrafirm processes) and on a specific dependent variable (sourcing decisions).

Our objective in this chapter is to review and assess substantive areas of conceptual work and empirical research in the area of organizational buying behavior. Our goal is not to offer yet another conceptualization, but to characterize and analyze work in the field, and to note other streams of research that can contribute to the kinds of reorganization, operationalization, testing, and extensions that we believe hold considerable promise for theory building and management practice. Our intended audience is potential students and researchers in the field, who wish to have an overview of models and research in the area.

We will structure our review in essentially chronological terms, beginning with early models of organizational buying behavior (OBB) and progressing through successive models that reflect important conceptual shifts in the field. One caveat is in order. As some authors put it: "If a reader wades into the literature on industrial buying behavior looking for structure, he will very likely come out reeling" (Bonoma, Zaltman, and Johnston 1977). Research and writing in the area constitute a formidable volume of work, and if one goes beyond literature dealing directly with OBB into related fields (such as organizational behavior

---

[1]The phrase "theories of the middle range" was coined by the sociologist Robert K. Merton to refer to theories that lie between the simple hypothesis found in abundance in day-to-day research efforts and to all inclusive systematic efforts to develop a unified theory that will explain all the observed uniformities. (1968, p. 39).

in management, dyadic interaction in psychology and communications, and transaction cost analysis in microeconomics), the literature and problems of finding structure increase exponentially. Consequently, we focus this paper on the important substantive models and the major conceptual shifts they represent. Beyond the models, we seek to broadly cite relevant literature in enough detail to entice the interested researcher and to inform the interested spectator.

DEFINITIONS AND OVERVIEW OF THE FIELD

As an area of study, organizational buying behavior is most often understood as an aspect of "industrial" or "business-to-business" marketing as opposed to "consumer" marketing. "Organizations" include industrial, reseller, institutional, and government markets (Kotler 1987). The *raison d'être* for research in the area is that the decision processes of individuals in an organizational context are different from decision processes in other contexts in which group dynamics are less important—a notion that is well supported in behavioral research.

Intuitively, organizational buying differs from consumer buying, but the differences may not be as clear as they appear. For example, organizational buying typically involves many individuals in the buying process, whereas consumer behavior often focuses on individual processes. However, consumer choices are often influenced by others, such as family members. Organizational purchases are thought to be more deliberate or "rational" than consumer decisions, but organizational decisions are also influenced by personal relationships, company and brand images, and other factors that many people would not consider "rational." It is true that organizational buying often involves more explicit procedures and criteria than typical consumer buying. And it involves more personal selling, reciprocity arrangements, limited product lines, and other features of industrial marketing, but these are differentiating characteristics rather than important conceptual differences.

Virtually all marketing management textbooks, as well as texts in consumer behavior and industrial marketing, include a chapter focussing on organizational buying behavior. In consumer behavior texts, the entire field of organizational buying behavior is often treated in a single chapter, whereas subareas of consumer behavior are treated in many chapters—some of them having relevance to organizational buying behavior. The single-chapter phenomenon may indicate that there is a great deal of focus in the area, and to a large extent this is true. There are few central concepts in the field, and they are relatively well-known.

The relatively sharp focus of the field is attributable to the predilection of researchers in the area for studying buying transactions between business organizations, in spite of the fact that other forms of organizations, such as families, can be fruitfully studied with the same concepts, for example, dyadic communication, coalition formation and functioning, and conflict resolution. Despite these opportunities for conceptual expansion of the domain of OBB, researchers and theorists have usually chosen to limit their interests to formal organizations—most often for-profit businesses—and to discuss behavioral phenomena and concepts such as those discussed previously in that context. Webster and Wind (1972), for example, define organizational buying behavior in the following way:

Organizational Buying Behavior is the decision-making process by which formal organizations establish the need for purchased products and services, and identify, evaluate, and choose among alternative brands and suppliers.

This definition posits that OBB is a process rather than a static event; it also suggests some nature of that process by identifying steps between "need" and choice behavior. Of note, the definition implies choice, and purchase. Today's business environment might include other kinds of choices, such as strategic alliances or joint ventures. Webster and Wind's definition is also slanted toward processes in the buying firm; clearly, processes in vendor firms are also relevant, as is the interaction process between vendor and potential buyer organizations. Several years after Webster and Wind's early conceptualization of organizational buying behavior, Bonoma, Zaltman, and Johnston (1977) also posited a decision-oriented and purchase-oriented process to define the field, but they stress that the process involves transactions and interaction:

Industrial buying behavior . . . [is] an explicit or implicit transactional decision-making interaction through which formal or informal profit centers represented by authorized delegates:
1. establish the need for products or services;
2. search among and identify potential suppliers;
3. evaluate the marketing mix, product, price, promotion, and distribution of potential suppliers;
4. negotiate for and enter into agreement about purchase terms;
5. complete a purchase; and,
6. evaluate the purchaser's utility in facilitating organizational goals.

This definition is deliberately limited to industrial groups, with its "profit center" stipulation, and it features role specialization ("authorized delegates") as well as transactional behavior. It also adds postpurchase evaluative activity, but stops short of defining that activity as an interactive process in which decision outcomes are linked to altered perceptions and the probabilities of future behavior between buying and selling firms as a function of previous interaction.

The dimensions that underlie these definitions of "industrial" or "organizational buying behavior" are broad ones. As we discussed, virtually all consumer behavior involves some kind of exchange or transaction; joint decision-making and role specialization occur in family groups as well as in organizations, and choice behavior is a dominant concern of consumer researchers. Consequently, definitions of organizational buying behavior reflect the deliberate choices of researchers to focus the field of interest.

For our purposes, we shall reflect the orientation of most research in the field and focus on transactions having economic importance for organizations. We will not arbitrarily limit our review to industrial firms, or only to purchasing behavior, since organizations can engage in many other behaviors, such as strategic alliances and joint ventures. In this chapter, "organization" most often refers to for-profit business organizations, since that is the focus of most research. The implications of that research, in our view, hold for other types of organizations as well, but are best treated separately from them (e.g., family units). We also define the field to include variables and influences from the larger environment of organizational transaction behavior, from such areas as the technological environment, the corporate culture, and the like, and we will briefly review aspects of organizational behavior that are "downstream" from the transactional behavior itself, such as the dyadic interaction that occurs between a salesperson and a purchasing agent, and the outcomes of decisions that influence later interorganization interaction.

From a management perspective, the academic field of "organizational buying behavior" is understood in terms of the critical activities of buying and selling. American firms invest heavily in the most tangible and measurable aspect of OBB: sales training programs, in which individuals are exposed to some OBB concepts as the basis for acquiring specific selling techniques. More generally, research in the field should be helpful to firms in understanding the behavioral dimensions underlying the larger processes of selling and purchasing. Such understanding can be translated to specific procurement procedures on the buying side, as well as to specific sales procedures on the vendor side. For example, the practice of "team-selling" reflects an understanding of the multiple-person buying center in customer firms, requiring a sales team composed of specialists to deal with the concerns of their counterparts in buying firms.

Profound changes in American business in recent years may drive a shifting focus in OBB research, which may begin to reflect very different relationships between organizations that interact in ways far beyond merely "buying" and "selling." Wilson and Mummalaneni (1988) point out that U.S. firms have downsized, entered into international arrangements of various sorts, and Webster (in a forthcoming work) observes that the strategic environment of business is causing vendors and buyers to reassess buying and procurement strategies:

Customers demand much more complete response to their needs from their vendors and in many instances place greater reliance for quality and delivery, as well as competitive prices, on a small number of suppliers. The nature of the relationship with vendors becomes a subject for strategic analysis and decision-making: should the procurement be done as a single transaction, a long-term buyer-seller relationship, or a formal strategic alliance such as a joint venture?

APPROACHES TO THE STUDY OF ORGANIZATIONAL BUYING BEHAVIOR: PARADIGMS AND RESEARCH

The earliest concerns with what has come to be defined as the field of organizational buying behavior were voiced by practicing managers, reflected in marketing textbooks, and conceptualized by researchers in early "models" of the phenomenon. But our models of organizational buying behavior have changed dramatically over the years.

Early Models of Organizational Buying Behavior

In the beginning of this century, it is probably safe to say that neither vendors nor sellers had much concern with organizational buying behavior. Transactions were limited to buying and selling, although relationships between salespeople and purchasers surely developed and influenced buying patterns. The predominant "model" guiding industrial marketing approaches was rooted in microeconomics, and it assumed that firms seek to minimize prices paid

for goods and to maximize profits. This minimum price model gave way to the related "lowest *total* cost" model, expanding the cost idea to include nonprice variables, such as service and reliability. Both models assumed perfect competition, information, and product substitutability—all microeconomic assumptions that do not reflect the real world of industrial transactions. Microeconomic notions are the underpinnings of the "rational buyer" model (Copeland 1924) that portrays a sort of multiattribute decision-making process among industrial buyers—about fifty years before such models were borrowed from psychology and applied in consumer behavior research. Essentially, the rational buyer model assumes purchasers assess all buying alternatives, using rational or objective criteria, weigh the payoffs associated with each, and make the decision that will maximize profit. In this simple view, the purchase is an outcome of a process controlled exclusively by the buyer.

While such rational processes surely characterize some OBB some of the time, other less "rational" processes are also involved. Additionally, the rational buyer model fails to reflect that decisions often involve many individuals. Early attempts to capture the multiperson characteristic of OBB employed flow diagrams of activities and job functions involved in specific industrial purchasing decisions. While such early flow charts were useful in their designations of activities, work flows, and individuals, their shortcomings were apparent. The extent and nature of the influences of individuals were not specified; in fact, the content of the linkages between individuals was not clear. Moreover, these diagrams were simply snapshots of particular purchases. Whether the same or different events would occur for other purchases was not clear. Such models were totally atheoretical, and they failed to even hint at concepts that could be useful in building theory.

Other early models sought to identify a single dominant theme, or characteristic, to explain OBB—one that reflected the real world of industrial purchase decision-making more than the earlier models derived from microeconomics. For example, Webster and Wind

(1972) note the popularity of a "source loyalty" model, which stresses habitual behavior and the tendency to prefer established suppliers. It is interesting to note that most of these early models were borrowed or adapted from behavioral science disciplines of the day. The pattern of "borrowing" models from parent disciplines and applying them to marketing contexts dominated consumer behavior research at the time (see Ward and Robertson 1973). In time, however, researchers constructed models based on the phenomena of interest. The first OBB-specific models were those focussing on decision processes within buying firms.

DECISION-PROCESS MODELS

Progress from pictorial models to conceptual ones occurred as researchers sought powerful explanatory variables to characterize OBB. Robinson, Faris, and Wind (1967) reasoned that the processes portrayed in the pictorial models would vary depending on the buying situation. They conceptualized "buyclasses," which have become part of the standard lexicon in the study of OBB: new task, modified rebuy, and straight rebuy. This continuum of purchase situations reflects that the time frame, the amount and type of information, and the number and types of participants all vary, depending on the relative newness of a buying situation.

Straight rebuys refer to goods or services that have been bought before, and routinely repurchased. *Modified rebuys* include things purchased previously, but it implies an information search that is more extensive than in straight rebuy situations. *New task* situations are the most complex, involving more people and deliberation.

Others have offered modifications to this early scheme of buying situations, or *buyclasses*. Lehmann and O'Shaughnessy (1974) suggested four product-related dimensions that hint at very different characteristics of buying situations: (1) Routine order, (2) Procedural problem product, (3) Performance problem product, and (4) Political problem product.

Moriarty and Galper (1978) proposed a two-dimensional buying classification that suggested that individual buying depends both on the buyclass and on the actual product categories: raw materials, components, capital equipment, and supply items.

All of these early decision-process models can be characterized as what Webster and Wind first called "task models," which emphasized descriptive or explanatory variables directly related to the "work" or decision-making of the purchase task itself. Task models were accompanied by "nontask" models of OBB, defined as those " . . . based on a set of variables (such as buyer's motives) which do not have a direct bearing on the specific problem to be solved by the buying task, although they may be important determinants of the final purchasing decision" (Webster and Wind 1972). Among the earliest nontask models were those borrowed from perceived risk theory in psychology, an area that was already enjoying fruitful application in consumer behavior (Bauer 1960; Cox 1967). Researchers interested in OBB quickly adapted this stream of research to their interests. For example, Sweeney, Matthews, and Wilson (1973) suggested four risk reduction strategies in OBB based on whether risk was internal or external, and whether it pertained to uncertainty or to consequences. Webster and Wind also suggested tactical ways industrial marketers reduce risk, for example, gathering information and developing source loyalty.

Another nontask model borrowed from behavioral science and applied to organizational buying behavior is in the area of diffusion of innovations (Rogers 1962, 1969). Initially proposed by rural sociologists, who were interested in how and why some agricultural innovations are adopted more readily than others, the model has been applied to OBB, and constitutes a chapter of its own in the general field of consumer behavior research (see Chapter 9 in this volume). However, relatively little research has explicitly focussed on organizational buying behavior for new products from a diffusion standpoint (Webster 1972; Moore 1986), and this is a potential area for future research.

Task and nontask models were the precursors of attempts to characterize the decision processes involved in OBB. Earlier studies had explored these processes, including the seminal work of Cyert, Simon, and Trow (1956), who documented three aspects of decision processes in their case study of a single firm: recurring, routine processes; communication processes within the firm; and problem-solving processes. Building on these early process notions, Robinson, Faris, and Wind (1967) posed an eight-stage decision process:

1. Anticipation of the recognition of a problem (need) and a general solution;
2. Determination of characteristics and quantity of needed item;
3. Description of characteristics and quantity of needed item;
4. Search for a qualification of potential sources;
5. Acquisition and analysis of proposals;
6. Evaluation of proposals and selection of supplier(s);
7. Selection of an order routine;
8. Performance feedback and evaluation.

This conception of purchase-decision stages is important, since it posits behavioral motives and activities that are presumed to be functionally related to subsequent choice behaviors. Such purchase-decision stages notions are generally labeled the "DMP," or the decision-making process. The DMP is conceptually similar to "hierarchy of effects" notions in communications and the "stages of adoption" notions in the diffusion of innovation literature. The extensiveness of the DMP clearly varies with the particular buying situation, and this contingency was also addressed in the 1967 study. The authors relate the DMP to buyclasses in their "Buygrid" model (Figure 12.1).

In 1968, Ozane and Churchill posed a decision process model for new products that builds upon these earlier conceptualizations (see Figure 12.2). For these authors, the organizational buying decision is conceptually similar to the

BUYGRID Model	New Task	Modified Rebuy	Straight Rebuy
1. Anticipation or recognition of a problem (need).			
2. Determination of characteristics and quantity of needed item.			
3. Description of characteristics and quantity of needed item.			
4. Search for and qualification of potential sources.			
5. Acquisition and analysis of potential sources.			
6. Evaluation of proposals and selection of supplier(s).			
7. Selection of an order routine.			
8. Performance feedback and evaluation.			

FIGURE 12.1
The BUYGRID Model
(Source: Robinson, Faris, and Wind 1967.)

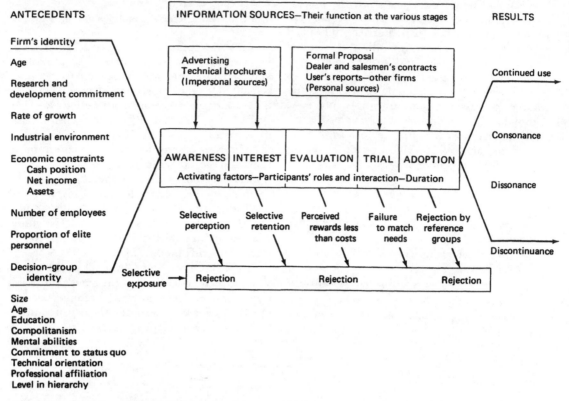

FIGURE 12.2 The Industrial Adoption Process Model
(Source: Ozanne and Churchill (1971).)

hierarchy of effects model in communications research (Colley 1961; Lavidge and Steiner 1961) and the diffusion of innovations model briefly discussed earlier. The model draws heavily from behavioral concepts, especially in the early stages, to explain reasons for the "rejection" of new products. Progress from awareness to adoption is influenced in the early stages by general information sources, and later by more specific media and personal influence.

Moriarty and Galper (1978) usefully integrate the early "buyphase" notions of Robinson, Faris, and Wind (1967) and Ozanne and Churchill's model (1968). Their integrative model notes that awareness and problem recognition both constitute a first stage in a DMP, since either may initiate the process, and both must be present to stimulate movement through later stages. For example, someone in a firm may become aware of a new product, process, vendor, etc., and that person may recognize an internal problem based on that knowledge; or, it may be that the problem is perceived first, leading to a search for a new product, process, or vendor, as portrayed in most of these decision-process models.

In the 1970s two other decision-process models were developed. Hiller (1975) proposed a three-part model of the buying decision process: (1) processes within an individual participant; (2) intercompany processes, between buyers and sellers; and (3) intracompany processes, among decision participants within the buying company. Buying decision process participants are characterized as a nucleus, the decision-making unit; the primary shell, those who place major policy constraints on the decision; and the secondary shell, those who are consulted and provide information. Corey (1978) offered a four-stage decision process model that, while managerially oriented, has broad behavioral implications:

1. *Defining the scope* of the procurement, including what is to be purchased and the scope of the buyer-seller commitment
2. *Supplier selection,* including the number and type of vendors
3. *Price-quantity determination,* the process by which prices will be agreed to: market price, competitive bidding, or cost-plus pricing; and the general issues of risk-sharing for matters such as inflation, changing buyer's requirements, and cost control
4. *Negotiating strategy,* which will be a function of the type of pricing, and includes decisions about the location of the negotiations and who will be involved.

Taken together, the decision-process models represented a useful step forward from earlier models. Complex processes were detailed and described, rather than assumed to occur as a function of some underlying process or variable. Concepts were posited to bring order and parsimony to early flowchart representations of decisions. However, the models generally did not do a good job of distinguishing between task and nontask variables, and they were silent on the issue of the interaction of multiple individuals involved in the DMP. Their strength was that they described a complex phenomenon well by breaking it down; however, their descriptive characteristic was also a weakness, since there was little basis to offer hypotheses or predictions, and the models provided little guidance in specifying functional relationships necessary to understand how the DMP affected, and was affected by, other OBB variables and processes.

Reflecting the descriptive nature of the early decision-process models, much empirical research attempts to validate the core concepts articulated in decision-process models, as well as to extend them by deriving testable hypotheses. For example, researchers have hypothe-

sized that different kinds of information should be important, depending on the buyclass. Lehmann and O'Shaughnessy (1974) found different attributes were important in vendor selection, depending on the type of buying situation: reliability of delivery and price were most important for routine order products, whereas technical service, ease of use, and training were most important for procedural problem products. Their study was replicated by Evans (1980), who found similar results.

Other researchers have employed protocol analysis (Doyle, Woodside, and Mitchell 1979; Matthyssens and Faes 1985) and cognitive scripts (Leigh and Rethans 1984) to test hypotheses regarding the activities and relative influence of individuals within and across buyclasses. Pingry (1976) found that purchasing agents dominate straight rebuy situations and engineers are most influential for new tasks. Brand (1972) found technical personnel were most important in new tasks and modified rebuys, but, contrary to the buyclass notion, they were also important in routine rebuys, as well. Jackson, Keith, and Burdick (1984), using data from purchasing agents in a role-playing task, report variations in influence across product classes, but not across buyclasses.

In an important recent study, Anderson, Chu, and Weitz (1987) found some support for the original buyclass model. They asked experienced field sales managers about buying decisions in customer organizations, focussing on the three dimensions that Robinson, Faris, and Wind (1967) suggest distinguish between buyclasses: newness of problem, information needs, and consideration of new alternatives. They found a strong association of newness with the amount of information desired by decision-makers, but only a weak correlation between these two measures and the tendency of buyers to consider new vendors. Their results suggest that newness of task and needs for information define buyclasses, but not a consideration of alternatives. They also found that the "buying centers," or the DMUs, for new tasks were characteristically large, slow to decide, uncertain about needs and appropriate solutions, more concerned about getting good solutions than getting a low price or an assured supply, more willing to consider vendors other than those currently used, and more apt to involve more technical personnel. In contrast, the direct opposite characteristics of DMU needs and behaviors were reported by these sales managers for straight and modified rebuys, where buying centers were likely to be small, quick to decide, confident in their appraisals of the problem and the possible solution, concerned about price and availability of supply, satisfied with "in" suppliers, and more influenced by purchasing agents (p. 82).

COMPREHENSIVE MODELS

By the 1970s, researchers had integrated research and conceptualizations into complex, comprehensive models that attempted to specify most of the variables characterizing OBB and to predict purchase decisions. Two of the best known were offered by Webster and Wind (1972) and Sheth (1973).

Webster and Wind's Model. Perhaps the most widely known generalized comprehensive model of OBB was developed by Webster and Wind (1972). This model (Figure 12.3) includes and extends earlier notions in Cyert and March's behavioral theory of the firm, which is focussed on decision-making among individuals within the organization. For these authors, a buying situation is created when a member of an organization perceives a problem that can be solved through purchasing. In response, a *buying center* is created, consisting of individuals who will be involved in the buying decision. The buying center consists of these individuals, who are seen as playing five roles: users, deciders, influencers, buyers, and gatekeepers. Gatekeepers control information flow and are usually purchasing agents, but many other job functions may be represented in the other roles. Other authors have added other roles, including Bonoma's "initiator" (1982), which was implied in Webster and Wind's definition of a buying situation. O'Shaughnessy (1977) reinterpreted and added some roles: initiator, advisor, liaison, monitor, authority, and decider—the latter with respect to specifications, sourcing, and/or vendor selection.

One individual may occupy several roles, and several individuals may occupy one role, such as the role of influencer. Each member of the buying center is likely to have unique expectations, perceptions, and objectives, reflecting his or her job function in the organization.

The Webster and Wind model specifies four sets of variables: environmental, organizational, interpersonal (the buying center), and individual. The relationships among these variables are summarized in Figure 12.3. Environmental variables include political, legal, cultural, technological, economic, and physical variables; their influence is exercised by social and economic institutions, such as governments and labor unions, as well as by supplier and competitor organizations.

Organizational variables are featured in Webster and Wind's model that distinguish it from Sheth's (1973) model (published a year later and discussed subsequently). Webster and Wind formulate four sets of these variables: technological, structural, goals and tasks, and actors, using a scheme developed by Leavitt (1964). A subset of each of these four sets of variables is relevant to particular buying situations, which have specific influence in terms of the composition and functioning of the buying center. For example, in centralized organizations, the buyer's job is influenced by defining geographical location, by establishing authority relationships between buyers and higher-level purchasing executives, by determining the formal nature of communication between buyers and users, and so forth.

The four organizational subsystems (technology, structure, tasks, and actors) interact with one another to determine organizational functioning and to define for individuals within the buying center the information, expectations, goals, attitudes, and assumptions used in their decision-making. Buying tasks are categorized in four dimensions: the organizational purpose served, the nature of demand (e.g., seasonality, derived demand, etc.), the extent of programming or routinization in the DMP,

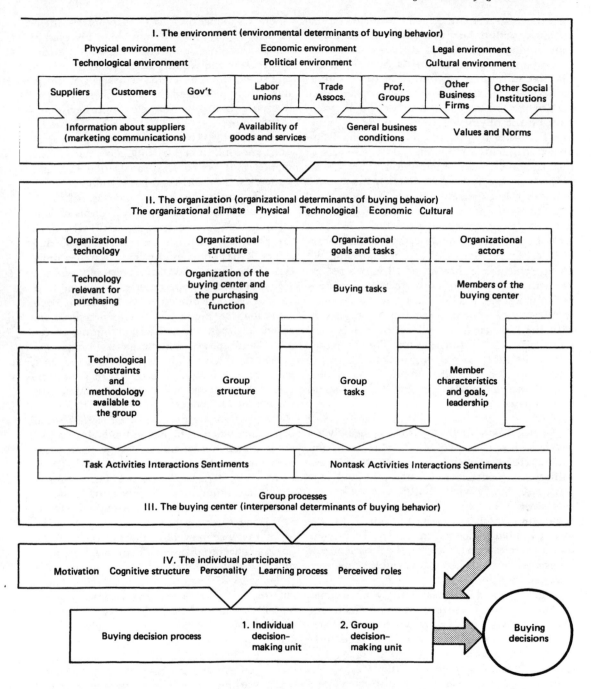

FIGURE 12.3 A General Model of Organizational Buying Behavior
(Source: Webster and Wind (1972).)

and the degree of decentralization of buying authority within the organization for the particular buying problem.

Organizational structure is further divided into five subsystems of communication, authority, status, rewards, and workflow; and each system is examined in the model for its influence on the buying decision process.

The functioning of the buying center is analyzed in terms of models and constructs of interpersonal (social) interaction. The role set of each of the individual participants, which includes role expectations, role behavior, and role relationships, is examined in detail. The nature of group functioning is influenced by the individual member's goals and personal characteristics, by the nature of group leadership, by group structure and tasks, and by external influences, including both organizational and environmental variables. Group processes include those activities and interactions having to do with the task itself, as well as the nontask dimensions of group functioning. Thus, the output of the DMP is not only a solution to the buying problem, but also provides nontask outcomes, such as satisfaction, for the group and its members.

Sheth's Model (1973). Drawing heavily on psychological concepts, Sheth does not detail the DMP or explicitly deal with buyclasses; rather, his model focuses on inputs and outputs, with the "buying decision process" as essentially the "black box" in traditional stimulus-organism-response (S-O-R) notions in behavioral psychology (see Figure 12.4). His focus is on inputs to the DMP, and on the interaction of influences on the dependent variable of discrete purchase decisions.

The range and level of specificity of variables in Sheth's model suggests the complexity of OBB processes—for example, "situational variables" include economic conditions, labor disputes, and so forth—and could include buyclasses. Variables such as "lifestyle," "role orientation," and "perceptual distortion" are also very general, with vast differences among them in the ease with which they may be operationalized and measured.

Sheth's model usefully conceptualizes differences in expectations of individuals involved in the purchase decision. These expectations, defined as the individual's perceptions of the extent to which each vendor or brand can satisfy the individual's needs and purchasing objectives, are shaped by marketer-controlled information sources, although they are modified by perceptual distortion. Additionally, expectations are conditioned by influences outside the marketer's direct control: satisfaction with past purchases and individual backgrounds.

Reflecting the notion of "buyclasses," Sheth distinguishes buying situations in terms of their inherent risk, and in terms of whether decisions are made jointly or autonomously. Following Bauer (1967) and Levitt (1965), risk is a function of the buyer's level of uncertainty and the seriousness of the consequences associated with various decision outcomes. Autonomous decisions may be made when time pressures are severe, or when the purchase is routine; on the other hand, the larger the organization and the greater the degree of decentralization, the more joint decision-making will occur. In joint decision making, participants in the buying process engage in conflict resolution.

The particular modes of conflict resolution depend on whether or not individuals disagree about available information with which to evaluate alternatives, and whether or not disagreement is about relevant criteria. The notion of conflict resolution modes is conceptually similar to research in family decision-making (Davis 1976) and to empirical studies of purchasing agent influence in organizations (Strauss 1962). Sheth's conceptualization of conflict resolution modes within the firm is also related to the earlier work of Cyert and March (1963). Those authors posit that there is latent conflict among organizational goals. Conflict may be resolved by breaking down problems into subparts and delegating issues to different parts of the organization ("local rationality"), by problematic search (information seeking), and by organizational learning (modifying future procedures based on past experience). Clearly, these notions are reflected in several aspects of Sheth's model.

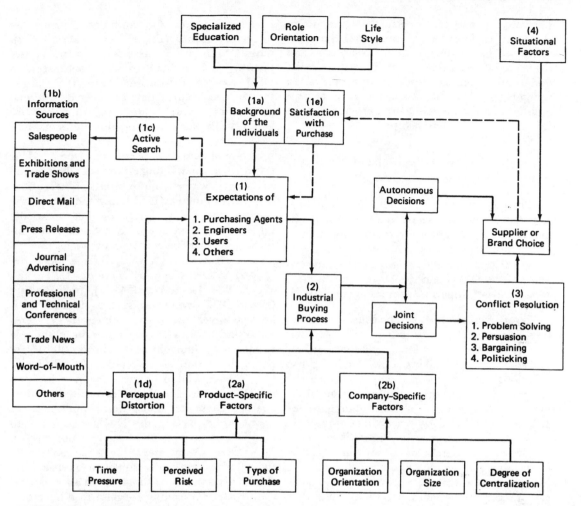

FIGURE 12.4 Sheth's Model of Industrial Buying
(Source: Sheth (1973).)

Choffray and Lilien's Model. Choffray and Lilien (1978 and 1980b) proposed a relatively quantitative model. Their industrial market response model consists of controllable variables (product design and marketing support), a decision process model, and external measures for parts of the DMP. The decision process model consists of four components: awareness, acceptance, individual evaluation, and group decision. The awareness component is the evoked set of possible vendors for each member of the decision-making unit; the evoked set is reduced by the acceptance stage and evaluated by indi-

viduals. The group-decision process is conceptualized as taking one of four potential forms: a weighted probability model, where the weight affects an individual's power; a proportionality model, where all members have equal weight; an unanimity model, where the process keeps going until all members agree; and an acceptability model, where the choice is the one least disturbing to the individual member's preferences.

Moriarty (1983) points out that the model rests on two key assumptions: that the DMU can be characterized by the job functions of participants, and that decision participants in the same category (e.g., engineers) share the same set of product evaluation criteria and the same information sources. Nonetheless, the quantitative characteristics of the model make it highly useful: It makes specific what are generalities in other models, and it provides a basis for testable interrelationships.

Empirical Research Stimulated by the Comprehensive Models

The comprehensive models have stimulated the most empirical research in OBB. Their conceptually rich variables and multivariate nature offer many opportunities for empirical analysis. Most research has been stimulated by the concepts of the DMU and the DMP, and we turn to a review of important studies in these areas.

Research on the DMU. The constructs of the buying center (Webster and Wind 1972), the buying task group (Spekman and Stern 1979), and the decision-making unit (Corey 1983) have long been the focus of empirical research. Cyert et al., (1956) first identified various individuals involved in a firm's major purchase decisions, and other early researchers in marketing (Dunkin 1940) recognized multiple-person involvement in purchases. Many other studies lend convergent validity to the proposition that the purchasing agent is rarely the single decision maker for purchase decisions, and that many other people are normally involved—particularly for different buyclasses, as we saw earlier in this chapter (*Scientific American* 1979; Harding 1966; O'Rourke, Shea, and Sulley 1973).

The DMU is "an informal, cross-sectional decision unit in which the primary objective is the acquisition, importation, and processing of purchase-related information" (Spekman and Stern 1979). DMUs may change from one purchasing situation to the next, and evolve during purchase decisions—different people may jump on, others may drop out. Although some DMUs may be called a "group" in the sense that they share a common vision of their purpose,

have specific roles, and exhibit other properties of formal groups (French and Raven 1959), most DMUs are far less formal, and consequently, more difficult to access and assess in OBB research. Bristor and Ryan (1988) argue that buying centers do not meet definitional criteria for "group" status, and that they are better studied as communication and social networks.

From a managerial perspective, the DMU is crucial, since marketing efforts must be tailored to the specific needs and interests of individuals identified in the DMU. Management must appreciate the group dynamics that make the DMU more than simply a collection of concerns among independent individuals.

The structure of the DMU has been described in terms of job functions (Lilien and Wong 1984; Jackson et al. 1984), job categories (Brand 1972), and roles, such as decider, gatekeeper, buyer, users, and influencers (Webster and Wind 1972). Gronhaug introduced the role of initiator. Ghingold and Wilson (1985) proposed the notion of "stakeholder," and Calder (1977) suggested over two dozen roles that might characteristically be involved in industrial purchase decisions. Some authors have posed other roles in the DMU that serve to involve other people and functions not directly in the DMU. Wind and Robertson (1982) identify a "linking pin" individual who exerts leadership in his or her own subgroup in an organization (such as a leading surgeon in a hospital), but who also maintains effective membership and influence in higher levels in the organization. Similarly, Spekman (1979) identifies a "boundary role person," and Krapfel (1982, 1985) describes this role in his advocacy model, discussed earlier. Essentially, he argues that some members of the DMU become advocates of the seller, a notion also suggested by Bruno (1982).

A few studies have attempted to identify determinants of buying group structures. For example, the size of the group is affected by perceived product importance, the resources available for handling buying problems, and the degree of routinization of the buying problems (Gronhaug 1975). Some of Gronhaug's characteristics appear conceptually similar to buyclasses. Patchen (1974) found that a person's "stake" in the purchase decision affected that person's participation in the DMU.

The concept of "role" has usefully been employed in research on DMU behavior. Stemming from the "interaction" or "relationship" tradition in OBB research, the concept of *role* refers to learned sets of behaviors associated with positions in groups that imply particular expectations and behaviors (Katz and Kahn 1966). Kernan and Sommers (1966) examined several dimensions of roles relating to industrial buying: types of roles, role commitment, and the maturity of occupational role types. This suggests probable ways that both buyers and sellers consider their roles and the implications of these perceptions for buying behavior.

Some authors have examined "role stress" as a feature of the work environment, and its impact on buying behavior. Thomas (1982), for example, found that role conflict, as well as role responsibility, mediate the influence a member of the DMU exerts in efforts to change others' buying decisions. Experimental results suggest that role stress affects buyer negotiation behavior and vendor selection (Clopton 1984; Puto, Patton, and King 1985). Industrial buyers were found to experience less ambiguity about their roles in OBB when the degree of formalization (explicit roles and policies, etc.) is high in the organization. However, high formalization is associated with high levels of role conflict — that is, individuals find themselves in roles that produce conflicting feelings and desires in the purchase decision. (For example, an individual's role may be to bring innovative products to the firm, but also to insure high quality and consistent supply, which may not always accompany new products.) Role ambiguity was found to be associated with both lower work satisfaction and lower levels of performance in organizational buying. However, role conflict was associated with lower work satisfaction, but with higher levels of job performance in one study (Michaels, Day, and Joachimsthaler 1987).

Other conceptualizations of the decision making unit have been proposed, such as coalitions (Bagozzi 1978) and networks (Bristor 1988), but little empirical research has been done on these concepts.

Research on the DMP. Much OBB research has focussed on the DMP, since a decision-making process is presumed to precede and be functionally related to vendor selection. Early "static" OBB models portray the DMP as a series of activities, or steps, whereas models in the interaction tradition portray DMPs as a complex series of transactions occurring over time. Despite the intuitive appeal of the idea of decision-making stages, studies indicate that there is considerable variation in procedures across organizations and products purchased (Choffray 1977; Johnston 1981; Johnston and Bonoma 1981; Moriarty and Galper 1978). Research also indicates that different areas within companies emphasize different criteria and objectives in purchasing (Choffray and Lilien 1980; Hutt and Speh 1981; Sheth 1973). Thus, three major areas of research are identified: studies that treat the DMP as a dependent variable, studies that examine variables mediating the DMP, and studies that examine the DMP itself.

ORGANIZATIONAL AND ENVIRONMENTAL INFLUENCES ON THE DMP. Studies have examined organizational "demographics" such as firm size, as well as variables pertaining to the organizational environment, in an attempt to predict differences in the DMP. For example, Crow and Lindquist (1982) report that the greater the organization's size, the less individuals report they are influential in buying decisions. Bellizi (1981) found different levels of influence depending on the size of firm, but he found similar patterns of influence among various job functions across the DMP, regardless of firm size. Other demographic variables, such as the firm's use of electronic data processing (EDP), has been related to the DMP. For example, increasing use of EDP and telecommunications may explain why two other organizational variables — geographics and communication separation — were not related to organizational buying patterns (Bellizi and Belonax 1982). Thomas and Grashof (1982) found that the DMP can be described by organizational rules when the internal and external environments of firms are stable.

In an important stream of research, Spekman and Stern (1979) utilized concepts from contingency theory in organizational behavior (Lawrence and Lorsch 1967) to explain buying group structure and decision-making processes. They found that greater participation by lower-level members of the DMU and a reduced importance of formal rules and procedures characterized DMPs when task uncertainty was high. Theoretical and empirical support of this contingency theory view has also been reported by Galbraith (1977), Duncan (1972), Sathe (1974), and Spekman (1977, 1978). Spekman and Stern's (1979) finding, based on contingency theory, is directly contrary to other views that hold that decisions will be made by fewer and more senior people when the buying task environment is uncertain (Cardozo 1980; Straw, Sandelands, and Dutton 1981; Corey 1971). This is called "constriction at the top."

In a test of these two competing predictions of the environmental effects of the decision-making unit and the decision-making process, McCabe found strong support of the "constriction at the top" logic (McCabe 1987, p. 96):

Top managers [tend] to centralize the DMP in response to high levels of decision-making uncertainty in the form of both product complexity and perceived task uncertainty.

The related concept of risk has been featured in various conceptualizations of OBB, as we have seen (Sheth 1973; Webster and Wind 1972), and research suggests that perceived risk affects vendor evaluation and selection (Levitt 1965), information seeking (Sweeney, Matthews, and Wilson 1973), and sourcing decisions (Sweeney, Matthews, and Wilson 1973). Another variable pertaining to the organizational environment that may affect the DMP is conflict. Perceived conflict during the DMP has

been related to the centralization of authority (Broughton 1980) and stages in the DMP (Broughton, Banville, and Lambert 1986). Robertson and Wind (1980) found that conflict was negatively related to innovativeness among hospital administrators but positively related to innovativeness for users. Ryan and Holbrook (1982) present nomological validity for the conceptualization of "decision-specific" conflict; that is, conflict is associated with each decision in a total consumption system, rather than as a function of organizational or individual variables. Comparatively little research has focussed on conflict resolution. O'Shaughnessy (1977) believes that buying decisions conform to formal or informal rules in organizations, including rules for resolving conflicts.

Barclay (1987) examined the impact of organizational contexts on interdepartmental conflict in organizational buying. Using a partial least squares approach, he found that the dominant antecedents to conflict in the DMP were barriers to interdepartmental communication, the practice of rewarding departments for meeting their own goals as opposed to wider organizational goals, ambiguity regarding departmental jurisdictions, rules and procedures that can reduce conflict, and the diversity of perspectives held by different departments due to different information sources, decision criteria, and interests.

Finally, aspects of an organization's orientation and position in its environment may influence the DMP. Gronhaug (1977) studied "product dependent" and "product independent" organizations. The former as firms that operate in competitive markets and depend upon exchange of output for survival; product independent firms, on the other hand, derive important parts of their revenues from contributing or regulatory groups. Product independent groups were found to initiate purchases because regulatory groups approved of the purchase, or because funds were available in the budget. Product dependent groups, on the other hand, initiate purchases because of actual need, and may be more likely to innovate—purchase a product primarily because it is new.

Campbell (1985) suggests that industry structure variables affect the DMP. He conceptualizes buying strategies or decision-making processes such as competitive bidding, or cooperative buying. Building on Porter (1980), he argues that organizational and environmental characteristics, including product, industry, company, and individual variables, all interact to determine which type of DMP is likely to characterize an organization. For example, competitive bidding is likely when a firm has a low frequency of purchases, when many suppliers exist, and when centralized buying and price are important.

VARIABLES THAT MEDIATE THE DMP. As noted previously, variables such as organizational size, departmental influences, and products purchased have been found to affect the nature of the decision-making process. Puto, Patton, and King (1985) identify more specific mediating variables: loyalty to existing suppliers, dominant attributes of the buying situation (such as price, quality, and service), and the buyer's perception of the procurement problem. Their findings, from a national survey of 2,000 industrial buyers, reinforce previous findings about the importance of source loyalty and the desire for certainty among buyers. However, their data suggest that risk handling is also related to how buyers "frame" the buying problem. The latter concept emanates from behavioral decision theory, and refers to "the decision maker's conception of the acts, outcomes, and contingencies associated with a particular choice" (Tversky and Kahneman, 1981, p. 453). In short, the decision frame is the complex scenario, and context, surrounding an industrial buying decision.

DECISION-MAKING PROCESSES. While much research has focussed on determinants of the DMP and the variables that mediate it, some studies have attempted to study the DMP itself. Moller (1985) classifies such studies in five methodological traditions. Decision systems analysis (DSA), as we have seen, is a process-tracing methodology, tracking the DMP through interviews with various individuals involved in the process (Vyas and Woodside 1984; Capon and Hulbert 1975; Capon, Farley, and Hulbert 1975; Woodside and Vyas 1981; Moller and Allos 1983). Structural role analysis is similar to DSA, but it is focussed more on individuals and their interrelationships, positions, and tasks (Calder 1977). Social influence analysis focuses on interpersonal relations within the buying center and, for Moller, includes conceptualizations and empirical research in the interaction tradition. Finally, information-processing analysis and multiattribute choice analysis focus on individuals' decision-making criteria and heuristics (Leigh and Rethans 1984; Clarkson 1963; Bettman 1977; Wildt and Bruno 1974).

In a pilot study of 15 organizational decisions, Wilson, Lilien, and Wilson (1988) examine seven formal group choice models that describe how organizational buying centers may make supplier choice decisions (based on the work of Choffray and Lilien 1980). Their findings support a contingency paradigm that states that particular choice processes, represented by the models, depend on the situation surrounding the decision. The situational, or contingent, conditions in the study were the degree of technical complexity, the cost, and the buyclass.

To summarize, the construct of a decision-making process is intended to account for activities functionally related to purchase decisions in organizations. Views of this process have progressed from early notions of a very simple and rational process to the specification of discrete stages, and on to the interaction view that the process cannot be specified by a series of discrete steps but occurs over the course of multiple transactions. Empirical studies suggest that, regardless of one's conceptual view, many factors mediate the process: At the broadest level, environmental and organizational characteristics exert significant influence on the DMP. Other mediating variables involve social processes of conflict reduction and risk reduction. Then there are specific situational variables, such as type of purchase, technical complexity, time pressure, cost and so forth. Each class of variables has significant effects on both the DMU and the DMP.

Conclusions on Comprehensive Models. Taken together, comprehensive models have stimulated much research and further conceptualization in the field. Each has strengths and weaknesses. For example, Webster and Wind are much more explicit about variables and processes that are only generally portrayed in Sheth's model; on the other hand, Sheth's model treats some microprocesses that are not included in Webster and Wind's model, such as perceptual distortion. In a comment that could apply to both of these early comprehensive models, Webster (1988) notes that the major strengths and weaknesses of the Webster and Wind model are due to its generality:

The model is comprehensive and identifies many key variables for consideration by the marketing strategist and provides an analytic framework for thinking about their interaction. But the model is weak on assertions about specific influence of these variables. One of the major benefits of the model is that . . . it has stimulated much high quality research and has provided an integrated framework for interpreting results and relating them to one another in such a way that a reasonably lively body of knowledge . . . has been developing . . . (1984, p. 39)

The relatively few comprehensive models have been followed in recent years by several more limited paradigms. These share a common focus on the interaction of individuals and organizations, and on the nature of the relationships that bond them. We now turn to the more recent research tradition in OBB.

INTERACTION AND RELATIONSHIP MODELS

In their 1977 monograph, Bonoma, Zaltman, and Johnston complain that most of the models and research in OBB, if not "all marketing," mistakenly focus on the unit paradigm (i.e., "models . . . limited to the behavior or actions of single actors or aggregates of actors or to the properties or characteristics of these actors") and are based on simplistic stimulus-response conceptualizations:

It is our strong belief that . . . S-R assumptions in the study of industrial buying behavior, with the corollary focus on individual choice processes and "rationality" characteristics, have misdirected both theory and explanation. The unit paradigm suffers from a number of failures to connect its basic structure with the readily observable bases of social action. First, the paradigm is mechanistic; actors and PAs (purchasing agents) are not so. Second, the unit paradigm takes a naive and unidirectional view of social causation in the industrial buying area as "moving" from stimulus to response; it does not acknowledge that responses also influence their stimuli, as in classic operant conditioning. Third, the paradigm has the classic problem of reductionism, of forcing a transactional sort of behavior into an individualistic mode. But the most basic and most serious problem is the unit paradigm's neglect of the social character of industrial buying behavior. (p. 20)

For these authors, the dyad is the appropriate level of analysis for understanding buying behavior, and they intend the dyadic paradigm to extend not only to two-person interaction (e.g., salesperson-purchasing agent), but also to the interacting organizational entities themselves (see Figure 12.5). Elsewhere, Bonoma, Bagozzi, and Zaltman (1978) posit a "system paradigm," consisting of an "embeddation model" in which dyadic relations are contained in an overall system context.

The broadly conceived dyadic paradigm has a number of characteristics:

1. Parties in the relationships have mutual interests;
2. The dyad contains instances of social influence;
3. Forces in the situation shape the relationship and outcomes;
4. Characteristics of the actors are important;
5. Normative factors are important;
6. Purposive behavior alters dyadic relations; and
7. There is uncertainty in the relationship.

Most of all, Bonoma et al. stress the characteristic of interdependence in dyadic relations:

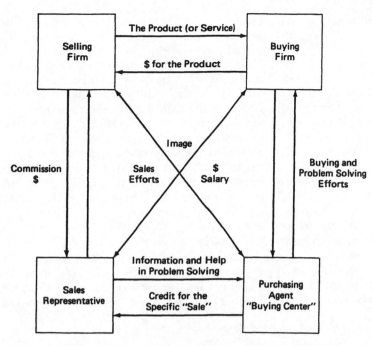

FIGURE 12.5 The Industrial Buying Process as an Exchange (Source: Bonoma, Zaltman, and Johnston (1977).)

The social or dyadic view of industrial buying behavior uncovers, emphasizes, and makes explicit the relational quality and character of interaction between the stimulus "provider" (the salesman, marketers, etc.), and the "recipient" (the consumer), and suggests that these relational, interactional properties of their joint behavior provide a much more powerful and consistent view of the character and outcome of the consumption act than does the "unit" paradigm of stimulus components. (p. 25)

Bonoma et al. review research and concepts relevant to intraorganizational influences on industrial buying process, using concepts and theories drawn mainly from psychology: motivation, learning and perception, role theory, word-of-mouth influences, group decision making, and dyadic communication. Interorganizational influences on buying processes are explained in terms of two-person (salesperson-buyer) interaction, source selection and loyalty, advertising, promotion and information sources, and other actors.

The "interaction" concept has generated considerable conceptual work, and some empirical studies. While most work has focussed on the interaction and social variables extolled by Bonoma et al., recent studies have broadened the interaction concept to focus on interorganization relationships, or "bonding" (Wilson and Mummalaneni 1988; Turner 1970). These concepts refer to stable, long-lasting corporate interdependencies such as joint ventures, just-in-time inventory arrangements, reciprocal arrangements, and the like. The changing nature of corporate relationships, stimulated by global marketing, industry concentration, and other factors, have important implications for the nature of OBB, and for research in the area. Arndt (1979) gives some indication of the implications in his definition of these changes as "domesticated markets":

Interorganizational systems . . . may be found under the labels conglomerates, franchising, vertical and horizontal integration, joint ventures, joint product development and marketing contract, joint physical distribution plans, and labor-management peace agreements. The resulting administered markets may be referred to as domesticated markets since transactions are moved inside a company (when, for instance, buyers and sellers actually merge) or inside the boundaries of a group of companies committed to long-term cooperation. (p. 70)

As we will see, research and conceptualization in the "interaction" tradition has progressed to what we call "relationship" paradigms, which attempt to take into account the behavioral dimensions of these new, long-lasting and stable relationships that transcend traditional "buying" and "selling" and occur in the contemporary business environment.

The IMP Model

An ambitious research program in the genre of the earlier conception of the "interaction" models is the IMP (Industrial Marketing and Purchasing) Group Interaction Model, based on the collaborative efforts of several European researchers (see Figure 12.6). Drawing heavily on the microeconomic notions of the "new institutionalists" (Williamson 1975), the IMP model reflects the idea that transaction costs may be reduced when a transaction is internalized in one unit—a notion consistent with the "domesticated markets" concept articulated by Arnad (1979). Thus, very high levels of commitment and trust must be built between buyers and vendors. In fact, the new relationships envisioned by the IMP model builders do not even use the terms "buyers" and "sellers," preferring to portray the two organizations as linked by short-term exchange episodes and long-term relationships. Besides these dimensions to the interaction process linking the two organizations, the relationship is influenced by its "atmospheres" (e.g., power/dependence, cooperation, and the like), and by the broader environment (e.g., market structure, internationalism, etc.).

Considerable qualitative data were gathered as the basis for the IMP model, and some research has been generated, but, as Wilson and Moller (1988) point out, much of the model is

FIGURE 12.6   An Illustration of the Interaction Model
(Source: Hakansson, (1982).)

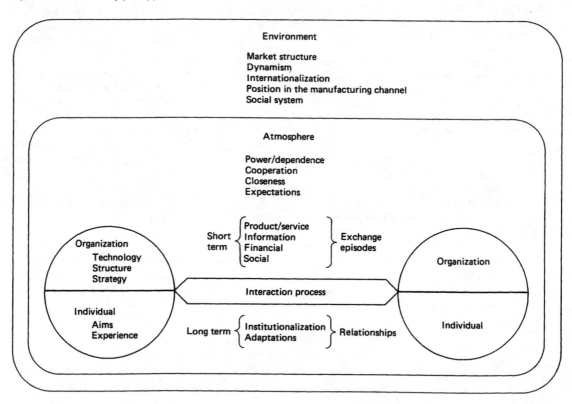

descriptive, and work toward testable theory has not occurred since propositions have not been derived and data have not been gathered to permit empirical testing of the model.

Models Based on Channel Relationships

While most OBB research focuses on vendor-buyer relations, some important conceptualizations and empirical research have focussed on the relations between sellers and organizations in the distribution channel.

Anderson and Narus (1984) use social exchange theory as a way to understand and evaluate manufacturer-distributor (and, more generally, seller-buyer) relationships. Working with concepts developed by Thibault and Kelley (1959) as bases for evaluating the outcomes of a relationship, Anderson and Narus define *comparison level* (CL) as a standard representing the expectations, based on general and specific experience, of the manufacturer and the distributor about the quality of outcomes from their relationship. This comparison defines the satisfaction of both parties and the attractiveness of the relationships to them. *Comparison*

level of alternative (CLAlt), by contrast, is a standard that represents the average quality of outcomes associated with the best alternative exchange relationship and, therefore, the minimum acceptable level of outcomes that will be tolerated by the parties and have them still remain in the relationship. These constructs, and others (such as relative dependence and communication), are functionally related to satisfaction in Anderson and Narus's model. Empirical testing of the model yielded promising results supporting the posited relationships.

Drawing on different theoretical sources, Anderson and Weitz (1987) constructed and tested a model similar to Anderson and Narus's (1984). For Anderson and Weitz, continuity in the manufacturer-distributor relationship is a mutually sought goal—an assertion well-grounded in previous work (Etgar 1979; Arndt 1979; Thorelli 1986; Williamson 1979). Building their theory on an eclectic array of sources, including channel research (Robicheaux and El-Ansary 1975; Stern and Reve 1980), negotiation, and structural economics, their model and the hypothesized relationships are shown in Figure 12.7. Empirical support was found for most of the hypothesized relationships.

FIGURE 12.7 Hypothesized Relationships
(Source: Anderson and Weitz (1987).)

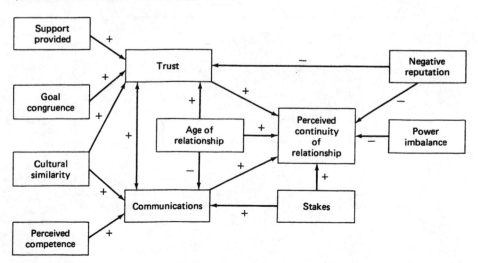

Buyer and Seller Models of Relationships

Another stream of research within the "interaction" perspective is what Wilson and Moller (1989) call "buyer and seller models of relationships." A conceptual model in this tradition is offered by Dwyer, Schurr, and Oh (1987), who seek to redirect research from treating buyer-seller exchanges as discrete events to understanding and studying them as ongoing relationships. As their model in Figure 12.8 shows, these authors pose that relationships develop in phases, each with particular characteristics and enabling subprocesses that lead to deepening

dependence. While the authors caution that their model "is built primarily on conceptual foundations and empirical evidence from exchange theory and its offspring—marital theory, bargaining theory, and power theory," their specification of developmental stages suggests some measurable variables that could be derived to test aspects of the model.

Another tradition in the area of buyer-seller relationships is represented in the work of Wilson and his colleagues (1985, 1988). Noting the changing environment of business markets (such as downsizing, international joint ventures, and the like), the emergence of trans-

FIGURE 12.8   The Relationship Development Process
(Source: Dwyer, Schurr, and Oh (1987).)

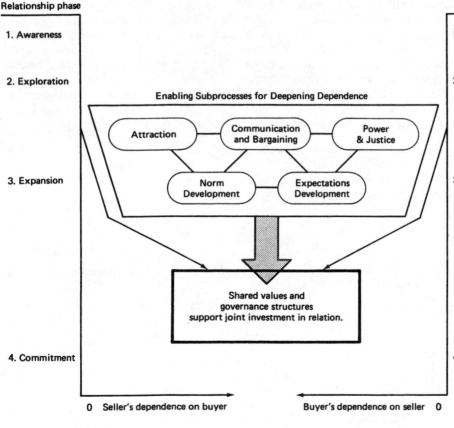

Relationship phase

1. Awareness
2. Exploration

Enabling Subprocesses for Deepening Dependence

Attraction   Communication and Bargaining   Power & Justice

Norm Development   Expectations Development

3. Expansion

Shared values and governance structures support joint investment in relation.

4. Commitment

0   Seller's dependence on buyer   Buyer's dependence on seller   0

Phase characteristics

1. Unilateral considerations of potential exchange partners.

2. Dynamic interaction occurs. A gradual increase in interdependence reflects bilateral testing and probing. Termination of the fragile association is simple.

3. A successful power source exercise marks the beginning of Expansions. Mutual satisfaction with customized role performance supports deepening interdependence. Additional gratifications are sought from the current exchange partner rather than from an alternative partner.

4. Contractual mechanisms and/or shared value systems ensure sustained interdependence. Mutual inputs are significant and consistent. Partners resolve conflict and adapt.

action or relationship orientations in OBB research, and the demise of the "discrete transaction paradigm" in economics (Williamson 1979), Wilson builds on his earlier dyadic sales process model (Wilson 1975, 1978) and posits a model of the "bonding process" between organizations (Turnbill and Wilson 1988). He also draws on the IMP model, discussed earlier, as well as research on bonding (Turner 1970; McCall 1970; Johnston 1982) and the psychological investment of the model of Rusbult (1980).

For Wilson, "bonding" is represented by the dependent variable of "commitment," defined as the dedication to the continuation of the relationship. In his model, the bonding process is initially driven by the complementary needs of two organizations. For example, Firm A may need Firm B's distribution network, while Firm B may need additional revenue from allowing Firm A to have access to its distribution network. Interaction exchanges between the firms lead to "social bonds" (the strength of the buyer-seller relationship) and "structural bonds" (the multiple economic and social factors that develop over the relationship). These two types of bonds are related to commitment, between the two firms. In an extended model (Wilson and Moller 1988), satisfaction is portrayed as a key determinant of commitment because it fosters strong social bonds between individuals and generates trust. In turn, trust leads to the willingness to make investments, which form structural bonds. As in the earlier model, social and structural bonds are then determinants of commitment.

Some other authors have examined particular instances of buyer-seller interaction. For example, Fraser, Spekman, and O'Neal (1988) pose a four-stage model to describe the managerial process for making a just-in-time decision and the internal and external factors that influence that decision process; similarly, Parkinson (1985) adopts an interaction perspective in examining buyer-seller relationships in the purchase of high-technology products. He finds customer involvement in the development of products, but the extent of the involvement varies with the structural characteristics, such as the organization's size.

Models of Selling Effectiveness

Some models in the broadly conceived area of organization buyer behavior focus as far "downstream" as you can go: on the dyadic, or two-person, interaction of one individual from the buying firm and one from the selling firm (or, in purely interactional terms, two individuals from firms seeking some kind of transaction). The literature on salesperson-buyer interaction is vast, most often focussing on selling effectiveness: What are the characteristics that predict success in sales interactions?

Research in this area developed in ways similar to the broader OBB research literature. Early models were simplistic and focussed on the sales side of the relationships, seeking one or two variables that could be used to identify the "great salesperson." Most often, these searches took the form of administering personality tests from the psychological testing literature, tests which were modified to seek personality characteristics associated with superior personal selling performance. These tests measured such enduring traits as empathy, forcefulness, sociability, and the like, while other researchers looked to demographic variables. The results were remarkably inconsistent. Some studies found positive associations between some variables and sales success — others found negative relationships with the same variables.

The underlying model here was similar to early OBB models, looking for one or two powerful variables that would predict buying behavior — at the organizational level in the OBB literature, and at the individual level in the salesperson-buyer literature. In each case, the implicit view is that of a one-way flow of information and influence. Some sales training seminars still exist that reflect this idea; if the salesperson will only act in a certain way, then sales success will result.

But just as the OBB literature turned away from static models portraying one-way flows of influence, salesperson-buyer researchers shifted from their early "salesmanship" conceptions to an interaction perspective. The transition was marked by two-dimensional grids, such as is seen in Blake and Mouton's (1970) levels of "concern for the customer" on one axis and "concern for the sale" on the other axis. Building on this typology, another framework classifies individuals based on their scores on personality tests and their performance in actual interaction situations: Merrill and Reid (1981) classify individuals in terms of their responsiveness ("remote" versus "control") and assertiveness ("ask" versus "tell"). The result is a typology of individuals who may be neatly designated in one of four categories: "analytical," "driver," "amiable," and "expansive." The problem with such approaches—and the sales training seminars on which they are based—is described by Robertson, Zellinski, and Ward (1986):

In addition to questions of reliability and validity . . . the strategic question about them is, what does one do with this kind of information? Would a salesforce manager assign a "driver" to work with . . . an "analytic?" Do "opposites attract," or do "birds of a feather flock together?" (p. 493)

Studies in psychology have long noted greater affect and attitude change as a function of similarity between interacting individuals, perhaps because similar individuals have common bases of experience and a greater pool of things to talk about (Zajonc 1980). Extending this finding to the salesperson-buyer dyad, marketing researchers have found positive relationships between sales success and the similarity of customers and salespeople. Many dimensions of similarity are involved: backgrounds, physical characteristics, and so forth. And customers who buy tend to perceive the salesperson as more like themselves than customers who do not buy (Evans 1963; Gadel 1964). Sometimes customer-buyer similarity is more important than expertise. Brock (1965) trained salespeople in a hardware store to use one of two approaches whenever the customer was interested in buying paint; he portrayed himself either as an expert or simply as having painting problems with needs similar to the customers. Greater sales success was achieved with the similarity approach.

There is a feature of convergent validity to these studies of similarity in the marketing context, in that they are consistent with much research in social psychology. However, many early studies have not been successfully replicated, and Weitz observes that "dyadic similarity studies have not demonstrated a meaningful relationship between similarity and effectiveness" (Weitz 1981, p. 88). He notes that many studies have not found a relationship (Doren, Emergy, and Switzer 1979) or have found that similarity explains little variance (Churchill, Collins, and Strang 1975). Correlational studies also do not control for the rival hypothesis that customers who made purchases perceived they were more similar to salespeople than customers who did not make purchases (Davis and Silk 1972). Nonetheless, experimental studies have shown similarity to be important, but not as important as expertise (Bambic 1978; Busch and Wilson 1976; Woodside and Davenport 1974).

Other researchers used interaction concepts to explain salesperson-buyer outcomes. For example, one study examined perceptions of "ideal" sales behavior versus "actual" sales behavior. The more salespeople and customers agreed on "ideal" behaviors, the greater their degree of role consensus. An experiment found that such consensus was unrelated to sales performance, but that expectation level (the difference between ideal and actual sales performance) was related to the number of suppliers used by customers (Tosi 1966). The greater the difference between the action and the expected levels of the salesperson's performance, the larger the number of suppliers used.

Building on leadership research in social psychology, Weitz (1981) proposed a contingency framework for sales effectiveness across different kinds of selling interactions. For Weitz, the effectiveness of the salesperson's behavior is contingent upon three sets of factors: (1) the salesperson's resources, (2) the customer's buying task, and (3) the characteristics of the customer-salesperson relationship. The second set of factors, the customer's buying task, explicitly links Weitz's framework with the larger body of OBB literature and research. Weitz began his research and conceptualizing further "downstream" when he examined actual behaviors in the dyad with his ISTEA framework (Weitz 1978). ISTEA is an acronym for "Impression formation," "Strategy formulation," "Transmission," and "Evaluation," which are elements of the dyadic sales process (see Figure 12.9). This framework combines the logic of decision stage models (viz., the ISTEA steps or stages) and interaction process models (viz., the "adjustments" that bring a process orientation to the model). Other researchers have combined notions from role theory, sales force management literature, and process conceptualizations (Walker, Churchill, and Ford 1977).

Models of Negotiation

Another perspective on dyadic processes in organizational buying behavior is represented in the negotiation literature. Again, interest in organizational buying behavior can lead one into a vast array of theory and research — in this case, game theory, decision sciences, and the like, as well as the more "macro" perspectives on negotiation in the organizational behavior literature.

Considering first perspectives on negotiation from the organizational behavior literature, Clopton (1984) points out that industrial buyers and sellers — as individuals — are boundary spanners, linking communication between the two firms; moreover, long-term relationships are usually sought, both parties are expected to emerge from negotiation with favorable outcomes, and conflict is prevalent. Negotiation is the mode to resolve conflict. Perdue, Day, and Michaels (1986) surveyed purchasing agents in an attempt to identify negotiation "styles," based on Thomas's typology of collaborative, competitive, sharing, accommodative, and avoidance negotiation styles (Thomas 1984). They found that purchasing agents most often perceive themselves as "collaborative" in their dealings with vendors. However, a social desirability bias may have influenced results. In any case, their measure was a global one and no attempt was made to specify conditions under which PAs might adopt one style or another.

From a game theory/decision science perspective, the topic of negotiation is treated in either "process" or "outcome" models of two-person negotiation. Process models attempt to model bargaining processes directly (Bartos 1974; Bush and Mosteller 1955; Chamberlain

FIGURE 12.9 The ISTEA Sales Process Model (Source: Weitz, (1978).)

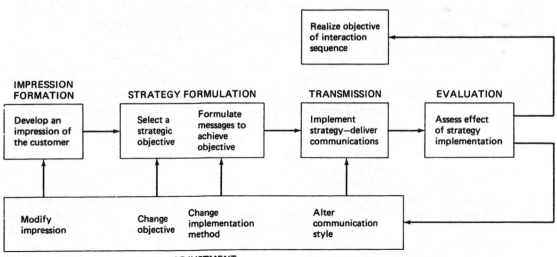

and Kuhn 1965), whereas outcome models attempt to predict results without attention to processes (Braithwaite 1955; Raiffa 1953). Neslin and Greenhaegh (1983) utilize Nash's outcome model (Nash 1950, 1953) in an attempt to predict some outcomes in industrial purchasing behavior — in their case, media purchasing. They argue, based on Webster (1979), that negotiation in the OBB context is most often a non–zero-sum two-person game, characterized by instances of conflict and assertions of power and influence, and involving long-term interdependent relationships. They argue that Nash's theory is predicated on most of these features of negotiation in OBB. They found that Nash's theory addresses the conflict factor, and that the theory predicted outcomes of one instance of buyer-seller negotiations. The authors caution that their model only addressed the conflict factor, and that it should not be applied to a variety of negotiations in OBB.

Gemunden (1985) approached the issue of buyer-seller negotiation from another point of view — the view of each party's efficiency in the negotiation. While not utilizing game theory perspectives, Gemunden conceptualizes efficiency in terms of six conflict-handling strategies — from "smoothing over conflicts" to "escalated confrontation." He purports to find differences in efficiency for each side depending on the strategies adopted to handle conflict. It is impossible to determine Gemunden's methodology, however, so results must be interpreted with extreme caution.

Soldow and Thomas (1984) attempt to integrate Weitz's contingency framework (discussed earlier) with ideas from the literature on negotiations. They refer to *relational communication* to mean "that part of a message beyond the actual content which allows communicators to negotiate their relative positions." Their conceptualization of the context of buyer-seller interaction is that either side can bid for a position of dominance, deference, or equality; in turn, the other side can either accept the bid or deny it.

To summarize, what we have called "sales effectiveness" or "negotiation" models are actually conceptualizations of dyadic interaction that are found implicitly or explicitly in most of the more comprehensive models of organizational buyer behavior. In fact, literature and research in this area is at the boundary of three conceptual and research traditions: organizational buying behavior, sales force management, and negotiation theory. There is intellectual appeal to such a boundary position; however, one must proceed with caution. For example, game theory approaches to negotiation — while clearly relevant to OBB — may not capture the complex multiple individuals, recursive DMPs, and changing values and preferences that occur over the time period of an industrial negotiation. Simply put, such models focus on particular aspects of the overall, complex process of OBB, and the danger for future research is that the processes portrayed may not fully reflect the broader context in which they occur or the dynamic nature of that process.

Finally, care must be exercised in the application of dyadic concepts to the more macro-level characteristics of organizational transactions. For example, conceptualizations of roles and role behavior were derived from studies of interindividual relationships, and may not easily be applied to characterize interorganizational relationships. This remains a core issue for the interaction perspective in OBB: What interactive concepts are relevant for the different levels of aspects of the organization-individuals, buying center, organizations themselves — and how can they be related?

Many other approaches to the study of OBB have been proposed that explicitly or implicitly reflect an interactive or relationship perspective. Some have been assessed with follow-up empirical research, but they have not yet received as much conceptual or empirical attention as the broad categories of approaches to study in the field we have treated to this point in the chapter. Some of these nascent models are purely conceptual, others derive from methodological approaches, and we turn now to a review of these models.

Exchange Models

Bagozzi reviews a number of conceptual and research areas pertinent to his broad "exchange" conceptualization of marketing (Bagozzi 1974), and he illustrates their applicability to problems in OBB (Bagozzi 1978). He reviews leadership and decision-making, group decision-making processes, communication network research, social influence processes (including research and theory in bargaining and negotiation), coalition and other group effects, and social power approaches. He also assesses the possible usefulness of social judgment theory and Coleman's model (1973) of social action. Similarly, Moller (1985), Wind and Thomas (1980), and Johnston and Spekman (1987) all review theoretical perspectives and research strategies in analyzing organizational buying processes.

Spekman (1977, 1978) reconceptualizes the Buying Center or Decision-Making Unit concept to more adequately account for the lateral relationship among members. He then offers a macrosociological perspective to research what he calls the "buying task group." Spekman's perspective is shaped by contingency theory, with its emphasis on understanding the interrelationships between subsystems within a firm, as well as the firm's interrelationships with its environment.

Adoption and Diffusion Models

Another conceptual approach is illustrated by researchers interested in new product adoption in industrial markets. For these researchers, key conceptualizations derive from the literature on adoption processes and the diffusion of innovations (see Chapter 9 of this volume). Some descriptive research illustrates that end users are often the members of the DMU who initiate interest in a new product (Berkowitz 1986). Other studies attempt to conceptualize developer/adoption relationships in the decision to buy new products. More (1986) proposes a generic model of the new product purchase process, which is derived from earlier decision process models, such as those proposed by Robinson, Faris, and Wind (1967), Ozanne and Churchill (1968), and Webster and Wind (1972), all discussed previously. More then suggests activities undertaken at both the buying firm ("adoption subprocesses") and at the selling firm ("development subprocesses"). Traditionally, the developing firm proceeds with little interaction with potential vendors until late in the purchase process—what More calls the traditional "developer-driven serial relationship." However, other relationships are possible that involve earlier and proactive codevelopment relationships. Such relationships have been reported elsewhere (von Hippel 1977).

While More does not offer behavioral propositions from his conceptualization, further work could suggest functional relationships regarding interfirm and intrafirm behavior that draw from research and theory in both the adoption/diffusion area and OBB.

Decision System Models

Other conceptualizations have emerged from methodological perspectives. The most important is decision system analysis (DSA). DSA is related to triangulation methodology, which demands a multimethod approach to studying behavioral phenomena (Denzin 1978). For example, Johnston and Spekman (1982) use subprocess analysis to examine buying processes, and Vyas and Woodside (1984) utilize protocol analysis. Bettman (1970) advocates direct observation, and Webb and Weick (1976) document analysis to assess supplier choice processes. DSA attempts to examine the interconnectedness of processes and subprocesses, typically through a series of interviews with several persons involved in a decision process (Capon and Hulbert 1975; Capon, Farley, and Hulbert 1975; Moller and Allos 1983; and Hulbert, Farley, and Howard 1972). DSA attempts to reveal the structure and decision-making nodes, including both decision criteria and heuristics, and to identify principal activities and participants over the course of the DMP. Farley, Hulbert, and Weinstein (1980) use the DSA approach to define an "activity-participant matrix," and use the matrix to suggest standardized measures to assess activities, participation, and similarity — the latter measure being used for comparing the same DMP in different companies.

Decision system analysis has been used by theorists most often identified with inductive approaches for studying interorganization decisions that are believed to be "unstructured" (viz., Minntzberg, Raisinghani, and Theoret 1976; Moore 1969). Vyas and Woodside (1984, 1981, 1982) and Woodside and Vyas (1981) provide comprehensive and detailed inductive modeling of industrial buying.

More interesting, the output of DSA research is often a series of flowcharts — characteristic of the earliest attempts to model OBB. The DSA approach is not simply "history repeating itself." Its use in OBB by the Columbia group in the 1980s, as well as by Moore and by Vyas and Woodside, has gone far beyond the simplistic flowchart modeling of an earlier era. For example, Vyas and Woodside's best known paper (1984) provides rich details and permits a reasonable basis for drawing inferences about organizational decision-making processes. There is a high price for DSA research, however. The multimethod data requirements, the level of detail, and the time required for data collection are intimidating. Nonetheless, DSA is an ideal tool for individuals who agree with Moore's belief that "valid description must precede proposed prescription, if the latter is to provide much in the way of practical application."

Script Theory Roles

Related to DSA, but drawing from roots in cognitive psychology, the conceptualization and methodology of script theory has been applied to organizational buying behavior (Leigh and Rethans 1984). This theory derives from Abelson's (1976) conceptualization of a cognitive script. The essential idea is that individuals hold a "hypothesized cognitive structure" in memory that can be used to direct behavior. Verbalization of such scripts is purported to reveal decision-making processes that "guide thinking and behavior in sales interactions" (Leigh and Rethans 1984). In Leigh and Rethans's study, 36 purchase managers responded with their "scripts" to an evoking context concerning the purchase of nonintelligent data terminals. After coding responses in terms of frequency of citation of specific activities and events, the authors validated the data with a follow-up questionnaire to a larger sample of PAs. They conclude that the script-theoretic approach has significant potential for inductive theory development in OBB, as well as applicability in buyer-seller negotiation and sales personnel training.

Finally, DSA and script-theoretic approaches to studying OBB have also been used in protocol analysis to study consumer information processing; conversely, consumer information-processing approaches have been applied to the OBB context (Stiles 1974; Crow 1984; Crow, Olshavsky, and Summers 1980). Multiattribute models have also been directly utilized to study both consumer and organizational buying behavior. A limitation of such models, which also suggests a strength of DSA and related approaches, is that buyers may use a combination of decision rules at various stages in the choice process. This is precisely a finding in Vyas and Woodside's study (1982), and it points out a limitation of linear attitude models when applied to the complexities of OBB.

Conclusions on Interaction and Relationship Models

We have described a number of conceptualizations under the general heading of "the interaction and relationship perspective," but work in this area is defined more by common criticisms of earlier "unit" conceptualizations than by a unified, coherent definition of just what the "interaction perspective" means. Indeed, Wilson and Moller's (1988) list of 35 sources of constructs and sources (Wilson 1975; see Figure 12.10) and Bonoma et al.'s (1978) list of 85 loosely conceptualized propositions pertaining to the "interaction perspective" suggest that we

Construct	IMP	AN	AW	DWO	HJ	WM & MW	FSO
Trust	X	X	X	X		X	
Power of Buyer		X	X	X			
Power of Seller		X	X	X			
Dependence on Buyer	X	X		X			
Dependence on Seller	X	X		X			
Stake			X				
Age of Relationship	X		X			X	
Communication		X	X	X			
Outcome of Value Performance					X	X	
Satisfaction						X	X
Transaction Costs					X	X	X
Transaction Specific Investment or Irretrievable Investment				X	X	X	X
Social Bonding Affective Relationship				X		X	
Cooperation	X	X					
Conflict	X	X					
CL		X					
CL/Alt						X	X
Replaceability					X		X
Satisfaction		X			X		
Functionality of Conflict Commitment		X					
Expectations	X			X			X
Social Distance Cultural Similarity	X		X				
Organizational Factors	X						X
Individual Factors	X						
Environmental Factors	X						X
Norm Development				X			X
Governance Structures				X			
Perceived Continuity of Relationship			X			X	
Negative Reputation			X				
Support Provided			X				
Perceived Competence			X				
Goal Congruence			X				
Social Pressure to Maintain Relationship					X	X	
Ease of Relationship Termination						X	
Exchange						X	X

Legend:

IMP	IMP Group
AN	Anderson and Narus
AW	Anderson and Weitz
DWO	Dwyer, Schurr, and Oh
HJ	Heide and John
WM & MW	Wilson & Mummalaneni and Mummalaneni & Wilson
FSO	Fraser, Spekman, and O'Neal

FIGURE 12.10 Constructs and Sources for OBB Studies Based on Interaction Perspectives (Source: Wilson and Moller (1988).)

have a broad, enticing perspective on OBB, rather than a coherent framework for theory and research development.

Clearly, the interaction perspective does suggest a framework for capturing the dynamic, social nature of OBB in contrast to earlier, comprehensive, or "unit" paradigms that portray OBB in terms of a set of one-way arrows. However, the earlier decision process and comprehensive models offer concepts and variables that are relatively easy to convert to operational variables, in contrast to the difficulty of operationalizing many constructs and variables by authors who cast their work in the "interaction perspective." The earlier comprehensive models suggested interaction processes in boxes (viz., "group decision-making"). The interaction perspective suggests specific processes that occur in those boxes.

The utility of "the interaction perspective" is perhaps best seen in the micro-level processes of the "dyadic" salesperson-buyer interaction in models such as Weitz's. At more macro-level units of analysis, such as those involved in the IMP conceptualization, discussed earlier, conceptualizations become more cumbersome and difficult to operationalize. At the most macro-level of analysis—in the notions of relationships between firms and "bonding"—the interaction perspective offers intriguing ways of understanding these new relationships in the contemporary business environment. Care must be taken, however, in applying concepts intended for one level analysis to another level. For example, concepts such as role behaviors, social comparison theory, and the like, were utilized in psychological studies of individual perceptions and behavior in social situations. It is not clear whether such concepts can be applied in valid ways to more molar kinds of relationships, such as those involving organizational entities. Indeed, the very idea of conceptualizing interorganizational and interpersonal interaction in the same way is a highly debatable proposition.

METHODOLOGICAL ISSUES IN ORGANIZATIONAL BUYING BEHAVIOR RESEARCH

We have provided a chronology of the conceptualizations that characterize the field of study of OBB, and we have briefly reviewed empirical studies pertaining to each of those conceptualizations. While we have not attempted to be exhaustive in our review, it should be clear to the reader that the volume of conceptualizations far exceeds the volume of follow-up empirical research. Indeed, it would appear that the volume of OBB research that tests and extends theories is far less than that found in consumer behavior research.

Moriarty (1983) believes this lag is due to the larger number of variables that often characterize organizational, as opposed to individual, decisions; additionally, decision participants in OBB are more difficult to identify and access than individual consumers, and the levels and units of analysis are difficult to specify. Moreover, it is difficult to apply sampling statistics to much OBB research, since it cannot be assumed that individuals, companies, or decisions are normally distributed in most research studies.

Most organizational buying behavior involves many people and recurring transactions, but many studies are based on data from a single participant—most often the purchasing agent—and many focus on a single decision. The gathering of data from multiple individuals, across multiple times and decisions, and perhaps in more than one organization, presents methodological and measurement problems that are, indeed, intimidating.

These issues result in serious questions about the validity of empirical studies in OBB. In an important assessment of the validity of many key studies in the field, Silk and Kalwani (1982) review eight studies of the composition and structure of organizational buying groups. They raise significant issues pertaining to the clarity of the types of decisions and organizations investigated, to the informant selection procedures, to the constructs measured, and to the measurement instruments. In particular, Silk and Kalwani note biases depending on the construct (participation versus influence in the buying decision) and on the measures of these constructs (global versus specific measures). They summarize their findings as follows (1982, pp. 168–170):

1. Respondents tend to attribute more participation and influence to themselves and/or the positions they hold than other informants attribute to them and/or the same positions.

2. Between-informant consensus about participation is high for measurement pertaining to specific stages in the purchase decision process which require dichotomous judgments about participation versus nonparticipation.
3. Consensus on influence, whether self-informant or between informant, is low for global measures involving relative judgments in the form of rankings or ratings.

Given the time frames and budgets of most researchers, and given the availability of research tools that can be practically applied, Silk and Kalwani's findings are disturbing indeed. There is no easy solution to the measurement and methodological problems they find. Researchers in the field would do well to consider the problem areas and find some possible solutions. In the area of respondent sampling and selection, for example, Moriarty and Bateson (1980) propose a "snowballing" technique to reliably identify and access multiple participants in organizational decision-making. Related approaches are reflected in the "key informant" procedure (Phillips 1980), and they have been employed in research in OBB (Brand 1972; Buckner 1967; Platten 1950) and in family decision-making (Davis 1971). Decision system models and script theory approaches may be useful in finding possible improvements in the measurement of influence in organizations. Their use in multivariate data analysis techniques, such as LISREL, may help researchers to adequately measure the complexity of OBB processes and effects.

Finally, in addition to these methodological and measurement issues, we have noted the dangers inherent in applying conceptualizations intended for a particular level or unit of analysis to other phenomena. This problem is particularly acute, given the changing nature of organizational buying behavior toward longer-term relationships, or "bonding." The temptation is to apply concepts and theories originally intended to understand and predicate individual or small-group phenomena to events and actions that characterize entire organizations. The perils of such uncritical "borrowing" have long been discussed in consumer behavior research (Ward and Robertson 1971).

SUMMARY

We asserted at the beginning of this chapter that OBB is a mature field of study, if one measures by the length of time it has attracted the attention, of researchers. However, it seems to us the field is still in the growth stage, and it invites considerably more research attention because we are still far from a set of acceptable, middle-range theories.

We have argued that progress toward theory development has not been hindered by a lack of conceptualizations (some might argue that it has been hindered by too many of them), but by the failure of researchers to design follow-up empirical research to extend and test some of them. This failure to do the follow-up research is due to many factors, but a core problem seems to be that it is difficult to specify relationships and pose hypotheses from some models, because the concepts are poorly defined and the models lack specifics. To be somewhat cynical, it may also be true that it is often easier to offer for publication a "new" conceptualization than to undertake empirical research. Finally, and probably most important, the failure to do the follow-up research toward theory building is most often due to the sheer complexity of OBB and the models in the field. Methodological and measurement issues are daunting, as we reviewed in the previous section in this chapter.

Nonetheless, some progress in theory and knowledge development has marked the field. The concepts of buyclasses, decision-making units, and decision-making processes have yielded important knowledge about decision processes in organizations. Comprehensive models have provided a basis for research to increase our understanding of functional relationships that explain organizational decisions. That many different conceptualizations compete to explain similar phenomena should not obscure the fact that data have been offered to increase our understanding. For example, studies that test the effects of different exogenous or mediating variables on phenomena such as the DMP do not mean that other conceptualizations and previous studies are wrong or irrelevant; rather, these studies incrementally add to our knowledge of complex phenomena.

In our opinion, future research in OBB should seek to integrate, extend, and test propositions derived from existing conceptualizations of phenomena in the field. While the task of selecting what propositions to offer from which conceptualizations is challenging, we believe that careful attention to the definition and selection of dependent variables will help to direct future research interests. For example, researchers interested in new product adoption may profitably draw from conceptualizations in the field of new product diffusion, and from parallel conceptualizations in OBB (e.g., Ozanne and Churchill 1968). The dependent variables may be interaction patterns in the DMU, aspects of the DMP, and/or the adoption decision itself. Such partitioning of phenomena (viz., the focus on new products), the

examination of linkages to existing conceptual frameworks, and the specification of dependent variables is precisely the kind of progress toward middle-range theory that we believe can move the field ahead.

Mindful of Bonoma, Zaltman, and Johnston's (1977) observation that, if you look for structure in OBB, you are likely to "come out reeling," we make a modest attempt to link major areas of research in the field with our conceptual approaches and representative research streams (Figure 12.11). Our intent is not to provide yet another conceptualization or model, but merely to suggest key areas of research (the top half of Figure 12.11) and the major conceptual approaches and representative research streams (the bottom half of Figure 12.11). The latter are characterized by "model orientation," ranging from relatively static to relatively dynamic portrayals of OBB phenom-

FIGURE 12.11 Conceptual Approaches and Representative Research Systems in OBB

Areas of OBB Research

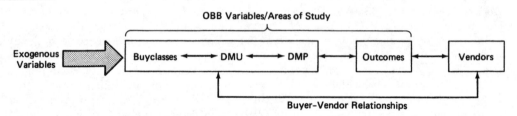

Conceptual Approaches to Research

(representative types of research)

	Model Orientation	
	Static	Dynamic
Dyad	• Personality characteristics of salespeople	• Interactive models of salesperson-buyer behavior
DMU	• DMU structure	• Network, coalition views of DMU functioning
Level of Analysis · **Organization**	• Micro-economics models	• Relationship-building, "bonding"
Comprehensive Models	Sheth Webster & Wind	• "Interaction" perspective viz., IMP model

ena, and by the level of analysis, ranging from the most "micro" focus on dyadic interaction to the DMU, to the larger organization. The final level of analysis attempts to represent all three levels: comprehensive models of OBB. Our intent is to help the reader focus his or her interests in the field by representing the major research thrusts and the major conceptual approaches. In this way, we hope that researchers can add to our knowledge, based on an understanding of what is known.

Finally, we note that the changing global business environment is forging new kinds of relationships, often called "strategic alliances," between organizations. The previous focus of most OBB research, on discrete buying decisions, seems increasingly myopic. Some researchers may wish to access the literature pertaining to organizational behavior and the strategic literature on interorganizational relationships. Some may wish to fruitfully study the "new look" in OBB, where "buying" takes on a variety of new meanings in the context of heightened buyer-seller interdependence and where single transactions are increasingly difficult to isolate in the new complex interorganizational relationships.

REFERENCES

ABELSON, ROBERT P. (1976). "Script Processing in Attitude Formation and Decision-Making," *Cognition and Social Behavior*, Eds. J. S. Carroll and J. W. Payne. Hillsdale, NJ: Erlbaum.

ANDERSON, ERIN, WUJIN CHU, and BARTON WEITZ (1987). "Industrial Purchasing: An Empirical Exploration of the Buyclass Framework," *Journal of Marketing*, 51 (July), 71–86.

ANDERSON, ERIN, and BARTON WEITZ (1987). "Determinants of Continuity in Conventional Industrial Channel Dyads," working paper, The University of Pennsylvania, Philadelphia, PA.

ANDERSON, JAMES C., and JAMES A. NARUS (1984). "A Model of the Distributor's Perspective of Distributor-Manufacturer Working Relationships," *Journal of Marketing*, 48 (4), 62–74.

ANDERSON, JAMES C. (1987). "A Model of Manufacturer and Distributor Working Partnerships,"

unpublished working paper, Evanston, IL: Northwestern University.

ANDERSON, PAUL F., and TERRY M. CHAMBERS (1985). "A Reward/Measurement Model of Organizational Buying Behavior," *Journal of Marketing*, 49 (2) (Spring), 7–23.

ARNDT, JOHAN (1979). "Toward a Theory of Domesticated Markets," *Journal of Marketing*, 43 (Fall), 69–75.

BAGOZZI, RICHARD P. (1974). "Marketing as an Organized Behavior System of Exchange," *Journal of Marketing*, 38 (October), 77–81.

BAGOZZI, RICHARD P. (1978). "Exchange and Decision Processes in the Buying Center," *Organizational Buying Behavior*, Eds. Thomas V. Bonoma and Gerald Zaltman. Chicago: American Marketing Association, 100–125.

BAMBIC, PETER (1978). "An Interpersonal Influence Study of Source Acceptance in Industrial Buyer-Seller Exchange Process: An Experimental Approach," unpublished Ph.D. dissertation, Graduate School of Business, Pennsylvania State University, University Park, PA.

BARCLAY, DONALD W. (1987). "Interdepartmental Conflict in Organizational Buying: The Impact of the Organizational Context," working paper, University of Western Ontario, London, Ont., No. 87-33.

BARCLAY, DONALD W. (1988). "Decision-Process Outcomes in Organizational Buying: A Conceptualization," working paper, University of Western Ontario, London, Ont., No. 88-4.

BARTOS, OTTOMAR J. (1974). *Process and Outcome of Negotiations*. New York: Columbia University Press.

BAUER, RAYMOND A. (1960). "Consumer Behavior as Risk Taking," *Proceedings of the American Marketing Association*, Ed. S. Hancock. Chicago: American Marketing Association.

BELLIZZI, JOSEPH A. (1981). "Organizational Size and Buying Influences," *Industrial Marketing Management*, 10, 17–21.

BELLIZZI, JOSEPH A. and JOSEPH J. BELONAX (1982). "Centralized and Decentralized Buying Influences," *Industrial Marketing Management*, 11, 111–115.

BELLIZZI, JOSEPH A. and PHILLIP McVEY (1983). "How Valid is the Buy-Grid Model?" *Industrial Marketing Management*, 12, 57–62.

BERKOWITZ, MARVIN (1986). "New Product Adoption by the Buying Organization: Who Are the

Real Influencers?" *Industrial Marketing Management,* 15, 33–43.

BETTMAN, JAMES (1970). *An Information Processing Theory of Consumer Choice.* Reading, MA: Addison-Wesley.

BLAKE, ROBERT R., and J. S. MOUTON (1970). *The Grid for Sales Excellence.* New York: McGraw-Hill.

BLAU, PETER (1955). *The Dynamics of Bureaucracy.* Chicago: University of Chicago Press.

BONOMA, THOMAS V. (1982). "Major Sales: Who Really Does the Buying?" *Harvard Business Review* (May/June), 111–119.

BONOMA, THOMAS V., RICHARD P. BAGOZZI, and GERALD ZALTMAN (1978). "The Dyadic Paradigm with Specific Application Toward Industrial Marketing," *Organizational Buying Behavior,* Eds. Thomas V. Bonoma and Gerald Zaltman. Chicago: American Marketing Association, 49–66.

BONOMA, THOMAS V., G. ZALTMAN, and W. JOHNSTON (1977). "Industrial Buying Behavior," working paper, No. 77-117. Cambridge, MA: Marketing Science Institute.

BRAITHWAITE, ROBERT B. (1955). *Theory of Games as a Tool for the Moral Philosopher.* Cambridge: Cambridge University Press.

BRAND, GORDON T. (1972). *The Industrial Buying Decisions.* New York: Wiley.

BRISTOR, JULIA M. (1988). "Influence in Organizational Buying Decisions: A Network Approach," working paper, University of Western Ontario, London, Ont., No. 88-21.

BRISTOR, JULIA M., and MICHAEL J. RYAN (1988). "The Buying Center is Dead, Long Live the Buying Center," *Advances in Consumer Research,* Eds. Paul F. Anderson and Melanie Wallendorf. Provo, UT: Association for Consumer Research, 255–258.

BROCK, TIMOTHY C. (1965). "Communicator-Recipient Similarity and Decision Change," *Journal of Personality and Social Psychology,* 1 (June), 650–654.

BROUGHTON, PAUL D. (1980). "An Empirical Investigation of Conflict in Organizational Buying Behavior," Ph.D. dissertation, Saint Louis University, St. Louis, MO.

BROUGHTON, PAUL D., GUY R. BANVILLE, and DAVID R. LAMBERT (1986). "Conflict in the Buying Center: A Study of Organizational Buying Behavior," *AMA Educators' Proceedings,* Eds. Ter-

ence A. Shimp et al. Chicago: American Marketing Association, 87–92.

BUCKNER, H. (1967). *How the British Industry Buys.* London: Hutchinson.

BUSCH, PAUL and DAVID T. WILSON (1976). "An Experimental Analysis of a Salesman's Expert and Referent Bases of Social Power in the Buyer-Seller Dyad," *Journal of Marketing Research,* 13 (February), 3–11.

BUSH, ROBERT R., and FREDERICK MOSTELLER (1955). *Stochastic Models for Learning.* New York: Wiley.

CALDER, BOBBY J. (1977). "Structural Role Analysis of Organizational Buying: A Preliminary Investigation," *Consumer and Industrial Buying Behavior,* Eds. Arch G. Woodside, Jagdish N. Sheth, and Peter D. Bennett. New York: North-Holland, 193–199.

CAMPBELL, N. C. G. (1985). "An Interaction Approach to Organizational Buying Behavior," *Journal of Business Research,* 13, 35–48.

CAPON, NOEL, and J. HULBERT (1975). "Decision Systems Analysis in Industrial Marketing," *Industrial Marketing Management,* 4, 143–160.

CAPON, NOEL, JOHN V. FARLEY, and J. HULBERT (1975). "Pricing and Forecasting in an Oligopoly Firm," *Journal of Management Studies,* 12 (May), 26–32.

CARDOZZO, RICHARD (1980). "Situational Segmentation of Industrial Markets," *European Journal of Marketing,* 14 (June, 264–276.

CARMAN, JAMES (1980). "Paradigms for Marketing Theory," *Research in Marketing,* 3, 1–36.

CHAMBERLAIN, N. W., and J. W. KUHN (1965). *Collective Bargaining,* 2nd ed. New York: McGraw-Hill.

CHOFFRAY, J. M. (1977). "A Methodology for Investigating the Nature of the Industrial Adoption Process and the Difference in Perceptions and Evaluation Criteria Among Decision Participants," unpublished Ph.D. dissertation, Mass. Institute of Technology, Cambridge, MA.

CHOFFRAY, J. M., and G. LILIEN (1978). "Assessing Response to Industrial Marketing Strategy," *Journal of Marketing,* 42 (April), 20–31.

CHOFFRAY, J. M., and G. LILIEN (1980a). "Industrial Market Segmentation by the Structure of the Buying Process," *Industrial Marketing Management,* 9 (October), 331–342.

CHOFFRAY, J. M., and G. LILIEN (1980b). *Marketing*

Planning for New Industrial Products. New York: Wiley.

CHURCHILL, GILBERT A. JR., ROBERT H. COLLINS, and WILLIAM A. STRANG (1975). "Should Retail Salespersons be Similar to Their Customers?" *Journal of Retailing,* 51 (Fall), 29–42.

CLARKSON, G. (1963). "A Model of Trust Investment Behavior," *A Behavioral Theory of the Firm,* Eds. R. M. Cyert and J. G. March. Englewood Cliffs, NJ: Prentice-Hall.

CLOPTON, STEPHEN W. (1984). "Seller and Buying Firm Factors Affecting Buyers' Negotiation Behavior and Outcomes," *Journal of Marketing Research,* 21 (February), 39–53.

COLEMAN, RICHARD (1973). *The Mathematics of Collective Action.* Chicago: A. W. Shaw.

COLLEY, RUSSELL E. (1961). *Defining Advertising Goals for Measured Advertising Results.* New York: Association of National Advertisers.

COPELAND, M. J. (1924). *Principles of Merchandising.* Chicago: A. W. Shaw.

COREY, E. R. (1971). "People Who Claim to be Opinion Leaders: Identifying Their Characteristics by Self Report," *Journal of Marketing,* 35 (October), 48–53.

COREY, E. R. (1978). *Procurement Management: Strategy, Organization and Decision Making.* Boston, MA: CBI.

COREY, E. R. (1983). *Industrial Marketing: Cases and Concepts.* Englewood Cliffs, NJ: Prentice-Hall.

COX, DONALD F., ED. (1967). *Risk Taking and Information Handling in Consumer Behavior.* Boston, MA: Division of Research, Graduate School of Business Administration, Harvard University.

CROW, L. E. (1974). "An Information Processing Approach to Industrial Buying: The Search and Choice Process," unpublished doctoral dissertation, Indiana University, Bloomington, IN.

CROW, L. E., and JAY D. LINDQUIST (1982). "Buyers Differ in Evaluating Suppliers," *Industrial Marketing Management,* 11, 205–214.

CROW, L. E. (1985). "Impact of Organizational and Buyer Characteristics on the Buying Center," *Industrial Marketing Management,* 14, 49–58.

CROW, L. E., RICHARD W. OLSHAVSKY, and JOHN O. SUMMERS (1980). "Industrial Buyer's Choice Strategies: A Protocol Analysis," *Journal of Marketing Research,* 17 (February), 34–44.

CYERT, R. M., and J. G. MARCH (1963). *A Behavioral Theory of the Firm.* Englewood Cliffs, NJ: Prentice-Hall.

CYERT, R. M., H. A. SIMON, and D. B. TROW (1956). "Observation of a Business Decision," *Journal of Business,* 29 (October), 237–248.

DAVIS, HARRY L. (1976). "Decision-Making Within the Household," *Journal of Consumer Research* (March), 255–260.

DAVIS, HARRY L., and ALVIN J. SILK (1972). "Interaction and Influence Processes in Personal Selling," *Sloan Management Review,* 13 (Winter), 56–76.

DENZIN, NORMAN K. (1978). *Sociological Methods: A Sourcebook.* New York: McGraw-Hill.

DOREEN, DALE, DONALD R. EMERGY, and ROBERT W. SWITZER (1979). "Selling as a Dyadic Relationship Revisited," paper presented at the 1979 AIDS Conference, New Orleans, LA.

DOYLE, PETER, ARCH WOODSIDE, and PAUL MITCHELL (1979). "Organizations Buying in New Task and Modified Rebuy Situations," *Industrial Marketing Management,* 8, 7–11.

DUNCAN, (1972). "Characteristics of Organizational Environments and Perceived Environmental Uncertainty," *Administrative Science Quarterly,* 17 (September), 313–327.

DUNKIN, D. J. (1940). "What Motivates Business Buyers," *Harvard Business Review,* 18 (Summer), 448–454.

DWYER, F. ROBERT, PAUL H. SCHURR, and SEJO OH (1987). "Developing Buyer-Seller Relationships," *Journal of Marketing,* 51 (April), 11–27.

ETGAR, MICHAEL (1979). "Sources and Types of Interchannel Conflict," *Journal of Retailing,* 55 (Spring), 76–78.

ETZIONI, A. (1961). *A Comparative Analysis of Complex Organizations: On Power, Involvement, and Their Correlates.* New York: The Free Press.

EVANS, FRANKLIN B. (1963). "Selling as a Dyadic Relationship—A New Approach," *American Behavioral Scientist,* 6 (May), 76–79.

EVANS, RICHARD H. (1980). "Choice Criteria Revisited," *Journal of Marketing,* 44 (1) (Winter), 55–56.

FARLEY, JOHN V., JAMES M. HULBERT, and D. WEINSTEIN (1980). "Price Setting and Volume Planning by Two European Industrial Companies: A Study of Comparison of Decision Processes," *Journal of Marketing,* 44 (Winter), 24–30.

FRAZIER, GARY L., ROBERT E. SPEKMAN, and C. R. O'NEAL (1988). "Just-in-Time Exchange Relationships in Industrial Markets," *Journal of Marketing,* 52 (October), 52–67.

FRENCH, JOHN R. P. JR., and BERTRAM RAVEN (1959). "The Bases of Social Power," *Studies in Social Power,* Ed. D. Cartwright. Ann Arbor, MI: University of Michigan, Institute for Social Research, 150–167.

GADEL, M. S. (1964). "Concentration by Salesmen on Congenial Prospects," *Journal of Marketing,* 28 (April), 64–66.

GALBRAITH, J. R. (1973). *Designing Complex Organizations.* Reading, MA: Addison-Wesley.

GEMUNDEN, HANS GEORG (1985). "Coping with Inter-Organizational Conflicts — Efficient Interaction Strategies for Buyer and Seller Organization," *Journal of Business Research,* 13, 405–420.

GINGOLD, MORRY, and DAVID T. WILSON (1988). "Buying Center Structure: An Extended Framework for Research," in R. Spekman, Ed., *A Strategic Approach to Business Markets.* Chicago, American Marketing Association. 1988, 180–193.

GRONHAUG, KJELL (1975). "Search Behavior in Organizational Buying," *Industrial Marketing Management,* 4, 15–23.

GRONHAUG, KJELL (1977). "Exploring a Complex Organizational Buying Decision," *Industrial Marketing Management,* 6 (December), 439–444.

HAKANSSON, HAKAN (1982). *International Marketing and Purchasing of Industrial Goods,* New York: Wiley.

HARDING, MURRAY (1966). "Who Really Makes the Purchase Decision?" *Industrial Marketing,* 51 (September), 76–81.

HILLIER, T. J. (1975). "Decision Making in the Corporate Industrial Buying Process," *Industrial Marketing Management,* 4, 99–106.

HOWARD, JOHN A., and JAGDISH N. SHETH (1969). *The Theory of Buyer Behavior.* New York: Wiley.

HULBERT, JAMES M., JOHN U. FARLEY, and JOHN A. HOWARD (1972). "Information Processing and Decision-Making in Marketing Organizations," *Journal of Marketing Research,* 9 (February), 75–77.

HUTT, MICHAEL D., and THOMAS W. SPEH (1981). *Industrial Marketing Management.* Chicago: Dryden Press.

JACKSON, DONALD W. JR., JANET E. KEITH, and RICHARD K. BURDICK (1984). "Purchasing Agents' Perceptions of Industrial Buying Center Influence: A Situational Approach," *Journal of Marketing,* 48 (4), 75–83.

JOHNSTON, M. P. (1982). "Social and Cognitive Features of the Dissolution of Commitment to Relationships," *Personal Relationships 4: Dissolving Personal Relationships,* Ed. S. Duck. London: Academic Press, 51–73.

JOHNSTON, WESLEY J. (1981). "Industrial Buying Behavior: A State of the Art Review," *Review of Marketing 1981,* Ed. K. J. Roering. Chicago: American Marketing Association, 75–88.

JOHNSTON, WESLEY J., and THOMAS V. BONOMA (1981). "The Buying Center: Structure and Interaction Patterns," *Journal of Marketing,* 45 (3) (Summer), 143–156.

JOHNSTON, WESLEY J., and ROBERT E. SPEKMAN (1982). "Industrial Buying Behavior: Where We Are and Where We Need to Go," *Research in Consumer Behavior,* Vol. 2, Ed. Jagdish N. Sheth. Greenwich, CT: JAI Press.

KASSARJIAN, HAROLD H. (1986). "Consumer Research: Some Recollections and a Commentary," *Advances in Consumer Research,* Vol. 13, Ed. Richard J. Lutz. Provo, UT: Association for Consumer Research, 6–8.

KATZ, D., and R. L. KAHN (1966). *The Social Psychology of Organizations.* New York: Wiley.

KELLY, J. P. (1974). "Functions Performed in Industrial Purchasing Decisions with Implications for Marketing Strategy," *Journal of Business Research,* 2 (October), 420–434.

KELLEY, HAROLD H., and JOHN W. THIBAUT (1978). *Interpersonal Relations: A Theory of Interdependence.* New York: Wiley.

KERNAN, JEROME B., and MONTROSE S. SOMMERS (1966). "The Behavioral Matrix: A Closer Look at the Industrial Buyer," *Business Horizons* (Summer), 63–64.

KOTLER, PHILLIP J. (1987). *Marketing Management: Analysis, Planning, and Control,* 6th ed. Englewood Cliffs, NJ: Prentice-Hall.

KRAPFEL, ROBERT E. JR. (1982). "An External Interpersonal Influence Model of Organizational Buyer Behavior," *Journal of Business Research,* 10, 147–157.

KRAPFEL, ROBERT E. JR. (1985). "An Advocacy Behavior Model of Organizational Buyers' Vendor Choice," *Journal of Marketing,* 49 (Fall), 51–59.

LAVIDGE, R. I., and G. A. STEINER (1961). "A Model for Predictive Measurements of Advertising Effectiveness," *Journal of Marketing,* 25 (October), 59–62.

LAWRENCE, PAUL R., and JAN W. LORSCH (1967). *Organization and Environment,* Homewood, IL: Irwin.

LEAVITT, HAROLD S. (1964). "Applied Organization Change in Industry: Structural, Technical, and Human Approaches," *New Perspectives in Organizational Research,* Eds. W. O. Cooper, J. J. Leavitt, and M. W. Shelly II. New York: Wiley, 55–71.

LEHMANN, DONALD R., and J. O'SHAUGHNESSY (1974). "Difference in Attribute Importance for Different Industrial Products," *Journal of Marketing,* 38 (2) (April), 36–42.

LEIGH, THOMAS W., and ARNO J. RETHANS (1984). "A Script-Theoretic Analysis of Industrial Purchasing Behavior," *Journal of Marketing,* 48 (1) (Fall), 22–32.

LEVITT, THEODORE (1965). *Industrial Purchasing Behavior: A Study of Communication Effects.* Boston, MA: Division of Research, Graduate School of Business Administration, Harvard University.

LILIEN, GARY L., and M. ANTHONY WONG (1984). "An Exploratory Investigation of the Structure of the Buying Center in the Metalworking Industry," *Journal of Marketing Research,* 21 (February), 1–11.

MATTHYSSENS, P., and W. FAES (1985). "OEM Buying Process for New Components: Purchasing and Marketing Implications," *Industrial Marketing Management,* 14, 145–157.

McCABE, DONALD L. (1987). "Buying Group Structure: Constriction at the Top," *Journal of Marketing,* 51 (October), 89–98.

McCALL, G. J. (1970). "The Social Organization of Relationships," in *Social Relationships,* Eds. G. J. McCall et al. Chicago: Aldine, 3–34.

MERRILL, D., and R. H. REID (1981). *Personal Styles and Effective Performance.* Radnor, PA: Chilton Books.

MERTON, ROBERT K. (1968). *Social Theory and Social Structure.* New York: The Free Press.

MICHAELS, RONALD, RALPH L. DAY, and ERICH A. JOACHIMSTHALER (1987). "Role Stress Among Industrial Buyers: An Integrative Model," *Journal of Marketing,* 51 (April), 28–45.

MINTZBERG, H., D. RAISINHANI, and A. THEORET (1976). "The Structure of 'Unstructured' Decision Processes," *Administrative Science Quarterly,* 21 (2), 246–275.

MOLLER, K., and E. KRISTIAN (1985). "Research Strategies in Analyzing the Organizational Buying Process," *Journal of Business Research,* 13, 3–17.

MOLLER, K., and J. ALLOS (1983). "Tuotannollisten komponenttien ostopaatosprosessi," (Summary: Buying of Production Materials: An Inten-

sive Study in Three Finnish Corporations). Helsinki: Helsinki School of Economics Publications, Series B-54.

MOORE, C. G. (1969). "A Descriptive Model of the Industrial Purchasing Process: The Supplier Selection Routine," *Management Action: Models of Administrative Decisions,* Eds. C. E. Weber and G. Peters. Scranton, PA: International Textbook, 76–114.

MORE, ROGER A. (1986). "Developer/Adopter Relationships in New Industrial Product Situations," *Journal of Business Research,* 14 (6) (December), 501–517.

MORIARTY, ROWLAND T. (1983). *Industrial Buying Behavior: Concepts, Issues, and Applications.* Lexington, MA: Lexington Books.

MORIARTY, ROWLAND J., and J. E. G. BATESON (1982). "Exploring Complex Decision Making Units: A New Approach," *Journal of Marketing Research,* 19 (May), 182–191.

MORIARTY, ROWLAND J., and MORTON GALPER (1978). "Organizational Buying Behavior: A State-of-the-Art Review and Conceptualization," working paper, Report No. 78-101, Cambridge, MA: Marketing Science Institute.

MORIARTY, ROWLAND J., and ROBERT E. SPEKMAN (1984). "An Empirical Investigation of the Information Sources Used During the Industrial Buying Process," *Journal of Marketing Research,* 21 (2) (May), 137–147.

NASH, JOHN F. (1950). "The Bargaining Problem," *Econometrica,* 18, 155–162.

NASH, JOHN F. (1953). "Two-Person Cooperative Games," *Econometrica,* 21, 128–140.

NESLIN, SCOTT A., and LEONARD GREENHALGH (1983). "Nash's Theory of Cooperative Games of a Predictor of the Outcomes of Buyer-Seller Negotiations: An Experiment in Media Purchasing," *Journal of Marketing Research,* 20 (4) (November), 368–379.

NEWCOMB, THEODORE M. (1959). "The Study of Consensus," *Sociology Today: Problems and Prospects,* Eds. R. K. Merton, et al. New York: Basic Books, 277–292.

O'ROURKE, MARY, JAMES M. SHEA, and WILLIAM SULLEY (1973). "Survey Shows Need for Increased Sales Calls, Advertising, and Updated Mailing Lists to Reach Buying Influences," *Industrial Marketing,* 58 (April).

O'SHAUGHNESSY, JOHN (1977). "Aspects of Industrial Buying Behavior Relevant to Supplier Account Strategies," *Industrial Marketing Management,* 6 (January), 15–22.

OZANNE, U. B., and G. A. CHURCHILL (1968). "Adoption Research: Information Sources in the Industrial Purchasing Decision," *Marketing and the New Science of Planning,* Ed. R. L. King. Chicago: American Marketing Association.

OZANNE, U. B. (1971). "Five Dimensions of the Industrial Adoption Process," *Journal of Marketing Research* (August), 322–328.

PARKINSON, S. T. (1955). "Factors Influencing Buyer-Seller Relationships in the Market for High-Technology Products," *Journal of Business Research,* 13, 49–60.

PATCHEN, MARTIN (1974). "The Locus and Basis of Influence in Organizational Decisions," *Organizational Behavior and Human Performance,* 11 (April), 195–211.

PERDUE, BARBARA C., RALPH L. DAY, and RONALD E. MICHAELS (1986). "Negotiation Styles of Industrial Buyers," *Industrial Marketing Management,* 15, 171–176.

PHILLIPS, LYNN W. (1981). "Assessing Measurement Error in Key Informant Reports: A Methodological Note on Organizational Analysis in Marketing," *Journal of Marketing Research,* 18, 395–415.

PINGRY, JACK R. (1976). "The Engineer and Purchasing Agent Compared," *Journal of Purchasing,* 10 (November), 33–45.

PLATTEN, J. H. JR. (1950). *How Industry Buys.* New York: Scientific American.

PORTER, MICHAEL E. (1980). *Competitive Strategy.* New York: The Free Press.

PUTO, CHRISTOPHER P., WESLEY E. PATTON, III, and RONALD H. KING (1985). "Risk Handling Strategies in Industrial Vendor Selection Decisions," *Journal of Marketing,* 49 (Winter), 89–98.

RAIFFA, HOWARD (1953). "Arbitration Schemes for Generalized Two-Person Games," *Contributions to the Theory of Games II: Annals of Mathematics Studies,* Eds. H. W. Kuhn and A. W. Tucker, Princeton, NJ: Princeton University Press.

RAY, MICHAEL L. (1978). "The Present and Potential Linkages Between the Microtheoretical Notions of Behavioral Science and the Problems of Advertising: A Proposal for a Research System," *Behavioral and Management Science in Marketing,* Eds. Harry L. Davis and Alvin Silk. New York: Ronald Press, 99–141.

ROBERTSON, THOMAS S., and YORAM WIND (1980). "Organizational Psychographics and Innovativeness," *Journal of Consumer Research* (June), 24–31.

ROBERTSON, THOMAS S., J. ZEILINSKI, and S. WARD (1986). *Consumer Behavior.* Glenview, IL: Scott, Foresman.

ROBICHEAUX, R. A., and A. I. EL-ANSARY (1975). "A General Model for Understanding Channel Member Behavior," *Journal of Retailing,* 52 (Winter), 13–30 and 93–94.

ROBINSON, P. J., C. W. FARIS, and Y. WIND (1967). *Industrial Buying Behavior and Creative Marketing.* Boston: Allyn and Bacon.

ROGERS, E. M. (1962). *Diffusion of Innovations.* New York: The Free Press.

ROGERS, E. M. (1969). *Modernization Among Peasants.* New York: Holt, Rinehart & Winston.

RUSBULT, C. E. (1980). "Commitment and Satisfaction in Romantic Associations: A Test of the Investment Model," *Journal of Experimental Social Psychology,* 16, 172–186.

RYAN, MICHAEL J., and MORRIS B. HOLBROOK (1982). "Decision-Specific Conflict in Organizational Buyer Behavior," *Journal of Marketing,* 46 (3) (Summer), 62–68.

SATHE, V. V. (1974). "Structural Adaptation in Environment: Study of Insurance Company Departments and Branch Banks," unpublished Ph.D. dissertation, Ohio State University, Columbus, OH.

Scientific American. "How Industry Buys—1970: A Study of the Systematic Procedure for Purchasing Materials, Component Parts, and Equipment," New York Scientific American, Inc. 1969, 4–20.

SHETH, J. N. (1973). "A Model of Industrial Buyer Behavior," *Journal of Marketing* (October), 50–53.

SILK, ALVIN J., and MANOHAR U. KALWANI (1982). "Measuring Influence in Organizational Purchase Decisions," *Journal of Marketing Research,* 19 (May), 165–181.

SILLS, D. L. (1957). *The Volunteers.* New York: The Free Press.

SOLDOW, GARY F., and GLORIA PENN THOMAS (1984). "Relational Communication: Form Versus Content in the Sales Interaction," *Journal of Marketing,* 48 (1) (Winter), 84–93.

SPEKMAN, ROBERT (1977). "A Contingency Approach to Power Relationships in the Organizational Buying Decision Unit," unpublished Ph.D. dissertation, Northwestern University, Evanston, IL.

SPEKMAN, ROBERT (1978a). "An Alternative Framework for Examining the Industrial Buying Process," *Organizational Buying Behavior*, Eds. T. V. Bonoma and G. Zaltman. Chicago: American Marketing Association.

SPEKMAN, ROBERT (1978b). "A Macro-Sociological Examination of the Industrial Buying Center: Promise or Problem," *Proceedings: 1978 Educators' Conference*, Series No. 43. Chicago: American Marketing Association, 111-115.

SPEKMAN, ROBERT (1979). "Influence and Information: An Exploratory Investigation of the Boundary Role Person's Basis of Power," *Academy of Management Journal*, 22 (1), 104-117.

SPEKMAN, ROBERT, and LOUIS W. STERN (1979). "Environmental Uncertainty and Buying Group Structure: An Empirical Investigation," *Journal of Marketing*, 43 (Spring), 54-64.

STERN, LOUIS W., and T. REVE (1980). "Distribution Channels as Political Economies: A Framework for Comparative Analysis," *Journal of Marketing*, 44 (Summer), 52-64.

STILES, G. W. (1974). "Determinants of the Industrial Buyer's Level of Information Processing," *Buyer/Consumer Information Processing*, Eds. G. D. Hughes and M. L. Ray. Chapel Hill, NC: University of North Carolina Press, 116-135.

STRAUSS, G. (1962). "Tactics of Lateral Relationship: The Purchasing Agent," *Administrative Science Quarterly*, 7 (September), 161-186.

SWEENEY, T. W., H. L. MATHEWS, and D. T. WILSON (1973). "An Analysis of Industrial Buyers' Risk Reducing Behavior: Some Personality Correlates," *AMA Proceedings*. Chicago: American Marketing Association, 217-221.

THIBAUT, J. W., and H. KELLEY (1959). *The Social Psychology of Groups*. New York: Wiley.

THOMAS, GLORIA P., and JOHN F. GRASHOF (1982). "Impact of Internal and External Environmental Stability on the Existence of Determinant Buying Rules," *Journal of Business Research*, 10, 159-168.

THOMAS, ROBERT J. (1982). "Correlates of Interpersonal Purchase Influence in Organizations," *Journal of Consumer Research*, 9, 171-182.

THOMAS, ROBERT J. (1984). "Bases of Power in Organizational Buying Decisions," *Industrial Marketing Management*, 13, 209-217.

THORELLI, HANS B. (1986). "Networks: Between Markets and Hierarchies," *Strategic Management Journal*, 7, 37-51.

TOSI, H. L. (1966). "The Effects of Expectation Levels and Role Consensus on the Buyer-Seller Dyad," *Journal of Business*, 39 (October).

TURNBULL, P. W., and D. T. WILSON (1988). "Strategic Advantage Through Buyer Relationship Management," Pennsylvania State University: Institute for the Study of Business Markets Report.

TURNER, RALPH H. (1970). *Family Interaction*. New York: Wiley.

TVERSKY, AMOS, and DANIEL KAHNEMAN (1981). "The Framing of Decisions and the Psychology of Choice," *Science*, 211 (January), 453-458.

VON HIPPEL, ERIC (1977). "Has a Customer Already Developed Your Next Product?" *Sloan Management Review*, 18 (Winter), 63-74.

VYAS, NIREN, and ARCH G. WOODSIDE (1981). "An Inductive Model of Industrial Supplier Choice Processes," unpublished paper, University of South Carolina, Columbia, SC.

VYAS, NIREN (1982). "Micro Analysis of Supplier Choice Strategies: Industrial Packaging Materials," working paper, College of Business Administration, University of South Carolina, Columbia, SC.

VYAS, NIREN (1984). "An Inductive Model of Industrial Supplier Choice Processes," *Journal of Marketing*, 48 (1) (Winter), 30-45.

WALKER, ORVILLE C. JR., GILBERT A. CHURCHILL, and W. M. FORD (1977). "Motivation and Performance in Industrial Selling: Existing Knowledge and Needed Research," *Journal of Marketing Research*, 14 (May), 156-168.

WARD, SCOTT, and THOMAS R. ROBERTSON (1973). *Consumer Behavior: Theoretical Sources*. Englewood Cliffs, NJ: Prentice-Hall.

WEBB, E., and K. E. WEICK (1976). "Unobtrusive Measures in Organizational Theory: A Reminder," *Administrative Science Quarterly*, 24 (December), 27-33.

WEBSTER, F. E. JR. (1965). "Modeling the Industrial Buying Process," *Journal of Marketing Research*, 2 (November), 370-376.

WEBSTER, F. E. JR. (1984). *Industrial Marketing Strategy*, 2nd ed. New York: Wiley.

WEBSTER, F. E. JR. (1972). "Communication and Diffusion Process in Industrial Market," *European Journal of Marketing*, 5 (Winter), 178-188.

WEBSTER, F. E. JR. (forthcoming). *Industrial Marketing Strategy*, 3rd ed. New York: Wiley.

WEBSTER, F. E. JR., and Y. WIND (1972). *Organizational Buying Behavior*. Englewood Cliffs, NJ: Prentice-Hall

WEITZ, BARTON A. (1978). "The Relationship Between Salesperson Performance and Understanding of Customer Decision-Making," *Journal of Marketing Research*, 15 (November), 501–516.

WEITZ, BARTON A. (1981). "Effectiveness in Sales Interactions: A Contingency Framework," *Journal of Marketing*, 45 (1) (Winter), 85–103.

WILDT, A. R., and A. V. BRUNO (1974). "Prediction of Preference for Capital Equipment Using Linear Attitude Models," *Journal of Marketing Research*, 11 (May), 203.

WILLIAMSON, O. E. (1975). *Markets and Hierarchies: Analysis and Antitrust Implications*. New York: The Free Press.

WILLIAMSON, O. E. (1979). "Transaction-Cost Economics: The Governance of Contractual Relations," *Journal of Law and Economics*, 22 (October), 3–61.

WILLIAMSON, O. E. (1985). *The Economic Institutions of Capitalism*. New York: The Free Press.

WILSON, DAVID T. (1975). "Dyadic Interaction: An Exchange Process," *Advances in Consumer Research*, Ed. B. Anderson, Cincinnati, OH: Association for Consumer Research, 394–397.

WILSON, DAVID T. (1978). "Dyadic Interaction: Some Conceptualizations," in *Organizational Buying Behavior*, Eds. T. V. Bonoma and G. Zaltman, Chicago: American Marketing Association.

WILSON, DAVID T. (1985). "Developing Organizational Buying Theory: A Small Sample Perspective," *Journal of Business Research*, 13, 177–185.

WILSON, DAVID T., and K. E. KRISTIAN MOLLER (1988). "Buyer-Seller Relationships: Alternative Conceptualizations," Penn State University, Institute for the Study of Business Markets, Report No. 10-1088, University Park, PA.

WILSON, DAVID T., and VENKATAPPARAO MUMMALANENI (1988). "Modeling and Measuring Buyer-Seller Relationships," Penn State University, Institute for the Study of Business Markets, Report No. 3-1988, University Park, PA.

WILSON, ELIZABETH J., GARY L. LILIEN, and DAVID T. WILSON (1988). "Formal Models of Group Choice in Organizational Buying: Toward a Contingency Paradigm," Penn State University, Institute for the Study of Business Markets, Report No. 7-1988, University Park, PA.

WIND, YORAM, and THOMAS S. ROBERTSON (1982). "The Linking Pin Role in Organizational Buying Centers," *Journal of Business Research*, 10, 169–184.

WIND, YORAM, and R. THOMAS (1980). "Conceptual and Methodological Issues in Organizational Buying Behavior," *European Journal of Business Research*, 14, 239–263.

WOODSIDE, ARCH G., and WILLIAM J. DAVENPORT (1974). "The Effects of Salesman Similarity and Expertise on Consumer Purchasing Behavior," *Journal of Marketing Research*, 11 (May), 198–202.

WOODSIDE, ARCH G., and N. VYAS (1981). "Industrial Buying Behavior of Fuel Oil: A Descriptive Model of a Firm's Decision Process," working paper, College of Business Administration, University of North Carolina, Chapel Hill, NC.

ZAJONC, ROBERT (1980). "Feeling and Thinking: Preferences Need No Inferences," *American Psychologist* 35 (February), 151–175.

13

CONSUMER BEHAVIOR RESEARCH AND SOCIAL POLICY

Alan R. Andreasen*
University of Connecticut

An issue of social policy arises in the field of consumer behavior whenever marketers attempt to influence target consumers in order to make a net material contribution to the society's collective goals. This chapter reviews research and theory on the extent to which marketing efforts achieve society's goals of (a) fairness, (b) equity, (c) safety, and (d) improved social and economic welfare. Recommendations are made for future research and for the promotion of further work in this important domain.

THE FRAMEWORK

Despite the centrality of consumer behavior in defining the character of a society, the intersection between consumer behavior and social policy has never become a prominent subspecialty within the academic discipline of consumer behavior. There have been flurries of interest in the specific issues of this topic from time to time, but the topic has not been the preoccupying interest of any significant "invisible college"

*The author wishes to thank David Horne, Jeff A. Kasmer, and Terrence Witkowski for comments on an earlier draft and Laurie Hayashi for her help in assembling the extensive set of references for this paper.

of consumer behavior researchers. Indeed, in many cases the life cycle of interest in topics like "ghetto marketing" or "energy conservation" have appeared more like those for fads than for lasting topics of serious intellectual concern (Andreasen 1978).

Nor is it even a preoccupation of the leaders of the field. In an analysis of presidential addresses of the Association for Consumer Research, Spiggle and Goodwin conclude quite simply that "public policy concerns are not a substantial focus" of addresses that, by tradition, are designed to take a measure of the discipline's state of the art (Spiggle and Goodwin 1987, p. 8).

459

A Narrow Conception of Social Policy

A review of the research and writing in the field makes it clear that a part of the problem is that the intersection between consumer behavior and social policy has been conceived too narrowly. When one seeks a list of social policy issues in the area of consumer behavior, the issues typically mentioned focus on one or another aspect of the following question: How do we make the marketplace work better *so that consumers can make better decisions about what to buy?* This position is unnecessarily narrow in two important respects. First, it ignores the fact that the field of marketing has "broadened" considerably since the early 1970s. It is now well accepted that consumer behavior involves more than economic goods and services. Second, consumer behavior is more than just "transactions." As Belk argued in his 1986 ACR presidential address, consumer researchers need to "recognize the full complexity of the relationship between consumption and the rest of life" (Belk 1986, p. 4).[1] Belk labels this enlarged perspective as "macro consumer behavior." Its study "concerns aspects of consumer behavior that are likely to have little interest to the decision making of a marketer or an advertiser, but have great interest to the members of society and to their individual and collective well-being" (Ibid.).

A broader view of the intersection of consumer behavior and social policy is, therefore, one that recognizes that consumer behavior:

1. encompasses more than economic transactions; and

2. has other meanings in people's lives beyond that which is typically of interest to marketing managers.

---

[1] Belk's view of macro consumer behavior includes dimensions beyond exchanges themselves (e.g., possession) that are not relevant in the present context.

The Intersection of Social Policy in Consumer Theory and Research

Definition of Social Policy. Social policy is, at base, simply "policy for the society." It is a codified expression of where and to what purposes a society believes it may properly intervene in the lives of individual corporations, groups, or persons in order to achieve some greater social good. With respect to consumer behavior theory and research, I would propose the following working definition: An issue of social policy arises in the field of consumer behavior whenever the society as a whole believes that intervention in the process or outcome of exchanges between (1) a marketer (individual, group, or organization) and (2) target consumers will make a net material contribution to that society's collective goals and where the desired outcome is unlikely to occur without such intervention. "Society" here denotes formal "representative" public organizations including federal, state, city, and neighborhood governments, and international bodies such as the United Nations, the World Bank, and the European Economic Community. It does not include informal societies such as clubs, unions, religious organizations, and the like. Similarly, "target consumers" denotes both individual consumers and collectivities such as companies and organizations.

Objectives of Social Policy. In determining whether or not to intervene in any given set of exchanges, a society will be concerned with both their *processes* and their *outcomes*. With respect to consumer exchanges, society has four major objectives. It may choose to intervene to insure that the exchanges:

1. Are *fair*: Do consumers have adequate, undistorted information to make choices? Are they subject to undue pressures? Do they have appropriate options for redress if things go wrong?

2. Are *equitable*: Are there segments of the population that are systematically discriminated against by the marketing process?

3. Are *safe*: Do marketing exchanges jeopardize the lives and physical well-being of the parties or of unsuspecting third parties?

4. Contribute to *improved economic and social welfare*: Do the outcomes of economic and social transactions lead to greater satisfaction with the goods and services the society consumes? Are there transactions that are not taking place that should, and transactions taking place that shouldn't?

Although Aaker and Day have suggested that *consumerism* can be "defined broadly as an organized expression for an improved quality of life" (Aaker and Day 1982, p. 8), the concept of social policy advocated in this paper differs from traditional approaches to consumerism. The latter focuses on protecting consumers, presumably from the effects of the possible *negative* impacts of marketing practices. The consumer social policy concept is broader in that it encompasses social policies that employ marketing practices to achieve *positive* impacts on society, for example, in promoting patronage of the arts, charitable giving, or the adoption of improved health practices.

Information Needs of Social Policymakers. In order to determine when and how to implement social policy, policymakers need both basic and applied research that will yield two broad types of information. First, they need to identify areas where there may be needs for social policy interventions. Identification would include not only detecting opportunities for intervention but also explaining their sources. Second, policymakers need information on just what types of interventions to employ. Interventions can take three possible forms:

1. *Regulation*: Policymakers can decide to *prevent* certain types of transactions (e.g., nonprescription sales of particular drugs) or transactions between certain parties (e.g., sales of alcohol to minors), or they can decide to *shape* transactions by requiring certain content (e.g., smoking is hazardous warnings) or by preventing other content (e.g., deceptive messages).

2. *Incentivization*: Policymakers can seek to promote certain kinds of transactions as being in the public interest by directly influencing the benefits involved (e.g., permitting income tax deductions for home mortgages to promote home ownership or subsidizing the cost of condoms in developing countries to promote family planning and to combat the spread of AIDS);

3. *Information and Persuasion*: Policymakers can also promote certain kinds of transactions by providing information about alternatives (e.g., publishing brochures on methods of quitting smoking or about how to complain about unsatisfactory products or services), or by actively seeking to convince target audiences that specific behaviors are desirable (e.g., wearing seatbelts or having regular cancer checkups) or *un*desirable (e.g., saying no to drugs or cutting down on cholesterol intake).

The relevance of these approaches to the four social policy objectives is not uniform. For example, regulation is the dominant intervention for achieving fairness and equity, while a combination of regulation and some persuasion is most appropriate for achieving safety. And *all three* can be used to improve economic and social welfare.

OUTLINE OF THE PAPER

Consumer behavior research and theory can make contributions toward meeting the information needs of consumer policymakers with respect to four broad social objectives. These objectives will provide the framework within which to assemble and categorize some of the *past* contributions of consumer researchers to social policy. It will also serve as the framework for outlining areas in which *future* research and theory might be developed.

It is, of course, impossible within a single paper to consider even a significant proportion of the existing work in a research area defined as broadly as the present one. Thus, the sections to follow will consider only some of the major research streams within each of the four policy domains. Further, the review will restrict its purview primarily to the United States, although references to issues or research in other cultures will be included in the sections on fairness and equity.[2]

ACHIEVING FAIRNESS

Historical Interest In Fairness

The question of whether the activities of marketers are fair in targeting consumers or to the society as a whole is perhaps the oldest issue of consumer social policy. Thoughtful scholars and researchers, as well as other social critics, have been concerned about the overall performance of the marketing system since at least the eighteenth century (e.g., in the work of Adam Smith). They have asked whether marketing costs too much (Cox, Goodman and Fichandler 1962), whether marketers are "hidden persuaders" (Packard 1957), whether marketers create artificial product obsolescence (Mayer 1959), and whether marketers collude and/or fix prices (Grether 1974).

Much of the research addressing these issues has been economic and has focussed on the marketing *firm* and its performance. Except for the occasional study of *opinions* about the marketplace and about marketers' practices (Bauer and Greyser 1968), there has been relatively little objective research on the fairness of the marketplace *as seen from the consumer's perspective*.

In general, attention to this perspective has ebbed and flowed with society's interest in consumerism. As Herrmann (1970), Aaker and Day (1982), and Nadel (1971) have pointed out, this interest has appeared in three distinct waves since the late nineteenth century.[3] These waves have had a number of features in common.

First, in each wave, there have been impor-

tant environmental and political conditions that set the stage for the rise in interest in consumerism, for example, the Great Depression and the rise of the New Deal in the 1930s. This general interest is then galvanized by serendipitous factors, such as a scandal (e.g., the Thalidomide drug case or General Motor's "bugging" of Ralph Nader), or the publication of a dramatic expose, such as Upton Sinclair's *The Jungle* (1906). It is then carried forward by a number of visible spokespeople such as Ralph Nader and Betty Furness. The latter are abetted by a small number of politicians who see consumerism as fitting their own career needs (e.g., Theodore Roosevelt in the 1890s and Warren Magnuson and Benjamin Rosenthal in the 1960s) and by journalists looking for good stories.

The problem of translating this general interest into specific regulations and statutes is then turned over to various legislative bodies. However, final action by these bodies is unlikely to take place without the intervention of other organizations that either "keep the heat on" the issues or help with the difficult legislative maneuvering necessary to translate consumer outrage into specific laws and regulations.

Role of Consumer Behavior Research

Since consumer behavior as a distinct discipline dates only from the mid-1960s, participation of *consumer behavior researchers* in the process of identifying and explaining examples of unfairness in the marketplace has been relatively recent. Interest in understanding and tracking *specific* consumer problems grew dramatically in the late 1970s under the broad label of consumer satisfaction/dissatisfaction (CS/D) research. Its growth coincided with (and was abetted by) a growing interest on the part of both government regulators and leaders within the consumer movement in making the policy formulation process more rational and systematic. Critics of past consumer policy formulation had argued that it was too often influenced by chance events, letter-writing campaigns, media publicity, and partisan political agendas (Cox,

---

[2]For excellent discussions of consumer policy issues in other developed countries, see Olander (1980; 1988) and in developing countries, see Thorelli (1988).

[3]The waves were (approximately) in the years 1890 to 1916, 1932 to 1939, and 1964 to 1980.

Fellmeth, and Schultz 1969; American Bar Association 1969). Three of the earliest comprehensive CS/D studies were, in fact, motivated by the policy planning needs of a public regulatory agency, the Federal Trade Commission (Technical Advisory Research Program 1979; Day and Landon 1976), and a private nonprofit sector organization, Ralph Nader's Center for Study of Responsive Law (Andreasen and Best 1977).

CS/D Research. The earliest work in CS/D research simply sought to develop measures of consumer satisfaction with varying market baskets of goods and services. For example, pioneering studies by Handy and Pfaff in the mid-1970s developed raw and weighted indexes of consumer satisfaction with food products across seven broad food categories (Handy and Pfaff 1975; Handy 1976; Pfaff 1977). After that point, research on the topic grew dramatically. Between 1975 and 1985, over 300 papers were prepared on the broad topic of consumer satisfaction and complaint behavior, and nine specialized conferences have been held in the United States.

Since 1985, two different patterns have emerged. First, there has been a considerable drop in CS/D research from a public policy perspective. At the same time, however, there has been a substantial growth in interest in the topic of consumer satisfaction research in the *private* sector. This has been driven primarily by the growth of the service sector of the economy where managers have realized that tracking satisfaction is crucial to success where intangibles such as personal attention and atmospheres are the "product." A number of private satisfaction tracking services have emerged (Brandt 1987). Many of these services have made extensive use of earlier methodological developments in *social policy* research.

A review of the early CS/D literature (Andreasen 1988) indicates that it has focused on three issues:

1. How often do consumers experience problems?
2. What have been their responses to these problems?

3. And more recently, what have been the principal institutional responses to voiced dissatisfaction?

As noted, initial studies on CS/D sought to calibrate the amount and types of dissatisfaction in the marketplace as a basis for policy planning.[4] Comprehensive studies of CS/D were carried out in the United States in the late 1970s by Day and his colleagues (Day and Bodur 1978; Day and Ash 1979; Leigh and Day 1981), by Andreasen and Best (1977), and by the Technical Assistance Research Project (TARP 1979). More recently, there also has been pioneering work carried out in Canada (Zussman 1983), Great Britain (Office of Fair Trading 1986), and West Germany (Meffert and Bruhn 1983).

This body of research has been largely descriptive. It indicates that, in a given year, about 40 to 50 percent of all consumers will report that they have experienced some form of dissatisfaction or problem. This will vary somewhat across countries and will depend on the "basket" of products and/or services included in the index. Wide variation in this figure is found across purchase categories, with the average likely to be between 15 and 25 percent. Among the categories with high levels of problems are autos, auto and appliance repairs, toys and mail order (Andreasen and Best 1977).

These findings, however, may be specific to Western and/or developed countries. Thorelli has found much higher levels of dissatisfaction in Thailand (Thorelli and Sentell 1982) and in the People's Republic of China (Thorelli 1983).

A difficulty in analyzing the data in these studies is their lack of careful conceptual development. The studies differ widely in the basic measure of dissatisfaction they use. Some focus on more or less objective measures of "problems," others on subjective feelings of "dissatisfaction." Some will count *any* negative experience whatever, some only "serious" dissatisfactions, and some only the most recent problem. Then there is the problem of *opportunity for problems*. Measures must control for

---

[4]The material in this section is largely drawn from Andreasen (1988).

frequency of purchase. Certainly those who buy often are more likely to experience problems than those who buy infrequently. Recent efforts by Day (1983), Ross (1985), and Ross and Oliver (1984) have made strides in the direction of standardization. However, definitional problems persist.

The studies noted in the preceding paragraph are typically based on some form of survey data. An alternative approach is to use *complaints data,* that is, data on the extent to which consumers voluntarily speak up about their dissatisfactions. Such data have the advantage that they do not require field surveys; they are already available within organizations. However, complaints data are not without their own difficulties. They are typically biased in two important ways. First, some types of problems in some types of industries are more likely to be voiced than others. For example, some problems are less serious and or less costly than others and do not merit the effort of complaining (Richins 1980). Some industries (e.g., physician services) receive relatively few complaints (where they are probably warranted) because the industry operates under what Hirschmann (1970) calls "loose monopoly" conditions that make them relatively immune to complaining except from a small elite (Andreasen 1986). Still other industries are more encouraging of complaints (Fornell 1976).

Complaints data are also biased in that not all consumers complain. As Best (1981) points out in rich detail, the impediments placed in the way of consumers are often quite formidable, even if the consumer knows where and how to complain and has the assertiveness to do so. These problems have led more marketers and researchers in recent years to fall back on the more costly, but more objective, survey research procedures.

Specific experiences of dissatisfaction can, of course, affect attitudes toward marketing and the marketplace in general. In turn, if consumers are generally upset with the system, they will be more supportive of interventions than if they are more contented. Tracking of consumer opinion toward the marketplace has been carried out since 1972 (Barksdale and

Darden 1972; Hustad and Pessemeir 1973). More recently, a number of researchers have attempted to develop general attitudinal measures. Allison (1978), Bearden and his colleagues (Bearden and Mason 1983; Bearden, Lichtenstein, and Teel 1983; Bearden, Mason, and Teel 1983), and Lambert (1980) have focused on the well-researched psychological concept of *alienation* (Seeman 1959).

On the other hand, Lundstrom and his colleagues (Lundstrom and Lamont 1976; Lundstrom, Skelly, and Sciglimpaglia 1980) and Lambert and Kniffin (1975) have focused on the more general concept of *consumer discontent.* Lundstrom and Lamont determined that there are six dimensions underlying the discontent: (1) general discontent; (2) general business attitude; (3) perceptions as to whether or not business induces unnecesary purchases; (4) perceptions of profits and prices; (5) perceptions of products and promotions; and (6) attitudes toward materialism.

More recent work by Gaski and Etzel has built upon earlier research by Barksdale, Darden, and Perrault (1976) to develop a general index of *consumer sentiment* toward marketing. This index is proposed to serve as a "continuing barometer of 'how marketing is doing' in the eyes of the consumer public" (Gaski and Etzel 1986, p. 72). The index has four components: price, advertising, retailing/selling, and products, and it comprises both evaluations of marketing and weights on each evaluation dimension. The index has been validated using a Market Facts panel, and the authors (and Market Facts) intend to replicate it annually.

These instruments may help describe atmospheres supportive of more social policy intervention and identify those who are more likely to support such interventions or to take action on their own. However, the instruments are only *potentially* helpful in identifying very broad areas where social policy is needed. They tell little about which practices need reforming and which consumers need specific help.

Materialism, Miscomprehension and Deception. Within the various functional areas of marketing, advertising has drawn the most attention of consumer researchers because of its considerable potential for unfairly influencing consumers and distorting their choices. One long-standing concern has been the extent to which the *cumulative effect* of advertising makes consumers more materialistic. This was one of the traits Lundstrom and Lamont (1976) found underlying much consumer discontent. The topic, however, has not seen systematic investigation in part because the most obvious social policy option for this problem, should it be deemed severe, is simply to reduce the quantity of advertising. This is probably unthinkable in advanced Western countries. However, it is not beyond the realm of possibility in developing countries where there is considerable concern that Western materialistic values may be antithetical to the retention of traditional values and cultures and, more directly, a threat to burgeoning local entrepreneurs.

A second major concern is whether advertising misleads consumers. Here, the social policy options are more palatable. Consumer researchers have addressed this topic by asking two basic questions: What is the extent of consumer misperception of advertising and to what extent do marketers contribute to this problem? The social policy questions then become: (1) What laws or regulations are needed to assure that the communicators of such information adhere to standards that will minimize such miscomprehension, or (2) what help do consumers themselves need to recognize and avoid marketer deceptions?

A principal focus of much of the research in this area has been on the detection issue; that is, defining and detecting marketer deception. It is recognized that often miscomprehension results from "deficiencies" in the consumer's own processing, for example, when they make incorrect inferences from a set of valid and objectively unambiguous data. On the other hand, a substantial body of literature, both scientific and anecdotal, exists that shows that deception on the part of marketers is not a rare occurrence.

The seminal study of miscomprehension was conducted by Jacoby, Hoyer, and Sheluga (1980), examining a large national sample's comprehension of 60 different 30-second televi-sion advertisements, program excerpts, and public service announcements. Each person in the sample saw two communications and was asked six true-false questions about each. The study found an overall miscomprehension rate of 29.6 percent. Only 4 percent of respondents answered all questions correctly. Demographic correlates of miscomprehension were modest, with higher rates for consumers who were younger or older, or who had less education. As Gates and Hoyer (1986) indicate, "these findings are in general agreement with those found by researchers in the broadcasting and journalism areas."

The Jacoby et al. study, however, has been criticized for inadequate attention to demand properties, yeasaying, and guessing (Mizerski 1981; Ford and Yalch 1982; Mizerski 1982). Schmittlien and Morrison (1983) reanalyzed the original data to eliminate these effects and estimated an overall miscomprehension rate of 46 percent.

It is clear that a major problem in estimating miscomprehension is the measurement methodology used. Typical recall and recognition methods confound possible negative effects of miscomprehension with those of memory loss. Mizerski (1982) reported that the FTC found miscomprehension rates varying from 2 percent to 40 percent depending on whether the measurement method was aided or unaided recall, or recognition. Ford and Yalch also suggested that differences may appear depending on whether true-false (Jacoby et al.) or multiple choice (FTC) tests were used. A study by Gates and Hoyer (1986) indicates that neither method is clearly superior. They propose that future analyses develop more specific hypotheses based upon cognitive theory about the likely nature of the miscomprehension. Then these expected miscomprehensions should be incorporated into multiple choice alternatives, rather than simply using tests to see whether consumers "got it right."

Whatever the methodology, it is unassailable that consumers have a *potential* to miscomprehend. Indeed, the existing research indicates that we *all* miscomprehend to a relatively significant degree. However, the important public policy issue is this: Do some marketers wittingly or unwittingly take advantage of this potential to gain unfair market advantage? Case experience at the Federal Trade Commission provides ample evidence of the existence of what Preston and Richards (1986) label *marketer-induced* miscomprehension of advertising messages, or *deception*. This evidence is confirmed in cases brought before the advertising industry's own self-regulatory bodies, the National Advertising Division, Council of Better Business Bureaus (NAD), the National Advertising Review Board (NARB) in the United States, and various self-regulatory bodies elsewhere in the world (Neelankavil and Stridsberg 1980).

Advertising deception is also matched by extensive deception in other areas of the marketing mix, such as deception in branding (Reece and Ducoffe 1987), endorsements and testimonials (Stern and Eovaldi 1984), sweepstakes and contests (Volner 1972), and personal selling (Federal Trade Commission 1982).

Gardner (1975) has identified three types of deception:

1. The unconscionable lie: a claim that is false ("Restores lost youth");
2. The claim-fact discrepancy: a claim from which consumers might reasonably draw an inference that is discrepant with the truth (this car is on sale; therefore, all models like it must be on sale);
3. The claim-belief interaction: a claim that the seller would have reason to expect consumers to misinterpret due to the consumers' previously held beliefs (e.g., to expect a customer to misread a carpet price per square foot as the more typical price per square *yard*).

Historically, the FTC has used this and similar definitions to judge ads on a case-by-case basis asking whether a given message had the "tendency or capacity to mislead or deceive." This requires that the commission consider what the advertisement *conveyed*, not what it said. The latter, as Preston and Richards (1986) point out, can be subject to tests of literal truth or falsity. However, the former can only be inferred by considering whether there is

likely to be miscomprehension. Traditionally, the FTC has used the judgments of its own commissioners and that of expert witnesses to determine what would tend to be conveyed. More recently, they have turned to specific field investigations with real target consumers to assess the potential to deceive. FTC hearings now routinely find both sides in a dispute presenting formal survey results supporting or denying claims of deception.

Grunert and Dedler (1985) argue, however, that these case-by-case approaches are situation-specific and do not permit the formation of general regulatory rules about deception. They urge that consumer behavior researchers focus less on the *existence* of miscomprehension and more on its causes. As they state (p. 158), "If we knew which components of an advertising message were most likely to mislead consumers, policymakers could act swiftly and rapidly whenever advertisement using such components appear, before consumers have been misled."

Several lists of potentially misleading components have been proposed by Harris (1977) and Preston (1977). Two of these have been "significantly researched" in the past (Grunert and Dedler 1985, p. 159). These are *incomplete comparisons* (Shimp 1978) and *unfounded superlatives* or puffery (Oliver 1979; Rotfeld and Rotzoll 1980). However, empirical research indicates that simply identifying a statement as an exemplar of these potentially deceptive components cannot be assumed to be primae facie evidence of a tendency to deceive. In a test of seven such components, Grunert and Dedler (1985) found the expected deception in three cases, no effects in two, and unexpected effects in the opposite direction in two. The authors speculate that in the last two cases respondents may have "recognized the tricks used (and formed) a worse judgment of the product attribute in question" (Grunert and Dedler 1985, p. 163).

Even if there are cognitive effects due to deception, it cannot be assumed that *consumption patterns* will be negatively affected. Research by Olson and Dover (1978) suggest that cognitive changes may not be determinative if they are eventually (or rapidly) superseded by behavioral experiences. These researchers found that, while a group exposed to a deceptive ad for coffee did exhibit "undesirable" changes in beliefs, these effects disappeared after the treatment group tasted the product.

Finally, it must be noted that for society to intervene to correct deception by sellers in the marketplace, it is also necessary to consider the *extent of the impact* of the deception on consumers, since impositions on business are not costless. Nor ought society to intervene excessively in the lives of its citizens (corporate and otherwise). One approach to assessing the likely impact of deception by sellers, short of conducting actual field experiments, is to consider the relative importance of the product or service attribute that is the subject of the deception. Armstrong, Gurol, and Russ (1983) propose a modification of the multiattribute attitude model as a framework for providing regulatory judges with a "salient deception score," which calibrates the extent to which a belief differs from "the truth" times the salience of the belief.

A second component of impact is *who* is being affected by the deception. It is not clear whether a level of distortion that might be tolerated if its target were a relatively affluent, educated audience might be the subject of societal restrictions if it affects more dramatically certain vulnerable populations, such as children, the poor, or the elderly. Relatively little theoretical or empirical investigation of this issue of *relative impact* has been undertaken to date.

Evaluation of Alternatives

Social policy alternatives for reducing or eliminating unfairness (as well as dealing with inequity and safety problems) are one of two types: (1) forms of regulation or informal social pressure that prevent or penalize continued wrongdoing; or (2) information and persuasion programs to help consumers help themselves. We shall consider one set of remedies under each heading: first, requiring marketers to engage in corrective advertising; second, urging consumers to engage in greater complaint behavior.

Corrective Advertising. When regulators have determined that a certain market practice is unfair, they face the problem of not only stopping the practice (often unnecessary after a lengthy hearing procedure), but also of how best to restructure a competitive situation that the unfair practice has created. This is particularly a problem with misleading advertising. If it has worked, misleading advertising has changed people's knowledge, attitudes, intentions, and, possibly, behavior. If a potentially unfair practice can be stopped before it is implemented, as in the FTC ad substantiation program (Cohen 1980), then harm is prevented. However, if the practice is implemented and presumably works, a residue remains, although subject to the normal processes of decay. How, then, to eliminate this residue?

One possibility investigated by a number of consumer behavior researchers has been to undertake corrective advertising.[5] Wilkie, McNeill, and Mazis (1984) summarized the results of eight experimental studies on the effects of corrective advertisements. The earliest of these eight studies focused on *overall* attitude measures and intentions to purchase, finding that corrective advertising did hold a potential for significantly affecting brand perceptions and eventually market shares. The impact of the corrective advertising was less affected by the source of the corrective message or its strength than by the simple fact that correction itself was required of the marketer.

In a series of papers in the mid-1970s, Wilkie argued for a shift in research focus to *specific beliefs* rather than global attitudes or intentions, a position consistent with the definitions of deception outlined previously (Wilkie 1973; 1974; 1975b). This, indeed, was the focus of the next round of corrective advertising studies, which also incorporated more sophisticated models of advertising effects. In particular, the studies identified both decay effects in the primary beliefs and also effects on related beliefs (although one study did not find examples of the latter effect).

---

[5]This section draws extensively from Wilkie, McNeill, and Mazis (1984).

Much of this research was done with students and/or in highly artificial situations. A parallel series of six *field* studies was carried out, attempting to assess the real-world effects of three corrective campaigns mandated by the FTC (for Listerine, STP, and Hawaiian Punch). Three of these studies were carried out by the FTC itself (Bernhardt et al. 1981; Mazis 1981; Mazis, McNeill, and Bernhardt 1983), and three by teams of academic researchers (Tyebjee 1982; Kinnear, Taylor, and Gur-Arie 1983; Armstrong, Gurol, and Russ 1983). These studies found that

1. Corrective ads are not uniformly effective. In one case, presumably as a result of the FTC corrective ads and the marketer's own efforts, misperceptions about Hawaiian Punch among panelists in Ann Arbor, Michigan fell from 80 percent in 1974 to 30 percent in 1982, *but did not disappear*. In the case of the Listerine corrective ads, " . . . the FTC remedy appears to have had an impact on consumers, (however) the approach used falls short of fully informing consumers. . . . The use of Listerine [for inappropriate purposes that were the subject of the corrective ads] is still quite prevalent." (Mazis 1981, p. 3)
2. If ad recall is low (as in the STP case), the true cause of shifts in perceptions may be difficult to discern.
3. Often the effects of the corrective advertisements cannot be separated from the effects of publicity.

Based on their review of these studies, Wilkie, McNeill, and Mazis (1984, p. 26) conclude the following:

Corrective ads have potential to provide consumers with useful information which may change beliefs or modify purchase behavior. They do not appear to have a substantial impact on company image, or on that of the general product category. They do seem capable of modifying consumers' views of key product attributes and of spreading such effects to closely related product beliefs. Minor variations in messages are not likely to strongly affect consumers. Major changes, however, such as Hunt's (1973) 'explicit attack' copy, can have significant effects. [Ironically,] future sales gains can accrue to a firm having to run corrective ads. . . . [Finally,] publicity may play a much more significant role than had previously been recognized.

The authors criticize correction efforts to date by pointing out that FTC decisions make minimal use of testing methods that have proved effective in private sector marketing, a problem that applies to many other areas in which attempts are made to secure socially desirable ends in the marketing arena (Wilkie, McNeill, and Mazis 1984, p. 30). Wilkie proposes using consumer information-processing models to guide investigations and policy making at the Federal Trade Commission with respect to affirmative disclosure strategies (Wilkie 1982; 1983; 1985; 1986; 1987).

Complaining Behavior. Albert O. Hirschman has proposed a model of market regulation that offers consumers two principal roles. First, as classical economic theory suggests, they can police bad marketing practices by their own "exiting" behavior, switching patronage from the offending product, retailer, or service establishment. Further, they can seek to widen their influence by negative word of mouth that encourages others to exit also.

However, as Hirschman points out, there are many situations in which a segment of consumers either does not have realistic alternatives (e.g., other postal services or power companies) or chooses not to seek other alternatives for reasons of loyalty (e.g., to a physician or a very convenient retail outlet). In such cases, the consumer's main option in the event of unfairness is to engage in "voicing" behavior. Hirschman argues that it may take only a few vocal customers to effectively police an entire industry.

Consumer researchers have not explored the extent to which exiting behavior (e.g., brand switching) is, in fact, undertaken as policing behavior. However, they have investigated voicing behavior. Overall, consumer complaints research appears to indicate that (1) consumers in developed Western countries voice complaints about 60 percent of the time when they have a problem; (2) these rates vary significantly across purchase categories with higher rates for repair services, mail order, television sets, and automobiles, and with lower rates for toys, medical/dental care, and low-cost nondurables; and (3) voicing may be much lower in other cultures (Bodur, Borak, and Kurtulus 1982).

Among the factors found to affect complaining are a number of characteristics of *the dissatisfaction itself*:

1. The purchase was expensive.
2. The purchase involved economic, social, or health risks.
3. The problem was expensive.
4. The negative disparity between performance and expectations was large.
5. The problem involved loss of use of the product.
6. The problem was manifest rather than a matter of judgment.
7. Blame for the problem could be attributed to the seller rather than the consumer.
8. Complaint channels were well understood.
9. The complaint handler is perceived to be likely to make a favorable response.
10. The problem involved a seller to whom the consumer was not particularly loyal.

Complaining is also affected by *the characteristics of consumers*. Consumers are more likely to voice a problem if *the consumer* has one or more of the following characteristics:

1. Higher than average income.
2. Higher than average education.
3. Younger age.
4. Non–Spanish-American ethnic status.
5. A favorable attitude toward complaining.
6. No fear of being seen as "hassling" the salesperson.
7. No fear of being labeled a "complainer."
8. Supportive of consumerism and other social actions.
9. Assertive.
10. Less trusting of others.
11. More experienced in the purchase category.

Building on work by Landon (1977), Richins (1980), and others, Andreasen (1988) hypothesized that voicing behavior may be explained by one or more of four models:

The Cost/Benefit Model. This model assumes that each problem occasion is unique and that dissatisfied consumers more or less objectively evaluate the extent of present dissatisfaction, the costs and benefits of complaining, and the probability of success. They decide to act or not on the basis of this analysis.

The Personality Model. This model assumes that, while consumers may objectively calculate what the costs and benefits of voicing might be, they are mainly driven to or restrained from action because of the kinds of people they are. They complain because they are assertive, attribute blame to others, have self-confidence about their own position, support this kind of social/consumerist intervention in other domains, and/or have few fears that complaining will lead to "hassles" or will stigmatize them as "cranks."

The Learning Model. This model has not been made explicit by researchers to date. It suggests that, like other consumer behaviors, complaining may be considered a learned response to dissatisfaction. Whatever it is that drove the first complaint — cost/benefit calculations or personality — subsequent attempts at complaining when dissatisfaction again occurs will be largely determined by how successful the outcome was for the earlier complaint.

The Restraints Model. This model suggests that the rate and type of complaining is driven not by what consumers wish to do but by what they are *able* to do. That is, consumers who are motivated to complain by cost/benefit calculations, personality, or learning, often do not do so because they either lack the personal health, income, or information to carry out their urge to complain in *this* case, or because they are effectively diverted or discouraged from doing so by the seller.

The relative explanatory power of these four models has yet to be explored. In general, research to date has not expressly looked at the means for *increasing* consumer complaining behavior.

Another implication of the Hirschman model, which has been the subject of some exploration, is the case where sellers possess what Hirschman labels a "loose monopoly." In such cases, the nature of the product or service is such that a number of consumers are more or less captives, either factually or psychologically, to a seller who, in effect, has monopoly power over them. There are, however, a small number of sophisticated elites who perceive themselves to have real alternatives and thus are not subject to the seller's monopoly power. In such markets, the sellers have the best of both worlds. If they choose to treat consumers unfairly, the elites will simply go elsewhere, while the rest of the captive market will remain and more or less servilely accept the unfair treatment. The seller loses a few sales to the decamping elites, but is spared their vocal abuse while at the same time reaping excessive profits from docile masses.

Andreasen (1985) suggests that the market for private physicians' services constitutes such a loose monopoly. In a pilot study, he found evidence that only a relatively small number of consumers perceived unsatisfactory service and these consumers were clearly of a higher socioeconomic status. Among those dissatisfied, 68 percent chose the "exiting" option. As Hirschman predicted, only a very small proportion voiced their concerns to physicians, whereas the remainder, about one-quarter, did nothing.

ACHIEVING EQUITY

A question that has preoccupied a subset of consumer behavior researchers since the early 1970s is whether or not the marketing system has operated to the disadvantage of specific population subsegments. In free market economies, it is considered acceptable social behavior for marketers to discriminate among consumers on the basis of tastes, ability to pay, and intensity of demand (e.g., to charge higher prices to early adopters). However, there is a point at which society has said that certain discriminatory practices applied to certain consumers are contrary to social policy.

The need to protect special consumers from predatory sellers stems from a social ethos that burdens the "stronger" members of society with the care and protection of its "weaker" members. This ethos gives rise to general social programs to protect the poor, the elderly, and the handicapped; for example, social security, unemployment insurance, and public access for the handicapped. It also motivates conscientious private sector firms to provide health and pension benefits to its workers and to show special concern for those affected by plant closings or industrial mishaps.

Inequity in the marketplace can be assumed to exist under two conditions:

1. There exists a uniquely identifiable segment of consumers who are vulnerable to the exploitative practices of marketers; and
2. There is at least one marketer willing to exploit them.

A considerable body of case law and regulatory experience suggests that inequity is, indeed, a distressingly common occurrence. (c.f. Kallent and Schlink 1933; Magnuson and Carper 1968; Andreasen 1975; Feldman 1980; Stern and Eovaldi 1984). This has been found to be the case for the poor, members of racial or ethnic minorities, children, the elderly, and women. And, more recently, attention has been paid to discrimination against the citizens of foreign countries, as in cases of product dumping, especially of chemical and pharmaceutical products, by U.S. firms (Kaikati 1984; Schulberg 1979).

Exploitation of the Poor

It is ironic that David Caplovitz, the first scholar to highlight the plight of the poor in the marketplace, was a sociologist rather than a researcher in the field of marketing. In his classic work, *The Poor Pay More* (1967), Caplovitz pointed out that the poor not only have less consumption resources than the rest of society, but also achieve less value for a given dollar of consumer expenditure. A long series of studies has reinforced this finding (Schrag 1972; Andreasen 1975; Magnuson and Carper 1968).

The sources of the poor's consumption problems are threefold (Andreasen 1975). First, they are victimized by their own characteristics, both poverty itself and several significant traits associated with it. Thus, whether one is poor depends largely on one's race, residence, age, and family structure. And, of course, these factors are associated. For example, if one had the bad luck to have been both a child *and* to have been living in a house headed by a female in 1988, one had a 54.4 percent chance of being poor. Or if one is a child, black, and is living in the South, one has a 44.8 percent chance of being poor (Statistical Abstract of the United States 1988).

At the simplest level, a lack of income affects the poor's ability to stretch their resources by buying large economy sizes or by taking advantage of bargains when they are available. Low and often *unsteady* income means that the poor must have access to credit in order to acquire the "standard package of consumption goods." This puts them at risk of losing their meager possessions through default or through having their wages garnished (and thereby putting their jobs also at risk). That access to credit is critical often means that they are reluctant to complain about discriminatory treatment because they fear losing what little chance they have for the credit they so desperately need (Schrag 1972; Caplovitz 1974).

A second source of the poor's problems is that poverty — and often their race — puts them in marketplaces that inevitably have limited merchandise assortments (usually only brand name goods) and charge higher prices (Federal Trade Commission 1968; Marion and Goodman 1972). Pressures from low-cost mass retailers are seldom available to keep prices in these markets down. Early studies investigating that the poor paid more for food found that this was mainly the result of their patronizing small, local Mom-and-Pop outlets in local neighborhoods rather than the result of chain stores charging higher prices in those locations than elsewhere (Sexton 1971).[6]

Living in poor areas is related to the third source of the poor's problems. It exposes them to the rapacious behavior of the sellers with whom they come in contact. These sellers have been known to take advantage of their lack of education, their limited shopping scope, and their reluctance to complain about overcharging. Selling shoddy merchandise, inducing buyers to sign unconscionable sales contracts, and refusing to honor product or service warranties is typical in these areas (Caplovitz 1967; Schrag 1972).

Consumer behavior researchers have been documenting many of the above charges and challenging misperceptions of the poor as consumers. In the latter regard, Andreasen (1975) challenged Richards's assertion that "on almost every count, the poor fail to use what many would call the rational solution" (Richards 1966, p. 82). Andreasen suggested that this is not the case.

Take for example the use of credit. Perhaps 70 percent of the take-home income of the poor is spent on necessities. . . . [I]t is inevitable that the poor have low or negative savings and high installment debt.

One may ask then: why do the poor not further scale down their discretionary needs [as Richards suggests they should]? One possible answer lies in the fact [that since] the incomes of the poor . . . are not only low but unstable. . . . [a rational] strategy of maximizing expected value . . . would lead to high debt accumulation under several conditions

1. Some . . . , those whom Bauer and his colleagues characterize as strivers (Bauer and Cunningham 1971) may believe that the odds of a substantial increase in income are high.

---

[6]It has also been hypothesized that the finding that the poor more often buy well-known nationally branded merchandise is not, as some suggest, because buying these brands is a means of achieving some modest psychological status or having some guarantee of not being cheated. Rather, it may be that the poor buy national brands simply because that is all that is available!

2. Others who may be temporarily well off, given what Martineau (1958) concludes is their short time horizon, may see this as permanent.

3. Others . . . may perceive the costs of being wrong (that is, of not securing a substantial increase in income to pay for the debts) as being relatively minor. This could occur for two reasons:

   a. Because [of their] limited education and market sophistication they may actually know less about the likely consequences of default, effect on credit ratings, effects on future employment prospects, court costs and the like (which are very real, cf. Caplovitz 1974).

   b. Although knowing the nature of the consequences, they may estimate the potential dollar losses to be small, arguing that they will have few possessions to repossess or wages to garnishee and, if worse comes to worse, they have no good jobs or careers to keep them from skipping out on their debts. (Andreasen 1976)

These conclusions, however, are necessarily speculative. Unfortunately, as noted previously, enthusiasm for research in this area waned long before this and other socially critical research questions could be resolved (Andreasen 1978).

Discrimination Against Racial and Ethnic Minorities

Certainly one of the most shameful features of the American experiment in democracy has been the magnitude and persistence of racial and ethnic discrimination (Kain 1965; Tumin 1967; Greeley 1976). The effects of discrimination in the marketplace are, in part, those already noted for the poor. Members of racial and ethnic minorities have suffered systematically with respect to key marketplace resources, including income (Wright 1978), employment opportunities (Blau and Duncan 1967; Becker 1980; Cummings 1980), and education (Coleman et al. 1966). Hirschman (1985) suggests four broad theories that can explain these disadvantages: Radical Economic Theory (Bonacich 1972; 1975); Ethnic Conflict Theory (Cummings 1980, p. 944); Minority

Group Theory (Allart and Letterman 1964); and Marxist Political Theory (Wright 1978). Hirschman, however, concludes from the available evidence that, whatever the cause, marketers do not reap excessive profits from racial and ethnic discrimination: "Although racial discrimination exists, it did not appear to enhance marketers' profits, and reductions in discrimination appear to be associated with increases in marketers' profits (Hirschman 1985, p. 184).

The effect of discrimination on consumption, of course, is not only to restrict the resources that can be brought to bear to meet consumption needs but also to restrict the alternatives that minorities are "allowed" to buy. The most obvious case is housing. Studies consistently show that residential segregation continues to be a fact in most areas of the United States (Fly and Reinhart 1980; Kantrowitz 1973). It affects not only where minorities can live but also whether they can own or rent. Residential segregation, in turn, compounds the minorities' employment problems by keeping them geographically distant from available employment. As noted, it also compounds their purchasing problems by placing them in markets with fewer low-cost outlets and more predatory sellers and lenders. In many communities where so-called red-lining exists, it may also mean that they must pay more for insurance — if they can get it at all.

Discrimination also negatively affects the consumption of minorities as follows:

1. It may restrict their shopping scope, since they often feel unwelcome in "foreign" neighborhoods or stores and (perhaps unrealistically) feel they would be treated more fairly, or at least in a more accepting manner, in outlets in their own neighborhoods and/or run by members of their own race or ethnic group (Caplovitz 1967).

2. It may encourage them to buy higher-priced brand name merchandise (1) to display economic status that is otherwise denied them (e.g., in housing, club membership and so forth) and/or (2) to protect them against being "ripped off" by unscrupulous off-brand merchants (Bullock 1961; Gibson 1969; Bauer and Cunningham 1970).

3. It may subject them to discriminatory treatment even while shopping outside their own neighbor-

hoods where they are easily identified as "different" (Sturdivant and Wilhelm 1968; Hanselman 1970). Such treatment may add significant psychological as well as economic costs to their consumption behavior.

A major problem with many analyses of the economic problems of ethnic and racial minorities, however, is that researchers do not always separate out all of the factors that are *associated* with minority status (Andreasen and Hodges 1977; Linhardt 1987). For example, U.S. Census Bureau data has consistently shown that black households allocate a substantially higher proportion of their income to clothing than do white households of similar incomes (Alexis 1962). Some have argued that this is an undesirable outcome in that it reflects either (1) compensatory consumption by minorities or (2) price gouging by merchants or (3) both. Others argue that it merely reflects differences in tastes that are not well understood by the majority community (Portis 1966). However, as Andreasen and Hodges (1977) noted, being black means also that one:

1. has more children who need more clothes;
2. is more likely to live in the South where one needs less clothing;
3. is more likely to be in a dual income family that needs more clothing;
4. is less likely to be in a white collar occupation which requires more expensive clothing.

Employing multiple regression to control for the effects of these associated variables, Hodges (1982) found *no* residual differences attributable just to race. It appears that the argument that minorities have special needs or tastes, or that they face different marketplace difficulties may be wrong, and that observed effects are merely the result of hidden variables. Spratlen and Choudhury (1987) have recently suggested that a similar explanation may account for blacks' greater consumption of cosmetics.

Sirgy and Samli (1987) point to another problem faced by ethnic and racial minorities: their portrayal (or lack of portrayal) in advertising. One of the areas where the marketing pro-

fession has, in the opinion of many, historically contributed to the problems of minorities is by systematically excluding them from mainstream advertising or representing them in ways that contributed to racial stereotypes (a problem minorities have shared with women and the elderly).

The earliest study of this problem by Shuey, King, and Griffith (1953) found blacks represented in fewer than 1 percent of all ads studied. Where they did appear, they were often seen as waiters or servants. In the 1960s, Kassarjian (1969) and Cox (1970) continued to find blacks in fewer than 1 percent of magazine ads. On the other hand, Cox did find some improvement over Shuey, King, and Griffith both in numbers and in role portrayals. Cox's conclusions, however, were challenged by Colfax and Stienberg (1972) and by O'Kelley and Bloomquist (1976).

Evidence in the 1970s indicated also that:

1. Blacks reacted more favorably to mainstream ads when they contained black models, especially if their inclusion did not appear to be "tokenism" (Schlinger and Plummer 1972; Kerin 1979);
2. While whites responded more favorable to ads with whites only (Cagley and Cardozo 1970; Schlinger and Plummer 1972), they also seemed to respond favorably to ads with black models (Stafford, Birdwell, and Van Tassel 1970; Muse 1971; Bush, Haire, and Solomon, 1979), especially if they are nonthreatening.

During the earliest period of black advertising, both male and female blacks in advertisements in *Ebony* "tended to be more white than black" (Snuggs and Qualls 1987). By the early 1970s, Chako (1976) found that *Ebony* male models had gotten darker in skin tone (although female models had gotten lighter). To isolate these effects, Kerin (1979) conducted an experiment in which he manipulated facial features, skin tone and the hair styles of black models and found that physical appearance did affect perceptions of product quality and the perceived suitability of some products for white consumers.

It is still not clear from this last set of research studies whether physiology is simply a code for the suitability of products for particular target audiences, or whether certain groups, clearly identified, represent threats to members of other groups. The problem here is that much of the empirical research is *not* driven by theory. This may be partly attributable to the newness of the consumer behavior discipline in the late 1960s and 1970s when the issues were of particular interest and partly due to the urgent need for descriptive information for marketers and policymakers about the most obvious effects of race.

It may be argued that the consumption problems for blacks are somewhat diminished from the 1960s (with the notable exception of housing discrimination). While this is still debatable, it is clear that a whole new set of ethnic minorities, mainly Asians and Hispanics, are becoming prominent in American society. They are important market targets, but they may be subject to the kind of marketplace discrimination and exploitation faced by blacks in the 1960s. Relatively little is known about these markets and what is reported often reflects little understanding of the subtle distinctions within specific ethnic groups. This is somewhat less true of the Hispanic markets where several researchers have attempted to explore what one research team called "the intensity of ethnic affiliation" (Deshpande, Hoyer, and Donthu 1986) and the relative role of cultural roots versus immediate environment in determining ethnic market behavior (Mirowski and Ross 1984).

Exploitation of Children

A third group for whom most societies profess special interest is composed of children. As with the elderly, there is special concern that their age may make them physiologically and psychologically vulnerable to specific marketing tactics.

Research and theory in this area is dominated by the debate on the question of what, in fact, is the process by which children learn to become consumers. The model underlying much of the research in this area is Piaget's theory that a child's development progresses through four clearly defined stages of cognitive growth (Piaget 1928, 1954). It is then hypothesized that

1. children's abilities to "properly" interpret marketing stimuli is limited by the capacities exhibited in the stage that they have currently reached; and
2. until they reach a prespecified stage of development they are in need of special societal attention.

A major problem in protecting children is that they derive much of their knowledge about products and services from the 25 or more hours of television that they watch per week. Yet, parents tend not to educate children about ads and often fight with them about their requests for advertised products (Goldberg and Gorn 1978). Until approximately ten years of age, children are not good at inferring the motives of advertisers (Wilkie 1986b, p. 436). Young children may assume that much of what they see on television is real. Below the age of eight, children "display little understanding of the persuasive intent of advertising and tend to trust the claims made in commercials" (Akins as quoted in Ward, 1979).

Piaget's model supports these conclusions, suggesting that the most vulnerable period for children is when they are under seven or eight years old. At this "preoperational" stage, they are unable to apply logical thought to concrete problems such as those needed in interpreting advertisements. Thus, for example, children in this age category can only separate ads from programs by noting that "commercials are funnier" or "commercials are shorter" (Ward, Reale, and Levinson 1972). This is especially the case when the ad is imbedded in the program rather than before or after it (Hoy, Young, and Mowen 1986).

Other consumer behavior researchers have proposed alternatives to the Piaget model. Building upon consumer research on cognitive processing, Deborah Roedder John has suggested a different model of cognitive development based on children's abilities to store and retrieve information about products. She distinguishes among:

1. Strategic Processors (10 years and older), who can process ads effectively;
2. Cued Processors (6 to 9 years), who often need assistance to store and to retrieve advertisements effectively;
3. Limited Processors (under 6), who are not effective processors of ads at all.

This model implies that children as old as nine may be vulnerable to undesirable influences by television.

If children are to be protected, several options are possible. Ads directed at children can be banned outright, as was the case in Quebec, Canada, in 1980. This position is typically based on Piaget's notion that children under six are inherently unable to comprehend the intent and meaning of commercials and that they are much more likely to consider *only* those products they see on TV (Goldberg in Ward 1979). An alternative strategy is to require affirmative disclosures within ads directed at children. However, as Piaget would predict, Atkin indicates that most young children "do not comprehend the standard disclaimers presented in contemporary toy commercials" (Ward 1979).

Atkin is more optimistic about a third societal strategy: airing or publishing public service messages outside the advertising context to educate children. Such announcements would teach children about the nature and role of advertising, about how to evaluate products in certain problem categories (e.g., toys and cereals), and about how to detect the hidden drawbacks of certain products. Atkin argues that "studies show that children pay close attention and learn the content of these messages: behavioral effects have also been demonstrated" (Ward 1979).

Goldberg (Ward 1979) supports this approach. He argues that more fundamental effects would be achieved if policy making and research did not focus on specific products but rather on children's choice rules. He suggests that, rather than impose choices on children

(e.g., by restricting the availability or the content of ads), public agencies should teach them to use "better" dimensions when they evaluate products. Thus, rather than restrict ads for sugared products, children should be urged to evaluate the healthiness of alternatives, but still be allowed to make their own decisions.

A relatively simple intervention supported by much of the research to date would be to make more explicit the separation of commercials from program content. This alternative is supported by both the FTC and the National Advertising Bureau. However, experimental research by Butter et al. (1981) and Stephens and Stutts (1982) show, at best, modest effects from several kinds of separators and that, even then, children do not understand the true differences between programs and commercials, only that they are different.

The least intrusive approach would be simply to let parents exert more influence. Ward, Wackman, and Wartella (1977) found that family environmental factors affected the rate of a child's cognitive development. Specifically, Robertson and Rossiter (1974) found that the level of parental education affected the point at which children understood advertisements. Wirman (1983) also found that understanding of commercials was related to the extent of parental control over television viewing. Reid (1979) also found that understanding of commercials was directly related to parents' efforts to explain commercials.

Exploitation of the Elderly

Most societies venerate their elderly and feel responsible for protecting them from dangers that the vulnerabilities of advanced age can bring. In marketing, this has led to two types of concerns.[7] One is — in a sense — protecting the elderly from themselves; the other is protecting them from the predations of marketers (Waddell 1975; Phillips and Sternthal 1977; Schiffman 1971; 1972; Burton and Hennon 1980;

---

[7]The material in this section is drawn largely from Smith and Moschis (1984).

Ross 1982). In the former case, research has shown that the elderly:

1. Use fewer information sources (Deshpande and Zaltman 1978). For example, they less often use unit pricing information (Mason and Bearden 1978), and therefore get less value than other consumers for their already constrained resources.
2. Watch more television (Real et al. 1980), and therefore may be more likely to buy advertised products (e.g., food products), which may be less valuable or healthful than some infrequently advertised products.[8]
3. Have decreased perceptual discrimination, and therefore may require specially designed packages and labels (Silvenis 1979) to prevent them from buying dangerous products.
4. Are significantly less likely to complain about consumer problems, despite being apparently subject to more fraud and deception in many purchase situations (Deshpande and Zaltman 1978, Bernhardt 1981).

With respect to vulnerability to marketer exploitation, research has suggested the following:

1. The elderly have been subject to stereotyping as infirm, senile, and fearful, whereas the true profile of the elderly shows them as rarely ill, frequently prosperous, and usually active. They are adventurous consumers well into their seventies and eighties (NRTA/AARP 1981).
2. The elderly apparently are more likely to be subjected to high-pressure, in-home sales tactics, especially in the sale of eyeglasses, hearing aids, and home repairs (NRTA/AARP 1981);
3. The elderly are likely to have less credit available and pay higher interest rates, even when their likelihood of defaulting is controlled (Meyers 1983).

Discrimination against Women

There are many areas of discrimination in the marketplace where society has been reluctant to intervene *formally* but where consider-

able informal pressure has been brought to bear on marketers to modify or abandon a set of practices. The most prominent example is the case of sex stereotyping.[9] A wide range of studies from the early 1970s onward (Courtney and Lockeretz 1971; Hennessey and Nicholson 1972; Dominick and Rausch 1972; Wagner and Banos 1973; Silverstien and Silverstien 1974; Dispenza 1975; Venkatesan and Losco 1975; Poe 1976; Pingree 1978; Belkaoui and Belkaoui 1976; Warren 1978; Slatton 1971; O'Donnell and O'Donnell 1978; Maracek et al. 1978; Kilbourne 1979; Posner 1981; Pesch et al. 1981; England and Gardner 1983) has documented that, at least until the mid-1980s, advertising in the United States and Canada has too often portrayed women

as young, slim, white, unflawed, and beautiful;

as weak and subservient;

as decoration or sex objects;

as not physically competitive;

as not in the workforce or in low status jobs

as experts on household purchases, but needing the sanction of men before acting on anything "major"; and

as not involved in high value, complex product purchases.

It is argued that portraying women in this way, among other things, alters women's occupational perceptions and preferences (Atkin 1975; O'Bryant and Corder-Bolz 1978; Jennings et al. 1980), as well as altering men's view of themselves, their "proper" attitudes and roles in life, and their relationships with the opposite sex.

The social response to such stereotyping has generally been to bring the "glare of publicity" to bear on the issue and to encourage marketers to reverse past practices. This has been effective, in part, because women have come to represent an important and growing consumer market, even in areas once considered the pro-

---

[8]This, obviously, is a debatable issue.

[9]The material in these paragraphs is largely drawn from Wyckham (1987).

vince of men (e.g., beer, automobiles). To combat stereotypes, private sector advisory committees have been formed (Wyckham 1987) and seminars and conferences held. There is considerable evidence that marketer attitudes and practices have, indeed, changed. As Lantos notes:

In today's commercials, Rosie (for Bounty towels) runs her own diner, in the Luv's commercial it is the father who diapers the baby, and in the Wisk commercials it is dad who worries about how to wash out his own "ring around the collar." Now it is not uncommon to see strong women, nurturing men, female executives, and male babysitters. (Lantos 1987, p. 115)

Still, Lantos notes that "advertising wasn't in the vanguard of change; rather, it was pressured into that change and lagged behind the culture which it depicted." He suggests that advertisers still have a way to go, quoting Meyers (1984, p. 131) as noting that "most advertisers have continued to reinforce the quickly vanishing attitudes of the traditional all-American housewife."

Although there appear to be fewer examples of sex discrimination in marketing *strategy,* a growing issue within the consumer behavior research community is whether there are gender biases in research methodology. Recent experimental research by Meyers-Levy suggests that the genders' "sex-role orientations can affect both the bases upon which [people] render judgments and the favorableness of their judgments" (Meyers-Levy 1988, p. 528). Such differences may well affect how men and women *respond* to research questions. Such differences, in turn, may depend on the issue and/or the sex of interviewer. Further, the sex-role orientations of the interviewers may affect the way they ask questions and/or interpret the responses. Warren has concluded that such differences do have major impacts on ethnographic qualitative research (Warren 1988). Presumably, a favorite marketing research technique, focus groups, may be similarly influenced.

ACHIEVING SAFETY

A great many of the products and services which we consume pose physical (and, sometimes, psychological) risks. Physical risks can range all the way from the dangers of a "paper cut" from a piece of quality stationery to the risks of a terrorist attack on an airliner. It is a continuing societal debate as to how much of this danger should be removed, how much should be left but made subject to consumer warnings, and how much should simply be ignored either because it is trivial or because treating it would incur other costs that exceed present benefits.

We shall consider first the nature of risk and then various societal strategies for managing it.

Risks and Warranties

Risk in consumer behavior has two connotations. First, risk is a synonym for *uncertainty* and connotes the probability that a product or service, although satisfactory, will not live up to one's expectations on one or more dimensions. Risk is also a synonym for *danger* and connotes the probability that a product or service will cause some harm to the consumer or, in some situations, to a consumer's household or to members of the general society. We shall focus here on the last connotation.

As Bauer and his colleagues noted in the formative years of the consumer behavior discipline (Bauer 1960), personal "danger" in a purchase can be (1) psychological (e.g., the risk that one will feel inadequate because one is unable to learn to use a new computer); (2) social (e.g., the risk that the acquisition of a certain style of clothing or model of car will disappoint or alienate friends or employers as being "too flashy," "too upscale," or otherwise inappropriate); (3) financial (e.g., the risk that the Florida land one might buy will turn out to be a swamp); or (4) physical (e.g., the risk that the purchase of an all-terrain vehicle will lead to a child's injury).

Society appears to agree that psychological and social risks are the consumers' to bear themselves, with the exception of the risk that an attempted purchase will expose a consumer to discrimination and the psychological and social costs this entails. Society expresses somewhat more concern about financial risks, including the risks of catastrophic medical expenses, bank failures, or stock market fraud. Thus, we support strict regulation of the banking industry, insurance companies, stock markets, and certain major sales transactions. Our society also supports interventions in the free market to force insurance companies to assist consumers to prepare themselves for certain kinds of dangers. Even so, regulations may not always be strong enough. The extremely high failure rates of Savings and Loan institutions in 1988 and 1989 would certainly have been minimized if there had been stricter regulation.

Our concern here is with the fourth class of danger, physical harm. Societies everywhere agree that they have a responsibility to protect their citizens from unreasonable physical risks. These risks can be substantial. For example, in the United States, 20 million people each year suffer injuries related to product usage. These result in 30,000 deaths, 110,000 permanent disabilities, and $5.5 billion in costs to the society (Luthans, Hodgetts, and Thompson 1980).

Despite the economic and human costs involved, in all countries it is not unusual for safety issues to have a relatively low priority on public agendas. As Mayer (1988, p. 83) points out, "consumer safety policy usually entails the protection of *unknown* individuals against *uncertain* risks in the *future* [as contrasted with] protecting known individuals against a clear and present danger." Thus, it is easier to get a society to provide more funds for police and fire departments than it is to get it to pass legislation to protect workers from possibly carcinogenic work conditions. Consumer safety problems are just not perceived as major risks by large, politically potent groups of individuals (Olson 1968; Nadel 1971). Even if these groups did perceive a major risk, there is the distinct possibility they will choose inaction, expecting to take advantage of what they perceive to be a free-ride opportunity (because they believe that others will act).

Societies also vary in the physical risks they consider particularly important in accord with cultural traditions, political priorities, and possibly chance events (e.g., the Thalidomide scandal of the 1960s or the Pinto crashes of the 1970s). Thus, smoking is currently a major public preoccupation in the United States and Canada, but it is of limited concern in France or in much of Asia.

Whenever a physical risk is recognized as significant enough to take action, society is still faced with a number of options. The least intrusive is a *voluntary* liability option (Gerner 1988). This option assumes that, given accurate information about the real risks of a purchase, consumers should be free to acquire (and sellers free to offer) dangerous goods and services at varying prices accompanied by greater or lesser levels of formal liability coverage. Encouraging industry to provide such alternatives would permit consumers the freedom to opt for their preferred risk portfolio (Buchanan 1970–1971; Oi 1977), an array of products with an array of warranties that each consumer judges is appropriate for his or her own situation. "Changes in risks are [then] registered in the decision-making calculus of consumers. When safety features are added to products, the consumer adjusts his 'risk portfolio' to take the added safety (reduced risk) associated with these features into account" (Gerner 1988, p. 51).

There are several difficulties with this seemingly rational model. First, it assumes that information is freely available. As the Ford Pinto case dramatically revealed (*Grimshaw* v. *Ford Motor Co.* 1981), there is ample evidence that marketers are not always predisposed to be candid about revealing to potential buyers known risks about their products. Second, it assumes that the acquisition of information about risks is costless or at least that consumers will judge the search benefit/cost ratio to be sufficiently positive to pursue it. Yet, we also have ample evidence that consumers very often do not conduct extensive searches, even when buying expensive or socially risky products (Newman 1977; Bloch, Sherrill and Ridgeway 1986).

Finally, the voluntary approach assumes that consumers are rational evaluators of risk information. The latter is perhaps the most serious problem. The work of Tversky and Kahneman (1974), and Nisbett and Ross (1980) make it clear that individuals tend to be biased in their evaluations of risk. Most important, they tend to underestimate low probabilities of major losses. It is in exactly such cases that society believes it ought to intercede on the consumer's behalf, rather than leave the solution to the free market.

Given the practical unworkability of the free market option, society has three major alternative approaches to mitigating consumers' physical risks (McKean 1970; Oi 1972; Peltzman 1975):

1. It can mandate minimum standards for product or service performance either through direct specification of product or service characteristics (e.g., insisting that children's pajamas be flame retardant) or through specification of certain performance levels (e.g., requiring that prescription drug caps be child-proof);

2. It can *require* buyers to acquire some form of liability insurance as a condition of ownership that permits compensation should physical injury actually occur (e.g., California's requirement that purchasers of motor vehicle permits acquire automobile insurance).

3. It can assist consumers to use products safely.

Evaluation of Alternatives

Mandated Standards. As noted at the outset of this paper, the consumer movement has gone through three waves of consumerism. Each wave saw a number of laws passed that were specifically designed to protect the health of consumers. In addition, several federal agencies have issued regulations that apply to specific products or entire industries. Most vigorous of these agencies are the Food and Drug Administration and the Consumer Products Safety Commission (CPSC).

Consumer behavior researchers have contributed to the analyses of the costs and benefits of these laws and regulations. Rogers (1984) found that, after a CPSC directive mandating three safety features on lawnmowers, prices rose an average of $22.00. Despite this price rise, Dudley and his colleagues found that manufacturers' shipments were higher after the regulation than before, and they concluded: "Clearly, the industry is able to make and sell a safer mower without disrupting the market" (Dudley, Dudley, and Phelps 1987, p. 189). Further, despite some government and industry fears that consumers would disable the new safety devices, a survey of 916 consumers in Lake Charles, Louisiana, found few cases of consumers circumventing the new features and that consumers in fact appreciated them (Dudley, Dudley, and Phelps 1987).

Warranties. There has been considerable research on the extent to which consumers use warranty information in the purchase of products. As the FTC staff noted in 1979, sellers are unlikely to promote reliability as a product feature if this trait is not easily perceived by consumers (Federal Trade Commission 1979). A potential role for voluntary warranties is that of making concrete the reliability of an offering—if consumers see it as such.

Research by Wiener (1985) indicates that, in fact, warranties *are* good indicators of reliability for a number of consumer durables (as measured by the *Consumer Reports'* ratings). Further, he found that warranties were better than other possible indicators of reliability such as price or country of manufacture. On the other hand, despite the value of warranty cues, an assessment of warranty language after passage of the key Magnuson-Moss Warranty Act of 1975 indicates that warranties remain very difficult to comprehend (Shuptrine and Moore 1980).

Consumer Self-Protection. Consumer education about risks is a two-part problem. First, consumers need to be educated to properly comprehend the risks in a purchase. Second, they need to act to protect themselves.[10] Former Consumer Product Safety Commission

---

[10]This is not to say that manufacturers would not still be liable if consumers failed to use reasonable caution. McGuire (1978), for example, reports the case of a man who sued a lawn mower manufacturer and won although he was injured while holding up a power mower to trim a hedge!

commissioner, David Pittle, is skeptical that consumer education can help *at all*. In a reflection on his experience at the commission, Pittle concluded:

It was my former belief that people who know more, behave better. . . . Today I view the education approach as unworkable. Indeed, I have become very vocal against the idea of wasting taxpayers' money to print and distribute bulletins/coloring books/demonstrations/other devices designed to teach people about the sudden kickback of chain saws. . . . For most people, there is no way that I can *now* warn you *effectively* against the possibility that, three years from now, the tip of your chain saw might hit a log and bounce back, seriously injuring you in a split second. (Pittle 1988, pp. 104–105; see also Staelin 1978; Adler and Pittle 1984)

Part of the problem is that consumers are not very good about understanding and using risk information (Nisbett and Ross 1980; Slovic, Fischhoff, and Lichtenstein 1978; Bettman, Payne, and Staelin 1986). Consumers overestimate some risks (e.g., being murdered, getting cancer, being caught in a flood) and underestimate others (e.g., dying of diabetes). Recent consumer behavior theory and research on information availability offers an explanation for this phenomenon. Bettman, Payne, and Staelin (1986) hypothesize that the overestimation of risks is a function of the availability of vivid or recent examples of risky situations stored in memory. Thus, sensational events lead to overestimates (Combs and Slovic 1979). On the other hand, events that have not happened recently are likely to be underestimated (Kates 1982). Because most common household hazards have not happened to individuals recently, consumers tend to think they will *never* happen (Slovic, Fischhoff, and Lichtenstein 1978).

A series of experiments confirms the potential of availability theory for explaining consumer perceptions of functional risk (Folkes 1988). Folkes concludes that increasing the *distinctiveness* of risk data can improve its availability to consumers when they undertake product decisions. Folkes urges further research on the exact process by which consumer heuristics bias risk data.

A second problem appears to be that consumers do not like to think about risks. They develop heuristics that often cause them either to assume that real risks are effectively *zero*, so they can avoid thinking about them, or to assume that the risks are very large, so they can also avoid thinking about them by foregoing the particular option.

In the face of this problem, marketers have explored two principal approaches. One is to provide information about risks in a "user-friendly" format. The other is to use fear appeals to secure attention to misperceived risks (e.g., from sidestream smoke) or to raise the level of perceived *personal* risk inherent in a given behavior (e.g., ingesting excessive amounts of high-cholesterol foods).

INFORMING CONSUMERS ABOUT RISKS. There is considerable research, again in the information-processing tradition, suggesting that better formatting of risk information can increase the probability that risk information is perceived correctly and used. This involves tailoring the information to what is known about how consumers process information. For example, Slovic, Fischhoff, and Lichtenstein (1978) found that information presented about the risks of automobile accidents stated in terms of *lifetime* risks rather than per trip risks would lead to more favorable attitudes towards seatbelt usage.

Bettman, Payne, and Staelin (1986) suggest that there are two basic approaches to improving individuals' use of risk information. The *reactive approach* adapts risk information formats to the strategies that consumers currently use to process information, for example, by using effective colors and dramatic type faces, by putting information consistently in the same prominent place, by using symbols wherever possible, and by reinforcing the information in several places (e.g., in advertisements, point-of-sale materials, and product labels). On the other hand, research has shown that it is important to base such strategies on a clear understanding of consumer heuristics. For example, Russo and his colleagues did *not* find that summary measures (which one would hypothesize should help consumers simplify processing) are more effective in communicating risk information than more detailed inputs (Russo et al. 1986). Other research suggests that this may depend on the medium used (Venkatesan, Lancaster, Kendall 1986).

The alternative is the *proactive approach,* which involves attempting to change consumers' processing strategies. One possibility would be to train consumers to more often explicitly *compare* the risks and benefits of specific choices.

USE OF FEAR APPEALS. An alternative set of strategies for increasing the use of risk information is to raise the affective content of that information by raising consumers' fears of the consequences of a particular course of action. Fear appeals have been advocated as a means to induce individuals to increase their own safety and, more generally, to take up healthier lifestyles. Fear is often incorporated in programs of *social marketing,* a subset of social policy considered subsequently (cf. Porter/Novelli 1988).

There is a long tradition of research on the use of fear appeals in propaganda and marketing reaching back to Janis and Feschbach's studies on toothbrushing in the 1950s (Janis and Feschbach 1953; 1954) and to various studies on smoking in the 1960s (Insko, Arkoff, and Insko 1965). This research suggests that using fear can be powerful or counterproductive depending on the situation of interest and on the way in which fear is used (Janis 1967). Rogers (1983) has outlined three theoretical perspectives that have been offered to explain the effects of fear on persuasion:

1. *Janis's Extension of the Drive Model.* This model was first proposed by Janis in 1967. It hypothesizes that the primary function of fear is to create arousal. A heightened drive state has both motivating and inhibiting effects. It can be *motivating* if consumers perceive and process the coping information into some form of attitude change. On the other hand, fear arousal can be *inhibiting* if it causes consumers to block out the message as being too threatening. Worse, it can cause a boomerang effect if it is so threatening that consumers adopt the psychologically self-protective strategy of concluding that the situation is even

less risky than they thought originally (so they will not have to think about the danger). It may also cause a boomerang effect if consumers intentionally reduce their future exposure to other sources of information on the subject. Janis concludes that the relationship between fear and persuasion is represented by an inverted "U" and that the optimum level of fear is "moderate" (see also Ray and Wilkie 1979). Janis's model has been criticized on formal grounds (Beck and Frankel 1981) and has been rejected by empirical data (Levanthal 1970).

2. *Levanthal's Parallel Response Model.* Levanthal (1970) hypothesized that fear provokes two potentially independent responses, one to cope with the danger implied in the message, the other to reduce the fear emotion itself. Levanthal's model introduced two key points: (1) that responses to fear can be emotional *and* cognitive and (2) that control of fear (an emotion) does not necessarily mean avoidance of the danger (a behavior).

3. *Rogers's Protection Motivation Theory.* Rogers's contribution was to focus on the content of the communication that provoked the fear and on the (cognitive) mediating processes that may or may not produce "protection motivation" (Rogers 1975). Rogers adapted the Fishbein and Ajzen (1975) expectancy-value model and hypothesized that "the three most crucial variables in a fear appeal are (1) the noxiousness of a depicted event (the value component), (2) the conditional probability that the event will occur provided that no adaptive activity is performed (an expectancy), and (3) the effectiveness of a coping response that might avert the noxious event (another expectancy)" (Rogers 1983, pp. 157–58).

In a more recent version of this model (Rogers 1983), Rogers introduced the crucial variable of efficacy, pointing out that the likelihood of someone engaging in coping behavior is strongly affected by the individual's perception of whether he or she can carry the behavior out *and* his or her perceptions that it will work. Rogers concluded that six conditions are *prerequisites* for protection motivation *and* coping behavior:

1. The threat is severe;
2. The target is vulnerable;
3. The target can perform the coping response;

4. The coping response is effective;

5. The rewards associated with the (alternative) maladaptive response (e.g., doing nothing) are outweighed by the factors decreasing the probability of the maladaptive response; and

6. The costs of the adaptive response are outweighed by the factors increasing the probability of making the adaptive response.

The difficulty in using fear appeals was well demonstrated in a classic study on seatbelt usage carried out in southern Ontario in the early 1970s (Robertson et al. 1974). In a split cable study, researchers bombarded test households with television commercials promoting seatbelt usage at the rate of two or three times a week over nine months. The messages were very powerful, showing pictures of crashes and scarred victims and using narratives that emphasized the tragedy of the experience. On the basis of unobtrusive, street corner observations, the researchers found *no effects* due to the commercials.[11] They concluded that approaches designed to *persuade* people to change behavior may not be cost-effective and that other *coercive* approaches (passive restraints or legal penalties) may be preferable. However, this research was conducted well before some of the more recent theoretical advances. Terry Belicha, Chief of the National Heart, Lung, and Blood Institute's Communications and Information Branch recently concluded: "The conventional wisdom for awhile was not to use fear strategies . . . There are indications now that the pendulum might be swinging back the other way. What's important is under what conditions and with what audiences fear will be effective" (Porter and Novelli 1988, p. 4).

IMPROVING ECONOMIC AND SOCIAL WELFARE

As we have seen, societies have major responsibilities to see that consumer behavior transactions, in effect, do no harm, that is, that they are not unfair, inequitable, or unsafe. Conservative theorists might argue that society ought to stop there and simply leave consumers alone to make their own free market choices. Unfortunately, this assumes that (1) marketers communicate the information consumers need; (2) consumers seek out the information and effectively process it and; (3) consumers are motivated to make choices and undertake behaviors that would be good for them and/or for society as a whole.

Most societies have decided that it is appropriate to intervene in all three areas. In the case of inadequate information, society has argued that sellers have not only an obligation not to distort information but also to actively communicate information that consumers *ought* to have and use (e.g., unit pricing information in supermarkets). Society has also deemed it part of its own general educational responsibilities to help teach its citizens not only how to read and write but also how to improve their economic welfare through better consumer decision making. Finally, society has long recognized that individuals often need pushing to adopt desirable behaviors (or to give up undesirable ones).

We shall consider briefly consumer behavior research in each of the three areas.

Information Disclosure

The earliest research on information disclosure on the part of marketers was a series of studies on unit pricing (Carman 1972–1973), open dating (Friedman 1972), nutrition labeling (Lenahan et al. 1973), and "truth in lending" (Day and Brandt 1974; Brandt, Day, and Deutscher 1975).

A major finding of this stream of research was that what seemed to *policymakers* to be potentially very valuable information, for example, about the nutritional components of products, was not used very much by consumers (Jeffrey et al. 1982; Levey et al. 1985; Olson, Bisogni, and Thonney 1982). This surprising outcome was a major contributor to subsequent intensive interest in just how consumers seek and use information and how information environments might be improved so that consumers

---

[11]Indeed, there was a *decline* in usage that reflected the onset of cold Canadian winters.

can more often make economically sound and safe choices.[12]

Much of this work has been spearheaded by Wilkie (Wilkie 1985; 1986; 1987) and Russo (Russo 1977a; 1977b; 1981; 1987; Russo et al. 1986). In general, the research uses consumer information-processing theory to help develop better techniques for information presentation in the marketplace. In a summary of much of this research, Russo (1988) focuses on a number of barriers that keep consumers from using more information to make better decisions. He notes that some of these barriers are inherent in the consumers themselves. Consumers are *limited in their knowledge* vis-à-vis sellers since their knowledge is domain specific. Sellers have a great incentive to be knowledgeable about how best to position and what to say or not say about their offerings. Consumers, who must choose among hundreds of product and service alternatives each week, do not have such an incentive to be knowledgeable.

Second, *consumers are limited in the effort* they can apply to information-seeking behavior (Andreasen and Ratchford 1975). And finally, they are *limited in their information processing capabilities*. The latter point is well established in cognitive psychology and implies that efforts should be made to limit the bites of information that consumers are expected to process to make better decisions. This is consistent with Jacoby's contention that too much information can "overload" consumers and cause them to make poorer decisions than if they had *less* information (Jacoby, Speller, and Kohn 1974; Jacoby 1977). Others, however, have argued that Jacoby's conclusions are flawed (Wilkie 1974; Russo 1974; Summers 1974). A number of replications and extensions of Jacoby's work have suggested that consumers are not overloaded but merely employing simplifying heuristics that yield less-than-optimal but still satisfying decisions (Staelin and Payne 1976; Scammon 1977; Malhotra 1982; Malhotra, Jain, and Lagakos 1982; Jacoby 1982; Malhotra 1984).

Russo (1988) also notes that consumers are constrained by other undesirable features of their information environment. Often information is *missing, irrelevant,* and/or *biased.* As noted earlier, information that policymakers think ought to be disclosed is not the information *consumers* want. For example, in the early 1970s, government agencies forced lenders to provide unambiguous credit interest information through "truth-in-lending" legislation. This legislation was intended primarily to help low-income consumers make better decisions by helping them shop for credit and, presumably, secure lower terms for loans. However, subsequent research indicated that the critical piece of information that this target group really needed was the *size of each payment* and not the interest rate. What was important to poor people was not some abstract investment concept but how big a chunk each payment took out of a limited budget (Day and Brandt 1974; Andreasen 1975). Policymakers had clearly lacked the depth of understanding needed to make the appropriate policy choices.

Similarly, it was found that if a proposed government energy-information disclosure program gave consumers information about the *annual* electricity costs of alternative appliances, this would make the consumers more knowledgeable but it would not affect their behavior (McNeill and Wilkie 1979). Subsequently, Hutton and Wilkie (1980) demonstrated that so-called life-cycle costing information[13] would be much more helpful and would significantly affect behavior. Hutton and Wilkie estimated that, if used, life-cycle costing information could save consumers over $4 billion a year.

It is clear from the preceding that public policymakers need information not on ideal models of consumer information processing but on the heuristics consumers use in the face of excessive, incomplete, or biased information. We know from such work as Kahnemann and Tversky's studies of individual risk assessments that consumers make "irrational" assessments.

---

[12]Much of the material in the following paragraphs draws from a summary prepared by J. Edward Russo (1988).

[13]Life-cycle costing calculates purchase, service, and energy costs over the life of an appliance, discounted to a present value.

However, we know relatively little about why they do so and what can be done to get them to behave more "rationally."[14]

Research is also needed on how consumers gather the information that they eventually process. Clearly, consumers could secure greater economic welfare if they simply put more information into what may be a less-than-optimal processing framework. However, it has been rather well established that consumers undertake much less search behavior than an objective observer would conclude is "rational." For example, studies have shown that about 25 percent of automobile buyers do no searching despite the assumed importance of the purchase (Furse, Punj, and Stewart 1984), and that only about one-half of all consumers purchasing major household appliances visit more than one retail outlet or consider more than one brand (Newman and Staelin 1972). On the other hand, researchers and theorists have argued that such findings do not take account of either the amount of information consumers have acquired from earlier experiences or the costs and benefits of further searching.

In the latter regard, researchers have noted that

1. Consumers explicitly consider both tangible and intangible or noneconomic costs and benefits in deciding how much to search. For example, Russo (1988) suggests that the following intangible factors are often relevant in the Search process:

Benefits of Searching	Costs of Searching
Reduced risk.	Effort to use the system.
Safe use of product.	
Knowledge for future purchases.	Effort to learn to use the system (e.g., videotex).
Satisfaction with completeness of information acquired.	Dissatisfaction with completeness of information acquired.
Ability to justify the decision process to oneself or others.	Inability to justify the decision process to oneself or others.
Entertainment value (e.g.) amusement, learning for its own sake, etc.	Negative use experiences (e.g.) annoyance, frustration, tedium, etc.

2. Many of the costs are the reverse of benefits (Capon and Lutz 1979: Sepstrup 1980; Maynes and Assum 1982; Russo 1987).

Some of the suggestions that have been offered for increasing search are the following:

1. Increase the benefits of the information *seeking* and processing by making the process more entertaining (as is done in *Consumers Reports* or in Consumers Union's edition for children, *Penny Saver*).
2. Reduce the costs of the process:
   Acquisition costs. For example, by providing charts of comparative information in popular media[15] or on interactive computer systems, such as CompuServe. Easily accessed comparative information can also be provided by sellers. Utility companies have found that consumers' energy usage can be altered by providing feedback on year-to-year changes in energy consumption on their utility invoices (Ritchie and McDougall 1985; Winett and Kagel 1984).
   Comprehension costs. Various price indexes are available as a technique for "predigesting" market information and making it more comprehensible. Russo and Staelin et al. (1986) have proposed the use of a Nutrition Quotient as a summary index of a food product's overall nutritional value. Carefully designed graphics can serve the same function. For example, Maynes (1978) has developed an economical procedure combining price and quality information in local markets to identify the "perfect information frontier." The latter is the lowest price a consumer ought to pay (with perfect information on available prices) for a desired level of quality.
   Processing costs. Again, simple charts that *order* information in ways that consumers would find helpful have the potential to increase the use of

---

[14]Rationality is, of course, usually defined in terms of objective standards. If one defines rationality as making optimal choices *given one's goals,* then often "irrational" consumer behavior may be rational *from the consumer's point of view* (Andreasen 1975).

[15]For example, many newspapers publish each week the lowest airline fares to selected destinations and the local mortgage interest rates and terms.

information. It has been suggested (Russo 1988) that an ordering of unit pricing information in stores would lead to greater use of it than would mere shelf tagging.

Several researchers have recently explored the potential for Videotex and on-line computer database systems as vehicles for reducing all three kinds of costs. France has successfully introduced Teletel, a national Videotex system run by the government that is used by over 2000 private companies (Mayer 1986). However, Videotex has had only limited success in other European countries (Grunert 1988; Sepstrup and Olander 1986) and in the United States (Talarzyk 1986).

Other technological innovations now being explored as means of reducing search costs are videodisks and computer-based expert systems (Russo 1987). They all have the potential of providing reduced processing costs while adding important tangible and intangible benefits (e.g., entertainment and the pleasure of mastering a new technology). However, as Grunert (1984) and Sharma, Bearden, and Teel (1983) have noted, the costs of acquiring and using such intimidating technologies are apparently too high for most consumers at present.

Consumer Education

A more general approach to giving consumers the skills to detect and combat unfair marketing practices is through consumer education. As Bannister and Monsma (1982) point out, consumer education can improve the quality of consumers' economic lives by aiding them in three broad areas: (1) decision making, (2) resource management, and (3) citizen participation. Consumer education can be provided *formally* in primary and secondary schools (Green 1988), cooperative extension programs (Turner 1988), and universities (Robinson 1988), often as part of other courses such as economics, and it can be provided *informally* through such media as newspapers, magazines (e.g., *Consumer Reports*), radio, and television (particularly cable television).

Consumer education in primary and secondary schools is surprisingly pervasive. A 1985 study found that

1. Twenty-seven states mandated some form of economics instruction;
2. Fifteen states required a semester of high school economics;
3. Four states required the offering of an economics elective;
4. Ten states mandated consumer education. (Brennan 1986)

Consumer education materials, textbooks, and curricula are available from a number of sources including the federal government (Mohr 1988), private businesses such as J. C. Penney (Bisbee 1981), and consumers unions (Baecher 1988). There is, in fact, a federal government agency, the Office of Consumers' Education, specifically mandated to assist those who wish to carry out such programs (Slagel 1982).

The extent of formal consumer education is, however, still relatively limited. Part of the problem is that consumer researchers have not been able to clearly identify "bottom-line" payoffs from such programs. One of the reasons is that much of the evaluation research to date has been quasi-experimental and typically carried out with student populations studied immediately after a consumer education program. The results have been very mixed. As reported by Green (1988), Langemehr and Garman et al. found positive effects of consumer education programs, whereas Bibb (1971), Clair (1973), Thomas (1969), and Waddell (1981) did not. Green argues that the major need in the area is for "a reliable valid instrument(s) that measures the commonly accepted concepts and objectives of consumer education" (Green 1988, p. 827).

Consumer researchers have not been active in the area of *general* educational testing. Further, with only a few exceptions, they have shown relatively little interest in a number of very important *normative* issues, such as how consumers *ought* to allocate their resources, how they *ought* to search for information, or how they *ought* to follow up episodes of dissatisfaction. Responsibility for the latter has apparently been relinquished to home economists.

Social Marketing

One of the major developments in the field of consumer behavior in the last fifteen years has been the broadening of the applications of marketing to a wide variety of topics outside the traditional economic domain. These topics include education, health, the arts, conservation, law, charitable giving, and politics. A great many of these applications of marketing are not matters of social policy but rather the product of conventional consulting relationships with profit-making organizations, such as hospitals and law firms. They become matters of social policy when they are carried out for government agencies like the U.S. Postal Service, the National Cancer Institute, or the Agency for International Development, or for "third sector" private agencies like the Roman Catholic Church or the United Way of America that are supported by society through tax benefits and voluntary contributions. Social marketing has saved U.S. taxpayers over $20 billion in losses due to forest fires through the Smokey the Bear campaign, helped the U.S. Postal Service compete effectively with new express-mail rivals, helped reduce infant mortality from diarrheal dehydration in Egypt and Honduras (Frost 1984), and made family planning products and services more accessible in Mexico, the Dominican Republic, Thailand, Ghana, and Bangladesh (Higgins 1983).

What differentiates these marketing interventions from traditional marketing is that they are intended to benefit either individual members of the target audience (as in antismoking or healthy heart campaigns) or the society as a whole (as in charity drives or energy conservation programs) and *not the sponsoring marketer*. The behavior change is the *end* of the marketing application, not (as in the private sector) the *means* to some organizational end (like profits). Because the objective of these applications is societal rather than organizational, this new domain is generally referred to as *social marketing* (Manoff 1985; Andreasen 1988).

The possibilities for positive interventions by marketers to address major social problems are almost limitless, especially when one includes the possible interventions to help solve problems in developing countries. The number and type of applications, therefore, are more a function of *supply* and *demand* factors; that is, the supply of marketers and researchers attracted to the newly expanded domain is determined by the demand for their services by public and nonprofit sponsors and managers. Demand is clearly rising as public and nonprofit managers perceive the potential value of marketing and are less inhibited by early fears that marketing would be too manipulative, intrusive, and unprofessional (Malcolm 1980; Clotfelter and Cook 1987). Social marketing is clearly in the growth phase of its life cycle (Fox and Kotler 1980; Manoff 1985; Kotler and Andreasen 1987).

The majority of consumer research in this broadened marketing domain has comprised relatively straightforward applications of existing models to new domains. Thus, we have had applications of lifestyle models to the arts (Andreasen and Belk 1980), energy conservation (Henion 1981), and alcohol abuse (Lastovicka et al. 1987); demographic segmentation models to charitable organizations (Mindak and Bybee 1966) and transportation (Lovelock 1975); and attitude models to blood donation behavior (Bagozzi 1981).

A case in point is the work on energy conservation. In addition to the lifestyle ("Conserver Society") research mentioned previously (cf. Leonard-Barton 1981), the literature has seen studies and theories about conservation that have applied

- Attribution theory (Belk, Painter, and Seminick 1981);
- Trade-off analysis (Bennett and Klein 1981);
- Logit econometric modeling (McDevitt and Peterson 1985);
- Adaptive consumer behavior models (Pitts, Wittenborg, and Sherrell 1981);
- Consumer decision process models (LaBay and Kinnear 1981); and
- Attitude theory (Heslop, Moran, and Cousineau 1981).

Studies of energy conservation behavior have also focused on vulnerable groups such as the elderly (Warriner 1981) and the poor (Tienda and Aborampah 1981).

What is significant about these applications of consumer behavior research in social marketing is that it has not been entirely a "one-way street." An argument can be made that attempts by consumer behavior researchers to stretch their concepts and methodologies to fit new domains has had a *major creative impact* on the basic discipline itself.

For example, the development of the exchange concept as a central paradigm for the consumer behavior process received major impetus from the work in social marketing. In this new domain, theorists and researchers were forced to consider how consumer decisions to give blood, to donate to a college, or to begin a diet were similar to decisions to buy a television set or a hamburger. They recognized that, at the most fundamental level, all of these decisions involve the exchange of bundles of costs for bundles of benefits. What differentiates the sale of traditional products and services from social marketing transactions is that one of the (many) costs of the former happens to be an economic price (Bagozzi 1978).

In a narrower realm, much of the development of self-perception theory as it applies to the foot-in-the-door techniques of consumer influence was carried out in the social marketing domain (Scott 1977; Reingen and Kernan 1979; Hansen and Robinson 1980; Mowen and Cialdini 1980). Early testing of the potential for both Fishbein's extended attitude model and LISREL was carried out in the context of promoting blood donation behavior (Bagozzi 1981; 1982).

It can be hypothesized that social marketing situations are of *such high involvement* that models which are difficult to test in traditional marketing settings will reveal themselves in the more highly charged social marketing contexts. In social marketing, one is asking parents to begin to regulate family size or a rural mother to regularly weigh her child and expose the fact that her family has little food. This is a much more serious issue for the target audience than asking them to buy a Toyota or new furniture. As a consequence, when behavior change *does* take place, one would expect it to be driven by very powerful, relatively easily discernible forces. Underlying linkages between attitudes, personality, lifestyle, memory, external influences, and behavioral intentions ought to be relatively stronger and more stable than is the case in the less involving choices where chance influences and/or basic structural instabilities can effectively mask the underlying true relationships.

As consumer behavior researchers come to recognize this potential—and several others suggested in the conclusions that follow—one may expect much more research in the social marketing domain, not only stretching the discipline but also "proving" heretofore obscure relationships.

RECOMMENDATIONS AND CONCLUSIONS

A number of theories and concepts have been introduced throughout this paper that can serve as a focus for further research on consumer behavior and social policy. This concluding section offers an additional set of research issues that appear to merit further investigation. They are organized in terms of the four major social policy objectives that have served as the framework for this paper.

Research on Fairness

Andreasen (1988) has identified several issues that remain unresolved with respect to consumer satisfaction/dissatisfaction and complaining behavior:

1. Studies to date have tended to focus on finding *the one best model* to explain a given set of complaining behaviors. Future research should attempt to discover the circumstances under which different models apply to different consumer segments. Andreasen (1988) proposes four alternative models that appear to merit further investigation in this regard: (1) the cost/benefit model; (2) the personality model; (3) the learning model; and (4) the restraints model.

2. It would appear that a relatively parsimonious behavioral conditioning model of CS/D behavior may be supportable, as it has been elsewhere (Nord and Peter 1980). Presumably, past successes and failures at complaining would have an important impact on attitudes and intentions toward future complaint actions.

3. It is known that CS/D behavior is driven by both perceived costs and benefits and the *probability* of their occurring. Future research is needed explicitly modeling the determinants of these probability vectors.

4. Surprisingly, attribution theory has been relatively infrequently explored in the CS/D context despite its obvious centrality. Blame is a concept that should be important in complaint research, yet it has been rarely introduced in complex models. One hypothesis drawn from the information-processing literature would be that self-blame for unsatisfactory performance may be associated with perceived depth of processing. Those who perceive that they have undergone a relatively shallow prepurchase evaluation of alternatives may be reluctant to blame others for a purchase breakdown.

5. Models of satisfaction tend to assume that ultimate satisfaction is a global construct. Yet attitude theory clearly implies that high-involvement consumer choices entail the evaluation of multiple attributes. Thus, satisfaction may be better conceived as satisfaction on several dimensions, some of which may give rise to global dissatisfaction and/or complaining, others of which may oppose it. Analysis models proposing multiattribute *outcomes* may yield better explanation of the nature of—and responses to—dissatisfaction than present approaches.

6. The extent to which brand or outlet switching is in fact *policing behavior* on the part of consumers has received little attention in the literature to date. For example, it is not clear when consumers report intentions to boycott a product or outlet whether the purpose of such an action is designed to be punitive or self-protective. These motivations may, in turn, be a function of situational and personality variables.

7. *Consumer*-normative modeling would help focus on the problem of how to make consumer complaining more effective.

Corrective Advertising. Corrective advertising has been explored in the for-profit context. Given the apparent increase in negative adver-

tising in the political sphere, it may be timely to explore the relevance of past research conclusions about corrective advertising to this arena. Since political campaigns move swiftly, more attention must necessarily be paid to *short-term* corrections, both those sponsored by rival candidates and those imposed by regulatory commissions. Recommended tactics for short-term effects may differ from those seeking long-term effects. For example, source influences, which research has shown often disappear in the longer run, may have important contributions for needed short-term market corrections.

Research on Equity

A major opportunity for studying a social policy issue and furthering our understanding of basic consumer behavior processes lies in the study of immigrants and their possible exposure to market discrimination. More generally, research on immigrants presents an opportunity to study broad processes of cultural adaptation, including the learning of new markets (Andreasen and Durkson 1968). We have the opportunity to study how immigrants learn new markets and become "American" consumers. What norms do they use? Who influences them? How quickly do they learn? How are previous consumer-culture norms accommodated—are they retained despite formidable obstacles, abandoned in hopes of rapid acculturation, or simply modified to suit individuals of "mixed cultures"? Are there differences across or within immigrant groups? Do Koreans adapt differently from Thais, or Mexicans from Nicaraguans (cf. Deshpande, Hoyer, and Donthu 1986)?

A second area for research on equity is with respect to the elderly. Much of the evidence about the elderly cited earlier is anecdotal (Smith and Moschis 1986, p. 110). However, several of the results to date appear to be plausible given the physiological and psychological changes that occur with advancing age. Yet, we have no research to date directly exploring the effects of such changes on consumer behavior. Over the past decade, we have learned a great deal about the marketing "education" of children as a function of their physical and mental development. Given the projected major growth in the elderly population in the next several decades, it would seem timely to study the opposite end of the aging process to learn how declines in physiological and cognitive functioning in the elderly affect their marketplace attitudes and behavior.

Research on Safety

A major area for further investigation with respect to safety is in the use of fear appeals. A recent conference on fear appeals has identified the following issues as still unresolved (Porter/Novelli 1988):

1. Since most laboratory studies of fear have involved written communications, it is not clear whether there would be different effects if fear was invoked on radio or television (although Robertson 1976 suggest that the impacts may be minimal).
2. There have been relatively few studies of long-term behavior change (e.g., recidivism in smoking) as a result of fear motivation. Most studies have focused on immediate attitude change or first behaviors (e.g., taking a stop-smoking course).
3. Messages are typically forced on subjects and so the potential for avoidance has not been adequately studied. The Ontario seatbelt study (Robertson 1976) did present messages in a natural setting, however they were unable to trace the relative role of avoidance versus, say, counterarguing.
4. Relatively little is known about individual differences in vulnerability to fear communications.

Research on Improving Welfare

For the next decade, a major forum for consumer research on social policy should be within the broad context of social marketing. As noted previously, a primary reason for emphasizing such research is that it can test models that have seemed plausible in the private sector but have not been supported or that have received mixed support. For example, consumer behavior researchers have had rela-

tively little success in linking personality to consumer choice (Kassarjian 1973). It is entirely possible that this may be because past research has focused on behaviors (e.g., automobile purchases) that were still not of sufficiently high involvement for the "true" effects of personality to appear. This may not be the case if one were studying family planning decisions, dieting plans, or cancer detection practices.

Social marketing decisions have a number of other attributes that have seen only limited attention in traditional consumer behavior research.[16]

NEGATIVE DEMAND. It is rare for a marketer in the private sector to be asked to market a product or service for which the target audience has a clear distaste. Yet, as Kotler and Andreasen (1987) note; "[Social marketers] must try to entice 'macho men' into wearing seat belts, timid souls into giving blood or taking medication around which swirl rumors about devastating effects on sexual potency, or aging citizens to finally admit they are infirm or otherwise need assistance." It is important to ask whether or not models that have been tested on behavioral changes between two positively valued alternatives are still valid when applied to changing a behavior from being negatively to positively valued.

INVISIBLE BENEFITS. It is usually relatively clear what benefits one is likely to get with a Hilton Hotel room or a new Timex. However, social marketers are often encouraging behaviors where *nothing happens*. Immunization is supposed to prevent disease "in the future." Individuals with high blood pressure are told it will be lowered if only they remember to take their pills, yet there are no obvious signs of such effects. Women are promised that taking a birth control pill means that a baby will not come. Mothers are told that oral rehydration therapy will prevent dehydration, a relationship many do not comprehend. The trouble is that the consumer has difficulty knowing whether the behavior worked! Often consumers

---

[16]Much of this material is drawn from Andreasen (forthcoming).

who agree to the behavior have the nagging feeling that the same outcome would have occurred if they *had not* taken the recommended course of action. We know little about how consumers can be persuaded to adopt such behaviors. Can behavior modification models work when rewards are difficult to make tangible?

THIRD PARTY BENEFICIARIES. Some of the behaviors advocated by social marketers have payoffs for third parties such as poor people or society in general and not to the person undertaking the advocated behavior. This is the case, for example, for energy conservation and obedience to speed laws. In these cases, most individuals consider the recommended behavior to be a personal inconvenience, but many will still act as recommended because they feel it is in the society's interest. We have few models of consumer decision making where consumers do not benefit (except perhaps indirectly) from a recommended action. Some of the work to date on altruistic behavior (Pomazal and Jaccard 1976), blood donations (Murphy 1985), and request compliance (Reingen and Kernan 1977) offer a starting point for such research.

HIGHLY RESISTANT BEHAVIOR. Securing fundamental behavioral change in individual lives presents social marketers with more daunting challenges than often found in the private sector. For this reason, it is important to explore more carefully the processes by which consumers overcome resistances to such major changes and to identify the factors that may make them vulnerable to the influences of social marketers. One possible line of exploration is Andreasen's theory suggesting that life status changes (marriages, divorces, residential moves, job advancements) may bring about a state of "behavioral disequilibrium" that can precipitate changes in routine life patterns and make the changing individual more open to marketer influence (Andreasen 1984).

DIFFICULT TO RESEARCH. It must be noted that, while the *opportunities* for conducting imaginative, discipline-stretching research abound in social marketing, there are often significant difficulties in conducting research on the desired behavior. As Bloom and Novelli (1981) have noted: "While people are generally willing to be interviewed about these [social marketing] topics, they are more likely to give inaccurate, self-serving, or socially desirable answers to such questions than to questions about cake mixes, soft drinks, or cereals." The resolution of these difficulties will require additional exploration of ways to improve our abilities to conduct deep research on sensitive topics (see also Rothschild 1979).

PROMOTING SOCIAL POLICY RESEARCH

The field of social policy research in many respects presents the best of all possible worlds to the research scholar. As demonstrated throughout this chapter, the field abounds in issues that are both fundamental to the discipline of consumer behavior and relevant to the information needs of public policymakers, who are eager to use consumer behavior theory and concepts to achieve social ends. The researcher who chooses to work in this arena thus finds a unique opportunity to pursue intellectually respectable basic or applied research often on the very frontiers of the consumer behavior discipline, while at the same time being able to feel that the results of this work may contribute, even if only in a small way, to the general welfare.

Those who find this prospect appealing should carefully monitor issues raised in the *Journal of Public Policy and Marketing* and the *Journal of Consumer Affairs,* in the trade press and official publications of regulatory agencies such as the Federal Trade Commission, and in reports in the popular and academic presses about the successes and failures of current major social marketing projects (such as the battle against the international AIDS epidemic). Attention to these sources will routinely yield a rich assortment of challenges for those who wish to combine personal and professional motivations in what is all too often a neglected consumer behavior research domain.

REFERENCES

AAKER, DAVID, and GEORGE S. DAY (1982). *Consumerism: Search for the Consumer Interest* (4th ed). New York: The Free Press.

ADLER, ROBERT S., and DAVID PITTLE (1984). "Cajolery or Command: Are Education Campaigns an Adequate Substitute for Regulation?" *Yale Journal of Regulation*, 1, 2, 159–193.

ALEXIS, MARCUS (1962). "Some Negro-White Differences in Consumption," *American Journal of Economics and Sociology*, 21 (January).

ALLARDT, ERIK, and YRJO LETTERMAN (1964). *Cleavages, Ideologies, and Party Systems*. Helinski: Academic Books.

ALLEN, CHRIS T., ROGER J. CALATONE, and CHARLES D. SCHEWE (1982). "Consumers' Attitudes about Energy Conservation in Sweden, Canada, and the United States, with Implications for Policymakers," *Journal of Public Policy and Marketing*, 1, 57–68.

ALLISON, NEIL K. (1978). "A Psychometric Development of a Test for Consumer Alienation from the Marketplace" *Journal of Marketing Research*, 15, 4 (November), 565–575.

AMERICAN BAR ASSOCIATION (1969). *Report of the ABA Commission to Study the Federal Trade Commission*. New York: American Bar Association.

ANDREASEN, ALAN R. (1975). *The Disadvantaged Consumer*. New York: The Free Press.

ANDREASEN, ALAN R. (1976). "The Differing Nature of Consumerism in the Ghetto," *Journal of Consumer Affairs*, 10, 2 (Winter), 179–190.

ANDREASEN, ALAN R. (1978). "The Ghetto Marketing Life Cycle: A Case of Underachievement," *Journal of Marketing Research*, 15, 1 (February), 20–28.

ANDREASEN, ALAN R. (1982). "Disadvantaged Hispanic Consumers: A Research Perspective and Agenda," *Journal of Consumer Affairs*, 16, 1 (Summer), 46–61.

ANDREASEN, ALAN R. (1984). "Life Status Changes and Changes in Consumer Preferences and Satisfaction," *Journal of Consumer Research*, 11, 3 (December), 784–794.

ANDREASEN, ALAN R. (1985). "Consumer Responses to Dissatisfaction in Loose Monopolies," *Journal of Consumer Research*, 12, 2 (September), 135–141.

ANDREASEN, ALAN R. (1986). "Disadvantaged Consumers in the 1980's," in Paul N. Bloom, and Ruth Page Smith (Eds.), *Perspectives on the Future of Consumerism*. Lexington, MA: Lexington Books, 113–128.

ANDREASEN, ALAN R. (1987). *Social Marketing: Its Potential Contribution to Child Survival*. Washington, DC: Academy for Educational Development.

ANDREASEN, ALAN R. (1988). "Consumer Complaints and Redress: What We Know and What We Don't Know," in E. Scott Maynes (Ed.), *Research in the Consumer Interest: The Frontier*, 675–722.

ANDREASEN, ALAN R., and RUSSELL W. BELK (1980), "Predictors of Attendance at the Performing Arts," *Journal of Consumer Research*, 7, 2 (September), 112–120.

ANDREASEN, ALAN R., and ARTHUR BEST (1977). "Consumers Complain—Does Business Respond?" *Harvard Business Review*, 55, 4 (July-August), 93–101.

ANDREASEN, ALAN R., and PETER G. DURKSON (1968). "Market Learning of New Residents," *Journal of Marketing Research*, 5, 2 (May), 166–177.

ANDREASEN, ALAN R., and LLOYD HODGES (1977). "Clothing, Race, and Consumer Decision Making," in Alan R. Andreasen, and Frederick D. Sturdivant (Eds.), *Minorities and Marketing: Research Challenges*. Chicago: American Marketing Association, 72–96.

ANDREASEN, ALAN R., and JEAN M. MANNING (1987). "Culture Conflict in Health Care Marketing," *Journal of Health Care Marketing*, 7, 1 (March), 2–8.

ANDREASEN, ALAN, R., and BRIAN T. RATCHFORD (1975). "Factors Affecting Consumers' Use of Information Sources," *Journal of Business Research* (August), 197–212.

ARMSTRONG, GARY M., M. N. GUROL, and FREDERICK RUSS (1983). "A Longitudinal Evaluation of the Listerine Corrective Advertising Campaign," *Journal of Public Policy and Marketing*, 2, 16–28.

ASSOCIATION OF COLLEGE, UNIVERSITY, and COMMUNITY ARTS ADMINISTRATORS (1984). *The Professional Performing Arts: Attendance Patterns, Preferences and Motives*. Madison, WI: Association of College, University, and Community Arts Administrators.

ATKIN, CHARLES K. (1975). *Effects of Television Advertising on Children: Second Year Experimental Evidence*, Report No. 2. East Lansing, MI: Michigan State University.

BAECHER, CHARLOTTE (1988). "The Role of Consumers Union (CU)," in E. Scott Maynes (Ed.), *The Frontier of Research in the Consumer Interest.* Columbia, MO: American Council on Consumer Interests, 843–848.

BAGOZZI, RICHARD P. (1978). "Marketing as Exchange: A Theory of Transactions in the Marketplace" *American Behavioral Scientist* (March/April), 535–556.

BAGOZZI, RICHARD P. (1981). "Attitudes, Intentions, and Behavior: A Test of Some Key Hypotheses," *Journal of Personality and Social Psychology,* 41 (October), 607–627.

BAGOZZI, RICHARD P. (1982). "A Field Investigation of the Causal Relations among Cognitions, Affect, Intentions, and Behavior," *Journal of Marketing Research,* 19, 4 (November), 562–584.

BANNISTER, ROSELLA, and CHARLES MONSMA (1982). *Classification of Concepts in Consumer Education,* Monograph 137. Cincinnati, OH: South-Western.

BARKSDALE, HIRAM C., and WILLIAM R. DARDEN (1972). "Consumer Attitudes Toward Marketing and Consumerism," *Journal of Marketing,* 36, 2 (October), 28–35.

BARKSDALE, HIRAM C., WILLIAM R. DARDEN, and WILLIAM D. PERRAULT, JR. (1976). "Changes in Consumer Attitudes Toward Marketing, Consumerism and Government Regulation: 1971–1975," *Journal of Consumer Affairs,* 10, 2 (Winter), 117–139.

BAUER, RAYMOND A. (1960). "Consumer Behavior as Risk Taking," in Robert S. Hancock (Ed.), *Dynamic Marketing for a Changing World.* Chicago: American Marketing Association.

BAUER, RAYMOND A., and SCOTT CUNNINGHAM (1971). *Studies in the Negro Market.* Boston: Marketing Science Institute.

BAUER, RAYMOND A., and STEPHEN A. GREYSER (1968). *Advertising in America: The Consumer View.* Cambridge, MA: Harvard University Press.

BEALES, HOWARD, RICHARD CRASWELL, and STEVEN SALOP (1981). "The Efficient Regulation of Consumer Information," *Journal of Law and Economics,* 24 (December), 491–539.

BEALES, HOWARD, MICHAEL B. MAZIS, STEVEN C. SALOP, and RICHARD STAELIN (1981). "Consumer Search and Public Policy," *Journal of Consumer Research,* 8, 1 (June), 11–22.

BEARDEN, WILLIAM O., DONALD R. LICHTENSTEIN, and JESSE E. TEEL (1983). "Reassessment of the Dimensionality, Internal Consistency and Validity of the Consumer Alienation Scale," Proceedings of The American Marketing Association Educators' Conference, 35–40.

BEARDEN, WILLIAM O., and J. BARRY MASON (1983). "Empirical Evidence of Marketplace Manipulation," *Journal of Macromarketing* (Fall), 6–20.

BEARDEN, WILLIAM, O., J. BARRY MASON, and JESSE E. TEEL (1983). "An Investigation of the Relationships Among Education, Income Adequacy, Consumer Alienation and Life Satisfaction," in Ralph L. Day and H. Keith Hunt (Eds.), *International Fare in Consumer Satisfaction and Complaining Behavior,* Bloomington, IN: Bureau of Business Research, Indiana University, 26–34.

BECK, K. H., and FRANKEL, A. (1981). "A Conceptualization of Threat Communications and Preventive Health Behavior," *Social Psychology Quarterly,* 44, 204–217.

BECKER, HENRY J. (1980). "Racial Segregation Among Places of Employment," *Social Forces,* 58 (March), 761–775.

BELK, RUSSELL W. (1986). "ACR Presidential Address: Happy Thought," in Melanie Wallendorf and Paul Anderson (Eds.), *Advances in Consumer Research,* Vol. 14, 1–4.

BELK, RUSSELL W., JOHN PAINTER, and RICHARD SEMENIK (1981). "Preferred Solutions to the Energy Crisis as a Function of Causal Attributions," *Journal of Consumer Research,* 8, 3 (December), 306–312.

BELKAOUI, AHMED, and JANIC J. BELKAOUI (1976). "A Comparative Analysis of the Roles Portrayed by Women in Print Advertisements, 1958, 1970, 1972," *Journal of Marketing Research,* 13, 2 (May), 168–172.

BENNETT, PETER D., and NOREEN KLEIN MOORE (1981). "Consumers' Preferences for Alternative Energy Conservation Policies: A Trade-Off Analysis," *Journal of Consumer Research,* 8, 3 (December), 313–321.

BERNHARDT, KENNETH L. (1981). "Consumer Problems and Complaint Actions of Older Americans: A National View," *Journal of Retailing,* 57, 3, 107–125.

BERNHARDT, KENNETH L., THOMAS C. KINNEAR, and MICHAEL B. MAZIS (1986). "A Field Study of Corrective Advertising Effectiveness," *Journal of Public Policy and Marketing,* 5, 146–162.

BERNHARDT, KENNETH L., THOMAS C. KINNEAR, MICHAEL B. MAZIS, and BONNIE REECE (1981).

"Impact of Publicity on Corrective Advertising Effects," *Advances in Consumer Research*, Vol. 8, 414-415.

BEST, ARTHUR (1981). *When Consumers Complain*. New York: Columbia University Press.

BEST, ROGER, and JIM McCULLOUGH (1977). "Evaluation of Food Labeling Policies Through Measurement of Consumer Utility," *Advances in Consumer Research*, Vol. 5. 213-219.

BETTMAN, JAMES R. (1975). "Issues in Designing Consumer Information Environments," *Journal of Consumer Research*, 2, 3 (December), 169-177.

BETTMAN, JAMES R., JOHN PAYNE, and RICHARD STAELIN (1986). "Cognitive Considerations in Designing Effective Labels for Presenting Risk Information," *Journal of Public Policy and Marketing*, 5, 1-28.

BIBB, F. G. (1971). "A Comparative Study of Knowledge of Three Aspects of Consumer Information Possessed by Selected Indiana, Illinois, and Wisconsin University Freshmen," unpublished doctoral dissertation. DeKalb, IL: Northern Illinois University, College of Business.

BISBEE, JOYCE E. (1981). "Business Sponsored Educational Materials: A Perspective," *The Teacher's Guide*. Buffalo, NY: National Association for Industry-Education Cooperation.

BLAU, PETER M., and OTIS DUDLEY DUNCAN (1967). *The American Occupational Structure*. New York: Wiley.

BLOCH, PETER H., DANIEL L. SHERRILL, and NANCY M. RIDGEWAY (1986). "Consumer Search: An Extended Framework," *Journal of Consumer Research*, 13, 1 (June), 119-128.

BLOOM, PAUL N., and GARY T. FORD (1979). "Evaluation of Consumer Education Programs," *Journal of Consumer Research*, 6, 3 (December), 270-279.

BLOOM, PAUL N., and WILLIAM D. NOVELLI (1981). "Problems and Challenges in Social Marketing," *Journal of Marketing*, 45, 2 (Spring), 79-82.

BODDEWYN, J. J. (1985). "Advertising Self-Regulation: Private Government and Agent of Public Policy," *Journal of Public Policy and Marketing*, 4, 129-141.

BODUR, MUZAFFER, ESER BORAK, and KEMAL KURTULUS (1982). "A Comparative Study of Satisfaction/Dissatisfaction and Complaining Behavior with Consumer Services: Bloomington and Istanbul," in Ralph L. Day and H. Keith Hunt (Eds.), *New Findings on Consumer Satisfaction and Complaining Behavior*, Bloomington, IN: Department of Marketing, Indiana University, 73-79.

BONACICH, EDNA (1972). "A Theory of Ethnic Antagonism: The Split Labor Market," *American Sociological Review*, 37 (October), 547-559.

BONACICH, EDNA (1975). "Abolition, the Extension of Slavery, and the Position of Free Blacks," *American Journal of Sociology*, 81 (November), 601-628.

BOURGEOIS, JACQUES, C., and JAMES G. BARNES (1976). "Consumer Activists: What Makes Them Different," *Advances in Consumer Research*, Vol. 3, 73-80.

BRANDT, D. RANDALL (1987, September). "A Procedure for Identifying Value-Enhancing Service Components Using Consumer Satisfaction Survey Data." Presented to the Sixth Annual Services Marketing Conference of the American Marketing Association, San Diego, 27-30.

BRANDT, MICHAEL T., and IVAN L. PRESTON (1977). "The Federal Trade Commission's Use of Evidence to Determine Deception," *Advances in Consumer Research*, Vol. 4, 197-203.

BRANDT, WILLIAM K., GEORGE S. DAY, and TERRY DEUTSCHER (1975). "Information Disclosure and Consumer Credit Knowledge: A Longitudinal Analysis," *Journal of Consumer Affairs*, 9, 1 (Summer), 15-32.

BRENNAN, DENNIS C. (1986). *A Survey of State Mandates for Economics Instruction 1985-86*. New York: Joint Council on Economic Education.

BRUCKS, MERRIE, GARY M. ARMSTRONG, and MARVIN E. GOLDBERG (1988). "Children's Use of Cognitive Defenses Against Television Advertising: A Cognitive Response Approach," *Journal of Consumer Research*, 14, 4 (March), 471-482.

BRUCKS, MERRIE, ANDREW A. MITCHELL, and RICHARD STAELIN (1984). "The Effect of Nutritional Information Disclosures in Advertising: An Information Processing Approach," *Journal of Public Policy and Marketing*, 3, 1-25.

BUCHANAN, JAMES M. (1970-1971). "In Defense of Caveat Emptor," *University of Chicago Law Review*, 64-73.

BULLOCK, HENRY A. (1961). "Consumer Motivation in Black and White: Part 1," *Harvard Business Review*, 39, 3 (May-June), 89-104.

BURTON, J. R., and C. B. HENNON (1980). "Consumer Concerns of Senior Citizen Participants," *Journal of Consumer Affairs*, 14, 2, 366-382.

BUSH, RONALD, JOSEPH HAIR, and PAUL SO-

LOMON (1979). "Consumers' Level of Prejudice and Response to Black Models in Advertisements," *Journal of Marketing Research*, 16, 3 (August), 341–345.

BUTTER, ELIOT J., PAULA M. POPOVICH, ROBERT H. STACKHOUSE, and ROGER K. GARDNER (1981). "Discrimination of Television Programs and Commercials by Preschool Children," *Journal of Advertising Research*, 21 (April), 53–56.

CAGLEY, JAMES W., and RICHARD CARDOZO (1970). "White Responses to Integrated Advertising," *Journal of Advertising Research*, 10 (April), 35–39.

CAPLOVITZ, DAVID (1967). *The Poor Pay More*. New York: The Free Press.

CAPLOVITZ, DAVID (1973). *The Merchants of Harlem: A Study of Small Business in a Black Community*, Vol. I, Sage Library of Social Research, Chapter 6, Beverly Hills, CA: Sage.

CAPLOVITZ, DAVID (1974). *Consumers in Trouble*. New York: The Free Press.

CAPON, NOEL, and RICHARD J. LUTZ (1979). "A Model and Methodology for the Development of Consumer Information Programs," *Journal of Marketing*, 43, 1 (January), 58–67.

CAPON, NOEL, and RICHARD J. LUTZ (1983). "The Marketing of Consumer Information," *Journal of Marketing*, 47, 3 (Summer), 108–112.

CARMAN, J. M. (1972–1973). "A Summary of Empirical Research on Unit Pricing in Supermarkets," *Journal of Retailing*, 48, 4 (Winter), 63–71.

CHAPKO, MICHAEL K. (1976). "Black Ads Are Getting Blacker," *Journal of Communication*, 26 (Autumn), 175–178.

CLAIR, R. C. (1973). "An Analysis of Economic Education and Consumer Education Knowledge of Kansas High School Seniors," unpublished doctoral dissertation. Manhattan, KS: Kansas State University.

CLOTFELTER, C. T., and P. J. COOK (1987). "The Unseemly 'Hard Sell' of Lotteries," *New York Times* (August 20), 27.

COHEN, DOROTHY (1980). "The FTC's Advertising Substantiation Program," *Journal of Marketing*, 44, 1 (January), 26–35.

COLEMAN, JAMES S. ET AL. (1966). *Equity of Educational Opportunity*. Washington, DC: U. S. Government Printing Office.

COLFAX, DAVID, and SUSAN STEINBERG (1972). "The Perpetuation of Racial Stereotypes: Blacks in Mass Circulation Magazine Advertisements," *Public Opinion Quarterly*, 36, 1 (Spring), 8–18.

COMBS, BARBARA, and PAUL SLOVIC (1979). "Causes of Death: Biased Newspaper Coverage and Biased Judgments," *Journalism Quarterly*, 56 (Winter), 837–843.

COURTNEY, ALICE E. (1978). *Canadian Perspectives on Sex Stereotyping in Advertising*, Canadian Advisory Council on the Status of Women, Ottawa.

COURTNEY, ALICE E. (1983). *Sex Stereotyping in Advertising*. Toronto: Lexington Books.

COURTNEY, ALICE E., and SARAH W. LOCKERETZ (1971). "Women's Place: An Analysis of the Roles Portrayed by Women in Magazine Advertisements," *Journal of Communications*, 21 (Spring), 110–118.

COX, EDWARD F., ROBERT C. FELLMETH, and JOHN E. SCHULTZ (1969). *The Nader Report on the Federal Trade Commission*. New York: Grove Press.

COX, KEITH K. (1969–1970). "Changes in Stereotyping of Negroes and Whites in Magazine Advertisements," *Public Opinion Quarterly*, 33 (Winter), 603–606.

COX, KEITH K. (1970). "Social Effects of Integrated Advertising," *Journal of Advertising Research*, 10 (April), 41–44.

COX, REAVIS, CHARLES S. GOODMAN, and THOMAS C. FICHANDLER (1962). *Distribution in a High-Level Economy*. Englewood Cliffs, NJ: Prentice-Hall, Inc.

CUMMINGS, SCOTT (1980). "White Ethnics, Racial Prejudice, and Labor Market Segmentation," *American Journal of Sociology*, 938–950.

DAY, GEORGE S., and WILLIAM K. BRANDT (1974). "Consumer Research and the Evaluation of Information Disclosure Requirements: The Case of Truth in Lending," *Journal of Consumer Research*, 1, 1 (June), 21–32.

DAY, RALPH L. (1983). "The Next Step: Commonly Accepted Constructs for Satisfaction Research," in Ralph L. Day and H. Keith Hunt (Eds.), *International Fare in Consumer Satisfaction and Complaining Behavior*. Bloomington, IN: Bureau of Business Research, Indiana University, 113–117.

DAY, RALPH L., and STEPHEN B. ASH (1979). "Comparison of Patterns of Satisfaction/Dissatisfaction and Complaining Behavior for Durables, Nondurables, and Services," in Ralph L. Day and H. Keith Hunt (Eds.), *New Dimensions of Consumer Satisfaction and Complaining Behavior*.

Bloomington, IN: Bureau of Business Research, Indiana University, 190–195.

DAY, RALPH L., and M. BODUR (1978). "Consumer Response to Dissatisfaction with Services and Intangibles," in *Advances in Consumer Research,* Vol. 5, 263–272.

DAY, RALPH L., and E. LAIRD LANDON, JR. (1976). "Collecting Comprehensive Consumer Complaint Data by Survey Research," in *Advances in Consumer Research,* Vol. 3, 263–68.

DESHPANDE, ROHIT, WAYNE D. HOYER, and NAVEEN DONTHU (1986). "The Intensity of Ethnic Affiliation: A Study of the Sociology of Hispanic Consumption," *Journal of Consumer Research,* 13, 2 (September), 214–220.

DESHPANDE, ROHIT, and GERALD ZALTMAN (1978). "The Impact of Elderly Consumer Dissatisfaction and Buying Experience on Information Search." Presented to third annual conference on Consumer Satisfaction/Dissatisfaction and Complaining Behavior, Chicago, IL.

DISPENZA, JOSEPH E. (1975). *Advertising the American Women.* Cincinnati, OH: Cabco/Standard Publishing.

DIXON, DONALD F., and DANIEL J. MCLAUGHLIN, JR. (1969). "Do the Inner City Poor Pay More for Food?" *Economic and Business Bulletin,* 20 (Spring), 6–12.

DOMINICK, JOSEPH R., and BRADLEY GREENBERG (1970). "Three Seasons of Blacks on Television," *Journal of Advertising Research,* 10 (April), 21–27.

DOMINICK, JOSEPH R., and GAIL E. RAUCH (1972). "The Image of Women in TV Commercials," *Journal of Broadcasting,* 16, 3 (Summer), 259–266.

DOWNS, PHILLIP E., and JON B. FRIEDEN (1983). "Investigating Potential Market Segments for Energy Conservation Strategies." *Journal of Public Policy and Marketing,* 2, 136–152.

DUDLEY, SID C., LOLA W. DUDLEY, and LONNIE D. PHELPS (1987). "Consumer Reactions to Walk-Behind Power Lawn Mower Safety Features," *Journal of Public Policy and Marketing,* 6, 181–191.

ENGLAND, PAULA, and TERESA GARDNER (1983). "Sex Differentiation in Magazine Advertisements: A Content Analysis Using Log-Linear Modeling," in James H. Leigh and Claude R. Martin (Eds.). *Current Issues and Research in Advertising,* Ann Arbor, MI: Division of Research,

Graduate School of Business, University of Michigan, 253–268.

FEDERAL TRADE COMMISSION (1968). *Economic Report on Installment Credit and Retail Sales Practices of District of Columbia Retailers.* Washington, DC: U.S. Government Printing Office.

FEDERAL TRADE COMMISSION (1979). *Consumer Information Remedies.* Washington, DC: U.S. Government Printing Office.

FEDERAL TRADE COMMISSION (1982). *Trade Regulation Rule: Cooling-Off Period for Door-to-Door Sales,* 16 C.F.R., Part 429.

FEICK, LAWRENCE F., ROBERT O. HERRMANN, and REX H. WARLAND (1986). "Search for Nutrition Information: A Probit Analysis of the Use of Different Information Sources," *Journal of Consumer Affairs,* 20, 2 (Winter), 173–192.

FELDMAN, LAURENCE P. (1980). *Consumer Protection: Problems and Prospects* (2nd Ed.), St. Paul, MN: West.

FISCHHOFF, BARUCH, PAUL SLOVIC, and SARAH LICHTENSTEIN (1980). "Knowing What You Want: Measuring Label Values" in Thomas S. Wallstein (Ed.), *Cognitive Processes in Choice and Decision Behavior.* Hillsdale, NJ: Erlbaum, 117–141.

FISHBEIN, MARTIN, and ITZAK AJZEN (1975). *Belief, Attitude, Intention, and Behavior.* Reading, MA: Addison-Wesley.

FLY, JERRY W., and GEORGE R. REINHARD (1980). "Racial Segregation During the 1970s," *Social Forces,* 58 (June), 1255–1262.

FOLKES, VALERIE S. (1988). "The Availability Heuristic and Perceived Risk," *Journal of Consumer Research,* 15, 1 (June), 13–23.

FORD, GARY T., and JOHN E. CALFEE (1986). "Recent Developments in FTC Policy on Deception," *Journal of Marketing,* 50, 3 (July), 82–103.

FORD, GARY T., and RICHARD YALCH (1982). "Viewer Miscomprehension Findings of Televised Communication—A Comment," *Journal of Marketing,* 46, 4 (Fall), 27–31.

FORNELL, CLAES (1976). *Consumer Input for Marketing Decisions: A Study of Corporate Departments of Consumer Affairs.* New York: Praeger.

FOX, KAREN F. A., and PHILIP KOTLER (1980). "The Marketing of Social Causes: The First Ten Years," *Journal of Marketing,* 44, 4 (Fall), 24–33.

FRIEDMAN, MONROE PETER (1972). "Consumer Responses to Unit Pricing, Open Dating and

Nutrient Labeling," in *Advances in Consumer Research*, Vol. 6, 361–369.

FROST, B. (1984). *Social Marketing of Oral Rehydration Therapy/Solution: A Workshop*. Washington, DC: Technologies for Primary Health Care Project.

FURSE, DAVID H., GIRISH N. PUNJ, and DAVID W. STEWART (1984). "A Typology of Individual Search Strategies Among Purchasers of New Automobiles," *Journal of Consumer Research*, 10, 4 (March), 417–443.

GAETH, GARY J., and TIMOTHY B. HEATH (1987). "The Cognitive Processing of Misleading Advertising in Young and Old Adults: Assessment and Training," *Journal of Consumer Research*, 14, 1 (June), 43–54.

GARDNER, DAVID M. (1975). "Deception in Advertising: A Conceptual Approach," *Journal of Marketing*, 39, 1 (January), 40–46.

GARMAN, E. T., J. S. MCLAUGHLIN, G. W. MCLAUGHLIN, and S. W. ECKERT (1983). "Measuring Change in Comprehension and Attitude in Consumer Education for Postsecondary Students," *Proceedings of the Twelfth Annual Southeastern Regional Family Economics-Home Management Conference*.

GASKI, JOHN F., and MICHAEL J. ETZEL (1986). "The Index of Consumer Sentiment Toward Marketing," *Journal of Marketing*, 50, 3 (July), 71–81.

GATES, FLIECE R., and WAYNE D. HOYER (1986). "Measuring Miscomprehension: A Comparison of Alternative Formats," *Advances in Consumer Research*, Vol. 13, 143–146.

GERNER, JENNIFER L. (1988). "Product Safety: A Review" in E. Scott Maynes (Ed.), *The Frontier of Research in the Consumer Interest*. Columbia, MO: American Council on Consumer Interests, 37–60.

GIBSON, D. PARKE (1969). *The $30 Billion Negro*. New York: Macmillan.

GITTER, A. GEORGE, STEPHEN M. O'CONNELL, and DAVID MOSTOFSKY (1972). "Trends in Appearance of Models in *Ebony* Ads Over 17 Years," *Journalism Quarterly*, 49 (Autumn), 547–550.

GOLDBERG, MARVIN E., and GERALD J. GORN (1978). "Some Unintended Consequences of TV Advertising to Children," *Journal of Consumer Research*, 5, 1 (June), 22–29.

GREELEY, ANDREW M. (1976). *Ethnicity, Denomination, and Inequality*. Beverly Hills, CA: Sage.

GREEN, D. HAYDEN (1988). "The Role of Secondary Schools," in E. Scott Maynes (Ed.), *The Frontier of Research in the Consumer Interest*. Columbia, MO: American Council on Consumer Interests, 819–829.

GRETHER, E. T. (1974). "Marketing and Public Policy: A Contemporary View," *Journal of Marketing*, 38, 2 (July), 2–7.

GRIMSHAW v. *FORD MOTOR COMPANY* (1981). 174 Cal. Rptr. 348 (Cal. A)

GRUNERT, KLAUS G. (1988). "Comments on J. Edward Russo," in E. Scott Maynes (Ed.), *The Frontier of Research in The Consumer Interest*. Columbia, MO: American Council on Consumer Interests, 219–224.

GRUNERT, KLAUS G., and KONRAD DEDLER (1985). "Misleading Advertising: In Search of a Measurement Methodology," *Journal of Public Policy and Marketing*, 4, 153–165.

GUERNICA, ANTONIO (1982). *Reaching the Hispanic Market Effectively*. New York: McGraw-Hill.

HANDY, CHARLES R. (1976). "Monitoring Consumer Satisfaction with Food Products," in H. Keith Hunt (Ed.), *Conceptualization and Measurement of Consumer Satisfaction and Dissatisfaction*. Cambridge, MA: Marketing Science Institute, 215–239.

HANDY, CHARLES R., and MARTIN PFAFF (1975). "Consumer Satisfaction with Food Products and Marketing Services," Agricultural Economics Report No. 281. Washington, DC: U.S. Department of Agriculture, Economic Research Service (March).

HANSELMAN, WILLIAM (1970). "The Basis for Market Discrimination: Race or Poverty," unpublished paper, Portland State University, Portland, OR.

HANSEN, R. A., and L. M. ROBINSON (1980). "Testing the Effectiveness of Alternative Foot-in-the-Door Manipulations," *Journal of Marketing Research*, 17, 3 (August), 359–364.

HARRIS, RICHARD J. (1977). "Comprehension of Pragmatic Implications in Advertising," *Journal of Applied Psychology*, 62, 603–608.

HENION II, KARL E. (1981). "Energy Usage and the Conserver Society: Review of the 1979 AMA Conference on Ecological Marketing," *Journal of Consumer Research*, 8, 3 (December), 339–342.

HENNESSEY, JUDITH ADLER, and JOAN NICHOLSON (1972). "NOW Says: Commercials Insult Women," *New York Times Magazine*, (May 28), 12.

HERMANN, ROBERT O. (1970). "The Consumer

Movement in Historical Perspective," *Agricultural Economics and Rural Sociology*, 88, (February).

HESLOP, LOUISE A., LORI MORAN, and AMY COUSINEAU (1981). " 'Consciousness' in Energy Conservation Behavior: An Exploratory Study," *Journal of Consumer Research*, 8, 3 (December), 299–305.

HIGGINS, K. (1983). "Marketing Enables Population Control Group to Boost Results," *Marketing News* (October 14), 2.

HIRSCHMAN, ALBERT O. (1970). *Exit, Voice and Loyalty: Responses to Decline in Firms, Organizations, and States*. Cambridge, MA: Harvard University Press.

HIRSCHMAN, ELIZABETH C. (1985). "Marketing, Minorities, and Consumption: Traditional and Neo-Marxist Perspectives," *Journal of Public Policy and Marketing*, 4, 179–193.

HODGES, LLOYD (1982). Unpublished doctoral dissertation. Champaign, IL: University of Illinois.

HOY, MARIEA GRUBBS, CLIFFORD E. YOUNG, and JOHN C. MOWEN (1986). "Animated Host-Selling Advertisements: Their Impact on Young Children's Recognition, Attitudes, and Behavior," *Journal of Public Policy and Marketing* 5, 171–185.

HUNT, H. KEITH (1973). "Effects of Corrective Advertising," *Journal of Advertising Research*, 13 (October), 15–24.

HUTTON, R. BRUCE, and WILLIAM L. WILKIE (1980). "Life Cycle Cost: A New Form of Consumer Information," *Journal of Consumer Research*, 6, 4 (March), 349–360.

INSKO, C. A., A. ARKOFF, and V. M. INSKO (1965). "Effects of High and Low Fear Arousing Communications upon Opinions Toward Smoking," *Journal of Experimental Social Psychology*, 1 (August), 256–266.

JACOBY, JACOB (1977). "Information Load and Decision Quality: Some Contested Issues," *Journal of Marketing Research*, 14, 4 (November), 569–577.

JACOBY, JACOB (1982). "Perspectives on Information Overload," *Journal of Consumer Research*, 10, 4 (March), 432–435.

JACOBY, JACOB, ROBERT W. CHESTNUT, and WILLIAM SILBERMAN (1977). "Consumer Use and Comprehension of Nutrition Information," *Journal of Consumer Research*, 4, 2 (September), 119–128.

JACOBY, JACOB, and WAYNE D. HOYER (1982). "On Miscomprehending Televised Communica-tion: A Rejoinder," *Journal of Marketing*, 46, 4 (Fall), 35–43.

JACOBY, JACOB, and WAYNE D. HOYER (1989). "The Comprehension/Miscomprehension of Print Communications: Selected Findings," *Journal of Consumer Research*, 15, 4 (March), 434–443.

JACOBY, JACOB, WAYNE D. HOYER, and DAVID A. SHELUGA (1980). *The Miscomprehension of Televised Communication*. New York: American Association of Advertising Agencies.

JACOBY, JACOB, DONALD E. SPELLER, and CAROL A. KOHN (1974). "Brand Choice Behaviors as a Function of Information Load," *Journal of Marketing Research*, 11, 63–69.

JANIS, IRVING L. (1967). "Effects of Fear Arousal on Attitude Change: Recent Developments in Theory and Experimental Research," in L. Berkowitz (Ed.), *Advances in Experimental Social Psychology*, Vol. 3. New York: Academic Press.

JANIS, IRVING L., and SEYMOUR FESCHBACH (1953). "Effects of Fear-Arousing Communications," *Journal of Abnormal and Social Psychology*, 48 (January), 78–92.

JANIS, IRVING L., and SEYMOUR FESCHBACH (1954). "Personality Differences Associated with Responsiveness to Fear-Arousing Communications," *Journal of Personality*, 23 (December), 154–166.

JEFFREY, ROBERT W., PHYLLIS L. PIRIE, BARBARA S. ROSENTHAL, WENDY M. GERBER, and DAVID S. MURRAY (1982). "Nutrition Education in Supermarkets: An Unsuccessful Attempt to Influence Knowledge and Product Sales," *Journal of Behavioral Medicine*, 5, 139–200.

JENNINGS, JOYCE, F. L. GEIS, and VIRGINIA BROWN (1980). "Influence of Television Commercials on Women's Self-Confidence and Independent Judgment," *Journal of Personality and Social Psychology*, 38, 2 (November), 203–210.

JOHN, DEBORAH ROEDDER, and CATHERINE A. COLE (1986). "Age Differences in Information Processing: Understanding Deficits in Young and Elderly Consumers," *Journal of Consumer Research*, 13, 3 (December), 297–315.

JOHN, DEBORAH ROEDDER (1985). "The Development of Knowledge Structures in Children," *Advances in Consumer Research*, Vol. 12, 329–333.

JOHN, DEBORAH ROEDDER, and JOHN C. WHITNEY, JR. (1986). "The Development of Consumer Knowledge in Children: A Cognitive

Structure Approach," *Journal of Consumer Research,* 12, 4 (March), 406–417.

KAHNEMAN, D., and TVERSKY, A. (1981). "The Framing of Decisions and the Psychology of Choice," *Science,* 211, 453–458.

KAIKATI, JACK G. (1984). "Domestically Banned Products: For Export Only," *Journal of Public Policy and Marketing,* 3, 125–133.

KAIN, JOHN F. (1965). "Race and Poverty: The Economics of Discrimination," in John F. Kain (Ed.), *Race and Poverty: The Economics of Discrimination.* Englewood Cliffs, NJ: Prentice-Hall, 1–32.

KALLENT, ARTHUR, and F. J. SCHLINK (1933). *100,000,000 Guinea Pigs.* New York: Grossett & Dunlap.

KANTROWITZ, NATHAN (1973). *Ethnic and Racial Segregation in the New York Metropolis.* New York: Praeger.

KASSARJIAN, HAROLD H. (1969). "The Negro and American Advertising 1946–1965," *Journal of Marketing Research,* 6, 1 (February), 29–39.

KASSARJIAN, HAROLD H. (1973). "Personality and Consumer Behavior: A Review" in Harold Kassarjian and Thomas Robertson (Eds.), *Perspective on Consumer Behavior* (rev. ed.), Glenview, IL: Scott, Foresman, 129–148.

KATES, ROBERT W. (1982). "Hazard and Choice Perception in Flood Plain Management," Research Paper No. 78, University of Chicago, Department of Geography.

KERIN, ROGER (1979). "Black Model Appearance and Product Evaluation," *Journal of Communication,* 29 (Winter), 123–128.

KILBOURNE, JEAN (1979). "Killing Us Softly: Advertising Images of Women," (film). Cambridge, MA: Cambridge Films.

KINNEAR, THOMAS C., JAMES R. TAYLOR, and ODED GUR-ARIE (1983). "Affirmative Disclosures: Long Term Monitoring of Residual Effects," *Journal of Public Policy and Marketing,* 2, 38–45.

KOTLER, PHILIP (1975). "Overview of Political Candidate Marketing," *Advances in Consumer Research,* Vol. 2, 761–769.

KOTLER, PHILIP (1979). "Strategies for Introducing Marketing into Nonprofit Organizations," *Journal of Marketing,* 43, 1 (January), 37–44.

KOTLER, PHILIP, and ALAN R. ANDREASEN (1987). *Strategic Marketing for Nonprofit Organization* (3rd ed.). Englewood Cliffs, NJ: Prentice-Hall.

LABAY, DUNCAN G., and THOMAS C. KINNEAR (1981). "Exploring the Consumer Decision Process in the Adoption of Solar Energy Systems," *Journal of Consumer Research,* 8, 3 (December), 271–278.

LAMBERT, ZARREL V. (1977). "Nutrition Information: A Look at Some Processing and Decision Making Difficulties," *Advances in Consumer Research,* Vol. 4, 126–132.

LAMBERT, ZARREL V. (1980). "Consumer Alienation, General Dissatisfaction, and Consumerism Issues: Conceptual and Managerial Perspectives," *Journal of Retailing,* 34, 2 (Summer), 3–24.

LAMBERT, ZARREL, V., and FRED W. KNIFFIN (1975). "Consumer Discontent: A Social Perspective," *California Management Review,* 18, 1 (Fall), 36–44.

LANDON, E. LAIRD (1977). "A Model of Consumer Complaint Behavior" in Ralph L. Day (Ed.), *Consumer Satisfaction, Dissatisfaction and Complaining Behavior.* Bloomington, IN: Bureau of Business Research, 31–35.

LANGREHR, FREDERICK W. (1979). "Consumer Education: Does It Change Students' Compentencies and Attitudes?" *Journal of Consumer Affairs,* 13, 1 (Summer).

LANTOS, GEOFFREY P. (1987). "Advertising: Looking Glass or Molder of the Masses?" *Journal of Public Policy and Marketing,* 6, 104–128.

LASTOVICKA, JOHN L., JOHN P. MURRY, JR., ERICJ A. JAOCHIMSTALER, GUARAV BHALLA, and JIM SCHEURICH (1987). "A Lifestyle Typology to Model Young Male Drinking and Driving," *Journal of Consumer Research,* 14, 2 (September), 257–263.

LEIGH, THOMAS W., and RALPH L. DAY (1981). "Satisfaction, Dissatisfaction and Complaint Behavior with Nondurable Products," in Ralph L. Day and H. Keith Hunt (Eds.), *New Dimensions of Consumer Satisfaction and Complaining Behavior.* Bloomington, IN: Bureau of Business Research, Indiana University, 170–183.

LENAHAN, R. S. ET AL. (1973). "Consumer Reaction to Nutritional Labels on Food Products," *Journal of Consumer Affairs,* 7, 1 (Summer), 1–12.

LEONARD-BARTON, DOROTHY (1981). "Voluntary Simplicity Lifestyles and Energy Conservation," *Journal of Consumer Research,* 8, 3 (December), 243–254.

LEVENTHAL, H. (1979). "Findings and Theory in the Study of Fear Communications," in L. Berkowitz (Ed.), *Advances in Experimental Social Psychology,* Vol. 5. New York: Academic Press.

LEVY, ALAN S., ODONNA MATHEWS, MARILYN STEPHENSON, JANET E. TENNEY, and RAYMOND E. SCHUCKER (1985). "The Impact of a Nutrition Information Program on Food Purchase," *Journal of Public Policy and Marketing,* 4, 1.

LINHARDT, WAYNE C. (1987). "Determining Black Expenditure Patterns Using Elasticity Coefficients: Developing a Profile" in Robert L. King (Ed.), *Minority Marketing: Issues and Prospects.* Charleston, SC: The Academy of Marketing Science, 18–22.

LOVELOCK, CHRISTOPHER H. (1975). "A Market Segmentation Approach to Transit Planning, Modeling and Management," *Proceedings, Sixteenth Annual Meeting Transportation Research Forum.*

LUNDSTROM, WILLIAM J., and LAWRENCE W. LAMONT (1976). "The Development of a Scale to Measure Consumer Discontent," *Journal of Marketing Research,* 13, 4 (November), 373–381.

LUNDSTROM, WILLIAM, GERALD U. SKELLY, and DONALD SCIGLIMPAGLIA (1980). "How Deep Are the Roots of Consumer Discontent: A Study of Rural Consumers" in Ralph L. Day and H. Keith Hunt (Eds.), *New Dimensions of Consumer Satisfaction and Complaining Behavior.* Bloomington, IN: Bureau of Business Research, Indiana University, 153–156.

LUTHANS, FRED, RICHARD M. HODGETTS, and KENNETH R. THOMPSON (1980). *Social Issues in Business.* New York: Macmillan.

MACKLIN, M. CAROLE (1987). "Preschoolers' Understanding of the Informational Function of Television Advertising," *Journal of Consumer Research,* 14, 2 (September), 229–239.

MAGNUSON, WARREN G., and JEAN CARPER (1968). *The Dark Side of the Marketplace.* Englewood Cliffs, NJ: Prentice-Hall.

MALCOLM, A. H. (1980). "Ottawa Runs into Protests Over Its Huge Advertising Costs," *New York Times* (November 1), 10.

MALHOTRA, NARESH K. (1982). "Information Load and Consumer Decision Making," *Journal of Consumer Research,* 8, 4 (March), 419–430.

MALHOTRA, NARESH K. (1984). "Reflections on the Information Overload Paradigm in Consumer Behavior," *Journal of Consumer Research,* 10, 4 (March), 436–440.

MALHOTRA, NARESH K., ARUN K. JAIN, and STEPHEN LAGAKOS (1982). "The Information Overload Controversy: An Alternative Viewpoint," *Journal of Marketing,* 46, 2 (Spring), 27–37.

MANOFF, RICHARD K. (1985). *Social Marketing.* New York: Praeger.

MARACEK, JEANNE, ET AL. (1978). "Women as TV Experts: The Voice of Authority," *Journal of Communication,* 28 (Winter), 159–168.

MARION, DONALD, and CHARLES GOODMAN (1972). "Operating Problems of Marketing Firms in Low-Income Areas," in Alan R. Andreasen (Ed.), *Improving Inner-City Marketing.* Chicago: American Marketing Association, 115–148.

MARTINEAU, PIERRE (1958). "Social Classes and Spending Behavior," *Journal of Marketing,* 23, 3 (October), 121–130.

MASON, J. BARRY, and WILLIAM O. BEARDEN (1978). "Satisfaction/Dissatisfaction with Food Shopping Among Elderly Consumers," *The Journal of Consumer Affairs,* 13, 2 (Winter), 359–369.

MAYER, MARTIN (1959). "Planned Obsolescence: Rx for Tired Markets," *Dun's Review and Modern Industry,* 73, 2 (February), 70–74.

MAYER, ROBERT N. (1986). *Videotex in France: The Other French Revolution.* Working Paper No. 86–5. Salt Lake City, UT: University of Utah, Department of Family and Consumer Studies.

MAYER, ROBERT N. (1988). "Consumer Safety and the Issue Emergence Process" in E. Scott Maynes (Ed.), *The Frontier of Research in the Consumer Interest.* Columbia, MO: American Council on Consumer Interests, 82–96.

MAYNES, E. SCOTT. (1977). "Informational Imperfection in Local Consumer Markets: Assessment and Implications," *Advances in Consumer Research,* Vol. 4, 288–296.

MAYNES, E. SCOTT (1978). "Information Imperfections in Local Consumer Markets," in Andrew A. Mitchell (Ed.), *The Effect of Information on Consumer and Market Behavior.* Chicago: American Marketing Association, 77–85.

MAYNES, E. SCOTT, and TERJE ASSUM (1982). "Informationally Imperfect Consumer Markets: Empirical Findings and Policy Implications," *Journal of Consumer Affairs,* 16, 1 (Summer), 62–87.

MAZIS, MICHAEL B. (1979). "Can and Should the FTC Restrict Advertising to Children," *Advances in Consumer Research,* Vol. 6, 3–6.

MAZIS, MICHAEL B. (1981). "The Effects of FTC's Listerine Corrective Advertising Order," A Report to the FTC, Washington, DC: Federal Trade Commission.

MAZIS, MICHAEL B., DENNIS L. MCNEILL, and KENNETH L. BERNHARDT (1983). "Day-After Recall of Listerine Corrective Commercials," *Journal of Public Policy and Marketing*, 2, 29–37.

MCCULLOUGH, JAMES, and ROGER BEST (1980). "Consumer Preferences for Food Label Information: A Basis for Segmentation," *Journal of Consumer Affairs*, 14, 1 (Summer), 180–192.

MCDEVITT, PAUL, and ROBIN PETERSON (1985). "Public Energy Conservation: An Investigation of the Post Tax Credit Era in the U.S.," *Journal of Public Policy and Marketing*, 4, 33–46.

MCGUIRE, E. PATRICK (1978). "Manufacturer's Malpractice," in Arthur Elkins and Dennis M. Callaghan (Eds.), *A Managerial Odyssey: Problems in Business and Its Environment*. Reading, MA: Addison-Wesley, 305–312.

MCKEAN, R. N. (1970). "Products Liability: Implications of Some Changing Property Rights," *Quarterly Journal of Economics*, 61, 4 (November), 611–626.

MCNEILL, D. L., and WILLIAM L. WILKIE (1979). "Public Policy and Consumer Information: Impact of the New Energy Labels," *Journal of Consumer Research*, 6, 1 (June).

MEFFERT, HERIBERT, and MANFRED BRUHN (1983). "Complaining Behavior and Satisfaction of Consumers — Results from an Empirical Study in Germany," in Ralph L. Day and H. Keith Hunt (Eds.), *International Fare in Consumer Satisfaction and Complaining Behavior*. Bloomington, IN: Bureau of Business Research, Indiana University, 35–48.

MEYERS, S. L. (1983). *Age Discrimination in Credit Markets*, Working Paper No. 99. Washington, DC: Federal Trade Commission, Bureau of Economics.

MEYERS, WILLIAM (1984). *The Image Makers*. New York: Times Books.

MEYERS-LEVY, JOAN (1988). "The Influence of Sex Roles on Judgment," *Journal of Consumer Research*, 14, 4 (March) 522–530.

MILSTEIN, JEFFREY S. (1975). "Consumer Research of the Office of Energy Conservation and Environment, Federal Energy Administration," *Advances in Consumer Research*, Vol. 2, 925–927.

MILSTEIN, JEFFREY S. (1977). "Attitudes, Knowledge and Behavior of American Consumers Regarding Energy Conservation with Some Implications for Governmental Action," *Advances in Consumer Research*, Vol. 4, 315–321.

MINDAK, WILLIAM A., and H. MALCOLM BYBEE (1971). "Marketing's Application to Fund Raising," *Journal of Marketing*, 35, 3 (July), 13–18.

MIROWSKY, JOHN, and CATHERINE ROSS (1984). "Mexican Culture and its Emotional Contradictions," *Journal of Health and Social Behavior*, 25 (March), 2–13.

MIZERSKI, RICHARD W. (1981). "Major Problems in 4As Pioneering Study of TV Miscomprehension," *Marketing News*, 14 (June 12), 7–8.

MIZERSKI, RICHARD W. (1982). "Viewer Miscomprehension Findings Are Measurement Bound," *Journal of Marketing*, 46, 4 (Fall), 32–34.

MOHR, LILLIAN A. (1988). "The Role of the Federal Government," in E. Scott Maynes (Ed.), *The Frontier of Research in the Consumer Interest*. Columbia, MO: American Council on Consumer Interests, 830–835.

MOWEN, JOHN C., and R. B. CIALDINI (1980). "On Implementing the Door-in-the-Face Compliance Technique in a Business Context," *Journal of Marketing Research*, 17, 2 (May), 253–258.

MURPHY, PATRICK E. (1985). "Recruiting Blood Donors: A Marketing and Consumer Behavior Perspective," in Russell W. Belk (Ed.), *Advances in Nonprofit Marketing*, Vol. 1. Greenwich CT: JAI Press, 207–245.

MUSE, WILLIAM V. (1971). "Product-Related Response to Use of Black Models in Advertising," *Journal of Marketing Research*, 8, 1 (February), 107–109.

NADEL, MARK V. (1971). *The Politics of Consumer Protection*. Indianapolis, IN: Bobbs-Merrill.

NADER, RALPH (1966). *Unsafe at Any Speed*, New York: Pocket Books.

NADER, RALPH (1968). "The Great American Gyp," *New York Review of Books*, 11 (November 21), 27.

NATIONAL RETIRED TEACHERS ASSOCIATION/ AMERICAN ASSOCIATION OF RETIRED PERSONS (1981). *Consumer Problems of Older Americans: New Directions for Government and Business*. Washington, DC: Consumer Affairs Section, American Association of Retired Persons.

NEELANKAVIL, JAMES P., and ALBERT B. STRIDSBERG (1980). *Advertising Self-Regulation: A Global Perspective*. New York: Hastings House.

NEWMAN, JOSEPH W. (1977). "Consumer External Search: Amount and Determinants," in Arch G. Woodside, Jagdish Sheth, and Peter D. Bennett (Eds.), *Consumer and Industrial Buying Behavior*. New York: North Holland.

NEWMAN, JOSEPH, and STAELIN, RICHARD (1972). "Prepurchase Information Seeking for New Cars and Major Household Appliances," *Journal of Marketing Research*, 9, 3 (August), 249–257.

NISBETT, RICHARD, and LEE ROSS (1980). *Human Inference: Strategies and Shortcomings of Social Judgment.* Englewood Cliffs, NJ: Prentice-Hall.

NORD, WALTER R., and J. PAUL PETER (1980). "A Behavior Modification Perspective on Marketing," *Journal of Marketing*, 44, 1 (Spring), 36–47.

O'BRYANT, SHIRLEY L., and CHARLES R. CORDER-BOLZ (1978). "The Effects of Television on Children's Stereotyping of Women's Work Roles," *Journal of Vocational Behavior* (April), 233–243.

O'DONNELL, WILLIAM J., and KAREN J. O'DONNELL (1978). "Update: Sex Role Message in TV Commercials," *Journal of Communication*, 28, 4 (Winter), 156–158.

OFFICE OF FAIR TRADING (1986). *Consumer Dissatisfaction.* London: Office of Fair Trading.

OI, WALTER Y. (1972). "The Economics of Product Safety," *The Bell Journal of Economics and Management Sciences*, 4, 1 (Spring), 3–28.

OI, WALTER Y. (1977). "Safety at Any Price?" *Regulation* (November/December).

O'KELLY, CHARLOTTE G., and LINDA EDWARDS BLOOMQUIST (1976). "Equality in Advertising: Women and Blacks on TV," *Journal of Communication*, 26, (Autumn), 179–184.

OLANDER, FOLKE (1988). "Salient Issues in Current European Consumer Policy Research," in E. Scott Maynes (Ed.), *The Frontier of Research in the Consumer Interest.* Columbia, MO: American Council on Consumer Interests, 547–584.

OLIVER, RICHARD L. (1979). "An Interpretation of the Attitudinal and Behavioral Effects of Puffery," *Journal of Consumer Affairs*, 13, 1 (Summer).

OLSON, CHRISTINE, CAROL A. BISOGNI, and PATRICIA F. THONNEY (1982). "Evaluation of a Supermarket Nutrition Education Program," *Journal of Nutrition Education*, 14, 141–45.

OLSON, JERRY C., and PHILIP A. DOVER (1978). "Cognitive Effects of Deceptive Advertising," *Journal of Marketing Research*, 15, 1 (February), 29–38.

OLSON, MANCUR, JR. (1968). *The Logic of Collective Action.* New York: Schoken Books.

PACKARD, VANCE (1957). *The Hidden Persuaders.* New York: Pocket Books.

PELTZMAN, SAM (1975). "The Effects of Automobile Safety Regulation," *Journal of Political Economy*, 83, 4 (August), 677–726.

PESCH, MARINA, ET AL. (1981). "Sex Role Stereotypes on the Airwaves of the Eighties," Annual Convention of the Eastern Communication Association, Pittsburgh, PA (April), 23–25.

PFAFF, MARTIN (1977). "The Index of Consumer Satisfaction: Measurement Problems and Opportunities," in H. Keith Hunt (Ed.), *Conceptualization Measurement of Consumer Satisfaction and Dissatisfaction 2nd.* Cambridge, MA: Marketing Science Institute, 36–72.

PHILLIPS, L., and B. STERNTHAL (1977). "Age Differences in Information Processing: A Perception on the Aged Consumer," *Journal of Marketing Research*, 14, 444–457.

PIAGET, JEAN (1928). *The Child's Conception of the World.* New York: Harcourt Brace.

PIAGET, JEAN (1954). *The Construction of Reality in the Child.* New York: Basic Books.

PINGREE, SUZANNE (1978). "The Effects of Nonsexist Television Commercials and Perceptions of Reality of Children's Attitudes about Women," *Psychology of Women Quarterly*, (Spring), 262–276.

PITTLE, R. DAVID (1988). "Product Safety: The Views of a Former Regulator," in E. Scott Maynes (Ed.), *The Frontier of Research in the Consumer Interest.* Columbia, MO: American Council on Consumer Interests, 102–110.

PITTS, ROBERT E., JOHN F. WILLENBORG, and DANIEL L. SHERRELL (1981). "Consumer Adaptation to Gasoline Price Increases," *Journal of Consumer Research*, 8, 3 (December), 322–330.

POE, ALISON (1976). "Active Women in Ads," *Journal of Communication*, 26 (Autumn), 185–192.

POMAZAL, RICHARD J., and JAMES J. JACCARD (1976). "An Informational Approach to Altruistic Behavior," *Journal of Personality and Social Psychology*, 33, 3, 317–326.

PORTER/NOVELLI (1988). *Seminar Results: Fear as a Persuasion Technique.* Washington, DC: Porter/Novelli and The National Heart, Lung and Blood Institute.

PORTIS, BERNARD (1966). "Negroes and Fashion Interests," *Journal of Business*, 39, 2 (April), 314–323.

POSNER, JUDITH (1981). "Sexual Sell Or We Do It All For You," Manuscript, Atkinson College, York University, Toronto, Ont.

Pratt, Robert W. Jr. (1974). "ACR: A Perspective," in *Advances in Consumer Research*, Vol. 1, 1–8.

Preston, Ivan L. (1976). "A Comment on 'Defining Misleading Advertising' and 'Deception in Advertising,'" *Journal of Marketing*, 35, 3 (July), 54–57.

Preston, Ivan L. (1977). "The FTC's Handling of Puffery and Other Selling Claims Made by Implication," *Journal of Business Research*, 5, 155–181.

Preston, Ivan L., and Jef I. Richards (1986). "The Relationship of Miscomprehension to Deceptiveness in FTC Cases," *Advances in Consumer Research*, Vol. 13, 138–142.

Ray, Michael L., and William L. Wilkie (1970). "Fear: The Potential of an Appeal Neglected by Marketing," *Journal of Marketing*, 34, 1 (January), 54–62.

Real, M. R., N. Anderson, and M. Harrington (1980). "Television Access for Older Adults," *Journal of Communications* 30, 74–76.

Reece, Bonnie B., and Robert H. Ducoffe (1987). "Deception in Brand Names," *Journal of Public Policy and Marketing*, 6, 93–103.

Reid, Leonard N. (1979). "The Impact of Family Group Interaction on Children's Understanding of Television Advertising," *Journal of Advertising*, 8 (Summer), 13–19.

Reingen, Peter H., and Jerome B. Kernan (1977). "Compliance with an Interview Request: A Foot-in-the-Door, Self-Perception Interpretation," *Journal of Marketing Research*, 14, 3 (August), 365–69.

Richards, Louise G. (1966). "Consumer Practices of the Poor," in Lola M. Ireland (Ed.), *Low Income Life Styles*. Washington, DC: U.S. Department of Health, Education and Welfare.

Richins, Marsha L. (1980). "Consumer Perspectives of Costs and Benefits Associated with Complaining," in H. Keith Hunt and Ralph L. Day (Eds.), *Refining Concepts and Measures of Consumer Satisfaction and Complaining Behavior*. Bloomington, IN: Bureau of Business Research, Indiana University, 50–53.

Ritchie, J. R. Brent, and Gordon H. G. McDougall (1985). "Designing and Marketing Consumer Energy Conservation Policies and Programs: Implications from a Decade of Research," *Journal of Public Policy and Marketing*, 4, 14–32.

Ritchie, J. R. Brent, Gordon H. G. McDougall, and John D. Claxton (1981).

"Complexities of Household Energy Consumption and Conservation," *Journal of Consumer Research*, 8, 3 (December), 233–242.

Robertson, Leon S. (1976). "Consumer Response to Seat Belt Use Campaigns and Inducements: Implications for Public Health Strategies," *Advances in Consumer Research*, Vol. 3, 287–289.

Robertson, Thomas S., and John R. Rossiter (1974). "Children and Commercial Persuasion: An Attribution Theory Analysis," *Journal of Consumer Research*, 1, 1 (June), 12–20.

Robinson, Jean R. (1988). "The Content of a College-University Course in Consumer Education," in E. Scott Maynes (Ed.), *The Frontier of Research in the Consumer Interest*. Columbia, MO: American Council on Consumer Interests, 857–873.

Rodgers, Gregory (1984). *The Amended Lawn Mower Standard: Effects on Consumers*. Washington, DC: Consumer Product Safety Commission.

Rogers, Ronald W. (1975). "A Protection Motivation Theory of Fear Appeals and Attitude Change," *Journal of Psychology*, 91, 93–114.

Rogers, Ronald W. (1983). "Cognitive and Physiological Processes in Fear Appeals and Attitude Change: A Revised Theory of Protection Motivation," in John T. Cacioppo and Richard E. Petty (Eds.), *Social Psychophysiology: A Sourcebook*. New York: Guilford Press, 153–176.

Ross, Ivan (1982). "Information Processing and the Older Consumer: Market and Public Policy Implications," *Advances in Consumer Research*, Vol. 9, 31–39.

Ross, Ivan (1985). "Consumer Initiated Information Audit," in H. Keith Hunt and Ralph L. Day (Eds.), *Consumer Satisfaction, Dissatisfaction and Complaining Behavior*. Bloomington, IN: Bureau of Business Research, Indiana University, 73–81.

Ross, Ivan, and Richard D. Oliver (1984). "The Accuracy of Unsolicited Consumer Communications as Indicators of 'True' Consumer Satisfaction/Dissatisfaction," *Advances in Consumer Research*, Vol. 11, 504–508.

Rotfeld, Herbert J., and Kim B. Rotzoll (1980). "Is Advertising Puffery Believed?" *Journal of Advertising*, 10, 16–20.

Rothschild, Michael D. (1979). "Marketing Communications in Nonbusiness Situations or Why It's So Hard to Sell Brotherhood Like Soap," *Journal of Marketing*, 43, 2 (Spring), 11–20.

Rudelius, William, Richard Weijo, and Gary Dodge (1984). "Marketing Energy Conservation to Homeowners: An Action Program from Public Policy Research," *Journal of Public Policy and Marketing*, 3, 149-166.

RUSSO, J. EDWARD (1974). "More Information is Better: A Reevaluation of Jacoby, Speller and Kohn," *Journal of Consumer Research*, 1, 68-72.

RUSSO, J. EDWARD (1977a). "The Value of Unit Price Information," *Journal of Marketing Research*, 14, 2 (May), 193-201.

RUSSO, J. EDWARD (1977b). "A Proposal to Increase Energy Conservation Through Provision of Consumption and Cost Information to Consumers," in Barnett A. Greenberg and Danny N. Bellenger (Eds.), *Contemporary Marketing Thought: 1977 Educator's Proceedings*. Chicago: American Marketing Association, 437-442.

RUSSO, J. EDWARD (1981). "The Decision to Use Product Information at the Point of Purchase," in Ron Stampfl and Elizabeth Hirschman (Eds.), *Theory in Retailing: Traditional and Nontraditional Sources*. Chicago: American Marketing Association.

RUSSO, J. EDWARD (1987). "Toward Intelligent Product Information Systems for Consumers," *Journal of Consumer Policy*, 10, 109-138.

RUSSO, J. EDWARD (1988). "Information Processing from the Consumer's Perspective," in E. Scott Maynes (Ed.), *The Frontier of Research in the Consumer Interest*. Columbia, MO: American Council on Consumer Interests, 185-218.

RUSSO, J. EDWARD, RICHARD STAELIN, CATHERINE A. NOLAN, GARY J. RUSSELL, and BARBARA L. METCALF (1986). "Nutrition Information in the Supermarket," *Journal of Consumer Research*, 13, 1 (June), 48-70.

SAEGERT, JOEL, ROBERT J. HOOVER, and MARYE THARP HILGER (1985). "Characteristics of Mexican American Consumers," *Journal of Consumer Research*, 12, 1 (June), 104-109.

SCAMMON, DEBRA L. (1977). "Information Load and Consumers," *Journal of Consumer Research*, 4, 3 (December), 148-155.

SCHIFFMAN, LEON (1971). "Sources of Information for the Elderly," *Journal of Advertising Research*, 11, 33-37.

SCHIFFMAN, LEON (1972). "Perceived Risk in New Product Trial by Elderly Consumers," *Journal of Marketing Research*, 9, 1 (February), 106-108.

SCHLINGER, MARY J., and JOSEPH PLUMMER (1972). "Advertising in Black and White," *Journal of Marketing Research*, 9 (May) 149-153.

SCHMITTLEIN, DAVID C., and DONALD MORRISON (1983). "Measuring Miscomprehension for Televised Communications Using True-False Questions," *Journal of Consumer Research*, 10, 2 (September), 147-156.

SCHRAG, PHILIP (1972). *Counsel for the Deceived*. New York: Pantheon Books.

SCHULBERG, FRANCINE (1979). "United States Export of Products Banned for Domestic Use," *Harvard International Law Journal* (Spring), 331-383.

SEEMAN, M. (1959). "On the Meaning of Alienation," *American Sociological Review*, 24, 783-791.

SEGAL, MADHAV N., and LIONEL SOSA (1983). "Marketing to the Hispanic Community," *California Management Review*, 26 (Fall), 120-134.

SEPSTRUP, PREBEN (1980). "Consumption of Mass Communication: On Construction of a Model of Information Consumption Behavior," in Jagdish Sheth (Ed.), *Research in Marketing*, Vol. 3. Greenwich, CT: JAI Press, 105-142.

SEPSTRUP, PREBEN, and FOLKE OLANDER (1986). "Consumer Information in the Electronic Media," Working Paper No. 4. Aarhus: Aarhus School of Business Administration and Economics, Department of Marketing.

SEXTON, DONALD E., JR. (1971). "Do Blacks Pay More?" *Journal of Marketing Research*, 8, 4 (November), 420-426.

SHARMA, SUBHASH, WILLIAM O. BEARDEN, and JESSE E. TEEL (1983). "Differential Effects of In-Home Shopping Methods," *Journal of Retailing*, 59, 4, 29-51.

SHIMP, TERENCE A. (1978). "Do Incomplete Comparisons Mislead?" *Journal of Advertising Research*, 18, 21-27.

SHUEY, AUDRED M., NANCY KING, and BARBARA GRIFFITH (1953). "Stereotyping of Negroes and Whites: An Analysis of Magazines Pictures," *Public Opinion Quarterly*, 17 (Summer), 281-287.

SHUPTRINE, F. K., and E. M. MOORE (1980). "Even After the Magnuson-Moss Act of 1975, Warranties Are not Easy to Understand," *Journal of Consumer Affairs*, 14, 2 (Winter).

SILVENIS, SCOTT (1979). "Packaging for the Elderly," *Modern Packaging*, 52 (October), 38-39.

SILVERSTEIN, ARTHUR, and REBECCA SILVERSTEIN (1974). "The Portrayal of Women in Television Advertising," *Federal Communications Bar Journal*, 27, 71-98.

SINCLAIR, UPTON (1906). *The Jungle.* New York: Bantam Books.

SIRGY, M. JOSEPH, and A. COSKUN SAMLI (1987). "Functional/Dysfunctional Consumer Behavior: A Normative Framework for Public Policy," in Robert L. King (Ed.), *Minority Marketing: Issues and Prospects.* Charleston, SC: Academy of Marketing Science, 78–82.

SLAGEL, MICHELLE L. (1982). "The Implementation of a Discretionary Project Program: A Case Study of the Office of Consumers' Education," unpublished doctoral dissertation. Washington, DC: George Washington University, School of Government and Business Administration.

SLATTON, YVONNE L. (1971). "The Role of Women in Sport as Depicted in Advertising in Selected Magazines, 1900–1968," unpublished doctoral dissertation. Iowa City, IA: University of Iowa.

SLOVIC, PAUL, BARUCH FISCHHOFF, and SARAH LICHTENSTEIN (1978). "Accident Probabilities and Seat Belt Usage: A Psychological Perspective," *Accident Analysis and Prevention,* 10, 281.

SMITH, RUTH B., and GEORGE T. BAKER (1986). "The Elderly Consumer: A Perspective on Present and Potential Sources of Consumer Activity," in Paul N. Bloom and Ruth Belk Smith (Eds.), *The Future of Consumerism.* Lexington, MA: Lexington Books, 99–112.

SMITH, RUTH B., and GEORGE P. MOSCHIS (1984). "Consumer Socialization of the Elderly: An Exploratory Study," in *Advances in Consumer Research,* Vol. 11, 548–52.

SNUGGS, THELMA L., and WILLIAM J. QUALLS (1987). "Portrayal of Blacks in Advertising: A Critical Review of the Literature," in Robert L. King (Ed.), *Minority Marketing: Issues and Prospects.* Charleston, SC: Academy of Marketing Science, 97–102.

SPIGGLE, SUSAN, and CATHY GOODWIN (1987). "Values and Issues in the Field of Consumer Research: A Content Analysis of ACR Presidential Addresses," *Advances in Consumer Research,* Vol. 15, 5–12.

SPRATLEN, THADDEUS H., and PRAVAT K. CHOUDURY (1987). "Black-White Differences in the Consumption of Cosmetics: Aggregate and Socio-Cultural Dimensions," in Robert L. King (Ed.), *Minority Marketing: Issues and Prospects.* Charleston, SC: Academy of Marketing Science, 41–45.

STAELIN, RICHARD (1978). "The Effects of Consumer Education on Consumer Product Safety Behavior," *Journal of Consumer Research,* 5, 1 (June), 30–40.

STAELIN, RICHARD, and JOHN W. PAYNE (1976). "Studies of the Information Seeking Behavior of Consumers" in Richard Staelin, and John W. Payne (Eds.), *Cognition and Social Behavior.* Hillsdale, NJ: Erlbaum, 185–201.

STAFFORD, JAMES, AL BIRDWELL, and CHARLES VAN TASSEL (1970). "Integrated Advertising-White Backlash," *Journal of Advertising Research,* 10 (April), 15–20.

Statistical Abstract of the United States, 1988. Washington, DC: U.S. Government Printing Office.

STEPHENS, NANCY, and MARY ANN STUTTS (1982). "Preschoolers' Ability to Distinguish Between Television Programming and Commercials," *Journal of Advertising,* 11, 23, 16–26.

STERN, LOUIS, and THOMAS EOVALDI (1984). *Legal Aspects of Marketing Strategy.* Englewood Cliffs, NJ: Prentice-Hall.

STURDIVANT, FREDERICK D., and WALTER T. WILHELM (1968). "Poverty, Minorities, and Consumer Exploitation," *Social Science Quarterly* (December), 643–650.

SUMMERS, JOHN O. (1974). "Less Information is Better," *Journal of Marketing Research,* 11, 4 (November), 467–468.

TALARZYK, W. WAYNE (1986). "Electronic Retailing in the United States: Trends and Potentials." Columbus, OH: Ohio State University. Working Paper Series No. 86–90.

TECHNICAL ADVISORY RESEARCH PROGRAM (TARP) (1979). *Consumer Complaint Handling in America: Final Report.* Washington, DC: United States Department of Health, Education and Welfare.

THOMAS, LILLIE RUTH (1969). "A Comparative Study of the Effects of Course Organization on Achievement in Consumer Education Concepts," unpublished doctoral dissertation. Tempe, AZ: Arizona State University, College of Education.

THORELLI, HANS B. (1983). "China: Consumer Voice and Exit," in Ralph L. Day and H. Keith Hunt (Eds.), *International Fare in Consumer Satisfaction and Complaining Behavior.* Bloomington, IN: Bureau of Business Research, Indiana University, 105–111.

THORELLI, HANS B. (1988). "Consumer Problems in Developed and Less Developed Countries," in E. Scott Maynes (Ed.), *The Frontier of Research in the Consumer Interest*. Columbia, MO: American Council on Consumer Interests, 523–546.

THORELLI, HANS B., and GERALD D. SENTELL (1982). *Consumer Emancipation and Economic Development: The Case of Thailand*. Greenwich, CT: JAI Press.

TIENDA, MARTA, and OSEI-MENSAH ABORAMPAH (1981). "Energy-Related Adaptations in Low-Income Nonmetropolitan Wisconsin Counties," *Journal of Consumer Research*, 8, 3 (December), 265–270.

TUMIN, MELVIN (1967). *Social Stratification: The Forms and Functions of Inequality*. Englewood Cliffs, NJ: Prentice-Hall.

TURNER, JOSEPHINE (1988). "The Role of Cooperative Education," in E. Scott Maynes (Ed.), *The Frontier of Research in the Consumer Interest*. Columbia, MO: American Council on Consumer Interests, 849–856.

TVERSKY, AMOS, and DANIEL KAHNEMAN (1974). "Judgment Under Uncertainty: Heuristics and Biases," *Science*, 185, 1124–1131.

TYEBJEE, TYZOON T. (1982). "The Role of Publicity in FTC Corrective Advertising Remedies," *Journal of Marketing & Public Policy*. 1, 111–122.

VENKATESAN, M., WADE LANCASTER, and KENNETH W. KENDALL (1986). "An Empirical Study of Alternative Formats for Nutritional Information Disclosure in Advertising," *Journal of Public Policy and Marketing*, 5, 29–43.

VENKATESAN, M., and JEAN LOSCO (1975). "Women in Magazine Ads" 1959–1971." *Journal of Advertising Research*, (October), 49–54.

VOLNER, R. (1972). "The Games Consumers Play: 'Give Away' and the Law—A Conflict of Policies," *Federal Communications Bureau Journal*, 121 ff.

WADDELL, F. W. (1975). "Consumer Research and Programs for the Elderly—The Forgotten Dimension," *Journal of Consumer Affairs*, 9, 164–175.

WADDELL, F. W. (1976). *The Elderly Consumer*. Columbia, MO: The Human Ecology Center, Antioch College.

WADDELL, F. W. (1981). "The Effects of Experimental Consumers Education on Subsequent Performance in the Marketplace," unpublished doctoral dissertation. Blacksburg, VA: Virginia Polytechnic Institute and State University.

WAGNER, LOUIS C., and JANIS B. BANOS (1973). "A Woman's Place: A Fellow-Up Analysis of the Roles Played by Women in Magazine Advertisements," *Journal of Marketing Research*, 10, 2 (May), 213–214.

WARD, SCOTT (1979). "Researchers Look at the 'KidVid' Rule: Overview of Session," *Advances in Consumer Research*, Vol. 6, 7–8.

WARD, SCOTT, GREG REALE, and DAVID LEVINSON (1972). "Children's Perceptions, Explanations and Judgments of Television Advertising: A Further Explanation," in Eli A. Rubinstein, George A. Comstock, and John P. Murray (Eds.), *Television and Social Behavior*. Washington, DC: U.S. Government Printing Office, 468–490.

WARD, SCOTT, and DANIEL B. WACKMAN (1973). "Children's Information Processing of Television Advertising," in Peter Clarke (Ed.) *New Models for Mass Communication Research*. Beverly Hills, CA: Sage, 199–246.

WARD, SCOTT, DANIEL B. WACKMAN, and ELLEN WARTELLA (1977). *How Children Learn to Buy*. Beverly Hills, CA: Sage.

WARREN, CAROL A. B. (1988). *Gender Issues in Field Research*. Newbury Park, CA: Sage.

WARREN, DENISE (1979). "Commercial Liberation," *Journal of Communication*, 28 (Winter), 169–173.

WARRINER, G. KEITH (1981). "Electricity Consumption by the Elderly: Policy Implications," *Journal of Consumer Research*, 8, 3 (December), 258–264.

WIENER, JOSHUA LYLE (1985). "Are Warranties Accurate Signals of Product Reliability?" *Journal of Consumer Research*, 12, 2 (September), 245–250.

WILKIE, WILLIAM L. (1973). *Consumer Research and Corrective Advertising*. Cambridge, MA: Marketing Science Institute.

WILKIE, WILLIAM, L. (1974). "Research on Counter and Corrective Advertising," in Sal V. Davita (Ed.), *Advertising and the Public Interest*. Chicago: American Marketing, 189–202.

WILKIE, WILLIAM L. (1975a). *Applying Attitude Research in Public Policy*. Cambridge, MA: Marketing Science Institute.

WILKIE, WILLIAM, L. (1975b). *How Consumers Use Information: An Assessment of Research in Relation to Public Policy Needs*. Washington, DC: National Science Foundation, Research Application Directorate.

WILKIE, WILLIAM, L. (1981). "Affirmative Disclosure: A Survey and Evaluation of FTC Orders Issued From 1970–1977." Washington, DC: Federal Trade Commission.

WILKIE, WILLIAM L. (1982). "Affirmative Disclosure: Perspectives on FTC Orders," *Journal of Public Policy and Marketing*, 1, 95–110.

WILKIE, WILLIAM L. (1983). "Affirmative Disclosures at the FTC: Theoretical Framework and Typology of Case Selection," *Journal of Public Policy and Marketing*, 2, 3–15.

WILKIE, WILLIAM L. (1985). "Affirmative Disclosures at the FTC: Objectives for the Remedy and Outcomes of Past Orders," *Journal of Public Policy and Marketing*, 4, 91–111.

WILKIE, WILLIAM L. (1986a). "Affirmative Disclosure at the FTC: Strategic Dimensions," *Journal of Public Policy and Marketing*, 5, 123–145.

WILKIE, WILLIAM, L. (1986b). *Consumer Behavior.* New York: Wiley.

WILKIE, WILLIAM L. (1987). "Affirmative Disclosures at the FTC: Communication Decisions," *Journal of Public Policy and Marketing*, 6, 33–42.

WILKIE, WILLIAM L., DENNIS L. MCNEILL, and MICHAEL B. MAZIS. (1984). "Marketing's 'Scarlet Letter': The Theory and Practice of Corrective Advertising," *Journal of Marketing*, 48, 2 (Spring), 11–31.

WILLIAMS, FLORA (1976). "The Food Problem and Income Adequacy," *Advances in Consumer Research* Vol. 3, 238–245.

WINETT, RICHARD A., and JOHN H. KAGEL (1984). "Effects of Information Presentation Format on Resource Use in Field Studies," *Journal of Consumer Research*, 11, 2 (September), 655–667.

WIRMAN, ALAN R. (1983). "Parental Influence and Children's Responses to Television Advertising," *Journal of Advertising*, 12, 1, 12–18.

WRIGHT, ERIC OLIN (1978). "Race, Class and Income Inequality," *American Journal of Sociology*, 83, 1368–1397.

WYCKHAM, ROBERT G. (1987). "Self-Regulation of Sex-Role Stereotyping in Advertising: The Canadian Experience," *Journal of Public Policy and Marketing*, 6, 76–92.

ZUSSMAN, D. (1983). "Consumer Complaint Behavior and Third Party Mediation," *Canadian Public Policy*, 9, 2.

14

BEHAVIORAL METHODS

Jerry Wind
University of Pennsylvania

Vithala R. Rao
Cornell University

Paul E. Green
University of Pennsylvania

Consumer researchers can be classified into five distinct segments: academic consumer researchers, marketing scientists, behavioral theorists, behavioral science methodologists, and consumer research practitioners. This chapter describes the differences among these segments with respect to their research approaches and research perspectives. Against this background, the chapter reviews the developments in the literature on three aspects of methodology of consumer research: research design, data collection, and data analysis and interpretation. Analytical methods suitable for different consumer research situations are identified.

The authors note a lack of methodological innovation and a paucity of truly creative methodological approaches. Some suggestions to improve this situation are offered in this chapter.

INTRODUCTION

Research methods employed in the study of consumer behavior have spanned virtually all aspects of social science research methods and applied statistics. Consumer researchers vary, however, greatly in their research approaches.

Although the classification system is not mutually exclusive and exhaustive, various consumer researchers can be identified as belonging to one of five "segments":

1. *THE ACADEMIC CONSUMER RESEARCHERS*—those who see consumer research as a separate discipline and who consider the Association for Consumer Research as their primary professional affiliation. Members of this segment are less concerned with practice. They have been publishing their work in recent years primarily in *The Journal of Consumer Research* (*JCR*) and in *Advances in Consumer Research*:

2. *THE MARKETING SCIENTISTS*—those academics whose primary academic pursuit is the prescriptive or normative modeling of marketing

phenomena, including the modeling of consumer behavior. This segment is eclectic in choosing its research methods; they conduct and apply consumer research to develop and validate their models of marketing behavior (managerial or consumer) and typically publish their work in *The Journal of Marketing Research (JMR)* and in *Marketing Science*.

3. *BEHAVIORAL THEORISTS*—those who develop and test theories of various facets of human behavior (e.g., psychologists, sociologists, economists, political scientists, communication researchers) related to their disciplines. While their focus on the study of consumer behavior is incidental, their seminal theoretical contributions to their respective disciplines have occasionally been the spring board for research on consumer behavior by those in Segment 1.

4. *BEHAVIORAL SCIENCE METHODOLOGISTS*—those who are methodologically oriented behavioral scientists and whose major concern is to develop sophisticated methodologies for testing and validating extant theories of behavioral science (e.g., those developed by Segment 3). Members in this segment include econometricians, mathematical psychologists, psychometricians, and mathematical sociologists. They contribute models and methods that can be (and are) adapted by consumer researchers.

5. *CONSUMER RESEARCH PRACTITIONERS*—those who include applied marketing researchers in business, government, or consulting firms; and consumer policy analysts, whose main focus is to tackle applied problems utilizing the results of consumer research.

The five segments vary in their concerns and research focus, and, as a result, in their dominant research methods. Given the veracity of one's research activity, particular individuals may be put in more than one segment; but, for the purposes of this chapter, it is convenient to think in terms of typical researchers in each of these segments. Whereas Table 14.1 outlines their differences, it is important to realize the enormous heterogeneity within segments and the similarity across segments. In fact, it is difficult to find any research method that has not been applied in some study of consumer behavior by at least someone in each of the five

segments. The categorization and differences shown in Table 14.1 are essentially subjective.

The reader may find of interest the distinctions with respect to the major research focus. While Segments 1 and 2 have been concerned with the same broad area over the last two decades, there have been very few attempts to synthesize these research streams. Given the eclectic use of research methods by all consumer researchers, this chapter will focus on research methods used in the study of consumer behavior by these first two segments. Our discussion will, however, include methods that are idiosyncratic to the other three segments, particularly as we outline our views on the expected future directions.

Choice processes are the primary focus of the two dominant segments for our discussion. While various approaches have been followed for studying choice processes by consumer researchers,[1] it will be of interest to identify our view of the consumer choice process. Several constructs relevant to the choice process and their interrelationships can be identified. Briefly stated, information on choice alternatives (as presented by marketers) enables consumers to develop perceptions about the alternatives. The utility function for the choice alternatives depends on the perceptions of the consumers and individual characteristics of the choices. The ultimate choice in the marketplace is determined by the utility function with necessary modifications due to the situational variables and budget constraints.

Thus, the consumer researcher has to identify and measure several constructs and estimate relationships between them for describing the consumer choice process; these are the following: product category (the *total* set of all items fulfilling predefined consumer needs or wants); choice set (brands deemed as alternatives for choice by an individual), brand information (all brand information available to a

---

[1]More recently, however, several academic consumer researchers have focused on various aspects of the consumption process (e.g., emotions, aesthetic responses, etc.). See, for example, Holbrook et al. (1984).

TABLE 14.1 The Five "Segments" of Consumer Researchers and Their Primary Focus

The Segments	Segment 1 *Academic* *Consumer* *Researcher*	Segment 2 *Marketing* *Scientist*	Segment 3 *Behavioral* *Theorist*	Segment 4 *Behavioral* *Science* *Methodologist*	Segment 5 *Consumer* *Research* *Practitioner*
Major Publication Outlets(s)	*JCR*	*JMR; MS*	Several Discipline Journals	*Econometrica Psychometrica JASA*	–
Major Research Concern	Choice Process	Choice and Determinants of Choice	Human Behavior	Techniques	Applied Problems
Primary Focus	Consumer Theory	Marketing Theory and Methods	Theories of Human Behavior	Methodologies	Practice
Dominant Types of Data Used	Experimental Data	Surveys and Longitudinal Panels	All Types of Data Including Observational Data	Experiments, Surveys, Longitudinal Panels	Surveys and Longitudinal Panels
Dominant Techniques of Data Analysis	Analysis of variance and covariance (ANOVA, ANOCOVA) Correlational Methods Factor Analysis	Multivariate Methods Econometric Methods Psychometric Methods Optimization Methods	Discipline Dependent (e.g., Network Analysis)	Multivariate Methods Econometric Methods Psychometric Methods Optimization Methods	Several; Follows Segment 2
Potential New Directions in Research	Methods for Observational Data and Qualitative Data	Integrative Methods Process Inferential Techniques	Incorporate Methods Developed by Segment 4	Continue Current Efforts	Follows Segment 2

consumer), individual characteristics (those relevant to the choice process), situational characteristics (those that describe the particular choice situation), brand perceptions (the result of an idiosyncratic transformation of all information available to an individual), brand preferences (an individual's ordering of brands in the choice set unique to the situation), and brand choice (the specific choice made). By suitable modifications, this view will also encompass consumer choices over time.

While the preceding description is very condensed, it does provide a way to differentiate the main research thrust of Segment 1 in comparison to that of Segment 2. As an aside, we may also note that Segment 5 seems to follow this paradigm for tackling applied problems, mainly, in marketing. While the marketing scientist (Segment 2) seems to focus upon empirical relationships between the several constructs noted (e.g., brand perceptions and brand preference; brand attributes and brand choice), the academic consumer researcher (Segment 1) seems to be concerned with the *internal process* that leads an individual from one stage to the next. As an example, consider the research problem of how an individual processes the enormous amount of information on brands for making preferential judgments about them. Other examples include the study of the effects of memory on the choice process and the processes by which an individual augments the set of brands being considered as new items offered in the market place.

Against this background, our review will focus on three aspects of methodology for consumer research: research design, data collection, and data analysis and interpretation.

This review is not intended as a comprehensive coverage; the studies included are illustrative of the types of studies used. There are many other excellent and creative studies of consumer research not included here. The discussion is intended to provide an overview of research methods used in consumer research[2] and to highlight the paradigm shifts that are shaping the nature of consumer research methods and impacting the value of their methods.

RESEARCH DESIGNS

Research designs of consumer behavior studies vary greatly. As noted earlier, members of all five segments have employed all available designs. Yet, one can see significant differences among the segments. During the 1980s, the academic consumer researchers who published in *JCR* tended to emphasize experimentation. Much of the consumer research by marketing scientists (Segment 2) and consumer research practitioners (Segment 5) focussed on survey research. Researchers outside the immediate field of consumer research (Segment 3) who occasionally study consumer behavior use the designs and methods common to their disciplinary origin; for example, the participant observational design is typically utilized by the cultural anthropologist.

A major difference between the academic consumer researchers and the marketing scientists and consumer research practitioners is the nature of their samples and respondents. Aca-

demic consumer researchers tend to use students as subjects; their focus is largely on understanding the internal dynamics of consumer choice. Given this objective, their apparent lack of concern for the generalizability and projectability of the results to the larger universe of consumers is perhaps understandable. In contrast, researchers in Segments 2 and 5 (marketing scientists and consumer research practitioners) tend to use "real consumers" as subjects, as well as larger and more representative samples. Their research, however, tends to be focussed on particular marketing problems and methodology development. Thus, one may argue that even these segments are not that concerned with various obstacles to the generalizability of results.

Experimentation

Laboratory and field experiments have long been used to establish consumers' responses to alternative stimuli and marketing strategies. Experiments have involved all individual marketing strategy variables (e.g., prices, advertising messages, product formulations, etc.) as well as overall marketing programs. Marketing scientists (Segment 2) have employed the methods of adaptive experimentation, especially in direct-mail marketing (Blattberg 1979) and (Allenby and Blattberg 1987). The objective here is to design a series of experiments such that the next experiment utilizes information obtained on the behavior of interest in the previous experiment. Thus, adaptive experimentation methods enable the researcher to optimize decisions over time.

Single factor experiments still dominate, but there is a steady increase in the use of factorial designs, randomized blocks, Latin, and Greco-Latin squares, and switch-over designs in both laboratory and field marketing experiments. For a description of the designs see Cochran and Cox (1957) and Raghavarao (1971). Analytically, analysis of variance (ANOVA) and analysis of covariance (ANCOVA) are the major techniques used (Scheffee 1970), with occasional applications of multivariate analysis of

---

[2]Much of the review of research methods is based on Green and Wind, "Statistics in Marketing," in Kotz and Johnson's *Encyclopedia of Statistical Sciences*, Vol. 5. (New York: Wiley, 1985).

variance (MANOVA) (Wind and Denny 1974) and multivariate analysis of covariance (MANCOVA) (see Roy et al. 1971; Searle 1971).

Laboratory experiments are especially popular among academic consumer researchers, as evidenced by the large number of experiments published in *JCR*. Laboratory experiments are also commonly used in marketing for testing consumers' reactions to alternative strategies of a single marketing variable or multiple marketing variables by consumer research practitioners (Segment 5). Copy testing procedures are available, for example, to evaluate alternative advertising messages. Similarly, consumer research practitioners often conduct product taste tests as lab experiments, comparing a number of alternative product formulations.[3] These types of experiments usually employ a number of evaluative measures (dependent variables) such as intentions to buy, attitudes toward the brand (which include overall liking as well as evaluations on specific attributes), and attitudes toward the advertisement (in the case of advertising experiments). Commercially, simulated test market studies have proliferated in the study of consumer reaction to new, frequently purchased products.

Typical simulated test market experiments involve a before-after type of design, with one interview prior to using the product (but after exposure to the advertising of the brand and that of its major competitors) and one or more interviews after using the product. It may be more appropriate to utilize a control group and randomization to enable unbiased estimation of the effects of advertising exposure in these test market experiments.

Data from such experiments are among the major inputs into new product forecasting models aimed at predicting both trial and repeat purchase, and at providing diagnostic insights into consumers' acceptance of the product (see Silk and Urban 1978; Urban et al.

---

[3]Some theories of discrimination can be used in the design of such experiments; see Buchanan and Morrison (1985).

1983). These can include the analysis and evaluation of brand switching patterns; the identification of the key demographic, psychographic, and purchase/usage patterns that discriminate between buyers and nonbuyers, satisfied or dissatisfied users, etc.; and the assessment of the perceived positioning of the brands by various segments (such as benefit or usage segments).

Field experiments, not unlike laboratory experiments, have included both the study of single variables and the examination of marketing programs. Two major types of field experiments are the minitest markets and the test market designs. Charlton, Ehrenberg, and Pymont (1972) report on a U.K. "minitest market" based on a panel of households, which were visited weekly. After exposure to a color brochure that displayed a set of available brands, respondents were asked to place orders, which immediately were filled from a mobile van, for brands from a variety of product categories. The procedure allows the assessment of the level of repeat buying, the cumulative penetration level (the percentage of households who buy the brand at least once in a given time period), and the average buying frequency (the average number of times the buyers buy the brand in the same time period).

The U.K. minitest market, which was validated by Ehrenberg (1971), is used primarily for the evaluation of new products and for measuring the effect, under controlled conditions, of alternative marketing strategies. Although such facilities are not common in the United States, a number of similar procedures are currently employed in this country.

Although the most commonly used field experiments are test markets—and often a mandatory stage in the new product development process of many firms—their use is on the decline due to their high costs and the time required to plan and implement them, their questionable projectability, and their vulnerability to competitive intervention. Nevertheless, they serve both as a vehicle to assess the market performance of a new product under alternative marketing strategies and as a pilot operation.

Two new technological developments are of special interest to the design of market experiments:

1. The availability of and tremendous growth in scanning data offers new opportunities for store and market experiments. The use of identification cards, which contain background information, issued to consumers at the retail outlets with scanning systems, and the development of "single source" data enable a consumer researcher to obtain detailed data on behavior related to each individual. This facility has enhanced the opportunities for consumer research. Alternative prices, coupons, shelf space, point of purchase promotion, advertising, and other marketing variables now can be evaluated faster and more easily. In addition, data from scanners have been employed to investigate such research problems as the identification of competitive sets (or market partitions), the estimation of price, advertising, and promotion elasticities, and the modeling of individual choice behavior.

2. The development of two-way cable TV systems such as the QUBE system, which have been in operation for a number of years in Columbus, Ohio, has provided some new possibilities for market experiments. While such systems facilitate more sensitive experiments with alternative strategies and almost instantaneous response, their use has been limited for consumer research.

These technological developments provide a number of valuable research opportunities not only for the marketing scientist, but also for the academic consumer researcher. (See Buzzell 1985, for a collection of readings on the electronic developments and their potential impact on marketing/consumer research.) The lack of use of these potential methodologies by Segment 1 (academic consumer researchers) may be partly due to the high costs and time involved in conducting such real-world experiments. Also, the academic researcher is often oriented toward obtaining data rather quickly by employing small scale experiments from convenient samples. Nevertheless, we expect that with these new kinds of data academic consumer researchers will conduct experiments outside the (student oriented) laboratory and begin to expand the focus of their research.

Sample Survey Methods

Sample surveys are the major source of primary data in marketing-based consumer research. Since the 1940s statistical procedures have been used both in selecting samples and in analyzing the survey results. In addition to simple random selection techniques, researchers have employed various kinds of stratified and cluster-sampling procedures.

Researchers in marketing have been influenced by the classic books of Hansen (1953), Sudman (1976), Cochran (1977), and Williams (1978). Of particular interest is the August, 1977, special issue of *JMR,* which included an excellent review article by Frankel and Frankel (1977). The review included a description of a number of methods for optimal sampling (i.e., a design for both the method of sampling and sample size so as to achieve the lowest possible standard errors of the estimates subject to cost constraints) in the presence of possible sources of bias.

Marketing scientists and consumer research practitioners also are becoming aware that in the design of complicated multistage samples (for which simple standard error formulas are not applicable) replicated designs often are essential. A number of methods, including balanced replication (McCarthy 1965), and jackknifing (Tukey 1977) have been proposed to select efficient sets of subsamples. Woodruff and Causey (1976) have compared these (and other approaches) with regard to computer time, reliability, and validity.

Developments in sampling and data collection procedures have also been closely linked to questionnaire design. Various experimental designs, such as orthogonal array designs, have been widely used in conjoint analysis type studies as a way to reduce the number of items presented to each respondent (Green and Carroll 1976). Sampling from a multivariate normal distribution has been proposed as an alternative (Parker and Srinivasan 1976), but most of the conjoint analysis type studies have relied on orthogonal main effects designs (Green and Srinivasan 1978, 1989). In these designs, the number of times a combination of Level i for

Factor A and Level j for Factor B is proportional to the product of the total number of times Level i of A occurs in the design and the total number of times Level j of B occurs in the design; this relationship will be true for all pairs of factors in the design. Such designs can estimate the main effects of all factors in an efficient manner. More recently, in response to the need to simplify the data collection task, Balanced Incomplete Block (BIB) designs have been utilized, allowing for the study of a large number of factors and levels, while requiring each respondent to evaluate only a few (typically less than ten) stimuli. In a BIB design, a group of respondents constitutes a block and each respondent evaluates only a small number of stimuli. Thus, in the block as a whole, each stimulus is evaluated the same number of times and each stimulus pair is evaluated by an equal number of respondents.

While survey research continues to include the use of open-ended questions, methods are now available to rigorously analyze such responses. For example, a matrix of stimuli by attributes can be constructed using open-ended evaluations of stimuli (brands, ads, etc.) and analyzed as any data matrix (see, for example, Green, Wind, and Jain 1973). Important developments in survey research methods continue to center on data collection methods, and on ways to elicit better quality responses. An interesting approach to the solicitation of information about sensitive topics is based on application of the randomized response technique (Warner 1965). For each sensitive question (e.g., Did you use marijuana last month?), a common question (e.g., Is your birth year odd or even?) is added and the respondent is asked to choose one of these two questions (sensitive and common) at random and answer it. At the outset, it is not clear which question is answered, but there is a statistical procedure to estimate the proportion answering yes to the sensitive question.

Since Warner's publication other researchers (Greenberg, Abernathy, and Horvitz 1969) have extended the technique beyond dichotomous questions (with yes or no responses) to questions that yield responses on a continuous scale such as the number of times a person has used marijuana or the amount consumed in a month. While this technique is useful for obtaining aggregate responses, it is not amenable to obtaining data at the individual level.

While the preceding topics by no means exhaust recent developments, they are illustrative of the kinds of survey problems being addressed and for which solutions have been proposed.

Longitudinal Designs

Experiments and surveys typically measure behavioral or other kinds of data at one point in time. Consumer researchers have utilized longitudinal designs to measure aspects of consumer behavior over time. In principle, a longitudinal study is the same as a survey implemented at various points in time. Typically, a panel of individuals is recruited at a point in time and their behavior is monitored (via questionnaires or diaries maintained by the individuals or obtained electronically) for several time periods. The panel tends to become less representative over time due to such problems as attrition and noncooperation, but care is taken to maintain the representative character of the panel members.

The use of panels for applied consumer research is quite extensive among the members of Segment 5, who have implemented various technological developments made by members of Segment 2. Given the focus of members of Segment 1, and the implicit cultural gap between them and members of Segments 2 and 5, those in Segment 1 tend not to use longitudinal panels in their research endeavors.

Data generated from longitudinal panels are valuable in developing models of dynamic market behavior both at the individual level and at the aggregate level. One could make a serious case for the study of the dynamics of choice in consumer research; in fact, this path was pursued in the past by such researchers as Nicosia (1966) and Day (1970). Farley and Ring (1970) have utilized longitudinal data collected in three waves to develop and estimate econometric models (simultaneous systems) for the purpose of testing the Howard-Sheth comprehensive theory of buyer behavior (1969). However, over time, research using longitudinal data has relied more heavily on sophisticated mathematical models developed from stochastic processes; this factor has contributed to its low incidence currently.

During the last ten years or so, several significant consumer research problems have been looked at with the help of longitudinal panel data. The majority of consumer researchers using panel data focussed on brand switching (Ehrenberg 1972). More recent applications include the identification of subsets of competing items (Kalwani and Morrison 1971; Grover and Rao 1988; Vilcassim 1989), variety seeking phenomena (Kahn 1986), effectiveness of short-term price promotions and other marketing variables (Neslin et al. 1985), and inference regarding choice process (Rao and Sabavala 1981). Many of these interesting ways of using longitudinal data for consumer research have been pursued by members of Segment 2.

Other Designs

Recent years have witnessed a number of other interesting and useful research designs for the study of consumer behavior. These have included:

- Observational, naturalistic, "humanistic research approaches" (Hirschman 1985; Belk, Wallendorf, and Sherry 1989)
- Cross-cultural comparative research designs (Graham et al. 1988; Sherry and Camargo 1987)
- The use of unobstrusive approaches (Webb 1966) such as the analysis of household refuse
- The use of semiotics in understanding the importance of signs and symbols in consumer research (Mick 1986; Holbrook and Grayson 1986)

We may summarize the previous discussion by noting that various research designs (experiments, surveys, and panels) have been employed in consumer research and that each design type has found a place in the repertoire of a consumer researcher. We strongly believe that research designs should be selected in accordance with the research problem under investigation and that a researcher should not be bound by designs that exist in the literature. Furthermore, it is desirable to develop research designs that follow the philosophy of "multitrait and multimethods" (Campbell and Fiske 1959). The field of consumer research offers significant opportunity for an investigator to be creative in the research design phase; for example, various cross-sectional designs can be complemented by data from longitudinal panels, and survey interviews supplemented by protocol analyses.

DATA COLLECTION

Related to both survey sampling procedures and the increasing number of laboratory experiments are developments in data-collection methods. Owing to the high costs of utilizing personal interviews, newer (and mostly cheaper) data-collection procedures involving telephone interviews, mail, or combinations of mail and telephone are being increasingly explored and implemented in surveys.

In both surveys and experiments, increasing attention has been given to computerized data collection whereby the respondent interacts with a terminal and the use of two-way cable TV, as seen in the QUBE system. The proliferation of home computers, consumers' increasing computer literacy, and the development of computerized interviewing procedures allow for varying the experimental stimuli presented to respondents as a function of earlier responses. The developments such as the Mouse Lab (Johnson et al. 1986) and a software for electronic questionnaire construction and data collection (Johnson 1987) are steps in this direction. These methods will enable a researcher to analyze order effects and sequential response processes. A natural application of these methods is in the determination of adaptive utilities. Of special interest in the area of data collection are the following

- The development of data-collection instruments that overcome the various response bias problems identified by researchers in the decision theory area; these biases include representativeness bias, framing effects, anchoring effects, etc.

- Efforts to use physiological measures to assess consumers' response to stimuli, typically advertising. Among the physiological measures used are heart rate—EKG, electromyographic (EMG) measures, and electroencyphalograph (EEG) brain devices (Rothschild et al. 1988).

The reliability and predictive validity of these measures in consumer research has yet to be determined.

DATA ANALYSIS AND INTERPRETATION

The diversity of data analysis employed in consumer research is no surprise and reflects the increased technological sophistication of consumer researchers and the increased popularity and recognized value of multivariate techniques, including econometrics and psychometric methods. Of the various frameworks for classifying data-analysis methods in consumer research, a framework with three descriptors is used here.[4] The descriptors and categories for each are as follows:

Descriptor	Categories
1. Number of variable sets	One set only, e.g., predictor set.
	Two sets, e.g., one predictor set and one criterion set.
	Three or more sets, e.g., predictor set, process descriptors, and outcome set.
2. Time dimension of data	Cross-sectional, i.e., one point or period in time.
	Time-series, i.e., observations at several points or periods in time.
3. Unit of observation and analysis	Micro-level, e.g., single consumer.
	Macro-level, e.g., a segment of consumers.

The first descriptor, number of variable sets, refers to the way variables are organized for testing relationships. If the focus is on the relationships within one set of variables, the analysis using factor analysis, multidimensional scaling, and similar procedures will be different from that used when two or more sets of variables are involved. The case of two variable sets is most often considered in consumer research, and is well known—multiple regression and analysis of variance are part of this case. Several situations with three or more sets of variables arise in consumer research; for example, consider the problem of relating a set of variables of background descriptors of a sample of consumers and a set of measures of media viewing/reading behavior with a set of measures of consumption of various product categories. Other situations that are relevant are the analysis of a data matrix of people by brands and by attributes in order to determine the underlying dependence structures among the three sets (people, brands, and attributes).

The second descriptor, the time dimension has major implications for the selection of the analysis methods. A cross-sectional study yields data at a single point in time, while time-series provide data at several points in time.[5] Time-series data are usually autocorrelated and require special techniques of analysis. Data collected from a longitudinal panel are also included in the time-series category, although they usually exhibit particular kinds of interdependence of observations (e.g., the correlation matrix among the errors will have a special structure due to the way the data are collected).

The distinction between micro and macro units of analysis requires more elaboration. In general, a micro unit is the smallest unit on which data on consumer choice or on other aspects of consumer behavior can be made. Typically, analysis is done on the same unit on which the data are collected. For example, households, individuals, and organizational decision makers can be conceived of as micro

---

[4]Much of this material is drawn from V. R. Rao, "Books on Quantitative Methods in Consumer Research," *Journal of Consumer Research*, 7 (September), 1980.

[5]While a cross-sectional study may extend over a period of time, only one observation is made on each micro unit during that period.

units.[6] Whenever aggregation is made of the data across a segment (however defined) the unit of analysis becomes a macro unit. As an example, product consumption or sales data reported for a city can be regarded as a macro unit, because city observations are aggregates of sales data that could be observed on smaller units, such as the households or businesses in each city. The reason for this distinction is largely due to the concern that a consumer decision model postulated at the level of a micro unit may not be easily translated into a corresponding model at the macro unit level. Thus, to postulate a micro unit model and estimate parameters using data on macro units can lead to a misleading inference.

Looking from the consumer research perspective, it may appear that the source of data — survey, experiment, or panel — should be separated in this taxonomy. But, there is no need for such additional descriptors since underlying statistical models are essentially the same. For example, denoting the predictor set of variables by X, the criterion variable by Y, and the set of variables describing the experi-

mental design by Z, an analysis model for the experimental data can be written as $Y = f(X, Z) + E$, where E is the set of residuals. Usually, the function, f, is linear in parameters. Depending on the design matrix described by Z, several simplifications can be made. A taxonomy of methods of analysis based on three descriptors — number of sets, time dimension, and level of aggregation — is shown in Figure 14.1. The panels at the bottom of this exhibit indicate major methods of analysis under each category.

The methods can be further classified according to the scale used for measuring the variables (i.e., the nominal, interval, ordinal, or ratio scales). In general, methods for analyzing relationships among variables measured on ordinal scales are technically more advanced than other types of scales. Further, data analysis techniques will also differ according to the distributional assumptions made for the variables. Although available in the literature, nonparametric techniques of data analysis (which do not require specific probability density assumptions) are not extensively employed in consumer research. The details for one such category of methods (Group B or "Dependence Structures") are described in Table 14.2. The multivariate methods shown here are generally available on various university computer systems (with such program systems as SAS) and are generally employed by consumer researchers of Segments 1, 2, and 5.

---

[6]We do recognize that in many buying situations there will be multiple respondents (i.e., the buying center) corresponding to a micro unit. In such cases, almost invariably, some form of aggregation will be necessary to arrive at observations for the micro unit. Processes involved for such aggregations are not considered in this paper.

TABLE 14.2 Multivariate Methods for Study of Relationships Between Two Sets of Variables Using Cross-Sectional Data

Number of Criterion Sets	*Variables in Predictor Set*	*Scale for Predictor Variables*	*SCALE FOR CRITERION VARIABLES*		
			Nominal	*Ordinal*	*Interval*
1	More than 1	Nominal	AID/AID-III	Monotone regression	ANOVA or dummy variable regression
1	More than 1	Interval	Discriminant analysis	Monotone regression	Multiple regression
More than 1	More than 1	Nominal	Canonical correlation with dummy variables	Transform and canonical correlation	Multivariate ANOVA or ANCOVA
More than 1	More than 1	Interval	Discriminant analysis	Transform and canonical correlation	Canonical correlation

Note: The methods of cluster analysis, principal component analysis, and multidimensional scaling of similarity data are not included in this table because they deal with relationships of variables among only one set. Also, the methods of logit, probit, etc. are covered in Group C (see Figure 14.1); they may be included here, if necessary.

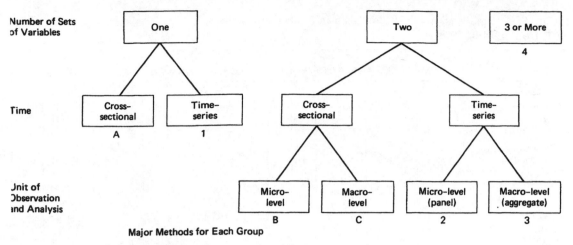

Number of Sets of Variables	One			Two			3 or More

Time	Cross-sectional	Time-series		Cross-sectional		Time-series	
	A	1					

Unit of Observation and Analysis				Micro-level	Macro-level	Micro-level (panel)	Macro-level (aggregate)
				B	C	2	3

Major Methods for Each Group

Group	Major Method
A	Factor analytic methods, including principal components analysis Cluster analysis Multidimensional scaling methods for similarity data Correspondence Analysis
B	Dependence Structure Methods
C	Multidimensional contingency analysis (e.g., loglinear model building, logit, probit, and tobit)
1	Time–series analysis
2	Stochastic modeling
3	Econometric techniques
4	Three mode factor analysis and three way methods

FIGURE 14.1 A Taxonomy of Data Analysis Situations for Consumer Research

Since the methodology of conjoint analysis[7] has been extensively used in consumer research, particularly by the consumer research practitioners, one may think that the underlying multivariate analysis methods are drastically different. This, however, is not the case. They are based on the methods of multivariate analysis covered in Table 14.2. But, the methodology of conjoint analysis is rather unique with respect to the design of the instrument for data collection (as noted earlier), and the way

these results are utilized for answering certain applied issues, such as the determination of characteristics of an optimal product. We will discuss these considerations later in the paper.

The diversity of data analysis methods employed in studies published in *JCR* since its inception in 1974 until 1989 is illustrated in Figure 14.2. It is clear from this exhibit that the *JCR* articles have relied quite extensively on two basic techniques—ANOVA and Regression—for analyzing the data reported. Further, the usage of other multivariate methods is quite sporadic; methods that call for knowledge of advanced statistics (e.g., canonical correlation and LISREL) have received limited use in the *JCR* articles. We believe that researchers have employed relevant methods of analysis for their

---

[7]Review papers have been prepared on both MDS (Green 1975) and conjoint analysis applications (Green and Srinivasan 1978, 1989). Marketing-oriented applications of MDS have been described in the book by Green and Rao (1972), and applications of MDS and conjoint analysis have appeared in the book by Green and Wind (1973).

FIGURE 14.2   Data Analysis Methods Used in Studies Published
in *JCR* from 1974 to 1989

Techniques	Year 1974	1975	1976	1977	1978	1979	1980	1981	1982	1983	1984	1985	1986	1987	1988	Total	%
Simple Methods																	
Cross tabs	2	1	2	3	5	1	1	3	3	3	2	6	—	—	—	32	8
T-test	—	2	1	1	1	—	1	—	1	1	1	1	2	4	1	17	4
Correlation Analysis	—	4	4	—	—	4	1	1	2	1	—	—	6	3	2	28	7
Methods in Group A																	
Factor Analysis	1	1	—	2	1	1	2	1	2	3	2	3	1	2	2	24	6
Cluster Analysis	2	—	—	—	—	—	—	—	—	—	1	—	1	—	1	5	1
MDS	3	1	2	—	—	1	—	—	1	1	—	—	1	—	—	10	2
Methods in Group B																	
Regression	4	2	5	6	2	3	12	12	6	8	9	5	6	7	5	92	22
ANOVA	4	3	4	5	4	2	7	3	7	3	10	12	5	9	17	95	23
ANCOVA	—	—	—	—	1	—	1	—	—	2	1	—	6	2	—	13	3
Discriminant Analysis	2	—	3	1	1	2	2	4	1	4	—	2	1	—	—	23	5
MANOVA, MANCOVA	—	2	1	—	1	2	1	2	6	1	2	1	4	5	5	33	8
Canonical Correlation	—	—	—	—	—	—	—	—	—	—	—	—	2	—	—	2	—
Path Analysis	—	2	—	1	2	2	—	1	—	2	—	—	—	1	—	11	3
Causal Modeling (LISREL)	—	—	—	—	2	—	2	1	1	1	3	1	3	1	1	16	4
Conjoint Analysis	—	1	1	1	2	3	—	5	4	—	—	1	1	—	—	19	4
Total	18	19	23	20	22	21	30	33	34	30	31	32	39	34	34	420	100

specific data analysis situations. It is also impressive that the *Journal of Consumer Research* has paid attention to the utilization of various data analytic methods for exploring the decision processes of consumers (e.g., MDS, cluster analysis, etc.).

The discussion in this section will be confined to the methods used in Groups A, B, and C. The time-series analysis techniques, methods of stochastic modeling, econometric methods, and three-way techniques referred to as Groups 1 through 4 respectively, are too broad to be covered in this chapter. The reader is referred to Massy et al. (1970), Thiel (1978), Box and Jenkins (1976), Tukey (1977), and Griliches and Intrilligator (1984).

Methods in Group A

In the analysis of interdependence structures (where one is interested in the mutual relationships among a set of variables and/or objects), consumer researchers have applied all the three major sets of techniques identified: factor analysis, cluster analysis, and multidimensional scaling of similarity data. The technique of correspondence analysis is only beginning to be applied in consumer research.

Factor analysis has a long tradition in consumer research, primarily due to the large number of variables on which buyer information is usually obtained. With the increased use in consumer research of the study of consumers' lifestyles, attitudes, interests, activities, and personality measures, factor analysis has achieved a new round of popularity (Wells 1974) typically among the members of Segment 5. In a typical psychographic study (or VALS/ Study), consumers are shown a large list of statements (e.g., "Friends usually come to me for advice on what kinds of hair care products to buy.") and are asked to indicate on a five- to seven-point scale how well each phrase describes them (from "not at all" to "very closely"). Factor analysis is then used to examine underlying groups of statements (i.e., factor loading patterns) and to compute factor scores of each respondent on the underlying dimensions of interest. The most commonly used version of factor analysis in consumer research is principal component analysis, followed by varimax rotation of retained components to approximate "simple structure," in which each variable correlates "highly" with one (and only one) factor.

Early applications of factor analysis to consumer research include studies by Ehrenberg (1968) on the identification of segments who watch different types of TV programs, by Sheth (1968) on brand loyalty measures, and by Stoetzel (1960) on liquor preferences. Consumer researchers have also been interested in various extensions of factor-analytic methods, including three-mode factor analysis (Tucker (1966), higher-order factor analysis (Wind, Green, and Jain 1973), confirmatory methods (Joreskog 1970), and asymmetric factor analysis (Harshman, Green, Wind, and Lundy 1982).

Cluster analysis also has received limited attention in consumer research, but is widely used in marketing research. Use of these techniques is a natural outgrowth of researchers' interest in market segmentation and product positioning. Recent methodological developments, such as overlapping clusters, have been adapted quickly for marketing research (Arabie, Carroll, DeSarbo, and Wind 1981). This methodology is of specific interest since it allows for the reexamination and relaxation of basic concepts, such as the time-honored belief that each consumer belongs to one and only one segment; consumers may belong to multiple segments once the use situation (or context of consumption) is brought into analysis. Another important approach is the DEDICOM method for the analysis of asymmetric data in marketing research Harshman (1981) and Harshman et al. (1982).

Multidimensional scaling methods are concerned with the representation of individuals' judgments regarding the relative similarities of pairs of objects (e.g., brands of automobiles) measured on interval or ordinal scales, as distance relations on points in a multidimensional space. Each point corresponds to a brand, and interpoint distances among the brands correspond in certain ways to the judged similarities data. In addition to the development of models for dealing with the analysis of data on judged similarities, algorithms[8] also have been prepared for analyzing preference data (Carroll 1972), using ideal point and vector models—models in which an individual's preference is highest at a finite value of an attribute of the object and in which preferences increase with the increasing (or the decreasing) value of the attribute. Researchers have also linked MDS methods with cluster analysis. Other MDS methods include the use of compositional approaches such as multiple discriminant analysis (Johnson 1971).

Cliff (1973) reviews developments prior to 1973 in both unidimensional and multidimensional scaling, while the Carroll and Arabie (1980) study focuses on MDS methods since 1973. Interestingly, Carroll and Arabie's definition of MDS is broad in that they do not limit the term to spatial distance models for similarities data; their purview includes nonspatial (e.g., discrete geometric models, such as tree structures) and nondistance (e.g., scalar product or projection) models. They also provide a useful taxonomy for organizing the diverse methodological developments in this field.

Consumer researchers were among the first to apply MDS to substantive problems; see Volume II of *Multidimensional Scaling* by Shepard et al. (1972). Since then, numerous applications have appeared, primarily in the *Journal of Marketing Research,* the *Journal of Marketing,* and the *Journal of Consumer Research.* Today, MDS methodology is a commonly used technique in market segmentation research and product positioning, primarily as a way to provide diagnostic information regarding consumers' perceptions of and preferences for a brand relative to its competitors. Moreover, the graphical aspects of the methodology, yielding perceptual and preference "maps" of competing products and services, has unquestionably contributed to its popularity in the study of consumer behavior, especially as it relates to marketing.

Until recently, MDS was geometric rather than statistical in nature; little was available in the form of statistical tests regarding appropri-

---

[8]Again, these methods come under Group B, where one set of variables is related to another set. In principle, these methods are akin to conjoint analysis.

ate dimensionality and the statistical stability of points in a particular configuration. Lately, however, Ramsay (1977, 1978) has developed a maximum likelihood procedure for MDS parameter estimation. Other researchers (Weinberg et al. 1981) have used jackknifing methods to establish confidence regions. Other developments in MDS include the introduction of scaling solutions for various types of data (such as "pick k out of n" and other hinds of choice data) and the constraining or reparameterizing of MDS solutions to stimulus and person characteristics (Green, Carroll, and Carmone 1976; DeSarbo and Hoffman 1987; DeSarbo and Rao 1986). These developments enable the researcher to conduct reverse mapping—determining the physical characteristics of an object that will correspond to a particular position in a perceptual space—an issue that has significantly limited the appeal of MDS for several practical consumer research problems.[9]

The technique of *correspondence analysis,* associated with the work of Benzecri (1973), is quite similar in principle to that of multidimensional scaling of similarities data. Using a distance measure, which is a modified version of a chi-square measure between any two rows (or columns), correspondence analysis develops a spatial representation of both the row points and column points in a two-way contingency table. The procedure is a compact way to represent relationships in a table. The method generalizes quite easily to multiway tables. An expository account (with associated algorithms) has been described by Greenacre (1984). In two papers, the relationships between correspondence analysis and multidimensional scaling are elaborated (Carroll, Green, and Schaffer 1986, 1987).

The methods described under this group offer continued potential for consumer research, owing to the possibility of condensing large amounts of data and providing for spatial rep-

resentations of relationships among constructs (e.g., attributes, brands, etc.). However, researchers should be concerned with their limitations. Validation of results is necessary not only for factor analysis but also for all of the methods. In addition, statistical properties of the results from MDS are not well investigated, and the researcher should be careful in interpreting the relationships between points from one set and points from a different set while using correspondence analysis.

Methods in Group B

Consumer researchers have employed all of the following techniques for the analysis of dependence structures[10] (i.e., relating one set to another set of variables):

- multiple regression;
- analysis of variance (ANOVA) and analysis of covariance (ANCOVA);
- discriminant analysis, two-group and multiple-group;
- canonical correlation, multivariate analysis of variance (MANOVA) and covariance (MANCOVA); and
- automatic interaction detection (AID) and the related procedures, such as THAID, MAID, MCA, and CHAID.

The focus in the consumer research literature (and especially in *JCR*) has been, however, on the application of these methods rather than on new methodological developments relating to these methods. In consumer research, as in most applied areas, *multiple regression* is still the workhorse technique. While employing regression analysis, the researcher has to make sure that the basic assumptions of the method are satisfied for the data analyzed: the linearity of parameters (usually the effects of the variables), the homoscedasticity of errors, a lack of multicollinearity, and a lack of serial correlation.

---

[9]While consumer and marketing researchers have not adopted these recent developments as yet, there is every reason to believe that more statistically based MDS methods will gain favor in consumer research, just as the precursor models have before them.

[10]The methods of the logit, probit, and tobit models may fall under this group, but they will be covered later under Group C. The only difference will be with respect to the level of aggregation.

When these assumptions are not satisfied, various extended methods of regression such as constrained regression, nonlinear regression, ridge regression, and robust regression should be considered and applied.

Applications of regression models run the gamut from econometrics-type applications to studies in the measurement of consumer attitudes (Ginter 1979). More methodologically based papers, dealing with discrete dependent variable regression and test reliability, have been published in marketing journals.

Analysis of variance and analysis of covariance (ANOVA and ANCOVA) have been used extensively in consumer research, primarily in analysis of experimental data. Virtually all classes of experimental design factorials, repeated measures, incomplete block designs, and partial factorials of various types have been utilized. Consumer researchers of Segment 1 have generally been utilizing ANOVA-type methods in order to detect interaction effects among the independent (or experimental) factors in an experiment. But, rescaling of the dependent variable (using some type of monotone transformation) before performing ANOVA can, in many cases, remove the presence of interactions. It is somewhat surprising that this monotone approach to analysis of variance (see Kruskal, 1964; Green and Rao, 1969) has not been systematically integrated into the repertoire of analysis methods used by members of Segment 1.

Discriminant analysis also has been applied to consumer behavior studies; a priori selected groups include loyal customers versus switchers, buyers of different brands in a product class, and so on. Canonical correlation has received less attention, primarily because of the difficulty in interpreting canonical variates.

On the other hand, *model-free methods,* such as Automatic Interaction Detection, Multiple Classification Analysis (Andrews, Morgan, and Sonquist 1971), THAID (Morgan and Messenger 1973), MAID (Maclachlan and Johansson 1981), CHAID (Perreault and Barksdale 1980), and CART (Breiman, Friedman, Olshen, and Stone (1984) have received more attention, especially in marketing. Automatic Interaction Detection, the prototype of methods of this type, takes an interval-scaled or dichotomous dependent variable and employs a binary splitting and search procedure that breaks down the total sample into more homogenous subgroups whose between-group sums of squares are large with respect to the dependent variable.

The popularity of such data analysis procedures is probably explained by the large data bases that marketing researchers are often faced with and by the paucity of substantive theory to guide the selection of appropriate predictor variables. Thus, the results from these analytical methods will invariably need to be validated. Also, most of these techniques incorporate simple ways to summarize and display the output, such as a tree diagram showing the sequence of binary splits, dependent-variable means, and group sample sizes.

Since the early 1980s, *covariance structure analysis* (also referred to as structural equation models, causal modeling, and multivariate analysis with latent variables) have been increasing in popularity among consumer researchers. The primary methodological developments have come from psychometricians (e.g., Joreskog 1970). An expository account from the viewpoint of a psychologist appears in the review by Bentler (1980). Bagozzi (1980) provides a comprehensive account of the methodology in applications to marketing and consumer research, and a special issue of *JMR* on the topic appeared in 1983. One of the major applications of LISREL has been the development of a measurement model when the variables measured contain error. The LISREL computer program package (Joreskog and Sorbom 1978) has been the methodology that most consumer and marketing researchers have applied.

As pointed out earlier, applications of ANOVA in consumer research may suffer from the need to rescale the dependent variable. This issue raises some fundamental problems in measurement. In addition, LISREL has not received extensive application, partly due to the technical sophistication needed for implementing the analysis. Further, there is room for using multiple methods in data analysis to ensure that the results are robust and are not susceptible to certain special assumptions of the specific techniques used.

Methods in Group C

The methods under this category refer to the analysis of aggregated data collected in a cross-section study (survey or experiment). The focus typically is on developing an aggregate relationship between the categorization of a unit on some variable of interest and certain descriptors of the unit. In that sense, the methods bear a significant resemblance to those in Group B. However, the approaches used are quite sophisticated and are relevant to variables measured on categorical scales. These techniques typically involve construction of multidimensional contingency tables and analysis using log-linear models; these have come to be known as discrete multivariate analysis (see Feinberg 1977; Bishop, Feinberg, and Holland 1975).

A related set of models that has become particularly popular consists of multinomial logit models. Here, the dependent variable is categorical and the predictor variables can be either categorical, continuous, or mixtures thereof. Essentially, logit models are being used to represent aspects of multiattribute choice in which the selection of some brands from a product class, or some transportation mode from a set of alternatives, are the types of behavior being modeled.

McFadden (1973; 1980) provided a random utility framework of an individual's choice that led to the multinomial logit model. Given this theoretical view, the model has received considerable attention in consumer research. Most applications of logit models in consumer research studies assume that the logit is a linear (in the parameters) function of a set of predictor variables that denote various attributes of the choice objects (e.g., brands) and choosers of the choice objects. Parameters are typically estimated by some type of maximum likelihood procedure. Other procedures that are relevant here are the multivariate probit model (Rao and Winter 1978), tobit model (Kinsey 1981),

and various extensions of the logit model (e.g., DOGIT developed by Gaudry and Dagenais 1977).

Conjoint Analysis

A detailed discussion of the technique of conjoint analysis is perhaps appropriate, owing to the considerable attention it has received in consumer and marketing research. With its origin in psychometrics, the method enables a researcher to decompose the evaluative judgments of a multiattributed item (obtained on an ordinal, categorical, or interval scale) to part-contributions (called part-worths) of each of the attributes. The seminal paper is that of Luce and Tukey (1964), dealing with conjoint measurement, which specifies the conditions under which there exist measurement scales for both the response and control variables, given the order of the joint effects of the control variables and a prespecified composition rule.

Consumer researchers, however, have been less interested in the axiomatic and hypothesis testing aspects of conjoint analysis than in the scaling procedure itself, assuming that a particular composition rule is applicable. Hence, Green and Srinivasan (1978) employ the term conjoint analysis to distinguish the scaling intention from the original motivation. Given its emphasis on the scaling aspects, conjoint analysis closely resembles other techniques proposed for modeling subjective judgments (Hoffman, Slovic, and Rorer 1968; Anderson 1970; Dawes and Corrigan 1974).

Not surprisingly, significant methodological developments have been made to this field by the same researchers (e.g., Kruskal 1965; Young 1969; Carroll 1969) who have contributed so importantly to MDS methodology. Since conjoint analysis was introduced to consumer and marketing research by Green and his colleagues in the early 1970s (Green and Rao 1971, 1972), followed by the special case of trade-off analysis (Johnson 1974), consumer and marketing researchers have enthusiastically applied these techniques to thousands of studies in industry and nonprofit organizations (Cattin and Wittink 1989).

As described by Green and Srinivasan (1978), the conjoint analysis model embraces the special cases of the vector model and the ideal point model of preferences.

Conjoint methods are used to obtain each individual's utility function. Through the use of highly fractionated designs, part-worths can be estimated for a fraction of all the combinations that would be implied by the full Cartesian product of all attribute levels employed in designing the stimulus profiles. The two most commonly used techniques for obtaining the part-worths are OLS and the LINMAP algorithm (Shocker and Srinivasan 1977). In a variety of empirical comparisons with competing algorithms, LINMAP has performed quite well.

Once the utility functions are obtained (one for each individual), a typical conjoint analysis study will employ a consumer choice simulator in which new product ideas are tested to see what share of choice each would receive if introduced as a competitor to existing products in the marketplace. This simulation posits one or more rules of consumer choice among alternatives offered to an individual. It is the choice simulation step that has contributed to the widespread popularity of the conjoint methodology.

Prompted by the apparent success of the methodology in choice simulation studies, marketing researchers have developed extensions to provide optimal product designs, rather than providing simply the best of a relatively few profiles that may be tested in the simulator. Contributions by Shocker and Srinivasan (1977), Urban (1975), Albers and Brockhoff (1977), Gavish et al. (1981), Hauser and Simmie (1981), Zufryden (1979), Pessemier (1982), Green and Wind (1973), and Green et al. (1983, 1989) illustrate efforts in this direction.

From a statistical standpoint, the last approach utilizes response surface methods (Box et al. 1978) to find a function that relates the criterion variable of interest (cash flow, sales, market share, etc.) to the product design variables. It is this function that is then optimized.

As a relatively inexpensive way to estimate consumer preferences for alternative product formulations and marketing strategy variables (e.g., different price levels, promotional messages, etc.), conjoint analysis already has demonstrated its value as a way of understanding consumer behavior and helping marketers improve their marketing decisions.

We may offer a few comments on the process of utilizing the vast array of behavioral methods available to a consumer researcher. First, it is essential that defensible conceptual bases be developed before selecting a particular method. Rather than being solely directed by the available methods, the researcher should first examine the assumptions needed for applying a particular method of analysis and evaluate the suitability of the method selected. The situations where assumptions are not satisfied will offer avenues not only for method development but also for developments in the substantive aspects of research. Finally, a researcher should evaluate the robustness of the results (if necessary by using Monte Carlo simulation techniques) obtained by the method in general and should provide validation of results reported for the particular problem on hand. The techniques such as split-half validation or jack-knife validation should become an integral part of behavioral research.

Other Emerging Methods

We will organize the discussion of emerging methods under two categories: (1) new approaches of data collection emerging in consumer research, and (2) new data-analysis approaches potentially valuable to consumer research. Table 14.3 lists some of the details for four of the five segments of consumer researchers identified earlier (the discussion for Segment 3, behavioral theorist, is too broad for inclusion in this chapter). While not intended to be comprehensive, we highlight some of the new trends, which in our opinion will have an impact on the field.

Increasingly, the academic consumer researchers have relied on protocol and content analysis, and its more recent offspring, the interpretive approach.

TABLE 14.3 Some Emerging Methods

Segment	Data Collection	Data Analysis
Academic Consumer Researcher	• Process Tracing Methods (e.g., protocol)	• Content Analysis and Other Interpretive Approaches • Meta Analysis
Marketing Scientist	• Analytic Hierarchy Process • Pattern Recognition	• Exploratory Data Analysis
Behavioral Science Methodologist	• Pattern Recognition	• Network Analysis • Duration Modeling • Even History Analysis • Cohort Analysis • Q-Methodology
Consumer Research Practitioner		• Exploratory Data Analysis

Process Tracing Methods (e.g., Protocol analysis) go back to the pioneering work of Clarkson (1963), and the Bettman developments of decision net models (1974). Protocol studies have been useful in describing and understanding the consumer decision process, but the complexity of such data-collection procedures has greatly reduced the use of this approach. More recently, a number of decision theory researchers have developed computer programs that use the computer as a way of gathering protocol type data (Johnson 1989). These developments are likely to increase the use and usefulness of protocol methods.

Content analysis, especially of ads, has been employed to evaluate how much information is available to consumers (Anderson 1970), the changing roles of women in society (Courtney and Lockertz 1971), the use of racial images in advertising (Kassarjian 1969, 1977), and advertising's contribution to various societal characteristics (and values) such as materialism (Belk and Pollay 1985a, 1985b; Tse, Belk, and Zhou 1989), and consumer behavior.

Many of the better content analysis studies have taken great care in the development of a set of definitions and in the careful conduct of the content analysis (by two independent researchers). This is followed by an analysis of the coding reliability of the judges, a reconciliation of differences between them, a recoding of the categories factor analyzing them, and the relating of the content categories to some behavior of interest (such as ad recall or attitude toward the ad introduced by the advertised product, etc.).

Interpretive approaches are a recent extension of the traditional content analysis. Hirschman (1988), for example, employed the approach to decode the consumption ideology embedded with the "Dallas" and "Dynasty" TV programs. Her approach is a hybrid of the structuralism of Levi-Strauss (1965, 1981) and the narrative syntactical method of Greimas (1970).

Holbrook (1987), another pioneer of interpretive approach to study consumption behavior and of the postpositivistic movement of consumer behavior, presents in a rejoinder (with O'Shaughnessy) to the Calder and Tybout (1987) reply to his original article a cogent and strong argument for the need for interpretive perspective in consumer research and even takes the extreme position that all knowledge and all science depends on interpretation. [See also the volume on this topic published by the Association of Consumer Research (1989) and the views of Hudson and Ozanne (1988)].

Meta-analysis is emerging as a viable method of analysis to seek generalizations across a diverse set of empirical studies in a particular subarea of consumer research. Johnson and Eagley (1989) present an illustration of this approach in evaluating the effects of involvement on persuasion. General references for meta-analysis include Hunter et al. (1982) and Farley and Lehmann (1986). Johnson (1989) has developed a software for conducting meta-analysis of research literatures.

PARADIGM SHIFTS IN CONSUMER RESEARCH

The dominant consumer research paradigm of the last two decades is changing. The changes encompass all segments of consumer researchers and may be related to the stage of maturation of the consumer research tradition in each segment.

The academic consumer researchers have gone through a significant narrowing of the scope of their research. During the first ten years of *JCR* (1974–1984), about 12 percent of the published articles focused on information processing. In contrast, in the last five years of the journal, about 44 percent of all published articles were on information processing. The emergence of the "postpositivist," humanistic, interpretive research approach as demonstrated, for example, in the work of Belk, Wallendorf, and Sherry (1989), Hirschman (1986), and Holbrook and O'Shaughnessy (1988) can be viewed as a healthy reaction to the "narrowing" of the discipline. The renewed interest in motivation (10 percent of the articles in the last five years versus 2 percent in the first ten years of *JCR*) may also be viewed as a healthy reaction against the dominance of cognitive psychology in consumer research.

The marketing scientists and consumer research practitioners have moved further away from the academic consumer researchers and, in general, are focussing on those aspects of consumer behavior that are of greater value to marketing decisions. Their research paradigm is thus shifting toward approaches that increase the reliability, validity, and value of their findings. This stream of research starts moving toward a design that incorporates the following:

- *More realistic unit of analysis.* From the traditional and almost exclusive focus on the individual to a focus on the family buying unit, this realistic unit also includes the assessment of the multiple roles of family members, by stages, in the buying and consumption decision process.
- *From single purchase to an assortment of products.* Most consumer research takes as the dependent variable a single purchase transaction. Yet, most households maintain inventories of brands for different family members, for variety purposes, or for consumption under different situations. Incorporating a product assortment perspective in consumer research is therefore a must.
- *From general behavior to situational specific purchase and consumption.* With a few notable exceptions, most consumer research studies do not take into account the situational factors that can affect purchase and consumption behavior. Incorporating situational variables in most consumer research would help improve the validity and value of the research.
- *From deterministic to stochastic modeling of consumer behavior.* Since the mid-1950s, considerable attention has been given to stochastic brand choice models. Yet, this modeling tradition has had little effect on the more traditional studies of consumer behavior. Realizing the stochasticity of consumer behavior would have significant implications for most consumer research approaches.
- *From a lopsided focus on the U.S. consumer to an understanding of consumer behavior around the world.* The globalization of the business environment requires greater focus on cross-cultural research instruments, which are both sensitive to idiosyncratic characteristics of the various cultures and capable of comparing and contrasting the results.
- *From a "low tech" environment of consumer behavior to a "high tech" environment, using advanced consumer research instruments.* Enormous and continual advances in computers and telecommunication technology are changing the nature of consumer behavior and also have significant implications for new innovative research methods.
- *From a single research approach to an integrated set of methods.* Whereas much of current research utilizes a single, dominant method, many of the more useful studies incorporate a number of methods. Conjoint analysis-based studies, which incorporate and link MDS and include clustering with a variety of multivariate statistical techniques and optimization models, are a good example of the type of research system that is emerging.

Consumer research conducted by researchers from other behavioral science disciplines is getting increased attention as many of the researchers find the rich context of consumer behavior to be an exciting domain for testing their concepts and methods. This is likely to lead to a new stream of new consumer research tools, providing for greater integration and cross-fertilization between consumer behavior and the other behavioral sciences.

CONCLUSIONS

The academic consumer research tradition has primarily concerned itself with applying (we hope in a competent and meticulous way) many of the available social science research methods. Its major shortcomings have been a lack of methodological innovation and a paucity of truly creative methodological approaches.

It is our hope that the invisible barriers that separate the segments of consumer researchers fall, and that greater intellectual exchange and openness takes place among the five segments. The resulting research will be of greater value to the academic and industrial clients of consumer researchers and of greater intellectual excitement.

REFERENCES

ALBERS, S., and K. BROCKHOFF (1977). "A Procedure for New Product Positioning in an Attribute Space," *European Journal Operation Research*, 1, 230–238.

ALLENBY, G. M., and R. C. BLATTBERG (1987). "A New Theory of Direct Market Testing: Why Rollout Results Do Not Match Test Results," *Journal of Direct Marketing* (Autumn), 24–37.

ALLISON, P. D. (1984). *Event History Analysis*. Beverly Hills, CA: Sage.

ANDERSON, N. H. (1970). "Functional Measurement and Psychophysical Judgment," *Psychology Review*, 77, 153–170.

ANDREWS, F. M., J. N. MORGAN, and J. A. SONQUIST (1971). *Multiple Classification Analysis*. Ann Arbor, MI: University of Michigan Press.

ANDREN, GUNNAR (1980). "The Rhetoric of Advertising," *Journal of Communications*, 30 (August), 74–80.

ARABIE, P., J. D. CARROLL, W. DESARBO, and Y. WIND (1981). "Overlapping Clustering: A New Method for Product Positioning," *Journal of Marketing Research*, 18, 310–317.

ASSOCIATION FOR CONSUMER RESEARCH (1989). *Interpretive Consumer Research*. Provo, UT: Association for Consumer Research.

BAGOZZI, R. P. (1980). *Causal Models in Marketing*. New York: Wiley.

BELK, RUSSELL W., and R. W. POLLAY (1985a). "Images of Ourselves: The Good Life in Twentieth Century Advertising," *Journal of Consumer Research*, 11, 887–897.

BELK, RUSSELL W., and R. W. POLLAY (1985b). "Materialism and Status Appeals in Japanese and U.S. Print Advertising: An Historical and Cross-Cultural Content Analysis," *International Marketing Review*, 2 (December), 38–47.

BELK, R. W., M. WALLENDORF, and J. F. SHERRY (1989). 'The Sacred and the Profane in Consumer Behaviory: Theodicy on the Odyssey," *Journal of Consumer Research*, 16, 1–38.

BENTLER, P. M. (1980). "Multivariate Analysis with Latent Variables: Casual Modeling," *Annual Review of Psychology*, 31, 419–456.

BENZERCI, J. (1973). *L'Analyse des Donnees*. Paris: Dunod.

BETTMAN, J. R. (1974). "Toward a Statistics for Consumer Decision Net Model," *Journal of Consumer Research*, 1, 71–80.

BISHOP, Y. M. M., S. E. FEINBERG, and P. W. HOLLAND (1977). *Discrete Multivariate Analysis*. Cambridge, MA: M.I.T. Press.

BLATTBERG, R. C. (1979). "The Decision of Advertising Experiments Using Statistical Decision Theory," *Journal of Marketing Research*, 16, 191–202.

BOX, G. E. P., W. G. HUNTER, and J. S. HUNTER (1978). *Statistics for Experimenters*. New York: Wiley.

BOX, G. E. P., and G. M. JENKINS (1976). *Time Series Analysis: Forecasting and Control*. Oakland, CA: Holden-Day.

BREIMAN, L., J. H. FRIEDMAN, R. A. OLSHEN, and C. J. STONE (1984). *Classification and Regression Trees*. Belmont, CA: Wadsworth International Group.

BUCHANAN, B. S., and D. G. MORRISON (1985). "Measuring Simple Preferences: An Approach to Blind, Forced Choice Product Testing," *Marketing Science*, 4, 93–109.

BURT, R. S. ET AL. (Forthcoming). *Applied Network Analysis: A Methodological Introduction*. Beverly Hills, CA: Sage.

BUZZELL, R. D. (ED.) (1985). *Marketing in an Electronic Age.* Boston, MA: Harvard Business School Press.

CALDER, B. J., and A. M. TYBOUT (1987). "What Consumer Research Is . . . ," *Journal of Consumer Research,* 114, 136–140.

CAMPBELL, D. T, and D. W. FISKE (1959). "Convergent and Discriminant Validity by the Multi-trait-Multimethod Matrix," *Psychological Bulletin,* 56, 81–105.

CARROLL, J. D. (69). "Categorical Conjoint Measurement," Meeting of Mathematical Psychology, Ann Arbor, MI.

CARROLL, J. D. (1972). "Individual Differences in Multidimensional Scaling," in *Multidimensional Scaling.* Vol. I. R. N. Shepard, A. K. Romney, and S. B. Nerlove, Eds. New York: Seminar Press, 105–157.

CARROLL, J. D., P. E. GREEN, and C. M. SCHAFFER (1986). "Interpoint Distance Comparisons in Correspondence Analysis," *Journal of Marketing Research,* 23, 271–280.

CARROLL, J. D., P. E. GREEN, and C. M. SCHAFFER (1987). "Comparing Interpoint Distances in Correspondence Analysis: A Clarification," *Journal of Marketing Research,* 26, 445–450.

CARROLL, J. D., and P. ARABIE (1980). "Multidimensional Scaling," in *Annual Review of Psychology,* M. R. Rosenzweig and L. W. Porters, Eds. Palo Alto, CA: Annual Reviews.

CARROLL, J. D., and J. J. CHANG (1970). "Analysis of Individual Differences in Multidimensional Scaling via an N-Way Generalization of Eckart-Young Decomposition," *Psychometrika,* 35, 283–319.

CATTIN, P., and D. R. WITTINK (1989). " Commercial Use of Conjoint Analysis: An Update," *Journal of Marketing,* 53 (July), 21–96.

CATTIN, P., and D. R. WITTINK (1981). "A Monte-Carlo Study of Metric and Nonmetric Estimation Methods for Multiattribute Models," *Journal of Marketing Research,* 18, 101–106.

CHARLTON, P., A. S. C. EHRENBERG, and B. PYMONT (1972). "Buyer Behavior Under Mini-Test Conditions," *Journal of Market Research Society,* 14, 171–183.

CLIFF, N. (1973). "Scaling," in *Annual Review of Psychology,* P. H. Mussen and M. R. Rosenzweig, Eds. Palo Alto, CA: Annual Reviews.

COCHRAN, W. G. (1977). *Sampling Techniques,* 3rd. ed. New York: Wiley.

COCHRAN, W. G., and G. M. COX, (1957). *Experimental Designs.* New York: Wiley.

COOMBS, C. H. (1964). *A Theory of Data.* New York: Wiley.

COURTNEY, ALICE, E., and SARAH W. LOCKERTZ (1971). "A Woman's Place: An Analysis of the Roles Portrayed by Women in Magazine Advertisements," *Journal of Marketing Research,* 8, 92–95.

CUSTER, S., and J. T. PLUMMER (1986). "Trend Setters Can't Afford to Await Traditional Data," *Marketing News,* 20, No. 16 (August 1).

DAWES, R. M., and B. CORRIGAN (1974). "Linear Models in Decision Making," *Psychology Bulletin,* 81, 95–106.

DAY, GEORGE S. (1970). *Buyer Attitudes and Brand Choice Behavior.* New York: The Free Press.

DeSARBO, W., and D. HOFFMAN (1987). "Constructing MDS Joint Spaces from Binary Choice Data: A Multidimensional Unfolding Threshold Model for Marketing Research," 24, 40–54.

DeSARBO, W., and V. R. RAO (1986). "A Constrained Unfolding Methodology for Product Positioning," *Marketing Science,* 1, 1–19.

EHRENBERG, A. S. C. (1968). "On Methods: The Factor Analysis Search for Program Types," *Journal of Advertising Research,* 8, 55–70.

EHRENBERG, A. S. C. (1971). "Predicting the Performance of New Brands," *Journal of Advertising Research,* 17, 11–17.

EHRENBERG, A. S. C. (1972). *Repeat-Buying: Theory and Applications.* Amsterdam-London: North-Holland.

FARLEY, J. U., and D. R. LEHMANN (1986). *Meta-Analysis in Marketing: Generalization of Response Models.* Lexington, MA: Lexington.

FARLEY, J. U., and L. W. RING (1970). "An Empirical Test of the Howard-Sheth Model of Buyer Behavior," *Journal of Marketing Research,* 7 (November), 427–438.

FEINBERG, S. E. (1977). *The Analysis of Cross-Classified Categorical Data.* Cambridge, MA: The MIT Press.

FORNELL, C., and D. F. LARCKER (1981). "Evaluating Structural Equation Models with Unobservable Variables and Measurement Error," *Journal of Marketing Research,* 18, 9–50.

FRANKEL, M. R., and L. R. FRANKEL (1977). "Some Recent Development in Sample Survey Design," *Journal of Marketing Research,* 14, 280–293.

FREEMAN, L. C., D. R. WHITE, and A. K. ROMNEY, EDS. (1986). *Research Methods in Social Network Analysis.* Fairfax, VA: George Mason University Press.

GAUDRY, M., and M. DAGENAIS (1977). The DOGIT Model. Montreal, Que.: Centre de Recherche sur les Transports, University of Montreal.

GAVISH, B., D. HORSKY, and K. SRIKANTH (1981). "Optimal Positioning of a New Product," *Management Science, 29,* 1277–1297.

GINTER, J. L. (1979). "A Discussion of Methodological Developments," *Advances,* 6, 589–591.

GINTER, J. L. (1974). "An Experimental Investigation of Attitude Change and Choice of a New Brand," *Journal of Marketing Research,* 11, 30–40.

GOODMAN, L. A. (1984). *The Analysis of Cross-Classified Data Having Ordered Categories.* Cambridge, MA: Harvard University Press.

GRAHAM, JOHN L., DONG KI KIM, CHI-YUAN LIN, and MICHAEL ROBINSON (1988). "Buyer-Seller Negotiations Around the Pacific Rim: Differences in Fundamental Exchange Processes," 15, 48–54.

GREEN, P. E., and A. M. KRIEGER (1989). "Recent Contributions to Optimal Product Positioning and Buyer Segmentation," Working Paper, Wharton School, University of Pennsylvania, PA.

GREEN, P. E. (1963). "Bayesian Statistics and Product Decision," *Business Horizons,* 5, 101–109.

GREEN, P. E., and J. D. CARROLL (1976). *Mathematical Tools for Applied Multivariate Analysis.* New York: Academic Press.

GREEN, P. E. (1975). "Marketing Applications of MDS: Assessment and Outlook." *Journal of Marketing,* 38, 24–31.

GREEN, P. E., S. M. GOLDBERG, and J. B. WILEY (1983). "A Cross-Validation Test of Hybrid Conjoint Models," *Advances,* 10, 147–150.

GREEN, P. E., and V. R. RAO (1972). *Applied Multidimensional Scaling: A Comparison of Approaches and Algorithms.* New York: Holt, Rinehart & Winston.

GREEN, P. E., and V. R. RAO (1977). "Nonmetric Approaches to Multivariate Analysis in Marketing," in *Multivariate Methods for Market and Survey Research.* J. N. Sheth, Ed. Chicago: American Marketing Association.

GREEN, P. E., and V. SRINIVASAN (1978). "Conjoint Analysis in Consumer Research: Issues and Outlook," *Journal of Consumer Research,* 5, 103–123.

GREEN, P. E., and V. SRINIVASAN (1989). "Conjoint Analysis in Marketing Research: A Review of New Developments," Working Paper, Wharton School, University of Pennsylvania, Philadelphia, PA.

GREEN, P. E., Y. WIND, and A. K. JAIN (1973). "Analyzing Free-Response Data in Marketing Research," *Journal of Marketing Research* (February), 45–52.

GREEN, P. E., and Y. WIND (1973). *Multivariate Decisions in Marketing.* Hinsdale, IL: The Dryden Press.

GREENACRE, M. J. (1984). *Theory and Application of Correspondence Analysis.* London: Academic Press.

GREENBERG, B. G., J. R. ABERNATHY, and D. G. JORVITZ (1969). "Application of the Randomized Response Technique in Obtaining Quantitative Data," *Proceedings of the Social Statistics Section,* American Statistical Association, 37, (August), 40–43.

GREIMAS, A. JULIAN (1970). *Signs, Language, Culture.* The Hague, The Netherlands: Mouton.

GRILICHES, Z. and M. D. INTRILLIGATOR (1984). *Handbook of Econometrics.* Amsterdam and New York: North-Holland.

GROVER, R., and V. R. RAO (1988). "Inferring Competitive Market Structure Based on a Model of Interpurchase Intervals," *International Journal of Research in Marketing,* 5, 55–72.

GUTTMAN, L. (1968). "A General Monetric Technique for Finding the Smallest Coordinate Space for a Configuration of Points," *Psychometrika,* 33, 469–506.

HANSEN, M. H., W. N. HURWITZ, and W. G. MADOW (1953). *Sample Survey Methods and Theory,* Vols. I and II, New York: Wiley.

HARSHMAN, R., P. E. GREEN, Y. WIND, and M. J. LUNDY (1982). "A Model for the Analysis of Asymmetric Data in Marketing Research," *Marketing Science,* 1, 205–242.

HAUSER, J. R., and P. SIMMIE (1981). "Profit Maximizing Perceptual Positions: An Integrated Theory for the Selection of Product Features and Price," *Management Science,* 27, 38–56.

HIRSCHMAN, E. C. (1985). "Primitive Aspects of Consumption in Modern American Society," *Journal of Consumer Research* 12, 142–154.

HIRSCHMAN, E. C. (1988). "The Ideology of Consumption: A Structural-Syntatical Analysis of

'Dallas' and 'Dynasty.' " *Journal of Consumer Research* 15 (December), 344–359.

HIRSCHMAN, E. C. (1986). "Humanistic Inquiry in Marketing Research: Philosophy, Method and Criteria," *Journal of Marketing Research*, 23, 3, (August).

HOFFMAN, P. J., P. SLOVIC, and L. G. RORER (1968). "An Analysis of Variance Model for the Assessment of Configural Cue Utilization in Clinical Judgment," *Psychology Bulletin*, 69, 338–349.

HOLBROOK, M. B., R. B. CHESTNUT, T. A. OLIVA, and E. A. GREENLEAF (1984). "Play as a Consumption Experience: The Roles of Emotions, Performances, and Personality in the Enjoyment of Games," *Journal of Consumer Research*, 11, 728–739.

HOLBROOK, M. B. (1987). "From the Log of a Consumer Researcher: Reflections on the Odyssey," in *Advances in Consumer Research*, Vol. 14. M. Wallendorf and P. Anderson (Eds.). Provo, UT: Association for Consumer Research, 365–369.

HOLBROOK, M. B., and JOHN O'SHAUGHNESSY (1988). "On the Scientific Status of Consumer Research and the Need for an Interpretive Approach to Studying Consumption Behavior," *Journal of Consumer Research* (December), 398–402.

HOLBROOK, M. B., and M. W. GRAYSON (1986). "The Semiology of Cinematic Consumption: Symbolic Consumer Behavior in *Out of Africa*," *Journal of Consumer Research*, 13, 374–381.

HOUT, M. (1983). *Mobility Tables*. Beverly Hills, CA: Sage.

HOWARD, J. A., and J. N. SHETH (1969). *The Theory of Buyer Behavior*. New York: Wiley.

HUDSON, L. A., and J. L. OZANNE (1988). "Alternative Ways of Seeking Knowledge in Consumer Research," *Journal of Consumer Research*, 14, 508–521.

HUNTER, J. E., F. L. SCHMIDT, and G. B. JACKSON (1982). *Meta-Analysis: Cumulating Research Findings Across Studies*. Beverly Hills, CA: Sage.

INTRILLIGATOR, M. (1978). *Econometric Models, Techniques and Applications*. Englewood Cliffs, NJ: Prentice-Hall.

JOHNSON, B. T. (1989). *DSTAT: Software for the Meta-Analytic Review of Research Literature*. Hillsdale, NJ: Erlbaum.

JOHNSON, B. T., and A. H. EAGLEY (1989). "The Effects of Involvement on Persuasion: A Meta-Analysis," *Psychological Bulletin*.

JOHNSON, E. J., J. W. PAYNE, D. A. SCHKADE, and J. R. BETTMAN (1986). "Monitoring Information Processing and Decisions: The Mouselab System," Duke University, Center for Decision Studies.

JOHNSON, E. J., J. W. PAYNE, D. A. SCHKADE, and J. R. BETTMAN (1988) "Monitoring Information Acquisitions and Decisions: A Process Tracing Methodology for Decision Research," Office of Naval Research Tech Report, September 1988.

JOHNSON, R. M. (1987). "Adaptive Conjoint Analysis," *Sawtooth Software Conference on Perceptual Mapping Conjoint Analysis, and Computer Interviewing*. Ketchum, ID: Sawtooth Software.

JOHNSON, R. M. (1974). "Trade-off Analysis of Consumer Values," *Journal of Marketing Research*, 11, 121–127.

JORESKOG, J. G. (1967). "Some Contributions to Maximum Likelihood Factor Analysis," *Psychometrika*, 32, 443–482.

JORESKOG, J. G. (1969). "A General Approach to Confirmatory Maximum Likelihood Factor Analysis," *Psychometrika*, 34, 183–202.

JORESKOG, J. G., and D. SORBOM (1978). *LISREL: Analysis of Linear Structural Relationships by the Method of Maximum Likelihood*. Chicago, IL: Educational Resources.

KAHN, B., M. U. KALWANI, and D. G. MORRISON (1986). "Measuring Variety-Seeking and Reinforcement Behaviors Using Panel Data," *Journal of Marketing Research*, Vol. 23, Issue 2 (May).

KALWANI, M. U., and D. G. MORRISON (1971). "A Parsimonious Description of the Hendry System," *Management Science*, 23, 467–477.

KASSARJIAN, H. H. (1969). "The Negro and American Advertising: 1946–1965," *Journal of Marketing Research*, 6, 29–39.

KASSARJIAN, H. H. (1977). "Content Analysis in Consumer Research," *Journal of Consumer Research*, 4 (June).

KINSEY, J. (1981). "Determinants of Credit Card Accounts: An Application of Tobit Analysis," *Journal of Consumer Research*, 8 (September), 172–182.

KNOKE, D., and J. H. KUKLINSKI (1982). *Network Analysis*. Beverly Hills, CA: Sage.

KRUSKAL, J. B. (1964a). "Multidimensional Scaling by Optimizing Goodness of Fit to a Nonmetric Hypothesis," *Psychometrika*, 29, 1–27.

KRUSKAL, J. B. (1965). "Analysis of Factorial Experiments by Estimating Monotone Transformations of the Data," *Journal of Royal Statistical Society, Series B.,* 27, 251–263.

LEVI-STRAUSS, CLAUDE (1965). "The Structural Study of Myth," in *Myth: A Symposium.* Thomas A. Sebeok, Ed. Bloomington, IN: Indiana University Press, 81–106.

LEVI-STRAUSS, CLAUDE (1981). "Interpreting Consumer Mythology: A Structural Approach to Consumer Behavior," *Journal of Marketing,* 45 (Summer), 49–61.

LINGOES, J. C. (1972). "A General Survey of the Guttman-Lingoes Non-Metric Program Series," in *Multidimensional Scaling,* Vol. I, R. N. Shepard, A. K. Romney, and S. B. Nerlove, Eds. New York: Seminar, 52–68.

LITTLE, J. D. C., and L. M. LODISH (1969). "A Media Planning Calculus," *Operations Research* (January/February), 17,1–35.

LUCE, R. D., and J. W. TUKEY (1964). "Simultaneous Conjoint Measurement: A New Type of Fundamental Measurement," *Journal of Mathematical Psychology,* 1, 1–27.

MACLACHLAN, D. L., and J. K. JOHANSSON (1981). "Market Segmentation with Multivariate Aid," *Journal of Marketing* (Winter), 45, 74–84.

MASON, W. M., and S. E. FEINBERG, EDS. (1985). *Cohort Analysis in Social Research: Beyond the Identification Problem.* New York: Springer-Verlag.

MASSY, W. F., D. B. MONTGOMERY, and D. G. MORRISON (1970). *Stochastic Models of Buying Behavior.* Cambridge, MA: MIT Press, 21–48.

MCCARTHY, P. J. (1965). *Rev. International Statist. Inst.,* 37, 239–264.

MCFADDEN, D. (1973). "Conditional Logit Analysis of Qualitative Choice Behavior," in *Frontiers in Econometrics,* P. Zarembka, Ed. New York: American Press, 105–141.

MCFADDEN, D. (1976). "Quantal Choice Analysis: A Survey," *Annals of Economic and Social Measurement,* 5/4. 363–390.

MCFADDEN, D. (1980). "Econometric Models for Probabilistic Choice Among Products," *Journal of Business,* 53, 3, Part 2 (July), 513–530.

MCKEOWN, B., and D. THOMAS (1988). *Q-Methodology.* Beverly Hills, CA: Sage.

MICK, D. G. (1986). "Consumer Research and Semiotics: Exploring the Morphology of Signs, Symbols, and Significance," *Journal of Consumer Research,* 13, 196–213.

MORGAN. J. N., and R. C. MESSENGER (1973). *THAID: A Sequential Analysis Program for the Analysis of Nominal Scale Dependent Variables.* Ann Arbor, MI: University of Michigan Press.

NESLIN, S. A., C. HENDERSON, and J. QUELCH (1985). "Consumer Promotions and the Acceleration of Product Purchases," *Marketing Science,* 4, 2 (Spring).

NESLIN, S. A., and R. W. SHOEMAKER (1983). "A Model for Evaluating the Profitability of Coupon Promotions," *Marketing Science,* Vol. 2, No. 4, Fall.

NICOSIA, F. M. (1966). *Consumer Decision Processes.* Englewood Cliffs, NJ: Prentice-Hall.

PARKER, B. R., and V. SRINIVASAN (1976). "A Consumer Preference Approach to the Planning of Rural Primary Health Care Facilities," *Operations Research,* Vol. 24., 991–1025.

PERREAULT, W. D., and H. C. BARKSDALE, JR. (1980). "A Model-Free Approach for Analysis of Complex Contingency Data in Survey Research," *Journal of Marketing Research,* Vol. 16, 503–515.

PESSEMIER, E. A. (1982). *Product Management: Strategy and Organization,* 2nd ed. New York: Wiley.

RAGHAVARAO, D. (1971). *Construction and Combinatorial Problems in the Design of Experiments.* New York: Wiley.

RAO, V. R., and F. W. WINTER (1978). "An Application of the Multivariate Probit Model to Market Segmentation and Product Design," *Journal of Marketing Research,* Vol. 15, 361–368.

RAO, V. R., and D. SABAVALA (1981). "Inference of Hierarchical Choice Processes from Panel Data," *Journal of Consumer Research,* 8 (June), 85–96.

RAMSAY, J. O. (1977)" Maximum Likelihood Estimation in Multidimensional Scaling," *Psychometrika,* Vol. 42, 241–266.

RAMSAY, J. O. (1978). "Confidence Regions for Multidimensional Scaling Analysis," *Psychometrika,* Vol. 43, 145–160.

ROTHSCHILD, M. L. ET AL. (1988). "Hemispherically Lateralized EEG as a Response to Television Commercials," *Journal of Consumer Research* (September), 185–198.

ROY, S. N., R. GNANADESIKAN, and J. N. SRIVASTAVA (1971). *Analysis and Design of Certain Quantitative Multiresponse Experiments.* New York: Pergamon Press.

SAATY, T. L. (1980) *The Analytic Hierarchy Process.* New York: McGraw-Hill.

SCHEFFE, H. (1970). *The Analysis of Variance.* New York: Wiley.

SCHMITTLEIN, D. C. (1982). "Assessing Validity and Test-Retest Reliability for 'Pick K of N' Data," Working Paper, Wharton School, University of Pennsylvania, Philadelphia, PA.

SEARLE, S. R. (1971). *Linear Models.* New York: Wiley.

SHEPARD, R. N. (1962). "The Analysis of Proximities: Multidimensional Scaling with an Unknown Distance Function; I, II," *Psychometrika,* Vol. 27, 125–140; 219–246.

SHEPARD, R. N., A. K. ROMNEY, and S. B. NERLOVE (1972). *Multidimensional Scaling,* Vol. II, New York: Seminar Press.

SHERRY, J. F., and E. G. CAMARGO (1987). "May Your Life be Marvelous: English Language Labeling and the Semiotics of Japanese Promotion," *Journal of Consumer Research,* 14, 2, (September) 174–188.

SHETH, J. N. (1968). "A Factor Analytic Model of Bank Loyalty," *Journal of Marketing Research,* Vol. 4, 395–404.

SHOCKER, A. D., and V. SRINIVASAN (1977). "LIN-MAP (Version II): A FORTRAN IV Computer Program for Analyzing Ordinal Preference (Dominance) Judgments via Linear Programming Techniques and for Conjoint Measurement," *Journal of Marketing Research,* Vol. 15, 101–103.

SILK, A. J. and G. L. URBAN (1978). "Pre-test Market Evaluation of New Packaged Goods: A Model and Measurement Methodology," *Journal of Marketing Research,* 15 (May), 171–191.

STOETZEL, J. (1960), "A Factor Analysis of the Liquor Preferences of French Consumers," *Journal of Advertising Research,* Vol. 1, 7–11.

SUDMAN, S. (1976). *Applied Sampling.* New York: Academic Press.

TAKANE, Y., F. W. YOUNG, and J. DELEEUW (1977). "Nonmetric Individual Differences Multidimensional Scaling: An Alternating Least Square Method with Optimal Scaling Features," *Psychometrika,* Vol. 17, 7–11.

THEIL, H. (1978). *Introduction to Econometrics.* Englewood Cliffs, NJ: Prentice-Hall.

TORGERSON, W. S. (1952). "Multidimensional Scaling: I Theory and Method," *Psychometrika,* Vol. 17, 401–419.

TSE, D. K., R. W. BELK, and N. ZHOU (1989). "Becoming a Consumer Society: A Longitudinal and Cross-Cultural Content Analysis of Print Ads from Hong Kong, the People's Republic of China and Taiwan," *Journal of Consumer Research* (March), 457–472.

TUCKER, L. R. (1966). "Some Mathematical Notes on Three Mode Factor Analysis," *Psychometrika,* Vol. 31, 279–311.

TUKEY, J. W. (1977). *Exploratory Data Analysis.* Reading, MA: Addison-Wesley.

TUKEY, J. W. (1958). "Bias and Confidence in Not-Quite Large Samples: Abstract," *Annals of Mathematical Statistics,* 29, 614.

TUMA, N. B., and M. T. HANNAN (1984). *Social Dynamics,* Orlando, FL: Academic Press.

TWEDT, S. W. (1952). "A Multiple Factor Analysis of Advertising Readership," *Journal of Applied Psychology,* 36, 207–215.

URBAN, G. L. (1975). "PERCEPTOR: A Model for Product Positioning," *Management Science,* 21 (April), 858–871.

URBAN, G. L., G. M. KATZ, T. E. HATCH, and A. J. SILK (1983). "The ASSESSOR Pre-test Market Evaluation System," *Interfaces,* 13 (December), 38–59.

VILCASSIM, N. (1989). "Extending the Rotterdam Model to Test Hierarchical Market Structures," *Marketing Science,* 8, 2 (Spring).

WARNER, S. L. (1965). "Randomized Response: A Survey Technique for Eliminating Evasive Answer Bias," *Journal of American Statistical Association,* 60, 63–69.

WASSERMAN AND FAUST (Forthcoming). *Social Network Analysis: Methods and Allocations.* Cambridge University Press.

WEBB, E. J., D. T. CAMPBELL, R. D. SCHWARTZ, and L. SEECHREST (1966). *Unobtrusive Measures: Non-Reactive Research in the Social Sciences.* Chicago: Rand McNally.

WEINBERG, S. L., J. D. CARROLL, and H. S. COHEN (1981). "Estimating Confidence Regions for INDSCAL-Derived Group Stimulus Points Using Jackknifing," Working Paper, Bell Laboratories, Murry Hill, NJ.

WELLS, W. D. (1974). *Lifestyle and Psychographics.* Chicago: AMA.

WILLIAMS, W. (1978). *A Sampler on Sampling.* New York: Wiley.

WIND, Y., and J. DENNY (1974). "Multivariate

Analysis of Variance in Research on the Effectiveness of TV Commercials," *Journal of Marketing Research,* 10 (May), 136–142.

WIND, Y., P. E. GREEN, and A. K. JAIN (1973). "Higher Order Factor Analysis in the Classification of Psychographic Variables," *Journal of Marketing Research Society,* 15, 224–232.

WIND, Y., and P. E. GREEN (1985). "Statistics in Marketing," in S. Kotz and N. Johnson, *Encyclopedia of Statistical Sciences,* 5, 227–248.

WOLF, F. M. (1986). *Meta-Analysis.* Beverly Hills, CA: Sage.

WOODRUFF, R. S., and B. D. CAUSEY (1976). "Computerized Method for Approximating the Variance of a Complicated Estimate," *Journal of the American Statistical Association,* 71 (June), 315–321.

YOUNG, F. W. (1969). "Polynomial Conjoint Analysis of Similarities: Definitions for a Special Algorithm," Research Paper No. 76, Psychometric Laboratory, University of North Carolina, Chapel Hill, NC.

YOUNG, F. W. (1972). "A Model for Polynomial Conjoint Analysis Algorithm," in *Multidimensional Scaling,* Vol. I, R. N. Shepard, A. K. Romney, and S. B. Nerlove, Eds. New York: Seminar Press, 69–104.

YOUNG, G., and A. S. HOUSEHOLDER (1938). "Discussion of a Set of Points in Terms of Their Mutual Distances," *Psychometrika,* 3, 19–22.

ZUFRYDEN, F. S. (1979). "A Conjoint Measurement-Based Approach for Optimal New Product Design and Market Segmentation," in *Analytic Approaches to Product and Marketing Planning,* A. D. Shocker, Ed. Cambridge, MA: Marketing Science Institute, 100–114.

15

PHILOSOPHICAL TENSIONS
IN CONSUMER INQUIRY

J. Paul Peter
University of Wisconsin–Madison

This paper presents an overview of a variety of philosophical positions and evaluates their value as foundations for consumer inquiry. Three positivistic accounts of science (logical empiricism, naive falsification, and sophisticated methodological falsification) are found to be logically inadequate and historically inaccurate. A relativistic view is then advocated as a philosophical foundation for the field, which could lead to the development of more useful knowledge. The implications of adopting relativistic views for practicing consumer researchers are also discussed.

INTRODUCTION

Consumer inquiry has many difficulties that make it a challenging vocation. For example, the field has never set any obtainable objectives by which progress could be measured, nor has it agreed upon the appropriate benefactors of its efforts. Agreement has not been reached on what aspects of the human condition, if any, qualify for exclusion from consideration, leaving the field with an infinite number of phenomena to account for. Other social sciences, which provide the majority of the field's intellectual grist, are commonly considered by their leaders to be in various states of disarray, if not outright crisis, leaving them questionable sources for research ideas and methods. Integrating these diverse and often incommensurable borrowings is a challenge far greater than any faced by Newton. If immutable laws or empirical generalizations are considered to be the standards for judgment, then consumer inquiry must be considered ineffectual.

It is not surprising, then, that consumer inquirers have turned to yet other fields in seeking solutions to their problems or at least solace for their condition. These fields include the philosophy of science, the history of science, and the sociology of science, which collectively are called the "science studies." It is likely that most consumer inquirers look to the science studies literature in hopes of finding better ways of doing science.

Certainly, much has been learned about the nature of science from the excursion into the science studies literature. However, simple answers to the question of how to do science better were not found. Rather, one of the major lessons learned has been that the philosophy of science is in a state of disarray and that there is much disagreement about the nature of science and how it works. In fact, Laudan states the condition quite clearly when he writes:

Unfortunately, of course, the efforts of philosophers to identify precisely the components of the scientific method have fallen on hard times. So gloomy is the situation these days that few active philosophers of science would still venture to claim that they knew what the scientific method was. But to put it that way is to give too rosy a picture of the present state of disarray in my field, for what I really mean to say is that many philosophers of science, present company included, would go so far as to deny that there was anything corresponding to a unified set of methods which characterized what we customarily call science. (1984, p. 1)

Given this situation, it is not surprising that there are different, conflicting philosophical views concerning the nature of science and that a number of them have been advocated as the appropriate foundation for consumer inquiry.

The purpose of this paper is to review and evaluate the major philosophical positions advanced in consumer inquiry and to suggest implications for practicing researchers. The paper is divided into three sections. In the first section, three positivistic accounts of science are reviewed and evaluated. These include logical empiricism, naive falsification, and sophisticated methodological falsification. It is the premise of this paper that these accounts are fundamentally defective and do not provide a sound philosophical foundation for consumer inquiry. In the second section, a relativistic account of science is described and evaluated. It is the position of this paper that a relativistic

view provides the best account of science that is currently available and the most useful philosophical foundation for consumer inquiry. The final section discusses general implications for practicing consumer researchers for adopting various philosophical positions.

POSITIVISTIC ACCOUNTS OF SCIENCE

Logical positivism was created by the mathematicians and philosophers of the Vienna Circle in the 1920s and dominated the philosophical landscape for the next thirty years. This approach was often discussed by its developers as though it provided a description of how scientific theories develop, or as though it detailed an explication of what constitutes a scientific theory. However, these scholars became so enamored with developing stringent criteria for scientific theories that their work lost sight of what was humanly possible. In fact, in spite of exemplary developments in many areas of science, there are likely no theories ever created by earthlings that could satisfy the requirements of the positivistic Received View.

There have been a number of attempts to modify logical positivism while still maintaining a number of its major tenets. These attempts share in common a strong belief in the objectivity of empirical data and its power to sort out truth (or something like it, such as verisimilitude or confirmation) from falsity, or at least to refute false theories. These positivistic accounts of science advocate a single scientific method. Although the particulars of this method have not been detailed, it is this method that is assumed to differentiate science from nonscience. These views focus on the processes involved in attempts to justify knowledge claims, and they do not seriously consider the processes by which theories are created.

Logical Empiricism

Logical empiricism is usually considered a moderate version of logical positivism that attempts to avoid the "problem of induction." The induction problem refers to the fact that no matter how many empirical observations support a statement, it can not be concluded that the statement is universally true. Thus, unlike logical positivists, logical empiricists reject the idea that scientific theories can be conclusively verified. However, they do argue that theories can be increasingly confirmed through empirical research and logical analysis.

In marketing and consumer inquiry, Hunt has written extensively on his interpretations of this perspective (e.g., 1976, 1983a, 1983b, 1984, 1989; Hunt and Speck 1985), and he has been its major advocate. While these accounts are sometimes contradictory, below is an attempt to summarize several of the major points in Hunt's interpretation.

According to Hunt, logical empiricists believe that the world is real, and that there are real phenomena which have an existence independent of the observer. The purpose of science is, therefore, to increase understanding of these real phenomena. While all scientific activity is not completely objective, objectivity as a goal for science is and ought to be a valuable norm (Hunt and Speck, 1985, pp. 30–31). The difference between science and nonscience is the open empirical testing of knowledge claims. This testing is called "intersubjective certification" (Hunt 1983a).

Logical empiricism holds that explanation is central to science and that the occurrence of a phenomenon is explained by showing that the phenomenon was expected to occur as a result of some regularity or "lawlike generalization." Scientific prediction has the same logical structure as scientific explanation, the major difference being the time frame. Theories and lawlike generalizations are used to explain past events and to predict future events (Hunt and Speck, 1985, p. 31).

According to Hunt, "Theories are systematically related sets of statements, including some lawlike generalizations, that are empirically testable . . . *lawlike* denotes nothing more than the observed regularity in the occurrence of two or more phenomena" (1983b, p. 10). Hunt argues that the deductive-nomological model (with the additional requirement of

causal mechanisms or causal laws in the explanans) and the inductive-statistical model (without the requirement that premises suggest a conclusion with "high probability") "remain the most viable models available for explaining phenomena" (Hunt 1983a, p. 99). Hunt also notes that the discovery/justification, the analytic/synthetic, and the observational/theoretical dichotomies play central roles in logical empiricism:

The discovery/justification dichotomy reminds us that it is useful to distinguish between procedures that scientists use to create or *discover* hypotheses, lawlike generalizations, and theories from the procedures that are used to evaluate [justify] the truth-content of these same theories, lawlike generalizations, and hypotheses . . .

The analytic/synthetic dichotomy proposes that the truth content of different kinds of sentences is ascertained in different ways. Some statements (analytical statements) are true or false depending *solely* on how certain terms in the statements are defined. For example, consider the statement "all department stores that have 81,000 square feet of floor space have 900 square yards of floor space." This statement is true by virtue of our definitions of "square feet" and "square yards." It is *analytically* true. On the other hand, the truth-content of other statements can be determined only by comparing them with certain aspects of the real world. For example, "all department stores that have 81,000 square feet of floor space will have at least ten separate departments" is *synthetic* and its truth content must be determined by examining actual characteristics of department stores.

The observational/theoretical dichotomy points out that some of the terms in science (observables) have relatively direct empirical referents whereas other terms (theoreticals) seem "far removed" from the empirical world . . . (Hunt and Speck, 1985, pp. 31–32).

Evaluation of Logical Empiricism. There are many reasons why logical empiricism has long been rejected in the science studies literature. (Only a few of them will be mentioned here. Chalmars 1976, Lincoln and Guba 1985, and Suppe 1977 provide more detailed accounts.) First, it fails to overcome the problem of induction, since it still depends on a finite number of observations to support the assertion that a universal statement is "probably true" (see Anderson 1983). In fact, philosophers have long agreed that there is no defensible method for determining the truth-content of statements.

Second, no defensible criterion has ever been found that differentiates science from non-science. Hunt's criteria of empirical testability and intersubjective certification are notoriously ambiguous and met by a variety of nonscientific areas (see Laudan 1983).

Third, the supposed symmetry between explanation and prediction has been severely criticized, leading even Hempel (1965) to change his views, and Bromberger (1966) demonstrated the deductive-nomological model to be seriously defective. Suppe (1977, p. 623) concluded that both the deductive-nomological and inductive-statistical models are defective. Hunt's requirement of causal laws in the explanans of the deductive-nomological model makes it impossible to create such explanations. This is because causal laws that meet the requirements of logical empiricism cannot be developed (see, for example, Hunt 1983, pp. 96–97; 125). In terms of Hunt's suggestion for dropping the "highly probable" statement from the inductive-statistical model, it should be clear that this leaves the model with no criterion for judgment. Thus, the value of these models has not been demonstrated.

Further, if "lawlike" denotes nothing more than "observed regularity," as proposed by Hunt, then a correlation of any kind can be considered a lawlike generalization. For example, a correlation between hemline lengths and the stock market prices meets his criterion, yet it seems unlikely that many people would accept this as a lawlike generalization. Similarly, Hunt's definition of theory fails to distinguish scientific theories from other forms of statements. For example, astrology, parapsychology and witchcraft can be shown to meet his requirements, yet few people accept these areas as scientific.

Finally, the analytic/synthetic distinction was shown to be untenable, as was the observa-tional/theoretical dichotomy (see Suppe 1977). Without these distinctions, logical empiricism must be viewed as inadequate.

Although this discussion provides only a brief sketch and evaluation of logical or modern empiricism, it should be clear that the approach has been repudiated in the science studies literature. One positivistic attempt to provide an alternative to logical empiricism is naive falsification. Rather than seeking gradual confirmation of theories through induction as advocated by logical empiricism, naive falsification emphasizes the refutation of deductively derived hypotheses.

Naive Falsification

Among empirical researchers in consumer inquiry, particularly those who advocate laboratory experimentation, naive falsification is often championed. For example, while there were serious disagreements in a recent debate on external validity (Calder, et al. 1981, 1982, 1983; Lynch 1982, 1983), apparently the participants agreed that ". . . Popper's falsification principle is at the heart of the process by which we advance both our scientific knowledge and our confidence in that knowledge" (McGrath and Brinberg 1983, p. 116).

While not providing a detailed account of Popper's views, the Calder-Lynch debate did provide an interpretation of some of its tenets. For example, Calder et al. (1981) argue that

Theory applications call for falsification test procedures. These procedures are used to test a theory by creating a context and measuring effects within that context that have the potential to disprove or refute the theory . . . Theories that repeatedly survive rigorous falsification attempts are accepted as scientific explanations (subject to more stringent testing) and are candidates for application. (p. 198)

They further point out that studies should be done to provide the most rigorous possible tests for a theory. Theories that do not pass these tests are to be ruthlessly rejected. Any disconfirming evidence falsifies a theory, as Lynch (1983) explains:

> In an earlier paper, Calder et al. (1981) argued from the standpoint of a falsification philosophy of science (Popper 1959) and quite correctly noted that theories can be rejected if their predictions can be shown to be false for *any* subjects, settings, and events within their domain. (p. 109)

Thus, we have the main elements of naive falsification as interpreted in consumer inquiry. Theories are to be proposed and then rigorous empirical research is done to try to falsify them. Since science seeks universal propositions, any nonsupportive finding leads to immediate rejection of a theory. Supportive findings do not confirm a theory but give it a stature of a theory that "has not yet been falsified."

Evaluation of Naive Falsification. It is easy to demonstrate why this form of falsification is naive. According to this view a theory is falsified if predictions are disconfirmed for *any* subjects, settings, or events within the domain of the theory. Clearly, almost all theories would be immediately falsified if this criterion were applied. For example, consider a theory that states that there is a particular difference between two groups. Even with a reasonably large effect size, a large percentage of individuals in the two groups will be essentially similar or ordered contrary to the direction of the overall group mean. For example, a difference of 0.8 of a standard deviation is considered large for much social research (Cohen 1977). With such a difference, however, 52.6 percent of the two populations overlap (see Sawyer and Peter 1983). Thus, according to naive falsification, since some of the subjects are ordered contrary to the hypothesis, the hypothesis and theory must be rejected. Clearly, few theories would survive even a single empirical study if scientists took naive falsification seriously! Additional problems with this perspective are discussed in a later section of this paper.

Sophisticated Methodological Falsification

Although many would argue that sophisticated methodological falsification is not a positivistic view, it is commonly interpreted as such in consumer inquiry (e.g., see Calder and Tybout 1987). This approach to falsification was developed by Lakatos (1970) in part to overcome the problem with naive falsification outlined previously. The main difference between it and naive falsification, according to Lakatos, is that

> . . . in my conception criticism does not—and must not—kill as fast as Popper imagined. Purely negative, destructive criticism, like "refutation" or demonstration of an inconsistency does not eliminate a research programme. Criticism of a programme is a long and often frustrating process and one must treat budding programmes leniently. One may, of course, show up the degeneration of a research programme, but it is only *constructive criticism* which, with the help of rival research programmes, can achieve real success. (quoted in Suppe 1977, pp. 660–661)

In this view the focus is not on a single theory but on a sequence of ever improving theories, which are the research programs that, according to Lakatos, characterize mature sciences. Research programs have both a "positive heuristic," which directs the path of inquiry, and a "negative heuristic," which indicates which paths not to follow. Research programs also have an irrefutable "hard core" of fundamental assumptions that are determined by methodological decisions and are insulated from refutation by a "protective belt" of auxiliary hypotheses.

Research programs follow the positive heuristic and successively attempt to falsify theories. The theories consist of the negative heuristic and auxiliary hypotheses and, when falsified, are modified by the addition of new hypotheses, making a new theory. Each such cycle is a "problem shift" and is "theoretically progressive" if each successor predicts some novel, unexpected fact. A problem shift is "empirically progressive" if it leads to the discovery of a new fact. A problem shift that is not both theoretically and (at least intermittently) empirically progressive is degenerating and should be stopped (Suppe 1977, pp. 662–663).

Evaluation of Sophisticated Methodological Falsification. Both Leong (1985, pp. 36–37) and Suppe (1977, pp. 664–670) provide detailed criticisms of sophisticated methodological falsification. These criticisms generally focus on the idea that Lakatos has failed to explain how scientists could a priori choose a research program that would be progressive. Further, his work ignores the facts that many other factors besides theoretical and empirical progressiveness are involved in scientific theorizing and that what is theoretically reasonable is conditioned by the subject matter of the science. These and other criticisms led Suppe to conclude that this perspective is a "seriously defective account" (p. 669) and that

In short, we can conclude that Lakatos has exposed *partially* one reasoning pattern in the growth of scientific knowledge which in some circumstances, *is* characteristic of good reasoning in science; but even in the cases he examines, much of the reasoning involved is not reflected in his account. Moreover, it is at best a pattern of good reasoning, and very often science does, and ought to, employ other, incompatible, patterns in proceeding rationally. Other than this limited achievement, Lakatos's work does little to illuminate the role of rationality in the growth of scientific knowledge. (1977, p. 670)

General Evaluation of Falsification

There are many reasons why falsification in all of its forms has been rejected as an adequate philosophy of science. One of the most telling problems is that while falsificationists recognize that theories cannot be proven to be true, they typically accept the idea that theories can be proven to be false. However, Duhem (1953), Laudan (1977), and others have demonstrated that it is not possible to prove a theory to be false. This is because there is much more involved in any empirical study than the substan-

tive hypothesis of interest. There are a whole set of assumptions about initial conditions, auxiliary hypotheses, and the validity of measuring instruments, of sampling, and of data analysis procedures. No study can completely unravel these and "test" only the substantive hypothesis of interest. Thus, any attempt to conclude that a theory has been falsified can easily be deflected by suggesting that something else in the maze of assumptions and premises caused the "falsifying" result (Laudan 1977, Anderson 1983).

In addition, imaginative researchers can make ad hoc modifications to a theory to dispute the inconsistent results or to argue that any unsupportive results demonstrate certain boundary conditions to the theory, but do not falsify it. They may also produce another set of empirical results that again support their favored theory, and they may attempt to persuade the research community that their theory remains valid.

The early history of psychology provides an interesting example of scientists rejecting empirical results that disagreed with their theories. Although Wündt and Tichener disagreed about the content of consciousness, both believed that thinking depended on mental images and their introspective research supported this idea. However, in a series of association experiments performed by Külpe at the University of Würzburg, subjects reported they were able to make associations and decisions without having any images in their consciousness. Kendler explains what happened:

Neither Wündt nor Tichener was willing to accept the conclusion that the Würzburg studies were damaging to their respective positions. Wündt rejected the results because they were due to a faulty methodology; one cannot observe thought without thinking. In addition, thinking cannot be studied by rigorous experimental methods because an introspector cannot repeatedly observe the mental processes associated with the original presentation of a problem . . .

Tichener rejected the results of the Würzburgers, not because thought could not be introspectively observed but, instead, because their observations were faulty. When thoughts were analyzed at Cornell, images were always reported. This encouraged Tichener to conclude that the unanalyzable imageless thought experiences reported by the Würzburgers were really unanalyzed. When observed at Cornell, imageless thought was revealed to be complexes of kinesthetic sensations and images. (1987, p. 74)

Thus, theories cannot be falsified by empirical data alone. It would be most unusual for advocates for a theory to simply abandon it because someone produced a set of empirical results that were inconsistent with the theory. In fact, Mitroff (1974) found in his research on the NASA moon scientists that the most respected scientists believed strongly in their theories and ignored data that did not support them.

The history of science provides many other examples of theories that survived and prospered in spite of the availability of empirical data that refuted them. Some common examples include Newtonian theory, relativity theory, Copernican astronomy, the theory of oxidation, natural selection, kinetic theory, and continental drift (see Chalmers 1976, Anderson 1983). Thus, it is clear that falsification does not provide a viable descriptive model of how some of the greatest scientific achievements in history came about. Further, if the greatest scientists in history did not follow falsification tenets, then it is unreasonable to accept falsification as the only model for science.

In consumer inquiry, some researchers have argued that falsification provides the only methodology for scientific knowledge (Calder and Tybout 1987, 1989). However, such a position is untenable (see Laudan 1983), and it should be clear that few social science researchers seriously attempt to falsify theories. Rather, in most cases, they attempt to falsify the null hypothesis in order to claim support for their favored theory (Peter 1983). Greenwald et al. (1986) have discussed at length the strong confirmation bias in social science and have pointed out that publication practices overwhelmingly favor supportive results. In fact, Greenwald et al. argue that researchers who do

not obtain supportive results are unlikely to even try to publish the work. In many cases, then, there is little chance that a "falsifying" result will be widely disseminated in the field and become part of scientific knowledge.

In consumer inquiry, it is clear that theories survive and prosper with either no or only marginal empirical research support. Familiar examples include need theory, a number of personality theories, and theories of the attitude-behavior relationship. In addition, many of the procedures advocated for conducting empirical research are biased against the null hypothesis and are designed to create supportive results (see Peter 1984). Also, statistical criteria used to judge the adequacy of empirical results, such as p-values less than 0.05, provide almost no hurdle for empirical results to surmount in order to be judged supportive. This is because obtaining a small p-value depends only on factors controlled by the researcher (see Sawyer and Peter 1983). Finally, it is clear that researchers fail to reject theories that have only a modicum of empirical support (see Peterson et al. 1985). Thus, it is clear that falsification does not provide an adequate description of consumer inquiry.

As a normative model, falsification also fails for several reasons. First, as noted previously, the history of science demonstrates that falsification cannot account for the activities of many great scientists and the acceptance of many great theories. Thus, to argue that the field should follow falsification tenets is to constrain the field to a single method when the history of science shows that a variety of methods have been productive.

Second, it is not clear operationally how the field could follow falsification tenets. If the "any subject, settings, or events" criterion was applied, then almost all theories in the field must be rejected, leaving the field essentially void of content. However, if this criterion is not used, then how much disconfirming evidence is enough to conclude that a theory is falsified? If ten studies support the theory, and two studies refute the theory, is the theory falsified or supported, overall? Falsificationists have no solution to this problem that is consistent with their analysis of science.

Finally, there are serious logical inconsistencies in the recently advocated position of those claiming to be falsificationists in consumer inquiry. For example, these writers argue that

It is our position that a falsificationist orientation (in the very simple sense of continuing to subject theories to tests in which they *could* fail or have their weaknesses revealed) coupled with a commitment to selecting theories comparatively (i.e., preferring ones that provide the most complete yet parsimonious account of available data) can and should be the general methodology for generating scientific knowledge. Note that these principles do not assume that theories can be demonstrated to be either true or unequivocally false, nor is there any inductive implication that the greater the number of tests a theory has survived the "better" it is. . . . All we suggest is that a process of ongoing testing, and a preference at any point in time for theories that provide a better explanation than their rivals offers the *possibility* of scientific progress. This is the best we can hope for. (Calder and Tybout 1989, p. 202).

If it is to be argued that theories cannot be shown to be true or false, then it is not clear what role empirical "testing" plays in this account of falsification. Theories cannot "fail or have their weaknesses revealed" since nonsupportive results cannot lead to the conclusion that the theory is false. Similarly, supportive results cannot lead to the conclusion that the theory is true. Empirical results also cannot be used to conclude that one theory is "better" than another in this account. This is because (1) it is denied in the preceding quotation that "the greater the number of tests a theory [survives] the 'better' it is" and (2) no empirical method is offered for determining the degree to which empirical results must differ to determine that one theory is superior to another. Apparently, then, empirical testing has no valuable role to play in this account, yet "ongoing testing" is encouraged.

This account of falsification differs from previous accounts. Subjective judgments are now seen to play an important role in science. For example, subjective judgments are required for

such things as determining how complete a theory is, how parsimonious it is, and whether it is superior to another theory. In fact, this view of "falsification" shares much common ground with relativistic accounts of science.

RELATIVISTIC ACCOUNTS OF SCIENCE

Several factors led a group of scholars interested in consumer inquiry to adopt relativistic views of science. First, having read a good deal of the science studies literature in the late 1970s and early 1980s, it became increasingly clear to these scholars that positivistic accounts of science were repudiated by contemporary philosophies of science. Second, there is no question that books by Kuhn (1970), Feyerabend (1975), and Laudan (1977) had a profound impact on shaping new perspectives advocated for the field. In addition, work in the cognitive sociology of science, such as Bloor (1976), Barnes (1977), Latour and Woolgar (1979), and Zukav (1979), were very influential. Third, the lack of progress in the field and the search for better ways of doing science led to interest in these views.

Perhaps the two best known relativistic accounts of science are critical relativism (Anderson 1983, 1986, 1988b) and the relativistic/constructionist perspective (Olson 1982, Olson and Peter 1984, Peter 1983, 1984, Peter and Olson 1983, 1989). Although there are differences in these perspectives, this paper will focus on the major tenets that underlie both views.

Fundamental Tenets of Relativism

Relativists in consumer inquiry believe that while there may be (or may not be) a reality independent of the observer, there is no way to know such a reality. In other words, scientists create views of reality and attempt to develop social consensus about these views. What counts as knowledge and the standards by which it is judged are relative to particular times in history, particular research communities, and particular contexts. For example, most of the early studies in our field would be unlikely to meet today's publication standards in terms of theoretical development or methodological sophistication. Similarly, mathematical modelers, behavioral researchers, and interpretive researchers typically use different standards for judging the quality of the work in their domains. Thus, relativists reject the positivistic idea that there are universal standards for judging knowledge claims.

To relativists, science is clearly a social process performed by interacting human beings. Thus, much more is involved in the acceptance of rejection of theories than the logic involved or the empirical evidence collected. As Kuhn (1970) noted, "the superiority of one theory to another is something that cannot be proved in debate. Instead, I have insisted, each party must try, *by persuasion,* to convert the other" (p. 198; emphasis added). Thus, relativists recognize that both psychological and sociological phenomena have strong influences on the acceptance of scientific knowledge.

As a social process, science is clearly subjective. In fact, any statement of objectivity must be based on a subjective belief. Since perceptions are governed by sense impressions and previous learning, humans can only "see" what they have been taught to see. For example, medical students do not see cancer or other diseases in lung X-rays until they are taught to do so. Children do not see "tables" or "chairs" until they are taught to associate these concepts with various pieces of furniture. Similarly, previous knowledge and beliefs determine what researchers perceive when creating and interpreting empirical data (see Arndt 1985).

A major difference between relativistic and positivistic views concerns the nature of empirical data. While positivistic researchers recognize that data have measurement error, they typically view data as being objective and independent of the researcher. As such, data are assumed to be the reality against which theories are tested.

However, relativists recognize that there is no purely observational language, i.e., all data are theory-laden. This means that at least implicit theories are involved in the construction of all empirical data. Any attempt to attach a meaning to a set of numbers also involves theory. Thus, empirical data do not represent a reality independent of the scientist. The scientist selects the theory, the specific hypotheses to be examined, the research setting, the test stimuli, the subjects, the measures, the statistics to be used, and he or she provides the interpretation of the results. In fact, the entire production of research is completely controlled by the scientist (Peter 1984). Further, scientists typically have biases concerning what they want the data to demonstrate, and, in the long-run, perseverance often yields the desired results (Greenwald et al. 1986). From this viewpoint, it is small wonder that McGuire (1973) referred to laboratory experimenters as "stage managers."

Relativists recognize that a theory has meaning only within its own context, i.e., theories are not universal. In fact, no universal laws or theories have ever been advanced that meet positivistic requirements (see Feyerabend 1975, Munevar 1981). Thus, relativists view knowledge as context-dependent.

Relativists accept the idea that there is no way to prove the truth or falsity of theories with empirical data. Thus, various types of heuristic power or usefulness are recommended for judging theories (see Peter and Olson 1983, 1989). In addition, it is recognized that the particular beliefs, values, standards, methods, and cognitive aims of the scientists in a research community strongly influence what is accepted as scientific knowledge (see Anderson 1986).

Evaluations of Relativistic Views. Since the publication of Anderson (1983) and Peter and Olson (1983), a number of comments have been published critiquing relativistic views. Hunt (1984) argues that intersubjective certification demarcates science from nonscience and that there is a single scientific method; however, he provides no proof of these assertions. He also argues that many philosophers today do not accept relativism, which seems to be an accurate assessment.

Of course, many philosophers do not accept relativism, nor can they, if they wish to maintain the importance of the philosophy of science. Since relativism recognizes that science is subjective, and that perceptions and consensus generation processes are critical to understanding science, the role of philosophers of science is sharply downgraded. Thus, many philosophers of science may have a vested interest in maintaining that science has a particular form of rationality, as well as in advocating realism and in rejecting relativism.

Muncy and Fisk (1985) critique versions of relativism that are, for the most part, far removed from the positions advocated for consumer inquiry, and their work will therefore not be discussed. Cooper (1987) presented his opinion that "the truth of an assertion can be evaluated against the collective evidence in the domain" (p. 127) and suggested that, although there are practical impediments, there is a truth worth seeking. No support is offered for these contentions, however.

As noted previously, Calder and Tybout (1987) champion falsification as the only method of doing science and treat relativism as a philosophy useful only for nonscientific, interpretive work. This position was refuted by Anderson (1988b) and Peter and Olson (1989). Siegel (1988) argues that Anderson's critical relativism is not really relativistic because it implicitly has standards that cut across different research programs. He argues that Anderson's position should be called "critical pluralism." Anderson (1988a) offers a defense of his position noting that his view is relativistic in terms of both objectives and time frames.

Hunt (1989) repeats his opinion that science differs from nonscience in its method of verifying knowledge claims, but again provides no evidence. He also misconstrues relativistic views on the nature of science. Hunt (1989, p. 188) claims that relativists argue that "there are no fundamental differences separating the sciences and the nonsciences," and that this statement logically implies that "the knowledge claims of the nonsciences have as much epistemological warrant as the sciences." Hunt goes on to argue that the second statement implies that "if a palmist should diagnose a person as

not having bone cancer (an example of a nonscience knowledge claim), such a diagnosis would have equal warrant as the diagnosis of a medical doctor that the person did have bone cancer (an example of a science knowledge claim)."

Of course, such an argument misstates the relativistic position in consumer inquiry. Surely, relativists in consumer inquiry recognize, as do most philosophers of science, that universal criteria that successfully demarcate sciences from nonsciences have not been created and that neither science nor nonscience can produce objective truth. This logically implies that the acceptance of knowledge claims depends on many factors and that in some cases, some people will and should accept the knowledge claims of science, but in other cases, nonscience claims will and should be accepted. For example, it seems likely that most people in Western cultures would accept the diagnosis of a medical doctor rather than that of a palmist in the situation outlined by Hunt. However, this does not mean that the medical doctor is always right and the palmist is always wrong; certainly there are many cases where medical doctors misdiagnose diseases.

It should be clear that science does not always offer more useful knowledge claims. For example, chiropractic medicine and acupuncture are considered by many to be nonscientific, yet many consumers believe in these therapies and claim to have been healed by them when traditional medical science failed to do so. Thus, the acceptance or rejection of knowledge claims is relative to particular contexts, research communities, and historical periods.

IMPLICATIONS FOR CONSUMER INQUIRY

Although the differences in positions discussed previously are of great interest to philosophically minded consumer inquirers, they have had little influence on many empirical researchers in the field. Following their positivistic training, these researchers seem primarily concerned with how to do science "correctly" at the operational level. To them, the primary question seems to be "what difference does it make which philosophy of science I choose when I design my research?"

In that aspects of philosophy undergird all methods and approaches to seeking knowledge, philosophical issues have both direct and indirect influences on workbench level researchers. These issues influence what researchers think they are doing, what they think research is capable of achieving, what topics they choose to study, and what methods they choose to use.

Empirical researchers in social science tend to advocate positivistic views for a number of reasons. First, these views typically champion empirical research as the sole arbitrator of truth and falsity, thus apparently giving empirical researchers a privileged status in the scientific community. Second, these views provide sets of operational rules that, while of questionable epistemological value, do simplify the process of doing and evaluating research. Third, these views have long been taught in doctoral programs as the accepted framework for science and are consistent with the ordinary person's view of science. Fourth, these views underlie traditional research methods that are strongly ingrained in social science. Fifth, these views relegate the insight and creativity necessary to construct theories to a secondary role, making science a comfortable job for even the dullest of minds. Thus, even though it can be demonstrated that positivistic views are untenable and positivistic practices have played a strong role in the current crisis in social science, it is unlikely that many empirical researchers will abandon them or change their views or practices.

Philosophical beliefs can either constrain or free scientists in a research community. Many consumer inquirers have chosen to constrain themselves to following the tenets of various positivistic views. While relativism is still an emerging view, listed subsequently are some tentative suggestions for freeing researchers in consumer inquiry.

Theory Construction

Perhaps because of a positivistic concern with "testing" theories, consumer researchers have done little in the way of creating useful theories. A clear implication of relativism is that theory construction is a critical activity in science and one worthy of much greater attention in the field. Works by Zaltman et al. (1982) and Wicker (1985) should provide useful starting points for developing more creative and more useful theories.

Type of Research

Positivistic views may well be responsible for establishing basic research as the most prestigious type of science. However, since the truth or falsity of theories cannot be determined in basic research, then other criteria and other types of research deserve greater attention.

One criterion for considering the usefulness of research concerns its contribution to society and society's welfare. At present, it is unlikely that much consumer research would score high marks according to this criterion. There are many important social problems that involve consumption issues that are ignored in the field. For example, issues concerning the problems and responsibilities for delivering a reasonable standard of living to the poor and homeless are ignored in our literature. We should direct our attention to the question of why our society has one of the highest standards of living in the world yet has the largest number of people stealing and killing others in order to obtain various products. Issues concerning the distribution of surplus food to starving Third World countries deserve consideration. Even a partial, tentative solution to one of these problems would far outweigh a complete solution to many of the trivial issues addressed in current consumer inquiry. Positivistic views may discourage such research since it is not of the basic, more "scientific" type. Frankly, positivistic methods are often not well suited for dealing with highly complex social phenomena in natural settings. Relativistic views, however, encourage consumer researchers to expand their research agendas to include meaningful, applied research and to avoid denigrating such research as something less "scientific," and therefore less important, than basic research.

Research Methods

While positivistic researchers believe there is a single scientific method, relativists recognize that no single method can be universally applied to guarantee scientific knowledge. Relativistic researchers recognize many approaches to creating scientific knowledge, including qualitative, quantitative, and interpretive approaches, and they recognize that no single method is always better than another for constructing scientific knowledge.

One obvious implication of this view is that researchers have complete freedom to select whatever methods are appropriate for achieving their objectives. However, there is more to it. Frankly, positivistic methods in consumer research are commonly used to "justify" theories that are already supported in other fields and already accepted by many consumer researchers. These theories are already accepted by many consumer researchers because they are consistent with the ideology underlying the cognitive paradigm that dominates the field. Relativists would encourage more creative use of these methods, greater use of qualitative and interpretive methods, and the creation of new methods that are not constrained to reaffirming existing beliefs and practices in the field and in society (see Peter 1983, Sampson 1981).

A final issue in research design concerns the status of methodology developed under the guidance of positivism to achieve positivistic goals. This includes the research directives of such areas as sampling theory, measurement theory, experimentation, and inferential statistics. The problem is determining the logical status and value of these methods when the philosophy they are based on has been repudi-ated. While it is unlikely that these methods will soon be abandoned, serious consideration should be given to determining what "scientific goals" these methods are capable of achieving.

Research Reporting Practices

The reporting practices and language used in consumer inquiry make the research appear as though it followed a particular sequence and is capable of achieving positivistic goals. Typically, research reports are created to appear as though they were hypothesis-testing, falsification attempts that either support or refute the validity of a theory.

Relativists recognize that empirical data and results are constructed by scientists and constitute only a part of an overall argument for a theory. They have no special, privileged status beyond this. Thus, there should be much more open reporting of what was done to create such results. For example, if the results were created by fishing through a correlation matrix, it should be reported as such without fear of rejection. Similarly, it is common practice in some areas of social science to not report such things as how many "pretests" were done before the desired result was obtained, how many subjects were dropped (called "aberrant data" or "outliers") in order to make the results come out favorably, or how many different manipulations were tried before finding one that worked. Relativists would encourage researchers to report such information and be open concerning how their research was conceptualized and conducted.

From a relativistic viewpoint, the language of research is laden with misleading positivistic terms. For example, theories cannot be "tested" by data, nor can they be "proven" or "confirmed." All studies are case studies that are constrained to particular times and circumstances and the value of inferential statistics is greatly overestimated. Thus, a less pretentious language and a more honest reporting of research practices could free the field from the hypocrisy created when researchers prepare research reports to look like positivistic science.

Research Evaluation

Relativists argue that there is no single criterion or set of criteria that can be universally applied to judge theories, research results, or scientific knowledge. Rather, which criteria are or should be applied depends on the particular context and the relevant goals and values of individual researchers and research communities. For example, mathematical modelers, laboratory experimenters, survey researchers, and interpretive researchers vary in the emphasis they place on criteria such as managerial relevance, mathematical sophistication, theoretical significance, generalizability, and simply whether or not the research is interesting. It is likely that even researchers claiming to be falsificationists recognize that more is involved in assessing scientific knowledge than extant empirical results, and that relativism provides a superior description of research evaluation.

SUMMARY

This paper investigated a variety of philosophical positions and suggested the implications of accepting them for consumer researchers. Three positivistic accounts of science, including logical empiricism, naive falsification, and sophisticated methodological falsification were reviewed and evaluated. It was argued that these approaches are defective and have been eschewed in the science studies literature. A relativistic account of science was presented, evaluated, and offered as an appropriate philosophy of science for consumer inquiry. Although relativistic views are still emerging and have not answered all of the questions about science, several implications of adopting them were suggested.

REFERENCES

ANDERSON, PAUL F. (1983). "Marketing, Scientific Progress, and Scientific Method," *Journal of Marketing*, 47 (Fall), 18–31.

ANDERSON, PAUL F. (1986). "On Method in Consumer Research: A Critical Relativist Perspective," *Journal of Consumer Research*, 13 (September) 155–173.

ANDERSON, PAUL F. (1988a). "Relative to What—That is the Question: A Reply to Siegel," *Journal of Consumer Research*, 15 (June), 133–137.

ANDERSON, PAUL F. (1988b). "Relativism Revidivus: In Defense of Critical Relativism," *Journal of Consumer Research*, 15 (December), 403–406.

ARNDT, JOHAN (1985). "On Making Marketing Science More Scientific: Role of Orientations, Paradigms, Metaphors, and Puzzle Solving," *Journal of Marketing*, 49 (Summer), 11–23.

BARNES, BARRY (1977). *Interests and the Growth of Knowledge.* London: Routledge & Kegan Paul.

BLOOR, DAVID (1976). *Knowledge and Social Imagery.* London: Routledge & Kegan Paul.

BROMBERGER, S. (1966). "Why Questions," in R. Colodny (Ed.), *Mind and Cosmos: Explorations in the Philosophy of Science.* Pittsburgh, PA: University of Pittsburgh Press, 86–111.

CALDER, BOBBY J., LYNN W. PHILLIPS, and ALICE M. TYBOUT (1981). "Designing Research for Application," *Journal of Consumer Research*, 8 (September), 197–207.

CALDER, BOBBY J., LYNN W. PHILLIPS, and ALICE M. TYBOUT (1982). "The Concept of External Validity," *Journal of Consumer Research*, 9 (December), 240–244.

CALDER, BOBBY J., LYNN W. PHILLIPS, and ALICE M. TYBOUT (1983). "Beyond External Validity," *Journal of Consumer Research*, 10 (June), 112–114.

CALDER, BOBBY J., and ALICE M. TYBOUT (1987). "What Consumer Research is . . ." *Journal of Consumer Research*, 14 (June), 136–140.

CALDER, BOBBY J., and ALICE M. TYBOUT (1989). "Interpretive, Qualitative, and Traditional Scientific Empirical Consumer Behavior Research," in Elizabeth C. Hirschman (Ed.), *Interpretive Consumer Research.* Provo, UT: Association for Consumer Research, 199–208.

CHALMARS, A. F. (1976). *What Is This Thing Called Science?* St. Lucia, Queensland: University of Queensland Press.

COHEN, JACOB (1977). *Statistical Power Analysis for the Behavioral Sciences,* New York: Academic Press.

COOPER, LEE G. (1987). "Do We Need Critical Relativism? Comments on 'On Method in Consumer Research,' " *Journal of Consumer Research*, 14 (June), pp. 126–127.

DUHEM, PIERRE (1953). "Physical Theory and Experiment," in Herbert Feigl and May Brodbeck (Eds.), *Readings in Philosophy of Science*. New York: Appleton-Century-Crofts, 235–252.

FEYERABEND, PAUL (1975). *Against Method*. London: Redwood Burn.

GREENWALD, ANTHONY G., ANTHONY R. PRATKANIS, MICHAEL R. LEIPPE, and MICHAEL H. BAUMGARDNER (1986). "Under What Conditions Does Theory Obstruct Research Progress?" *Psychological Review*, 93, No. 2, 216–229.

HEMPEL, CARL G. (1965). *Aspects of Scientific Explanation and Other Essays in the Philosophy of Science*. New York: The Free Press.

HUDSON, LAUREL ANDERSON, and JULIE L. OZANNE (1988). "Alternative Ways of Seeking Knowledge in Consumer Research," *Journal of Consumer Research*, 14 (March), 508–521.

HUNT, SHELBY D. (1976). *Marketing Theory: Conceptual Foundations of Research in Marketing*. Columbus, OH: Grid.

HUNT, SHELBY D. (1983a). *Marketing Theory: The Philosophy of Marketing Science*. Homewood, IL: Irwin.

HUNT, SHELBY D. (1983b). "General Theories and the Fundamental Explananda of Marketing," *Journal of Marketing*, 47 (Fall), 9–17.

HUNT, SHELBY D. (1984). "Should Marketing Adopt Relativism?" in Paul F. Anderson and Michael J. Ryan (Eds.), *Scientific Method in Marketing*. Chicago: American Marketing Association, 30–34.

HUNT, SHELBY D. (1989), "Naturalistic, Humanistic, and Interpretive Inquiry: Challenges and Ultimate Potential," in Elizabeth C. Hirschman (Ed.), *Interpretive Consumer Research*. Provo, UT: Association for Consumer Research, 185–198.

HUNT, SHELBY D., and PAUL S. SPECK (1985). "Does Logical Empiricism Imprison Marketing?" in Nikhilesh Dholakia and Johan Arndt (Eds.), *Changing the Course of Marketing: Alternative Paradigms for Widening Marketing Theory, Research in Marketing, Supplement 2*. Greenwich, CT: JAI Press, 27–35.

KENDLER, HOWARD H. (1987). *Historical Foundations of Modern Psychology*. Chicago: Dorsey Press.

KUHN, THOMAS S. (1970). *The Structure of Scientific Theories*, 2nd ed. Chicago: University of Chicago Press.

LAKATOS, IMRE (1970). "Falsification and the Methodology of Science Research Programs," in Imre Lakatos and Alan Musgrave (Eds.), *Criticisms and the Growth of Knowledge*. London: Cambridge University Press, 91–195.

LATOUR, BRUNO, and STEVE WOOLGAR (1979). *Laboratory Life*. Beverly Hills, CA: Sage.

LAUDAN, LARRY (1977). *Progress and Its Problems*. Berkeley, CA: University of California Press.

LAUDAN, LARRY (1983). "The Demise of the Demarcation Problem," in Rachael Laudan (Ed.), *The Demarcation Between Science and Pseudo-Science*, Vol. 2. Blacksburg, VA: Center for the Study of Science in Society, Virginia Polytechnic Institute.

LAUDAN, LARRY (1984). "Reconstructing Methodology," in Paul F. Anderson and Michael J. Ryan (Eds.), *Scientific Method in Marketing*. Chicago: American Marketing Association, 1–4.

LEONG, SIEW MING (1985). "Metatheory and Metamethodology in Marketing: A Lakatosian Reconstruction," *Journal of Marketing*, 49 (Fall), 23–40.

LINCOLN, YVONNA S., and EGON G. GUBA (1985). *Naturalistic Inquiry*. Beverly Hills, CA: Sage.

LYNCH, JOHN G., JR. (1982). "On the External Validity of Experiments in Consumer Research," *Journal of Consumer Research*, 9 (March), 225–239.

LYNCH, JOHN G., JR. (1983). "The Role of External Validity in Theoretical Research," *Journal of Consumer Research*, 10 (June), 109–111.

MCGRATH, JOSEPH E., and DAVID BRINBERG (1983). "External Validity and the Research Process: A Comment on the Calder/Lynch Debate," *Journal of Consumer Research*, 10 (June), 115–124.

MCGUIRE, WILLIAM J. (1973). "The Yin and Yang of Progress in Social Psychology: Seven Koan," *Journal of Personality and Social Psychology*, 26 (June), 446–456.

MITROFF, IAN (1974). "Norms and Counter-Norms in a Select Group of Apollo Moon Scientists: A Case Study of the Ambivalence of Scientists," *American Sociological Review*, 39 (August), 579–595.

MUNCY, JAMES A., and RAYMOND P. FISK (1985). "Cognitive Relativism and the Practice of Marketing Science," *Journal of Marketing*, 51 (January), 20–33.

MUNEVAR, GONZALO (1981). *Radical Knowledge: A Philosophical Inquiry into the Nature and Limits of Science*. Indianapolis, IN: Hackett.

OLSON, JERRY C. (1982). "Presidential Address—1981: Toward a Science of Consumer Behavior," in A. Mitchell (Ed.), *Advances in Consumer Re-*

search, Vol. 9. Chicago: Association for Consumer Research, v–x.

OLSON, JERRY C., and J. PAUL PETER (1984). "External Validity?" in Paul F. Anderson and Michael J. Ryan (Eds.), *Scientific Method in Marketing.* Chicago: American Marketing Association, 81–84.

PETER, J. PAUL (1983). "Some Philosophical and Methodological Issues in Consumer Research," in Shelby D. Hunt, *Marketing Theory: The Philosophy of Marketing Science.* Homewood, IL: Irwin, 382–394.

PETER, J. PAUL (1984). "On Ignoring a Research Education," in Stephen W. Brown and Raymond P. Fisk (Eds.), *Marketing Theory: Distinguished Contributions.* New York: Wiley, 324–327.

PETER, J. PAUL, and JERRY C. OLSON (1983). "Is Science Marketing?" *Journal of Marketing,* 47 (Fall), 111–125

PETER, J. PAUL, and JERRY C. OLSON (1989). "The Relativistic/Constructionist Perspective on Scientific Knowledge and Consumer Research," in Elizabeth C. Hirschman (Ed.), *Interpretive Consumer Research.* Provo, UT: Association for Consumer Research, 24–29.

PETERSON, ROBERT A., GERALD ALBAUM, and RICHARD F. BELTRAMINI (1985). "A Meta-Analysis of Effect Sizes in Consumer Behavior Experiments," *Journal of Consumer Research,* 12 (June), 97–103.

POPPER, KARL R. (1959). *The Logic of Scientific Discovery.* New York: Harper Torchbooks.

SAMPSON, EDWARD E. (1981). "Cognitive Psychology as Ideology," *American Psychologist,* 36 (July). 730–743.

SAWYER, ALAN G., and J. PAUL PETER (1983). "The Significance of Statistical Significance Tests in Marketing Research," *Journal of Marketing Research,* 20 (May), 122–133.

SIEGEL, HARVEY (1988). "Relativism for Consumer Research (Comments on Anderson)," *Journal of Consumer Research,* 15 (June), 129–132.

SUPPE, FREDERICK (1977). *The Structure of Scientific Theories,* 2nd ed. Urbana, IL: University of Illinois Press.

WICKER, ALLAN W. (1985). "Getting Out of Our Conceptual Ruts," *American Psychologist,* 40 (October), 1094–1103.

ZALTMAN, GERALD, KAREN LEMASTERS, and MICHAEL HEFFRING (1982). *Theory Construction in Marketing: Some Thoughts on Thinking.* New York: Wiley.

ZUKAV, GARY (1979). *The Dancing Wu Li Masters: An Overview of the New Physics.* New York: Bantam.

POSTMODERN ALTERNATIVES: THE INTERPRETIVE TURN IN CONSUMER RESEARCH

16

John F. Sherry, Jr.*
Northwestern University

This chapter explores the postmodern perspective in consumer research. The viewpoint is evaluated in terms of its connotations and denotations. It is examined also in terms of its sociopolitical context in conventional consumer research. Nonconventional or "alternative" perspectives, such as the sociocultural, the semiotic, the humanistic, the critical theoretical, and the like, are examined in a literature review. Prospects for these eclectic perspectives are assessed, and programmatic research recommendations are made.

APOLOGIA

As a participant observer in the culture of consumer research, I am aware of an "experimental moment" (Marcus and Fischer 1986) occurring in the sociology of the profession. Whether this moment portends a paradigm shift in the discipline, or merely reflects a healthy recognition of the "tyranny of paradigms" and their rhetorical bases (Arndt 1985a, 1985b), it has fostered a

politicization of the very issue of pluralism itself (Sherry 1987a). A close reading of essays published in the *Journal of Consumer Research,* which explores some of the boundaries of the discipline (Calder and Tybout 1987; Cooper 1987; Holbrook 1987a; Kernan 1987), of rejoinders to controversial treatments of consumer behavior (e.g., Anderson 1988a; Holbrook and O'Shaughnessy 1988) or of the *Journal of Consumer Research* style sheet (Lutz 1988a), reveals something of the tension animating the conduct of inquiry in recent years. It is important to treat both the substantive and political dimensions of this moment, since each potentiates and retards the other. In this chapter, I con-

*The author is grateful for comments made by Nikhilesh Dholakia, Morris Holbrook, Grant McCracken, David Mick, Julie Ozanne, Melanie Wallendorf, and one anonymous reviewer on earlier drafts of this chapter.

sider the pursuit of "alternative" perspectives (Hudson and Ozanne 1988) in consumer research not only as a clinical or evolutionary development of the discipline (a life cycle issue), but also as a social drama (Sherry 1986; Turner 1974) that might as well be construed as a revitalization movement (Wallace 1956).

Alternative Ways of Knowing

While the biases of this chapter should be evident, I will alert the reader to the perspective guiding this review. Rorty (1980) divides philosophy into "systematic and edifying" categories. Systematic philosophy—our central academic focus, grounded in epistemology—has advocated "knowing" as the master paradigm by which all human agency is limned. Knowing is characterized by beliefs so intrinsically persuasive that their justification is deemed unnecessary. Edifying philosophy revolves around skepticism of the unexamined claims of epistemology, and advocates a perpetual search for other "vocabularies" through which phenomena may be construed. It is just such an edifying philosophy that will permit consumer research to radiate adaptively into new niches (Belk 1987a; Holbrook 1987b; Tucker 1967; Sherry 1987a).

The term "alternative" is applied in this chapter to perspectives and methods in the service of skeptical search. Whether such alternatives merely supplement or eventually supplant conventional approaches, they are presented in this chapter as a complement to orthodoxy. As Peirce (1935–1936) observed, philosophy should

. . . trust rather to the multitude and variety of its arguments than to the conclusiveness of any one. Its reasoning should not form a chain which is no stronger than its weakest link, but a cable whose fibers may be ever so slender, provided they are sufficiently numerous and intimately connected. (Vol. 5, p. 264)

This statement is echoed by Bateson (Bateson and Bateson 1987, p. 200) in his advocacy of "double description," a process intended to cap-

ture the "richest" knowledge about phenomena; myth *and* botany tell us more about trees than either perspective does alone. Gardner's (1978) use of Norse mythology to proselytize for "interpretive completeness," cited approvingly by Rodman (1987), is instructive:

It was said in the old days that every year Thor made a circle around Middle-earth, beating back the enemies of order. Thor got older every year, and the circle occupied by gods and men grew smaller. The wisdom god, Woden, went out to the King of the trolls, got him in an armlock, and demanded to know of him how order might triumph over chaos. "Give me your left eye," said the King of the trolls, "and I'll tell you."

Without hesitation, Woden gave up his left eye. "Now tell me."

The troll said, "The secret is *'Watch with both eyes!'*"

Seen in cross-cultural perspective, and denied its honorific—some (Berman 1984) would say hegemonic—status, "science" means merely "disciplined inquiry" (McCloskey 1985, p. 54). That is, any rigorously systematic conceptual framework—including those arising in the field generally glossed as "humanities"—that provides a "profounder or more adequate *knowledge of* what we already 'know' in a factual sense," is scientific (Howe 1960, pp. ix; xiv). McCloskey believes the hallmark of good and bad in learned discourse to be the "earnest and intelligent attempt to contribute to a conversation" (1985, p. 27). His rhetorical analysis of learned discourse has spread from economics (see especially Klamer, McCloskey, and Solow 1988) from whence our first consumer behavior constructs were borrowed, to others of the human sciences, where equally useful constructs are emerging (Nelson, Megill, and McCloskey 1988). If self-correction (or empirical vulnerability) is seen to be the key to responsible inquiry (Lett 1987), then the adoption of an alternative ethos should enhance our understanding of consumer behavior, and catalyze this disciplinary advance envisioned by some of its founders (Tucker 1967).

Our scholarly conversation, whether construed as a dialogue (Levy 1978) or a polylogue (Sherry 1988a), will be the livelier for its incorporation of other voices. The fear of "anarchy and paroxysms of self-expression" as potential consequences of alternative approaches to consumer behavior expressed by some researchers (Calder and Tybout 1987, p. 139)—intimations of Yeats's (1921) "Things fall apart; the center will not hold/Mere anarchy is loosed upon the world," are detectable here—is a predictable sociopsychological response of a maturing discipline. Thus, even as incontravertibly scientific an approach to ethnography as the one proposed by Werner and Schoepfle (1987a,b) can be rejected by gatekeepers whose own ethnocentrism and impoverished conceptual frameworks (Keown 1988) serve as stopgap measures to delay the sanctioning of pluralism. I envision a similar response to Bernard's (1988) efforts. (Interestingly enough, the Werner and Schoepfle [1987a,b] approach to ethnoscience has been criticized within anthropology as being uncritically or unreflectively positivistic [Briggs 1988]). The equally exaggerated concern— "Thou shalt not sit/With statisticians nor commit/A social science" (Auden 1946)—voiced by some alternative researchers (Belk's [1987b] lampoon being an implicit illustration) is likewise a predictable response to perceived complacency. Perhaps, as Nietzsche (1913, p. 3) suggested, our century is distinguished not by the triumph of science, but by the triumph of the scientific method over science. If this is the case, then it is time to promote the kind of "guerilla science" advocated by Cooper and Levine (1985). Social science can thus be understood as seeking discursive strategies that help us to resist power and keep conversations alive: "creating interpretive frames and enacting inquiries that provide more coherence with existing values, that help to enable collective action, and that offer mechanisms for transaction across disciplinary and institutional boundaries" (Shapiro 1988, p. 378). In this chapter, I hope to steer between the Scylla of positivist materialism and the Charybdis of romantic idealism (Brown 1987) to arrive at a simple affirmation of paradigmatic pluralism.

Postmodernism and Consumer Research

The need exists to cast alternative approaches in the semantic scheme of postneologisms. While the tempocentric "post" prefix is generally glossed as "contemporary," it is connotatively much richer in our culture of consumer research. Semantically, "post" conjures up images both military and mercantile; it hints at the siege mentality attending our theories and practices of trade. It suggests something of the coursing involved in our careers, and of the epistolary campaigns waged by outraged authors and disciplinary watchdogs against journal editors and conference chairs. Affixing "post" to an appropriate root is a worthy challenge.

Gellner (1985, p. 4) has observed that every "philosophical baby that is born alive" is either a "little positivist" or a "little Hegelian," and that the image that each of these sides has of the other is "simple and damning." Drawing from the works of Popper and Adorno, Gellner casts this opposition in emic terms as "an army of verbiage-intoxicated, pseudorebellious windbags, meeting a horde of inwardly vacuous, conformist, impotent Babbits" (1985, p. 6). The tone of this encounter suits much of the current exchange on alternative perspectives in consumer research, whether conducted through journal pages or at cocktail parties. While persuasive criticisms have been leveled against the positivist philosophy of science (Caldwell 1982; Haan et al. 1983; McCloskey 1985; McMullin 1988; Miller 1987; Ryan 1986; Woolgar 1988; see also Peter in this volume), sometimes in the service of methodological pluralism, it seems clear that the rumors of the death of logical positivism have been greatly exaggerated. Consequently, I am reluctant to affix the label "postpositivist" to the alternative perspectives and methods described in this chapter. Some of the approaches are based in or are refinements of positivism, some antedate positivism by millennia, and some are either actively antagonistic or entirely indifferent toward positivism. Rather, I prefer to label such alternatives as "postmodern," to link consumer research with parallel developments in contiguous disciplines.

Postmodernism is a cross-disciplinary trend encouraging sensitivity to differences and tolerance of the incommensurable (Lyotard 1984, 1979). This trend challenges the hold of "specific totalizing visions" and the "general paradigmatic style of organizing research" over "fragmented scholarly communities" (Marcus and Fischer 1986, p. 8). Contextuality, texture, native perspectives, and outliers are significant postmodern considerations. Assumptions undergirding the validity of entrenched paradigms are called into question, prompting a reexamination of our notions of appropriate inquiry (Berman 1984; Marcus and Fischer 1986; Sherry 1987a; Shweder and Fiske 1986), and a search for models capable of incorporating the ambiguity and uncertainty of social life (Barrett 1984; Levine 1985; Sherry 1987a). Rhetoric of inquiry replaces logic of inquiry, in postmodern epistemology, by "pluralizing, incorporating, and contextualizing modern grounds of research — not by eliminating them" (Nelson 1988). Geertz's (1973) discussion of the refiguration of social thought captures the postmodern ethos now touching consumer research, while Anderson's and Venkatesan's (1987) cautionary essay on interdisciplinary borrowing alerts us to some of the perils of such refiguration.

Postmodern inquiry has often taken an "interpretive turn" (Rabinow and Sullivan 1987); hermeneutic social science, which has had a venerable past, has acquired a "new lease on life" (Haan et al. 1983). Whether this resurgence is a market correction that will restore texture and everyday phenomenology to a prominent position within consumer research, or a countercultural movement that will eventually coalesce into a subdiscipline of consumer research, the "interpretive" social science, which is providing models for the understanding of consumer behavior (for example, see O'Shaughnessy 1987), is also providing a lexicon that is potentially divisive. The adjective "interpretive" is alternately honorific (Hudson and Ozanne 1988) and pejorative (Calder and Tybout 1987). It is ultimately misleading, since

"interpretation" is a fundamental activity of positivist inquiry (as is recognized by anyone who has conducted conjoint or discriminant analysis, administered projective tests, or otherwise massaged data). Indeed, Berger and Berry (1988, p. 165) have shown that "objectivity is not generally possible in statistics." The "nerve of interpretation" (Levy 1985, p. 81) being steeled by qualitative researchers has long been calmed by their quantitative counterparts. The theory-ladenness of scientific observation ensures that all of consumer research is an interpretive quest, and makes Frankel's (1987, p. 170) resignation eminently sensible: "It seems to me that if we can't get away from it, we might as well get on with it and do the work of interpretation as rigorously and honestly as we can." The forging of a postmodern science has begun in a number of disciplines (Griffin 1988), and its effects are being felt in our own. In keeping with the opportunities afforded by postmodern inquiry, and with the back to the future motif that characterizes much interdisciplinary borrowing, I employ the adjective "alternative" to characterize the perspectives and methods diffusing into consumer research from disciplines previously underrepresented in our inquiry (Belk, Zaltman et al. 1987; Hudson and Ozanne 1988). It is instructive to view these contributions as embedded in the sociopolitical context of contemporary consumer research.

POLITICIZATION OF PLURALISM

According to Turner (1974), a social drama is a unit of aharmonic or disharmonic process that arises in a conflict situation, for example, in market protectionism (Sherry 1986). Such drama is a contest between influential paradigm-bearers. The paradigms, and the rules for social action which they embody, are conventionally represented through metaphor. "Foundation" or "root" metaphors (Turner 1974, p. 28), that is, conceptual archetypes that structure our understanding of paradigms, are the vehicles through which protagonist and antagonist contend. Over the last five years, a fascinating social drama has been unfolding in the theatre of consumer research. The protagonist has been variously construed as "positivism," "sophisticated falsificationism," "traditional" or "conventional" research; the antagonist has been billed as "interpretivism," "humanism," "naturalistic inquiry," or "alternative" research (Calder and Tybout 1987; Hirschman 1986; Hudson and Ozanne 1986; Belk, Sherry, and Wallendorf 1988). Whether staged as objective versus subjective, dispassionate versus passionate, or scientific versus artistic (Belk 1986), the drama has been well attended and promoted, its plot and characters being as often commented upon as its disciplinary significance. That this dissensus had not been formally examined in Association for Consumer Research Presidential addresses (Spiggle and Goodwin 1988), until Lutz (1989) broached the issue in 1988, is itself symbolic of the highly charged political milieu in which the social drama unfolds.

Social Drama and Revitalization

Recognizing that ancestral shoulders provide the perch for contemporary visionaries (Wallendorf and Belk 1988), I locate the watershed for consumer research in 1986. The work of scholars antedating this watershed, which I review in subsequent paragraphs, constitutes a collective "prologue" to our social drama. Following Turner (1974), the social drama in consumer research unfolds in four acts. In Act I, a publicly signalled *breach* in social relations occurs between influential paradigm-bearers. The influx of new disciplinary perspectives into consumer research, mirroring the succession of psychology in a discipline formerly dominated by economics, culminated in a set of keynote addresses that challenged the professional membership of the Association for Consumer Research to alter the course of inquiry in radical ways. Belk's (1987a) Presidential Address urged researchers to investigate "macro consumer behavior" along a number of explicit dimensions. Rogers's (1987) Fellows' Address also exhorted researchers to cast a broader epistemological net by incorporating tenets of the

critical school of social science into their regimes. Each of these addresses was delivered in the wake of the Consumer Behavior Odyssey, a well-funded and well-publicized transcontinental, interdisciplinary naturalistic inquiry into consumption broadly construed (Wallendorf and Belk 1988). The Odyssey was designed, executed, and marketed as an alternative both to experiment- and survey-driven research, and to research oriented to managerial practice. It became a controversial political vehicle, part vision quest, part paradigm shift, the published record of which has just begun to emerge (Belk 1987c; Holbrook 1987c; Kassarjian 1987; Sherry 1987a).

In Act II, a *crisis* supervenes and threatens to escalate. The breach is widened to become coextensive with a dominant cleavage in social relations between actors. Again, I locate the crisis in the events of 1986. Three events in particular marked this crisis. The publication of an article by Holbrook and Grayson (1986), a semiotic analysis of cinematic consumption that may well have been "the single most reviewed paper in the annals of *JCR*" (Kassarjian, personal communication), proved to be as controversial among readers as it was among reviewers, and it intensified the debate about the nature of consumer research. Second, the program of the Annual Conference of the Association for Consumer Research contained an unprecedented number of "nontraditional" research presentations, prompting guarded optimism in one camp of researchers and outspoken skepticism in the other. Finally, the deliberations attending the appointment of a new editor to the *Journal of Consumer Research* unfolded in an environment of heated gossip and considerable trepidation, as the appointee was widely believed to be able to influence profoundly the direction of the discipline for years to come. Such belief is well founded (Cummings and Frost 1987). As symbols become most potent under conditions of uncertainty, the political agendas of the candidates were emically characterized along a continuum from "dog food managerialism" to "weird science," with each research camp fearing the worst if its paradigm-bearer were to lose the nod. Together with the solicitation of papers for a tract on "Alternative Ways of Knowing" of the upcoming AMA Winter Educators' Conference (Belk et al. 1987), the success of the first International Conference on Marketing and Semiotics (Umiker-Sebeok 1987; Mick 1988), and the recommendation by (and the subsequent rejection of) a publications committee to the ACR Board of Directors of a proposal to launch two new journals that would broaden the scope of consumer research, these events of 1986 constituted a crisis that widened the rift between positivist and nonpositivist camps in the discipline.

Redressive action takes place in Act III of the social drama. Such action serves to dampen the escalating crisis. Turner (1974) maintains that pragmatism and symbolism reach their fullest expression during this phase. Significantly, social change is most profoundly affected in Act III. Once again, multiple events constitute the adjustive mechanism at work in consumer research. The reconstitution of the editorial review board and the redrafting of the review philosophy and style sheet of the *Journal of Consumer Research* created an environment more tolerant of postmodern research. The designation of McCracken's (1986) theoretical article on culture and consumption as the winner of the inaugural "best contribution" to the *Journal of Consumer Research* award delivered an impactful message to the field at large. Further, submission of Hirschman's (1989) edited volume on "interpretive" consumer research as the first in a series of monographs to be considered by the publications committee of the Association for Consumer Research served as an important sanctioning of postmodern approaches. The completion of the Odyssey monograph (Belk 1990) should consolidate this gain. Finally, the inclusion of the present chapter in this handbook is a recognition of the promises such postmodern approaches hold for the evolution of the discipline of consumer research.

The social drama concludes in Act IV with *reintegration or irreparable schism*. The former outcome is presaged by a journal whose "facelift is not entirely cosmetic" (Lutz 1988b, p. i), by annual conferences whose purviews grow increasingly wide, and by a longitudinal if irregu-

lar kind of presidential oscillation across the camps in the Association for Consumer Research. The latter outcome will be characterized by the rise of alternative journals and proliferation of monographs, by the creation and joint sponsorship of "separate but equal" or "specialty" conferences, and by the eventual founding of a new professional society. Either of these outcomes will be catalyzed by the escalating interest in consumer behavior in disciplines such as anthropology (Appadurai 1986a; McCracken 1988a; Spencer-Wood 1987), sociology (Campbell 1987; Mukerji 1983), history (Agnew 1988; Fox and Lears 1983; Macfarlane 1987; McCracken 1987; Schama 1988), semiotics (Umiker-Sebeok 1987), and popular culture (Hine 1986), among others. The rise of "K-Mart realism" in contemporary American literature will soon bring literary critics more directly into the orbit of consumer research, Stern's (1988a,b,c) literary evaluations of advertising having provided them the requisite sanction. Work emerging at the intersection of these disciplines, such as Brown's (1987) treatment of agoraphobia and related consumption disorders, Culver's (1988) discussion of the paradox of enlightened consumption in American child lore, Stewart's (1984) essays on longing, Bolwby's (1981) exploration of window shopping, and Belk's (1987d) hagiography of Santa Claus, suggests something of the synergistic potential of consumer research. Whether the discipline will be able to radiate adaptively to new niches by incorporating "new" methods and perspectives into its orientation, or whether it will elect a more circumscribed, parochial course and thereby help balkanize the study of consumer behavior, depends largely upon the productivity of postmodern researchers, and the integrity of the peer review process so insightfully articulated by Morgan (1987).

Some observers may view the postmodern movement in consumer research as a collective form of reactance, wherein particular individuals negotiate their own life crises by individuating in response to the perceived excessiveness of disciplinary compliance attempts. Others may cast the movement as a "ritual of rebellion" (Gluckman 1956) in which a group of researchers protests against conventional disciplinary order and questions the established principles of the discipline. These rituals ultimately result in the reaffirmation of the status quo. My preference is to view postmodern alternatives collectively as a revitalization movement (Wallace 1986), mounted deliberately and consciously by researchers to create a more satisfying "culture." Revitalization movements arise under conditions of high stress for individuals and general disillusionment with a distorted cultural gestalt (Sherry 1986). Spread initially by charisma and commitment, the principles of such movements are eventually routinized if the new paradigm provides adequate stress reduction. With the increasing availability and variety of published postmodern research, the charismatic dimension of the movement will fade, no longer to be seen as an epiphenomenon of a Levy, a Holbrook, or a Belk. Just as important as published exemplars of alternative research to the reshaping of the discipline is the programmatic drafting of frontier research issues. The conversion of "getting there from here" from prospect to practice will be greatly facilitated by such guidance. Thus, the alternative research reviewed in this chapter should be judged in good measure by its ability to inspire additional inquiry.

AN OVERVIEW OF LITERATURES

The following pages present a very circumscribed view of postmodern developments in consumer research. The discussion is focussed principally on material available in sources conventionally consulted by consumer researchers, which results in bias toward the field which has regarded consumer behavior as a subdiscipline: marketing. In fact, scholars such as Belk (1987b) and Ryan (1986) have suggested that a discipline of consumer research does not yet exist. Nonetheless, in addition to those borrowed constructs imported by cosmopolitan consumer researchers, I have included work in parallel disciplines whose universes of discourse suggest no awareness of the very existence of consumer research sui generis. Further, many

of the authors identified subsequently have incorporated their own histories-of-ideas and programmatic regimes into their texts, as befits the kind of frontier research that unfolds under discontinuous disciplinary precedents. Thus the reader is urged to consult the references cited in the articles I identify: given the recency of postmodern developments in consumer research, the historical value of these citations is eclipsed by their potential impact upon the direction of future research. Estimating such impact is fraught with difficulty, but one of these postmodern alternatives—Levy's (1981) article on consumer mythology—has already been designated a marketing "megawork" (Robinson and Adler 1987).

My overview of postmodern alternatives is sketched in broad strokes. First, I review the critical thought that has fueled the search for alternatives in consumer research. Second, I explore some culturological dimensions of postmodern developments, focussing specifically on anthropological, sociological, and historical modes of inquiry typically slighted in conventional consumer research. Third, I examine the fascination of postmodern consumer researchers with the communication of meaning, dwelling in particular upon macro, structural, and semiotic treatments of consumption. Finally, I describe some of the contending correctives in consumer research as shaped by two emerging vehicles: naturalistic inquiry stemming from the Consumer Behavior Odyssey (Belk 1990) and humanistic inquiry associated with interpretive consumer research (Hirschman 1989). The review is based primarily upon published sources, but numerous working papers are cited as well. Readers will recognize immediately that I have slighted such fields as philosophy, aesthetics, literary criticism, and popular culture studies, among others. Lowenstein's (1985) study of the impact of the marketplace on the evolution of the bibliographic ego, existing as it does at the intersection of many of these disciplines, is an example of the kind of relevant work that I will not undertake to review in this chapter. Neither do I treat geography, although its relevance to consumer research (see for example Sack 1988) continues to grow. As the perspective of these fields are drawn increasingly into the orbit of consumer research, I trust a companion piece to my present effort will straightaway be constructed. I have limited my overview to those fields which I believe have impacted consumer research most directly, and with which I have some immediate familiarity.

Critical Perspectives

Although there is probably no researcher who has not lamented the failure of the discipline to adopt his or her own orientation and approaches as its own, there have been relatively few thoroughgoing and programmatic critical overviews of consumer research. The evaluative framework proposed by Sheth (1982) is an exceptional examination of the shortages and surpluses in consumer research along the dimensions of focus, process, and purpose. Sheth finds our knowledge of group behavior and non–problem-solving behavior limited, our theorizing guided by constructs that are descriptive and borrowed rather than normative and native, and our purpose turned to managerial rather than disciplinary ends. Critics such as Zielinski and Robertson (1982) fault the field for its failure to be interdisciplinary and integrative, while Kassarjian (1982) bemoans the "fragmented" nature of the discipline. Belk's (1984) call for attention to consuming rather than buying, and his reminder of the importance of context, is just now being heeded. Jacoby's (1978) satirical review of the consumer research literature remains timely today. The irony of this timeliness is striking. These initial, insightful calls for reform have generated little empirical enthusiasm, but seem to have inspired a new wave of critical reflection, which may in turn prompt the kind of empirical inquiry that will further advance the discipline.

As a stepping stone toward the eventual creation of an outlet that might be called the *Journal of Radical Marketing Thought,* Firat, Dholakia, and Bagozzi (1987) have compiled a volume of essays to catalyze innovative research into marketing and consumer behavior. The perceived need for such a journal is as remarkable as the substantive issues addressed in the volume. This book is itself a lineal descendent of the Dholakia and Arndt (1985) collection — notable in the present case for its critique of the ideology of consumer choice (Dholakia and Dholakia 1985) and its recognition of alternative approaches to consumer research (Benton 1985) — purporting to challenge the course of conventional marketing. The editors' lament that the implicit assumptions that regard a certain worldview, historic juncture, and social system as perpetual (1987, p. xii) have gone largely uncriticized in the two disciplines, is an accurate one. Further, the prescription for radicalizing the disciplines, synthesized from the volume's contributors is provocatively stated: Scholars must infuse humanistic values into their work, foster enlightened, reasoned practices, adopt macrosystemic perspectives, use comprehensive causal models, develop holistic and integrative frameworks, and deepen the historical basis of investigation (1987, p. 374).

While each of the essays in this volume has implications for consumer behavior, the editors have bracketed several chapters in particular as consumption-centered. Holbrook (1987d) has insightfully considered the neglect of introspection as a research strategy, experience as a research focus, and narrative as an expository vehicle in the discipline of consumer research. Sherry (1987b) has adopted a cultural criticism perspective to explore the ideology of consumption and attendant dysfunctions, arguing the need for a canon of propriety to guide such directed intervention programs as contemporary marketing. The meanings of consumption as shaped by marketing practice are explored by Moorman (1987). That consumer behavior is critical to self-actualization, but that a radical reordering of the individual's relation to consumption processes is necessary to avert the harmful psychic consequences of unreflective false consciousness is detailed by Kilbourne (1987). Benton's (1987) account of the succession of the culture of production by the culture of consumption has made apparent the wisdom of reorienting marketing according to traditional social criticism and aligning the discipline with other contemporary social change movements, in the service of the search for an improved quality of life. Firat's (1987) concern with macro consumption phenomena has prompted his discussion of the "Structure of Available Alternatives for Consumption," a socially constructed framework he believes determines consumer choice, and whose infrastructural and superstructural determinants themselves are poorly understood. Belk's (1987b) modest proposal "for creating a discipline that actually investigated consumer behavior," cited at the beginning of my essay, serves as a capstone summary and criticism of the field that the Firat, Dholakia, and Bagozzi (1987) volume seeks to radicalize.

Of the many correctives proposed by researchers concerned with broadening the discipline, two in particular, one ontological, the other methodological, have helped catalyze postmodern developments in consumer research. The first of these is the advocacy of research into hedonic and experiential dimensions of consumer behavior (Hirschman and Holbrook 1982; Holbrook and Hirschman 1982). This advocacy has fostered inquiry into phenomenological dimensions of consumption previously slighted by consumer researchers, and challenged the hegemony of the information-processing perspective. By focussing on the multisensory, fantasy, and emotive aspects of consumer behavior, by offering a range of propositions on issues such as mental constructs, product classes, product usages, and individual differences, and by complementing existing models of consumption through an emphasis on experience, these authors have extended the depth inquiry begun by their motivation research forebears. They have broadened their central constructs and suggested techniques for probing dimensions of consumer experience (Hirschman and Holbrook 1986). Their perseverance has helped legitimize the search for balance in understanding consumer behavior.

The second proposed corrective is the advocacy of a critical relativist perspective of methodology (Anderson 1986, 1988b). This critique of the ways in which knowledge is generated and evaluated in consumer research has challenged positivist orthodoxy and suggested that conventional workbench issues more rigorously pursued would advance the discipline appreciably. Anderson's revisionism has prompted considerable debate across research camps (Cooper 1987; Calder and Tybout 1987; Siegel 1988). He has also set the tone for debate within the emerging circle of nonpositivist researchers, as Hirschman's (1986) version of humanistic inquiry was dissected shortly after publication in a set of widely circulated working papers (Belk and Wallendorf 1987; Brinberg and Kumar 1987; Sherry 1987c; see also Wallendorf and Belk 1988). That dissensus has emerged simultaneously with alternative perspectives is itself a persuasive argument against the reifying of diverse approaches into an "interpretive" paradigm. The naturalistic inquiry espoused by Belk, Sherry, and Wallendorf (1988), itself informed by the critical perspective, awaits its own critical reception. The broad-based assault on traditional consumer research methods has drawn from fields as far flung as hermeneutics (Ryan and Bristor 1987; Ozanne and Hinson 1987), Austrian economics (Boettke 1987), mythology (Speck 1987), and theology (Kavanaugh 1981; Mascarenhas 1987; Tamari 1987). This exploration of "new" methods and "alternative" ontologies is one of the hallmarks of postmodern inquiry in consumer research. It has culminated in the examination of ways by which consumption is employed as a vehicle to achieve transcendent experience (Belk, Wallendorf, and Sherry 1989).

Culturological Perspectives

In contrast to the distinct cast that cognitive social psychology has imparted to contemporary consumer research, a macro-orientation has arisen over the past half decade that seeks a more comprehensive and embedded understanding of consumer behavior. This orientation is shaped chiefly by anthropological, sociological, and historical viewpoints, which are diffusing into consumer research, carried by newcomers to the discipline and imported by natives seeking wider interpretive frames. Work representative of each of these viewpoints and channels is sampled in the following pages.

Anthropology. Initially touted by Winick (1961) and championed by Levy (1978), the anthropological perspective began its sustained diffusion into consumer research with Sherry's (1983) modeling of the process of gift exchange and call for ethnographic inquiry. In subsequent cognate articles treating the two disciplines, Sherry (1987d, 1988b) has examined the history and sources of mutual neglect, identified areas of conceptual and empirical compatibility, described the major anthropological research orientations and ethnographic methodology, and laid out programmatic research directives based upon a comprehensive anthropological framework. He has also explored the utility of the culture concept in consumer behavior (Sherry 1986b). Applications of an economic anthropological perspective to issues such as the globalization and development (Sherry 1988c) of a folkloric perspective to word-of-mouth and complaint behavior (Sherry 1984), of a linguistic perspective to market pitching (1988d), and of a symbolic anthropological perspective to brand loyalty (Sherry 1986c) have helped demonstrate the breadth of relevance each discipline has for the other. Ethnographic analyses of flea markets (Sherry 1988a), farmers' markets (Heisley, McGrath, and Sherry 1988), and gift shops (Sherry and McGrath 1988; McGrath 1989) have consolidated this demonstration.

Contributing to the establishment of this anthropological beachhead is the historically and symbolically focussed work of McCracken (1988a). His timely volume is the culmination of numerous inquiries into the nature of material culture, the most highly regarded of which (McCracken 1986) has explored some of the mechanisms that effect the transfer of meaning from the categories of the culturally constituted world to consumer goods themselves, and from thence to consumers. In cognate literature reviews (1987, 1988b), McCracken has described modern consumption as a historical artifact,

evaluating the consumer revolution in terms of the cultural, sociological, psychological, political, intellectual, marketing, and consumer contexts in which it unfolded. His discussion of the evocative power of objects (1988c) as a bridge to displaced meaning, of the consistent complementarity of goods that both enables and constrains choice (1988d), and of the role of goods in cultural continuity and change (1988e) has deepened our understanding of material culture and suggested novel avenues of research. Whether dealing with the social symbolics of patina (1988f), of clothing (1988g), or of collections (1988h), McCracken has emphasized the capacity of goods to mobilize behavior.

A third stream of anthropological inquiry into consumer behavior is the cross-cultural investigations of Arnould and Wilk. In a jointly authored paper (1984), they have explored the diffusion of Western consumer goods into the ritual orbit of nonwestern societies, noting the difference in social dynamics between commercial and gift economies. This issue was subsequently examined individually, in Arnould's (1989) revision and refinement of diffusion theory, and Wilk's (1988) examination of the micro- and macro-level implications of the diffusion of American baseball. Family decision making in cross-cultural perspective has also been examined (Wilk 1987). In an early paper, Arnould (1983) had called for the explication of intersubjective, phenomenological experience, rather than the scaling and operationalizing of variables characteristic of consumer research. His collaborative investigation of object attachment and social linkage (Wallendorf and Arnould 1988), in effect, has answered that call through its use of a mixed research design to capture the richness of context attending consumers' involvement with objects.

Anthropological inquiry paralleling and potentiating the work in progress within consumer research has begun to accelerate. A call for an anthropology of consumption was formally issued by Douglas (1976), whose communications theory of goods was elaborated later (Douglas and Isherwood 1979) into a fully articulated semiotic framework, which equated consumption with the creation of intelligibility, with power relations, and with the manipulation of periodicity. Sahlins has also (1976) adopted a semiotic perspective in his explication and critique of contemporary Western consumption; his discussion of object codes and the totemic dimension of consumer behavior has proven especially intriguing to anthropologists working within the discipline of consumer research. Mintz's (1982, 1985) seminal treatments of the social dynamics and cross-cultural impact attending the diffusion of sugar, including the politics of overconsumption, as well as his provocative speculation that profoundly compulsive behavior frequently masquerades as freedom of choice (1987a), have grounded the semiotic perspective in biology and history. The inquiry into the social life of things launched by Appadurai (1986a) and his colleagues has just begun diffusing into consumer research. In particular, Appadurai's (1986b) treatment of the shaping of consumption by the politics of valuation, Kopytoff's (1986) call for a cultural biography of things that would capture the range and depth of consumer-object relations, and Gell's (1986) description of the transformation of consumption in developing economies have immediate relevance to current work in consumer research.

The concern anthropologists once had for the histories of things (Mintz 1987b) has been renewed, with Wolf's (1982) volume on world system dynamics being a particularly successful instance. Object-specific explorations by anthropologists — cloth, for instance, has fascinated researchers (Bayley 1986, Schneider 1987) — which are an inevitable outgrowth of the study of material culture (Babcock 1986, Clark 1987, Schlereth 1982, Shanks and Tilley 1987, Spenser-Wood 1987b), promise to contribute to the nascent work on consumer-object relations in consumer research (Belk 1988a; Belk et al. 1988; Kelly 1987; McCracken 1988i; Shimp and Madden 1988). So also does the historico-philosophical treatment of the role of the object in the revision of the theory of consumption developed by Miller (1987). The significance of consumption in archaeological perspective (Brumfiel 1987; Hodder 1989) grows increasingly apparent.

Perrin's (1988) sensitive and detailed accounts of the levels of social setting in which consumption is embedded, coupled with Newman's (1988) examination of lifestyle degradation in the contemporary United States, have provided a compelling new agenda for researchers interested in the situational dimensions of consumer behavior. Collaborative work between anthropologists and consumer researchers (e.g., Heskel and Semenik 1983; Heisley and Holmes 1987) has also begun to fulfill important bridging functions. Finally, volumes produced by the Society for Economic Anthropology (Plattner 1985; Rutz and Orlove 1988) have begun to address consumer behavior issues, albeit within traditional field venues. Such volumes will undoubtedly accelerate the shift in anthropological focus to contemporary industrial consumption settings.

Sociology. Acknowledging the scattered and uneven precedents for a sociology of consumption, Nicosia and Mayer (1976) have proposed a conceptual framework that recognizes the social embeddedness of consumer behavior, and have illustrated the practicality of an approach unmoored from individual decision making. However, programmatic sociological research into consumption of the kind advocated by Robertson and Zielinski (1982) — a "key perspectives" approach of eminent utility — has not progressed appreciably. The investigation, prompted by Rogers's (1976) examination of new product adoption and diffusion, by Gatignon and Robertson (1985), is one notable exception; Coleman's (1983) work on social class is another.

The principal proponents and practitioners of sociologically informed consumer research have been Zaltman and his colleagues. An early paper (Zaltman and Wallendorf 1977), which sampled such neglected topics as social roles, societal level analysis, collective decision making, demography, lifestyle, social class, and illegal exchange, coupled with both a textbook (Zaltman and Wallendorf 1983) and a reader

(Wallendorf and Zaltman 1984), which devoted considerable attention to social dimensions of consumption, have imparted impetus to sociological research emerging within the discipline. Advocacy of "heretical" perspectives (Zaltman and Bonoma 1979) that facilitate discovery of "hidden events" (Zaltman 1983) underlying consumption patterns has reached fruition in the postmodern climate of consumer research. Studies of assimilation and acculturation (O'Guinn, Lee, and Faber 1985; Reilly and Wallendorf 1984, 1987; Wallendorf and Reilly 1982, 1983), of ethnic affiliation (Deshpande, Hoyer, and Donthu 1986) and innovativeness (Hirschman 1981), of social class (Fisher 1987), and of metatheoretical bias (Deshpande 1983, 1984; Haas 1986; Hirschman 1985; Redmond and Wallendorf 1984; Tetreault 1987; Zaltman and Price 1984) have stemmed directly from this advocacy. Zaltman's sociological perspective has been complemented indirectly by that of Howie Becker (1979, 1982, for example), whose championing of photography as a research technique has begun to have an impact on the field through the work of Heisley (Heisley and Levy 1985; Heisley, McGrath, and Sherry 1988a) and Wallendorf (Wallendorf and Arnould 1988; Belk, Sherry, and Wallendorf 1988; Wallendorf and Westbrook 1985).

Several sociological approaches in particular have been proposed as "alternative" methods for exploring consumer behavior. Ethnomethodology has been espoused by Spiggle and Sanders (1983), while Sanders (1985, 1987, 1988) has demonstrated the usefulness of ethnographic methods in complementing conventional survey research. Symbolic interactionism has been applied to such issues as discipline building (Prus 1987; Prus and Frisby 1987), subcultural coding (Durgee 1986a), and consumer-object relations (Solomon 1983). Phenomenology—an area I view as a philosophical clinical zone between psychology and sociology (Churchill and Wertz 1984)—has been used to enhance researchers' interviewing and interpretation skills (Durgee 1987a, 1987b) to explore consumer-object relations (Myers 1985), to probe the psychology of buying (Wertz and Greenhut 1985),

to evaluate emergent trends (Mruck 1985), and to explicate marketing practice (Fennell 1985). Durgee (1986b, 1988; Durgee and Stuart 1987) has used his sociological perspective to nurture a variant of motivation research among marketing practitioners. Content analytic approaches to consumption phenomena, such as those employed by Spiggle (1986) and Belk (1987c) to study comic strips and comic books, by Belk and Pollay (1985) to study advertising, and by Spiggle (1987) to study shopping lists, have been sociologically informed. Prus's investigations (1984, 1985, 1986a, 1986b) of relationship management, pricing, sales, and trust, each of which has employed participant observation and interviewing as principal methods, have influenced postmodern consumer researchers. His volumes on the interpersonal dimensions of sales interactions (Prus 1989a) and ethnographic approaches to marketing (Prus 1989b) have a similar impact. His newsletter *Marketplace Exchange* has proven to be a valuable nexus of information exchange among sociologically inclined consumer researchers.

Sociological investigation ongoing outside the boundaries of consumer research promises to shape the reorientation of our field. Gary Becker's (1976, 1981) economic perspective of social dynamics has heartened some researchers and alienated others, but it has influenced significantly the way we construe consumer interactions. Sociologists have figured prominently in reevaluations of the nature of advertising (Barthel 1988; Goffman 1976; MacCannell 1987; Schudson 1984). Rogers's work on Silicon Valley (Rogers and Lawron 1984) is among the few grounded studies upon which a meaningful investigation of corporate culture will eventually be based. Mukerji (1983) has demonstrated convincingly that mass consumption antedates the development of capitalism, which in turn will help liberate the study of consumption from marketing-bound conceptions. In fact, the very nature of consumer behavior itself has been provocatively and persuasively redefined by Campbell (1987), whose discussion of "modern autonomous imaginative hedonism" as the engine of consumption has received an enthusiastic hearing from postmodern consumer researchers. Ewen's (1988) intriguing and wide-ranging examination of the semiotics of design with particular attention to the concept of "style" contributes to this redefinition. The culture-critical perspective of consumer behavior advanced by Williams (1981), coupled with the normative implications of Etzioni's (1988) deontological critique of neopositivist economics, provide the kind of integration needed for an effective reorientation of this kind to occur. Bourdieu's (1984) survey of middle-class consumer behavior in France, a species of social psychoanalysis that explores the linkages of lifestyle patterns with class-conditioned cultural competence, has demonstrated the value of subjecting reputedly generalizable constructs to local scrutiny. The emerging subdiscipline of consumer-object relations is being catalyzed by sociologists such as Rochberg-Holton (1986). The rise of visual sociology (see, for example, recent issues of the *Journal of Visual Sociology* and *Visual Anthropology)* is abetting this emergence. Work on the phenomenology of sales interactions (Pinch and Clark 1986; Clark and Pinch 1987), of financial markets (Adler and Adler 1984), and of auctions (Smith 1986) has gradually diffused into consumer research (Sherry 1988a). Finally, gift giving has reemerged as a focus of sociological attention (Cheal 1988). With their capstone essay on cultural sociology, Wuthnow and Witten (1988) provide consumer researchers a point of entry into a number of research agendas of importance in the postmodern climate.

History. Fullerton's (1987a) eloquent discussion of the poverty of ahistorical analysis in contemporary marketing thought is readily generalizable to the field of consumer research. Our lack of attention to "complex flux" and "uniqueness" of consumption phenomena in time, and our unexamined belief in "uniformitarianism" (Fullerton 1987a, p. 98, p. 103) have been critical disciplinary shortcomings. His debunking of the "catastrophic" and "continuity" models of evolution upon which conventional marketing history has rested, and his introduction of a "complex flux" model that

conforms more precisely to known facts (Fullerton 1988), suggests that our understanding of consumption may be severely time-bound as well. Mager and Helgeson (1987) have helped direct our attention to the changing cultural forces that have shaped some of our conceptions of consumption. Kumcu's (1987a) succinct comparison of historical method with conventional positivism and his assessment of the benefits of historical analysis have provided consumer researchers with a useful introduction to the field. Savitt's (1980) overview is similarly instructive. With the institutionalization of Michigan State University's annual "Workshop on Historical Research in Marketing" (see volumes by Hollander and Standley 1983, and Hollander and Nevett 1985, for examples), and with the growing significance of the annual Macromarketing Conference, we can expect the historical investigation of consumer behavior to accelerate.

Several recent tutorial articles have contributed to this acceleration. Firat (1987) has examined several historiographical traditions — the *Annales* school, the hermeneutic perspective, and Marxian analysis — for the light to be shed on consumption phenomena that do not lend themselves to probing by experiment or survey. His historically based critique of positivist inquiry (Firat 1988a) and his call for the founding of a historically grounded discipline to study needs (Firat 1988b) have amplified researchers' dissatisfaction with synchronic perspective. Fullerton (1987b) has continued his critique of positivist inquiry in a useful sketch of German historicism, which details both the philosophical assumptions and disciplinary goals of the school, as well as their implications for consumer research. Kumcu's (1987b) application of historical perspective to consumer behavior, with particular regard to retailing systems, is a further challenge to conventional positivist inquiry. The historical perspective of advertising issues presented by Pollay (1986, 1987a, 1987b) and critiqued by Holbrook (1987c) has helped shape the introspective disciplinary climate developing in consumer research. Pollay's (1987c) ethnohistorical meditative case study of his becoming an advertising archivist has contributed to a psychohistorical introspective tradition emerging within the discipline (Holbrook 1988d). Finally, in an essay combining work-bench suggestions with programmatic research directives, Rassuli and Hollander (1987) have provided some historical grounding for what may become one of the discipline's most productive new avenues of inquiry: comparative studies.

If we accept the premise that the past is a foreign country (Lowenthal 1985), the merger of historical and cross-cultural studies into a comparative perspective of consumer behavior is readily understandable. A volume of research edited by Tan and Sheth (1985) has demonstrated the multistrandedness of this merger. The advocacy of a philosophy of contextualization (Engel 1985) has called our attention to ethnocentric and tempocentric biases that have characterized consumer research. The impending bifurcation of consumer research into pure and applied disciplines (Sheth 1985) as a result of historical forces impacting marketing is a further testimony to the tumultuous nature of the postmodern environment. The "consumer revolution" discussed by McCracken (1985) may well have a twentieth-century analog in the work of postmodern consumer researchers. The potential discontinuity and aimlessness of consumer research projected by Helgeson, Mager, and Kluge (1985) in the face of the current research environment can be averted by viewing postmodern developments in historical perspective, and by linking these developments both to antecedent research and to each other as the postmodern tradition emerges. Thus, whether research is focussed on cultural area or country, on ethnicity or nationality, or on substantive or methodological issues, as are the sixty-odd papers in the Tan and Sheth (1985) volume, an historically informed comparative perspective of consumer behavior can become a unifying principle within the discipline. Kaufman's (1987) study of marketing in Han dynasty China is a step in this direction.

Three volumes in particular are evidence of increasing interest in such comparative perspectives. Although each is focussed upon marketing—one on "broadening" the discipline

(Shapiro and Walle 1988), the others on applying the discipline to economic development (Kumcu and Firat 1988; Littlefield and Csath 1988)—a number of the contributors deal explicitly with consumer behavior. Historical and macro-level dimensions, and to a lesser extent cross-cultural dimensions, of consumer behavior are treated in the Shapiro and Walle (1988) volume. Consumption patterns in transitional societies and their managerial implications are discussed in some depth in the Kumcu and Firat (1988) volume. The essays in the Littlefield and Csath (1988) volume, although terse and primarily driven by their applications, illustrate something of the cross-cultural diversity both of consumer behaviors and analytic interpretation. Each of these three contributions presages a return to the kind of comparative contextuality that will permit our understanding of consumption to grow more comprehensive.

As with the anthropological and sociological traditions I have already considered, historical inquiry into consumer behavior being conducted beyond the disciplinary boundaries of consumer research is continuing apace. McCracken's (1987, 1988b) cognate reviews are the best single introduction to this historical work, and obviate the need for extended discussion in this chapter. However, a number of particular treatments deserve recognition for the impact they are having on contemporary consumer research. An edited volume of essays on the "culture of consumption" by Fox and Lears (1983) has helped fuel much critical reflection among consumer researchers (Dholakia and Sherry 1987; Sherry 1987b). Macfarlane's provocative volumes on individualism (1978) and the culture of capitalism (1987), each of which is a stimulating exercise in anthropologically informed social history, have contributed to this critical reflection. Agnew's (1986) examination of the "inescapably dialectical" relationship between commerciality and theatricality has greatly facilitated exploration of the experiential dimension of consumer behavior. Our understanding of the evolution of contemporary consumer behavior has been shaped by the historical accounts of Braudel

(1979a, 1979b, 1979c), McKendrick, Brewer, and Plumb (1982), and Williams (1982), while scholars such as de Certeau (1984), Foucault (1970), and White (1978) have influenced our notions of the critical purposes toward which historical inquiry itself may be fashioned. Numerous historical case studies have begun to have a cumulative impact upon the field. Geary's (1986) examination of the medieval consumption of sacred relics, Cassanelli's (1986) investigation of quasilegal drug consumption in Africa, and Reddy's (1986) exploration of the adoption of capitalist modes of evaluating commodities in postrevolutionary France have each demonstrated the value of ethnohistorical approaches to understanding consumer behavior. Schama's (1987) meticulous examination of the multileveled role played by consumption in Dutch ethnogenesis — in particular, the anxieties of superabundance and the ordeal of prosperity — has methodological and culture critical implications for consumer researchers beyond its sheer thickness of description of a historical epoch. So also does Apple's (1987) investigation of the "commercialization and medicalization" of infant care.

Communicative Perspectives

Much of the postmodern research into consumer behavior has focussed on symbolic communication. This focus has revealed something of the mutually constituting nature of consumption and communication. Generally speaking, postmodern consumer researchers have adopted three approaches in interpreting the significance of communication. A macro-level perspective has been used to explore the ways in which symbolism is shaped and reflected by the culture in which it is embedded. The "packing" process by which symbols are infused with meaning is of interest here. A structural perspective has been used to interpret the significance of that embeddedness. From this viewpoint, the "deep structure" or symbolic infrastructure of a culture is at issue. A semiotic perspective has been used as an omnibus framework to explore all manners of symbolic behavior. This perspective has served as a conceptual

cachement basin for issues ranging from cognitive process to cultural movement as each impacts upon meaning. While these perspectives inevitably and inexorably intergrade, I have selected a number of works that represent each of these approaches to illustrate something of the range and diversity of the postmodern exploration of consumption and communication.

Macro Perspectives. The macro-level or "cultural studies" approach adopted by a number of contemporary consumer researchers has its roots in a counter-Enlightenment shift away from notions of rationality as objective to a critique of ideology that explores the antecedents to and consequences of thought control in consumer culture (Alvesson 1987; Christians 1986; Grossberg 1983; Rabinow and Sullivan 1987). A triangulated reading of Geertz's (1964) essay on ideology as a cultural system, Real's (1986) indispensable review of critical and institutional theories of communication, and Carey's (1988a,b) volumes on the multistranded relationship of culture and communication reveals the dense interpenetration of scholarly traditions (whose disentanglement is beyond the scope of my essay) that has culminated in the recent desire of some consumer researchers to move beyond "the narrow concern for empirically measuring media effects" (Real 1986, p. 477), which I construe as the micro-orientation, to the study of the cultural significance of communication. This work has been largely confined to studies of advertising, although there are indications that the inquiry is being extended to other dimensions of persuasive communication. For example, even such ostensibly innocuous vehicles as "Sesame Street" have been evaluated for their efficacy in perpetuating the hegemonic character of consumer culture (Mattelart, Delcourt, and Mattelart 1984, pp. 97–98).

Leiss (1976) and his colleagues have been the principal contributors to the emerging macro-level perspective in consumer research to date. By defining the "real" importance of contemporary advertising as "the privileged discourse for the circulation of messages and social cues about the interplay between persons and objects" (Leiss, Kline, and Jhally 1986, p. 47), these scholars have reoriented the plane of inquiry to a sociocultural level. Their discussion of the commodification of consumers, of the evolution of advertising as both a unique cultural form and a model for the entire field of communications, of consumption as an articulated communication system, of basic advertising formats, and, most important, of the cultural frames by which the significance of goods is ultimately construed, has empowered consumer researchers to broaden the scope of legitimate inquiry. Their provocative assertion that advertising is written to achieve test results rather than sales results (1986, p. 138) is itself enough to fuel a powerful new research regime. Jhally's (1987) subsequent investigation of the meaning of commodities in mass-mediated society—in particular his treatment of compulsion and alienation and his resurrection of advertising-as-religion construals—has further incentivized researchers to grapple with meaning and significance.

Several consumer researchers have extended this probing into the social significance of advertising. Sherry (1987e) has employed a cultural systems perspective to interpret advertising as a way of knowing, a way of discerning, and a way of creating meaning that structures experience semiotically and semiologically into distinct patterns. The shortcomings of information processing-based models of advertising have been evaluated by McCracken (1987b), who has advocated a cultural perspective capable of viewing advertising as one conduit in the transfer of meaning from the cultural world to consumer goods (McCracken 1986). Belk and Pollay (1985b) have presented a historical analysis of the ways in which advertising reflects and influences values in the United States, while Sherry and Camargo (1987) have explored the way in which linguistic borrowing creates a promotional patois by which Japanese consumers are able to negotiate cultural continuity and change. Moving beyond advertising to study other forms of mass-mediated communication, Belk (1987e) has investigated themes of materialism in U.S. comic books, and Spiggle (1986) has contrasted the conventional comic with the countercultural "comix" to reveal a uniform embracing of materialism across ideological camps. Each of these latter studies has raised issues regarding core cultural values and noncommercial materialism that are in urgent need of further exploration. Emerging work on acculturation into consumer society (O'Guinn, Lee, and Faber 1986; O'Guinn and Faber 1985) has an especially urgent appeal given the recent fragmentation of our domestic marketplace. Finally Levy (1984) has used consumers' perceptions of products themselves to make inferences about the stability of cultural categories and values over time.

Structuralist Perspectives. Structural approaches to consumer behavior have derived chiefly, although not exclusively, from the work of Levi-Strauss (1963, 1969), and they have sought to discover the basic meaning beneath consumption phenomena construed as myths. The principle proponents of structuralist approaches have been Leymore, Levy, and Hirschman. Predictably enough, the earliest structuralist forays into consumer behavior have concentrated upon advertising. Leymore (1975, 1987, 1988) has usefully interpreted advertising as the mythology of consumer culture, and has detailed the rules by which the codes of advertising can be transformed to reveal their culturally significant meanings. Levy (1981) has employed personal narrative as a projective vehicle from which to elicit insight into fundamental categories such as values, status, gender, and age from informants' accounts of foodways. This study was the precursor to contemporary deep structural examinations of consumer behavior. In a series of articles, Hirschman (1987a, 1987b, 1988) has sifted cinema and television productions for their respective consumption codes, by which cultural categories, ramifying through metaphysics, cosmology, sociology, and psychology, are reproduced and reinforced for American consumers.

Semiotic Perspectives. In a pair of didactic essays, Mick (1986, 1988a) has catalyzed the formal diffusion of semiotics into consumer research and has assessed the extent of that diffusion to date. These essays bracket a period that has witnessed the meeting of the First International Conference on Marketing and Semiotics (Umiker-Sebeok 1987) and the publication of a special edition of the *International Journal of Research in Marketing* on semiotics (Pinson 1988). Mick's essays have demonstrated the degree to which consumer research has been influenced by the habit of mind, if not the formal vocabulary and techniques, of semiotic analyses. These essays have also suggested something of the breadth of the semiotic purview in consumer research. Of those works that do not explicitly employ the scholarly apparatus of semiotics, research into issues such as symbolism and secular ritual falls most directly into this purview. Because Mick's review essay (1988c) has obviated the need for much further accounting, I have confined my comments to a subset of the literature of particular interest.

Investigation of the ritual substratum of consumer research is in its infancy. Explored originally by Levy (1978b), interest in ritual consumer behavior has been revived by Rook (1984), whose studies of grooming (Rook 1985; Rook and Levy 1983) and threshold protection (1987b) have also revitalized the use of projective methods in consumer research. Pandya (1985) has treated gift giving within a semiotic framework. Fashion codes have been consumer research mainstays (Holman 1980, 1981), and recent studies have examined them in terms of power and gender displays (Solomon and Anand 1985). Sherry (1984) has probed the deep structural significance of consumer oral traditions such as rumor-mongering. Pollay (1987c) has employed the extended case study format to interpret the significance of specific U.S. Christmas practices. Interest in secular rituals that accompany holidays is building among consumer researchers (e.g., Arnould and Wallendorf 1988). Holbrook has created a virtual cottage industry of the study of aesthetic production and consumption, his essay on the semiology of consumer aesthetics (1987b) being an especially comprehensive overview. Dietary practices (Verba and Camden 1987) and mealtime behaviors (Heisley and Levy 1985) have received attention. Inquiries into the numinous dimension of consumer behavior (Hirschman

1985b; Belk, Wallendorf, and Sherry 1988) have sifted the secular rituals of contemporary culture for their semiotic import. Noth's (1988) proposal for the creation of a semiotics of consumer behavior arrives on the swell of critical interest in the ritual substratum of consumption.

Research into symbolic consumer behavior has quite often fallen into the purview of semiotics. While the long and venerable history of this topic renders it resistant to the compaction required in my essay, several contributions (themselves encapsulating much antecedent treatment of symbolism) are especially worthy of note. Principal among these is *Symbolic Consumer Behavior,* a volume edited by Hirschman and Holbrook (1981) whose eclectic essays on symbolics, aesthetics, and mass communication imparted much impetus to the renewed interest in extrafunctional dimensions of consumer behavior. The study of product constellations (Solomon and Assael 1987)—the symbolic complementarity and diagnosticity of sets of products —and the syntax of product use (Kehret-Ward 1987, 1988) have shed considerable light upon the nature of consumption systems. Investigations of consumption symbolism (e.g., Belk, Bahn, and Mayer 1982; Hirschman 1986b; Kleine and Kernan 1987) have added to this understanding. Application of this knowledge has been attempted in the field of design (Flock 1988; O. Solomon 1988). The production of symbolic vehicles by competing cultural production systems, and the brokering of these vehicles by cultural gatekeepers, have begun to come under more careful scrutiny in consumer research (M. Solomon 1988). Linguistic treatments of advertising, such as Mick's (1987) study of story grammars, Denny's (1988) observations on pragmatics, North's (1987) discussion of framing, and Durand's (1987) examination of rhetoric, have demonstrated the utility of semiotics to consumer research.

Integrating the Perspectives

Each of the integrating perspectives I have identified—the critical, the culturological, and the communicative—produces an orientation to research that is programmatic in its own right. These orientations can be briefly sketched. Critical researchers are interested in the articulation of moral and political economies. Further, their interest extends beyond the merely economic to embrace to ludic dimensions of consumer behavior. Culturological researchers are concerned with transforming our notion of externality by demonstrating the fundamental character of economic embeddedness. Their interest in the macro-level dimensions of consumption is grounded in contextuality, whether of a social or temporal nature. Finally, communicative researchers are absorbed with the venerable issues of encoding and decoding. Their principal interest is in the nature of meaning, its transmutation into consumption codes, and its translatability between communicants.

Thus, loosely disentangled, these orientations suggest collectively some general directions that postmodern inquiry might pursue:

- Investigation of the macrofoundations of consumption phenomena such as needs and choice (Dholakia, McIntyre, and Joy 1988; Firat and Dholakia 1982), and expansion of the microfoci of consumer research to embrace extra-economic features (Hudson and Murray 1986).

- Recognition of the cultural biases that inform (and deform) theory construction (Joy 1988; Rexeisen 1982; Roth and Moorman 1988).

- Comparison of research findings across social and temporal boundaries (Belk 1984b; Belk and Zhou 1987; Jolibert and Fernandez-Moreno 1983; O'Connor, Sullivan, and Pogorzelski 1985; Tse, Belk, and Zhou 1989).

- Shift to discourse-centered investigations of consumer behavior and to hermeneutic approaches in understanding meaning (Levy 1986; O'Shaughnessy 1985; Parker 1988; Traube 1986).

- Development of enlightened directed intervention programs that take into account culturally patterned consumer behaviors (Firat 1988c) and the cultural contradictions engendered by the diffusion of market capitalism (Belk 1988c; Dholakia and Firat 1988; see also Peter in this volume).

Clearly, these research directions are quite general and by no means exhaustive. They do indicate, however, the habit of mind resulting

from the merger of perspectives I have explored. In an era of increasing contact, if not outright collision, of disciplines with one another, of cultures with one another, and of each of these singular creations with the other, the embeddedness of the researcher becomes as much a liability as an asset to productive inquiry. As this embeddedness is more rigorously scrutinized, consumer researchers will challenge both the fundamental constructs of their discipline and the unilinear evolution of the culture their efforts have helped to direct. Ontology, epistemology, axiology, and praxis are all affected by postmodern inquiry. We are discovering, just as Horatio grew to learn, that there are more things in heaven and earth than are dreamt of in our philosophy. Before lodging specific research recommendations, I find it helpful to consider some of the recent work whose explicit agenda includes the promotion of just such a habit of mind.

SOME CONTENDING CORRECTIVES

At the time of this writing, I am aware of two vehicles that attempt to capture and package the kinds of postmodern alternatives described in this chapter for an audience explicitly composed of consumer researchers. Each vehicle is a monograph, whose collective papers provide readers with a sense of the variety of postmodern alternatives and of the complementary and conflictual orientations held by researchers in this emerging tradition. One volume in progress stems directly from a single multidisciplinary research project, the other from a number of independent projects related in spirit as interpretive. Given their early stages of production, I have treated some of these efforts in an unconscionably cursory fashion. However, the emergent nature of the postmodern tradition and the summary mission of this chapter dictates such as expedient approach.

The Consumer Behavior Odyssey

Because the history of the Consumer Behavior Odyssey—a transcontinental interdisciplinary naturalistic inquiry into consumer behavior broadly construed—has been detailed by a number of chroniclers (Kassarjian 1987; Wallendorf, Belk, and Heisley 1988), and because the disciplinary impact of the project has been tentatively (and by no means uniformly) assessed by several of its principals (Cote and Foxman 1987; Holbrook 1987c, 1988c; Sherry 1987a; Wallendorf 1987), I have not recounted these issues here. Rather, a substantive accounting of the project's output is more germane to my purpose. The Odyssey data archive, housed at the Marketing Science Institute in Cambridge, Massachusetts, consists of approximately 800 pages of field notes and journals, 137 videotapes, about a dozen audiotapes, 4000 photographs, and a heterogeneous artifact file. Odyssey researchers have published numerous papers and one videotape, and have made dozens of professional presentations from the data collected during the project (Wallendorf 1988). Among the issues addressed in this work have been naturalistic methodology (Belk, Sherry, and Wallendorf 1988; Belk 1988c), consumer-object relations (Belk, Wallendorf, Sherry, Holbrook, and Roberts 1987; Holbrook 1988c), periodic market system dynamics (Belk, Sherry, and Wallendorf 1988; Sherry 1987d), and experiential dimensions of consumption (O'Guinn 1987a, 1987b, 1987c).

An edited volume entitled *Highways and Buyways: Naturalistic Research From the Consumer Behavior Odyssey* (Wallendorf and Belk 1990) is currently in production. (The book will be published by the Association for Consumer Research as part of its monograph series.) The book examines the philosophy and methods of naturalistic inquiry, the conceptual leitmotifs that shape and reflect the project itself, and the numerous consumption phenomena (in extended case study format) investigated by the researchers. Extensive use is made of photographic illustrations. Wallendorf and Belk (1988) have provided a detailed account of the origin, development, and launching of the project. Jaworski and MacInnis (1988) have reflected upon their roles as informants to the project, and upon their reactions to the methodological techniques to which they were subjected. Holbrook (1988d) has used the psycho-

analytic analysis of his own consumer-object relations to meditate upon the nature of motivation research. The ways in which consumer behavior shapes and reflects the contemporary processes of secularization and sacralization are explored in a reprinted chapter by Belk, Wallendorf, and Sherry (1989). A synchronic analysis of a farmers' market, excerpted from a long-term ethnographic investigation that made extensive use of photographic research methods, has been prepared by Heisley, McGrath, and Sherry (1988). A chapter on collectors and collecting, based upon an initial work by Belk, Wallendorf, Sherry, Holbrook, and Roberts (1987), is underway. Additional chapters on researcher-informant relations, research-program evaluation, consumer-object relations, transcendent experience, performative consumption, and living beings as possessions are currently being drafted.

Humanistic Consumer Research

In the wake of the interest and controversy created by Hirschman's (1986) essay on humanistic inquiry, a number of consumer researchers have pooled their efforts to create a volume of "alternative" papers to serve as a primary reference source for postmodern investigators. Entitled *Interpretive Consumer Research* (Hirschman 1989), the volume includes, as well, a set of ostensibly evaluative chapters written by conventionally positivist consumer researchers (Hunt 1989; Calder and Tybout 1989). This inclusion mirrors the tension in the discipline I have described, but it fails to provide readers with a semblance of balance missing from traditional, single-orientation treatments of consumer behavior. However unfortunate this shortcoming, the reader is able to glean insight into the politics of disciplinary evolution, into logocentrism and the rhetorical bases of positivist inquiry, and into the intimate relationship of comprehensive close readings of primary texts to scholarly integrity. One imagines that the reader's fervent wish will be for a shift from circled wagons to hermeneutic circles.

The volume explores philosophical and

methodological issues in interpretive research, and includes a variety of studies shaped by approaches contained within the rubric of "humanism": ethnography, literary criticism, history, semiotics, and popular culture. Anderson (1989) has continued his development of the critical relativist orientation by exploring the relationship of this paradigm to interpretivism, by probing the notion of "understanding" in contrast to "explanation," and by countering conventional criticisms of interpretivism. Peter and Olson (1989) have also taken exception to the Calder and Tybout (1987) construal of scientific inquiry, and have affirmed the need for a constructionist perspective of science. Ozanne and Hudson (1989) have cast positivism and interpretivism in a dialectical relationship that reveals, through the bridging of their contradictory orientations, a number of alternative approaches to consumption phenomena. By focussing on the contrasting axiology, ontology, and epistemology of these orientations as applied to a phenomenon of special interest to consumer researchers — emotion — and by proposing that critical theory be viewed as a resolution of the positivist-interpretivist conflict, the authors have made a cogent appeal for paradigmatic pluralism. In their examination of naturalistic research techniques, Wallendorf and Belk (1989) have proposed criteria for evaluating the "trustworthiness" — as clearly distinguished from "quality" — of inquirers' data collection, interpretation, and presentation techniques. Building upon the work of Lincoln and Guba (1985), the authors have introduced the notion of "integrity" as an evaluative criterion, and have explored the dynamics of misinformation in researcher-informant relations to useful effect.

Applications of interpretivist perspectives are distributed across a range of concerns, and often combine quantitative with qualitative techniques. Lavin and Archdeacon (1989) have examined the relevance of historiography to the study of the relationship of marketing and ethnicity. In broadening the notion of humanism beyond the current social scientific applications in consumer research, Holbrook, Bell, and Grayson (1989) have shown the utility of merging the idiographic perspective of the artist and critic with the nomothetic perspective of the experimentalist through their use of projective technique to explore consumption symbolism, and through their close reading of the consumption code of a particular Broadway production. The partially ironic intent of this piece is itself consistent with the role of irony in postmodern literary texts. Mick and Politi (1989) have used their protocol-based study of connotative meaning in advertising imagery to demonstrate the effectiveness of interpretive methods as a logic of justification, rather than merely as a logic of discovery. The semiotic perspective employed by McQuarrie (1989) has revealed a previously uninvestigated rhetorical trope — resonance — that serves as a cue to enhance the meaning and communicative efficacy of advertisements. The methodological excursus into literary explication employed by Stern (1989) to analyze advertising has demonstrated the virtually unrecognized limits our conventionally framed construals of persuasive communication have placed upon our insight. McCracken's (1989) ethnographic investigation of "homeyness," a condition created by urban Canadians who manipulate consumption in the service of domestic ambience, has extended the study of product constellations into the domain of culture.

Apropos of the volume's projected distribution date, a number of contributors have focussed their attention on holiday consumption practices. In this regard, Belk (1989) has explored, through the analysis of popular cultural sources in historical perspective, the interpretation of values which characterizes the commercial and Christian celebration of Christmas in the United States. So also have Hirschman and LaBarbera (1989) probed the meaning of Christmas in the United States, and have described the dialectical tensions between sacred and secular, and the positive and the negative dimensions of the holiday as experienced by their respondents. Finally, in an ethnographic comparison of activities unfolding during Christmas and Hanukkah in two midwestern American gift stores, Sherry and McGrath (1989) have examined the semiotic significance of and deep structural motivation for the gift search, the impact of retail ambience on relationship management, and the gendered nature of secular ritual.

Toward Interpretive Closure

Despite the summary treatment I have accorded them, it is apparent that the papers in each of these volumes (Belk 1990; Hirschman 1989) represent a diversity of perspectives and methods too complex to permit grouping into anything other than a historically grounded common category. Such is the "seemingly irreducible variety" (Jameson 1987, p. 352) of the postmodern. The combination of quantitative with qualitative methods, the shift from text to field, the contrast between introspection and extroversion as research strategies, and the tension between synchronic and diachronic perspectives are just a few of the oppositions embodied in these works that render the label "interpretivist" ironic. Collectively, these papers embody a skeptical impulse inherent in all authentic inquiry. They indicate the many directions that inquiry can legitimately take in a postmodern environment. Clearly, each of these studies carries within it the seeds of future studies and the prospect of cross-pollination with other studies. It remains for me to delineate some broad dimensions along which postmodern inquiry might productively radiate.

SOME DIRECTIONS FOR FUTURE RESEARCH

In contrast to Holbrook's (1989) repeated admonition to young scholars to eschew alternative research approaches—a politically wise but disciplinarily perverse bit of advice despite the subtle irony in which it is usually couched—I recommend an enthusiastic, rigorous, and playful exploration of postmodern alternatives by novices and veterans alike. A multidimensional provoking of curiosity is the surest way to promote the paradigmatic pluralism I espoused in the opening pages of this chapter. Such provocation, whether induced through collaboration with colleagues outside the discipline or

through systematic cross-training during the individual's workcourse, can be institutionalized, to the great gain of consumer research. Despite its need for updating in an era of gender neutrality and computer literacy, Mills's essay "On Intellectual Craftsmanship" (1975/1959, pp. 211–212) remains a provocative and inspiring admonition to researchers. As valuable as his workbench suggestions for stimulating the sociological imagination is his meditation on the role of the academic as technician, which speaks directly to our postmodern era of consumer researchers:

Perhaps [we are] too well trained, too precisely trained. Since one can be *trained* only in what is already known, training sometimes incapacitates one from learning new ways; it makes one rebel against what at first is bound to be loose and even sloppy. But you must cling to such vague images and notions, if they are yours, and you must work them out. For it is in such forms that original ideas, if any, almost always first appear.

Indeed, Levy's advice can be appended as a code to my review of postmodern alternatives:

Having survived my ideas being called banal, excessive, destructive, irrelevant, obscure, and immature, I discover today that that is the way to become a distinguished educator. The message I learn from this history is to take heart, to be daring in having your ideas, to be persistent in putting them forth, to be courageous in struggling with adverse reviewers, and to hope for the best. (1988)

Recognizing once again the numerous research regimes suggested by the authors whose works I have noted, and the richness of the citation bases upon which these works are founded, and emphasizing the need for individual initiative in examining the implications of these rich sources, I recommend five avenues of inquiry to be pursued.

1. Approach-Avoidance: Marketing

In its struggle to become an independent discipline, consumer research has been both nurtured and stifled by its association with marketing. Marketers have provided the subdiscipline with roots, but not with wings. The postmodern climate can empower researchers to explore consumption in two alternative directions. The first direction is the path of least resistance. Researchers need to probe much more deeply into marketing-based consumer behaviors with alternative perspectives and methods. The topics treated in each of the chapters of this handbook are amenable to reinterpretation, reevaluation, and perhaps reorientation, within the alternative frameworks I have explored. Brand loyalty (Sherry 1986c), diffusion (Arnould 1988), and motivation (Campbell 1987), for example, have been subjected to such probing. This is equally true with respect to marketing practice, where applications of ethnography, semiotics, and other so-called interpretive approaches have gained currency (Sherry 1986d). The second direction is more problematic, yet potentially more rewarding. Researchers need to examine consumption as if it were not merely an epiphenomenon of marketing. Consumption is a biobasic behavior whose significance antedates that of marketing. Further, there are aspects of consumer behavior that are either beyond the current purview of marketing or which have not yet been fully marketized. Examinations of the sacred and profane dimensions of consumption (Belk, Wallendorf, and Sherry 1988) or of love as an arbiter of consumer-object relations (Shimp and Madden 1988) are examples of such expanded inquiry.

2. Triangulation

More than a decade ago Reichardt and Cook (1979) outlined the advantages of moving beyond the quantitative *versus* qualitative debate in social scientific research in their advocacy of paradigmatic pluralism. That their appeal was not persuasive among consumer researchers is attributable in part to the dearth of exemplars of "interpretive" inquiry at the time they wrote their essay. Since that time, a body of alternative literature has accumulated, making triangulation a practical possibility, perhaps to an unprecedented degree. Thus, the remaining

barriers to investigation of common phenomena from radically multimethodological perspectives are functions of disciplinary politics, of expediency, or of entropy. Triangulation would appear to be one of the most pressing needs facing consumer researchers. Triangulation *across* research traditions is one appropriate avenue. For example, imagine the design challenge and wealth of data that would be involved in a triangulated, comparative study of the relationship of ethnicity to consumer behavior. Begin with ethnographic investigations in an ethnically diverse urban area, construct and administer surveys through active negotiation and collaboration with the natives, design and execute experiments or conduct focus groups with subjects drawn from a population with which the inquirer is intimately familiar, create and analyze projective instruments with emic sensitivity to cultural nuance, and integrate the entire investigation with an ongoing discussion of the findings with informants as well as professional colleagues. Our notions of ethnicity as well as consumption would profit from such study. Mick's recent attempts to enlarge our conceptions of marketing communication by revising our notions of basic constructs such as "schema" (1988b) and "comprehension" (1988c) through the merging of semiotic and cultural perspectives with those of cognitive science are representative of this kind of triangulation. Similarly, triangulation *within* the emerging postmodern tradition is clearly warranted. Both Wallendorf and Belk (1988) and Mick (1988) have drawn attention to the many points of difference and disagreement among so-called interpretive consumer researchers. For example, the utility (or futility) of an auditing procedure has proven to be a point of contention (Parker 1988, p. 223). So also has the utility of member checking been disputed (Emerson and Pollner 1988). Imagine again the richness of a multidimensional study that would examine historically and ethnographically the production of advertising by a particular agency and its consumption by clients and prospects. Such a study would analyze semiotically and semiologically the actual advertisements comparatively across product categories, brands, target segments, and time, and it would interpret critically the impact of the agency upon the industry and the culture. Such study would fuse the best of Jhally (1987) and Marchand (1985), of Dyer (1982) and Williamson (1978), and of Schudson (1984) and Vestergaard and Schroder (1985), and it would impart some of the "passion" inspired by Henry (1963).

3. Outreach and Collaboration

The forging of alliances with other disciplines should be given a prominent place on the agenda of consumer research. I have demonstrated something of the breadth of interest in consumption that exists outside of our discipline, as well as the maddeningly parallel nature of this interest. The interdisciplinary fervor of conference track chairs will be institutionalized among the editorial review boards of journals principally through such alliances that move the field beyond its current "comfort zones" (Zaltman 1983). Some of this institution building has been begun by the "newcomers" to consumer research, some by those cross-trained beyond the field, and some by "borrowers" in search of greater interpretive adequacy. The encouragement of cross-attendance at conferences, the reading of journals outside of one's field, the joint sponsorship of conferences and journals, and the expansion of invisible colleges will help consumer research move in this direction.

4. Empirical and Critical Schools

The efforts of Rogers (1987) and Poster and Venkatesh (1987) to accelerate the diffusion of critical school social science into consumer research urgently require support and expansion. The normative dimensions of consumer behavior, with the possible exception of some of the public policy literature, is sorely underdeveloped. The ideology of consumption, the power dynamics underwriting that ideology and its cross-cultural diffusion, and the moral economy affected by that diffusion are most worthy of investigation. These topics are more accessible to postmodern perspectives and

methods than to our traditional empiricist ones. We also need to explore the range of consumer "misbehavior" (Holbrook 1985; Zaltman and Wallendorf 1977), those dysfunctional consequences of the ideology of consumption that plague contemporary society. Rook's (1987) examination of the buying "impulse" is a step in this direction. So also is the recent work on compulsive consumption (Faber, O'Guinn, and Krych 1987). Haug's (1987) critique of commodity aesthetics is ripe for diffusion into consumer research. A critical school perspective of consumer behavior enables (and perhaps demands) a different kind of activism than the traditional applications orientation of consumer researchers; assessing the socioenvironmental impact of consumer behaviors is no mere demarketing or macromarketing task. Duesenberry's (1960) famous quip that "economics is all about why people make choices, while sociology is all about why they don't have any choices to make," is an implicit challenge to consumer research to develop a critique of the ideology of choice and to question the hegemony of decision making in the scheme of things.

5. New Presentation Modes

Among the most exciting and controversial developments of the emerging postmodern research tradition is the experimentation with nonconventional modes of conveying the researcher's understanding of a phenomenon (Clifford and Marcus 1986; Sapir 1988; Tyler 1987). These modes range from works that purport to be faithful cultural representations which restore meaning, to those wherein the researcher's interpretation exceeds and disputes the "conscious knowledge" of subjects (Traube 1986). Standardized research articles and monographs, themselves rhetorical vehicles or artifacts of a particular paradigm (Bazerman 1988; Thornton 1988), may well be insufficient vessels for containing our varied experiences of consumer behavior. Something of this insufficiency is conveyed by the increasing use of video recording and photography among consumer researchers (see Belk, Sherry, and Wallendorf 1987 for precedents and applications), and by the publication of a videocassette on "deep meaning in possessions" (Wallendorf and Belk 1987) by the Marketing Science Institute. Parallel video research is emerging on the other side of the Atlantic as well (Pinch and Clark 1988). Our resistance to book-length treatments of consumption objects and systems (e.g., Fields 1983; Kira 1966; Rossi 1976) may also be on the wane. Essays, such as Wills's (1989) meditation on a deodorant bottle, constitute another potential vehicle. Other alternative modes or genres readily suggest themselves. Friedman's (1985, 1987) fascinating accounts of the impact of consumer behavior on popular culture prompt direct speculation: Are there consumer researchers among us who are able to write novels based upon that research? Delia Ephron's novel *Funny Sauce* (1986) is as carefully drawn a portrait of consumption and contemporary family life cycle issues as is available in our academic "literature," as well as being more impactful and widely targeted. In a similar fashion, Ishmael Reed's *The Terrible Twos* (1988) complements the many Christmas-focussed accounts of consumer behavior I have noted in this chapter. The central conceit of John Rolfe Gardiner's *In the Heart of the Whole World* (1988) — that the shopping mall mediates the relationship between sacred and profane dimensions of contemporary culture — is latent in much of our critical academic literature. Tom Miller's *The Panama Hat Trail*, a delightful depiction of aspects of a particular consumption system, is another such illustration. Might not such novels be as readily aspired to as exemplars as are the natural science treatises that are our current models? The Farmers' brave effort to novelize as arcane a field as international finance (Farmer and Farmer 1985) is an implicit challenge to consumer researchers. So also is Coles's (1987) literary approach to business ethics. Who is it among us, writer of the occasional poem or short story, who might be turned toward the illumination of consumer behavior? As researchers we have studied film (Holbrook and Grayson 1986; Holbrook 1988b) and television (Hirschman 1988b), sometimes triangulating between the two media

(Belk 1988b). We have not yet created *with* these media, rather than *from* them, despite the existence of cinematographers in our midst. Films such as the one by Aibel et al. (1984) on estate sales might serve as appropriate exemplars. So also do we harbor painters and musicians, but the relationship of their work to consumer behavior has not been publicly (or perhaps even privately) scrutinized. Here again, Holbrook has suggested some of the ways in which such artistically driven scholarship might develop, through his use of stories (1988d, 1987d), drawings (1983; Holbrook and Zirlin 1985), and music (1987f, 1986) to probe experiential dimensions of consumer behavior. From the chrysalis of such scholarship will autonomous consumer art emerge.

CONCLUSION

Having ranged across the disparate quarters of postmodern geography, the reader has earned an interpretive summary. While numerous manuals (see, for example, the inaugural volume edited by R. F. Ellen 1984) and an enterprising miniseries (directed by John Van Maanen for Sage Publications) now clamor for our methodological attention, much of the essence of nonpositivist research has been neatly summed up by Christians and Carey (1981) in just four criteria. *Naturalistic observation* permits the analyst access to a native world view. *Contextualization* forces the researcher to recognize the embeddedness and multiplicity of meaning and to acknowledge the linkages between and the interpretations of meanings. *Maximized comparisons* that range across cultural, psychological, situational, or temporal boundaries encourage the construction of a "cumulative perspective" that renders interpretation "more penetrating and coherent." Finally, researchers seek to create *sensitized concepts*, whether models or metaphors, which are faithful to native categories but which also are sufficiently powerful to interpret larger domains of experience (Christians and Carey 1981).

The precision and accuracy of this cogent summation are commendable, but the authors do not attempt to account for one of the most problematic features of postmodern inquiry as evaluated by conventional consumer researchers—the idiosyncrasy of the inquirer. To paraphrase Murray's (1943, p. 6) assessment of thematic apperception testing, the future of postmodern inquiry in consumer research depends upon the possibility of perfecting the interpreter (consumer research's "forgotten instrument") more than it does on perfecting techniques. Consumer research has not encouraged the honing of the kind of intraceptive intuition (Murray 1943) requisite to plumbing consumer worldview and ethos. We have not learned to use "the subjectivity inherent in all observations as the royal road to an authentic, rather than fictitious, objectivity" (Devereux 1967, p. xvii). Postmodernism will flourish or languish in the discipline to the extent that the acuity of the researcher-as-instrument is valued and sharpened. Lacking such a tradition of valuation, consumer researchers must seek out the mavens of postmodernism (Feick and Price 1987), yet be hypercritical of the surrogate consumers (Solomon 1986) mediating the diffusion of this movement into the discipline, until such time as instruction in alternative paradigms is incorporated into the initiation of our neophyte scholars.

In this chapter I have sketched the principal sociopolitical and disciplinary implications of postmodern inquiry in consumer research. In glossing most of the works that have contributed to the emergence of postmodern inquiry, I have identified the range of alternatives consumer researchers appear ready to tolerate, if not celebrate, as well as a handful of issues that future researchers might constructively address. Because of the highly volatile nature of this experimental moment, it is difficult to predict the shape postmodern alternatives will assume in our history of ideas. Such alternative approaches have the potential to balance and integrate the discipline of consumer research, as well to balkanize it even further. Adherents of these approaches may as easily be assimilated into contiguous disciplines as accepted into the mainstream of consumer research. If the discipline is earnest in its attempt to eradicate meta-theoretical bias and foster paradigmatic pluralism—"to enlarge the sense of how life can go" in an intellectual era in which it is "increasingly difficult to get out of each other's way" in Geertz's (1988, p. 139, p. 147) phrase—we can expect the emerging postmodern tradition to be nurtured, in doctoral seminars as well as journal pages. I hope this chapter will foster just such nurturing and challenge novices to forsake a comfortable apprenticeship in favor of a broader perspective.

REFERENCES

ADLER, PATRICIA, and PETER ADLER, Eds. (1984). *The Social Dynamics of Financial Markets*. Greenwich, CT: JAI Press.

AGNEW, JEAN-CHRISTOPHE (1986). *Worlds Apart: The Market and the Theatre in Anglo-American Thought, 1550–1750*. New York: Cambridge University Press.

AIBEL, ROBERT, BEN LEVIN, CHRIS MUSELLO, and JAY RUBY (1984). "A Country Auction: The Paul V. Leitzel Estate Sale," film. University Park, PA: Pennsylvania State University, Audio Visual Services.

ALVESSON, MATS (1987). *Organization Theory and Technocratic Consciousness: Rationality, Ideology and Quality of Work*. Berlin: Mouton de Gruyter.

ANDERSON, BEVERLEE, and M. VENKATESAN (1987). "Interdisciplinary Borrowing in Consumer Behavior: Legitimate Offspring?" in *Marketing Theory*, Eds. R. Belk, G. Zaltman, R. Bagozzi, D. Brinberg, R. Deshpande, A. F. Firat, M. Holbrook, J. Olson, J. Sherry, and B. Weitz. Chicago: American Marketing Association, 276–279.

ANDERSON, PAUL (1986). "On Method in Consumer Research: A Critical Relativist Perspective," *Journal of Consumer Research*, 13(2), 155–173.

ANDERSON, PAUL (1988b). "Relative to What— That is the Question: A Reply to Siegel," *Journal of Consumer Research*, 15(1), 133–137.

ANDERSON, PAUL (1988a). "Relativism Revidivus: In Defense of Critical Relativism," *Journal of Consumer Research*, 15(3), 403–406.

ANDERSON, PAUL (1989). "On Relativism and Interpretivism—With a Prolegemenon to the 'Why' Question," in *Interpretive Consumer Research*, Ed.

Elizabeth Hirschman. Provo, UT: Association for Consumer Research, 10–23.

APPADURAI, ARJUN, Ed. (1986a). *The Social Life of Things.* New York: Cambridge University Press.

APPADURAI, ARJUN (1986b). "Introduction: Commodities and the Politics of Value," in *The Social Life of Things,* Ed. Arjun Appadurai. New York: Cambridge University Press, 3–63.

APPLE, RIMA (1987). *Mothers and Medicine: A Social History of Infant Feeding, 1890–1950.* Madison, WI: University of Wisconsin Press.

ARNDT, JOHAN (1985a). "The Tyranny of Paradigms: The Case for Paradigmatic Pluralism in Marketing," in *Changing the Course of Marketing,* Eds. Nikhilesh Dholakia and Johan Arndt. Greenwich, CT: JAI Press, 1–25.

ARNDT, JOHAN (1985b). "On Making Marketing More Scientific: The Role of Orientations, Paradigms, Metaphors, and Puzzle Solving," *Journal of Marketing,* 49(3), 11–23.

ARNOULD, ERIC (1983). "Fancies and Glimmers: Culture and Consumer Behavior," in *Advances in Consumer Research,* Vol. 10, Eds. Richard Bagozzi and Alice Tybout. Ann Arbor, MI: Association for Consumer Research, 702–704.

ARNOULD, ERIC (1989). "Preference Formation and the Diffusion of Innovations: The Case of Hausa-Speaking Niger," *Journal of Consumer Research,* 16(2).

ARNOULD, ERIC, and MELANIE WALLENDORF (1988). "Oh Give Thanks for We Are One: A Cross-Cultural Comparison of the Meaning of Participation in Thanksgiving Rituals," paper presented at the Annual Conference of the Association of Consumer Research, Honolulu, HI.

ARNOULD, ERIC, and RICHARD WILK (1984). "Why Do the Natives Wear Adidas," *Advances in Consumer Research,* Vol. 11, Ed. Thomas Kinnear. Provo, UT: Association for Consumer Research, 748–752.

AUDEN, W. H. (1946). "Under Which Lyre: A Reactionary Tract for the Times," in *W. H. Auden: Collected Poems,* Ed. Edward Mendelsen, 1976. New York: Random House, 259–263.

BABCOCK, BARBARA (1986). "Modeled Selves: Helen Cordero's 'Little People,'" in *The Anthropology of Experience,* Eds. Victor Turner and Edward Bruner. Urbana, IL: University of Illinois Press, 316–343.

BARRETT, STANLEY (1984). *The Rebirth of Anthro-*

pological Theory. Toronto: University of Toronto Press.

BARTHEL, DIANE (1988). *Putting on Appearances: Gender and Advertising.* Philadelphia: Temple University Press.

BATESON, GREGORY, and MARY C. BATESON (1987). *Angels Fear: Toward an Epistemology of the Sacred.* New York: Macmillan.

BAZERMAN, CHARLES (1988). *Shaping Written Knowledge: The Genre and Activity of the Experimental Article in Science.* Madison, WI: University of Wisconsin Press.

BAYLY, C. A. (1986). "The Origins of Swadeshi (Home Industry): Cloth and Indian Society, 1700–1930," in *The Social Life of Things,* Ed. Arjun Appadurai. New York: Cambridge University Press, 285–321.

BECKER, GARY (1976). *The Economic Approach to Human Behavior.* Chicago: University of Chicago Press.

BECKER, GARY (1981). *A Treatise on the Family.* Cambridge, MA: Harvard University Press.

BECKER, HOWARD (1979). "Do Photographers Tell the Truth?" in *Qualitative and Quantitative Methods in Evaluation Research,* Eds. Thomas Cook and Charles Reichardt. Beverly Hills, CA: Sage, 99–117.

BECKER, HOWARD (1982). *Art Worlds.* Berkeley, CA: University of California Press.

BELK, RUSSELL (1984a). "Manifesto for a Consumer Behavior of Consumer Behavior," paper presented at the AMA Winter Conference on Marketing Theory, Fort Lauderdale, FL.

BELK, RUSSELL (1984b). "Cultural and Historical Differences in Concepts of Self and Their Effects on Attitudes Toward Having and Giving," in *Advances in Consumer Research,* Vol. 11, Ed. Thomas Kinnear. Provo, UT: Association for Consumer Research, 753–760.

BELK, RUSSELL (1986). "Art versus Science as Ways of Generating Knowledge About Materialism," in *Perspectives on Methodology in Consumer Research,* Eds. David Brinberg and Richard Lutz. New York: Springer-Verlag, 3–36.

BELK, RUSSELL (1987a). "ACR Presidential Address: Happy Thought," in *Advances in Consumer Research,* Vol. 14, Eds. Melanie Wallendorf and Paul Anderson. Provo, UT: Association for Consumer Research, 1–4.

BELK, RUSSELL (1987b). "A Modest Proposal for Creating Verisimilitude in Consumer-Information-Processing Models, and Some Suggestions for Establishing a Discipline to Study Consumer Behavior," in *Philosophical and Radical Thought in Marketing*, Eds. A. F. Firat, N. Dholakia, and R. Bagozzi. Lexington, MA: Lexington Books, 361–372.

BELK, RUSSELL (1987c). "The Role of the Odyssey in Consumer Behavior and in Consumer Research," in *Advances in Consumer Research*, Vol. 14, Eds. Melanie Wallendorf and Paul Anderson. Provo, UT: Association for Consumer Research, 357–361.

BELK, RUSSELL (1987d). "A Child's Christmas in America: Santa Claus as Deity, Consumption as Religion," *Journal of American Culture* (Spring), 87–100.

BELK, RUSSELL (1987e). "Material Values in the Comics," *Journal of Consumer Research*, 14(1), 26–42.

BELK, RUSSELL (1988a). "Possessions and the Extended Self," *Journal of Consumer Research*, 15(2).

BELK, RUSSELL (1988b). "Third World Consumer Culture," in *Marketing and Development: Toward Broader Dimensions*, Eds. E. Kumcu and A. F. Firat (*Research in Marketing*, Supplement 4, Eds. Jagdish Sheth). Greenwich, CT: JAI Press.

BELK, RUSSELL (1989). "Materialism and the Modern U.S. Christmas," in *Interpretive Consumer Research*, Ed. Elizabeth Hirschman. Provo, UT: Association for Consumer Research, 115–135.

BELK, RUSSELL (1990). *Highways and Buyways: Naturalistic Research From the Consumer Behavior Odyssey*, unpublished monograph, University of Utah, Salt Lake City, UT.

BELK, RUSSELL, KENNETH BAHN, and ROBERT MAYER (1982). "Developmental Recognition of Consumption Symbolism," *Journal of Consumer Research*, 9(2), 4–17.

BELK, RUSSELL, and RICHARD POLLAY (1985a). "Materialism and Magazine Advertising during the Twentieth Century," in *Advances in Consumer Research*, Vol. 12, Eds. Elizabeth Hirschman and Morris Holbrook. Provo: UT: Association for Consumer Research, 394–403.

BELK, RUSSELL, and RICHARD POLLAY (1985b). "Images of Ourselves: The Good Life in Twentieth Century Advertising," *Journal of Consumer Research*, 11(4), 887–897.

BELK, RUSSELL, JOHN F. SHERRY, JR., and MELANIE WALLENDORF (1988). "A Naturalistic Inquiry into Buyer and Seller Behavior at a Swap Meet," *Journal of Consumer Research*, 14(4), 449–470.

BELK, RUSSELL, and MELANIE WALLENDORF (1987). "Humanistic Inquiry: A Comment," working paper, University of Utah, Salt Lake City, UT.

BELK, RUSSELL, MELANIE WALLENDORF, and JOHN F. SHERRY, JR. (1989). "The Sacred and Profane in Consumer Behavior: Theodicy on the Odyssey," *Journal of Consumer Research*, 16(1), 1–38.

BELK, RUSSELL, MELANIE WALLENDORF, JOHN F. SHERRY, JR., MORRIS HOLBROOK, and SCOTT ROBERTS (1988). "Collectors and Collecting," in *Advances in Consumer Research*, Vol. 15, Ed. Michael Houston. Provo, UT: Association for Consumer Research, 548–553.

BELK, RUSSELL, and NON ZHOU (1987). "Learning To Want Things," in *Advances in Consumer Research*, Vol. 14, Eds. Melanie Wallendorf and Paul Anderson. Provo, UT: Association for Consumer Research, 478–481.

BELK, RUSSELL, GERALD ZALTMAN, RICHARD BAGOZZI, DAVID BRINBERG, ROHIT DESHPANDE, A. FUAT FIRAT, MORRIS HOLBROOK, JERRY OLSON, JOHN SHERRY, and BARTON WEITZ, EDS. (1987). *Marketing Theory*. Chicago: American Marketing Association.

BELL, RUDOLPH (1985). *Holy Anorexia*. Chicago: University of Chicago Press.

BERGER, JAMES, and DONALD BERRY (1988). "Statistical Analysis and the Illusion of Objectivity," *American Scientist*, 76(2), 159–165.

BENTON, RAYMOND (1985). "Alternative Approaches to Consumer Behavior," *Research in Marketing, Supplement 2: Changing the Course of Marketing: Alternative Paradigms for Widening Marketing Theory*, Eds. Nikhilesh Dholakia and Johan Arndt. Greenwich, CT: JAI Press, 197–218.

BENTON, RAYMOND (1987). "Work, Consumption and the Joyless Consumer," in *Philosophical and Radical Thought in Marketing*, Eds. A. F. Firat, N. Dholakia, and R. Bagozzi. Lexington, MA: Lexington Books, 235–250.

BERMAN, MORRIS (1984). *The Reenchantment of the World*. Toronto: Bantam Books.

BERNARD, H. RUSSELL (1988). *Research Methods in Cultural Anthropology*. Beverly Hills, CA: Sage.

BOETTKE, PETER (1987). "Understanding Market Processes: An Austrian View of 'Knowing,' " in *Marketing Theory*, Eds. R. Belk, G. Zaltman, R.

Bagozzi, D. Brinberg, R. Deshpande, A. F. Firat, M. Holbrook, J. Olson, J. Sherry, and B. Weitz. Chicago: American Marketing Association, 195–199.

BOLWBY, RACHEL (1981). *Just Looking: Consumer Culture in Dreiser, Gissing and Zola.* New York: Methuen.

BOURDIEU, PIERRE (1984). *Distinction: A Critique of the Judgment of Taste.* Cambridge, MA: Harvard University Press.

BRAUDEL, FERNAND (1979a). *The Structures of Everyday Life,* trans. Sian Reynolds. New York: Harper & Row.

BRAUDEL, FERNAND (1979b). *The Wheels of Commerce.* New York: Harper & Row.

BRAUDEL, FERNAND (1979c). *The Perspective of the World.* New York: Harper & Row.

BRIGGS, CHARLES (1988). "Review of Werner and Schoepfle (1987a,b)," *American Anthropologist,* 90(4), 1001–1003.

BRINBERG, DAVID, and AJITH KUMAR (1987). "Validity Issues in Experimental and Naturalistic Inquiry," working paper, State University of New York at Albany, NY.

BROWN, GILLIAN (1987). "The Empire of Agoraphobia," *Representations,* 20(Fall), 134–157.

BROWN, RICHARD (1987). "Positivism, Relativism, and Narrative in the Logic of the Historical Sciences," *American History Review,* 92(4), 908–920.

BRUMFIEL, ELIZABETH (1987). "Consumption and Politics at Aztec Huexotla," *American Anthropologist,* 89(3), 676–686.

CALDER, BOBBY, and ALICE TYBOUT (1987). "What Consumer Research Is . . . ," *Journal of Consumer Research,* 14(1), 136–140.

CALDER, BOBBY, and ALICE TYBOUT (1989). "Interpretive, Qualitative and Traditional Scientific Empirical Consumer Behavior Research," in *Interpretive Consumer Research,* Ed. Elizabeth Hirschman. Provo, UT: Association for Consumer Research, 199–208.

CALDWELL, BRUCE (1982). *Beyond Positivism: Economic Methodology in the Twentieth Century.* Boston: Allen and Unwin.

CAMPBELL, COLIN (1987). *The Romantic Ethic and the Spirit of Modern Consumerism.* New York: Basic Blackwell.

CAREY, JAMES, ED. (1988a). *Media, Myths, and Narratives: Television and the Press.* Newbury Park, CA: Sage.

CAREY, JAMES (1988b). *Communication as Culture: Essays on Media and Society.* Chester, MA: Unwin Hyman.

CASSANELLI, LEE (1986). "Qat: Changes in the Production and Consumption of a Quasilegal Commodity in Northeast Africa," in *The Social Life of Things,* Ed. Arjun Appadurai. New York: Cambridge University Press, 236–257.

DE CERTEAU, MICHEL (1984). *The Practice of Everyday Life,* trans. Steven Rendall. Berkeley, CA: University of California Press.

CHEAL, DAVID (1988). *The Gift Economy.* London: Routledge.

CHRISTIANS, CLIFFORD (1986). "Dialogic Communication Theory and Cultural Studies," in *Studies in Symbolic Interaction,* Vol. 9, Ed. Norman Denzin. Greenwich, CT: JAI Press.

CHRISTIANS, CLIFFORD, and JAMES CAREY (1981). "The Logic and Aims of Qualitative Research," in *Research Methods in Mass Communication,* Eds. Guido Stempel and Bruce Westley. Englewood Cliffs, NJ: Prentice-Hall, 342–362.

CHURCHILL, SCOTT, and FREDERICK WERTZ (1985). "An Introduction to Phenomenological Psychology for Consumer Research: Historical, Conceptual, and Methodological Foundations," in *Advances in Consumer Research,* Vol. 12, Eds. Elizabeth Hirschman and Morris Holbrook. Provo, UT: Association for Consumer Research, 550–555.

CLARK, LYNN (1987). "Gravestones: Reflectors of Ethnicity or Class?" in *Consumer Choice in Historical Archaeology,* Ed. Suzanne Spenser-Wood. New York: Plenum, 383–395.

CLIFFORD, JAMES, and GEORGE MARCUS (1986). *Writing Culture: The Poetics and Politics of Ethnography.* Berkeley, CA: University of California Press.

COLEMAN, RICHARD (1983). "The Continuing Significance of Social Class to Marketing," *Journal of Consumer Research,* 10(3), 265–280.

COLES, ROBERT (1987). "Storytellers' Ethics," *Harvard Business Review,* 65(2), 8–14.

COOPER, LEE (1987). "Do We Need Critical Relativism? Comments on 'On Method in Consumer Research,'" *Journal of Consumer Research,* 14(1), 126–127.

COOPER, LEE, and HAROLD LEVINE (1985). "Guerrilla Science: An Epistemology for the Applied Behavioral Sciences," in *Human Systems Development,* Eds. Robert Tannenbaum, Newton Marguhes, Fred Massarik, et al. San Francisco: Jossey-Bass, 489–519.

COTE, JOSEPH, and ELLEN FOXMAN (1987). "A Positivist's Reactions to a Naturalistic Inquiry Experience," in *Advances in Consumer Research,* Vol. 14, Eds. Melanie Wallendorf and Paul Anderson. Provo, UT: Association for Consumer Research, 362–364.

CULVER, STUART (1988). "What Manikins Want: The Wonderful Wizard of Oz and The Art of Decorating Dry Goods Windows," *Representatives,* 21(Winter), 97–116.

CUMMINGS, LARRY, and PETER FROST (1985). *Publishing in the Organizational Sciences.* Homewood, IL: Irwin.

DENNY, RITA (1988). "Pragmatic Dimensions of Advertising," *Advances in Consumer Research,* Vol. 15, Ed. Michael Houston. Provo, UT: Association for Consumer Research, 260–261.

DESHPANDE, ROHIT (1983). "Paradigms Lost': On Theory and Method in Research in Marketing," *Journal of Marketing,* 47(Fall), 101–110.

DESHPANDE, ROHIT (1984). "Theoretical Myopia: The Discipline of Marketing and the Hierarchy of the Sciences," *Scientific Methods in Marketing: Proceedings of the 1984 AMA Winter Educators' Conference,* Eds. Paul Anderson and Michael Ryan. Chicago: American Marketing Association, 18–21.

DESHPANDE, ROHIT, WAYNE HOYER, and NAVEEN DONTHU (1986). "The Intensity of Ethnic Affiliation: A Study of the Sociology of Hispanic Consumption," *Journal of Consumer Research,* 13(2), 214–220.

DEVEREUX, GEORGE (1967). *From Anxiety to Method in the Behavioral Sciences.* The Hague, The Netherlands: Mouton.

DHOLAKIA, NIKHILESH, and JOHAN ARNDT, EDS. (1985). *Changing the Course of Marketing: Alternative Paradigms for Widening Marketing Theory,* in *Research in Marketing, Supplement 2.* Greenwich, CT: JAI Press.

DHOLAKIA, NIKHILESH, and RUBY ROY DHOLAKIA (1985). "Choice and Choicelessness in the Paradigm of Marketing," *Research in Marketing, Supplement 2: Changing the Course of Marketing: Alternative Paradigms for Widening Marketing Theory,* Eds. Nikhilesh Dholakia and Johan Arndt. Greenwich, CT: JAI Press, 173–185.

DHOLAKIA, NIKHILESH, and A. FUAT FIRAT (1988). "Global Marketing and Development in the Era of Globalizing Markets and Consumption Patterns," in *The Role of Marketing in Development,* Eds. E. Kumcu and A. F. Firat. Greenwich, CT: JAI Press.

DHOLAKIA, NIKHILESH, RICHARD MCINTYRE, and ANNAMMA JOY (1988). "The Choice of Needs and the Needs of Choice: Alternative Frameworks," in *Marketing: A Return to the Broader Dimension,* Eds. Stanley Shapiro and A. H. Walle. Chicago, IL: American Marketing Association, 286–288.

DHOLAKIA, NIKHILESH, and JOHN F. SHERRY, JR. (1987). "Marketing and Development: A Resynthesis of Knowledge," *Research in Marketing,* Vol. 9, Ed. Jagdish Sheth. Greenwich, CT: JAI Press, 119–143.

DOUGLAS, MARY (1976). "Relative Poverty—Relative Communication," in *Traditions of Social Policy: Essays in Honor of Violet Butter,* Ed. A. H. Halsey. Oxford: Basil Blackwell, 197–215.

DOUGLAS, MARY, and BARON ISHERWOOD (1979). *The World of Goods.* New York: Basic Books.

DUESENBERRY, J. (1960). "Comments on 'An Economic Analysis of Fertility' by Gary S. Becker," in *Demography and Economic Change in Developed Countries.* Princeton, NJ: Universities National Bureau Conference Series, 2, 231–240.

DURAND, JACQUES (1987). "Rhetorical Figures in the Advertising Image," in *Marketing and Semiotics: New Directions in the Study of Signs for Sale,* Ed. Jean Umiker-Sebeok. Berlin: Mouton de Gruyter, 295–318.

DURGEE, JEFFREY (1986a). "Richer Findings From Qualitative Research," *Journal of Advertising Research* (August/September), 36–44.

DURGEE, JEFFREY (1986b). "Self-Esteem Advertising," *Journal of Advertising,* 15(4), 21–28.

DURGEE, JEFFREY (1987a). "Phenomenology: New Methods for Asking Questions and Interpreting Results," in *Advances in Consumer Research,* Vol. 14, Eds. Melanie Wallendorf and Paul Anderson. Provo, UT: Association for Consumer Research, 561.

DURGEE, JEFFREY (1987b). "Point of View: Using Creative Writing Techniques in Focus Groups," *Journal of Advertising Research* (December/January), 57–65.

DURGEE, JEFFREY (1988). "Point of View: Product Drama," *Journal of Advertising Research,* 28(1), 42–49.

DURGEE, JEFFREY, and ROBERT STUART (1987).

"Advertising Symbols and Brand Names That Best Represent Key Product Meanings," *Journal of Consumer Marketing,* 4(3), 15–24.

DYER, GILLIAN (1982). *Advertising as Communication.* New York: Methuen.

ELLEN, R. F. (1984). *Ethnographic Research: A Guide to General Conduct.* New York: Academic Press.

EMERSON, ROBERT, and MELVIN POLLNER (1988). "On the Uses of Members' Responses to Researchers' Accounts," *Human Organization,* 47(3), 189–198.

ENGEL, JAMES (1985). "Toward the Contextualization of Consumer Behavior," in *Historical Perspective in Consumer Research: National and International Perspectives,* Eds. Chin Tiong Tan and Jagdish Sheth. Singapore: School of Management, National University of Singapore, 1–4.

EPHRON, DELIA (1986). *Funny Sauce.* New York: Penguin.

ETZIONI, AMITAI (1988). *The Moral Dimension: Toward a New Economics.* New York: The Free Press.

EWEN, STUART (1988). *All Consuming Images: The Politics of Style in Contemporary Culture.* New York: Basic Books.

FABER, RONALD, THOMAS O'GUINN, and RAYMOND KRYCH (1987). "Compulsive Consumption," in *Advances in Consumer Research,* Vol. 14, Eds. Melanie Wallendorf and Paul Anderson. Provo, UT: Association for Consumer Research, 132–135.

FARMER, RICHARD, and JEAN FARMER (1986). *Lust for Lucre: Explorations in International Finance.* Bloomington, IN: Cedarwood Press.

FEICK, LAWRENCE, and LINDA PRICE (1987). "The Market Maven: A Diffuser of Marketplace Information," *Journal of Marketing,* 51(1), 83–97.

FENNELL, GERALDINE (1985). "Things of Heaven and Earth: Phenomenology, Marketing and Consumer Research," in *Advances in Consumer Research,* Vol. 12, Eds. Elizabeth Hirschman and Morris Holbrook. Provo, UT: Association for Consumer Research, 544–549.

FIELDS, GEORGE (1983). *From Bonsai to Levis.* New York: New American Library.

FIRAT, A. FUAT (1987a). "The Social Construction of Consumption Patterns: Understanding Macro Consumption Phenomena," in *Philosophical and Radical Thought in Marketing,* Eds. A. F. Firat, N. Dholakia, and R. Bagozzi. Lexington, MA: Lexington Books, 251–267.

FIRAT, A. FUAT (1987b). "Historiography, Scientific Method, and Exceptional Historical Events," in *Advances in Consumer Research,* Vol. 14, Eds. Melanie Wallendorf and Paul Anderson. Provo, UT: Association for Consumer Research, 435–438.

FIRAT, A. FUAT (1988a). "The Inevitability of Historical Evidence in Generating Macromarketing Knowledge," in *Marketing: A Return to the Broader Dimensions,* Eds. Stanley Shapiro and A. H. Walle. Chicago: American Marketing Association, 98–103.

FIRAT, A. FUAT (1988b). "A Critical Historical Perspective on Needs: The Macro or the Micro Rationale?" in *Marketing: A Return to the Broader Dimensions,* Eds. Stanley Shapiro and A. H. Walle. Chicago: American Marketing Association, 289–295.

FIRAT, A. FUAT (1988c). "Consumption Experiences and Consumption Patterns: Towards a Deeper Understanding of Underlying Dimensions," working paper, Appalachian State University, Boone, NC.

FIRAT, A. FUAT, NIKHILESH DHOLAKIA, and RICHARD BAGOZZI, EDS. (1987). *Philosophical and Radical Thought in Marketing.* Lexington, MA: Lexington Books.

FIRAT, A. FUAT, and NIKHILESH DHOLAKIA (1988). "Consumption Choices at the Macro Level," *Journal of Macromarketing,* 2(Fall), 6–15.

FISHER, JAMES (1987). "Social Class and Consumer Behavior: The Relevance of Class and Status," in *Advances in Consumer Research,* Vol. 14; Eds. Melanie Wallendorf and Paul Anderson. Provo, UT: Association for Consumer Research, 492–496.

FISK, GEORGE, Ed. (1986). *Marketing Management Technology as a Social Process,* New York: Praeger.

FLOCH, JEAN-MARIE (1988). "The Contribution of Structural Semiotics to the Design of a Hypermarket," *International Journal of Research in Marketing,* 4(3), 233–252.

FOUCAULT, MICHEL (1970). *The Order of Things: An Archaeology of the Human Sciences.* New York: Vintage Books.

FOX, RICHARD, and T. J. JACKSON LEARS, Eds. (1983). *The Culture of Consumption: Critical Essays in American History, 1880–1980.* New York: Pantheon.

FRANKEL, BARBARA (1987). "Comment on Keesing's 'Anthropology as Interpretive Quest,' " *Current Anthropology,* 28(2), 169–170.

FRIEDMAN, MONROE (1985). "The Changing Language of a Consumer Society: Brand Name Usage in Popular American Novels in the Postwar Era," *Journal of Consumer Research*, 11(4), 927–938.

FRIEDMAN, MONROE (1987). "Word-of-Author Advertising and the Consumer: An Empirical Analysis of the Quality of Product Brands Noted by Authors of Popular Cultural Works," *Journal of Consumer Policy*, 10(3), 307–318.

FULLERTON, RONALD (1987a). "The Poverty of Ahistorical Analysis: Present Weakness and Future Cure in U.S. Marketing Thought," in *Philosophical and Radical Thought in Marketing*, Eds. A. F. Firat, N. Dholakia, and R. Bagozzi. Lexington, MA: Lexington Books, 97–116.

FULLERTON, RONALD (1987b). "Historicism: What It Is, And What It Means For Consumer Research," in *Advances in Consumer Research*, Vol. 14, Eds. Melanie Wallendorf and Paul Anderson. Provo, UT: Association for Consumer Research, 431–434.

FULLERTON, RONALD (1988). "How Modern is Modern Marketing? Marketing's Evolution and the Myth of the 'Production Era,' " *Journal of Marketing*, 52(1), 108–125.

GARDINER, JOHN ROLFE (1988). *In the Heart of the Whole World*. New York: Alfred Knopf.

GARDNER, JOHN (1978). *On Moral Fiction*. New York: Basic Books.

GATIGNON, HUBERT, and THOMAS ROBERTSON (1985). "A Propositional Inventory for New Diffusion Research," *Journal of Consumer Research*, 11(4), 849–867.

GEARY, PATRICK (1986). "Sacred Commodities: The Circulation of Medieval Relics," in *The Social Life of Things*, Ed. Arjun Appadurai. New York: Cambridge University Press, 169–191.

GEERTZ, CLIFFORD (1964). "Ideology as a Cultural System," in *Ideology and Discontent*, Ed. D. Apter. Glencoe, IL: The Free Press, 47–56.

GEERTZ, CLIFFORD (1973). *The Interpretation of Cultures*. New York: Basic Books.

GEERTZ, CLIFFORD (1988). *Works and Lives: The Anthropologist as Author*. Stanford, CA: Stanford University Press.

GELL, ALFRED (1986). "Newcomers to the World of Goods: Consumption Among the Muria Gonds," in *The Social Life of Things*, Ed. Arjun Appadurai. New York: Cambridge University Press, 110–138.

GELLNER, ERNEST (1985). *Relativism and the Social Sciences*. New York: Cambridge University Press.

GLUCKMAN, MAX (1956). "The License in Ritual," in *Custom and Conflict in Africa*. London: Basil Blackwell, 109–136.

GOFFMAN, ERVING (1976). *Gender Advertisements*. New York: Harper and Colophon Books.

GRIFFIN, DAVID (1988). *The Reenchantment of Science: Postmodern Proposals*. Albany, NY: State University of New York Press.

GROSSBERG, LAWRENCE (1983). "Cultural Studies Revisited and Revised," in *Communications in Transition*, Ed. Marya Mander. New York: Praeger, 39–70.

HAAN, NORMAN, ROBERT BELLAH, PAUL RABINOW, and WILLIAM SULLIVAN, EDS. (1983). *Social Science as Moral Inquiry*. New York: Columbia University Press.

HAAS, JACK (1986). "Prospects for Consumer Research," in *Advances in Consumer Research*, Vol. 14, Eds. Melanie Wallendorf and Paul Anderson. Provo, UT: Association for Consumer Research, 76–78.

HAUG, WOLFGANG (1987). *Commodity Aesthetics: Ideology and Culture*. New York: International General.

HEISLEY, DEBORAH, and PAULA HOLMES (1987). "A Review of Family Consumption Research: The Need for a More Anthropological Perspective," in *Advances in Consumer Research*, Vol. 14, Eds. Melanie Wallendorf and Paul Anderson. Provo, UT: Association for Consumer Research, 453–457.

HEISLEY, DEBORAH, and SIDNEY LEVY (1985). "Familiar Interlude: Autodriving in Consumer Analysis," paper presented at the 1985 Association for Consumer Research Conference, Las Vegas, NV.

HEISLEY, DEBORAH, MARY ANN MCGRATH, and JOHN SHERRY (1988). "To Everything There is a Season: A Photoessay of a Farmers' Market," in *Highways and Buyways: Naturalistic Research From the Consumer Behavior Odyssey*, Eds. Russell Belk and Melanie Wallendorf, unpublished monograph, University of Utah, Salt Lake City, UT.

HELGESON, JAMES, JOHN MAGER, and ALAN KLUGE (1985). "Consumer Research: Some History, Trends and Thoughts," in *Historical Perspective in Consumer Research: National and International Perspectives*, Eds. Chin Tiong Tan and Jagdish

Sheth. Singapore: School of Management, National University of Singapore, 155–159.

HENRY, JULES (1963). *Culture Against Man.* New York: Vintage Books.

HESKEL, DENNIS, and RICHARD SEMENIK (1983). "An Anthropological Perspective for Consumer Research Issues," in *AMA Educators' Conference Proceedings,* Eds. Patrick Murphy, O. C. Ferrell, Gene Laczniak, Robert Lusch, Paul Anderson, Terrence Shimp, Russell Belk, and Charles Weinberg. Chicago: American Marketing Association, 118–122.

HINE, THOMAS (1986). *Populuxe.* New York: Alfred Knopf.

HIRSCHMAN, ELIZABETH (1985a). "Scientific Style and the Conduct of Consumer Research," *Journal of Consumer Research,* 12(2), 225–239.

HIRSCHMAN, ELIZABETH (1985b). "Primitive Aspects of Consumption in Modern American Society," *Journal of Consumer Research,* 12(2), 142–154.

HIRSCHMAN, ELIZABETH (1986a). "Humanistic Inquiry in Marketing Research: Philosophy, Method, and Criteria," *Journal of Marketing Research* (August), 237–249.

HIRSCHMAN, ELIZABETH (1986b). "The Creation of Product Symbolism," in *Advances in Consumer Research,* Vol. 13, Ed. Richard Lutz. Provo,UT: Association for Consumer Research, 327–331.

HIRSCHMAN, ELIZABETH (1987a). "Movies as Myths: An Interpretation of Motion Picture Mythology," in *Marketing and Semiotics: New Directions in the Study of Signs for Sale,* Ed. Jean Umiker-Sebeok. Berlin: Mouton de Gruyter, 335–373.

HIRSCHMAN, ELIZABETH (1987b). " 'Beverly Hills Cop' and Consumer Behavior," in *Marketing Theory,* Eds. R. Belk, G. Zaltman, R. Bagozzi, D. Brinberg, R. Deshpande, A. F. Firat, M. Holbrook, J. Olson, J. Sherry, and B. Weitz. Chicago: American Marketing Association, 136–141.

HIRSCHMAN, ELIZABETH (1988). "The Ideology of Consumption: A Structural-Syntactic Analysis of *Dallas* and *Dynasty,*" *Journal of Consumer Research,* 15(3), 344–359.

HIRSCHMAN, ELIZABETH, Ed. (1989). *Interpretive Consumer Research.* Provo, UT: Association for Consumer Research.

HIRSCHMAN, ELIZABETH, and MORRIS HOLBROOK (1981). *Symbolic Consumer Behavior.* Ann Arbor, MI: Association for Consumer Research.

HIRSCHMAN, ELIZABETH, and MORRIS HOLBROOK (1982). "Hedonic Consumption: Emerging Concepts, Methods, and Propositions," *Journal of Marketing,* 46(3), 92–101.

HIRSCHMAN, ELIZABETH, and MORRIS HOLBROOK (1986). "Expanding the Ontology and Methodology of Research on the Consumption Experience," in *Perspectives on Methodology in Consumer Research,* Eds. David Brinberg and Richard Lutz. New York: Springer-Verlag, 213–251.

HIRSCHMAN, ELIZABETH and PRISCILLA LA BARBERA (1989). "The Meaning of Christmas," in *Interpretive Consumer Research,* Ed. Elizabeth Hirschman. Provo, UT: Association for Consumer Research, 136–147.

HODDER, IAN (1989). *The Meaning of Things: Material Culture and Symbolic Expression.* Boston: Unwin Hyman.

HOLBROOK, MORRIS (1983). "Product Imagery and the Illusion of Reality: Some Insights from Consumer Esthetics," in *Advances in Consumer Research,* Vol. 10, Eds. Alice Tybout and Richard Bagozzi. Ann Arbor, MI: Association for Consumer Research, 65–71.

HOLBROOK, MORRIS (1985). "Consumer Misbehavior: The Nature of Irregular, Irrational, Illegal, and Immoral Consumption," working paper, Columbia University, New York, NY.

HOLBROOK, MORRIS (1986). "I'm Hip: An Autobiographical Account of Some Musical Consumption Experiences," in *Advances in Consumer Research,* Vol. 13, Ed. Richard Lutz. Provo, UT: Association for Consumer Research, 614–618.

HOLBROOK, MORRIS (1987a). "What Is Consumer Research?" *Journal of Consumer Research,* 14(1), 128–132.

HOLBROOK, MORRIS (1987b). "The Study of Signs in Consumer Esthetics: An Egocentric Review," in *Marketing and Semiotics: New Directions in the Study of Signs for Sale,* Ed. Jean Umiker-Sebeok. New York: Mouton de Gruyter, 73–121.

HOLBROOK, MORRIS (1987c). "From the Log of a Consumer Researcher: Reflections on the Odyssey," in *Advances in Consumer Research,* Vol. 14, Eds. Melanie Wallendorf and Paul Anderson. Provo, UT: Association for Consumer Research, 365–369.

HOLBROOK, MORRIS (1987d). "O, Consumer, How You've Changed: Some Radical Reflections on the Roots of Consumption," in *Philosophical and*

Radical Thought in Marketing, Eds. A. F. Firat, N. Dholakia, and R. Bagozzi, Lexington, MA: Lexington Books.

HOLBROOK, MORRIS (1987e). "Mirror, Mirror on the Wall: What's Unfair in the Reflections on Advertising," *Journal of Marketing,* 51(3), 95–103.

HOLBROOK, MORRIS (1987f). "An Audiovisual Inventory of Some Fanatic Consumer Behavior: The 25-Cent Tour of a Jazz Collector's Home," in *Advances in Consumer Research,* Vol. 14, Eds. Melanie Wallendorf and Paul Anderson. Provo, UT: Association for Consumer Research, 144–149.

HOLBROOK, MORRIS (1988b). "An Interpretation: *Gremlins,* as Metaphors for Materialism," *Journal of Macromarketing,* 8(1), 54–59.

HOLBROOK, MORRIS (1988c). "Steps Toward a Psychoanalytic Interpretation of Consumption: A Meta-Meta-Meta-Analysis of Some Issues Raised by the Consumer Behavior Odyssey," in *Advances in Consumer Research,* Vol. 15, Ed. Michael Houston. Provo, UT: Association for Consumer Research, 537–542.

HOLBROOK, MORRIS (1988d). "The Psychoanalytic Interpretation of Consumer Behavior: I Am an Animal," in *Highways and Buyways: Naturalistic Research From the Consumer Behavior Odyssey,* Eds. Melanie Wallendorf and Russell Belk, unpublished monograph, University of Utah: Salt Lake City, UT.

HOLBROOK, MORRIS (1989). "Seven Routes to Facilitating the Semiological Interpretation of Consumption Symbolism and Marketing Imagery in Works of Art," in *Advances in Consumer Research,* Vol. 16, Ed. Thomas Srull. Provo, UT: Association for Consumer Research.

HOLBROOK, MORRIS, and MARK GRAYSON (1986). "The Semiology of Cinematic Consumption: Symbolic Consumer Behavior in *Out of Africa,*" *Journal of Consumer Research,* 13(3), 374–381.

HOLBROOK, MORRIS, and ELIZABETH HIRSCHMAN (1982). "The Experiential Aspects of Consumption: Consumer Fantasies, Feelings, and Fun," *Journal of Consumer Research,* 9(2), 132–140.

HOLBROOK, MORRIS, STEPHEN BELL, and MARK GRAYSON (1989). "The Role of Humanities in Consumer Research: Close Encounters and Coastal Disturbances," in *Interpretive Consumer Research,* Ed. Elizabeth Hirschman. Provo, UT: Association for Consumer Research, 29–47.

HOLBROOK, MORRIS, and JOHN O'SHAUGHNESSY (1988). "On the Scientific Status of Consumer Research and the Need for an Interpretive Approach to Studying Consumption Behavior," *Journal of Consumer Research,* 15(3) 398–402.

HOLBROOK, MORRIS, and ROBERT ZIRLIN (1985). "Artistic Creation, Artworks and Aesthetic Appreciation: Some Philosophical Contributions to Nonprofit Marketing," in *Advances in Nonprofit Marketing,* Vol. 1, Ed. Russell Belk. Greenwich, CT: JAI Press, 1–54.

HOLLANDER, STANLEY, and RONALD SAVITT, Eds. (1983). *First North American Workshop on Historical Research in Marketing Proceedings.* East Lansing, MI: Michigan State University.

HOLLANDER, STANLEY, and TERRENCE NEVETT, Eds. (1985). *Marketing in the Long Run: Proceedings of the Second Workshop on Historical Research in Marketing.* East Lansing, MI: Michigan State University.

HOLMAN, REBECCA (1980). "Apparel as Communication," in *Symbolic Consumer Behavior,* Eds. Elizabeth Hirschman and Morris Holbrook. Ann Arbor, MI: Association for Consumer Research, 16–25.

HOLMAN, REBECCA (1981). "Product Use as Communication: A Fresh Appraisal of a Venerable Topic," in *Review of Marketing 1981,* Eds. Ben Enis and Kenneth Roering. Chicago: American Marketing Association, 106–119.

HOWE, CLARENCE (1960). "Translator's Foreword" in *The Logic of the Humanities,* Ernst Cassirer. New Haven, CT: Yale University Press, vii–xviii.

HUDSON, LAUREL, and JEFF MURRAY (1986). "Methodological Limitations of the Hedonic Consumption Paradigm and a Possible Alternative: A Subjectivist Approach," in *Advances in Consumer Research,* Vol. 13, Ed. Richard Lutz. Provo, UT: Association for Consumer Research, 343–348.

HUDSON, LAUREL, and JULIE OZANNE (1988). "Alternative Ways of Seeking Knowledge in Consumer Research," *Journal of Consumer Research,* 14(4), 508–521.

HUNT, SHELBY (1989). "Naturalistic Humanistic, and Interpretive Inquiry: Challenges and Ultimate Potential," in *Interpretive Consumer Research,* Ed. Elizabeth Hirschman. Provo, UT: Association for Consumer Research, 185–198.

JACOBY, JACOB (1978). "Consumer Research: A State of the Art Review," *Journal of Marketing,* 42(April), 87–96.

JAMESON, FREDERIC (1987). "The Politics of Theory: Ideological Positions in the Postmodern Debate," in *Interpretive Social Science: A Second Look,* Eds. Paul Rabinow and William Sullivan. Berkeley, CA: University of California Press, 351–364.

JAWORSKI, BERNARD, and DEBORAH MACINNIS (1988). "On Being an Informant in the Consumer Behavior Odyssey," in *Highways and Buyways: Naturalistic Research From the Consumer Behavior Odyssey,* Eds. Melanie Wallendorf and Russell Belk, unpublished manuscript, University of Arizona, Tuscon.

JHALLY, SUT (1987). *The Codes of Advertising: Fetishism and the Political Economy of Meaning in the Consumer Society.* New York: St. Martin's Press.

JOLIBERT, ALAIN, and CARLOS FERNANDEZ MORENO (1983). "A Comparison of French and Mexican Gift Giving Practices," in *Advances in Consumer Research,* Vol. 10, Eds. Richard Bagozzi and Alice Tybout. Ann Arbor, MI: Association for Consumer Research, 191–196.

JOY, ANNAMMA (1988). "Marketing and Culture: An Epistemological Critique," in *Marketing: A Return to the Broader Dimensions,* Eds. Stanley Shapiro and A. H. Walle. Chicago, IL: American Marketing Association, 389–394.

KASSARJIAN, HAROLD H. (1982). "The Development of Consumer Behavior Theory," in *Advances in Consumer Research,* Vol. 9, Ed. Andrew Mitchell. Ann Arbor, MI: Association for Consumer Research, 20–22.

KASSARJIAN, HAROLD H. (1987). "How We Spent Our Summer Vacation: A Preliminary Report on the 1986 Consumer Behavior Odyssey," in *Advances in Consumer Research,* Vol. 14, Eds. Melanie Wallendorf and Paul Anderson. Provo, UT: Association for Consumer Research, 376–377.

KAUFMAN, CAROL (1987). "The Evaluation of Marketing in a Society: The Han Dynasty of Ancient China," *Journal of Macromarketing,* 7 (Fall), 52–64.

KAVANAUGH, JOHN (1981). *Following Christ in a Consumer Society.* Maryknoll, NY: Orbis Books.

KEHRET-WARD, TRUDY (1987). "Combining Products in Use: How the Syntax of Product Use Affects Marketing Decisions," in *Marketing and Semiotics: New Directions in the Study of Signs for Sale,"* Ed. Jean Umiker-Sebeok. Berlin: Mouton de Gruyter, 219–238.

KEHRET-WARD, TRUDY (1988). "Using a Semiotic Approach to Study the Consumption of Functionally Related Products," *International Journal of Research in Marketing,* 4(3), 187–200.

KELLY, ROBERT (1987). "Culture as Commodity:

The Marketing of Cultural Objects and Cultural Encounters," in *Advances in Consumer Research,* Vol. 14, Eds. Melanie Wallendorf and Paul Anderson. Provo, UT: Association for Consumer Research, 347–351.

KEOWN, CHARLES (1988). "Review of Werner and Schoepfle (1987), *Systematic Fieldwork,"* *Journal of Marketing Research,* 25(1), 116–117.

KERNAN, JEROME (1987). "Chasing the Holy Grail: Reflections on 'What Is Consumer Research,' " *Journal of Consumer Research,* 14(1), 133–135.

KILBOURNE, WILLIAM (1987). "Self-Actualization and the Consumption Process: Can You Get There From Here?" in *Philosophical and Radical Thought in Marketing,* Eds. A. F. Firat, N. Dholakia, and R. Bagozzi. Lexington, MA: Lexington Books, 217–234.

KIRA, ALEXANDER (1966). *The Bathroom: Criteria for Design.* New York: Bantam Books.

KLAMER, ARJO, DONALD MCCLOSKEY, and ROBERT SOLOW, Eds. (1988). *The Consequences of Economic Rhetoric.* New York: Cambridge University Press.

KLEINE, ROBERT, and JEROME KERNAN (1987). "Toward an Epistemology of Consumption Symbolism: Some Preliminary Considerations," in *Advances in Consumer Research,* Vol. 14, Eds. Melanie Wallendorf and Paul Anderson. Provo, UT: Association for Consumer Research, 573.

KOPYTOFF, IGOR (1986). "The Cultural Biography of Things: Commoditization as Process," in *The Social Life of Things,* Ed. Arjun Appadurai. New York: Cambridge University Press, 64–91.

KUMCU, ERDOGAN (1987a). "Historical Method: Toward a Relevant Analysis of Marketing Systems," in *Philosophical and Radical Thought in Marketing,* Eds. A. F. Firat, N. Dholakia, and R. Bagozzi. Lexington, MA: Lexington Books, 117–133.

KUMCU, ERDOGAN (1987b). "A Historical Perspective Framework to Study Consumer Behavior and Retailing Systems," in *Advances in Consumer Research,* Vol. 14, Eds. Melanie Wallendorf and Paul Anderson. Provo, UT: Association for Consumer Research, 439–441.

KUMCU, ERDOGAN, and A. F. FIRAT, Eds. (1988). *Marketing and Development: Toward Broader Dimensions* in *Research in Marketing,* Supplement 4, Ed. Jagdish Sheth. Greenwich, CT: JAI Press.

LAVIN, MARILYN, and THOMAS ARCHDEACON (1989). "The Relevance of Historical Method for

Marketing Research," in *Interpretive Consumer Research*, Ed. Elizabeth Hirschman. Provo, UT: Association for Consumer Research, 60–68.

LEISS, WILLIAM (1976). *The Limits to Satisfaction: An Essay on the Problem of Needs and Commodities*. Toronto: University of Toronto Press.

LEISS, WILLIAM, STEPHEN KLINE, and SUT JHALLY (1986). *Social Communication in Advertising: Persons, Products, and Images of Well-Being*. New York: Methuen.

LETT, JAMES (1987). *The Human Enterprise: A Critical Introduction to Anthropological Theory*. Boulder, CO: Westview Press.

LEVI-STRAUSS, CLAUDE (1963). *Structural Anthropology*. New York: Basic Books.

LEVI-STRAUSS, CLAUDE (1969). *The Raw and the Cooked*. New York: Harper & Row.

LEVINE, DAVID (1985). *The Flight From Ambiguity: Essays in Social and Cultural Theory*. Chicago: University of Chicago Press.

LEVY, SIDNEY J. (1978a). *Marketing Behavior: Its Meaning for Management*. New York: AMACOM.

LEVY, SIDNEY J. (1978b). "Hunger and Work in a Civilized Tribe: Or, the Anthropology of Market Transactions," *American Behavioral Scientist*, 21(March/April), 557–570.

LEVY, SIDNEY J. (1981). "Interpreting Consumer Mythology: A Structural Approach to Consumer Behavior," *Journal of Marketing*, 45(Summer), 49–61.

LEVY, SIDNEY J. (1984). "Synchrony and Diachrony in Product Perception," unpublished manuscript, J. L. Kellogg Graduate School of Management, Northwestern University, Evanston, IL.

LEVY, SIDNEY J. (1985). "Dreams, Fairy Tales, Animals, and Cars," *Psychology and Marketing*, 2(2), 67–81.

LEVY, SIDNEY J. (1986). "Meanings in Advertising Stimuli," in *Advertising and Consumer Psychology*, Vol. 3, Eds. Jerry Olson and Keith Sentis. New York: Praeger, 214–226.

LEVY, SIDNEY J. (1988). "Acceptance Speech: AMA Marketing Educator of the Year," talk presented at the 1988 American Marketing Association Summer Conference, San Francisco, CA.

LEYMORE, VARDA (1975). *Hidden Myth*. New York: Basic Books.

LEYMORE, VARDA (1987). "The Structure is the Message—The Case of Advertising," in *Marketing and Semiotics: New Directions in the Study of Signs for Sale*, Ed. Jean Umiker-Sebeok. Berlin: Mouton de Gruyter, 319–331.

LEYMORE, VARDA (1988). "Inside Information: Structure and Effectivity in Advertising," *International Journal of Research in Marketing*, 4(3), 217–232.

LINCOLN, YVONNA, and EGON GUBA (1985). *Naturalistic Inquiry*. Beverly Hills, CA: Sage.

LITTLEFIELD, JAMES and MAGDOLNA CSATH, EDS. (1988). *Marketing and Economic Development: Issues and Opinions*. Blacksburg, VA: Virginia Polytechnic Institute and State University.

LOWENSTEIN, JOSEPH (1985). "The Script in the Marketplace," *Representations*, 12(Fall), 101–114.

LOWENTHAL, DAVID (1985). *The Past is a Foreign Country*. Cambridge University Press.

LUTZ, RICHARD (1988a). "JCR Style Sheet," *Journal of Consumer Research*, 15(1), 146–152.

LUTZ, RICHARD (1988b). "Editorial," *Journal of Consumer Research*, 15(1), ii–iii.

LUTZ, RICHARD (1989). "Positivism, Naturalism and Pluralism in Consumer Research: Paradigms in Paradise," in *Advances in Consumer Research*, Vol. 16, Ed. Thomas Srull. Provo, UT: Association for Consumer Research, 1–7.

LYOTARD, JEAN-FRANCOIS (1984/1979). *The Postmodern Condition: A Report on Knowledge*. Minneapolis, MN: University of Minnesota Press.

MacCANNELL, DEAN (1987). " 'Sex Sells': Comment on Gender Images and Myth in Advertising," in *Marketing and Semiotics: New Directions in the Study of Signs for Sale*, Ed. Jean Umiker-Sebeok. Berlin: Mouton de Gruyter, 521–531.

MACFARLANE, ALAN (1978). *The Origins of English Individualism*. New York: Basil Blackwell.

MACFARLANE, ALAN (1987). *The Culture of Capitalism*. New York: Basil Blackwell.

MAGER, JOHN, and JAMES HELGESON (1987). "The Developments of Marketing Thought: Cultural Changes and Marketing Evolution," in *Marketing Theory*, Eds. R. Belk, G. Zaltman, R. Bagozzi, D. Brinberg, R. Deshpande, A. F. Firat, M. Holbrook, J. Olson, J. Sherry, and B. Weitz. Chicago: American Marketing Association, 326–331.

MARCHAND, ROLAND (1985). *Advertising the American Dream: Making Way for Modernity, 1920–1940*. Berkeley, CA: University of California Press.

MARCUS, GEORGE, and MICHAEL FISCHER (1986). *Anthropology as Cultural Critique: An Experimental*

Moment in the Human Sciences. Chicago: University of Chicago Press.

MASCARENHAS, OSWALD (1987). "Toward a Theology of Consumption," in *Marketing Theory*, Eds. R. Belk, G. Zaltman, R. Bagozzi, D. Brinberg, R. Deshpande, A. F. Firat, M. Holbrook, J. Olson, J. Sherry, and B. Weitz. Chicago: American Marketing Association, 71–76.

MATTELART, ARMAND, XAVIER DELCOURT, and MICHELE MATTELART (1984). *International Image Markets: In Search of an Alternative Perspective*. London: Comedia.

McCLOSKEY, DONALD (1985). *The Rhetoric of Economics*. Madison, WI: University of Wisconsin Press.

McCRACKEN, GRANT (1985). "Clio in the Marketplace: Theoretical and Methodological Issues in the History of Consumption," in *Historical Perspective in Consumer Research: National and International Perspectives*, Eds. Chin Tiong Tan and Jagdish Sheth. Singapore: School of Management, National University of Singapore, 151–154.

McCRACKEN, GRANT (1986). "Culture and Consumption: A Theoretical Account of the Structure and Movement of the Cultural Meaning of Consumer Goods," *Journal of Consumer Research*, 13(1), 71–84.

McCRACKEN, GRANT (1987a). "The History of Consumption: A Literature Review and Consumer Guide," *Journal of Consumer Policy*, 10, 139–166.

McCRACKEN, GRANT (1987b). "Advertising: Meaning or Information?" in *Advances in Consumer Research*, Vol. 14, Eds. Melanie Wallendorf and Paul Anderson. Provo, UT: Association for Consumer Research, 121–124.

McCRACKEN, GRANT (1988a). *Culture and Consumption: New Approaches to the Symbolic Character of Consumer Goods and Activities*. Bloomington, IN: Indiana University Press.

McCRACKEN, GRANT (1988b). "The Making of Modern Consumption," in *Culture and Consumption: New Approaches to the Symbolic Character of Consumer Goods and Activities*. Bloomington, IN: Indiana University Press, 3–20.

McCRACKEN, GRANT (1988c). "The Evocative Power of Things: Consumer Goods and the Preservation of Hopes and Ideals," in *Culture and Consumption: New Approaches to the Symbolic Character of Consumer Goods and Activities*. Bloomington, IN: Indiana University Press, 104–117.

McCRACKEN, GRANT (1988d). "Diderot Unities and the Diderot Effect: Neglected Cultural Aspects of Consumption," in *Culture and Consumption: New Approaches to the Symbolic Character of Consumer Goods and Activities*. Bloomington, IN: Indiana University Press, 118–129.

McCRACKEN, GRANT (1988e). "Consumption, Change and Continuity," in *Culture and Consumption: New Approaches to the Symbolic Character of Consumer Goods and Activities*. Bloomington, IN: Indiana University Press, 130–137.

McCRACKEN, GRANT (1988f). " 'Ever Dearer in our Thoughts': Patina and the Representation of Status Before and After the Eighteenth Century," in *Culture and Consumption: New Approaches to the Symbolic Character of Consumer Goods and Activities*. Bloomington, IN: Indiana University Press, 31–43.

McCRACKEN, GRANT (1988g). "Clothing as Language: An Object Lesson in the Study of the Expressive Properties of Material Culture," in *Culture and Consumption: New Approaches to the Symbolic Character of Consumer Goods and Activities*. Bloomington, IN: Indiana University Press, 57–70.

McCRACKEN, GRANT (1988h). "Lois Roget: Curatorial Consumer in a Modern World," in *Culture and Consumption: New Approaches to the Symbolic Character of Consumer Goods and Activities*. Bloomington, IN: Indiana University Press, 44–53.

McCRACKEN, GRANT (1988i). "Marketing Material Cultures: Person-Object Relations Inside and Outside the North American Museum," in *Advances in Nonprofit Marketing*, Vol. 4, Ed. Russell Belk. Greenwich, CT: JAI Press.

McCRACKEN, GRANT (1989). "Homeyness: A Cultural Account of One Constellation of Consumer Goods and Meaning," in *Interpretive Consumer Research*, Ed. Elizabeth Hirschman. Provo, UT: Association for Consumer Research, 168–183.

McGRATH, MARY ANN (1989). "A Natural History of Gift Giving: The Perspective from a Gift Store," working paper, Loyola University of Chicago, Chicago, IL.

McKENDRICK, N., J. BREWER, and J. PLUMB (1982). *The Birth of a Consumer Society: The Commercialization of Eighteenth Century England*. Bloomington, IN: Indiana University Press.

McMULLIN, ERNAN, ED. (1988). *Construction and Constraint: The Shaping of Scientific Rationality*. Notre Dame, IN: University of Notre Dame Press.

McQuarie, Edward (1989). "Advertising Resonance: A Semiological Perspective," in *Interpretive Consumer Research,* Ed. Elizabeth Hirschman. Provo, UT: Association for Consumer Research, 97–114.

Mick, David (1986). "Consumer Research and Semiotics: Exploring the Morphology of Signs, Symbols, and Significance," *Journal of Consumer Research,* 13(2), 196–213.

Mick, David (1987). "Towards a Semiotic of Advertising Story Grammars," in *Marketing and Semiotics: New Directions in the Study of Signs for Sale,* Ed. Jean Umiker-Sebeok. Berlin: Mouton de Gruyter, 249–278.

Mick, David (1988a). "Contributions to the Semiotics of Marketing and Consumer Behavior," in *The Semiotic Web: A Yearbook of Semiotics,* Eds. Thomas Sebeok and Jean Umiker-Sebeok. Berlin: Mouton de Gruyter.

Mick, David (1988b). "Schema-Theoretics and Semiotics: Toward More Holistic, Programmatic Research on Marketing Communications," *Semiotics,* 70(1–2), 1–26.

Mick, David (1988c). "A Critical Review of the Comprehension Construct in Marketing Communications Research," working paper, University of Florida, Gainesville, FL.

Mick, David, and Laura Politi (1989). "Consumers' Interpretations of Advertising Imagery: A Visit to the Hell of Connotation," in *Interpretive Consumer Research,* Ed. Elizabeth Hirschman. Provo, UT: Association for Consumer Research, 85–96.

Miller, Daniel (1987). *Material Culture and Mass Consumption.* New York: Basil Blackwell.

Miller, Richard (1987). *Fact and Method: Explanation, Confirmation and Reality in the Natural and Social Sciences.* Princeton, NJ: Princeton University Press.

Miller, Tom (1986). *The Panama Hat Trail.* New York: Vintage Books.

Mills, C. Wright (1975/1959). "On Intellectual Craftsmanship," in *The Sociological Imagination,* Ed. C. W. Mills. New York: Oxford University Press. 195–226.

Mintz, Sidney (1982). "Choice and Occasion: Sweet Moments," in *The Psychology of Human Food Selection,* Ed. Lewis Barker, Westport, CT: Avi.

Mintz, Sidney (1985). *Sweetness and Power.* New York: Viking Press.

Mintz, Sidney (1987a). "Choosing Freely," paper presented at the Annual Meetings of the American Anthropological Association, Chicago, IL.

Mintz, Sidney (1987b). "Author's Rejoinder," *Food and Foodways,* Vol. 2. London: Harwood Academic, 171–197.

Moorman, Christine (1987). "Marketing as Technique: The Influence of Marketing on the Meaning of Consumption," in *Philosophical and Radical Thought in Marketing,* Eds. A. F. Firat, N. Dholakia, and R. Bagozzi. Lexington, MA: Lexington Books, 193–215.

Morgan, Gareth (1987). "Journals and the Control of Knowledge: A Critical Perspective," in *Publishing in the Organizational Sciences,* Eds. Larry Cummings and Peter Frost. Homewood, IL: Irwin, 63–75.

Mruk, Christopher (1985). "Integrated Description: A Phenomenologically Oriented Technique for Researching Large Scale, Emerging Human Experience and Trends," in *Advances in Consumer Research,* Vol. 12, Eds. Elizabeth Hirschman and Morris Holbrook. Provo, UT: Association for Consumer Research, 556–559.

Mukerji, Chandra (1983). *From Graven Images: Patterns of Modern Materialism.* New York: Columbia University Press.

Murray, Henry (1943). *Thematic Apperception Test Manual.* Cambridge, MA: Harvard University Press.

Myers, Elizabeth (1985). "Phenomenological Analysis of the Importance of Special Possessions: An Exploratory Study," in *Advances in Consumer Research,* Vol. 12, Eds. Elizabeth Hirschman and Morris Holbrook. Provo, UT: Association for Consumer Research, 560–565.

Nelson, John (1988). "Seven Rhetorics of Inquiry: A Provocation," in *The Rhetoric of the Human Sciences: Language and Argument in Scholarship and Public Affairs,* Eds. John Nelson, Allan Megill, and Donald McCloskey. Madison, WI: University of Wisconsin Press, 407–434.

Nelson, John, Allan Megill, and Donald McCloskey, Eds. (1988). *The Rhetoric of the Human Sciences: Language and Argument in Scholarship and the Human Sciences.* Madison, WI: University of Wisconsin Press.

Newman, Katherine (1988). *Falling From Grace: The Experience of Downward Mobility in the American Middle Class.* New York: The Free Press.

Nicosia, Francesco, and Robert Mayer (1976).

"Toward a Sociology of Consumption," *Journal of Consumer Research,* 3(3), 65–76.

NIETZSCHE, FRIEDRICH (1913). *The Will to Power,* in *The Complete Works of F. Nietzsche,* Vol. 15, Ed. O. Levy. Edinburgh: Foulis.

NOTH, WINFRED (1987). "Advertising: The Frame Message," in *Marketing and Semiotics: New Directions in the Study of Signs for Sale,* Ed. Jean Umiker-Sebeok. Berlin: Mouton de Gruyter, 279–294.

NOTH, WINFRED (1988). "The Language of Commodities: Groundwork for a Semiotics of Consumer Goods," *International Journal of Research in Marketing,* 4(3), 173–186.

O'CONNOR, P. J., GARY SULLIVAN, and DANA POGORZELSKI (1985). "Cross Cultural Family Purchasing Decisions: A Literature Review," in *Advances in Consumer Research,* Vol. 12, Eds. Elizabeth Hirschman and Morris Holbrook. Provo, UT: Association for Consumer Research, 59–64.

O'GUINN, THOMAS (1987a). "The Marketing of the Consumption of Religion," paper presented at the AMA Winter Educators' Conference, San Antonio, TX.

O'GUINN, THOMAS (1987b). "Touching Greatness: Some Aspects of Star Worship Examined Within Naturalistic Context," paper presented at the American Psychological Association Conference, New York, NY.

O'GUINN, THOMAS (1987c). "To Be Like Them: Emulating Stars, Observations in Naturalistic Settings," paper presented at the Annual Conference of the Association for Consumer Research, Boston, MA.

O'GUINN, THOMAS, WEI-NA LEE, and RONALD FABER (1986). "Acculturation: The Impact of Divergent Paths of Buyer Behavior," in *Advances in Consumer Research,* Vol. 13, Ed. Richard Lutz. Provo, UT: Association for Consumer Research, 579–583.

O'GUINN, THOMAS, and RONALD FABER (1985). "New Perspectives on Acculturation: The Relationship of General and Role Specific Acculturation with Hispanics' Consumer Attitudes," in *Advances in Consumer Research,* Vol. 12, Eds. Elizabeth Hirschman and Morris Holbrook. Provo, UT: Association for Consumer Research, 113–117.

O'SHAUGHNESSY, JOHN (1985). "A Return to Reason in Consumer Behavior: An Hermeneutical Approach," in *Advances in Consumer Research,* Vol. 12, Eds. Elizabeth Hirschman and Morris Holbrook. Provo, UT: Association for Consumer Research, 305–311.

O'SHAUGHNESSY, JOHN (1987). *Why People Buy.* New York: Oxford University Press.

OZANNE, JULIE, and CATHY HINSON (1987). "Hermeneutics as a Method for Studying Social Phenomena," paper presented at the 1988 AMA Winter Educators' Conference, San Diego, CA.

OZANNE, JULIE, and LAUREL HUDSON (1989). "Exploring Diversity in Consumer Research," in *Interpretive Consumer Research,* Ed. Elizabeth Hirschman. Provo, UT: Association for Consumer Research, 1–9.

PANDYA, ANIL (1985). "Symbolic Communication Among Consumers," *Marketing Communications — Theory and Research,* Ed. Michael Houston and Richard Lutz. Chicago: American Marketing Association, 89–92.

PARKER, RICHARD (1988). "Conversational Interaction: Directions for Qualitative Marketing and Consumer Research," in *Research in Consumer Behavior,* Vol. 3, Ed. Elizabeth Hirschman. Greenwich, CT: JAI Press, 211–245.

PEIRCE, CHARLES (1935–1966). *Collected Papers of Charles Sanders Peirce.* Cambridge, MA: Harvard University Press [reference is to volume and page].

PERRIN, CONSTANCE (1988). *Belonging in America: Reading Between the Lines.* Madison, WI: University of Wisconsin Press.

PETER, J. PAUL (1989). "Philosophical Tensions in Consumer Inquiry," in *Handbook of Consumer Theory and Research,* Eds. Harold Kassarjian and Thomas Robertson. Englewood Cliffs, NJ: Prentice-Hall.

PETER, J. PAUL, and JERRY OLSON (1989). "The Relativistic/Constructionist Perspective on Scientific Knowledge and Consumer Research," in *Interpretive Consumer Research,* Ed. Elizabeth Hirschman. Provo, UT: Association for Consumer Research, 24–28.

PINCH, TREVOR, and COLIN CLARK (1986). "The Hard Sell: 'Patter Merchanting' and the Strategic (Re)Production and Local Management of Economic Reasoning in the Sales Routines of Market Pitchers," *Sociology,* 20(2), 169–191.

PINCH, TREVOR, and COLIN CLARK (1988). "The Hard Sell: A Study of the Sales Techniques of Market Traders," videocassette, York University, U.K.

PINSON, CHRISTIAN (1988). "Special Issue: Semiotics and Marketing," *Journal of International Research in Marketing,* 4(3).

PLATTNER, STUART, Ed. (1985). *Markets and Marketing.* New York: University Press of America.

POLLAY, RICHARD (1986). "The Distorted Mirror: Reflections on the Unintended Consequences of Advertising," *Journal of Marketing,* 50(2), 18–36.

POLLAY, RICHARD (1987a). "On the Wall of Reflections on the Values in the 'Distorted Mirror,'" *Journal of Marketing,* 51(3).

POLLAY, RICHARD (1987b). "Insights Into Consumer Behavior From Historical Studies of Advertising," *Advances in Consumer Research,* Vol. 14, Eds. Melanie Wallendorf and Paul Anderson. Provo, UT: Association for Consumer Research, 447–450.

POLLAY, RICHARD (1987c). "The History of Advertising Archives: Confessions of a Professional Pac-Rat," in *Advances in Consumer Research,* Vol. 14, Eds. Melanie Wallendorf and Paul Anderson. Provo, UT: Association for Consumer Research, 136–159.

POSTER, MARK, and ALLADI VENKATESH (1987). "From Marx to Foucault—An Intellectual Journal Through Critical Theory," in *Marketing Theory,* Eds. R. Belk, G. Zaltman, R. Bagozzi, D. Brinberg, R. Deshpande, A. F. Firat, M. Holbrook, J. Olson, J. Sherry, and B. Weitz. Chicago, IL: American Marketing Association, 20–26.

PRUS, ROBERT (1984). "Purchasing Products for Resale: Assessing Suppliers as 'Partners-in-Trade,'" *Symbolic Interaction,* 7(2), 249–278.

PRUS, ROBERT (1985). "Price-Setting As Social Activity: Defining Price, Value, and Profit in the Marketplace," *Urban Life,* 14(1), 59–93.

PRUS, ROBERT (1986a). "It's on 'Sale!': An Examination of Vendor Perspectives, Activities, and Dilemmas," *Canadian Review of Sociology and Anthropology,* 23(1), 72–96.

PRUS, ROBERT (1986b). "Laying the Groundwork for Buyer Commitments. The Social Production of Trust," paper presented at the Ethnographic Research: An Interactionist/Interpretive Inquiry Conference, Waterloo, Ont.

PRUS, ROBERT (1987). "Generic Social Processes. Implications of a Processual Theory of Action for Research on Marketplace Exchanges," in *Advances in Consumer Research,* Vol. 14, Eds. Melanie Wallendorf and Paul Anderson. Provo, UT: Association for Consumer Research, 66–70.

PRUS, ROBERT (1989a). *Making Sales: Influence as Interpersonal Accomplishment.* Beverly Hills, CA: Sage.

PRUS, ROBERT (1989b). *Pursuing Customers: An Ethnography of Marketing Activities.* Beverly Hills, CA: Sage.

PRUS, ROBERT, and WENDY FRISBY (1987). "Marketplace Dynamics: The P's of 'People' and 'Process,'" in *Advances in Consumer Research,* Vol. 14, Eds. Melanie Wallendorf and Paul Anderson. Provo, UT: Association for Consumer Research, 61–65.

RABINOW, PAUL, and WILLIAM SULLIVAN (1987). "The Interpretive Turn: A Second Look," in *Interpretive Social Science: A Second Look,* Eds. Paul Rabinow and William Sullivan. Berkeley, CA: University of California Press, 1–30.

RASSULI, KATHLEEN, and STANLEY HOLLANDER (1987). "Comparative History as a Research Tool in Consumer Behavior," in *Advances in Consumer Research,* Vol. 14, Eds. Melanie Wallendorf and Paul Anderson. Provo, UT: Association for Consumer Research, 442–446.

REAL, MICHAEL (1986). "Demythologizing Media: Recent Writings in Critical and Institutional Theory," *Critical Studies in Mass Communication,* 3, 459–496.

REDDY, WILLIAM (1986). "The Structure of a Cultural Crisis: Thinking About Cloth in France Before and After the Revolution," in *The Social Life of Things,* Ed. Arjun Appadurai. New York: Cambridge University Press, 261–284.

REDMOND, WILLIAM and MELANIE WALLENDORF (1984). "Marketing and the Scientific Enterprise: A Sociological Analysis," in *Scientific Method in Marketing,* Eds. Paul Anderson and Michael Ryan. Chicago: American Marketing Association, 10–13.

REED, ISHMAEL (1988). *The Terrible Twos.* New York: Atheneum.

REICHARDT, CHARLES, and THOMAS COOK (1979). "Beyond Qualitative *Versus* Quantitative Methods," in *Qualitative and Quantitative Methods in Evaluation Research,* Eds. Thomas Cook and Charles Reichardt. Beverly Hills, CA: Sage, 7–32.

REILLY, MICHAEL, and MELANIE WALLENDORF (1984). "A Longitudinal Study of Mexican-American Assimilation," in *Advances in Consumer Research,* Vol. 11, Ed. Thomas Kinnear. Provo, UT: Association for Consumer Research, 735–740.

REILLY, MICHAEL, and MELANIE WALLENDORF (1987). "A Comparison of Group Differences in Food Consumption Using Household Refuse," *Journal of Consumer Research,* 14(2), 289–294.

REXEISEN, RICHARD (1984). "Theory Development in Perspective: Exposing the Cultural Bias," *Advances in Consumer Research,* Vol. 11, Ed. Thomas Kinnear. Provo, UT: Association for Consumer Research, 329–332.

ROBERTSON, THOMAS, and JOAN ZIELINSKI (1982). "Sociological Perspectives for Consumer Research," unpublished manuscript, The Wharton School, University of Pennsylvania, Philadelphia, PA.

ROBINSON, LARRY, and ROY ADLER (1987). *Marketing Megaworks: The Top 150 Books and Articles.* New York: Praeger.

ROCHBERG-HALTON, EUGENE (1986). *Meaning and Modernity: Social Theory in the Pragmatic Attitude.* Chicago: University of Chicago Press.

RODMAN, WILLIAM (1987). "Watching With Both Eyes: Ethnography and Moral Fiction," paper presented at the Annual Conference of the American Anthropological Association, Chicago, IL.

ROGERS, EVERETT (1976). "New Product Adoption and Diffusion," *Journal of Consumer Research,* 2(2), 290–301.

ROGERS, EVERETT, and JUDITH LAWRON (1984). *Silicon Valley Fever: Growth of High Technology Culture.* New York: Basic Books.

ROGERS, EVERETT (1987). "The Critical School and Consumer Research," in *Advances in Consumer Research,* Vol. 14, Eds. Melanie Wallendorf and Paul Anderson. Provo, UT: Association for Consumer Research, 7–11.

ROOK, DENNIS (1984). "Ritual Behavior and Consumer Behavior," in *Advances in Consumer Research,* Vol. 11, Ed. Thomas Kinnear. Provo, UT: Association for Consumer Research, 279–284.

ROOK, DENNIS (1985). "The Ritual Dimension of Consumption," *Journal of Consumer Research,* 12(3), 251–264.

ROOK, DENNIS (1987a). "The Buying Impulse," *Journal of Consumer Research,* 14(2), 189–199.

ROOK, DENNIS (1987b). "Modern Hex Signs and Symbols of Security," in *Marketing and Semiotics: New Directions in the Study of Signs for Sale,* Ed. Jean Umiker-Sebeok, Berlin: Mouton de Gruyter, 239–246.

ROOK, DENNIS, and SIDNEY LEVY (1983). "Psychosocial Themes in Consumer Grooming Rituals," *Journal of Consumer Research,* Vol. 10, Eds. Richard Bagozzi and Alice Tybout. Provo, UT: Association for Consumer Research, 329–333.

RORTY, RICHARD (1980). *Philosophy and the Mirror of Nature.* Princeton, NJ: Princeton University Press.

ROSSI, WILLIAM (1976). *The Sex Life of the Foot and Shoe.* New York: Dutton.

ROTH, MARTIN, and CHRISTINE MOORMAN (1988). "The Cultural Content of Cognition and the Cognitive Content of Culture: Implications for Consumer Research," in *Advances in Consumer Research,* Vol. 15, Ed. Michael Houston. Provo, UT: Association for Consumer Research, 403–410.

RUTZ, HENRY, and BENJAMIN ORLOVE, Eds. (1988). *The Social Economy of Consumption.* New York: University Presses of America.

RYAN, MICHAEL (1986). "Implications From the 'Old' and the 'New' Physics for Studying Buyer Behavior," in *Perspectives on Methodology in Consumer Research,* Eds. David Brinberg and Richard Lutz. New York: Springer-Verlag, 37–63.

SACK, ROBERT (1988). "The Consumer's World: Place as Context," *Annals of the Association of American Geographers,* 78(4), 642–664.

SAHLINS, MARSHALL (1976). *Culture and Practical Reason.* Chicago, IL: University of Chicago Press.

SANDERS, CLINT (1985). "Tattoo Consumption: Risk and Regret in the Purchase of a Socially Marginal Service," in *Advances in Consumer Research,* Vol. 13, Eds. Elizabeth Hirschman and Morris Holbrook. Provo, UT: Association for Consumer Research, 17–22.

SANDERS, CLINT (1987). "Consuming as Social Action: Ethnographic Methods in Consumer Research," in *Advances in Consumer Research,* Vol. 14, Eds. Melanie Wallendorf and Paul Anderson. Provo, UT: Association for Consumer Research, 71–75.

SANDERS, CLINT (1988). "Marks of Mischief: Becoming and Being Tattooed," *Journal of Contemporary Ethnography,* 16(4), 395–432.

SAPIR, J. DAVID (1988). "Review of Prattis, Ed. (1985). *Reflections: The Anthropological Muse,*" *American Anthropologist,* 90(2), 445–446.

SAVITT, RONALD (1980). "Historical Research in Marketing," *Journal of Marketing,*" 44(Fall), 52–58.

SCHAMA, SIMON (1988). *The Embarrassment of Riches:*

An Interpretation of Dutch Culture in the Golden Age. New York: Knopf.

SCHLERETH, THOMAS, Ed. (1982). *Material Culture Studies in America.* Nashville, TN: The American Association for State and Local History.

SCHNEIDER, JANE (1987). "The Anthropology of Cloth," *Annual Review of Anthropology,* 16, 409–448.

SCHUDSON, MICHAEL (1984). *Advertising, The Uneasy Persuasion.* New York: Basic Books.

SHANKS, MICHAEL, and CHRISTOPHER TILLEY (1987). *Social Theory and Archaeology.* Albuquerque, NM: University of New Mexico Press.

SHAPIRO, MICHAEL (1988). "The Rhetoric of Social Science: The Political Responsibilities of the Scholar," in *The Rhetoric of the Human Sciences: Language and Argument in Scholarship and Public Affairs,* Eds. John Nelson, Allan Megill, and Donald McCloskey. Madison, WI: University of Wisconsin Press, 363–380.

SHAPIRO, STANLEY, and A. H. WALLE, Eds. (1988). *Marketing: A Return to the Broad Dimensions.* Chicago: American Marketing Association.

SHERRY, JOHN F., JR. (1983). "Gift Giving in Anthropological Perspective," *Journal of Consumer Research,* 10(2), 157–168.

SHERRY, JOHN F., JR. (1984). "Some Implications of Consumer Tradition for Reactive Marketing," in *Advances in Consumer Research,* Vol. 11, Ed. Thomas Kinnear. Provo, UT: Association for Consumer Research, 741–747.

SHERRY, JOHN F., JR. (1986a). "Some Cultural Correlates of U.S.–Japanese Protectionism," in *Protectionism: Can American Business Overcome It?* Ed. Douglas Lamont. Indianapolis, IN: Books Craft, 79–91.

SHERRY, JOHN F., JR. (1986b). "The Cultural Perspective in Consumer Research," in *Advances in Consumer Research,* Vol. 13, Ed. R. Lutz. Provo, UT: Association for Consumer Research, 573–975.

SHERRY, JOHN F., JR. (1986c). "Cereal Monogamy: Brand Loyalty as Secular Ritual in Consumer Culture," paper presented at the Seventeenth Annual Conference of the Association for Consumer Research, Toronto, Ont.

SHERRY, JOHN F., JR. (1986d). "Interpreting Data From the Field," paper presented at the Seventeenth Annual Conference of the Association for Consumer Research, Toronto, Ont.

SHERRY, JOHN F., JR. (1987a). "Keeping the Monkeys Away From the Typewriters: An Anthropologist's View of the Consumer Behavior Odyssey," in *Advances in Consumer Research,* Vol. 14, Eds. Melanie Wallendorf and Paul Anderson. Provo, UT: Association for Consumer Research, 370–373.

SHERRY, JOHN F., JR. (1987b). "Cultural Propriety in a Global Marketplace," in *Philosophical and Radical Thought in Marketing,* Eds. A. F. Firat, N. Dholakia, and R. Bagozzi. Lexington, MA: Lexington Books, 179–191.

SHERRY, JOHN F., JR. (1987c). "A Comment on Hirschman's Humanistic Inquiring in Marketing Research," working paper, Northwestern University, Evanston, IL.

SHERRY, JOHN F., JR. (1987d). "Heresy and the Useful Miracle: Rethinking Anthropology's Contributions to Marketing," in *Research in Marketing,* Vol. 9, Ed. J. Sheth. Greenwich, CT: JAI Press, 285–306.

SHERRY, JOHN F., JR. (1987e). "Advertising as a Cultural System," in *Marketing and Semiotics: New Directions in the Study of Signs for Sale,* Ed. Jean Umiker-Sebeok. Berlin: Mouton de Gruyter, 441–461.

SHERRY, JOHN F., JR. (1988a). "A Sociocultural Interpretation of the Flea Market," working paper, Northwestern University, Evanston, IL.

SHERRY, JOHN F., JR. (1988b). "Marketing and Consumer Behavior: Windows of Opportunity for Anthropology," *Journal of the Steward Anthropological Society,* 16(1).

SHERRY, JOHN F., JR. (1988c). "Market Pitching and the Ethnography of Speaking," in *Advances in Consumer Research,* Vol. 15, Ed. Michael Houston. Provo, UT: Association for Consumer Research, 543–547.

SHERRY, JOHN F., JR. (1989). "Observations on Marketing and Consumption: An Anthropological Note," in *Advances in Consumer Research,* Vol. 16, Ed. Thomas Srull. Provo, UT: Association for Consumer Research.

SHERRY, JOHN F., JR., and EDUARDO CAMARGO (1987). " 'May Your Life Be Marvelous': English Language Labelling and the Semiotics of Japanese Promotion," *Journal of Consumer Research,* 14(2), 174–188.

SHERRY, JOHN F., JR., and MARY ANN MCGRATH (1989). "Unpacking the Holiday Presence: A Comparative Ethnography of Two Gift Stores," in *Interpretive Consumer Research,* Ed. Elizabeth

Hirschman. Provo, UT: Association for Consumer Research, 148–167.

SHETH, JAGDISH (1982). "Consumer Behavior: Shortages and Surpluses," in *Advances in Consumer Research*, Vol. 9, Ed. Andrew Mitchell. Ann Arbor, MI: Association for Consumer Research, 13–16.

SHIMP, TERRENCE, and THOMAS MADDEN (1988). "Consumer-Object Relations: A Conceptual Framework Based Analogously on Sternberg's Triangular Theory of Love," in *Advances in Consumer Research*, Vol. 15, Ed. Michael Houston. Provo, UT: Association for Consumer Research, 163–168.

SHWEDER, RICHARD, and DONALD FISKE, Eds. (1986). *Metatheory in Social Science: Pluralisms and Subjectivities*. Chicago: University of Chicago Press.

SIEGEL, HARVEY (1988). "Relativism for Consumer Research?" *Journal of Consumer Research*, 15(1), 129–132.

SOLOMON, MICHAEL (1983). "The Role of Products as Social Stimuli: A Symbolic Interactionism Perspective," *Journal of Consumer Research*, 10(3), 319–329.

SOLOMON, MICHAEL (1986). "The Missing Link: Surrogate Consumers in the Marketing Chain," *Journal of Marketing*, 50(4), 208–218.

SOLOMON, MICHAEL (1988). "Building Up and Breaking Down: The Impact of Cultural Sorting on Consumption Symbolism," *Research in Consumer Behavior*, Vol. 3, Ed. Elizabeth Hirschman. Greenwich, CT: JAI Press.

SOLOMON, MICHAEL, and PUNAM ANAND (1985). "Ritual Costumes and Status Transition: The Female Business Suit as Totemic Emblem," in *Advances in Consumer Research*, Vol. 13, Eds. Elizabeth Hirschman and Morris Holbrook. Provo, UT: Association for Consumer Research, 315–318.

SOLOMON, MICHAEL, and HENRY ASSAEL (1987). "The Forest or the Trees? A Gestalt Approach to Symbolic Consumption," in *Marketing and Semiotics: New Directions in the Study of Signs for Sale*, Ed. Jean Umiker-Sebeok. Berlin: Mouton de Gruyter, 189–218.

SOLOMON, ODILE (1988). "Semiotics and Marketing: New Directions in Industrial Design Applications," *International Journal of Research in Marketing*, 4(3), 201–216.

SPECK, PAUL (1987). "Relativism and Positivism: The Mythic and Ritualistic Dimensions of Contemporary Marketing Science," in *Marketing Theory*, Eds. R. Belk, G. Zaltman, R. Bagozzi, D. Brinberg, R. Deshpande, A. F. Firat, M. Holbrook, J. Olson, J. Sherry, and B. Weitz. Chicago, IL: American Marketing Association, 200–203.

SPENCER-WOOD, SUZANNE, ED. (1987a). *Consumer Choice in Historical Archaeology*. New York: Plenum Press.

SPENCER-WOOD, SUZANNE (1987b). "Introduction," in *Consumer Choice in Historical Archaeology*, Ed. Suzanne Spenser-Wood. New York: Plenum Press, 1–24.

SPIGGLE, SUSAN (1986). "Measuring Social Values: A Content Analysis of Sunday Comics and Underground Comix," *Journal of Consumer Research*, 13(1), 100–113.

SPIGGLE, SUSAN (1987). "Grocery Shopping Lists: What Do Consumers Write?" in *Advances in Consumer Research*, Vol. 14, Eds. Melanie Wallendorf and Paul Anderson. Provo, UT: Association for Consumer Research, 241–245.

SPIGGLE, SUSAN, and CLINT SANDERS (1984). "The Construction of Consumer Typologies: Scientific and Ethnomethods," in *Advances in Consumer Research*, Vol. 11, Ed. Thomas Kinnear. Provo, UT: Association for Consumer Research, 337–342.

SPIGGLE, SUSAN, and CATHY GOODWIN (1988). "Values and Issues in the Field of Consumer Research: A Content Analysis of ACR Presidential Addresses," in *Advances in Consumer Research*, Vol, 15, Ed. Michael Houston. Provo, UT: Association for Consumer Research, 5–9.

STERN, BARBARA (1988a). "Medieval Allegory: Roots of Advertising Strategy for the Mass Market," *Journal of Marketing*, 52(3), 84–94.

STERN, BARBARA (1988b). "Figurative Language in Services Advertising: The Nature and Uses of Imagery," in *Advances in Consumer Research*, Vol. 15, Ed. Michael Houston. Provo, UT: Association for Consumer Research, 185–190.

STERN, BARBARA (1988c). "How Does an Ad Mean," *Journal of Advertising*.

STERN, BARBARA (1989). "Literary Explication: A Methodology for Consumer Research," in *Interpretive Consumer Research*, Ed. Elizabeth Hirschman. Provo, UT: Association for Consumer Research, 48–59.

STEWART, SUSAN (1984). *On Longing*. Baltimore, MD: Johns Hopkins University Press.

TAMARI, MEIR (1987). *"With All Your Possessions": Jewish Ethics and Economic Life*. New York: The Free Press.

TAN, CHIN TIONG, and JAGDISH SHETH, Eds. (1985). *Historical Perspective in Consumer Research: National and International Perspectives*. Singapore: School of Management, National University of Singapore.

TETREAULT, MARY (1987). "Speculations on the Sociology of Marketing," in *Marketing Theory*, Eds. R. Belk, G. Zaltman, R. Bagozzi, D. Brinberg, Rohit Deshpande, A. F. Firat, M. Holbrook. J. Olson, J. Sherry, and B. Weitz. Chicago: American Marketing Association. 166–168.

THORNTON, ROBERT (1988). "The Rhetoric of Ethnographic Holism," *Cultural Anthropology*, 3(3), 285–303.

TRAUBE, ELIZABETH (1986). "The Question of Interpretive Anthropology," paper presented at the Annual Meeting of the American Anthropology Association, Philadelphia, PA.

TSE, DAVID, RUSSELL BELK, and NAN ZHOU (1989). "Becoming a Consumer Society: A Longitudinal and Cross-Cultural Content Analysis of Print Ads from Hong Kong, the People's Republic of China, and Taiwan," *Journal of Consumer Research*, 15(4), 457–472.

TUCKER, WILLIAM (1967). *Foundations for a Theory of Consumer Behavior*. New York: Holt, Rinehart & Winston.

TURNER, VICTOR (1974). *Dramas, Fields, and Metaphors*. Ithaca: Cornell University Press.

TYLER, STEPHEN (1987). *The Unspeakable: Discourse, Dialogue and Rhetoric in the Postmodern World*. Madison, WI: University of Wisconsin Press.

UMIKER-SEBEOK, JEAN, Ed. (1987). *Marketing and Semiotics: New Directions in the Study of Signs for Sale*. New York: Mouton de Gruyter.

VERBA, STEPHEN, and CARL CAMDEN (1987). "Writing With Flesh: A Semiotic Interpretation of Research Findings on Body Image Attitudes and Behaviors in the U.S.," in *Marketing and Semiotics: New Directions in the Study of Signs for Sale*, Ed. Jean Umiker-Sebeok. Berlin: Mouton de Gruyter, 165–186.

VESTERGAARD, TORBEN, and KIM SCHRODER (1987). *The Language of Advertising*. New York: Basil Blackwell.

WALLACE, ANTHONY (1956). "Revitalization Movements," *American Anthropologist*, 58, 264–281.

WALLENDORF, MELANIE (1987). " 'On the Road Again': The Nature of Qualitative Research on the Consumer Behavior Odyssey," in *Advances in Consumer Research*, Vol. 14, Eds. Melanie Wallendorf and Paul Anderson. Provo, UT: Association for Consumer Research, 374–375.

WALLENDORF, MELANIE (1988). "Odyssey Publications, Presentations, and Work in Progress," unpublished manuscript, University of Arizona, Tucson, AZ.

WALLENDORF, MELANIE, and ERIC ARNOULD (1988). " 'My Favorite Things': A Cross Cultural Inquiry Into Object Attachment, Possessiveness, and Social Linkage," *Journal of Consumer Research*, 14(4), 531–547.

WALLENDORF, MELANIE, and RUSSELL BELK (1987). "Deep Meaning in Possessions," videotape. Cambridge, MA: Marketing Science Institute.

WALLENDORF, MELANIE, and RUSSELL BELK (1988). "The History and Development of the Consumer Behavior Odyssey," in *Highways and Buyways: Naturalistic Research from the Consumer Behavior Odyssey*, Eds. Melanie Wallendorf and Russell Belk, unpublished monograph, University of Utah, Salt Lake City, UT.

WALLENDORF, MELANIE, and RUSSELL BELK (1989). "Assessing Trustworthiness in Naturalistic Consumer Research," in *Interpretive Consumer Research*, Ed. Elizabeth Hirschman. Provo, UT: Association for Consumer Research, 69–84.

WALLENDORF, MELANIE, RUSSELL BELK, and DEBORAH HEISLEY (1988). "Deep Meaning in Possessions: The Paper," in *Advances in Consumer Research*, Vol. 15, Ed. Michael Houston. Provo, UT: Association for Consumer Research, 528–530.

WALLENDORF, MELANIE, and MICHAEL REILLY (1983a). "Distinguishing Culture of Origin From Culture of Residence," in *Advances in Consumer Research*, Vol. 10, Eds. Richard Bagozzi and Alice Tybout. Ann Arbor, MI: Association for Consumer Research, 699–701.

WALLENDORF, MELANIE, and MICHAEL REILLY (1983b). "Ethnic Migration, Assimilation and Consumption," *Journal of Consumer Research*, 10(3), 292–302.

WALLENDORF, MELANIE, and ROBERT WESTBROOK (1985). "Emotions and Clothing Disposition," paper presented at the Annual Conference of the Association for Consumer Research, Las Vegas, NV.

WALLENDORF, MELANIE, and GERALD ZALTMAN, Eds. (1984). *Readings in Consumer Behavior: Individuals, Groups, and Organizations.* New York: Wiley.

WERNER, OSWALD, and MARK SCHOEPFLE (1987a). *Systematic Fieldwork, Volume 1: Foundations of Ethnography and Interviewing.* Newbury Park, CA: Sage.

WERNER, OSWALD, and MARK SCHOEPFLE (1987b). *Systematic Fieldwork, Volume II: Ethnographic Analysis and Data Management.* Newbury Park, CA: Sage.

WERTZ, FREDERICK, and JOAN GREENHUT (1985). "A Psychology of Buying: Demonstration of Phenomenological Approach in Consumer Research," in *Advances in Consumer Research*, Vol. 12, Eds. Elizabeth Hirschman and Morris Holbrook. Provo, UT: Association for Consumer Research, 566–570.

WHITE, HAYDEN (1978). *Topics of Discourse: Essays in Cultural Criticism.* Baltimore, MD: Johns Hopkins University Press.

WILK, RICHARD (1987). "House, Home, and Consumer Decision Making in Two Cultures," in *Advances in Consumer Research*, Vol. 14, Eds. Melanie Wallendorf and Paul Anderson. Provo, UT: Association for Consumer Research, 303–307.

WILK, RICHARD (1988). "Colonial Time and TV Time: Baseball and Consciousness in Belize," working paper, New Mexico State University, Las Cruces, NM.

WILLIAMS, RAYMOND (1981). *Problems in Materialism and Culture.* London: NCB.

WILLIAMS, R. (1982). *Dream Worlds: Mass Consumption in Late Nineteenth Century France.* Berkeley, CA: University of California Press.

WILLIAMSON, JUDITH (1978). "Decoding Advertisements: Ideology and *Meaning in Advertising.*" New York: Marion Boyars.

WILLS, GARRY (1989). "Message in the Deodorant Bottle: Inventing Time," *Critical Inquiry*, 15(Spring), 497–509.

WINICK, CHARLES (1961). "Anthropology's Contributions to Marketing," *Journal of Marketing*, 24(5), 53–60.

WOLF, ERIC (1981). *Europe and the People Without History.* Berkeley, CA: University of California Press.

WOOLGAR, STEVE (1988). *Science: The Very Idea.* New York: Tavistock.

WUTHNOW, ROBERT, and MARSHA WITTEN (1988). "New Directions in the Study of Culture," *Annual Review of Sociology*, 14, 49–67.

YEATS, WILLIAM B. (1921). "The Second Coming," in *The Norton Anthology of Poetry.* (1970). Eds. A. Eastman, A. Allison, H. Barrows, C. Blake, A. Carr, and H. English. New York: Norton, 914–915.

ZALTMAN, GERALD (1983). "Presidential Address," in *Advances in Consumer Research*, Vol. 10, Eds. Richard Bagozzi and Alice Tybout. Ann Arbor, MI: Association for Consumer Research, 1–5.

ZALTMAN, GERALD, and LINDA PRICE (1984). "The Sociology and Psychology of Comfort Zones," in *Scientific Method in Marketing*, Eds. Paul Anderson and Michael Ryan. Chicago: American Marketing Association, 39–43.

ZALTMAN, GERALD, and MELANIE WALLENDORF (1977). "The Missing Chunk or How We've Missed the Boat," in *Contemporary Marketing Thought.* Eds. Barnett Greenberg and Danny Bellender. Chicago, American Marketing Association, 235–238.

ZALTMAN, GERALD, RUSSELL BELK, RICHARD BAGOZZI, DAVID BRINBERG, ROHIT DESHPANDE, A. FUAT FIRAT, MORRIS HOLBROOK, JERRY OLSON, JOHN SHERRY, AND BARTON WEITZ, Eds. (1987). *Marketing Theory.* Chicago: American Marketing.

ZIELINSKI, JOAN, and THOMAS ROBERTSON (1982). "Consumer Behavior Theory: Excesses and Limitations," in *Advances in Consumer Research*, Vol. 9, Ed. Andrew Mitchell. Ann Arbor, MI: Association for Consumer Research, 8–12.

NAME INDEX

SUBJECT INDEX